THE CHURCHILL DOCUMENTS

Books by Martin Gilbert

The Churchill Biography

Volume III: The Challenge of War, 1914–1916
Document Volume III* (in two parts)
Volume IV: World in Torment, 1917–1922
Document Volume IV* (in three parts)
Volume V: Prophet of Truth, 1922–1939
Document Volume V*: The Exchequer Years, 1922–1929
Document Volume V*: The Wilderness Years, 1929–1935
Document Volume V*: The Coming of War, 1936–1939
Volume VI: Finest Hour, 1939–1941
Churchill War Papers I*: At the Admiralty, September 1939–May 1940
Churchill War Papers II*: Never Surrender, May–December 1940
Churchill War Papers III*: The Ever-Widening War, 1941
Volume VII: Road to Victory, 1941–1945
Volume VIII: Never Despair, 1945–1965
Churchill: A Photographic Portrait
Churchill: A Life

*The document volumes are also being published by Hillsdale College Press as *The Churchill Documents*

Other Books

The Appeasers (with Richard Gott)
The European Powers, 1900–1945
The Roots of Appeasement
Children's Illustrated Bible Atlas
Atlas of British Charities
Atlas of American History
Atlas of the Arab-Israeli Conflict
Atlas of British History
Atlas of the First World War
Atlas of the Second World War
Atlas of the Holocaust
Atlas of Jewish History
Atlas of Russian History
The Jews of Russia: Their History in Maps
Jerusalem Illustrated History Atlas
Sir Horace Rumbold: Portrait of a Diplomat
Jerusalem: Rebirth of a City, 1800–1900
Jerusalem in the Twentieth Century
Exile and Return: The Struggle for
Jewish Statehood
Auschwitz and the Allies
The Jews of Hope:
The Plight of Soviet Jewry Today
Shcharansky: Hero of Our Time

The Holocaust: The Jewish Tragedy
The Boys: Triumph over Adversity
The First World War
The Battle of the Somme
The Second World War
D-Day
The Day the War Ended
In Search of Churchill
A History of the Twentieth Century,
1900–1933: Empires in Conflict
A History of the Twentieth Century,
1934–1951: Descent into Barbarism
A History of the Twentieth Century,
1952–1999: Challenge to Civilization
Never Again: A History of the Holocaust
The Jews in the Twentieth Century
Letters to Auntie Fori: The 5,000-Year
History of the Jewish People
Israel: A History
The Righteous: The Unsung Christian
Heroes of the Holocaust
Kristallnacht: Prelude to Destruction
Churchill and America
Churchill and the Jews

In Ishmael's House: A History of Jews under Muslim Rule

Editions of Documents

Britain and Germany Between the Wars
Plough My Own Furrow: The Life of Lord Allen of Hurtwood
Servant of India: Diaries of the Viceroy's Private Secretary, 1905–1910

THE CHURCHILL DOCUMENTS

Martin Gilbert

Volume 15
Never Surrender
May 1940–December 1940

Hillsdale College Press, Hillsdale, Michigan

Dedicated to the memory of
Emery Reves
who helped to carry the books
of Sir Winston Churchill
to the world

Hillsdale College Press
33 East College Street
Hillsdale, Michigan 49242
www.hillsdale.edu

© C & T Publications Limited
All rights reserved. No part of this publication may be reproduced, transmitted, or stored in a retrieval system, in any form or by any means, without the prior written permission of the copyright holder.

Originally published in 1994 by William Heinemann Ltd. in Great Britain and in 1995 by W. W. Norton in the United States as *The Churchill War Papers*, Volume II.

Printed in the United States of America

Printed and bound by Sheridan Books, Chelsea, Michigan

Cover design by Hesseltine & DeMason, Ann Arbor, Michigan

THE CHURCHILL DOCUMENTS
Volume 15: *Never Surrender, May 1940–December 1940*

Library of Congress Control Number: 2006934101

ISBN: 978-0-916308-33-9

First printing 2011
Second printing 2014
Third printing 2020

Contents

Note to the New Edition	vi
Preface	vii
Acknowledgements to the New Edition	xxv
Acknowledgements	xxvii
11–31 May 1940	1
JUNE 1940	221
JULY 1940	449
AUGUST 1940	596
SEPTEMBER 1940	753
OCTOBER 1940	890
NOVEMBER 1940	1018
DECEMBER 1940	1165
APPENDICES	1315
MAPS	1323
INDEX	1335

Note
to the New Edition

Winston Churchill's personal papers are among the most comprehensive ever assembled relating to the life and times of one man. They are so extensive that it was only possible to include in the narrative volumes of his biography a part of the relevant documents.

The Companion Volumes, now titled *The Churchill Documents*, were planned to run parallel with the narrative volumes, and with them to form a whole. When an extract or quotation appears in a narrative volume, the complete document appears in an accompanying volume of *The Churchill Documents*. Where space prevented the inclusion of a contemporary letter in the narrative volume, it is included in the document volume.

In these three volumes of *The Churchill Documents*—Volume 14: *At the Admiralty, September 1939–1940,* Volume 15: *Never Surrender, May 1940–December 1940,* and Volume 16: *The Ever-Widening War, 1941*—are set out all the documents relevant to *Winston S. Churchill*, Volume VI: *Finest Hour, 1939–1941*. Mention in these texts of the "Main Volume" refers to this sixth volume of the biography.

Preface

This second volume of Churchill's War Papers is compiled principally from Churchill's own papers at Churchill College, Cambridge, and from the British Government archives at Kew. In addition, I have used a variety of private archives and published volumes of diaries and recollections, which I have listed in the acknowledgements. The period covered, May to December 1940, is one of the decisive periods in British history, ranking with the Norman conquest of 1066, the Spanish Armada of 1588, the defeat of the combined French and Spanish fleets at Trafalgar in 1805, and the German breakthrough on the Western Front in March 1918. This volume begins with another attempted German breakthrough in France, this time completely successful, and with the Battle of Britain and the Blitz, two of the main weapons in Hitler's attempt to prepare for invasion, or to force Britain to sue for peace.

The emergence of Churchill as Prime Minister took place a few hours after the German onslaught on Holland and Belgium. The first eight and a half months of his Premiership saw Britain struggling against considerable odds on land, at sea and in the air, the situation grievously intensified by the fall of France. This volume documents Churchill's views and actions, thoughts and exhortations, methods of work and government, and shows the heavy pressures on him of unexpected, and often potentially disastrous, events and possibilities.

In the early part of this volume, set-backs and defeats marked the almost daily bombardment of bad news: the rapid German thrust through Holland, Belgium and northern France, the Belgian capitulation, the French inability to go onto the offensive as the German armies reached the Channel Coast, the retreat of the British Expeditionary Force to Dunkirk, the entry of Italy into the war as Germany's ally, and the divided counsels at the centre of French policy-making, culminating in the fall of France, and made even more anguished, for Churchill, by American hesitations in providing essential supplies, including planes and destroyers. Between the Dunkirk evacuation and the fall of France, Churchill instructed the British Ambassador in Washington (*pages 270–1*) to talk to President Roosevelt, 'and discourage any complacent assumption on United States' part that they will pick up the debris of the British Empire by their present policy'. Adding to his anger were American suggestions that, should Britain be overrun, the British Fleet should be transferred to the United States.

Within a few weeks of becoming Prime Minister, Churchill had emerged as a pillar of morale at a time when the threat of invasion was ever-present. A week before the Dunkirk evacuation, at a testing time for Britain, his interpreter Captain Berkeley wrote in his diary (*page 94*): 'The grave anxiety has continued, without more ups and downs to relieve it. The PM gave a magnificent broadcast address last night, which has at last put the true position before the people. He is being "sublime" at every stage and after narrowly averting a serious collapse in Paris four days ago has been galvanising everybody here.' During that visit to Paris, and on three subsequent visits before the fall of France, Churchill took up a position, soon to be reflected in his speeches and broadcasts, that Britain would not surrender. 'I sang my usual song', he later recalled (*page 219*),'we would fight on whatever happened or whatever fell out.' This determination found a response in the British public that was as remarkable, and as dramatic, as it was unforeseen.

The middle sections of the volume are dominated by the possibility of a German invasion of Britain, and by the Battle of Britain and the Blitz. Further afield there were other worries which had to absorb a great deal of Churchill's efforts: the Italian threat to Britain in Egypt, the naval dangers in the Mediterranean, the possibility of German action in Spain or the Balkans, the intensification of the U-boat war, the transatlantic convoys bringing to Britain the essential rifles and other munitions purchased in the United States, and the daily search for yet more weapons of war, military supplies, aircraft, and new weapons, especially anti-aircraft weapons. So urgent did the need become to find the weaponry to reduce nightly bomber assault that in

August 1940 Churchill was forced to tell his advisers (*page 653*): 'It was essential that time and energy should not be wasted on trying to achieve perfection.'

By the final sections of the volume, it is clear that although Britain had averted defeat, her ability to remain at war would be fiercely and continuously challenged by Germany, and that Hitler's determination to destroy British power and morale would not abate. The volume ends with Britain's first victory, at Sidi Barrani in the Western Desert, over the Italians, but with German air and sea power still inflicting heavy losses, and with the economic burden of warmaking threatening to become intolerable. Churchill's appeals to President Roosevelt, first for destroyers and then for financial credit, were not answered as quickly, or initially as positively, as he had hoped, or as Britain needed.

This volume of the Churchill War Papers contains 1,720 documents. As in the previous volumes of documents, they set out Churchill's ideas and proposals over the wide range of subjects with which he was concerned, and for which, in the period covered by this volume, he held ultimate responsibility. Arranged in chronological order, these documents also put Churchill's thought and action in the context of the daily events, changes, pressures and uncertainties of the war. As well as the letters that he wrote, the telegrams he sent, and the minutes he circulated to his Ministers and secretariat, I have included every speech he made, both in the House of Commons and outside it, and the full text of each of his broadcasts. I have also printed each of his interventions at the War Cabinet and at the Chiefs of Staff Committee of which, as Minister of Defence, he was Chairman, and all his interventions at the meetings of the Supreme War Council between 16 May and 13 June 1940.

During his visits to France for the Supreme War Council, and when specially called across the Channel by the French Prime Minister, Paul Reynaud, Churchill tried to sustain those French leaders who wished to remain at war, and whose demands for British help, especially in the air, seemed at times a determining factor in their will to resist. Churchill had to balance French needs, and Britain's desire to continue the fight in France, with the growing danger of a German invasion of Britain. The perils of invasion, and the preparations to meet it, were central to his efforts throughout the summer and autumn.

On becoming Prime Minister, Churchill gave his predecessor, Neville Chamberlain, the opportunity to continue living at 10 Downing Street. Thus it was that for the first weeks of his Premiership, Churchill lived at Admiralty House, where he had taken up residence on becoming First Lord of the Admiralty in September 1939. Hardly had he moved to Downing Street than the intensity of the German air raids on London forced him to sleep elsewhere: mostly at Down Street, a converted underground station on the Piccadilly Line, and for three nights at the Central (also known as the Cabinet) War Rooms. Even Chequers, the Prime Minister's country home in Buckinghamshire, was judged unsafe during full-moon weekends, and he had to move further west, to Ditchley Park in Oxfordshire. Eventually he found a secure above-ground residence a few minutes' walk from Downing Street. Known as 'No. 10 Annexe', it was strengthened with iron girders and metal shutters, and became his main place of work, overlooking St James's Park. For two-thirds of the period covered in this volume, the dangers of the Blitz were real, and bombs fell in and around Whitehall. One of the documents that I have included shows Churchill's concern that even the water on the St James's Park and Buckingham Palace garden lakes might serve as a guide to German bombers. Surely it would be possible, he asked his advisers (*pages 995–6*), to camouflage the lakes 'by spreading wires across and steel wool camouflage nets, or by some other method. If it did not cost too much it would be worth trying'.

Churchill was sixty-one years old when he became Prime Minister. He reached his sixty-second birthday in November 1940, after the danger of invasion had begun to recede, but while the Blitz was still intense. Many of the documents in this volume, particularly the diary entries of those who saw him at work, and during rare moments of relaxation, show every aspect of his character: I have pointed to some of these, under 'characteristics of, and moods, as seen by his contemporaries', in the Churchill index entry. John Colville, his most junior Private Secretary in 1940, let me see his diary while I was writing the wartime narrative volumes of the biography (volume six, *Finest Hour* and volume seven, *Road to Victory*). It contains many glimpses of Churchill in different moods and circumstances. Other diaries from which I have published extracts include those of Captain Berkeley, his interpreter when he was in France, of his Secretary of State for War, Anthony Eden (later Foreign Secretary), of two Members of Parliament, Henry Channon and Harold Nicolson, of the Commander-in-Chief, Home Forces (later Chief of the Imperial General Staff), General Alan Brooke, and of a Labour member of his administration, Hugh Dalton.

In addition to diaries and letters written at the time, I have included recollections from several published memoirs, including those of Harold Macmillan, one of Churchill's junior ministers (and later Prime Minister); General Edward Louis Spears, his emissary to France, and later to de Gaulle; and General Hastings Ismay, the head of his Defence Office. In 1948, General Ismay also sent Churchill a series of recollections of Churchill's visits to France, and of the Blitz, when Churchill was writing his war memoirs. Diarists, memoir writers and contemporary correspondents testify to Churchill's enormous energy, good nature and courage, even at times of accumulated adversity, and of burdens greater than those borne by Lloyd George in the First World War. Like the younger Pitt in the war against Napoleon, Churchill was able, by his character as well as his policies, to inspire the nation at times of doubt and fear, and to see a way forward to survival and military success. A member of his Private Office, John Martin, wrote home on 30 May 1940 (*page 196*): 'The PM's confidence and energy are amazing. "Nobody ever left his presence without feeling a braver man" was said of Pitt; but it is no less true of him.'

During the dangerous weeks following the fall of France, and when the Blitz was at its height, Churchill kept a careful watch for expressions of defeatist opinion. In a document which I have reproduced in facsimile (*page 464*), he informed all senior civil servants and officials that they 'should not hesitate to report, and if necessary remove, any officers or officials who are found to be consciously exercising a disturbing or depressing influence, or whose talk is calculated to spread alarm and despondency'.

Churchill's effort to reflect what he saw as the determination of the British people not to give in to the threat of military defeat was seen most clearly in his intervention in the War Cabinet on 27 and 28 May 1940. The French Government, then fearful of imminent collapse, was eager to promote a joint Anglo-French approach to Mussolini, to prevent Italy joining the conflict. In the War Cabinet on May 27, Lord Halifax wanted an effort made to see whether such a peace initiative was possible, and suggested that, in return for Mussolini bringing about a general European settlement in which British independence would be preserved, Britain would agree to recognise Italy's claims in the Mediterranean. In Churchill's Private Office, John Colville wrote in his diary that day that there were 'signs that Halifax is being defeatist' (*page 169*).

On the following day, May 28, Halifax told the War Cabinet that he believed Britain could get better terms from Germany if negotiations were begun before France was defeated, and before Britain's own aircraft factories were bombed. Churchill rejected this, stating (*page 180*) that once Britain got to the conference table with Hitler 'we should then find that the terms offered us touched our independence and integrity'. When, at that point, 'we got up to leave the Conference table, we should find that all the forces of resolution which were now at our disposal would have vanished'. When Halifax pressed his point, and was supported in part by Neville Chamberlain, who also said that it was 'right to remember that the alternative to fighting on nevertheless involved a considerable gamble', Churchill declared that 'the nations which went down fighting rose again, but those which surrendered tamely were finished.' On a severely practical note, he added 'that the chances of decent terms being offered to us at the present time were a thousand to one against'.

At this crucial moment, the War Cabinet broke off to enable Churchill to fulfil a long-standing engagement to meet the non-War Cabinet members of his Government. He told them, as Hugh Dalton, who was present, noted in his diary (*page 183*): 'We shall go on, and we shall fight it out, here or elsewhere, and if at last the long story is to end, it were better it should end, not through surrender, but only when we are rolling senseless on the ground.' The ministers and junior ministers crowded around him, patting him on the back and expressing their approval. He returned to the War Cabinet inspired by this unexpected and unprecedented demonstration. The minutes of the War Cabinet recorded his remarks (*page 185*), that the ministers had 'expressed the greatest satisfaction when he had told them that there was no chance of our giving up the struggle. He did not remember ever before having heard a gathering of persons occupying high places in political life express themselves so emphatically.'

It was a turning point in Churchill's conduct of affairs. Inspired by the demonstration, he answered Halifax's reference to a new French request for an Anglo-French approach, to be made this time through President Roosevelt, with the words: 'An appeal to the United States at the present time would be altogether premature. If we made a bold stand against Germany, that would command their admiration and respect; but a grovelling appeal, if made now, would have the worst possible effect.' The possibility of enlisting Mussolini or Roosevelt as a mediator was dropped. But Churchill did warn President Roosevelt two weeks later (*page 338*) that a time might come 'when the present ministers no longer have control of affairs and when very easy terms could be obtained for the British Empire by their becoming a vassal state of the Hitler Empire. A pro-German Government would certainly be called into being to make peace, Churchill warned the President, 'and might present to a shattered or a starving nation an almost irresistible case for entire submission to the Nazi will.' Churchill ended this stark appraisal with a request for the immediate despatch, for the use of the Royal Navy, of thirty-five First World War American destroyers. His request was not granted for several months.

It was not just inspiration and morale, but each area of war policy, with which Churchill was involved. As Prime Minister and Minister of Defence his responsibilities covered every aspect of warmaking, for the defence of Britain, for any overseas initiatives, military, naval and air, and for the sphere of diplomacy: trying to keep Italy out of the Axis camp, encouraging Spain and Turkey to maintain their neutrality, and, in the case of Vichy France, trying to convince them to turn their back on the Axis.

The composition, effective working, and inter-departmental cooperation within the government itself, was another central factor in Churchill's daily work. Disputes between Ministers could end on his desk, as did that between the Secretary of State for Air, Sir Archibald Sinclair, and the Minister of Aircraft Production, Lord Beaverbrook. He had also to intervene when Ministers were upset by offensive cartoons in the newspapers. Inefficiency, incompetence and negative attitudes roused his ire: I have indicated some examples of this in the Churchill index entry, under 'rebukes by'. He did not take kindly to what he called 'a drizzle of carping criticism', or to those officials, military or civilian, who, as he expressed it, 'failed to rise to the height of circumstances'. Among his injunctions to his Ministers were, 'Don't let this matter sleep', and, 'I never "worry" about action, but only about inaction.'

Examples of this 'worry' abound. While agreeing with the War Cabinet after the failure of the Anglo-French expedition against Dakar in September 1940 'that we should be careful of embarking upon new adventures with inadequate preparations', Churchill went on to tell his colleagues (*page 873*): 'But nothing was easier or more fatal than to relapse into a policy of negation.' His own search for the offensive, and for active measures, was continuous. A typical example was his determination to mount 14-inch naval guns on the cliffs at Dover in order to bombard German fortifications across the Channel. Another example was his efforts at the end of 1940 to persuade General Wavell to follow up his victory over the Italians in the Western Desert with further action. On one occasion he minuted to his advisers (*page 1140*), about a West African force then in Kenya: 'The proposals to keep the Brigade and not fight is most depressing.'

Hardly a week went by without Churchill suggesting some military, naval or air initiative, whereby Britain might take the offensive, or forestall the offensives of others. The Churchill index entry 'offensive operations' points to several such proposals. In mid-July, he was complaining to the Secretary of State for War (*page 515*) about 'the dead-alive way in which the Middle East campaign is being run' on the eve of a possible Italian attack. A day later he was asking Air Marshal Sir Richard Peirse, the head of Bomber Command (*page 522*), to do more in the way of disrupting the Kiel Canal, through which invasion barges might be brought.

Churchill's vigilance was unremitting and wide-ranging. By his nightly reading of the national newspapers, he followed the public mood, and was on the alert for a wide variety of problems, from breaches of security to over-harsh punishments. In August he wrote to the Postmaster-General (*page 685, note 1*): 'There are, as you will see from *The Times* today, considerable complaints about the Post Office during air raids. Perhaps you will give me a report on what you are doing.' Churchill's statistical office, headed by Professor Lindemann, was continually asked to check facts with regard to munitions production, imports and shipping losses, aircraft losses and aircraft production. Remembering the terrible problems and suffering caused in the First World War by offensives not backed by adequate weapons, by the failure to introduce the convoy system until 1917, and by the lack of scrutiny of production and supply, Churchill used his statistical office as a window onto the workings of all government departments, examining the crucial minutiae of warmaking, including the daily pattern of the importation of rifles essential for the defence of Britain against invasion, and the relaxation of food rationing with a view to boosting morale at home.

In the third week of June 1940, with France being overrun by Germany, Churchill appealed direct to Hitler's new ally, Stalin. In his letter (*pages 417–8*) he expressed to the Soviet leader Britain's willingness 'to discuss fully with the Soviet Government any of the vast problems created by Germany's present attempts to pursue in Europe a methodical process by successive stages of conquest and absorption'. He received no reply, but when, twelve months later almost to the day, Hitler invaded the Soviet Union, Churchill offered Russia whatever help Britain could give.

At the very moment when the threat of invasion was at its height, Churchill was looking ahead to offensive operations against the Germans, telling his naval advisers in mid-September (*page 812*): 'Great efforts should be made to produce the landing craft as soon as possible,' and he went on to ask: 'Are the Joint Planning Committee satisfied that these numbers are sufficient?' He was already thinking of a number of possible amphibious landings for 1941, among them (*page 745*) the capture of Oslo (Hitler's first western conquest), the cutting off of the Cherbourg Peninsula, and a landing in the Low Countries for an attack on the Ruhr, or the seizure of some north German territory, 'so that the enemy may be made to experience war in his own land'.

Following Germany's European conquests of the spring and summer of 1940, London had become the headquarters of several governments in exile, and of groups of patriots determined to continue the fight. With characteristic imagination, and anxious also to have as many troops as possible under arms in Britain, Churchill gave his support to the employment of Polish forces, and wanted enemy aliens, who were then being interned, to be formed into a Foreign Legion, to help in the defence of Britain. He endorsed the establishment of a Dutch Brigade, stressing the importance (*page 259*) 'of furnishing them with as much equipment as possible'. His support for de Gaulle was also persistent and practical. There is a considerable amount of material in this volume on the Free French cause. When Churchill and de Gaulle first met, France was still fighting. Churchill told the War Cabinet that the General made a 'favourable impression of French morale and determination' (*page 273*). From the moment de Gaulle came to Britain, Churchill helped him build up a Free French force, establish his authority, and see military action. In the case of the joint operation against Dakar, on the coast of West Africa, this was unsuccessful. Churchill then gave his support to de Gaulle's plans to attack the Vichy authorities at Duala. 'Nothing is to be done meanwhile,' Churchill told the Chiefs of Staff, 'which would prevent us from giving effect to his reasonable requests' (*page 879*).

Churchill was persistent in his efforts to provide de Gaulle with the resources, and the political backing, that he needed. When Britain seized all French warships and sailors in English ports, Churchill wrote to his naval advisers: 'I think it important that de Gaulle should have one or two or three ships, even perhaps a battleship, where the Frenchmen predominate and which fly the French flag' (*page 481*). At the same time Churchill made several attempts to see if the Vichy Government could be persuaded to abandon its loyalty to Germany. His messages and contacts with Vichy included efforts to sound out General

Weygand, the former Commander-in-Chief of the French forces. Considerable attention was paid to winning back French North Africa, particularly Morocco, to the former Anglo-French cause.

Churchill and his advisers knew of German pressure on Spain, and of a German plan to close the Strait of Gibraltar, even to capture Gibraltar itself: this made the search for an arrangement with Vichy both prudent and urgent. In October 1940, the possibility that the Vichy Government would hand over Toulon and the French warships there to the Germans made Churchill 'particularly uneasy', spurring him to seek means of influencing Vichy against such a move. Two months later, he was to write direct to Marshal Pétain, offering Britain's military help if the Vichy Government, in its vexation and anger with the Germans, sought to establish itself as a pro-Allied government in North Africa.

These approaches to Vichy came against a background of total hostility and mistrust. In July 1940, the imminent transfer of the French Fleet to German control, under the terms of the Franco-German armistice, had seemed an immediate threat to Britain's survival. Hitler would then have been able to use the considerable French naval forces to augment his invasion plans. The British attack on those French warships at anchor in their naval base at Mers el-Kébir, Oran, when 1,500 sailors were killed, was one of the most difficult decisions Churchill took in the whole war. It was one which served as a signal, particularly to the still-sceptical United States, of Britain's ability to be ruthless in self-defence.

Another area of ruthlessness was that of bombing policy. Envisaging Hitler being unable to invade Britain and turning against Russia, Churchill wrote to the Minister of Aircraft Production in July 1940 (*pages 492–3*) that there was 'one thing that will bring him back and bring him down, and that is an absolutely devastating, exterminating attack by very heavy bombers from this country upon the Nazi homeland'. Churchill went on to explain: 'We must be able to overwhelm them by this means, without which I do not see a way through.' To build the bombers was the task of the Minister concerned, Lord Beaverbrook. Five days later, Churchill told one of his Private Secretaries (*page 513*) that when Hitler did come back from

Russia, even if he reached as far as the Caspian Sea, he would find 'a fire in his own backyard, and we will make Germany a desert, yes a desert'.

Until this could be done, bombing had more immediate and urgent aims. These included the earlier attempt to help the Anglo-French armies in France, the attack on Italian munitions supplies when Italy entered the land war against France, and the destruction of German shipping, and especially the barges being assembled for a possible invasion in the late summer. One bombing aim, that was carried out in December 1940, was a reprisal for the continuing severity of the Blitz: Operation Abigail, the singling out of a German town for massive attack (*see page 1263, note 1*).

Many documents in this volume relate to appointments, both ministerial and military. Churchill was never reluctant to praise those whose work seemed to him effective: one such was General Barker, in charge of the 'vulnerable points' along the British coast. Another was Sir Michael Palairet, British Ambassador to Greece at a time when Greece was under Italian pressure. 'I have been deeply interested in the whole series of excellent telegrams you have sent from Athens . . .', Churchill wrote (*page 1284*), 'and admire the deep and wide appreciation of the whole scene which they display.'

Despite his efforts, Churchill was not entirely successful, in overcoming the Air Ministry's animus against the head of Fighter Command, Air Chief Marshal Sir Hugh Dowding. He did manage to persuade the Secretary of State for Air not to remove Dowding at the height of the Battle of Britain, but he was unable to persuade the Air Council to prolong Dowding's appointment, or to have him given an active command after 1940. Churchill was more successful, although he made himself unpopular, in pushing for the appointment of two officers whom he regarded as of particular ability – 'real men in the real places' was a phrase he used on another occasion – the weapons expert Major Jefferis, and the tank expert General Hobart. The future of tank warfare, and the need for new weaponry, were two areas where Churchill pushed particularly hard for effective action. Several documents also testify to his determination not to see a repeat of what he called (*page 688*) 'the sombre mass slaughters' of the Somme and Passchendaele.

Not all Churchill's ideas for offensive action passed the scrutiny of his advisers: his desire to use British naval, air and military forces in the Mediterranean to seize the Italian island of Pantellaria, between North Africa and Sicily, was turned down by the Chiefs of Staff, over whom he had no ultimate powers of veto or control. 'Winston unhappy at his plan being turned down,' was Anthony Eden's comment (*page 1180*) in his diary.

One consistent aspect of Churchill's vigilance and involvement was the need to maintain secrecy, to reduce to an essential minimum the circulation of secret documents, and to respond to information acquired from the Germans' own top secret Enigma radio communications. These 'golden eggs', as Churchill called them, began to be of importance during the autumn of 1940, and remained so for the rest of the war. Enigma could be a mixed blessing: while revealing that German plans to invade Britain were being put in abeyance, it also revealed German designs on Greece, a British ally on whose behalf considerable diversion of resources was then made. Churchill and his advisers could piece together with considerable accuracy the German military build-up in the Balkans. 'The great thing is to get the true picture, whatever it is,' he told one of his senior advisers, as Britain, with her limited resources, prepared for the possibility of action in a new war zone.

The most difficult 'true picture' for Churchill to acquire was that regarding the United States, and the contribution it would make. From his first days as Prime Minister he understood the indispensable nature of American help in the long-term, and also sought such help, at the request of his most senior advisers, in the short term, especially with regard to destroyers. But the frustrations, uncertainties and set-backs in the search for American help were continuous throughout the first eight and a half months of his premiership. 'I must say I am a little impatient about the American scepticism,' he wrote in August 1940 (*page 701*), when American journalists had doubted the scale of British success during the Battle of Britain. 'There is something rather obnoxious in bringing correspondents down to air squadrons in order that they may assure the American public that the fighter pilots are not bragging.'

In his many messages to Roosevelt, Churchill tried to encourage the President with regard to Britain's ability to resist, and to accelerate the flow of supplies to Britain. He was not always successful. Seventeen days after he became Prime Minister he told the War Cabinet (*page 163*): 'The United States had given us practically no help in the war, and now that they saw how great was the danger, their attitude was that they wanted to keep everything which would help us for their own defence.' A few days later he telegraphed to the Canadian Prime Minister, William Mackenzie King, hoping to enlist his help with Roosevelt (*page 255*): 'Although President is our best friend, no practical help has been forthcoming from the United States as yet. We have not expected them to send military aid, but they have not even sent any worthy contribution in destroyers or planes.'

Churchill expended considerable energy in the matter of the American destroyers, explaining their need to Roosevelt and pressing for them when they were not forthcoming. When the destroyers eventually came, in return for American leases on British naval and air bases in the West Indies and Newfoundland, Churchill was obliged to send on to Roosevelt an Admiralty memorandum about the destroyers' lack of seaworthiness for war service. 'Please do not suppose we are making any complaints about the conditions of these vessels,' he wrote (*pages 1296–7*). 'It may however be an advantage to your yards to know the kind of things that happen when ships that have been laid up so long are put into the hardest service in the Atlantic.'

During the discussion about destroyers, Churchill resisted the suggestion that a condition for their despatch should be that in the event of a German victory, the British Fleet should be transferred to the Americans. 'Such a discussion, perhaps on the eve of an invasion, would be injurious to public morale, now so high,' Churchill told the Foreign Secretary in August 1940 (*pages 668–9*).

Shortly after the fall of France, Churchill had written with some bitterness to the British Ambassador in Washington, about the policy of the United States (*page 436*): 'Up till April they were so sure the Allies would win that they did not think help necessary. Now they are so sure that we shall lose that they do not think it possible.' He saw no point in making a broadcast appeal to the Americans. 'I don't think words count for much now,' he explained, and added, in his distress: 'We really have not had any help worth speaking of from the United States so far.' A few weeks later he commented bitterly to one of his staff that the United States was 'very good in applauding the valiant deeds done by others'. Throughout those days of danger, Churchill resented the influence of the American Ambassador in Britain, Joseph Kennedy (the father of the future President), who cast doubt on Britain's staying power, and on the value of any direct American military participation. 'It is astonishing', Churchill wrote to the Foreign Secretary in October 1940 (*page 901*), 'how this misleading stuff put out by Kennedy that we should do better with a neutral United States than with her warring at our side should have travelled so far.'

In December 1940, Churchill wrote what was arguably his most important letter to Roosevelt. Several documents in this volume show how the letter evolved. Churchill realised the importance of explaining to the President the very real danger facing Britain of German submarine strangulation, as well as the essential part which American shipping help would have to play if that danger was to be met in the coming year. In his letter, Churchill explained (*pages 1190–1*) that whereas the danger of Britain 'being destroyed by a swift, overwhelming blow' had for the time being greatly receded, 'In its place, there is a long, gradually-maturing danger, less sudden and less spectacular. This mortal danger is the steady and increasing diminution of sea tonnage.' The letter set out in detail what Churchill hoped the United States would do, and ended with a plea (*page 1196*) that Roosevelt would not restrict American assistance 'only to such munitions of war and commodities as could be immediately paid for'.

The threat of American aid coming to an end when Britain's ability to pay ran out, as, in December 1940, it was about to do, was a real one. In a further letter to Roosevelt three weeks later, on the last day of 1940, Churchill addressed this issue. I have included those draft sections of this letter, which on reflection Churchill felt it better not to send. In one of them, Churchill had wanted to react to the American demand to acquire what remained of Britain's gold reserves with the words (*page 1311*): 'It is not fitting that any nation should put itself wholly in the hands of another, least of all a nation which is fighting under increasingly severe conditions for what is proclaimed to be a cause of general concern.'

The documents assembled in this volume show many aspects of Churchill's war leadership that are often overlooked. His vigilant personal involvement in the day-to-day problems of invasion was continuous. Then, too, there was his concern for adequate air raid shelters, and his search for financial compensation for those who had lost their homes in the bombing.

Churchill's moods can be traced through the fortunes, ill-fortunes and frustrations of the war itself. When pressures were heavy, and the difficulties mounted, his anger could make itself felt and even those close to him could be bruised. Lord Halifax complained to a friend that Churchill was 'very arrogant and hates criticism of any kind' (*pages 483–4*). That same day, however, a general who visited him wrote in his diary: 'One cannot help Winston enough, although he seems to have courage for everybody.' Arrogance and courage were not incompatible, though during the first eight and a half months of his premiership, when his burdens were as heavy as they could be, arrogance was seldom in evidence, frustration and exhortation much more so.

There were other days on which, by chance, evidence survives of different, apparently conflicting moods. At the end of a day during which a Private Secretary found the Prime Minister (*page 558*) 'in a cantankerous frame of mind, demanding papers which were not available', the Commander-in-Chief, Home Forces, wrote in his diary: 'Just by ourselves at the end of a long day's work was rather trying. But he was very nice and I got a good insight into the way his brain is working. He is most interesting to listen to and full of the most marvellous courage, considering the burden he is bearing.' On one occasion, one of those close to the Prime Minister complained about his character to Clementine Churchill. She decided to send her husband a letter (she tore it up before sending it, then pieced it together again and sent it), warning him (*pages 425–6*) that 'there is a danger of your being generally disliked by your colleagues & subordinates because of your rough sarcastic & overbearing manner'. This was the same man who had been described three weeks earlier (*page 248*) as 'a mountain of energy and good nature', and within the following few weeks as (*page 523*) 'in wonderful spirits . . . full of offensive plans,' and (*page 651*) 'most genial'.

The background to all Churchill's moods was the uneven, often perilous course of the war: 'You must indeed have had a terrible time during the last fortnight,' the British Ambassador in Madrid wrote to Churchill a week after Clementine's letter of rebuke. The burdens could arise out of the blue, and in any aspect of war policy: a new war zone being opened up, as with Italy's entry into the conflict, the defeat of an ally, the build-up of German invasion preparations, the secret knowledge, derived from Enigma, of a possible new offensive or a new adversary, the close-run call of the Battle of Britain, the intensity and prolonged nature of the Blitz, deficiencies in arms and ammunition, the slow pace of American help: each was among the factors adding to the strains under which Churchill had to work, and which for him, and those closest to him in the War Cabinet and the Chiefs of Staff Committee, were a daily anxiety.

There is an example of this accumulation of anxieties in October 1940, when thirty-two British merchant ships were sunk in a single week. Churchill wrote to the Minister of Shipping (*page 993*): 'I follow these losses daily: and also the invasion risk. . . . Everything in our power will be done.' But that power was always limited, sometimes severely so, by the realities of Britain's military, naval and air weaknesses, the lessening of which was a central part of Churchill's daily activity. The documents in this volume, many of them from the most secret circles of government knowledge and discussion, show how many were the set-backs, how vast the areas of need, and how few were the avenues of hope, during the first eight and a half months of Churchill's Premiership. Not all the difficulties were known to the public: but all of them were known to the Prime Minister. Yet his exhortation 'Never Surrender', intended to raise the morale of the British people, was also a self-admonition. As he told one of his Private Secretaries (*page 735*): 'Each night I try myself by Court Martial to see if I have done anything effective during the day. I don't mean just pawing the ground, anyone can go through the motions, but something really effective.' The documents in this volume are a testimony to that effectiveness.

Martin Gilbert
Merton College
Oxford
9 June 1994

Acknowledgements
to the New Edition

The following foundations and individuals gave generous support for the publication of *Winston S. Churchill*, Volume VI: *Finest Hour, 1939–1941*, and volumes 14, 15, and 16 of *The Churchill Documents*: the Lynde and Harry Bradley Foundation, Milwaukee, Wisconsin; the Earhart Foundation, Ann Arbor, Michigan; the late George B. Ferguson, Peoria, Arizona; Mr. and Mrs. Thomas N. Jordan, Jr., Healdsburg, California; Mr. and Mrs. Tim M. Roudebush, Lenexa, Kansas; Mr. and Mrs. Emil A. Voelz, Jr., Akron, Ohio; and the Saul N. Silbert Charitable Trust, Sun City, Arizona.

Acknowledgements

I am grateful to all those who have responded to my request for material, or have answered my queries, in particular:

Miss P. M. Andrews, Cabinet Office, Historical and Records Section; Larry Arnn, Julie Kessler and Daniel Palm, the Claremont Institute, California; Joan Astley; Anna J. M. Azoulay, Secretary to the Military Attaché, Royal Netherlands Embassy;

Dr B. S. Benedikz, the University of Birmingham, University Library; Jeanne Berkeley; N. R. Bomford, Head Master, Harrow School; Commodore Jan Bring, Defence and Naval Attaché, Embassy of Sweden; Rosemary Buckley, Administrative Assistant, the Lord Mayor's Parlour, Birmingham;

Michael Chapman, Whitehall Library, Ministry of Defence; Professor Terry Copp, Wilfrid Laurier University, Waterloo, Ontario;

His Excellency Baron H. Dehennin, Belgian Embassy; Joan Delin; Minister-Counsellor M. Den Doncker, Belgian Embassy; Dr Christopher Dowling, Imperial War Museum;

His Excellency Lennart Eckerberg, The Ambassador, Swedish Embassy;

Lord Freyberg; Ray Funnell, Department of Research and Information Service, Royal Air Force Museum, Hendon;

Colonel Paul Gaujac, Chef du Service Historique de l'Armée de Terre, Ministry of Defence, Vincennes;

Marion Harding, Department of Archives, Photographs, Film and Sound, National Army Museum; M. L'Hévéder, French Embassy, London; Andrew Ingleby, Economics Division, Bank of England; Captain Claude Huan;

Neil Johannessen, Manager, British Telecommunications Museum; P. A. Judd, Assistant Librarian, Pembroke College, Cambridge;

Jacqueline Kavanagh, Written Archivist, BBC Written

Archives Centre; E. P. Kay, Welsh Office; Jill Kelsey, Assistant Registrar, Royal Archives, Windsor Castle;

David Littman;

Dr Alan McGowan, College Archivist, Royal Naval College, Greenwich; Len Mader, External Affairs, Ottawa; Brigadier B.S. Malik, Military Adviser, The High Commission of India; Joyce Markham, Library and Records Department, Foreign and Commonwealth Office; Alastair Massie, Department of Archives, Photographs, Film and Sound, National Army Museum; Lieutenant-Colonel Anthony Mather, Central Chancery of the Orders of Knighthood; Julia Mather, Editorial Assistant, Whitaker's Almanack; Captain Milewski, the Sikorski Institute;

Verne W. Newton, Director, Franklin D. Roosevelt Library; Claire Nutt, Library and Records Department, Foreign and Commonwealth Office;

Kate O'Brien, Military Archivist, King's College London; His Excellency Candemir Önhon, Ambassador of Turkey;

Penny Prior, Library and Records Department, Foreign and Commonwealth Office;

Gordon Ramsay; Christopher Reith; Denis Richards; Squadron-Leader David J. Richardson, RAAF, Assistant Air Attaché, Australian High Commission; General Robineau, Directeur du Service Historique de l'Armée de l'Air, Ministry of Defence, Vincennes;

Ivor Samuels; Richard Searle, Chief Librarian, Whitehall Library, Ministry of Defence;

Martin Taylor, Search Room Assistant, Churchill Archives Centre, Churchill College, Cambridge; Dr Vittorio Rocco di Torrepadula, Italian Embassy; Edward Thomas;

Pierre Waksman, Conservateur et Chef des Archives, Service historique de la Marine, Vincennes; Jeff Walden, BBC Written Archives Centre; Penny Ward, Heritage Officer, Thanet; Maria Warwick, Mayor's Secretary, Ramsgate; Lord Williams of Elvel; John S. Williams, City Archivist, Bristol City Council; Gillian Woodrow, Foreign and Commonwealth Office, Library Services; Enid Wurtman;

Dr Ronald W. Zweig.

For the preparation of the footnotes and the completion of the text, Elizabeth Jay, Rachelle Gryn and Abe Eisenstat each undertook research which helped to unravel some of the historical granny knots. During my work on the footnotes, I gained a great deal from the scrutiny of Adam O'Riordan, who until his untimely death gave me the benefit of his wide knowledge of grammar, syntax, history and literature.

The book was read in typescript by Elaine Donaldson and in proof by Frank Dunn, to both of whom my thanks are due. My editor at Heinemann, Lynne Drew, has been a pillar of strength throughout the work on this volume, and its predecessor, *At the Admiralty*. I am also grateful to Clare Blackwell, Production Controller, Reed Books. The considerable task of correspondence, including the search for the more elusive items of information, was carried out by Kay Thomson, both for this volume and its predecessor.

The publication of this volume, like its predecessor *At the Admiralty*, was made possible by the exceptional generosity of Wendy Reves, and by the determination of the International Churchill Society, and its United States president, Richard Langworth, to bring the Churchill document series, known as the companion volumes, back into production. I was also helped by the Hollinger Foundation, to whose Chairman, Conrad Black, himself a biographer, my thanks are due. I would like to thank the custodians, editors, authors and copyright holders of material in the following archives and books which I have used in the compilation of this volume:

The Royal Archives, Windsor; the Public Record Office, Kew, for the papers of the Cabinet Office, Prime Minister's Office, Ministry of Defence, Foreign Office, War Office, Air Ministry and Admiralty; Hansard (Parliamentary debates); Archives of *The Times*; BBC Written Archives Centre; Harrow School Archive.

The Earl of Avon papers (Anthony Eden) (Birmingham University Library), the Churchill papers (the Churchill Trust and Churchill College, Cambridge), Baldwin papers (Cambridge University Library), Balfour of Inchyre papers (Harold Balfour), Beaverbook papers, Captain Berkeley papers, Neville Chamberlain papers (Birmingham University Library), Camrose papers, Cherwell papers (Professor Lindemann) (Nuffield College, Oxford), Randolph Churchill papers, John Colville papers, G. M. O. Davy papers, Freyberg papers, Henley papers (Michael Eden), Marshall-Cornwall papers, John Martin papers, Harold Nicolson papers, John Peck papers, Richard Pim papers, Viscount Quickswood papers (Lord Hugh Cecil), Lord Reith papers (BBC Written Archives Centre); Franklin D. Roosevelt papers (Roosevelt Library), Eric Seal papers, Baroness Spencer-Churchill papers, Ronald Storrs papers (Pembroke College, Cambridge), G. R. Storry papers, Viscount Templewood papers (Sir Samuel Hoare) and Josiah Wedgwood papers.

I have also quoted from letters which I received from Samuel Battersby, Anthony Goldsmith, Grace Hamblin, Pamela Harriman, Squadron-Leader J. R. Kayll, Sir John Martin, Sir John Peck, General Sir Harold Redman and Sir Anthony Royle; from a conversation with Kathleen Hill; and from the following publications:

Lord Avon, *The Eden Memoirs, The Reckoning*, London, 1965.
Harold Balfour, *Wings over Westminster*. London, 1973.
The Private Diaries of Paul Baudouin, London, 1948.
Lord Birkenhead, *The Life of Lord Halifax*, London, 1965.
Michael Bloch, *The Duke of Windsor's War*, London, 1982.
Arthur Bryant, *The Turn of the Tide, 1939–1943, A Study based on the Diaries and Autobiographical Notes of Field Marshal the Viscount Alanbrooke*, London, 1957.
Barbara Cartland, *Ronald Cartland*, London, 1942.
Mary Churchill, *Clementine Churchill*, London, 1979.
Winston S. Churchill, *Great Contemporaries*, London, 1937.
Winston S. Churchill, *Into Battle* (compiled by Randolph S. Churchill), London, 1941.
Winston S. Churchill, *The Second World War* (volume two, *Their Finest Hour*), London, 1949.
Winston S. Churchill, *Secret Session Speeches* (edited by Charles Eade), London, 1946.
Lord Citrine, *Two Careers*, London, 1967.
John Colville, *Man of Valour, Field Marshal Lord Gort*, London, 1972.
John Colville, *The Fringes of Power, Downing Street Diaries 1939–1955*, London, 1985.

R. Coupland (editor), *The War Speeches of William Pitt the Younger*, third edition, Oxford, 1940.
Charles de Gaulle, *The Call to Honour, 1940–1942*, London, 1955.
David Dilks (editor), *The Diaries of Sir Alexander Cadogan, OM, 1938–1945*, London, 1971.
Paul Freyberg, *Bernard Freyberg VC, Soldier of Two Nations*, London, 1991.
Roy Harrod, *The Prof, A Personal Memoir of Lord Cherwell*, London, 1953.
Robert Rhodes James (editor), *Victor Cazalet, a Portrait*, London, 1976.
Robert Rhodes James (editor), *Chips, The Diaries of Sir Henry Channon*, London, 1967.
J. G. Lockhart, *Cosmo Gordon Lang*, London, 1949.
Ben Pimlott, *The Second World War Diary of Hugh Dalton*, London, 1986.
Colonel Roderick Macleod and Denis Kelly (editors), *The Ironside Diaries, 1937–1940*, London, 1962.
The Memoirs of General the Lord Ismay, London, 1960.
R. V. Jones, *Most Secret War*, London, 1978.
Paul Maze, *A Frenchman in Khaki*, London, 1934.
The Memoirs of Field Marshal the Viscount Montgomery of Alamein, London, 1958.
Lord Moran, *Winston Churchill, The Struggle for Survival*, London, 1966.
Malcolm Muggeridge (editor), *Ciano's Diaries, 1939–1943*, London, 1947.
Nigel Nicolson (editor), *Harold Nicolson, Diaries and Letters, 1939–1945*, London, 1967.
General Pile, *Ack-Ack*, London, 1949.
Paul Reynaud, *In the Thick of the Fight*, London, 1955.
Samuel I. Rosenman (editor), *The Public Papers and Addresses of Franklin D. Roosevelt*, volume for 1940, New York, 1941.
Captain S. W. Roskill, *The War at Sea 1939–1945*, volume one, London, 1954.
William Shirer, *Berlin Diary*, London, 1941.
Hugh Skillen, *Spies of the Airwaves*, London, 1989.
E. L. Spears, *Assignment to Catastrophe*, volume one, *Prelude to Dunkirk*, London, 1954.

E. L. Spears, *Assignment to Catastrophe*, volume two, *The Fall of France, June 1940*, London, 1954.
John Spencer-Churchill, *Crowded Canvas*, London, 1961.
Charles Stuart, *The Reith Diaries*, London, 1975.
V. E. Tarrant, *King George V Class Battleships*, London, 1991.
H. G. Wells, *Men like Gods*, London, 1923.
John Wheeler-Bennett, *King George VI*, London, 1958.
John Wheeler-Bennett (editor), *Action This Day, Working with Churchill*, London, 1968.
Evelyn Wrench, *Geoffrey Dawson and our Times*, London, 1955.

I have also quoted contemporary reports from the following newspapers: *The Times, Atlantic Monthly, Daily Express, Daily Mail, Evening Standard, Isle of Thanet Gazette, Listener, Sunday Dispatch* and *Sunday Express*. The cartoons reproduced in this volume first appeared in the *Evening Standard, Punch, Daily Express, Daily Mail* and the *Daily Mirror*.

As the last thank you, soaring above all others, I would like to acknowledge the help, encouragement and enthusiasm of my wife Susie, the staunch supporter of my Churchill efforts for more than twenty years.

May 1940

ON THE EVENING of Friday, 10 May 1940, Churchill became Prime Minister. The news was announced by his predecessor, Neville Chamberlain, when he spoke on the wireless that night. It was overshadowed in most of the morning newspapers on Saturday, 11 May, by the news that German forces had invaded Belgium, Holland and France.

Lord Cranborne[1] to Winston S. Churchill
(*Churchill papers, 2/393*)

11 May 1940

My dear Winston,

Very warmest congratulations on the news, which we heard on the wireless last night. You have, I am afraid, got a very tough job, but at any rate the very fact that you are in charge will carry, both to our friends and our enemies abroad, a conviction of British resolution, in a way nothing else could do. If only you had been listened to sooner; but, in the words of Sir Archibald Southby,[2] it's no good gobbing back.

---

[1] Robert Arthur James Gascoyne-Cecil, Viscount Cranborne, 1893–1972, known as 'Bobbety'. Eldest son of the 4th Marquess of Salisbury. Conservative MP for South Dorset, 1929–41. Parliamentary Secretary of State for Foreign Affairs, 1935–8; resigned with Anthony Eden, February 1938. Paymaster-General, 1940. Privy Councillor, 1940. Summoned to the House of Lords in his father's barony of Cecil of Essendon, 1941. Secretary of State for Dominion Affairs, 1940–2 and 1943–5; for the Colonies, 1942. Leader of the House of Lords, 1942–5. Knight of the Garter, 1946. Succeeded his father as 5th Marquess, 1947. Lord Privy Seal, 1951–2. Secretary of State for Commonwealth Relations, 1952. Lord President of the Council, 1952–7. Leader of the House of Lords, 1951–7. In 1937 he was elected to the Other Club (founded by Churchill and F. E. Smith in 1911).

[2] Archibald Richard James Southby, 1886–1969. Entered the Royal Navy, 1901; Commander, 1920. Conservative MP, 1928–47. Assistant Government Whip, 1931–5. Junior Lord of the Treasury, 1935–7. Created Baronet, 1937. A member of the Parliamentary Delegation to Buchenwald concentration camp, April 1945.

May 1940

Alice, Lady Wimborne[1] to Winston S. Churchill
(*Churchill papers, 2/399*)

11 May 1940
Ashby St Ledgers, Rugby

Dearest Winston,

In this moment of stress you should not be burdened with letters. But the ties of gratitude and affection of a life time are too strong for even such a reason preventing me from adding my loving congratulations to the myriad of them you will receive. I look back to the days when you were so much here, you and Ivor[2] little more than boys when he and I were first married. And all our plots for the discomfiture of St John Brodrick! which duly took place in the House the day the present Ivor[3] was born. Now you are Prime Minister of England. The young eagle of those days soared quickly to great heights – & finally is perched upon the summit of the greatest mountain in the world.

The other one so gifted so forceful too in his way has left us . . .

Lady Violet Bonham Carter[4] to Winston Churchill
(*Churchill papers, 2/392*)

11 May 1940

Dearest Winston,

My wish is realized – I can now face all that is to come with faith & confidence.

I know, as you do, that the wind has been sown, & that, we must all reap the whirlwind. But you will ride it – instead of being driven before it – Thank

---

[1] Alice Katherine Sibell Grosvenor, 1880–1948. Younger daughter of the 2nd Baron Ebury. She married Ivor Guest (later 1st Viscount of Wimborne) in 1902. On the death of the 1st Viscount, on 14 June 1939, their only son Ivor succeeded as 2nd Viscount Wimborne. Born in 1903, he had been Conservative MP for Brecon and Radnor, 1935–9; he was to be Parliamentary Under-Secretary of State for Air, 1943–5, and Liberal Whip in the House of Lords, 1944–8.

[2] Ivor Churchill Guest, 1873–1939. Son of Ivor Bertie Guest and Lady Cornelia Spencer Churchill (Churchill's aunt). On active service in South Africa, 1900. Conservative MP for Plymouth, 1900–6. Liberal MP for Cardiff, 1906–10. Created Baron Ashby St Ledgers, 1910. Paymaster-General, 1910–12. Succeeded his father as 2nd Baron Wimborne, 1914. Lord Lieutenant of Ireland, 1915–18. Created Viscount, 1918.

[3] Ivor Grosvenor Guest, 1903–67. Eldest son of Churchill's cousin the 1st Viscount Wimborne. Educated at Eton and Trinity College, Cambridge. Liberal MP for Brecon and Radnor, November 1935 to June 1939. Succeeded his father as 2nd Viscount, June 1939. On active service in the Second World War; Major, Royal Armoured Corps, 1943. Parliamentary Private Secretary to the Under-Secretary of State for Air (Lord Sherwood), 1943–5. Liberal Whip in the House of Lords, 1944–8. Chairman of the Governors of Stowe School, 1952–60. OBE, 1953.

[4] Helen Violet Asquith, 1887–1969. Elder daughter of H. H. Asquith. Educated in Dresden and Paris. Married, 1915, Sir Maurice Bonham Carter (who died in 1960). President of the Women's Liberal Federation, 1923–5 and 1939–45; President of the Liberal Party Organisation, 1945–7. A Governor of the BBC, 1941–6. Member of the Royal Commission on the Press, 1947–9. Unsuccessful Liberal candidate, 1945 and 1951. DBE, 1953; created Baroness Asquith of Yarnbury, 1964. Published *Winston Churchill as I Knew Him*, 1965.

Heaven that you are there, & at the helm of our destiny – & may the nation's spirit be kindled by your own.

God bless & keep you – & England

Ever your
Violet

Venetia Montagu[1] to Winston S. Churchill
(Churchill papers, 2/396)

11 May 1940　　　　　　　　　　　　　　　　　　Beccles Hall, Norfolk

Darling I want to add my voice to the great paean of joy which has gone up all over the civilized world when you became PM. Thank God at last.

As one of your oldest friends (for I am almost getting to be that now) I must tell you how I rejoice that you have been given the chance of saving us all.

Don't please answer, or I shall feel I shouldn't have written.

Much love
Venetia

Incidentally how nice to have No. 10 once more occupied by someone one loves.[2]

Nellie Romilly[3] to Winston S. Churchill
(Churchill papers, 1/355)

11 May 1940　　　　　　　　　　　　　　　　　　　　Huntington Park
　　　　　　　　　　　　　　　　　　　　　　　　　　　　Kington
　　　　　　　　　　　　　　　　　　　　　　　　　　Herefordshire

Dearest Winston,

I can't forbear sending you my dearest love that you have at last taken control, at the grandest & most awful moment in the world's history.

I could have wished that my Bertram could have lived to know it – but he had reached the highest peak of human suffering before peace came. His heart

---

[1] Beatrice Venetia Stanley, 1887–1948. Clementine Churchill's cousin. The confidante of Asquith from 1912 to 1915, she married Edwin Montagu in July 1915. Her London house was at 62 Onslow Gardens, Kensington, and her country house, Beccles Hall, in Norfolk. Her husband died in 1924.

[2] Churchill replied by telegram: 'Thank you so much dear Venetia, Winston.'

[3] Nellie Hozier, 1888–1957. Clementine Churchill's sister. Served as a nurse in Belgium, 1914. Captured by the Germans, but released almost immediately. In 1915 she married Colonel Bertram Romilly.

was broken because he couldn't serve his country. He often said to me 'I am only struggling to live as I don't want to waste Winston's 100 guineas for my operation'.[1]

It was v sweet of you to have let Clemmie[2] come down just when you needed her so much. No one here will ever forget your visit here. Keep strong.

Best love from
Nellie R

Vic Oliver[3] to Winston S. Churchill
(*Churchill papers, 1/355*)

11 May 1940

Dear Mr Churchill,

Sarah[4] and I are thrilled beyond words, not only because we know how happy you must be, but also because we feel the same as the entire nation feels; that the right man is in the right job.

---

[1] The 1993 equivalent of 100 guineas in 1940 was somewhat more than £2,000.

[2] Clementine Hozier, 1885–1977. Daughter of Lady Blanche Ogilvy (eldest daughter of the 10th Earl of Airlie) and Colonel Henry Hozier, soldier, war correspondent and (from 1874) Secretary to the Corporation of Lloyd's of London, insurance underwriters. She married Churchill in 1908; they had five children, Diana (born 1909), Randolph (born 1911), Sarah (born 1914), Marigold (born 1919) and Mary (born 1922). In the First World War Clementine Churchill was active providing, through the YWCA, canteens for munitions workers; in the Second World War she presided over the Red Cross Aid to Russia Fund and the Fulmer Chase Maternity Home. From 1914 to 1947 she was also President of the YWCA War and National Fund, and from 1949 to 1951 Chairman of the YWCA National Hostels Committee. Created Baroness Spencer-Churchill, 1965; she took her seat on the cross benches, and not only attended the House of Lords thirteen times in seven months, but voted in favour of the abolition of the death penalty on 20 July 1965. A Trustee of Lord Attlee's Memorial Foundation, 1966. President of the National Benevolent Fund for the Aged, 1972. For a comprehensive account of her life, see Mary Soames, *Clementine Churchill*, London 1976.

[3] Victor Samek, 1898–1964. Born in Austria, the son of Baron Victor von Samek. Educated at the University of Vienna. Relinquished his father's title, 1922. A concert pianist, he worked in the United States from 1933 to 1935 under the stage name Vic Oliver; subsequently he worked on the stage and in revues in Britain and America. Married, as his third wife, Sarah Churchill, 1936 (from whom he obtained a divorce in 1945).

[4] Sarah Millicent Hermione Spencer Churchill, 1914–83. Born while her father was returning from the siege of Antwerp, 7 October 1914. Edward Marsh was her godfather. She married Vic Oliver on 25 December 1936 (divorced, 1945). On stage in Birmingham, Southampton, Weston-super-Mare and London, 1937–9; on tour with Vic Oliver in the play *Idiot's Delight*, 1938. Playing on the London stage in *Quiet Wedding*, 1939; in J. M. Barrie's *Mary Rose*, 1940. Appeared in the film *Spring Meeting*, 1940. Entered the Women's Auxiliary Air Force, October 1941; Assistant Section Officer (later Section Officer) at the Photographic Interpretation Unit, Medmenham, 1941–5. Accompanied her father (as ADC), to the Teheran Conference, November 1943, and to Yalta, February 1945. In 1949 she married Anthony Beauchamp, who died in 1957. In April 1962 she married the 23rd Baron Audley, MBE, who died in July 1963. In 1951 she appeared on the stage in the United States in *Grammercy Ghost*. She published *The Empty Spaces* (poems) in 1966, and *A Thread in the Tapestry* (recollections) in 1967, *Collected Poems* in 1974 and *Keep on Dancing* (further recollections) in 1981.

May 1940

We are sending you all our love, affection and admiration. May you be completely successful!

Yours
Vic & Sarah

Major-General Sir Hugh Tudor[1] to Winston S. Churchill
(*Churchill papers, 2/399*)

11 May 1940

My dear Winston,

Nobody can be more glad than I am that you are Prime Minister at last. I have always believed you should and would be; and now, in these tragic days, it is obvious to everybody that you are the man for the job.

That a soldier[2] should be head of the Government in this war is a good omen – for the first time in History I think![3]

Wishing you complete success and victory.

Yours ever
Hugh Tudor

Major-General Sir Reginald Barnes[4] to Winston S. Churchill
(*Churchill papers, 2/392*)

11 May 1940

My dear old Winston,

As your very old & admiring Friend I must add my little song to the chorus of congratulations which you are no doubt getting. I am so glad dear old pal,

---

[1] Henry Hugh Tudor, 1871–1965. 2nd Lieutenant, Royal Artillery, 1890. On active service in South Africa, 1899–1902. Brigadier-General commanding the Artillery of the 9th (Scottish) Division, 1916–18. Major-General commanding the 9th Division, 21–24 March 1918. Major-General commanding the Irregular Forces in Ireland (the 'Black and Tans'), 1920–1. General Officer Commanding the special gendarmerie in Palestine (known as 'Tudor's lambs'), 1922, with the rank of Air Vice-Marshal. Knighted, 1923. Retired, 1923, and lived in Newfoundland. In 1959 he published his First World War diaries, entitled *The Fog of War*.

[2] Churchill had been gazetted Second Lieutenant in 1895. He had seen action as a Lieutenant on the North-West Frontier of India, in the Sudan and in South Africa. For six months in 1916 he had been Lieutenant-Colonel commanding the 6th Royal Scots Fusiliers on the Western Front.

[3] The Duke of Wellington had been Prime Minister only in peacetime. Neither of the First World War prime ministers, Asquith and Lloyd George, had any military experience.

[4] Reginald Walter Ralph Barnes, 1871–1946. Joined the 4th Hussars, 1890. Travelled with Churchill to Cuba, to witness the Spanish struggle against the Cuban insurgents, 1895. Adjutant, 4th Hussars, 1896–1900. On active service in South Africa, 1899–1902 (severely wounded, despatches, DSO), and in the European War, 1914–18 (wounded twice, despatches seven times, promoted Major-General). Knighted, 1919. Retired from the Army, 1920.

the country could not be in better hands, & I only wish there was any small way in which I could help you ? in your immense task.

I have always felt it in my bones that the Huns would use the same old battleground.[1]

Every success & all luck to you.

Reggie

Admiral of the Fleet Sir Charles Forbes[2] to Winston S. Churchill
(*Churchill papers, 2/405*)

11 May 1940

My dear Prime Minister,

You were good enough to congratulate me on my promotion a fortnight or so ago; allow me to return the compliment & congratulate you most heartily on becoming Prime Minister but I am sorry you have left the Admiralty.

May I also thank you for your speech on Wednesday.[3] In spite of the way our adventure in the middle of Norway ended I am still of opinion, like you, that provided we get firmly established in the Narvik area the Hun will be very sorry he ever went in to Norway.

There is no getting over the fact that unless an Army is underground it cannot function if the enemy has control of the air but it has not yet come to that as regards Naval Forces. The little ships were magnificent & they are going to give a good account of themselves down South.

I hope you will go on with the 'Marines'.[4]

Good luck to you in your difficult task & my best wishes.

Yours sincerely,
Charles Forbes

---

[1] As in 1914, the German Army was advancing through Belgium, in order to strike at France from the north-east and avoid the French fortifications along the Rhine and the Maginot Line.

[2] Charles Morton Forbes, 1880–1960. Entered the Royal Navy, 1894. Served at Jutland, 1916 (DSO). Director of Naval Ordnance, 1925–8. Third Sea Lord and Controller of the Navy, 1932–4. Vice-Admiral, 1st Battle Squadron, 1934–6. Knighted, 1935. Commander-in-Chief, Home Fleet, 1938–40; Plymouth, 1941–3.

[3] Churchill's speech on 8 May 1940, at the conclusion of the Norway debate, is published in full in the previous volume of the Churchill War Papers, *At the Admiralty*.

[4] 'Marines', or more usually 'Royal Marine', was a code name for the plan to drop mines in the River Rhine and its tributaries, and also in the Danube, to disrupt German barge traffic. The mining of the Rhine began that day (11 May 1940).

May 1940

Winston S. Churchill to Neville Chamberlain[1]
(Churchill papers, 20/11)

11 May 1940

My dear Neville,

I had a long talk last night with Attlee[2] and Greenwood,[3] and they made it clear that in a War Cabinet of six or seven they would both expect places. I indicated that I should want Alexander,[4] Morrison[5] and Bevin,[6] as well

---

[1] Arthur Neville Chamberlain, 1869–1940. Son of Joseph Chamberlain, his mother died in childbirth in 1875. Educated at Rugby and Mason College, Birmingham. In business in the Bahamas, 1890–7. Lord Mayor of Birmingham, 1915–16. Director-General of National Service, 1916–17 (when his cousin Norman, to whom he was devoted, was killed in action on the Western Front). Conservative MP for Ladywood, 1918–29; for Edgbaston, 1929–40. Postmaster-General, 1922–3. Paymaster-General, 1923. Minister of Health, 1923, 1924–9 and 1931. Chancellor of the Exchequer, 1923–4 and 1931–7. Leader of the Conservative Party, 1937. Prime Minister, 1937–40. Lord President of the Council, May–November 1940.

[2] Clement Richard Attlee, 1883–1967. Educated at Haileybury and University College, Oxford. Called to the Bar, 1906. Tutor and lecturer, London School of Economics, 1913–23. On active service at Gallipoli, Mesopotamia (wounded) and France, 1914–19; Major, 1917. First Labour Mayor of Stepney, 1919, 1920; Alderman, 1920–7. Labour MP for Limehouse, 1922–50; for West Walthamstow, 1950–5. Parliamentary Private Secretary to Ramsay MacDonald, 1922–4. Under-Secretary of State for War, 1924. Chancellor of the Duchy of Lancaster, 1930–1. Postmaster-General, 1931. Deputy Leader of the Labour Party in the House of Commons, 1931–5. Leader of the Opposition, 1935–40. Lord Privy Seal, 1940–2. Deputy Prime Minister, 1942–5. Lord President of the Council, 1943–5. Prime Minister, 1945–51 (Minister of Defence, 1945–6). Leader of the Opposition, 1951–5. Created Earl, 1955.

[3] Arthur Greenwood, 1880–1954. Lecturer in economics, Leeds University, and Chairman of the Yorkshire District Workers' Educational Association. Assistant Secretary, Ministry of Reconstruction, 1917–19. Labour MP for Nelson and Colne, 1922–31; for Wakefield, 1932–54. Parliamentary Secretary, Ministry of Health, 1924. Minister of Health, 1929–31. Privy Councillor, 1929; Deputy Leader of the Labour Party, 1935. Member of the War Cabinet, 1940–2. Lord Privy Seal, 1945–7. Chairman of the Labour Party, 1952.

[4] Albert Victor Alexander, 1885–1965. Educated at an elementary school, and technical classes, in Bristol. Labour (Co-operative) MP for Hillsborough, 1922–31 and 1935–50. Parliamentary Secretary, Board of Trade, 1924. First Lord of the Admiralty in Ramsay MacDonald's second Labour Government, 1929–31; in Churchill's wartime Coalition Government, 1940–5; and in Attlee's Labour Government, 1945–6. Member of the Cabinet Delegation to India, 1946. Minister of Defence, 1947–50. Created Viscount, 1950. Chancellor of the Duchy of Lancaster, 1950–1. Leader of the Labour Peers in the House of Lords, 1955–65. Created Earl, 1963. Knight of the Garter, 1964.

[5] Herbert Stanley Morrison, 1888–1965. Errand boy, shop assistant, telephone operator, newspaper circulation manager. Secretary to the London Labour Party, 1915–47. Mayor of Hackney, 1920–1. Labour MP, 1923–4, 1929–31 and 1935–51. Minister of Transport, 1929–31. Member, National Service Committee for London, 1939–40; London Regional Council for Civil Defence, 1939–40. Minister of Supply, 12 May to October 1940. Home Secretary and Minister of Home Security, 1940–5. Member of the War Cabinet, 1942–5. Deputy Prime Minister (under Clement Attlee), 1945–51 (also Lord President of the Council and Leader of the House of Commons). Secretary of State for Foreign Affairs, 1951. Deputy Leader of the Opposition, 1951–5. Created Baron, 1959.

[6] Ernest Bevin, 1881–1951. National Organiser, Dockers' Union, 1910–21. General Secretary, Transport and General Workers' Union, 1921–40. Member of the Trades Union Congress General Council, 1925–40. Labour MP for Central Wandsworth, 1940–50; for East Woolwich, 1950–1. Minister of Labour and National Service, 1940–5. Privy Councillor, 1940. Secretary of State for Foreign Affairs, 1945–51. Lord Privy Seal, 1951.

as their proportion of Under-Secretaries. Dalton[1] also will have to be considered. They mentioned the Trades Disputes Act, but agreed that I was right in refusing any condition of that character.[2]

Sinclair[3] would like very much to take the Air Ministry, but Party dignity requires him to hold out for a seat in the War Cabinet, and I do not see at present how this can be arranged without adding to our numbers unduly.

I hope to have the War Cabinet and the Fighting Services complete to-night for the King.[4] The haste is necessitated by the battle.

I should be most grateful to you if you would lead the House of Commons as Lord President of the Council, and as we must work so closely together, I hope you will not find it inconvenient to occupy once again your old quarters, which we both know so well, in No. 11.[5]

I do not think there is any necessity for a Cabinet to-day, as the Armies and other Services are fighting in accordance with pre-arranged plans. I should be very glad, however, if you and Edward[6] would come to the Admiralty War

---

[1] Edward Hugh John Neale Dalton, 1887–1962. Educated at Eton and King's College, Cambridge: Barrister, 1914. On active service in France and Italy, 1914–18. Lecturer, London School of Economics, 1919. Reader in Commerce, University of London, 1920–5; Reader in Economics, 1925–6. Labour MP for Camberwell, 1924–9; for Bishop Auckland, 1929–31 and 1935–59. Parliamentary Under-Secretary, Foreign Office, 1929–31. Chairman, National Executive of the Labour Party, 1936–7. Minister of Economic Warfare, 1940–2. President of the Board of Trade, 1942–5. Chancellor of the Exchequer, 1945–7; resigned over a Budget leak, 1947. Minister of Town and Country Planning, 1950–1. Created Baron, 1960.

[2] The Trades Disputes and Trade Unions Act of 1927 was not repealed until 1946, when Labour was in power. The 1927 Act made illegal a sympathetic strike or a lockout designed to coerce the Government. It also severed the connection between civil service organisations and other unions, and it imposed restrictions on the unions' political activities and their conduct of trade disputes. The political levy could only be raised from workers who 'contracted in'.

[3] Archibald Henry Macdonald Sinclair, 1890–1970. Educated at Eton and Sandhurst. Entered the Army, 1910. 4th Baronet, 1912. Captain, 1915. Second-in-Command of the 6th Royal Scots Fusiliers while Churchill was in command, January–May 1916. Squadron-Commander, 2nd Life Guards, 1916–18. Elected to the Other Club, 1917. Major, Guards Machine Gun Regiment, 1918. Private Secretary to Churchill, Ministry of Munitions, 1918–19. Churchill's personal Military Secretary, War Office, 1919–21. Churchill's Private Secretary, Colonial Office, 1921–2. Liberal MP for Caithness and Sutherland, 1922–45. Secretary of State for Scotland, 1931–3. Leader of the Parliamentary Liberal Party, 1935–45. Secretary of State for Air in Churchill's wartime Coalition Government, 1940–5. Knight of the Thistle, 1941. Created Viscount Thurso, 1952.

[4] Albert Frederick Arthur George, 1895–1952. Second son of King George V. Educated at the Royal Naval Colleges, Osborne and Dartmouth; Lieutenant, 1918. Succeeded his brother as King, December 1936. Crowned (as George VI), May 1937.

[5] As Chancellor of the Exchequer, Churchill had lived at 11 Downing Street from 1924 to 1929, Chamberlain from 1931 to 1937.

[6] Edward Frederick Lindley Wood, 1881–1959. Educated at Eton and Christ Church, Oxford. Conservative MP for Ripon, 1910–25. Parliamentary Under-Secretary of State for the Colonies, 1921–2. President of the Board of Education, 1922–4. Minister of Agriculture, 1924–5. Created Baron Irwin, 1925. Viceroy of India, 1926–31. President of the Board of Education, 1931–4. Succeeded his father as 3rd Viscount Halifax, 1934. Secretary of State for War, 1935. Lord Privy Seal, 1935–7. Lord President of the Council, 1937–8. Foreign Secretary, 1938–40. Ambassador in Washington, 1941–6. Order of Merit, 1946. One of his three sons was killed in action in Egypt in October 1942.

Room at 12.30 p.m., so that we could look at the maps and talk things over.

British and French advanced forces are already on the Antwerp–Namur line, and there seems to be very good hopes that this line will be strongly occupied by the Allied Armies before it can be assailed. This should be achieved in about 48 hours, and might be thought to be very important. Meanwhile the Germans have not yet forced the Albert Canal, and the Belgians are reported to be fighting well. The Dutch also are making a stubborn resistance.

Yours very sincerely,
Winston S. Churchill

Neville Chamberlain to Winston S. Churchill
(Churchill papers, 20/11)

11 May 1940   10 Downing Street
Private

My dear Winston,

Thank you very much for your letter of this morning.

As regards myself, I shall gladly fall in with your suggestion that I should lead in the Commons as Lord President of the Council. In my judgment I can help you best in an office of this kind.

The Labour Party are, I think, not unreasonable in asking for a prominent position in the War Cabinet, but it is the personalities that matter, and although Greenwood would be amiable and agreeable enough I do not think he could contribute much else.

I hope you will take particular care how you fill the Ministry of Supply.[1] This is a key post in the war and it is of the first importance to your own position that it should be carried by a man who will give confidence.

I will come over to the Admiralty with Edward at 12.30. Until you get your places filled we three will have to take the responsibility of directing the war.

Yours ever
Neville Chamberlain

---

[1] That day Churchill appointed the Labour Party stalwart Herbert Morrison as Minister of Supply. He was replaced five months later by a businessman, Sir Andrew Duncan. In January 1941 the position went to Lord Beaverbrook, who had previously been Minister of Aircraft Production. Andrew Duncan returned in February 1942 and remained at Supply until the end of the war.

May 1940

Lord Halifax to Winston S. Churchill
(*Churchill papers, 20/11*)

11 May 1940

My dear Winston,

I know how great is the burden that you have courageously taken upon yourself. And if I can lighten it in any degree by helping out on this FO side of the work, of course I will readily do so. You know me well enough to feel sure that if you ever come to think otherwise, you need never hesitate to do so. In these critical hours, I shall be happy to feel as you said the other afternoon that you, Neville and I can be together.

But I don't think you really mean me to lead the H/L.[1] That is impossible & I had to give up when I came to the FO, for it means being in the H/L every day. So I would beg you to think again about that! I fear the two are really incompatible.

I need not tell you how wholly my thoughts & wishes are with you in the leadership it now falls to you to give to us all. God bless you always.

Yrs ever
Edward

Meeting of Ministers[2]: minutes
(*Cabinet papers, 65/7*)

11 May 1940   Admiralty
12.30 p.m.

NORWAY

The Chief of the Imperial General Staff[3] said that two reports had been received of parachute troops being dropped by the enemy in Northern Norway.

---

[1] House of Lords.

[2] The three members of the War Cabinet present at this first Ministerial meeting of Churchill's premiership were Churchill (Prime Minister, in the Chair), Neville Chamberlain, and Lord Halifax (Secretary of State for Foreign Affairs). Also present were Air Chief Marshal Sir Cyril L. N. Newall (Chief of the Air Staff), General Sir W. Edmund Ironside (Chief of the Imperial General Staff), Admiral of the Fleet Sir Dudley Pound (First Sea Lord and Chief of Naval Staff), and General Sir John Dill (Vice-Chief of the Imperial General Staff). The two members of the Secretariat present were Sir Edward Bridges and Major-General H. L. Ismay.

[3] William Edmund Ironside, 1880–1959. 2nd Lieutenant, Royal Artillery, 1899. On active service in South Africa, 1899–1902. Major, 1914. Staff Officer, 4th Canadian Division, 1916–17. Took part in the battles for Vimy Ridge and Passchendaele. Commandant of the Machine Gun Corps School, France, 1918. Brigadier-General commanding the 99th Infantry Brigade, 1918. Major-General commanding the Allied Troops, Archangel, October 1918 to October 1919. Knighted, 1919. Head of the British Military Mission to Hungary, 1920. Commanded the Ismid Force, Turkey, 1920; the North Persian Force, 1920–1. Lieutenant-General, 1931. Quartermaster-General, India, 1933–6. General, 1935. General Officer Commanding-in-Chief, Eastern

MAY 1940

'ROYAL MARINE'

The Prime Minister said that the 'Royal Marine' Operation had been started. The first of the fluvial mines ought to reach Mannheim in the course of that afternoon.

INVASION OF GREAT BRITAIN

The Prime Minister raised the question whether the Police should be armed.

General Ismay[1] was instructed to take up this point with the Minister of Home Security[2] and the Secretary of State for War.[3]

SWEDEN

The Prime Minister referred to the probable effect on public opinion in Sweden of the invasion of Holland and Belgium. Was it not worth while to try to make Sweden realise that Germany had no regard for the interests of small

Command, 1936–8. Governor and Commander-in-Chief, Gibraltar, 1938–9. Head of the British Military Mission to Poland, August 1939. Chief of the Imperial General Staff, 1939–40. Commander-in-Chief, Home Forces, May to July 1940. Field Marshal, 1940. Created Baron, 1941. On 4 July 1938 Churchill wrote of Ironside, to Sir Abe Bailey: 'He is the finest military brain in the Army at the present time.'

[1] Hastings Lionel Ismay, 1887–1965. Known as 'Pug'. Educated at Charterhouse and Sandhurst. 2nd Lieutenant, 1905; Captain, 1914. On active service in India, 1908, and Somaliland, 1914–20 (DSO). Staff College, Quetta, 1922. Assistant Secretary, Committee of Imperial Defence, 1925–30. Military Secretary to the Viceroy of India (Lord Willingdon), 1931–3. Colonel, 1932. Deputy Secretary, Committee of Imperial Defence, 1936–8; Secretary (in succession to Sir Maurice Hankey), 1938. Major-General, 1939. Chief of Staff to the Minister of Defence (Churchill), 1940–5. Knighted, 1940. Deputy Secretary (military) to the War Cabinet, 1940–5. Lieutenant-General, 1942. General, 1944. Chief of Staff to the Viceroy of India (Lord Mountbatten), 1947. Created Baron, 1947. Secretary of State for Commonwealth Relations, 1951–2. Secretary-General of NATO, 1952–7. Knight of the Garter, 1957. He published his memoirs in 1960.

[2] John Anderson, 1882–1958. Educated at Edinburgh and Leipzig Universities. Entered the Colonial Office, 1905; Secretary, Northern Nigeria Lands Committee, 1909. Secretary to the Insurance Commissioners, London, 1913. Secretary, Ministry of Shipping, 1917–19. Knighted, 1919. Chairman of the Board of Inland Revenue, 1919–20. Joint Under-Secretary of State in the Government of Ireland, 1920. Permanent Under-Secretary of State, Home Office, 1922–32. Governor of Bengal, 1932–7. MP for the Scottish Universities, 1928–50. Lord Privy Seal, 1938–9. Home Secretary and Minister of Home Security, 1939–40. (The Anderson Shelter was named after him: every household was encouraged to have one.) Lord President of the Council, 1940–3. Chancellor of the Exchequer, 1943–5. Chairman of the Port of London Authority, 1946–58. Created Viscount Waverley, 1952. Order of Merit, 1957. Member of the BBC General Advisory Council.

[3] Robert Anthony Eden, 1897–1977. Educated at Eton and Christ Church, Oxford. Served on the Western Front, 1915–18, when he was awarded the Military Cross. Conservative MP, 1923–57. Parliamentary Under-Secretary, Foreign Office, 1931–3. Lord Privy Seal, 1934–5. Minister for League of Nations Affairs, 1935. Foreign Secretary, 1935–8. Secretary of State for Dominion Affairs, September 1939 to May 1940. Secretary of State for War, May–December 1940. Foreign Secretary, December 1940 to July 1945, and October 1951 to April 1955. Knight of the Garter, 1954. Prime Minister, 1955–7. Created Earl of Avon, 1961. One of his brothers was killed near Ypres in October 1914, another in 1916 at the Battle of Jutland. His elder son was killed in action in Burma on 23 June 1945, aged twenty.

nations? If Sweden could be induced to come into the war on our side, the whole position in Scandinavia would be changed.

The Secretary of State for Foreign Affairs[1] undertook to put this point forcibly to the Swedish Minister,[2] but without much hope that it would affect Sweden's attitude.

It was agreed to meet again at 10 p.m. that night.

Meeting of Ministers: minutes
(*Cabinet papers, 65/7*)

11 May 1940　　　　　　　　　　　　　　　　　　　　　　　　　Admiralty
10.30 p.m.

Ministers were given the latest information in regard to operations in Holland and Belgium.

Discussion ensued as to the prospects of a German thrust reaching the Dyle line before our forces had succeeded in establishing themselves.

John Colville[3]: diary
(*Colville papers*)

11 May 1940

There seems to be some inclination in Whitehall to believe that Winston will be a complete failure and that Neville will return.

---

[1] Lord Halifax.

[2] Bjorn Prytz, 1887–1976. Managing Director of the Swedish company SKF (Swedish Ballbearings), 1919–37. Swedish Minister to London, 1938–47.

[3] John Rupert Colville, 1915–87. Educated at Harrow and Trinity College, Cambridge. Entered the Diplomatic Service, 1937. Assistant Private Secretary to Neville Chamberlain, 1939–40; to Churchill, 1940–1 and 1943–5; to Clement Attlee, 1945. Private Secretary to Princess Elizabeth, 1947–9. CVO, 1949. First Secretary, British Embassy, Lisbon, 1949–51. Joint Principal Private Secretary to the Prime Minister (Churchill), 1951–5. CB, 1955. Active in the creation of Churchill College, Cambridge. Director of Hill Samuel, merchant bankers, 1955–80. Knighted, 1974. Author of *Fool's Pleasure*, 1935. Contributor to *Action This Day: Working with Churchill*, 1968. Biographer of Lord Gort, *Man of Valour*, 1972. In 1985 he published his war and post-war diaries, *The Fringes of Power*. Jock, as he was known, gave me access to his diaries when they were in typescript, and was an unfailing source of guidance and information for each of the main volumes of the Churchill biography, and for the previous document volumes.

May 1940

Sir John Reith[1]: diary
(*The Reith Diaries*)

11 May 1940

War Cabinet announced tonight, Churchill being defence minister as well as PM. Heaven help us. The three Service departments are Sinclair, Eden and Alexander. This is obviously so that Churchill can ignore them more or less and deal direct with the chiefs of staff. Awful.

Winston S. Churchill to Sir John Reith
(*Churchill papers, 2/398*)

12 May 1940

My dear Reith,

By the time you receive this letter, you will have been informed of the change which is taking place in the office you have so capably fulfilled at the Ministry of Information.

I take this opportunity of expressing my high sense of appreciation of the services you have rendered.

I am sure you will forgive me for not giving you previous intimation of the change I have thought it necessary to make. It is a matter of extreme national importance that the new Administration should be installed with the least possible delay; and I have been overlaid not only with the difficult task of forming a new Government, but with the course of a battle of considerable importance.

Yours sincerely,
Winston S. Churchill

---

[1] John Charles Walsham Reith, 1889–1971. Educated Royal Technical College, Glasgow. Engineer's apprentice; then joined S. Pearson & Son Ltd as an engineer, 1913. On active service, Royal Engineers, 1914–15 (seriously wounded in the head). Major, 1915. Mission to America, for munitions contracts, 1916–17. Admiralty Engineer-in-Chief's Department, 1918. In charge of liquidation of munitions engineering contracts, 1919. First General Manager, BBC, 1922; Managing Director, 1923; Director-General, 1927–38. Knighted, 1927. Chairman, BOAC, 1939–40. Minister of Information, 1939–40. Minister of Transport, 1940. National MP for Southampton, 1940. Created Baron, 1940. Minister of Works, 1940–2. Lieutenant-Commander, RNVR, 1942. Director of Combined Operations, Material Department, Admiralty, 1943–5. Member, Commonwealth Telecommunications Board, 1946–50.

14 MAY 1940

Sir John Sinclair[1]*: recollection*
(*Davy papers*)

12 May 1940

I was sleeping in the War Room and on 12th May was shaving at 7 a.m. when I was told by the duty office that the Prime Minister wanted someone to go round and tell him about the situation. I found him in bed, smoking a cigar, which made my stomach queasy at that time of the morning. I laid the map on his tummy, when it stopped wobbling, and told him how the British were disposed on the line of the Dyle. He did not seem very interested, but ran his finger along the line of the Meuse and said 'What have the French got there?' I told him they were very thin because they looked on the Meuse as an insuperable tank obstacle and the Ardennes Forest as impassable for armour by its rough tracks. I told him the Howard-Vyse[2] mission had pressed the French on this and had been unable to convince them that there was any threat on that sector, and that this had been reported several times to the War Office in written reports and orally on visits from the mission. He grunted.

Lord Hankey[3] *to Sir Samuel Hoare*[4]
(*Beaverbrook papers*)

12 May 1940

I found complete chaos this morning. No one was gripping the war in its crisis. The Dictator, instead of dictating, was engaged in a sordid wrangle

---

[1] John Alexander Sinclair, 1897–1977. Midshipman, Royal Navy, 1914–16. Royal Field Artillery, 1919. Instructor, Staff College, 1938–9. Operations Section, War Office, 1939–40. OBE, 1940. Deputy Director of Military Operations, 1941. Commandant Royal Artillery, First Division, 1942. Director of Military Intelligence, 1944–5. CB, 1945. Colonel Commandant Royal Artillery, 1952–62. Knighted, 1953.

[2] Richard Granville Hylton Howard-Vyse, 1883–1962. Entered the Army, 1902. On active service, 1914–18 (despatches, DSO, Chief Staff Officer, Desert Mounted Corps, Palestine, 1917–18). Inspector of Cavalry, 1930–4. Retired pay, 1935. Knighted, 1935. Recalled, as Head of the Military Mission with the French High Command, 1939–40. Chairman, Prisoner-of-War Department, Red Cross, 1941–5. Chairman of the British Legion, 1950–3; President, 1958–62.

[3] Maurice Pascal Alers Hankey, 1877–1963. Entered Royal Marine Artillery, 1895. Captain, 1899. Retired, 1912. Secretary to the Committee of Imperial Defence, 1912–38. Lieutenant-Colonel, Royal Marines, 1914. Knighted, February 1916. Secretary to the War Cabinet, 1916–18; to the Cabinet, 1919–38. Created Baron, 1939. Minister without Portfolio, September 1939 to May 1940. Chancellor of the Duchy of Lancaster, 1940–1. Paymaster-General, 1941–2. His brother Hugh was killed in action in South Africa in March 1900. His brother Donald was killed in action on the Western Front in October 1916.

[4] Samuel John Gurney Hoare, 1880–1959. Educated at Harrow and New College, Oxford. Conservative MP for Chelsea, 1910–44. Succeeded his father as 2nd Baronet, 1915. Lieutenant-Colonel, British Military Mission to Russia, 1916–17, and to Italy, 1917–18. Deputy High Commissioner, League of Nations, for care of Russian refugees, 1921. Secretary of State for Air, October 1922 to January 1924 and 1924–9. Secretary of State for India, 1931–5; for Foreign Affairs, 1935. First Lord of the Admiralty, 1936–7; Home Secretary, 1937–9; Lord Privy Seal,

with the politicians of the left about the secondary offices. NC[1] was in a state of despair about it all.

The only hope lies in the solid core of Churchill, Chamberlain and Halifax, but whether the wise old elephants will ever be able to hold the Rogue Elephant, I doubt.

Lord Beaverbrook[2] to Winston S. Churchill
(*Churchill papers, 20/4*)

12 May 1940

My dear Winston,

The list goes well because you carry everything before you now with the British public.

I remember a train load of Blue Jackets at Victoria Station cheering you wildly after you were dismissed from the Admiralty in 1915.

Your popularity has reached the same high again.

Maybe you might think it worth while to show me your names for other offices before you issue your list.

I might have useful ideas on the publicity side.

Yours ever
Max

1939–40; Secretary of State for Air, April–May 1940. Ambassador to Spain, 1940–4. Created Viscount Templewood, 1944.

[1] Neville Chamberlain.

[2] William Maxwell Aitken, 1879–1964. Known as 'Max'. A Canadian financier. Conservative MP, 1910–16. Knighted, 1911. Elected to the Other Club, 1912. Canadian Expeditionary Force Eye-Witness in France, May–August 1915; Canadian Government Representative at the Front, September 1915 to 1916. Newspaper proprietor: bought the *Daily Express*, his largest circulation newspaper, in December 1916. Created Baron Beaverbrook, 1917. Chancellor of the Duchy of Lancaster and Minister of Information, 1918. Minister for Aircraft Production, 1940–1. Minister of State, 1941. Minister of Supply, 1941–2. Lord Privy Seal, 1943–5. On 28 May 1915, when Churchill's fortunes were at their lowest ebb following his removal as First Lord of the Admiralty at the height of the Gallipoli campaign, Beaverbrook (then Sir Max Aitken) had written, in an article commissioned by Lord Northcliffe but never published: 'Nor need Mr Churchill despair of his future. It will undoubtedly be high and even splendid, for he possesses many qualities which no other public man can claim. If his future were as dark as I believe it to be bright he would I think encounter it with the same composure' (*Churchill papers: 2/237*).

16   MAY 1940

Brigadier-General Reginald Hoare[1] to Winston S. Churchill
(*Churchill papers, 2/395*)

12 May 1940

My dear Winston,

I feel I must write you a few lines to offer you my sincere and hearty congratulations on having reached the highest pinnacle of your political ambition. Well done my old No. 1 of the polo team!

I hope you will act up to the old regimental motto 'Mente et Manu',[2] and put some 'brains and brawn' into your very onerous task, and may success crown your efforts.

With every good wish
    from
Your old polo captain

                                                                                 Reginald Hoare

Randolph S. Churchill[3] to Winston S. Churchill
(*Churchill papers, 1/355*)

12 May 1940

My dear Papa,

At last you have the power & authority out of which the caucus have cheated you & England for nine long years!

I cannot tell you how proud & happy I am. I only hope that it is not too late. It is certainly a tremendous moment at which to take over. I send you all my deepest wishes for good fortune in the anxious days ahead.

                                                                                Your loving son
                                                                                   Randolph

---

[1] Reginald Hoare, 1865–1947. An officer in the 4th Hussars, which he later commanded. In 1897 he served with Churchill in India, and was a fellow-member of the regimental polo team. On active service in South Africa, 1899–1901 and in the European War, 1914–18 (wounded, despatches, DSO, CMG). Brigadier-General.

[2] 'With Heart and Hand' (literally 'With Mind and Hand').

[3] Randolph Frederick Edward Spencer Churchill, 1911–68. Churchill's only son. His godfathers were F. E. Smith and Sir Edward Grey. Educated at Eton and Christ Church, Oxford. On leaving Oxford in 1932, without taking his degree, he worked briefly for Imperial Chemical Industries as assistant editor of their house magazine. Joined the staff of the *Sunday Graphic*, 1932; wrote subsequently for many newspapers, including the *Evening Standard* (1937–9). Reported during Hitler's election campaign of 1932, the Chaco War of 1935 and Spanish Civil War; accompanied the Duke of Windsor on his tour of Germany, 1937. Unsuccessful Parliamentary candidate 1935 (twice), 1936, 1945, 1950 and 1951. Conservative MP for Preston, 1940–5. On active service, North Africa and Italy, 1941–3. Major, British Mission to the Yugoslav Army of National Liberation, 1943–4 (MBE, Military, 1944). Historian; author of the first two volumes of this biography, and editor of the first two sets of documents.

May 1940

War Cabinet: Confidential Annex[1]
(*Cabinet papers, 65/13*)

12 May 1940   Admiralty
10.30 p.m.

BOMBING POLICY

Sir Cyril Newall[2] said that the Chiefs of Staff had given further and careful consideration to the question of the employment of our heavy bombers and had reached the following conclusions: –

(i) That it was desirable in principle, on military grounds, to attack the enemy in his vitals i.e. the Ruhr, as soon as possible, subject to (iii) below.

(iii) That, when presenting the case to Ministers, the Chief of the Air Staff should point out that moon conditions would not be favourable for attacking the oil refineries until about 16th or 17th May.

In his (Sir Cyril Newall's) view, we had now reached a vital stage in the war, and it had always been accepted that when that stage was reached we should be prepared to take decisive action. We were not yet able to forecast with precision the enemy's intentions, but it was possible that the land operations in Belgium and Luxembourg were subsidiary to the operations in Holland, which country the Germans intended to seize at all costs so as to gain air bases from which they could launch an intensive air attack on Great Britain.

Sir Edmund Ironside said that he agreed, in general, with the views put forward by the Chief of the Air Staff. If the heavy bombers were unable to attack the very difficult targets in the immediate rear of the land battle, he would prefer to see the Ruhr plan carried out rather than that these bombers should be held back and do nothing. The Royal Air Force, by their operations

---

[1] The minutes of the discussions at the War Cabinet (known as Conclusions, but usually containing fairly full details of what different Ministers said) were printed and circulated each day, marked 'Secret', to members of the War Cabinet. Matters of particular secrecy were recorded in the Cabinet Secretary's Standard File, and kept in the Cabinet Office. Known as the 'Confidential Annex', and marked 'Most Secret', they were not circulated, and form a separate category of documents now available at the Public Record Office, Kew.

[2] Cyril Louis Norton Newall, 1886–1963. 2nd Lieutenant, Royal Warwickshire Regiment, 1905; Indian Army, 1909; Royal Flying Corps, 1914. On active service in India, 1908, and on the Western Front, 1914–18 (despatches thrice; Major). Royal Air Force, 1919. Deputy Director of Personnel, Air Ministry, 1919–22. Director of Operations and Intelligence, and Deputy Chief of the Air Staff, 1926–31. Air Officer Commanding the RAF, Middle East, 1931–4. Knighted, 1935. Member of the Air Council for Supply and Organisation, 1935–7. Air Chief Marshal, 1937. Chief of the Air Staff, 1937–40. Marshal of the Royal Air Force, 1940. Order of Merit, 1940. Governor-General and Commander-in-Chief, New Zealand, 1941–6. Created Baron, 1946.

during the previous 48 hours, had given our advancing troops a most valued respite. In his view, the position should be squarely faced, that a great land battle was about to commence and if our line cracked we might indeed lose our all. The Ruhr plan could not have an effect upon the course of the land battle for a considerable period – which had been given as three weeks – from the time the attack commenced. Nevertheless, in all the circumstances he (Sir Edmund Ironside) agreed that the right policy was to take the initiative while we yet could. If we did not use our heavy bomber force now, there was a grave danger that we might not be able to use it at all.

Sir Dudley Pound[1] expressed full agreement with the views put forward by his colleagues.

In the course of further discussion there was general agreement that on moral grounds we had full justification for carrying the air war into the enemy's country. In the light of events, neutral opinion and, in particular, that of the USA, would probably welcome such action rather than condemn it. Nevertheless the decision was a most vital one and the arguments finely balanced between taking action immediately, and waiting till the situation clarified as regards the land battle. Amongst other points, the constant drain on our fighter aircraft to France, the anti-aircraft situation in the United Kingdom and the new production figures for bombers and fighters, were discussed as directly relevant to the problem.

The Prime Minister, summing up, said that we were no longer bound by our previously held scruples as to initiating 'unrestricted' air warfare. The enemy had already given us ample justification for retaliation on his country. Opinion in the United States of America would not now be adverse if we carried out the operations proposed. The Germans would attack us in this country when, and where, it suited them. From the arguments put forward by the Chiefs of Staff it seemed that our position would be worse the longer we waited. It was, moreover, significant that the Germans had so far held off, and the reason for this could be interpreted as being because it was not in their interests to be attacked in their own country.

After hearing all the arguments he (the Prime Minister) agreed, in principle, with the view taken by the Chiefs of Staff. Nevertheless it would hardly be right for an immediate decision to be taken until the Lord Privy Seal

---

[1] Alfred Dudley Pickman Rogers Pound, 1877–1943. Entered the Royal Navy, 1891. Torpedo Lieutenant, 1902. Captain, 1914. Second Naval Assistant to Lord Fisher, December 1914 to May 1915. Flag Captain, HMS *Colossus*, 1915–17. Took part in the Battle of Jutland. Served on the Admiralty Staff, 1917–19. Director of Plans Division, Admiralty, 1922. Commanded the Battle Cruiser Squadron, 1929–32. Knighted, 1933. Second Sea Lord, 1932–5. Commander-in-Chief, Mediterranean, 1936–9. Admiral of the Fleet, 1939. First Sea Lord and Chief of the Naval Staff, 1939–43. He declined a peerage in 1943. Order of Merit, 1943.

May 1940

and the Minister without Portfolio[1] had been consulted, and put in possession of all the implications of the problem. The three members of the War Cabinet present were fully conversant with all aspects of this question, and the best course would be for the Chief of the Air Staff to explain the whole problem on the following day to Mr Attlee and, if possible, to Mr Greenwood, after which the matter could again be discussed at a meeting of the War Cabinet in the evening.

It was agreed:—
(i) That this question should again be considered at a meeting of the War Cabinet to be held at 6.30 p.m. on 13th May.
(ii) To request the Chief of the Air Staff to explain on Monday, 13th May, to the Lord Privy Seal and, if possible, to the Minister without Portfolio, in advance of the Meeting of the War Cabinet, the main considerations involved in the question of the employment of our heavy bomber force.

General Ismay: recollection
(*'The Memoirs of General the Lord Ismay'*, page 116)

13 May 1940

Two or three days after he became Prime Minister, I walked with him from Downing Street to the Admiralty. A number of people waiting outside the private entrance greeted him with cries of 'Good luck, Winnie. God bless you.' He was visibly moved, and as soon as we were inside the building, he dissolved into tears. 'Poor people,' he said, 'poor people. They trust me, and I can give them nothing but disaster for quite a long time.'

John Colville: diary
(*Colville papers*)

13 May 1940

Winston is still in his lair at the Admiralty, but will begin to work at No. 10 this afternoon. He looks like keeping a double establishment until the Chamberlains move out of No. 11 as they will do in about a month's time.

---

[1] On the previous day, Clement Attlee had become Lord Privy Seal, and Arthur Greenwood Minister without Portfolio.

Chiefs of Staff Committee[1]: *minutes*
(*Cabinet papers, 79/4*)

13 May 1940
11.30 a.m.

The Prime Minister said that although we should not reduce our home defence resources below a minimum safety figure, there was a great deal to be said for making further efforts to give additional support to the Allied armies who were establishing themselves on the Dyle. He invited the Chief of the Air Staff to consider, in consultation with the Secretary of State for Air, whether any further measures could be taken, and to inform him of their conclusions as soon as possible.

Harold Nicolson[2]: *diary*
(*'Diaries and Letters, 1939–1945'*)

13 May 1940

When Chamberlain enters the House, he gets a terrific reception, and when Churchill comes in the applause is less. Winston sits there between Chamberlain and Attlee, and it is odd to see the Labour Ministers sitting on the Government Bench. Winston makes a very short statement, but to the point.

Winston S. Churchill: statement
(*Hansard*)

13 May 1940   House of Commons
2.54 p.m.

HIS MAJESTY'S GOVERNMENT

The Prime Minister (Mr Churchill): I beg to move,
 'That this House welcomes the formation of a Government representing the united and inflexible resolve of the nation to prosecute the war with Germany to a victorious conclusion.'

---

[1] The Chiefs of Staff Committee consisted of Churchill (in the Chair), Air Chief Marshal Newall, General Ironside and Admiral of the Fleet Sir Dudley Pound. The member of the Secretariat present at this meeting was Lieutenant-Colonel Ian Jacob.

[2] Harold George Nicolson, 1886–1968. Son of Sir Arthur Nicolson (1st Baron Carnock). Educated at Wellington and Balliol College, Oxford. Entered Foreign Office, 1909; Counsellor, 1925. Served at the Paris Peace Conference, 1919, Teheran, 1925–7, and Berlin, 1927–9. On the editorial staff of the *Evening Standard*, 1930. National Labour MP for West Leicester, 1935–45. Parliamentary Secretary, Ministry of Information, 1940–1. A Governor of the BBC, 1941–6. Joined the Labour Party, 1947. Author and biographer. Knighted, 1953.

MAY 1940

On Friday evening last I received His Majesty's Commission to form a new Administration. It was the evident wish and will of Parliament and the nation that this should be conceived on the broadest possible basis and that it should include all parties, both those who supported the late Government and also the parties of the Opposition. I have completed the most important part of this task. A War Cabinet has been formed of five Members, representing, with the Opposition Liberals, the unity of the nation. The three party Leaders have agreed to serve, either in the War Cabinet or in high executive office.[1] The three Fighting Services have been filled. It was necessary that this should be done in one single day, on account of the extreme urgency and rigour of events. A number of other positions, key positions, were filled yesterday, and I am submitting a further list to His Majesty to-night. I hope to complete the appointment of the principal Ministers during to-morrow. The appointment of the other Ministers usually takes a little longer, but I trust that, when Parliament meets again, this part of my task will be completed, and that the administration will be complete in all respects.[2]

I considered it in the public interest to suggest that the House should be summoned to meet to-day. Mr Speaker[3] agreed, and took the necessary steps, in accordance with the powers conferred upon him by the Resolution of the House. At the end of the proceedings to-day, the Adjournment of the House will be proposed until Tuesday, 21st May, with, of course, provision for earlier meeting, if need be. The business to be considered during that week will be notified to Members at the earliest opportunity. I now invite the House, by the Motion which stands in my name, to record its approval of the steps taken and to declare its confidence in the new Government.

To form an Administration of this scale and complexity is a serious undertaking in itself, but it must be remembered that we are in the preliminary stage of one of the greatest battles in history, that we are in action at many other points in Norway and in Holland, that we have to be prepared in the Mediterranean, that the air battle is continuous and that many preparations, such as have been indicated by my hon. Friend below the Gangway,[4] have to be made here at home. In this crisis I hope I may be

---

[1] Neville Chamberlain, leader of the Conservative Party, as Lord President of the Council; Clement Attlee, leader of the Labour Party, as Lord Privy Seal; and Sir Archibald Sinclair, leader of the Liberal Party, as Secretary of State for Air.

[2] For the complete list of Churchill's Government, see Appendix C.

[3] Edward Algernon Fitzroy, 1869–1943. Son of the 3rd Baron Southampton. Educated at Eton and Sandhurst. A page of honour to Queen Victoria. Conservative MP for Daventry, 1900–6 and 1910–43. Captain, 1st Life Guards, 1914 (wounded at the First Battle of Ypres). Commanded the mounted troops of the Guards Division, 1915–16. Deputy Chairman of Committees, House of Commons, 1922–8. Privy Councillor, 1924. Speaker of the House of Commons from 1928 until his death. His widow was created Viscountess Daventry in 1943. Their son Michael (born 1895) was killed in action on 15 April 1915.

[4] I have not been able to find out who this Member was.

pardoned if I do not address the House at any length to-day. I hope that any of my friends and colleagues, or former colleagues, who are affected by the political reconstruction, will make allowance, all allowance, for any lack of ceremony with which it has been necessary to act. I would say to the House, as I said to those who have joined this Government: 'I have nothing to offer but blood, toil, tears and sweat.'

We have before us an ordeal of the most grievous kind. We have before us many, many long months of struggle and of suffering. You ask, what is our policy? I will say: It is to wage war, by sea, land and air, with all our might and with all the strength that God can give us; to wage war against a monstrous tyranny, never surpassed in the dark, lamentable catalogue of human crime. That is our policy. You ask, what is our aim? I can answer in one word: It is victory, victory at all costs, victory in spite of all terror, victory, however long and hard the road may be; for without victory, there is no survival. Let that be realised; no survival for the British Empire, no survival for all that the British Empire has stood for, no survival for the urge and impulse of the ages, that mankind will move forward towards its goal. But I take up my task with buoyancy and hope. I feel sure that our cause will not be suffered to fail among men. At this time I feel entitled to claim the aid of all, and I say, 'Come then, let us go forward together with our united strength.'

BUSINESS OF THE HOUSE

4.32 p.m.

The Prime Minister: I beg to move,

'That this House do now adjourn until Tuesday, 21st May.'

Sir Richard Acland[1] (Barnstaple): To-day we have been paying compliments and expressing good wishes, which we all sincerely feel. The Prime Minister will be aware, however, that hon. Members have a number of questions which they will want to ask at some time. They cannot be asked to-day, and they cannot all be asked except in a general discussion. We cannot expect such a discussion next week. Can the right hon. Gentleman give us some indication that, unless something unusual happens, there is likely to be a general discussion in the following week?

The Prime Minister: I am myself most anxious and, indeed, resolved to carry the House of Commons along with the Government at every stage in our fortunes as they unfold. The House of Commons has fought long and resolute wars for freedom in the past, and it is by the strength of the House of Commons that we shall largely be sustained in this conflict. At the present time we are in the preliminaries of a very great battle, and I do not know what

[1] Richard Thomas Dyke Acland, 1906–90. Son of the Liberal politician Sir Francis Acland. Stood unsuccessfully for Parliament as a Liberal, 1929 and 1931. Liberal MP, 1935–40. Succeeded his father as 15th Baronet, 1939. Labour MP, 1947–55. Senior Lecturer, St Luke's College of Education, 1959–74.

the position will be when we meet again. Obviously, if there is any general desire at any time in the near future for a statement on the military situation, if it is felt to be a suitable moment to make such a statement, and if there is a desire to have a debate on general policy, arrangements can be made for it, and I, personally, should be very glad to receive representations if necessary upon that matter.

Mr Maxton[1]: I would not like the Prime Minister to assume that everybody in the House thinks that a general debate ranging over the whole globe, in which all the amateur strategists tell the heads of Service Departments how they should be doing their jobs, is the most profitable way in which the House of Commons can conduct its business. If I have any influence with the Prime Minister, I hope he will take my advice and proceed with the ordinary routine business of the House of Commons.

The Prime Minister: Certainly, I shall be very much influenced by my hon. Friend's opinion, and I will do my utmost to conciliate him and his party.

Sir I. Albery[2] (Gravesend): Can my right hon. Friend give the House any information about the Government's proposals with reference to the Finance Bill?

The Prime Minister: Not to-day.

John Colville: diary
(*Colville papers*)

13 May 1940

Went down to the House with Seal[3] to hear the new PM ask for a vote of confidence in his Government. He made a brilliant little speech.

---

[1] James Maxton, 1885–1946. Known as 'Jimmy'. A leading Scottish radical. Labour MP for Glasgow (Bridgeton) from 1922 until his death. Chairman of the Independent Labour Party (ILP), 1926–31 and 1934–9. Biographer of Lenin.

[2] Irving James Albery, 1879–1967. Member of the Stock Exchange, 1902–64. On active service in South Africa, 1900, and on the Western Front 1914–18 (Military Cross, despatches). Conservative MP, 1934–45. Knighted, 1936.

[3] Eric Arthur Seal, 1898–1972. Served in the Royal Air Force, 1918–19. Entered the Patent Office, 1921; transferred to the Admiralty, 1925. Principal Private Secretary to the First Lord of the Admiralty (Lord Stanhope, then Churchill), 1938–40. Principal Private Secretary to the Prime Minister (Churchill), 1940–1. CB, 1941. Deputy Secretary of the Admiralty, North America, 1941–3. Member of the British Supply Council, Washington, 1943. Under-Secretary of the Admiralty (London), 1943–5. Director of Building Materials, Ministry of Works, 1947–8. Deputy Under-Secretary of State, Foreign Office (German Division), 1948–51. Deputy Secretary, Ministry of Works, 1951–9. Knighted, 1955.

Lloyd George[1] also spoke and was afterwards invited into the PM's room and offered the Ministry of Agriculture (for which the cheap press has always tipped him). He refused it because he thinks the country is in a hopeless position and he is generally despondent.

War Cabinet: minutes
(Cabinet papers, 65/7)

13 May 1940 10 Downing Street
6 p.m.

The general situation on the whole front showed strong German mechanised forces advancing in a number of directions, but as yet no signs of infantry columns. The French were not yet certain whether the main German effort was directed through Luxemburg against the left of the Maginot Line, or through Maastricht. The first phase of the movement of the French and British armies would be complete by 7 o'clock the following morning, and they would be engaged in consolidating their positions. The Belgian army did not appear to be putting up a strong resistance, and Liège was probably isolated.

The Secretary of State for War[2] said that General Gamelin[3] had now wired to say that, in view of the situation in Holland, he did not think any good purpose would be served by moving the Light Division now at Brest to assist the Dutch. He (the Secretary of State) would like to be given discretion to withdraw the British battalion from The Hook if, after consultation with the Admiralty, it appeared desirable to do so.

The Prime Minister hoped that the battalion would not be withdrawn, if it were successfully providing a nucleus to rally Dutch resistance. He agreed,

[1] David Lloyd George, 1863–1945. Educated at a Welsh church school. Solicitor, 1884. Liberal MP for Caernarvon, 1890–1931. President of the Board of Trade, 1905–8. Privy Councillor, 1905. Chancellor of the Exchequer, 1908–15. An original member of the Other Club, 1911. Minister of Munitions, May 1915 to July 1916. Secretary of State for War, July–December 1916. Prime Minister, December 1916 to October, 1922. Order of Merit, 1919. Independent Liberal MP, 1931–45. Created Earl, 1945.

[2] Anthony Eden, who had last held Cabinet office as Secretary of State for Foreign Affairs, from which he resigned in February 1938 in protest against Neville Chamberlain's approaches to Italy and neglect of the United States.

[3] Maurice Gustave Gamelin, 1872–1958. Born in Paris. 2nd Lieutenant, 1893. Lieutenant-Colonel, 1914. Served on General Joffre's staff, 1911–17; drafted the principal directives at the Battle of the Marne, 1914. Commanded a brigade during the Battle of the Somme, 1916. Commanded the 9th Infantry Division, 1917–18. Military Assistant to the Syrian High Commissioner, 1925–8, when he defeated the Druse rebellion. Commanded the 20th Army Corps (Nancy), 1929. Army Chief of Staff, 1931. Inspector-General of the Army and Vice-President of the War Council, 1935–7. Chief of the General Staff of National Defence, January 1938 to September 1939. Honorary knighthood, 1938. Generalissimo, commanding the French Land Forces, September 1939 to May 1940, when he was superseded and later interned by the Vichy regime. Tried for having 'weakened the spirit of the French armies', 1941. Deported to Buchenwald concentration camp, 1943–5. Liberated by American troops, May 1945.

however, that the matter should be left to the discretion of the Secretary of State for War.

The Prime Minister said that the picture which had been placed before the War Cabinet of the present situation showed that there were two alternatives. The Germans might either be launching their great land attack with the object of trying to defeat the Franco-British armies, or they might content themselves with making contact along the line which the Allied armies had taken up in Belgium, and with consolidating their position in Holland preparatory to their great attack on this country.

The Chief of the Imperial General Staff agreed with this view of the situation, but thought that the extent to which the Germans had committed their air and mechanised resources indicated that the land battle was beginning. Once the penetrations made by the German mechanised forces had been widened, the advance of their main columns might be expected to begin.

The Prime Minister said that, if his colleagues approved, he proposed to send a personal message to President Roosevelt,[1] informing him of the seriousness of the situation.

This suggestion met with approval.

Discussion ensued as to what action President Roosevelt could take to help the Allies.

War Cabinet: Confidential Annex
(*Cabinet papers, 65/13*)

13 May 1940　　　　　　　　　　　　　　　　　　　　　　10 Downing Street
6 p.m.

The Prime Minister said that the War Cabinet would have to decide whether the heavy bombers of the Royal Air Force should engage the oil refineries and marshalling yards in the Ruhr starting on the night of 14th/15th May, as provisionally agreed at a Meeting of Ministers held the previous evening at which the Lord Privy Seal and the Minister without Portfolio[2]

---

[1] Franklin Delano Roosevelt, 1882–1945. United States Assistant Secretary of the Navy, 1913–20. Governor of New York State, 1929–33. President of the United States, 1933–45. Churchill's support for Roosevelt was frequently repeated in his articles in both Britain and America. 'I am,' he wrote in *Collier's* magazine in the first year of Roosevelt's presidency, 'though a foreigner, an ardent admirer of the main drift and impulse which President Roosevelt has given to the economic and financial policy of the United States.' And when, at Oxford, an undergraduate echoed the prevailing anti-American feeling by asking Churchill if he approved Roosevelt's policy 'of neglecting the affairs of the rest of the world for the especial benefit of the United States', Churchill replied with feeling: 'The President is a bold fellow, I like his spirit' (*G. R. Storry papers*, note of 23 February 1934).

[2] Attlee and Greenwood.

had not been able to be present. He would summarise the arguments for and against this course of action as follows:–
- (a) The enemy, by the many atrocities he had already committed, had given ample justification in the eyes of the world for an attack upon the Ruhr.
- (b) The Germans would undoubtedly attack vital objectives in this country as soon as they were ready to do so. This would be when they had established themselves in Holland and secured air bases from which they could bring their fighters and short range bombers to bear on this country.
- (c) Once the Germans had got well forward into Holland and Belgium, they would have secured depth to their air defences.
- (d) An attack now would force the Germans to retaliate at a time when they were not ready to do so, and before our fighter and bomber strength had been worn down by prolonged operations.

On the other hand –
- (a) If the land battle, which might be decisive, was now opening it might be better to concentrate the whole resources of our Air Force in an effort to defeat the German Armies.
- (b) If it were not certain that the Germans proposed to attack industrial objectives in this country it would be unwise to provoke them into doing so. Moreover, the greater relative strength of the German Air Force at the present time would increase the power of their retaliation.
- (c) If it were decided to postpone the attack, it could be made at a later stage though of course under far less favourable conditions.

The Minister without Portfolio said that he thought that the arguments in favour of making the attack were very strong.

The Prime Minister felt that air attack on this country was inevitable. Whatever course the war in France took, we could not afford to use up our fighters day by day, until the defences of this country were seriously impaired. It was true that our fighters would find it difficult to deal with German attacks by night, but, on the other hand, the Germans would be unable to bomb our vital points with any degree of accuracy. If, however, our fighter strength was seriously weakened, we would lay ourselves open to the far greater accuracy of daylight attack. Such reinforcements as could be spared would be sent to the Army, but it must not be thought that in any circumstances it would be possible to send large numbers of fighters to France. Similarly, we should not allow our heavy bomber force to be frittered away, and thus deprive ourselves of its powerful deterrent effect, and of the ability to deliver its heavy blow. The Army, therefore, must not expect great assistance from the bomber force, any more than from the fighters.

He was by no means sure that the great battle was developing. No great masses of German troops had yet come forward, and the position was quite compatible with German anxiety not to engage the full strength of their army, but only to use specialised troops.

The Chief of the Imperial General Staff pointed out that mechanised forces could not be stabilised. The Germans had so far only used mechanised forces and we would inevitably be able to compel these forces to retire unless the Germans moved their main army forward. The retirement of the Germans from the positions they had at present reached would mean a considerable moral loss and no doubt the German High Command would be very reluctant to withdraw them. It seemed fairly certain that we should know one way or the other within the next 48 hours.

The Prime Minister said that in view of the balanced nature of the arguments for and against attack on the Ruhr, he would prefer to put off a decision for three or four days, in order to make sure whether the great battle had started or not.

The War Cabinet would, of course, review the situation from day to day, but it was most important that the heavy bomber squadrons should no longer be kept in a state of tension expecting daily to get the order to attack, only to have it postponed at the last moment.

The Prime Minister thought that it was important not to waste our aircraft in France on unprofitable attacks on German tanks, which had given a very good account of themselves against air attack. German tanks should be met by our own tanks and artillery.

Summing up the discussion, he thought that it was the general view of the War Cabinet that it would be only prudent to defer a decision for three or four days, while daily reviewing the position in the light of the Military situation. In the meantime we should conserve the heavy bomber force as much as possible, and personnel should not be kept keyed up for an attack on the Ruhr.

The War Cabinet agreed:—

(a) To postpone a decision on the question of bombing military targets in the Ruhr for, say, three or four days until it was seen how the military situation was developing. The position should, however, be reviewed daily by the War Cabinet.

(b) That, in the meantime, the strength of the heavy bomber force should be conserved, and the state of readiness of individual squadrons relaxed as far as practicable.

John Colville: diary
(*Colville papers*)

14 May 1940

There is still a certain air of 'malaise' about No. 10, which is largely due to the contrast between the fixity of the late PM's habits and the inconsequential nature of Winston's. I suppose we shall get used to it; but the prospect of constant late nights – 2.00 a.m. or later – is depressing.

War Cabinet: minutes
(*Cabinet papers, 65/7*)

14 May 1940   10 Downing Street
11.30 a.m.

The Prime Minister pointed out that, if the Dutch resistance was being continued, it was very important that the Guards Battalion, which had been landed at the Hook of Holland, should not be withdrawn too hastily, though it must be left to the Secretary of State for War to decide as to the actual time of withdrawal in the light of events.

The Lord President of the Council[1] raised the question of the action which should be taken if, in the meantime, an Italian ship escorted by an Italian warship tried to evade our Contraband Control at Gibraltar.

The Prime Minister said that in the first instance, at any rate, we should leave such a ship alone.[2]

---

[1] Neville Chamberlain.
[2] That evening, in a letter published next to the Low cartoon in the *Evening Standard*, a group of Italian ex-servicemen appealed to Mussolini to refrain from entering the war on the side of Germany. One sentence read: 'Our wounds will bleed again, and we will all remember the hundreds of thousands of our dead who perished in a noble cause that united Italy, England and France as brothers in arms against German aggression.'

May 1940

David Low[1]: cartoon[2]
(*'Evening Standard'*)

14 May 1940

ALL BEHIND YOU, WINSTON

---

[1] David Low, 1891–1963. Born in New Zealand. A political cartoonist. Came to London, where he was cartoonist on the *Star* from 1919, the *Evening Standard* from 1927 and the *Daily Herald* from 1950. Knighted, 1962. Author of more than 25 volumes of cartoons.

[2] Front row: Churchill, Attlee, Bevin, Morrison (with glasses) and Amery; second row: Chamberlain, Greenwood, Halifax, Sinclair, Duff Cooper, A. V. Alexander, Eden.

30   MAY 1940

Captain Berkeley[1]: *diary*
(*Berkeley papers*)

14 May 1940

Winston has a government – Eden, Amery,[2] Beaverbrook, etc. And rows of Labour people. The effect on the population seems to have been first rate, there is positive relief in the streets. So I suppose the whole shabby business was right and proper, and I am no politician. Now perhaps we ought to liquidate the COS[3] as well. I'm not sure they're not far more in need of it than the old government: CIGS[4] has the oddest sallies now and then.

Chiefs of Staff Committee: minutes
(*Cabinet papers, 79/4*)

14 May 1940
6 p.m.

The Prime Minister said that he had called the meeting to consider a telephone message from M. Reynaud,[5] which read as follows:–

'Germany intends to deliver a mortal blow towards Paris. The German Army has broken through our fortified line south of Sedan. The reason is that we cannot resist the combined attacks of heavy tanks and bomber squadrons. To stop the German drive whilst there is still time and to allow our counter attack to succeed it is necessary to cut off the German tanks and the bombers supporting them. It can only be done by an enormous force of fighters. You were kind enough to send four squadrons which is

---

[1] Claude Berkeley, an Army officer, was a member of the War Cabinet Secretariat, and interpreter, from September 1939. Described by General Spears as 'a brilliant linguist' (*Prelude to Dunkirk*, page 294). He was subsequently in Washington with the Joint Chiefs of Staff.

[2] Leopold Charles Maurice Stennett Amery, 1873–1955. Known as 'Leo'. A contemporary of Churchill at Harrow. Fellow of All Souls College, Oxford, 1897. *Manchester Guardian* correspondent in the Balkans and Turkey, 1897–9. Served on the editorial staff of *The Times*, 1899–1909. Conservative MP, 1911–45. Intelligence Officer in the Balkans and eastern Mediterranean, 1915–16. Assistant Secretary, War Cabinet Secretariat, 1917–18. Parliamentary Under-Secretary, Colonial Office, 1919–21. First Lord of the Admiralty, 1922–4. Colonial Secretary, 1924–9. Secretary of State for India and Burma, 1940–5.

[3] The Chiefs of Staff.

[4] The Chief of the Imperial General Staff (General Ironside).

[5] Paul Reynaud, 1878–1966. On active service, 1914–18 (twice decorated). Entered the Chamber of Deputies, 1919. Minister of Colonies, 1931–2. Minister of Justice, April–November 1938. Minister of Finance, 1930, and November 1938 to March 1940. Prime Minister, 21 March to 17 June 1940 (Foreign Minister, 21 March to 18 May and 6 June to 17 June 1940). Arrested by the Vichy Government, September 1940. Deported to Germany, 1943–5. Released, 1945. Minister of Finance, 1948. Deputy Prime Minister, 1953. President of the Finance Committee of the National Assembly, 1958.

more than you promised, but if we are to win this battle, which might be decisive for the whole war, it is necessary to send at once, if possible to-day, ten more squadrons. Without such support we cannot be sure of stopping the German advance between Sedan and Paris. Between Sedan and Paris there are no fortifications left to be compared with the line to be re-established at almost any cost.

'I am confident that in this crisis English help will not fail us.'

The Prime Minister said that the enemy's break through on a comparatively narrow front would be difficult to sustain, as the forts on the flanks should be able to hold firm, and the Maginot Line was self-contained. He was not yet convinced that we could afford to divert more resources from this country. He had summoned the War Cabinet, with the Service Ministers, to meet at 7 p.m. to give further consideration to this vital matter.

War Cabinet: minutes
(*Cabinet papers, 65/7*)

14 May 1940
7 p.m.

10 Downing Street

The Prime Minister read to the War Cabinet a message which he had received over the telephone from M. Reynaud and on which he had had some preliminary discussion with the Chiefs of Staff.

The Prime Minister said that M. Reynaud had told him that the French were bringing back fighters from North Africa. M. Reynaud had said that his request for fighters had the authority of Generals Gamelin and Georges.[1] The French naturally had their whole attention fixed on the battle which was taking place on their front. He thought, however, that we should hesitate before we denuded still further the heart of the Empire. A penetration of the line by mechanised units could not be decisive against a large army unless

---

[1] Joseph Georges, 1875–1951. Entered the French Infantry, 1897. Chief of Staff to Marshal Foch, 1918. Head of the French Economic Service in the Ruhr, 1923. Chief of Staff to Marshal Pétain, 1925–6. Chef de Cabinet in the Maginot Government, 1929. Commanded the 19th Corps in Algeria, 1931. Wounded in Marseilles at the time of the assassination of King Alexander of Yugoslavia, 1934. Created Generalissimo, 1934. Commander of the Forces and Operations in the North East, 1939–40. A member of the French Committee of National Liberation, 1943.

heavily reinforced from the rear. The columns of motor vehicles would require petrol. The essential point was probably to support the coming counter-attack.

The Chief of the Imperial General Staff agreed and said that he hoped to know that night at what time the counter-attack would take place. If necessary, one of the Chiefs of Staff could go over to see General Gamelin.

Winston S. Churchill to Paul Reynaud
(*Premier papers, 3/188/1*)

14 May 1940

The War Cabinet and Staffs have given earnest consideration to the request which you made to me this afternoon, and no time is being lost in studying what we can do to meet the situation.

We have sent for Staff Officers from France who will be able to give us the latest picture, in order that we may be sure that available resources are used to the best advantage of our cause.

Winston S. Churchill to General Ismay
(*Churchill papers, 20/17*)

14 May 1940

OPERATION 'PAUL'[1]

Bring to the notice of the Chiefs of Staff Committee[2] the importance of planting vegetables in the approaches to Lulea. This is one of the most important objects for which we have gone to Narvik. Pains should be taken to ascertain the earliest arrivals of German ships, and then to obstruct them in the harbour, or outside it, with every suitable variety of mine. The whole of these approaches should be rendered unsafe to navigation. If possible, some

---

[1] Operation 'Paul' was the plan, devised by Churchill while he was at the Admiralty, for the planting of mines ('vegetables') in the approaches to the Swedish Baltic port of Luleå, in order to prevent the movement of Swedish iron ore to Germany during the summer, ice-free months.

[2] Henceforth, Churchill was to send all his minutes for the Chiefs of Staff Committee, and his comments on the Chiefs of Staff discussions and memoranda, through General Ismay.

loaded ore ships should be sunk in the fairway. FO must be consulted on questions of neutrality, but this does not matter so much now. Let a good plan be prepared to be used in about three weeks. When it is ready I will bring it before the Cabinet myself.

WSC

Winston S. Churchill to Lord Cork[1]
(*Admiralty papers, 199/1929*)

14 May 1940
5.29 p.m.

Although I am leaving the Admiralty I shall as Minister of Defence preserve that close personal contact with you which has I trust been a help. I hope you will get Narvik cleaned up as soon as possible, and then work southwards with increasing force. All good wishes.[2]

John Colville: diary
(*Colville papers*)

14 May 1940

After dinner I went to Admiralty House, where Winston proposes to work at night. He has fitted up the ground floor for this purpose: the dining-room in which the private secretary and one of Winston's specially trained night-women-typists sit; the lovely drawing-room with its curious ugly dolphin furniture, which is used as a kind of promenade; and an inner room in which the Great Man himself sits. At the side of his desk stands a table laden with bottles of whisky, etc. On the desk itself are all manner of things: toothpicks, gold medals (which he uses as paper-weights), special cuffs to save his coatsleeves from becoming dirty, and innumerable pills and powders.

---

[1] William Henry Dudley Boyle, 12th Earl of Cork and Orrery, 1873–1967. Entered the Royal Navy as a cadet, 1887. Commanded HMS *Repulse*, 1916–18. Commander-in-Chief, Home Fleet, 1933–5; Portsmouth, 1937–9. Admiral of the Fleet, 1938. Served at the Admiralty, charged by Churchill with preparing plans for a naval expedition into the Baltic (Plan 'Catherine'), October 1939 to March 1940. Commanded the combined expedition for the capture of Narvik, April to June 1940. Retired from active service, 1940. Home Guard, 1941–2.

[2] In his reply on the following day, Lord Cork reported that the landing at Bjervik, near Narvik, on 13 May, had gone well. With regard to the town of Mo, further south, which was to have been evacuated, Cork wrote that 'we must hold on and fight'. If Mo were overrun, 'the whole Narvik situation becomes precarious.'

Peck[1] and I arrived at about 9.15 and waited till 10.30 before anything happened. In the meanwhile I read some of W's correspondence which we had ready for him. There was a letter from the King, two or three days old, urging that Lord Beaverbrook should not be made Minister of Aircraft Production in view of the effect likely to be produced in Canada. Also a large number of letters suggesting various appointments. A note by Brendan Bracken[2] referred to a number of 'our friends' disliked by 'the parachutist', by whom he meant David Margesson[3] (who, owing to the reconstruction, has landed in the enemy camp, I suppose).

At about 10.30 Winston came down, and then by degrees a motley gathering appeared. David Margesson, Sinclair, Eden, Beaverbrook, the American Ambassador[4] (who told me the most disquieting evidence of Italy's intention to enter the war) and Pug Ismay. Strange bedfellows indeed! They walked about talking to each other while Winston popped in and out first through one door and then through the next, appointing Under Secretaries with David, talking about the German thrust at Sedan with Eden and listening to the alarmist and, I think, untrustworthy opinions of Mr Kennedy. Eventually Tony Bevir[5] came in to relieve me, Peck having gone home early, and I walked home through the warm night at about 1 a.m.

---

[1] John Howard Peck, 1913–. An Assistant Private Secretary to the First Lord of the Admiralty (Lord Stanhope), 1937–9; to the Minister for Co-ordination of Defence (Lord Chatfield), 1939–40; to the First Lord of the Admiralty (Churchill), April–May 1940; to the Prime Minister (Churchill), 1940–5. Transferred to the Foreign Service, 1946. Ambassador to Senegal, 1962–6, and Mauritania, 1962–5. Under-Secretary of State, 1966–70. Ambassador to the Republic of Ireland, 1970–3. Knighted, 1971. He published his memoirs, *Dublin from Downing Street*, in 1978.
[2] Brendan Bracken, 1901–58. Educated in Australia and at Sedbergh School. Journalist and financier. Conservative MP for North Paddington, 1929–45; for Bournemouth, 1950–1. Elected to the Other Club, 1932. Chairman of the *Financial News*. Managing Director of the *Economist*. Chairman of the *Financial Times*. Parliamentary Private Secretary to the Prime Minister (Churchill), 1940–1. Privy Councillor, 1940. Minister of Information, 1941–5. First Lord of the Admiralty, 1945. Created Viscount, 1952.
[3] Henry David Reginald Margesson, 1890–1965. Educated at Harrow and Magdalene College, Cambridge. On active service, 1914–18 (Military Cross). Captain, 1918. Conservative MP for Upton, 1922–3; for Rugby, 1924–42. Assistant Government Whip, 1924. Junior Lord of the Treasury, 1926, 1926–9 and 1931. Chief Government Whip, 1931–40. Privy Councillor, 1933. Secretary of State for War, 1940–2. Created Viscount, 1942.
[4] Joseph Patrick Kennedy, 1888–1969. Born in Boston. Graduated from Harvard, 1912. Assistant General Manager, Fore River Plant, Bethlehem Shipbuilding Corporation, 1917–19. Investment banker. Chairman of the Securities Exchange Commission, 1934–5, and of the US Marine Commission, 1937. Ambassador to London, 1937–41. Of his four sons, Joseph was killed in action in 1944; John (President of the United States) was assassinated in 1963; and Robert (a Senator) was assassinated in 1968.
[5] Anthony Bevir, 1895–1977. On active service, 1915–18 (despatches twice). Entered the Colonial Office, 1921. Assistant Secretary, War Cabinet Office, 1939. Private Secretary to Neville Chamberlain, 1940; to Churchill, 1940–5; to Clement Attlee, 1945–51; to Churchill, 1951–5, and to Anthony Eden, 1955–6; Secretary for Appointments, 1947–56. CBE, 1944. CVO, 1946. Knighted, 1952.

Winston S. Churchill: telephone conversation with Paul Reynaud[1]
(*Premier papers, 3/188/1*)

15 May 1940
Most Secret

The Prime Minister spoke to M. Reynaud over the telephone shortly after 7 a.m. this morning.

M. Reynaud was apparently in a very excited mood. He said that the counter-attack last night on the Germans who had broken through South of Sedan had failed and that the road to Paris was open and the battle was lost. He talked even of giving up the struggle. The Prime Minister told him in reply that he must not be misled by panic-stricken messages of this kind; that only a small proportion of the French Army was yet engaged and that the Germans who had broken through would be in a vulnerable position. He also said several times that, whatever the French did, we would continue to fight to the last.

M. Reynaud asked that we might send further troops to their assistance. The Prime Minister pointed out that, as he well knew, this was impossible.

The Prime Minister asked and obtained M. Reynaud's permission to speak direct to General Georges. General Georges rang up later on, shortly after 9 a.m.

Chiefs of Staff Committee: minutes
(*Cabinet papers, 79/4*)

15 May 1940
10 a.m.

THE SITUATION ON THE WESTERN FRONT

The Prime Minister said that he had been rung up at 8.30 a.m. by M. Reynaud, whose confidence appeared to be considerably shaken, and who said that the battle was lost, and the road to Paris open. He pointed to the small number of British troops in France, and begged for immediate assistance.

In reply, he (the Prime Minister) had said that the German penetration was on a narrow front, and could not possibly be rapidly exploited in strength. We

---

[1] A note by Churchill's Principal Private Secretary, E. A. Seal, at the bottom of this document, states: 'I did not listen in to the conversation. The above account is reconstructed from the Prime Minister's remarks which I overheard as they were made and the account he subsequently gave me of M. Reynaud's words' (*Premier papers, 3/188/1*).

could not send troops to France quicker than the schedule to which we were working, and in any case nothing could arrive in time to influence the present battle. He had found it necessary to point out to M. Reynaud that whatever the French might do, we should continue the fight – if necessary alone. M. Reynaud had then pulled himself together, and had said that the French too would fight to the end. He had then demanded to speak direct to General Georges, and at about 10 a.m. he had done so.

He had found General Georges calm, and had received an account of the situation. There had been undoubtedly a serious breach of more than 15 kilos on the front at Sedan, but it was now plugged. He had been very warm in his praise of the assistance given by the Royal Air Force, and had asked for nothing. He (the Prime Minister) had told General Georges that we would continue to give full assistance, but could not unguard ourselves beyond a certain point. This General Georges had quite understood.

Sir Edmund Ironside said that he had also spoken to General Georges' and General Gamelin's Headquarters, and had received the same account. He had received a wire from General Georges saying that German elements had crossed the Meuse at a number of points between Givet and Namur, and that the 9th Army was falling back. It might therefore be necessary for the 1st Army to bend back to the line Wavre–Charleroi – which would mean a slight adjustment of the right wing of the BEF.[1] He hoped that the enemy were now held South of Sedan.

The serious part of the situation was that, up to the present, the French had not stood firm under pressure. The Germans had as yet only brought forward six or seven Armoured Divisions, and 17 Infantry Divisions. The first shock of impact of the Armoured Division had undoubtedly been very severe, and in places the French had failed to withstand it; but up to the present only a very small proportion of the French Army had been engaged. It appeared likely that, owing to the enemy's passage of the Meuse, we might have to fall back on to our old line on the frontier.

He had also spoken to Lord Gort.[2] The 1st Corps expected to be attacked today. A part of the 48th Division had had to come into line on the right of the British Expeditionary Force to relieve certain French units. The 2nd Corps on the left were well established. The 12th Lancers and the Divisional cavalry

---

[1] The British Expeditionary Force, commanded by Lord Gort.
[2] John Standish Surtees Prendergast Vereker, 1886–1946. Succeeded his father as 6th Viscount Gort, 1902. Educated at Harrow and Sandhurst. 2nd Lieutenant, 1905; Captain, 1914. On active service, 1914–18 (despatches nine times, Victoria Cross, Military Cross, DSO and two bars). General, 1937. Chief of the Imperial General Staff, 1937–9. Commander-in-Chief of the British Field Force, 1939–40. Inspector-General to the Forces for Training, 1940. Governor and Commander-in-Chief, Gibraltar, 1941–2; Malta, 1942–4. High Commissioner and Commander-in-Chief, Palestine, 1944–5. In 1938 he became a member of the Other Club.

May 1940

regiments had been withdrawn into reserve. The Commander-in-Chief's chief anxiety was his right flank, on account of the French withdrawal. . . .

The Prime Minister said that he might have to go to Paris during the day to sustain the French Government. In the meanwhile, he thought it would be advisable for the Chiefs of Staff to study the possible effects of a German break through.

(NOTE:– At this point Air Chief Marshal Sir Hugh Dowding[1] and Air Marshal Peirse[2] entered the meeting.)

Air Marshal Peirse said that the demand which had come the previous day from M. Reynaud for 10 fighter squadrons had been made without any reference to the Air Officer Commanding-in-Chief, in France.[3] The latter had now reported that he was short of fighters, having suffered casualties in the squadrons of the Advanced Air Striking Force. He had temporarily diverted three squadrons from the Air Component of the British Expeditionary Force on to the Sedan front the previous afternoon, but these had now gone back to their proper task. The fighters were required to escort our day bombers who, in face of the very heavy anti-aircraft fire which they were now encountering, would be forced to fly higher. They would also be employed in shooting down the German bombers which were flying at will over France, though they were not doing much damage.

The Prime Minister said that the time had now come to reconsider the employment of the heavy bombers, and, if the Chiefs of Staff agreed, he proposed to raise the matter at the War Cabinet.

Sir Cyril Newall said that he had received a message from General Gamelin, in which he said that he hoped the Royal Air Force would strike deep into Germany.

---

[1] Hugh Caswall Tremenheere Dowding, 1882–1970. Educated at Winchester. Joined the Royal Artillery, 1900; Royal Flying Corps, 1914. On active service, 1914–19 (despatches). Director of Training, Air Ministry, 1926–9. Commander the Fighting Area, Air Defence of Great Britain, 1929–30. Air Member for Research and Development, 1930–6. Knighted, 1933. Air Officer Commanding-in-Chief, Fighter Command, 1936–40. Mission to the USA for the Ministry of Aircraft Production, 1940–1. Created Baron, 1943.

[2] Richard Edmund Charles Peirse, 1892–1970. A pilot in the Royal Naval Air Service, 1913–14, and one of Churchill's flying instructors at that time. On active service, 1914–18 (DSO, AFC). Deputy Director of Operations and Intelligence, Air Ministry, 30–3. Air Officer Commanding British Forces, Palestine and Transjordan, 1933–6. Deputy Chief of the Air Staff, 1937–40. Knighted, 1940. Vice-Chief of the Air Staff, April–October 1940. Air Officer Commanding-in-Chief, Bomber Command, 1940–2; India, 1942–3; Allied Air Commander-in-Chief, South-East Asia, 1943–4.

[3] Arthur Sheridan Barratt, 1891–1966. Royal Flying Corps, 1914. On active service, 1914–18. CMG, 1919. Director of Staff Duties, Air Ministry, 1935. Commandant, RAF Staff College, 1936–9. CB, 1937. Air Officer Commanding-in-Chief, British Air Forces in France (BAAF), 1940 (despatches, Military Cross); Army Co-operation Command, 1940–3; Technical Training Command, 1943–5. Knighted, 1940. Inspector-General of the RAF, 1945–7. Air Chief Marshal, 1946.

Sir Hugh Dowding said that we were faced with a tremendously important decision in view of the situation developing in France. How matters would end there he was not in a position to judge, but if things went badly we would then have to face an attack directed against this country, possibly from France in addition to Holland and Germany. Provided no more fighters were removed from ADGB,[1] he was confident that the Navy and the Royal Air Force would be able to keep the Germans out of this country. If more fighters were taken from him, however, they would not achieve decisive results in France, and he would be left too weak to carry on over here. He was absolutely opposed to parting with a single additional Hurricane. If he were not further weakened, he would be prepared for any German attack here in retaliation for action by our bombers.

In reply to the Prime Minister, Air Marshal Peirse said that there was no doubt the German Air Force were not pressing home their attacks so hard now, but numerically they could afford heavy losses.

Sir Cyril Newall said that he was having the possibility examined of withdrawing additional aircraft from training to reinforce the first line, but he was anxious not to interrupt the advanced training of pilots and crews.

War Cabinet: minutes
(*Cabinet papers, 65/7*)

15 May 1940 10 Downing Street
11 a.m.

The Prime Minister said that he had had an alarmist message from M. Reynaud earlier in the morning. M. Reynaud had said that the Germans had broken through at Sedan, and that the road to Paris was open. He had made an urgent appeal for British help. He (the Prime Minister) had refused to accept so gloomy a picture of the situation. He had pointed out that it was impossible for us to send any more divisions to France at the present moment; and even if we had been ready to denude this country of troops, it would be quite impossible to get them quickly to the scene of action.

He had then spoken to General Georges who had seemed quite calm. General Georges' view of the position was that in the North things were fairly satisfactory; pressure was considerable in the centre; in the South, the situation was undoubtedly serious. The Germans had broken through on a

---

[1] The Air Defence of Great Britain.

May 1940

fairly wide front, but this was now plugged ('colmaté'). General Georges had paid a tribute to the wonderful assistance of the Royal Air Force. He had made no direct request for further help. He (the Prime Minister) had said that we would do everything we could, but we could not denude England of her essential defences.

The Prime Minister said that he had also had a telegram from General Gamelin, who had said that, although the position was serious between Namur and Sedan, he viewed the situation with calm. He had asked for all possible air assistance.

The Prime Minister said that he had received a message from Admiral Keyes[1] to the effect that the Belgian Government had not yet decided to evacuate Brussels. The Belgian Army had withdrawn to a new line and he was confident that they could hold their position provided that they obtained strong air co-operation. He anticipated a strong German attack on Antwerp from the North. He suggested that, if practicable, two destroyers should be sent to the mouth of the Scheldt to provide supporting fire.

OPERATION 'ROYAL MARINE'

The Prime Minister reported that air photographs of the barrier at Karlsruhe showed very considerable damage, which would permit of the passage of mines. Some difficulty had been experienced during the first and second nights in streaming mines into the tributaries, and the mines were now being streamed direct into the Rhine. At Thionville, leading into the Moselle, 40 mines had been captured owing to the rapid advance of the enemy's troops. Steps were to be taken to place mines in the Meuse that night.

The Prime Minister said that it should be made clear that the action announced in General Winkelman's proclamation[2] amounted to no more than a military capitulation in a particular area.

---

[1] Roger John Brownlow Keyes, 1872–1945. Entered the Royal Navy, 1885, Naval Attaché, Athens and Constantinople, 1905–7. Commodore in charge of submarines, North Sea and adjacent waters, August 1914 to February 1915. Chief of Staff, Eastern Mediterranean Squadron (Dardanelles), 1915. Director of Plans, Admiralty, 1917. Vice-Admiral in command of the Dover Patrol (and Zeebrugge raid), 1918. Knighted, 1918. Created Baronet, 1919. Deputy Chief of the Naval Staff, 1921–5. Commander-in-Chief, Mediterranean, 1925–8; Portsmouth, 1929–31. Admiral of the Fleet, 1930. Elected to the Other Club, 1930. National Conservative MP, 1934–43. Director of Combined Operations, 1940–1. Created Baron, 1943. Churchill wrote the foreword to his memoirs, *Adventures Ashore & Afloat* (1939). His elder son was killed in action in Libya, leading a raid on Rommel's headquarters, 18 November 1941.

[2] General Winkelman, the Netherlands Commander-in-Chief, had announced the surrender of Rotterdam and Utrecht, 'in order to save further useless loss of life'.

ITALY

Continuing, the Foreign Secretary said that it might be of value if the Prime Minister, on assuming office, were to send a communication to Signor Mussolini.[1] Perhaps the general heads of the message might be communicated to Sir Percy Loraine[2] by telegram, with authority for him to cast the message into the most appropriate form, having regard to the situation in Rome.

The Prime Minister said that he was quite ready to send such a message, and had already thought of doing so. He would propose to say that, on assuming the office of Prime Minister, he wished to assure Signor Mussolini of his hope that this country and Italy should not be divided by bloodshed; we were finding the war hard, but we were confident of ultimate victory; it would be a disaster of the first magnitude if any irrevocable step were taken, but, if this should happen, we should have no choice but to pursue the matter to the end, and this we should do. The Prime Minister said that he would draft a message and then consult with the Foreign Secretary.

The War Cabinet took note –
(a) Of the statement by the Secretary of State for Foreign Affairs.
(b) That the Prime Minister proposed to send a personal message to Signor Mussolini on the lines indicated in the discussion.

ENEMY ALIENS

The Prime Minister said that in existing circumstances he thought it important that there should be a very large round-up of enemy aliens and suspect persons in this country.[3] It was much better that these persons should be behind barbed-wire, and internment would probably be much safer for all German-speaking persons themselves since, when air attacks developed, public temper in this country would be such that such persons would be in great danger if at liberty.

In reply to a question by the Prime Minister, the Chief of the Imperial General Staff said that between seven and eight hundred enemy parachutist

---

[1] Benito Mussolini, 1883–1945. A journalist and active Socialist. Served on the Austrian front, 1917. Founded the Fascist Party at the end of the war and led it to power in 1922. President of the Council of Ministers, 1922–6. Head of State from 1926. Fled from Rome in 1943. Head of the German-controlled government of northern Italy, 1944–5. Killed by Italian partisans while attempting to flee to Switzerland, 28 April 1945.

[2] Percy Lyham Loraine, 1880–1961. Served as a 2nd Lieutenant in the South African War, 1900–1. Entered the Diplomatic Service as an Attaché at Constantinople, 1904. 12th Baronet, 1917. 1st Secretary, Warsaw, October 1919. Minister to Teheran, 1921–6; to Athens, 1926–9. High Commissioner for Egypt and the Sudan, 1929–33. Privy Councillor, 1933. Ambassador in Ankara, 1933–9; in Rome, 1939–40.

[3] The Minister of Home Security, Sir John Anderson, had listed for the War Cabinet the groups to be interned: 'i, Italians and British subjects of Italian origin. ii, Czech refugees in this country who were not enemy aliens. iii, Refugees from the Netherlands and Belgium, some of whom might be German agents. iv, the British Fascists. v, the Communists in this country'.

prisoners had been examined. They were men of all ages ranging from a General of 50 to a boy of 19. Some of them thought that they had landed in England.

The Prime Minister said that the matter was urgent, and he invited the Lord Privy Seal and the Minister without Portfolio[1] to collaborate with the Minister of Home Security in the manner suggested. He hoped it would be possible for the War Cabinet to receive a report on the whole subject in a few days' time.

The War Cabinet approved the Prime Minister's proposal.

War Cabinet: Confidential Annex
(*Cabinet papers, 65/13*)

15 May 1940
11 a.m.

The Prime Minister said that there remained two important questions to be decided that morning in regard to air operations:–
  (1) Whether we should send any more fighter squadrons to France in response to M. Reynaud's appeal.
  (2) Whether we should attack military objectives in the Ruhr and elsewhere in Germany east of the Rhine.

As regards the former, he suggested that the War Cabinet would have little difficulty in deciding against the despatch of further fighter squadrons in view of the fact that no demand for these had been received from the Military authorities in France.

The Prime Minister asked the Secretary of State for Air for his views on the question of an attack against military objectives in the Ruhr and other similar targets.

The Secretary of State for Air said that the experience of the last few days in France pointed to the fact that, at the present rate of losses, it would be extremely difficult for the Royal Air Force to maintain its present effort in support of the land battle by daylight bombing operations.

The Air Officer Commanding-in-Chief, Fighter Command,[2] welcomed the proposal to attack the Ruhr. He considered that it was the soundest action which we could take in the present situation. We should not be deterred by the fear of attacks from Germany since these, in his opinion, were bound to come sooner or later.

The Prime Minister agreed that we must expect this country to be hit in

[1] Clement Attlee and Arthur Greenwood.
[2] Sir Hugh Dowding.

return. The attraction of German bombers to this country would, however, have the advantage of relieving the pressure on France.

The Vice Chief of the Air Staff[1] said that the General and Air Staffs had already been in consultation on the question of the most suitable marshalling yards for attack.

The Prime Minister said that, apart from the purely military aspect, there was the important consideration of neutral opinion which would have to be taken into account. American sympathy had recently been veering very much in our favour. Would the operations in view produce a revulsion of feeling, or would they be accepted by the United States as a reasonable and justifiable retaliation for German methods of warfare?

The Lord Privy Seal[2] considered that the moment had arrived when it was essential that we should counter-attack. The proposed attack on the German railways and oil refineries seemed to provide the best means of doing this, and he was accordingly in favour of our carrying out these operations forthwith.

The Prime Minister said that it was clear that the War Cabinet were united in favour of taking immediate action in delivering a hard blow at Germany. He considered that the proposed operations would cut Germany at its tap root, and was hopeful that they might even provide an immediate contribution to the land battle. They should dispel French doubts about our willingness to suffer and also have a salutary effect on Italy. Finally, he considered that this was the psychological moment to strike Germany in her own country and convince the German people that we had both the will and the power to hit them hard. He accordingly suggested that the operations should be carried out that evening. There was no need to consult the French Government as they had given us full authority, at the Supreme War Council, to carry out this operation.[3]

It would therefore merely be necessary to inform them through the usual channels.

The Prime Minister asked the Minister of Information[4] to arrange that

---

[1] Air Marshal Richard Peirse.
[2] Clement Attlee.
[3] The Supreme War Council had last met, in Paris, on 27 April 1940.
[4] Alfred Duff Cooper, 1890–1954. Known as 'Duff'. Educated at Eton and New College, Oxford. Entered the Foreign Office as a clerk, 1913. On active service, Grenadier Guards, 1917–18 (DSO, despatches). Conservative MP for Oldham (Churchill's first constituency), 1924–9. Financial Secretary, War Office, 1928–9 and 1931–4. MP for St George's, Westminster, 1931–45. Financial Secretary, Treasury, 1934–5. Privy Councillor, 1935. Secretary of State for War, 1935–7. First Lord of the Admiralty, 1937–8. Minister of Information, 1940–1. British Representative, Singapore, 1941. Chancellor of the Duchy of Lancaster, 1941–3. British Representative, French Committee of National Liberation, 1943–4. Ambassador to France, 1944–7. Knighted, 1948. Created Viscount Norwich, 1952. In 1919 he married Lady Diana Manners. In 1928 he was elected to the Other Club.

discreet reference should be made in the press to the killing of civilians in France and the Low Countries, in the course of German air attacks. No reference should, however, be made to the possibility of retaliation on our part.

The War Cabinet agreed:–
(1) That no further fighter squadrons should for the present be sent to France, and to invite the Prime Minister so to inform Monsieur Reynaud.
(2) To authorise the Chief of the Air Staff to order Bomber Command to carry out attacks on suitable military[1] objectives (including marshalling yards and oil refineries) in the Ruhr as well as elsewhere in Germany; and that these attacks should begin that night with approximately 100 heavy bombers.
(3) That the French Government should be informed, through the normal channels, of our intention to carry out these operations.

Lord Camrose[2]: notes of a conversation with General Ironside
(*Camrose papers*)

15 May 1940

This morning Reynaud was on the 'phone to Winston, begging him to send more men and saying there was nothing between the Germans and Paris. Ironside described Reynaud as 'collapsed'. Winston handled him splendidly. The difference since Winston came into power in the way of saving time and making quick decisions has been wonderful. Chamberlain was a fine fellow, splendid character, but so much time was wasted in explaining things to him. They had decided two very important things at a meeting of the Staffs this morning, and when the War Cabinet met at 11 o'clock Winston got their sanction in ten minutes although last night the Cabinet was practically unanimous against both proposals.

---

[1] All words underlined in this volume were underlined in the original document.
[2] William Ewart Berry, 1879–1954. Newspaper proprietor. Founder of *Advertising World*, 1901. Editor-in-Chief of the *Sunday Times*, 1915–36. Chairman, Financial Times Limited, 1919–45; Allied Newspapers Limited, 1924–36. Created Baron Camrose, 1929. Chief Proprietor and Editor-in-Chief of the *Daily Telegraph and Morning Post*, 1936–54. Principal Adviser, Ministry of Information, 1939. Advanced to a Viscountcy, 1941. One of Churchill's close friends (he was elected to the Other Club in 1926), and from 1945 a principal financial adviser; in 1946 he negotiated both the sale of Churchill's war memoirs, and also the purchase of Chartwell by a group of Churchill's friends and its conveyance to the National Trust (Camrose himself contributing £15,000 and sixteen other friends £5,000 each).

Winston S. Churchill to Sir Roger Keyes
(*Churchill papers, 20/14*)

15 May 1940

Many thanks for your excellent reports. We are doing our best to help in the air in accordance with General Gamelin's request. He is commanding the whole battle and alone has the complete view. Pray give my warm regards to our friend.[1] Be careful what you say on the 'phone. Better to telegraph unless time of vital importance.

Henry Channon[2]: *diary*
(*Robert Rhodes James (editor), 'Chips'*)

15 May 1940

Harold[3] and Rab[4] have both been sent for by the Prime Minister and asked to continue in their present jobs; both gleefully accepted. Rab tells me that he had a characteristic five minutes with Winston: when he reminded

---

[1] Leopold, 1901–83. Married, 1926, Princess Astrid of Sweden. Succeeded his father (King Albert) as King of the Belgians in 1934. Queen Astrid was killed in a car crash in Switzerland in 1935. In September 1939 Leopold reasserted Belgian neutrality. On the German invasion, 10 May 1940, he assumed command of the Belgian Army. Surrendered, 28 May 1940. Detained by the Germans, as a technical prisoner of war, with his mother, Queen Elisabeth, in the royal palace of Laeken, 1940–5. Prevented from returning to the throne in 1945. In 1951 he abdicated in favour of his son King Baudouin.

[2] Henry Channon, 1897–1958. Known as 'Chips'. An American by birth. Educated privately, and at Christ Church, Oxford. In 1933 he married Lady Honor Guinness, elder daughter of the 2nd Earl of Iveagh. Conservative MP for Southend-on-Sea, 1935–50; for Southend-on-Sea (West), 1950–8. Parliamentary Private Secretary to the Under-Secretary of State for Foreign Affairs (R. A. Butler), 1938–41. Knighted, 1957.

[3] Harold Harington Balfour, 1897–1988. On active service, 1914–18 (Military Cross and bar). Royal Flying Corps, 1915. Royal Air Force, 1918–23. Conservative MP, 1929–45. Parliamentary Under-Secretary of State for Air, 1938–44. Privy Councillor, 1941. Member of the Beaverbrook–Harriman Mission to Moscow, 1941. Minister Resident in West Africa, 1944–5. Created Baron (Balfour of Inchyre), 1945. President of the Federation of Chambers of Commerce of the British Empire, 1946–9; of the Commonwealth and Empire Industries Association, 1956–60.

[4] Richard Austen Butler, 1902–82. Known as 'Rab'. Educated at Marlborough and Pembroke College, Cambridge. President of the Cambridge Union, 1924. Conservative MP for Saffron Walden, 1929–65. Under-Secretary of State, India Office, 1932–7. Parliamentary Secretary, Ministry of Labour, 1937–8. Under-Secretary of State for Foreign Affairs, 1938–41. Privy Councillor, 1939. Minister of Education, 1941–5. Minister of Labour, 1945. Chancellor of the Exchequer, 1951–5. Lord Privy Seal, 1955–61. Home Secretary, 1957–62. Deputy Prime Minister, 1962–3. Secretary of State for Foreign Affairs, 1963–4. Created Baron Butler of Saffron Walden, 1965. Master of Trinity College, Cambridge, 1965–78.

him that they had often sparred in the past, and disagreed on many things, 'Yes', Winston stuttered, 'but you have invited me to your private residence'.[1]

Winston S. Churchill to President Roosevelt
(Churchill papers, 20/14)

15 May 1940

Although I have changed my office, I am sure you would not wish me to discontinue our intimate, private correspondence. As you are no doubt aware, the scene has darkened swiftly. The enemy have a marked preponderance in the air, and their new technique is making a deep impression upon the French. I think myself the battle on land has only just begun, and I should like to see the masses engage. Up to the present, Hitler is working with specialized units in tanks and air. The small countries are simply smashed up, one by one, like matchwood. We must expect, though it is not yet certain, that Mussolini will hurry in to share the loot of civilisation. We expect to be attacked here ourselves, both from the air and by parachute and air-borne troops in the near future, and are getting ready for them. If necessary, we shall continue the war alone, and we are not afraid of that. But I trust you realise, Mr President, that the voice and force of the United States may count for nothing if they are withheld too long. You may have a completely subjugated Nazified Europe established with astonishing swiftness, and the weight may be more than we can bear. All I ask now is that you should proclaim non-belligerency, which would mean that you would help us with everything short of actually engaging armed forces. Immediate needs are: First of all, the loan of 40 or 50 of your older destroyers to bridge gap between what we have now and the large new construction we put in hand at the beginning of the war. This time next year we shall have plenty. But if in the interval Italy comes in against us with another 100 submarines, we may be strained to breaking-point. Secondly, we want several hundred of the latest types of aircraft, of which you are now getting delivery. These can be repaid by those now being constructed in the United States for us. Thirdly, anti-aircraft equipment and ammunition, of which again there will be plenty next year, if we are alive to see it. Fourthly,

---

[1] Between 4.30 and 6.30 p.m. on 15 May, at five-minute intervals, Churchill saw nineteen of the Junior Ministers to be appointed, and spoke to six more on the telephone. The only one to refuse office was the Labour MP Emanuel Shinwell, whom Churchill proposed as Under-Secretary of State at the Ministry of Food. The position was accepted by Robert Boothby. Colville noted in his diary that day: 'It was my difficult job to explain on the telephone to Kenneth Lindsay, the Duke of Devonshire, Lord Denham and Captain McEwen that their services were no longer required.'

the fact that our ore supply is being compromised from Sweden, from North Africa, and perhaps from Northern Spain makes it necessary to purchase steel in the United States. This also applies to other materials. We shall go on paying dollars for as long as we can, but I should like to feel reasonably sure that when we can pay no more, you will give us the stuff all the same. Fifthly, we have many reports of possible German parachute or air-borne descents in Ireland. The visit of a United States Squadron to Irish ports, which might well be prolonged, would be invaluable. Sixthly, I am looking to you to keep that Japanese dog quiet in the Pacific, using Singapore in any way convenient. The details of the material which we have in hand will be communicated to you separately.

With all good wishes and respect.

Winston S. Churchill to all Royal Naval units
(*Admiralty papers, 1/10570*)

15 May 1940

On leaving the Admiralty I desire to convey to all officers and men of His Majesty's Fleet an expression of my personal admiration for the work which they have accomplished during these first eight months of war.

The ever increasing demands made on personnel and ships have been and I am convinced will continue to be met with unrelaxing devotion to duty. The several gallant actions which have been fought are a source of inspiration; but I understand the ceaseless toil of those many to whom the chance of battle has not come, but who daily face danger and strain in carrying out their duties.

The kindness and help of the Navy has been a comfort to me.

I was proud after many years to come again to the Admiralty in the hour of peril and the sorrow which I feel on leaving is tempered by feeling I shall not be far away. I leave you in good hands both afloat and ashore. As Prime Minister and Minister of Defence it will be my duty to watch over your interests and your proceedings.

To all in His Majesty's Fleet and Auxiliaries and the Merchant Navy I wish Godspeed victory and peace.

Winston S. Churchill

May 1940

Lord Ivor Spencer-Churchill[1] to Winston S. Churchill
(*Churchill papers, 1/355*)

15 May 1940

My dear Winston,

I need hardly say with what emotion I have followed recent events and with what deep satisfaction I have viewed their outcome.

I know you will be, to the nation, in the days before us, the same source of inspiration you have always been to those who, like myself, felt that sooner or later you would be called to guide our destinies. I wish, for your sake, that this could have been at a time when the burden was less severe – but Fate has willed it otherwise and has reserved for you the supreme time of trial. I pray that God will bless your efforts, and preserve your health and strength.

With deep affection.

Yrs
Ivor

Major George Cornwallis-West[2] to Winston S. Churchill
(*Churchill papers, 1/355*)

15 May 1940

My dear Winston,

May I be one of many to congratulate you on your appointment as Prime Minister. Next to the Sovereign the highest position in the Kingdom. I always felt you'd get there. It brings back memories of the old days at Salisbury Hall. I so well remember you saying 'to become PM of this country, there must be a certain combination of circumstances and a definite occasion'. Both are present only too overwhelmingly in the present case. May God speed you & give you all the success you deserve. You have been the only front bench politician who, quâ Germany, has been right all along.[3]

---

[1] Lord Ivor Charles Spencer-Churchill, 1898–1956. Younger son of Churchill's cousin the 9th Duke of Marlborough. Educated at Eton and Magdalen College, Oxford. On active service, 1917–18. Lieutenant, Royal Army Service Corps.

[2] George Frederick Myddelton Cornwallis-West, 1874–1951. Joined the Scots Guards, 1895. On active service in South Africa, 1899–1901. Married, 1900 (as his first wife), Churchill's mother, Lady Randolph Churchill, with whom he lived at Salisbury Hall near St Albans. The marriage was dissolved in 1913. Married (second) Mrs Patrick Campbell, the actress, in 1914. Lieutenant-Colonel commanding the Anson Division, Royal Naval Division, Antwerp, 1914. Present at the siege of Antwerp. Succeeded to his family estates on the death of his father in 1919. Lord Lieutenant of Denbigh. Author of several one-act plays and of several books, including *Two Wives* (1929). In 1940 he married, as his third wife, Georgette, the widow of Adolph Hirsch.

[3] Churchill replied by telegram: 'Thank you so much my dear George for your kind letter' (*Churchill papers, 1/355*).

Lord Hugh Cecil[1] to Winston S. Churchill
(*Churchill papers, 2/393*)

15 May 1940

My dear Winston,
 I congratulate. The bluebottle has become a Purple Emperor. Let us rejoice.
 No answer of course.

Ever yours
Hugh Cecil

The Purp: Emp: is a very beautiful butterfly, not often seen because it usually flies high among the tops of trees.

Violet Pearman[2] to Winston S. Churchill
(*Churchill papers, 2/397*)

15 May 1940 Edenbridge
Personal Kent

My dear Mr Churchill,
 May I wish you success, and also health and strength to go forward in your gigantic and noble task. You have the whole of the nation with you; we have tremendous confidence in you, and any appeal you make to us, I am sure will have immediate and overwhelming response.
 The wisdom and knowledge with which you have selected your Cabinet is

---

[1] Lord Hugh Richard Heathcote Gascoyne Cecil, 1869–1956. Known as 'Linky'. Fifth son of the 3rd Marquess of Salisbury. Educated at Eton and University College, Oxford. Conservative MP for Greenwich, 1895–1906; for Oxford University, 1910–37. A prominent member of the Church Assembly. Provost of Eton, 1936–44. Created Baron Quickswood, 1941. In 1908 he was the 'best man' at Churchill's wedding.

[2] Violet Constance Evelyn Williams, 1896–1941. Began secretarial work at the Treasury, 1915; worked subsequently in the Cabinet Office, Home Office and Irish Office (during the 'Troubles'). During the war she married George Edward Pearman (known as 'Alan'), a chartered accountant. He enlisted, falsely declaring himself to be old enough to serve. Both his legs were blown off during fighting on the Western Front, and he suffered also from severe shell-shock. After the war he became a lift attendant. With one daughter aged nine and another of only two months, Mrs Pearman began part-time work at Chartwell in July 1929, and became Churchill's principal full-time secretary on 11 November 1929. In 1938 she was forced to retire, through illness, but continued to do part-time work for Churchill. Following her death on 17 March 1941, Churchill arranged for her monthly salary (of £12 a week) to be paid to her daughter Rosemary, then aged eleven; then for seven years from July 1943, Churchill paid £100 a year towards Rosemary Pearman's education. Violet Pearman's elder daughter, Marguerite, born in 1919, served first in a munitions factory (1940), then in the Women's Auxiliary Air Force (1940–5), first with barrage balloons, then as a wireless operator with Coastal Command, Norfolk, and Ismailia.

great. No other man could have done it. You and you alone can get the best out of that 'team' of mixed men and ideas. Especially do I know with what affection the Labour men regard you – personal affection and respect – from what various leaders have said to me in the past. (As you know I always tried to get Liberal and Labour views and ideas in order to preserve a balanced and just mind to deal with constituents etc. in my work for you).

May God bless you in your work, which seems not only national, but for the salvation of all we hold dear – life, liberty and civilisation throughout the world.

May I remind you to have a strict watch over refugees, and to deal ruthlessly with aliens. England (or rather Britain) must never have a suspicion of the treachery which undermined Denmark and Norway, and which is undermining Holland.

Would to God that Parliament had listened to your warnings in the past. Britain's 'woolliness' and weakness has been the cause of this. Thank God you are in complete control now!!

Sincerely yours,
Violet Pearman

Winston S. Churchill to Neville Chamberlain
(*Churchill papers, 2/402*)

16 May 1940

My dear Neville,

You have been good enough to consult me about the Leadership of the Conservative Party. I am of course a Conservative. But as Prime Minister of a National Government, formed on the widest basis, and comprising the three Parties, I feel that it would be better for me not to undertake the Leadership of any one political Party. I therefore express the hope that your own Leadership of our Party will remain undisturbed by the change of Government or Premiership, and I feel sure that by this arrangement the cause of national unity will best be served.

The relations of perfect confidence which have grown up between us makes this division of duties and responsibilities very agreeable to me.

Yours ever,
Winston S. Churchill

Winston S. Churchill to Benito Mussolini
(*Churchill papers, 20/14*)

16 May 1940

Now that I have taken up my office as Prime Minister and Minister of Defence I look back to our meetings in Rome and feel a desire to speak words of goodwill to you as chief of the Italian nation across what seems to be a swiftly-widening gulf. Is it too late to stop a river of blood from flowing between the British and Italian peoples? We can no doubt inflict grievous injuries upon one another and maul each other cruelly, and darken the Mediterranean with our strife.[1] If you so decree it must be so; but I declare that I have never been the enemy of Italian greatness, nor ever at heart the foe of the Italian law-giver. It is idle to predict the course of the great battles now raging in Europe, but I am sure that whatever may happen on the Continent, England will go on to the end, even quite alone, as we have done before, and I believe with some assurance that we shall be aided in increasing measure by the United States, and, indeed, by all the Americas.

I beg you to believe that it is in no spirit of weakness or of fear that I make this solemn appeal which will remain on record. Down the ages above all other calls comes the cry that the joint heirs of Latin and Christian civilisation must not be ranged against one another in mortal strife. Hearken to it I beseech you in all honour and respect before the dread signal is given. It will never be given by us.[2]

Chiefs of Staff Committee: minutes
(*Cabinet papers, 73/4*)

16 May 1940
10.15 a.m.

The Prime Minister agreed that in the circumstances with which we were now faced, it was right to send further fighters to France.[3] In his view we

[1] At the 11.30 a.m. War Cabinet, in discussing a 7 May War Cabinet decision that British merchant ships should continue 'to be allowed to pass through the Mediterranean in both directions', Churchill said: 'Reports were so frequent and contradictory about the intentions of Italy that it was impossible to do more than watch the situation and continue to thin out the shipping as much as possible' (*Cabinet papers, 65–7*).

[2] For the full text of Mussolini's reply, sent on 18 May 1940, see Churchill's broadcast to the Italian people on 23 December 1940. On receiving Churchill's message, the Italian Foreign Minister Count Ciano, who was Mussolini's son-in-law, noted in his diary: 'It is a message of goodwill, couched in vague terms, but none the less dignified and noble.' Ciano noted that even Mussolini 'appreciated the tone', but that his reply was 'needlessly harsh in tone' (Malcolm Muggeridge, editor, *Ciano's Diaries, 1939–43*, London 1947, pages 251–2).

[3] The Chiefs of Staff had just approved a request from Air Marshal Barratt for four additional fighter squadrons to be sent 'at once' to France. According to Barratt, the German use of bombers, in support of their infantry advance, 'had destroyed the French morale to such an extent

ought to send six squadrons, two of which might be sent from Wick, the defence of the Fleet at Scapa being left to the Anti-Aircraft guns. Alternatively, the Fleet might be based on the Clyde. Sir Cyril Newall reiterated the considered opinion of the Chiefs of Staff that four squadrons was the limit to which we should go in sending further fighters to France at the present time.

It was agreed that the matter should be referred to the meeting of the War Cabinet that same morning.

War Cabinet: minutes
(*Cabinet papers, 65/7*)

16 May 1940   10 Downing Street
11.30 a.m.

NARVIK

The Prime Minister read out a telegram from Lord Cork, reporting that the landing at Bjervik had been successfully carried out; that the German forces had suffered a number of casualties, including 70 prisoners; and that the operations in this area were proceeding satisfactorily.

WESTERN FRONT

The Prime Minister took an extremely grave view of this news.[1] He considered that a withdrawal from our line on account of the penetration of the French line by a force of some 120 German armoured vehicles was quite unjustifiable and would expose the British Army to far more serious risks than if they remained in their present position and fought. He therefore felt that the order to withdraw was one which could not possibly be accepted without further consultation, and he accordingly proposed that he should himself go to France that very afternoon to discuss the matter with the French.

The War Cabinet expressed general agreement with this view and invited the Prime Minister to proceed that afternoon to France, with a view to ascertaining the position and representing strong objections to such a withdrawal.

---

that the German troops had been able to advance almost without the loss of a man'. If these extra British planes were sent, Barratt felt able 'to stop the "rot" '.

[1] The Vice-Chief of the Imperial General Staff, General Sir John Dill, had reported a telephone call with the Chief of the General Staff, British Expeditionary Force, from which he had learned (from a conversation 'perforce to be conducted in parables') that 'the Germans had made a deep penetration with armoured forces' from the direction of Mézières, had captured Hirson, were reported to be pressing towards La Capelle, were believed to have reached Vervins, 'and might be advancing in the direction of Laon'; that orders 'had been issued' for a French withdrawal to a line running through Trelon–Marpent–Brussels–Malines–Antwerp.

May 1940

War Cabinet: Confidential Annex
(*Cabinet papers, 65/13*)

16 May 1940　　　　　　　　　　　　　　　　　　　　　10 Downing Street
11.30 a.m.

The Prime Minister said that an urgent appeal had been received from France for the despatch of additional fighter aircraft. The War Cabinet would have to decide, as a matter of urgency, whether this request should be met. German armoured fighting vehicles appeared to have broken through and reached the area Hirson–Montcornet–Neufchâtel.

The Prime Minister said that to despatch fighter aircraft from this country at a time when we were most likely to be attacked ourselves in response to the attacks on military targets in the Ruhr the previous night, was taking a very grave risk, but it seemed essential to do something to bolster up the French. Armoured fighting vehicles could not conquer the whole of France, but there was a danger of their spreading panic behind the lines. The first necessity, therefore, was to support the French morale and give them a chance to recover themselves and deal with German armoured forces by the use of their own Army. He favoured withdrawing the two fighter squadrons allocated to the defence of Scapa, and sending six squadrons in all. More than that we could not do. If the fighters were taken away from Scapa the Fleet might have to be sent round to the Clyde, but Scapa was heavily defended by anti-aircraft artillery in addition to the ships' batteries.

The Prime Minister said that the main reason for the despatch of fighters was to give the French moral support. Provided their ground troops further back put up some opposition against them, it should be possible to deal with German armoured forces in comparatively small numbers. They would surely not be allowed to reach Paris altogether unopposed.

The War Cabinet agreed:–
(i) That arrangements should be made for the immediate despatch of the equivalent of four fighter squadrons to France.
(ii) That preparations should be made for the despatch of two additional fighter squadrons, at very short notice, if it was so decided.
(iii) That a decision whether to send the two additional squadrons to France should be taken in the light of Air Marshal Joubert de la Ferté's[1] report later in the day.
(iv) That the French should be informed of the decision at (i) only.

---

[1] Philip Bennet Joubert de la Ferté, 1887–1965. Joined the Royal Field Artillery, 1907; the Royal Flying Corps, 1913. On active service in France, Egypt and Italy, 1914–18 (despatches six times, DSO). Air Officer Commanding-in-Chief, Royal Air Force, India, 1937–9. Knighted, 1938. Assistant Chief of the Air Staff, 1939–40. In charge of radar and radar counter-measures, 1939–40. Adviser to the Admiralty on Combined Operations, 1940. Officer Commanding-in-

MAY 1940

Sir Alexander Cadogan[1]: diary
(*'The Diaries of Sir Alexander Cadogan'*)

16 May 1940

Cabinet in morning at which we received blacker and blacker news from France. Finally Dill[2] explained plans for withdrawal in Belgium. This infuriated Winston, who said we couldn't agree to that, which could jeopardise our whole army. Sprang up and said he would go to France – it was ridiculous to think that France could be conquered by 120 tanks (but it may be!). He said he would leave after lunch, and asked NC[3] to 'mind the shop!'

FOLLOWING the War Cabinet of Thursday, 16 May 1940, Churchill flew from London to Paris, accompanied by the Vice-Chief of the Imperial General Staff, General Dill, and the head of his Defence Office, General Ismay.

General Ismay: recollection[4]
(*Churchill papers, 4/44*)

16 May 1940

From the moment that we got out of the Flamingo[5] at Le Bourget, it was obvious that the situation was far more critical than we had suspected. The

Chief, Coastal Command, 1941–3. Inspector General of the Royal Air Force, 1943. Director of Public Relations, Air Ministry, 1946–7.

[1] Alexander George Montagu Cadogan, 1884–1968. Seventh son of the 5th Earl Cadogan. Educated at Eton and Balliol College, Oxford. Attaché, Diplomatic Service, 1908. British Minister to China, 1933–5; Ambassador, 1935–6. Knighted, 1934. Deputy Under-Secretary of State for Foreign Affairs, 1936–7; Permanent Under-Secretary, January 1938 to February 1946. Permanent British Representative at the United Nations, 1946–50. Government Director, Suez Canal Company, 1951–7. Chairman of the BBC, 1952–7. One brother, William George Sydney Cadogan, born in 1879, was killed in action in France on 14 November 1914. Another brother, Edward Cecil George Cadogan, was a Conservative MP from 1922 to 1945 and largely responsible for the abolition of judicial corporal punishment.

[2] John Greer Dill, 1881–1944. Born in Northern Ireland. Entered the Army, 1901. On active service, 1914–18 (DSO). Commanded the British Forces in Palestine, 1936–7. Knighted, 1937. General Officer Commanding Aldershot Command, 1937–9. Commanded the 1st Army Corps, France, 1939–40. Vice-Chief of the Imperial General Staff, 1940. Chief of the Imperial General Staff, 1940–1. Head of the British Joint Staff Mission, Washington, from 1941 until his death.

[3] Neville Chamberlain.

[4] Ismay set down the recollections printed here and on pages 60 and 64, at Churchill's request, in 1946, when Churchill was writing his war memoirs and had sent Ismay the draft typescript. (Letter of 20 May 1946, and enclosure.)

[5] One of a number of De Havilland aircraft put at the disposal of senior Government Ministers and Service personnel. It was usually accompanied on overseas flights by an escort of Hurricane fighters.

officers who met us said that the Germans were expected in Paris in a few days at most. With the memory of 1914–18 in our minds, none of us could believe it.

I have never forgotten the complete dejection on the faces of Reynaud, Daladier[1] and Gamelin as we entered the room at the Quai d'Orsay. I remember saying to myself 'The French High Command are beaten already.'

Supreme War Council: minutes[2]
(*Cabinet papers, 99/3*)

16 May 1940
5.30 p.m.
Quai d'Orsay

Note by the Secretary – The meeting took place informally in the study of M. Reynaud. Notes of the first few minutes of the meeting are not available, but the meeting began with a brief statement of the existing situation and an indication by the French of the possibility of having to withdraw from the line Namur/Wavre at present held in Belgium.[3]

Mr Churchill said that we had always been told that the object of getting the line Namur/Antwerp was that by so doing we would shorten our front and economise 20 Divisions. Now we had got there, why should we retire? Let us fight on that line.

M. Reynaud said the point was that we had lost Namur.

General Gamelin said that we had not been able to bring troops from the north because of the strike in Belgium.

Mr Churchill said 'shoot the strikers.'[4]

---

[1] Edouard Daladier, 1884–1970. Entered the Chamber of Deputies, 1919. Minister for Colonies, 1924. Prime Minister, 1933 and again in 1934 (for two months). Minister of War and Defence, 1932–4 and again from June 1936 to 18 May 1940. Prime Minister (for the third time), April 1938 to March 1940. An opponent of Vichy, he was held in custody in Germany from 1943 to 1945, including some months at Buchenwald concentration camp.

[2] Britain was represented by Churchill, France by Reynaud and Daladier. Also present, for Britain, were the Ambassador to France, Sir Ronald Campbell, General Dill, Air Marshal Joubert de la Ferté, General Ismay and Brigadier O. M. Lund. The British Secretariat consisted of Lieutenant-Colonel H. Redman and Lieutenant-Commander R. D. Coleridge. The French team consisted of General Gamelin, General Bergeret (representing General Vuillemin) and Paul Baudouin, with Roland de Margerie as the Secretariat.

[3] No record was kept of General Gamelin's remarks or of Churchill's response, as the officer who was to take the notes, Colonel Redman, 'joined the meeting after it had been in progress about ten minutes' (Letter from General Ismay to Churchill, 8 September 1948). In his war memoirs, Churchill wrote: 'In front of Gamelin on a student's easel was a map, about two yards square, with a black ink line purporting to show the Allied front' (Winston S. Churchill, *Their Finest Hour*, London 1949, page 42).

[4] While preparing his war memoirs in 1948 Churchill read this remark in the minutes of the Supreme War Council. He wrote in the margin: 'No.' But Ismay, to whom he sent the minutes, replied that he was 'ready to swear' that Churchill had said 'Shoot the strikers'. Ismay added: 'You had in fact made this same observation at Le Bourget airfield, when the officers who met us told us of the railway strike' (Letter of 8 September 1948, *Churchill papers, 4/44*).

May 1940

General Gamelin said that we had already moved four divisions to the threatened front.

Mr Churchill asked whether Lord Gort had actually been given the order to retire.

General Gamelin said that he was not sure whether General Georges had actually given that order or not. He said that, actually, the front of the BEF was small compared with the rest of the line. He explained that he had been taking reserves from the right to fill the gap, and had begun to collect divisions forward of Paris.

Mr Churchill said that, in that case, we should attack.

General Gamelin said that yes, the French could attack, but mechanised forces were needed. There were only three Armoured Divisions, and these were very exhausted. Two had been fighting from the beginning and had lost two-thirds of their light and one-third of their heavy tanks. They had stopped the Germans and done a great deal of damage to them.

Mr Churchill asked what about the Infantry Divisions.

General Gamelin said that, owing to attack from the air and by armoured fighting vehicles, all those engaged had suffered very heavily.

Mr Churchill asked whether the Germans had armoured fighting vehicles everywhere.

General Gamelin said that the Germans had about eight of their ten armoured divisions engaged in this battle. The spearhead of the thrust appeared to consist of two armoured divisions and two infantry divisions.

Mr Churchill said that it was clear that two armoured divisions and two infantry divisions were not going to penetrate very greatly into France.

General Gamelin said that that was the question. The whole German army in motors was coming along. Naturally, the French hope was that the enemy armoured forces would exhaust themselves.

Mr Churchill said that the Germans could not yet have brought much of their strength across the Meuse.

General Gamelin said that the constant bombing of railways by the Germans was holding up our reinforcements. He said that we needed a lot of bombardment aircraft to engage targets both close to the battle front and also in rear on the lines of communication. Also, there must be fighters to protect the infantry.

Mr Churchill said that the British had only 39 Squadrons of Fighters for the protection of England. These were the life of the country and guarded our vitals from attack. We must conserve them. As regards bombing, the British had sent four Squadrons which had attacked near Sedan. We had taken great risks in order to destroy the bridges over the Meuse and had lost 36 aircraft in doing so. You can replace bridges, he said, but not Fighters. The losses were much to be regretted, and it seemed wrong to destroy the whole British effort unless targets were very well worth-while. He said that the Royal Air Force had been attacking oil refineries and marshalling yards, and would go on attacking them. As regards Fighters, the British War Cabinet had that morning decided to give four more Squadrons, which would arrive in the course of the day. They were also arranging to fill up existing Squadrons to their original strength.

General Gamelin said that the French had begun the battle with 650 Fighters, and they now had only 150 left.

Mr Churchill said that we must not waste heavy bombers in the land battle. Attack on bridges means great losses.

General Gamelin said that the Germans had not unlimited bridging material and could not go on building fresh bridges.

Mr Churchill said that we had bombarded all the places we had been asked to, and were anxious to attack only such vital objectives as would stop the enemy from attacking by day. It was not reasonable that the British aircraft should be required to take on German armoured fighting vehicles. This should be done by ground action.

General Gamelin said that the French feeling was that we simply must stop the present advance of the armoured force. It was getting at our rear where we were completely vulnerable. The difference between 1918 and now, he said, was that then infantry met infantry whenever a break occurred. We were now, he said, at the period of the mêlée. In order to meet such an attack as the present we needed armoured fighting vehicles to meet armoured fighting vehicles.

General Dill asked what the answer was. Did General Gamelin think that counter-attack on the flanks could succeed?

General Gamelin said that he hoped so. He thought that the enemy armoured force must have had a very difficult time. If they could be stopped by air attack, the attacks from the flanks could be put in with good chance of success.

Mr Churchill said that on the other hand, aircraft attacking armoured fighting vehicles were very vulnerable and they were not suited for such attack.

General Gamelin did not seem to agree.

Mr Churchill said that the question was whether the vigour of this offensive would diminish.

M. Daladier said that it would be wrong to think so, and that the power of the attack would increase as the attack continued.

General Dill said that surely petrol would run out.

M. Daladier said that they brought up petrol with them.

Mr Churchill asked what the French 75's could do against the heavy tanks.

General Gamelin said that weapons below 47 mm were not of much use, but above that were effective.

Mr Churchill asked whether we could not find guns to take on the enemy armoured fighting vehicles.

M. Daladier said that the best of our forces were in Belgium.

General Gamelin said that the French had lost much of their best artillery.

Mr Churchill said that to deal with a daylight attack we must have Fighters. He said that the French had asked for ten Fighter Squadrons. The British had given four instead of the two originally promised, and yet another four as a result of this morning's decision. This meant that six more were now asked for.

General Gamelin said that the French had taken every Fighter they had. For instance, only one Squadron of Fighters was protecting Paris at present, and none were protecting the French factories.

Mr Churchill said that he did not think that six more Squadrons of Fighters would make the difference.

M. Daladier said that the French believed the contrary. If the infantry could feel that the Fighters were above protecting them, they would be given confidence and would not be taking cover when the tanks came along.

Air Marshal Joubert de la Ferté asked whether each French Army had its own Fighters.

General Gamelin said each group of Armies had.

Air Marshal Joubert de la Ferté said this was important for flexible application of Fighter effort.

M. Daladier said that many French Fighters had been damaged on the ground. Many others were worn out through continual use. In practice, they only had a little over 100 in working condition.

M. Reynaud said that we must choose between two big risks: Either we must leave the English factories without Fighter protection – like the French factories – or we must be prepared to see the German armies continue their advance towards Paris.

Mr Churchill said that as long as the British could hold command of the air over England and could control the seas of the world, they were confident of the ultimate results, and it would always be possible to carry on.

General Gamelin said where shall we be able to find another French Army?

Mr Churchill asked where the rest of the French Army was.

M. Daladier said that the whole of the French Army was now engaged, excepting for that portion in Alsace and Lorraine. The best part was in Belgium now.

Mr Churchill asked General Dill whether he thought it would be possible to withdraw the British line towards the canal lines without being broken up.

General Dill said yes, if this were done by night, by stages, but it would be difficult and costly.

Mr Churchill said that if the French thought that the fate of this battle depended on Fighter Squadrons, the four new Fighter Squadrons that would be arriving to-morrow should be of great help for the counter-attack.

Air Marshal Joubert de la Ferté asked General Gamelin whether he had said that not only Fighter support but Bomber support also was wanted by them from the Royal Air Force.

General Gamelin said yes.

Mr Churchill said that we could carry out bombardments from England. He did not know quite what results could be achieved by bombing.

Air Marshal Joubert de la Ferté said that the CAS[1] would insist on bombers being used to attack objectives in the rear. He emphasised the importance to the enemy of supplies, particularly of petrol.

M. Daladier said that for the present battle it was only possible to look a very short distance back from the front, as immediate effect was required.

General Gamelin said that the bottle-necks of the bridges were very important. There were always vulnerable targets to be found in their vicinity.

Mr Churchill said that if we could achieve useful results we should use the four Fighter Squadrons, but if it was only to save a day he was doubtful whether it was a practical proposition.

General Gamelin said that the more time we saved the more Divisions we could bring forward from the reserve.

Mr Churchill said that he did not think that the use of these Squadrons would make this difference.

Mr Churchill asked what Squadrons the RAF had out here.

Air Marshal Joubert de la Ferté said a total of 30 Squadrons, of which 16 were Fighters. Of course, there had been many losses.

Mr Churchill said that if we added the French and British strength together they would still be very inferior, and six or ten Squadrons would not make the difference.

Mr Churchill said that we had lost half of what we had put in in the way of air strength in four days of fighting.

M. Daladier said that the French were collecting all they could in the way of old weapons to stop the German advance. The French would fight to the end. He asked what the British would do when the Germans reached the channel ports.

Mr Churchill asked what would reach there, and whether it would just be armoured forces.

General Gamelin said at present it would only be parts of the armoured force, but later motorised divisions would be coming up.

---

[1] The Chief of the Air Staff, Sir Cyril Newall.

M. Daladier said that if the Germans were to get into Paris he thought the war would be lost.

Mr Churchill asked why we could not attack on other parts of the front.

M. Reynaud said that inferiority in numbers was responsible.

M. Daladier said that the German thrust was covered on its flanks, not in front: it was like attacking a beast – it objected much more to an attack on its muzzle than on its flanks.

Mr Churchill asked how many Divisions had been used by the French.

General Gamelin said that out of 96 Divisions, the French had used half, and on a small front.

Mr Churchill said that the Germans could not have mechanised forces everywhere.

General Gamelin said that they had nine or ten armoured divisions, and each division had double the number of heavy tanks that the French did.

Mr Churchill said that certain pre-war prophets had been proved wrong as the offensive was coming into its own again.

He thanked M. Reynaud very much for the clear idea that had been given of the gravity of the situation, of which the British were not previously aware. It had seemed not in the least possible that great Armies in fortified positions could be pierced and thrust aside.

Winston S. Churchill: recollection[1]
(*'Their Finest Hour'*, *page 42*)

16 May 1940

The Commander-in-Chief[2] briefly explained what had happened. North and south of Sedan, on a front of fifty or sixty miles, the Germans had broken through. The French army in front of them was destroyed or scattered. A heavy onrush of armoured vehicles was advancing with unheard-of speed towards Amiens and Arras, with the intention, apparently, of reaching the coast at Abbeville or thereabouts. Alternatively they might make for Paris. Behind the armour, he said, eight or ten German divisions, all motorised, were driving onwards, making flanks for themselves as they advanced against the two disconnected French armies on either side. The General talked perhaps five minutes without anyone saying a word. When he stopped there

---

[1] Churchill began writing his memoirs in the late summer of 1945, when Field Marshal Alexander put a villa on Lake Como at his disposal. The main work on the second volume, *Their Finest Hour*, was done at Chartwell in the twelve months prior to the book's publication in 1949.

[2] Lord Gort.

was a considerable silence. I then asked: 'Where is the strategic reserve?' and, breaking into French, which I used indifferently (in every sense): '*Où est la masse de manoeuvre?*' General Gamelin turned to me and, with a shake of the head and a shrug, said: '*Aucune.*'

There was another long pause. Outside in the garden of the Quai d'Orsay clouds of smoke arose from large bonfires, and I saw from the window venerable officials pushing wheel-barrows of archives on to them. Already therefore the evacuation of Paris was being prepared.

General Ismay to Winston S. Churchill[1]
(*Churchill papers, 4/44*)

16 May 1940

M. Reynaud cheered up under your influence, but Daladier and Gamelin remained the picture of misery and despair throughout.

A feature of the map which you describe on page 30 was a black line which purported to show the Allied front. In this line there was a small but deadly ominous bulge at Sedan.

The following is typical of General Gamelin's state of mind throughout the meeting. You asked him when and where he proposed to counter attack the flanks of the bulge. His reply was: 'Inferiority of numbers, inferiority of equipment, inferiority of method' – and then a hopeless shrug of the shoulders.

The burden of General Gamelin's, and indeed of all the French High Command's subsequent remarks was insistence on their inferiority in the air and earnest entreaties for more squadrons of the Royal Air Force – bomber as well as fighter, but chiefly the latter. This prayer for fighter support was destined to be repeated at every subsequent Conference until France fell.

In the course of his appeal, General Gamelin remarked that fighters were needed not only to give confidence to the French Army, but also to stop the tanks. At this you said: 'No: it is the business of the artillery to stop the tanks. It is the business of the fighters to cleanse the skies (nettoyer le ciel) over the battle'.

The one solid conclusion that emerged from the meeting was your undertaking to ask the Cabinet to sanction the despatch of six squadrons of fighters in addition to the four which had been approved at the meeting over which you had presided in the morning before leaving for France.

---

[1] See page 53, footnote 4.

Lieutenant-General Sir Harold Redman[1]: recollection
(*Letter to the author, 14 July 1980*)

16 May 1940

Mr Churchill quite certainly was the figure, & personality, round whom the proceedings revolved. This was but natural, as he was the head of a visiting delegation, and newly come to power, and aggressively seeking to find out the exact state of affairs – which Reynaud, Gamelin & the others hardly knew themselves.

The truth of the matter was, that after several months of complete inactivity on the western front, the violence & strength of the air attacks & armoured thrusts of the Germans, had caught them unprepared; & after the first rude shock, all the French could think of, was that air reinforcements, particularly in fighter aircraft, simply must be found, & at once, & where could they come from but from Britain, who must stand or fall with France.

But you will have all of this sized up better than I ever could.

I can only add, that while this meeting was indeed rather crucial, and although it has been dignified with the title of 'Supreme War Cabinet', it was in fact just a hurried get-together of principals, called at the instigation of an over-optimistic newly appointed Prime Minister, rightly determined to go & find out for himself, at the chief danger point, the exact state of affairs.

What a wonderful man he was.

Winston S. Churchill to the War Cabinet
(*Churchill papers, 4/149*)

16 May 1940
9 p.m.

I shall be glad if the Cabinet could meet immediately to consider following. Situation grave in the last degree. Furious German thrust through Sedan finds French Armies ill-grouped many in North, others in Alsace. At least four days required to bring twenty divisions to cover Paris and strike at the flanks of the Bulge, which is now fifty kilometres wide.

Three armoured divisions with two or three infantry divisions have

---

[1] Harold Redman, 1899–1986. Entered the Royal Artillery, 1917; on active service, 1918. Lieutenant-Colonel, 1939. War Cabinet Secretariat, Anglo-French Liaison Section, 1939–40. General Staff, Eighth Army (Brigadier), 1941–2. Secretary to the Combined Chiefs of Staff, 1943–4. CBE, 1944. Deputy Commander, French Forces of the Interior (Major-General), August–September 1944. Head of the British Military Mission to France, 1945–6. CB, 1947. Director of Military Operations, War Office, 1948–51. Principal Staff Officer to the Deputy Supreme Allied Commander Europe, 1952–5. Knighted, 1953. Governor and Commander-in-Chief, Gibraltar, 1955–8. Director and Secretary, the Wolfson Foundation, 1958–67.

advanced through gap and large masses hurrying forward behind them. Two great dangers therefore threaten. First that BEF will be largely left in the air in taking no action to make a difficult disengagement and retreat to the old line. Secondly that the German thrust will wear down the French resistance before it can be fully gathered.

Orders given to defend Paris at all costs, but archives of the Quai d'Orsay already burning in the garden. I consider the next two three or four days decisive for Paris and probably for the French Army. Therefore the question we must face is whether we can give further aid in fighters above four squadrons for which the French are very grateful and whether a larger part of our long range heavy bombers should be employed tomorrow and following nights upon the German masses crossing the Meuse and flowing into the Bulge. Even so results cannot be guaranteed: but the French resistance may be broken up as rapidly as that of Poland unless this battle of the Bulge is won. I personally feel that we should send squadrons of fighters demanded (i.e. six more) tomorrow and, concentrating all available French and British aviation, dominate the air above the Bulge for the next two or three days, not for any local purpose but to give the last chance to the French Army to rally its bravery and strength. It would not be good historically if their requests were denied and their ruin resulted. Also night bombardment by a strong force of heavy bombers can no doubt be arranged. It looks as if the enemy was, by now, fully extended both in the air and tanks. We must not under-rate the increasing difficulties of his advance if strongly counter-attacked. I imagine that if all fails here we could still shift what is left of own air striking force to assist BEF should it be forced to withdraw. I again emphasise the mortal gravity of the hour, and express my opinion as above. Kindly inform me what you will do. Dill agrees. I must have answer by midnight in order to encourage the French. Telephone to Ismay at Embassy in Hindustani.

War Cabinet: minutes[1]
(*Cabinet papers, 65/7*)

16 May 1940　　　　　　　　　　　　　　　　　　　　10 Downing Street
11 p.m.

The War Cabinet were informed that, according to reports received from various sources, the situation in France appeared to be less critical than it had been in the afternoon.

The War Cabinet then discussed a message received from the Prime Minister in Paris (Paris telegram No. 206, DIPP), in which he urged that six

[1] During Churchill's absence in France, Neville Chamberlain took the Chair at this meeting of the War Cabinet.

more squadrons of fighters should be sent to France in addition to the four already promised in answer to the last French request, and that a larger part of our heavy bombers should be employed on the following nights upon the German masses crossing the Meuse into the bulge in the French line. They were informed that of the four squadrons already promised two had left during the day and the other two were leaving at dawn. If six more were sent, we should be down to 29 squadrons in all in the United Kingdom. Everything was being done to make up fighter aircraft received from production with the necessary accessories, which were being stripped from aircraft which had been damaged in action.

The Chief of the Air Staff said that there would be no difficulty in putting heavy bombers on to the Meuse crossings. The provision of the additional fighter squadrons was more difficult. We had at present seven fighter squadrons operating in the north of France and three in the south, but the latter had moved their bases and were somewhat disorganised. The bases in the north could not receive six more squadrons; three was the most they could take. There remained in the United Kingdom at the present time only six *complete*[1] Hurricane squadrons. He proposed to move all these down to aerodromes in Kent, and to send servicing parties over to the aerodromes in northern France used by the Air Component. Three of the six squadrons to be sent to Kent would work in France from dawn until noon, and then return to Kent, being relieved by the other three for the afternoon. The effect would be the same as if the whole of the six squadrons were sent to work from French aerodromes, but they would be in less danger of attack on the ground in Kent and the crews would have better facilities for rest. The timings of the move would have to be worked out, and it would not be possible to get them all down to Kent to-morrow, since some squadrons would have to move in from distant parts.

The War Cabinet instructed the Chief of the Air Staff –

(a) To put in hand immediate arrangements, on the lines which he had proposed, for making available six Hurricane squadrons for operations in France as early as possible.
(b) To arrange for heavy bombers to attack the Meuse crossings on the night 17th-18th May, and following nights.

John Colville: diary
(*Colville papers*)

16 May 1940

The Cabinet met at 11.00 p.m. to discuss a terrifying telegram Winston had sent from Paris and to decide whether seriously to weaken our defences by

[1] Italicised in the original.

sending out fighters from this country. I will not describe the situation: it will be in every history book of the future; but evidently there has been lamentable staff work on the French side and Paris has been left undefended by reserves. We had hoped that only armoured divisions had penetrated the French defences, but it now seems that infantry divisions are pouring through the gap on a fifty-kilometre front.

Winston's telegram was decyphered in driblets and I rushed it into the Cabinet by instalments. W wants us to mass all our air strength to stop the advance in order to save the collapsing French morale. He speaks of 'the mortal gravity of the hour' – which made Arthur Rucker[1] say 'He is still thinking of his books' and Seal talk of his 'blasted rhetoric'. Everybody is on edge, except the soldiers.

W wants a reply from the Cabinet by midnight and Cornwall-Jones,[2] of the Cabinet Offices, is to give it to Ismay, who is with Churchill, in Hindustani.

General Ismay to Winston S. Churchill[3]
(*Churchill papers, 4/44*)

16 May 1940

At about 11.30 p.m. I received a telephone message in Hindustani that the Cabinet's answer was 'Yes'. You immediately took me off in a car to M. Reynaud's flat. We found it more or less in darkness, the only sign of life in the sitting room being a lady's fur coat. M. Reynaud emerged from his bedroom in his dressing gown and you told him the glad news. You then persuaded him to send for M. Daladier, who was duly woken up and brought to the flat to hear the decision of the British Cabinet.

---

[1] Arthur Nevil Rucker, 1895–1991. On active service, 1915–18. Entered the Civil Service, 1920. Private Secretary to successive Ministers of Health (including Neville Chamberlain). CBE, 1937. Principal Private Secretary to the Prime Minister (Neville Chamberlain), 1939–40. Knighted, 1942. Deputy Secretary, Ministry of Health, 1943. Member of the Commonwealth War Graves Commission, 1956–69.

[2] Arthur Thomas Cornwall-Jones, 1900–80. Indian Army, 1920–47. Seconded to the War Cabinet and Minister of Defence, 1939–40 and 1941–3. Secretary, Middle East Defence Committee, 1941–3. OBE, 1943. British Secretary, Combined Chiefs of Staff, 1944–6. CBE, 1945. Senior Assistant Secretary (Military) to the Cabinet, 1946–50. CMG, 1949.

[3] See page 53, footnote 4.

May 1940

John Colville: diary
(*Colville papers*)

17 May 1940

Rose at 6.00 to go down to Hendon to meet the PM on his return from France. He looked quite cheerful, having slept and breakfasted well at the Embassy. However Dill, Ismay and the rest of the unfortunate staff had had a miserable time. Winston had told them to be ready by 5.45, and it then transpired that he did not wish to leave until 7.00 and he had gone on sleeping while they wandered about aimlessly and could get no breakfast. He is very inconsiderate with his staff.

War Cabinet: minutes
(*Cabinet papers, 65/7*)

17 May 1940   10 Downing Street
10 a.m.

The Prime Minister gave the War Cabinet an account of his visit to France on the previous day.

He had found M. Daladier and General Gamelin depressed, but M. Reynaud in rather better heart. There was no doubt that the 9th French Army had sustained a heavy defeat. Their smaller anti-tank guns were unable to stop the German tanks and the German tanks' flame-throwing gun was effective to a range of about 300 yards, even against block houses. Some of the French troops, however, had retreated without sufficient cause.

The Germans had some 30 to 40 divisions massed behind the gap. It was now plain why the Allied troops had not been bombed in their advance into Belgium; the Germans had wanted to get us into forward positions in order to effect a break through and turn our flanks.

The German advance had now slowed down, probably to re-form and re-fuel. French divisions were being brought up from Alsace, and down from the North. General Giraud[1] had been put in command of the 9th Army, the commander of which had been superseded.

---

[1] Henri-Honoré Giraud, 1879–1949. Military Governor of Metz and commander of the 6th Military Region, 1936–40. Commanded the French Seventh Army, based on Dunkirk, 1940: advanced into Holland, 10 May 1940. Taken prisoner, May 1940, but escaped in 1942; he was brought out of Vichy France by a British submarine. Commander-in-Chief of the United French Armed Forces, 1943–4.

The Prime Minister had also seen General Swayne[1] who had reported that General Georges was dealing calmly with the situation.

The Prime Minister said that he had made it clear to the French that, unless they made a supreme effort, we would not feel justified in accepting the grave risk to the safety of this country which would be entailed by the despatch of more fighters to France. If the French would fight their hardest, we would do everything possible to help them.

He had also seen Air Vice-Marshal Evill,[2] who had given a most encouraging account of the air fighting, in which the German losses had been four or five times as great as our own. The total German losses had been so heavy that there was little doubt that the disparity between the Allied and German air strength had now been appreciably lessened. The Germans, however, escorted their bombing attacks with such heavy fighter protection that it was difficult for our fighters to get at the German bombers.

He felt that the War Cabinet had been faced with the gravest decision that a British Cabinet had ever had to take. On receiving their decision (telegram No. 159) he had at once visited M. Reynaud and General Gamelin. He had first of all shown them the telegram (No. 206 DIPP), which had been before the War Cabinet at their Meeting the previous evening. He had then shown them the War Cabinet's reply which had heartened them to a very considerable degree.

He had told Air Marshal Joubert de la Ferté to remain with Air Marshal Barratt, who was very tired and must obtain some rest. Both Air Marshals were at General Georges' headquarters. He had told them that they must make supreme efforts to settle 'The Battle of the Bulge' – 'la Poche' – on which the fate of Europe depended. With the arrangements which had now been made, he thought that we should be able to dominate the air over the Bulge. There was a reasonable hope that, with a four or five days' respite from air attack, the French Army would be able to rally and re-establish the position.

The situation on the rest of the front seemed fairly satisfactory. A plan had been prepared for the withdrawal of the British Army in stages, if necessary, but he felt that we ought not to yield an inch of ground without fighting.

He had been told that the French had sustained very heavy losses in fighter aircraft and that only one-quarter of the force with which they had started the campaign remained serviceable.

---

[1] John George des Réaux Swayne, 1890–1964. On active service, Western Front, 1914–18; prisoner of war. Chief Instructor, Staff College, 1937–9. Head of British Military Mission to French General Headquarters, 1939–40. CBE, 1940. General Officer Commanding 4th Division, 1940–2, being responsible for the defence of fifty miles of coastline in the Southampton–Portsmouth–Gosport–Isle of Wight area. Chief of General Staff, India, 1944–6. Knighted, 1944. Retired with the rank of Lieutenant-General.

[2] Douglas Claude Strathern Evill, 1892–1971. A naval cadet. On active service, 1914–18 (Distinguished Service Cross, Air Force Cross). Air Vice-Marshal, 1939. CB, 1940. Head of the Royal Air Force delegation in Washington, 1942. Vice-Chief of the Air Staff, 1943–6. Knighted, 1943. Air Chief Marshal, 1946.

The Minister of Information[1] suggested that more should be done to inform the general public of the seriousness of the situation, about which most people were in complete ignorance.

The Prime Minister agreed. The French communiqués and commentaries were framed with this in view. The public in this country should likewise be made to realise that the British and French Armies were engaged in a most critical battle which was approaching its climax.

The Prime Minister drew attention to the urgent need for replacing the heavy losses which the Royal Air Force had sustained, particularly in respect of Fighter aircraft. Could another 12 Squadrons of Fighters be raised within the next month?

The Chief of the Air Staff explained that special steps were being taken to bring existing Fighter squadrons up to strength, and to form new squadrons. These steps included the salvage of all serviceable material and instruments from crashed and damaged aircraft. Despite this, he considered that it would be impossible to form as many as 12 new squadrons within a month. He would prefer that the War Cabinet should not, at the moment, take a decision to withdraw the Fighter Squadrons covering Scapa.

The Prime Minister suggested that consideration should be given to the bearing of the new situation in France on our operations at Narvik. On the one hand, we knew that the Germans had a complete *Geschwader*[2] in Norway, which was a welcome diversion. On the other hand, we should consider whether Narvik was eating up what we needed for our own defence, particularly in destroyers, anti-aircraft guns and Fighters.

The Chief of the Imperial General Staff said that the Chiefs of Staff had already reviewed our operations at Narvik in the larger setting mentioned by the Prime Minister. As a result, a telegram had been sent to Lord Cork, informing him that he must deal with the situation with the forces at his disposal and that he could expect no more, and asking for his views. Meanwhile, the situation in Northern Norway appeared to be satisfactory. A number of German prisoners had been taken, with comparatively few casualties among the British forces, and it seemed likely that Narvik would be captured at any moment.

The Prime Minister read to his colleagues a communication which he had received from President Roosevelt in reply to his personal message.[3]

[1] Alfred Duff Cooper.
[2] A *Geschwader* normally consisted of three *Gruppen*, each of about 30 aircraft (that is, 90 aircraft in all). The total German operational forces in Norway in mid-May 1940 consisted of 360 long-range bombers, 120 coastal (float) planes, 70 twin-engined fighters, 60 long-range reconnaissance planes, 50 dive-bombers and 50 single-engined fighters.
[3] See pages 69–70.

68 MAY 1940

Harold Nicolson: diary
('*Diaries and Letters, 1939–1945*')

17 May 1940

At 12.40 the telephone rings, and Mac[1] in an awed voice says, 'The Prime Minister's Private Secretary'. I lift the receiver and wait without hearing anything. Then after about two minutes' silence, a voice says, 'Mr Nicolson?' I say, 'Yes'. 'Please hold on. The Prime Minister wishes to speak to you.' Another long pause and then Winston's voice: 'Harold, I think it would be very nice if you joined the Government and helped Duff at the Ministry of Information.' 'There is nothing that I should like better.' 'Well, fall in tomorrow. The list will be out tonight. That all right?' 'Very much all right.' 'OK', says Winston, and rings off.

Winston S. Churchill to Neville Chamberlain
('*Their Finest Hour*', *page 48*)

17 May 1940

I am very much obliged to you for undertaking to examine to-night the consequences of the withdrawal of the French Government from Paris or the fall of that city, as well as the problems which would arise if it were necessary to withdraw the BEF from France, either along its communications or by the Belgian and Channel ports. It is quite understood that in the first instance this report could be no more than an enumeration of the main considerations which arise, and which could thereafter be remitted to the Staffs. I am myself seeing the military authorities at 6.30.

Winston S. Churchill to Sir Edward Bridges[2]
(*Churchill papers, 20/13*)

17 May 1940

Prepare at once an outline for a revision of the existing system of dealing with economic problems and placing it under the Lord President.[3] I had in

---

[1] Miss Macmillan was Harold Nicolson's secretary. In 1964, while I was preparing my book *The Roots of Appeasement*, Harold Nicolson let me see, and take with me to Scotland, the original typescript of his diary. Having read it, I urged him to publish it. At the time, he said he was reluctant to see it in print. Eventually it was edited in three volumes by his son Nigel.

[2] Edward Bridges, 1892–1969. Only son of the Poet Laureate Robert Bridges. On active service, 1914–18 (Military Cross). Home Civil Service (Treasury), 1919–38. Secretary to the Cabinet, 1938–46. Knighted, 1939. Permanent Secretary to the Treasury, 1945–56. Created Baron, 1957. Chairman of the British Council, 1959–67. Knight of the Garter, 1965. Contributed a chapter to *Action This Day: Working with Churchill* (1968).

[3] Neville Chamberlain.

May 1940

mind that trade, transport, shipping, MEW,[1] food, agriculture, would all come into a general group, over which he would exercise a large measure of executive control. How would this fit in with the present Home Affairs Committee? Let me have this to-night or to-morrow early. About two sheets of paper would be sufficient.

WSC

Winston S. Churchill to Alfred Duff Cooper[2]
(*Churchill papers, 20/13*)

17 May 1940

I should be glad to receive some proposals from you for establishing a more effective control over the BBC. Now that we have a Government representing the Opposition as well as the Majority, we should have a much freer hand in this respect.

WSC

President Roosevelt to Winston S. Churchill
(*Premier papers, 3/468*)

17 May 1940

I have just received your message and I am sure it is unnecessary for me to say that I am most happy to continue our private correspondence as we have in the past. I am of course giving every possible consideration to the suggestions made in your message. I shall take up your specific proposals one by one.

First: With regard to the possible loan of 40 or 50 of our older destroyers. As you know a step of that kind could not be taken except with the specific authorization of the Congress and I am not certain that it would be wise for that suggestion to be made to the Congress at this moment. Furthermore, it seems to me doubtful from the standpoint of our own defense requirements which must inevitably be linked with the defense requirements of this hemisphere and with our obligations in the Pacific whether we could dispose even temporarily of these destroyers. Furthermore, even if we were able to take the step you suggest, it would be at least six or seven weeks as a

---

[1] The Ministry of Economic Warfare, headed, since 15 May 1940, by Dr Hugh Dalton.
[2] Minister of Information since 12 May 1940.

minimum, as I see it, before these vessels could undertake active service under the British flag.

Second: We are now doing everything within our power to make it possible for the Allied Governments to obtain the latest type of anti-aircraft in the United States.

Third: If Mr Purvis[1] may receive immediately instructions to discuss the question of anti-aircraft equipment and ammunition with the appropriate authorities here in Washington, the most favorable consideration will be given to the request made in the light of our own defense needs and requirements.

Fourth: Mr Purvis has already taken up with the appropriate authorities here the purchase of steel in the United States and I understand that satisfactory arrangements have been made.

Fifth: I shall give further consideration to your suggestion with regard to the visit of the United States squadron to Irish ports.

Sixth: As you know the American fleet is now concentrated at Hawaii where it will remain at least for the time being. I shall communicate with you again as soon as I feel able to make a final decision with regard to some of the other matters dealt with in your message and I hope you will feel free to communicate with me in this way at any time.

The best of luck to you.

Franklin D. Roosevelt

Randolph S. Churchill: recollection
(*Randolph Churchill papers*)

18 May 1940

A week or so later I got leave from my unit and leaving on an early train arrived at Admiralty House about 8.30 in the morning (my father had not, of course, knocked Chamberlain out of 10 Downing Street in an indecent hurry). I went up to my father's bedroom. He was standing in front of his basin and was shaving with his old fashioned Valet razor. He had a tough beard, and as usual he was hacking away.

WSC: 'Sit down, dear boy, and read the papers while I finish shaving.' I did

---

[1] Arthur Blaikie Purvis, 1890–1941. Born in London. Worked for the Nobel Explosives Company, Glasgow, 1910–24. Moved to Canada, becoming President of Canadian Industries Ltd (manufacturers of chemicals). A leading industrialist in Canada between the wars; Chairman of the National Employment Commission, 1936–8. Director-General of the British Purchasing Commission (New York and Washington), 1939–40. Chairman of the Anglo-French Purchasing Board, Washington, December 1939 to June 1940. Privy Councillor, 1940. Chairman of the British Supply Council in North America, 1941. Killed in an air crash, 14 August 1941.

as told. After two or three minutes of hacking away, WSC half turned and said: 'I think I see my way through.' He resumed his shaving. RSC was astounded, and said: 'Do you mean that we can avoid defeat?' (which seemed credible) 'or beat the bastards' (which seemed incredible).

WSC flung his Valet razor in to the basin, swung around, and said:– 'Of course I mean we can beat them.'

RSC: 'Well, I'm all for it, but I don't see how you can do it.'

By this time WSC had dried and sponged his face and turning round to RSC, said with great intensity:– 'I shall drag the United States in,' which he did.[1]

Winston S. Churchill to President Roosevelt
(*Churchill papers, 20/14*)

18 May 1940

Many thanks for your message, for which I am grateful. I do not need to tell you about the gravity of what has happened. We are determined to persevere to the very end whatever the result of the great battle raging in France may be. We must expect in any case to be attacked here on the Dutch model before very long, and we hope to give a good account of ourselves. But if American assistance is to play any part it must be available soon.

War Cabinet: minutes
(*Cabinet papers, 65/7*)

18 May 1940
11.30 a.m.

The Prime Minister said that on the whole the military situation in France was better. The French were bringing up troops, and French artillery had had some success in destroying German tanks. The Royal Air Force had covered themselves with glory.

The First Sea Lord[2] said that, in accordance with the Prime Minister's orders, the blockships for Zeebrugge and Ostend had not carried out their

---

[1] Or did not. It was Germany's declaration of war on the United States in December 1941, shortly after Pearl Harbor, that finally brought America in, as a belligerent, to the war in Europe.

[2] Admiral Pound.

operation the previous night, but would be held in home waters in immediate readiness. Demolitions at Flushing had been begun on the previous evening.

The Prime Minister said that the blocking operations should be postponed from day to day, but that the ships should be ready to carry them out immediately if the situation so demanded. The French should be informed that this task would be our sole responsibility.

The Secretary of State for Foreign Affairs said that he felt that the Soviet Government were uneasy at the German advance, and that it might be possible to make some arrangement with them. We should at least find out if this was possible.

He (the Foreign Secretary) had had a long conversation with Sir Stafford Cripps[1] who, it would be recalled, had flown from China to Moscow, where he had had long discussions with M. Molotov.[2] Sir Stafford Cripps took the view that we had been at fault in our handling of the Soviet Government and felt convinced that we could reach agreement with them on trade and possibly on political questions. For this purpose, personal discussions were essential. Sir Stafford did not ask to be entrusted with this task, but if the Government felt he could be of service and chose to send him to Moscow to find out what the possibilities were, no harm would be done and the Soviet Government would see that we were in earnest.

After consultation with the Prime Minister, he (the Foreign Secretary) had discussed the matter further with the Minister for Economic Warfare[3] the previous afternoon, and had agreed that it would be of advantage to invite Sir Stafford Cripps to undertake this mission, provided it was clearly understood by him that his functions were to ascertain from the Soviet Government their attitude on various questions in which the Ministry of Economic Warfare and other Departments were interested, and to report as to the possibility of

---

[1] Richard Stafford Cripps, 1889–1952. Educated at Winchester. Barrister, 1913. Red Cross, France, 1914. Assistant Superintendent, Queen's Ferry Munitions Factory, 1915–18. Labour MP, 1931–50. Solicitor-General, 1930–1. Knighted, 1930. Ambassador to Moscow, 1940–2. Minister of Aircraft Production, 1942–5. President of the Board of Trade, 1945. Minister for Economic Affairs, 1947. Chancellor of the Exchequer, 1947–50.

[2] Vyacheslav Mikhailovich Scriabin, 1890–1986. Used the underground name Molotov. Took part in the first Russian revolution of 1905 as a student; arrested and deported to Siberia. Secretary of *Pravda*, 1911. Exiled for a second time, 1915. Member of the Executive of the Petrograd Soviet, 1917. Chairman of the Council of People's Commissars, 1930–41. People's Commissar for Foreign Affairs, 1939–46. Deputy Chairman of the State Defence Committee, 1941–5. Took part in the Teheran, Yalta, and Potsdam conferences, 1943–5. Foreign Minister, 1946–9 and 1953–6. First Deputy Chairman, Council of Ministers, 1953–7. Soviet Ambassador to Mongolia, 1957–60; to the International Atomic Energy Agency, Vienna, 1960–2.

[3] Dr Dalton.

overcoming the various difficulties which had arisen in regard to these matters.

The Prime Minister said that there was general agreement in the Cabinet that it would be of advantage to invite Sir Stafford Cripps to undertake an exploratory mission on the lines suggested. He doubted, however, whether it would be desirable at the same time to announce our intention of sending an Ambassador to Moscow. This could be left till a later stage.

The Prime Minister said that he thought that it was essential that we should concentrate our efforts on ensuring the most effective Air force to meet the events of the next few months, even though this might involve some risk to long-term schemes. It was essential that every endeavour should be concentrated on ensuring that our large reserves of aircraft were put into a condition in which they could all be used for active operations as quickly as possible. It was clear that the most essential step was to accelerate the production of the items of equipment in which there were shortages. The points raised in regard to control of aircraft storage units and of RAF repair depots should be further discussed between the two Departments and points of difficulty resolved.

In regard to the proposal to withhold delivery of training aircraft to Canada, he thought that it would be unwise to take an immediate decision, and that this matter also should be further discussed. He therefore suggested that the two Ministers should meet together that afternoon in order to discuss the questions at issue, under the Chairmanship of the Lord Privy Seal,[1] who would act as arbiter in the event of disagreement.

General Swayne: message
(*Premier papers, 3/188/3*)

18 May 1940
5 p.m.

'Patient[2] is rather lower and depressed. The lower part of the wound continues to heal, but as I expected, the upper part has started to suppurate again, though they tell me that so far they have not seen much pus. The effect of the injection will not be known for some time, but I have asked the Doctors to let me know as soon as possible the general effect which, as you will realise, must be the combined result of many local injections.'

This is the end of General Swayne's message. He said in addition that the situation was rather obscure this afternoon, but that there had been a number of incidents (which probably mean air raids on headquarters, etc.). If General

[1] Clement Attlee.
[2] France.

Swayne has anything to report tomorrow morning, he will ring you up in the War Room between 8 and 9 a.m.

He will be standing by for the next ¼-hr. in case you have anything to ask him, but he says that there is really nothing to add to what has been said above.

War Cabinet: minutes
(*Cabinet papers, 65/7*)

18 May 1940 10 Downing Street
5.30 p.m.

The Lord President of the Council[1] drew attention to the first recommendation, namely, that no attempt should be made to arrange for voluntary dispersal of population until there had been such air attack on this country as would bring home clearly to people the dangers to which they were exposed. Events on the Continent might have a rapid and considerable effect upon public opinion in this respect.

The Prime Minister thought that the Germans would not adopt a policy of indiscriminate bombing. Their action in Norway and Poland could not be taken as a guide. In attacking this country they would find it far more profitable to concentrate on specific military targets.

War Cabinet: Confidential Annex
(*Cabinet papers, 65/13*)

18 May 1940
5.30 p.m.

The Permanent Secretary to the Ministry of Labour[2] said that, in discussion that morning, the Minister of Labour had stressed the point that authority to apply measures for the control of labour would have to be vested in the Ministry of Labour if they were to be practicable, and that they should not be distributed among a number of Departments, as in the case of the measures which applied to the control of property. The Minister of Labour had also taken the view that it would be essential that the control of profits should be put into operation simultaneously with that of labour.

[1] Neville Chamberlain.
[2] Thomas Williams Phillips, 1883–1966. Entered the Civil Service, 1906. Assistant Secretary, Ministry of Labour, 1919; Permanent Under-Secretary of State, Ministry of Labour, 1935–44. Knighted, 1934. Permanent Under-Secretary of State, Ministry of National Insurance, 1944–8. Chairman, War Damage Commission, 1949–59.

The Prime Minister said that the proposed powers would be transitory and would be related to the declaration of a supreme emergency. When this emergency arose, the Government would claim the right to take service and property as it might think right. When the emergency had passed, the reinstatement of former rights would be considered in accordance with the constitutional usages of this country. He considered that the request for the necessary powers should be presented to Parliament in the simplest terms and that the details of the scheme should be left to be worked out under the guidance of the Lord President of the Council, in association with the Ministers and officials concerned.

The War Cabinet:–
(1) Invited the Lord President of the Council to proceed with the working out of a scheme conferring on the Government drastic powers for the control of property, business, labour and services, on the lines indicated in his Report (attached to this Annex)[1].
(2) Agreed that the institution of these measures should be linked to a declaration of a supreme emergency.
(3) Agreed that the draft Bill, containing the necessary powers, should be couched in the simplest terms.
(4) Invited the Prime Minister to broadcast a statement on the following day, on the lines suggested by the Lord President, indicating the seriousness of the situation, in order to pave the way for the acceptance of these measures by the country.

Neville Chamberlain to Winston S. Churchill
(*Churchill papers, 9/176*)

18 May 1940   Privy Council Office

NOTES FOR PRIME MINISTER'S BROADCAST

It is suggested that the Prime Minister should make in his broadcast an urgent call for a great intensification of effort on the part of everyone who can contribute to the winning of the war. The hour is grave. A great and critical battle is being fought in France and Flanders. The men of the BEF and of the armies of our Allies are withstanding with magnificent courage the shock of a fierce and bitter assault. Their self-sacrifice and resolution must be matched by equal constancy and sacrifice at home.

It is vital that we should win the battle now in progress. We are confident

[1] Not printed.

that we shall win it, but we must not underestimate the sternness of the test or the magnitude of the effort we are called upon to make.

If the battle is to be won, we must provide our men with ever-increasing quantities of the weapons and ammunition they need. We must have, and have quickly, more aeroplanes, more tanks, more guns, more shells. There is urgent need of these essential munitions, not only to increase our strength against a powerfully-armed enemy and to replace the losses which must be incurred in so fierce a struggle, but also to enable us to call more readily upon reserves in the knowledge that they will be speedily replaced.

There is a further point. The battle now raging is critical indeed, but it is not all that we have to consider. It will have its aftermath. Our task is not merely to win the battle but to win the war. When the battle is over we must continue no less urgently to hasten the production of munitions.

It may be that drastic steps will be necessary to achieve the results essential to our safety, and if so they will be taken. Today it is the clear duty of every man and woman to make the full contribution of which they are capable to the national need. It is their duty to give all the material help in their power, grudging neither their property nor their wealth.

It is their duty to work with all their might to save their country, forgetful of themselves and remembering only the sterner tasks and greater sacrifice of the men in the Armies overseas.

NC

Winston S. Churchill to General Ismay
(*Churchill papers, 20/13*)

18 May 1940

1. I cannot feel that we have enough trustworthy troops in England, in view of the very large numbers that may be landed from air-carriers preceded by parachutists. I do not consider this danger is imminent at the present time, as the great battle in France has yet to be decided.

I wish the following moves to be considered with a view to immediate action:
  (i) The transports which brought the Australians to Suez should bring home eight battalions of Regular infantry from Palestine properly conveyed, even at some risk, by whatever route is thought best. I hope it will be possible to use the Mediterranean.
  (ii) The Australian fast convoy arrives early in June with 14,000 men.
  (iii) These ships should be immediately filled with eight battalions of

Territorials and sent to India, where they should pick up eight more Regular battalions. The speed of this fast convey should be accelerated.

2. Everything must be done to carry out the recommendations for the control of aliens put forward by the Committee[1] and minuted by me on another paper. Action should also be taken against Communists and Fascists, and very considerable numbers should be put in protective or preventive internment, including the leaders. These measures must, of course, be brought before the Cabinet before action.

3. The Chiefs of Staff must consider whether it would not be well to send only half of the so-called Armoured Division to France. One must always be prepared for the fact that the French may be offered very advantageous terms of peace, and the whole weight be thrown on us.

Winston S. Churchill to General Ismay[2]
(*Churchill papers, 20/13*)

18 May 1940

The proximity fuse and the necessary rocket projectors have hitherto been treated as important protection for ships, but even larger numbers will be needed, even some perhaps more urgently, for the protection of aircraft factories and other exceptionally important points. What is being done about this? Let proposals be made to-morrow for setting up the necessary manufacture. Are any modifications in the design of the projectors necessary? DNO[3] can go on with the ship side of the business, but be careful no hold-up takes place in the supply for the vulnerable points ashore. Report tomorrow night what organisation or measures are required to procure this production.

WSC

---

[1] On 16 May 1940 the Joint Intelligence Committee recommended that internment be extended to all enemy aliens, male and female, between the ages of sixteen and seventy. This conclusion was endorsed by the Chiefs of Staff. There is an account of its effect on the Jewish refugees then in Britain in Miriam Kochan, *Britain's Internees in the Second World War*, London, 1983.

[2] Churchill asked Ismay to send copies of this minute to Admiral Pound, Anthony Eden, Sir Archibald Sinclair, Herbert Morrison and Professor Lindemann.

[3] The Director of Naval Ordnance, Captain Leach, RN.

May 1940

Neville Chamberlain to Winston S. Churchill
(*Churchill papers, 2/402*)

18 May 1940
Privy Council Office

My dear Winston,

Thank you for your letter about the Leadership of the Conservative Party. I can quite understand that in your present position as Prime Minister in a Government embracing all three parties it might seem inappropriate that you should at the same time be Leader of one Party, even though that Party be your own.

I shall therefore very gladly fall in with your suggestion that I should retain the Leadership, in the belief that this course will best enable me to help you in serving the cause of national unity, to which we both attach primary importance.

Yours ever
Neville Chamberlain

John Colville: diary
(*Colville papers*)

18 May 1940

Winston, who is full of fight and thrives on crisis and adversity, dictated a few brief notes, containing questions on strategical points for the people concerned to answer, and then wrote a letter to General Georges about the situation in France. Referring to the rapid advance of the German army he said, 'The tortoise is thrusting his head very far beyond his carapace.' In reality I think we are the tortoise, and Germany the hare. The tortoise will win in the end, but the hare is 'making the going'.

A. V. Alexander, the new First Lord, came in and W showed him the sharp and uncompromising reply Mussolini today sent to his firm but very polite telegram on becoming PM. Alexander thought that as Italy's participation in the war was now virtually certain (which I do not believe) we should seize the initiative and occupy Crete. Winston answered that our hands were too full elsewhere to enable us to embark on adventures: such is the change that high office can work in a man's inherent love of rash and spectacular action.

Anthony Eden: diary
(*'The Reckoning'*)

18 May 1940
10 p.m.

The German thrust towards the sea continues and the French 1st and 9th Armies seem badly broken up. No counter-attack has materialized or made progress except one from Laon which appears to have met no opposition. Meeting with Winston and Chiefs of Staff at Admiralty 10.30. Decided to send Dill tomorrow at dawn to see Reynaud and Georges to try to learn latter's plan and give him our view.

War Cabinet: minutes
(*Cabinet papers, 65/7*)

19 May 1940   10 Downing Street
10 a.m.

In accordance with the instructions of the Prime Minister, General Dill had now gone to France to spend the next four or five days with General Georges. An Officer would be returning that evening with a report from General Dill as to the position.

The Chief of the Imperial General Staff said that he had also telephoned to Lord Gort and had asked him to consider whether he could concentrate some part of the British Expeditionary Force in the Arras area.

The Prime Minister said that he felt sure the War Cabinet would approve the action taken by the Chief of the Imperial General Staff. While the British Army was under the orders of General Georges, it was right that the Chief of the Imperial General Staff and Lord Gort should concert as to the plans which should be taken in various eventualities to safeguard the position of the British Expeditionary Force, and that these plans should be communicated to General Georges, who would take them into account in giving his orders for the conduct of the battle.

The Secretary of State for Foreign Affairs read to the War Cabinet a telegram, No. 759, which he had just received, reporting a conversation between Lord Lothian[1] and President Roosevelt on the previous evening.

---

[1] Philip Henry Kerr, 1882–1940. Educated at the Oratory School, Birmingham, and New College, Oxford. Worked as a civil servant in South Africa, 1905–8. Editor, *The Round Table*, 1910–16. Secretary to Lloyd George, 1916–21. Secretary of the Rhodes Trust, 1925–39. Succeeded his cousin as 11th Marquess of Lothian, 1930. Chancellor of the Duchy of Lancaster, 1931. Chairman of the Indian Franchise Committee, 1932. Ambassador in Washington from 1939 until his death.

President Roosevelt had, of course, shown himself very friendly and had emphasised the efforts which he was making to keep Italy from entering the war. He had, however, said nothing which showed that he recognised our pressing need for immediate aircraft supplies; nor had he mentioned the suggestion that the United States Government should let us have aircraft at once from their own supplies, to be replaced later from orders already placed in the United States.

The Prime Minister said that in these circumstances he proposed to send a telegram to President Roosevelt at once making clear our immediate needs.

The War Cabinet invited the Secretary of State for Air to furnish the Prime Minister before 5 p.m. that day with information for inclusion in such a telegram.

John Colville: diary
(*Colville papers*)

19 May 1940

After the Cabinet I went to Admiralty House and found Mrs Churchill who said that the preacher at St Martin-in-the-Fields had preached such a pacifist sermon that morning that she got up and left. 'You ought to have cried "Shame",' said Winston, 'desecrating the House of God with lies!' Then he came back and said to me, 'Tell the Minister of Information with a view to having the man pilloried.' It is refreshing to work with somebody who refuses to be depressed even by the most formidable danger that has ever threatened this country.

After lunch came the astounding and, if true, nerve-racking news that the French army south of the BEF has melted away and left a vast gap on the British right. Winston was summoned back from Chartwell, where he had gone for a few hours' sunshine and to write his broadcast speech for tonight.

John Colville: recollection
(*'Man of Valour', page 204*)

19 May 1940

This vital decision[1] once taken, to the lasting credit both of Dowding and of Churchill, the Prime Minister, after a gruelling week, retired to Chartwell on the morning of Trinity Sunday for a few hours' sunshine and sought distraction by feeding his surviving black swan (the remainder had been eaten by foxes) and his greatly cherished goldfish. Almost before the last ant's egg

---

[1] Not to send over to France any further British fighter aircraft.

had been offered, the telephone rang to inform him, quite erroneously as it turned out, that the French 1st Army had melted away entirely and had left a vast gap on the right of the BEF. With the police car's bell ringing incessantly and a total disregard of red traffic lights or Belisha beacons, the Prime Minister returned post-haste to Downing Street, only to be informed that the report was exaggerated but that Pownall[1] had telephoned to say Gort was contemplating a retreat to the sea. Churchill had himself, two days previously, given instructions that plans for such an eventuality should be made, and Ironside had made similar provisions in consultation with the Admiralty; but both of them had considered this a mere precaution against disastrous necessities which still seemed far away.

War Cabinet: Confidential Annex
(*Cabinet papers, 65/13*)

19 May 1940
4.30 p.m.

The Chief of the Imperial General Staff informed the War Cabinet that the British were in touch on their left with the Belgians about Oudenard, but on the right in the St Amand area the French were not holding well at all. The Chief of the General Staff at General Headquarters[2] had rung up the War Office and said that if the gap on the right of the BEF widened, the Commander-in-Chief had it in mind to withdraw towards Dunkerque, resting his right on the canal running through St Omer, and to fight it out there.

The Chief of the Imperial General Staff said that he had replied that this proposal could not be accepted at all. We might at a pinch be able to supply the BEF in a bridgehead resting on the Channel ports for a limited time, but we could certainly never evacuate the force complete. He had already suggested on the previous evening that the BEF should advance south-west through the Béthune–Arras area, with its left somewhat reformed in order to get back on to its lines of communication, and fight its way through to join up

---

[1] Henry Royds Pownall, 1887–1961. Entered the Army, 1906. On active service, 1914–18 (DSO, Military Cross). Director of Military Operations and Intelligence, War Office, 1938–9. Chief of the General Staff, British Expeditionary Force, 1939–40. Knighted, 1940. Inspector-General of the Home Guard, 1940. General Officer Commanding the British Troops in Northern Ireland, 1940–1. Vice-Chief of the Imperial General Staff, 1941. Commander-in-Chief, Far East, 1941–2. General Officer Commanding the Forces in Ceylon, 1942–3. General Officer Commanding-in-Chief, Persia, 1943. Chief of Staff to the Supreme Allied Commander, South-East Asia (Lord Mountbatten), 1943–4. Chief Commissioner, St John's Ambulance Brigade, 1947–9. Chancellor, Order of St John, 1951. Churchill's principal helper on the military aspects of his war memoirs, 1945–55.

[2] General Pownall.

with the French. If we could get on to the line of the Somme and regain touch with the French there, we might secure our position.

The Prime Minister said that he fully agreed with the objection of the Chief of the Imperial General Staff to the proposal to fall back on the Channel ports. In such a position the British Expeditionary Force would be closely invested in a bomb-trap, and its total loss would be only a matter of time. Our forces must therefore at all costs move back towards Amiens. If necessary we could continue the retirement back through Rouen, moving always towards our bases and reserves. Admittedly this would uncover the Channel ports, but the Germans would in any case be able to operate against this country from aerodromes in the Low Countries. The loss of the ports was therefore comparatively less serious than in the last war, when aircraft had not had such a long range. We must face the fact that the Belgian Army might be lost altogether, but we should do them no service by sacrificing our own Army. They should be urged to try and conform with the movement of the British Expeditionary Force. At the worst we would make every endeavour to evacuate as many of them as we could.

Defence Committee[1]: *minutes*
(*Cabinet papers, 69/1*)

19 May 1940 Upper War Room
8.15 p.m. Admiralty

The Prime Minister emphasised that the withdrawal of the British Expeditionary Force on to the Amiens line was the last chance of retrieving the position. It was a matter of hours. The Order must, therefore, be given at once and no considerations of civilities must stand in the way. Since it was clear that the French took the same view of what was necessary as did the War Cabinet, there should be no difficulty in convincing them of the advantage of a plan which sought to bring back a fine and intact army of nine Divisions over a distance of 70 miles along its own communications for the purpose of ranging it alongside the French Army at Amiens. He accordingly suggested that the Chief of the Imperial General Staff should proceed forthwith to France bearing instructions which he (the Prime Minister) dictated as follows:–

(1) The War Cabinet decided that the Chief of the Imperial General Staff was to direct the Commander-in-Chief, British Expeditionary Force, to move southwards upon Amiens attacking all enemy forces encountered and to take station on the left of the French Army.

[1] Consisting of Churchill (as Minister of Defence), the three Service Ministers (A. V. Alexander, Eden and Sinclair) and the three Service chiefs (Pound, Ironside and Newall).

May 1940

(2) The Chief of the Imperial General Staff will inform General Billotte[1] and the Belgian Command, making it clear to the Belgians that their best chance is to move tonight between the British Expeditionary Force and the Coast.

(3) The War Office will inform General Georges in this sense.

John Colville: diary
(*Colville papers*)

19 May 1940

The Cabinet met at 4.30 and decided that the BEF must fight its way southwards towards Amiens to make contact with the French. Winston decided to fly to GHQ to see Gort and to visit the front line, and I was to have gone with him. To my bitter disappointment the project was abandoned just as I had reached home to pick up some clothes.

Winston S. Churchill: broadcast[2]
(*Churchill papers, 9/144*)

19 May 1940

I speak to you for the first time as Prime Minister
  in a solemn hour
    for the life of our country,
      of our Empire,
        of our Allies and – above all –

    of the cause of freedom.

---

[1] Gaston Billotte, –1940. Commander of the First Army Group, 1939, situated on the Belgian border. In a memorandum on 6 December 1939 he warned Generals Gamelin and Georges of the German superiority in mechanised divisions, and their ability to sweep through Belgium as they had done through Poland; his warning led to the formation of the first French heavy armoured division ten days later. Advanced into Belgium, to Namur, 10 May 1940. Driven back into France and towards Dunkirk, and cut off from the main French forces. Commander-in-Chief of the French, Belgian and British forces in the North, on 19 May 1940 he was unable to carry out Gamelin's orders to drive southward and link up with the main French armies on the Somme. Died as a result of a car crash, 21 May 1940.

[2] Churchill's broadcast is set out here in the layout from which he delivered it, the system he had used for forty years. It was known to his staff as 'speech form' or 'psalm form'.

A tremendous battle is raging in France and Flanders.

The Germans, by a remarkable combination of air-bombing and heavily-armoured tanks,

 have broken through the French defences north of the Maginot Line
 and strong columns of their armoured vehicles

 are ravaging the open country which,
  for the first day or two,

  was without defenders.

They have penetrated deeply

 and spread alarm and confusion in their track.

Behind them there are now appearing Infantry in lorries

 and behind them again the large masses are moving forward.

The re-groupment of the French armies to make head against,

 and also to strike at this intruding wedge,

 has been proceeding for several days,

  largely assisted by the magnificent efforts of the RAF.

We must not allow ourselves to be intimidated

 by the presence of these armoured vehicles in unexpected places behind our lines.

If they are behind our Front,

 the French are also at many points fighting actively behind theirs.

Both sides are therefore in an extremely dangerous position,

 and if the French Army and our own Army are well-handled –

  as I believe they will be –

 if the French retain that genius for recovery and counter-attack for which they have been so long famous,

May 1940

    and if the British Army shows the dogged endurance
    and solid fighting power of which there have been
    so many examples in the past,

a sudden transformation of the scene might spring into being.

It would be foolish to disguise the gravity of the hour.

It would be still more foolish to lose heart and courage

    or to suppose that well-trained,
        well-equipped armies,

    numbering three or four millions of men –

can be overcome in the space of a few weeks or even months

    by a scoop or raid of mechanised vehicles,
        however formidable.

We may look with confidence to the stabilization of the Front in France,

    and to the general engagement of the masses

        which will enable the qualities
        of the French and British soldiers

        to be marched squarely against those
        of their adversaries.

For myself I have invincible confidence in the French Army and its leaders.

Only a very small part of that splendid army has yet been engaged;

    only a very small part of France has yet been invaded.

There is good evidence to show that practically the whole

    of the specialized and mechanized forces of the enemy

        have been already thrown into the battle,

        and we know that very heavy losses have been inflicted upon them.

No officer or man,
> no brigade or division
>> which grapples at close quarters with the
>>> enemy
>> wherever encountered
> can fail to make a worthy contribution to the
>> general result.

The Armies must cast away the idea of resisting attack
> behind concrete lines or natural obstacles,
> and must realise that mastery can only be regained
> by furious and unrelenting attack;
> and this spirit must not only animate the High Command
> but must inspire every fighting man.

In the air – often at serious odds –
> we have been clawing down three or four to one
> and the relative balance of the British and German
>> Air Forces
> is now considerbly more favourable to us
> than at the beginning of the battle.

In cutting down the German bombers
> we are fighting our own battle
>> as well as that of France.

My confidence in our ability to fight it out to the finish
> with the German Air Force
>> has been strengthened by the fierce encounters
>> which have taken place and are taking place.

At the same time

May 1940

our heavy bombers are striking nightly

   at the tap-root of German mechanized power,

     and have already inflicted serious damage upon the oil refineries on which the Nazi effort to

        dominate the world directly depends.

We must expect that as soon as stability is reached on the Western Front,

   the bulk of that hideous apparatus of aggression which dashed Holland into ruin and slavery in a few days,

     will be turned upon us.

I am sure I speak for all when I say we are ready to face it,

   to endure it and to retaliate against it

     to any extent that the unwritten laws of war permit.

There will be many men and many women in this Island

   who when the ordeal comes upon them –

     as come it will –

   will feel comfort and even a pride that they are sharing

     the perils of our lads at the Front –

       soldiers, sailors and airmen –

        God bless them! –

and drawing away from them a part at least of the onslaught they have to bear.

Is not this the appointed time for all to make the utmost

       exertions in their power?

If the battle is to be won,

     we must provide our men with ever-increasing quantities

       of the weapons and ammunition they need.

We must have – and have quickly –

    more aeroplanes,
        more tanks,
            more guns,
                more shells.

There is imperious need for these vital munitions.

They increase our strength against the powerfully-armed enemy;

    they replace the wastage of the obstinate struggle;

        and the knowledge that wastage will be speedily replaced

            enables us to draw more readily upon our
                                  reserves,

    and throw them in now that everything counts so much.

Our task is not only to win the battle,
        but to win the war.

After this battle in France abates its force,

        there will come the battle for our Islands,

            for all that Britain is and all that Britain means.

In that supreme emergency

    we shall not hesitate to take every step –

        even the most drastic –

    to call forth from our people the last ounce and
        inch of effort of which they are capable.

The interests of property,

    the hours of labour,

        are nothing compared to the struggle for life and
                                  honour,

            for right and freedom, to which we have
                            vowed ourselves.

I have received from the Chiefs of the French Republic[1]

---

[1] Before delivering the speech, Churchill noted in his text at this point the words '& Reynaud'. While speaking, he added the phrase 'and in particular from its indomitable Prime Minister, M. Reynaud'.

May 1940

    the most sacred pledges that whatever happens

        they will fight to the end –

        be it bitter or be it glorious –

    nay if we fight to the end it can only be glorious.

Having received His Majesty's commission

        I have formed an Administration of men and women
                of every Party,

        and of almost every point of view.

We have differed and quarrelled in the past,

        but now one bond unites us all.

To wage war until victory is won

        and never to surrender ourselves to servitude
                          and shame

            whatever the cost and the agony may be.

If this is one of the most awe-striking periods in the long

    history of France and Britain

    it is also beyond all doubt the most sublime.

Side by side,
        unaided except by their kith and kin in the great
                          Dominions,

        and by the wide Empires which rest beneath their
                              shield,

        the British and French peoples have advanced
        to rescue not Europe only but mankind

            from the foulest and most soul-destroying
                          tyranny

which has ever darkened and stained the pages of history.

Behind them gather a group of shattered States and bludgeoned
                                                            races,

   the Czechs,
    the Poles,
     the Norwegians,
      the Danes,
       the Dutch,
        the Belgians –

upon all of whom the long night of barbarism will

 descend unbroken by even a star of hope,

  unless we conquer – as conquer we must –

   as conquer we shall.

Today is Trinity Sunday.
 Centuries ago words were written to be a call and
  a spur to the faithful servants
   of Truth and Justice:

' Arm yourselves and be ye men of valour, and

be in readiness for the conflict: for it is

better for us to perish in battle than to

look upon the outrage of our nation and our

altars. As the Will of God is in Heaven,

even so let Him do.'[1]

---

[1] This quotation had been sent to Churchill, on the day before his speech, by Andrew Stewart, of the Broadcasting Division of the Ministry of Information. Stewart, who had joined the BBC in Glasgow in 1926, served as Scottish Programme Director from 1935 to 1948. Created CBE in 1954, from 1968 to 1977 he was Director of Scottish Television.

Anthony Eden to Winston S. Churchill
(*Churchill papers, 2/394*)

19 May 1940

My dear Winston,
  You have never done anything as good or as great. Thank you, & thank God for you.

Yours
Anthony

Winston S. Churchill to General Ismay
(*Cherwell papers*)

19 May 1940

General Ismay,
  Let me have an air state of the actual strength of the fighter squadrons in GB. No more squadrons of fighters will leave the country whatever the need in France. If it becomes necessary to evacuate the BEF a very strong covering operation will be necessary from English bases against the German bombers who will most certainly do their best to prevent re-embarkation. This should be studied today. From the point of view of the future resistance it makes no difference whether we strike down German bombers here or in France. Indeed the latter is to be preferred so long as the home bases are not voided. AOC in C[1] should be told the above and make his plans accordingly.
  2. But I also request that within a month from today at least ten squadrons of fighters for home defence shall be formed from the Schools[2] from spare machines. Also that plans should be made to use the Battles[3] etc. to bombard German factories if it is possible to reach them.
  3. In the event of a withdrawal of the BEF or a collapse in France we ought to get a good many of our aircraft, now fighting there, back. It must be borne in mind that since the battle began the Germans have lost far more heavily in

---

[1] Air Marshal Barratt.
[2] The flying schools at which pilots and air crew received their training.
[3] From the outbreak of war, all ten squadrons of the Advanced Air Striking Force consisted of Battle bombers. These did not have the range or carrying capacity to make any effective contribution to the strategic air offensive. As early as 1937 Battles had been recognised by the Air Ministry as 'not really capable of being usefully employed in a war against Germany'. In all, 3,000 were manufactured. In France in 1940 they were used exclusively to support the Army in the field.

aircraft than we, and that the actual proportion of strength has moved in our favour.

I see no reason why with these resources we should not fight it out with them on better terms than were possible at the beginning of the war. Once individual and unit superiority is established very great advantages will follow.

The utmost available AA strength should be concentrated on the aircraft factories. These are more important than anything else at the moment.

WSC

John Colville: diary
(*Colville papers*)

19 May 1940

The PM started writing his speech at 6.00 to broadcast at 9.00. I heard it from home, where I dined. It was good and it brought out the full seriousness of the hour, but it was not Winston at his best, nor quite the clarion-call I had expected.

At Admiralty House there was the usual 'evening party', the Chiefs of Staff, Beaverbrook, Eden, etc. The PM sent a telegram to Roosevelt asking for fighter aircraft and implying that without them we should be in a parlous state, even though this country would never give up the struggle. Considering the soothing words he always uses to America, and in particular to the President, I was somewhat taken aback when he said to me, 'Here's a telegram for those bloody Yankees. Send it off tonight.' I duly sent it to Herschel Johnson[1] at the American Embassy and was somewhat annoyed to be woken up at 2.30 a.m. and told that the PM wanted it back to review what he had said – particularly as he made no alteration after all. In telegraphing to the President he always calls himself 'A former Naval Person'.

Winston also dictated a telegram to Reynaud, expressing his distress at the plight of the French army and insinuating that we had been rather let down. I gather the French Government are in a deplorable state of pessimism and depression.

---

[1] Herschel V. Johnson, 1894–1966. Served with the United States Army in France, 1917–18. Entered the US Foreign Service, 1919. First Secretary and Counsellor, London, 1937–41. Minister to Sweden, 1941–6. Deputy US Representative, United Nations Security Council, 1946–8. Ambassador to Brazil, 1948–53.

Winston S. Churchill to President Roosevelt
(*Churchill papers, 20/14*)

20 May 1940

Lothian has reported his conversation with you. I understand your difficulties, but I am very sorry about the destroyers. If they were here in six weeks they would play an invaluable part. The battle in France is full of danger to both sides. Though we have taken heavy toll of enemy in the air and are clawing down two or three to one of their planes, they have still a formidable numerical superiority. Our most vital need is, therefore, the delivery at the earliest possible date of the largest possible number of Curtiss P40 fighters now in course of delivery to your Army.

With regard to the closing part of your talk with Lothian, our intention is, whatever happens, to fight on to the end in this Island, and, provided we can get the help for which we ask, we hope to run them very close in the air battles in view of individual superiority. Members of the present Administration would likely go down during this process should it result adversely, but in no conceivable circumstances will we consent to surrender. If members of the present Administration were finished and others came in to parley amid the ruins, you must not be blind to the fact that the sole remaining bargaining counter with Germany would be the Fleet, and, if this country was left by the United States to its fate, no one would have the right to blame those then responsible if they made the best terms they could for the surviving inhabitants. Excuse me, Mr President, putting this nightmare bluntly. Evidently I could not answer for my successors, who in utter despair and helplessness might well have to accommodate themselves to the German will. However, there is happily no need at present to dwell upon such ideas. Once more thanking you for your goodwill.[1]

---

[1] On the day that Churchill sent this telegram, British Military Intelligence arrested an employee of the United States Embassy, Tyler Kent, in whose flat they found thirty folders containing 1,500 secret documents which Kent had stolen from the Embassy. The most recent of these documents was a copy of this telegram to Roosevelt. Kent's intention had been to smuggle his documents back to the United States, to serve as ammunition for the isolationist organisations opposed to Roosevelt's pro-British policies. Kent had been posted to the London Embassy in October 1939, after five years in the Embassy in Moscow. A violent anti-Semite, he believed that the Jews were 'basically responsible for the establishment of world communism' (Robert Harris, 'The American tearoom spy', *The Times*, 4 December 1982). Tried at the Old Bailey in October 1939, and sentenced to seven years' imprisonment, Kent was deported back to the United States at the end of the war.

Captain Berkeley: diary
(*Berkeley papers*)

20 May 1940

The grave anxiety has continued, without more ups and downs to relieve it. The PM gave a magnificent broadcast address last night, which has at last put the true position before the people. He is being 'sublime' at every stage and after narrowly averting a serious collapse in Paris four days ago has been galvanising everybody here.

Earl Baldwin of Bewdley[1] to Winston S. Churchill
(*Churchill papers, 20/1*)

20 May 1940

My dear PM,

I listened to your well known voice last night and I should have liked to have shaken your hand for a brief moment and to tell you that from the bottom of my heart I wish you all that is good – health and strength of mind and body – for the intolerable burden that now lies on you.

Yours always sincerely,
SB

Chiefs of Staff Committee: minutes
(*Cabinet papers, 79/4*)

20 May 1940
10.15 a.m.

NARVIK

The Committee had before them a draft of a telegram which the Prime Minister proposed to send to Admiral of the Fleet Lord Cork, in continuation of the telegram which had been despatched to him from the Admiralty the previous night.

The Committee expressed their approval of the terms of the proposed telegram.

---

[1] Stanley Baldwin, 1867–1947. Educated at Harrow and Trinity College, Cambridge. Conservative MP for Bewdley, 1908–37. Financial Secretary to the Treasury, 1917–21. President of the Board of Trade, 1921–2. Chancellor of the Exchequer, 1922–3. Prime Minister, 1923–4 and 1924–9. Lord President of the Council, 1931–5. Prime Minister (for the third time), 1935–7. Created Earl, and Knight of the Garter, 1937.

The Prime Minister said he had spoken on the telephone to General Dill, and to General Swayne. They had said that, in principle, the French were pushing up from the South, particularly in the Cambrai-le-Câteau area. General Weygand[1] was shortly expected at General Georges' Headquarters to confer on the situation. It was difficult to get a clear picture over the telephone, and written Reports should be obtained from General Dill as soon as the Conference with General Weygand was over, and from the Chief of the Imperial General Staff when he had seen Lord Gort and General Billotte, and the Belgian Commander-in-Chief.[2] In the meanwhile, the orders to the BEF, in accordance with the decision taken by the War Cabinet the night before, must stand.

War Cabinet: minutes
(*Cabinet papers, 65/7*)

20 May 1940 10 Downing Street
11.30 a.m.

The Prime Minister said that the War Cabinet would have seen the Minutes of the Meeting held in the Admiralty Upper War Room, at 8.15 p.m. the previous evening (DO (40) 4th Meeting)[3]. These Minutes contained the text of the letter received from General Dill, and of the message which the Chief of the Imperial General Staff had taken to Lord Gort.

The Prime Minister said that he had spoken to General Ironside on the telephone that morning. The latter had given the War Cabinet's message to Lord Gort. Everything possible would be done to help the Belgian Army which would have to conform to the British movements.

The Prime Minister had also had a message from General Swayne at General Georges' headquarters, who had been very glad to hear of the British decision. It was not clear what orders General Georges had intended to give as regards the movement of the BEF. It was possible that the matter had been left in the hands of General Billotte, who was in command of the French left, but with whom Lord Gort did not appear to be in touch at the moment. Lord Gort was moving three divisions down to the Lens area, but anticipated that it would take 48 hours to complete the move. The roads were very badly congested with refugees.

[1] Maxime Weygand, 1867–1965. Chief of Staff to Marshal Foch, 1914–23. Honorary British knighthood, 1918. French High Commissioner for Syria, 1923–4. Commander-in-Chief of the French Army, 1931–5. Chief of the General Staff of National Defence and Commander-in-Chief (for the second time) from 19 May 1940, in place of General Gamelin, until the armistice a month later. Governor-General of Algeria and Delegate-General of the Vichy Government in French Africa, 1941. A prisoner of the Germans in Germany, 1942–5; a prisoner of the French in France, 1945–6. The third volume of his memoirs was published in English as *Recalled to Service*.
[2] Major-General F. Michiels.
[3] The Defence Committee meeting of 19 May 1940, see pages 82–3.

The First Lord of the Admiralty added that Havre had been subjected to intense air attack. Many fires had been started in the town and the docks had been seriously damaged. All traffic on the river between Rouen and the coast was held up owing to magnetic mines.

The Prime Minister thought that as a precautionary measure the Admiralty should assemble a large number of small vessels in readiness to proceed to ports and inlets on the French coast.

The Prime Minister expressed disappointment with the progress of operations at Narvik, which were causing a heavy drain on our resources in equipment and shipping. In his view, the operations were not being pressed hard enough, and the War Cabinet should perhaps consider the despatch of a direct order to Lord Cork to take Narvik by assault.

The First Lord of the Admiralty read a signal which had been despatched to Lord Cork the previous day giving him a strong indication of the urgency of clearing up Narvik at the earliest possible moment. He suggested that the reply to this signal should be awaited before any decision was taken to send a direct order to Lord Cork.

The Secretary of State for War said that the slowness of the operations was due to weather conditions. Three feet of melting snow handicapped all movement. The Germans, who were holding defensive positions, were less impeded by this than assaulting troops.

The Secretary of State for Foreign Affairs and the Prime Minister suggested that the Chiefs of Staff should now consider carefully whether we were likely to get a dividend out of our occupation of Narvik, even after we had succeeded in capturing it. It was clear that the troops, ships and equipment occupied in the operation were urgently needed elsewhere.

The Chief of the Air Staff said that the whole problem was now under examination by the Chiefs of Staff.

May 1940

War Cabinet: Confidential Annex
(*Cabinet papers, 65/13*)

20 May 1940
11.30 a.m.

The War Cabinet had before them a Report by the Chiefs of Staff (WP (40) 159).[1]

The Prime Minister said that he had minuted on the Chiefs of Staff Report suggesting:–

(i) A study of the covering operations which would be necessary from English bases, in the event of it being necessary to withdraw the British Expeditionary Force from France.

(ii) Attacks on German bombers over France were no less valuable than operations against them over this country.

(iii) Ten squadrons of fighters should be formed within a month from spare aircraft used for training purposes.

(iv) Plans should be made to use Battle aircraft to bombard German factories if possible.

(v) Arrangements should be made to get back as many of our aircraft as possible from France in the event of a withdrawal of the British Expeditionary Force or a collapse in France.

(vi) AA defences should be concentrated to protect the aircraft factories in this country.

The Prime Minister agreed that we had reached the limit of the air assistance which we could send to France, and that we could not consider despatching further resources permanently to France, thus denuding our defences at home.

---

[1] In their report of 18 May 1940, 'The Air Defence of Great Britain', Newall, Pound and Ironside had written: 'If we decline to send any further fighter assistance to France or to continue the support which we are now affording with these squadrons in England for more than a few days at a time at most, then it is not beyond the bounds of possibility that the French Army may give up the struggle. If, on the other hand, we continue to accept this constant drain on the vital defences of this country in order to sustain French resistance, then a time will arrive when our ability to defend this country will disappear. We do not believe that to throw in a few more squadrons, whose loss might vitally weaken the fighter line at home, would make the difference between victory and defeat in France' (*Cabinet papers, 66/7*).

Winston S. Churchill to Lord Cork
(*Admiralty papers, 199/1929*)

20 May 1940
6.48 p.m.
Personal and Private

I am increasingly disappointed by the stagnation which appears to rule in the military operations round Narvik, and at the delay in occupying the town itself. According to all reports there are very few Germans in Narvik, and only forces of about 1,500 in the surrounding country. Yet these seem to hold up three or four times their number, who refrain from coming to grips with them and keeping them under constant fire at close quarters. It is necessary to reach a decision in this theatre in view of larger events. Expedition is eating up large quantities of shipping and other essential supplies. More destroyers will be needed in the South very soon. It is indeed lamentable that slowness in repairing Bardu Aerodrome has forced *Glorious* to return to Scapa to refuel. Delay is costing more men and ships than vigorous action. I should be much obliged if you would enable me to understand what is holding you back.

A. V. Alexander to Winston S. Churchill
(*Admiralty papers, 116/4471*)

20 May 1940

My dear Prime Minister,

I was more than grateful to you for your personal signal to the Earl of Cork in support of the Admiralty's telegram. I am however exercised in my mind as a result of our discussions to-day on the Narvik position, so I was glad that you took the view that nothing further should be done until there was a reply to our signal and your personal message. I have gathered from the First Sea Lord that he agrees with your instruction as to preparation of plans in certain eventualities. Whilst I think the preparation of these plans is a wise precaution, I desire to submit to you my own assessment of the position in the enclosed personal memorandum.[1]

Yours sincerely,
A. V. Alexander

[1] In his memorandum to Churchill, A. V. Alexander listed several reasons for not evacuating Narvik: (i) Britain's promise that she would do 'all within our power' to help Norway against German aggression. (ii) The importance of Swedish iron ore if Britain were left to fight Germany alone after the fall of France. (iii) The drain on German military and air strength by having to fight on in Norway. (iv) The continuing mobilisation of Norwegian citizens and their ability to effect 'coastal hindrances' of the Germans. (v) The possibility of influencing Sweden 'to resist any dictated terms'. (vi) 'What would be the situation if within the next three or four days, or even the next two or three weeks, we reach the situation in France comparable to the Battle of the Marne in 1914, and the tide was turned, if in the meantime we had fled from our commitments in Norway,

May 1940

Defence Committee: minutes
(*Cabinet papers, 69/1*)

20 May 1940 10 Downing Street
6.30 p.m.

NARVIK

The Committee discussed the present position at Narvik and the future action which should be taken in that area.

The Prime Minister informed the Committee that he had despatched a telegram to Lord Cork urging energetic action to clear up the situation and asking what was delaying matters. This followed a telegram from the Chiefs of Staff asking Lord Cork what action could be taken with his existing forces. It would be unwise to take any definite decision until answers to these telegrams were received, but there were a number of factors which pointed in the direction of evacuating Narvik after the town had been captured and the railway rendered unserviceable. The Germans might now feel themselves strong enough to make demands on Sweden for the passage of troops and in view of recent happenings on the Western Front it was now doubtful whether the Swedes would resist. It would thus be impossible for us ever to make a land advance towards the ore fields. The expedition was consuming our resources and would not result in our getting any ore at any rate for a long time. Narvik was not essential to us as a Naval base.

Mr Alexander said that from the point of view of the Norwegians, who were still mobilising forces and fighting the Germans, it was most important to hold on to Narvik. Moreover, the Germans evidently desired to take the place judging by the exertions they were making in the air and over land.

After some further discussion, the Committee decided to defer any decision until a reply had been received from Lord Cork to the telegrams which had been sent to him, but considered that in the meanwhile all aspects of withdrawal should be studied by the Staffs.

INVASION

There were three platoons of infantry and some 300 RAF personnel armed with rifles on all aerodromes, most of which had also concrete pill-boxes completed. Some of the military guards were half-trained soldiers from infantry depots, who might not have fired a musketry course.

The Prime Minister said that all such men should be exercised in the firing of a few rounds of ball ammunition, even if they could not do a full course.

---

and if we had then to settle down to a long economic struggle, not with the support but with the enmity of peoples we had promised to assist?' (*Admiralty papers, 116/4471*).

The Chief of the Air Staff said that the Advanced Air Striking Force had already been moved from Rheims to Troyes. The total numbers of personnel in the Advanced Air Striking Force was very considerable, and he was anxious to move it all as soon as possible right out to the west of France and then up to the south of the Seine, where they would be in a position to support the BEF south of Amiens. The Advanced Air Striking Force had never been entirely at the disposal of the French High Command and was not under their command, but Air Marshal Barratt feared that to move it now might have an unfortunate effect on French morale.

The Prime Minister said that owing to the effect on the French it would be out of the question to move the whole Advanced Air Striking Force out to the west now, though there would be no objection to some transference of ancillary personnel, provided the French raised no objection and the fighting efficiency of the force was not impaired.

The Committee agreed that Air Marshal Barratt should be authorised to discuss with the French, as if on his own initiative, a thinning out of the commitment of the Advanced Air Striking Force in the Troyes area, with the proviso that nothing should be said to the French which would give rise to misunderstanding as to our intentions.

General Percival[1] raised the question of the despatch to France of the two motor battalions of Regular infantry which formed part of the Armoured Division. It had been intended that these should join the Division overseas if the situation at home permitted, but he knew that the Chief of the Imperial General Staff was anxious to keep these battalions in the United Kingdom at the present time.

The Prime Minister thought there could be no question of despatching these valuable units overseas at this juncture, but the matter would have to be discussed after the return of the Chief of the Imperial General Staff from France.

---

[1] Arthur Ernest Percival, 1887–1966. A clerk in a City office in London, 1907–14. On active service, 1914–18 (DSO, Military Cross, wounded). Served in North Russia, 1919 (bar to DSO), and in Ireland, 1920–2 (OBE, despatches twice). General Staff Officer, Malaya, 1936–8. Brigadier, General Staff, 1st Corps, British Expeditionary Force, France, September 1939 to February 1940. Assistant Chief of the Imperial General Staff, 1940. General Officer Commanding 44th (Home Counties) Division, 1940–1. CB, 1941. General Officer Commanding, Malaya, May 1941. Surrendered to the Japanese, 15 February 1942. Released from captivity in Manchuria, August 1945. Present on board USS *Missouri* for the Japanese surrender. In 1947 he published *The War in Malaya*.

May 1940

Paul Reynaud to Winston S. Churchill
(*Premier papers, 3/188/1*)

20 May 1940   Paris
7.35 p.m. (by telephone)

General Weygand begs, in view of necessity of holding up of advance of German divisions towards the sea, Air Marshal Newall be authorised to carry out such bombing operations over the battlefield as may be requested by General Billotte who is co-ordinating the operations of the French, British and Belgian armies in Belgium.

Winston S. Churchill to Paul Reynaud
(*Premier papers, 3/188/1*)

20 May 1940
8.10 p.m.

Chief of the Air Staff has the authorisation which General Weygand has requested and the RAF Bomber Command is exerting the maximum bombing effort by day and night in support of the land battle. In accordance with the arrangements previously agreed the RAF bombing plan is concerted with General Georges through Air Marshal Barratt.

Winston S. Churchill to Sir Roger Keyes
(*Churchill papers, 20/14*)

20 May 1940

Cannot understand what sort of solution you have in mind. BEF will make every effort to sustain and shield the Belgian Army during the movements which are indispensable to its life and further action.

Winston S. Churchill to Sir Roger Keyes
(*Churchill papers, 20/14*)

21 May 1940

Weygand is coming up your way to-morrow to concert action of all forces. Essential to secure our communications southward and strike at small bodies intruding upon them. Use all your influence to persuade your friends to conform to our movements. We must preserve power to advance southwards and make effort to regain local initiative. Belgian army should keep hold of our seaward flank. No question of capitulation for anyone. We greatly admire

King's attitude. German thrust towards coast must not succeed in separating us from main French forces. Have complete confidence in Gort and Weygand, who embody offensive spirit vital to success.

Winston S. Churchill to A. V. Alexander
(Premier papers, 3/475/1)

21 May 1940

Many thanks for your letter of May 20 in which you suggest an immediate exchange of technical information with the United States.[1]

I do of course appreciate very forcibly the importance of retaining the good will of the United States authorities and of extracting from them all the material assistance they can give; but I should prefer to wait a few days before reaching a decision upon the proposal you make. I do not think a wholesale offer of military secrets will count for much at the moment. I made an offer previously to give them the secret of the Asdics[2] in exchange for their bomber sight, but it was not accepted. However I will keep this new suggestion in mind until the moment is ripe.

Winston S. Churchill to Paul Reynaud
(Foreign Office papers, 800/312)

21 May 1940
Personal and Private

Many congratulations upon appointing Weygand, in whom we have entire confidence here.[3] It is not possible to stop columns of tanks from piercing thin lines and penetrating deeply. All ideas of stopping holes and hemming in these intruders are vicious. Principle should be, on the contrary, to punch holes. Undue importance should not be attached to the arrival of a few tanks at any

---

[1] In a letter marked 'Most Secret and Urgent' on 20 May, Alexander had written: 'In the circumstances of our present situation I feel that we should do everything we can to show our good-will towards the United States of America. I think that the time has come when we might greatly influence the American attitude in the right direction by making them an unrestricted offer to pool technical information. Our war experience will have made this a good bargain for the Americans' (*Premier papers, 3/475/1*).

[2] An anti-submarine radar device which had been installed in British ships shortly before the outbreak of war.

[3] Weygand has been appointed Commander-in-Chief of the French Army, and Chief of the General Staff of National Defence (in succession to Gamelin).

particular point. What can they do if they enter a town? Towns should be held with riflemen, and tank personnel should be fired upon should they attempt to leave vehicles. If they cannot get food or drink or petrol, they can only make a mess and depart. Where possible, buildings should be blown down upon them. Every town with valuable cross-roads should be held in this fashion. Secondly, the tank columns in the open must be hunted down and attacked in the open country by numbers of small mobile columns with a few cannon. Their tracks must be wearing out, and their energy must abate. This is the one way to deal with the armoured intruders. As for the main body, which does not seem to be coming on very quickly, the only method is to drive in upon the flanks. The confusion of this battle can only be cleared by being aggravated, so that it becomes a mêlée. They strike at our communications; we should strike at theirs. I feel more confident than I did at the beginning of the battle; but all the Armies must fight at the same time, and I hope the British will have a chance soon. Above is only my personal view, and I trust it will give no offence if I state it to you.

Every good wish.

Chiefs of Staff Committee: minutes
(*Cabinet papers, 79/4*)

21 May 1940
10.15 a.m.

General Ismay said that the Prime Minister was about to issue orders for a study to be made of possible German methods in an attack on this country. The technique employed in Norway had differed from that employed in Holland and there was no doubt that the Germans would attempt to spring new surprises. It would be advisable therefore to study all reports which had been received, however fantastic, so that we could adapt our defences to meet any method which the enemy might employ.

It was agreed, in anticipation of the instructions of the Prime Minister, that representatives of each of the three Services should be appointed to examine all available data which might throw light on the methods which the Germans might employ in an attack on this country and to report all the various possibilities so that our defensive plans could be perfected to meet all eventualities.

General Ismay said that the Prime Minister wished attention to be paid to the possibility of enemy aircraft landing on straight stretches of arterial roads, particularly in East Anglia. Steps had been taken in Holland to guard against this risk and it would be worth studying what action could be taken here on the same lines.

It was agreed to draw the attention of the Home Defence Executive to the danger specified by the Prime Minister and to instruct them to take such steps as might be practicable to guard against it.

War Cabinet: minutes
(*Cabinet papers, 65/7*)

21 May 1940 10 Downing Street
11.30 a.m.

The Prime Minister said that the Chief of the Imperial General Staff, who had just returned from Flanders, would give the War Cabinet his appreciation of the present state of affairs on the Western Front. General Ironside had had a narrow escape the previous night when his hotel at Calais had received a direct hit from a German bomb.

The Prime Minister said that the situation was more favourable than certain of the more obvious symptoms would indicate. The most dangerous of these symptoms was that a German armoured column, which had been reported in strength at Amiens, had now entered Abbeville, and held that town. Another armoured column had been seen passing Frévent. It was probably making for Boulogne. Two battalions of Guards were being sent to Boulogne in destroyers in order to hold that town against the German column.

Our forces still enjoyed an overwhelming superiority of numbers in this theatre of operations. We must now be ready to fight hard under open warfare conditions.

The Germans had probably left very small forces, if any, behind to hold the towns through which they had passed. Cambrai was believed to be practically empty of Germans. We had held Arras, although German armoured fighting vehicles were reported on all the roads round the town. Two British divisions were now operating in this theatre to the south and west of Arras; it was hoped that a third division would join them that day.

The Chief of the Imperial General Staff had found General Billotte, who was in command of the French left, in a state of indecision, but had galvanised him into giving orders for a counter-attack southwards from the Douai–Valenciennes area, in which he had some eight French divisions at his disposal. There seemed no reason why the counter-attack should not result in retaking Cambrai. General Weygand was visiting Flanders that day and would see both Lord Gort and General Billotte.

The Prime Minister expressed the gratitude of the War Cabinet to the Chief of the Imperial General Staff for dealing so promptly and vigorously with the situation in France. He suggested that the Chief of the Imperial General Staff and the Chief of the Air Staff should concert together arrangements for ensuring that prompt and adequate air support could be provided to the operations of our forces in the Amiens–Arras area.

The Prime Minister said that Battle aircraft were being used on the front to-day, and that they were likely to be increasingly useful in the course of the next two months, if the enemy were to establish bases closer to the United Kingdom and were to obtain a foothold on the French coast. The types of aircraft now in question were not those of the first efficiency, but if we ran short of the better types it would be unwise to deprive ourselves of the second-best in the life-and-death struggle which we might have to face in the next few weeks. Although the number of machines involved was inconsiderable, he thought that it would be dangerous to send away from the country even a small number of aircraft, if they could be used for operational purposes in the near future. The supply of pilots, though of immense value, was remote in comparison with the needs of the moment, when the enemy appeared to be staking everything on reaching a quick decision. He was therefore inclined to suspend the despatch of these aircraft until after the immediate crisis, and felt confident that the Dominions would understand the position.

Winston S. Churchill: statement
(*Hansard*)

21 May 1940   House of Commons

The Prime Minister: With regard to the Business of the House, to-morrow, as already announced, we shall take the Second Reading of the Treachery Bill.[1] I think it is desirable that we should ask the House not only to take the Second Reading, but the Committee and remaining stages so that the Bill may become law as early as possible. It will also be necessary, in connection with the formation of the Local Defence Volunteer Force, to have a small Bill to amend the National Service (Armed Forces) Act. We shall ask leave to bring in this Bill to-morrow, and, in view of its urgency, we desire to pass it through all its stages on the same day. The text of the Bill will be made available to hon. Members as soon as the House meets to-morrow.

---

[1] Passed through the House of Commons without dissent on the evening of 22 May 1940, the second sitting day after Labour and the Liberals had joined the Government, the Treason Act made it possible to detain without trial anyone suspected of treasonable activities. As a result, many German spies were arrested and subsequently shot (with the exception of those who agreed to work against their first masters). Also that evening an amendment to Regulation 18B of the First World War Defence of the Realm Act (DORA) was passed, which made possible the arrest of Sir Oswald Mosley and other members of the British Union of Fascists.

Winston S. Churchill to Neville Chamberlain
(*Churchill papers, 20/13*)

21 May 1940

1. This grave document[1] was placed in my hands last night. I discussed it with the Home Secretary,[2] who already had a copy, and invited him to make proposals for action on it at the end of Cabinet to-morrow. Would you kindly bring it to the notice of our colleagues, either by circulating it from hand to hand, or by reading it to them at the Cabinet, and take the necessary decisions. In my view if there is any doubt, dangerous elements should be interned without further delay, but I will agree to whatever the Cabinet thinks best.

2. It is now thought better that we should meet to-morrow in Paris, as Weygand will have almost certainly returned there by ten o'clock. He reaches Cherbourg at 3 a.m. and will have his train. I shall take a good sweep to the southward.

WSC

John Colville: diary
(*Colville papers*)

21 May 1940   Admiralty House

At Admiralty House there was chaos owing to the lack of information being received, because communications have broken down. I have not seen Winston so depressed, and while I stood by him, trying to get M. Reynaud on the telephone, he said: 'In all the history of war, I have never seen such mismanagement.' Against the advice of the Chiefs of Staff and all present, he decided to go to Paris early tomorrow morning to see Weygand and Reynaud and to impress upon them that it is no use concentrating on the destruction of German motorised columns which have penetrated far into France, but that we must withstand the main German advance and ourselves attack. Sir C. Newall, the Chief of Air Staff, told me he thought the BEF was in grave danger; but at least they seem to be fighting well, unlike their French allies.

At about 1.30 a.m., just after the PM had gone upstairs, the Air Ministry

---

[1] A Secret Service report about the treasonable activities of Anna Wolkoff, Tyler Kent, and the Right Club (headed by Captain Ramsay, a Conservative Member of Parliament since 1931, who was to spend the rest of the war in detention).

[2] Sir John Anderson.

rang up to say that General Billotte, whose weakness and vacillation are thought to have contributed to much of our discomfiture, had been seriously injured in a motor smash. They thought the PM would be relieved. I found him in his bedroom, a comic sight clad in nothing but a vest. All he said was 'Poor man, poor man' – but without much sign of grief in his tones!

Lord Cork to Winston S. Churchill
(*Admiralty papers, 199/1929*)

21 May 1940
2.56 p.m. (sent)
5.31 p.m. (received)
Personal

Regret that you are disappointed but realize it is inevitable. I have tried to make clear my views that what is going on here is not a struggle for town of Narvik but whether or not we can establish ourselves in this country. That depends upon being able to counter German air attack as quickly as possible. All energies are temporarily devoted to doing that and to securing position at Bodo. I do not admit stagnation. French troops have been carrying out an arduous campaign far from shirking close grips. The Germans retreated before their advance which is necessarily slow and subjected to air attack. They are now waiting for direct attack but require tanks and for these landing craft are necessary. The landing craft however are in demand for getting stores and guns ashore to complete aerodromes and I have chosen this as most important work of the moment. It should be completed in four or five days.

Nothing holds me back but desire to get fighters established which indeed under present conditions ought to be available for a landing on any scale. I quite agree it is deplorable that HMS *Glorious* has to return to fuel but I would observe the preparation of an aerodrome in this country is not easy: starting with three or four feet of snow to clear away does not facilitate estimating time required. I had hoped she could have spent more time. The devoted help of Skuas acting under great disadvantages only slightly bettered the situation. Harstad was subjected to incendiary bombs yesterday, oil tanks fired, two ships burnt out, several casualties and many houses burnt or ruined.

I deplore decision not to send any bombers here which means we cannot delay enemy advance North by road, and, apparent to all, have no means of striking back.

I assure you desire not to fail you is uppermost in my mind. I do not require spurring for I am doing my best in order to attain object and do not doubt achieving it.

Punch cartoon

22 May 1940

AT THE HELM
THE PRIME MINISTER

May 1940

Winston S. Churchill to Lord Cork
(*Admiralty papers, 199/1929*)

22 May 1940
2.18 a.m.
Personal

I am very grateful for your 1506/21 and realise your many difficulties and your desire to achieve results as soon as possible.

The capture of Narvik town will have a special significance and I note your intention to achieve this as soon as you have established the aerodromes.

War Cabinet: minutes
(*Cabinet papers, 65/7*)

22 May 1940   10 Downing Street
10.30 a.m.

The Lord President of the Council[1] informed the War Cabinet that, in view of the very grave news from France and of the difficulty of knowing exactly what was taking place in that country, the Prime Minister had decided to go to France, and was now on his way to Paris to meet M. Reynaud and General Weygand. During his absence, the Prime Minister had requested that he (the Lord President of the Council) should take his place.

The Lord President of the Council said that the Prime Minister had authorised him to say that he would endorse whatever decision might be taken in his absence in regard to the assumption of such additional powers by the Government as might be considered necessary to meet the present situation.

The first of these powers concerned the approval of Defence Regulation No. 54B giving powers over local authorities. This matter had been discussed on the previous evening by a Committee which included all the Members of the War Cabinet, with the exception of the Prime Minister, and it had been unanimously agreed to submit the Regulation to His Majesty for approval. All that was required, therefore, was that the War Cabinet should formally endorse this decision.

---

[1] Neville Chamberlain.

Winston S. Churchill: recollection
(*'Their Finest Hour'*, page 57)

22 May 1940

When I arrived in Paris on May 22 there was a new setting. Gamelin was gone; Daladier was gone from the war scene. Reynaud was both Prime Minister and Minister of War. As the German thrust had definitely turned seaward, Paris was not immediately threatened. Grand-Quartier-Général (GQG) was still at Vincennes. M. Reynaud drove me down there about noon. In the garden some of those figures I had seen round Gamelin – one a very tall cavalry officer – were pacing moodily up and down. '*C'est l'ancien régime,*' remarked the aide-de-camp. Reynaud and I were brought into Weygand's room, and afterwards to the map room, where we had the great maps of the Supreme Command. Weygand met us. In spite of his physical exertions and a night of travel, he was brisk, buoyant, and incisive. He made an excellent impression upon all. He unfolded his plan of war.

Supreme War Council: minutes
(*Cabinet papers, 99/3*)

22 May 1940   Vincennes
midday

Mr Churchill reached GQG about noon, accompanied by the British Ambassador,[1] General Sir John Dill, Air Vice-Marshal Peirse, and General Ismay. M. Paul Reynaud was accompanied by Captain de Margerie.[2] General Weygand welcomed the two Prime Ministers to his General Staff Headquarters and conducted them to the Map Room, where he requested Colonel Simon[3] to describe in general terms the order of battle of the Allied forces.

---

[1] Ronald Hugh Campbell, 1883–1953. Entered the Foreign Office in 1907. Private Secretary to Lord Carnock, 1913–16; to Lord Hardinge of Penshurst, 1916–19; and to Lord Curzon, 1919–20. British Minister in Paris, 1929–35; at Belgrade, 1935–9. Knighted, 1936. Ambassador to France, 1939–40; to Portugal, 1940–5.

[2] Roland de Margerie, 1899–1991. Joined the French Foreign Office, 1917. First Secretary, French Embassy, London, 1933–9; Counsellor of Embassy, 1939. Captain, 152nd Regiment of the Line, September 1939 to February 1940. ADC to General Gamelin, February–March 1940. Cabinet Secretary, April–June 1940. French Consul-General, Shanghai, 1940–4. Ambassador to the Holy See, 1956–9; to Spain, 1959–62; to the Federal Republic of Germany, 1962–5. His son Emmanuel was later Ambassador in Madrid, London and Washington.

[3] Paul Simon, a member of the French delegation to the Supreme War Council. After the fall of France, as a supporter of de Gaulle, he acted as liaison between the Free French in London and the Occupied Zone. Of this period, de Gaulle wrote: 'Simon brought to bear his keen intelligence and cold determination, and was to render signal services' (*The Call to Honour*, page 274). He was killed on the eve of the liberation of France in 1944.

MAY 1940   111

Colonel Simon said that there were two French divisions under the orders of General Fagalde[1] in the extreme North, along the Scheldt and in Zeeland. The Belgian forces came next, down to the neighbourhood of Audenarde. Further to the South came the British Expeditionary Force with four divisions, completed by three further divisions in the neighbourhood of Arras. There were two further British divisions in the Lille area. On the right flank of the latter came the first French Army, supported by the Cavalry Corps. General Billotte, the Commander-in-Chief of the British, French and Belgian forces in the North, was now in hospital as a result of a serious motor-car accident; he had handed over his command to General Blanchard,[2] who had himself been replaced by General Prioux[3] who had just distinguished himself signally at the head of the Cavalry Corps.

Mr Churchill observed that a column of German armoured forces had set out from Abbeville on the previous morning, and had crossed Etaples in the direction of Boulogne. A wounded British officer had watched this German force moving past and estimated its strength at from 4,000 to 5,000 men. About one half of this body moving Northwards had been attacked at about 1630 hours by British aircraft sent out from England and had by this means been held up at Etaples. Two Guards battalions – the last units of the active Army still in England – had been landed at Boulogne with forty-eight AA mobile guns to organise the defence of the town against any possible German incursion. Steps had been taken to protect Calais and Dunkerque. It seemed therefore that these three harbours could be considered secure against any raid similar to that which had been carried out at Abbeville.

General Weygand confirmed the British Prime Minister's statement. He added that there were at Calais three French infantry battalions and that the command at Dunkerque was in the hands of a particularly vigorous Admiral,[4] who had sufficient forces at his disposal to protect the town.

[1] Marie Bertrand Alfred Fagalde, 1878–1966. Born in Algeria. On active service on the Western Front, 1914–18. Liaison Officer with the British Army, 1917. Military Attaché in London, 1919. Colonel, 1925. Commanded an infantry brigade in Algeria, 1931. General, commanding an Army corps, 1938–40. Prisoner of war from 18 June 1940 until 9 May 1945.

[2] General Blanchard, who was born in 1877, fought throughout the First World War, receiving two citations for bravery. He was gassed in May 1918. In the 1920s he served with the French Army of the Rhine. Commanded the 1st Army from 10 May to 22 May 1940 (when he replaced General Billotte as Commander-in-Chief of the French and British Forces in the North).

[3] René Jacques Adolphe Prioux, 1879–1953. Born in Bordeaux. On active service in Algeria (1909–12), Tunisia (1912), Algeria (1912–14), the Western Front (1914–18, being wounded in the first month of the war), Morocco (1925–8) and Tunisia (1932–6). Commanded the Cavalry Corps, 1939–40. Prisoner of war, 30 May 1940 to 16 April 1942.

[4] Jean-Marie Charles Abrial, 1879–1962. Entered the French Navy in 1896. Member of the Supreme Naval Council, 1937. Admiral Commanding the French Naval Forces in the North, 1940. On 21 May he was given responsibility for the French land forces defending the bridgehead at Dunkirk. The embarkation of so many Allied troops 'was attributed in large measure to his courage and energy' (*The Times*, 21 December 1962). From Dunkirk he transferred to Cherbourg (10 June). Nine days later he was taken prisoner by the Germans, but released a month later when the Vichy Government appointed him Governor-General of Algeria. Secretary of State for the

Replying to Mr Churchill, General Weygand explained that large numbers of enemy infantry were already in contact with the Huntziger Army.[1] They had been witnessing, and were still witnessing, a first German attack conducted according to a new formula and by new methods. He believed that this first attack would later be followed by an offensive of the classic type, supported by large masses of artillery. When the first problem had been settled, therefore, they would have to face the second, which would be no whit less arduous, all the more since there was every reason to believe that the enemy would make vigorous attempts to proceed Southward against the Armies linked to the Maginot Line.

General Weygand then gave an outline of the conclusions at which he had arrived as a result of his tour of the Front. He believed that there could be no question of asking the Anglo-Franco-Belgian forces in the North, consisting of over forty divisions, simply to retreat Southwards in an attempt to join up with the main French Army. Such a movement would be bound to fail and the forces would be condemned to certain disaster. The situation required, on the contrary, that the available French and British forces should, under the protection of the Belgian Army, which would provide cover to the East and in certain circumstances to the North, take offensive action Southwards in the Cambrai and Arras area and in the general direction of St Quentin, in such a manner as to fall on the flank of the armoured German divisions at present engaged in the St Quentin–Amiens bulge.

Throughout General Weygand's survey, Mr Churchill and General Sir John Dill gave numerous signs of approval, and showed by their questions and comments that their own conception of the battle was in exact correlation with that of the Commander-in-Chief, particularly in the matter of the task to be assigned to the Belgian army.[2] Mr Churchill repeatedly stated that the restoring of communications between the armies in the north and the main forces in the south, through Arras, was essential; that the British forces under General Gort had no more than four days' food left, that all the supplies and war stores of the BEF were concentrated along the coast from Calais southwards towards St Nazaire; and that General Gort's paramount concern was to preserve this line of communication, which was absolutely vital for him. Accordingly General Gort had begun two days previously to move certain forces behind the line towards his right flank with the object of proceeding gradually towards Arras and Bapaume. The outcome of the battle

---

Navy, 1942. Convicted of treason by the French High Court of Justice after the war. Sentenced to ten years in prison (of which he served two) and national degradation.

[1] General Charles Huntziger was commanding the centre group of armies, with his headquarters at Arcis-sur-Aube.

[2] Weygand had told the Supreme War Council that 'the Belgian Army should withdraw gradually from the Scheldt to the Yser, while at the same time providing cover for the Anglo-French forces moving towards St Quentin'.

was vital to the further conduct of the war, for the maintenance of the British forces through the channel ports was becoming exceedingly hazardous and the Cambrai–St Quentin area therefore assumed decisive importance.

(Mr Churchill later explained privately to the French Prime Minister and to General Weygand that relations between General Billotte and the British Commander-in-Chief were not entirely satisfactory; in particular General Gort had been left without instructions for four days on end. In this connection, General Weygand explained that General Billotte had been incapacitated owing to a serious motor car accident, and had now been replaced by General Blanchard.)

After an exchange of views between Air Vice-Marshal Peirse and General Weygand, in which Mr Churchill took part, it was agreed that General Weygand's wishes would be met and that the Metropolitan British Air Forces would be wholly employed in the battle. The bomber squadrons, which sometimes had difficulty in finding definite objectives, particularly in the previous two days, on the line of battle itself, would harry lines of communication between the front and the River Meuse; the fighter squadrons, which, since they operated from bases in England could hardly remain on the scene for more than 20 minutes, would act in relays or successive waves of attack.

General Weygand then laid stress upon the danger to national defence now being constituted by the influx of refugees from the Netherlands, Belgium and Northern France. Masses of refugees moving along the roads impeded troop movements, allowed German units to mingle with them and, moreover, affected the morale of the troops. It was absolutely essential to put a stop to these movements, to prevent any further refugees from entering into France and to divert the columns of refugees away from the main lines of communication for a certain operation on each day by parking them in fields and imposing certain conditions upon their movements. General Weygand had been extremely firm with the King of Belgium on this point and hoped that the Allied Governments would adopt a similarly firm attitude.

Mr Churchill and M. Reynaud expressed complete agreement with the views of General Weygand.

General Weygand then explained briefly that during the previous night he had had conversations with three staff officers of the Giraud Army, who had given him very favourable information regarding the methods employed by the German Army in the course of the battle. On his instructions a brief note had been prepared on the subject, which he read to the meeting.

Mr Churchill drew the conclusion that if suitable methods were applied and if a calm determination was maintained, it should be possible to resist attacks by the armoured German units even when they were supported by bomber activity. The question was now to hold on everywhere at every single point where an Allied force was in possession.

General Weygand added that it was also necessary to act and that every time an attack was launched some part of the enemy force found itself faced with difficulties.

The meeting concluded at 1.15 p.m.

Winston S. Churchill to Lord Gort
(*Churchill papers, 20/14*)

22 May 1940

I flew to Paris this morning with Dill and others. The conclusions which were reached between Reynaud, Weygand and ourselves are summarised below. They accord exactly with general directions you have received from War Office. You have our best wishes in the vital battle now opening towards Bapaume and Cambrai.

It was agreed[1] –

1. That the Belgian Army should withdraw to the line of the Yser and stand there, the sluices being opened.

2. That the British Army and the French First Army should attack south-west towards Bapaume and Cambrai at the earliest moment – certainly tomorrow, with about eight Divisions – and with the Belgian Cavalry Corps on the right of the British.

3. That as this battle is vital to both Armies and the British communications depend upon freeing Amiens, the British Air Force should give the utmost possible help, both by day and by night, while it is going on.

4. That the new French Army group which is advancing upon Amiens and forming a line along the Somme should strike northwards and join hands with the British Divisions who are attacking southwards in the general direction of Bapaume.

War Cabinet: Confidential Annex
(*Cabinet papers, 65/13*)

22 May 1940
7.30 p.m.

The Prime Minister gave the War Cabinet an account of his visit to France with the Vice Chiefs of Staff and General Ismay. He had first seen M. Reynaud. He had gathered that M. Daladier was considerably shaken by the serious defects which had been disclosed in the French military machine, particularly in view of the fact that he had been Minister for War for the past

---

[1] These were the four official conclusions of the Supreme War Council, and had been appended to the transcript of the discussion.

MAY 1940

four years. The party had then gone on to see General Weygand, who had made a most favourable impression by his vigour and confidence.

General Weygand had given them his full appreciation of the situation and it was clear that his views coincided exactly with those which the Chief of the Imperial General Staff had expounded to the War Cabinet. During his visit to the armies in the north on the previous day, General Weygand had, unfortunately, missed seeing Lord Gort; but he had spent a considerable time with the King of the Belgians and the Belgian Commanders-in-Chief. He had told them that it was essential for them to withdraw. They had demurred on the grounds that by doing so they would give up the whole of their country. The moral effect would be bad, and the Belgian forces might question whether there was anything left for them to fight for. The King had suggested that the Belgians, in contact with the British, should fall back towards the coast and fight it out on a roughly semi-circular line with their backs to the sea. General Weygand had pointed out to them the hopelessness of such a plan from the strategical point of view, but had not left them convinced. Nevertheless, just before the Prime Minister had reached General Weygand, a message had been received to the effect that the Belgians had agreed to withdraw to the line of the Yser. General Weygand had issued orders for the sluices in that area to be opened in order to cover the Belgian front.

The Prime Minister read to the War Cabinet the conclusions which he had drawn up after his discussion with General Weygand. M. Reynaud had concurred in the draft. A copy of these conclusions had been despatched to Lord Gort for his information. The orders based on these conclusions would, of course, reach Lord Gort through the normal channels.

It was intended that the attacks by the British Army and the French Army to the South-West and by the French Army Group northward in the Amiens direction, should take place on the following day, 23rd May.

The Chief of the Imperial General Staff observed that, so far as was known, no preparations had been made for these attacks at noon that day, and he thought that the attacks would take some time to mount.

The Prime Minister said that General Weygand had informed him that all German armoured divisions were operating in the Arras–Bapaume area, where, unfortunately, the country was particularly favourable to them. On the southern front, along the line of the Aisne, the Germans appeared to be preparing for an infantry attack in the 'classic style'. Air Marshal Peirse had explained to General Weygand the difficulties with which our bombers had to contend in attacking the German armoured columns by day. He had, however, undertaken that the Royal Air Force would do everything possible to assist the proposed attacks by the British and French Armies, both by day and night. Provided the French fought well, there seemed a good prospect of success.

The Vice Chief of the Imperial General Staff said that General Weygand had told him that he was doing everything possible to raise the morale of the French troops. There was certainly a weakness in the French Commanders, but from the fact that the French forces had not fought much anywhere it seemed likely that the morale of the units as well was not too good.

The Prime Minister said that General Weygand had issued a stern order regarding refugees, who were to be driven into the fields and to be forbidden the use of the roads except for very limited and stated hours. Furthermore the populace had been instructed to remain in their homes.

General Ironside: diary
(*'The Ironside Diaries, 1937–1940'*)

22 May 1940

Winston came back from Paris about 6.30 p.m. and we had a Cabinet at 7.30 p.m. He was almost in buoyant spirits, having been impressed by Weygand. Said that he looked like a man of fifty. But when it came down to things it was still all *projets*. The BEF has lost a chance of extricating itself and is very short of food and ammunition. I am trying to square up this end to clear the Channel ports for Gort.

Winston S. Churchill to General Ismay and General Ironside
(*Churchill papers, 4/150*)

23 May 1940

Apart from the general order issued, I trust, last night by Weygand, for assuring the southward movement of the Armies via Amiens, it is imperative that a clear line of supply should be opened up at the earliest moment to Gort's Army by Dunkirk, Calais or Boulogne. Gort cannot remain insensible to the peril in which he is now placed, and he must detach even a Division or whatever lesser force is necessary, to meet our force pushing through from the coast. If the Regiment of armoured vehicles, including cruiser tanks, has actually landed at Calais this should improve the situation, and should encourage us to send the rest of the Second Brigade of that Armoured Division in there. This coastal area must be cleaned up if the major operation of withdrawal is to have any chance. The intruders behind the Line must be struck at and brought to bay. The refugees should be driven into the fields and parked there, as proposed by General Weygand, so that the roads can be kept

May 1940

clear. Are you in touch with Gort by telephone and telegraph, and how long does it take to send him a cyphered message? Will you kindly tell one of your Staff Officers to send a map to Downing Street with the position, so far as it is known to-day, of the nine British Divisions. Do not reply to this yourself.

WSC

War Cabinet: minutes
(*Cabinet papers, 65/7*)

23 May 1940　　　　　　　　　　　　　　　　　　　　　　10 Downing Street
11.30 a.m.

The Prime Minister said that the situation which had developed round the Channel Ports had become so critical that he had instructed the Chief of the Imperial General Staff to remain at the War Office in order that he might in person supervise the conduct of these operations. It appeared that very much larger German forces had succeeded in getting through the gap than had at first been supposed. General Reichenau's[1] statement purporting to warn the German Armies against a determined stand by the Allied Armies in the North was clearly intended to deceive; and was an indication of how imperative it was that the British and Belgian Armies should extricate themselves from their present trap.

The Prime Minister said that he had received a telegram from the British Ambassador in Paris stating that General Weygand and M. Reynaud had confirmed their agreement with the plan of operations in the North which had been agreed upon the previous day. General Weygand had said that the conditions for this were more favourable at the present than on the previous day, but had emphasised the vital necessity for holding Boulogne and especially Calais.

The whole success of the plan agreed with the French depended on the French forces taking the offensive. At present they showed no signs of doing so.

He had accordingly sent the following telegram to M. Reynaud –

'Strong enemy armoured forces have cut communications of northern armies. Salvation of these armies can only be obtained by immediate execution of Weygand's plan. I demand that French Commanders in North and South and Belgian General Headquarters be given most stringent orders to carry this out and turn defeat into victory. Time vital as supplies are short.'

[1] Walther von Reichenau, 1884–1942. On active service, 1914–18. Chief of Staff to the Commander-in-Chief of the German Army, 1933. General, 1935. Commanded Army Group IV, 1939. Unlike some generals, he supported Hitler in his war plans against Poland. Served in Poland and France. Promoted Field Marshal, June 1940. Killed in an air crash on 17 January 1942.

A copy of this telegram had been sent to Lord Gort.

Continuing, the Prime Minister said that he had been in touch with Sir Roger Keyes on the telephone. Sir Roger said that the Belgians would co-operate in the plan agreed upon with the French the previous day.

If General Weygand's plan succeeded, it would mean the release of 35 Allied Divisions from their present serious predicament. If it failed, it would be necessary to make a fresh plan with the object of saving and bringing back to this country as many of our best troops and weapons with as little loss as possible. These would prove a valuable addition to the defence of these islands against the attack on them which was likely to be the next phase of the war.

The plans to guard against the latter contingency were to be reviewed at a meeting of Ministers and Chiefs of Staff to be held that afternoon.

The Prime Minister said that he would be making a statement on the situation in the House that afternoon and the Minister of Information might use this to guide him as to what he should say to the Press.

The Prime Minister read to his colleagues a telegram (unnumbered, dated the 23rd May 1940), which he had received from the Prime Minister of the Australian Commonwealth,[1] suggesting that in view of the gravity of the situation, the Dominion Governments should severally address appeals to President Roosevelt for the release of every available aircraft, and that they should also appeal for American volunteer pilots. Mr Menzies had asked the other Dominion Prime Ministers to give their views on this suggestion, and the Prime Minister of New Zealand[2] had already sent a telegram (No. 189, Most Secret, dated the 23rd May, 1940) to say that his Government would only support the proposed approach if (a) the military situation required it, and (b) informal enquiries at Washington had made it clear that it would not be unwelcome to the Administration and would, in their opinion, be likely to lead to useful results. Telegram No. 441, dated the 23rd May, had just been received from General Smuts[3] expressing the opinion that it was for the

---

[1] Robert Gordon Menzies, 1894–1978. Prime Minister of Australia, 1939–41. Minister for Co-ordination of Defence, 1939–42. Minister for Information and Minister for Munitions, 1940. Leader of the Opposition, 1943–9. Prime Minister, 1949–66. Knight of the Garter, 1963.

[2] Peter Fraser, 1884–1950. Born in Scotland. Joined the Independent Labour Party in London, 1908. Emigrated to New Zealand, 1910. Prominent in the New Zealand Labour Party. Prime Minister of New Zealand, 1940–9. Privy Councillor, 1940. Companion of Honour, 1945.

[3] Jan Christian Smuts, 1870–1950. Born in Cape Colony. General commanding Boer Commando Forces, Cape Colony, 1901. Colonial Secretary, Transvaal, 1907. Minister of Defence, Union of South Africa, 1910–20. Second-in-Command of the South African forces that defeated the Germans in South-West Africa, July 1915. Honorary Lieutenant-General commanding the imperial forces in East Africa, 1916–17. South African Representative at the Imperial War Cabinet, 1917 and 1918. Prime Minister of South Africa, 1919–24. Minister of Justice, 1933–9. Prime Minister, 1939–48. Field Marshal, 1941. OM, 1947. In 1917 he was made an honorary member of the Other Club. One of Churchill's last public speeches was at the unveiling of Smuts' statue in Parliament Square in 1956.

May 1940

Government in the United Kingdom to advise, in the light of their knowledge of the military situation, whether the suggested representations should be made.

The Prime Minister read out a reply which he had in mind to send to Mr Menzies (with copies to the other Dominion Prime Ministers), giving an appreciation of the situation, describing the messages which had already been sent to President Roosevelt, and expressing the opinion that we had not yet reached a situation in which a public appeal would be justified.

The War Cabinet expressed general agreement with the lines on which the Prime Minister proposed to reply to the Prime Minister of the Commonwealth of Australia.

Winston S. Churchill to Robert Menzies
(*Premier papers, 4/43B/1*)

23 May 1940

Your appreciation is concurred in, and in addition we must expect early heavy attack on these Islands. For this we are preparing, and we hope that our naval defence will be effective against large bodies, and that our land defence will deal with any sea-borne survivors after some rough work. Evidently final result will depend on ability of our Air Force to make head against superior numbers, and help destroy airborne descents. Our Air Force will be far more effective in this country, for many technical reasons which I cannot give, than operating overseas, and we believe we are capable of limiting daylight raids on ports and factories to manageable proportions on account of the number of casualties we shall inflict on German aviation being out of all proportion to our own Air losses. Night raids far less dangerous to precise targets. Anyhow everyone here resolved to fight it out. Very glad to see fast convoy of Australians approaching. Canadians already here will be used.

Every form of intimate, personal appeal and most cogent arguments have already been sent to Roosevelt, and we have demanded all the aids you mention. He is doing his best, but must carry Congress and public opinion still much diverted by impending Presidential Election. In these circumstances I should not recommend a public appeal at this moment, for it would give President an impression of weakness.[1] You will understand we have

---

[1] Churchill deleted the phrase 'beyond what situation in France, grave though it be, yet justifies'.

been acting in France under General Gamelin's orders, and conforming to the French plans. I saw Weygand yesterday, who is attempting to execute important operations in entire accord with us. Weygand made an excellent impression upon us, and has full control.

Churchill

War Cabinet: Confidential Annex
(*Cabinet papers, 65/13*)

23 May 1940   10 Downing Street
11.30 a.m.

The Chief of the Air Staff[1] said that, to summarize the Appreciation in the briefest possible terms, it recommended that we should capture Narvik and then withdraw from Norway.

The Prime Minister deprecated asking troops to incur heavy losses in assaulting a town which it was proposed to evacuate immediately afterwards.

The First Lord of the Admiralty hoped that no decision would be taken at that meeting to abandon Norway. He felt that there were grave political considerations which needed full consideration.

The Prime Minister said that he did not ask for an immediate decision. Plans for evacuating Norway should, however, be worked out at once, both by the Service Staffs in this country, and by Lord Cork. He had no doubt that this country would shortly be subjected to very heavy attack. The guns, destroyers, aircraft carriers, shipping and troops at present devoted to the Norwegian project were urgently needed for our own defence.

The Lord Privy Seal[2] said that he shared the Prime Minister's views.

The Prime Minister said that, even if it was decided at once to withdraw from Northern Norway, it would be some weeks before withdrawal could be effected. He hoped that in the interval we should take every advantage of our position in Northern Norway to mine the approaches to Lulea to the maximum possible extent.[3] We should, on no account, mention withdrawal to the Norwegians until it had actually begun. We should then offer the King of Norway and his entourage asylum in this country.

The War Cabinet agreed that the Commander at Narvik and the Service Staffs in this country should at once be instructed to prepare plans for a complete withdrawal from Northern Norway.

[1] Sir Cyril Newall.
[2] Clement Attlee.
[3] This was Operation 'Paul'.

May 1940

Winston S. Churchill to Lord Lloyd[1]
(*Churchill papers, 20/13*)

23 May 1940

I am in full agreement with the answer you propose to Wedgwood's[2] Questions, and I do not want Jewish forces raised to serve outside Palestine. The main and almost the sole aim in Palestine at the present time is to liberate the eleven battalions of excellent Regular troops who are now tethered there. For this purpose the Jews should be armed in their own defence, and properly organised as speedily as possible. We can always prevent them from attacking the Arabs by our sea-power, which cuts them off from the outer world, and by other friendly influences. On the other hand, we cannot leave them unarmed when our troops leave, as leave they must at a very early date.

Winston S. Churchill to General Ismay
(*Churchill papers, 3/348*)

23 May 1940

The following decisions seem indispensable in view of the impending danger to Great Britain, and the situation existing in Belgium:
1. Narvik must be wound up at once. Lord Cork should be ordered to prepare scheme for evacuation. At the same time a parallel project should be worked out here by the Planning Committee. This should be ready in three days, which will give time for the present operations at Narvik to reach a conclusion, if they have any chance of doing so.

---

[1] George Ambrose Lloyd, 1879–1941. Educated at Eton and Cambridge. Travelled widely in the East as a young man. Honorary Attaché, Constantinople Embassy, 1905. Special Trade Commissioner to Turkey, including Mesopotamia, 1907. Conservative MP for West Staffordshire, 1910–18. A director of Lloyds Bank, 1911–18. Captain, 1914. On active service in Gallipoli, Mesopotamia and the Hedjaz; he accompanied T. E. Lawrence on one of his desert raids. Present at the capture of Gaza, 1917. Knighted, 1918. Governor of Bombay, 1918–23. Conservative MP for Eastbourne, 1924–5. Privy Councillor, 1924. Created Baron, 1925. High Commissioner for Egypt and the Sudan, 1925–9. One of the Vice-Presidents (with Churchill) of the India Defence League, 1933–5. Chairman, British Council, 1936. Elected to the Other Club, 1936. Secretary of State for the Colonies, 1940–1. His son, Alexander David Frederick Lloyd, was on active service in Palestine, the Middle East, and Europe, 1939–45; Parliamentary Under-Secretary of State, Home Office, 1952–4; Colonial Office, 1954–7; then President of the Commonwealth and British Empire Chambers of Commerce.

[2] Josiah Clement Wedgwood, 1872–1943. Known as 'Josh'. Naval architect, 1896–1900. On active service in South Africa, 1900. Liberal MP for Newcastle-under-Lyme, 1906–19. Commanded armoured cars in France, Antwerp, Gallipoli and East Africa, 1914–17 (DSO, wounded, despatches twice). Assistant Director, Trench Warfare Department, Ministry of Munitions, 1917. War Office Mission to Siberia, 1918. Elected to the Other Club, 1918 (resigned, 1930). Granted the Labour Whip, May 1919. Labour MP, 1919–42. Vice-Chairman of the Labour Party, 1921–4. Chancellor of the Duchy of Lancaster, 1924. Created Baron, 1942.

2. At least eight Battalions of British Regular Infantry must come at once from Palestine. It is no use talking about a strategic reserve for the Middle East when we are in our present position at home. Even if these troops go round by the Cape, they could be here in six weeks.

3. The convoy bringing the Australians in the big ship should be speeded up as fast as possible. It could surely make 25 knots.

4. I will this afternoon at 5 p.m. view the defence of Great Britain. CIGS is not to be disturbed from his conduct of the operation at Calais and Boulogne. General Ismay should let me have a brief statement of the plan, on which I attach a few notes.

WSC

Winston S. Churchill: statement
(*Hansard*)

23 May 1940
3 p.m.

House of Commons

THE WAR

The Prime Minister (Mr Churchill): The German armoured forces which made their way through the breach in the French Army have penetrated into the rear of the Allied Armies in Belgium and are now attempting to derange their communications. Abbeville is in enemy hands and heavy fighting is proceeding around and in Boulogne. It is too early yet to say what the result of this coastal fighting may be; but it evidently carries with it implications of a serious character. Meanwhile, General Weygand, who is in supreme command, is conducting operations involving all the Allied Armies with a view to restoring and reconstituting their combined front.

PEACE TERMS

Mr Gurney Braithwaite[1] asked the Prime Minister whether His Majesty's Government renews and reiterates the pledge of its predecessor that no peace will be concluded with the enemy except in agreement and co-operation with the Government of the French Republic?

The Prime Minister: Yes, Sir.

---

[1] Joseph Gurney Braithwaite, 1895–1958. Sub-Lieutenant, Royal Navy Volunteer Reserve, 1914. Served at Gallipoli (Suvla Bay landing), 1915, and in the advance from Gaza to Jerusalem (1917). Resident Naval Officer, Port Said, 1919. Became a stockbroker after the war; Member of the Stock Exchange, 1926. Conservative MP, 1931–5 and 1939–55. Parliamentary Secretary, Ministry of Transport and Civil Aviation, in Churchill's second premiership, 1951–3. Created Baronet, 1954.

May 1940

John Martin[1]: recollection
(*Letter to the author, 22 December 1981*)

23 May 1940

I was taken into his room at the House of Commons. There was no conversation, but I remember his geniality and air of brisk confidence. He told me to stand over in the window and looked me up and down searchingly, then without further ado said, 'I understand that you are to be one of my Private Secretaries.' With a friendly smile I was dismissed.[2]

John Colville: diary
(*Colville papers*)

23 May 1940

A dramatic afternoon, mostly spent in the Upper War Room at the Admiralty. It began with the news that the Germans were in Boulogne, that the BEF could not break through southwards to join up with the French, and that they only had two days' food left. It seemed all but certain that our army would have to retire precipitously and try to embark, under Herculean difficulties, for England. Then the PM spoke on the telephone to Reynaud and Weygand. The latter claimed that the French had recaptured Amiens and Peronne. If true the news is stupendous, although the position of the BEF still remains critical and they will have to fight their way southwards against heavy odds.

---

[1] John Miller Martin, 1904–91. Entered the Dominions Office, 1927. Seconded to the Malayan Civil Service, 1931–4. Secretary, Palestine Royal Commission, 1936–7. Private Secretary to the Prime Minister (Winston Churchill), 1940–1; Principal Private Secretary, 1941–5. Assistant Under-Secretary of State, Colonial Office, 1945–56. Deputy Under-Secretary of State, 1956–65. Knighted, 1952. High Commissioner, Malta, 1965–7. His memoir, *Downing Street, The War Years*, was published shortly after his death in 1991.

[2] John Martin added: 'Churchill believed he could sum up a man in such a swift scrutiny. Later I was to see him reject a candidate after an equally abrupt examination. In the ordinary way candidates for such vacancies at No. 10 were nominated by the Treasury, but Churchill would not have accepted Sir Horace Wilson's nominations and I suspect that I owed my selection to Brendan Bracken, who often showed admiration for the Palestine Royal Commission and indicated that he was familiar with the Commissioners' tribute to me as their Private Secretary.' Martin was then thirty-six years old. The age of Churchill's other Private Secretaries at that time was: Anthony Bevir, responsible for Civil List Pensions (later the Patronage Secretary) forty-four, Eric Seal forty-two, John Peck twenty-seven and John Colville twenty-five.

Defence Committee: minutes
(*Cabinet papers, 69/1*)

23 May 1940
5 p.m.

Some delay was being caused, however, in the provision of holding-down bolts for the guns, which would take three weeks to manufacture. A further limiting factor was the provision of Officers and skilled men to supervise the working of the guns.

The Prime Minister said that urgent steps should be taken to expedite the holding-down bolts. He could not believe that if an effort were made, the time for their manufacture could not be reduced.

Sir Hugh Elles[1] said that the evacuation of the civil population presented a formidable problem. He had had the evacuation of 60 per cent of the population of Yarmouth, Lowestoft, Harwich, and Felixstowe studied. It could be carried out within a period of from 36 to 48 hours. If, however, for military reasons, it were desired to deal with the South and East coasts as well, the problem might assume unmanageable proportions.

The Prime Minister said that he appreciated the force of the arguments in favour of stopping the week-end traffic to the coasts, but he was not at all convinced of the desirability of evacuating any of the population. When the time came they could be ordered to stay in their homes, and the people on the coast at points at which the enemy was not landing would be in no great danger, since the enemy would strike inland at important objectives. Arrangements would have to be made to control the population where operations were taking place. He thought that these problems should be further studied, and brought before the War Cabinet for consideration.

War Cabinet: minutes
(*Cabinet papers, 65/7*)

23 May 1940　　　　　　　　　　　　　　　　　　　　　　　　　　　Admiralty
7 p.m.

The Prime Minister said that he had been giving further consideration to the observations made by the Lord Privy Seal that morning on the danger of

---

[1] Hugh Jamieson Elles, 1880–1945. Entered the Royal Engineers, 1899. Served in the South African War, 1901–2. Deputy Assistant Quartermaster-General, 4th Division, 1914. Brigade Major, 10th Division, 1915. Wounded in action, 1915. Lieutenant-Colonel commanding the Tank Corps in France, 1916–19. Promoted Brigadier-General, 1917; Major-General, 1918. Knighted, 1919. Commandant of the Tank Corps Training Centre, 1919–23. Director of Military Training, War Office, 1930–3. Master General of Ordnance, War Office, 1934–7. General, 1938. Regional Commissioner for South-East England, 1939–45.

falling between two stools, and that it might be best for the BEF to fall back on the Channel Ports. He had spoken to M. Reynaud and had told him that the position of the BEF was very difficult. M. Reynaud had replied that the French operations were continuing.[1] He had then spoken to General Weygand at 6 p.m., and General Weygand had also had a conversation with the Chief of the Imperial General Staff. The gist of the latter conversation had been summarised by the Chief of the Imperial General Staff as follows:–

(1) He (General Weygand) had taken Amiens, Albert and Péronne, and the manoeuvre was continuing under good conditions.
(2) He considered that the only solution was to continue the manoeuvre. The rest was disaster.
(3) He was quite unmoved when I told him of the weight of the forces moving up on the line Béthune–St Omer. He said that the German Armoured Divisions were reduced by casualties.
(4) He talked of studying the question of feeding Blanchard from the sea. I told him that we knew the difficulties and had little chance of doing much.
(5) Weygand was confident.

General Weygand had demanded that the operation should continue. The Chief of the Imperial General Staff and the Vice-Chief of the Imperial General Staff[2] had both been of the view that it was better that the operation should continue, since, if the BEF were to retire on the Channel ports, it was unlikely that more than a small part of the force could be got away.

The Prime Minister said that there had been reports of a catastrophic situation at Boulogne. It had been reported that the Germans had captured one of the forts and were shelling the town. A signal had been sent from the Admiralty ordering the evacuation, and stating that destroyers were being sent to take off the troops. This signal, however, had crossed a signal from the Senior Naval Officer at Boulogne,[3] stating that the situation was considerably easier, and that the British troops were holding on, although they were being fairly heavily bombed. The fact that the Germans were bombing the town was a clear indication that they had not captured it. The orders to evacuate Boulogne had accordingly been cancelled. There was no doubt that our troops were undergoing a great ordeal and he would suggest that it might be of the greatest help to them if even a few hundred marines could be landed to reinforce them.

---

[1] According to Reynaud, he had told Churchill: 'Weygand is satisfied. We ought not to change anything. We must follow the path which we have traced out. *We must go on*' (Paul Reynaud, *In the Thick of the Fight*, London, 1955, page 369). The italics were Reynaud's own.
[2] General Ironside and General Dill.
[3] Captain D. J. R. Simpson, the senior officer of the destroyer flotilla at Boulogne, had been made Senior Naval Officer in the port during the evacuation. He was killed on 23 May 1940, when his task was taken over by Commander E. R. Conder, who was subsequently awarded the DSC for his work.

The Chief of Naval Staff[1] was invited to find out whether a party of marines was available.

The Chief of the Imperial General Staff undertook to enquire whether the Officer in Command at Boulogne was anxious to receive a reinforcement. A decision whether to send a reinforcement should depend on his reply, provided trained troops were available.

The Prime Minister said that a Tank Regiment had disembarked at Calais and had been placed under Lord Gort. They had been ordered to clear the route to St Omer, but had encountered enemy forces three miles out of Calais. No details of the fighting had yet been received. The remainder of the armoured division had been disembarked at Cherbourg and had now reached a point south of Abbeville.

The Chief of the Imperial General Staff said that 250,000 rations had been landed at Calais. He was hopeful that means would be found to get them through to the army. The ammunition position, however, was serious.

Summing up the position, the Prime Minister thought that, even regarding the latest news in its most favourable light, there was as yet little ground for confidence. He felt, however, that we had no choice in the matter but to do our best to conform to General Weygand's plan. Any other course would wreck the chance of General Weygand's plan succeeding.

According to a message from Sir Roger Keyes, the King of the Belgians had said that he would fully understand if the BEF was being withdrawn, but that it could only have one result for the Belgian Army, i.e., capitulation. So long as we adhered to the plan, the Belgians would conform to it. The Belgian army would have fallen back to the line of the Yser by the following day.[2]

King George VI: diary
(*John Wheeler-Bennett, 'King George VI'*)

23 May 1940   Buckingham Palace
10.30 p.m.

The Prime Minister came at 10.30 p.m. He told me that if the French plan made out by Weygand did not come off, he would have to order the BEF back to England. This operation would mean the loss of all guns, tanks, ammunition, & all stores in France. The question was whether we could get the troops back from Calais & Dunkirk. The very thought of having to order this movement is appalling, as the loss of life will probably be immense.

---

[1] Admiral Pound.
[2] The War Cabinet's attention was also drawn to a telegram from Geneva, reporting that 'popular feeling in Germany was not elated, and that the situation was considered serious. A very high official in the German Ministry for Foreign Affairs had said that, if the present attack could be held for a few weeks, there was danger of a complete collapse.'

Lord Camrose: notes of a conversation with Lord Trenchard[1]
(*Camrose papers*)

23 May 1940

The Prime Minister asked Trenchard to dine with him last night.[2] On the doorstep he met Eden. The party consisted of the latter, Mrs Churchill, Mary Churchill,[3] and the PM.

Despite the presence of the ladies, the discussion ranged far and wide. Eden stated that we had no low-dive bombers and had not practised diving on tanks. This aroused Trenchard's wrath and he stated very emphatically that the suggestions were quite untrue, and, so far as I could gather, he practically told Eden he did not know what he was talking about.

Winston was summoned to the telephone on several occasions and apparently was giving instructions direct to officers in command at Boulogne. Roger Keyes also came through from some place in Belgium.

Both ladies took part quite freely in the discussion and all seemed to have combined to irritate Trenchard. Winston complained of the way in which certain people were working and, either as the result of this or something else which was said, Trenchard retorted with the remark that, while it might be convenient and perhaps necessary for the Prime Minister to sleep two or three hours in the afternoon and work at night, it was impossible for everybody else engaged in the war to arrange their doings accordingly.

After the ladies had retired Winston demanded to know from Trenchard in a very heated way what he proposed to do about the office of GOC[4] for Home Defence which had been suggested to him. Trenchard said that before answering that he must inform him what his conception of the job would be and what was the actual way in which he (Trenchard) could be of use in such a position. (He told me that he felt all the time he was doing badly in the discussion and the presence of Eden irritated him enormously.) He then told

[1] Hugh Montague Trenchard, 1873–1956. Entered the Army, 1893. Active service, South Africa, 1899–1902 (dangerously wounded). Major, 1902. Assistant Commandant, Central Flying School, 1913–14. Lieutenant-Colonel, 1915. General Officer Commanding the Royal Flying Corps in the Field, 1915–17. Major-General, 1916. Knighted, 1918. Chief of the Air Staff, 1918–29. Air Marshal, 1919. Created Baronet, 1919. Air Chief Marshal, 1922. Marshal of the Royal Air Force, 1927. Created Baron, 1930. Commissioner, Metropolitan Police, 1931–5. Created Viscount, 1936. Trustee of the Imperial War Museum, 1937–45. A member of the Other Club from 1926. His elder son, and both his stepsons, were killed in action in the Second World War.

[2] The dinner took place on Thursday, 23 May 1940. Lord Camrose wrote up this note on the following day.

[3] Mary Churchill, 1922– . Churchill's fifth and youngest child. Served with the Auxiliary Territorial Service, 1940–5; accompanied her father on several of his wartime journeys. In 1947 she married Captain Christopher Soames (later Lord Soames, died 1987). They had five children. In 1978 her husband was created a Life Peer, and in 1979 she published *Clementine Churchill*, a biography of her mother. Created DBE, 1980, after her husband's term as Governor of Rhodesia. In 1982 she published *A Churchill Family Album*, and in 1990 *Winston Churchill, His Life as a Painter*. Chairman, Royal National Theatre Board, since 1989.

[4] General Officer Commanding.

the PM that it was sheer waste of time to appoint a GOC who had to consult the staffs of each of the Services, then the Ministers, and then the PM before he had power to do anything. It would mean conference after conference after conference, and in war there was no time for this waste of energy and thought. The PM seized on the reference to the conferences and hotly denied that he wasted time in any conference he ever held. He then abruptly got up and said 'Let us join the ladies'. Trenchard asked to be excused and came away.

In the course of the dinner conversation (in one of Winston's absences on the telephone) Trenchard said something to Mrs Churchill to the effect that he did not want to worry the Prime Minister in the middle of all his other troubles, whereupon Mrs Churchill replied that she wished he (Trenchard) and Roger (Keyes) could be sewn up in a bag and thrown into the sea!

Trenchard this morning sent a letter to Winston (copy of which he showed me) practically amounting to an apology for being irritated last night, recalling the fact that he and Winston had always worked together in the past, and renewing his offer to help in any position where he felt he would be worth while.

The actual position, so far as I can understand it, is that Kirke[1] is now recognised as being of little value, and Trenchard has been offered Kirke's position with just the same limited powers that the latter possesses. Trenchard contends that GOC for Home Defence is only workable with powers which make him assistant to the Prime Minister in his capacity of Minister for Home Defence. Energetic and prompt measures are demanded by the situation, and he feels that without powers of this sort nothing decisive can be done.

My own feeling is that Winston is afraid of employing Trenchard because he is a man of decided opinions and strong character. It will be a disaster if his services are not employed at the present time.

Ronald Cartland[2] to his mother
(Barbara Cartland, 'Ronald Cartland')

23 May 1940

From all I hear Winston is proving simply first-rate. I am delighted about it – a Government at last which I can wholeheartedly support.

---

[1] Walter Mervyn St George Kirke, 1877–1949. Entered the Royal Artillery, 1896. On active service, 1914–18 (DSO, despatches six times). CMG, 1918. CB, 1919. Deputy Director of Military Operations, 1919–21 (when Churchill was Secretary of State for War). General Officer Commanding-in-Chief, Western Command, 1933–6. Knighted, 1934. General, 1936. Director-General of the Territorial Army, 1936–9. Inspector-General of Home Defences, 1939. Commander-in-Chief of Home Forces, 1939–40.

[2] John Ronald Hamilton Cartland, 1907–40. Brother of Barbara Cartland. Their father was killed in action on the Western Front on 27 May 1918. Educated at Charterhouse. Worked at the Conservative Central Office, 1927–35. Conservative MP for King's Norton, 1935–40. Captain, 53rd Anti-Tank Regiment, Royal Artillery, British Expeditionary Force, 1940. Killed in action in

May 1940

Winston S. Churchill to General Weygand
(*Churchill papers, 20/14*)

23 May 1940

General Gort wires that co-ordination of Northern front is essential with armies of three different nations. He says he cannot undertake this co-ordination, as he is already fighting north and south and is threatened on his lines of communications. At the same time, Sir Roger Keyes tells me that up to 3 p.m. to-day (23rd) Belgian headquarters and King had received no directive. How does this agree with your statement that Blanchard and Gort are *main dans la main*? Appreciate fully difficulties of communication but feel no effective concert of operations in northern area against which enemy are concentrating. Trust you will be able to rectify this. Gort further says that any advance by him must be in the nature of sortie, and that relief must come from south, as he has not (repeat not) ammunition for serious attack. Nevertheless, we are instructing him to persevere in carrying out your plan. We have not here even seen your own directive, and have no knowledge of the details of your northern operations. Will you kindly have this sent through French Mission at earliest? All good wishes.

Winston S. Churchill to Paul Reynaud
(*Churchill papers, 20/14*)

23 May 1940

Communications of Northern Armies have been cut by strong enemy armoured forces. Salvation of these armies can only be obtained by immediate execution of Weygand's plan. I demand the issue to the French commanders in north and south and Belgian GHQ of the most stringent orders to carry this out and turn defeat into victory. Time is vital as supplies are short.

Winston S. Churchill to General Ismay
(*Churchill papers, 20/17*)

24 May 1940

Before Narvik is evacuated, it is essential that the largest possible number of mines should be laid in the approaches to Lulea. Let a plan be prepared for laying these by flights from aircraft-carriers. The evacuation would, I presume, be covered not only with Gladiators at Bardufoss, but by Skuas from

---

France, 30 May 1940. Churchill wrote of him, on 7 November 1941 (in the preface to Barbara Cartland's book *Ronald Cartland*): 'At a time when our political life had become feckless and dull, he spoke fearlessly for Britain. His words and acts were instinct with the sense of our country's

the carriers. From this point of view it would be regrettable if our only armoured carrier, *Illustrious*, should be absent at Dakar.

WSC

John Colville: diary
(*Colville papers*)

24 May 1940

Went early to Admiralty House and met the PM, dressed in the most brilliant of flowery dressing-gowns and puffing a long cigar as he ascended from the Upper War Room to his bedroom. He had one or two telephone conversations with the CIGS and Sir Roger Keyes (from Belgium), emerging from his bath in a towel in order to do so.

Winston S. Churchill to Paul Reynaud
(*Churchill papers, 20/2*)

24 May 1940

As we agreed on Wednesday it is of the first importance that you and I should keep in the closest possible touch on defence matters. It is not easy for either of us to leave our posts frequently in order to visit each other, and I have therefore appointed an old friend of yours Major-General Spears,[1] by whose hand I send this letter, to be the personal liaison officer between us on matters relating to defence.

This appointment will leave existing liaisons between our respective High

---

traditions and duty. His courage and bearing inspired those who met him or heard him.' Ronald Cartland's brother Anthony was killed in action on the previous day, 29 May 1940.

[1] Edward Louis Spears, 1886–1974. Joined the Kildare Militia, 1903. Captain, 11th Hussars, 1914. Four times wounded, 1914–15 (Military Cross). Liaison officer with French 10th Army, 1915–16. Head of the British Military Mission to Paris, 1917–20. Brigadier-General, 1918. National Liberal MP for Loughborough, 1922–4; Conservative MP for Carlisle, 1931–45. Churchill's Personal Representative with the French Prime Minister, May–June 1940. Head of British Mission to de Gaulle, 1940. Head of Mission to Syria and the Lebanon, 1941. First Minister to Syria and the Lebanon, 1942–4. Knighted, 1942; created Baronet, 1953. Elected to the Other Club, 1954. Chairman of Ashanti Goldfields. Chairman (later President) of the Institute of Directors.

Commands, and between our respective Navies, Armies and Air Forces, undisturbed.

I would propose that General Spears should normally live in Paris, and pay occasional visits to London whenever you or I so desire.

I am sure that you have full confidence in General Spears, whose special qualifications for this appointment are already well known to you.

Winston S. Churchill to Paul Reynaud
(<i>Churchill papers, 20/14</i>)</div>

24 May 1940

Points one, two and three[1] are agreed, and we are still trying our best. Point four: We were very glad to hear that Fagalde had been given General Command instead of Blanchard, but your telegram leaves this in doubt. For the moment Dunkirk route is open, and we are supplying Gort thereby. Point five: Alas, no more troops exist. Point six: We know nothing of any evacuation of Arras. It is entirely contrary to our wishes. Point seven: Only material evacuated from Havre was gas shells, which it seemed indiscreet to leave there: also some material was moved to the South bank for safety. Anyhow, it is a matter for us. Point eight: Am much in favour of unity of Command, and we have faithfully conformed to it, but believe me, my friend, until Weygand took control there has been no Command in the North worthy of the name since the retreat began.

We have sent General Dill over to-day to see Belgians, Blanchard and Gort. As soon as I receive his report, I will wire you further. All good wishes, and excuse candour.

Winston S. Churchill to Ernest Bevin
(<i>Churchill papers, 20/2</i>)</div>

24 May 1940

My dear Mr Bevin,

I shall be glad if you will give to the Conference of Trade Union Executives an assurance of my deep and active interest in the purpose of their assembly, and let them know how much I should have welcomed, under conditions of less urgency and pressure of manifold dangers, an opportunity to speak to

[1] Points one, two and three in Reynaud's telegram were explanations of the Weygand plan, whereby the encircled Anglo-French armies in northern France 'make a desperate effort to advance and effect a junction with the French forces which are marching from the south to the north'. Reynaud added: 'General Weygand is convinced that his plan can only succeed if the Belgian Army, and those of Blanchard and Gort, are inspired by a grim intention to make a sortie, which alone can save them.'

them personally. The Conference, I am sure, will appreciate the nature of the responsibility which falls upon you, as a Minister of State in this severe crisis of our fortunes, in explaining to the Unions the necessity which has caused Parliament to enact the new Emergency legislation, and how the Government plans to use its exceptional powers for the prompt and complete organization of the country's industrial resources to help us to meet the imminent perils that face us.

The country's needs are imperative, inescapable and imperious, and we shall pay dearly if we fail to meet them. We can meet them now as a Government founded upon a new unity of national purpose, and with the creative energies of a people awakened to the magnitude of the task. We have the fullest confidence in the readiness of the organized workers to accept the obligations arising out of the demands which the State is compelled to make upon their endurance and their capacity for sacrifice. We look with equal confidence to the Trade Union Executives called into Conference by their General Council to assist the State by using their widespread organization to serve the purposes you will unfold at the Conference.

The gravity of the situation deepens hour by hour and we are all called upon to make a supreme effort to defend the country, to preserve our liberties, and to win the war. Trade unionists, with their tradition of sacrifice in the service of freedom, cannot hesitate to throw their full strength into the struggle.

WSC

John Peck to Winston S. Churchill
(*Churchill papers, 20/30*)

24 May 1940   10 Downing Street

Prime Minister

Mr J. H. Thomas[1] telephoned to give you the following message:–
'You have definitely won the first round.'

JP

[1] James Henry Thomas, 1874–1949. Began work as an errand boy at the age of nine. Later an engine-cleaner, fireman and engine-driver. A founder member of the National Union of Railwaymen; General Secretary, 1918–24 and 1925–31. Labour MP, 1910–31; National Labour MP, 1931–6. Privy Councillor, 1917. Secretary of State for the Colonies, 1924 and 1931. Lord Privy Seal and Minister of Employment, 1929–30. Secretary of State for the Dominions, 1930–5; for the Colonies, 1935–6.

May 1940

War Cabinet: minutes
(*Cabinet papers, 65/7*)

24 May 1940 10 Downing Street
11.30 a.m.

BOULOGNE

(1) The Prime Minister said that Boulogne had been evacuated on the previous night. 1,000 had been got away, but 200 had been left behind.

(2) Our destroyers taking part in the operations at Boulogne the previous day had suffered a certain amount of damage from bombing, and machine-gun and battery fire. They had been fired at by some twenty German field-guns north of the harbour. The destroyers had replied, and believed they had succeeded in putting seven of these guns out of action.

CALAIS

(3) We had the following troops in Calais:–
1 Tank Regiment, including cruiser and light tanks;
2 Rifle Battalions, the majority of whose equipment had now been landed; and
1 Battalion of Queen Victoria Rifles.

These were holding a position through the town, which was being shelled. The tanks had had an engagement with German tanks on the previous afternoon which had resulted in a stalemate. Their instructions had been to try to clear the forward roads, but this they had been unable to do, and in consequence the food convoy from Calais had failed to get through to St Omer.

(4) As regards the Naval 12-pounder guns which were being prepared for use at Calais, the First Lord of the Admiralty said that mountings were being improvised, and that all possible steps were being taken to accelerate the necessary work. It was hoped to have six of the guns ready by the following afternoon, i.e., they might reach Calais in the evening.

The Prime Minister suggested that the 3·7-inch Naval guns, which had proved so useful at Andalsnes, might come in useful again, and that steps should be taken to have them in readiness.

DUNKIRK

(5) Considerable numbers of French troops were in Dunkirk, but no English troops had as yet been sent there, with the exception of certain small units sent back to this area from the BEF. The port was functioning quite well. One supply ship had been unloaded on the previous day. An ammunition ship was due to arrive there that day.

(6) The Chief of the Imperial General Staff said that he was waiting to receive a report from General McNaughten[1] on his return from Dunkirk, in

---

[1] Andrew George Latta McNaughten, 1887–1966. Born in Canada. On active service, 1914–18 (wounded twice, despatches thrice). Chief of the Canadian General Staff, 1929–35. Commanded the 1st Division, Canadian Overseas Force, 1939–40. Lieutenant-General, 1940. General Officer

order to decide whether to send the Canadians to that place. It was possible that Dunkirk already contained as many troops as it could hold.

REPORT BY SIR R. KEYES

(7) The Prime Minister said he had that morning spoken to Sir Roger Keyes, who had reported that two French Divisions under General Fagalde – including the Division which had been at Walcheren – were now on the left of the Belgians. The Belgians had endeavoured to persuade these Divisions to go down and occupy the Gravelines line, but, on hearing that the German tanks were in the vicinity, the French had turned back. Sir Roger Keyes had said that communications were open between Ostend and the British Expeditionary Force, and that it would be perfectly feasible to send supplies along this route.

The Prime Minister said that he had been considering whether it would not be advisable to suggest to General Weygand that General Dill might be appointed to co-ordinate the British, French and Belgian operations in the North of France.

EMPLOYMENT OF ENEMY ALIENS[1]

The Prime Minister said that his view on this matter had greatly hardened since the events of the last few weeks. He thought it would be better to employ no Germans in any position of responsibility. The proper method by which Germans opposed to the Nazi régime could contribute to the common cause was by work in the factories or fields of this country, or, best of all, under discipline in the Pioneer Corps. The German technique in the occupation of the Low Countries had shown the weaknesses to which we were exposed, and he was strongly in favour of removing all internees out of the United Kingdom.

War Cabinet: Confidential Annex
(*Cabinet papers, 65/13*)

24 May 1940　　　　　　　　　　　　　　　　　　　　　10 Downing Street
11.30 a.m.

The Secretary of State for Foreign Affairs said that just before the meeting he had seen the Belgian Ambassador[2] who had been accompanied by a

---

Commanding the Canadian Corps, 1940–2. General Officer Commanding-in-Chief, the First Canadian Army, 1942–4. General, 1944. President, Canadian Atomic Energy Control Board, 1946–9. His younger son, a Squadron Leader, Royal Canadian Air Force, was killed in action over Germany in 1942.

[1] The item under discussion was 'Invasion of Great Britain, Security measures, Control of Aliens'. The previous speaker, the Home Secretary, Sir John Anderson, had suggested that German enemy aliens who were 'employed in useful productive work, the conditions of whose employment made it necessary for them to be away from their homes during the night', should be exempt from the requirement to remain at home during the night.

[2] Emile Cartier, Baron de Marchienne, 1871–1946. Belgian Ambassador to the United States, 1920–7; to London from 1927 until his death. Created an honorary GCVO, 1934; honorary GBE, 1937.

Belgian Minister. They had brought an urgent message pointing out that it was imperative that the King of the Belgians should not be captured. They suggested that the situation was such that arrangements should be made, if necessary, to bring him and his staff, comprising 30 or 40 persons, to England that night. Before the King would consent to leave, however, it would be necessary that a message should be sent to him by the British Government. They had suggested that his departure should be made either by boat or plane from Ostend, Nieuport, or Dunkirk. He (the Foreign Secretary) was certainly of the opinion that the King of the Belgians should on no account run the risk of being taken prisoner.

The Prime Minister considered that such a move would be premature. The Belgian Army was still holding the line of the Scheldt, and it would be regrettable that the King should leave his Army at this stage. When the time came, however, it would be perfectly possible to send a message which would clear the King's conscience.

The Chief of the Imperial General Staff agreed. There was no sign as yet of any break in the Belgian Army, and therefore no grounds for immediate alarm.

The War Cabinet agreed to invite the Foreign Secretary to inform the Belgian Ambassador that in the opinion of His Majesty's Government the situation was not yet so critical as to justify the proposed departure of the King of the Belgians, but meanwhile, that close touch would be kept with Sir Roger Keyes, and all arrangements would be made to evacuate the King of the Belgians and his Staff at short notice should this become necessary.

Winston S. Churchill to Sir Roger Keyes
(*Churchill papers, 20/14*)

24 May 1940

We are naturally much concerned to ensure the safety if things go badly of the King, Queen[1] and members of Belgian Government still in Belgium.

Necessity has not yet arisen, but if and when it does it will no doubt be necessary to act very promptly.

We can, of course, understand what must be the King's feeling about the position he holds in relation to the Army, but from wider international point of view and from point of view of carrying on the war, we would emphasise

---

[1] Queen Elisabeth of the Belgians, King Leopold's mother.

that it would be essential in circumstances contemplated that King should move to place of greater safety. We earnestly hope he would take same view, and would be prepared to take decision quickly should need arise. Please impress on him importance we attach to this.

We shall have arrangements ready for evacuation at short notice.

Sir Charles Wilson[1]: diary[2]
(Lord Moran, 'The Struggle for Survival')

24 May 1940

Though it was noon, I found him in bed reading a document. He went on reading while I stood by the bedside. After what seemed quite a long time, he put down his papers and said impatiently:

'I don't know why they are making such a fuss. There's nothing wrong with me.'

He picked up the papers and resumed his reading. At last he pushed his bed-rest away and, throwing back the bed-clothes, said abruptly:

'I suffer from dyspepsia, and this is the treatment.'

With that he proceeded to demonstrate to me some breathing exercises. His big white belly was moving up and down when there was a knock on the door, and the PM grabbed at the sheet as Mrs Hill[3] came into the room.

Soon after I look my leave.

Winston S. Churchill to Sir Edward Bridges
(Churchill papers, 20/13)

24 May 1940

I am sure there are far too many Committees of one kind and another which Ministers have to attend, and which do not yield a sufficient result. These should be reduced by suppression or amalgamation. Secondly, an effort should be made to reduce the returns with which the Cabinet is oppressed to a smaller compass and smaller number. Pray let proposals be made by the Cabinet Office staff for effecting these simplifications.

---

[1] Charles McMoran Wilson, 1882–1977. A physician. On active service as a Medical Officer, 1914–18; Major, Royal Army Medical Corps (Military Cross, despatches twice). Dean of St Mary's Hospital Medical School, 1920–45. Knighted, 1938. Churchill's doctor for fifteen years, from 1940 to 1955. President of the Royal College of Physicians, 1941–50. Created Baron Moran, 1943. In 1965, immediately after Churchill's death, he published *Winston Churchill, The Struggle for Survival*.

[2] Churchill's doctor kept no diary, nor have any notes been found among his papers for 24 May 1940, despite the fullness of this particular entry. Even the notes that do exist, according to their custodian, 'are not altogether a contemporary record'. The 'diary extracts' are therefore, more properly speaking, recollections.

[3] Kathleen Hill, Churchill's secretary, see page 342, note 1.

May 1940

Winston S. Churchill to Professor Lindemann[1]
(*Churchill papers, 20/13*)

24 May 1940

Let me have on one sheet of paper a statement about the tanks. How many have we got with the Army? How many of each kind are being made each month? How many are there with the manufacturers? What are the forecasts? What are the plans for heavier tanks?

NOTE. – The present form of warfare, and the proof that tanks can overrun fortifications, will affect the plans for the 'Cultivator',[2] and it seems very likely that only a reduced number will be required.

Winston S. Churchill to Lord Beaverbrook
(*Churchill papers, 20/13*)

24 May 1940

I should be much obliged if you would have a talk with Lindemann, so as to get at some agreed figures upon aircraft outputs, both recent and prospective. I have for a long time been convinced that the Air Ministry do not make enough of the deliveries with which they are supplied, and Lindemann is obtaining for me returns of all aircraft in their hands, so that one can see what use is made of them.

It is of the highest importance that all aircraft in storage and reserve should not only be made available for service, but that these should be organised in Squadrons with their pilots. Now that the war is coming so close, the object

---

[1] Frederick Alexander Lindemann, 1886–1957. Known as 'the Prof.' Born at Baden-Baden (where his mother was taking the cure); son of an Alsatian father who had emigrated to Britain in the early 1870s, and an American mother. Educated at Blair Lodge, Scotland; Darmstadt, 1902–5, and Berlin University, 1906–10. Doctor of Philosophy, Berlin, 1910. Studied physical chemistry in Paris, 1912–14. Worked at the Physical Laboratory, RAF, 1915–18, when he helped to organise the kite balloon barrage. Learned to fly, 1916. Personally investigated the aerodynamic effects of aircraft spin. Professor of Experimental Philosophy (physics), Oxford, 1919–56. Student of Christ Church (where he subsequently resided), 1921. Elected to the Other Club, 1927. Published his *Physical Significance of the Quantum Theory*, 1932. Member of the Expert Committee on Air Defence Research, Committee of Imperial Defence, 1935–9. Unsuccessful by-election candidate, Oxford University, 1937. Personal Assistant to the Prime Minister (Churchill), 1940–1; in 1953 Churchill's Private Secretary, John Martin, wrote to him, about the war years: 'Those without experience in the inner circle will never know the size of Winston's debt to you and how much stimulus and inspiration of ideas flowed from your office.' Created Baron Cherwell, 1941. Paymaster-General, 1942–5 and 1951–3. Privy Councillor, 1943. Viscount, 1956. His brother-in-law, Lieutenant Noel Musgrave Vickers (a barrister, born 1880, who had married Linda Lindemann in 1910), was killed in action on 24 March 1918, leaving a two-year-old son.

[2] 'Cultivator', or 'Cultivator No. 6', was the code name for a trench-digging machine, work on the design of which Churchill had instituted while at the Admiralty.

must be to prepare the largest number of aircraft, even, as you said, training and civil aircraft, to carry bombs to enemy aerodromes on the Dutch, Belgian and French coasts. I must get a full view of the figures, both of delivery and employment, and this can be kept up to date weekly.

WSC

Winston S. Churchill to General Ismay
(*Churchill papers, 4/150*)

24 May 1940

VCNS[1] informs me that order was sent at 2 a.m. to Calais saying that evacuation was decided in principle, but this is surely madness. The only effect of evacuating Calais would be to transfer the forces now blocking it to Dunkirk. Calais must be held for many reasons, but specially to hold the enemy on its front. The Admiralty say they are preparing 24 naval 12-pounders, which with SAP[2] will pierce any tank. Some of these will be ready this evening.

WSC

Winston S. Churchill to General Ismay
(*Churchill papers, 4/150*)

24 May 1940

I cannot understand the situation around Calais. The Germans are blocking all exits, and our regiment of Tanks is boxed up in the town because it cannot face the field guns planted on the outskirts. Yet I expect the forces achieving this are very modest. Why, then, are they not attacked? Why does not Lord Gort attack them from the rear at the same time that we make a sortie from Calais? Surely Gort can spare a Brigade or two to clear his communications and to secure the supplies vital to his Army. Here is a General with nine Divisions about to be starved out, and yet he cannot send a force to clear his communications. What else can be so important as this? Where could a Reserve be better employed? This force blockading Calais should be attacked at once by Gort, by the Canadians from Dunkirk and by a

[1] Tom Spencer Vaughan Phillips, 1888–1941. Entered the Royal Navy, 1903. Director of Plans, Admiralty, 1935–8. Commodore Commanding the Home Fleet Destroyer Flotillas, 1938–9. Rear-Admiral, 1939. Vice-Chief of the Naval Staff, 1939–41. Knighted, 1941. Commander-in-Chief of the Eastern Fleet, 1941. Drowned when his flagship, the *Prince of Wales*, was sunk by Japanese torpedo bombers on 10 December 1941.

[2] Sonic Armour Piercing ammunition.

sortie of our boxed-up Tanks. Apparently the Germans can go anywhere and do anything, and their Tanks can act in twos and threes all over our rear, and even when they are located they are not attacked. Also our tanks recoil before their field guns, but our field guns do not like to take on their tanks. If their motorized artillery, far from its base, can block us, why cannot we, with the artillery of a great Army, block them? Of course if one side fights and the other does not, the war is apt to become somewhat unequal. The responsibility for cleansing the communications with Calais and keeping them open, rests primarily with the BEF.

WSC

Defence Committee: minutes
(*Cabinet papers, 69/1*)

24 May 1940
5 p.m.

The Prime Minister urged that every effort should be made to carry out Operation 'Paul'[1] and thereby deprive the Germans of at least a part of the iron ore which they would hope to get out through Lulea during the summer months. No political considerations should stand in the way of this operation. The operation should be begun just before the end of the evacuation from Narvik.

The Chief of the Imperial General Staff read out a message which had just been received to the effect that German tanks had penetrated past the forts on the west side of Calais and had got between the town and the sea. The Brigadier[2] was organising his forces on an inner line of defence. He thought that it would be useless to dribble more infantry reinforcements into Calais, since they would not have the weapons with which to deal with the heavy tanks. The brigade which was already there and the tank regiment had been ordered to fight it out in their present positions.

The Prime Minister agreed that this force must fight it out in the town and endeavour to engage the Germans in street fighting, which they would be very anxious to avoid if possible.

The Prime Minister stressed the importance of finding some means of dealing with the enemy's tanks, possibly some form of mine. Nevertheless, short of the sea passage being made in fog, the Royal Navy and Royal Air Force should be able to deal with a sea-borne expedition.

[1] The mining of the approaches to the Swedish Baltic port of Luleå.
[2] Brigadier C. N. Nicholson. Commanding the four battalions of the 30th Brigade, Calais, 1940. Captured by the Germans on the late afternoon of 26 May. Taken prisoner, he died in a German prisoner-of-war camp.

Captain Berkeley: diary
(*Berkeley papers*)

24 May 1940

Spent two hours at No. 10 this evening as Winston wanted to talk to Weygand on the phone. Weygand couldn't be got till 1.40, and then wouldn't talk. Anyhow the telephone was appallingly faint, and after Ismay and Redman had screamed at each other for a long time. I took a hand and shouted 'the PM says "d'accord" '. Saw Eden, rather fussed, CIGS, calm as usual, Dill, who looks very fine, Morton,[1] who is now a great man, and a nice bunch of PS's. Brendan Bracken is throwing himself about a great deal, it seems.

Desmond Morton to Winston S. Churchill
(*Premier papers, 7/2*)

25 May 1940

I strongly recommend you to pay at least one visit a day to the Map Room in the Cabinet War Room. The most up to date information about the fighting in France is shown on this map, compared to which the one in the Upper War Room in the Admiralty is in my opinion definitely misleading.

Winston S. Churchill to Paul Reynaud
(*Churchill papers, 20/14*)

25 May 1940

We have every reason to believe that Gort is still persevering in southward move. All we know is that he has been forced by the pressure on his western flank, and to keep communication with Dunkirk for indispensable supplies, to place parts of two divisions between himself and the increasing pressure of the German armoured forces, which in apparently irresistible strength have

---

[1] Desmond Morton, 1891–1971. 2nd Lieutenant, Royal Artillery, 1911. Converted to Roman Catholicism shortly before the First World War. Shot through the heart while commanding a field battery at the Battle of Arras, April 1917, but survived the wound. Later awarded the Military Cross. ADC to Sir Douglas Haig, 1917–18. Seconded to the Foreign Office, 1919. Head of the Committee of Imperial Defence's Industrial Intelligence Centre, January 1929 to September 1939; its terms of reference were 'To discover and report the plans for manufacture of armaments and war stores in foreign countries'. A member of the Committee of Imperial Defence sub-committee on Economic Warfare, 1930–9. Principal Assistant Secretary, Ministry of Economic Warfare, 1939. Personal Assistant to Churchill, 1940–45. Knighted, 1945. Economic Survey Mission, Middle East, 1949. Seconded to the Ministry of Civil Aviation, 1950–3.

successively captured Abbeville and Boulogne, are menacing Calais and Dunkirk, and which have taken St Omer. How can he move southward and disengage his northern front unless he throws out this shield on his right hand? Nothing in the movements of the BEF of which we are aware can be any excuse for the abandonment of the strong pressure of your northward move across the Somme, which we trust will develop.

Secondly, you complained of heavy materials being moved from Havre. Only materials moved away were gas shells, which it was indiscreet to leave. Also some of the stores have been moved from the north to the south side of the river at Havre.

Thirdly, should I become aware that extreme pressure of events have compelled any departure from the plan agreed, I shall immediately inform you. Dill, who was this morning wholly convinced that the sole hope of any effective extrication of our Army lies in the southward move and in the active advance of General Frère,[1] is now with Gort. You must understand that, having waited for the southward move for a week after it became obvious, we find ourselves now ripped from the coast by the mass of the enemy's armoured vehicles. We therefore have no choice but to continue the southward move, using such flank guard protection to the westward as is necessary.

General Spears will be with you to-morrow morning, and it will probably be quickest to send him back when the position is clear.

Winston S. Churchill to Anthony Eden and General Ironside
(*Churchill papers, 4/150*)

25 May 1940

Pray find out who was the Officer responsible for sending the order to evacuate Calais yesterday, and by whom was this very lukewarm telegram I saw this morning drafted, in which mention is made of 'for the sake of Allied solidarity.' This is not the way to encourage men to fight to the end. Are you sure there is no streak of defeatist opinion in the General Staff?

WSC

---

[1] General Frère, commander of the French VIIth Army, 1940. De Gaulle, whose division was in his zone, recalled of 5 June 1940: 'As alarming reports were being opened all around him and doubts and reticences could be seen under the outward professional calm, that excellent soldier said to me: "We're sick. Rumour has it that you are to be Minister. It's certainly late in the day for a cure. Ah! At least let's save our honour!" ' (*The Call to Honour*, page 532). Paul Reynaud wrote: 'This magnificent soldier, seriously wounded during the previous war, was arrested on 13 June 1943 by the Gestapo because of his participation in the Resistance Movement. It was he who, in 1942, had assumed charge of the Organisation of Army Resistance (ORN). Imprisoned in Strutthof camp in Alsace, he died in 1944 as a result of his cruel treatment' (*In the Thick of the Fight*, page 263, footnote 2).

Winston S. Churchill to General Ironside
(*Churchill papers, 4/150*)

25 May 1940

I must know at earliest why Gort gave up Arras, and what actually he is doing with the rest of his Army. Is he still persevering in Weygand's plan, or has he become largely stationary? If the latter, what do you consider the probable course of events in the next few days, and what course do you recommend? Clearly, he must not allow himself to be encircled and surrender without fighting a battle. Should he not do this by fighting his way to the coast and destroying the armoured troops which stand between him and the sea with overwhelming force of artillery, while covering himself and the Belgian Front, which would also curl back, by strong rearguards? To-morrow at latest this decision must be taken.

It should surely be possible for Dill to fly home from any aerodrome momentarily clear, and RAF should send a whole Squadron to escort him.

WSC

Winston S. Churchill to Paul Reynaud
(*Churchill papers, 20/14*)

25 May 1940

My telegram last night told you all we knew over here, and we have still heard nothing from Lord Gort to contradict it. But I must tell you that a Staff Officer has reported to the War Office confirming the withdrawal of two Divisions from Arras region, which your telegram to me mentioned. General Dill, who should be with Lord Gort, has been told to send a Staff Officer by Air at the earliest moment. As soon as we know what has happened I will report fully. It is clear, however, that the Northern Army are practically surrounded and that all its communications are cut except through Dunkirk and Ostend.

War Cabinet: minutes
(*Cabinet papers, 65/7*)

25 May 1940   10 Downing Street
11.30 a.m.

The Prime Minister said that at about midnight on the previous night he had had a telegram from M. Reynaud (No. 271 DIPP) saying that the British Army was no longer conforming to General Weygand's plan and had withdrawn towards the Channel ports. At that time we had had no information of any such move on Lord Gort's part. After consulting the Chief of the Imperial General Staff, he had sent a reply to M. Reynaud (telegram No. 200 DIPP) to the following effect:–

We believed that Lord Gort was still persevering in the southward move. All we knew was that he had been forced by pressure on his right flank to place parts of two divisions between himself and the German armoured forces. Should we become aware that extreme pressure had compelled any departure from the agreed plan, we should at once inform M. Reynaud.

Later, however, a Staff Officer had reported to the War Office confirming the withdrawal of two Divisions from the Arras area. No doubt the action taken had been forced on Lord Gort by the position in which he had found himself. Nevertheless, he should at once have informed us of the action which he had taken, and the French had grounds for complaint. But this was no time for recriminations. General Dill had been instructed to send a Staff Officer back to this country with a report at the earliest possible moment. In the meantime, we must tell the French that the reported withdrawal had now been confirmed.

(A telegram in this sense was drafted and despatched to M. Reynaud (No. 205 DIPP).

The Prime Minister said that he had had a conversation with Vice-Admiral Sir James Somerville,[1] who had landed at Calais the previous night from a destroyer which had also landed 60 Royal Marines and a quantity of ammunition. He had seen the Senior Naval and Military Officers, who had been in good heart and were putting up a stout defence. Only three of our tanks remained, but we had accounted for a large number of German tanks. It was imperative that we should hold on to Calais, and he had arranged for a heartening message to be sent to our forces.

Admiral Somerville was returning to Calais that night with additional supplies, including trench mortars.

The Secretary of State for War referred to the French official statement that they were still holding Calais. As there were 3,000 British troops and only 800 French troops in the port, it was only fair to the British public that they should be told that British troops were playing a big part in the gallant defence of Calais. He suggested that an announcement should be made that Calais was strongly held by an Anglo-French Force.

---

[1] James Fownes Somerville, 1882–1949. Entered the Royal Navy, 1898. On active service at the Dardanelles, 1915 (despatches, DSO). Commanded the Destroyer Flotillas, Mediterranean Fleet, 1936–8. Commander-in-Chief, East Indies, 1938–9. Retired list, 1939. Knighted, 1939. On special services at the Admiralty, 1939–40, including the Dunkirk evacuation. Officer Commanding Force H, 1940–2. Commander-in-Chief, Eastern Fleet, 1942–4. Head of British Admiralty Delegation, Washington, 1944–5. Admiral of the Fleet, 1945.

In connection with the discussion recorded in Minute 2,[1] the Prime Minister said that the bombing by the enemy of targets in this country should give a welcome stimulus to air-raid precautions activities. He had noticed several reports in the Press that Anderson shelters were not being properly used by the public.

The Minister of Home Security[2] said that the number of such cases was almost negligible, and the Press reports were much exaggerated. Some cases had occurred of the materials for shelters being left lying about while awaiting missing components. In other cases, there had been no able-bodied person in the household who could erect the shelter. Local authorities had been given stringent instructions to remove shelters which were not erected, and to give them to other householders who were in need of them.

The Prime Minister urged that this was not enough; the persons responsible should be punished in some way. The Government had the necessary powers under the new Act.

The Prime Minister said that he saw no objection to an approach of the character suggested.[3] It must not, of course, be accompanied by any publicity, since that would amount to a confession of weakness. It was very probable that at any moment Signor Mussolini might put very strong pressure on the French, with a view to obtaining concessions from them. The fact that the French were denuding their Italian frontier of troops put them in a very weak bargaining position.

The Prime Minister reminded his colleagues that the following day, Sunday, the 26th May, had been appointed as a National Day of Prayer. There was to be a service in Westminster Abbey, attended by the King and Queen. For security reasons, however, the attendance of Their Majesties was not being announced in advance, nor were any special arrangements being made to invite the attendance of members of both Houses of Parliament.

It was, however, desired to arrange for the attendance of as many members of His Majesty's Government as possible. The Secretary of the War Cabinet would, therefore, send a written notification of the time of the service to all Ministers, including Under-Secretaries, and inform the Dean of Westminster[4] how many places should be reserved.

---

[1] Sir Cyril Newall had told the War Cabinet that German bombs had fallen on aerodromes in Yorkshire and East Anglia, and also in Middlesbrough, 'but the damage and casualties were very slight'. He noted that 'they had not been recognized as enemy aircraft until they had actually dropped their bombs'.

[2] Sir John Anderson.

[3] Lord Halifax had told the War Cabinet of a French proposal to approach Mussolini, through President Roosevelt, 'with a view to exploring the possibilities of a friendly settlement'.

[4] Paul De Labilliere, Dean of Westminster from 1938 until his death in 1946.

War Cabinet: Confidential Annex
(*Cabinet papers, 65/13*)

25 May 1940
11.30 a.m.

The First Sea Lord said that HMS *Glorious* with 16 Hurricanes, had left Scapa for Narvik on the afternoon of the 24th May.

The Prime Minister informed the War Cabinet that the question of the evacuation of Narvik had been discussed at a meeting of the Defence Committee the previous evening. The Chief of the Air Staff had submitted that the Hurricanes in HMS *Glorious* would be essential for the successful and speedy evacuation of our forces at Narvik. It was recognised that these aircraft would be lost when we evacuated, but we should probably be able to get the pilots away. The Defence Committee had agreed that Lord Cork should be informed that it was our intention, in view of developments on the Western Front, to evacuate Narvik as early as possible. He read to the War Cabinet the telegram which had been despatched to Lord Cork containing instructions on this matter.[1]

Winston S. Churchill to William Mackenzie King[2]
(*Churchill papers, 20/14*)

25 May 1940

I should like you to know how greatly impressed and touched my colleagues and I have been by the great response which Canada is making to the urgent needs of the present situation in respect of naval, army and air assistance alike.[3] Though the prompt and ready reply to the suggestions made by us came as no surprise, I desire to emphasise our deep appreciation and ask you and your colleagues to believe that these further proofs of Canada's readiness to stand with us at all costs against our determined and ruthless enemy are a source of the greatest encouragement.

[1] At 7.17 that morning (25 May 1940) a telegram had reached London from Lord Cork, in which he stated: 'I regret to have to say that attack on Narvik which was to have taken place on the night of 26th–May 27th has had to be postponed for some days on account of situation at Bodo which is not developing too well and reinforcements of guns and stores are urgently required. I cannot manage both at once, and must give Bodo immediate attention.' Cork added: 'French and Norwegian troops are making good progress on Eidfjord Peninsula and have now forced Germans back to Haugfjelded' (*Admiralty papers, 199/1929*).

[2] William Mackenzie King, 1874–1950. Entered the Canadian Parliament in 1908. Appointed to his first ministerial post, as Minister of Labour, 1909. Elected Leader of the Liberal Party of Canada, 1919. Prime Minister, 1921–6, 1926–30 and 1935–48 (also Secretary of State for External Affairs, 1935–46. Privy Councillor (United Kingdom), 1922. Order of Merit, 1947.

[3] At the War Cabinet on 25 May, reference was made to a Canadian Government decision to send four destroyers to Britain.

146   MAY 1940

Defence Committee: minutes
(*Cabinet papers, 69/1*)

25 May 1940   10 Downing Street
5.30 p.m.

There was a general discussion on the situation, in the course of which the Prime Minister expressed the view that General Dill's message at any rate showed that the plan was being co-ordinated, and that independent action was at an end. He had had a telegram from Sir Roger Keyes, who had said that the Belgians considered the Germans much inferior to their forerunners of 1914. The Belgian cavalry Division, which was in excellent order, was in position to cover the gap caused by the German attack on the Courtrai front. He enquired whether it would not be possible for the combined Armies in the Northern area to march Southward together, breaking a way through the enemy's Armoured Divisions by force of numbers, and covering their march by flank guards and rear guards.

General Dewing[1] doubted whether this would be possible. The march would be in very vulnerable formation, and would probably be held up by the enemy in front, which would give the enemy following behind a chance to penetrate. It was very hard for an Army to move when subject to attack on three sides simultaneously.

General Dewing said that 3.7-inch Howitzers would not be of great value in Calais, where street fighting was in progress. The troops were in possession of mortars, and demands were being made to send them more mortar ammunition by trawler. It was believed that the trawler with the ammunition had sailed from Dover, but there was no news yet of its arrival.

The Prime Minister thought it most important to try and get the ammunition in to the port at all costs during the night.

The Prime Minister hoped that the Fleet would adopt a vigorously offensive attitude against the Italians if they came into the war. Referring to the possibility of withdrawing eight Regular battalions from Palestine, he expressed the view that the transports should proceed singly, unescorted, through the Mediterranean if they were sent at all.

---

[1] Richard Henry Dewing, 1891–1981. Entered the Royal Engineers, 1911. On active service in Mesopotamia and Persia, 1915–18 (Military Cross, DSO). Army Instructor, Imperial Defence College, 1936–9. Director of Military Operations, War Office, 1939–40. Chief of Staff, Far East, 1940–1. CB, 1941. Military Mission, Washington, 1942. Chief of Army–RAF Liaison, Australia, 1943–4. Allied Military Mission to Denmark, 1945. One of his two sons was killed in action in Libya in 1942.

Defence Committee: minutes
(*Cabinet papers, 69/1*)

25 May 1940   Admiralty
10 p.m.

The Prime Minister read to the Meeting a letter from General Spears, written after his meeting with M. Reynaud and General Weygand. The latter had apologised for having accused Lord Gort of having fallen back without warning and without order. It was clear that there was no chance of General Weygand striking North in sufficient strength to disengage the Blanchard Group in the North. General Weygand had only eight Divisions stretched out over 130 kilometres south of the Somme. General Weygand's opinion was that attacks to the South by the group of armies in the North, including the British Army, could serve no other purpose than to gain breathing-space before falling back to a line covering the harbours.

The Prime Minister then read to the Meeting a message which he had received from M. Reynaud, giving the latest position in regard to the orders given to General Blanchard by General Weygand.

The Prime Minister also read a message received from Sir Roger Keyes in regard to the decision of the King of the Belgians to remain with his army.

(At this point General Dill entered the Meeting and was given a résumé of the position as seen from this side.)

The Prime Minister asked General Dill why Lord Gort had retired from Arras, and whether he had had General Georges' consent.

General Dill said that Lord Gort had found that the enemy were round his right flank, and he had had no option but to withdraw his forces in this area.

The Prime Minister then asked General Dill for his views as to the prospect of the drive to the South.

In discussion, the following points emerged:–
(1) General Dill said that before the Fifth Division had been diverted to Ypres, he had told General Blanchard that the attack must succeed, and General Blanchard had agreed.
(2) Another alternative to the proposed plan would be to strike South with even stronger forces than at present contemplated, leaving only thin rearguards behind.
(3) If, however, the drive to the South was tried and failed, then Lord Gort would be in a far worse position than at present, and would not have sufficient strength to try the other course open to him, namely, to cut his way North to the coast. If this alternative were also to fail, he would be surrounded and would have to capitulate.

The Prime Minister then put the points in favour of an advance North to the ports and the beaches.

Having regard to the practical certainty that no effective French offensive was likely to be launched from South of the Somme for some considerable time, the view was generally expressed that an immediate march to the coast was the right course.

General Dill was then called to speak to Lord Gort on the telephone. The line was so unsatisfactory, however, that it was impossible to conduct a reasonable conversation. General Dill said that he felt sure that Lord Gort would wish an expression of views from home as to what course he should adopt in the position in which he found himself.

In the light of this discussion, the following conclusions were reached:–

Calais

At all costs it was essential to hold on to Calais for as long as possible. If we attempted to withdraw our garrison from Calais, the German troops in Calais would immediately march on Dunkirk. A message should be sent to our troops in Calais telling them that every hour that they could hold out would be of immeasurable value to the British Army. Every effort should be made to provide air and naval support.

Dunkirk

If we were now to decide on a move to the ports, we must make certain of Dunkirk. There were said to be two French Divisions in Dunkirk, but they were neither of them reliable, and the Canadian Brigade should be put into Dunkirk.

Ostend

General Dill said that Ostend had had a very deserted appearance when he had been there that morning.

It was agreed that the War Office should consider steps to ensure that Ostend was not captured by *coup-de-main*.

General Karslake[1] reported that Brigadier Swayne thought that the French were very down-hearted and did not mean to stay in the war.

In this connection the Prime Minister said that the fact that M. Reynaud had asked that he should not meet the War Cabinet as a whole, but should only meet the Prime Minister and perhaps one other Minister when he came to London the next day, might possibly be somewhat significant.

---

[1] Henry Karslake, 1879–1942. Royal Artillery, 1898. On active service in South Africa (despatches twice, DSO) and 1914–18 (despatches, GMG); Brigadier-General, Tank Corps, 1918. Commanded the Baluchistan District, India, 1933–5. Knighted, 1935. Colonel Commandant, Royal Artillery, from 1937 until his death. Retired from active service, with the rank of Lieutenant-General, 1938. Recalled, 1939. General Officer Commanding the British Forces in France following Lord Gort's return at the end of May 1940.

The Prime Minister said that he would not be at all surprised if a peace offer was made to the French, having regard to their weak position and to the likelihood of an attack on France by Italy. If France went out of the war, she must, however, make it a condition that our Army was allowed to leave France intact, and to take away its munitions, and that the soil of France was not used for an attack on England. Further, France must retain her Fleet. If an offer were made on these terms, he (the Prime Minister) would accept it, and he thought that we could hold out in this country once we had got our Army back from France.

The Prime Minister directed that a Meeting of the War Cabinet should be held at 9 o'clock on the morning of Sunday, 26th May.

March to the Coast

The Prime Minister summed up the plans outlined in discussion as follows:–

(1) Lord Gort should march north to the coast, in battle order, under strong rearguards, striking at all forces between himself and the sea. This plan should, if possible, be prepared in conjunction with General Blanchard, and the Belgians should be informed.
(2) A plan should at once be prepared on these lines, and the Navy should prepare all possible means for re-embarkation, not only at the ports but on the beaches.
(3) The RAF should dominate the air above the area involved.
(4) A warning telegram should at once be sent by the War Office to Lord Gort to draw up a scheme on these lines, on the assumption that the march would start on the night of the 26/27th, but informing him not to give effect to this plan without further orders from the War Cabinet.
(5) The first six Divisions now in this country should be mobilised, i.e., brought to full strength and provided with equipment.
(6) The stores at Havre, Rouen, Rennes, St Nazaire and Nantes, or at least a proportion of them, should be evacuated.

Winston S. Churchill to General Ironside
(*Churchill papers, 4/150*)

25 May 1940

Something like this should be said to the Brigadier defending Calais: Defence of Calais to the utmost is of the highest importance to our country and our Army now. First, it occupies a large part of the enemy's armoured forces, and keeps them from attacking our line of communication. Secondly, it preserves a sally port from which portions of the British Army may make their way home. Lord Gort has already sent troops to your aid, and the Navy will do all possible to keep you supplied. The eyes of the Empire are upon the defence of Calais, and His Majesty's Government are confident you and your gallant Regiment[1] will perform an exploit worthy of the British name.

WSC

Winston S. Churchill to Paul Reynaud
(*Churchill papers, 20/14*)

25 May 1940

Cannot send formula[2] till to-morrow as must consult others. Will do my best but feel convinced only safety lies in ability to fight. All here most grateful for your visit and admire your calm courage amid these storms.

Winston S. Churchill: recollection
(*'Their Finest Hour', page 65*)

25 May 1940

As the adverse battle drew to its climax I and my colleagues greatly desired that Sir John Dill should become CIGS. We had also to choose a Commander-in-Chief for the British Island, if we were invaded. Late at night on May 25 Ironside, Dill, Ismay, myself, and one or two others in my room at Admiralty House were trying to measure the position. General Ironside volunteered the proposal that he should cease to be CIGS, but declared himself quite willing to command the British Home Forces. Considering the unpromising task that such a command was at the time thought to involve, this was a spirited and selfless offer. I therefore accepted General Ironside's proposal; and the high dignities and honours which were later conferred upon him arose from my appreciation of his bearing at this moment in our affairs. Sir John Dill became CIGS on May 27. The changes were generally judged appropriate for the time being.

---

[1] Nicholson's Brigade (the 30th) consisted of single battalions of the King's Royal Rifle Corps, the Rifle Brigade, the Royal Tank Regiment and Queen Victoria's Rifles.

[2] Lord Halifax's formula, that if Mussolini would help secure a European settlement which would safeguard British and French independence, Britain would be prepared to discuss Italy's claims in the Mediterranean (see pages 185–7).

Winston S. Churchill to Sir Roger Keyes
(*Churchill papers, 20/14*)

26 May 1940

Impart following to your friend.[1] Presume he knows that British and French are fighting their way to coast between Gravelines and Ostend inclusive and that we propose to give fullest support from Navy and Air Force during hazardous embarkation. What can we do for him? Certainly we cannot serve Belgium's cause by being hemmed in and starved out. Only hope is victory, and England will never quit the war whatever happens till Hitler is beat or we cease to be a State. Trust you will make sure he leaves with you by aeroplane before too late. Should our operation prosper and we establish an effective bridgehead, we would try if desired to carry some Belgian divisions to France by sea. Vitally important Belgium should continue in war, and safety King's person essential.

War Cabinet: Confidential Annex
(*Cabinet papers, 65/13*)

26 May 1940 10 Downing Street
9 a.m.

The Prime Minister informed the War Cabinet that the previous night he had received a letter from General Spears, describing an interview he had had with what had been to all intents and purposes a War Council of France, and also a message from M. Reynaud.

He read these two documents to the War Cabinet. The letter from General Spears may be summarised as follows:–

(i) The suggestion that Lord Gort had fallen back on the 24th May without warning and without orders had been cleared up. General Weygand had apologised with good grace.

(ii) On the strength of a report brought in from General Blanchard by Commandant Fauvel,[2] General Weygand had been inclined to alter his instructions to General Blanchard in the sense of inviting him to fall

---

[1] King Leopold of the Belgians.
[2] Commandant (Major) Fauvelle, a Staff Officer from General Blanchard's Group of Armies. He had been sent by Blanchard from Dunkirk to Paris two days earlier, to report on the situation. Unable to fly from Dunkirk to Paris, he had gone by sea to London and flown to Paris from there. Reynaud has written: 'According to him there was no longer any hope of Blanchard being able to carry out the offensive movement that Weygand had ordered' (*In the Thick of the Fight*, page 374, footnote 2). Spears, who was present when Fauvelle made his report to Reynaud, wrote: 'He was the very embodiment of catastrophe. . . . In my view nothing short of throwing Fauvelle out of the window would have been adequate' (*Prelude to Dunkirk*, page 189).

back to the Channel harbours, but in view of the fact that he had had later information from General Blanchard, he had finally determined to allow General Blanchard to use his own discretion.
(iii) General Weygand did not consider that attacks to the southward by the Blanchard group of armies could serve any other purpose than to gain breathing space to fall back to a line covering the harbours. (It had been the original intention to try and break through with a force of five French and two British Divisions, but one of the British Divisions had since had to be put into the line between Menin and Ypres to resist a thrust from the East.)
(iv) There seemed no chance whatever of any French attack from the south across the Somme to disengage the Blanchard group. There were only eight Divisions spread over a very wide front.
(v) Commandant Fauvel had been extremely pessimistic. The Blanchard group had lost all their heavy guns; they had no armoured vehicles; and movements were very much hampered by refugees.

The message from M. Paul Reynaud set out the conclusions which had been reached at the meeting which General Spears had attended. The principal point was that discretion was given to General Blanchard as to his action.

The Prime Minister also read a telegram received from Sir Roger Keyes relating to the evacuation of the King of the Belgians, which could be summarised as follows:–

The King was being urged by his Ministers to fly with them, but he was determined not to desert his army at a time when a stern battle was in progress. If the King were to leave, this would inevitably hasten the capitulation of the Belgian Army and endanger the BEF. King Leopold had written to King George VI to explain his motive in remaining with his army and people if the Belgian Army became encircled and the capitulation of the Belgian Army became inevitable.

The Prime Minister said that the above communications and other information which had been received had been considered at a meeting the previous night of the Service Ministers and Chiefs of Staff. General Karslake, who had seen General Swayne, reported that the latter thought that the French seemed unlikely to take any effective action from the south. M. Reynaud had telegraphed that he was arriving in this country that day and wished to meet the Prime Minister alone, or perhaps with one other Minister present only. It seemed from all the evidence available that we might have to face a situation in which the French were going to collapse, and that we must do our best to extricate the British Expeditionary Force from northern France.

The Prime Minister read to the War Cabinet the conclusions which had been reached at the meeting of Ministers and Chiefs of Staff the previous night. On the basis of these conclusions a telegram had been despatched to

Lord Gort, warning him that he might be faced with a situation in which the safety of the British Expeditionary Force would be the predominant consideration, and that every endeavour would be made to provide ships for the evacuation, and aircraft to cover it. Preliminary plans were accordingly to be prepared at once.

The Prime Minister expressed the opinion that, although we could not foresee the outcome of the battle, there was a good chance of getting off a considerable proportion of the British Expeditionary Force. We must, however, be prepared for M. Reynaud in his interview that day to say that the French could not carry on the fight. He would make every endeavour to induce M. Reynaud to carry on, and he would point out that they were at least in honour bound required to provide, as far as lay in their power, for the safe withdrawal of the British Expeditionary Force. He asked the War Cabinet to be ready to meet again at 2 p.m. to receive his report of his discussion with M. Reynaud. He hoped that M. Reynaud would be willing to meet the War Cabinet. There was some indication that M. Reynaud might bring with him a military expert, in which case the discussions might be extended in their scope.

In order to be prepared to meet all eventualities he had asked the Chiefs of Staff to consider the situation which would arise if the French did drop out of the war, on the following terms of reference:—

'In the event of France being unable to continue in the war and becoming neutral, with the Germans holding their present position, and the Belgian army being forced to capitulate after assisting the British Expeditionary Force to reach the coast; in the event of terms being offered to Britain which would place her entirely at the mercy of Germany through disarmament, cession of naval bases in the Orkneys etc.; what are the prospects of our continuing the war alone against Germany and probably Italy. Can the Navy and the Air Force hold out reasonable hopes of preventing serious invasion, and could the forces gathered in this Island cope with raids from the air involving detachments not greater than 10,000 men; it being observed that a prolongation of British resistance might be very dangerous for Germany engaged in holding down the greater part of Europe.'

The Prime Minister said that peace and security might be achieved under a German domination of Europe. That we could never accept. We must ensure our complete liberty and independence. He was opposed to any negotiations which might lead to a derogation of our rights and power.

The Secretary of State for Foreign Affairs suggested that in the last resort we should ask the French to put their factories out of gear.

The Lord President of the Council[1] felt that whatever undertakings of this character we might extract from the French would be worthless, since the terms of peace which the Germans would propose would inevitably prevent their fulfilment.

The Prime Minister agreed. It was to be expected, moreover, that the Germans would make the terms of any peace offer as attractive as possible to the French, and lay emphasis on the fact that their quarrel was not with France but with England.

On 26 May 1940 Churchill lunched with Reynaud at Admiralty House, before going to 10 Downing Street for a further meeting of the War Cabinet.

War Cabinet: Confidential Annex
(*Cabinet papers, 65/13*)

26 May 1940   10 Downing Street
2 p.m.

The Prime Minister said that he did not think that M. Reynaud would object to the British Expeditionary Force being ordered to march to the coast, although this matter had not yet been finally settled with him.

The Prime Minister then gave an account of M. Reynaud's discussion with him over lunch.

M. Reynaud had given an *exposé* of France's position. Apart from the troops in the Maginot Line, including the fortress troops, the French had 50 divisions between Malmédy and the coast. Against these the Germans could put 150 divisions. The French Ministers had asked General Weygand for his views on the position. They would defend Paris as long as possible, but if Paris was taken they would retire to the south-west. General Weygand had made it clear, however, that the Germans with their superiority of numbers and tanks, could pierce the line and pass through it. While he would obey orders and fight it out as long as he was told to do so, and would be prepared to go down fighting for the honour of the Flag, he did not think that France's resistance was likely to last very long against a determined German onslaught.

The French Ministers therefore concluded that, with 50 divisions against 150, it was clear that the war could not be won on land. On sea we had good fleets which had established a superiority over Germany; but if Germany had command of resources from Brest to Vladivostok it did not look as though the

---

[1] Neville Chamberlain.

blockade could win the war. It was clear that this country would take a long time to build up a big army, and that we could not make a big effort in 1941 on land.

This left the Air. If the Germans took Paris they would have the air factories in that neighbourhood, as well as those in Belgium and Holland.

What of the United States of America? The munitions industry in that country was feeble.

Where, then, could France look for salvation? Someone had suggested that a further approach should be made to Italy. This would release 10 French divisions. There were said to be a number of people in Italy, such as Grandi[1] and Balbo,[2] and the like, who thought that to stab France in the back when she was in a mortal struggle with Germany was rather too like the action which Russia had taken in regard to Poland.

If an approach was made to Italy, what sort of terms would Italy ask? Probably the neutralisation of Gibraltar and the Suez Canal, the demilitarisation of Malta, and the limitation of naval forces in the Mediterranean. Some alteration in the status of Tunis would also be asked for, and the Dodecanese would have to be put right. The Prime Minister said that he had not understood what was meant by this.

Apparently the French suggestion was that the offer of such terms might keep Italy out of the war.

M. Reynaud realised that the Germans would probably not keep any terms which they agreed to. He had hinted that he himself would not sign peace terms imposed upon France, but that he might be forced to resign, or might feel that he ought to resign.

The Prime Minister said that he had then put the other side of the case, and suggested that as soon as the situation in North-eastern France had been cleared up, the Germans would make no further attacks on the French line and would immediately start attacking this country. M. Reynaud thought that the dream of all Germans was to conquer Paris, and that they would march on Paris.

---

[1] Dino Grandi, 1895–1988. Born at Mordano (Bologna). On active service, 1915–18 (three Military Crosses for valour). Graduated in law, Bologna University, 1919. Journalist and political organiser; led the Fascist movement in the north of Italy, 1920–1. Chief of the Fascist General Staff, 1921. Elected to the Chamber of Deputies, 1921; Deputy President of the Chamber, 1924. Under-Secretary of State for Foreign Affairs, 1925–9. Foreign Minister, 1929–32. Italian Ambassador in London, 1932–9. Member of the Fascist Grand Council. Created Count, 1937. A member of several London clubs, including the St James's, the Athenaeum and the Travellers'. President of the Chamber of Fasci and Corporazioni, Italy, 1939–43. Minister of Justice, Rome, 1939–43. On 24 July 1943 he moved the resolution in the Fascist Grand Council which was the direct cause of the overthrow of Mussolini.

[2] Italo Balbo, 1896–1940. A pioneer aviator. One of the more flamboyant Italian Fascist leaders. Minister of Aviation, 1936, and subsequently Governor of Libya. He opposed Italy's alliance with Hitler and urged Mussolini not to enter the war in 1940. He was killed when accidentally shot down over Libya by Italian anti-aircraft gunners.

The Prime Minister had said that we were not prepared to give in on any account. We would rather go down fighting than be enslaved to Germany. But in any case we were confident that we had a good chance of surviving the German onslaught. France, however, must stay in the war. If only we could stick things out for another three months, the position would be entirely different. He had asked M. Reynaud if any peace terms had been offered to him. M. Reynaud had said 'No,' but that they knew they could get an offer if they wanted one. He repeated that General Weygand was prepared to fight on, but could hold out no hope that France had sufficient power of resistance.

The Prime Minister said that he suggested that the Foreign Secretary should now go over and see M. Reynaud, who was at Admiralty House, and that he himself, the Lord President of the Council and the Lord Privy Seal[1] should come over a few minutes later.

A short further discussion ensued on whether we should make any approach to Italy.

The Foreign Secretary favoured this course, and thought that the last thing that Signor Mussolini wanted was to see Herr Hitler dominating Europe. He would be anxious, if he could, to persuade Herr Hitler to take a more reasonable attitude.

The Prime Minister doubted whether anything would come of an approach to Italy, but said that the matter was one which the War Cabinet would have to consider.

The Minister without Portfolio said that if we could maintain the struggle for some further weeks he thought that we could make use of our economic power in regard to raw materials, textiles, and oil. Stocks in Germany were very depleted.[2] In any event, he hoped that France would take steps to see that valuable stocks and manufacturing capacity in France did not fall into German hands.

The Prime Minister said that he thought the only point to be settled that day was to persuade M. Reynaud that General Weygand should be instructed to issue orders for the BEF to march to the coast. It was important to make sure that the French had no complaint against us on the score that, by cutting

---

[1] Neville Chamberlain and Clement Attlee.

[2] Arthur Greenwood, the Minister without Portfolio, argued in a memorandum for the War Cabinet that day, 26 May 1940 (War Cabinet Paper 171 of 1940, 'British Strategy in the near future'), that Germany could be harmed by a 'tight economic blockade' and her war effort thereby 'seriously reduced and her industrial manpower made impotent'. He also argued for full economic co-operation with the United States. He wrote: 'I suggest that immediate steps should be taken through diplomatic channels to press for active economic assistance and that a strong mission should be sent out to America without delay to secure economic and financial allies for the prosecution of the blockade with the utmost vigour' (*Cabinet papers, 66/8*).

our way to the coast, we were letting them down militarily. At the same time it was important that the orders for the march to the coast should be issued as soon as possible. He asked the Secretary of State for War[1] to prepare a draft telegram for despatch, which should be brought over to Admiralty House at 3.15 p.m.

CHURCHILL, Neville Chamberlain and Arthur Greenwood left 10 Downing Street for Admiralty House to see Reynaud, who was already with Lord Halifax. After Reynaud had left for France, they continued with their discussion.

War Cabinet: Confidential Annex[2]
(*Cabinet papers, 65/13*)

26 May 1940
5 p.m.

The Prime Minister said that we were in a different position from France. In the first place, we still had powers of resistance and attack, which they had not. In the second place, they would be likely to be offered decent terms by Germany, which we should not. If France could not defend herself, it was better that she should get out of the war rather than that she should drag us into a settlement which involved intolerable terms. There was no limit to the terms which Germany would impose upon us if she had her way. From one point of view, he would rather France was out of the war before she was broken up, and retained the position of a strong neutral whose factories could not be used against us.

The Lord Privy Seal said that Herr Hitler was working to a time-limit, and he had to win by the end of the year.

The Lord President of the Council thought that he would have to win by the beginning of the winter.

The Lord Privy Seal said that if France now went out of the war, Herr Hitler would be able to turn on us the sooner.

The Prime Minister said that he hoped that France would hang on. At the same time we must take care not to be forced into a weak position in which we went to Signor Mussolini and invited him to go to Herr Hitler and ask him to treat us nicely. We must not get tangled in a position of that kind before we had been involved in any serious fighting.

[1] Anthony Eden.
[2] This meeting was described in the War Cabinet papers as 'an informal Meeting of War Cabinet Ministers'.

The Foreign Secretary said that he did not disagree with this view, but that he attached perhaps rather more importance than the Prime Minister to the desirability of allowing France to try out the possibilities of European equilibrium. He was not quite convinced that the Prime Minister's diagnosis was correct and that it was in Herr Hitler's interest to insist on outrageous terms. After all, he knew his own internal weaknesses. On this lay-out it might be possible to save France from the wreck. He would not like to see France subjected to the Gestapo.

The Prime Minister did not think that Germany was likely to attempt this in regard to France.

The Foreign Secretary said that he was not so sure.

The Prime Minister had said that it was undesirable that France should be in a position to say that we had stood between her and a tolerable settlement.

He referred to the Prime Minister's statement that we might be better off without France. That meant, provided we could obtain safeguards on particular points. This was certainly a point of view which deserved serious consideration.

The Prime Minister thought that it was best to decide nothing until we saw how much of the Army we could re-embark from France. The operation might be a great failure. On the other hand, our troops might well fight magnificently, and we might save a considerable portion of the Force. A good deal of the re-embarkation would be carried out by day. This would afford a real test of air superiority, since the Germans would attempt to bomb the ships and boats.

The Prime Minister said that his general comment on the suggested approach to Signor Mussolini was that it implied that if we were prepared to give Germany back her colonies and to make certain concessions in the Mediterranean, it was possible for us to get out of our present difficulties. He thought that no such option was open to us. For example, the terms offered would certainly prevent us from completing our re-armament.

The Foreign Secretary said that, if so, the terms would be refused, but he felt sure that Signor Mussolini must feel in a most uncomfortable position.

The Prime Minister said that Herr Hitler thought that he had the whip hand. The only thing to do was to show him that he could not conquer this country. If, on M. Reynaud's showing, France could not continue, we must part company. At the same time, he did not raise objection to some approach being made to Signor Mussolini.

During the latter part of this discussion the Prime Minister was called out of the room to speak to Sir Roger Keyes, who had a message from the King of the Belgians. The King was determined to stay with his Army. There was, perhaps, a chance that he might be persuaded to leave at the last minute. The Belgians were determined to act as the left flank to assist our re-embarkation.

Sir Roger Keyes said there was still nothing in Ostend to prevent it being taken. The Menin Gate was being shelled that afternoon.[1] He had been at Lord Gort's headquarters when orders had come to march to the coast. It was clear that these orders had been received with acclamation at GHQ, where it was held that the march to the South held out no prospect of success.

The Lord President of the Council asked what information should be given to the Dominions.

The Prime Minister thought that nothing should be said to them in regard to the discussions with M. Reynaud. At the same time, they should be told that we had now obtained the formal assent of the French Government to falling back on the coast, and that the position was a serious one.

Sir Alexander Cadogan: diary
(*'The Diaries of Sir Alexander Cadogan'*)

26 May 1940

Summoned to Admiralty at 5. Found WSC, H,[2] Neville, Greenwood and Attlee. Discussed situation. WSC seemed to think we might almost be better off if France *did* pull out and we could concentrate on defence here. Not sure he's right. He against final appeal, which Reynaud wanted, to Muss[3]. He may be right there. Settled nothing much. WSC too rambling and romantic and sentimental and temperamental. Old Neville still the best of the lot. I suggested *immediate* withdrawal of best troops and Bofors guns from Narvik. But this wasn't smiled on.

Captain Berkeley: diary
(*Berkeley papers*)

26 May 1940

Reynaud was over on Sunday and I spent some hours in Admiralty House with Morton, Bevir, etc., while he argued back and forth with the Cabinet and service ministers. The upshot was that the forces on the Somme could not move beyond it, and that no thrust southward by the forces in Belgium was therefore practicable. Orders were therefore at once given to fall back on the

---

[1] In the aftermath of the First World War, the Menin Gate at Ypres had been rebuilt as a memorial to British war dead who had no known grave. When German troops reached the Menin Gate in May 1940, British stonemasons were still at work carving the last of the 56,000 names of those who fell in the Ypres salient from October 1914 to August 1917. The stonemasons were taken prisoner, but subsequently repatriated.
[2] Lord Halifax.
[3] Mussolini

ports, but the situation there was already parlous and is now far worse. Reynaud was not impressive. The PM was terrific, hurling himself about, getting his staff into hopeless tangles by dashing across to Downing St without a word of warning, shouting that we would never give in, etc. Eden looked most unhappy and for a while was, I think, inclined to rebel against the decision to give up the attempt to cut off the German thrust.

General Ismay: recollection
(*'The Memoirs of Lord Ismay'*, page 131)

26 May 1940

On the night of 26 May, a telegram was sent to the commander at Calais, Brigadier Nicholson, telling him that his force would not be withdrawn, and that he must fight it out to the bitter end.[1] The number of troops involved was relatively small, but it is a terrible thing to condemn a body of splendid men to death or captivity. The decision affected us all very deeply, especially perhaps Churchill. He was unusually silent during dinner that evening, and he ate and drank with evident distaste. As we rose from the table, he said, 'I feel physically sick.' He has quoted these words in his memoirs, but he does not mention how sad he looked as he uttered them.

Vice-Admiral Sir James Somerville to Winston S. Churchill
(*Premier papers, 3/175*)

27 May 1940
7.15 a.m.
telephoned from Dover

A bad situation is developing between Calais and Dunkirk. The enemy have mounted 40 guns as far as Gravelines and are shelling shipping approaching Dunkirk. This message has been passed to the War Office.

---

[1] Brigadier Nicholson's only comment, on receiving this order, was, as recorded by Admiral Sir James Somerville (who visited him that night): 'Given more guns which were urgently needed, he was confident he could hold on for a time.'

Winston S. Churchill to Lord Gort
(*Churchill papers, 20/14*)

27 May 1940

At this solemn moment I cannot help sending you my good wishes. No one can tell how it will go. But anything is better than being cooped up and starved out. I venture these few remarks. First, cannon ought to kill tanks, and they may as well be lost doing that as any other way. Second, I feel very anxious about Ostend till it is occupied by a brigade with artillery. Third, very likely the enemy tanks attacking Calais are tired and, anyhow, busy on Calais. A column directed upon Calais while it is still holding out might have a good chance. Perhaps they will be less formidable when attacked themselves.

2. It is now necessary to tell the Belgians. I am sending following telegram to Keyes, but your personal contact with King is desirable. Keyes will help. We are asking them to sacrifice themselves for us.

3. Presume troops know they are cutting their way home to Blighty. Never was there such a spur for fighting. We shall give you all that the Navy and Air Force can do. Anthony Eden is with me now and joins his good wishes to mine.

Winston S. Churchill to Sir Roger Keyes
(*Churchill papers, 20/14*)

27 May 1940

Belgian Embassy here assume from King's decision to remain that he regards war as lost and contemplates separate peace. It is in order to dissociate itself from this that constitutional Belgian Government has reassembled on foreign soil. Even if present Belgian Army has to lay down its arms, there are 200,000 Belgians of military age in France and greater resources than Belgium had in 1914 on which to fight back. By his present decision the King is dividing the nation and delivering it into Hitler's protection. Please convey these considerations to the King, and impress on him the disastrous consequences on the Allies and to Belgium of his present choice.

162 MAY 1940

Desmond Morton to Winston S. Churchill
(*Premier papers, 3/222/5*)

27 May 1940

You asked for a report as to what was done to render the alleged landing grounds in Norfolk unserviceable.

Air Commodore Boyle,[1] Director of Air Intelligence, informs me on the telephone that work began at the end of last week under the Local Authorities in Norfolk ploughing up certain parts of the land and scattering suitable obstacles over other parts. He is satisfied that the steps taken are adequate.

DM

Winston S. Churchill: note[2]
(*Premier papers, 4/43B/1*)

27 May 1940

Reply. It will be a splendid episode in the history of the Empire if Australia, New Zealand & Canadian troops defend the Motherland against invasion.

War Cabinet: minutes
(*Cabinet papers, 65/7*)

27 May 1940
11.30 a.m.

Various suggestions had been made that we should cede some of our possessions in the New World to the United States in part payment of our war debt, but suggestions of this kind had always been discouraged by President Roosevelt.

Lord Lothian[3] thought that we should consider making a formal offer to

---

[1] John David Boyle, 1884–1974. Fourth son of the 7th Earl of Glasgow. 2nd Lieutenant, Rifle Brigade, 1906. Royal Flying Corps, 1912. On active service, 1914–18 (despatches twice, DSO 1917). Wing-Commander, Royal Air Force (on its formation), 1918. CBE, 1919. Aerodrome Board, Air Ministry, 1934–6. Director of Air Intelligence, 1939–41. His elder son, a Major in the Black Watch, was killed on active service in 1945. His younger son, a Squadron Leader in the Royal Air Force, was killed while on flying duty, 1960.

[2] The Prime Minister of Australia, Robert Menzies, had telegraphed to Churchill on the morning of 27 May 1940, asking 'what use the United Kingdom Government desire should be made of Commonwealth troops both trained and in training'. He added that 'the Commonwealth Government will pledge the whole of their resources to victory'.

[3] In his telegram No. 814 from Washington, sent on 24 May 1940.

the United States Government that, while we were not prepared to discuss any question of sovereignty, we were prepared to lease to the United States landing grounds on British territory, in view of the importance of such facilities to USA security. Lord Lothian mentioned particularly Trinidad, Newfoundland and Bermuda.

Lord Lothian believed that an offer of this kind made by us would make a deep impression in the United States and add to our security. If we acted quickly, our action would have the advantage also of spontaneity. If this proposal were to be pursued, it was very desirable that Congress should vote the necessary appropriations before its adjournment in early June.

The Prime Minister said that he would be opposed to a proposal that we should offer such facilities except as part of a deal. The United States had given us practically no help in the war, and now that they saw how great was the danger, their attitude was that they wanted to keep everything which would help us for their own defence.

War Cabinet: Confidential Annex
(*Cabinet papers, 65/13*)

27 May 1940
11.30 a.m.

The Prime Minister said that at the meeting with M. Reynaud the previous afternoon, complete agreement had been reached that the British Expeditionary Force must be withdrawn to the coast. The BEF was being pressed on both flanks, and the Germans had made a break in the line East of Courtrai. It was clear that we could not allow the security of our Army to be compromised in order to save the First French Army. He asked the Chief of the Imperial General Staff[1] to make the position in this respect clear to Lord Gort.

The Prime Minister thought that it would be as well that he should issue a general injunction to Ministers to use confident language. He was convinced that the bulk of the people of the country would refuse to accept the possibility of defeat.

The Prime Minister dealt with the main Report by the Chiefs of Staff[2] first. In his opinion this Report did not give a true picture of the position. In particular he challenged the Tables of the British and German air strengths, which gave a misleading impression. He had caused a statistical examination of the comparative position of the two Air Forces to be made, and although it

---

[1] Sir John Dill had succeeded Sir Edmund Ironside as Chief of the Imperial General Staff that same day (27 May 1940).
[2] War Cabinet Paper No. 168 of 1940.

had been extremely difficult to arrive at a true comparison, there were certain observations which he wished to make.

(i) During the last three years, according to the figures provided by the Air Ministry, the Germans had turned out 25,000 aircraft and we had produced 15,000 i.e. a ratio of 5 to 3. On this basis it was quite misleading to say that the Germans had a superiority of 4 to 1 over us. Either we credited the Germans with getting a much greater operational strength out of a given production than ourselves, or we made insufficient allowance for all the difficulties which, if our own experience was to be any guide, they must have encountered in expanding their air force.

(ii) We knew the very large requirements of our own training establishments and formations. If the German Air Force was really four times as large as ours, presumably their training requirements must similarly be four times as great and would amount to an enormous total. Unless we believed that the Germans succeeded in carrying out their training with a far smaller proportion of wastage than ourselves (which seemed unlikely), we must accept the fact that training requirements made far greater inroads into their operational strength than was shown in the tables.

(iii) In January, 1940, the Air Ministry had estimated that Germany was turning out 2,000 aircraft per month. A detailed examination of this estimate had been carried out by the Ministry of Economic Warfare, however, and as a result of this the Air Ministry had finally accepted a very much lower estimate of only 1,000 aircraft per month. Our whole policy might depend on our assessment of the German air strength, and it was therefore essential that all estimates should be subjected to the most detailed scrutiny.

(iv) With regard to the figures for the Metropolitan Air Force given in Appendix 'C', the late Secretary of State for Air[1] had given as his forecast of first-line strength on the 30th June, 1940, a figure of 2,150 aircraft. The figure given in the Tables, however, amounted only to 1,256, to which must be added some 200 to 300 aircraft in France, a

---

[1] Kingsley Wood, 1881–1943. Member of the London County Council, 1911–19. Chairman, London Insurance Committee, 1917–18. Conservative MP for Woolwich West, 1918–43. Knighted, 1918. Parliamentary Private Secretary to the Minister of Health, 1919–22. Parliamentary Secretary, Ministry of Health, 1924–9 (when Neville Chamberlain was Minister); Board of Education, 1931. Privy Councillor, 1928. Chairman, Executive Committee of the National Conservative and Unionist Association, 1930–2. Postmaster-General, 1931–5. Minister of Health, 1935–8. Secretary of State for Air, 1938–40. Lord Privy Seal, April–May 1940. Chancellor of the Exchequer from May 1940 until his death.

May 1940

total of, say, 1,550. If these figures were correct, they would imply that we had lost two-fifths of our effective force since active operations had begun on Western Front. The figures of our losses up to the 24th May were 360, but against this must be offset the new intake since May 12th of 610 machines.

The Prime Minister said that he proposed to go into these Tables of comparative strengths himself and try to obtain agreed figures on a truly comparable basis. The German bombing force might be four times as great as ours, but he did not believe the ratio was anything like so great in respect of our total air force.

The Vice Chief of the Air Staff[1] agreed that Appendices 'B' and 'C' were not drawn up on comparable bases. The British figures referred to operational strength, and the German figures to first-line strength. An attempt had been made to arrive at a true basis of comparison, and he handed to the War Cabinet a comparative Table drawn up on these lines.

The Prime Minister observed that from this Table it appeared that the odds against us were only $2\frac{1}{2}$ to 1. If our airmen were shooting down 3 to 1, the balance was on our side.

The Chief of the Air Staff[2] pointed out that at night the balance would be very much less favourable for us. It was only in the day fighting that we were able to inflict such heavy losses on the enemy.

The Secretary of State for Air[3] drew attention to the importance of the factors of morale and superior equipment. One of our fighter squadrons operating from Kent had given battle to a crack German squadron equipped with Me.110s. The Germans had fought extremely well, but their losses had been very much greater than ours.

The Prime Minister paid tribute to the skill of the Air Ministry's designers which had produced such a fine fighting machine as the Hurricane.

Continuing, he observed that the Chiefs of Staff Report was based on the assumption that French resistance would collapse completely, and that we should be exposed at short range to the concentrated attack of the whole of the German naval and air forces, operating from bases extending from Norway to the North-west of France. If France went out of the war, it did not necessarily follow that this assumption was correct; France might become a neutral, and it was not certain that Germany would insist on retaining all the ports in Northern France. She might be so anxious to divide France from us that she would offer France very favourable terms of peace.

---

[1] Air Marshal Richard Peirse.
[2] Air Chief Marshal Sir Cyril Newall.
[3] Sir Archibald Sinclair.

Winston S. Churchill to General Ismay
(*Churchill papers, 20/13*)

27 May 1940

The Chiefs of Staff Committee and the Vice-Chiefs should together examine this afternoon the following question and report upon it:–

In the event of France being unable to continue in the war and becoming neutral with the Germans holding their present position and the Belgian army being forced to capitulate after assisting the British Expeditionary Force to reach the coast; in the event of terms being offered to Britain which would place her entirely at the mercy of Germany through disarmament, cession of naval bases in the Orkneys, &c.; what are the prospects of our continuing the war alone against Germany and probably Italy. Can the Navy and the Air Force hold out reasonable hopes of preventing serious invasion, and could the forces gathered in this Island cope with raids from the air involving detachments not greater than 10,000 men; it being observed that a prolongation of British resistance might be very dangerous for Germany engaged in holding down the greater part of Europe.

WSC

War Cabinet: Confidential Annex
(*Cabinet papers, 65/13*)

27 May 1940
4.30 p.m.

The Prime Minister said that the Foreign Secretary's Note[1] set out the kind of approach to Signor Mussolini which M. Reynaud wanted the French and British Governments to make. While M. Reynaud was prepared to fight on for honour's sake, he was afraid that France was in danger of collapsing. If Italy undertook to stay out of the war, the French could remove ten Divisions from the Italian front. An attack by Italy at this juncture would give the *coup-de-grâce* to their existence. If France collapsed, Germany would probably give her good terms, but would expect the French to have the kind of Ministers who were acceptable to the Germans.

---

[1] War Cabinet Paper No. 170 of 1940.

MAY 1940   167

The Prime Minister said that it might be argued that an approach on the lines proposed by M. Reynaud was not unlike the approach which we had asked President Roosevelt to make to Signor Mussolini. There was, however, a good deal of difference between making the approach ourselves and allowing one to be made by President Roosevelt ostensibly on his own initiative.

The Lord President[1] thought that the completely misleading account of military operations in Northern France, coupled with the share of praise which the French were claiming for themselves in connection with events in which they had taken no part, must have some explanation. Was it that they intended to say that the French had had a magnificent scheme, but that, owing to the withdrawal of the BEF, they had been unable to carry it out and the poor French had been let down by their allies and must take the best chance available to them to get out of things. It would be unfortunate if they were to add to this that we had been unwilling even to allow them the chance of negotiations with Italy.

The Prime Minister said that the Lord President's argument amounted to this, that nothing would come of the approach, but that it was worth doing to sweeten relations with a failing ally. He read the following telegram, which he had received from M. Reynaud that morning (No. 283 DIPP):–

'I thank you for your cordial welcome and for your telegram. Your friendship is precious to me. As for Italy, that (?ultimate)[2] argument which to my mind carries most weight is that the assistance given by your country to mine through the approach we are making at this tragic hour will help to strengthen an alliance of hearts which I believe to be essential.'

The Prime Minister said that he was increasingly oppressed with the futility of the suggested approach to Signor Mussolini, which the latter would certainly regard with contempt. Such an approach would do M. Reynaud far less good than if he made a firm stand. Further, the approach would ruin the integrity of our fighting position in this country. Even if we did not include geographical precision and mentioned no names, everybody would know what we had in mind. Personally he doubted whether France was so willing to give up the struggle as M. Reynaud had represented. Anyway, let us not be dragged down with France. If the French were not prepared to go on with the struggle, let them give up, though he doubted whether they would do so. If this country was beaten, France became a vassal State; but if we won, we might save them. The best help we could give to M. Reynaud was to let him

---

[1] Neville Chamberlain.
[2] Words that could not be properly or fully deciphered were indicated in this way in the War Cabinet's minutes, with a bracket and a question mark.

feel that, whatever happened to France, we were going to fight it out to the end. This manoeuvre was a suggestion to get France out of the difficulty that she might have to make a separate peace, notwithstanding her bargain not to do so.

At the moment our prestige in Europe was very low. The only way we could get it back was by showing the world that Germany had not beaten us. If, after two or three months, we could show that we were still unbeaten, our prestige would return. Even if we were beaten, we should be no worse off than we should be if we were now to abandon the struggle. Let us therefore avoid being dragged down the slippery slope with France. The whole of this manoeuvre was intended to get us so deeply involved in negotiations that we should be unable to turn back. We had gone a long way already in our approach to Italy, but let us not allow M. Reynaud to get us involved in a confused situation. The approach proposed was not only futile, but involved us in a deadly danger.

The Secretary of State for Air thought that it might help matters if the Prime Minister were to go to Paris and see other French Ministers.

The Prime Minister said that General Spears was in Paris. France had got to settle this matter for herself. It was a question of her word and her army's honour. He had heard that day that there had been some change for the better in the fighting spirit of the French troops. There might be some hope in this. Otherwise everything would rest on us. If the worst came to the worst, it would not be a bad thing for this country to go down fighting for the other countries which had been overcome by the Nazi tyranny.

The Secretary of State for Foreign Affairs said that he saw no particular difficulty in taking the line suggested by the Lord President. Nevertheless, he was conscious of certain rather profound differences of points of view which he would like to make clear.

In the first place, he would have thought that, if we could persuade them to do so, there would have been some positive value in getting the French Government to say that they would fight to the end for their independence.

In the second place, he could not recognise any resemblance between the action which he proposed, and the suggestion that we were suing for terms and following a line which would lead us to disaster. In the discussion the previous day he had asked the Prime Minister whether, if he was satisfied that matters vital to the independence of this country were unaffected, he would be prepared to discuss terms. The Prime Minister had said that he would be thankful to get out of our present difficulties on such terms, provided we retain the essentials and the elements of our vital strength, even at the cost of some cession of territory. On the present occasion, however, the Prime Minister seemed to suggest that under no conditions would we contemplate any course except fighting to a finish. The issue was probably academic, since we were unlikely to receive any offer which would not come up against the fundamental conditions which were essential to us. If, however, it was possible to obtain a settlement which did not impair those conditions, he, for his part, doubted if he would be able to accept the view now put forward by the Prime Minister. The Prime Minister had said that two or three months would show whether we were able to stand up against the air risk. This meant that the future of the country turned on whether the enemy's bombs happened to hit our aircraft factories. He was prepared to take that risk if our independence was at stake; but if it was not at stake he would think it right to accept an offer which would save the country from avoidable disaster.

The Prime Minister said that he thought the issue which the War Cabinet was called upon to settle was difficult enough without getting involved in the discussion of an issue which was quite unreal and was most unlikely to arise. If Herr Hitler was prepared to make peace on the terms of the restoration of German colonies and the overlordship of Central Europe, that was one thing. But it was quite unlikely that he would make any such offer.

The Foreign Secretary said he would like to put the following question. Suppose the French Army collapsed and Herr Hitler made an offer of peace terms. Suppose the French Government said 'We are unable to deal with an offer made to France alone and you must deal with the Allies together.' Suppose Herr Hitler, being anxious to end the war through knowledge of his own internal weaknesses, offered terms to France and England, would the Prime Minister be prepared to discuss them?

The Prime Minister said that he would not join France in asking for terms; but if he were told what the terms offered were, he would be prepared to consider them.

John Colville: diary
(*Colville papers*)

27 May 1940

The Cabinet are feverishly considering our ability to carry on the war alone in such circumstances, and there are signs that Halifax is being defeatist. He says that our aim can no longer be to crush Germany but rather to preserve our own integrity and independence.

Lord Halifax: diary
(*Lord Birkenhead, 'Halifax'*)

27 May 1940

At the 4.30 Cabinet we had a long and rather confused discussion about, nominally, the approach to Italy, but also largely about general policy in the event of things going really badly in France. I thought Winston talked the most frightful rot, also Greenwood,[1] and after bearing it for some time I said exactly what I thought of them, adding that if that was really their view, and if it came to the point, our ways must separate. Winston, surprised and mellowed, and, when I repeated the same thing in the garden, was full of apologies and affection. But it does drive me to despair when he works himself up into a passion of emotion when he ought to make his brain think and reason.

Defence Committee: minutes
(*Cabinet papers, 69/1*)

27 May 1940
7 p.m.

THE SITUATION IN FRANCE

The Prime Minister described to the Meeting the disturbing news which had been received from Sir Roger Keyes. This news made the situation of the British Expeditionary Force even more desperate, and their only choice would be to fight their way back to the coast, taking as heavy a toll of the enemy as they could on the way.

Although the situation was critical and desperate, we had no reason to reproach ourselves for the terrible ordeal which now faced the British Expeditionary Force. We had agreed unreservedly before the war to place the British Expeditionary Force under the orders of the French. Immediately the Germans invaded Holland and Belgium Lord Gort, under the orders of the French High Command, had moved his force forward into Belgium to the assistance of that country. Then had come the German break through on the Meuse, and the complete inability of the great French Army to stem the German advance. There had been no mass of manoeuvre in the rear of the

---

[1] Minister without Portfolio: the second most senior Labour member of the War Cabinet after Attlee.

advance French troops, which we had reason to expect General Gamelin would immediately pour into the gap. If, when the enemy advance had continued, the British Expeditionary Force had been ordered to fall back, Lord Gort would have carried the order out. No such order had been given. When the German thrust had turned North West, Lord Gort had withdrawn gradually so as to maintain touch with the French First Army and with the Belgians.

Continuing, the Prime Minister recalled that he had visited Paris and had used every effort to put heart into the French Prime Minister and the French High Command. Then had followed the removal of General Gamelin and his replacement by General Weygand. It would also be recalled that at this juncture Lord Gort had mooted the idea that the British Expeditionary Force should fall back to the coast and form a bridgehead. The War Cabinet, hardly believing that the French Army would not stage a vigorous counter-offensive at an early date, had not favoured the British Commander-in-Chief's plan and General Weygand had been strongly opposed to it. General Weygand had promised a French offensive from the South, with which it was agreed should be synchronised an advance from the North against the 'gap' by the British Expeditionary Force. It would be remembered that General Billotte, who had been charged with the task of co-ordinating the action of the British and Belgian Armies and the French First Army, had proved himself supine and useless. He had been relieved by General Blanchard, who, while showing greater initiative, had arrived too late on the scene to rally the French First Army. The French counter-offensive from the South had never materialised.

The Belgians, who had shown such folly in resisting all our efforts to help when time was still on our side, were now paying the price for their folly and contributing to the disaster with which our Army was faced. While the King of the Belgians could not be reproached for the action which he was now taking, this action completed the full circle of misfortune into which our Allies had landed us while we had loyally carried out our obligations and undertakings to them.

In conclusion the Prime Minister informed the Meeting that he intended to make a statement at the Cabinet on the following day in the sense of the foregoing observations.

As a result of the ensuing discussion on the situation in France the following decisions were taken –

(a) That all army stores now accumulated at Le Havre, particularly guns and ammunition, should be got back to England as rapidly as possible.
(b) That the Advance Air Striking Force should be moved back to the Le Mans area as soon as possible.
(c) That blocking operations at Ostend should be carried out as soon as practicable.

ALIENS

Sir John Dill reported that the Military Authorities in the Eastern Command were being hampered by lack of co-operation on the part of local Civil Authorities to deal effectively with aliens in the Eastern Counties.

The Prime Minister directed that the Chief of the Imperial General Staff should forward to General Ismay a note on this subject which should immediately be despatched to the Home Secretary carrying instructions from the Prime Minister that the Civil Authorities in the Eastern Counties were to be ordered to afford the fullest co-operation to the Military Authorities in taking any steps considered necessary for controlling aliens in that area.

General Spears: telephone conversation with Winston S. Churchill
(*Cabinet papers, 65/7*)

27 May 1940
8.20 p.m.

Major-General Spears said that the French High Command had received a message from General Champon (French Mission to the Belgian Army) to the effect that the King of the Belgians had telegraphed to his Chief of Staff to send a plenipotentiary to the Germans to ascertain under what conditions an armistice could be arranged, and had suggested 'cease fire' at midnight tonight, the 27th–28th May. General Champon had said that he had taken note of this communication, and had added that these conditions could not be settled without getting into touch with Paris. Inasmuch as the three Armies, the Belgian, French and British, formed one block, the Belgians could not act alone. General Champon concluded by saying that he was making contact with General Blanchard, and would be grateful for the instructions of General Weygand.

To this communication General Weygand had replied as follows:–
(1) I will advise my Government immediately.
(2) Whilst awaiting new instructions, I am ordering General Blanchard to dissociate himself from the Belgian surrender.
(3) General Blanchard will take all urgent decisions in agreement with General Lord Gort to counter this act of desertion.

General Spears then said that General Weygand desired the immediate agreement of the Prime Minister to the despatch of the following telegram to General Blanchard:–

'The French and British Governments have agreed to instruct their Commanders-in-Chief, Generals Blanchard and Lord Gort, to defend the honour of their flags by dissociating themselves totally from the Belgian armistice.'

The Prime Minister replied to General Spears that he was in full agreement

MAY 1940   173

with the above telegram, and that instructions were being given to Lord Gort to continue his operation in conjunction with General Blanchard.

In conclusion, General Spears said that the Belgian Government were dissociating themselves from the act of the King of the Belgians, and that M. Pierlot[1] was going to announce this fact on the wireless to-night.

War Cabinet: minutes
(*Cabinet papers, 65/7*)

27 May 1940   10 Downing Street
10 p.m.

The Prime Minister informed the War Cabinet that a message had been received from Sir Roger Keyes to the effect that the King of the Belgians had ordered his Commander-in-Chief to send a plenipotentiary to the Germans to ask for an armistice for the Belgian Army to take effect from midnight that night.

News of this had been received in Paris and General Spears had rung up to say that General Weygand had advised the French Government to dissociate themselves from the Belgians in this matter and to order General Blanchard and Lord Gort to fight on. He had asked for the Prime Minister's support in this advice.

The Prime Minister said that he had acceded immediately to this request.

The Prime Minister said that he had telegraphed to Sir Roger Keyes in the early hours of that morning that the British Expeditionary Force was withdrawing towards the ports, and that we should do our best to evacuate such of the Belgian Army as could get back to the coast. He had emphasised the importance of ensuring the King's safety, and had made it clear that we should fight on to the end. This message should not have affected the King's determination to continue the struggle, although, perhaps, he could not altogether be blamed now for the action he was taking. Nevertheless, he had been very precipitate in seeking an armistice. Apparently the collapse of the Belgians was due to the heavy bombing to which they had been subjected that day. Any grounds for recrimination lay rather in the Belgian action on the outbreak of war than in the more immediate past. At the time when there had been only fifteen German divisions on their Western frontier, and the bulk of the German Army had been engaged in Poland, if Belgium had then invited us to enter their country, we could have established ourselves in a strong

---

[1] Hubert Pierlot, Prime Minister of Belgium from February 1939 until February 1945. In exile with the Belgian Government in London from June 1940.

defensive position or invaded Germany. The King's action was certainly not heroic. Presumably, he would now make a separate peace with the Germans and carry on as a puppet monarch. This might well be the best that he could do for his country, but we had to face the fact that it had the most serious consequences for the British Expeditionary Force. It was possible, of course, that the four divisions in the Lille area might manage to draw back and cut their way out to the coast. Our formations were practically intact and the troops were in excellent heart. They did not realise the plight in which they had been placed.

The Chief of the Imperial General Staff said that the collapse of the Belgians would undoubtedly place the British Expeditionary Force in the most serious peril. Lord Gort had no troops with which to close the gap and prevent the Germans breaking through to Dunkirk. No information had yet been received by the War Office as to the casualties which our Army had suffered. Some personnel had been withdrawn from France that day, but a ship leaving Dunkirk that afternoon had been heavily attacked from the air and had suffered some casualties from machine-gun fire.

The Prime Minister said that General Spears had reported that the feeling in Paris was better than it had been a short time ago. This might perhaps be attributed in part to the results of M. Reynaud's visit to London the previous day. As for the effect of the Belgian defection on French resistance, the French had probably already written off Blanchard's army as a dead loss. The action of the Belgians might sting the French to anger, in which case they would be very much more formidable opponents to the Germans than in their present stunned and bewildered state.

Our chief preoccupation now was to get off as much of the British Expeditionary Force as possible. There would be very confused fighting in the area of operations. The bombers on both sides would be able to do little, as the opposing troops would be very much intermingled. The German bombers, however, would get their opportunity when our men reached the coast.

The Minister of Information suggested that a statement should be issued referring to the gallant defence by the British troops.

The Prime Minister agreed, but thought that for the sake of relatives no names of regiments should be given at present.

The Minister of Information suggested that the public should be given some indication of the serious position in which the BEF had been placed. The French communiqués still had a cheerful tone. There was no doubt that the public were, at the moment, quite unprepared for the shock of realisation of the true position.

The Prime Minister thought that the seriousness of the situation should be emphasised; but he would deprecate any detailed statement or attempt to assess the results of the battle, until the situation had been further cleared up.

The announcement of the Belgian Armistice would go a long way to prepare the public for bad news.

The Minister of Information said that he realised the danger of announcements which appeared to contradict the French communiqués, and he thought that it would be as well to remind the public of the constant German efforts to drive a wedge between the two peoples. At the same time editors could be asked to tone down the French announcements.

The Prime Minister thought that it would be necessary for him to make a full statement in Parliament, although it might be another week before the situation had cleared sufficiently to allow him to do so. He proposed to say that the essential dangers which had menaced this country in the first days of the war had not been greatly increased by what had happened. Our means of meeting them, on the other hand, had increased since the beginning of the war; moreover, we could take heart from the superior quality and morale of our Air Force which had been so clearly demonstrated.

John Colville: diary
(*Colville papers*)

27 May 1940

After the Cabinet I went over to Admiralty House with the PM. He said he did not think the French would give in and that at any rate they ought not to do so. At midnight, after reading a few papers and saying 'Pour me out a whisky and soda, very weak, there's a good boy', he went to bed.

Winston S. Churchill to General Ismay
(*Churchill papers, 20/13*)

28 May 1940

1. Pray bring the following before the COS Committee:

What measures have been taken, in the event of Italy's going to war, to attack Italian forces in Abyssinia, sending rifles and money to the Abyssinian insurgents, and generally to disturb that country?

I understand General Smuts has sent a Union brigade to East Africa. Is it there yet? When will it be? What other arrangements are made? What is the strength of the Khartoum garrison, including troops in the Blue Nile Province? This is the opportunity for the Abyssinians to liberate themselves, with Allied help.

2. If France is still our ally after an Italian declaration of war, it would

appear extremely desirable that the combined Fleets, acting from opposite ends of the Mediterranean, should pursue an active offensive against Italy. It is important that at the outset collision should take place both with the Italian Navy and Air Force, in order that we can see what their quality really is, and whether it has changed at all since the last war. The purely defensive strategy contemplated by Commander-in-Chief Mediterranean[1] ought not to be accepted. Unless it is found that the fighting qualities of the Italians are high, it will be much better that the Fleet at Alexandria should sally forth and run some risks than that it should remain in a posture so markedly defensive. Risks must be run at this juncture in all theatres.

3. I presume that the Admiralty have a plan in the event of France becoming neutral.

War Cabinet: minutes
(*Cabinet papers, 65/7*)

28 May 1940
11.30 a.m.
10 Downing Street

The Prime Minister said that the Belgian Army had ceased fire at 0400 hours that morning. He invited Admiral Sir Roger Keyes, who had just returned from Belgium, to give the War Cabinet his appreciation of the present situation.

Sir Roger Keyes said that the Belgian Army had been completely demoralised by incessant bombing from large numbers of German aircraft. The Germans appeared to have maintained a ring of fighter patrols round the battle area and, although our fighters had been seen in many engagements with the German fighters, they had been unable to break through the ring in order to attack the German bombers, which had circled round at low altitudes, bombing the Belgian troops with impunity.

Sir Roger Keyes commented on the precipitate flight of the Belgian Government. King Leopold had said that he wished to have nothing more to

---

[1] Andrew Browne Cunningham, 1883–1963. Entered the Royal Navy, 1898. On active service, 1914–18 (DSO and two bars). Vice-Admiral Commanding the Battle Cruiser Squadron, 1937–8. Deputy Chief of the Naval Staff, 1938–9. Knighted, 1939. Commander-in-Chief, Mediterranean, 1939–42. Head of the British Admiralty Delegation, Washington, 1942. Naval Commander-in-Chief, Expeditionary Force, North Africa, 1942. Commander-in-Chief, Mediterranean, 1943. Admiral of the Fleet, 1943. First Sea Lord and Chief of the Naval Staff, 1943–6. Created Baron, 1945; Viscount, 1946. In 1951 he published his memoirs, *A Sailor's Odyssey*.

do with them. In his (Sir Roger Keyes's) view the Belgian Government were entirely responsible for the chaos caused by the evacuation of the civil population, who had been told that asylum would be found for them in England or France. It had been noticeable that the Local Authorities had in most cases been the first to get away.

The Prime Minister expressed the War Cabinet's warm appreciation of what Sir Roger Keyes had done in such difficult and dangerous circumstances. He did not think, however, that Sir Roger Keyes should return to Belgium, at any rate for the moment.
(At this point Sir Roger Keyes withdrew).
The Prime Minister said that the King of the Belgians would now presumably become the puppet of Hitler, and might possibly obtain better treatment for his people than if he had left the country and continued to resist from foreign soil. No doubt history would criticise the King for having involved us and the French in Belgium's ruin. But it was not for us to pass judgment on him.

The Prime Minister then read to the War Cabinet the terms of the armistice which the Belgians had agreed with the enemy, as follows:–
(1) All Belgian troop movements forbidden. Belgian troops must line up on the side of the road to await orders. They must make known their presence by means of white signs, flags, &c.
(2) Orders must be given forbidding destruction of war material and stores.
(3) German troops must be allowed to proceed to the coast.
(4) Free passage to Ostend is demanded and no destruction permitted.
(5) All resistance will be overcome.

The Minister of Information read to the War Cabinet a message he had just received from Sir Walter Monckton[1] pressing for a frank statement of the desperate situation of the British Expeditionary Force. He feared that, unless this was given out, public confidence would be badly shaken and the civil population would not be ready to accept the assurances of the Government of

---

[1] Walter Turner Monckton, 1891–1965. Educated at Harrow and Balliol College, Oxford. President of the Oxford Union Society, 1913. On active service, 1915–19 (Military Cross). Called to the Bar, 1919. King's Counsel, 1930. Attorney-General to the Prince of Wales, 1932–6. Knighted, 1937. Director-General of the Press Censorship Bureau, 1939–40. Director-General, Ministry of Information, 1940–1; British Propaganda and Information Services, Cairo, 1941–2. Solicitor-General, 1945. Conservative MP for Bristol West, 1951–7. Minister of Labour and National Service, 1951–5. Minister of Defence, 1955–6. Paymaster-General, 1956–7. Created Viscount, 1957.

the chances of our ultimate victory. The Minister suggested that he should make a short statement in the 1 o'clock news of the BBC.

The Prime Minister said that he would also make a statement in the House of Commons in the afternoon to the effect that the British Expeditionary Force was fighting its way back to the coast under the protection of the Royal Air Force, and that the Navy was embarking the troops[1]. It would be idle to try to forecast the success of this operation at this stage.

The Prime Minister observed that the enemy might perhaps take advantage of the situation to send in a heavy attack against the United Kingdom. Our fighter defences might have to be redisposed to meet it, but no doubt the enemy was fully extended like ourselves.

Winston S. Churchill: statement
(*Hansard*)

28 May 1940   House of Commons

WAR SITUATION

The Prime Minister (Mr Churchill): The House will be aware that the King of the Belgians yesterday sent a plenipotentiary to the German Command asking for a suspension of arms on the Belgian front. The British and French Governments instructed their generals immediately to dissociate themselves from this procedure and to persevere in the operations in which they are now engaged. However, the German Command has agreed to the Belgian proposals and the Belgian Army ceased to resist the enemy's will at four o'clock this morning. I have no intention of suggesting to the House that we should attempt at this moment to pass judgment[2] upon the action of the King of the Belgians in his capacity as Commander-in-Chief of the Belgian Army. This Army has fought very bravely and has both suffered and inflicted heavy losses. The Belgian Government has dissociated itself from the action of

---

[1] This was the Dunkirk evacuation, Operation 'Dynamo', which had been authorised by the Admiralty on the evening of May 26.

[2] This phrase had been suggested to Churchill by Lieutenant-Colonel G. M. O. Davy, who had been brought into the War Cabinet to give an account of the Belgian capitulation, and had persuaded Churchill, he later recalled, to 'cut all references to treachery and the absence of warning'. After Churchill had redrafted his statement, 'He then looked at me and said, "How about that, Colonel Davy?" "That's better, Sir," I replied, and everyone laughed. The PM smiled at me and I went out' (Colonel Davy, recollection, *Davy papers*).

the King and declaring itself to be the only legal Government of Belgium, has formally announced its resolve to continue the war at the side of the Allies who have come to the aid of Belgium at her urgent appeal. Whatever our feelings may be upon the facts so far as they are known to us, we must remember that the sense of brotherhood between the many peoples who have fallen into the power of the aggressor, and those who still confront him, will play its part in better days than those through which we are passing.

The situation of the British and French Armies now engaged in a most severe battle and beset on three sides and from the air, is evidently extremely grave. The surrender of the Belgian Army in this manner adds appreciably to their grievous peril. But the troops are in good heart, and are fighting with the utmost discipline and tenacity, and I shall, of course, abstain from giving any particulars of what, with the powerful assistance of the Royal Navy and the Royal Air Force, they are doing or hope to do. I expect to make a statement to the House on the general position when the result of the intense struggle now going on can be known and measured. This will not, perhaps, be until the beginning of next week.

Meanwhile, the House should prepare itself for hard and heavy tidings. I have only to add that nothing which may happen in this battle can in any way relieve us of our duty to defend the world cause to which we have vowed ourselves; nor should it destroy our confidence in our power to make our way, as on former occasions in our history, through disaster and through grief to the ultimate defeat of our enemies.

Mr Lees-Smith[1]: I thank the Prime Minister for the statement which he has given to the House. As he is to make a further statement next week this is not the time for any discussion at all. I will, therefore, confine myself to a single observation. Whatever he may have to tell us in the next few days or weeks or months, we have not yet touched the fringe of the resolution of this country.

Sir Percy Harris[2]: All I want to say is that the dignified statement of the Prime Minister reflects not only the feeling of the whole House but the feeling of the whole nation.

---

[1] Hastings Bertrand Lees-Smith, 1878–1941. Labour MP, 1910–18 and 1920–3, 1924–31 and from 1935 until his death. Postmaster-General, 1929–31. President of the Board of Education, 1931. Privy Councillor, 1931. Acting Chairman of the Parliamentary Labour Party, 1940–1.

[2] Percy Alfred Harris, 1876–1952. Barrister. Member of the London County Council, 1907–34 and from 1946 until his death. Assistant Director, Volunteer Services, War Office, 1916. Liberal MP, 1916–18 and 1922–45. Created Baronet, 1932. Chief Whip, Liberal Parliamentary Party, 1935–45; Deputy Leader, 1940–5. Privy Councillor, 1940. Author of *Forty Years In and Out of Parliament*.

War Cabinet: Confidential Annex
(*Cabinet papers, 65/13*)

28 May 1940
4 p.m.

The Foreign Secretary said that Sir Robert Vansittart[1] had now discovered what the Italian Embassy had in mind, namely, that we should give a clear indication that we should like to see mediation by Italy.

The Prime Minister said that it was clear that the French purpose was to see Signor Mussolini acting as intermediary between ourselves and Herr Hitler. He was determined not to get into this position.

The Foreign Secretary said that the proposal which had been discussed with M. Reynaud on Sunday had been as follows: that we should say that we were prepared to fight to the death for our independence, but that, provided this could be secured, there were certain concessions that we were prepared to make to Italy.

The Prime Minister thought that the French were trying to get us on to the slippery slope. The position would be entirely different when Germany had made an unsuccessful attempt to invade this country.

The Foreign Secretary said that we must not ignore the fact that we might get better terms before France went out of the war and our aircraft factories were bombed, than we might get in three months' time.

The various possibilities now under development of countering night-bombing were referred to.

The Prime Minister then read out a draft which expressed his views. To him the essential point was that M. Reynaud wanted to get us to the Conference-table with Herr Hitler. If we once got to the table, we should then find that the terms offered us touched our independence and integrity. When, at this point, we got up to leave the Conference-table, we should find that all the forces of resolution which were now at our disposal would have vanished. M. Reynaud had said that if he could save the independence of France, he would continue the fight. It was clear, therefore, that M. Reynaud's aim was to end the war.

The Foreign Secretary said that M. Reynaud also wanted the Allies to address an appeal to the President of the United States.

---

[1] Robert Gilbert Vansittart, 1881–1957. Educated at Eton. Entered the Diplomatic Service, 1902. Assistant Clerk, Foreign Office, 1914; 1st Secretary, 1918; Counsellor, 1920. Secretary to Lord Curzon, 1920–4. Principal Private Secretary to Ramsay MacDonald, 1928–30. Knighted, 1929. Permanent Under-Secretary of State for Foreign Affairs, 1930–8. Elected to the Other Club, 1933. Chief Diplomatic Adviser to the Foreign Secretary, 1938–41. Privy Councillor, 1940. Created Baron, 1941. His autobiography, *The Mist Procession*, was published posthumously, in 1958. His brother Arnold was killed in action in 1915.

The Prime Minister thought that a paragraph might be added to the draft outlined by the Lord President[1] to the effect that we were ready in principle to associate ourselves with such an appeal.

The Minister without Portfolio[2] thought that M. Reynaud was too much inclined to hawk round appeals. This was another attempt to run out.

The Prime Minister said that he came back to the point that the French wanted to get out of the war, but did not want to break their Treaty obligations to us. Signor Mussolini, if he came in as mediator, would take his whack out of us. It was impossible to imagine that Herr Hitler would be so foolish as to let us continue our re-armament. In effect, his terms would put us completely at his mercy. We should get no worse terms if we went on fighting, even if we were beaten, than were open to us now. If, however, we continued the war and Germany attacked us, no doubt we should suffer some damage, but they also would suffer severe losses. Their oil supplies might be reduced. A time might come when we felt that we had to put an end to the struggle, but the terms would not then be more mortal than those offered to us now.

The Foreign Secretary said that he still did not see what there was in the French suggestion of trying out the possibilities of mediation which the Prime Minister felt was so wrong.

The Lord President said that, on a dispassionate survey, it was right to remember that the alternative to fighting on nevertheless involved a considerable gamble.

The War Cabinet agreed that this was a true statement of the case.

The Prime Minister said that the nations which went down fighting rose again, but those which surrendered tamely were finished.

The Foreign Secretary said that nothing in his suggestion could even remotely be described as ultimate capitulation.

The Prime Minister thought that the chances of decent terms being offered to us at the present time were a thousand to one against.

AT THIS POINT the War Cabinet broke off its discussion, to enable Churchill to meet the full Cabinet, a meeting that had been arranged earlier in the day.

---

[1] Neville Chamberlain.
[2] Arthur Greenwood.

Hugh Dalton: diary[1]
(*Ben Pimlott, 'The Second World War Diary of Hugh Dalton'*)

28 May 1940

In the afternoon all ministers are asked to meet the PM. He is quite magnificent. The man, and the only man we have, for this hour. He gives a full, frank and completely calm account of events in France. When the Germans broke through on the Meuse, French morale for the moment collapsed. Therefore, he flew to France and saw Reynaud and Gamelin. The latter said, 'We have been defeated by German superiority in numbers, in material and in methods.' Churchill said, 'What then are you going to do?' Gamelin merely shrugged his shoulders. Churchill said, 'Will you please leave the room', and then, alone with Reynaud, they went into everything, including the High Command. The French, before this war, had given up all ideas of the offensive. They were hypnotised by the Maginot Line. General Billotte commanding the forces north of the Somme, including our own, had given no important or significant order for four days! Since then he had been killed in a motor accident and succeeded by Blanchard. The French had failed to make a push northwards from the Somme. They had had too few Divisions between the sea and Amiens and their communications had been badly bombed. Therefore, though we had done our best from the north, it had been impossible to close the gap, and we were in grave danger of being surrounded. Now, therefore, it was necessary to fight our way through to the Channel Ports and get away all we could.

The act of the King of the Belgians had opened our flank, but this was not so grave as might have been supposed, owing to the inundations on the Ysère, which were perhaps a better defence than the Belgian Army! How many would get away we could not tell. We should certainly be able to get 50,000 away. If we could get 100,000 away, that would be a magnificent performance. Only Dunkirk was left to us. Calais had been defended by a British force which had refused to surrender, and it was said that there were no survivors. We could only use the beaches east and west of Dunkirk in addition to the port itself. Dunkirk was under a great pall of black smoke, to which our ships were adding artificial smoke so as to screen our embarkations from the air. The Air Force were maintaining the most powerful possible fighter patrols over this scene, and the Germans were suffering immense losses in the air, as on the ground, in their attempts to interfere with the embarkation. The superiority of our fighters was once again being manifested, and on two

---

[1] The editor of Hugh Dalton's diaries, Ben Pimlott, writes in an editorial note: 'Although there is an entry for virtually every day for much of the period of the Coalition, Dalton did not compose his diary daily. His usual practice was to dictate a week's material at a single sitting.' From internal evidence, this entry for 28 May was written at least two days later.

occasions great flights of German bombers had turned away and declined battle when they saw our fighter patrols.

The PM went on to say that our clawing-down rate was gradually rising, taking an average of one day with another, to 3:1, to 4:1, and lately to 5:1. It was clear that we had killed off most of the best Nazi pilots, unless, which seemed unlikely, they had been holding some of their best in reserve. 'They're cold meat,' our airmen say.

He was determined to prepare public opinion for bad tidings, and it would of course be said, and with some truth, that what was now happening in Northern France would be the greatest British military defeat for many centuries. We must now be prepared for the sudden turning of the war against this island, and prepared also for other events of great gravity in Europe. No countenance should be given publicly to the view that France might soon collapse, but we must not allow ourselves to be taken by surprise by any events. It might indeed be said that it would be easier to defend this island alone than to defend this island plus France, and if it was seen throughout the world that it was the former, there would be an immense wave of feeling, not least in the USA which, having done nothing much to help us so far, might even enter the war. But all this was speculative. Attempts to invade us would no doubt be made, but they would be beset with immense difficulty. We should mine all round our coast; our Navy was immensely strong; our air defences were much more easily organised from this island than across the Channel; our supplies of food, oil, etc., were ample; we had good troops in this island, others were on the way by sea, both British army units coming from remote garrisons and excellent Dominion troops, and, as to aircraft, we were now more than making good our current losses, and the Germans were not.

It was idle to think that, if we tried to make peace now, we should get better terms from Germany than if we went on and fought it out. The Germans would demand our fleet – that would be called 'disarmament' – our naval bases, and much else. We should become a slave state, though a British Government which would be Hitler's puppet would be set up – 'under Mosley[1] or some such person'. And where should we be at the end of all that? On the other side, we had immense reserves and advantages. Therefore, he said, 'We shall go on and we shall fight it out, here or elsewhere, and if at last the long story is to end, it were better it should end, not through surrender, but only when we are rolling senseless on the ground.'[2] There was a murmur of

[1] Oswald Ernald Mosley, 1896–1980. Educated at Sandhurst. On active service, 1917–18. A Conservative MP, 1918–22, he sat as an Independent, 1922–4 and as a Labour member, 1924 and 1926–31. Succeeded his father as 6th Baronet, 1928. Labour Chancellor of the Duchy of Lancaster, 1929–30. Founded the British Union of Fascists, 1932. Imprisoned, 1940–5. He published his autobiography, *My Life*, in 1968. Mosley was married to Clementine Churchill's cousin Diana Mitford.

[2] Dalton later set down another version of Churchill's words in the margin of this diary entry: 'If this long island story of ours is to end at last, let it end only when each one of us lies choking in his own blood upon the ground.'

approval round the table, in which I think Amery, Lord Lloyd and I were loudest. Not much more was said. No one expressed even the faintest flicker of dissent. Herbert Morrison asked about evacuation of the Government, and hoped that it would not be hurried. The PM said Certainly not, he was all against evacuation unless things really became utterly impossible in London, 'but mere bombing will not make us go'.

It is quite clear that whereas the Old Umbrella[1] – neither he nor other members of the War Cabinet were at this meeting – wanted to run very early, Winston's bias is all the other way. When we separate, several go up and speak to him, and I, patting him on the shoulder, from my physically greater height, say, 'You ought to get that Cartoon of Low showing us all rolling up our sleeves, and frame it and stick it up in front of you here.' He says, with a broad grin, 'Yes, that was a good one, wasn't it.'[2] He is a darling!

Winston S. Churchill: recollection
('Their Finest Hour', page 88)

28 May 1940

I had not seen many of my colleagues outside the War Cabinet, except individually, since the formation of the Government, and I thought it right to have a meeting in my room at the House of Commons of all Ministers of Cabinet rank other than the War Cabinet Members. We were perhaps twenty-five round the table. I described the course of events, and I showed them plainly where we were, and all that was in the balance. Then I said quite casually, and not treating it as a point of special significance:

'Of course, whatever happens at Dunkirk, we shall fight on.'

There occurred a demonstration which, considering the character of the gathering – twenty-five experienced politicians and Parliament men, who represented all the different points of view, whether right or wrong, before the war – surprised me. Quite a number seemed to jump up from the table and come running to my chair, shouting and patting me on the back. There is no doubt that had I at this juncture faltered at all in the leading of the nation I should have been hurled out of office. I was sure that every Minister was ready to be killed quite soon, and have all his family and possessions destroyed, rather than give in. In this they represented the House of Commons and almost all the people. It fell to me in these coming days and months to express their sentiments on suitable occasions. This I was able to do because they were mine also. There was a white glow, overpowering, sublime, which ran through our Island from end to end.

[1] Neville Chamberlain.
[2] It is reproduced on page 29.

War Cabinet: Confidential Annex
(*Cabinet papers, 65/13*)

28 May 1940
7 p.m.

The Prime Minister said that in the interval he had seen the Ministers not in the War Cabinet. He had told them the latest news. They had not expressed alarm at the position in France, but had expressed the greatest satisfaction when he had told them that there was no chance of our giving up the struggle. He did not remember having ever before heard a gathering of persons occupying high places in political life express themselves so emphatically.

The Foreign Secretary again referred to the proposed appeal to the United States. It appeared that Mr Bullitt[1] had told M. Reynaud that he favoured the plan, but thought that Lord Lothian should be consulted before anything was done. This differed somewhat from what M. Reynaud had said.

The Prime Minister thought that an appeal to the United States at the present time would be altogether premature. If we made a bold stand against Germany, that would command their admiration and respect; but a grovelling appeal, if made now, would have the worst possible effect. He therefore did not favour making any approach on the subject at the present time.

Winston S. Churchill to Paul Reynaud
(*Churchill papers, 4/152*)

28 May 1940
11.40 p.m.
By telephone

I have with my colleagues examined with the most careful and sympathetic attention the proposal for an approach by way of precise offer of concessions to Signor Mussolini that you have forwarded to me today, fully realising the terrible situation with which we are both faced at this moment.

2. Since we last discussed this matter the new fact which has occurred, namely the capitulation of the Belgian Army, has greatly changed our

---

[1] William Christian Bullitt, 1891–1967. Entered the State Department, 1917. President Wilson's special emissary to Russia, 1919. United States Ambassador to the Soviet Union, 1933–6; to France, 1936–41. President Roosevelt's special representative in the Far East, 1941. Special Assistant Secretary of the Navy, 1942–3. Served as a Major in the French armed forces, 1944.

position for the worse, for it is evident that the chance of withdrawing the armies of Generals Blanchard and Gort from the Channel ports has become very problematical. The first effect of such a disaster must be to make it impossible at such a moment for Germany to put forward any terms likely to be acceptable and neither we nor you would be prepared to give up our independence without fighting for it to the end.

3. In the formula prepared last Sunday by Lord Halifax it was suggested that if Signor Mussolini would co-operate with us in securing a settlement of all European questions which would safeguard our independence and form the basis of a just and durable peace for Europe, we would be prepared to discuss his claims in the Mediterranean. You now propose to add certain specific offers, which I cannot suppose would have any chance of moving Signor Mussolini, and which once made could not be subsequently withdrawn, in order to induce him to undertake the role of mediator, which the formula discussed on Sunday contemplated.

4. I and my colleagues believe that Signor Mussolini has long had it in mind that he might eventually fill this role, no doubt counting upon substantial advantages for Italy in the process. But we are convinced that at this moment when Hitler is flushed with victory and certainly counts on early and complete collapse of Allied resistance, it would be impossible for Signor Mussolini to put forward proposals for a conference with any success. I may remind you also that the President of the USA has received a wholly negative reply to the proposal which we jointly asked him to make and that no response has been made to the approach of Lord Halifax, made to the Italian Ambassador[1] here last Saturday.

5. Therefore, without excluding the possibility of an approach to Signor Mussolini at some time, we cannot feel that this would be the right moment and I am bound to add that in my opinion the effect on the morale of our people, which is now firm and resolute, would be extremely dangerous. You yourself can best judge what would be the effect in France.

6. You will ask, then, how is the situation to be improved. My reply is that by showing that after the loss of our two armies and the support of our Belgian Ally, we still have stout hearts and confidence in ourselves, we shall at once strengthen our hands in negotiations and draw to ourselves the admiration and perhaps the material help of the USA. Moreover, we feel that as long as we stand together, our undefeated Navy and our Air Force which is daily destroying German fighters and bombers at a formidable rate, afford us the means of exercising in our common interest a continuous pressure upon Germany's internal life.

7. We have reason to believe that the Germans too are working to a timetable and that their losses and the hardships imposed on them together with

---

[1] Giuseppe Bastianini.

the fear of our air raids is undermining their courage. It would indeed be a tragedy if by too hasty an acceptance of defeat we throw away a chance that was almost within our grasp of securing an honourable issue from the struggle.

8. In my view if we both stand out we may yet save ourselves from the fate of Denmark or Poland. Our success must depend first on our unity, then on our courage and endurance.

Winston S. Churchill: note to Cabinet Ministers and senior officials
(*Premier papers, 4/68/9*)

29 May 1940
Strictly Confidential
10 Downing Street

In these dark days the Prime Minister would be grateful if all his colleagues in the Government, as well as high officials, would maintain a high morale in their circles; not minimising the gravity of events, but showing confidence in our ability and inflexible resolve to continue the war till we have broken the will of the enemy to bring all Europe under his domination.

No tolerance should be given to the idea that France will make a separate peace; but whatever may happen on the Continent, we cannot doubt our duty and we shall certainly use all our power to defend the Island, the Empire and our Cause.

WSC

Winston S. Churchill to Anthony Eden, General Ismay and General Dill[1]
(*Premier papers, 3/175*)

29 May 1940

It is essential that the French should share in such evacuations from Dunkirk as may be possible. Nor must they be dependent only upon their own shipping resources. Arrangements must be concerted at once with the French Missions in this country, or if necessary with the French Government, so that no reproaches, or as few as possible, arise. It might perhaps be well if we evacuated the two French Divisions from Dunkirk, and replaced them *pro tem* with our own troops, thus simplifying the Command. But let me have the best proposals possible, and advise me whether there is any action I should take.

WSC

[1] Churchill affixed a red ACTION THIS DAY label to this minute. This was to be a frequent addition each day to urgent requests.

Winston S. Churchill to General Ismay and General Dill
(*Churchill papers, 20/13*)

29 May 1940

The change which has come over the war affects decisively the usefulness of Cultivator No. 6.[1] It may play its part in various operations, defensive and offensive, but it can no longer be considered the only method of breaking a fortified line. I suggest that the Minister of Supply[2] should to-day be instructed to reduce the scheme by one-half. Probably in a few days it will be to one-quarter. The spare available capacity could be turned over to Tanks. If the Germans can make Tanks in nine months, surely we can do so. Let me have your general proposals for the priority construction of an additional thousand Tanks capable of engaging the improved enemy pattern likely to be working in 1941.

There should also be formed, if it does not already exist, an anti-Tank Committee to study and devise all methods of attacking the latest German Tanks. Pray let me have suggested list of names.

WSC

Winston S. Churchill to General Spears
(*Foreign Office papers, 800/312*)

29 May 1940

Your reports most interesting, and Ambassador strongly praises your work. Continue report constantly. Meanwhile reiterate our inflexible resolve to continue whatever they do. Margerie made a remark in my presence last week which made me doubtful of his zeal. It would be inexpedient to give all the figures Reynaud wants at present.

WSC

War Cabinet: minutes
(*Cabinet papers, 65/7*)

29 May 1940   10 Downing Street
11.30 a.m.

The Prime Minister said that the latest information from the Admiralty was that 40,000 troops from the BEF had so far been landed in this country, and that evacuation was now taking place at the rate of about 2,000 an hour.

---

[1] A trench-crossing device which Churchill had sponsored while at the Admiralty.
[2] Herbert Morrison.

The Prime Minister said that the Air Force had changed its method of giving protection to the evacuation operations and, instead of continuous patrols over the area, the Air Force was now providing occasional patrols of much greater strength. The War Cabinet had asked for the maximum air protection to be given, and he thought that the Air Staff must be left to provide this in whatever manner they thought best.

The Prime Minister said that Narvik had been occupied by French and Norwegian troops at 10 p.m. the previous evening.

Some discussion took place on the suggestion that eight Regular battalions should be withdrawn from Palestine to this country.

The Prime Minister said that, in his view, the vital need at the present time was to protect this country, and that this must take precedence over all other needs.

The War Cabinet had before them a Report by the Chiefs of Staff[1] (WP (40) 177) submitting proposals for the control of operations and forces in the event of an attempted invasion of this country.

The Prime Minister observed that there was no reason why the Commander-in-Chief[2] should not have direct access to him before operations began. This would be a matter of convenience, but need not be formally recorded in the Report.

War Cabinet: Confidential Annex
(*Cabinet papers, 65/13*)

29 May 1940
11.30 a.m.

The Prime Minister said that British troops should on no account delay their withdrawal to conform with the French, otherwise there would be a danger of getting no troops off. Any French troops that arrived at the coast should, of course, be embarked with our own. Lord Gort had been sent an order to continue the struggle with the object of gaining time for the evacuation of as many troops as possible, and of inflicting the maximum amount of damage on the Germans.

[1] War Cabinet Paper No. 177 of 1940.
[2] Lord Gort.

The Prime Minister said that in a desperate situation any brave man was entitled, in the absence of precise orders to the contrary, to use his own discretion, and that therefore he would prefer not to modify the instructions to Lord Gort. Our object was to ensure the evacuation of every possible man, and then the infliction of the maximum possible damage on the enemy. A day gained now might well mean a further 40,000 men taken off. A Commander, in circumstances as desperate and distressing as those in which Lord Gort now found himself, should not be offered the difficult choice between resistance and capitulation.

The Prime Minister said that the instructions sent to Lord Gort had not been intended to convey the impression that troops which were cut off from hope of relief and were without food or without water or without ammunition should attempt to continue the struggle. He would consider sending a telegram containing modified instructions on the lines of the suggestion made by the Lord Privy Seal.

The Secretary of State for War suggested that the Prime Minister might like to send, through Ministerial channels, a communication to the Allied Commander-in-Chief on the lines of the communications which had already passed between the French and British Staff as to the future employment of British troops in France.

The War Cabinet –
  (i) Took note that the Prime Minister proposed to send a further telegram to Lord Gort modifying the instructions already sent in the light of the above discussion.
  (ii) Invited the Prime Minister to send a telegram to M. Reynaud, for transmission to General Weygand, as to the future employment of British troops in France.

The Secretary of State for Foreign Affairs raised the question as to when and by what method we should inform the Norwegian Government of our decision to evacuate Narvik.

The Prime Minister said that Lord Cork attached great importance to secrecy in regard to withdrawal and he (the Prime Minister) was in favour of waiting a few days before taking a decision. We must, of course, offer to evacuate any Norwegian troops who wished to be taken away.

Sir Alexander Cadogan: diary
(*'The Diaries of Sir Alexander Cadogan'*)

29 May 1940

Cabinet 11.30. News unpleasant. We have got off 40,000 men and taking them, at present, at rate of 2,000 an hr. But the end will be awful. A horrible discussion of what instructions to send to Gort. WSC rather theatrically bulldoggish. Opposed by NC and H[1] and yielded to a reasonable extent. Fear relations will become rather strained. That is Winston's fault – theatricality.

Winston S. Churchill to Lord Gort
(*Premier papers, 3/175*)

29 May 1940
9.40 p.m.
Personal

If you are cut from all communication with us, and all evacuation from Dunkirk and beaches had in your judgement been finally prevented, after every attempt to re-open it had failed, you would become the sole judge of when it was impossible to inflict further damage upon the enemy. His Majesty's Government are sure that the repute of the British Army is safe in your hands.

Winston S. Churchill to General Ismay
(*Churchill papers, 20/13*)

29 May 1940

We must have eight battalions from Palestine home at the earliest moment. I regard the Mediterranean as closed to troop-ships. The choice is therefore between the Red Sea and the Persian Gulf. Let this alternative route be examined this afternoon, and Admiralty be consulted, and report to me on relative times and safety. The Australians can be left in Palestine for the moment, but the High Commissioner,[2] like others, must conform to the supreme requirements of the State.

[1] Neville Chamberlain and Lord Halifax.
[2] Harold Alfred MacMichael, 1882–1969. Winner of the Public Schools Fencing Championship, 1901. Joined the Sudan Political Service, 1905. On active service in the Sudan, 1916 (despatches three times, DSO). Civil Secretary, Sudan. Knighted, 1932. Governor and Commander-in-Chief, Tanganyika, 1934–8. High Commissioner and Commander-in-Chief, Palestine, and High Commissioner for Transjordan, 1938–44. Narrowly escaped assassination, 1944. Special Representative, Malaysia, 1945. Constitutional Commissioner, Malta, 1946–7.

Admiralty should say whether it would be possible to pick these men up at the Cape in the big liners for extra speed.

Winston S. Churchill to Lord Halifax
(Foreign Office papers, 800/310)

29 May 1940

We should surely take a strong line with the Egyptian Government, who must not be allowed to hamper our military measures when we are their sole defence against Italian annexation.[1] We ought on no account to tolerate any Egyptian efforts to contract themselves out of the war.[2]

John Colville: diary
(Colville papers)

29 May 1940

Winston's ceaseless industry is impressive. He is always having ideas which he puts down on paper in the form of questions and despatches to Ismay or the CIGS for examination. Sometimes they relate to matters of major importance, such as the measures to be taken against invasion, or the provision of more aeroplanes, and sometimes they relate to quite trivial questions. This is the sort of thing: 'General Ismay. Inquire into the number of German guns now trophies in this country and whether any can be reconditioned for blocking exits from beaches against tanks conceivably landed thereon.' Another today asked whether wax could be supplied to troops to put in their ears in order to deaden the noise of warfare.

---

[1] Sir Miles Lampson, British Ambassador in Egypt, had reported to Lord Halifax, who circulated his telegram to the War Cabinet, on the desire of the Egyptian Government to declare Cairo an 'open city', and, in order to do so to the satisfaction of the Italians, to remove from the city all British military units and headquarters. Lampson commented: 'We all feel declaration, if feasible, would have no value unless accompanied by the assurance from the Allies that if Cairo were subjected to air attack by any foreign power there would be immediate retaliation in kind against that power' (*Foreign Office papers, 800/310*).

[2] On reading this minute when it was presented to him for initialling, Churchill added in his own hand: 'I hope you do not mind my sending you "chits" like this. There is so much going on.' Having added this, and initialled the minute, Churchill then added a postscript: 'I have only just seen No. 348. I am so glad you are acting already.'

General Ironside: diary
(*'The Ironside Diaries, 1937–1940'*)

29 May 1940

I dined with Winston in the evening with him and his wife alone. He was in great form. He showed me Louis Spears' letter that had come in from Paris. There is a good deal of defeatist attitude amongst the French. Weygand is a good hard conscientious worker. Georges is purely 'negative' and does not function very much.

Captain Pim[1]: recollection
(*Pim papers*)

29 May 1940

It was late on the evening of the 29th May while on duty in the War Room that I had an opportunity of asking Mr Churchill, who although then Prime Minister, was still residing at Admiralty House and who was in the War Room eight and ten times a day, for four days leave to enable me to give a hand in the evacuation. Mr Churchill not only approved my request but said, and I remember his words, 'God bless you; I wish I were going with you myself.' There is no doubt that service of this sort was dear to his heart – it was at once an action outside any known rules and such as he always particularly loved.

Winston S. Churchill to Paul Reynaud
(*Premier papers, 3/175*)

29 May 1940
11.45 p.m.

We have evacuated nearly 50,000 from Dunkirk and beaches, and hope another 30,000 tonight. Front may be beaten in at any time or piers, beaches and shipping rendered unusable by air attack and also by artillery fire from the South-West. No one can tell how long present good flow will last, or how much we can save for future. We wish French troops to share in evacuation to

---

[1] Richard Pike Pim, 1900–87. An Ulsterman. Served in the Royal Navy Volunteer Reserve, 1916–18. Royal Irish Constabulary, 1921. Civil Service, Northern Ireland, 1922. On the staff of the Northern Ireland Prime Minister, 1938. In charge of Churchill's map room at the Admiralty, at 10 Downing Street, and during the Prime Minister's travels overseas, 1939–45. Knighted, 1945. Inspector-General, Royal Ulster Constabulary. Member of Council, Winston Churchill Memorial Trust, 1965–9. In 1968 he generously gave me access to his unpublished diaries of the war years.

fullest possible extent, and Admiralty have been instructed to aid French Marine as required. We do not know how many will be forced to capitulate, but we must share this loss together as best we can, and above all bear it without reproaches arising from inevitable confusion, stresses and strains.

As soon as we have reorganised our evacuated troops, and prepared forces necessary to safeguard our life against threatened and perhaps imminent invasion we shall build up a new BEF from St Nazaire. I am bringing regulars from India and Palestine. Australians and Canadians are arriving soon. At present we are removing equipment South of Amiens beyond what is needed for five Divisions. But this is only to get into order and meet impending shock, and we shall shortly send you new scheme for reinforcement of our troops in France. I send this in all comradeship. Do not hesitate to speak frankly to me.

David Lloyd George to Winston S. Churchill
(*Churchill papers, 20/111*)

29 May 1940
Secret and Personal

My dear Winston,

You were good enough yesterday to ask me if I would be prepared to enter the War Cabinet if you secured the adhesion of Mr Chamberlain to the proposal. It is the first time you have approached me personally on the subject and I can well understand the reason for your hesitancy, for, in the course of our interview, you made it quite clear that if Chamberlain interposed his veto on the ground of personal resentment over past differences you could not proceed with the offer. This is not a firm offer. Until it is definite I cannot consider it.

I am sure you will be just enough to realise that the experience I have already had in this war justifies my reply to your conditional inquiry. Since the war began I have in public thrice offered to help the Government in any capacity, however humble. No notice has been taken of my tenders. I have never been consulted. I have never been invited even to sit on a committee. Since you became Prime Minister I offered to do my best to help in organising the food supplies of this country. I have acquired considerable knowledge and experience both in Peace as well as in War in that line. At the request of your personal friends I put forward alternative proposals for the intensive production of food in this country, and I suggested the part I might play in directing this essential branch of national service. Nothing came of this scheme. I have not even been informed of the reason for its rejection. I say this in order to show that it was due to no unwillingness on my part that you found it impossible to utilise my services. I apprehend that Party and personal considerations frustrated your wishes. I cannot be put in that position again. I am no office seeker. I am genuinely anxious to help to extricate my country from the most terrible disaster into which it has ever been plunged by the ineptitude of her rulers. Several of the architects of this catastrophe are still leading members of your Government, and two of them are in the Cabinet that directs the war.

Like millions of my fellow-countrymen I say to you that, if in any way you think I can help, I am at your call. But if that call is tentative and qualified I shall not know what answer to give.

Believe me,
Ever sincerely,
D. Lloyd George

Winston S. Churchill to David Lloyd George
(Churchill papers, 20/11)

29 May 1940

My dear LG,

I have just received your letter of to-day. I am sorry that the same difficulties in regard to persons which you mentioned to me are also only too present elsewhere. I cannot complain in any way of what you say in your letter. The Government I have formed is founded upon the Leaders of the three Parties, and like you I have no Party of my own. I have received a very great deal of help from Chamberlain; his kindness and courtesy to me in our new relation have touched me. I have joined hands with him, and must act with perfect loyalty. As you say, the inquiry I made of you yesterday could only be indeterminate, and I could not ask you to go further than you have done in your letter.

With regard to the organization of the food supplies of this country, of which my personal friends had some talk with you, I can assure you that no personal or Party difficulties have frustrated its consideration. The Ministry of Agriculture was discussed and one of my friends made representations to you. It was only after you had taken the decision that you did not at that time contemplate sharing responsibilities involved in joining the administration, that I made another selection, without making any stipulations with the new Minister.[1] The alternative project of organization of Food Supplies could well be taken up on another occasion. I have simply been so over-pressed by terrible events, that I have not had life or strength to address myself to it.

Thank you very much for what you say in your last paragraph and I trust

---

[1] Robert Hudson, see page 1220, note 3.

that we shall keep in personal contact, so that I may acquaint you with the situation as it deepens. I always have the warmest feelings of regard and respect for you.

Yours ever
Winston S. Churchill

John Martin to his wife
(*Martin papers*)

30 May 1940

The PM's confidence and energy are amazing. 'Nobody left his presence without feeling a braver man' was said of Pitt; but it is no less true of him.

John George Spencer-Churchill[1]: *recollection*
(*'Crowded Canvas', pages 162–3*)

30 May 1940

Still soaking wet, and in full battle kit, I got on a train at Dover and travelled up to London. I noticed two Staff officers in the same railway coach. They were General Pownall and Captain Lord Munster,[2] ADC to General Lord Gort, who looked very smartly dressed and 'Staff'. I felt terribly unkempt by comparison, especially considering that my mission was to the Prime Minister.

Not knowing Lord Munster very well, I did not talk to him on the journey. On arrival at Victoria Station I went straight to the adjoining Grosvenor Hotel and shaved. Then, without wasting further time, I took a taxi to the Admiralty. I arrived and stepped into the lift for the Prime Minister's

---

[1] John George Spencer-Churchill, 1910–92. Known as 'Johnny'. Churchill's nephew; elder son of Jack and Lady Gwendeline Churchill. Educated at Harrow. In 1929 he travelled with his uncle (and his cousin Randolph) to Canada and the United States. Artist and designer of murals; in 1938 he painted the Marlborough Pavilion at Chartwell. Served in the Royal Engineers, 1939–45. Major, 1945. In 1961 he published his memoirs, *Crowded Canvas*.

[2] Geoffrey William Richard Hugh FitzClarence, 1906–75. Succeeded his uncle as 5th Earl of Munster, 1928, while still at school. Paymaster-General, 1938–9. Parliamentary Under-Secretary of State for War, February–September 1939. Captain, Grenadier Guards. ADC and Military Assistant to Lord Gort, 1939–41. Parliamentary Under-Secretary of State for India and Burma, 1943–4; at the Home Office, 1944–5; at the Colonial Office, 1951–4. Minister without Portfolio, 1954–7. Privy Councillor, 1954. HM Lieutenant, Surrey, 1955–7.

apartments at the same moment as Lord Munster who, it turned out, had been sent over by Lord Gort on a similar mission.

Our reception at 8 a.m. by my uncle and aunt, both of whom were in dressing gowns, was a moment never to be forgotten. The contrast between Lord Munster's uniform and mine was rather acute because he, I recollect, was in jackboots and Staff dress appropriate to his function as ADC to the Commander-in-Chief of the BEF, and dry, having been put aboard a special boat I suppose. I was in ordinary battledress, absolutely sodden and thoroughly shaken by my ordeals.

'Johnny!' exclaimed my uncle delightedly, 'I see you have come straight from battle!'

Preferring to give way to my fellow-emissary, whom I considered to be far more important, I replied: 'I think Lord Munster has also come . . .' But my uncle was determined to hear my story first. 'Who sent you and what have you got to say about the situation?' he asked. 'I believe we have taken off about eighty thousand men and still have another two hundred and fifty thousand.'

'I have been sent by General Alexander,[1] 1st Division Commander,' I said, 'to say that in his opinion the most urgent need is for small boats to get the troops off the beaches out to the bigger ships.'

My uncle next wanted to know why I was so wet. 'Have you come straight out of the sea?' he asked.

'Yes,' I told him, 'and I will be pleased to go back again in a fast motor-boat to give everyone encouragement.'

At long last Lord Munster was able to get a word in edgeways, 'I have exactly the same message to report,' he said. 'The C in C thinks that the small boats can be our salvation.'

Defence Committee: minutes
(*Cabinet papers, 69/1*)

30 May 1940   Admiralty
10.15 a.m.

The Prime Minister said that the principle must be established that the British and French share the available shipping. He recognised that the embarkation of French soldiers might reduce the number of British who could be saved, but for the good of the common cause this must be accepted.

The Prime Minister suggested that a number of men who had been cut off might fight their way down to the shore at points between Dunkirk and the Somme.

[1] Lieutenant-General Harold Alexander (see page 210, note 2).

Lieutenant-Colonel Ian Jacob[1]: *recollection*
('The Atlantic', March 1965, page 82)

30 May 1940

The Prime Minister questioned General Pownall and listened to the plans. No one in the room imagined that they could be successful if the German armoured divisions supported by the Luftwaffe pressed their attack. The perimeter would be broken as it thinned out, and there would be carnage on the beaches. Churchill never gave a sign of weakness. Nothing but encouragement and resolve showed in his face or his voice.

We felt that he would have liked to be fighting on the beaches himself.

War Cabinet: minutes
(*Cabinet papers, 65/7*)

30 May 1940
12.30 p.m.
10 Downing Street

The Prime Minister said that the latest information was that 77,000 officers and men withdrawn from the BEF had reached this country, and that another 4,000 were en route. Withdrawal was proceeding all the time, but the conditions were difficult. The Admiralty had made a great effort to provide a large number of small boats, but still more were needed.

He had discussed the whole matter that morning with the Service Ministers, the Chiefs of Staff and Lieutenant-General Pownall, who had returned to this country on Lord Gort's directions. It was thought that not more than 60,000 British troops were now left behind the line of perimeter defence which ran from a point between Gravelines and Dunkirk to Nieuport. Practically all our troops were now behind this line; small rearguards might have been cut off, but it was not thought that many troops had been lost in this way.

The position in regard to the French was that one French Corps had withdrawn within the perimeter defence. The other French Divisions had said that they were too tired to continue the march to the coast, and must be regarded as cut off. It was clear that if our troops had waited any longer for the French they would have suffered the same fate.

The perimeter defence was, of course, being held to enable French troops as well as our own, to be withdrawn. There had been a conference on the matter

---

[1] Edward Ian Claud Jacob, 1899–1993. Second Lieutenant, Royal Engineers, 1918. Military Assistant Secretary, Committee of Imperial Defence, 1938. Lieutenant-Colonel, 1939. Military Assistant Secretary to the War Cabinet, 1939–45. CBE, 1942. Retired from the Army, 1946, with the rank of Lieutenant-General. Controller, European Services, BBC, 1946. Knighted, 1946. Chief Staff Officer to the Minister of Defence, and Deputy Secretary to the Cabinet, 1952. Director-General of the BBC, 1952–60.

May 1940

with the French authorities on the previous day, and the beaches west of Dunkirk had been allotted to the French. Later, owing to the French troops near Gravelines having been driven back, these beaches had come under shell-fire, and a third of the beaches east of Dunkirk had been allotted to the French. The French troops on the beaches were not in formed bodies. At one time the position in regard to the embarkation of French troops had threatened serious trouble; but matters had been eased.

The troops first evacuated had consisted mainly of line of communication troops, but a considerable number of fighting troops had now been successfully embarked. It was, of course, necessary to leave good troops to hold the perimeter line, since, if this was forced, further evacuation would be impossible. It was thought that the perimeter line might be held for, say, another two or three days. After that time the enemy would probably bring up artillery, and the beaches would be under fire.

The Prime Minister read to his colleagues the telegram which he had sent to M. Reynaud on the previous night with regard to the progress of evacuation and the steps to be taken, when we had reorganised our evacuated troops, to build up a new British Expeditionary Force in France.

Attention was drawn to a further message from M. Reynaud, reporting General Weygand's views on the position (telegram No. 308 DIPP from Paris).

In discussion, it was suggested that it might be well that the Prime Minister should send a further message to M. Reynaud drawing attention to the number of encouraging features in the situation. The following were mentioned:–

(1) The very great successes achieved by the RAF on the 29th May. The enemy losses had been 70 aircraft (confirmed) shot down, against a loss of 14 of our machines. Thirty-seven aircraft had been shot down by a single squadron of Defiants,[1] without loss.

(2) The encouraging figures of production of aircraft engines from the Rolls-Royce factory.

(3) Telegram No. 269 DIPP from Belgrade, which reported that an important Yugoslav, who had just returned from Germany, said that conditions there were terribly bad, and that Austria was crowded with wounded, which was having a serious effect on the morale of the people.

(4) Telegram No. 707 from Rome reporting that a German, before leaving for Germany, had stated that, although Germany was winning the war easily, her losses were so heavy that she could not continue for long at such a rate.

The War Cabinet agreed that the Prime Minister should send an encouraging message to M. Reynaud on the lines suggested.

[1] The Defiant was a fighter with a power-operated turret.

Sir Alexander Cadogan: diary
(*'The Diaries of Sir Alexander Cadogan'*)

30 May 1940

Cabinet 12.30. WSC produced much better instructions to Gort, ordering him to come away before the end and giving some latitude about final capitulation.

Winston S. Churchill to Lord Gort
(*Cabinet papers, 65/7*)

30 May 1940
2 p.m.

Continue to defend the present perimeter to the utmost in order to cover maximum evacuation now proceeding well. Report every three hours through La Panne. If we can still communicate we shall send you an order to return to England with such Officers as you may choose at the moment when we deem your Command so reduced that it can be handed over to a Corps Commander. You should now nominate this Commander. If communications are broken you are to hand over and return as specified when your effective fighting force does not exceed the equivalent of three Divisions. This is in accordance with correct military procedure, and no personal discretion is left to you in the matter. On Political grounds it would be a needless triumph to the enemy to capture you when only a small force remained under your orders. The Corps Commander chosen by you should be ordered to carry on the defence, in conjunction with the French, and evacuation whether from Dunkirk or the beaches, but when in his judgment no further organised evacuation is possible and no further proportionate damage can be inflicted upon the enemy, he is authorised in consultation with the Senior French Commander to capitulate formally to avoid useless slaughter.

The Cabinet have approved this telegram.

John Colville: diary
(*Colville papers*)

30 May 1940
4 p.m.

Back to No. 10 by four o'clock and heard that half the BEF were now away but that Dunkirk, the port of embarkation, was scarcely usable any more.

Winston S. Churchill to A. V. Alexander
(*Churchill papers, 20/13*)

30 May 1940

What measures have been taken to seize all Italian ships at the moment of war? How many are there in British ports, and what can be done about them on the seas or in foreign ports? Will you kindly pass this to the proper Department immediately?

WSC

War Cabinet: minutes
(*Cabinet papers, 65/7*)

30 May 1940
5.30 p.m.

The Prime Minister said that he had received conflicting accounts of the numbers of the British Expeditionary Force who had been evacuated. The War Office figure of the numbers evacuated to Dover, Ramsgate, Margate and Harwich since the 20th May were as follows:–

British fit	92,642
British wounded	8,152
Allies	4,447
Total	105,241

The Admiralty had given a figure of 86,000.

Later in the Meeting the First Lord of the Admiralty said that the Admiralty figure for the number landed at all the ports up to 12 noon that day was 101,154.

The Prime Minister asked that the War Office and the Admiralty should, in future, collaborate in computing the numbers of British and other troops evacuated from France, with a view to submitting an agreed report to the War Cabinet.

The Prime Minister read a report from Dunkirk stating that a ship had been sunk there that afternoon under conditions which suggested that it might be difficult to continue to use the harbour; that fog was seriously interfering with the evacuation; and that progress was being delayed by the withdrawal of the more modern destroyers.

The Chief of Naval Staff[1] said that he had no knowledge of this report and that every available destroyer was being used.

[1] Admiral Pound.

The Chief of Naval Staff said that there had been definite signs of German activity on the Norwegian coast. There were also indications that motor-boats had been collected at Bremen and Hamburg. Meanwhile, the Germans were known to have an organised force of ships at Vigo. The dispositions to deal with this latter threat were described. It might also be significant that the Germans had left one particular stretch opposite our coast clear of mines. The position in this matter had been brought to the notice of the Commander-in-Chief, Home Forces.[1] It was hoped that the production of anti-tank mines for laying on beaches would start in a week's time.

The Prime Minister doubted whether a raid on a large scale could be carried out by fast motor-boats. These craft would have to come over in flotillas, if they were to put ashore any useful number of men at any one point. The Navy would have to make every endeavour to intercept such raids on the high seas.

The Prime Minister thought that we should not hesitate to contaminate our beaches with gas if this course would be to our advantage. We had the right to do what we liked with our own territory.

War Cabinet: Confidential Annex
(*Cabinet papers, 65/13*)

30 May 1940
5.30 p.m.

The Prime Minister read a report which he had received from General Spears on the condition of the French Army South of Amiens. The French troops here had been fighting hard for eight days and were very hard pressed. The French black troops had proved unsatisfactory. General Weygand had given the odds as three to one against the French. Time had never been so precious, and he (General Weygand) had begged that the British should send every possible soldier to the Somme. One British Division would make all the difference. General Spears had pointed out that this was quite impossible, but General Weygand had again repeated his fear of the certainty of an onslaught on the French Army, concluding with the words 'Nous sommes à la limite'.

---

[1] On 27 May 1940 General Ironside had become Commander-in-Chief, Home Forces.

The Prime Minister drew the attention of the War Cabinet to the requests which were being received from the French for further Divisions to help on the Somme Front, for RAF assistance, for co-operation in appeals to President Roosevelt and for concessions to Italy, and said that he could not resist the conclusion that, when we refused these requests, as we must, the French would use these refusals as an excuse for giving up the struggle.

In his own view, it would be quite unreasonable to denude the essential defences of this country to send such small fully trained and equipped forces as were available to fight on the Somme front, where they could not possibly make any appreciable effect in relation to the large German forces which would be shortly available for pressing an attack. When we were able to organise and re-equip the men now being withdrawn from France; when the regular battalions now being withdrawn from overseas had arrived; when further Dominion forces had reached this country; then indeed we should not need all our available forces for home defence. We should therefore certainly tell the French that, if they could hold out in the meantime, we should send them help as soon as we were able to do so, but we should make it quite clear that we had no forces that we could send at the present moment. He suggested that he and the Lord Privy Seal, accompanied by the Chief of the Imperial General Staff, should go to Paris the next day to explain the position to the French on these lines. The meeting should be treated as a meeting of the Supreme War Council.

There was general agreement with this view.

Winston S. Churchill: recollection
(*'Their Finest Hour'*, page 95)

30 May 1940
11 p.m.

On the 30th I held a meeting of the three Service Ministers and the Chiefs of Staff in the Admiralty War Room. We considered the events of the day on the Belgian coast. The total number of troops brought off had risen to 120,000, including only 6,000 French; 860 vessels of all kinds were at work.

A message from Admiral Wake-Walker[1] at Dunkirk said that, in spite of intense bombardment and air attack, 4,000 men had been embarked in the previous hour. He also thought that Dunkirk itself would probably be untenable by the next day.

---

[1] William Frederic Wake-Walker, 1888–1945. On active service, 1914–18. Captain, 1927. Rear-Admiral, Minelaying, 1939–40. CBE, 1941. Vice-Admiral, 1942. Third Sea Lord and Controller, Admiralty, from 1942 to his death. Knighted, 1943. Admiral, 1945.

Defence Committee: minutes
(*Cabinet papers, 69/1*)

30 May 1940 Admiralty
11 p.m.

The Prime Minister emphasized the urgent necessity of getting off more French troops. If we failed to do so it might do irreparable harm to the relations between ourselves and our Allies. When the British strength was reduced to that of a corps it would be desirable to tell Lord Gort to embark and return to England, leaving a Corps Commander in charge. The British Army would have to stick it out as long as possible so that the evacuation of the French could continue. General Blanchard should if possible be embarked with Lord Gort.

President Roosevelt to Winston S. Churchill
(*Premier papers, 3/476/1*)

30 May 1940 The White House

My dear Churchill:–
Ever so many thanks for that remarkably interesting story of the Battle of the River Plate – a grand job by your three cruisers.[1]

You are much in my thoughts. I need not tell you that.

As ever yours,
Franklin D. Roosevelt

Winston S. Churchill to General Ismay
(*Churchill papers, 20/13*)

31 May 1940

A civil war in Ireland arising out of a German descent would bring various advantages to us:–

1. We should bomb and fight the German Air Force under conditions specially favourable to us, and costly to them.

2. We should take Berehaven, &c., for our own use.

3. We should have split the Sein Feiners effectively and should have the greater part of the population on our side for the first time in history.

---

[1] On 7 May 1940, three days before becoming Prime Minister, Churchill had sent Roosevelt an advance copy of the official account of the Battle of the River Plate in December 1939, in which the German pocket battleship *Admiral Graf Spee* had been forced out of action by *Achilles*, *Ajax* and *Exeter*. She scuttled herself in Uruguayan water in the River Plate, off Montevideo.

MAY 1940   205

But much depends on prompt attack upon the enemy Air Force, who have invaded, or on the way there.

AT 8.30 ON THE MORNING of 31 May 1940, Churchill left London by air for Paris, for a meeting of the Supreme War Council.

Captain Berkeley: diary
(*Berkeley papers*)

31 May 1940[1]

We left at 8.30 from Hendon. PM introduced me to his wife and plastered me with compliments before an assembly of some 20 ministers and generals! We put our eggs in two Flamingoes: PM, Ismay and Tommy Thompson[2] in one, Attlee, CIGS and myself in the other. We have to go a long way round now: down to Weymouth to pick an escort of nine Hurricanes (lovely darting hornets), across to Jersey landfall west of St Malo, then due east to Villacoublay near Versailles, where we got lost at the wrong end of the vast aerodrome. Embassy at 1, a hurried lunch with Thompson and our liaison detachment, then SWC at the Ministère de la Guerre at 2.30, preceded by a private talk between Winston and Reynaud.

The atmosphere was bad: utterances unexceptional except one or two moments when recriminations were very near the surface and almost audible, but no sort of good spirit on the French side. They looked, said Ismay, 'spent' – even Weygand, who is the last hope. Pétain[3] looks his 84 years, and took little part. Chief items were Narvik, Dunkirk (time-table for last stages of evacuation), further British collaboration on the continent (PM refusing to

---

[1] Captain Berkeley wrote this diary entry five days later.
[2] Charles Ralfe Thompson, 1894–1966. Known as 'Tommy'. Midshipman, 1911. Served mainly in submarines, 1915–31. Flag Lieutenant and Flag Commander to the Board of Admiralty, 1936–40. OBE, 1938. Retired with the rank of Commander, 1939. Personal Assistant to the Minister of Defence (Churchill), 1940–5. CMG, 1945.
[3] Henri Philippe Pétain, 1856–1951. Entered the French Army, 1878. Colonel, August 1914. Commanded the 6th Division of Infantry at the Battle of the Marne. Commanded the 2nd Army, 1915. In charge of the defence of Verdun, 1916. General-in-Chief, 1917–18; he impressed Churchill in April 1918 by his determination to throw back the German onslaught. Marshal of France, 1918. Inspector-General of the French Army, 1922–31. Minister of War, 1934. Ambassador to Spain, March 1939 to May 1940. Minister of State and Vice-President of the Council, May–June 1940. Chief of the French State (with the seat of government at Vichy), June 1940 to June 1944. Detained by the Germans after he tried to cross into France in the summer of 1944. Brought to trial in France in 1945 and sentenced to death; his sentence having been commuted to life imprisonment, he died in prison six years later.

commit himself), Italy. The discussion was appallingly untidy, and PM resolutely spoke bad French all the way through (he does even when talking things over with HE[1] and Ismay in the embassy!). We wound up with mutual assurances that we would never give in and parted, Ismay, Redman[2] and I to draft conclusions in the Crillon, Beit[3] and Coleridge[4] to draft a record. Later Ismay returned from the Embassy and we all dined together. But he had to go back and sit with Winston at 1.30 a.m.

Winston was ebullient as ever. When we started back he insisted on pacing round the aerodrome to review our nine Hurricanes, tramping through the tall grass in the flurry of propellers with his cigar like a pennant. Spears attended the meeting and was much in evidence. He is muscling in on a very high plane and causing tremendous indignation. An agreeable person but, it seems, a ruffian. I hear sad accounts of Desmond Morton, Prof. Lindemann and Brendan Bracken also. PM does like glib imposters!

General Ismay: recollection
(*'The Memoirs of Lord Ismay'*, page 133)

31 May 1940

As we were standing round the table waiting for the discussion to begin, a dejected-looking old man in plain clothes shuffled towards me, stretched out his hand and said: 'Pétain'. It was hard to believe that this was the great Marshal of France whose name was associated with the epic of Verdun and who had done more than anyone else to restore the morale of the French Army after the mutinies of 1917. He now looked senile, uninspiring and defeatist.

---

[1] His Excellency (the British Ambassador to France, Sir Ronald Campbell).

[2] A member of the War Cabinet Secretariat.

[3] Alfred Beit, 1903–94. Son of Churchill's friend Sir Alfred Beit, whom he succeeded as 2nd Baronet in 1930, and himself a Conservative MP, 1931–45. In 1939 he married Clementine Mitford, a cousin of Clementine Churchill. Air Ministry representative on the three-service mission to Paris, 1940 (with Colonel Redman and Commander Coleridge, RN). Resident in the Republic of Ireland since the war. Trustee of the Beit Foundation for scientific research.

[4] Richard Duke Coleridge, 1905–84. Entered the Royal Navy, 1919. Seconded to the Offices of the War Cabinet and Ministry of Defence, French General Headquarters, Vincennes, May–June 1940; War Cabinet Offices, London, July 1940 to May 1941. Joint Staff Mission, Washington, 1941. British Joint Staff and Combined Chiefs of Staff, 1942–5 (attended the conferences in Washington, 1942, and Quebec, 1943). OBE, 1944. British Joint Services Mission, Washington, 1948. CBE, 1951. Executive Secretary, North Atlantic Treaty Organisation, 1952–70. Succeeded his father as 4th Baron, 1955.

May 1940

Supreme War Council: minutes
(*Cabinet papers, 99/3*)

31 May 1940

Mr Winston Churchill said that there were several urgent questions which must be decided at once. The first was the question of Narvik. At Narvik there were 4,000 Poles, two Battalions of the French Foreign Legion and one division of Chasseurs Alpins – a total of about 16,000 men, or perhaps a few more. In addition, the British had one Brigade of Guards and a few non-divisional units at Bodo. Narvik had now been captured with small loss to the Allies, while some 200 Germans had been taken prisoner. But the British Government was nevertheless of the considered opinion that the Narvik area should be evacuated at once. It would be very difficult to maintain our troops there; naval losses were being suffered daily; and the destroyers immobilized in Northern Norway, as well as some 100 anti-aircraft guns, were badly wanted elsewhere. Provisional arrangements had therefore been made for an evacuation, beginning on the 2nd June. If the French Government agreed, this plan would be proceeded with, the French force being repatriated by the British Navy. It would be necessary to bring the King of Norway from Tromso to Great Britain, and also to bring away such Norwegian troops as desired to leave, or alternatively to enable them to move into the hills and disperse. It was very important that the Allies should not be hindered in their life-and-death struggle in France by operations in Norway.

M. Reynaud said that the French Government agreed to the evacuation of the Allied forces from Norway. The destroyers would be urgently required in the Mediterranean in the event of war with Italy. The 16,000 men would be very valuable on the line of the Aisne and the Somme, and the anti-aircraft equipment was also urgently needed.

From the political standpoint, a useful purpose would doubtless be served if two or three Norwegian Regiments could be brought back to fight in France. This would have great symbolical value.

Mr Churchill said that during the last few days there had been considerable losses in destroyers. Four had been sunk off Dunkirk, and eight or nine others damaged. Destroyers were very much in demand at the moment, and it would therefore not be possible to guarantee the destination of those that would be set free by the evacuation of Narvik. Presumably they would be urgently required off the north-western coasts of France.

As the French and British Governments were in agreement about Narvik, telegrams should be sent at once to Lord Cork and to the Norwegians, informing them of this decision.

M. Reynaud agreed. He asked what arrangements were proposed regarding the transport of troops from Norway.

Mr Churchill said that the British would undertake this task and provide the necessary transport. The French troops would be transported direct to France as far as possible; but there might have to be some re-organisation in the Clyde owing to the probable confusion at the moment of embarkation.

M. Reynaud explained that if he insisted on the return of French troops direct to France, it was because the battle of the Aisne and the Somme was a race against time.

Mr Churchill then turned to the situation at Dunkirk. The position there, as far as he knew it, was that up to noon on that day, 165,000 men had been evacuated by sea. This was an extraordinary feat. It proved the non-existence of German sea-power and the limitations of German air-power. The Germans had done their best to hinder the evacuation by air action; there had been terrible scenes at the ports and on the beaches. Nevertheless, the German Air Force had been held off or beaten. The total of evacuated included 10,000 wounded, but so far only 15,000 French soldiers.

M. Reynaud drew attention to the disparity in numbers as between the French and the British. Of 220,000 British troops in the Low Countries, 150,000 had been evacuated, whereas of 200,000 French troops only 15,000 had been taken off. He was most anxious, from the point of view of French public opinion, that the French should be withdrawn in greater numbers; otherwise the public might draw unfortunate conclusions.

Mr Churchill said that he was very much aware of this factor. But they had to realise the great difficulties that arose when Armies were thus forced to retire; these difficulties had been greatly enhanced by the Belgian desertion, which had forced the British to cover the whole left flank. The Allied troops were now formed in a semi-circle, with the equivalent of three British Divisions in the central segment, and French troops on either flank. The British troops were regular divisions, among the best troops in the BEF. They had suffered some casualties, but were far from broken. They would act as a rear-guard. The French troops consisted of two divisions of General Fagalde's Corps and two much-reduced divisions under General de la Laurencie.[1] Orders had now been given that the evacuation of French troops should as from to-day take precedence over that of British troops.

M. Reynaud said that the French were fully conscious of the disastrous consequences of the Belgian defection; he would be glad if the British Government could see their way to laying greater emphasis upon them.

Mr Churchill said that he would like the French to understand that the

---

[1] General de Laurencie commanded the French Third Corps immediately to the south of the British Expeditionary Force. A Captain during the Battle of the Somme in 1916, when he met General Spears, who described him as 'certainly the quickest-witted Frenchman I have ever met, which is saying a great deal' (*Prelude to Dunkirk*, page 76). Opposed to the Vichy Government and imprisoned.

chief reason why the British had got a lot of their people off first was because there had been many Line-of-Communication troops and other rear units in the back area who were available for immediate evacuation. The proportion of fighting troops evacuated was much smaller. In addition, as far as he knew, the French troops had, up to the present, had no orders to evacuate. One of the chief reasons why he had come to Paris was to make sure that the same orders were now given to the French troops as had been given to the British. The three divisions who were now holding the centre would cover the evacuation of all the Allied forces within the perimeter; those that remained outside must already be considered as lost.

M. Reynaud said that he had nothing to add, provided that there was no great disproportion between the numbers of French and British troops evacuated. The point was of considerable political significance.

Mr Churchill said that he had spoken to Lord Gort on the telephone yesterday and had laid stress on this factor, which was of equal political and military significance.

General Dill had already informed General Weygand that Lord Gort had been ordered to continue to hold the position as long as possible, in order to cover the evacuation of the maximum number of Allied troops. But Dunkirk could not be held for more than another 48 hours at the most, if only on account of the growing shortage of water, food and ammunition. Orders had therefore been given for an evacuation, and he would be glad if similar orders could be given to the French Commanders-in-Chief at Dunkirk.

General Weygand said that instructions in this sense were already being acted upon. General Blanchard and Lord Gort were in close touch, and Admiral Abrial, the Commander-in-Chief at Dunkirk, was also co-operating closely. All three were doing their utmost to ensure that Dunkirk would be covered and defended as long as possible, with a view to facilitating the evacuation.

Mr Churchill said that we had now a hope of avoiding anything in the nature of a capitulation, although the Germans might at any moment shatter that hope. The British intended to fight their way back to the very edge of the sea. No doubt part of the rear-guard would be crushed, but there was a good hope that all except the rear-guard would be evacuated.

General Weygand said that he heartily shared this hope. But the French troops were the furthest removed from Dunkirk, since they were holding the southern area of the perimeter. One part had succeeded in crossing the line of hills about Cassel; the other part had not crossed this barrier. The Germans now claimed that they had taken General Prioux prisoner. They had captured Mont des Cats, and it was most unlikely that the troops south of the Mont Kemmel line would be able to escape, although those north of the line had a good chance. The French Commanders south of the line had proclaimed that they would fight to the end. Their troops would probably be exterminated.

Mr Churchill said that the British would keep their three divisions on the perimeter in order to enable as many French troops to get away as possible. This would be the British contribution to the heavy Allied losses that must inevitably be suffered under such conditions. There would, he hoped, be no reproaches as between comrades-in-arms faced with a great disaster.

General Weygand put in a plea that the British should hold out as long as they possibly could, even after the four French divisions within the perimeter had been embarked, in order that those troops still outside the perimeter should have every possible chance of getting away too. He urged that the coast should not be cleared until there was no more hope, that is, until the French force in the south had either fought its way to the sea or been exterminated.

Mr Churchill said that in that case, some help would be needed from the two French divisions now on the perimeter.

General Weygand said that those divisions were under the orders of Admiral Abrial, who was co-ordinating the defence.

Mr Churchill asked whether they would still be available as a garrison at Dunkirk after all other troops within the perimeter had been evacuated.

General Weygand said that they would be available until it was no longer humanly possible to stay or to save any more troops. The naval authorities would then try to take the garrison off.

Admiral Darlan[1] said that that would be the moment for carrying out demolitions and blocking the harbour.

Mr Churchill said that there was a secondary point which he would like to bring forward: as the British troops within the perimeter were now of a strength hardly above that of an Army Corps, the British authorities had decided that it would be better to evacuate their Army Commander and to hand the command to a very competent Army Corps commander[2] who was

---

[1] Jean Louis Xavier François Darlan, 1881–1942. Entered the French Navy as a cadet, 1899. On active service, 1914–18 (three citations). Captain, 1918. Admiral, 1932. Honorary British knighthood, 1938. Commander-in-Chief of all French naval forces, April 1939 to June 1940. Minister of the Navy and Mercantile Marine, following the establishment of the French Government in Vichy, June 1940 to April 1942; also, under Marshal Pétain, Vice-President of the Council of Ministers, Secretary of State for Foreign Affairs, February 1941 to April 1942, and Minister for National Defence, 1942. Gave his support to the Allied landings in North Africa (which he was visiting by chance, to see his sick son), 8 November 1942. Chief of State in French Africa, 11 November until his assassination in Algiers, 24 December 1942.

[2] Harold Rupert Leofric George Alexander, 1891–1969. Educated at Harrow and Sandhurst. On active service, 1914–18 (wounded three times, despatches five times, DSO, Military Cross). Lieutenant-General commanding 1st Corps, 1940 (despatches). General Officer Commanding Southern Command, 1940–2; Burma, 1942; the Middle East, 1942–3. Commander-in-Chief, 18th Army Group, North Africa, 1943; Allied Armies in Italy (15th Army Group), 1943–4. Knighted, 1942. Field Marshal, 1944. Supreme Allied Commander, Mediterranean Theatre, 1944–5. Created Viscount, 1946. Knight of the Garter, 1946. Governor-General of Canada, 1946–52. Created Earl Alexander of Tunis, 1952. Minister of Defence (in Churchill's second premiership), 1952–4. Order of Merit, 1959. In 1962 he published *The Alexander Memoirs, 1940–1945*.

now on the spot. Lord Gort would leave that same night. He suggested that similar orders might be given to General Blanchard.

General Weygand said that this would be more difficult for the French, as they had many troops south of the Kemmel line, under the orders of two Army Corps Commanders. He must leave it to General Blanchard to decide who should take over the command from him. He suggested giving General Blanchard orders analogous to those given to Lord Gort; General Blanchard and Admiral Abrial would then consult as to which Corps Commander should take over. General Blanchard might decide to leave two Corps Commanders in charge, one north and one south of the danger area.

Mr Churchill said that the British Government had found itself compelled to order Lord Gort to evacuate the fighting troops before the wounded, of which there were many thousands within the perimeter. It was only the dire circumstances of the war that had made such an order necessary for the sake of the future: the able-bodied could be taken off in greater numbers than stretcher cases, and numbers were vital for continuing the struggle. It was hoped, however, that American aid might perhaps be enlisted to look after and succour the wounded left behind.

It must be understood that at any time the process of evacuation might be cut short by a breach of the flanks covering Dunkirk, or by heavy bombardment of the port. They were up against the fortunes of war. If present hopes were confirmed, 200,000 able-bodied troops might be got away. This would be almost a miracle: four days ago he would not have wagered on more than 50,000 as a maximum. He must add, however, that the British would lose all their equipment with the exception of small arms and personal equipment. Some 1,000 British field guns, all the heavy guns, and all the mechanical transport would have to be left behind: everything except what an Infantry soldier could carry with him. Yet it was precisely equipment of which the British were so terribly short; for example, they had now lost more than double the number of guns that existed in the United Kingdom.

M. Reynaud said that he would like, on behalf of the French Government, to thank and praise the British Navy and the Royal Air Force for their wonderful work in connection with the evacuation.

Mr Churchill thanked M. Reynaud warmly for this tribute. It was clear, he hoped, that the British intended to fight on alongside the French with what resources were left to them. But until the troops had been evacuated it would not be possible to say what their value might be, nor to what extent they could be re-equipped. Many of those who had got away were L of C troops or rear units; the proportion of fighting troops was not yet known. Re-organisation and re-arming would be necessary, and some interval for this purpose was imperative.

The troops that had returned to England were in good spirits, of high morale, and anxious to return to the fight. Everyone had been immensely struck with their bearing. They felt that despite the confusion, they had dealt the enemy a severe blow and proved themselves superior whenever they had come face to face on fair terms. This must indeed have been the case or they could not have got back to the coast, and the gap caused by the Belgian desertion could not otherwise have been filled.

He wished to emphasise that great injury had been done to the German might. Large numbers of tanks had been destroyed. The German armoured divisions were exhausted and thrown out of gear. The Germans must have suffered heavy losses, otherwise they would have come sweeping on. The anti-tank regiment of the 48th Division had destroyed 44 tanks; one officer, with one two-pounder, had knocked out seven. He felt convinced that the Germans had suffered severely, and that a pause was likely.

The picture would not be complete without mention of the air aspect. This operation had been a trial of strength between the British and the German Air Forces. The British home air forces had intervened to the utmost, especially with fighters. We had found our Hurricanes much superior to the enemy's best machines. Frequently our losses had been in the proportion of 1 to 4, or even 1 to 5, of the enemy's. Two days before 70 German aeroplanes had been brought down at the cost of 14 of ours. The Defiant fighter with its power-operated turret had been particularly remarkable. On the 29th May one squadron of 12 of these aircraft had, in two sorties, destroyed 37 enemy aircraft without losing a single machine. These Defiants were coming forward slowly, and held out great hopes for the future.

M. Reynaud said that the German losses in heavy material must have been far less than those of the Allies. Moreover, the Germans had a great industrial superiority: thus they had been able to build 3,000 heavy tanks since the outbreak of the war.

As to the future, he felt convinced that once the situation on the North-Eastern front had been liquidated, Germany would at once, despite her recent losses, undertake an attack southwards against the line of the Somme and the Aisne, perhaps accompanied by a flanking movement from Basle through Switzerland. The British Air Forces could make a powerful contribution to the holding of the line of the Somme and the Aisne, and he need not stress the vital need of holding that line. The French Government therefore wished to ask that as soon as the operation in the north was ended, the full strength of the Royal Air Force should be made available on the new front, together with such troops as Great Britain could spare. In the latter connection, he did not believe that the Germans would as yet attempt an invasion of the United Kingdom. He therefore begged the British Government to send out the largest possible number of troops to the new front, possibly re-equipping and re-organising them in France itself to save time.

Mr Churchill said that it would be impossible to determine what British land forces could be sent out until a clear picture had been obtained of what total forces had been retrieved from the North. Of the 11 Divisions previously constituting the BEF there might perhaps be 4 or 5 Divisions left, which would, however, have to be reconstituted, and for which it would be very difficult to find fresh equipment.

As for further forces, in the last three weeks one Regiment of Guards had been sent to Belgium, of which one half had been lost; and of two Rifle Brigades, some three thousand men strong, sent to Calais, only 30 men had survived. There were now no forces left that could be sent at once. Something had to be kept within the United Kingdom to deal with a possible invasion by sea or by air. In this connection the danger had become much more pressing, since Germany could now debouch not only from the mouths of the German rivers but from ports in Holland, Belgium and, within a matter of days, France itself.

M. Reynaud said that he fully appreciated this danger. He was, however, convinced that the German plan was to turn the full force of the onslaught upon the new French front of the Somme and the Aisne.

Mr Churchill turned to the air aspect of the new situation. When sending 10 further Fighter Squadrons to France two weeks previously, he had said that these squadrons were the last reserve with which Great Britain might have to defend her life. Although the British Air Forces, and the French, had the advantage in quality and fighting spirit, they were faced with a grave inferiority in numbers. The ratio was certainly not less unfavourable than $2\frac{1}{2}$ to 1.

The Advanced Air Striking Force, consisting of 6 Bomber and 3 Fighter Squadrons, would be kept in being in its new bases west of Paris and its recent losses made good. He was not certain that the Lower Somme area was within reach of Fighter Squadrons operating from the United Kingdom. Much of the success of the British Air Forces in the Dunkirk area had been due to close proximity to the English bases. The new requirements would, of course, be closely studied at once.

Of the 39 Squadrons allotted to the Air Defence of Great Britain, 10 had been sent to France, originally for a few days only; but as matters had turned out there was now very little of these 10 Squadrons left. Great Britain was, therefore, left with only 29 Squadrons to meet a concentrated attack, not so much upon the civilian population of the islands – for such an attack would be stoutly resisted and he did not fear it – as upon the factories engaged in the production of new aircraft. He felt confident that the Royal Air Force would continue to give a good account of itself against the present heavy odds; but if the factories were put out of action, then the situation would indeed become hopeless. It was impossible to run any further risk; he was neither authorised, nor would he be willing, to expose the vital British aircraft industry to greater danger than was already being run.

M. Reynaud said that France was deeply grateful for the recent despatch of the 10 Squadrons, which represented a substantial proportion of British defence in the air. France, for her part, had, perhaps unwisely, thrown the whole of her air force into the battle; she would do so again in the coming battle of the Somme, as she considered that the outcome of that battle would be of decisive importance for the Allied cause.

Mr Churchill said that unless he was mistaken, the French losses in the air had, most fortunately, not been heavy.

M. Reynaud said that unfortunately, the French air force had been considerably weakened; there was now an insufficient number of fully-trained pilots to man the aircraft that were still available.

Mr Churchill said that he proposed in a few days, after a survey of what was left of the BEF, to give to the French Government some idea of the size of the land force the British might hope to build up in Western France. There were at present already two Divisions, one of them Armoured, in position on the new front.

General Sir John Dill said that there were only three Divisions, not fully equipped, left in Great Britain. Everything had been poured into the BEF as soon as it was ready.

Mr Churchill added that further Divisions might become available at an increasing *tempo* in the future. There were at present 14 Divisions undergoing training, equipped only with rifles and therefore totally unfit for modern warfare. When guns, anti-tank equipment and other supplies began to come in, the situation would alter very rapidly. Meanwhile, every effort was being made to draw as fully as possible upon the Empire. Eight battalions were now being brought home from Palestine, to be replaced by Indian battalions, and a further 8 battalions were on their way from India itself. A further force of some 14,000 Australian troops was due on the 12th June, and the second Canadian division would be landing in about a month's time. Both the latter forces were of the highest quality, but not fully trained or equipped.

The present emergency could not have arisen at a worse moment; there was nothing ready, though a great deal was on its way. If a minimum of troops was not kept in the United Kingdom to resist an invasion, then all would be lost.

M. Reynaud said that he need not stress further the urgent character of the demands he had to make. The British Government certainly understood how vital the battle of the Somme was going to be. The French High Command were now bringing back troops from Tunisia, despite the imminent danger of an Italian attack, and were proposing to call up two further classes of youths aged $18\frac{1}{2}$ to $20\frac{1}{2}$. These would be sent to take the place of the forces withdrawn from Tunisia. Largely owing to the over-running of the industrial area in North-Eastern France, there was no cloth for uniforms for these classes, and he therefore hoped that Great Britain might be in a position to supply cloth. There was also a shortage of small arms for the new classes, and efforts were being made to purchase weapons in the United States and Spain.

Mr Churchill said that the request for cloth for uniforms would at once be examined with the utmost goodwill.

As to the general situation, he could only ask M. Reynaud to give him a few days to think it over before deciding what it would be possible for Great Britain to contribute in the way of further land forces. He felt bound at once to utter the warning that the immediate contribution would of necessity be small.

M. Reynaud read the following draft telegram which Admiral Darlan proposed to send to Admiral Abrial at Dunkirk:–

'The Supreme War Council has just taken the following decisions:–

'1. A bridgehead shall be held round Dunkirk with the divisions under your command, and those under British command, for the purpose of enabling the Allied troops to embark.

'2. As soon as you are convinced that no troops outside the bridgehead can make their way to the points of embarkation, the troops holding the bridgehead shall withdraw and embark, the British forces embarking first.'

Mr Churchill intervened to say that the British would not embark first, but that the evacuation should proceed on equal terms between the British and the French, 'bras dessus bras dessous.'

M. Reynaud amended the draft accordingly and continued:

'3. Once Dunkirk has been completely evacuated of land and naval units, the harbour shall be blocked; the British Admiralty shall be responsible for this operation, subject to due notice being given to it by you in good time.

'4. The evacuation operations at Dunkirk shall be carried out under your orders.'

Mr Churchill agreed. He added that the British accepted responsibility for the rearguard action. Some confusion was, however, inevitable, and he could only say that every effort would be made to restore equilibrium by getting the French off first from now on.

General Dill said that General Gort, at La Panne, was experiencing difficulty in communicating with Dunkirk and had telephoned at lunch time to say that a German attack at La Panne was now menacing the perimeter. He also enquired about the troops still outside the perimeter: in view of the decision not to evacuate until all outside troops that could be saved had been brought in, the timing of the final embarkation could not be fixed yet.

M. Reynaud said that Admiral Abrial must decide about these troops and about the moment after which they would be considered lost. It was impossible to decide the matter in Paris.

General Weygand asked if a copy of the instructions to General Gort could be given to General Blanchard.

General Dill said that the instructions were now to the effect that until the

BEF had been reduced to one Army Corps General Gort was to be in three-hourly contact with the War Office; when the force fell below Corps strength, General Gort must leave and hand over his command to another officer. He was in fact embarking that night, though he had not wanted to leave.

Mr Churchill hoped that similar instructions would be given to General Blanchard.

M. Reynaud said that the decision must be left to General Blanchard himself, as he still had a much larger force under his command.

Mr Churchill said that the British view was that if Italy came in against the Allies we should strike at her at once in the most effective manner. Many Italians were opposed to war, and all should be made to realise its severity. He proposed that we should strike at the North-Western industrial triangle enclosed by the three cities of Milan, Turin and Genoa. Such an attack could be delivered without undue hardship to civilians. The British had four heavy Bomber Squadrons available for the purpose and the French Government had already authorised the sending of an advance party, which had in fact left England for South-Eastern France. The Royal Air Force believed strongly that great results would be gained by making this attack: Would M. Reynaud now agree to it, or did he still fear retaliation on French territory? He (Mr Churchill) did not think that the retaliation would be as serious as the damage the Royal Air Force could inflict.

M. Reynaud agreed that from the political point of view it was important to strike hard, to bring home to the Italian people the mistake they had made in entering the war when it was quite unnecessary for them to do so. As for the damage that might be inflicted on France, consultations might take place; but he agreed that the Allies must strike at once.

Admiral Darlan said that along the coast between the Italo-French frontier and Naples, one-third of Italy's oil supplies was stored. A Naval and aerial bombardment of these stores would cripple Italy seriously. The French Admiralty had a plan ready.

M. Reynaud suggested that representatives of the two Admiralties and Air Forces should meet to plan this operation. Agreement already existed between the two Admiralties, but there were no arrangements as yet for a combined operation.

Mr Churchill said that he would send the Deputy Chief of the Air Staff[1] and an Admiralty representative immediately to plan the operation.

He added that he was anxious that Ministers of the Administration he had just formed should become acquainted with their French opposite numbers as

[1] William Sholto Douglas, 1893–1969. On active service, 1914–18 (despatches thrice, Military Cross, DFC). Commanded Nos. 43 and 85 (fighter) squadrons, 1917–18. Assistant Chief of the Air Staff, 1938–40. Deputy Chief of the Air Staff, 1940. Air Officer Commanding-in-Chief, Fighter Command, 1940–2; Middle East Command, 1943–4; Coastal Command, 1944–5. Knighted, 1941. Commanding the British Air Forces of Occupation, Germany, 1945–6. Governor, British Zone of Germany, 1946–7. Created Baron, 1948. Chairman, British European Airways, 1949–64.

soon as possible. For instance, he would like Mr Bevin, the Minister of Labour and Trade Union leader, to visit Paris. Mr Bevin was showing great energy; under his leadership the British working class was now giving up holidays and privileges to a far greater extent than in the last war. Mr Duff Cooper, the new Minister of Information, was coming over shortly, and he would also like Lord Lloyd to visit the French Minister for the Colonies.[1]

M. Reynaud said that he and his Ministers would be delighted to receive all British Ministers.

Reverting to the question of war with Italy, he said that certain problems arose in regard to the Eastern Mediterranean, especially in connection with the control of certain Islands.

Admiral Darlan thought that there was a slight difference in the French and British instructions regarding Crete. He himself was to move on receipt of orders from the French Government, but Admiral Cunningham was apparently authorised to move against Crete directly war broke out with Italy.

Sir Ronald Campbell pointed out that this was not quite correct. The British instructions were that no action should be taken to occupy Crete unless Italy attacked Greek territory; otherwise we might be giving the Italians the very pretext for which they were looking.

Mr Churchill said that he was anxious for this move to be made, if only to give the British and French Navies an opportunity of making contact with the Italian Navy, in order to see if it was as good as in the last war.

M. Reynaud suggested that the question of the moment at which the Crete operation might be begun should be discussed through the diplomatic channel.

Mr Churchill accepted this suggestion.

Mr Churchill, reverting to the general outlook, thought that the Germans were being very hard pressed. In spite of their great successes they had, behind the technical troops so largely responsible for the recent advance, an army which was very far from the standard of 1914. Conscription had only been in force in Germany for five years, and he could not believe that the German Army was as good as the French. If the Allies could hold out through the summer, Britain would emerge as a most important factor. In the meanwhile, she would do what she could to help, but her contribution would be limited for some time to come; it was useless to send out troops without weapons.

The Allies must maintain an unflinching front against all their enemies. The United States had been roused by recent events, and even if they did not enter the war, they would soon be prepared to give us powerful aid. Payment should be no obstacle; steel and other essential materials should be ordered in

[1] Louis Rollin, who had succeeded Georges Mandel as Minister of the Colonies on 18 May 1940.

vast quantities; if we were unable to pay, America would nevertheless continue to deliver.

An invasion of England, if it took place, would have a still profounder effect on the United States, especially in those many towns in the New World which bore the same names as towns in the British Isles. England did not fear invasion, and would resist it most fiercely in every village and hamlet. To put up a stout resistance she must have troops, and it was only after her essential and urgent needs had been met that the balance of her armed forces could be put at the disposal of her French ally.

In the present emergency, it was vital that England and France should remain in the closest accord. By doing so, they could best ensure that their spirits remained high. He was absolutely convinced that they had only to carry on the fight to conquer. Even if one of them should be struck down, the other must not abandon the struggle. The British Government were prepared to wage war from the New World if, through some disaster, England herself was laid waste. It must be realised that if Germany defeated either Ally, or both, she would give no quarter: they would be reduced to the status of vassals and slaves for ever. It would be better far that the civilisation of Western Europe, with all its achievements, should come to a tragic but splendid end, than that the two great Democracies should linger on, stripped of all that made life worth living. That, he knew, was the deep conviction of the whole British people, and he would himself be proclaiming it in the British Parliament within a few days.

Mr Attlee said that he entirely agreed with everything Mr Churchill had said. The British people now realised the danger with which they were faced, and knew that in the event of a German victory everything they had built up would be destroyed: for the Germans killed not only men, but ideas. Our people were resolved as never before in their history.

M. Reynaud thanked the two British Ministers for these inspiring words, which fully accorded with French convictions. He was sure that the morale of the German people was not up to the level of the momentary triumphs of their Army. If France could hold the Somme, with the help of Britain, and if American industry came in to make good the disparity in arms, now aggravated by the occupation of a great part of France's industrial areas, then they could be certain of victory. If one country went under, the other would not abandon the struggle; he was most grateful for Mr Churchill's renewed assurance on this point. Never before had their two countries been so united and determined as in the present hour of danger.

CONCLUSIONS

1. Norway

The Supreme War Council agreed that the allied forces now in the Narvik area should be evacuated at the earliest possible moment.

2. Evacuation from Dunkirk

The Supreme War Council took note that up to the present, owing to the order in which the armies had reached the perimeter, the number of French troops which it had been possible to evacuate was small as compared with the number of British, and that orders had already been issued by the British Government that every effort should be made, in the hours or days that may remain, to reduce this disproportion.

3. Future British Assistance to France

The Supreme War Council took note that the British Government, without making any definite promise, would consider immediately, in the light of the discussion which had taken place –

(a) What reinforcements could be sent to France, with particular reference to the impending battle on the Somme and the Aisne, and how soon they could be made available. It is a fight against time;

(b) What air support could be afforded to this battle;

and that they would communicate the results of this consideration to the French Government at the earliest possible moment.

Winston S. Churchill: recollection
(*'Their Finest Hour', page 100*)

31 May 1940

After we rose from the table some of the principals talked together in the bay window in a somewhat different atmosphere. Chief among these was Marshal Pétain. Spears was with me, helping me out with my French and speaking himself. The young Frenchman, Captain de Margerie, had already spoken about fighting it out in Africa. But Marshal Pétain's attitude, detached and sombre, gave me the feeling that he would face a separate peace. The influence of his personality, his reputation, his serene acceptance of the march of adverse events, apart from any words he used, was almost overpowering to those under his spell. One of the Frenchmen, I cannot remember who, said in their polished way that a continuance of military reverses might in certain eventualities enforce a modification of foreign policy upon France. Here Spears rose to the occasion, and, addressing himself particularly to Marshal Pétain, said in perfect French: 'I suppose you understand, M. le Maréchal, that that would mean blockade?' Someone else said: 'That would perhaps be inevitable.' But then Spears to Pétain's face: 'That would not only mean blockade, but *bombardment* of all French ports in German hands.' I was glad to have this said. I sang my usual song: we would fight on whatever happened or whoever fell out.

Sir Ronald Campbell to Lord Halifax
(*Foreign Office papers, 800/312*)

31 May 1940

The Prime Minister has come and gone. He came at a psychological moment and his visit was of supreme value. He handled the French magnificently. He will give you a much better account of it than I could do by letter. All I need say is that at the end of the Supreme War Council meeting he made the most magnificent peroration on the implacable will of the British people to fight on to the bitter end, and to go down fighting rather than succumb to bondage. M. Reynaud responded in the same vein but one felt that it came rather from his head than his heart.

Hugh Dalton: diary
(*'The Second World War Diary of Hugh Dalton'*)

31 May 1940

The King says he has had to remind Winston that he is only PM in England and not in France as well!

June 1940

Winston S. Churchill to Desmond Morton
(*Premier papers, 7/2*)

1 June 1940

I believe we shall make them rue the day they try to invade our island. No such discussion can be permitted.[1]

WSC

Winston S. Churchill: note
(*Colville papers*)

1 June 1940

No. Bury them in caves and cellars. None must go.[2] We are going to beat them.

John Colville: diary
(*Colville papers*)

1 June 1940

I had a somewhat stormy passage this afternoon with the PM, because the Chiefs of Staff were not at Admiralty House when he wanted them. He rated me soundly, but I did not mind as my conscience was, in this case, clear and as

---

[1] On 28 May the Foreign Office had suggested that 'most secret plans' should be considered both for the evacuation of the Royal Family and the Government 'to some part of the Overseas Empire, whence the war could continue to be waged if circumstances prevented its continuation from the United Kingdom', and for 'the removal now' from Britain 'to another part of the Empire' of the Crown Jewels, the Coronation Chair, gold bullion, securities and precious stones.

[2] The Director of the National Gallery, Kenneth Clark, had suggested sending the paintings from the National Gallery to a safe haven in Canada.

he always pitches upon the first available person to display his wrath, irrespective of who is to blame. But he bears no grudge.

War Cabinet: minutes
(*Cabinet papers, 65/7*)

1 June 1940
11.30 a.m.

The Prime Minister gave an account of the Meeting of the Supreme War Council held on the previous day. The French Government had been represented by M. Reynaud, Marshal Pétain and General Weygand. Considering how critical the situation was, the results of the Meeting had been very satisfactory. He read over the Resolutions which had been agreed after the Meeting.

A satisfactory agreement had been reached on the policy for the evacuation of the Allied forces from Dunkirk.

The French had accepted in full our proposals regarding the future of operations in Norway.

The French expected a further attack on the French Armies in the west very shortly and had made an urgent plea that we should despatch reinforcements of land and air forces as early as possible. They had emphasised that their formations were only able to hold the present line very thinly. The Prime Minister's own view was that, now that we had got off such a large proportion of the British Expeditionary Force, we should send some additional troops to France, complete with the necessary air component. Every endeavour should also be made to reopen our long-range air attacks on German industry.

M. Reynaud had been told that we would send down some heavy bomber squadrons to assist the French in attacking Italian industries, and that servicing units were already proceeding. Reference was also made to naval plans.

The Prime Minister thought that it would be necessary for the Vice-Chief of the Air Staff and a member of the Naval Staff to go over to Paris and concert the plans in detail with the French authorities.

The Chief of the Air Staff said that a complete plan had been worked out for air attack on the Italian industries. He fully agreed that it was <u>most</u> important to hit Italy a very hard blow right at the outset of the war.

The Lord President of the Council suggested that it would be sufficient if the Italians were informed that we had made all preparations to start air attacks on their industry immediately after the outbreak of war. The despatch of the servicing units to southern France would be an earnest of these intentions.

The Prime Minister thought that a very much deeper impression would be made on Mussolini if the bomber squadrons themselves were sent. He might not otherwise believe that we were in earnest. Moreover, if the squadrons were already there, the first blow could be struck within an hour or so of the opening of hostilities.

The Prime Minister explained that, in the discussions the previous day at the Supreme War Council in Paris, the French had been told that the Germans could not be held off for more than 24 or at the very most 48 hours. They had accepted the fact that the remains of General Blanchard's army, which was still near Armentières, was now definitely cut off by the German forces in the neighbourhood of Cassel; but they had thought that other French troops, which were believed to be between Cassel and the perimeter, ought to be given a chance to enter the perimeter and to join the forces that were being evacuated. It had therefore been agreed in Paris to send instructions to Admiral Abrial at Dunkirk that the forces within the perimeter should embark as soon as there were no more troops outside who could make their way inside; on the suggestion of the British representatives, a sentence had been added to the effect that the British were to form a rearguard for the operation of embarkation. He (the Prime Minister) was now clear that the embarkation must be finished that night and that there was no hope for any French troops that were still outside the perimeter.

The Prime Minister urged that we should bear in mind that we were in fact finding it possible to evacuate to this country a very high proportion of the British troops engaged in the Flanders operations, while the number of French troops lost would be very much greater than our own.

The Prime Minister said that the operations for the evacuation of the Allied forces from Dunkirk had been the first real trial of strength between the British and German Air Forces. The Germans had a perfect target in the masses of ships and men at Dunkirk, which they would certainly have made every effort possible to destroy. Nevertheless, they had failed conspicuously in the attempt and had suffered losses far heavier than our own. We had achieved our purpose and saved our Army, and there could be no doubt that this constituted a signal victory for the Royal Air Force, which gave cause for high hopes of our success in the future. The whole operation reflected the very highest credit on the Air Ministry and on the Royal Air Force, and he hoped that a special Order of the Day would be issued to the Royal Air Force, impressing upon all personnel the great success which had been achieved and the severity of the blow which they had struck at the enemy.

Chiefs of Staff Committee: minutes
(*Cabinet papers, 79/1*)

1 June 1940
3.30 p.m.

The Prime Minister emphasised the importance of holding on as long as possible. The Germans might not break through, and it might be possible to continue for another night. The success or failure of our efforts to rescue the remnants of the French Army might have great results on the Alliance. As long as the front held, the evacuation should be continued – even at the cost of naval losses.[1] If necessary the flow of ships must be maintained, at any rate at certain periods, during the following day.

In the course of further discussion, it was agreed that nobody but the Commander on the spot could decide whether the time had come to go, or whether the position could be held to allow evacuation to continue longer.

Winston S. Churchill to General Weygand
(*Premier papers, 3/175*)

1 June 1940
6.45 p.m.
Most Immediate

Crisis in evacuation now reached. Five Fighter Squadrons acting almost continuously is most we can do, but six ships several filled with troops sunk by bombing this morning. Artillery fire menacing only practicable channel. Enemy closing in on reduced bridgehead. By trying to hold on till tomorrow we may lose all. By going tonight, much may certainly be saved, though much will be lost.

---

[1] In all, six destroyers (out of forty-four engaged in the evacuation) and twenty-four smaller Royal Navy vessels were sunk.

Situation cannot be fully judged only by Admiral Abrial in the fortress, nor by you, nor by us here. We have therefore ordered General Alexander commanding British Sector of Bridgehead to judge in consultation with Admiral Abrial whether to try to stay over tomorrow or not. Trust you will agree.

Winston S. Churchill to President Roosevelt
(*Premier papers, 3/468*)

1 June 1940

I hope you will not mind if I refer again to the question of aircraft. As you know, we have communicated details of our urgent needs through Mr Purvis, as you suggested, and are now beginning to receive reports from him.

I understand your position regarding additional aircraft priorities, as explained by Mr Morgenthau[1] to Mr Purvis. Nevertheless, I feel justified in asking for the release to us of 200 Curtiss P40 fighters now being delivered to your Army. The courage and success of our pilots against numerical superiority are a guarantee that they will be well used. At the present rate of comparative losses, they would account for something like 800 German machines.

I also understand your difficulties, legal, political and financial, regarding destroyers. But the need is extreme.

John Martin: diary
(*Martin papers*)

2 June 1940

We have worked out an elaborate arrangement of shifts which ought to make it possible for each PS to have a 'weekend' once, if not twice, a fortnight. It is really necessary for any but supermen like the PM himself (though even he goes to sleep most days for about an hour after lunch). He has a boxful of papers left outside his room each night and works through this in bed in the

---

[1] Henry Morgenthau Junior, 1891–1967. A gentleman farmer in New York State before the First World War. Lieutenant, United States Navy, 1918. A neighbour and early supporter of Governor (later President) Roosevelt. New York State Conservation Commissioner, 1931. Chairman of the Federal Farm Board, 1933. Secretary of the Treasury, 1934–45. A strong supporter of active American defence preparations, and of Lend Lease. His plan in 1944 to reduce post-war Germany to a pastoral condition, with almost no industry, was rejected by President Truman, who would not take him to the Potsdam Conference, whereupon he resigned.

morning, dictating to a shorthand-writer, and generally does not get up and dress till quite late. About 11 he comes over to No 10 for the daily Cabinet meeting, which lasts till about 2. There is much coming and going of Ministers and Chiefs of Staff etc. for this. (Yesterday we had Lord Gort on his return from France.) Then the PM returns to Admiralty House for lunch and rest, usually working in Downing Street (or having another meeting of Ministers there or in the House of Commons) from about 4.30 until dinner time. He dines at Admiralty House and there sees a succession of Ministers until bed-time not much before midnight and may be a good deal later.

The chief difficulty is understanding what he says and great skill is required in interpreting inarticulate grunts or single words thrown out without explanation. I think he is consciously odd in these ways. Anyhow he is certainly a 'character' and I shan't soon forget an interview with him in his bedroom walking about clad only in a vest.

It has been an anxious week, waiting hour by hour for the latest news of the BEF. Their successful evacuation is an incredible achievement which could not have been hoped for a week ago.

Winston S. Churchill to Sir Archibald Sinclair and Sir Cyril Newall
(*Churchill papers, 20/13*)

2 June 1940

It is of the utmost importance, in view of the raids on Lyons and Marseilles, that we should be able to strike back with our heavy bombers at Italy the moment she enters the war. I consider therefore that these squadrons should be flown to their aerodromes in Southern France at the earliest moment when French permission can be obtained and when the servicing units are ready for their reception.

Pray let me know at our meeting to-night what you propose.

WSC

Winston S. Churchill to General Ismay
(*Churchill papers, 20/13*)

2 June 1940

The successful evacuation of the BEF has revolutionized the Home Defence position. As soon as the BEF units can be reformed on a Home Defence basis, we have a mass of trained troops in the country which would require a raid to be executed on a prohibitively large scale. Even 200,000 men would not be beyond our compass. The difficulties of a descent and its risks and losses increase with every addition to the first 10,000. We must at once take a new view of the situation. Certain questions must be considered, chiefly by the War Office, but also by the Joint Staffs:—

1. What is the shortest time in which the BEF can be given a new fighting value?

2. Upon what scheme would they be organized? Will it be for service at Home in the first instance and only secondarily despatch to France? On the whole, I prefer this.

3. The BEF in France must immediately be reconstituted, otherwise the French will not continue in the war. Even if Paris is lost, they must be adjured to continue a gigantic guerrilla. A scheme should be considered for a bridgehead and area of disembarkation in Brittany, where a large army can be developed. We must have plans worked out which will show the French that there is a way through if they will only be steadfast.

4. As soon as the BEF is reconstituted for Home Defence, three Divisions should be sent to join our two Divisions South of the Somme, or wherever the French left may be by then. It is for consideration whether the Canadian Division should not go at once. Pray let me have a scheme.

5. Had we known a week ago what we now know about the Dunkirk evacuation, Narvik would have presented itself in a different light. Even now the question of maintaining a garrison there for some weeks on a self-contained basis should be reconsidered. I am deeply impressed with the vice and peril of chopping and changing. The letter attached of the Minister of Economic Warfare[1] as well as the telegram of some days ago from the C-in-C must, however, receive one final weighing.

6. Ask Admiralty to supply a latest return of the state of the destroyer flotillas, showing what reinforcements have arrived or are expected within the month of June, and how many will come from repair.

7. It should now be possible to allow the eight regular battalions in Palestine to be relieved by the eight native battalions from India, before they are brought home, as brought home they must be, to constitute the cadres of the new BEF.

8. As soon as the Australians land, the big ships should be turned round and should carry eight or ten territorial battalions to Bombay. They should

[1] Dalton's letter stressed the stock of 450,000 tons of Swedish iron ore then at Narvik: 'This is a high grade ore which it is most desirable to have for oxidising in steel furnaces.' He added: 'This ore would be a prize of first-class importance to Germany, since no ore for making comparable steels is at present available to her.' Lord Cork, in his telegram of 26 May 1940, wrote: '(a) The moral effect and the effect on our prestige which I need not stress. (b) Our forces in the Narvik area are tying down a very much greater force of enemy in men, mechanised material, petrol and aircraft. (c) The Naval effort during evacuation will of necessity be large and prolonged unless a disaster is courted and will take place at a time when our naval effort might well be required in the North Sea one thousand miles away. (d) The port of Narvik and the railway to the Swedish border cannot be destroyed sufficiently to prevent the enemy putting it into working order by the winter with the forced labour and mechanical resources they have at their command' (*Premier papers, 3/328/4*).

bring back a second eight Regular battalions from India, and afterwards carry to India a second eight or ten territorial battalions from England. It is for consideration how far the same principle should not be applied to batteries in India.

9. Our losses in equipment must be expected to delay the fruition of our expansion of the BEF from the twenty Divisions formerly aimed at by 2 + 12, to no more than fifteen Divisions by 2 + 18; but we must have a project to put before the French. The essence of this should be the armoured Division, the 51st, the Canadians and two territorial Divisions under Lord Gort by mid-July, and the augmenting of this force by six Divisions formed from the twenty-four regular battalions in conjunction with territorials, a second Canadian Division, an Australian Division and two territorial Divisions by 2 + 18. Perhaps we may even be able to improve on this.

10. It is of the highest urgency to have at least half a dozen Brigade groups formed from the regulars of the BEF for Home Defence.

11. What Air co-operation is arranged to cover the final evacuation tonight? It ought to be possible to reduce the pressure on the rear guard at this critical moment.

I close with a general observation. As I have personally felt less afraid of a German attempt at invasion than of the piercing of the French line on the Somme or Aisne and the fall of Paris, I have naturally believed the Germans would choose the latter. This probability is greatly increased by the fact that they will realise that the armed forces in Great Britain are now far stronger than they have ever been, and that their raiding parties would not have to meet half-trained formations, but the men whose mettle they have already tested, and from whom they have recoiled, not daring seriously to molest their departure. The next few days, before the BEF or any substantial portion of it can be reorganized, must be considered as still critical.

WSC

War Cabinet: minutes
(*Cabinet papers, 65/7*)

2 June 1940
6.30 p.m.

The Prime Minister said that he hoped that the General Staff was giving the most intensive study to the problem of defeating tanks. It was of the utmost urgency that solutions to this problem should be devised. On the one hand, there was the possibility of adapting special weapons for this purpose, while, on the other hand, it should be possible to devise some system for harrying and pursuing tanks. It should be possible to cut off tank crews from supplies of food, water and petrol.

The Chief of the Imperial General Staff said that all these problems were being intensively examined.

War Cabinet: Confidential Annex
(*Cabinet papers, 65/13*)

2 June 1940
6.30 p.m.

The Prime Minister said that the effect of M. Reynaud's telegram was that a battle of capital importance was impending on the Somme and Oise Front.[1] The French Government expected that the three British Divisions which it had been intended to send to France in the next few weeks should be sent to France at once, and that these Divisions should be followed as soon as possible by units reconstituted from the personnel of the BEF which had been evacuated from Dunkirk to this country. In addition, it would be essential that fighter aircraft based on French soil should be available for the support of the French army.

General Weygand and General Vuillemin[2] also asked that the maximum British air strength should immediately be based in France, General Vuillemin asking that 320 British fighter aircraft should be based in France.

A preliminary discussion ensued as to the forces which could immediately be sent to reinforce the French Front.

On the one hand it was argued that with the considerable accession to the strength of our Home Forces, represented by the 200,000 troops withdrawn from Dunkirk, even without their heavy equipment, the risk of a successful invasion of this country was greatly lessened. The difficulties of re-equipping the BEF were, however, very great. Time would be taken in re-equipping the units, and sending them overseas again. It would almost certainly be impossible in the time available to send to the assistance of the French a force

---

[1] In his telegram, which reached London at 12.30 p.m. on 2 June 1940, a copy of which was circulated to the War Cabinet, Reynaud asked for three more British divisions to be sent to France, and the despatch of both 'bombing and fighting aircraft'. The telegram ended: 'We have indications of an imminent attack on various points of the Front' (*Cabinet papers, 79/4*).

[2] Joseph Vuillemin, 1883–1963. Joined the French Army, 1909. A pilot from 1914, he saw distinguished service as an aviator throughout the First World War (Croix de Guerre with thirteen palms and five stars). Colonel, 1924, organising aviation in Algeria. Brigadier-General, 1933, in charge of organising air lines across the Sahara, having them marked and lighted. Inspector of Bombardment Aviation, 1934. Major-General, 1936. Chief of the Air General Staff, 1938–9. Commander-in-Chief of the French Air Forces, 1939–40. Awarded the Médaille Militaire, July 1940.

of sufficient strength to play a decisive part in the battle which the French were now awaiting on the Somme.

At the same time it was pointed out that if we were to decline to respond to M. Reynaud's appeal there was a considerable danger that a point might be reached at which French resistance might collapse; and if Paris fell, they might be tempted to conclude a separate peace. This would mean the establishment in France of a Government friendly to the Nazis. Then we should have to bomb aerodromes in France, occupied by German air forces, and to exercise economic pressure against France. We might eventually be faced with a French Government, not merely out of the war, but actually hostile to us.

The Secretary of State for Foreign Affairs said that, while he did not exclude the possibility of giving further assistance to the French, he thought that the Cabinet would wish to have an opportunity of seeing the considered view of the Chiefs of Staff before reaching a decision on this vital matter.

The Prime Minister said that he would wait for the appreciation of the situation from the Chiefs of Staff before asking the Cabinet to come to a decision but would now give, for the benefit of the Chiefs of Staff, an outline of a course of action that he asked them to consider.

He would like to tell the French that we would send three divisions as quickly as we could; we would send the Canadians first and would hope to have the three divisions in France within five/six weeks. We would use the full strength of our long-range bombers to bombard by night, and when possible by day, targets as indicated by the French Commander-in-Chief. This task should have preference whenever necessary over the bombardment of the Ruhr area. The Advanced Air Striking Force would remain in action in France. Lord Gort would be sent back to re-form the Headquarters of a reconstituted British Expeditionary Force. If we sent over fresh British divisions, we should likewise reconstitute an appropriate Air Component. But, unless we found that Fighter Squadrons could operate from this country on the lower Somme, fighter support should be limited to the Fighter Squadrons in the Advanced Air Striking Force and the Air Component. Additional fighter squadrons would not be sent across the Channel unless it was found possible to operate them from west of Abbeville.

The French would thus, by the middle of July, receive reinforcements corresponding to ten Divisions made up as follows:– Three British Divisions, the equivalent of two Divisions from Narvik (which should reach France by the middle of June), and 60,000–80,000 French troops which were being evacuated from Dunkirk – the equivalent of, say, five Divisions.

The Chiefs of Staff should consider a solution to the problem on these lines giving the greatest possible support to France without leaving the defence forces of the United Kingdom dangerously reduced in face of the risk of invasion.

The Prime Minister said that he had been giving further consideration to the question of the withdrawal of the Allied forces from Narvik. He had been hoping that now that we had succeeded in withdrawing so large a proportion of the BEF from France it might be possible to re-consider the decision to withdraw all our forces from Narvik and to maintain a garrison there for some weeks on a self-contained basis. He had now reached the conclusion that the decision to withdraw must stand.[1]

Randolph S. Churchill to his father
(<i>Churchill papers, 1/355</i>)</center>

2 June 1940

My dear Papa,

It was indeed generous of you to say that you would meet £100 of my bills. I do hope it is not very inconvenient for you to do this. I enclose the two most urgent.

Reading between the lines of the communiqués it is difficult to persuade oneself that matters are going very well in France. Pamela[2] and I are thinking of you constantly at this grim moment. We pray that you will find strength to sustain you so that you may continue to lead us heroically to whatever may befall.

Your loving son
Randolph

Winston S. Churchill to Sir Alexander Hardinge[3]
(<i>Churchill papers, 20/7</i>)</center>

2 June 1940

My dear Hardinge,

I much regret to receive your letter of May 30. I should have thought that in the terrible circumstances which press upon us, and the burden of disaster

---

[1] The evacuation from Narvik began on the evening of 3 June 1940, having been delayed for twenty-four hours to allow Norwegian troops in Northern Norway to regroup.

[2] Pamela Digby, born 1920. Daughter of the 11th Baron Digby. In 1939 she married Randolph Churchill, from whom she obtained a divorce in 1946; their son Winston was born at Chequers in 1940. She subsequently married Leyland Hayward, and then Averell Harriman. Appointed by President Clinton to be United States Ambassador to Paris, 1993.

[3] Alexander Henry Louis Hardinge, 1894–1960. Educated at Harrow and Trinity College, Cambridge. On active service, 1915–18 (wounded, Military Cross). Adjutant, Grenadier Guards, 1919–20. Assistant Private Secretary to King George V, 1920–36. Private Secretary to King Edward VIII, 1936; and to King George VI, 1936–43. Privy Councillor, 1936. Knighted, 1937. Succeeded his father as 2nd Baron Hardinge of Penshurst, 1944 (his elder brother having died of wounds received in action on 18 December 1914).

and responsibility which has been cast upon me after my warnings have been so long rejected, I might be helped as much as possible. I had it in mind to submit Mr Bracken's name to the King for a post in the Government, which would have carried with it a Privy Councillorship. But he preferred to remain a private member, giving me the personal assistance as my Parliamentary Private Secretary which he has done for so many years. In these circumstances and as he is privy necessarily to many secret matters I counted with confidence upon His Majesty's gracious favour in making the submission. One precedent which rises in my mind is that of Mr Balfour's Private Secretary, Mr Sandars,[1] who was not even a Member of Parliament, but in 1902 was sworn to the Privy Council in the reign of King Edward VII. In Mr Bracken's case the Committee of the Privy Council has seen no objection to the proposal.

Mr Bracken is a Member of Parliament of distinguished standing and exceptional ability. He has sometimes been almost my sole supporter in the years when I have been striving to get this country properly defended, especially from the air. He has suffered as I have done every form of official hostility. Had he joined the ranks of the time-servers and careerists who were assuring the public that our Air Force was larger than that of Germany, I have no doubt he would long ago have attained High Office. The fact that this is known to the public will be one of the reasons why his name will receive widespread approval.[2]

Yours sincerely
Winston S. Churchill

War Cabinet: minutes
(*Cabinet papers, 65/7*)

3 June 1940　　　　　　　　　　　　　　　　　　　　　　　　10 Downing Street
11.30 a.m.

The Prime Minister informed the War Cabinet that the personnel of the BEF had now been withdrawn to this country practically intact, except for their losses through casualties in action. The French had not made anything like full use of the facilities available for the evacuation of their troops on the previous day and night. He proposed therefore to telegraph to M. Reynaud, urging the French to make every effort in co-operation with us to evacuate their men as quickly as possible.

[1] John Satterfield Sandars, 1853–1934. Private Secretary to A. J. Balfour, 1892–1905 (Balfour was Leader of the Opposition, 1892–5, and Prime Minister, 1902–5).

[2] The King agreed to Brendan Bracken becoming a Privy Councillor. In his reply on 3 June, Sir Alexander Hardinge wrote: 'The last thing that His Majesty wants to do is to create difficulties for you when you are bearing such an overwhelming burden of responsibility and anxiety – indeed his sympathy for you is beyond measure.' For Churchill's letter to the King, see 4 June 1940.

JUNE 1940 233

War Cabinet: Confidential Annex
(*Cabinet papers, 65/7*)

3 June 1940
11.30 a.m.

The War Cabinet had before them a Report by the Chiefs of Staff putting forward recommendations as to the reply which should be given to the French demands for assistance on the Western Front (WP (40) 189).[1]

The Prime Minister thought that the Report accurately set out the arguments for and against the despatch of forces to France, but his personal view was that the proposed assistance was not sufficient. It was recommended in the report that we should send two divisions; but he thought that we should promise to send a third division, provided that the French could supply the artillery for it. During the interval before the third division could sail, we should have received from production 150 field guns and 80 anti-tank guns. The position would therefore be somewhat better than that stated in paragraph 11 of the Report.[2]

The Secretary of State for War said that he was anxious to withdraw the drafts for the BEF divisions who were, at present, in France, South of the Somme. Their proper function was to effect replacements in the divisions of the BEF.

The Prime Minister pointed out that, from the political point of view, it would be very difficult to withdraw any considerable number of men from France, at a moment when the French were urging us so desperately to send reinforcements.

Summing up the discussion in connection with military reinforcements, the Prime Minister said that he was in full agreement with the view of the Chiefs of Staff that it would be a mistake to send the Canadian division to France forthwith. He proposed that we should tell the French that it was, of course, our intention to re-constitute the BEF. The loss of the great bulk of our equipment would mean delay, but we hoped to fulfil our undertakings within

---

[1] The proposed assistance was: (i) to re-establish a British Expeditionary Force headquarters in France 'at once'; (ii) the despatch of two divisions and a proportion of Corps troops to France 'as soon as possible' starting 'within about a week', the 43rd Division following about ten days later, and (iii) the despatch of further divisions to be contingent upon the general situation 'when they become nearer readiness for despatch'. As to air forces, the Chiefs of Staff recommended that the six bomber and three Hurricane squadrons then in France 'will be brought up to operational strength as soon as possible, and will be supplemented by Army Co-Operation Squadrons which will be sent from the United Kingdom. The Metropolitan Bomber Force will be ready to give support as necessary from Great Britain' (Chiefs of Staff Paper No. 421, War Cabinet Paper 189 of 1940, 3 June 1940, *Cabinet papers, 66/8*).

[2] 'After the despatch of the artillery for this force, only about 450 field guns and 42 anti-tank guns will remain in this country' (War Cabinet Paper 193 of 1940, Memorandum by the Chiefs of Staff, 'Productive Programmes', *Cabinet papers, 66/8*).

six months of the dates originally given. In the meanwhile, we were sending two divisions at once and a third would follow, provided that the French could supply artillery.

Turning to the question of air forces, the Prime Minister recalled that on the 10th May we had had the following air forces in France.

In the Air Component
4 Squadrons of Hurricanes.
5 Army Co-operation Squadrons.
    (Lysanders).
2 Squadrons of Blenheim Bombers.[1]
2 Army Co-operation Squadrons.
    (Blenheims).

In the Panther Force
2 Squadrons of Hurricanes.
8   "   " Battles.
2   "   " Blenheim Bombers.

If the recommendations in the Report were adopted, we would have a smaller air force in France than at the beginning of the battle.

The Prime Minister mentioned the heavy strain on the German Air Force.

The Air Officer Commanding-in-Chief[2] agreed that we had inflicted heavy losses on the Germans, and he hoped that if an attack was launched on this country we should be able to withstand it as a result of the greater fighting spirit of our pilots.

The Prime Minister considered that all possible pressure on objectives in Germany should continue to be applied by the Metropolitan Air Force up to the opening of the land battle, but it would then be necessary to give priority to the needs of the latter. Any forces not employed in the battle could be used to attack targets in Germany.

Continuing, he suggested that the French should be told of the air support which we could send to France in the first instance, and that the matter should then be reconsidered in ten days. To them it looked as if we had some 500 fighters of incomparable quality which we would be withholding at a moment when they would be making a supreme effort on land. It would therefore have to be pointed out to them that we were at this moment staggering under the enormous strain of the recent operations in France and would recover if we

---

[1] The Bristol Blenheim bomber, of which 5,400 were manufactured, but which proved too slow for daytime use. It was later more effective as a night-fighter and night-bomber, but was withdrawn altogether in the summer of 1942.
[2] Air Marshal Barratt.

were given sufficient respite. Until then, however, we could not do more than bring up to strength the six bomber and three Hurricane squadrons now in France. The despatch of any more fighter squadrons at this moment would be uneconomical, because it would be impossible to maintain them.

Winston S. Churchill to Sir Archibald Sinclair
(Churchill papers, 4/201)

3 June 1940

My dear Archie,

The Cabinet were distressed to hear from you that you were now running short of pilots for fighters, and that they had now become the limiting factor.

This is the first time that this particular admission of failure has been made by the Air Ministry. We know that immense masses of aircraft are devoted to the making of pilots, far beyond the proportion adopted by the Germans. We heard some months ago of many thousands of pilots for whom the Air Ministry declared they had no machines, and who consequently had to be 're-mustered': as many as 7,000 were mentioned, all of whom had done many more hours of flying than those done by German pilots now frequently captured. How then, therefore, is this new shortage to be explained?

Lord Beaverbrook has made a surprising improvement in the supply and repair of aeroplanes, and in clearing up the muddle and scandal of the aircraft production branch. I greatly hope that you will be able to do as much on the Personnel side, for it will indeed be lamentable if we have machines standing idle for want of pilots to fly them.

Yours ever
WSC

Winston S. Churchill to Lord Halifax
(Churchill papers, 4/201)

3 June 1940

My dear Edward

The situation has been changed so far as Home Defence is concerned by the fact that the greater part of the Expeditionary Force, including many highly-trained units, is now safely back in this Island. Moreover, there are difficulties of transportation for these battalions in Palestine which have not yet been overcome. I am proposing to have them replaced by eight native Indian battalions which Amery has been good enough to arrange.

I consider I have a large measure of responsibility as Minister of Defence for advising the Cabinet upon the main groupings and development of our Forces. If France goes out of the war it will be largely because we are unable to make anything like the military effort which we made in the first year of the last war. The moment the invasion danger has been parried it will be indispensable to try to build up a new and stronger Expeditionary Force. For this I must have all the regular British cadres.

I hope I may be given some help in this, and be allowed to view the War situation as a whole.

Winston S. Churchill to Paul Reynaud and General Weygand
(*Churchill papers, 20/14*)

3 June 1940

We have been most carefully considering your telegram of yesterday requesting military and air assistance. We will, of course, begin at once rebuilding the BEF as fast as our lack of equipment allows. Even greater difficulties arise in air fighters, on account of the intensity of recent fighting and new strategic positions created by enemy occupation of channel ports. I hope to telegraph you to-morrow, Tuesday, final decision of Cabinet. Meanwhile, no time is being lost.

Winston S. Churchill to General Spears
(*Churchill papers, 20/14*)

3 June 1940
Private

You should prepare them for favourable response Army but disappointment about Air.

Winston S. Churchill to Paul Reynaud and General Weygand
(*Premier papers, 3/175*)

3 June 1940

We are coming back for your men to-night. Pray make sure that all facilities are used promptly. Last night, for three hours, many ships waited idly at much cost and danger.

Winston S. Churchill to General Weygand
(*Churchill papers, 20/14*)

3 June 1940

Prime Minister would be glad to know why you deprecate his mentioning in his speech to-morrow in the House of Commons the figure of 300,000 as having been successfully evacuated, providing that nationalities are not specified.

Prime Minister, on the contrary, thinks it would be helpful.

Winston S. Churchill to Sir Edward Bridges
(*Churchill papers, 20/13*)

3 June 1940

Has anything been done about shipping 20,000 internees to Newfoundland or St Helena? Is this one of the matters that the Lord President has in hand? If so would you please ask him about it. I should like to get them on the high seas as soon as possible, but I suppose considerable arrangements have to be made at the other end. Is it all going forward?

WSC

Winston S. Churchill to Professor Lindemann
(*Churchill papers, 20/13*)

3 June 1940

See attached paper[1] which seems to contain a lot of loose thinking. Evidently we must 'pull forward' everything that can be made effective in the next five months, and accept the consequent retardation of later production, but there is no reason whatever to alter so far as I can see the existing approved schemes for a three years' war. Indeed, they will be more necessary than ever if France drops out.

Pray let me have your views.

---

[1] War Cabinet Paper 193 of 1940, Memorandum by the Chiefs of Staff, 'Productive Programmes'.

Winston S. Churchill to Professor Lindemann
(*Churchill papers, 20/13*)

3 June 1940

You are not presenting me as I should like every few days, or every week, with a short clear statement of the falling off or improvement of munitions production. I am not able to form a clear view unless you do this.

Hugh Dalton: diary
('*The Second World War Diary of Hugh Dalton*')

3 June 1940

The PM has a squash of ministers. Things are very much better than last week. We have got out more than 300,000 men. He had thought of nothing but dead, wounded, and long dreary processions making their way to prison camps and starvation in Germany. The French? They will ask us for help, and we must give them more than we can spare, which will still be not all that they ask. We must not denude this island. 'We've got the men away but we've lost the luggage.' This will take some time to make up from our aircraft and munition factories. The French insisted on the post of honour at the end, and so 'after a seemly wrangle we brought the Cameron Highlanders away. Otherwise they were to have stayed and died at the end.'[1]

PM is much more confident against invasion than he was a week ago. After all, we have the BEF in this country now, hardened veterans.

The PM wants to be able to say to the House tomorrow, 'If I wavered for a moment, all my colleagues in the Government would turn and rend me.' No one raised any objection to this.

Winston S. Churchill to Paul Reynaud
(*Cabinet papers, 65/13*)

4 June 1940

In reply to the message which you gave General Spears to deliver to me on the 2nd June, I gave you my assurance last Friday that we would immediately consider, without making any definite promise, what reinforcements we could send to France at once, and what air support we could afford to you in the impending battle.

2. Let me first emphasise certain general points. (i) That portion of the

---

[1] The Cameron Highlanders were taken off from Dunkirk at 11.50 p.m. on 30 May 1940.

British Expeditionary Force which has been recovered from the Northern Front will have to be entirely re-equipped before it can be used. (ii) The three divisions which you mention as being available in your message are not yet fully equipped. Under our original programme the first of them would have been despatched to France towards the end of this month. (iii) Almost the entire fighter force has been engaged in the recent battle. The operations have been of an intensity never before contemplated, and the losses in aircraft and particularly in pilots have been correspondingly high. I would most earnestly ask you to appreciate that the above points materially affect the assistance that we can immediately render.

3. Our proposals are as follows. As regards land forces, we will re-establish a BEF headquarters in France and build up a new BEF as fast as we can. One division is being prepared for immediate despatch, and will begin to proceed overseas within seven days. A second division, one of the seasoned regular divisions recovered from Dunkirk, is being re-equipped with greatest urgency, in order that it may follow the first division as quickly as possible. A proportion of Corps troops will also be despatched within this period. It is not possible to give you the precise date at which a third division could be despatched, but we will press it forward as fast as possible. The date at which this division will be ready may well depend largely on the date when its artillery can be provided. Could you help in this respect? The appropriate component of Army co-operation aircraft will also be despatched to France.

4. As regards fighters, the three squadrons now in France are being brought up to strength immediately. In view of the very serious losses of the last three weeks it must take some little time to overhaul our squadrons, seek to replace our losses, and determine what further help we can send and when. We fully appreciate need for extreme urgency, and I will communicate with you further on the subject at the earliest possible moment.

5. As regards bomber aircraft, we intend to bring the six squadrons now in France up to full operational strength as soon as possible. The remainder of the Metropolitan Bomber Force will remain based on this country, but will continue to give support as in the past – priority being given to the land battle, and to action against objectives selected by your High Command.

War Cabinet: Confidential Annex
(*Cabinet papers, 65/13*)

4 June 1940
11.30 a.m.

The War Cabinet had before them a draft telegram to the French prepared in accordance with the conclusions reached at the meeting of the War Cabinet on the previous day.

The Prime Minister said that after further consideration he had decided to suspend its despatch until the War Cabinet had had an opportunity to review the matter once more. In the meantime he had sent an interim reply to M. Reynaud, through General Spears, who had been warned for his own information that we should have particular difficulty in meeting the French demands for further air support. His own view was that we could not refuse to maintain in France the same number of squadrons as we had had there before the last battle started, while keeping a larger number of squadrons than ever in this country. At one time during the battle we had been down to 29 fighter squadrons in the Air Defence of Great Britain whereas now we had about 45. According to figures produced by the Minister of Aircraft Production we had now more aircraft available in this country than we had had before the German invasion of the Low Countries began. We could never keep all that we wanted for our own defence while the French were fighting for their lives.

The Prime Minister agreed with the terms of an amendment to paragraph 4 of the draft telegram proposed by the Secretary of State for War, at least as a preliminary reply to the French. He felt strongly that, from the psychological point of view, it would be very much better to send a larger number of squadrons to France than to increase the strength of squadrons by sending the equivalent number of aircraft.

The Prime Minister drew attention to Paris Telegram No. 339 DIPP in which Sir Ronald Campbell reported that M. Reynaud had demurred to the suggestion that the French Air Force were not pulling their weight. He had said that they were losing aircraft at the rate of 37 a day, and their daily intake only amounted to 18, which included 8 from America. These figures had been confirmed by Air Marshal Barratt.

Winston S. Churchill: speech
(*Hansard*)

4 June 1940   House of Commons
3.40 p.m.

WAR SITUATION

The Prime Minister (Mr Churchill): From the moment that the French defences at Sedan and on the Meuse were broken at the end of the second week of May, only a rapid retreat to Amiens and the south could have saved the British and French Armies who had entered Belgium at the appeal of the Belgian King, but this strategic fact was not immediately realised. The

French High Command hoped they would be able to close the gap, and the Armies of the north were under their orders. Moreover, a retirement of this kind would have involved almost certainly the destruction of the fine Belgian Army of over 20 divisions and the abandonment of the whole of Belgium. Therefore, when the force and scope of the German penetration were realised and when a new French Generalissimo, General Weygand, assumed command in place of General Gamelin, an effort was made by the French and British Armies in Belgium to keep on holding the right hand of the Belgians and to give their own right hand to a newly created French Army which was to have advanced across the Somme in great strength to grasp it.

However, the German eruption swept like a sharp scythe around the right and rear of the Armies of the north. Eight or nine armoured divisions, each of about 400 armoured vehicles of different kinds, but carefully assorted to be complementary and divisible into small self-contained units, cut off all communications between us and the main French Armies. It severed our own communications for food and ammunition, which ran first to Amiens and afterwards through Abbeville, and it shore its way up the coast to Boulogne and Calais, and almost to Dunkirk. Behind this armoured and mechanised onslaught came a number of German divisions in lorries, and behind them again there plodded comparatively slowly the dull brute mass of the ordinary German Army and German people, always so ready to be led to the trampling down in other lands of liberties and comforts which they have never known in their own.

I have said this armoured scythe-stroke almost reached Dunkirk – almost but not quite. Boulogne and Calais were the scenes of desperate fighting. The Guards defended Boulogne for a while and were then withdrawn by orders from this country. The Rifle Brigade, the 60th Rifles, and the Queen Victoria's Rifles, with a battalion of British tanks and 1,000 Frenchmen, in all about 4,000 strong, defended Calais to the last. The British Brigadier was given an hour to surrender. He spurned the offer, and four days of intense street fighting passed before silence reigned over Calais, which marked the end of a memorable resistance. Only 30 unwounded survivors were brought off by the Navy and we do not know the fate of their comrades. Their sacrifice, however, was not in vain. At least two armoured divisions, which otherwise would have been turned against the British Expeditionary Force, had to be sent for to overcome them. They have added another page to the glories of the Light Division, and the time gained enabled the Graveline waterlines to be flooded and to be held by the French troops.

Thus it was that the port of Dunkirk was kept open. When it was found impossible for the Armies of the north to reopen their communications to Amiens with the main French Armies, only one choice remained. It seemed, indeed, forlorn. The Belgian, British and French Armies were almost surrounded. Their sole line of retreat was to a single port and to its neighbouring beaches. They were pressed on every side by heavy attacks and far outnumbered in the air.

When a week ago to-day I asked the House to fix this afternoon as the occasion for a statement, I feared it would be my hard lot to announce the greatest military disaster in our long history. I thought – and some good judges agreed with me – that perhaps 20,000 or 30,000 men might be re-embarked. But it certainly seemed that the whole of the French First Army and the whole of the British Expeditionary Force north of the Amiens–Abbeville gap, would be broken up in the open field or else would have to capitulate for lack of food and ammunition. These were the hard and heavy tidings for which I called upon the House and the nation to prepare themselves a week ago. The whole root and core and brain of the British Army, on which and around which we were to build, and are to build, the great British Armies in the later years of the war, seemed about to perish upon the field or to be led into an ignominious and starving captivity.

That was the prospect a week ago. But another blow which might well have proved final was yet to fall upon us. The King of the Belgians had called upon us to come to his aid. Had not this Ruler and his Government severed themselves from the Allies, who rescued their country from extinction in the late war, and had they not sought refuge in what has proved to be a fatal neutrality, the French and British Armies might well at the outset have saved not only Belgium but perhaps even Poland. Yet at the last moment, when Belgium was already invaded, King Leopold called upon us to come to his aid, and even at the last moment we came. He and his brave, efficient Army, nearly half a million strong, guarded our eastern flank and thus kept open our only line of retreat to the sea. Suddenly, without prior consultation, with the least possible notice, without the advice of his Ministers and upon his own personal act, he sent a plenipotentiary to the German Command, surrendered his Army and exposed our whole flank and means of retreat.

I asked the House a week ago to suspend its judgment because the facts were not clear, but I do not feel that any reason now exists why we should not form our own opinions upon this pitiful episode. The surrender of the Belgian Army compelled the British at the shortest notice to cover a flank to the sea more than 30 miles in length. Otherwise all would have been cut off, and all would have shared the fate to which King Leopold had condemned the finest Army his country had ever formed. So in doing this and in exposing this flank, as anyone who followed the operations on the map will see, contact was lost between the British and two out of the three corps forming the First French Army, who were still further from the coast than we were, and it seemed impossible that any large number of Allied troops could reach the coast.

The enemy attacked on all sides with great strength and fierceness, and their main power, the power of their far more numerous air force, was thrown into the battle or else concentrated upon Dunkirk and the beaches. Pressing in upon the narrow exit, both from the east and from the west, the enemy began to fire with cannon upon the beaches by which alone the shipping could approach or depart. They sowed magnetic mines in the channels and seas; they sent repeated waves of hostile aircraft, sometimes more than 100 strong in one formation, to cast their bombs upon the single pier that remained, and upon the sand dunes upon which the troops had their eyes for shelter. Their U-boats, one of which was sunk, and their motor launches took their toll of the vast traffic which now began. For four or five days an intense struggle reigned. All their armoured divisions – or what was left of them – together with great masses of German infantry and artillery, hurled themselves in vain upon the ever-narrowing, ever-contracting appendix within which the British and French Armies fought.

Meanwhile, the Royal Navy, with the willing help of countless merchant seamen, strained every nerve to embark the British and Allied troops. Two hundred and twenty light warships and 650 other vessels were engaged. They had to operate upon the difficult coast, often in adverse weather, under an almost ceaseless hail of bombs and an increasing concentration of artillery fire. Nor were the seas, as I have said, themselves free from mines and torpedoes. It was in conditions such as these that our men carried on, with little or no rest, for days and nights on end, making trip after trip across the dangerous waters, bringing with them always men whom they had rescued. The numbers they have brought back are the measure of their devotion and their courage. The hospital ships, which brought off many thousands of British and French wounded, being so plainly marked were a special target for Nazi bombs; but the men and women on board them never faltered in their duty.

Meanwhile, the Royal Air Force, which had already been intervening in the battle, so far as its range would allow, from home bases, now used part of its main metropolitan fighter strength, and struck at the German bombers, and at the fighters which in large numbers protected them. This struggle was protracted and fierce. Suddenly the scene has cleared, the crash and thunder has for the moment – but only for the moment – died away. A miracle of deliverance, achieved by valour, by perseverance, by perfect discipline, by faultless service, by resource, by skill, by unconquerable fidelity, is manifest to us all. The enemy was hurled back by the retreating British and French troops. He was so roughly handled that he did not harry their departure seriously. The Royal Air Force engaged the main strength of the German Air Force, and inflicted upon them losses of at least four to one; and the Navy, using nearly 1,000 ships of all kinds, carried over 335,000 men, French and British, out of the jaws of death and shame, to their native land and to the tasks which lie immediately ahead. We must be very careful not to assign to this deliverance the attributes of a victory. Wars are not won by evacuations. But there was a victory inside this deliverance, which should be noted. It was gained by the Air Force. Many of our soldiers coming back have not seen the

Air Force at work; they saw only the bombers which escaped its protective attack. They underrate its achievements. I have heard much talk of this; that is why I go out of my way to say this. I will tell you about it.

This was a great trial of strength between the British and German Air Forces. Can you conceive a greater objective for the Germans in the air than to make evacuation from these beaches impossible, and to sink all these ships which were displayed, almost to the extent of thousands? Could there have been an objective of greater military importance and significance for the whole purpose of the war than this? They tried hard, and they were beaten back; they were frustrated in their task. We got the Army away; and they have paid fourfold for any losses which they have inflicted. Very large formations of German aeroplanes – and we know that they are a very brave race – have turned on several occasions from the attack of one-quarter of their number of the Royal Air Force, and have dispersed in different directions. Twelve aeroplanes have been hunted by two. One aeroplane was driven into the water and cast away, by the mere charge of a British aeroplane, which had no more ammunition. All of our types – the Hurricane, the Spitfire and the new Defiant – and all our pilots have been vindicated as superior to what they have at present to face.

When we consider how much greater would be our advantage in defending the air above this island against an overseas attack, I must say that I find in these facts a sure basis upon which practical and reassuring thoughts may rest. I will pay my tribute to these young airmen. The great French Army was very largely, for the time being, cast back and disturbed by the onrush of a few thousands of armoured vehicles. May it not also be that the cause of civilisation itself will be defended by the skill and devotion of a few thousand airmen? There never had been, I suppose, in all the world, in all the history of war, such an opportunity for youth. The Knights of the Round Table, the Crusaders, all fall back into a prosaic past: not only distant but prosaic; but these young men, going forth every morn to guard their native land and all that we stand for, holding in their hands these instruments of colossal and shattering power, of whom it may be said that

> 'When every morning brought a noble chance,
> And every chance brought out a noble knight,'

deserve our gratitude, as do all of the brave men who, in so many ways and on so many occasions, are ready, and continue ready, to give life and all for their native land.

I return to the Army. In the long series of very fierce battles, now on this front, now on that, fighting on three fronts at once, battles fought by two or three divisions against an equal or somewhat larger number of the enemy, and fought fiercely on some of the old grounds that so many of us knew so well, in these battles our losses in men have exceeded 30,000 killed, wounded and missing. I take occasion to express the sympathy of the House to all who have suffered bereavement or who are still anxious. The President of the Board of Trade[1] is not here to-day. His son has been killed, and many in the House have felt the pangs of affliction in the sharpest form. But I will say this about the missing. We have had a large number of wounded come home safely to this country – the greater part – but I would say about the missing that there may be very many reported missing who will come back home, some day, in one way or another. In the confusion of this fight it is inevitable that many have been left in positions where honour required no further resistance from them.

Against this loss of over 30,000 men, we can set a far heavier loss certainly inflicted upon the enemy. But our losses in material are enormous. We have perhaps lost one-third of the men we lost in the opening days of the battle of 21st March, 1918, but we have lost nearly as many guns – nearly 1,000 guns – and all our transport, all the armoured vehicles that were with the Army in the North. This loss will impose a further delay on the expansion of our military strength. That expansion had not been proceeding as fast as we had hoped. The best of all we had to give had gone to the British Expeditionary Force, and although they had not the numbers of tanks and some articles of equipment which were desirable, they were a very well and finely equipped Army. They had the first-fruits of all that our industry had to give, and that is gone. And now here is this further delay. How long it will be, how long it will last, depends upon the exertions which we make in this island. An effort the like of which has never been seen in our records is now being made. Work is proceeding everywhere, night and day, Sundays and week-days. Capital and labour have cast aside their interests, rights, and customs and put them into the common stock. Already the flow of munitions has leapt forward. There is no reason why we should not in a few months overtake the sudden and serious loss that has come upon us, without retarding the development of our general programme.

Nevertheless, our thankfulness at the escape of our Army and so many men,

---

[1] Andrew Rae Duncan, 1884–1952. Coal Controller, 1919–20. Chairman of the Advisory Committee of the Mines Department, 1920–9. Vice-President, Shipbuilding Employers' Federation, 1920–7. Knighted, 1921. Chairman of the Central Electricity Board, 1927–35. A director of the Bank of England, 1929–40. Chairman of the Executive Committee of the British Iron and Steel Federations, 1935–40 and 1945–52. MP for the City of London, 1940–50. President of the Board of Trade, 1940 and 1941. Minister of Supply, 1940–1 and 1942–5. A Director of Imperial Chemical Industries, and of the Dunlop Rubber Company. One of his two sons was killed in action in the Second World War.

whose loved ones have passed through an agonising week, must not blind us to the fact that what has happened in France and Belgium is a colossal military disaster. The French Army has been weakened, the Belgian Army has been lost, a large part of those fortified lines upon which so much faith had been reposed is gone, many valuable mining districts and factories have passed into the enemy's possession, the whole of the Channel ports are in his hands, with all the tragic consequences that follow from that, and we must expect another blow to be struck almost immediately at us or at France. We are told that Herr Hitler has a plan for invading the British Isles. This has often been thought of before. When Napoleon lay at Boulogne for a year with his flat-bottomed boats and his Grand Army, he was told by someone, 'There are bitter weeds in England.' There are certainly a great many more of them since the British Expeditionary Force returned.

The whole question of home defence against invasion is, of course, powerfully affected by the fact that we have for the time being in this island incomparably more powerful military forces than we have ever had at any moment in this war or the last. But this will not continue. We shall not be content with a defensive war. We have our duty to our Ally. We have to reconstitute and build up the British Expeditionary Force once again, under its gallant Commander-in-Chief, Lord Gort. All this is in train; but in the interval we must put our defences in this island into such a high state of organisation that the fewest possible numbers will be required to give effective security and that the largest possible potential of offensive effort may be realised. On this we are now engaged. It will be very convenient, if it be the desire of the House, to enter upon this subject in a secret Session. Not that the Government would necessarily be able to reveal in very great detail military secrets, but we like to have our discussions free, without the restraint imposed by the fact that they will be read the next day by the enemy, and the Government would benefit by views freely expressed in all parts of the House by Members with their knowledge of so many different parts of the country. I understand that some request is to be made upon this subject, which will be readily acceded to by His Majesty's Government.

We have found it necessary to take measures of increasing stringency, not only against enemy aliens and suspicious characters of other nationalities, but also against British subjects who may become a danger or a nuisance should the war be transported to the United Kingdom. I know there are a great many people affected by the orders which we have made who are the passionate enemies of Nazi Germany. I am very sorry for them, but we cannot, at the present time and under the present stress, draw all the distinctions which we should like to do. If parachute landings were attempted and fierce fighting attendant upon them followed, these unfortunate people would be far better out of the way, for their own sakes as well as for ours. There is, however, another class, for which I feel not the slightest sympathy. Parliament has given us the powers to put down Fifth Column activities with a strong hand, and we shall use those powers, subject to the supervision and correction of the House, without the slightest hesitation until we are satisfied, and more than satisfied, that this malignancy in our midst has been effectively stamped out.

Turning once again, and this time more generally, to the question of invasion, I would observe that there has never been a period in all these long centuries of which we boast when an absolute guarantee against invasion, still less against serious raids, could have been given to our people. In the days of Napoleon, of which I was speaking just now, the same wind which would have carried his transports across the Channel might have driven away the blockading fleet. There was always the chance, and it is that chance which has excited and befooled the imaginations of many Continental tyrants. Many are the tales that are told. We are assured that novel methods will be adopted, and when we see the originality of malice, the ingenuity of aggression, which our enemy displays, we may certainly prepare ourselves for every kind of novel stratagem and every kind of brutal and treacherous manoeuvre. I think that no idea is so outlandish that it should not be considered and viewed with a searching, but at the same time, I hope, with a steady eye. We must never forget the solid assurances of sea power and those which belong to air power if it can be locally exercised.

I have, myself, full confidence that if all do their duty, if nothing is neglected, and if the best arrangements are made, as they are being made, we shall prove ourselves once again able to defend our island home, to ride out the storm of war, and to outlive the menace of tyranny, if necessary for years, if necessary alone. At any rate, that is what we are going to try to do. That is the resolve of His Majesty's Government – every man of them. That is the will of Parliament and the nation. The British Empire and the French Republic, linked together in their cause and in their need, will defend to the death their native soil, aiding each other like good comrades to the utmost of their strength. Even though large tracts of Europe and many old and famous States have fallen or may fall into the grip of the Gestapo and all the odious apparatus of Nazi rule, we shall not flag or fail. We shall go on to the end. We shall fight in France, we shall fight on the seas and oceans, we shall fight with growing confidence and growing strength in the air, we shall defend our island, whatever the cost may be. We shall fight on the beaches, we shall fight on the landing grounds, we shall fight in the fields and in the streets, we shall fight in the hills; we shall never surrender, and even if, which I do not for a moment believe, this island or a large part of it were subjugated and starving, then our Empire beyond the seas, armed and guarded by the British Fleet, would carry on the struggle, until, in God's good time, the new world, with all its power and might, steps forth to the rescue and the liberation of the old.

Henry Channon: diary
('Chips')

4 June 1940

The Prime Minister made an important and moving statement. I sat behind him (he was next to Neville who looked tiny and fragile), and he was eloquent, and oratorical, and used magnificent English; several Labour Members cried. He hinted that we might be obliged to fight alone, without France, and that England might well be invaded. How the atmosphere has changed from only a few weeks ago when idiotic MPs were talking academic nonsense about our restoring independence to Warsaw and Prague.

Jock Colville tells me that the Admiralty is fantastic now; people who were at each other's throats a few weeks ago are now intimate and on the best of terms. Winston darts in and out, a mountain of energy and good-nature, the Labour leaders, Brendan Bracken and Prof. Lindemann, sometimes Randolph, Beaverbrook, the Defence Ministers, etc. – the new racket all much in evidence, but no Neville and no Horace Wilson.[1]

Colonel Josiah Wedgwood to Winston S. Churchill
(*Churchill papers, 2/399*)

4 June 1940

That was worth 1,000 guns & the speech of 1,000 years.

Yours
Jos

Winston S. Churchill to Stanley Baldwin
(*Baldwin papers*)

4 June 1940   10 Downing Street

My dear SB,

I have not till now found a moment to thank you for yr vy kind letter & good wishes wh reached me – I am ashamed to say – nearly a fortnight ago. We are going through vy hard times & I expect worse to come: but I feel sure that better days will come: though whether we shall live to see them is more doubtful.

---

[1] Horace John Wilson, 1882–1972. Entered the Civil Service, 1900; Permanent Secretary, Ministry of Labour, 1921–30. Knighted, 1924. Chief Industrial Adviser to the Government, 1930–9. Seconded to the Treasury for special service with Stanley Baldwin, 1935–7, and with Neville Chamberlain, 1937–40 (when he had a room at 10 Downing Street). Permanent Secretary to the Treasury and Head of the Civil Service, 1939–42.

I do not feel the burden weigh too heavily, but I cannot say that I have enjoyed being Prime Minister vy much so far.

Yours sincerely
Winston S. Churchill

Winston S. Churchill to King George VI
(*Churchill papers, 20/7*)

4 June 1940   10 Downing Street

Sir,

I am very grateful to Your Majesty for so graciously meeting my wishes in respect of the new Privy Councillorships. I feel very much encouraged by your Majesty's kindness to me.

Better days will come – though not yet.

Your Majesty's faithful & devoted servant and subject
Winston S. Churchill

Winston S. Churchill to General Ismay
(*Churchill papers, 20/13*)

4 June 1940

We are greatly concerned – and it is certainly wise to be so – with the dangers of the German landing in England in spite of our possessing the command of the seas and having very strong defence by fighters in the Air. Every creek, every beach, every harbour has become to us a source of anxiety. Besides this the parachutists may swoop over and take Liverpool or Ireland and so forth. All this mood is very good if it engenders energy. But if it is so easy for the Germans to invade us in spite of sea-power some may feel inclined to ask the question – why should it be thought impossible for us to do anything of the same kind to them? The completely defensive habit of mind, which has ruined the French, must not be allowed to ruin all our initiative. It is of the highest consequence to keep the largest numbers of German forces all along the coasts of the countries they have conquered and we should immediately set to work to organise raiding forces on these coasts where the populations are friendly. Such forces might be composed of the self-contained, thoroughly equipped units of say 1,000 up to not less than 10,000 when combined. Surprise would be ensured by the fact that the destination would be concealed until the last moment. What we have seen at Dunkirk shows how quickly troops can be moved off (and I suppose on) to selected points if need be. How wonderful it would be if the Germans could be made to wonder where they were going to be struck next instead of forcing us to try to wall in the Island and roof it over. An effort must be made to shake off the mental and moral prostration to the will and initiative of the enemy from which we suffer.

WSC

John Colville: diary
(*Colville papers*)

4 June 1940

At Admiralty House[1] after dinner Winston was a little on edge. He kept on ringing the bell and complaining that we were making too much noise. The last time he did so, he said, 'What is all this bloody jaw? Who is it?' I said, 'It's the First Lord, sir,' and he smiled, saying, 'Well, you've got me this time.'

Lord Cork to Winston S. Churchill
(*Admiralty papers, 199/1929*)

4 June 1940   Narvik
10.04 p.m.

Embarkation of 4,500 troops carried out last night Monday without incident, continuing to-night Tuesday under favourable conditions of low cloud and rain.

Vita Sackville-West[2] *to Harold Nicolson*
(*'Harold Nicolson, Diaries and Letters, 1939–1945'*)

5 June 1940   Sissinghurst

I wish I had heard Winston making that magnificent speech! Even repeated by the announcer it sent shivers (not of fear) down my spine. I think that one of the reasons why one is stirred by his Elizabethan phrases is that one feels the whole massive backing of power and resolve behind them, like a great fortress: they are never words for words' sake.

---

[1] On becoming Prime Minister on 10 May 1940, Churchill told Neville Chamberlain he could continue to live in the flat at 10 Downing Street until he was ready to leave. Churchill continued to live at Admiralty House, and to work in Downing Street, until 14 June 1940 (see page 331).

[2] Vita Sackville-West, 1892–1962. Daughter of the 3rd Baron Sackville. Authoress. Married Harold Nicolson in 1913. In 1940 she published *Country Notes in Wartime*. Companion of Honour, 1948.

Winston S. Churchill to General Ismay
(*Churchill papers, 20/13*)

5 June 1940

Further to my minute of yesterday about offensive action, when the Australians arrive it is a question whether they should not be organized in detachments of 250, equipped with grenades, trench mortars, tommy guns, armoured vehicles and the like, capable of acting against an attack in this country, but also capable of landing on the friendly coasts now held by the enemy. We have got to get out of our minds the idea that the Channel ports and all the country between them are enemy territory. What arrangements are being made for good agents in Denmark, Holland, Belgium, and along the French coast? Enterprises must be prepared, with specially trained troops of the hunter class, who can develop a reign of terror down these coasts, first of all on the 'butcher and bolt' policy, but later on, or perhaps as soon as we are organized, we should surprise Calais or Boulogne, kill and capture the Hun garrison and hold the place until all the preparations to reduce it by siege or heavy storm have been made, and then away. The passive resistance war, which we have acquitted ourselves so well in, must come to an end. I look to the Joint Chiefs of the Staff to propose me measures for a vigorous, enterprising and ceaseless offensive against the whole German-occupied coastline. Tanks and AFVs[1] must be made in flat-bottomed boats, out of which they can crawl ashore, do a deep raid inland, cutting a vital communication, and then back, leaving a trail of German corpses behind them. It is probable that, when the best troops go on to the attack of Paris, only the ordinary German troops of the line will be left. The lives of these must be made an intense torment. The following measures should be taken:-
(1) Proposals for organizing the striking Companies.
(2) Proposals for transporting and landing Tanks on the beach, observing that we are supposed to have the command of the sea, while the enemy have not.
(3) A proper system of espionage and intelligence along the whole coasts.
(4) Deployment of parachute troops on a scale equal to 5,000.
(5) Half a dozen of our 15-inch guns should be lined up immediately to fire 50 or 60 miles, and should be mounted either on railway mountings or on steel and concrete platforms, so as to break up the fire of the German guns that will certainly in less than four months be firing across the Channel.

WSC

---

[1] Armoured Fighting Vehicles.

Randolph S. Churchill to his father
(*Churchill papers, 1/355*)

5 June 1940   Retford

I cannot tell you how stimulating & reassuring it was to see you again & to find you so full of courage and determination.

Your loving son
Randolph

Notes of a Meeting[1]
(*Cabinet papers, 127/13*)

5 June 1940   10 Downing Street
11 a.m.

PM: How can we help the French in the battle? without hurting ourselves mortally, and in a way that will encourage the French to feel that we are doing all in our power.[2]

Winston S. Churchill to General Ismay
(*Churchill papers, 20/13*)

5 June 1940

How was it that when I went to Paris and asked for the ten additional Squadrons I was told we had only 39, so that the ten reduced them to 29? Please look up the papers on this point. The Air Ministry change their figures every single day.

Winston S. Churchill to General Weygand and Paul Reynaud
(*Premier papers, 3/188/1*)

5 June 1940
4.15 p.m.

We have had this morning a request in general terms for air assistance in the land battle now developing on the Abbeville–Rheims front: but we have

---

[1] These notes were kept by General Ismay. Those present were Churchill, Sinclair, Beaverbrook, Newall, Peirse, Dowding and Ismay.

[2] In reply to Churchill's question, Dowding opposed the despatch of any more fighters to France. Following Churchill's persistent questioning as to the numbers of planes and pilots available, or in prospect, Dowding agreed to produce the detailed figures early that same afternoon.

June 1940 253

had no precise information as to the form this assistance should take nor where.

We are holding four squadrons of bombers and two squadrons of fighters at full strength ready to intervene from this country. To do this we have had to break up many squadrons and suspend the whole process of re-organisation after the stress and confusion of Dunkirk.

Meanwhile we are dispatching reconnaissance aircraft into the Abbeville–Amiens area. If this reconnaissance shows good targets the bombers will be dispatched to attack escorted by fighters. If no suitable targets are found the fighters will in any case be dispatched to intervene in the battle area.

The above relates to day operation in addition to those undertaken by British Air Force in France.

We also have strong bomber forces detailed for the attack tonight of objectives already specified by you.

Sir Ronald Campbell to Lord Halifax
(*Cabinet papers, 65/13*)

5 June 1940
8.55 p.m.

M. Reynaud when I saw him this evening told me that Marshal Pétain on learning of the Prime Minister's reply to the latest French appeal for further help in the air had exclaimed 'well, there is nothing left but to make peace. If you do not want to do it you can hand over to me'.

M. Reynaud had of course scouted the idea and said he only mentioned it to me to show how grave the situation was. He asked whether I thought that His Majesty's Government completely realised it. I said that I was quite certain they did and that they were going, and would continue to go, as far as was possible. If they denuded British Isles of all their air defences on the eve of invasion by all of the enemy's devices they would incur an unforgivable responsibility.

I am deeply distressed by the reiteration of these appeals at a time when I know you are doing all you can, but the very grave danger in which the French stand in this hour must be their excuse.

Winston S. Churchill to Paul Reynaud and General Weygand
(*Churchill papers, 20/14*)

5 June 1940

Your comments will be examined by General Staff, who have orders to send the two divisions as soon as possible.

Permit me to observe that your divisions picked out of Dunkirk are not to enter the line for a month. We are trying to send one of our seasoned divisions in in a fortnight.

Fighter Aircraft. – General Vuillemin's demand was altogether unreasonable and his letter made the worst impression on everyone here and greatly increased my difficulties. Kindly look at the paragraph in which he refers to the assistance we gave in the recent battle. You don't seem to understand at all that British fighter aviation has been worn to a shred and frightfully mixed up by the need of maintaining standing patrols of forty-eight fighters over Dunkirk without which the evacuation would have been impossible. The mere sorting out of the aeroplanes from the different squadrons practically paralyses the force for four or five days. However, I have sent you this morning a telegram saying that we would hold four squadrons of day bombers and two of Hurricane fighters available for operations this afternoon in addition to the nine squadrons you have already and I shall try to maintain the same to-morrow, when I will telegraph again.

Winston S. Churchill to William Mackenzie King
(*Premier papers, 4/43B/1*)

5 June 1940　　　　　　　　　　　　　　　　　　　　　　10 Downing Street
Most Secret
Personal

All the matters in your telegram of May 30[1] have been for some time in my mind. British situation vastly improved by miraculous evacuation of BEF which gives us an army in the Island more than capable, when re-equipped, of coping with any invading force likely to be landed. Also evacuation was a main trial of strength between British and German Air Forces. Germans have been unable to prevent evacuation, and though largely superior in numbers have suffered at least three times our loss. For technical reasons, British Air Force would have many more advantages in defending the Air above the Island than in operating overseas. Principal remaining danger is, of course, Air factories, but if our Air defence is so strong that enemy can only come on dark nights precision will not be easy. I therefore feel solid confidence in British ability to continue the war, defend the Island and the Empire, and maintain the blockade.

I do not know whether it would be possible to keep France in the war or not. I hope they will, even at the worst, maintain a gigantic guerilla. We are reconstituting the BEF out of other units.

---

[1] Not found.

We must be careful not to let Americans view too complacently prospect of a British collapse, out of which they would get the British Fleet and the guardianship of the British Empire, minus Great Britain. If United States were in the war and England conquered locally, it would be natural that events should follow line you describe. But if America continued neutral, and we were overpowered, I cannot tell what policy might be adopted by a pro-German administration such as would undoubtedly be set up.

Although President is our best friend, no practical help has been forthcoming from the United States as yet. We have not expected them to send military aid, but they have not even sent any worthy contribution in destroyers or planes, or by a visit of a squadron of their Fleet to Southern Irish ports. Any pressure which you can supply in this direction would be invaluable.

We are most deeply grateful to you for all your help and for destroyers, which have already gone into action against a U-Boat. Kindest regards.

Winston S. Churchill to Neville Chamberlain
(*Churchill papers, 20/11*)

6 June 1940   10 Downing Street
Private

My dear Neville,

I was much encouraged by the line you took yesterday about LG. I feel he will be a valuable counsellor, and a help to me and to the Cabinet. I am sure he would bring added strength to the Government, and that otherwise, being treated as an outcast, he will become the focus for regathering discontents. Whatever happens you and I will continue to work together, but I should be very grateful to you if you felt able to work officially with him, and not make your assistance, which I value so highly, dependent upon his exclusion. I believe that you would find him ready to put aside all personal feuds or prejudices; and this is also Beaverbrook's opinion, who has seen him frequently. In this terrible hour, with all that impends, the country ought to be satisfied that all its ablest and best-known leaders are playing their part, and I certainly do not think that one should be set against another. I know the sacrifices of personal interest and position which you have made arise solely from your public spirit and our cruel need, and I venture to hope that you will aid and ease me in this matter, which I regard as very important for the general cohesion of the Government. I will guarantee that he will work fairly and honourably with you, failing which please count as always upon

Your sincere friend,
Winston S. Churchill

Winston S. Churchill: statement
(*Hansard*)

6 June 1940   House of Commons

The Prime Minister (Mr Churchill): His Majesty's Government in the United Kingdom recognise the Belgian Government at present established in France as the only legal Government of Belgium, and as therefore entitled to exercise in the name of Belgium all due authority. I need hardly add that it is the unswerving aim of His Majesty's Government, and, I am sure, also of the French Government, to secure for Belgium the effective restoration of her freedom and independence.

John Colville: diary
(*Colville papers*)

6 June 1940

The PM went to a cinema, to see the Dunkirk film, and returned to Admiralty House in rather a bad temper. He bade me light the fire, although it was the hottest of hot nights, and then proceeded to work till 1.30. He was cross with the French, who are being persistent in their demands for further air support. Pétain and Weygand are saying that if we do not send fighters, the present battle will be lost and France will have to capitulate. Pétain told Reynaud that if he had not the courage to do so, he, Pétain, would undertake the task. I think the French are trying to frighten us, for bargaining purposes, but Winston is justifiably angry with Vuillemin who referred to our tremendous air efforts in the first battle as 'tardy, inadequate but nevertheless of value'.

The PM was in an impatient frame of mind. He was angry with the First Sea Lord, who is being excessively cautious about Winston's cherished Operation 'Paul' (which is to interrupt by mine-laying the Lulea iron-ore traffic), and with the Secretary of State for War (Anthony Eden) who is making difficulties about bringing battalions of trained troops back from Palestine.

Winston S. Churchill: recollection
(*'Their Finest Hour', page 144*)

6 June 1940

'Depend upon it,' said Dr Johnson, 'when a man knows he is going to be hanged in a fortnight, it concentrates his mind wonderfully.' I was always sure we should win, but nevertheless I was highly geared up by the situation, and very thankful to be able to make my views effective. June 6 seems to have been for me an active and not barren day. My minutes, dictated as I lay in bed in the morning and pondered on the dark horizon, show the variety of topics upon which it was necessary to give directions.[1]

Winston S. Churchill to General Ismay
(*Churchill papers, 20/13*)

6 June 1940

It is of the utmost importance to find some projectile which can be fired from a rifle at a Tank like a rifle grenade, or from an anti-Tank rifle, like a trench-mortar bomb. The sticky bomb[2] seems to be useful for the first of these, but perhaps this is not so. Anyhow, concentrate attention upon finding something that can be fired from AT rifles or from ordinary rifles.

WSC

Winston S. Churchill to Herbert Morrison
(*Churchill papers, 20/13*)

6 June 1940

I should be grateful if I might be supplied each week, beginning this Saturday, with reports on the progress made with the Proximity Fuse and the UP weapon.[3] Please let these reports be quite short, if possible not exceeding one sheet of paper.

WSC

Winston S. Churchill to Sir Archibald Sinclair and Sir Cyril Newall
(*Churchill papers, 20/13*)

6 June 1940

What was the result of the discussion yesterday with Admiral Royle, Fifth Sea Lord,[4] about transferring temporarily some trained and half-trained

[1] I have been able to find eleven minutes dictated by Churchill on 6 June, each of which is printed here.
[2] The Sticky Bomb was a British anti-tank grenade. Its adhesive outer covering was designed to stick to the surface of a tank. There were times, however, not all that infrequent, when it stuck to the hand of the thrower, which did not enhance its popularity. Its official designation was 'Grenade, hand, Anti-Tank, No. 74 (ST)'.
[3] The Unrotated Projectile anti-aircraft rocket.
[4] Guy Charles Cecil Royle, 1885–1954. Midshipman, 1900. On active service in the Royal Navy, 1914–18 (Battle of Jutland, despatches, CMG). Naval Attaché, Tokyo, 1924–7. Naval Secretary to the First Lord of the Admiralty, 1934–7. Vice-Admiral, Aircraft Carriers, 1937–9.

pilots from the Fleet Air Arm to the Fighter Force? I was considering that at least fifty should be found at once as a minimum. Pray let me know what has happened. Was Air Marshal Dowding consulted and is he satisfied?

WSC

Winston S. Churchill to Herbert Morrison
(*Churchill papers, 20/13*)

6 June 1940

In your examination of the points raised in the discussion on WP (G) (40) 143 (Development of Timber Production in this country and France), I should like you to consider and report to me upon the following points:–

(1) We have standing timber capable of producing about 27 million tons of soft wood. Lest we jeopardise future reserves the Forestry Commission has limited the amount to be felled to 9 million tons, of which we are at present only felling 2·1 million a year. The plan here put forward proposes to fell 3·4 million tons in the coming year. This is a very modest proposal which from the timber point of view might well be exceeded in present circumstances.

(2) To fulfil the programme, extra labour will be required. It is not quite clear why we need two skilled workers to every unskilled worker, while the French are satisfied with one skilled worker to every three unskilled workers. If it is suggested that the quality of our unskilled workers would be inferior, our volunteers of the 18–20 class could be employed as woodsmen for part of their time. These would presumably be as efficient as any unskilled labour available to the French.

(3) Would it not be well to make some special commissioner responsible for the execution of the British plan in lieu of the Forestry Commission?

Would you please make the necessary contacts with other Departments and report to me accordingly?

WSC

Winston S. Churchill to Lord Beaverbrook
(*Churchill papers, 20/13*)

6 June 1940

I should be grateful if I might be supplied each Saturday with weekly reports, beginning this Saturday, on –
1. the stabilisation of the automatic bombsights.

Naval Secretary to the First Lord (Churchill), September–November 1939. Fifth Sea Lord and Chief of Naval Air Services, 1939–41. Knighted, 1941. First Naval Member, Commonwealth Naval Board, 1941–5. Admiral, 1942.

June 1940

2. the production of the provisional stabilised bombsights.
3. low altitude RDF and the AI.[1]

These reports should be quite short, not exceeding one sheet of paper in length.

WSC

Winston S. Churchill to Lord Halifax and Anthony Eden
(*Churchill papers, 20/13*)

6 June 1940

The Dutch Ministers[2] yesterday stressed the importance of forming a Dutch Brigade, and of furnishing them with as much equipment as possible. If there is no Foreign Office objection, it seems very important to get on with this as quickly as possible, and I shall be very glad to receive a weekly report.

WSC

Winston S. Churchill to Sir Archibald Sinclair and Sir Cyril Newall
(*Churchill papers, 20/13*)

6 June 1940

It is of the highest importance that we should strike at Italy the moment war breaks out, or an overbearing ultimatum is received. Please let me know the exact position of the servicing Units which are on their way to the southern Aerodromes in France.

WSC

Winston S. Churchill to Admiral Pound
(*Churchill papers, 20/13*)

6 June 1940

There seem to be a lot of valuable ships in Malta harbour under various conditions of repair. Can I have a nominal list of them, and the dates when they will be ready for sea. What is the position of the *Monitor*? Apparently she will be thrown away. Admiral Cunningham does not seem to have been much concerned about the fate of all these ships.

---

[1] Radio Direction Finding (radar) and Air Interception (a radar device, code name 'Smeller').
[2] Following the German occupation of Holland, the Dutch Queen and Government had moved to London, where they were to remain until the last weeks of the war.

Winston S. Churchill to Admiral Pound
(*Churchill papers, 20/13*)

6 June 1940

The Aerodromes at Bardufoss and Skaarnland should be rendered unusable for three or four months by means of delay action bombs buried in different parts of the Aerodrome. Have we got these bombs? And can they be sent to Lord Cork in time? This ought to have been thought of before. The greatest importance is attached to the operation 'Paul.' Pray let me have a report of how this is progressing, and when it is intended to begin.

Winston S. Churchill to Lord Halifax
(*Churchill papers, 20/13*)

6 June 1940

The Belgian Minister, M. Spaak,[1] spoke yesterday of the desire of his country that an explicit public declaration should be made by Great Britain that we recognise the Belgian Government apart from the King as the sole constitutional Belgian authority.

I was very glad to hear from you yesterday that you had this in hand.

WSC

Winston S. Churchill to Lord Halifax
(*Churchill papers, 20/13*)

6 June 1940
Private

I have hitherto argued against going to war with Italy because she attacked Yugoslavia, and have wished to see whether it was a serious attack upon Yugoslavian independence or merely taking some naval bases in the Adriatic. However, this situation has changed. Italy is continually threatening to go to war with England and France, and not by 'the back door.' We are so near a break with Italy on grounds which have nothing to do with Yugoslavia that it

---

[1] Paul-Henri Spaak, 1899–1972. Socialist Deputy for Brussels, 1932. Belgian Minister of Transport, Posts and Telegraphs, 1935–6. Minister of Foreign Affairs and Trade, 1936–8; Prime Minister, May 1938 to February 1939. Minister for Foreign Affairs, September 1939 to August 1949 (in London, 1940–5). Prime Minister and Minister for Foreign Affairs, 1947–9. Chairman, Council for European Recovery, 1948. Belgian Minister for Foreign Affairs, 1954–7. Secretary-General of the North Atlantic Treaty Organisation, 1957–61. Deputy Prime Minister, Minister of Foreign Affairs and African Affairs, Belgium, 1961–6. Companion of Honour (CH), 1963.

would seem that our main aim might well be now to procure this Balkan mobilisation. Will you think this over?

WSC

Winston S. Churchill to Anthony Eden
(*Churchill papers, 20/13*)

6 June 1940

1. I am much disappointed with your letter, which shows how everything gets smaller and is slowed down so far as British action is concerned. It is more than a fortnight ago since I was told that eight battalions could leave India and arrive in this country in forty-two days from the order being given. The order was given. Now it is not till June 6 that the first eight battalions leave India on their voyage round the Cape, arriving only July 25.

2. The Australians are coming in the big ships, but they seem to have wasted a week at Capetown, and are now only proceeding at eighteen knots, instead of the twenty I was assured were possible. It is hoped they will be here about the 15th. Is this so? At any rate, whenever they arrive the big ships should be immediately filled with territorials – the more the better – preferably twelve battalions, and sent off to India at full speed. As soon as they arrive in India they should embark another eight regular battalions for this country, making the voyage again at full speed. They should then take another batch of territorials to India. Future transferences can be discussed later. There can be no question of the shipping situation obstructing these moves, as the big ships can go to and fro on their business. Of course, if you were able to propose me a more rapid sailing from India of the second eight battalions, I should be pleased. But all I am asking now is that the big ships should go to and fro at full speed.

3. I am very sorry indeed, to find the virtual deadlock which local objections have imposed upon the battalions from Palestine. It is quite natural that General Wavell[1] should look at the situation only from his own viewpoint. Here we have to think of building up a good army in order to make up, as far as possible, for the lamentable failure to support the French by an adequate BEF during the first year of the war. Do you realise that in the first year of the late war we brought forty-seven Divisions into action, and that

[1] Archibald Percival Wavell, 1883–1950. On active service in South Africa, 1901, and on the Western Front, 1914–16 (wounded, Military Cross). Military Attaché with the Russian Army in the Caucasus, 1916–17, and with the Egyptian Expeditionary Force, Palestine, 1917–18. CMG, 1919. Commanded the troops in Palestine and Transjordan, 1937–8. General Officer Commanding-in-Chief, Southern Command, 1938–9. Knighted, 1939. Commander-in-Chief, Middle East, 1940–1; India, 1941–3. Field Marshal, 1943. Created Earl, 1947. Biographer of Field Marshal Allenby.

these were Divisions of twelve battalions plus one Pioneer battalion, not nine as now? We are, indeed, the victims of a feeble and weary Departmentalism.

4. Owing to the saving of the BEF, I have been willing to wait for the relief of the eight battalions from Palestine by eight native Indian battalions, provided these latter were sent at once; but you give me no time-table for this. I have not yet received any report on whether it is possible to send these British battalions and their Indian relief via Basra and the Persian Gulf.

Perhaps you would very kindly let me have this in the first instance.

5. I am prepared also to consider as an alternative, or an immediate step, the sending home of the rest of the Australian corps. Perhaps you will let me have a note on this, showing especially dates at which the moves can be made.

6. You must not think I am ignoring the position in the Middle East. On the contrary, it seems to me that we should draw upon India much more largely, and that a ceaseless stream of Indian units should be passing into Palestine and Egypt via Bombay and Karachi across the desert route. India is doing nothing worth speaking of at the present time. In the last war not only did we have all the regular troops out in the first nine months (many more than are there now), but also an Indian Corps fought by Christmas in France. Our weakness, slowness, lack of grip and drive are very apparent on the background of what was done twenty-five years ago. I really think that you, Lloyd and Amery ought to be able to lift our affairs in the East and Middle East out of the catalepsy by which they are smitten.

7. If you will very kindly consider these matters together and be ready to discuss them with me and your two colleagues on Monday next, I shall be most grateful.

Winston S. Churchill to Paul Reynaud
(*Churchill papers, 20/14*)

6 June 1940

Movement of 52nd Division being accelerated to utmost. It starts embarkation to-morrow and by using two ports should complete disembarkation by 13th. In order to send you help quicker than could be done by a re-formed Dunkirk Division, we are sending the Canadians, who start embarkation on 11th. A third Division will follow as soon as possible if you can provide artillery. Please let me know.

Our Air Forces, both bomber and fighter, are again intervening from this country to-day in the Somme battle. Fighters are refuelling in France and thus able to operate for longer periods. In addition considerable heavy bomber forces will to-night continue their attacks against objectives specified by your High Command.

Good wishes.

General Ismay to General Spears
(*Premier papers, 3/188/3*)

7 June 1940
12 noon

Prime Minister strongly deprecates the disclosure to Army Committee Senate of precise strengths employed in yesterday's battle, and considers that to disclose the strength which it is proposed to employ today is still more to be deprecated.

In order, however, that M. Reynaud may be aware of the scale of our effort, he may be told for his personal information that 144 British fighters were engaged in France yesterday, and that a still larger number will be operating today.

War Cabinet: Confidential Annex
(*Cabinet papers, 65/3*)

7 June 1940　　　　　　　　　　　　　　　　　　　　　　　10 Downing Street
12.30 p.m.

The Prime Minister said that the French seemed to be resisting the German attack fairly well in spite of the weight of the enemy's assault. The 51st Division, however, was over matched, and no reinforcements could arrive for it for two or three days. The French were pressing us hard all the time to send additional air support, and M. Monnet[1] had come to see him the previous evening to make a special appeal. It was clear that they would try and put the blame on us if they lost this critical battle.

In point of fact we had had 144 fighters operating over France the previous day, mainly from home aerodromes, but using advanced landing grounds in France. This was the equivalent of 12 squadrons, and more than they had originally asked for. An even larger number would be operating today. Our heavy bombers had also been active in attacking the targets which had been indicated by the French High Command. He proposed, therefore, to send a further telegram to M. Reynaud emphasising the great efforts which we were making on their behalf.

The reorganisation of Fighter Command was proceeding faster than had been previously expected. The Air Officer Commanding-in-Chief had

[1] Jean Monnet, 1888–1979. French representative on the Allied Executive Committee for the relocation of common resources, 1916–18. Deputy Secretary-General of the League of Nations, 1919. Chairman of the Franco-British Economic Co-ordination Committee, 1939. Member of the British Supply Council, Washington, 1940–3. Commissioner for Armament, Supplies and Reconstruction, French National Committee, Algiers, 1943–4. General Commissioner, Plan for the Modernisation and Equipment of France (Monnet Plan), 1946. Honorary GBE, 1947. President of the European Coal and Steel Community, 1952–5. Chairman of the Action Committee for the United States of Europe, 1956–75. Honorary Companion of Honour, 1972.

reported that, out of 21 Hurricane squadrons, 14 were fit to operate the previous day from bases in the United Kingdom. This implied that all these squadrons had 12 or more pilots and 12 aircraft fit to fly. Squadrons based in France would have to have 16. Great efforts were being made to provide additional pilots. Some were being obtained from the Fleet Air Arm, and all suitable pilots under 30 years of age in the Air Ministry and the Ministry of Aircraft Production were being combed out. It was hoped to produce 50 from among the ferry pilots employed under the Ministry of Aircraft Production. The flow of aircraft was very satisfactory, and the Minister of Aircraft Production had managed to lay his hands on some Dutch aircraft in transit from the United States. There was also a possibility of his getting hold of some American aircraft consigned to Sweden.

The small arm ammunition position was less unsatisfactory than had at first appeared. We had a certain margin until August, when production would broaden out. There would, however, be a shortage of special natures, such as armour-piercing.

Winston S. Churchill to the Dominion Prime Ministers
(*Premier papers, 4/43B/1*)

7 June 1940
10 p.m.
Most Secret and Personal

1. We emphasised that that portion of BEF evacuated from northern France must be completely re-equipped before employed again, and that considerable replacements in personnel and equipment would also be necessary in our air fighter force, whole of which has been most intensively engaged.

2. BEF Headquarters would be re-established in France and new BEF built up as quickly as possible. Two divisions and proportion of Corps troops would be sent over within a period of days. Third division would be despatched as rapidly as possible, but this depends largely on when its artillery can be provided. French asked if they can help in this respect. Appropriate proportion of Army Co-operation aircraft would accompany above formations.

3. Fighter squadrons now in France are being brought up to strength immediately, and every effort would be made to send further help immediately recent losses have been replaced.

4. Bomber squadrons now in France would be brought up to full strength as soon as possible, and remainder of bomber force in United Kingdom would continue support as in the past, priority being given to action against objectives selected by French High Command.

June 1940

Winston S. Churchill to Paul Reynaud and General Weygand
(*Premier papers, 3/188/1*)

7 June 1940
11.15 p.m.

I am now able to tell you that during the last 24 hours, we have increased our effort in the air for the assistance of France. During the night, our heavy bombers attacked in strength (59 tons of bombs) all the targets indicated by the French High Command. In addition to-day the medium bombers from Britain have so far undertaken 60 sorties.

2. The fighters working from this country and using forward landing grounds south of the Somme have operated for the purpose of escorts to medium bombers and as independent fighter patrols at a strength of 192 aircraft sorties, exclusive of protection for troop transport movements between Southampton and Cherbourg, etc.

3. To-morrow, it is proposed by amalgamating three fighter squadrons to send two additional fighter squadrons at full strength to be based in France in the Advance Air Striking Force area under the orders of Commander-in-Chief BAFF.[1] This will bring his strength up to five full fighter squadrons. In addition, we hope to be able to operate four fighter squadrons daily based in this country from the advanced refuelling landing grounds south of the Somme.

4. Our recent experience has shown that we cannot at present maintain more than this number of squadrons at the high battle wastage experienced in the Flanders battle.

5. In consequence of the improvement in communications which has been apparent to-day between Commander-in-Chief, BAFF, and this country, it is now possible to place eight medium bomber squadrons in England at the disposal of Commander-in-Chief, BAFF, for co-operation with the French and British forces in the battle. The heavy bomber squadrons will continue to be available for the attack of targets by night indicated by the French High Command.

6. I understand that there has been a request via the French Air Attaché in London[2] for some barrage balloons, complete with winches, &c., for the defence of Paris. We are allotting forthwith 24 complete balloon outfits with crews for this purpose.

7. It may be relevant to observe that attacks on objectives in this country

---

[1] Air Marshal Barratt.
[2] Colonel Pierre Fournier.

have been undertaken during the last two nights at a strength of approximately 100 aircraft per night, exclusive of extensive mining operation by aircraft.

8. I am referring your complaint about General Fortune[1] to the War Office. He has a wide front to hold and has had very heavy losses.

Sir Ronald Campbell to Lord Halifax
(Foreign Office papers, 800/362)

7 June 1940
Paris

I have just had the Prime Minister's latest telegram about the help we are giving the French in the air. It is a <u>magnificent</u> effort.

Winston S. Churchill to Professor Lindemann
(Churchill papers, 20/13)

7 June 1940
Secret

I am much grieved to hear of the further delay in the proximity fuse.

Considering the enormous importance of this, and the directions I have given that all possible pressure should be put behind it, it would surely have been right to have two or three firms simultaneously making the experimental pattern, so that if one failed, the other could go on.

Please report to me what has been done.

You have not given me yet either a full statement of the production which is already ordered in UP and in rockets for the proximity fuse and in rockets for the ordinary fuse before we get the PF.

It is of the utmost importance that you should go forward with the stabilising bomb sight, as we must knock out their aircraft factories at the same rate that they affect ours. If you will gather together (a) all the people interested in the PF, and (b) all those interested in the stabilised bomb sight, I will next week receive their reports and urge them on.

WSC

---

[1] Victor Morven Fortune, 1883–1949. On active service, 1914–18 (despatches, DSO). Major-General, 1935. Commanded the 51st (Highland) Division, 1937–40. Prisoner of war, June 1940 to May 1945. Knighted, 1945.

8 June 1940　　　　　　　　　　　　　　　　　　　　Daily Express

Winston S. Churchill to Paul Reynaud
(*Premier papers, 3/188/1*)

8 June 1940

We are giving you all the support we can in this great battle short of ruining the capacity of this country to continue the war. We have had very heavy and disproportionate loss in the air to-day, but we shall continue to-morrow.

Winston S. Churchill to Anthony Eden
(*Churchill papers, 20/13*)

8 June 1940

1. I should be very glad to see, during the week-end, the outlines of your plan for reconstituting the BEF. Probably you will have to reduce the Divisions from nine to seven, and I am sure you are right to begin by forming Brigade Groups. How do you propose to use the sixteen Battalions we are getting from India? Can you make two Divisions, or four Divisions out of them? I hope the latter. Or again, would you use them in part to reconstitute the two lost Divisions of the BEF?

2. The attached note[1] is very interesting, and I agree with it, except that one cannot make a rule in a war of this kind that only men who have been under fire can command those who have been out already. There is a great opportunity now for picking leaders, not only among those who have had the opportunity of meeting the enemy, but also in those who have prepared themselves to do so. Men of force and intelligence and personality, who would make their way to leading positions in civil life, should be given their chance as soon as they have acquired the minimum of training. We want live wires, and not conventional types. Qualities shown in action, however, take precedence and give fine opportunities for promoting men in the twenties to the Command of Battalions.

Defence Committee: minutes
(*Cabinet papers, 69/1*)

8 June 1940
5.15 p.m.

The Prime Minister said that there were two alternatives open to us at the present time. We could regard the present battle as decisive for France and

---

[1] A memorandum, dated 6 June 1940, by the Vice-Chief of the Imperial General Staff, Lieutenant-General Sir R. H. Haining.

ourselves, and throw in the whole of our fighter resources in an attempt to save the situation, and bring about victory. If we failed, we should then have to surrender. Alternatively, we should recognise that whereas the present land battle was of great importance, it would not be decisive one way or the other for Great Britain. If it were lost, and France was forced to submit, we could continue the struggle with good hopes of ultimate victory, provided we ensured that our fighter defences in this country were not impaired: but if we cast away our defence the war would be lost, even if the front in France were stabilised, since Germany would be free to turn her air force against this country, and would have us at her mercy.

One thing was certain. If this country were defeated, the war would be lost for France no less than for ourselves, whereas, provided we were strong ourselves, we could win the war, and, in so doing, restore France to her position. He felt it would be fatal to yield to the French demands and jeopardise our own safety.

Unanimous agreement was expressed with this view, and a telegram was drafted by the Prime Minister, and amended in discussion, for despatch to M. Reynaud. This telegram was reconsidered at the conclusion of the meeting, and another was drafted in substitution.

Winston S. Churchill to Paul Reynaud
(*Premier papers, 3/188/1*)

8 June 1940   10 Downing Street

We hope to continue the very great effort made at heavy & disproportionate loss yesterday and now being renewed at even heavier loss to-day. The additional fighter aircraft for which you press me cannot decide the fate of this great land battle. They might give temporary relief for a few days, and then they would be burnt up and cast away; whereas if not cast away they afford the means by which we expect to prolong the war till the United States comes in, or even indefinitely, thus saving in the end not only ourselves but France. I understand your feelings and Weygand's and am doing my utmost to help, but there is no reason why this battle should be decisive for France, and certainly it must not be the end of the resistance of England, for then all hope of final victory would be gone.

We believe that if we do not by an act of strategic folly leave ourselves utterly defenceless Hitler will break his Air weapon in trying to invade us. The score of Squadrons or so which you would like to have melted down in the next few days as a mere makeweight or episode in your splendid struggle will we believe if properly used in this country, enable us to break his Air attack, and thus break him. It would be madness for us to cast aside the entire future, and the surest hope of our common victory, for the sake of what could only be a comparatively minor intervention. I have not an Officer or colleague who would remain with me if I took so improvident a step. But even if it rested with me alone, I would not be guilty of such weakness and despair.

Winston S. Churchill to Desmond Morton and Professor Lindemann
(*Premier papers, 7/2*)

9 June 1940

Go to it, both of you, & report to me what we sh'd put out for full blast production.

Winston S. Churchill to Lord Lothian
(*Churchill papers, 20/14*)

9 June 1940

My last words in speech were, of course, addressed primarily to Germany and Italy, to whom the idea of a war of Continents and a long war are at present obnoxious; also to Dominions, for whom we are trustees. I have nevertheless always had in mind your point and have raised it in various telegrams to President as well as to Mackenzie King. If Great Britain broke under invasion, a pro-German Government might obtain far easier terms from Germany by surrendering the Fleet, thus making Germany and Japan masters of the new world. This dastard deed would not be done by His Majesty's present advisers, but, if Mosley were Prime Minister or some other Quisling[1] Government set up, it is exactly what they would do, and perhaps the only thing they could do, and the President should bear this very clearly in mind. You should talk to him in this sense and thus discourage any

---

[1] Vidkun Quisling, 1887–1945. Norwegian General Staff Officer, 1911. Retired from the Army, 1923, with the rank of Major. Entered the Norwegian Parliament, 1925. Minister of Defence, 1931. Resigned, 1933, to found a National Unity movement similar to the Nazi movement in Germany. Six days before the German attack on Norway in April 1940 he travelled to Copenhagen, where he confided Norwegian defence plans to a German agent. Helped the Germans to establish their administration in Norway, May 1940. Prime Minister of Norway, 1942–5. Charged with high treason, 1945, and executed (October 1945). His name became an eponym for the leader of any enemy-sponsored puppet regime.

complacent assumption on United States part that they will pick up the debris of the British Empire by their present policy. On the contrary, they run the terrible risk that their sea power will be completely over-matched. Moreover, islands and naval bases to hold the United States in awe would certainly be claimed by the Nazis. If we go down, Hitler has a very good chance of conquering the world.

I hope the foregoing will be a help to you in your conversations.

Winston S. Churchill to General Smuts
(*Premier papers, 4/43B/1*)

9 June 1940

We are of course doing all we can both from the Air and by sending Divisions as fast as they can be equipped to France. It would be wrong to send the bulk of our fighters to this battle and, when it was lost, as is probable, be left with no means of carrying on the war. I think we have a harder, longer and more hopeful duty to perform. Advantages of resisting German air attack in this Island, where we can concentrate very powerful fighter strength, and hope to knock out four or five hostiles to one of ours, are far superior to fighting in France, where we are inevitably out-numbered, rarely exceed two to one ratio of destruction, and where our aircraft are often destroyed at exposed aerodromes. This battle does not turn on the score or so of fighting Squadrons we could transport with their plant in the next month. Even if by using them up we held the enemy, Hitler could immediately throw his whole strength against our undefended Island and destroy our means of future production by daylight attack. The classical principles of war which you mention are in this case modified by the actual quantitative data. I see only one sure way through now, to wit, that Hitler should attack this country and in so doing break his Air weapon. If this happens he will be left to face the winter with Europe writhing under his heel and probably with the United States against him after the Presidential election is over.

Am most grateful to you for cable.[1] Please always give me your counsel, my old and valiant friend.

---

[1] In a telegram to Churchill decyphered at 5 p.m. on 8 June 1940, Smuts stressed the need for Britain to concentrate 'all available resources' in France. 'If this battle is won by France,' he explained, 'chances of attack on Britain will correspondingly lessen. I also do not think, while this battle is on, there is much danger of a really formidable attack on Britain, and certainly risks must in any case be run' (*Premier papers, 4/43B/1*).

Winston S. Churchill to General Ismay
(*Churchill papers, 20/17*)

9 June 1940

OPERATION 'PAUL'

We have been ill-served over this and the operation needlessly delayed. The best chances have been lost. The *Illustrious* is being wasted. I am very much grieved that the Admiralty have not taken care of this most important operation and tried to fit it in earlier.

Now at last the moment has come when the complete evacuation of Narvik is in sight, if not indeed already achieved, and when the situation at home is improved by the rescue of the BEF. I understood from the First Sea Lord that the operation would be carried out at once. What is the position about this? The sooner it is over the better. Thereafter the aircraft carriers can go to America to pick up aeroplanes. I cannot approve the *Illustrious* being sent round the Cape to Alexandria. Pray let me have proposals for action together with time table.

Winston S. Churchill to General Ismay
(*Premier papers, 3/93/1*)

9 June 1940
10 Downing Street

It is impossible to provide protection everywhere against mere threats of possible descent by parachute. The only sound principle of defence is to have vigilant, widespread local watch and such protection as can be organized on the spot, and to hold well-organized, mobile forces at hand at short notice to attack the assailants. The Commander-in-Chief, Home Forces,[1] should be supported in his sound decision not to dissipate or distribute his striking force. Unless he is sustained you will presently have no army at all, only a vast swarm of sentries. No universal protection can be given, but examples can be made of assailants. The key aircraft factories set out in appendix 'A'[2] Lists (a) and (b) seem to me to be almost the sole exception to this general rule. I presume some of the mobile columns are very close to these areas. They might live in the handiest places.

I should like to know what arrangements are possible without deviating from the general principle of no dispersion. Surely defence parties can be organized from the working staff, and also from the local parashooters. This last method will also apply to unoccupied aerodromes, coal-mines etc. <u>Don't disperse the army</u>. Keep strong strike forces in hand. Have good communications.

[1] General Ironside.
[2] In Chiefs of Staff Paper No. 370 of 1940.

War Cabinet: minutes
(*Cabinet papers, 65/7*)

9 June 1940　　　　　　　　　　　　　　　　　　　10 Downing Street
7 p.m.

The Prime Minister alluded to a case which had come to his notice of an Air Force Officer having been insulted by troops at Dover. He requested the Chief of the Imperial General Staff to carry out a vigorous campaign, which should include propaganda, in all units to ensure that the gallantry and heroism shown by the Royal Air Force in recent operations were known and appreciated.

The Prime Minister described a conversation which he had had that afternoon with General de Gaulle,[1] who had recently been appointed to an important position on General Weygand's Staff. He had given the Prime Minister a more favourable impression of French morale and determination. He had said that with the personnel withdrawn from Dunkirk and arriving from other sources three new armoured divisions would be formed, ready to go into action by the 12th June, and thereafter six or seven new divisions would be built up to increase the French reserves. He had urged that the further British divisions which were being moved to France should be sent as rapidly as possible. The Prime Minister had outlined our plans and had told him that General Weygand would be receiving a definite programme through the normal liaison channels. He had also explained to General de Gaulle why we could not engage the whole of our Air Force in the battle in France, and the latter had said that, speaking for himself, he agreed with our policy.

The Prime Minister also read to the War Cabinet telegram No. 373 DIPP, which had just been received from His Majesty's Ambassador in Paris, conveying a personal message from M. Reynaud. This was in a more cheerful tone than some of his earlier messages; but its main burden was to request the despatch of our divisions as rapidly as possible and to offer to provide them with artillery and anti-tank guns.

---

[1] Charles de Gaulle, 1890–1970. On active service on the Western Front, 1914–16 (three times wounded, mentioned in despatches). Prisoner of war, 1916–18 (he made five attempts to escape). An advocate between the wars of armoured divisions as an essential part of warfare. Commanded the 4th Armoured Brigade, 5th Army, September 1939; the 4th Armoured Division, May 1940. Under-Secretary for War and National Defence, 6 June 1940. Chief of the Free French (later President of the French National Committee), London and Brazzaville, 1940–2. President of the French Committee of National Liberation, Algiers, 1943. President of the Provisional Government of the French Republic, and head of its armed forces, November 1943 to January 1946. Prime Minister, June 1958 to January 1959. President, December 1958 to June 1969.

274   JUNE 1940

The Prime Minister referred to a photograph which he had seen, which clearly showed that the barrage on the Rhine had been broken by the fluvial mines. The report stated that the river traffic had been completely stopped between Karlsruhe and Mainz. Meanwhile, the French had suggested that we should withdraw Admiral Fitzgerald's[1] party. In reply, he had drafted a telegram, which he read to the War Cabinet, pointing out the success which had attended this manoeuvre and strongly urging that yet further operations of this nature should be undertaken. The Prime Minister handed the draft to the Chief of the Air Staff, and requested him to despatch it after making any amendments on points of detail, in consultation with the Fifth Sea Lord.

The Prime Minister read to the War Cabinet the figures showing the large increase in the number of fighter aircraft on the strength of operational units as compared with the previous week, and the large numbers of fully equipped aircraft now ready for service in the Aircraft Storage units. These figures represented a remarkable achievement on the part of the Minister of Aircraft Production, and he thought that the War Cabinet would wish to place on record their appreciation of it.

Winston S. Churchill to General Weygand and General Georges
(*Premier papers, 3/375*)

9 June 1940
Secret

Am surprised to hear you wish to send back the Naval party laying fluvial mines in the Rhine. Why should you do this?[2] Our aerial reconnaissance shows that all traffic on the Rhine between Karlsruhe and Mainz is stopped. Not one barge was seen in transit by our aviators. Why not keep it stopped? We have not hitherto been able owing to battle needs to lay the air fluvials in the lower reaches, especially from Mainz to Coblenz and Cologne. Traffic on this section is vital to the enemy's industry and military supplies. It requires only a squadron or two of night-bombers, and will not affect our night support of your army. The moon is getting good. Propose therefore to continue

---

[1] John Uniake Penrose Fitzgerald. Entered the Royal Navy, 1904. Captain, 1929. Director of the Department of Torpedoes and Mining, Admiralty, 1938–40. A French and Spanish speaker. Retired, 1940.

[2] In the final version of this telegram, as sent to France at 2 a.m. on 11 June 1940, Churchill replaced this first paragraph with the words: 'As General Georges no longer requires the British naval party or the fluvial mines for anti-tank operations, I strongly press for the resumption of the Rhine operation. Mines should be laid continuously and at the maximum rate.' The final telegram also ended: 'Operations on the Seine should also be considered' (*Premier papers, 3/375*).

streaming into the Rhine from French territory continually to poison river down to Mainz, and open up by air the attack on lower reaches. Pray let me know what reasons you have to the contrary. It would be most improvident to throw this attack on pontoon bridges and munition traffic away.

WSC

Defence Committee: minutes
(*Cabinet papers, 69/1*)

9 June 1940
10.30 a.m.

The Prime Minister said that there was evidently considerable feeling in certain circles in France that we had given inadequate support on land, and had only paid attention to rescuing our own Army from Dunkirk. We, on the other hand, had some reason to feel that matters had not been very well handled by the French; and recent events on the left flank in France had been a repetition of what had occurred in Flanders. It was nevertheless essential that nothing should be said here which might be construed as criticism of the French.

After further discussion, the terms of the message were agreed upon to be broadcast at 1 p.m. that day, a copy of which is annexed.

War Cabinet: minutes
(*Cabinet papers, 65/7*)

10 June 1940
12.30 p.m.

The Prime Minister said that news of the Allied evacuation of Narvik was already becoming known, and it was therefore desirable that a statement on the subject should be issued by the Ministry of Information.

The Prime Minister said that the Germans and Italians were putting out propaganda with the object of convincing the French that now was the time for them to make peace, as they had been led astray by the British, who were not giving them any support. He thought that the best reply to this propaganda would be a statement to be broadcast at 1 p.m. that day in the form of a message from the Prime Minister to M. Reynaud showing that all available means were being used to give help on land and sea and in the air.

The Prime Minister said that he had considered whether he ought to go to Paris at once to an early Meeting of the Supreme War Council. No doubt a Meeting would be necessary in the next few days. But if he went to Paris now the French would almost certainly press us to give them help with fighter squadrons beyond what we could agree to. He therefore favoured entrusting General Spears with a personal message to give to M. Reynaud.

At the end of the discussion the Prime Minister said that he thought the best course would be for General Spears to proceed to Paris that afternoon with a communication for M. Reynaud, explaining the action which we were taking and the forces which we hoped to develop, expressing the hope that M. Reynaud would himself answer Signor Ansaldo's broadcast[1] as soon as possible, and saying that he (the Prime Minister) would be prepared also to broadcast that evening.

The Prime Minister added that he hoped that the Foreign Secretary would assist him in drafting the portion of the message relating to Signor Ansaldo's broadcast.

The War Cabinet expressed general agreement with the procedure proposed by the Prime Minister.

The War Cabinet had before them a Memorandum by the Secretary of State for War giving proposals for the reorganisation of the 12 Divisions evacuated from Dunkirk.[2]

The Prime Minister drew attention to the advantages to be obtained from telescoping two divisions into one. It would be economical in Headquarters Staff and in ancillary troops, and would enable the maximum number of infantry units to be incorporated within divisions. Some of the infantry units left over would be available to relieve the 'holding battalions' from coast defence duties, and to enable them to revert to their original rôle. He hoped that it would be possible to increase the number of infantry battalions in each brigade from three to four, thereby increasing the proportion of fighting troops to administrative units.

---

[1] In a radio broadcast, Giovanni Ansaldo, the editor of Count Ciano's newspaper *Il Telegrafo*, had invited France to use Italy as a go-between in reaching a settlement which would free Germany's hands to attack Britain. In the War Cabinet discussion it was agreed that 'this should be answered as soon as possible'.
[2] War Cabinet Paper No. 196 of 1940.

War Cabinet: Confidential Annex
(*Cabinet papers, 65/13*)

10 June 1940
12.30 p.m.

The Prime Minister asked whether consideration had been given to the possibility that HMS *Rodney* and other capital ships should go in and attack the German cruisers in Trondhjem Harbour.

The Chief of Naval Staff replied that careful thought had been given to this possibility, but that it was open to very serious disadvantages which he summarized as follows:–

(a) Our capital ships would almost certainly be located by air reconnaissances under the existing conditions of continuous daylight. They would then be subjected to ten-hour bombing on their way in, and to another ten-hour bombing on their way out.
(b) The entrance to the Harbour would undoubtedly have been mined.
(c) Attack would have to be expected from shore defences.
(d) The German ships were anchored inland under conditions which would make it extremely difficult to carry out a fleet action.
(e) U-boats would be lying in wait in the approaches, and it would be impossible to count on dealing with them before they fire their torpedoes.

Consideration had been given to the possibility of sending in one of our submarines, but in the absence of any cover of darkness at night, the chances of her getting in were thought to be so remote as to make the success of such an operation impossible.

The Prime Minister suggested that the War Cabinet could not but accept these as good reasons. He asked whether it would be possible to bottle the German cruisers in Trondhjem by mining.

The Chief of Naval Staff said that arrangements for this were being made. There were three entrances. A submarine was at present off one of them and a mine-layer was operating in one of the others. Mine-laying by surface craft was not possible at this time of year since it was light all night.

The Prime Minister had expressed grave doubts as to the wisdom of the proposed operation by the Fleet Air Arm. Neither the Swordfish nor the Skua would be a match for the very strong opposition which they would be likely to encounter from German aircraft bases at Trondhjem. It would be a gallant operation, but one which, in his opinion, might well prove far too costly.

The Chief of the Air Staff advised strongly against the operation. There were believed to be a large number of Messerschmitts at Trondhjem, and our losses would be extremely heavy, with the possibility of little or no return. The same argument would apply to any suggestion of sending Hampdens. There was no night and Trondhjem would be the extremity of their range.

The Lord President of the Council considered that such an operation would be very injudicious having regard to the heavy losses of pilots and aircraft which it might involve at a time when these were so urgently needed for other purposes.

After further discussion the War Cabinet agreed:–

(a) That instructions should be issued forthwith by the Admiralty to the Commander-in-Chief of the Home Fleet,[1] informing him that the proposed operation against Trondhjem with the Fleet Air Arm and HMS *Rodney* was not approved by the War Cabinet at present on account of the undue preponderance of shore based aircraft:

(b) That the Admiralty should give urgent consideration to other methods of dealing with the German men-of-war in Trondhjem harbour.

Sir Alexander Cadogan: diary
(*'The Diaries of Sir Alexander Cadogan'*)

10 June 1940

WSC said he was going over to France after lunch, but subsequently cancelled it – largely, I suspect, because French Government are packing up and leaving today.

Winston S. Churchill to Paul Reynaud
(*Cabinet papers, 69/1*)

10 June 1940

The maximum possible support is being given by British Forces in the great battle which the French Armies are now conducting with such undaunted courage.

All available means are being used to give help on land, sea, and in the air. The RAF has been continually engaged over the battlefield and within the last few days fresh British forces have landed in France to take their place with those already engaged in the common struggle, whilst further extensive reinforcements are being rapidly organised, and will shortly be available.

---

[1] Admiral of the Fleet Sir Charles Forbes.

June 1940

John Colville: diary
(*Colville papers*)

10 June 1940

In the afternoon there was chaos at Admiralty House. Winston made one of his lightning decisions to go to Paris, and just as he was about to leave for Hendon, a telegram was thrust into my hand to say that the French Government were going to leave Paris. 'What the Hell?' was all the PM said, but subsequently as there was no aerodrome available at which he could land he reluctantly concluded that 'there was no perch on which he could alight' and gave up the plan.

Mussolini decided to come into the war, and we had to wake up Winston from his afternoon slumber and tell him of this added complication.

At Admiralty House the possibility of the French giving in, or being defeated, was of greater interest to all present than the approaching entry of Italy into the war. All Winston said about the latter event was, 'People who go to Italy to look at ruins won't have to go as far as Naples and Pompeii in future.' He was in a very bad temper, snapped almost everybody's head off, wrote angry minutes to the First Sea Lord, and refused to pay any attention to messages given him orally.

Winston S. Churchill: recollection
(*'Their Finest Hour', page 116*)

10 June 1940

A speech from President Roosevelt had been announced for the night of the 10th. About midnight I listened to it with a group of officers in the Admiralty War Room, where I still worked. When he uttered the scathing words about Italy, 'On this 10th day of June, 1940, the hand that held the dagger has struck it into the back of its neighbour,' there was a deep growl of satisfaction. I wondered about the Italian vote in the approaching Presidential Election; but I knew that Roosevelt was a most experienced American party politician, although never afraid to run risks for the sake of his resolves. It was a magnificent speech, instinct with passion and carrying to us a message of hope.

Winston S. Churchill[1] to William Mackenzie King
(Premier papers, 4/44/4)

11 June 1940

Of Canada's own thoughts it is not for me to speak, but I know well the profound emotion with which in due time the people of this country will learn of the Canadians' arrival in France.[2]

Winston S. Churchill to Lord Hankey
(Premier papers, 3/188/2)

11 June 1940

A memorandum should be prepared in typescript this morning setting out the considerations which arise and the demands we should have to make if the contingency contemplated occurs. There is I think no need to anticipate an immediate collapse, but the matter must be watched by someone from day to day who has access to Darlan and Reynaud. I do not know at present where our Ambassador has gone to, or what means of communication exist. If we have to go to France this afternoon, I will take the memorandum with me.[3]

WSC

---

[1] This message, written as if by Churchill in the first person, was in fact drafted by Norman Archer, Assistant Secretary, Dominions Office, and approved by Churchill as drafted. Henceforth, almost all Churchill's messages to the Dominions were Archer's drafts, accepted like this one without change. I have made every effort to include in this volume, as in all the document volumes, only those letters, minutes and memoranda that Churchill either dictated or wrote himself. Where contributions to letters were made by others, I have done my best to ascertain this and indicate it. The message of 15 June 1940 (pages 339–41) was Churchill's own.

[2] Norman Archer also drafted a telegram to the Prime Minister of Australia, thanking him for placing three warships at Britain's disposal; Churchill (in fact Archer) praised Australia's determination 'to support our efforts by every means in her power in these critical hours' (*Churchill papers, 20/14*).

[3] Hankey's memorandum 'Action by His Majesty's Government in the event of a French military collapse', stated that the Government's aim would be to follow the Dutch and Belgian precedent of offering the French Government asylum in England. If France were felt to be about to sign an armistice with Germany, however, it was the opinion of the First Sea Lord (Admiral Pound) that 'it would be better if the French Fleet were sunk before that emergency arises', and that he, Pound, would 'get in touch with Admiral Darlan with a view to inducing him to sink the French Fleet'. Stocks of oil had already been destroyed at the Channel ports 'and within the last day or two at Rouen and Havre, in co-operation with the local authorities'. The French themselves had already destroyed oil stocks at the main refinery inland from Dunkirk: elsewhere 'it would be as well to remind them of the importance of making the necessary arrangements in advance' (*Premier papers, 3/188/2*).

Lord Beaverbrook to Sir Samuel Hoare
(*Beaverbrook papers*)

11 June 1940

Winston is standing up to the strain very well. He is like Atlas with two worlds to carry. With one hand he bears up the British Empire, with the other he sustains the French Republic. And the French Republic takes a bit of supporting too, let me tell you.

Lord Halifax to Sir Samuel Hoare
(*Foreign Office papers, 800/323*)

11 June 1940

There has been a lot of domestic chatter hostile to those whom certain sections wish to hold responsible for shortage of equipment and the like, but which, in fact, is the continuing vendetta against Neville. Winston has spoken strongly to Attlee and Archie[1] upon the importance of keeping their respective press organs in order, and I think opinion is setting against this kind of heresy hunting.

Winston S. Churchill to A. V. Alexander
(*Churchill papers, 20/13*)

11 June 1940

It is most important that the use of aluminium by the Admiralty should be reduced to the absolute minimum in order to give the Air Force the full benefit of the supply. Will you ask the Controller[2] to give you a report on the subject for my consideration thereafter.

There are several points about the Fleet distribution leading up to the loss of a certain ship which require examination. First, the Narvik exodus was known to be in progress by the enemy, and therefore its protection against

---

[1] Sir Archibald Sinclair, Secretary of State for Air and leader of the Liberal Party.
[2] Rear-Admiral Bruce Fraser.

surface ships was the first charge on the Home Fleet. How was it at this juncture that two battle-cruisers – *Renown* and *Repulse* – were sent off to the Faroes entirely out of relation to the important business the Admiralty were carrying out from Narvik? Why was it necessary to send two battle-cruisers on the vague reports of . . .[1]

Winston S. Churchill to Admiral Pound
(*Churchill papers, 20/13*)

11 June 1940

I trust that the restrictive orders about bombardment on the French coast do not mean that this service to the Army is being neglected. The fire from the sea has a great moral effect, both on the enemy whose flank is turned, and upon our retreating troops. I am astonished that the Germans have been allowed to establish a battery of motor-drawn artillery at Fécamp and that this battery has shelled and driven off a British destroyer with casualties. Why has a cruiser not been sent, or other suitable bombarding vessel, and why is this battery that is in the track of our retreating troops not knocked out or driven away? It is the duty of the Navy to give proper support at the present time.

WSC

Winston S. Churchill to Sir Archibald Sinclair and Sir Cyril Newall
(*Churchill papers, 20/13*)

11 June 1940

This report[2] is most interesting and I shall be glad if you will arrange to use the Squadron you mentioned yesterday for the purpose of infecting the reaches mentioned where the traffic is reported to be so heavy. We do not need to ask the French permission for this, but only for the continuous streaming of the Naval fluvials. This I am doing. Meanwhile you should act as soon as you can on the lower reaches. Kindly report what you will do.

WSC

Lord President would, I am sure, like to see these photographs and this report.

WSC

---

[1] This document is incomplete.
[2] On the mining of the Rhine (Operation 'Royal Marine').

Winston S. Churchill to Lord Beaverbrook
(*Churchill papers, 20/13*)

11 June 1940
Secret

Remember that the photographic machines are of tremendous value in enabling us to find out if any expedition is preparing in the German harbours and river mouths. We are greatly dependent upon their reconnaissance reports, and also upon photographs which far exceed what the human eye can discern.

Winston S. Churchill to Lord Beaverbrook
(*Churchill papers, 20/13*)

11 June 1940

It was decided on December 22 at a Conference on Bombsight Design at the RAE[1] that urgent action should be taken to convert 2,600 ABs,[2] Mark II, into stabilised high altitude bombsights, over 90 per cent of the drawings then being completed. Please let me know exactly what followed. How is it that only one bombsight was converted? I should be very glad if you would look at the files and ascertain who was responsible for stifling action.

Winston S. Churchill to Lord Halifax and General Ismay
(*Churchill papers, 20/13*)

11 June 1940

What is the attitude of Egypt to be in view of Mussolini's references? I presume he means that if she declared herself neutral she would have to send all British troops out of the country, and intern all British ships in her harbours. This would clearly bring Egypt into the war. Would it be wise to extract a definite declaration of war? Or would it not be better to let Italy interpret Egypt's failure of neutrality as an excuse for war? It would certainly be quite a good excuse. I should like to know what is thought about this.

---

[1] The Royal Aircraft Establishment at Farnborough.
[2] Aerial bombsights.

2. It is vital that nothing should hamper our defence arrangements, and that the Egyptian Forces should bear their part in them. For Egypt everything depends in the first instance upon the Fleet at Alexandria. I am told that there are a number of AA guns there which are in Egyptian hands, and may be moved to Cairo. This should be prevented. What matters is the Fleet. As long as we can get all military facilities and assistance from Egypt would there be serious objection to Cairo being declared an open town? The troops in the cantonments around the city could readily re-enter to preserve order. Have we not already evacuated the Kasr-el-Nil barracks and the Citadel, and handed them over to Egyptian troops? I am not sure how this stands.

3. At the moment, subject to your advice, I am inclined to make sure that Egypt gives us all facilities of a military character, including, of course, the active help of her armed forces, and to let Italy pick the quarrel with Egypt, which she must do as the consequence of these facilities.

WSC

Defence Committee: minutes
(*Cabinet papers, 70/1*)

11 June 1940
10.30 a.m.

The Prime Minister enquired for details about the tank proposed by Sir Albert Stern,[1] and asked the Minister of Supply to arrange for a meeting at which he could hear the views put forward on behalf of this tank.

The Prime Minister said that he required a programme whereby 500 to 600 heavy tanks could be produced, and in the hands of troops by the end of March, 1941. Every consideration should be sacrificed to speed up production, all refinements being eliminated. In the meanwhile every effort should be made to press on with the production of existing types, and no modification should be accepted which would delay in the slightest degree their production.

---

[1] Albert Stern, 1878–1966. Lieutenant, Royal Naval Volunteer Reserve, Armoured Car Division, 1914. Secretary, Landship Committee, Admiralty, 1915. Chairman of the Tank Committee, 1916. Lieutenant-Colonel, 1916. Director of Tank Supply, Ministry of Munitions, 1916; Director-General, Mechanical Warfare Department, Ministry of Munitions (under Churchill), 1916–18. Knighted, 1918. Member of the London Committee of the Ottoman Bank, 1921–64. Chairman, Special Vehicle Development Committee, Ministry of Supply, 1939–43. Member of the Tank Board, 1941.

JUNE 1940

Winston S. Churchill: recollection
('*Their Finest Hour*', page 135)

11 June 1940

About eleven o'clock on the morning of June 11 there was a message from Reynaud, who had also cabled to the President. The French tragedy had moved and slid downward. For several days past I had pressed for a meeting of the Supreme Council. We could no longer meet in Paris. We were not told what were the conditions there. Certainly the German spearheads were very close. I had had some difficulty in obtaining a rendezvous, but this was no time to stand on ceremony. We must know what the French were going to do. Reynaud now told me that he could receive us at Briare, near Orleans. The seat of government was moving from Paris to Tours. Grand-Quartier-Général was near Briare. He specified the airfield to which I should come. Nothing loth, I ordered the Flamingo to be ready at Hendon after luncheon, and, having obtained the approval of my colleagues at the morning Cabinet, we started about two o'clock.

Winston S. Churchill to President Roosevelt
(*Premier papers, 3/468*)

11 June 1940
Secret and Personal

French have sent for me again, which means that crisis has arrived. Am just off. Anything you can say or do to help them now may make the difference.

We are also worried about Ireland. An American Squadron at Berehaven would do no end of good I am sure.

War Cabinet: minutes
(*Cabinet papers, 65/7*)

11 June 1940　　　　　　　　　　　　　　　　　　　　10 Downing Street
12.30 p.m.

The Prime Minister said that M. Reynaud had at first rather discouraged the suggestion of an early meeting. The reason had perhaps been that he had been visiting the front. A second telegram had then been sent suggesting that the meeting should be held at GQG, and this had now been agreed to. The meeting had therefore been fixed for 6 p.m. that evening.

The Prime Minister said that he might well have to remain in France for more than one day, since there were a large number of matters which would have to be discussed with the French. We should have to concert with them a grand strategic plan for the future conduct of the war and to find out what their intentions were. The despatch of additional forces to France, and their destination, would have to be examined. It seemed as if the French would be prepared to fight on in the more difficult country to the south of Paris if they were driven right back. He would, of course, give them every encouragement to continue the struggle and discourage any signs of a movement towards making a separate peace. He would impress on them that if they could keep going, and thus prevent the enemy achieving the quick decision which he required, we should hold out, even if the whole resources of the enemy were turned on to the United Kingdom.

The Prime Minister said that he felt sure that his colleagues had welcomed the tone of President Roosevelt's broadcast the previous night. He read out a draft personal message which he proposed to send to the President.

The War Cabinet expressed their warm approval of the terms of the message.

The Prime Minister said that on the previous day he had instructed the Minister of Home Security[1] to arrange for a general internment of male Italians.

The Secretary of State for Foreign Affairs urged that the arrangements previously made with the Italian Government for reciprocal deportation should not be upset by demands that certain isolated individuals should be held in custody in this country. It was to our advantage to get rid of as many Italians as possible. Italy would have to feed them, and they would probably form centres of disaffection in Italy, since many of them had no desire to return to that country. We should try to get the French to follow the same policy.

The Prime Minister agreed with the policy outlined, but thought that, as a general principle, we should endeavour to round up all enemy aliens as quickly as possible, so as to place them out of harm's way, and that we should subsequently examine individual cases and release those who were found to be well-disposed to this country.

The Secretary of State for Foreign Affairs said that the Prime Minister had suggested to him that there was something to be said for not forcing the Egyptian Government to declare war on Italy so long as our own military effort was not in any way impeded. He agreed that it would be a great advantage to us if a state of war between Egypt and Italy could be brought

---

[1] Sir John Anderson.

about by the direct action of Italy, rather than that we should seem to force it on Egypt. He therefore proposed to advise His Majesty's Ambassador at Cairo[1] to deal with the Egyptian Government on these lines, always on the understanding that our military, naval and air operations would be in no way hampered. Egypt must not, of course, declare her neutrality, but might adopt the status of a non-belligerent ally.

The Prime Minister suggested that it might also be desirable to accede to the wish of the Egyptian Government that Cairo should be declared an open town. If the Italians were, nevertheless, to bomb it, then we should be entitled to bomb Rome. It was important that anti-aircraft guns manned by Egyptians and required for the defence of the fleet at Alexandria should not be moved to Cairo.

Winston S. Churchill to President Roosevelt
(*Churchill papers, 20/14*)

11 June 1940

We all listened to you last night and were fortified by the grand scope of your declaration. Your statement that the material aid of the United States will be given to the Allies in their struggle is a strong encouragement in a dark but not unhopeful hour. Everything must be done to keep France in the fight and to prevent any idea of the fall of Paris, should it occur, becoming the occasion of any kind of parley. The hope with which you inspire them may give them the strength to persevere. They should continue to defend every yard of their soil and use the full fighting force of their army. Hitler, thus baffled of quick results, will turn upon us and we are preparing ourselves to resist his fury and defend our Island. Having saved the BEF, we do not lack troops at home and as soon as Divisions can be equipped on the much higher scale needed for Continental service they will be despatched to France. Our intention is to have a strong army fighting in France for the campaign of 1941. I have already cabled you about airplanes, including flying-boats, which are so needful to us in the impending struggle for the life of Great Britain. But even more pressing is the need for destroyers. The Italian outrage makes it necessary for us to cope with a much larger number of submarines which may come out into the Atlantic and perhaps be based on Spanish ports. To this the only counter is destroyers. Nothing is so important as for us to have the thirty or forty old destroyers you have already had reconditioned. We can fit them

---

[1] Miles Wedderburn Lampson, 1880–1964. Entered the Foreign Office, 1903. British Minister to China, 1926–33. Knighted, 1927. High Commissioner for Egypt and the Sudan, 1934–6; Ambassador to Egypt and High Commissioner for the Sudan, 1936–46. Privy Councillor, 1941. Created Baron Killearn, 1943. Special Commissioner in South-East Asia, 1946–8.

very rapidly with our asdics and they will bridge the gap of six months before our war-time new construction comes into play. We will return them or their equivalents to you, without fail, at six months' notice if at any time you need them. The next six months are vital. If while we have to guard the East Coast against invasion a new heavy German-Italian submarine attack is launched against our commerce, the strain may be beyond our resources; and the ocean traffic by which we live may be strangled. Not a day should be lost. I send you my heartfelt thanks and those of my colleagues for all you are doing and seeking to do for what we may now, indeed, call the Common Cause.

General Spears: recollection
(*'The Fall of France, June 1940'*, pages 137–8)

11 June 1940

After several changes in the time of our departure, we finally took off at 2.30 p.m. in the Flamingo. It was escorted by twelve Hurricanes. In the plane were Anthony Eden, General Dill, Pug Ismay, Brigadier Lund,[1] Captain Berkeley, Pug's assistant and matchless translator, and myself.

Winston brooded in his arm-chair, his eyes on the horizon. Occasionally he beckoned to one of us to ask a question, then relapsed into silence.

Most of the time, Eden and Dill, heads together, were discussing endless tables and columns of figures. What pleasant well-bred faces they had, I thought, in spite of their puckered brows.

Ismay, too, had an enormous number of folders in his dispatch-cases. He never took his eyes off them save when called by Churchill or Dill, when he would look up, wide-eyed, put his hand to his ear to hear through the vibrations of the machine, and smile as soon as he had grasped what was wanted of him.

We arrived at Briare late in the afternoon, having made a considerable detour. Aerodromes seldom give an impression of being over-populated, but this one seemed particularly flat and deserted. Winston, in black, leaning on his stick, strolled about beaming as if he had left all his preoccupations in the plane and had reached the one spot in the world he most wished to visit at that particular moment. He conveyed the impression that the long journey had been well worth while since at last it was vouchsafed to him to walk about the aerodrome of Briare.

[1] Otto Marling Lund, 1891–1956. Royal Artillery, 1911. On active service on the Western Front, 1914–18 (DSO, despatches four times). Deputy Director of Operations and Plans, War Office, 1939–40. Major-General, Royal Artillery, Home Forces, and 21st Army Group, 1941–4. Director, Royal Artillery, War Office, 1944–6. General Officer Commanding-in-Chief, Anti-Aircraft Command, 1946–8. Knighted, 1948.

Three or four cars drove up at intervals, and the Prime Minister left in the first with a French Colonel, who, from his expression, might have been welcoming poor relations at a funeral reception.

We drove a few kilometres to a hideous house, the sort of building the *nouveau riche* French *bourgeoisie* delight in, a villa expanded by successful business in groceries or indifferent champagne into a large monstrosity of red lobster-coloured brick, and stone the hue of unripe Camembert.

This was Weygand's abode, where the Prime Minister was to sleep.

The place, to which I took an instant dislike, had, I was glad to hear, a ridiculous name: *Le Château du Muguet* – Lily of the Valley Castle.

Supreme War Council: minutes
(*Cabinet papers, 99/3*)

11 June 1940
7 p.m.

Briare

Mr Churchill[1] explained that he had come to France with his colleagues to survey the situation with unclouded eyes and, in conjunction with M. Reynaud and his advisers,[2] to make the best possible plan in the existing circumstances. He desired to make it clear at the outset that Britain would continue the struggle in all circumstances. It was his expectation, and even hope, that as soon as the Germans had stabilised a position in France they would turn against the United Kingdom and give the RAF an opportunity of breaking Germany's might in the air. He felt confident that they would succeed.

He then gave details of the dates of despatch of British Divisions in France in the next few weeks. He realised that these were small numbers in the light of the present emergency. If the French could nevertheless hold out, the British participation would grow apace and the immediate problem was one of tiding over the lean weeks until the potential strength of the Allies became actual.[3]

M. Reynaud invited General Weygand to report on the present military situation.

General Weygand said that the battle was now engaged on the whole front, which was occupied by the totality of the French Forces with nothing

---

[1] General Spears later recalled: 'The Prime Minister then spoke; the words came slowly, carefully selected but hammered together sharply into a vivid mosaic.'

[2] The French leaders present with Reynaud when the Briare meeting began were Marshal Pétain, General Weygand and General de Gaulle.

[3] General Spears later recalled: 'He stopped. Reynaud thanked him, but I felt his suppressed irritation and that of the other Frenchmen at the inadequacy of this trickle to halt a conflagration whose flames were fast spreading from the Channel to the Atlantic.'

whatever left in reserve. On the extreme left, where the battle had first begun, the French troops had been fighting for over six days without any rest. On the eastward sector as far as the Meuse, the battle had now been raging for 48 hours. Thus active operations were in progress along the whole of the new front, consisting of positions hastily built up in the last few days. The Maginot Line was as yet quiet, but a frontal attack was expected at any moment, probably in the extreme south near the Swiss Border.

General Spears: recollection
(*'The Fall of France', pages 143–5*)

11 June 1940

Weygand: 'There is nothing to prevent the enemy reaching Paris. We are fighting on our last line and it has been breached.' His tone now as dramatic as his words, he rapped out: 'I am helpless, I cannot intervene for I have no reserves, there are no reserves. *C'est la dislocation*' – the break-up.

I looked round and read consternation on all the English faces. My own mouth was so dry I could not swallow. I wrote quickly to make up for lost time as I found I had stopped to listen, for the picture evoked was slow to take shape in my mind.

I looked at Reynaud. Eyebrows raised, he was gazing at the middle of the table. Churchill, hunched over the table, his face flushed, was watching Weygand intently. His expression was not benevolent. But Weygand was now launched on his favourite theme, the folly of having embarked on the war at all. 'I wish to place on record that I consider that those responsible embarked upon the war very lightly and without any conception of the power of German armaments. As it is, we have lost something like two-fifths of our initial strength.'[1]

Weygand had finished. He was drained dry like a squeezed lemon. Not an idea, not a suggestion was to be wrung out of him. This must have been Churchill's conclusion, for he put him no questions, did not even look at him again, and merely asked that General Georges should be summoned. During the short interval before Georges appeared, Churchill said nothing, but sat flushed and preoccupied, playing with his ring. I looked at de Gaulle. I had noted that he had been ceaselessly smoking cigarettes, lighting one from

---

[1] These remarks are not in the Supreme War Council minutes, which are copious but not complete. The task of the minute-taker was to jot down headings of what was said, with a summary of the argument, while the discussion was in progress, and then to transcribe it as fully as possible afterwards.

another, his lips pursed and rounded in the characteristic movement I had already observed. Not a muscle of his face had moved. Nothing had been said that had caused his expression to change. The Prime Minister had looked at him several times. He was searching for something he had failed to find in the other French faces. The fact that he returned several times to a study of de Gaulle made me think he had detected in him the thing he was looking for.

Supreme War Council: minutes
(*Cabinet papers, 99/3*)

11 June 1940   Briare

General Georges, who joined the Meeting at this stage, gave a description of the military situation which closely coincided with that given by General Weygand. Of their original 103 Divisions, the Allies had lost, when the present battle opened, 35 including the bulk of their mechanised forces and at least one armoured Division. The infantry Divisions lost were certainly amongst the best the Allies possessed since they had been earmarked for offensive operations in open country. In preparation for the new battle between Montmédy and the Channel, the French Command had rushed everything that could be spared from the Eastern and South-Eastern France and all their reserves without exception, but that movement had been impeded by the rapidity of the German advance and the activity of the enemy's bombers. This explained why the Germans had succeeded in obtaining bridgeheads on the Lower Somme. The French armies had failed to drive the enemy back in the West, and now the battle had been raging for six days along the whole of the new Front without interruption.

The French losses had been heavy. General Georges enumerated eight or ten Divisions which had by now been reduced to two Battalions and a few guns. Half-trained troops had been put in to fill gaps, but there was now nothing left to put in, and the line was held by nothing more than a light screen of reduced and weary Divisions with no reserves behind them. They were, therefore, at the mercy of any concentrated attack by the Germans, and despite the splendid valour of the troops he could only describe the situation as extremely precarious. The situation was as menacing now on the Eastern part of the new line as in the centre and on the West.[1]

Mr Churchill gave some details of the British and other additional forces that would soon become available. The Allied forces withdrawn from Narvik,

[1] General Spears later recalled: 'Not a single positive suggestion had been made, nor had the hint of a plan emerged. The Prime Minister may have sensed this, and felt that it was time he intervened again. His mouth had been working, an indication that he was pouring an idea into the mould of words.'

equivalent to one small Division, would soon be ready for action in France. The British 52nd Division was at that moment deploying from Le Mans, with its 36 guns. The Canadian Division, of very fine troops, was landing that night with 72 guns and corps artillery. A regular Division withdrawn from Dunkirk would begin disembarkation on the 20th. A further regular Division, which still lacked guns but which the French had undertaken to supply with artillery, would be available by the 1st July, and further reconstituted Divisions from the North would be put in steadily thereafter. Everything that could be sent would be sent, excepting only a small force which it was considered essential to keep in the United Kingdom to guard in some measure against invasion. There were at the moment, in fact, no fully equipped forces anywhere in the British Isles, although there were at least 20 Divisions in active training awaiting equipment.

General Georges said that the problem was entirely one of numbers. The Allies were facing a preponderance of something like three to one. Although the losses in men and material had been heavy on both sides, the German numbers were bound to tell at this critical stage. The entry of Italy into the war further complicated the problem in the air; the French had only some 175 fighters left on the Northern Front altogether.

Mr Churchill said that he must at that stage express Great Britain's immense admiration for the manner in which the French armies were now defending their territory, and her grief at finding that she could give so little help at such a moment. The hard fact was that what remained of the BEF had come out of Flanders literally naked, and could only resume the struggle once it had been re-armed; else there would have been 13 or 14 British Divisions now fighting by the side of the French.

He would venture to express the opinion that the German armies also were now in a state of extreme exhaustion, and that with their immensely long lines of communication they also must be feeling the strain greatly. If the line could be held for the next few days, he hoped that it would be possible to organise a counter-attack with the help of the British forces that would then be in position, e.g., in the Rouen area. If the line held for another three or four weeks, moreover, there would be a substantial British force available to attack the enemy's flank. He was convinced that Germany was feeling her losses acutely; there was no sign of a victorious spirit within Germany. Every hour, every day gained was a step further.

General Weygand agreed, but reiterated that it was a question of hours not days or weeks. The new German technique of mass attacks with tanks and aircraft and of advances of anything up to 50 kilometres in one day was one which called for immense reserves if it was to be checked effectively. He had, as already stated, no reserves whatever, and he had himself seen on the previous day in the neighbourhood of Rouen what was the result of that situation.

June 1940

General Sir John Dill wished to make it clear that General Weygand was entirely free to make use of the British units now landing in whatever manner he considered most useful. There was no thought in his mind that the 52nd Division must be used as a complete unit or not at all.

General Weygand thanked Sir John Dill for this statement.

Marshal Pétain pointed out[1] that in the worst days of 1918, when a breach had been made in the front belt by the 5th Army, he had been able to rush 20 Divisions to the rescue, followed shortly afterwards with an equally large second reserve. To-day the situation was completely different, as there was not a single reserve company to put in. Similarly, at the height of the Verdun battle, the French had still been able to relieve each unit after four days; to-day the French troops were fighting continuously with no hope of relief within measurable time.

Mr Churchill explained that every day the British Government considered anew whether further British fighters could be put into the battle. The whole fighter force had been completely disorganised and confused as a result of the Dunkirk operation. Gradually this confusion was being remedied. Meanwhile six or eight squadrons took part in the battle every single day, refuelling at French bases. The BAAF was being kept up to full strength.

He would again, on the following day, examine whether anything further could be done. He hoped that the French representatives would understand that this was not a matter of selfishness on the part of the British. It was merely their deep conviction that if they broke up their fighter defence then they would be unable to carry on the war. The British fighter force was the only weapon with which they could hope – and he was confident that they would succeed – to break the might of Germany, when the time came, that is, when the onslaught against the British Isles began.

M. Reynaud realised that the British fighter defence must be kept in being. He urged, however, that it was equally important to prevent the smashing up of the last line of defence in France. British fighters, operating from the United Kingdom, were necessarily less efficacious against the German bombers than those based on French soil. In the present circumstances, he doubted whether the risk to Great Britain would be materially increased by basing further fighting squadrons in France. Heavy losses had already been inflicted on the German bomber forces, and they would continue. If an emergency arose the British fighters could quickly regain their native bases. It was the considered view of the French High Command that a large-scale air attack upon the advancing German forces might completely reverse the situation and save the

---

[1] On reading the official minutes while writing his war memoirs in 1948, Churchill noted at this point: 'I appealed to Pétain, reminding him of Beauvais 1918.' This was when Churchill had gone to the front with Clemenceau, and both men had been struck by Pétain's determination to halt the German advance and to counter-attack.

day. Limited air actions in the past few weeks had had very considerable effects. Their Air Forces were the only weapons left in the hands of the Allied Governments to influence the outcome of the battle and the future course of the war. Great Britain could, therefore, to-day swing the scales if she wished.

General Georges said that he fully concurred in these views. Further air operations were, in fact, the only asset on the Allied balance sheet.

Mr Churchill explained that in the British view the attack on the United Kingdom, when it came, would in all probability bring in the United States, who were already near the point of intervention. The attack would, of course, be fiercely resisted, and he was confident that tremendous losses would be inflicted upon the German Air Force. That might well swing the scales. It followed that it would be a fault of major strategy to jeopardise the only instrument with which that result could be achieved, namely, the British fighter strength, especially as it was not certain that a contrary decision would have the effect of reversing the position in France.

Again, the losses inflicted upon the enemy in the air rose in proportion as the British fighters operated nearer their home bases. Nevertheless, he would willingly examine again what more could be done to give the French greater support in the air. He could affirm truthfully that he longed to give France his further aid, but that the giving of it might in his view destroy the last hope the Allies had of breaking the back of Germany's might.[1]

M. Reynaud said that, if the present battle in France was lost, history would certainly ascribe the defeat to the lack of aircraft. It was the German bombers that had so gravely affected the spirit of the French troops, and the German bombers could only be opposed by Allied fighters.

Mr Churchill pointed out that the German tanks and their preponderance in numbers of Divisions had also played a great part. The British soldiers who had fought in Flanders, like the French, had expressed anger at the fact that they had not been helped by the RAF. That was, in fact, wholly untrue, though comprehensible: the RAF had acted deep within the German lines and had undoubtedly saved the BEF. But that was not realised by soldiers fighting under the continuous terror of the German bombers.

One difficulty about sending British fighters to French bases was that the losses in aircraft destroyed on the ground were so heavy. Nevertheless, the BAAF had achieved much and would continue to do so; it would remain, of course, at the complete disposal of the French High Command and would obey the latter's every request.

General de Gaulle wished to make a suggestion. The British armoured

---

[1] In his memoirs, *The Fall of France*, General Spears recalled how, at this point, he was 'struck by Churchill's words about the French Navy', but no such words appear in the minutes (nor does Spears say what they were). Churchill told the War Cabinet on his return to London that Darlan had said he would never surrender the Fleet but would in the last resort send it to Canada.

Division under General Evans[1] was equipped with light and thinly-protected tanks. The French tanks were of a heavier type, and there was a great lack on the French side of lighter vehicles for reconnaissance duties. He therefore felt that, if the British tank force could be associated or amalgamated with the French, the result would be a much higher effectiveness.

Mr Churchill said that this suggestion would be examined at once.

General Weygand wished to say a few words about the consequences of an unfavourable outcome of the present battle. There was still a hope that the outcome would not be unfavourable. If, however, the last line of defence broke, what would be the result? He could see no hope whatever of constituting with another line of defence since he had nothing left with which to build up such a line. Hence, in his view, nothing could prevent an invasion of the whole of French territory by the enemy. Not only Paris but every large town would be occupied. Doubtless the remnants of the French forces would continue to fight until not a man remained. But that would be uncoordinated warfare, and he himself, as Commander-in-Chief, would find himself completely powerless.

Mr Churchill asked whether the French Command had studied the possibility of holding one or more bridgeheads on the Atlantic seaboard. Through these, British Divisions would gradually and with increasing tempo be put in, and the United States would, he felt certain, also soon be taking their share.

General Weygand said that the possibility was now being studied. Strategically, however, it would be a most difficult task to continue the fight and at the same time to bring forces back into the Redoubt in Brittany, which was the plan now under study. As regards supply, moreover, Brittany had no industries whatever and the French forces in the Redoubt would be wholly dependent upon the United Kingdom. Meanwhile, there could be no doubt that the Germans would revenge themselves by systematically destroying every town, village and factory in the occupied parts of France. It was, therefore, a most grievous prospect to contemplate.

M. Reynaud concurred in this view. The military difficulties of such a project were immense; but he fully appreciated the great political importance it might have.

Mr Churchill wished to make a further suggestion, though he did so with some hesitation in the presence of the Commander-in-Chief of the French armies, whose great experience must be the judge of its practicability. Nevertheless, he thought that if co-ordinated defence, as General Weygand had described it, broke down, there would be immense advantages in conducting what he might describe as guerrilla warfare on a gigantic scale

---

[1] Roger Evans, 1886–1968. On active service in Mesopotamia, 1917–18 (Military Cross, despatches). Major-General, 1938. Commanded an armoured division, 1938–40. CB, 1941.

throughout France. The difficulties of the enemy would be tremendous, with his units scattered, his lines of communication immensely extended and precarious, and opponents on the watch for him at every turn. He felt confident that provided some effective means of dealing with the German tanks could be devised, and provided some secure bridgehead could be held on the Atlantic sea-board, such tactics might well save the situation during the few months that still would have to elapse before Britain's strength increased at a tremendous pace and before the United States came in on a full scale.

He realised, of course, that the prospect for France would be a terrible one. The United Kingdom had not yet suffered as France had suffered. Britain was, however, ready and willing to face the same horrors. She was indeed anxious to draw on to herself the full malice of the Nazis' tyranny and, however tremendous the German fury might prove to be, she would never give in.

The alternative of France accepting defeat was equally terrible. If it came, Great Britain would nevertheless carry on, if necessary for years. Her difficulties would be immensely increased, but he still felt that if she could survive the next three or four months then she would be in a position to wage war for as long as was necessary to smash the German domination. She would fight in the air, she would fight with her unbeaten navy, and she would fight with the blockade weapon. It might well become a war of Continents and although the collapse of France opened up the most distressing picture, yet he felt certain that even then Germany could at least be brought to her knees. He hoped, however, that the disaster of a French collapse would never happen.

M. Reynaud said that France's determination to carry on was no less than Britain's. If the last line of defence broke, a political question would arise. In the meantime they could only place all their hopes and confidence in the French army.

Mr Churchill said that Great Britain had the utmost confidence in the French High Command. Every Englishman was profoundly grieved that fuller military help could not be given to France in this grave hour. But they were not far now from the time of harvest of effectives and weapons.

He suggested that General Weygand and Sir John Dill should at once discuss the possibility of organising a counter-attack with the help of the strong and fresh British Divisions now on their way.

M. Reynaud agreed to this proposal.

With regard to the question of bridgeheads on the Atlantic sea-board, he explained that General Altmeyer[1] (the younger of two Generals bearing the

---

[1] Robert Altmeyer, younger brother of René Altmeyer (commander of the French Tenth Army, which extended from the sea to a point south-east of Péronne: the British forces in France formed a part of René's army). After visiting Brittany to study the possibility of military resistance there, Robert was convinced that the peninsula could be held.

same name) had been appointed by General Weygand to draw up a plan, and that he was already actively engaged on this task. The technical difficulties were immense but the political advantages were equally great.

Mr Churchill expressed pleasure at this appointment.

This was indeed the darkest hour for the Allied cause, but he could only repeat that he had in no way lost confidence in the ultimate smashing of a régime created and kept in being by a small group of evil men.

M. Reynaud said that he was equally confident.

CONCLUSIONS OF MEETING ON 11TH JUNE, 1940, AT 7 P.M.

(1) Air Support for France

The Prime Minister agreed to give immediate consideration to the question of providing further fighter support for the French, either by basing further British squadrons in France or in any other way.[1]

General Spears: recollection
(*'The Fall of France'*, page 158)

11 June 1940   Briare

I have a memory, but a vague one, of an interlude in which Weygand said something about the Germans having a hundred divisions to spare to invade Britain. Churchill's answer (which he gives in his book[2]) to Weygand's question 'What would you do then?' was that he was no military expert; but his technical advisers were of opinion that the best method of dealing with the German invasion of the island of Britain was to drown as many as possible on the way over and knock the others on the head as they crawled ashore.

I remember more clearly than the words Winston's chuckle as he said it, and I have a clear memory of Weygand's answer: 'I must admit you have a very good anti-tank ditch.'

The discussion seemed to trail off. Churchill, evidently haunted and tortured at watching the martyrdom of the people he liked so well, and in whom we had placed such implicit military trust, was distressed over the

---

[1] It was also agreed (2) to give 'immediate consideration' to a suggestion by de Gaulle that the light armoured vehicle force under General Evans 'should combine or associate itself for the purpose of combined operations with the French armoured divisions equipped with heavy armoured vehicles'; (3) to encourage the French plan then being examined to organise a redoubt in Brittany which would provide 'bridgeheads through which British and other assistance in the form of men and supplies could be brought in to carry on the struggle'; and (4) that Gort and Weygand 'should consult together as to the possibility of launching a counter-attack, perhaps in the Rouen area, as soon as sufficient British forces had taken up their positions in the west of the line of battle'.

[2] *The Second World War*, volume 2, pages 136–8.

meagre contribution which was all we were able to make. Churchill, being Churchill, was bound to say so. Years had been lost, but soon we should be able to garner what we had sown in the last few months, and he repeated his deep regrets that we were not able to have more fighting units alongside the French.[1]

'It is like talking of rain to a man in the Sahara,' said Reynaud, and he repeated that history would record that if this battle was lost, it would have been owing to lack of air forces. The Prime Minister did not take this up.

Anthony Eden: recollection
(*'The Reckoning', page 116*)

11 June 1940   Briare

When the moment came for Mr Churchill to tell the French that we would go on with the struggle, if necessary alone, I watched the expressions opposite. Reynaud was inscrutable and Weygand polite, concealing with difficulty his scepticism. Marshal Pétain was mockingly incredulous. Though he said nothing, his attitude was obviously *C'est de la blague*. Once in our discussion, Churchill, in his eagerness to convey his meaning, broke into French, at the same time looking earnestly at Reynaud. Since Reynaud spoke good English, the manoeuvre was of doubtful effect, but it led to a moment of some confusion when, at the end of one such passage, Reynaud murmured absently: '*Traduction.*'

General Ismay: recollection[2]
(*Churchill papers, 4/44*)

11 June 1940

Just after we sat down to dinner, a Staff Officer came up to General Weygand, who was sitting on my right, and told him that Air Marshal Barratt wanted to speak to me very urgently. I left the table and went to the only telephone in the building (situated in the Gents' lavatory) and found the Air Marshal in a state of rage. He said that the 48 bombers, which had been sent to the vicinity of Marseilles at great trouble some days previously, were not

---

[1] In his diary, written on the following morning, Captain Berkeley recalled Churchill's actual words as 'We grieve that we cannot help more, but we cannot' (Berkeley diary, 12 June 1940, *Berkeley papers*).

[2] Ismay set down these recollections in a letter of 18 March 1948, while he was helping Churchill with volume 2 of his war memoirs.

being allowed to take off by the local French authorities for fear of retaliation by the Italian Air Force on the unprotected towns in the South of France. I told Barratt that he need not worry. 'The Prime Minister is here', I said, 'and so is Reynaud, who himself promised us these facilities only a few days ago in Paris. I will go and get their orders. But for goodness sake don't let go of this telephone, otherwise I will never get you again.' I went back to the dining room and asked you, M. Reynaud, Mr Eden and General Weygand to leave the table, and I told the story. M. Reynaud was somewhat shamefaced, but, on being pressed by you, gave me authority to tell Barratt that he might inform the local authorities that the French High Command were agreeable to the operation. Barratt was highly relieved. But his relief was short lived; as the French local authorities, in complete disregard of the orders of their High Command, proceeded to drag carts and lorries on to the airfield, and thus to prevent our bombers taking off. A very tired, very angry Barratt burst in on me at dawn next day, and together we told you what had happened, while you were dressing. You reported it at the meeting which took place a few minutes later. M. Reynaud expressed his regrets, but in view of the terrible plight of the French, you did not press the matter.

General Spears: recollection
(*'The Fall of France', pages 161–2*)

12 June 1940   Briare

When I arrived at the château I went straight to the Prime Minister's bedroom and found him finishing dressing. He was very cross.

'Don't point that revolver at me,' he barked as I fumbled in strapping my revolver to my belt; then added with a half chuckle: 'Do you remember when mine went off at Vimy?' and I remembered of course. He was then commanding a battalion[1] and had come to visit me. He was always testing out new forms of trench clothing and weapons. On this occasion he had shown me before we started for the trenches a complicated automatic revolver with which he was very pleased. I was leading the way down a communication trench when I heard a burst of fire literally in my ear. I dived behind the next traverse thinking we had been surprised by a daylight raid. I peered round cautiously, revolver in hand. There was Winston, his patent automatic firing dangerously and continuously in the direction of his feet as it dangled at the end of its lanyard, which he held at arm's length. He danced like a cat on hot bricks in his attempts to get out of the unpredictable line of fire as the barrel pointed this way and that. I collapsed on the duckboards laughing until I could laugh no longer.

[1] The 6th Battalion, Royal Scots Fusiliers, which Churchill commanded on the Western Front from January to June 1916.

'Go on reiterating that we shall carry on, whatever they do,' he told me. 'If they have lost their faith in themselves let them develop faith in us and in our determination. We will carry them as well as everything else, or,' he added characteristically, 'we will carry those who will let themselves be carried. You are of course to stay on. I am sorry now you were not here these last few days.'

Churchill said nothing as he went downstairs, but he looked very stern, with the expression of deep concentration he always wears when he is utterly absorbed in the contemplation of a problem.

The Frenchmen were standing about in the hall and conference room waiting for the Prime Minister; so was the British contingent, which had been joined by Air Marshal Barratt.

Churchill took Reynaud aside for a few minutes. It was evident he was doing most of the talking. Then we trooped into the dining-room. It was about 8 o'clock. On the French side Pétain's absence left an obvious gap. It was difficult to avoid the impression that he had kept away because he disapproved of the proceedings of the night before. Georges was not there either. He had had his say and his continued absence from his headquarters could hardly have been justified.

I was sorry to see that another absentee was de Gaulle. He had gone to Brittany to investigate how the matter of the bridgehead stood. Darlan had joined the party. Rubicund and nautical, he was complete with bulldog pipe, hands thrust in his monkey-jacket. If he looked ill-at-ease the impression conveyed was that this was because he was so far from the sea.

Supreme War Council: minutes
(*Cabinet papers, 99/3*)

12 June 1940   Briare
8 a.m.

The Prime Minister opened the meeting by asking what particular form of help the French had in mind. At present we had eleven squadrons in France under Air Marshal Barratt – six squadrons of bombers and five squadrons of fighters. The British felt that the best way of helping was to keep these squadrons right up to strength so far as possible.

Air Marshal Barratt said that the approximate numbers of aircraft fit for operations at the present time were as follows:–

Fighters	50–60
Bombers	70–80

Air Marshal Barratt, continuing, said that his bombers were all Battles, and that they were less suited for day work than for night work.

M. Reynaud said that he had asked for four squadrons of fighters to be based in France, in addition to the five squadrons already there. The French officers back from the front line had told him that the morale of the troops would be very high if they did not feel that they were dominated in the air.

The Prime Minister explained that we had two sets of bombers operating in France, namely:–
(1) The bombers under Air Marshal Barratt.
(2) The bombers of the Bomber Command, on which Air Marshal Barratt had a call for employment in France.

Air Marshal Barratt said that the latter had been operating at considerable strength throughout the operations on the very targets that General Weygand had suggested.

He added that in addition to this day's bombing work, anything up to 100 bombers of Bomber Command were employed by night on the rearward communications of the German Army.

The Prime Minister gave the French an assurance that he would have the whole matter of increased air support for France examined carefully and sympathetically by the War Cabinet immediately he got back to London. So far as bombers were concerned, he would see whether it was possible to send Air Marshal Barratt some Blenheims. At the same time he entered a caveat that it would be a fatal mistake to denude the United Kingdom of its essential home defences.

The Prime Minister said that in accordance with the decision of the Supreme War Council, servicing units had been sent to the South of France and preparations had been made to bomb Northern Italy from there. In addition, it had been arranged that three squadrons of Whitleys should fly direct to Northern Italy from England. These had started before Air Marshal Barratt had notified us of the French objections to the operation and it was too late to stop them. The Prime Minister added that in any announcement of these operations it would be made clear that they had been carried out by British forces based on England.

The Prime Minister, in reply to a question from M. Reynaud, said that the British Government thought that it was better not to occupy Crete unless the Italians were to commit an act of aggression against Greece; and that even then we should only do so with Greek consent. GHQ were, however, quite prepared to reconsider the matter if the French had other views.

M. Reynaud said that he thought that it was all the more necessary that we should not take the initiative in Crete in view of Signor Mussolini's undertaking not to attack the Balkan States.

M. Reynaud asked whether it was thought that the Italians would employ Fifth Columnists and/or parachutists against Suez.

The Prime Minister said that we had taken all precautions, and Mr Eden added that four battalions had recently been sent from Palestine to Egypt to deal with the security problem.

General Weygand received a question on Cyprus. He thought it very important that we should not lose this important outpost to Italy.

The Prime Minister said that cover would be given to Cyprus by the naval movements undertaken immediately Italy declared war.

General Dill added that the Cyprus garrison had been increased.

The meeting then reverted to a discussion of the general situation in France, and the Prime Minister put the following questions:–

(i) Will not the mass of Paris and its suburbs present an obstacle dividing and delaying the enemy as in 1914, or like Madrid?

(ii) May this not enable a counter-stroke to be organised with British and French forces across the Lower Seine?

(iii) If the period of co-ordinated war ends, will that not mean an almost equal dispersion of the enemy forces? Would not a war of columns and [attacks] upon the enemy communications be possible? Are the enemy resources sufficient to hold down all the countries at present conquered as well as a large part of France, while they are fighting the French Army and Great Britain?

(iv) Is it not possible thus to prolong the resistance until the United States come in?

M. Reynaud said that the Germans had raised 55 divisions and built 4,000–5,000 heavy tanks since the outbreak of war. The problem confronting Great Britain and France was an industrial one, and the only hope of its solution lay in exploiting the industrial resources of the United States of America.

The Prime Minister said that they already were in close contact with the USA, and would continue to press them in the matter. He would send President Roosevelt a special message.

The Prime Minister expressed the hope that if there was any change in the situation, the French Government would let the British Government know at once, in order that they might come over and see them at any convenient spot, before they took any final decisions which would govern their action in the second phase of the war.

The Prime Minister repeated his request in the most formal manner, and M. Reynaud agreed to it.

FOLLOWING the meeting on the morning of Wednesday, 12 June 1940, Churchill flew back to London.

Antony Goldsmith[1]: recollection
(*Letter to the author, 11 November 1991*)

12 June 1940   Briare

There were problems about a return Spitfire escort as high octane petrol was not available at Briare, F/Lt Blennerhassett[2] assured Mr Churchill and his staff, that there would be cloud cover for most of the journey to Hendon. However on leaving the French coast the skies cleared, and at 8,000 ft we could clearly see French town of Le Havre burning. At this point in the flight we noticed two unidentified aircraft several miles away so we thought it judicious to go down to sea level to avoid contact, the Spitfire escort picked us up shortly afterwards. The rest of the flight home was uneventful.

Winston S. Churchill to Paul Reynaud and General Weygand
(*Premier papers, 3/188/1*)

12 June 1940

The Royal Air Force will make a further increased effort to render assistance to your valiant hard-pressed forces to-morrow and onwards. During the daylight hours to-morrow all available Blenheims, to the number of sixty, will be ready to attack targets indicated by General Georges through Air-Marshal Barratt. Ten Squadrons of Fighters will also work from England within the limits of their range. To-morrow night (13th–14th) 182 heavy Bombers will be available to attack targets as desired by General Georges.

In addition to above support from this country you will, of course, have the six Bomber and five Fighter Squadrons of the Advanced Air Striking Force under the orders of Air-Marshal Barratt. Special instructions have been issued to ensure that these Squadrons are kept up to full strength in aircraft, pilots and crews.

---

[1] One of the aircrew who flew the Flamingo special De Havilland aircraft to France.
[2] The pilot of Churchill's Flamingo on the flight to and from Briare.

JUNE 1940

Lord Lothian to Winston S. Churchill
(*Premier papers, 3/468*)

12 June 1940 Washington
10 a.m. (received)

Have just learned from authoritative source that the President is not convinced that our need for destroyers is serious, and is therefore concentrating on the Allies' other needs. I think it imperative that the Prime Minister should as soon as possible inform him confidentially through me of the numbers, types and tonnages of destroyers lost, the number damaged and time needed for repair and any other information necessary to convince him of our case. The press has been carrying statement here that we have already made good all destroyers lost.

War Cabinet: minutes
(*Cabinet papers, 65/7*)

12 June 1940 10 Downing Street
5 p.m.

The Chief of the Air Staff summarised the information concerning Air Operations given to the War Cabinet that morning. Seven Whitley bombers had succeeded in attacking the Fiat works at Turin, and three had attacked targets at Genoa. It had now been ascertained that the troubles experienced by our aircraft had been due to their having run into storms and encountered bad icing conditions.

As to the press report that Geneva had been bombed, it was known that one of our aircraft, owing to icing, had had to release its bombs in order to gain height to get over the mountains.[1]

The Prime Minister said that M. Reynaud and General Weygand had agreed to the air operation being carried out against targets in Northern Italy by RAF aircraft starting from aerodromes in France, as well as from aerodromes in this country. Nevertheless, General Vuillemin had, on his own initiative, stopped the Wellingtons in France from getting off the aerodrome. Evidently the French feared Italian reprisals. It was also reported that the French and Italian troops were fraternising at the Col de Larche. It was clear that any further air attacks on Italy would have to be carried out from aerodromes in this country. As soon as the scattered aircraft had returned to this country, we should repeat the operation, and it would be wise to do this without delay.

[1] On the night of 11/12 June thirteen British bombs fell on Switzerland, seven on Renens near Lausanne and six on Geneva. Four Swiss were killed, including Fernand Chollet, a soldier who was asleep in his barracks at Champel when the bomb fell.

June 1940

The First Sea Lord said that it had not been possible to get ships in to take off the 51st Division the previous night owing to fog. There were still ships lying off the coast, however, to evacuate any men who might still be able to get away.

The Prime Minister said that the British Commanders in the Havre peninsula must not accept any further orders from the French, who had let us down badly. They had not allowed the 51st Division to retire on Rouen, and had then kept it waiting until it was no longer possible for it to reach Havre; finally, they had compelled it to capitulate with their own troops.[1] Any remaining troops must be evacuated from Havre that night without fail.

The Prime Minister then gave the War Cabinet a report of his meeting with M. Reynaud, Marshal Pétain and General Weygand. They had been studiously polite and dignified, but it was clear that France was near the end of organised resistance.

Continuing, the Prime Minister said that General de Gaulle, who was sitting with M. Reynaud, was all in favour of carrying on a guerrilla warfare. He was young and energetic and had made a very favourable impression. He did not believe in a 'war of fronts' and thought that new methods must be adopted. It seemed probable that, if the present line collapsed, M. Reynaud would turn to General de Gaulle to take command.

M. Reynaud had said that Marshal Pétain had quite made up his mind that peace must be made with the Germans. His view was that all France was being systematically destroyed by the Germans and that it was his duty to save the rest of the country from this fate. He had gone so far as to write a memorandum on the subject, which he had shown to M. Reynaud, but had not left it with him. There could be no doubt that Marshal Pétain was a dangerous man at this juncture; he had always been a defeatist, even in the last war.

The Prime Minister said that he had put certain questions to the French as follows:–

(a) Would not the large built-up area of Paris form a good centre of resistance to the advance of the enemy's tanks, like Madrid?

General Weygand had replied that he had already informed the Paris deputies that the city would be declared an open town and that no attempt at resistance would be made in it. It was full of defenceless people and he could not see it destroyed by German bombardment.

(b) Was there not a chance of making a counter-attack across the Lower Seine to cut in on to the German communications leading towards Paris? We might be able to gather together some eight or nine divisions within a week or so, if we put in the French Chasseurs Alpins and the

---

[1] The capitulation had taken place that morning, 12 June 1940 (see page 308, note 1).

British troops from Narvik, the 52nd Division, the Canadian Division and the 3rd Division, which would be ready in this country about the 20th. There were also two French Divisions which were being reconstituted in the area.

General Weygand had replied that the conception was sound strategically, but the question was whether they could hold out long enough to collect the reserves for this counter-attack. He evidently had not thought so himself and it was on these grounds that the Chief of the Imperial General Staff had been authorised to agree to put in the British reinforcements piece-meal by brigades as they arrived.

(c) If the period of co-ordinated defence came to an end, would it not be possible to carry on a 'war of columns'? This would force the Germans to expend a very large number of troops in combating these tactics, and might enable the French to hold out until the United States came into the war on our side.

General Weygand had replied that he did not himself feel that it would be possible for the French to hold out so long, but he had repeated that he would be willing to serve under any other General who would undertake the task of command.

The Prime Minister said that M. Reynaud seemed quite determined to fight on, and Admiral Darlan had declared emphatically that he would never surrender the French Navy to the enemy. In the last resort, he would send it over to Canada. Nevertheless, there was, of course, the danger that he might be overruled by the politicians.

The Prime Minister had emphasised to the French that, if there was any grave deterioration in the situation on which they felt they had to take decisions of great moment, we must be informed immediately and given an opportunity to consult with them before such decisions were taken.

Some discussion then took place as to how the Germans managed to keep such a tremendous offensive effort going without relaxation.

The Prime Minister said that for six years they had been preparing their offensive war, and the whole Army was imbued with the spirit to press forward at all costs.

The Prime Minister said that he had promised to send a further message to the President of the United States, placing before him clearly the present situation.

The Secretary of State for War quoted extracts from the discussion which had taken place at the meeting in France, in which M. Reynaud and General Weygand had emphasised the decisive effect of air power, and had expressed the view that a great attack by the Allied air forces – which was the only reserve left to the Allied Governments – might even now turn the scale.

The Prime Minister said that he could not believe that this was so, but he had nevertheless promised that the War Cabinet would earnestly consider what air support we could give, and would certainly not in any way lessen the amount which had hitherto been given.

The Secretary of State for War enquired whether a considerable psychological effect might not be achieved if the Royal Air Force in some way could make their presence visible to the French troops on extensive areas of the front.

The Prime Minister thought that this could at any rate be done by action on the Lower Seine, from which the most dangerous attack was developing, and where it would be worth while making our greatest effort. Summing up the position, he thought that a chapter in the war was now closing. The French might continue the struggle; there might even be two French Governments, one which made peace, and one which organised resistance in the Colonies and with the Fleet, and carried on a guerrilla warfare – it was too early yet to tell; but effective resistance as a great land Power was coming to an end. We must now concentrate everything on the defence of this island, though for a period we might still have to send a measure of support to France. He viewed the new phase with confidence. A declaration that we were firmly resolved to continue the war in all circumstances would prove the best invitation to the United States of America to lend us their support. We should maintain the blockade, and win through, though at the cost of ruin and starvation throughout Europe. In the meanwhile, the flow of our forces to France must continue, and the Air Staff must consider how great an effort we could put in during the following two or three days to support the battle.

Winston S. Churchill to President Roosevelt
(*Premier papers, 3/468*)

12 June 1940 10 Downing Street
Personal & Secret

I spent last night and this morning at the French GQG where the situation was explained to me in the gravest terms by Generals Weygand and Georges. You have no doubt received full particulars from Mr Bullitt. The practical point is what will happen when and if the French Front breaks, Paris is taken, and General Weygand reports formally to his Government that France can no longer continue what he calls 'coordinated war'. The aged Marshal Pétain who was none too good in April and July 1918, is I fear ready to lend his name and prestige to a treaty of peace for France. Reynaud on the other hand is for fighting on, and he has a young General de Gaulle who believes much can be done. Admiral Darlan declares he will send the French Fleet to Canada. It would be disastrous if the two big modern ships fell into bad hands. It seems to me that there must be many elements in France who will wish to continue the struggle either in France or in the French Colonies, or in both. This therefore is the moment for you to strengthen Reynaud the utmost you can, and try to tip the balance in favour of the best and longest possible French resistance. I venture to put this point before you although I know you must understand it as well as I do.

Of course I made it clear to the French that we should continue whatever happened, and that we thought Hitler could not win the war or the mastery of the world until he has disposed of us, which has not been found easy in the past, and which perhaps will not be found easy now. I made it clear to the French that we had good hopes of victory, and anyhow had no doubts whatever of what our duty was. If there is anything you can say publicly or privately to the French, now is the time.

John Colville: diary
(*Colville papers*)

12 June 1940

After midnight Reynaud rang up. Winston could not hear him, because the line was so bad and eventually de Margerie and I had to carry on a conversation through the intermediary of telephone operators. Reynaud asked that Winston should go back to France tomorrow, arriving at the Prefecture at Tours by 2.45. This looks as if the French mean to give in, because Reynaud promised to consult Winston again before any fundamental decision was taken, and this sudden summons is ominous. Perhaps W will be able to persuade them to carry on the war, west of Paris, on a guerrilla basis. The Germans must be exhausted and their lines of communication are immense, so if only the French could hold yet a few days the skies might clear.

Winston was furious because Reynaud would talk of the hour of arrival and destination over an open line: he thought it very dangerous and spent a long time considering how to deceive the Germans who had, he felt sure, listened to the conversation. Finally he decided to go very early in the morning with a strong escort of fighters; but at one moment he was ordering me to ring up de Margerie and say, untruthfully, that it was impossible for him to go. This would have caused chaos at the other end and, at the risk of having my head bitten off, I dissuaded him.

Speaking of the surrender of the 51st Division, W said it was the most 'brutal disaster' we had yet suffered.[1]

---

[1] The 51st Division (8,000), commanded by General Fortune, was forced to surrender to General Rommel at St Valéry-en-Caux when the much larger French force (38,000) at the port surrendered. German artillery, firing directly on to the beaches, had prevented more than 3,000 British and French from being evacuated by sea. Rommel later wrote: 'No less than twelve generals were brought in as prisoners, among them four divisional commanders.'

Antony Goldsmith: recollection
(*Letter to the author, 11 November 1991*)

13 June 1940

On arrival at Tours airfield at about 1 p.m. it was raining heavily and what with the airfield having been bombed overnight it was not the most comfortable of landings. Then to top it all off there was nobody to meet the aircraft and quite frankly nobody seemed the slightest bit interested in the fact that the Prime Minister of England had just landed. By this time The Master looked as though he was trying to chew a mouthful of nuts and bolts. But all was resolved by commandeering the station commander's Citroën, and Mr Churchill disappeared down the road muttering about his lunch and being very hungry.

Winston S. Churchill: recollection
(*'Their Finest Hour', pages 158–9*)

13 June 1940   Tours

Arrived over Tours, we found the airport had been heavily bombed the night before, but we and all our escort landed smoothly in spite of the craters. Immediately one sensed the increasing degeneration of affairs. No one came to meet us or seemed to expect us. We borrowed a service car from the station commander and motored into the city, making for the Prefecture, where it was said the French Government had their headquarters. No one of consequence was there, but Reynaud was reported to be motoring in from the country, and Mandel[1] was also to arrive soon.

It being already nearly two o'clock, I insisted upon luncheon, and after some parleyings we drove through streets crowded with refugees' cars, most of them with a mattress on top and crammed with luggage. We found a café, which was closed, but after explanations we obtained a meal.[2] During

---

[1] Georges Mandel (born Louis Rothschild) 1885–1944. Of Jewish parentage, born near Paris. A journalist, he took the name of Georges Mandel. Joined Clemenceau's staff on *L'Aurore*, 1903. Chef de Cabinet to Clemenceau, 1906–9 and 1917–19 (during Clemenceau's two premierships). In charge of the trials dealing with treason and defeatism, 1917–18. Elected to the Chamber of Deputies, 1920. Minister of Posts and Telegraphs, 1934–6 (when he introduced the first French television broadcast, in November 1935). Minister of Colonies, April 1938 to May 1940. Minister of the Interior, May–June 1940 (when he arrested many Nazi sympathisers). Churchill's choice to lead a Free French movement in Britain, but refused to leave France, June 1940. Imprisoned in France, 1940–2; in Germany, 1943–4. Sent back to France, 4 July 1944. Assassinated by Vichy militia, 7 July 1944.

[2] Captain Berkeley noted in his diary: 'Winston in superb form, cracking jokes right and left' (*Berkeley papers*).

luncheon I was visited by M. Baudouin,[1] whose influence had risen in these latter days. He began at once in his soft, silky manner about the hopelessness of the French resistance. If the United States would declare war on Germany it might be possible for France to continue. What did I think about this? I did not discuss the question further than to say that I hoped America would come in, and that we should certainly fight on. He afterwards, I was told, spread it about that I had agreed that France should surrender unless the United States came in.

We then returned to the Prefecture, where Mandel, Minister of the Interior, awaited us. This faithful former secretary of Clemenceau, and a bearer forward of his life's message, seemed in the best of spirits. He was energy and defiance personified. His luncheon, an attractive chicken, was uneaten on the tray before him. He was a ray of sunshine. He had a telephone in each hand, through which he was constantly giving orders and decisions. His ideas were simple: fight on to the end in France, in order to cover the largest possible movement into Africa. This was the last time I saw this valiant Frenchman. The restored French Republic rightly shot to death the hirelings who murdered him. His memory is honoured by his countrymen and their allies.

Presently M. Reynaud arrived. At first he seemed depressed. General Weygand had reported to him that the French armies were exhausted. The line was pierced in many places; refugees were pouring along all the roads through the country, and many of the troops were in disorder. The Generalissimo felt it was necessary to ask for an armistice while there were still enough French troops to keep order until peace could be made. Such was the military advice. He would send that day a further message to Mr Roosevelt saying that the last hour had come and that the fate of the Allied cause lay in America's hands. Hence arose the alternative of armistice and peace.

Supreme War Council: minutes
(*Cabinet papers, 99/3*)

13 June 1940 Prefecture
3.30 p.m. Tours

M. Reynaud described the most recent situation on the French front as reported by General Weygand. The French armies were at their last gasp, and

[1] Paul Baudouin. Director of the Bank of Indo-China, 1930. Inspector of Finance, 1937 (Léon Blum): head of a committee for controlling currency exchange. Sent to Rome to seek a Franco-Italian rapprochment, 1939 (Daladier). Secretary to the War Cabinet, April–May 1940, and Under-Secretary of State to the President of the Council (Reynaud), May–June 1940. Under-Secretary for Foreign Affairs, 6 June 1940, when he became a leading advocate of an armistice. Foreign Minister (under Pétain), June–October 1940. Tried for treason, 1947. In 1948 he published *The Private Diaries of Paul Baudouin*.

the Commander-in-Chief had stated that it would soon be necessary to plead for armistice to save the soil and structure of France. M. Reynaud had replied that he did not consider the situation yet desperate. Great losses had been inflicted on the enemy, and if the armies could fight on yet awhile, help would soon come from Great Britain and from the United States.

What was imperative now was to have definite proof that America would come in with sufficient speed and force. That very morning M. Reynaud had received the proposal from President Roosevelt that the message sent by him to the latter on the previous Monday, 10th June, should be made public in both countries. This was encouraging, as was the promise of an increase in the immediate supply of aircraft and guns. M. Reynaud's message of 10th June had said that the enemy was at the gates of Paris but that the French would continue the fight from the last province left them, and if necessary, from Africa or the overseas Empire. 'Tell your people,' the message had gone on, 'that France is sacrificing everything in the cause of freedom. We desperately need at once every form of material and moral help you can give us short of an expeditionary force. The fate of 90 per cent of the world's population is at stake and France, the advance post of democracy, is in mortal peril.'

M. Reynaud proposed that day to send a further message to Mr Roosevelt saying that the last hour had come, that the fate of the Allied cause lay in America's hands.

He explained that he would be unable to carry the French Government with him in a resolve to carry on unless President Roosevelt's reply conveyed a firm assurance of immediate aid. His colleagues would reply, 'Why carry on with the certain result of an occupation of the whole of France, accompanied by systematic corruption and adulteration by Hitler's propaganda machine of the spirit and essence of the French people?' The Government itself could, of course, retreat and carry on. But the population would remain, be subtly but thoroughly transformed, and France would cease to exist.

Hence arose the alternative of armistice and peace. The Council of Ministers had on the previous day instructed M. Reynaud to enquire what would be Britain's attitude should the worst come. He himself was well aware of the solemn pledge that no separate peace would be entered into by either Ally. General Weygand and others pointed out that France had already sacrificed everything in the common cause. She had nothing left; but she had succeeded in greatly weakening the common foe. It would in those circumstances be a shock if Britain failed to concede that France was physically unable to carry on, if France was still expected to fight on and thus deliver up her people to the certainty of corruption and evil transformation at the heads of ruthless specialists in the art of bringing conquered peoples to heel.

That then was the question which he had to put. Would Great Britain realise the hard facts with which France was faced?

Mr Churchill said that Great Britain realised how much France had suffered and was suffering. Her own turn would come, and she was ready. She grieved to find that her contribution to the land struggle was at present so small owing to the reverses which had been met with as a result of applying an agreed strategy in the North. The British had not yet felt the German lash but were aware of its force. They nevertheless had but one thought: to win the war and destroy Hitlerism. Everything was subordinate to that aim; no difficulties, no regrets could stand in the way. He was well assured of their capacity for enduring and persisting, for striking back till the foe was beaten.[1]

They would therefore hope that France would carry on, fighting South of Paris down to the sea, and, if need be, from North Africa. At all costs time must be gained. The period of waiting was not limitless: a pledge from the United States would make it quite short.

The alternative course meant destruction for France quite as certainly. Hitler would abide by no pledges. If, on the other hand, France remained in the struggle with her fine Navy, her great Empire, her army still able to carry on guerrilla warfare on a gigantic scale, and if Germany failed to destroy England, which she must do or go under, if then her might in the air was broken, then the whole hateful edifice of Nazidom would topple over. Given immediate help from America, perhaps even a declaration of war, victory was not so far off.

At all events England would fight on. She had not and would not alter her resolve: no terms, no surrender. The alternatives for her were death or victory. That was his answer to M. Reynaud's question.

M. Reynaud said that he had never doubted England's determination. He was, however, anxious to know how the British Government would react in a certain contingency. The French Government – the present one or another – might say 'We know you will carry on. We would also, if we saw any hope of a victory soon enough to enable us to re-create France as she was and desires to be. But we see no sufficient hopes of an early victory. We cannot count on American help. There is no light at the end of the tunnel. We cannot abandon our people to indefinite German domination. We must come to terms. We have no choice.'

This would be a most grave decision for a French Government to take. But it might be the only one. It was already too late to organise a redoubt in Brittany. Nowhere would a genuine French Government have a hope of escaping capture on French soil, and Hitler's puppet Government would at once begin its task of undermining and corruption.

The question to Britain would therefore take the form: 'Will you acknowledge that France has given her best, her youth and lifeblood; that she can do

---

[1] General Spears later recalled: 'Winston was gathering momentum as he went, his eyes flashed, his hands were clenched as if grasping a double-handed sword. The picture he was drawing made him splutter with rage as he contemplated it' (*The Fall of France*, page 205).

no more; and that she is entitled, having nothing further to contribute to the common cause, to enter into a separate peace while maintaining solidarity implicit in the solemn agreement entered into three months previously?

Mr Churchill said that in no case would Britain waste time and energy in reproaches and recriminations. That was, however, a different matter and did not mean that she would consent to action contrary to the recent agreement.

He considered that the first step ought to be M. Reynaud's further message putting the present position squarely to President Roosevelt. Let them await the answer before considering anything else. Let the position be put in the strongest terms by M. Reynaud. He would himself back up the message with another, in continuation of recent despatches pleading for France. Meanwhile, M. Reynaud could rest assured that there would be no reproaches whatever happened, that England would continue to cherish the cause of France, and that if she herself triumphed, France would be restored in her greatness.

Let President Roosevelt's reply be awaited before anything was said regarding British consent to a departure from the solemn undertaking.

M. Reynaud agreed to this course, and outlined the contents of the message he would address to the President. The French Army had been the vanguard of the forces of democracy. It had weakened the enemy, but now had come the time of the main forces. Would they come, or would they await their turn to be destroyed piecemeal? The Allies had committed grievous errors, and it was manifestly Hitler's hope to annihilate them one by one, including America herself once England had been disposed of. Would any United States citizen dare to hold his head high if both France and England were overwhelmed and his country did nothing?

Mr Churchill said that a firm promise from America would introduce a tremendous new factor in the situation the French Government would have to face. The decision would rest with them, with or without Britain's consent. But there would be many other factors to consider also. The war would certainly continue. The blockade, if need be of the whole of Europe, would become increasingly effective. Famine and desperate suffering would ensue. These were very terrible, but inescapable prospects. France, if she were occupied by the Germans, could not hope to be spared, unless England, too, fell. There might arise bitter antagonism between the French and English people.

There would, in fact, be many matters to be considered if President Roosevelt's reply was of a negative character.

Meanwhile, he was anxious to know how long France could hope to hold out before General Weygand found himself obliged to sue for armistice. Was another week possible, or less?

M. Reynaud said that he viewed with horror the prospect that Great

Britain might inflict the immense suffering of an effective blockade upon the French people. He was convinced that a separation of the two countries would be a great disaster, and that neither could hope for independence thereafter. Even if the worst came, if President Roosevelt's reply held out insufficient hope, if he himself was compelled to abandon the position to which he was desperately clinging, he hoped that Great Britain would, in recognition of the untold sacrifices of French men and women, make some gesture that would obviate the risk of an antagonism, the later consequences of which he considered fatal.

Mr Churchill said that this question would have to be examined with many others that would arise if France decided to enter into an armistice and Treaty. The issue to-day was to put the position before the American President in its full brutal reality.

M. Reynaud agreed.

General Spears: recollection
(*'The Fall of France'*, pages 213–14)

13 June 1940   Tours

Remembering how, when confronted with a difficult situation at the Peace Conference, Lloyd George often asked for an adjournment to consult his colleagues, I scribbled a note to Churchill suggesting he should do likewise, and leant over and handed it to him as he was speaking. He stopped, read it, nodded and went on with what he had been saying, which was in fact a repetition. 'We shall have to consider the whole position after the receipt of the American answer. We shall have to examine many things if France decides to ask for an armistice and a treaty. The American answer can be expected within twenty-four hours. For the moment the only move open to us is to put the situation to the American President with the greatest frankness.'

Churchill then said he hoped Reynaud would not mind his conferring with his colleagues. Turning round he looked out of the window at the now sunny garden, and feeling no doubt that this was the most likely place where it would be possible to talk quietly without being overheard, he said: '*Dans le jardin.*' So to the garden we went.[1]

---

[1] Churchill, Halifax, Beaverbrook, Sir Alexander Cadogan, Sir Ronald Campbell, General Ismay and General Spears.

Beaverbrook and Halifax at once expressed complete support of Churchill. The diplomats tended to form a bunch round Halifax a little way behind, though the Ambassador drew up to the Prime Minister several times to answer questions. I believe that everyone was too stunned to speak. I certainly was. I felt completely at sea, rather savage and greatly bewildered as well as frustrated and useless, being unable to cast any light on Reynaud's mood, or even guess at an explanation of what seemed a new and defeatist policy on his part. All I could say was that Reynaud had been completely different that morning when he had described how at the Cabinet meeting the night before he had resisted the 'armisticers' and been supported by most of his colleagues in opposing Weygand's peace offensive.

There followed some speculation as to what Reynaud had meant to imply. Would he finally decide to go to North Africa? Had he got it in him to brave Pétain and Weygand, or would he slide out, do a Pontius Pilate and leave the way clear for someone else to make peace?

Then suddenly Beaverbrook spoke. His dynamism was immediately felt. 'There is nothing to do but to repeat what you have already said, Winston. Telegraph to Roosevelt and await the answer. Tell Reynaud that we have nothing to say or discuss until Roosevelt's answer is received. Don't commit yourself to anything. We shall gain a little time and see how those Frenchmen sort themselves out. We are doing no good here. In fact, listening to these declarations of Reynaud's only does harm. Let's get along home.' It was as simple as that, but it was what everyone felt to be the voice of common sense, and so, up the garden path, back we went to the Prefecture. The promenade had taken about twenty minutes.

Supreme War Council: minutes
(Cabinet papers, 99/3)

13 June 1940 Prefecture
Tours

After a brief adjournment, Mr Churchill said that discussion with his colleagues had not altered his views, which were certainly shared by the whole British Government.

M. Reynaud summarised what he proposed to say in his message to President Roosevelt as follows: 'The position of the armies has gravely deteriorated since my previous message. It is essential that I should have some sign of hope from you to give to the French Government and people. I ask you to take a further step forward, to declare war if you can, but in any event to send us every form of help short of an expeditionary force.'

That, M. Reynaud went on, would secure for the Allies the powerful support of the American Navy and Air Force. For his own part, he felt convinced that America would take a further step forward, a step sufficient to allow him to reach agreement with the British Government regarding the conditions which should govern their joint future conduct of the war, when, with the full help of America, they would be able to march on to victory.

Those were his personal convictions; everything he had said previously represented the views expressed at the Council of Ministers on the previous day.

Mr Churchill said that his own telegram to President Roosevelt would also describe the situation bluntly. He would include in it a reference to the question M. Reynaud had put to him earlier in the meeting which expressed that the British Government was unable to give an answer until it was acquainted with the terms of President Roosevelt's reply to M. Reynaud's own message. All this might occupy one day or two. The two Prime Ministers could then consider together the terms of the reply and what decisions were called for. If America came in they could be certain of victory; but if she did not and the French people had for a while to suffer Nazi domination, he felt convinced that their spirit would not break and that they would not grow to love Hitler's works however strong the efforts of the German propaganda machine.

M. Reynaud agreed to all these proposals and expressed his confidence that when they met again it would be ways and means of continuing their joint war effort that they would have to discuss.

Mr Churchill had one concrete point of detail to raise before the meeting broke. There were at present in France several hundred German pilots held prisoner. They constituted a great danger and he hoped very much that M. Reynaud would agree forthwith that they should be despatched to England, where they would be kept out of harm's way. He considered this matter urgent.

M. Reynaud said that he would take action forthwith.

Mr Churchill said until their next meeting, the British programme of disembarkations in France would continue as arranged.

M. Reynaud expressed gratitude for this assurance. Everything that he had discussed earlier in the meeting was, of course, only a hypothesis which would arise if President Roosevelt's final answer was of a negative character.

Mr Churchill said that this was certainly the darkest hour for the Allied cause. Nevertheless, its confidence that Hitlerism would be smashed and that Nazidom could not and would not over-rule Europe remained absolutely unshaken.

M. Reynaud said that his confidence remained equally firm; else he could not endure to go on living.

June 1940

Winston S. Churchill: recollection
(*'Their Finest Hour'*, page 162)

13 June 1940

As we went down the crowded passage into the courtyard I saw General de Gaulle standing stolid and expressionless at the doorway. Greeting him, I said in a low tone, in French: '*L'homme du destin*'. He remained impassive. In the courtyard there must have been more than a hundred leading Frenchmen in frightful misery. Clemenceau's son was brought up to me. I wrung his hand.[1]

General Spears: recollection
(*'The Fall of France'*, pages 218-19)

13 June 1940   Tours

As I stood in the doorway, de Gaulle appeared. He had, as I have noted, joined the conference late, but had taken no part in the discussion. He called me aside and said that Baudouin was putting it about to all and sundry, notably to the journalists, that Churchill had shown complete comprehension of the French situation and would understand if France concluded an armistice and a separate peace. I noted his words: '. . . *que l'Angleterre comprendrait si la France faisait un armistice et une paix séparée.*' Had Churchill really said that? de Gaulle asked. It would be most unfortunate if he had, for it would give the defeatists the right to say: 'What is the good of fighting on when even the French do not expect us to?' And also it would deeply affect others who were not prepared to break unilaterally France's pledge to England not to make a separate peace.

I asserted that the Prime Minister could not have made anything approaching such a statement after the conference, for at it he had clearly indicated the contrary. What he had said in French, when the idea was indicated by Reynaud, was '*Je comprends*' (I understand) in the sense of 'I understand what you say,' not in the sense of 'I agree'.

'Well, that's what Baudouin is saying. He is putting it about that France is now released from her engagement to England. It is unfortunate.'

'I will see if I can catch the Prime Minister before he leaves,' I said and, running out, I found my car and pelted after the English party. At the aerodrome all the planes were revving up against the dismal background of smashed hangars and a bomb-pitted runway.

---

[1] Churchill had been with Clemenceau after the German breakthrough of March 1918, and had greatly admired his stamina and resolve. In his book *Great Contemporaries* (1937), he wrote: 'Happy the nation which when its fate quivers in the balance can find such a tyrant and such a champion.' Clemenceau's son, Michel, was a member of the French Parliament.

I told Churchill of Baudouin's effort, and got from him absolute and categorical confirmation that at no time had he given to anyone the least indication of his consenting to the French concluding a separate armistice. 'When I said "*Je comprends*", I meant I understand. *Comprendre* means understand in French, doesn't it? Well,' said Winston, 'when for once I use exactly the right word in their own language, it is going rather far to assume that I intended it to mean something quite different. Tell them my French is not so bad as that.'[1]

He beamed. 'Shay—' But I did not hear the rest, lost in the roar of the engine. He clutched his hat, bent his head to the draught of the propellers, waved his stick, and the precious, lovable man was off. I gazed upward, in a moment the Flamingo and its escort had disappeared.

General Ismay: recollection
(*'The memoirs of Lord Ismay', page 145*)

13 June 1940   Tours

We left the battered airfield that afternoon, and by 10 p.m. the Cabinet was assembled to be told the sad story. Thus ended our fifth visit to France since the battle started. The physical and mental strain on all of us had been intense, but the Prime Minister, who had had by far the most grievous burden to carry, never looked harassed or tired. He had, as he afterwards admitted, suffered real agony of soul; but he never gave a sign of it.[2]

---

[1] As Spears noted in his memoirs, Baudouin continued to assert that Churchill's use of 'Je comprends' meant 'I agree' rather than 'I understand'. Spears added: 'This was reflected in Admiral Darlan's telegram to all French warships on 23 June 1940 when he stated: "It should not be forgotten that the British Prime Minister, informed on June 11th (*in fact, the 13th*) of the necessity in which France found herself of bringing the struggle to an end, declared that he *understood* (*my emphasis*) that necessity and accepted it without withdrawing his sympathy from our country. He is therefore not qualified to speak otherwise." ' (The words in brackets are printed here as they appear in Spears' memoirs.)

[2] While Churchill was returning to London, Reynaud was on his way to Cagney, where the French Cabinet was in session. After the war it was learned there was some criticism, among those ministers who had wished to continue the fight, that Churchill and his colleagues had not gone to Cagney to stiffen the resolve of Reynaud's ministers along the lines of his strong words at Tours. In fact, Churchill had been unaware of the Cagney meeting, nor did Reynaud invite him to it. Reflecting on this after the war, Churchill wrote: 'Perhaps the harassed Premier did not think I should be stern enough. In this fierce French quarrel I might well have done more harm than good. There was too much in my memory for me to be a harsh claimant. I lay under the impression of twenty years of history – the United States withdrawal from the League of Nations; the MacDonald efforts to reduce the French Army to equality with Germany; our inadequate contribution to the awful battle. All these burdens would have hampered my advocacy' (Churchill draft memoirs, *Churchill papers, 4/155*).

War Cabinet: minutes
(*Cabinet papers, 65/7*)

13 June 1940 10 Downing Street
10.15 p.m.

The Prime Minister gave the War Cabinet an account of the Meeting which he and the Foreign Secretary had had with M. Reynaud that afternoon at Tours. There had been considerable signs of disorganisation, and refugees had been streaming through the town. The Meeting had been held in a room in the Prefecture.

M. Reynaud had at first seemed very depressed. General Weygand had reported to him that the French Armies were exhausted. Their line was pierced in many places; refugees were pouring through the country; and many of the troops were considerably disordered. He felt that it was necessary to ask for an armistice while there were still enough French troops left to keep order in the country until peace could be made. M. Reynaud had said that the French had suffered as much as they could bear and had done their best as a loyal ally. He now asked whether Great Britain would release France from the pledge which she had made not to make a separate peace.

In reply, he (the Prime Minister) had said that he felt on rather weak ground as we had so few troops taking part in the battle. We would have had fourteen divisions, but for reverses met with as a result of applying an agreed strategy in the North. Nevertheless, we were determined to continue to give all the help in our power, and believed that Hitler could not win the war without overcoming us. Our war aim still remained the total defeat of Hitler, and we felt that we could still bring this about. We were, therefore, not in a position to release France from her obligation. Whatever happened, we would level no reproaches or recriminations at France; but that was a different matter from consenting to release her from her pledge.

The discussion had then turned to the American situation. M. Reynaud's message of the 10th June, in which he had said that France would fight on even if it meant continuing the struggle from French Possessions in America, had just been published, and M. Reynaud was evidently much heartened by the fact that President Roosevelt had consented to this. He (the Prime Minister) said that the French must now send a new demand to President Roosevelt, urging him to intervene. This appeal would be backed up from here by a statement of the position and a request for assistance to France. M. Reynaud agreed to do this and proposed to make an appeal for the maximum help which the President could give short of sending an expeditionary force.

Matters were finally left that the French would hold on until the result of this final appeal was known.

The meeting had then ended, and he had gone into another room where he had seen a number of Ministers, including M. Herriot[1] and M. Mandel. The former had shown himself resolutely determined to continue the struggle.

Since returning to this country a further remarkable message had been received from President Roosevelt. The Prime Minister then read to the War Cabinet this message, a copy of which is appended to these Minutes.[2] This message, he said, came as near as possible to a declaration of war and was probably as much as the President could do without Congress. The President could hardly urge the French to continue the struggle, and to undergo further torture, if he did not intend to enter the war to support them. If the President were not disavowed by his country, then it was clear that he would bring them in on our side in the near future. This message would have been quite sufficient as an answer to M. Reynaud's final appeal, but it would be observed that it had come in advance of it, which made the effect even more striking.

The Prime Minister suggested that he should say to M. Reynaud that President Roosevelt's message fulfilled every hope and could only mean that the United States intended to enter the war on our side. If the French continued the struggle, Hitler would enter Paris within a day or so, but he would find the capital a mere empty shell. Though he might occupy much of her country, the soul of France would have gone beyond his reach. No doubt he would offer very specious terms to the French, but these we could not permit them to accept. When Hitler found that he could get no peace in this way, his only course would be to try and smash this island. He would probably make the attempt very quickly, perhaps within a fortnight; but before that the United States of America would be in the war on our side.

The Lord Privy Seal urged that a statement in dramatic terms should be

---

[1] Edouard Herriot, 1872–1957. French writer and politician. Mayor of Lyons, 1905. Minister of Supplies, 1916. A Socialist-Radical deputy from 1919. Prime Minister and Foreign Minister, June 1924 to April 1925, July 1926 (for one day), and June–December 1932. Minister of Education, 1926–8. An elder statesman in 1940, he had just published *The Well-Springs of Liberty*. Interned by the Germans, 1943–5. On Victory-in-Europe Day, 8 May 1945, he was at the British Embassy in Moscow, having recently been liberated by the Soviet Army. President of the Socialist-Radical Party, 1945. President of the National Assembly, 1947–54.

[2] This was Roosevelt's telegram to Reynaud of 13 June 1940, in which the President told the French Prime Minister: 'Your message of 10th June has moved me very deeply. As I have already stated to you and to Mr Churchill, this government is doing everything in its power to make available to the Allied Governments the material they so urgently require, and our efforts to do still more are being redoubled. This is so because of our faith in and support of the ideals for which the Allies are fighting. The magnificent resistance of the French and British armies has profoundly impressed the American people. I am, personally, particularly impressed by your declaration that France will continue to fight on behalf of Democracy, even if it means slow withdrawal, even to North Africa and the Atlantic. It is most important to remember that the French and British fleets continue mastery of the Atlantic and other oceans; also to remember that vital materials from the outside world are necessary to maintain all armies. I am also greatly heartened by what Prime Minister Churchill said a few days ago about the continued resistance of the British Empire, and that determination would seem to apply equally to the great French Empire all over the world. Naval power in world affairs still carries the lessons of history, as Admiral Darlan well knows' (*Cabinet papers, 65/7*).

issued to hearten the people of France. It was not enough merely to send messages of encouragement to the French Government.

The Prime Minister said that he made it quite clear at the meeting that we should never desert France, and that, if we won through, as we believed we should, the wrongs of France would be righted. We should fight on and never quit the struggle until France had been fully restored.

There was general agreement that an announcement in dramatic terms of the solidarity of France and Great Britain should be issued. We might say that 'France and Great Britain were one.'

Her Majesty the Queen[1] might be invited to include this sentiment in her forthcoming broadcast to the women of France.

The Secretary of State for Dominion Affairs[2] then raised the question of the line we should take with Dominion Governments. He stressed that it was not enough to tell them all that had passed. They must be treated as full partners and their assent must not be taken for granted.

The Prime Minister proposed that we should communicate to the Dominions our announcement to the French people on our solidarity with them, and also the latest message which had been received from President Roosevelt. We should then add that it had always been our intention to fight on to the bitter end, and suggest that now was the time for Dominion Governments to make a similar declaration.

The Prime Minister summarised the immediate action which should be taken as follows:–

(a) He would send a telegram to M. Reynaud making clear that President Roosevelt's message of the 13th June was the answer to M. Reynaud's appeal of the 10th June, and gave the latter the assurance of further support which he considered essential if France was to continue the struggle. It was important to make clear to M. Reynaud the full implications of the President's message as we understood it.

(b) A statement should be issued, in the form of a message to the French Government from His Majesty's Government, proclaiming the indis-

---

[1] Lady Elizabeth Bowes-Lyon, 1900– . Daughter of the 14th Earl of Strathmore. In 1923 she married the Duke of York, who succeeded his brother (King Edward VIII) as King George VI in 1936, when she became Queen Elizabeth. On the accession to the throne of her daughter Elizabeth as Queen Elizabeth II in 1952, she was styled Her Majesty Queen Elizabeth the Queen Mother.

[2] Thomas Walker Hobart Inskip, 1879–1947. Educated at Clifton and King's College, Cambridge. Barrister, 1899. Served in the Naval Intelligence Division, Admiralty, 1915–18. Conservative MP for Central Bristol, 1918–29, and for Fareham, 1931–9. Knighted, 1922. Solicitor-General, October 1922 to January 1924, November 1924 to March 1928, and September 1931 to January 1932. Attorney-General, 1928–9 and 1932–6. Minister for the Co-ordination of Defence, 1936–9. Secretary of State for Dominion Affairs, January–September 1939 and May–October 1940. Lord Chancellor, September 1939 to May 1940. Created Viscount Caldecote, 1939. Lord Chief Justice, 1940–6.

soluble union of our two peoples and of our two Empires.[1] This statement should be given the widest possible publicity.

(c) He would send a telegram to President Roosevelt seeking his consent to the publication of his last message, and supporting the further appeal made by M. Reynaud.

(d) A telegram should be sent to the Dominions informing them of the position and asking them publicly to endorse our policy.

The Prime Minister then left the room to speak to the American Ambassador. During his absence a summary of M. Reynaud's broadcast appeal to President Roosevelt, as reported on the tape, was brought in and read.

On his return, the Prime Minister said that Mr Kennedy had spoken to the President, who was agreeable to publication of his message, but that Mr Hull[2] was opposed to it. The President had heard that the meeting at Tours had been very successful, and it seemed that he did not realise how critical the situation was. Mr Kennedy had gone back to the American Embassy in order to communicate to the President a full account of the meeting, based on notes supplied to him by the Prime Minister. He was then returning to No. 10 Downing Street.

The Prime Minister read to the War Cabinet the drafts of the following:–

(a) A telegram from himself to M. Reynaud.

(b) The message to the French Government from His Majesty's Government, proclaiming the indissoluble union of our two peoples and our two Empires.

(c) A telegram from himself to President Roosevelt.

Winston S. Churchill to Paul Reynaud
(*Cabinet papers, 65/7*)

13 June 1940

On returning here we received copy of President Roosevelt's answer to your appeal of 10th June. Cabinet is united in considering this magnificent document as decisive in favour of the continued resistance of France in accordance with your own declaration of 10th June about fighting before Paris, behind Paris, in a Province or, if necessary, in Africa or across the

---

[1] The idea of a Franco-British union came from Jean Monnet and was supported by General de Gaulle, who believed that it might strengthen Reynaud's hand. Neville Chamberlain also supported it, as did Sir Robert Vansittart. Churchill was at first sceptical, but eventually agreed to it at a meeting of the War Cabinet on 16 June.

[2] Cordell Hull, 1871–1955. Elected to the United States Congress for Tennessee, 1907–21 and 1923–31; Senator, 1931–3. Secretary of State, 1933–44. Nobel Peace Prize, 1945. He published *The Memoirs of Cordell Hull* (two volumes) in 1948.

Atlantic. The promise of redoubled material aid is coupled with definite advice and exhortation to France to continue the struggle even under the grievous conditions which you mentioned. If France on this message of President Roosevelt's continues in the field and in the war, we feel that the United States is committed beyond recall to take the only remaining step, namely, becoming a belligerent in form as she already has constituted herself in fact. Constitution of United States makes it impossible, as you foresaw, for President to declare war himself, but, if you act on his reply now received, we sincerely believe that this must inevitably follow. We are asking President to allow publication of message, but even if he does not agree to this for a day or two, it is on the record and can afford the basis for your action. I do beg you and your colleagues, whose resolution we so much admired to-day, not to miss this sovereign opportunity of bringing about the world-wide oceanic and economic coalition which must be fatal to Nazi domination. We see before us a definite plan of campaign, and the light which you spoke of shines at the end of the tunnel.

Message to the French Government from the British Government[1]
(*Cabinet papers, 65/7*)

13 June 1940

In this solemn hour for the British and French nations and for the cause of freedom and Democracy to which they have vowed themselves, His Majesty's Government desire to pay to the Government of the French Republic the tribute which is due to the heroic fortitude and constancy of the French armies in battle against enormous odds. Their effort is worthy of the most glorious traditions of France and has inflicted deep and long-lasting injury upon the enemy's strength. Great Britain will continue to give the utmost aid in her power. We take this opportunity of proclaiming the indissoluble union of our two peoples and of our two Empires. We cannot measure the various forms of tribulation which will fall upon our peoples in the near future. We are sure that the ordeal by fire will only fuse them together into one unconquerable whole. We renew to the French Republic our pledge and resolve to continue the struggle at all costs in France, in this Island, upon the oceans, and in the air, wherever it may lead us, using all our resources to the utmost limit and sharing together the burden of repairing the ravages of war. We shall never turn from the conflict until France stands safe and erect in all her grandeur, until the wronged and enslaved States and peoples have been liberated, and until civilisation is freed from the nightmare of Nazidom. That this day will dawn we are more sure than ever. It may dawn sooner than we now have the right to expect.

[1] This message was almost certainly drafted by Churchill.

Winston S. Churchill to President Roosevelt
(*Cabinet papers, 65/13*)

14 June 1940
early hours
Secret and Personal

Ambassador Kennedy will have told you about the British meeting today with the French at Tours of which I showed him our record. I cannot exaggerate its critical character. They were very nearly gone. Weygand had advocated an armistice while he still had enough troops to prevent France from lapsing into anarchy. Reynaud asked us whether in view of the sacrifice and sufferings of France we would release her from the obligation about not making a separate peace. Although the fact that we have unavoidably been largely out of this terrible battle weighed with us, I did not hesitate in the name of the British Government to refuse consent to an armistice or separate peace. I urged that this issue should not be discussed until a further appeal had been made by Reynaud to you and the United States, which I undertook to second. Agreement was reached on this and a much better mood prevailed for the moment with Reynaud and his Ministers.

Reynaud felt strongly that it would be beyond his power to encourage his people to fight on without hope of ultimate victory, and that that hope could only be kindled by American intervention up to the extreme limit open to you. As he put it, they wanted to see light at the end of the tunnel.

While we were flying back here your magnificent message was sent and Ambassador Kennedy brought it to me on my arrival. The British Cabinet was profoundly impressed and desire me to express their gratitude for it, but Mr President I must tell you that it seems to me absolutely vital that this message should be published tomorrow 14th June in order that it may play the decisive part in turning the course of world history. It will I am sure decide the French to deny Hitler a patched-up peace with France. He needs this peace in order to destroy us and take a long step forward to world mastery. All the far-reaching plans strategic, economic, political and moral which your message expounds may be still-born if the French cut out now. Therefore I urge that the message should be published now. We realise fully that the moment Hitler finds he cannot dictate a Nazi peace in Paris he will turn his fury on to us. We shall do our best to withstand it and if we succeed wide new doors are opened upon the future and all will come out even at the end of the day.

JUNE 1940 325

War Cabinet: minutes
(*Cabinet papers, 65/7*)

14 June 1940　　　　　　　　　　　　　　　　　　　　　　10 Downing Street
12.30 p.m.

The Prime Minister said that a message had now been received from the American Ambassador to say that President Roosevelt was unwilling that his message of the 13th June, in answer to M. Reynaud's appeal, should be published. Mr Kennedy had asked whether he (the Prime Minister) would explain the position to M. Reynaud. He had declined to do so, and had stressed strongly that, if President Roosevelt appeared now to be holding back, this would have a disastrous effect on French resistance.

Reference was made to telegram No. 405 from Sir R. Campbell, referring to pernicious reports that Britain would liberate France from her engagements if America should not declare war. The question was discussed whether it was necessary to take steps to deny these rumours. The Prime Minister suggested that the Foreign Secretary should send a message to Sir R. Campbell pointing out that, in our view, President Roosevelt's message of the 13th June gave M. Reynaud the assurance of further support which he considered essential. In this telegram reference might also be made to these rumours, and an opportunity taken of denying them.

War Cabinet: Confidential Annex
(*Cabinet papers, 65/13*)

14 June 1940　　　　　　　　　　　　　　　　　　　　　　10 Downing Street
12.30 p.m.

The Prime Minister said that while every effort should be made to keep alive French resistance, so long as it continued, by the despatch of fresh troops, we must now go ahead with the wholesale withdrawal of our Lines of Communication personnel at the bases. The indications were that the Germans were preparing to attack Le Mans and advance towards Nantes. If the French defence should crumble, our position there would be serious. The situation would require to be very carefully watched.

The Prime Minister asked that he should be furnished with a priority list of the material which was being withdrawn, and a time-table of the plans for the evacuation of material and personnel.

Hugh Dalton: diary
(*'The Second World War Diary of Hugh Dalton'*)

14 June 1940
5 p.m.

Winston has one of his ministers' squashes. Gives an account of his last visit to France and a very vivid appreciation.

French organised resistance is at an end. The Government and the High Command still give orders, but they are not effectively transmitted nor obeyed. You meet men who can talk to you, but have no telephone. General Georges supported Weygand's advice to Reynaud that he should ask for an armistice. Reynaud refused.

Reynaud had asked Churchill 'most solemnly and formally' to relieve France from her promise not to make a separate peace. Churchill had refused. This, he thinks, was the answer Reynaud wanted from him. Reynaud had put this question after a long meeting of the Cabinet.

The French Army has lost the battle. They have no reserves left. Their Divisions have been reduced to the strength of two battalions. In some parts soldiers are wandering in the woods, taking food from passers-by. They state that if they had had twelve more Divisions, they could have won. That may be true, but that sort of thing is true of almost every battle.

Hitler will soon make the French a peace offer. It will be made to sound very generous. A French government may be found to accept it. The French fleet raises a number of problems and there may be great temptation. There should be a France across the Water. Reynaud and Mandel would be for this. Only too much recrimination is possible on both sides, French and British. But what good would it do? Very few British Divisions have fought in France. At the end, very few indeed. French losses have been out of all proportion to ours, in every sphere.

We here must strike a still more defiant note. We shall defend this island. Weygand said to him, 'You have a very good anti-tank trap in the Channel.' We must intensify the blockade and show great activity in the air. We have more troops here than we have ever had before. All forms of home defence are being vigorously pushed forward. It is a long-standing doctrine that raids may succeed but that large-scale invasion of this island is impossible. Our fighter strength is now greater than before the offensive began. There have been prodigies both of production and repair of aircraft. There will now be very violent attacks made upon this island, but, if they are beaten off at first, they cannot succeed later. Nazidom will lie like a dark pall over all Europe, but, after only a few months, it may dissolve like the snow in spring.

There is no alternative before us except to fight it out; else we shall be first despoiled and then enslaved.

June 1940

Defence Committee: minutes
(*Cabinet papers, 69/1*)

14 June 1940 10 Downing Street
6.30 p.m.

The Meeting had been summoned to consider a telegram received from General Brooke[1] stating that he had been informed by General Weygand that organised resistance by the French was at an end.

A draft telegram to the Howard-Vyse Mission stating that in view of this development General Brooke was being ordered to act independently, but in co-operation with French forces fighting in his vicinity, was first considered.

The Prime Minister said that naval operations in connection with the immediate situation in France could be divided into two main categories. Firstly, naval assistance in keeping open French sea communications with North Africa via the Mediterranean and Atlantic ports. Secondly, measures to prevent the French fleet falling into the hands of the enemy.

The discussion then turned on the detailed instructions which should be sent to General Brooke regarding the evacuation of British troops from France and his own retirement.

The Prime Minister said that although organised resistance by the French Armies might be coming to an end, the French Government were not suing for an armistice as we had feared. They were apparently falling back further into the country and continuing to fight, although action was unco-ordinated. It was essential, therefore, that if the French Tenth Army was still fighting, General Brooke should co-operate with them as long as they were putting up any resistance at all. He should, however, get rid of all line of communication personnel and valuable military stores with as little delay as possible. The disembarkation of all further reinforcements in France should be held up and the ships returned to this country.

The Chief of the Imperial General Staff pointed out that this was in effect General Brooke's plan. He was, however, sending back the two brigades now in the Le Mans area at once to the ports.

---

[1] Alan Francis Brooke, 1883–1963. Entered the Army, 1902. On active service, 1914–18 (DSO and bar, despatches six times). General Officer Commanding-in-Chief, Anti-Aircraft Command, 1939. Commanded the 2nd Army Corps, British Expeditionary Force, 1939–40. Knighted, 1940. General Officer Commanding-in-Chief, Home Forces, 1940–1. Chief of the Imperial General Staff, 1941–6. Field Marshal, 1944. Created Baron, 1945; Viscount Alanbrooke, 1946. Order of Merit, 1946. Master Gunner, St James's Park, 1946–56. His statue in Whitehall was unveiled by the Queen in 1993.

The Prime Minister thought that these two brigades should be put into the battle if the French were still continuing to fight. They would surely be of great assistance to the French Tenth Army, which was retiring back on Le Mans. The first brigade of the Canadians, however, which had only just disembarked, should be re-embarked at once.

At the conclusion of the meeting at 8.20 p.m., the Prime Minister and CIGS spoke to General Brooke personally on the telephone.

General Brooke said that he proposed to move back the two Brigades now at Le Mans to the ports at once. It was suggested to him, both by the Prime Minister and CIGS, that he should leave these two Brigades in their present position, to assist the retirement of the forward Brigade and the L of C[1] troops. It was emphasised that we were in honour bound to fight alongside the French as long as we possibly could.

General Brooke said that, in view of the gap on his right flank, to maintain the two Brigades in their present position was to run the risk of losing them altogether.

In these circumstances, the Prime Minister agreed that the Brigades should be moved back, but that this operation should be regarded not as one of general policy, but as one imposed by local conditions.

Winston S. Churchill to Paul Reynaud
(*Cabinet papers, 69/1*)

14 June 1940
Most Secret

General Brooke has informed CIGS that General Weygand has told him that organised French resistance has ceased.

In these circumstances I feel sure you will agree that the Allied Cause would best be served by our stopping the disembarkation of any further British Forces in France till the situation is more clear. Orders have therefore been issued to this effect and also to evacuate the very large L of C personnel between Rennes and Nantes.

Meanwhile General Brooke has been ordered to act in conjunction with any French Forces which may be fighting in his vicinity and to retire with the French Tenth Army upon Le Mans.

---

[1] Lines of Communication.

JUNE 1940

Winston S. Churchill: recollection
(*'Their Finest Hour'*, page 171)

14 June 1940

General Brooke, after his talk with the French commanders, and having measured from his own headquarters a scene which was getting worse every hour, reported to the War Office and by telephone to Mr Eden that the position was hopeless. All further reinforcements should be stopped, and the remainder of the British Expeditionary Force, now amounting to a hundred and fifty thousand men, should be re-embarked at once. On the night of June 14, as I was thought to be obdurate, he rang me up on a telephone line which by luck and effort was open, and pressed this view upon me. I could hear quite well, and after ten minutes I was convinced that he was right and we must go. Orders were given accordingly. He was released from French command. The back loading of great quantities of stores, equipment, and men began.

General Brooke: recollection[1]
(*'The Turn of the Tide'*, pages 172-3)

14 June 1940

The telephone bell rang and I found myself talking to Dill on that very indifferent line which had been kept going between Le Mans and London. I naturally thought he was calling up from the War Office, but as a matter of fact he was with Churchill at 10 Downing Street. He asked me what I was doing with the 52nd Division, and I gave him an account of the dispositions which I have just described and which I had agreed with him on my previous talk. He replied: 'The Prime Minister does not want you to do that.' And I think I answered: 'What the hell does he want?' At any rate, Dill's next reply was: 'He wants to speak to you,' and he handed the receiver over to him. To my surprise, I found myself talking to Churchill on this very bad line of communication. I had never met him, I had never talked to him, but I had heard a good deal about him!

He asked me what I was doing with the 52nd Division, and, after I had informed him, he told me that that was not what he wanted. I had been sent to France to make the French feel that we were supporting them. I replied that it was impossible to make a corpse feel, and that the French Army was, to all

---

[1] General Brooke set out these recollections for the editor of his diary, the historian Sir Arthur Bryant, in 1956. They were based upon his diary entry for 14 June 1940, which read: 'Just before dinner (around 8 p.m.) called up by Dill who was at 10 Downing Street and put PM on to me. I had a difficult discussion with him as regards the evacuation of the 2nd Brigade of 52nd Division. He considered they might be used to assist the French or fill the gap between Tenth Army and the Army on its right (some 30 miles!). At last I got him to agree to what I was doing.'

intents and purposes, dead, and certainly incapable of registering what was being done for it. However, he insisted that we should make them feel that we were supporting them, and I insisted that this was quite impossible and would only result in throwing away good troops to no avail. He then asked me whether I had not got a gap in front of me. When I replied that this was correct, he asked whether the division could not be put into the gap. I told him that, as the gap was some thirty to forty miles broad at that time, and would probably be some forty to sixty miles to-morrow the remainder of the 52nd Division would be of little avail in trying to block this widening chasm. I said that it would again inevitably result in the throwing away of good troops with no hope of achieving any results.

Our talk lasted for close on half an hour, and on many occasions his arguments were so formed as to give me the impression that he considered that I was suffering from 'cold feet' because I did not wish to comply with his wishes. This was so infuriating that I was repeatedly on the verge of losing my temper. Fortunately, while I was talking to him I was looking through the window at Drew[1] and Kennedy[2] sitting on a garden seat under a tree. Their presence there acted as a continual reminder of the human element of the 52nd Division and of the unwarrantable decision to sacrifice them with no attainable object in view.

At last, when I was in an exhausted condition, he said: 'All right, I agree with you.'

Winston S. Churchill to Anthony Eden
(*Premier papers, 3/328/10*)

14 June 1940

I hope before any fresh appointment is given to General Auchinleck,[3] the whole story of the slack and feeble manner in which the operations at Narvik were conducted, and the failure to make an earlier assault on Narvik Town, will be considered. Let me know the dates when General Auchinleck was in effective command of the military. I regard the operations at Narvik as a

[1] James Syme Drew, 1883–1955. Entered the Army, 1902. On active service, 1914–18 (DSO, Military Cross). Commanded the 52nd (Lowland) Division, 1938–40. Major-General, Training, Combined Operations, 1941. Director-General of the Home Guard and the Territorial Army, 1944. Knighted, 1944.

[2] John Noble Kennedy, 1893–1970. Royal Navy, 1911. Royal Artillery, 1915. On active service, 1915–18 (despatches, Military Cross); South Russian campaign, 1919 (despatches). Deputy Director of Military Operations, War Office, 1938; Director of Plans, 1939. Commander, Royal Artillery, 52nd Division, France, 1940. Director of Military Operations, War Office, 1940–3. Assistant Chief of the Imperial General Staff (Operations and Intelligence), 1943–5. Knighted, 1945. Governor of Southern Rhodesia, 1946–54. Chairman, National Convention of Southern Rhodesia, 1960. In 1959 he published his memoirs, *The Business of War*.

[3] Claude John Eyre Auchinleck, 1884–1981. 2nd Lieutenant, Indian Army, 1903. On active service in Mesopotamia, 1916–18 (DSO). Held various active and staff appointments in India,

June 1940

shocking example of costly over-caution and feebleness, all the more lamentable in contrast with German fortitude in defence and vigour in attack.[1]

When the whole story is complete, the question of disciplinary action against General Mackesy[2] must also be considered. Rewards to brave and skilful Officers have no meaning unless severe and public punishment is also inflicted on those who fall below the standard of determination without which we cannot win this war.

John Colville: diary
(*Colville papers*)

14 June 1940

The Churchills are moving into No. 10 today, but the PM thought it best to spend the night with Lord Beaverbrook. He came to No. 10 after dinner and had a long conference with David Margesson, Desmond Morton, Brendan Bracken and Duncan Sandys[3] (who shows no *gêne* about sitting here and drinking in all the most secret information) regarding the suggestion that 250,000 French troops should be brought here with their equipment in order to make this Island stiff with soldiers and lessen the likelihood of a successful invasion.

1919–39. General Officer Commanding-in-Chief, Northern Norway, 1940 (knighted); India, 1941 (when he secured the Iraqi port of Basra during the Rashid Ali revolt); Middle East, 1941–2 (when he succeeded Wavell); and India (for the second time), 1943–7. Field Marshal, 1946. Supreme Commander, India and Pakistan, 1947. Known as 'the Auk'.

[1] A year later, Churchill was so impressed by Auchinleck's rapid and successful response to the revolt of Rashid Ali in Baghdad that he chose him as Wavell's successor as Commander-in-Chief, Middle East.

[2] Pierse Joseph Mackesy, 1883–1956. Commissioned in the Royal Engineers, 1902. Served in Togoland and the Cameroons, 1914–15; in France, 1916–18 (DSO); and at Murmansk, 1919. Commanded the Third Infantry Brigade in Palestine, 1935–7. Major-General, 1937. CB, 1938. Commander of the Land Forces destined for Narvik, April 1940. In charge of a War Cabinet survey of possible enemy operations, 1941.

[3] Duncan Edwin Sandys, 1908–87. Educated at Eton and Magdalen College, Oxford. 3rd Secretary, British Embassy, Berlin, 1930. Conservative MP for Norwood, 1935–45; for Streatham, 1950–74. Political columnist, *Sunday Chronicle*, 1937–9. Member of the National Executive of the Conservative Party, 1938–9. Elected to the Other Club, 1939. On active service in Norway, 1940 (disabled; Lieutenant-Colonel, 1941). Financial Secretary, War Office, 1941–3. Chairman, War Cabinet Committee for defence against flying bombs and rockets, 1943–5. Privy Councillor, 1944. Minister of Works, 1944–5; of Supply, 1951–4; of Housing and Local Government, 1954–7; of Defence, 1957–9; of Aviation, 1959–60. Secretary of State for Commonwealth Relations, 1960–4 (and for Colonies, 1962–4). Created Baron Duncan-Sandys, 1974. In 1935 he married Churchill's daughter Diana (marriage dissolved, 1960). Companion of Honour, 1973.

June 1940

Winston S. Churchill to Sir Archibald Sinclair
(*Premier papers, 3/24/2*)

15 June 1940

My dear Secretary of State for Air,

Thank you for your letter of June 5th enclosing the Air Ministry's Memorandum on Fighter Pilots.[1]

The figures which you sent me at the end of May suggest that if we are already short of pilots, the Germans must be suffering from an even worse shortage. You give us 9,000 pilots with recent flying experience but less than 5,000 operational machines, at the same time giving the Germans 12,000 pilots and about 12,000 machines. The fact that the Germans are flying mainly over occupied territory cannot reduce their losses of airmen appreciably. I understand that recent experience shows that only one in ten British airmen lost on operational fights is captured alive, and even if the Germans take to their parachutes somewhat readily it seems unlikely that a much greater fraction survive to fly another day.

Again, either we devote too many machines to the training of each pilot, (and should search for economies), or German pilots are inadequately trained. Over the last year our training organization absorbed 4,000 aircraft and only produced 2,500 pilots. In previous estimates, your Dept have calculated that the Germans produce roughly one pilot for each aircraft absorbed into the training pool.

The Air Staff complain that they lack modern single-engined training aircraft. I should be glad to see further particulars on this point, for I understand that we have since war began produced more training aircraft than the Germans.

Pray let me have your views on these matters.

Yours sincerely,
Winston S. Churchill

---

[1] The Air Ministry memorandum 'Fighter Pilot Deficiencies, June 1940' stated: 'The basic deficiency of pilots in Fighter Command on 31st May amounted to 178. This arises partly from the recent formation of new fighter squadrons, and partly from the excess of wastage over replacements which is due to general fighting over enemy territory instead of over United Kingdom as was expected.' As to the shortage of advanced single-engine trainers, this, Sinclair told Churchill, 'is due to delays and disappointments in the delivery of the Master. As long ago as 1938, when the prospective deficiencies came to light, the Air Ministry placed orders in America for the Harvard to supplement the Master, but out of 2,500 trainers delivered between April 1939 and March 1940, only 430 were of advanced single-engine trainer types' (*Premier papers, 3/24/2*).

War Cabinet: minutes
(*Cabinet papers, 65/7*)

15 June 1940 10 Downing Street
10 a.m.

The Prime Minister said that a further message had been received from President Roosevelt, the main points of which were as follows:–

The President said that he hoped it was realised that the United States were doing all they could to furnish materials and supplies. His message of the 13th had in no sense been intended to commit the United States of America to military participation. This could only be done by Congress. He was unable to agree to publication of his message, since it was desirable to avoid any possible misunderstanding. The Senate had already voted $50 millions for relief of refugees in France. He also referred to the Fleet position.

The Prime Minister read a draft reply which he had prepared. In this draft he stressed his disappointment that the President had not seen his way to agree to publication of the message of the 13th June. He pointed out that events were now moving very fast, and that nothing short of a declaration of war by the United States would be likely to sustain the French much longer. The draft also stressed the importance of our receiving immediate help in destroyers.

The following points were made in discussion:–

(1) The Lord President of the Council thought that the Prime Minister might stress the moral and psychological effect of an American declaration of war.

(2) It was agreed that our need for destroyers should be even more strongly pressed.

The Prime Minister said that things had gone badly in France on the previous day. A message had been received from General Brooke, saying that General Weygand had stated that organised French resistance had come to an end, and that the French Army, while continuing to fight, was disintegrating into disconnected groups. General Brooke had asked permission to send back two Brigades of the 52nd Division, as they could not at the moment play any useful part in the struggle. After speaking to General Brooke on the telephone he had agreed to this course, not as a matter of policy but as a matter of local military necessity. He had also stopped the further movement to France of the Canadian Division, one Brigade of which had already crossed.

The Prime Minister then read the telegrams which had been sent to M. Reynaud and to General Brooke as the result of decisions taken late the night before.

JUNE 1940

The Prime Minister emphasised that General Brooke, though no longer under French Command, should try to co-operate with any French Forces that were still fighting and should make every effort to sustain French resistance. The withdrawal of the two Brigades of the 52nd Division should not be taken as a sign that all British Forces were about to withdraw.

The Prime Minister said that he had made it clear in his telegram to M. Reynaud the reasons for our withdrawal. He suggested that for the time being our troops should remain at Cherbourg, so that if a fresh opportunity arose they could be ordered to proceed elsewhere in France.

The Chief of Naval Staff informed the War Cabinet that a brief message had been received at the Admiralty to say that the French Navy had carried out a bombardment of objectives at Genoa, but no details were as yet available.

The Prime Minister suggested that now that this operation had been carried out, further consideration should be given to action on the same lines by the British Navy against Italian objectives.

It was pointed out that an attack on the West Coast of Italy was a different matter from an attack on the East Coast, both as regards the risks from Italian aircraft, the strength of which had not yet been tried, and as regards the dividend to be obtained. Broadly, there were hardly any worth-while targets on the East coast of Italy.

IRAQ

The Prime Minister, in summing up the discussion,[1] said that he saw no reason to give an immediate reply to General Nuri's[2] enquiry. Iraq had done nothing to deserve special consideration from us, and would be far more likely to be impressed by military successes achieved against Italy. The present was

---

[1] The Iraqi Foreign Minister, General Nuri, had asked the British Government to confirm its 1939 Palestine White Paper policy restricting Jewish immigration to Palestine. Speaking before Churchill, Arthur Greenwood, the Minister without Portfolio, told the War Cabinet that 'An announcement of the kind proposed might have serious repercussions on opinion in America, where the influence of the Jewish community was out of all proportion to their numbers.' But the Colonial Secretary, Lord Lloyd, countered with the argument: 'Unless some plain reassurance was given regarding our policy in Palestine, there was a risk that the situation in Iraq and the Middle East, which was already unsatisfactory, might flare up dangerously.'

[2] Nuri Pasha es Said, 1888–1958. Born in Baghdad. Entered the Military Academy, Istanbul, 1903. Captured by the British, 1915, he joined the Arab revolt. Personal envoy to the Emir Feisal in Europe, 1920. Minister of Defence, Iraq, 1922. Prime Minister, 1930. Minister for Foreign Affairs, 1932. Again Prime Minister, 1938–40. Withdrew from Iraq during the pro-German revolt, 1941. Prime Minister, 1941–5 and 1949–52. Minister of Defence, 1953. Active in the foundation of the Arab League, 1954. Broke off relations with the Soviet Union, and signed the Baghdad Pact (linking Iraq and Turkey, and later Pakistan and Persia, with Britain). Prime Minister for the seventeenth time, 1958. Assassinated (together with the King and the Crown Prince) during the Baghdad uprising, 14 June 1958.

a most critical moment for the development of American opinion. Important events might soon take place which would affect our power to carry out any promise we might give.

War Cabinet: Confidential Annex
(*Cabinet papers, 65/13*)

15 June 1940
10 a.m.

The Secretary of State for War said that a similar problem arose in the case of 4,000 French troops who were now on their way back from the Clyde to Brest.

The Prime Minister said that no immediate decision could be reached on these matters. The position might be clearer after the interview which he would be having later that day with General de Gaulle.

The Prime Minister said that the main point was to secure the French Fleet. He thought that as soon as the French Government was established at Bordeaux it would be necessary for him, and one or two members of the War Cabinet, to fly over to Bordeaux. He would take opportunity of consultation with the French Ministers in regard to such vitally important matters as the French Fleet.

Winston S. Churchill to Sir Archibald Sinclair
(*Churchill papers, 20/13*)

15 June 1940

I notice from the report of June 14 that 355 bombing aircraft are available in Squadrons, and 220 within two or three days, total 575. For these the crews available are only 343. This shows a lamentable lag in the pilots, and I should be very glad if you would let me know exactly what you are doing to correct it, and when we may expect an improvement. As long as the Air Ministry is behind production in the pilots it has ready trained, it is a serious default.

WSC

John Colville: diary
(*Colville papers*)

15 June 1940

After tea Winston dictated long telegrams to Roosevelt and to the Dominions (whose premiers had all sent the most touching and encouraging messages) pointing out that we had now got to face the most trying ordeal of heavy bombing and saying to all that he personally was convinced that the carnage and destruction in this country would bring the US into the war. He said that the French condition for carrying on had been a promise of active US support: the promise of redoubled supplies which had been received was not sufficient, and though France might fight on from her Colonies her resistance at home would now almost certainly come to an end. 'If words counted, we should win this war,' he said, as a comment on his own telegraphic efforts.

We arrived at Chequers in time to dine at 9.30. The party consisted of Winston, Duncan and Diana Sandys,[1] Lindemann and myself. It was at once the most dramatic and the most fantastic evening I have ever spent. Before going into the dining-room Tony Bevir told me on the telephone that telegrams had been received from Bordeaux to the effect that the position was deteriorating fast and the request to be allowed to make a separate peace was being put in a more brutal form. I imparted this to Winston who was immediately very depressed. Dinner began lugubriously, W eating fast and greedily, his face almost in his plate, and every now and then firing some technical question at Lindemann, who was quietly consuming his vegetarian diet. The Sandyses and I sat silent, because our spasmodic efforts at conversation were not well received. However champagne and brandy and cigars did their work and we soon became talkative, even garrulous. Winston, in order to cheer himself and us up, read aloud the messages he had received from the Dominions and the replies he had sent to them and to Roosevelt. 'The war is bound to become a bloody one for us now,' he said, 'but I hope our people will stand up to bombing and the Huns aren't liking what we are giving them. But what a tragedy that our victory in the last war should have been snatched from us by a lot of softies.'

Winston and Duncan Sandys paced up and down the rose garden in the moonlight while Diana, Lindemann and I walked on the other side of the house. It was light and deliciously warm, but the sentries, with tin helmets and fixed bayonets, who were placed all round the house, kept us fully alive to the horrors of reality. I spent most of the time telephoning, searching for Winston among the roses and listening to his comments on the war. I told him that fuller information had now been received about the French attitude, which appeared to be slipping. 'Tell them,' he said, 'that if they let us have

---

[1] Diana Churchill, 1909–63. Churchill's eldest child. In 1932 she married the eldest son of Sir Abe Bailey, John Milner Bailey (from whom she obtained a divorce in 1935). In 1935 she married Duncan Sandys, MP. She had three children, Julian (born 1936), Edwina (born 1938) and Celia (born 1943).

their fleet we shall never forget, but that if they surrender without consulting us we shall never forgive. We shall blacken their name for a thousand years!' Then, half afraid that I might take him seriously, he added: 'Don't, of course, do that just yet.' He was in high spirits, repeating poetry, dilating on the drama of the present situation, maintaining that he and Hitler only had one thing in common – a horror of whistling – offering everybody cigars, and spasmodically murmuring, 'Bang, Bang, Bang, goes the farmer's gun, run rabbit, run rabbit, run, run, run.'

Kennedy[1] telephoned and Winston, becoming serious for a minute, poured into his ears a flood of eloquence about the part that America could and should play in saving civilisation. Referring to promises of industrial and financial support, he said such an offer 'would be a laughing-stock on the stage of history', and he begged that 'we should not let our friend's (President R) efforts peter out in grimaces and futility'.

About 1.00 a.m. Winston came in from the garden and we all stood in the central hall while the Great Man lay on the sofa, puffed his cigar, discoursed on the building up of our fighter strength, and told one or two dirty stories. Finally, saying 'Goodnight, my children', he went to bed at 1.30.

Winston S. Churchill to President Roosevelt
(*Churchill papers, 20/14*)

15 June 1940

I am grateful to you for your telegram and I have reported its operative passages to Reynaud to whom I had imparted a rather more sanguine view. He will, I am sure, be disappointed at non-publication. I understand all your difficulties with American public opinion and Congress, but events are moving downward at a pace where they will pass beyond the control of American public opinion when at last it is ripened. Have you considered what offers Hitler may choose to make to France? He may say, 'surrender the Fleet intact and I will leave you Alsace-Lorraine,' or alternatively, 'if you do not give me your ships I will destroy your towns.' I am personally convinced that America will in the end go to all lengths, but this moment is supremely critical for France. A declaration that the United States will if necessary enter the war

---

[1] United States Ambassador.

might save France. Failing that, in a few days French resistance may have crumbled and we shall be left alone.

Although the present Government and I personally would never fail to send the Fleet across the Atlantic if resistance was beaten down here, a point may be reached in the struggle where the present ministers no longer have control of affairs and when very easy terms could be obtained for the British Islands by their becoming a vassal state of the Hitler empire. A pro-German Government would certainly be called into being to make peace and might present to a shattered or a starving nation an almost irresistible case for entire submission to the Nazi will. The fate of the British Fleet, as I have already mentioned to you, would be decisive on the future of the United States, because if it were joined to the Fleets of Japan, France and Italy and the great resources of German industry, overwhelming sea-power would be in Hitler's hands. He might, of course, use it with a merciful moderation. On the other hand, he might not. This revolution in sea-power might happen very quickly and certainly long before the United States would be able to prepare against it. If we go down you may have a United States of Europe under the Nazi command far more numerous, far stronger, far better armed than the New World.

I know well, Mr President, that your eye will already have searched these depths, but I feel I have the right to place on record the vital manner in which American interests are at stake in our battle and that of France.

I am sending you through Ambassador Kennedy a paper on Destroyer strength prepared by the Naval Staff for your information.[1] If we have to keep as we shall the bulk of our Destroyers on the East Coast to guard against invasion, how shall we be able to cope with a German-Italian attack on the food and trade by which we live? The sending of the thirty-five destroyers as I have already described will bridge the gap until our new construction comes in at the end of the year. Here is a definite practical and possibly decisive step which can be taken at once and I urge most earnestly that you will weigh my words.

---

[1] The Naval Staff paper on destroyer strength gave the combined British and French destroyer losses since the outbreak of war as 32, of which 25 had been lost since 1 February 1940. It noted that of the 133 destroyers then in commission in Home Waters, only 68 were 'fit for service'. If a German invasion took place, 'it will almost certainly be in the form of dispersed landings from a large number of small craft, and the only effective counter to such a move is to maintain numerous and effective destroyer patrols'. To meet this threat 'we have only the sixty-eight destroyers mentioned above. Only ten small-type new construction destroyers are due to complete in next four months.' The position became 'still worse,' the paper noted, 'when we have to contemplate diverting further destroyer forces to the Mediterranean, as we may be forced to do when the sea war there is intensified.'

Winston S. Churchill to the Dominion Prime Ministers
(Churchill papers, 20/14)

15 June 1940

To (1).[1]

I am deeply touched by your message, which is only in keeping with all that the Mother Country has ever received in peace or war from New Zealand.

To (2).[2]

I am deeply touched by your message, which is only in keeping with all that the Mother Country has ever received in peace or war from Australia.

To (3).[3]

I am very grateful for your message.[4] Suggestions which it makes are receiving urgent consideration. In the meantime, I should like to let you know how I myself see the position.

To (4).[5]

You may like to know how I myself see the position.

To all.

I do not regard the situation as having passed beyond our strength. It is by no means certain that the French will not fight on in Africa and at sea, but, whatever they do, Hitler will have to break us in this Island or lose the war. Our principal danger is his concentrated air attack by bombing, coupled with parachute and air-borne landings and attempts to run an invading force across the sea. This danger has faced us ever since the beginning of the war, and the French could never have saved us from it, as he could always switch on to us. Undoubtedly, it is aggravated by the conquests Hitler has made upon the European coast close to our shores. Nevertheless, in principle the danger is the same. I do not see why we should not be able to meet it. The Navy has never pretended to prevent a raid of five or ten thousand men, but we do not see how a force of, say, eighty to a hundred thousand could be transported across the

---

[1] Peter Fraser.
[2] Robert Menzies.
[3] General Smuts.
[4] Among the suggestions that Smuts had made was that Britain occupy the three Irish Atlantic coast ports (Berehaven, Queenstown and Loch Swilly) which Churchill had secured as British naval bases under the Irish Treaty of 1922. Chamberlain had returned these ports to Eire in 1938. On that occasion Churchill had told the House of Commons: 'You are casting away real and important means of security and survival for vain shadows and for ease' (*Hansard*, 5 May 1938).
[5] William Mackenzie King.

sea, and still less maintained in the teeth of superior sea power. As long as our Air Force is in being it provides a powerful aid to the Fleet in preventing sea-borne landings and will take a very heavy toll of air-borne landings. Although we have suffered heavy losses by assisting the French and during the Dunkirk evacuation, we have managed to husband our air-fighter strength in spite of poignant appeals from France to throw it improvidently into the great land battle which it could not have turned decisively. I am happy to tell you that it is now as strong as it has ever been and that the flow of machines is coming forward far more rapidly than ever before; in fact, pilots have now become the limiting factor at the moment. Our fighter aircraft have been wont to inflict a loss of two or two and a half to one even when fighting under the adverse conditions in France. During the evacuation of Dunkirk, which was a sort of No-Man's land, we have inflicted a loss of three or four to one, and often saw German formations turn away from a quarter of their numbers of our planes. But all Air authorities agree that the advantage in defending this country against an oversea air attack will be still greater because, first, we shall know pretty well by our various devices where they are coming, and because our squadrons lie close enough together to enable us to concentrate against the attackers and provide enough to attack both the bombers and the protecting fighters at the same time. All their shot-down machines will be total losses; many of ours and their pilots will fight again. Therefore, do not think it by any means impossible that we may so maul them that they will find daylight attacks too expensive. The major danger will be from night attack on our aircraft factories, but this, again, is far less accurate than daylight attack, and we have many plans for minimising its effect. Of course, their numbers are much greater than ours, but not so much greater as to deprive us of a good and reasonable prospect of wearing them out after some weeks or even months of air struggle. Meanwhile, of course, our bomber force will be striking continually at their key points, especially oil and oil refineries and air factories and at their congested and centralized war industry in the Ruhr. We hope our people will stand up to this bombardment as well as the enemy. It will, on both sides, be on an unprecedented scale. All our information goes to show that the Germans have not liked what they have got so far.

It must be remembered that, now that the BEF is home and largely re-armed or re-arming, if not upon a Continental scale at any rate good enough for Home defence, we have far stronger military forces in this Island than we have ever had in the late war or in this war. Therefore, we hope that such numbers of the enemy as may be landed from the air or by sea-borne raid will be destroyed and be an example to those who try to follow. No doubt we must expect novel forms of attack and attempts to bring tanks across the sea. We are preparing ourselves to deal with these as far as we can foresee them. No one can predict or guarantee the course of a life and death struggle of this character, but we shall certainly enter upon it in good heart.

I have given you this full explanation to show you that there are solid reasons behind our resolve not to allow the fate of France, whatever it may be, to deter us from going on to the end. I personally believe that the spectacle of the fierce struggle and carnage in our Island will draw the United States into the war, and even if we should be beaten down through the superior numbers of the enemy's air force it will always be possible, as I indicated to the House of Commons in my last Speech, to send our Fleets across the oceans, where they will protect the Empire and enable it to continue the war and the blockade, I trust, in conjunction with the United States, until the Hitler régime breaks under the strain. We shall let you know at every stage how you can help, being assured that you will do all in human power as we, for our part, are entirely resolved to do.

Winston S. Churchill to President Roosevelt
(*Premier papers, 3/468*)

15 June 1940
10.45 p.m.

Since sending you my message this afternoon I have heard that M. Reynaud, in a telegram which he has just sent to you, has practically said that the decision of France to continue the war from overseas depends on your being able to assure the French Government that the USA will come into the war at a very early date.

When I sent you my message just now I did not know that M. Reynaud had stated the dilemma in these terms, but I am afraid there is no getting away from the fact that this is the choice before us now.

Indeed, the British Ambassador in Bordeaux[1] tells me that if your reply does not contain the assurance asked for, the French will very quickly ask for an armistice, and I much doubt whether it will be possible in that event for us to keep the French Fleet out of German hands.

When I speak of the United States entering the war I am of course not thinking in terms of an expeditionary force, which I know is out of the question. What I have in mind is the tremendous moral effect that such an American decision would produce, not merely in France but also in all the democratic countries of the world, and, in the opposite sense, on the German and Italian peoples.

---

[1] Sir Ronald Campbell, who had moved to Bordeaux with the French Government.

JUNE 1940

John Colville: diary
(*Colville papers*)

16 June 1940

Woken at 6.30 by the telephone and shortly afterwards by a despatch rider who brought the full facts about the French from London. When I heard that the PM was awake, about 7.30, I took them to his room and found him lying in bed, looking just like a rather nice pig, clad in a silk vest. He ruminated for some time and then decided to call the Cabinet in London at 10.15.

On the way to London the PM dictated a number of minutes to Mrs Hill[1] and did enough work to keep us all busy during the morning. It is one of the great differences between Chamberlain and Churchill that whereas the former, in reading Cabinet papers, seldom made any comments and only on questions of the highest policy, Churchill scrutinises every document which has anything to do with the war and does not disdain to enquire into the most trivial point.

War Cabinet: minutes
(*Cabinet papers, 65/7*)

16 June 1940
10.15 a.m.

In the course of the Meeting two messages were received from Sir R. Campbell, supported by another from General Spears, indicating that M. Reynaud would welcome a meeting with the Prime Minister in France that afternoon. The reply sent was that a message was on its way from the Prime Minister to M. Reynaud and that the question of a meeting could be considered later.

The Prime Minister referred to telegrams which had been received from each of the Dominions expressing their staunch support of the Mother Country in her determination to continue the struggle. He read out the replies which had been sent, which met with the warm approval of the War Cabinet.

The Prime Minister referred to the suggestion contained in General Smuts'

---

[1] Rose Ethel Kathleen Hill, 1900–92. Chief Clerk, Automobile Association and Motor Union Insurance Company, Portsmouth, 1917–24, and a member of the Portsmouth Philharmonic Society (first violins), 1918–24. District Commissioner of Girl Guides, Bengal–Nagpur Railway, 1928–30. Secretary to the Chief Commissioner of Girl Guides for All-India, 1930–2. Broadcast as a solo violinist; Calcutta, Bombay and Delhi, 1935–6. Returned to England, 1937. Churchill's first Residential Secretary, July 1937; lived at Chartwell from July 1937 to September 1939. Churchill's Personal Private Secretary from 1939 to 1946. MBE, 1941. Curator of Chequers, 1946–69.

telegram that the Irish Atlantic ports should be occupied at once, even in the face of Irish opposition, in order to prevent them suffering the same fate as the Norwegian ports.

The Prime Minister welcomed Mr MacDonald's[1] proposed visit to Mr de Valera[2] and agreed that, although as a last resort we should not hesitate to secure the ports by force, it would be unwise at this moment to take any action that might compromise our position with the United States of America, in view of the present delicate developments.

The Secretary of State for War said that he had seen a report prepared for the Ministry of Information on the state of public opinion up and down the country. This report was not very encouraging. Bearing in mind the stern times ahead of us, he would like to have seen a firmer note of resolution in the people of this country.

In the discussion which ensued, reference was made to the attitude of the Press. While on the whole the attitude of the Press had been helpful, it was unfortunate that there was a certain tendency to encourage inquests rather than to concentrate on the tasks ahead. It was important that steps should be taken to make the Press realise that demands for inquests could only engender a spirit of doubt as to our strength, and that such demands ought therefore to be sternly discouraged.

The Prime Minister informed the War Cabinet that he intended to make a statement in the House on Tuesday, which he would follow up by a broadcast on Tuesday night.

---

[1] Malcolm John MacDonald, 1901–81. Son of Ramsay MacDonald. Educated at Bedales and Queen's College, Oxford. Labour MP for Bassetlaw, 1929–31 (National Labour, 1931–5); for Ross and Cromarty, 1936–45. Parliamentary Under-Secretary, Dominions Office, 1931–5. Privy Councillor, 1935. Secretary of State for Dominion Affairs, 1935–8 and 1938–9; Colonial Secretary, 1935 and 1938–40. Minister of Health, 1940–1. High Commissioner, Canada, 1941–6. Governor-General of Malaya, Singapore and British Borneo, 1946–8. Commissioner-General for South-East Asia, 1948–55. High Commissioner, India, 1955–60. Governor-General of Kenya, 1963–4; High Commissioner, 1964–5. British Special Representative in East and Central Africa, 1965–6; in Africa, 1966–9. Order of Merit, 1969.
[2] Eamon de Valera, 1882–1975. Born in New York. A leading figure in the Easter Rebellion, 1916. Sentenced to death; sentence commuted to life penal servitude on account of his American birth. Released under the general amnesty, June 1917. President of the Sinn Fein, 1917–26. Elected to Parliament as a Sinn Fein MP, 1918. Imprisoned with other Sinn Fein leaders, 1918; escaped from Lincoln Jail, February 1919. 'President' of the Irish Republic, 1919–22. Rejected the Irish Treaty and fought with the Irregulars against the Free State Army, 1922–3. President of Fianna Fail, 1926–59. Leader of the Opposition in the Free State Parliament, 1927–32. Prime Minister and Minister for External Affairs, 1932–48. Prime Minister for a second and third time, 1951–4 and 1957–9. President of the Republic of Ireland, 1959–73.

344   JUNE 1940

War Cabinet: Confidential Annex
(*Cabinet papers, 65/13*)

16 June 1940
10.15 a.m.

The Prime Minister said that the issue put to us by M. Reynaud was a perfectly plain one. The French Government were insisting that before they left French soil they must at least find out what the enemy's terms for an armistice would be. This seemed to imply that there was some possibility that if the terms were too harsh, the French Government might be willing to carry on the struggle from outside France. We had now to decide whether we should release them from their obligations to us not to enter into any discussion of terms. The question of their acceptance or refusal of such terms would arise later when the terms themselves were known.

Some discussion followed on the wording of the terms of our consent to the French request and whether we should refuse to give our formal assent. It was suggested that a refusal of such formal assent might give M. Reynaud an excuse for resigning, and this it was most important to avoid.

The Prime Minister thought that we should make it an absolute condition for the granting of our consent that the French Fleet should sail forthwith for British ports pending any discussion of armistice terms. We should add that until these terms were known, the further question of peace terms could not, of course, arise, but that in no circumstances whatsoever would the British Government participate in any negotiations for armistice or peace. He pointed out that it would be very dangerous to assent to the French request with the French Fleet in an indeterminate condition. It would be important also not to give any impression that by the mere resignation of M. Reynaud the French Government were cleared of their obligations to us. We had the most solemn treaty obligations by the French Government as a whole that neither party during the present war would either negotiate or conclude an armistice or treaty of peace except by mutual agreement. President Roosevelt should be sent a copy of our reply, and urged not to act as a mediator in any circumstances unless the safety of the French Fleet was previously secured.

The Prime Minister suggested that it might be convenient if at this stage the War Cabinet were placed in possession of the views of the Service Ministers.

The First Sea Lord said that the First Lord of the Admiralty was unable to attend the present meeting, as he was in Scotland. The First Lord would undoubtedly wish to insist on the condition that while the French were making their inquiries, or contracting negotiations for an armistice, their Fleet should be away from France and in harbours where we could safeguard it.

The Secretary of State for Air entirely agreed with the course proposed. Our right course was to demand from France what was essential (namely the taking of steps to safeguard their Fleet), but no more than was essential. By so doing we should strengthen the hands of M. Mandel and the more resolute elements in France.

The Secretary of State for War also entirely concurred in the course proposed by the Prime Minister. He assumed that our message would confine itself to dealing with the actual French request, and would contain no hint or suggestion of the likelihood of peace negotiations between France and Germany.

The Prime Minister said that the view of the War Cabinet was now clear. We should send a brief message to the French Government which would make it clear that our Treaty was not with M. Reynaud or any other individual Prime Minister but with France herself. We were prepared to release France from that Treaty to the limited extent necessary to allow of the enquiry as to Germany's armistice terms which the present French Cabinet wished to make, but only provided that the French Fleet was immediately ordered to sail for a British harbour.

In addition, we should have to see to it that there was no kind of suggestion that the United Kingdom had any part or lot in the enquiries or negotiations. These were initiated by France alone on her sole responsibility.

Discussion ensued as to whether the French Government's intention was to invite President Roosevelt to act as a go-between? The view was expressed that if the French invoked President Roosevelt as an intermediary and he accepted that office, it would be easier for them to save their Fleet from Germany's clutches. It was not, however, for us to make the suggestion that President Roosevelt should be asked to become the French Government's channel of communications.

The Prime Minister said that one danger of invoking President Roosevelt was that he might give advice which was of application to the United Kingdom as well as to France. He might, for example, issue an appeal to all the belligerent Governments to call the war off. This might to some extent shake some sections of British public opinion, the whole of which was at present united and inflexible. At the present juncture all thoughts of coming to terms with the enemy must be dismissed so far as Britain was concerned. We were fighting for our lives and it was vital that we should allow no chink to appear in our armour.

In the course of discussion the Chief of the Air Staff suggested that the reply to the French should also include a proposal for the custody of the French Air Force, particularly their Fighter Force – the proposal being put not as a condition but as a request. French aircraft could be very easily flown to this country.

The Prime Minister felt that, at the present moment, this would introduce a dangerous complication. Admiral Darlan, at the head of the French Fleet, had a far greater name and position than General Vuillemin, the head of the French Air Force. Moreover, the Air Force differed from the Navy in being an essential adjunct to the French Army, and it would therefore be difficult to argue that they should be separated at this juncture. The proposal was however one that might follow later.

The Secretary of State for Foreign Affairs read the draft of a telegram it was proposed to send to His Majesty's Ambassador at Washington, informing him of the reply that was being sent to the French Government. It was possible that the President might be asked to take some part in the negotiations and it would be desirable for him to have the British point of view.

The Prime Minister emphasised that the President must be clearly informed of the point we had made in our message to the French Government concerning the French Fleet. It should be made clear also that if the French Fleet were in our hands and the Germans made any threat to torture France in order to bring about the surrender of her Fleet, then the United States should play its trump card by threatening a declaration of war.

War Cabinet to Paul Reynaud[1]
(*Churchill papers, 20/14*)

16 June 1940
12.35 p.m.

Our agreement forbidding separate negotiations, whether for armistice or peace, was made with the French Republic, and not with any particular French Administration or statesman. It therefore involves the honour of France. Nevertheless, provided, but only provided, that the French Fleet is sailed forthwith for British harbours pending negotiations, His Majesty's Government give their full consent to enquiry by the French Government to ascertain the terms of an armistice for France. His Majesty's Government, being resolved to continue the war, wholly exclude themselves from all part in the above-mentioned enquiry concerning an armistice.

---

[1] This telegram was sent through Sir Ronald Campbell, who was then with the French Government at Bordeaux.

June 1940

Winston S. Churchill: recollection
(*'Their Finest Hour'*, page 189)

16 June 1940

On the afternoon of June 16 M. Monnet and General de Gaulle visited me in the Cabinet Room. The General in his capacity of Under-Secretary of State for National Defence had just ordered the French ship *Pasteur*, which was carrying weapons to Bordeaux from America, to proceed instead to a British port. Monnet was very active upon a plan to transfer all French contracts for munitions in America to Britain if France made a separate peace. He evidently expected this, and wished to save as much as possible from what seemed to him to be the wreck of the world. His whole attitude in this respect was most helpful. Then he turned to our sending all our remaining fighter air squadrons to share in the final battle in France, which was of course already over. I told him that there was no possibility of this being done. Even at this stage he used the usual arguments – 'the decisive battle', 'now or never', 'if France falls all falls', and so forth. But I could not do anything to oblige him in this field. My two French visitors then got up and moved towards the door, Monnet leading. As they reached it, de Gaulle, who had hitherto scarcely uttered a single word, turned back, and, taking two or three paces towards me, said in English: 'I think you are quite right.' Under an impassive, unperturbable demeanour he seemed to me to have a remarkable capacity for feeling pain. I preserved the impression, in contact with this very tall phlegmatic man: 'Here is the Constable of France.' He returned that afternoon in a British aeroplane, which I had placed at his disposal, to Bordeaux. But not for long.

War Cabinet: minutes
(*Cabinet papers, 65/7*)

16 June 1940   10 Downing Street
3 p.m.

The Prime Minister recalled that at the conclusion of the meeting held the previous day, there had been some discussion on a proposal for the issue of some further declaration of closer union between the countries of France and Great Britain. He had that day seen General de Gaulle who had impressed on him that some very dramatic move was essential to give M. Reynaud the support which he needed to keep his Government in the war, and he had suggested that a proclamation of the indissoluble union of the French and

British peoples would serve the purpose. Both he and M. Corbin[1] had been concerned at the decision reached by the War Cabinet that morning and embodied in telegram No. 368 DIPP to France. He (the Prime Minister) had then heard that a new declaration had been drafted for consideration, and General de Gaulle had telephoned to M. Reynaud. As a result it had seemed advisable to suspend action for the moment. Accordingly a second telegram had been sent to Sir Ronald Campbell instructing him to suspend action on telegram No. 368 DIPP.

The Secretary of State for Foreign Affairs said that after the morning meeting of the War Cabinet he had seen Sir Robert Vansittart, whom he had previously asked to draft some dramatic announcement which might strengthen M. Reynaud's hand. Sir Robert Vansittart had been in consultation with General de Gaulle, M. Monnet, M. Pleven[2] and Mr Morton. Between them they had drafted a proclamation. General de Gaulle had impressed upon him the need for publishing the document as quickly as possible, and wished to take the draft back with him to France that night. He had also suggested that the Prime Minister should meet M. Reynaud next day.

The draft proclamation which had been prepared was then read to the War Cabinet. It was recognised that such a proclamation raised some very big questions with which it was difficult to deal at such short notice.

The Prime Minister said that his first instinct had been against the idea, but in this grave crisis we must not let ourselves be accused of a lack of imagination. Some dramatic announcement was clearly necessary to keep the French going. The proposal could not be lightly brushed aside, and he was encouraged to find such a body of opinion in the War Cabinet in favour of it.

(Note. – at 3.55 p.m. news was received:–

(a) That it had been announced on the French wireless that the Council of

---

[1] André Charles Corbin, 1881–1970. Attaché, 1906; Chief of the Press Service, French Foreign Office, 1920. French Ambassador to Madrid, 1929–31; to Brussels, 1931–3; to London, 1933–40. Honorary knighthood, 1938.

[2] René Pleven, 1901–93. A banker and businessman. In June 1940 he was in England on a purchasing mission for the French Government. One of the first Frenchmen to join de Gaulle in London, he was placed in charge of the finances of the fledgling Free French movement. Sent by de Gaulle to Chad, he won over the rest of French Equatorial Africa to the Free French movement. Negotiated the first Franco-American lend-lease agreement, and the withdrawal of British forces from Madagascar. Minister of Colonies, 1943–4. Minister of Finance, 1944–6. Twice Prime Minister of France: July 1950 to March 1951 and August 1951 to January 1952. Minister of Defence, 1952–4. Author of the 'Pleven Plan' for a European Army including full German participation (rejected by the French Assembly, 1954). Foreign Minister, 13–30 May 1958.

Ministers would meet at 5 p.m. to decide whether further resistance was possible.

(b) That General de Gaulle had been informed by M. Reynaud on the telephone that if a favourable answer on the proposed proclamation of unity was received by 5 p.m. M. Reynaud felt that he would be able to hold the position.)

Foreign Office to Sir Ronald Campbell
(*'Their Finest Hour'*, page 185)

16 June 1940
6.45 p.m.

The PM, accompanied by the Lord Privy Seal, Secretary of State for Air, and the three Chiefs of Staff[1] and certain others, arrives at Concarneau[2] at twelve noon to-morrow, the 17th, in a cruiser[3] for a meeting with M. Reynaud. General de Gaulle has been informed of the above, and has expressed the view that time and rendezvous would be convenient. We suggest the meeting be held on board as arousing less attention. HMS *Berkeley* has been warned to be at the disposal of M. Reynaud and party if desired.

Lord Halifax to Sir Ronald Campbell
(*'Their Finest Hour'*, pages 185–6)

16 June 1940
8 p.m.
by telephone

After consultation with General de Gaulle, PM has decided to meet M. Reynaud to-morrow in Brittany to make a further attempt to dissuade the French Government from asking for an armistice. For this purpose, on the advice of General de Gaulle, he will offer to M. Reynaud to join in issuing forthwith a declaration announcing immediate constitution of closest Anglo-French Union in all spheres in order to carry on the war. Text of draft

---

[1] Clement Attlee, Sir Archibald Sinclair, Admiral Pound, Air Chief Marshal Newall and General Dill.
[2] A small port on the coast of Brittany.
[3] HMS *Galatea*.

350 JUNE 1940

declaration as authorised by HMG is contained in my immediately following telegram. You should read this text to M. Reynaud at once.

An outline of this proposed declaration has already been telephoned by General de Gaulle to M. Reynaud, who has replied that such a declaration by the two Governments would make all the difference to the decision of the French Government. General is returning to-night with copy.

Captain Berkeley: diary
(*Berkeley papers*)

16 June 1940

Towards evening a meeting was fixed up for the next day in Brittany, the party travelling by cruiser. The purpose was, on the assumption that France would fight on, to implement the act of union.

Just as we were leaving, however, came a telegram 'Meeting cancelled, message follows'. Winston refused to be put off, and drove down to Waterloo, sat in his compartment, and stuck there for half an hour while Ismay and CNS[1] in turn begged him to be reasonable.[2] Finally he went back to Downing Street to await further news. When it came at 11.30 the message said that a ministerial crisis had broken out and that the meeting was therefore impossible.[3]

Winston S. Churchill: recollection
(*'Their Finest Hour', page 186*)

16 June 1940

Our War Cabinet sat until six o'clock on the 16th, and thereafter I set out on my mission. I took with me the Leaders of the Labour and Liberal Parties, the three Chiefs of Staff, and various important officers and officials. A special train was waiting at Waterloo. We could reach Southampton in two hours, and a night of steaming at thirty knots in the cruiser would bring us to

---

[1] Chief of the Naval Staff (Admiral Pound).
[2] In his account to the Commons nine days later, Churchill said that the message reached him only when he was in the train.
[3] It is clear from Captain Berkeley's diary that a message cancelling the rendezvous off Concarneau had reached Churchill before he set off for the station. Berkeley wrote up his diary for 16 June two days later. Churchill's account was written eight years after the event. Reflecting on the episode some years later, Berkeley wrote: 'I believe Winston should have gone all the same. And if he had gone twenty-four hours previously as he wanted to do, there would perhaps have been no crisis. Reynaud certainly fought well and was only narrowly defeated.'

the rendezvous by noon on the 17th. We had taken our seats in the train. My wife had come to see me off. There was an odd delay in starting. Evidently some hitch had occurred. Presently my private secretary arrived from Downing Street breathless with the following message from Campbell at Bordeaux:

'Ministerial crisis has opened. . . . Hope to have news by midnight. Meanwhile meeting arranged for to-morrow impossible.'

On this I returned to Downing Street with a heavy heart.

Although vain, the process of trying to imagine what would have happened if some important event or decision had been different is often tempting and sometimes instructive. The manner of the fall of France was decided on June 16 by a dozen chances, each measured by a hair's-breadth. If Paul Reynaud had survived the 16th, I should have been with him at noon on the 17th, accompanied by the most powerful delegation that has ever left our shores, armed with plenary powers in the name of the British nation. Certainly we should have confronted Pétain, Weygand, Chautemps,[1] and the rest with our blunt proposition: 'No release from the obligation of Marsh 28 unless the French Fleet is sailed to British ports. On the other hand, we offer an indissoluble Anglo-French Union. Go to Africa and let us fight it out together.' Surely we should have been aided by the President of the Republic, by the Presidents of the two French Chambers, and by all that resolute band who gathered behind Reynaud, Mandel, and de Gaulle. It seems to me probable that we should have uplifted and converted the French bases, could have moved both troops and air forces into Morocco and Algeria quicker than he, and in greater strength. We should certainly have welcomed in the autumn and winter of 1940 a vehement campaign in or from a friendly French North-West Africa.

---

[1] Camille Chautemps, 1885–1963. A lawyer, son of a former Minister of the Colonies. Mayor of Tours, and a leading French Freemason. Elected as a Socialist Radical Deputy, 1919. Minister of the Interior, 1924; of Justice, 1925; of the Interior, 1925 and 1926. Prime Minister for three days in 1930. Minister of the Interior, 1932 and 1933. Prime Minister, November 1933 to January 1934. Minister of Public Works, January 1936; Minister of State, June 1936; Prime Minister, June 1937 to March 1938. Honorary knighthood, 1938. A member of the Reynaud Cabinet, 1940; as Vice-President of the Council, he continued to hold this office for a brief period in Marshal Pétain's Vichy Government. While on a mission, for Vichy, to the United States, in the late autumn of 1940, he broke with the Vichy Government, and on 10 March 1944 he offered his services to General de Gaulle's Free French Provisional Government in Algiers. No position of trust was offered to him. In 1946 he was sentenced to five years' imprisonment, and national degradation for life, for 'collaboration with the enemy', but he was already living in the United States. The sentence was later annulled. He died in the United States.

Winston S. Churchill to General Ismay
(*Churchill papers, 20/13*)

16 June 1940

Who is responsible for making the 'sticky' bomb? I am told that a great sloth is being shown in pressing this forward. Ask General Carr[1] to report today upon the position, and to let me have on one sheet of paper the back history of the subject from the moment when the question was first raised.

The matter is to be pressed forward from day to day, and I wish to receive a report every three days.

WSC

Winston S. Churchill to General Ismay
(*Premier papers, 3/331/9*)

16 June 1940
Secret

Nobody suggested destroying the petrol supplies unless their permanent seizure by the enemy was imminent. It is, however, essential that all preparations should be made, and I do not feel the measures set out in your second paragraph (marked by me in red) are sufficient for this purpose.

Let me have a fuller report.

WSC

Winston S. Churchill to Malcolm MacDonald
(*Churchill papers, 20/13*)

16 June 1940

Have you considered the advisability of raising a West Indies Regiment? It might have three battalions strongly officered by British Officers, and be representative of most of the Islands; to be available for Imperial Service; to give an outlet for the loyalty of the Negroes, and bring money into these poor Islands.

At present we are short of weapons, but these will come along.[2]

WSC

[1] Laurence Carr, 1886–1954. On active service, 1914–18 (DSO). Commanded the 2nd Infantry Brigade, 1936–8. Director of Staff Duties, War Office, 1938–9. Assistant Chief of the Imperial General Staff, 1939–40. CB, 1939. General Officer Commanding 1st Corps, 1940–1; Eastern Command, 1941–2. Senior Military Assistant, Ministry of Supply, 1943–4.

[2] The 1st Caribbean Regiment was raised from volunteers in the West Indies. It served in Egypt.

Winston S. Churchill: War Cabinet paper
(*Cabinet papers, 120/10*)

16 June 1940   10 Downing Street
Secret

INVASION BY AIR

We are asked to consider many plans of possible invasion by Germany. Some of these seem to me very absurd. I have, however, always had anxiety about the Tyne, and I should be glad if the points made in the attached paper, which I wrote some time ago, could be reviewed in the light of our present situation. We now know to some extent the resources of the enemy in parachute troops, &c., but our own forces and preparations have greatly advanced, and I presume that an attack on Newcastle could not succeed. I should be glad, however, if the Home Defence authorities would trace out what the reactions which would now follow such an attempt would be, and how they would deal with it.

WSC

INVASION BY AIR
Note by the Right Hon. Winston S. Churchill, CH, MP
June 1936

The idea would be that having tired out the British Air Force by repeated small scale attacks upon London, the Aggressor State would send say, two hundred troop machines carrying fifty soldiers each, and one hundred store carrying machines across the North Sea towards (say) Newcastle. The local aerodromes and landing grounds would be seized at dawn by men descending in parachutes, and an hour later the troop-carrying planes would arrive. There is no reason why they should not come back for a second or third contingent, unless the British air force was strong enough to master them, while at the same time defending London against continuous attack. Once landed, the invaders would occupy an extended area carefully studied beforehand, and put it into a state of defence. At the same time they would expel all the population except those required as hostages or for forced labour on the defences. As in every large city there is always at least a week's food in the shops and stores, and as the invaders would only be (say) a twentieth of the former population, they would have many weeks' supplies available. They would then ring the changes upon the bombing of London and the south, and reinforcements or further munitions from the air to their northern lodgement, and would be very likely able to reinforce the latter continually.

Besides this large-scale invasion, the landing of small raiding parties to break up communications or destroy important munition centres should be considered.

In a country where every man is a soldier and every town the headquarters of a division or corps these descents would not exercise decisive influence; but in a country like Great Britain with such very weak land forces, twenty or thirty thousand well-trained, highly-disciplined storm troops in our midst would become a major preoccupation. Certainly it would put an end to any intervention by British troops upon the Continent in the early stages of a war.

A largely superior Air Force is the same kind of remedy as a largely superior Fleet used to be. In addition, however, and more especially in default, three or four strong perfectly equipped mechanised Regular divisions, and a Territorial force at full strength and far better trained, would probably prove an effective deterrent upon such descents. Perhaps if the people were told of their dangers they would consent to make the necessary sacrifices.

Winston S. Churchill to A. V. Alexander
(*Churchill papers, 20/13*)

17 June 1940

I am content with your proposed disposition of the heavy ships in the West, namely, *Repulse* and *Renown* to maintain the blockade at Scapa; *Rodney*, *Nelson* and *Valiant* at Rosyth to cover the Island; *Hood* and *Ark Royal* to join *Resolution* at Gibraltar, to watch over the fate of the French Fleet.

2. It is of the utmost importance that the Fleet at Alexandria should remain to cover Egypt from an Italian invasion which would otherwise destroy prematurely all our position in the East. This Fleet is well placed to sustain our interests in Turkey, to guard Egypt and the Canal and can, if the situation changes, either fight its way westward or go through the Canal to guard the Empire or come round the Cape on to our trade routes.

3. The position of the Eastern Fleet must be constantly watched and can be reviewed when we know what happens to the French Fleet and whether Spain declares war or not.

4. Even if Spain declares war it does not follow that we should quit the Eastern Mediterranean. If we have to quit Gibraltar we must immediately take the Canaries, which will serve as a very good base to control the Western entrance to the Mediterranean.

WSC

Winston S. Churchill to A. V. Alexander
(*Churchill papers, 20/13*)

17 June 1940

It is most important that the use of aluminium by the Admiralty should be reduced to the absolute minimum in order to give the Air Force the full benefit of the supply. Will you ask the Controller to give you a report on the subject for my consideration thereafter.

2. There are several points about the Fleet distribution leading up to the loss of a certain ship which require examination. First, the Narvik exodus was known to be in progress by the enemy, and therefore its protection against surface ships was the first charge on the Home Fleet. How was it at this juncture that two battle-cruisers – *Renown* and *Repulse* – were sent off to the Faroes entirely out of relation to the important business that Admiralty were carrying out from Narvik? Why was it necessary to send two battle-cruisers on the vague reports of two transports having been seen moving towards Iceland? Surely a couple of light cruisers or one eight-inch would have been quite sufficient for this. A German descent upon Iceland, though objectionable, is not urgently serious and certainly not irremediable. On the other hand, the proper and sure execution of the Narvik withdrawal was a major task. Perhaps you would ask the Naval Staff to report on this matter, on which Parliament will certainly concern itself. The loss was very grievous and even more vexing is it that the enemy retired without injury or interception. I am afraid that it will be felt that the Navy has bungled this, and certainly the Germans have had a remarkable success. Considering the very few ships they had and the enormous forces which we dispose, it is astonishing how we are bedevilled by them. I am quite sure this story will require very severe scrutiny.

WSC

Winston S. Churchill to Herbert Morrison
(*Churchill papers, 20/13*)

17 June 1940

Whether France continues in the war or not our policy must be to produce in the UK and North America as many field guns and shells as possible without interfering with programmes for the manufacture and supply of other equally essential war stores.

This can only be achieved by the adoption in the British Army of two types of field guns, the 25-pr and the 75-mm. There are objections to having two types in one army, but we are not in a position to indulge them.

Steps should be taken at once to start large scale production of 75-mm guns and ammunition in North America. Immediate steps should also be taken to produce this gun and ammunition for it in the UK without interfering with the present programme for 25-pr guns and shells.

For many months to come the scale of the North American and UK production will not depend in practice upon the number of divisions which it is proposed to form in the British Army. There is now a far larger Army already in Britain than can be equipped with artillery. Additional field guns will be required for anti-tank and local defence and for the supply of French troops should France continue in the war.

All the preparations which you are able to make for the execution of the present programme of arming 55 divisions should go forward on paper so that no time is lost. Anything you can do to accelerate delivery will be of immense benefit. An immediate speed-up of delivery is everything.

War Cabinet: minutes
(*Cabinet papers, 65/7*)

17 June 1940
11 a.m.
10 Downing Street

The Prime Minister was reluctant to see the plans for continuing air attack on North Italy abandoned and thought that orders for evacuating the Air Force from the South of France should be held up until the matter had been investigated further.

There was some discussion whether General Brooke should remain in France, either at Nantes or Cherbourg, or return to this country.

The Chief of the Imperial General Staff felt that no useful purpose would be served by General Brooke's remaining in France.

The Prime Minister hoped that the War Office would not recall General Brooke so long as his presence in France could be of value to the difficult withdrawal with which our troops were faced.

The Prime Minister said that he had had a telephone conversation with General Spears, who was returning to England, as he did not think he could perform any useful service in the present situation. General de Gaulle was also coming back with him, as he had apparently been warned that, as things were developing, it might be as well for him to leave France.

Reference was made to the telegram which had been despatched to M. Reynaud on the previous day (No. 368 DIPP) in which it was stated that the sailing of the French Fleet for British harbours was a condition of our assenting to the French enquiring as to the terms of an armistice for France. This telegram had been delivered to M. Reynaud, but he had then been asked to suspend action on it, and it was not certain whether he had shown it to the other members of the French Government. Sir R. Campbell had therefore been instructed to deliver the telegram to Marshal Pétain.

The Prime Minister suggested that a further telegram should be sent, pointing out that, if the French Government sought an armistice without fulfilling this condition, our consent would not be forthcoming.

The Secretary of State for Foreign Affairs said that the Belgian Minister for Foreign Affairs[1] had told our Chargé d'Affaires that the Belgian Government wished to be entirely associated with His Majesty's Government. He had asked if facilities could be given for the evacuation of some 900 Belgian Officers and 30 to 35 thousand troops, including 7,000 at Brest.

The Prime Minister suggested that a reply should be sent to the Belgians as follows:

(1) Their troops should be told to proceed to the ports, and we would do our best to continue evacuation as long as possible.
(2) They should be informed as to the ports from which they could most conveniently be taken off.
  (The Admiralty would advise the Foreign Office on this point.)
(3) The Belgians should be asked to inform us as early as possible as to the number of their troops likely to reach each port.

The War Cabinet invited the Foreign Secretary to reply to the Belgian Government on the above lines.

The Prime Minister strongly urged the selection and rapid promotion of men who had made their mark in action.

The Secretary of State[2] said that the LDV's[3] were at the moment largely a 'broomstick' Army. Rifles were being provided for them as quickly as possible. We had a supply of rifles which had been kept in store since the last war, and which were now being reconditioned. Another 500,000 rifles were ready to leave the United States. According to the original intention, these would have been divided equally between this country and France, but arrangements were now being made which would ensure that the whole consignment came to us.

The Prime Minister emphasised the importance of getting these rifles shipped at the earliest possible moment. Nothing must be left undone to get these rifles as quickly as possible.

---

[1] Paul-Henri Spaak.
[2] Anthony Eden, Secretary of State for War.
[3] The Local Defence Volunteers, later called, at Churchill's suggestion (first made when he was at the Admiralty), the Home Guard.

Winston S. Churchill: recollection
(*'Their Finest Hour'*, page 172)

17 June 1940

At Brest and the western ports the evacuations were numerous. The German air attack on the transports was heavy. One frightful incident occurred on the 17th at St Nazaire. The 20,000-ton liner *Lancastria*, with five thousand men on board, was bombed and set on fire just as she was about to leave. A mass of flaming oil spread over the water round the ship, and upwards of three thousand men perished. The rest were rescued under continued air attack by the devotion of the small craft. When this news came to me in the quiet Cabinet Room during the afternoon I forbade its publication, saying: 'The newspapers have got quite enough disaster for today at least.' I had intended to release the news a few days later, but events crowded upon us so black and so quickly that I forgot to lift the ban, and it was some years before the knowledge of this horror became public.[1]

John Colville: diary
(*Colville papers*)

17 June 1940

After the Cabinet the PM paced backwards and forwards in the garden, alone, his head bowed, his hands behind his back. He was doubtless considering how best the French fleet, the air force and the Colonies could be saved. He, I am sure, will remain undaunted.

Winston S. Churchill: broadcast
(*Churchill papers, 9/176*)

17 June 1940
9 p.m.

The news from France is very bad and I grieve for the gallant French people who have fallen into this terrible misfortune. Nothing will alter our feelings towards them or our faith that the genius of France will rise again. What has happened in France makes no difference to our actions and purpose. We have become the sole champions now in arms to defend the world cause. We shall do our best to be worthy of this high honour. We shall defend our Island

---

[1] In fact, the news of the sinking of the *Lancastria* was made public six weeks later, following several reports of it in newspapers throughout the United States. The precise death toll has never been ascertained, but was greater than that of the *Titanic* (1,513) and the *Lusitania* (1,198) combined.

home, and with the British Empire we shall fight on unconquerable until the curse of Hitler is lifted from the brows of mankind. We are sure that in the end all will come right.

Sir Alexander Cadogan: diary
(*'The Diaries of Sir Alexander Cadogan'*)

17 June 1940

About 11 p.m. summoned by PM. Found him storming at Corbin – who was singing in chorus. PM had a scorching message to Pétain and Weygand. I tried to tone it down a bit, but failed. So sent it off. Showed him a snorter which I had drafted, but he wouldn't read, but he said 'send it off at once, minutes count'. So off it went.

Winston S. Churchill to Marshal Pétain and General Weygand
(*Churchill papers, 20/14*)

17 June 1940

I wish to repeat to you my profound conviction that the illustrious Marshal Pétain and the famous General Weygand, our comrades in two great wars against the Germans, will not injure their ally by delivering over to the enemy the fine French Fleet. Such an act would scarify their names for a thousand years of history. Yet this result may easily come by frittering away these few precious hours when the Fleet can be sailed to safety in British or American ports, carrying with it the hope of the future and the honour of France.[1]

General Ironside: diary
(*'The Ironside Diaries'*)

17 June 1940

There is no doubt that Winston has any amount of courage and experience. Thrown with his back to the wall, he may lose some of his lack of balance. He is quite undismayed by the state of affairs.

[1] Copies of this telegram were also sent to President Lebrun and Admiral Darlan. 'In order that these appeals might not lack personal reinforcement on the spot,' Churchill later recalled, 'we sent the First Sea Lord, who believed himself to be in intimate personal and professional touch with Admiral Darlan; the First Lord, Mr A. V. Alexander; and Lord Lloyd, Secretary of State for the Colonies, so long known as a friend of France. All these three laboured to make what contacts they could with the new Ministers during the 19th. They received many solemn assurances that the Fleet would never be allowed to fall into German hands. But no more French warships moved beyond the reach of the swiftly approaching German power' (*Their Finest Hour*, page 191).

John Martin: diary
(*Martin papers*)

17 June 1940

The PM gave me such a kind and human goodnight when he went up to bed at 1 o'clock this morning – put his hand on my arm and said he was sorry there had been no time in all the rush of these days to get to know me.

Air Chief Marshal Sir Hugh Dowding to Winston S. Churchill
(*Churchill papers, 2/393*)

17 June 1940

Headquarters, Fighter Command,
Royal Air Force, Bentley Priory
Stanmore, Middlesex

My dear Prime Minister,

Thank you very much for sending me your book.[1] It was very good of you to remember among all the businesses and worries which beset you, and I shall keep it among my most valued possessions.

Well! now it is England against Germany, and I don't envy them their job. With all best wishes to you in your tremendous task –

Yours very sincerely
H. C. J. Dowding

Sir Alexander Cadogan: diary
(*'The Diaries of Sir Alexander Cadogan'*)

18 June 1940

Cabinet 12.30. Winston not there – writing his speech.

Winston S. Churchill: speech
(*Hansard*)

18 June 1940
3.49 p.m.

House of Commons

The Prime Minister (Mr Churchill): I spoke the other day of the colossal military disaster which occurred when the French High Command failed to withdraw the Northern Armies from Belgium at the moment when they knew that the French front was decisively broken at Sedan and on the Meuse. This

---

[1] It is not clear which book Churchill had sent: his most recently re-issued book was a volume of his pre-war speeches entitled *Arms and the Covenant*, first published in 1938 (see page 377, note 2).

delay entailed the loss of 15 or 16 French divisions and threw out of action for the critical period the whole of the British Expeditionary Force. Our Army and 120,000 French troops were indeed rescued by the British Navy from Dunkirk but only with the loss of their cannon, vehicles and modern equipment. This loss inevitably took some weeks to repair, and in the first two of those weeks the battle in France has been lost. When we consider the heroic resistance made by the French Army against heavy odds in this battle, the enormous losses inflicted upon the enemy and the evident exhaustion of the enemy, it may well be thought that these 25 divisions of the best trained and best equipped troops might have turned the scale. However, General Weygand had to fight without them. Only three British divisions or their equivalent were able to stand in the line with their French comrades. They have suffered severely, but they have fought well. We sent every man we could to France as fast as we could re-equip and transport their formations.

I am not reciting these facts for the purpose of recrimination. That, I judge, to be utterly futile and even harmful. We cannot afford it. I recite them in order to explain why it was we did not have, as we could have had, between 12 and 14 British divisions fighting in the line in this great battle instead of only three. Now I put all this aside. I put it on the shelf, from which the historians, when they have time, will select their documents to tell their stories. We have to think of the future and not of the past. This also applies in a small way to our own affairs at home. There are many who would hold an inquest in the House of Commons on the conduct of the Governments – and of Parliaments, for they are in it, too – during the years which led up to this catastrophe. They seek to indict those who were responsible for the guidance of our affairs. This also would be a foolish and pernicious process. There are too many in it. Let each man search his conscience and search his speeches. I frequently search mine.

Of this I am quite sure, that if we open a quarrel between the past and the present, we shall find that we have lost the future. Therefore, I cannot accept the drawing of any distinctions between Members of the present Government. It was formed at a moment of crisis in order to unite all the parties and all sections of opinion. It has received the almost unanimous support of both Houses of Parliament. Its Members are going to stand together, and, subject to the authority of the House of Commons, we are going to govern the country and fight the war. It is absolutely necessary at a time like this that every Minister who tries each day to do his duty shall be respected, and their subordinates must know that their chiefs are not threatened men, men who are here to-day and gone to-morrow, but that their directions must be punctually and faithfully obeyed. Without this concentrated power we cannot face what lies before us. I should not think it would be very advantageous for the House to prolong this Debate this afternoon under conditions of public stress. Many facts are not clear that will be clear in a short time. We are to have a Secret Session on Thursday, and I should think that would be a better opportunity for the many earnest expressions of opinion which Members will desire to make and for the House to discuss vital matters, as I have said before, without having everything read the next morning by our dangerous foes.

The military events which have happened during the past fortnight have not come to me with any sense of surprise. Indeed, I indicated a fortnight ago as clearly as I could to the House that the worst possibilities were open, and I made it perfectly clear then that whatever happened in France would make no differnce to the resolve of Britain and the British Empire to fight on, 'if necessary for years, if necessary alone.' During the last few days we have successfully brought off the great majority of troops we had on the lines of communication in France – a very large number, scores of thousands – and seven-eighths of the troops we have sent to France since the beginning of the war, that is to say, about 350,000 out of 400,000 men, are safely back in this country. Others are still fighting with the French, and fighting with considerable success in their local encounters with the enemy. We have also brought back a great mass of stores, rifles and munitions of all kinds which had been accumulated in France during the last nine months.

We have, therefore, in this island to-day a very large and powerful military force. This force includes all our best trained and finest troops and includes scores of thousands of those who have already measured their quality against the Germans and found themselves at no disadvantage. We have under arms at the present time in this island over a million and a quarter men. Behind these we have the Local Defence Volunteers, numbering half a million, only a portion of whom, however, are yet armed with rifles or other firearms. We have incorporated into our Defence Forces every man for whom we have a weapon. We expect a very large addition to our weapons in the near future, and in preparation for this we intend to call up, drill and train further large numbers at once. Those who are not called up or employed upon the vast business of munitions production in all its branches – and it runs through every kind of grade – serve their country best by remaining at their ordinary work until they are required.

We also have Dominions Armies here. The Canadians had actually landed in France but have now been safely withdrawn, much disappointed, but in perfect order, with all their artillery and equipment. These very high-class forces from the Dominions will now take part in the defence of the Mother Country. Lest the account which I have given of these very large forces should raise the question why they did not take part in the great battle in France, I must make it clear that, apart from the divisions training and organising at home, only 12 divisions were equipped to fight upon a scale which justified their being sent abroad. This was fully up to the number which the French had been led to expect would be available in France at the ninth month of the war. The rest of our forces at home have a fighting value for home defence which will, of course, steadily increase every week that passes. Thus, the invasion of Great Britain would at this time require the transportation across the sea of hostile armies upon a very large scale and, after they had been so transported, they would have to be continually maintained with all the masses of munitions and supplies which are required for continuous battle, as continuous battle it would be.

Here is where we come to the Navy. After all, we have a Navy. Some people seem to forget that. We must remind them. For the last 30 years I have been concerned in discussions about the possibilities of oversea invasion, and I took the responsibility on behalf of the Admiralty, at the beginning of the last war, of allowing all Regular troops to be sent out of the country, although our Territorials had only just been called up and were quite untrained. Therefore, this island was for several months practically denuded of fighting troops. The Admiralty had confidence at that time in their ability to prevent a mass invasion, even though at that time the Germans had a magnificent battle fleet in the proportion of 10 to 16, even though they were capable of fighting a general engagement every day and any day, whereas now they have only a couple of heavy ships worth speaking of. We are also told that the Italian Navy is to come to gain sea superiority in these waters. If they seriously intend it, I shall only say that we shall be delighted to offer Signor Mussolini a free and safeguarded passage through the Straits of Gibraltar in order that he may play the part which he aspires to do. There is general curiosity in the British Fleet to find out whether the Italians are up to the level they were at in the last war or whether they have fallen off at all.

Therefore, it seems to me that as far as seaborne invasion on a great scale is concerned, we are far more capable of meeting it to-day than we were at many periods in the last war and during the early months of this war, before our other troops were trained, and while the BEF was already abroad and still abroad. The Navy have never pretended to be able to prevent raids by bodies of 5,000 or 10,000 men flung suddenly across and thrown ashore at several points on the coast some dark night or foggy morning.

The efficacy of sea-power, especially under modern conditions, depends upon the invading force being of large size. It has to be of large size, in view of our military strength, to be of any use. If it is of large size, then the Navy have something they can find and meet and, as it were, bite on. Now we must remember that even five divisions, however lightly equipped, would require 200 to 250 ships, and with modern air reconnaissance and photography, it would not be easy to collect such an armada, marshal it and conduct it across the sea without any powerful naval forces to escort it, and with the very great possibility that it would be intercepted long before it reached the coast, and the men all drowned in the sea or, at the worst, blown to pieces with their equipment while they were trying to land. We also have a great system of minefields, recently strongly reinforced, through which we alone know the channel. If the enemy tries to sweep passages through these minefields, it will be the task of the Navy to destroy the minesweepers and any other forces employed to protect them. There should be no difficulty in this, owing to our great superiority at sea.

Those are the regular, well-tested, well-proved arguments on which we have relied during many years in peace and war. But the question is whether there are any new methods by which those solid assurances can be circumvented. Odd as it may seem, some attention has been given to this by the Admiralty, whose prime duty and responsibility it is to destroy any large seaborne expedition before it reaches or at the moment when it reaches these shores. It would not be useful to go into details. It might even suggest ideas to other people which they have not thought of, and they would not be likely to give us any of their ideas in exchange. All I will say is that untiring vigilance and mind-searching must be devoted to the subject, because the enemy is crafty and cunning and full of novel treacheries and stratagems. The House may be assured that the utmost ingenuity is being displayed and imagination is being evoked from large numbers of competent officers, well-trained in tactics and thoroughly up to date, to measure and counterwork novel possibilities, of which many are suggested, some very absurd and some by no means utterly irrational.

Some people will ask why, then, was it that the British Navy was not able to prevent the movement of a large army from Germany into Norway across the Skaggerak? But the conditions in the Channel and in the North Sea are in no way like those which prevail in the Skaggerak. In the Skaggerak, because of the distance, we could give no air support to our surface ships, and consequently, lying as we did close to the enemy's main air power, in those waters we were compelled to use only our submarines. We could not enforce the decisive blockade or interruption which is possible from surface vessels. Our submarines took a heavy toll but could not, by themselves, prevent the invasion of Norway. In the Channel and in the North Sea, on the other hand, our superior naval surface forces, aided by our submarines, will operate with close and effective air assistance.

This brings me, naturally, to the great question of invasion from the air and of the impending struggle between the British and German air forces. It seems quite clear that no invasion on a scale beyond the capacity of our land forces to crush speedily is likely to take place from the air until our Air Force has been definitely overpowered. In the meantime, there may be raids by parachute· troops and attempted descents of airborne soldiers. We should be able to give those gentry a warm reception both in the air and if they reach the ground in any condition to continue the dispute. But the great question is, Can we break Hitler's air weapon? Now, of course, it is a very great pity that we have not got an Air Force at least equal to that of the most powerful enemy within striking distance of these shores.[1] But we have a very powerful Air Force which has proved itself far superior in quality, both in men and in many types of machine, to what we have met so far in the numerous fierce air battles which have been fought. In France, where we were at a considerable disadvantage and lost many machines on the ground, we were accustomed to inflict losses of as much as two to two and a half to one. In the fighting over Dunkirk, which was a sort of no man's land, we undoubtedly beat the German air force, and this gave us the mastery locally in the air, and we inflicted losses of three or four to one. Anyone who looks at the photographs which were published a week or so ago of the re-embarkation, showing the masses of troops assembled on the beach and forming an ideal target for hours at a time, must realise that this re-embarkation would not have been possible unless the enemy had resigned all hope of recovering air superiority at that point.

In the defence of this island the advantages to the defenders will be very great. We hope to improve on the rate of three or four to one which was realised at Dunkirk, and in addition all our injured machines and their crews which get down safely – and, surprisingly, a very great many injured machines and men do get down safely in modern air fighting – all of these will fall, in an attack upon these islands, on friendly soil and live to fight another day, whereas all injured enemy machines and their complements will be total losses as far as the war is concerned. During the great battle in France, we gave very powerful and continuous aid to the French Army both by fighters and bombers, but in spite of every kind of pressure we never would allow the entire Metropolitan strength of the Air Force, in fighters, to be consumed. This decision was painful, but it was also right, because the fortunes of the battle in France could not have been decisively affected, even if we had thrown in our entire fighter force. The battle was lost by the unfortunate strategical opening, by the extraordinary and unforeseen power of the armoured columns, and by the great preponderance of the German Army in numbers. Our fighter Air Force might easily have been exhausted as a mere accident in that great struggle, and we should have found ourselves at the present time in a very serious plight. But, as it is, I am happy to inform the House that our fighter air strength is stronger at the present time, relatively to the Germans, who have suffered terrible losses, than it has ever been, and consequently we believe ourselves to possess the capacity to continue the war in the air under better conditions than we have ever experienced before. I look forward confidently to the exploits of our fighter pilots, who will have the glory of saving their native land, their island home, and all they love, from the most deadly of all attacks.

[1] When Churchill had argued in favour of such an air policy (of doubling, and then redoubling the Air Force) in 1934, he had been denounced by the then Liberal Party leader, Sir Herbert Samuel, as using the language of 'a Malay run amok'. Clement Attlee had commented that Churchill's proposal was unnecessary as Hitler's dictatorship was even then 'falling down'.

There remains the danger of bombing attacks, which will certainly be made very soon upon us by the bomber forces of the enemy. It is true that the German bomber force is superior in numbers to ours, but we have a very large bomber force also which we shall use to strike at military targets in Germany without intermission. I do not at all underrate the severity of the ordeal which lies before us, but I believe our countrymen will show themselves capable of standing up to it, like the brave men of Barcelona,[1] and will be able to stand up to it, and carry on in spite of it, at least as well as any other people in the world. Much will depend upon this, and every man and every woman will have the chance to show the finest qualities of their race and render the highest service to their cause. For all of us at this time, whatever our sphere, our station, our occupation, our duties, it will be a help to remember the famous lines:

' He nothing common did, or mean,
Upon that memorable scene.'[2]

I have thought it right upon this occasion to give the House and the country some indication of the solid, practical grounds upon which we base our inflexible resolve to continue the war, and I can assure them that our professional advisers of the three Services unitedly advise that we should do so, and that there are good and reasonable hopes of final victory. We have also fully informed and consulted all the self-governing Dominions, and I have received from their Prime Ministers, Mr Mackenzie King, Mr Menzies, Mr Fraser and General Smuts, messages couched in the most moving terms in which they endorse our decision and declare themselves ready to share our fortunes and to persevere to the end.

We may now ask ourselves, In what ways is our position worsened since the beginning of the war? It is worsened by the fact that the Germans have conquered a large part of the coastline of Western Europe, and many small countries have been overrun by them. This aggravates the possibilities of air attack and adds to our naval preoccupations. It in no way diminishes, but on the contrary definitely increases, the power of our long-distance blockade. Should military resistance come to an end in France, which is not yet certain, though it will in any case be greatly diminished, the Germans can concentrate their forces, both military and industrial, upon us. But for the reasons I have

[1] Reflecting on the bombing of Republican-held cities in Spain during the Spanish Civil War, Churchill wrote on 1 September 1938: 'As to the psychological effects upon the civil populations of Madrid, Barcelona and Valencia, these have been exactly the opposite of what the German and Italian air bombers expected. So far from producing panic and the wish to surrender, they have aroused a spirit of unyielding resistance among all classes. They have united whole communities, otherwise deeply sundered, in a common hatred of such base and barbarous methods. I, therefore, remain convinced, that where the strength of the air forces is equal, the side which consumes its energy upon the slaughter of the civil population is likely to encounter surprising disappointments' ('Is Air Power Decisive in War?' *Evening Standard*, 1 September 1938).

[2] Andrew Marvell's lines on the execution of King Charles I.

given to the House these will not be found so easy to apply. If invasion becomes more imminent, we, being relieved from the task of maintaining a large army in France, have far larger and more efficient forces here to meet them. If Hitler can bring under his despotic control the industries of the countries he has conquered, this will add greatly to his already vast armament output. On the other hand, this will not happen immediately, and we are now assured of immense, continuous and increasing support in supplies and munitions of all kinds from the United States, and especially of aeroplanes and pilots from the Dominions and across the oceans, coming from regions which are beyond the reach of enemy bombers.

I do not see how any of these factors can operate to our detriment on balance before the winter comes, and the winter will impose a strain upon the Nazi régime, with almost all Europe writhing and starving under their heel which, for all their ruthlessness, will run them very hard. We must not forget that from the moment when we declared war on the 3rd September it was always possible for Germany to turn all her air force upon this country, together with any other devices of invasion she might conceive, and that France could do little or nothing to prevent her doing so. We have, therefore, lived under this danger, in principle and in a slightly modified form, during all these months. In the meanwhile, however, we have enormously improved our methods of defence, and we have learned, what we had no right to assume at the beginning, namely, the individual superiority of our aircraft and pilots.

Therefore, in casting up this dread balance-sheet, contemplating our dangers with a disillusioned eye, I see great reason for intense vigilance and exertion, but none whatever for panic or despair. During the first four years of the last war the Allies experienced, as my right hon. Friend opposite the Member for Carnarvon Boroughs (Mr Lloyd George) will remember, nothing but disaster and disappointment, and yet at the end their morale was higher than that of the Germans, who had moved from one aggressive triumph to another. During that war we repeatedly asked ourselves the question, 'How are we going to win?' and no one was able ever to answer it with much precision, until at the end, quite suddenly, quite unexpectedly, our terrible foe collapsed before us, and we were so glutted with victory that in our folly we cast it away.

We do not yet know what will happen in France or whether the French resistance will be prolonged, both in France and in the French Empire overseas. The French Government will be throwing away great opportunities and casting away their future if they do not continue the war in accordance with their Treaty obligations, from which we have not felt able to release them. The House will have read the historic declaration in which, at the desire of many Frenchmen, and of our own hearts, we have proclaimed our willingness to conclude at the darkest hour in French history a union of common citizenship. However matters may go in France or with the French

Government, we in this island and in the British Empire will never lose our sense of comradeship with the French people. If we are now called upon to endure what they have suffered we shall emulate their courage, and if final victory rewards our toils they shall share the gains, aye, and freedom shall be restored to all. We abate nothing of our just demands – Czechs, Poles, Norwegians, Dutch, Belgians, all who have joined their causes to our own shall be restored.

What General Weygand called the 'Battle of France' is over. I expect that the battle of Britain is about to begin. Upon this battle depends the survival of Christian civilisation. Upon it depends our own British life and the long continuity of our institutions and our Empire. The whole fury and might of the enemy must very soon be turned on us. Hitler knows that he will have to break us in this island or lose the war. If we can stand up to him, all Europe may be free, and the life of the world may move forward into broad, sunlit uplands; but if we fail then the whole world, including the United States, and all that we have known and cared for, will sink into the abyss of a new dark age made more sinister, and perhaps more prolonged, by the lights of a perverted science. Let us therefore brace ourselves to our duty and so bear ourselves that if the British Commonwealth and Empire lasts for a thousand years, men will still say, 'This was their finest hour.'

Hugh Dalton: diary
(*'The Second World War Diary of Hugh Dalton'*)

18 June 1940

Winston again makes a grand speech – defiant, reasoned, and confident. It is noticeable that he is much more loudly cheered by the Labour Party than by the general body of Tory supporters.

John Colville: diary
(*Colville papers*)

18 June 1940

After the speech I told him Attlee wanted to see him. He was performing his toilet (!) and said: 'So does Amery; he is very tiresome, always wanting to air his views about how to win the war, on behalf of the Junior Ministers, instead of getting on with his work at the India Office.'

Later in the afternoon Vansittart and Morton insisted on my going up to wake Winston, who had just taken to his bed: they wanted to urge on him a new scheme of Van's which entailed Lord Lloyd flying out to Bordeaux to put

HMG's views fairly and squarely to the French Government. Van thought that this would be preferable to, and would exclude, de Gaulle broadcasting.

I went up to the PM's bedroom. The blinds were drawn and Winston himself was right under the bedclothes. When he emerged he had a bandage over his eyes to keep out the light. Finally it was agreed that Van's project, which Halifax and Morton think a forlorn hope, should be put into effect <u>and</u> that de Gaulle should broadcast.

On a minute about the proposal to take away the King of Italy's[1] Garter, the PM has scribbled: 'I think there should be the utmost ignominy and publicity in the case of this miserable puppet.'

Winston S. Churchill to Sir Alexander Cadogan
(*Premier papers, 3/69A*)

18 June 1940

The most strenuous efforts should be made to rally the Belgians to their duty. There can be no question of their going out of the war. If they do, we will wash our hands of their interests altogether, and they must clearly understand that their Colonies will not be allowed to form part of the German system as long as we can prevent this by sea action. Have steps been taken by the Admiralty to lay forcible hands on all Belgian shipping within our reach? Will you very kindly put this all in motion. I regard Mr Jaspar's telegram[2] as most objectionable.

WSC

---

[1] Victor Emmanuel III, 1869–1947. Became King of Italy in 1900 (when his father was assassinated). Appointed Mussolini as Prime Minister, 1922. Participated in the overthrow of Mussolini, 1943. Abdicated, 1946: he had hoped that his abdication would lead to a referendum upholding the monarchy for his son Umberto, but three weeks after his abdication the Italian people voted for a Republic (by 12½ million votes to 10½).

[2] At 12.10 p.m. the Foreign Office had received a telegram from Sir Ronald Campbell in Bordeaux, which was immediately marked for special distribution to the War Cabinet. It read: 'M. Jaspar, Belgian Minister of Public Health, informed me confidentially that the Belgian Government have decided not, repeat not, to continue the struggle.' Jaspar added that 'He said he alone opposed the decision' (*Foreign Office papers, 371/24275*). Within a few days the Belgian Government had reached London, where it was headed for the rest of the war by Hubert Pierlot.

Winston S. Churchill to General Ismay
(*Cabinet papers, 69/1*)

18 June 1940
Secret

10 Downing Street

General Ismay.

To-morrow morning at 10 a.m. here in the Cabinet Room, would it be convenient for me to see C-in-C Home Forces, General Paget,[1] the Chief Engineer,[2] and CIGS or VCIGS.[3] Please arrange and let me know.

I should like to be informed upon (1) the coastal watch and coastal batteries. (2) The gorges of the harbours and defended inlets. (3) The troops held in immediate support of the foregoing. (4) The mobile columns and Brigade Groups. (5) The General Reserve.

Someone should explain to me the state of these different Forces, including the guns available in each area. I gave directions that the 8th Tank Regiment should be immediately equipped with the supply of infantry and cruiser Tanks until they have 52 new Tanks, all well-armoured and well-gunned. What has been done with the output of this month and last month? Make sure it is not languishing in depots but passes swiftly to troops. General Carr is responsible for this. Let him report.

I minuted three days ago about the 'sticky' bomb. All preparations for manufacture should proceed in anticipation that the further trials will be successful. Let me have a timetable showing why it is that delay has crept in all this process which is so urgent.

What are the ideas of the C-in-C HF[4] about Storm Troops? We have always set our faces against this idea, but the Germans certainly gained in the last War by adopting it, and this time it has been a leading cause of their victory. There ought to be at least 20,000 Storm Troops or 'Leopards' drawn from existing Units, ready to spring at the throat of any small landings or descents.

---

[1] Bernard Charles Tolver Paget, 1887–1961. Son of Francis Paget, Bishop of Oxford. On active service, 1914–18 (wounded twice, despatches, DSO, Military Cross). Major-General, 1937. On active service in Norway, April 1940, when he extracted two brigades during a seven-day action that won specific praise from Churchill in the House of Commons. CB, 1940. Chief of the General Staff, Home Forces, May 1940 to May 1941. Lieutenant-General, 1941. Commander-in-Chief, South Eastern Command, 1941; Commander-in-Chief, Home Forces, 1941–3. Commander-in-Chief, 21st Army Group, June–December 1943. Commander-in-Chief, Middle East Force, 1944–6. Knighted, 1942. His younger son died of wounds received in action in Germany in 1945 (posthumous DSO).

[2] Albert Robert Valon, 1885–1971. Entered the Army, 1906. On active service, 1914–18 (Military Cross). Major-General, 1939: Director of Ordnance Services (Engineering), War Office, 1939–40. Inspector of Army Ordnance Workshops, 1940–2. Inspector, Royal Electrical and Mechanical Engineers (REME), 1942–3. CB, 1943.

[3] General Dill and General Haining.

[4] Commander-in-Chief, Home Forces, General Ironside.

These Officers and men should be armed with the latest equipment, tommy guns, grenades, etc., and should be given great facilities in motorcycles and armoured cars.

Pray assure me that the available good Tanks and the available anti-Tank guns are kept handy at central depots, whence they can be transported by the most rapid means to points of attack.

I shall be glad to discuss all these matters to-morrow with the Home Command.

WSC

Winston S. Churchill to Ernest Bevin[1]
(*Premier papers, 4/53/2*)

18 June 1940

Minister for Labour

I certainly sh'd welcome any approach to Irish unity; but I have forty years experience of its difficulties. I c'd never be a party to the coercion of Ulster to join the Southern counties: but I am much in favour of their being persuaded. The key to this is de Valera showing some loyalty to Crown & Empire.

WSC

John Colville: diary
(*Colville papers*)

18 June 1940

Just before dinner a telegram came in from Campbell, saying that the French thought it would be dishonourable to negotiate an armistice unless their armed forces were still intact, but it seemed likely that the fleet would be denied to the Germans. I took this telegram up to the PM, who was dressing. When he saw me coming with a telegram he said: 'Another bloody country gone west, I'll bet.'

---

[1] In a letter to Churchill that day, Ernest Bevin had proposed an agreement on a new constitution 'on the basis of a united Ireland at the end of hostilities', and suggested that the chairman of the constitutional negotiations be appointed by President Roosevelt.

Defence Committee: minutes
(*Cabinet papers, 69/1*)

19 June 1940
10 a.m.

10 Downing Street

STORM TROOPS

The Prime Minister enquired whether the idea of storm troops, which had been made use of so successfully by the Germans, had been accepted by the Army, and, if so, what progress had been made.

The Commander-in-Chief, Home Forces, said that he was averse to turning any particular Division into a Division of Storm Troops. He was, however, proceeding on the principle that there should be a large number of smaller units in the nature of Storm Troops . . .[1]

RIFLES

525,000 rifles had been secured in the USA, and it had been intended to split these with the French on a fifty-fifty basis. Of our share, a small number had been shipped on the *Eastern Prince*, which sailed on 13th June. The remainder, i.e. over 200,000, were believed to have been loaded on the *Pacific Shipper*, which was sailing this week, and would take ten days on the crossing. A telegram had been sent to get confirmation of this fact. The French had now made over all their orders to us,[2] and a telegram had been sent off to find out what arrangements were being made for shipping their share. A further 200,000 were also being secured.

The Prime Minister drew attention to the great danger of shipping large quantities of rifles in one ship. Immediate steps should be taken to ensure that any further shipments were dispersed among a number of cargoes.

THE STICKY BOMB

The Prime Minister enquired why there had been so much delay in taking up the idea of the sticky bomb, which appeared to be so promising. He had himself seen the bomb a week or two previously, and he thought that much time had been lost through not preparing the organisation for producing it on a large scale as soon as the design was completed. He directed that a Report

---

[1] Ironside listed at this point Tank-Hunting Platoons, Independent Companies (five of which had returned from Norway), and Special Irregular Units (one of which was commanded by Brigadier Wingate, and another of which was made up of American volunteers).

[2] On 16 June 1940, in Washington, an agreement had been signed by J. Frédéric Bloch-Lainé, Vice-Chairman of the Anglo-French Purchasing Board, and Arthur Purvis, the Board's Chairman, transferring to Britain the 132 principal French arms contracts with the United States, including orders for aircraft engines, spares, essential parts, instruments, machine guns, and 965 bombers. These contracts were valued at more than $90 million. There were also further contracts for machine tools worth more than $86 million, and other contracts for substantial quantities of petrol, brass and zinc. ('Assignment of French Contracts', 16 June 1940, *Cabinet papers, 115/735*.)

should be made to him on the following day to show the progress which had been achieved.

Winston S. Churchill to A. V. Alexander and Admiral Pound
(*Churchill papers, 20/13*)

19 June 1940

I wish to draw the attention of the Admiralty to the immense importance of the French ship which is bringing us 275,000 rifles. Her safety should be one of the first charges on the Navy. The ships carrying 75's artillery are also important.

WSC

War Cabinet: minutes
(*Cabinet papers, 65/7*)

19 June 1940　　　　　　　　　　　　　　　　　　　10 Downing Street
12.30 p.m.

The Prime Minister hoped that a careful watch would be kept on the expenditure of AA ammunition.

The Chief of the Air Staff undertook to impress this point on the Air Officer Commanding-in-Chief, Fighter Command.

The Prime Minister said that the proportion of anti-aircraft guns brought off from Narvik appeared very unsatisfactory. He hoped that the War Office and the Admiralty would arrange for an informal inquiry to be carried out in both these cases, and that disciplinary action should be taken if any officers were found to have failed in their duty.

The Prime Minister said that he had received a telegram from the First Lord of the Admiralty who was at Bordeaux with the Chief of Naval Staff,[1] which gave a more encouraging picture of the general situation than we had been led to believe possible. Apparently, the fighting was continuing and the French Navy was in good heart. They had bombarded the Italian coast and had sunk two Italian submarines. The First Lord had been favourably impressed with Admiral Darlan, who was confident that the French Fleet

---

[1] A.V. Alexander and Admiral Pound had gone to Bordeaux to see if the French fleet was likely to remain actively at war.

would obey him. He seemed determined to ensure that the French ships did not fall into the hands of the Germans.[1] The Battleship *Richelieu* was already on her way to Dakar and the *Jean Bart* would be sunk if she could not be towed to England. Demolitions of oil stocks and harbour facilities would be carried out and ships unable to put to sea would be destroyed (telegram No. 459 from Bordeaux).

The First Lord proposed to remain at Bordeaux for the time being. The Chief of Naval Staff was on his way back.

The Prime Minister said that he had been approached on the previous day by M. Monnet who had urged that another member of the Government should fly out to Bordeaux.

The Prime Minister had agreed that Lord Lloyd should go and the latter was on his way accompanied by M. Monnet, and a member of the French Embassy Staff. M. Corbin had strongly pressed this suggestion.

The Prime Minister said that he had that morning seen General Sikorski[2] who had just returned from France. The General had told him of his experiences during his 8–10 days on the French Front. The French troops had seemed paralysed in the face of the German onslaught, and had disappeared into houses before the advance of the German tanks. The German troops were not particularly formidable, but the French morale seemed to be low.

On the other hand the Polish troops had fought very well and had been highly complimented by General Weygand, who had said that with a few more Polish divisions he could have stemmed the tide.

Polish troops were now marching on Bordeaux and wished to be evacuated in order to continue fighting. If in any way possible, arrangements must be made to embark them. Polish pilots had been instructed to fly any machines they could get hold of to England, and they seemed to be experiencing no difficulty in flying off with French aircraft. There was a Brigade of Poles at Brest, but he was afraid that it was too late to get them away.

The Secretary of State for War said that arrangements had been put in hand at Bordeaux and Marseilles to take off any Czech troops who wished to

---

[1] Two hours before this War Cabinet, a telegram reached London from Lord Lothian in Washington, and was given special distribution to the War Cabinet, in which he wrote: 'It has been represented to me by a distinguished lawyer that if the French sign an armistice it is due to force majeure, and therefore from that moment we are entitled to capture or sink their fleet, as having yielded to enemy they are not in a position to act on their own free will and virtually become enemies of themselves' (*Premier papers, 3/476/10*).

[2] Wladyslaw Sikorski, 1881–1943. Organiser of pre-1914 Polish Military Organisation, 1909. Lieutenant-Colonel, Polish Legions, 1914–18. Commanded two Army corps in the defence of Poland against the Bolsheviks, 1920. Prime Minister of Poland, 1922–3. Minister of Military Affairs, 1923–5. Commander, Lwow Army Region (which he had defended against the Ukrainians in 1919), 1926–8. On half-pay, 1928–39. Recalled to service, 1939. Prime Minister of the Polish Government in exile (first in Paris, then in London) and Commander-in-Chief of the Polish Army, from the fall of Poland until his death in an air crash at Gibraltar on 4 July 1943.

leave, but he would much prefer to embark Polish troops. In view of the congestion at Bordeaux, however, embarkation might prove very difficult.

The Prime Minister suggested that the Foreign Office should send a telegram at once, drawing the attention of the French Government to their responsibility for the security of Allied troops who had been fighting on their soil. The honour of France was here at stake.

Steps must also be taken to ensure the safe return to this country of the Duke of Windsor.[1]

SWEDISH DESTROYERS[2]

The Lord President of the Council referred to the suggestion which had been made to the War Cabinet on the previous day, that steps should be taken to seize the four Swedish destroyers acquired from Italy which were on their way from Eire to the Faroe Islands. They could not reach Sweden, and it was thought that their intention was to proceed to Petsamo.

The Prime Minister said that it was of the highest importance to us to secure possession of these destroyers. Immediate steps should be taken to see that they did not slip through our fingers, and we could consider later what explanations we should offer.

The Prime Minister said that he had had a long talk that morning with the Commander-in-Chief, Home Forces. It was clear that our defences were getting stronger every day, and that the position was, on the whole, satisfactory.

The Prime Minister referred to the shipment of arms from the United States of America. It appeared that these arms had been unduly concentrated in a few ships.

It was explained that the loading had been carried out in accordance with instructions given in the United States, in some instances by the French. The attention of the Admiralty had been drawn to these cases, and arrangements were in hand to provide the necessary escort.

---

[1] Edward Albert Christian George Andrew Patrick David, 1894–1972. Entered the Royal Navy as a cadet, 1907. Prince of Wales, 1910–36. 2nd Lieutenant, Grenadier Guards, August 1914. Attached to Sir John French's staff, November 1914. Served in France and Italy, 1914–18. Major, 1918. Succeeded his father as King Edward VIII, January 1936. Abdicated, December 1936. Duke of Windsor, 1936. In 1937 he married Wallis Simpson, who became Duchess of Windsor. Resident in France, 1937–40. Governor–General and Commander-in-Chief, Bahamas, 1940–5. Returned to France in 1945, and lived there until his death.

[2] The four destroyers had been bought by Sweden from Italy earlier in 1940. Two had been built in 1926 and two in 1935. They were seized by the Royal Navy in Skaalefjord in the Faroe Islands on 22 June 1940, but released, and returned to Sweden on 10 July. From August 1940 they were employed by the Swedish Navy in neutrality guard operations.

The War Cabinet had before them a Memorandum by the Chiefs of Staff recommending the adoption of a policy of demilitarisation of the Channel Islands as soon as the aerodromes on them are no longer required.[1]

The Prime Minister said that it ought to be possible, by the use of our sea power, to prevent the invasion of the Islands by the enemy and that, if there was a chance of offering a successful resistance, we ought not to avoid giving him battle there. It was repugnant now to abandon British territory which had been in the possession of the Crown since the Norman Conquest.

Defence Committee: minutes
(*Cabinet papers, 70/1*)

19 June 1940   10 Downing Street
7 p.m.

The Meeting had before them a Joint Memorandum[2] by the Permanent Under-Secretary of State for War[3] and the Director-General of Army Requirements.[4] A copy of this Memorandum is appended to these Minutes.

The Prime Minister said that the scale of our effort had been defined as 55 Divisions, and he saw no reason why this programme should be reduced.

The Prime Minister said that he saw the matter as follows:–
(1) The highest priority should be assigned to everything that could be pulled forward in the next five months, namely, June–October, 1940.
(2) During the ensuing seven months every effort should be made to achieve highest production by the end of May, 1941.

---

[1] War Cabinet Paper No. 208 of 1940.

[2] Not printed; it concerned the problems that would be encountered in a 55-Division army, and proposed reducing the intended maximum strength to 36 Divisions.

[3] Percy James Grigg, 1890–1964. Educated at Bournemouth School and St John's College, Cambridge. Entered the Treasury, 1913. Served in the Royal Garrison Artillery, 1915–18. Principal Private Secretary to successive Chancellors of the Exchequer, 1921–30. Chairman, Board of Customs and Excise, 1930; Board of Inland Revenue, 1930–4. Knighted, 1932. Finance Member, Government of India, 1934–9. Elected to the Other Club, 1939. Permanent Under-Secretary of State for War, 1939–42. Secretary of State for War, 1942. Privy Councillor, 1942. National MP, East Cardiff, 1942–5. British Executive Director, International Bank for Reconstruction and Development, 1946–7. Subsequently Chairman of Bass, and a director of Imperial Tobacco, the Prudential Assurance Company and other companies.

[4] Robert John Sinclair, 1893–1979. On active service, 1914–15; served at Gallipoli (wounded, despatches). Deputy-Director of Munitions Inspection (under Churchill), 1917–18. MBE, 1919. Director of Imperial Tobacco, 1933–67 (Chairman, 1947–59). A member of the Prime Minister's Panel of Industrialists, January 1939. Director-General of Army Requirements, War Office, 1939–42. Member of the Supply Council, 1939–42. Member of the Army Council, 1940–2. Knighted, 1941. Chief Executive, Ministry of Production, 1943: Board of Trade, 1944–5. Created Baron, 1957. Member of the United Kingdom Permanent Security Commission, 1965–77. One of his two sons was killed in action in the Middle East in 1942.

(3) There remained the period from June, 1941, onwards. This was admittedly a long-term programme; but unless the fulfilment of this long-term programme impinged on the programme to be achieved by June, 1941, there was no reason why it should be interfered with.

At the end of the Meeting, reference was made to exchange of technical information with the United States of America.

The Prime Minister said that he had been considering this matter, but he would prefer that such exchange should be made as part of a general deal. He had no objection, however, to information being given on specific matters. For example, a sample 25-pdr gun and ammunition could be sent to the States.[1]

Winston S. Churchill to Desmond Morton
(*Churchill papers, 20/13*)

19 June 1940

I have always understood that we were working with 55 Divisions, though perhaps this could not be achieved by Z plus 24.

I see no reason whatever to narrow the scope to 36, and I do not understand where this figure originates. You should discuss this matter with Professor Lindemann, who has all the figures at his disposal. I have already ruled on priorities as follows: The next five months, including June, to be pressed forward at the expense, where necessary of anything that cannot mature by June 1941. The intervening period between November 1940 and June 1941 should not be cut, unless in exceptional cases.

General Dill to Winston S. Churchill
(*Churchill papers, 2/393*)

19 June 1940   War Office

My dear Prime Minister,

Thank you very much indeed for sending me a copy of *Arms & the Covenant*.[2] I am delighted to have it.

Your stupendous burden of today must to some small extent be lightened

---

[1] On 27 June 1940 Churchill wrote to Lord Beaverbrook about the exchange of technical and scientific information with the United States: 'I agree the situation has somewhat changed by the French collapse, and consequent exposure of many of our secrets.'

[2] *Arms and the Covenant*, a collection of Churchill's speeches on defence and foreign affairs made between 1932 and 1938, had been compiled by Randolph Churchill and published on 24 June 1938; 3,381 copies were sold. The book was reissued in June 1940 as a cheap 7s. 6d. edition, of which 1,382 were sold. A third edition was issued in 1947.

by the knowledge that your conscience is clear regarding the complete lack of preparedness of this country for war with Germany.

May I take this opportunity of saying how greatly I admire your courage and vitality in these dark days.

With my best wishes.

Yours very sincerely
J. G. Dill

War Cabinet: minutes
(*Cabinet papers, 65/7*)

20 June 1940 10 Downing Street
12 noon

The Prime Minister suggested that, as there seemed a serious risk that the French might scuttle a considerable part of their fleet instead of bringing it to British ports, they might be persuaded to make greater efforts to get the vessels away if the USA would make an offer to buy them. The money could be used for the maintenance of refugees or the rehabilitation of French territory. An immediate offer of this kind might do harm, as suggesting the assumption that the French were going to give up the struggle. But a telegram might be sent to our Ambassador at Washington putting the suggestion to him, asking him not to act on it immediately, but to be ready to put it to President Roosevelt if a suitable occasion should arise.

The Chief of the Imperial General Staff referred to a number of messages from the Governor and Commander-in-Chief at Gibraltar[1] urging the importance of sending British troops to stiffen French morale in North Africa. The Governor of Gibraltar had pointed out that, judging by the cold reception which the last party of British evacuees from Gibraltar had received at Casablanca, it was evident that anti-British propaganda was having some success.

The Prime Minister thought that it would be better to leave the question of sending troops to North Africa until we knew what the French Government were going to do.

---

[1] Clive Gerard Liddell, 1883–1956. Entered the Army, 1902. On active service, 1914–18 (despatches six times, DSO, CMG, CBE). Adjutant-General to the Forces, 1937–9. Knighted, 1939. Governor and Commander-in-Chief, Gibraltar, 1939–41. General, 1941. Inspector General for Training, 1941–2.

The Lord President had seen a preliminary draft of an *Aide-mémoire* from the Chiefs of Staff, which included the statement that there could be no security for Eire or the United Kingdom unless proper arrangements were made which included the presence of British or Dominion troops and Air forces in Eire, and His Majesty's Ships in Irish ports. It was further pointed out that the main, and perhaps the sole, obstacle to such collaboration was the partition question.

The Lord President said that, on the basis that help to Eire after invasion had taken place might well come too late, we were compelled to consider the question of entering the Irish ports by force.

The Prime Minister, while agreeing generally with the Lord President, said that we must avoid putting undue pressure on the loyal province of Ulster. He would not urge those who had worked self-government loyally within the Empire to join with those who wished to stay outside it. He was not convinced that the military situation was so serious as it had been represented. He was in favour of allowing the enemy to make the first move; if they succeeded in establishing themselves in Ireland our forces should then be ready to pounce upon them. The whole of Ireland, including Mr de Valera, would in those circumstances be on our side.

Winston S. Churchill: speech notes[1]
(*'Secret Session Speeches', pages 8–16*)

20 June 1940   House of Commons

Secret Session. House of Commons.

My reliance on it as an instrument for waging
                                                        war.

More active and direct part for its Members
L.D.V.

---

[1] No *Hansard* notes were taken during the Secret Session. Churchill made his speech from the notes that he had dictated to his secretary, Kathleen Hill, and to which he had added certain phrases in ink. The added phrases are printed here in bold lettering; phrases that Churchill decided to delete at the last moment are crossed through. Phrases that Churchill underlined are underlined here. This speech is set out here in the 'speech form' of Churchill's notes. In 1946 he published a facsimile of these notes in a small volume, *Secret Session Speeches*, edited by Charles Eade. No fuller version of this particular speech has survived. On 19 December 1945 Herbert Morrison, then Lord President of the Council and Leader of the House of Commons, moved the Resolution 'That no proceeding in this House during the last Parliament held in Secret Session be any longer secret.'

All this in accordance with past history.

This S.S.[1] a model of discretion.

My view always Govt. strengthened by S.S.

~~Quite ready to have others.~~

Agree with idea S.S. shd be quite a normal part
    of our procedure,
        not associated with any crisis.

Relief to be able to talk without enemy reading.

Quite ready to have other S.Ss.,
    especially on precise subjects.

But I hope not press Ministers engaged in
    conduct of war too hard.
                This week!

refreshed by
Mood of the House.
        Cool and robust.

Speeches most informative. **confidence & secrecy**
    Difficult to betray any secrets disclosed
                                today.

Moore-Brab (Wallasey)[2]   Praise.   **original**

He was sorry I mentioned expert advisers   **unexpected**
    favoured fighting on.   **wit**

Politicians and Generals, –

In last war and this.   **Generals cd do no wrong**
                                now – no right

Not put too much on the politicians:
    even they may err.

---

[1] Secret Session.

[2] John Theodore Cuthbert Moore-Brabazon, 1884–1964. Educated at Harrow and Trinity College, Cambridge. Pioneer motorist and aviator; holder of Pilot's Certificate No. 1. Won the *Daily Mail* £1,000 for flying a circular mile, 1909. Lieutenant-Colonel in charge of the Royal Flying Corps Photographic Section, 1914–18 (Military Cross, despatches thrice). Conservative MP for Chatham, 1918–29; for Wallasey, 1931–42. Chairman, Air Mails Committee, 1923. Elected to the Other Club, 1936. Parliamentary Private Secretary to the Lord Privy Seal, 1939–40. Minister of Transport, 1940–1. Minister of Aircraft Production, 1941–2. Created Baron, 1942. He published *The Brabazon Story* in 1956.

JUNE 1940

Noel Baker. Derby.[1]

Goering.[2] How do you class him?
    He was an airman turned politician.

I like him better as an airman.
    Not very much anyway.

> **ruthless in changing military & naval, air leaders**
>
> **young ones are you sure they are all so bad?**

Moore-Brab tells us of his wonderful brain,
    and the vast dictatorial powers and plans

Anyhow he did not produce the best pilots
    or the best machines,
        or perhaps, as we may see presently,
            the best Science.

M.B. said 250 nights in the year
    when no defence against night bombing.

~~I hope it is not so~~

This is one of those things you can only tell
        by finding out.

We have had a couple of nights of bombing,
    evidently much worse than that.

Folly underrate gravity attack impending.

But if 100 to 150 bombers employed
    entitled to remark:

    Not very cleverly employed.

Hardly paid expenses.

[1] Philip John Noel-Baker, 1889–1982. A Quaker; First Commandant, Friends Ambulance Unit, France, 1914–15 (subsequently on the Italian front). League of Nations Secretariat, 1919–22; active in publicising and supporting the work of the League of Nations. Labour MP, 1929–31 (for Coventry) and 1936–70 (for Derby). Parliamentary Secretary, Ministry of War Transport, 1942–5. Secretary of State for Air, 1946–7; for Commonwealth Relations, 1947–50. British delegate to the United Nations Preparatory Commission, 1945; member of the British Delegation to the UN General Assembly, 1946–7. Minister of Fuel and Power, 1950–1. Nobel Peace Prize, 1959. Created Baron, 1977.

[2] Hermann Goering, 1893–1946. Served as a Lieutenant in the German Infantry, 1914. Commander of the Richthofen fighter squadron, 1918. A follower of Hitler from 1923. Wounded during the unsuccessful Munich putsch of November 1923, after which he lived in Austria, Italy and Sweden. Air Adviser in Denmark and Sweden, 1924–8. Returned to Germany, and elected to the Reichstag, 1928. President of the Reichstag, 1932–3. Prime Minister of Prussia, 1933. Commander-in-Chief of the German Air Force, 1933–45. Air Chief Marshal, 1935. Commissioner for the Four-Year Plan, 1936. Field Marshal, 1938. President of the General Council for the War Economy, 1940. Sentenced to death at Nuremberg, October 1946, but committed suicide the night before his intended execution.

Learn to get used to it.

    Eels get used to skinning.

Steady continuous bombing,
    probably rising to great intensity
                      occasionally,
    must be regular condition of our life.

The utmost importance preserve morale of
                              people,
    especially in the night work of factories.

A test of our nerve against theirs.

Our bombing incomparably superior.
    More precise, and so far more effective.

Indiscriminate bombing v. selected targets.

Enemy have a great preponderance numbers.
    but their industry
        much more concentrated.

No one can tell result.

This supreme battle depends upon
    the courage of the ordinary man and woman.

Whatever happens, keep a stiff upper lip.

Duty of all M.Ps. to uphold confidence
    and speed production.

Bellenger's[1] speech.

Failure of French war conception.

The Maginot line. The defensive theory.
    Brilliant military achievement of Hitler.
        Triumph of the offensive spirit.

Triumph of long-prepared machinery.

Original strategic failure
    advance into Belgium

---

[1] Frederick John Bellenger, 1894–1968. On active service as a Lieutenant, Royal Artillery, 1914–18 (twice wounded). Labour MP from 1935 until his death. Captain, Royal Artillery, France, 1940. Financial Secretary, War Office, 1945–6. Privy Councillor, 1946. Secretary of State for War, 1946–7. No record was kept of Bellenger's speech in the Secret Session, nor of Moore-Brabazon's, other than Churchill's reference to them.

without making sure of the sub-
 Maginot line,

and without having a strategic reserve
 to plug a gap.

Fate of Northern Armies sealed when
 the G. armoured Divisions curled round
 their whole communication.
 Abbeville, Boulogne, Calais.

Not 2 days' food.
 only ammunition one battle.
Question of forming Torres-Vedras line.

Quite impossible with Air attack on ports.
 One in three supply ships sunk.

All experience shows danger of detachments
Situation looked terrible,
 especially when Belgium gave in.

Give all credit to all three Forces.

Army fought its way back;
 Navy showed its wonderful reserve power;
  Air Force rendered naval work possible.

B.E.F. a fine Army. Only 10 Divisions

Without proper armoured Divisions
 well-equipped,
  but placed in a hopeless
   strategic situation.

Much to be thankful for.

Melancholy position of the French Govt.

We have to make the best of them.

No criticisms, no recriminations.
 We cannot afford it, in public.

Pétain. Reynaud. Darlan.

5 precious days largely wasted.

Surprise if mercy shown by Germany.

The French Fleet.   The French Empire.
   Our policy.

Urge them to continue
   but all depends upon the battle of Britain

I have good confidence.

Some remarks about <u>Home Defence</u>.

Belisha[1] spoke of 'man the defences
   and resist the enemy.'

That will play its part;
   but essence of defence of Britain
      is to attack the landed enemy at once,

  leap at his throat
    and keep the grip until the life is out
                          of him.

We have a powerful Army
  growing in strength and equipment
                  every day.

Many very fine Divisions.
  ~~Mobile Brigades~~

Vigilant coast watch. Strong defence of
   ports and inlets.
Mobile Brigades acting on interior lines
    Good prospects of winning a victory
    radial lines
   Quantity not quality

If Hitler fails to invade
  or destroy Britain
     he has lost the war.

---

[1] Leslie Hore-Belisha, 1893–1957. His father, an Army officer, died when Hore-Belisha was nine months old. Known, on account of his Jewish origins, as 'Horeb Elisha'. Educated at Clifton and St John's College, Oxford. On active service in France, 1915–16, and at Salonica, 1916–18. President of the Oxford Union, 1919. Liberal MP for Plymouth Devonport, 1923–42 (National Liberal from 1931; Independent from 1942 to 1945). Parliamentary Secretary, Board of Trade, 1931–2. Financial Secretary, Treasurey, 1932–4. Minister of Transport, 1934–7 (with a seat in the Cabinet from October 1936). Privy Councillor, 1935. Secretary of State for War, 1937–40 (Member of the War Cabinet, 1939–40). Minister of National Insurance, !945. Created Baron, 1954.

June 1940

I do not consider only the severities
    of the winter in Europe.

I look to superiority in Air power
                      in the future.

Transatlantic reinforcements.

If get through next 3 months
    get through next 3 years.

It may well be our fine Armies
    have not said goodbye to the Continent
                              of Europe.

If enemy coastline extends from the Arctic
    to the Mediterranean

        and we retain sea-power
             and a growing Air power

        it is evident that Hitler
            master of a starving, agonized and
                surging Europe;

    will have his dangers as well as we.

But all depends upon winning this battle
    here in Britain, now this summer.

If we do, the prospects of the future
                        will expand,
  and we may look forward
    and make our plans for 1941 and 1942

    and that is what we are doing.

Attitude of United States.
    Nothing will stir them like fighting
                      in England.

No good suggesting **to them** we are down and out.

The heroic struggle of Britain
    best chance of bringing them in.

Anyhow they have promised fullest aid
    in materials, munitions.

A tribute to Roosevelt.

Knox[1] **& Stimson**[2]
All depends upon our resolute bearing
   and holding out until Election issues
      are settled there.

If we can do so, I cannot doubt
   a whole English-speaking world
      will be in line together

~~and with all the Continents except Europe~~
   and with the Oceans and with the Air
      and all the Continents except Europe
         (RUSSIA)

I do not see why we should not find our way
                      through
   this time, as we did last.

Question of Ireland.
   Greatly influenced by a great Army
      developing here.

Germans would fight in Ireland
   under great disadvantages.

Much rather they break Irish neutrality
      than we.

Lastly, say a word about ourselves.

How the new Govt. was formed.

Tell the story Chamberlain's actions.

Imperative there should be loyalty, union
   among men who have joined hands.

Otherwise no means of standing
   the shocks and strains which are coming.

---

[1] W. Frank Knox, 1874–1944. A Republican. Secretary for the Navy from July 1940 until his death in April 1944.

[2] Henry Lewis Stimson, 1867–1950. Born in New York City. Admitted to the Bar, 1891. Secretary of War, 1911–13 (under President Taft). Colonel, American Expeditionary Force, France, 1917–18. Governor-General of the Philippines, 1927–9 (under Coolidge). Secretary of State, 1929–32 (under Hoover). Member of Panel, Permanent Court of Arbitration, The Hague, 1938–48. Secretary of War (under Roosevelt), 1940–5. No other politician has served in the Cabinets of two Republican and two Democratic presidents.

> I have a right to depend loyalty
> to the administration
> and feel we have only one enemy to face,
> the foul foe who ~~menace~~ threatens
> our freedom and our life,
> and bars the upward march of man.

Winston S. Churchill
(*Churchill papers, 20/13*)

20 June 1940

Surely this is great nonsense?[1] Evacuating civilians from Iceland. Should not Mr Smith[2] be encouraged to make the Icelanders stand up to the trifling dangers they suffer. Anyhow they have a large island and plenty of places to run into.

Winston S. Churchill to Sir John Anderson
(*Churchill papers, 20/13*)

20 June 1940

I understand that it was settled last Saturday that your Department was to take on the executive control of smoke as a means of hiding factories and similar industrial targets.

I would be glad to know who you have put in charge of this work, which I regard as of the highest importance, and the progress which he has made.

John Colville: diary
(*Colville papers*)

20 June 1940

At about 11.30 p.m. Winston went back to No. 10 taking Alexander[3] and Duff Cooper with him: 'two dreadnoughts and a battleship', as he described the party on getting into the car.

---

[1] A telegram from the British Minister in Iceland, sent on 17 June 1940, advising the evacuation of civilians from the island.

[2] Charles Howard Smith, 1888–1942. Entered the Foreign Office, 1912. Assistant Under-Secretary of State, 1933–9. Minister at Copenhagen, October 1939 to April 1940. Minister at Reykjavik from 1940 until his death.

[3] A. V. Alexander, First Lord of the Admiralty.

JUNE 1940

R. V. Jones[1]: recollection
('Most Secret War', pages 101-2 and 108)

21 June 1940

I listened for a time while some of those around the table[2] made comments which suggested that they had not fully grasped the situation; only then did Churchill address a question to me on some point of detail. Instead of dealing with it, I said, 'Would it help, sir, if I told you the story right from the start?'

Churchill seemed somewhat taken aback, but after a moment's hesitation said, 'Well, yes it would!' And so I told him the story. The fact that my call to the Cabinet Room had been so sudden had given me no time to rehearse, or even to become nervous. The few minutes of desultory discussion that had ensued after my entry showed me that nobody else there knew as much about the matter as I did myself and, although I was not conscious of my calmness at the time, the very gravity of the situation somehow seemed to generate the steady nerve for which it called. Although I was only 28, and everyone else round the table much my senior in every conventional way, the threat of the beams was too serious for our response to be spoilt by any nervousness on my part.[3]

I told him that the first thing was to confirm their existence by discovering and flying along the beams for ourselves, and that we could develop a variety of countermeasures ranging from putting in a false cross-beam to make the Germans drop their bombs early, or using forms of jamming ranging from crude to subtle. Churchill added all his weight to these suggestions. In addition, he said that if the Germans were to fly along beams, this would be the ideal case for our sowing fields of aerial mines, which he had been pressing on the Air Ministry for some years, adding as he angrily banged the table, 'All I get from the Air Ministry is files, files, files!'[4]

[1] Reginald Victor Jones, 1911– . Scientific Officer, Air Ministry, 1936; seconded to Admiralty, 1938–9. Air Ministry, Air Staff, 1939. Assistant Director of Intelligence, 1941; Director, 1946. Director of Scientific Intelligence, Ministry of Defence, 1952–3. Professor of Natural Philosophy, University of Aberdeen, 1946–81. Chairman of the Air Defence Working Party, 1963–4. Author of *Most Secret War*(1978).

[2] Churchill, Lindemann and Beaverbrook were on one side of the table; on the other were Sir Archibald Sinclair, Sir Cyril Newall, Sir Hugh Dowding, Sir Charles Portal, Sir Philip Joubert de la Ferté, Professor Tizard and Robert Watson-Watt.

[3] Jones had identified a pattern of German radio beams emanating from Northern France (Dieppe and Cherbourg) whereby German bombers were being directed on to targets in Britain. The existence of these beams had been confirmed by Signals Intelligence intercepts, where the Germans referred to them as *Knickebein* (Crooked Leg).

[4] Aerial mines had long been one of Churchill's special projects, both during his years in opposition (when he was a member of the Air Defence Research Sub-Committee of the Committee of Imperial Defence) and at the Admiralty, where the mines had been given the code name 'Egglayer'.

As I was speaking at the Knickebein meeting, I could sense the impession that I was making on him. One day after the war, when I was sitting at his bedside, he told me about it: having surveyed our position in the early weeks of June 1940, he thought that we ought just to be able to hold the Luftwaffe by day. And then, when this young man came in and told him that they could still bomb as accurately by night, when our nightfighters would still be almost powerless, it was for him one of the blackest moments of the war. But as the young man went on the load was once again lifted because he said that there could be ways of countering the beams and so preventing our more important targets being destroyed.

Winston S. Churchill: recollection
(*'Their Finest Hour'*, *page 342*)

21 June 1940

Being master, and not having to argue too much, once I was convinced about the principles of this queer and deadly game I gave all the necessary orders that very day in June for the existence of the beam to be assumed, and for all counter-measures to receive absolute priority. The slightest reluctance or deviation in carrying out this policy was to be reported to me. With so much going on I did not trouble the Cabinet, or even the Chiefs of Staff. If I had encountered any serious obstruction I should of course have appealed and told a long story to these friendly tribunals. This however was not necessary, as in this limited and at that time almost occult circle obedience was forthcoming with alacrity, and on the fringes all obstructions could be swept away.

Defence Committee: minutes
(*Cabinet papers, 69/1*)

21 June 1940   Upper War Room
11 a.m.   Admiralty

French bases on the mainland of Africa were also considered.[1] Casablanca had only a poor harbour. Oran had an excellent harbour, and if it could be provided with the necessary anti-aircraft and fighter defences, would be sufficient for all purposes. British troops would have to be sent into North Africa to secure this base whether or not the French co-operated.

---

[1] In order to re-route Britain's Atlantic trade along more secure routes, various bases were under consideration by the Chiefs of Staff, including the Canaries (Spanish), and the Azores and the Cape Verde Islands (Portuguese). The Chiefs of Staff believed that the 'most valuable base' would be Grand Canary.

The Prime Minister emphasised the great importance of detailed plans being worked out to seize and hold any bases we might require. The commanders should be appointed immediately, so that they would be fully conversant with the plans from their very inception. Surprise and boldness of action were essential. The special training which the troops detailed would receive would be of great value whichever expedition was ultimately undertaken. No delay should be incurred in getting the troops trained and making arrangements for embarkation at short notice irrespective of a decision as to their destination.

The Chief of the Air Staff said that the Chiefs of Staff at their meeting on the previous day had reached the conclusion that first priority should be given to the requirements for dealing with a German invasion of Eire, which in their opinion was the most serious menace outside the United Kingdom.

The Prime Minister said that we must accept the prospect of the Germans being able to get into Eire before us, but as soon as this took place we must be ready to pounce upon them with strong forces from every quarter at once with the least possible delay. In view of Mr de Valera's intransigent attitude we should not accede to any requests from the Eire Government to be supplied with munitions which we wanted for our own use. We should continue our pressure upon him to allow us to send in troops before the Germans made a move. He agreed that the possibility of inducing Mr de Valera to accept a Brigade of the London Irish should be explored.

The Prime Minister urged that the commander of the forces which were to operate in Ireland should be appointed immediately, in order that he might become acquainted with the task he had to fulfil and the troops which he would have under his command. All arrangements should be brought to the highest state of readiness, so that immediate action could be taken when the German invasion took place.

War Cabinet: minutes
(*Cabinet papers, 65/7*)

21 June 1940   10 Downing Street
12 noon

The Prime Minister said that the recommendations of this Meeting had been brought to his notice on the previous evening, and, in consultation with the First Lord of the Admiralty, he had agreed that French shipping should be allowed to proceed to colonial ports outside the Mediterranean.

The proposal to allow French ships to proceed to the remaining unoccupied ports in Metropolitan France was, however, generally felt to stand on a different footing. These ports might at any moment be occupied by the enemy. Further, while it would be difficult to justify holding up ship-loads of food destined for districts crowded with refugees, there was no evidence that food cargoes were being held up. It was believed that most of the vessels were coal ships.

It was agreed that no definite answer could be given to the French Ambassador until he could indicate more precisely what ships he had in mind, what the cargoes were, and to which ports it was intended that they should sail.

In connection with the discussion on the preceding item, the Prime Minister said that he was perturbed as to the way in which the scheme for evacuating children overseas was developing. It was one thing to allow a limited number of children to be sent to North America; but a scheme for the evacuation of very large numbers of children stood on a different footing and was attended by grave difficulties.

The Secretary of State for Foreign Affairs drew the attention of the War Cabinet to the fact that the Duke of Windsor was reported to have arrived at Barcelona.

The Prime Minister suggested that His Majesty's Ambassador at Madrid[1] should be instructed to get into touch with the Duke, to offer him hospitality and assistance, and to ascertain his wishes.

The Prime Minister asked that the War Office should again consider raising a Foreign Legion. Many enemy aliens had a great hatred of the Nazi régime, and it was unjust to treat our friends as foes. Equipment might not be available for such a force immediately, but it could be found in due course. It would be as well to have these men under discipline in the meantime. Their services might be used in, for example, Iceland.

The Prime Minister thought that it would be undesirable to call up men at a more rapid rate than was proposed by the Secretary of State for War in his Memorandum on Man-Power in the Army.[2] He suggested that the Minister of Information should take action to explain to the public the undesirability of swamping the military machine.

---

[1] Sir Samuel Hoare.
[2] War Cabinet Paper No. 210 of 1940.

Winston S. Churchill to General Ismay
(*Churchill papers, 20/13*)

21 June 1940

I must return to the question of the foreign troops in this country, and particularly of a foreign legion. I see no question why enemy aliens, wishing to fight against Germany, should not be incorporated in a military body where the discipline is strict, where the penalties are severe, and where they can be under constant observation. It is easy to have a Vigilance Committee of their own people to vet and re-vet these men, who would, of course, be volunteers. We should aim at 5,000 to begin with. The model of the French Foreign Legion should be studied in respect of Officers.

We are also to have in this country a Polish Division, and Dutch, Belgian and Norwegian Brigades. A period of three months' training without arms can, if necessary, be imposed, during which time they may to a certain extent be used on fortifications.

Pray have this matter thoroughly explored, and I will see the General Staff upon it as soon as proposals have been framed.

WSC

Winston S. Churchill to General Ismay
(*Churchill papers, 20/13*)

21 June 1940

Let me have a further report about these guns.[1] How are we getting on with the ones we are making?

I understood that one 14-inch was available in a few weeks. Has the emplacement been begun, and where? Don't let this matter sleep. Our guns must fire as soon as theirs. Let me have a report each week, beginning Saturday, 22.

WSC

---

[1] The naval guns intended to be set up on the cliffs near Dover.

June 1940

Admiralty meeting: minutes[1]
(*Admiralty papers, 205/7*)

21 June 1940
Upper War Room
Admiralty

LOSS AND RECRUDESCENCE OF U-BOAT CAMPAIGN

A list of losses was handed to the Prime Minister which showed that on the assumption that losses during the month of June 1940 continue for the last part of the month as for the first three weeks, the losses during this month would be the heaviest since the war started.[2] The Prime Minister said that he had not realised that the figures of losses had increased to such an extent.

DESPATCH OF ARMOURED DIVISIONS OVERSEAS

The Prime Minister directed that a small committee should be appointed to discuss the best method of moving armoured divisions overseas in an offensive phase of the war.

TANKS

The Prime Minister said he had recently had discussions with the War Office and Ministry of Supply and considerable results had been achieved. He had arranged for as much steel as possible to be purchased at once from the USA. It was hoped that 500 of a new type of tank, 33 tons in weight, would be available in nine months time. These would have $3\frac{1}{2}''$ armour, a high velocity turret gun, and a mortar. It was hoped also that there would be 2,500 Infantry and Valentine tanks by the Spring. This should result in five armoured divisions being ready for operations in the Spring of 1941. It had been originally intended that there should be 36 Divisions 24 months after the war started, but it was hoped now to have these after 21 months, and thereafter to push ahead until there were 55 divisions.

HEAVY GUNS

The Prime Minister directed that a copy of the Army programme in respect of heavy guns, as approved during the present week, should be sent to the Controller.[3]

---

[1] Those present were Churchill, A. V. Alexander (First Lord), Admiral Pound (First Sea Lord), Admiral Phillips (Vice-Chief of the Naval Staff) and Admiral Fraser (Controller).

[2] Between 1 and 20 June, German submarines had sunk forty-two British merchant ships. In the next ten days they were to sink a further ten.

[3] Bruce Austin Fraser, 1888–1981. Third Sea Lord and Controller of the Navy, 1939–42. Knighted, 1941. Second-in-Command, Home Fleet, 1942. Commander-in-Chief, Home Fleet, 1943–4. Commander-in-Chief, Eastern Fleet, 1944. Commander-in-Chief, British Pacific Fleet, 1944–5. Admiral, 1944. Created Baron Fraser of North Cape, 1946. First Sea Lord and Chief of the Naval Staff, 1948–51.

OVERSEAS POSSESSIONS

The Prime Minister asked what methods were being taken to counter the E-Boat[1] menace. The First Sea Lord said that plans were going ahead. The German boats were known to have bad hulls, and gunfire with any size gun would do considerable damage. If hunting craft such as Corvettes or trawlers could keep their bows on to these E-Boats and use their guns, he believed that they would inflict very considerable damage.

SUPPLIES FROM AMERICA

VCNS stressed the necessity for the provision of flying boats from the USA, and the Prime Minister asked that this point, together with any others, should be submitted to him as soon as possible as he proposed to send a communication to President Roosevelt at a very early date.

War Cabinet: minutes
(*Cabinet papers, 65/7*)

22 June 1940
10 a.m.
10 Downing Street

The Foreign Secretary was called away for a few minutes in order to speak on the telephone to the Prime Minister, who was at Chequers. On returning the Foreign Secretary said that the Prime Minister was anxious to send a further message to the French Government reminding them that His Majesty's Government were entitled to be taken fully into their confidence at this critical juncture. His Majesty's Government had not released France from the solemn obligations which she had undertaken. It would not be consistent with French honour to permit their resources to be used against us by Germany.

War Cabinet: minutes
(*Cabinet papers, 65/7*)

22 June 1940
9.30 p.m.
10 Downing Street

In the course of the previous discussion the Prime Minister suggested that another broadcast should be made on behalf of the Government, as soon as possible, dealing with terms which Germany had imposed on France. These could be described as being of the most murderous character, such as would make the French Government the tool of the enemy in striking down the late

---

[1] Armed German merchant ships.

ally of France. It should be made clear that the Bordeaux Government, in accepting these terms, had negotiated under duress and had been deprived of all liberty.

The Prime Minister prepared a draft which was read to the War Cabinet, and agreed to the amendment.

War Cabinet: Confidential Annex
(*Cabinet papers, 65/13*)

22 June 1940
9.30 p.m.

A signal had just been received from the British Naval Liaison Officer at Bizerta stating that information had been received from a French source that a committee of four Admirals including Admiral Abrial and Admiral Estéva[1] had been appointed by Admiral Darlan to take charge in the event of his not being permitted to continue to function. These Admirals had been enjoined by Admiral Darlan to carry out his original orders that the Fleet was to fight to a finish; that the defended ports were to be held against the enemy; and that the fleet was not to accept any orders from a foreign Government.

The First Sea Lord expressed the view that this information was in accordance with Admiral Darlan's previous assurances and showed that he had taken all possible steps to safeguard our interests.

The Prime Minister said that in a matter so vital to the safety of the whole British Empire we could not afford to rely on the word of Admiral Darlan. However good his intentions might be, he might be forced to resign and his place taken by another Minister who would not shrink from betraying us. The most important thing to do was to make certain of the two modern battleships *Richelieu* and *Jean Bart*. If these fell into the hands of the Germans, they would have a very formidable line of battle when the *Bismarck* was commissioned next August. Against these fast and powerful ships we should only have *Nelson*, *Rodney* and the older battleships like *Valiant*. *Strasbourg* and *Dunkirk* would certainly be a great nuisance if they fell into the hands of the enemy, but it was the two modern ships which might alter the whole course of the war.

---

[1] Admiral Estéva. Admiral Commanding the French Naval Forces at Oran (Mers el-Kebir). Appointed Resident-General in Tunisia by the Vichy Government, September 1940. Protested to the Germans about the despatch of 100 German bombers to Tunisia at the time of the Anglo-American landings further west, November 1942. Ordered the neutrality of Tunisia four days later. When the Allies reached Tunis the Germans flew him, under arrest, to Paris (protesting 'I do not accept orders from Berlin, I am a French official'). In Paris he was confined to the Ritz Hotel for twelve days.

Oran was a strongly defended harbour and it would be very difficult to sink the two battle-cruisers behind such strong defences. It was most unfortunate that we had not been able to catch them at sea. He enquired what action could be taken to make sure of *Richelieu* and *Jean Bart*.

The First Sea Lord said that Dakar, where *Richelieu* would be, was a strongly defended harbour covered by 9.4" guns and with all its defences modernised. The defences of Casablanca were weak, but there would not be room to use torpedo planes against a ship in the harbour. Bombardment by ships' guns would be difficult, since the ship would be protected on one side by the mole.

The Prime Minister said that at all costs *Richelieu* and *Jean Bart*, particularly the former, must not be allowed to get loose. It would have been better if we could have put our own ships alongside them on the high seas in order to open a parley with their captains, but this must now be done when the ships were in harbour. A strong force must be sent and *Richelieu* should be dealt with first. If the captains refused to parley, they must be treated as traitors to the Allied cause. The ships might have to be bombed by aircraft from *Ark Royal* or they must be mined into their harbours and naval forces stationed outside to prevent the minefields being swept up. In no circumstances whatever must these ships be allowed to escape.

The Minister of Information suggested that an appeal should be sent immediately to Admiral Darlan asking him to send a personal order to the ships' captains to sail their ships to British ports.

The Prime Minister doubted whether this would be of much use. Admiral Darlan would never be allowed by the present French Government to despatch such a message.

The Secretary of State for Foreign Affairs thought that we should exhaust every means of persuasion before using force. He therefore suggested that at this stage we should concentrate all our efforts on making the parleys a success. We should select as our envoy for these a naval counterpart of General de Gaulle. Concurrently we should foster the sympathy for the Allies which we had reason to believe now existed in the French Navy by feeding it with the right kind of propaganda.

The Prime Minister agreed but stressed that we must at all times keep in view our main object, which was that in no circumstances must we run the mortal risk of allowing these ships to fall into the hands of the enemy. Rather than that, we should have to fight and sink them.

The Prime Minister considered that we should address our appeals both to Admiral Estéva and to the French Captains. At the same time we should take every step to keep a close watch on the French ships.

The War Cabinet agreed, with a view to the vital need for obtaining control of the French Navy, the following action should be taken immediately:–
(a) A further appeal should be addressed to Admiral Darlan in the form of personal messages from the First Lord and the First Sea Lord.
(The terms of these messages were settled in the course of the Meeting.)
(b) Simultaneously an appeal should be made to Admiral Estéva at Oran. It was proposed that this appeal should be made by the Vice Chief of Naval Staff, who should fly out at once. It was also proposed that Lord Lloyd should accompany the Vice Chief of Naval Staff on his visit to Oran. Besides providing valuable support in connection with the discussion in regard to the Fleet, Lord Lloyd might later proceed to Tunis, and possibly Syria, with a view to stiffening French resistance in these Colonies.

Winston S. Churchill to L. S. Amery
(*Churchill papers, 20/13*)

22 June 1940
Secret

1. Yours of June 21.[1] We have already very large masses of troops in India of whom no use is being made for the general purposes of the war. The assistance of India this time is incomparably below that of 1914–18. The fact that we are somewhat reducing the quality of our British garrisons, makes it all the more desirable that a larger number of Indian troops should also be employed outside India. It seems to be very likely that the war will spread to the Middle East, and the climate of Iraq, Palestine and Egypt are well suited to Indian troops. I recommend their organisation in Brigade Groups, each with a proportion of artillery on the new British model. I should hope that six or eight of these Groups could be ready this winter. They should include some Brigades of Gurkhas.

2. The process of liberating the Regular British battalions must continue, and I much regret that a fortnight's delay has become inevitable in returning you the Territorial battalions in exchange. You should reassure the Viceroy[2] that it is going forward.

[1] Not printed.
[2] Victor Alexander John Hope, 1887–1952. Earl of Hopetoun until 1908. Known as 'Hopey'. Educated at Eton. Succeeded his father as 2nd Marquess of Linlithgow, 1908. On active service, 1914–18 (despatches). Commanded the Border Armoured Car Company, 1920–6. Civil Lord of Admiralty, 1922–4. Deputy Chairman of the Conservative Party Organisation, 1924–6. Chairman, Royal Commission on Indian Agriculture, 1926–8. Chairman, Joint Select Committee on Indian Constitutional Reform, 1933–4. Chairman, Medical Research Council, 1934–6. Privy Councillor, 1935. Viceroy of India, 1936–43. Knight of the Garter, 1943. Chairman of the Midland Bank. His country seat was Hopetoun House, South Queensferry, two miles west of the Forth Bridge.

3. The idea of raising large numbers of troops in India, through the agency of a Congress campaign for recruiting, appears to me to require very careful consideration, first as to whether the new troops will be efficient or loyal. A strong infusion of British Officers who speak the language is necessary, if any good results are to be obtained from Indian battalions. I doubt whether these Officers can be found or spared at the present time.

We need munitions from India, and not that they should be eaten up by a swollen Indian force in India.

WSC

Winston S. Churchill to Anthony Eden
(*Churchill papers, 20/13*)

22 June 1940

LOCAL DEFENCE VOLUNTEERS

Could I have a brief statement of the LDV position, showing the progress achieved in raising and arming them, and whether they are designed for observation or for serious fighting. What is their relationship to the police, the Military Command and the Regional Commissioners? From whom do they receive their orders, and to whom do they report? It would be a great comfort if this could be compressed on to one or two sheets of paper.

Winston S. Churchill to Anthony Eden
(*Churchill papers, 20/13*)

22 June 1940

Attached is an exceedingly woolly and wide-gaping telegram[1] from the Governor of Gibraltar. I heard from you and CIGS that you were not particularly impressed with his capacity, and that you were sending a highly-competent second in Command to sustain him. But surely this is the time to get the real men in the real places, and not have inadequacy bolstered up.

---

[1] Not printed. The Governor was Lieutenant-General Sir Clive Liddell (see page 378, note 1).

Winston S. Churchill to Sir John Anderson
(*Churchill papers, 20/11*)

22 June 1940　　　　　　　　　　　　　　　　　　　10 Downing Street
Personal and Secret

My dear Home Secretary,

I have for some time felt that Sir Hugh Elles[1] is not the man he was, and is not adequate for his task. His foolish broadcast of a few days ago confirms me in this. I have known him slightly for a long time, and his recent appearances in Council have not inspired me with confidence. He was a great failure as MGO,[2] and I was surprised to see him emerge in work of such remarkable importance. I had in mind that perhaps Moore-Brabazon, whose exceptional abilities are unharnessed at the present time, would be a far more forceful and effective figure. I am not sure at present whether his appointment should be Ministerial or non-Ministerial, if the former, whether legislation would be necessary, if the latter, whether he would have to vacate his Seat. Legislation would certainly raise no difficulties in the House. I have not of course approached Moore-Brabazon in any way.[3]

I am sending you this letter through the Lord President, who is presiding over the Committee which deals with Security questions.

　　　　　　　　　　　　　　　　　　　　　　　Yours vy sincerely
　　　　　　　　　　　　　　　　　　　　　　　Winston S. Churchill

Winston S. Churchill to the Duke of Windsor
(*Churchill papers, 20/9*)

22 June 1940　　　　　　　　　　　　　　　　　　　10 Downing Street

We should like your Royal Highness to come home as soon as possible. Arrangements will be made through Ambassador, Madrid, with whom you should communicate.

---

[1] Regional Commissioner for South-East England.
[2] Master-General of Ordnance.
[3] Chamberlain, the Lord President, advised Churchill three days later that Elles should not be moved: 'I do not find that his work in the Ministry of Home Security is the subject of criticism among those who have regular opportunites to observe it. On the contrary, he is said to have done well' (*Churchill papers, 20/11*).

War Cabinet: minutes
(*Cabinet papers, 65/7*)

23 June 1940					10 Downing Street
10 a.m.

The Prime Minister explained the circumstances in which he had decided early that morning, in consultation with the Foreign Secretary, that it would be wiser to defer the visit of the Secretary of State for the Colonies and the Vice-Chief of Naval Staff[1] to Oran pending information as to how the situation was developing.

The Foreign Secretary said that he had contemplated that the Secretary of State for the Colonies and the Vice-Chief of Naval Staff would hearten and encourage the French authorities in North Africa which might be in a twilight of uncertainty.

The War Cabinet were informed that the French aircraft-carrier *Bearn* which was bringing 50 aircraft from the United States and the *Emile Bertin* carrying £60 millions of gold had both been ordered to proceed to Martinique.

The First Sea Lord said that HMS *Dunedin* had been ordered to proceed to Martinique to meet these two French ships. *Dunedin* could get there quicker than any other ship in the area, but the French ships would probably arrive there before her.

The Prime Minister emphasised the importance of getting possession of these two ships, and in particular the gold. We could announce that we should keep the gold in trust for the French Empire, but that they must fight for it. *Dunedin* should proceed at full speed, and her captain should make contact with the Governor of Martinique and try to get him on our side. She should not let the two French ships out of her sight. If they stayed in Martinique well and good, but if they moved she should shadow them so that they could be intercepted. They might slip across to Dakar, which was the nearest point on the other side of the Atlantic.[2]

Later in the Meeting the Prime Minister read a letter which he had just received from General de Gaulle outlining the proposals for setting up a Council of Liberation (Comité National Français). He asked the British Government to recognise this Council. General de Gaulle was a fine fighting soldier, with a good reputation and a strong personality, and might be the right man to set up such a Council. Before, however, approving the proposal

---

[1] Alfred Duff Cooper and Admiral Tom Phillips.
[2] The official naval historian writes (of the *Bearn* and *Emile Bertin*): 'By witholding oil supplies and the application of American pressure the ships were finally kept satisfactorily immobilised.' (Captain S.W. Roskill, *The War at Sea 1939–45*, volume 1, page 276). British naval action against the ships was not possible as Martinique was within the American Defence Zone.

and giving it official recognition, it would be as well to ascertain what French personalities were available to serve on the Council and which of them, in particular, General de Gaulle had in mind.

The War Cabinet –
(1) Agreed in principle that His Majesty's Government should make a declaration recognising a Council of Liberation.
(2) Invited the Secretary of State for Foreign Affairs to examine the proposals in General de Gaulle's letter, and the Memorandum enclosed therewith, as a matter of great urgency.

Sir Alexander Cadogan: diary
(*'The Diaries of Sir Alexander Cadogan'*)

23 June 1940

After Cabinet – about 12.15 – PM, Neville, H[1] and I saw de Gaulle and agreed on declaration he should broadcast tonight, with corresponding declaration by HMG, about formation of 'National Committee'.

Winston S. Churchill to the Admiralty
(*Churchill papers, 20/13*)

23 June 1940

I do not think it would be a good thing to keep *Hood* and *Ark Royal* lolling about in Gibraltar Harbour, where they might be bombed at any time from the shore.

Surely when they have fuelled they should go to sea and come back only unexpectedly and for short visits.

What is being done?

Winston S. Churchill to his Private Office
(*Premier papers, 3/24/2*)

23 June 1940

Ask for a return of officers under thirty who have good flying qualifications who are still to be retained at the Air Ministry.

[1] Lord Halifax.

Winston S. Churchill to Lieutenant-General William Dobbie[1]
(*Churchill papers, 20/14*)

23 June 1940

The Cabinet watch with constant attention the resolute defence which your garrison and the people of Malta are making of that famous fortress and Island. I have the conviction that you will make that defence glorious in British military history, and also in the history of Malta itself. You are well fitted to rouse and sustain the spirit of all in enduring severe and prolonged ordeals for a righteous cause.

Winston S. Churchill to General Ismay
(*Churchill papers, 20/13*)

24 June 1940

I understand that the trials were not entirely successful and the bomb failed to stick on tanks which were covered with dust and mud. No doubt some more sticky mixture can be devised and Major Jefferis[2] should persevere.

Any chortling by officials who have been slothful in pushing this bomb over the fact that at present it has not succeeded will be viewed with great disfavour by me.

WSC

Winston S. Churchill to General Ismay
(*Churchill papers, 20/13*)

24 June 1940

Has any news been received of the German prisoner pilots in France, whose return to this country was solemnly promised by Monsieur Reynaud?

[1] William George Sheddon Dobbie, 1879–1964. On active service in South Africa, 1899–1902, and on the Western Front, 1914–18 (despatches seven times, Mons ribbon, DSO). Inspector of the Royal Engineers, 1930–35. General Officer Commanding Malaya, 1935–9. Governor and Commander-in-Chief, Malta, 1940–2. Lieutenant-General, 1940. Knighted, 1941. One of his two sons was killed in action in the Second World War.

[2] Millis Rowland Jefferis, 1899–1963. Joined the Royal Engineers, 1918. Major, 1939; that November he constructed a small floating mine to be used in rivers (for Churchill's 'Royal Marine' operation, mining the Rhine). Commanded the 1st Field Squadron in Norway, April–May 1940, on sabotage duties (despatches). In charge of rocket and bomb experimentation, first under the War Office, then, from August 1940 until the end of the war, under Churchill's direct auspices. Responsible for, among other weapons, the Scatter Bomb, anti-tank mortars, the CLAM magnetic explosive device to attach to tanks and ships, and the PIAT hand-held anti-tank rocket. Promoted Lieutenant-Colonel, August 1940, at Churchill's specific request. Brigadier, 1942. CB, 1942. Knighted, 1945. Deputy Engineer-in-Chief, India, 1946. Engineer-in-Chief, Pakistan (with the rank of Major-General), 1947–50. Returned to England to become Chief Superintendent, Military Engineering experimental establishment, 1950–3.

Winston S. Churchill to General Ismay
(*Churchill papers, 20/13*)

24 June 1940

I think it is necessary to constitute more precisely the secretariat which will assist me in my duties as Minister of Defence. This should be under your general superintendence. You should continue as at present to represent me at the Chiefs of Staffs meetings, and generally to act as my Staff Officer through whom I am accustomed to pass the bulk of my communications to the three fighting departments. As a branch of the above, I think it necessary at this time to have a special liaison with Home Defence and ARP,[1] and this Captain Sandys, MP, can discharge; his duties being to act as liaison and to keep me informed of the position, and to draw my attention to points requiring urgent attention. No alteration will be made in the circulation of papers, but Captain Sandys should simultaneously have a copy of such papers as are necessary for the above work. If time permits he should mark salient points or make short précis. I must keep in touch with these two large spheres without being hampered by the need of reading long papers.

On a different footing stand the reports from the Ministry of Supply. I think of appointing Mr Oliver Lyttelton[2] as my liaison with this great sphere, about which I am very anxious at the present time. His duties will be to become acquainted with the whole field of munition production, including statistics furnished by Sir Walter Layton,[3] and the Statistical Branch under Professor Lindemann; to read all the papers which reach me on these subjects; in this case also without disturbing or delaying the normal flow. He should be in a position to keep me constantly and correctly informed verbally

---

[1] Air Raid Precautions.

[2] Oliver Lyttelton, 1893–1972. The son of Alfred Lyttelton, Balfour's Colonial Secretary. Educated at Eton and Trinity College, Cambridge. 2nd Lieutenant, Grenadier Guards, December 1914; on active service on the Western Front, 1915–18 (Military Cross, DSO, despatches three times, wounded April 1918). Entered merchant banking, 1919. Joined the British Metal Corporation, 1920; later Managing Director. Elected to the Other Club at the beginning of 1939. Appointed Controller of Non-Ferrous Metals, September 1939. President of the Board of Trade, and Privy Councillor, July 1940. Conservative MP for Aldershot, 1940–54. Minister of State, Middle East (based in Cairo), and Member of the War Cabinet, June 1941. Minister of Production, March 1942 to May 1945. Chairman of Associated Electrical Industries, 1945–51 and 1954–63. Secretary of State for Colonial Affairs, 1951–4. Created Viscount Chandos, 1954. Chairman of the National Theatre Board, 1962; Life President, 1971. Knight of the Garter, 1970. One of his three sons was killed on active service in Italy in 1944.

[3] Walter Thomas Layton, 1884–1966. Lecturer in economics, University College, London, 1909–12. Represented the Ministry of Munitions on the Milner Mission to Russia, 1917. Statistical Adviser, Ministry of Munitions, 1917–18. Unsuccessful Liberal candidate at the elections of 1922 and 1923. Editor of *The Economist*, 1922–38. Knighted, 1930. Chairman, News Chronicle Ltd, 1930–50; Vice-Chairman, Daily News Ltd, 1930–63. Head of the Joint War Production Staff, 1942–3. Director, Reuters Ltd, 1945–53. Created Baron, 1947. Vice-President, Consultative Assembly of the Council of Europe, 1949–57. Deputy Leader of the Liberal Party in the House of Lords, 1952–5. Director, Tyne-Tees Television Ltd, 1958–61.

or by short notes of the whole progress, and to draw my attention to financial, departmental or other obstructions. Mr Lyttelton's position will be similar to that of Major Morton, though he will not have a room at No. 10. Major Morton keeps me informed of enemy war production; relations with the Foreign Office and the French Committee; Secret Service and Fifth Column activities. He is not charged with Military matters.

Think the above over and talk to me about it before I cast it in a more formal form.

Winston S. Churchill to General Ismay
(*Churchill papers, 20/13*)

24 June 1940

It seems most important to establish now before the trap closes an organization for enabling French officers and soldiers, as well as important technicians, who wish to fight to make their way to various ports. A sort of 'underground railway' as in the olden days of slavery should be established and a Scarlet Pimpernel[1] organization set up. I have no doubt there will be a steady flow of determined men and we need all we can get for the defence of the French colonies. The Admiralty and Air Force must co-operate. General de Gaulle and his Committee would, of course, be the operative authority.

WSC

Winston S. Churchill to Lord Halifax
(*Churchill papers, 20/13*)

24 June 1940

You have no doubt been considering what should be our relations with the Bordeaux Government. We shall, of course, recognise the de Gaulle Committee as the responsible constitutional representative of France. We shall not be allowed, I presume, by the enemy in any case to have representatives in occupied French territory. Therefore, it would seem that we should not accept any representative of the Bordeaux Government here. It would be convenient if Corbin[2] joined de Gaulle. He looks terribly shattered, but he is a man of

---

[1] A character in the novel of the same name, published in 1905 by the Hungarian-born British novelist Baroness Orczy (1865–1947). The Scarlet Pimpernel in the story (named after a small flower with scarlet leaves) was an Englishman, Sir Percy Blakeney, whose mission was smuggling French aristocrats out of France at the time of the French Revolution. The Baroness published two sequels, *The Elusive Pimpernel* (1908) and *The Way of the Scarlet Pimpernel* (1933).

[2] The French Ambassador in London since 1933.

high ability. As soon as a representative Cabinet has been formed by the de Gaulle Committee we should, I suppose, accredit an official diplomatic representative to it. Meanwhile, I daresay the group working under the superintendence of Sir Alexander Cadogan, including Sir Robert Vansittart and General Spears, would seem to offer a good liaison.

We should try to get the United States to recognise the French Liberation Government and to accredit an American Ambassador to it. Whether this would be compatible with leaving an American representative with the French Government in France is doubtful, but there would be advantages in America having an official agent in France.

It seems most important that the United States should withdraw countenance from the caitiff Government, because that will determine the destination of the French gold deposited in the United States. At the very least this gold should be frozen, so that the Germans cannot get it, but best of all would be for it to be put at the disposal of the new French Government.

I hope you will let me know your views on these points, on which my knowledge at present is rather vague.

WSC

War Cabinet: minutes
(*Cabinet papers, 65/7*)

24 June 1940
12 noon

10 Downing Street

The Prime Minister read a message from M. Reynaud which he had just received through the French Ambassador. M. Reynaud pleaded that there should be no recriminations against the present French Government, and attempted to argue that, notwithstanding the terms of the armistice, the British Government would be safeguarded against the enemy obtaining possession of the French Fleet.

It was clear from this message that M. Reynaud could be no more relied on than any of the other members of the Bordeaux Government. This Government had broken their solemn treaty obligations with us and were now completely under the thumb of Germany. They would allow all their resources to fall into the hands of the enemy and be used against their previous Allies. There was grave danger that the rot would spread from the top through the Fleet, the Army and the Air Force, and all the French Colonies. The Germans would put every form of pressure upon the Government to act to our detriment. They would inevitably be drawn more and more into making common cause with Germany, and we must expect that soon we should be the object of the deepest hatred of France. So long as the position of the French warships was unsecured, they would be used as a blackmailing threat against us. We must at all costs ensure that these ships either came under our control or were put out of the way for good.

In the near future we should have to solve the problem of our future relations with the present French Government. If it was to be located in an enclave surrounded on all sides by enemy-occupied territory, we could not maintain an Ambassador with it, since we should have no means of communicating with him. In such circumstances, it was difficult to see how we could accept a French Ambassador in London. Our relations might well approach very closely to those of two nations at war with each other.

The Secretary of State for Foreign Affairs said that the French Ambassador had expressed to him on the previous day the grave concern which he and M. Léger[1] felt over our action in supporting General de Gaulle. He was most anxious to do everything possible to keep French resistance alive, but insisted that we were not going the right way about it. He had asked that we should not allow General de Gaulle to make his broadcast on the previous night.

The position of M. Corbin was certainly a very difficult one, though it was disturbing to find that he was in opposition to General de Gaulle, who had mentioned him as the first of his backers. The problem of our relations with the Bordeaux Government was most difficult.

While he[2] agreed generally with the views expressed by the Prime Minister, he thought that it might be desirable that we should go rather slow for the present in withdrawing recognition from the Pétain Government. To do so would give food for enemy propaganda that we were treating France as an enemy, and might extinguish the will to resist, in co-operation with us, which existed among large numbers of French people.

The Prime Minister said that he would send a reply to M. Reynaud setting out the position as he saw it. He would make it clear that no trust could be put in the German word, and that there was no limit to the pressure which Germany would put on France. It was not a question of recrimination, but of things which were to us matters of life and death.

The Prime Minister then read out a telegram which had been sent by

---

[1] Alexis Saint-Léger Léger, 1887–1975. French writer (as St Jean Perse) and diplomat. Joined the French Foreign Service, 1914. Secretary-General, Ministry of Foreign Affairs, Paris, 1933–40. Left France for the United States, 1940. Nobel Prize for Literature, 1960.

[2] The Foreign Secretary, Lord Halifax.

General Weygand to General Lelong[1] in London instructing him to arrange for the French troops now in this country to be sent to Casablanca.

It was pointed out that these consisted of two battalions of the Foreign Legion and two of Chasseurs Alpins. It might very well turn out to be best that these men should be given the option of returning to France if they wished, or continuing the fight with us, but it was not possible or necessary to reach an immediate decision. It was easy to find excuses, e.g., lack of transport facilities.

The Minister of Information said that General de Gaulle's broadcast had now been given, and there was nothing more to be done on the matter for the moment. It had been made clear that we recognised him, not as head of an independent Government, but as the head of a Committee which had been established to facilitate the co-operation of French elements who were determined to continue to fight the common enemy.

Winston S. Churchill to Lord Halifax
(*Premier papers, 3/457*)

24 June 1940

It does not seem to be necessary to address the President again upon the subject of destroyers to-day or to-morrow. Evidently he will be influenced by what happened to the French Fleet, about which I am hopeful. I am doubtful about opening Staff talks at the present time. I think they would turn almost entirely from the American side upon the transfer of the British Fleet to trans-Atlantic bases. Any discussion of this is bound to weaken confidence here at the moment when all must brace themselves for the supreme struggle. I will send the President another personal telegram about destroyers and flying boats a little later on.

WSC

[1] Albert Lelong, 1880–1954. Entered the French Army in 1902. Attached to the Russian Army (in Russian Poland), 1914. Head of the French Military Mission in Russia, 1917–18. French Military Attaché in London, 1936, and 1939–40.

War Cabinet: minutes
(*Cabinet papers, 65/7*)

24 June 1940
6 p.m.

After a short discussion, the War Cabinet agreed as follows:–
(1) French shipping should not be allowed to sail from any British port.
(2) All French ships on the high seas should be diverted into British ports.
(3) Discretion should be given to the Naval authorities to allow French ships to sail in exceptional cases, provided that the Commanders of HM Ships were satisfied that the vessels were in a position to complete their voyage in safety; for example, shipping might be allowed to proceed to Indo-China, where the loyalty of the local Government to the Allied cause was above suspicion.
(4) Ships of any flag should be stopped from proceeding to German-occupied ports in France.
(5) The expedition to Le Verdon to cut out merchant vessels should proceed, subject to the proviso that French ships should not be taken if within the three-mile limit. There was, of course, no objection to such vessels being seized if outside the three-mile limit.

The Prime Minister said that he had received a cordial telegram from Mr Mackenzie King, referring among other matters, to the possibility that the British Fleet might be sent to North America if the situation deteriorated.

The Prime Minister read his draft reply, in which he expressed his confidence as to the final outcome of the war and that there was no reason to fear that the Royal Navy would have to be transferred to American waters.

The War Cabinet invited the Prime Minister to telegraph to Mr Mackenzie King on the lines suggested.

War Cabinet: Confidential Annex
(*Cabinet papers, 65/13*)

24 June 1940
6 p.m.

The Prime Minister said that he had just had some discussion with those who had been closely connected recently with General de Gaulle, including Sir R. Vansittart and General Spears. It had been suggested that the British declaration, following on General de Gaulle's broadcast, had gone too far, in that it implied an intention to sever relations with the Bordeaux Government.

The declaration had not, however, gone as far as this. But in any event those present at the discussion had agreed that we could not draw back. The waverers would be influenced only by strong action on our part. If we hesitated, they would give way all along the line. If they had no stomach for continuing, they would find plenty of other pretexts for withdrawing. In these circumstances, it would be best to continue to express our sympathy and to avoid recriminations, but to act solely in accordance with the dictates of our own safety.

He (the Prime Minister) agreed with this line, which he proposed to take in a statement to be made in Parliament. We could not be expected to release ships, aircraft and gold, all of which would be afterwards turned against us by the enemy.

Winston S. Churchill to William Mackenzie King
(*Premier papers, 4/43B/1*)

24 June 1940 10 Downing Street
Personal & Private

Many thanks for your message which I have studied attentively. If you will read again my telegram of June 5, you will see that there is no question of trying to make a bargain with the United States about their entry into the war and our despatch of the Fleet across the Atlantic should the Mother Country be defeated. On the other hand I doubt very much the wisdom of dwelling upon the last contingency at the present time. I have good confidence in our ability to defend this Island and I see no reason to make [the slightest][1] preparation for or give any countenance to the transfer of the British Fleet. I shall myself never enter into any peace negotiations with Hitler but obviously I cannot bind a future Government which if we were deserted by the United States and beaten down here might very easily be a kind of Quisling affair ready to accept German overlordship and protection. It would be a help if you would impress this danger upon the President as I have done in my telegrams to him.

All good wishes and we are very glad your grand Canadian division is with us in our fight for Britain.

WSC

---

[1] Churchill deleted these words before the telegram was sent.

410   JUNE 1940

War Cabinet: minutes
(*Cabinet papers, 65/7*)

24 June 1940   10 Downing Street
10.30 p.m.

The Prime Minister read a telegram that had just been received from Casablanca to the effect that General Noguès[1] had been summoned to Bordeaux. It was not stated whether he was complying with these instructions.

The Prime Minister said that he would gladly accept the offer made by the Minister of Information to fly out at once to North Africa. It was most important that a British Minister should see M. Reynaud, and if possible General Noguès, at the earliest possible moment.

War Cabinet: Confidential Annex
(*Cabinet papers, 65/13*)

24 June 1940   10 Downing Street
10.30 p.m.

The Prime Minister said that the ships that mattered most were the *Jean Bart* and *Richelieu* which were at present unarmed and should prove easy to secure once they left the shelter of the French ports. An operation to destroy the Force de Rade[2] would undoubtedly prove very costly and might not be successful.

The Minister of Information drew attention to the message reported to have been received by Sir Dudley North[3] to the effect that Admiral Darlan had given explicit assurances that in no circumstances would the French Government hand over their Fleet intact. It was pointed out that this was

[1] Auguste Noguès. Commander-in-Chief of the French Forces in North Africa and Resident-General, Morocco. On 19 June 1940 de Gaulle had telegraphed to him that he would be ready to serve under him if he would reject the armistice. On 25 June Noguès telegraphed to the Government at Bordeaux that he was ready to continue the war. Two days later he telegraphed again, giving his support to the armistice and to Pétain, who retained him in his North African command.
[2] A fast squadron, used principally for commerce raiding.
[3] Dudley Burton Napier North, 1881–1961. Entered the Royal Navy as a Cadet, 1896. Commanded a battle cruiser at the battles of Heligoland (1914), Dogger Bank (1915) and Jutland (1916). CMG, 1919. Knighted, 1937. Rear-Admiral commanding His Majesty's Yachts, 1934–9. Flag Admiral Commanding North Atlantic Station (based at Gibraltar), 1939–40. Relieved of his command, September 1940, for having allowed six French warships to pass through the Gibraltar Strait. Placed on the retired list, having been refused a court martial or court of enquiry (this stain on his reputation was removed by Harold Macmillan in 1957 when he stated in the House of Commons: 'Admiral North cannot be accused of any dereliction of duty'). From 1942 to 1945 he held the minor post of Flag Officer in charge of Great Yarmouth.

tantamount to an admission that the French Government had decided to break the terms of the Armistice as soon as they had signed them. Admiral Darlan's dilemma was that he had either to break faith with us or to expose himself to the charge that he had deliberately entered into an engagement which he had no intention of fulfilling. This, it was pointed out, was what the German Government had done on the conclusion of the Armistice in 1918.

The Prime Minister said that too much weight could not be attached to these private messages. The situation had to be faced in the light of public documents and in view of the terms of the Armistice to which the Bordeaux Government had agreed. The covert suggestion that the French authorities might scuttle their ships could not be relied on. It must be remembered that the protection given by the Armistice did not necessarily apply to the peace terms, although it might be expected that the peace terms would be framed on the basis of the Armistice. Once the German occupation of French territory was complete, and the French Government were entirely at their mercy, there was nothing to prevent Germany from imposing peace terms more onerous than those to which the French had agreed for the purpose of the Armistice.

Duke of Windsor to Winston S. Churchill
(Churchill papers, 20/9)

24 June 1940   Madrid
Personal

Your message and facilities for returning greatly appreciated but I ask you to consider the following seriously.

My visits to England since the war have proved my presence there is an embarrassment to all concerned, myself included, and I cannot see how any post offered me there, even at this time, can alter this situation.

I therefore suggest that as I am anxious to continue to serve the Empire, some useful employment, with more official backing than I have hitherto received, be found for me elsewhere.

Sir Samuel Hoare to Winston S. Churchill
(Churchill papers, 20/9)

24 June 1940   Madrid

Duke of Windsor is most anxious to have reply to his personal wire before leaving here.

He does not want to appear to be returning as a refugee with nothing to do. I hope you can help him with a friendly answer as soon as possible.

I have told him that if he fails to return to England in a few days, all sorts of mischievous rumours will circulate about him.¹

He is ready to leave Madrid provided his stay in Lisbon does not overlap with the Duke of Kent's.²

He would like an aeroplane at Lisbon on Tuesday 2nd July.

Winston S. Churchill to the Duke of Windsor
(*Churchill papers, 20/9*)

25 June 1940

It will be better for Your Royal Highness to come to England as arranged, when everything can be considered.

Winston S. Churchill to General Wavell
(*Churchill papers, 20/14*)

25 June 1940

Cabinet has been gratified by the numerous minor successes gained by your forces over the Italians and their levies in these early days of war with a boastful enemy.³

Winston S. Churchill: speech
(*Hansard*)

25 June 1940   House of Commons
3 p.m.

WAR SITUATION

The Prime Minister (Mr Churchill): The House will feel profound sorrow at the fate of the great French nation and people, to whom we have been joined so long in war and peace, and whom we have regarded as trustees with ourselves for the progress of a liberal, cultured and tolerant civilisation in

¹ Since the Duke of Windsor's departure from Paris to Madrid, it was rumoured that he was willing to make himself available, in the event of a British defeat, to return to Britain and resume his kingship, at the head of a government acceptable to Germany.

² George Edward Alexander Edmund, fourth son of King George V and Queen Mary. Born in 1902. Created Duke of Kent, 1934. Served in the Intelligence Divison of the Admiralty, 1939–40; with Training Command, RAF, 1940–2. Killed in an air accident while on a training flight in Scotland, 25 August 1942 (less than two months after the birth of his second son, Prince Michael).

³ From its bases in Egypt, Wavell's army was in action along the Libyan border. On 6 July 1940 British carrier-based aircraft attacked Italian naval targets in Tobruk. Following Vichy control of Tunisia, however, there could be no French advance from the west, and Wavell's force of 36,000 men faced 215,000 Italians without a French counterweight. In September Wavell was forced to fall back fifty miles inside Egypt.

Europe. There is no use or advantage in wasting strength and time upon hard words and reproaches. We hope that life and power will be given to us to rescue France from the ruin and bondage into which she has been cast by the might and fury of the enemy – [An Hon. Member: 'And by the politicians'] – and from other causes. We hope, however, that the French Empire, stretching all over the world, and still protected by sea power, will continue the struggle at the side of its Allies, that it may become the seat of a government which will strive steadfastly for victory, and will organise armies of liberation. These are matters which Frenchmen alone can decide. We find it difficult to believe that the destiny of France and the spirit of France will find no other expression than in the melancholy decisions which have been taken by the Government at Bordeaux. We shall certainly aid, to the best of our ability and resources, any movement or any action by Frenchmen outside the power of the enemy, to work for the defeat of Nazi German barbarism and for the freedom and restoration of France.

What our relations will be with the Bordeaux Government, I cannot tell. They have delivered themselves over to the enemy and lie wholly in his power. He may do much by blandishments or by severities, by propaganda, and by the choosing of pro-German Ministers to make our relations difficult. We do not know whether we shall be allowed to have any British representative in the restricted region called 'unoccupied France,' because that is entirely surrounded by and under the control of the enemy; but, relying upon the true genius of the French people, and their judgment upon what has happened to them when they are allowed to know the facts, we shall endeavour to keep such contacts as are possible through the bars of their prison. Meanwhile we must look to our own salvation and effectual defence, upon which not only British but French, European, and world-wide fortunes depend. The safety of Great Britain and the British Empire is powerfully, though not decisively, affected by what happens to the French Fleet.

When it became clear that the defeat and subjugation of France was imminent and that her fine Army, on which so many hopes were set, was reeling under the German flail, M. Reynaud, the courageous Prime Minister, asked me to come to Tours, which I did on 13th June, accompanied by the Foreign Secretary and the Minister for Aircraft Production, Lord Beaverbrook. I see that some accounts have been given of these conversations by the Bordeaux Government which do not at all correspond with the facts. We have, of course, a record kept by one of the Cabinet secretaries who came with us, and I do not propose to go into this now at any length. M. Reynaud, after dwelling on the conditions at the front and the state of the French Army, with which I was well acquainted, asked me whether Great Britain would release France from her obligations not to negotiate for an Armistice or peace without the consent of her British Ally. Although I knew how great French sufferings were, and that we had not so far endured equal trials or made an equal contribution in the field, I felt bound to say that I could not give consent. I said that there would be no use in adding mutual reproaches to the other miseries we might have to bear, but I could not give consent. We agreed that a further appeal should be made by M. Reynaud to the United States and that if the reply was not sufficient to enable M. Reynaud to go on fighting – and he, after all, was the fighting spirit – then we should meet again and take a decision in the light of the new factors.

On the 16th I received a message from M. Reynaud, who had then moved to Bordeaux, to say that the American response was not satisfactory, and requesting the formal release of France from her obligations under the Anglo-French Agreement. The Cabinet was immediately convened, and we sent a message, of which I do not give the exact text, but I give the general substance. Separate negotiations, whether for Armistice or peace, depend upon an agreement made with the French Republic and not with any particular French administration or statesman. They, therefore, involve the honour of France. However, in view of all they had suffered, and of the forces evidently working upon them, and provided that the French Fleet is despatched to British ports and remains there while the negotiations are conducted, His Majesty's Government will give their consent to the French Government asking what terms of armistice would be open to them. It was also made clear that His Majesty's Government were resolved to continue the war, altogether apart from French aid, and dissociated themselves from such inquiries about an Armistice.

The same evening, the 16th, when I was preparing, at M. Reynaud's invitation, to go to see him, and I was in fact in the train, I received news that he had been overthrown and that a new Government under Marshal Pétain had been formed, which Government had been formed for the prime purpose of seeking an Armistice with Germany. In these circumstances, we naturally did everything in our power to secure proper arrangements for the disposition of the French Fleet. We reminded the new Government that the condition indispensable to their release had not been complied with, the condition being that it should be sent to a British port. There was plenty of time to do it, and it would have made no difference to the negotiations: the terms could hardly have been more severe than they were. In order to reinforce the earnestness with which we held our views, we sent the First Sea Lord and the First Lord as well as Lord Lloyd to establish what contacts were possible with the new Ministers. Everything was, of course, fusing into collapse at that time, but many solemn assurances were given that the Fleet would never be allowed to fall into German hands. It was, therefore, 'with grief and amazement' – to quote the words of the Government statement which we issued on Sunday – that I read Article 8 of the Armistice terms.

This Article, to which the French Government have subscribed, says that the French Fleet, excepting that part left free for the safeguarding of French interests in the Colonial Empire, shall be collected in ports to be specified and there demobilised and disarmed under German or Italian control. From this text it is clear that the French war vessels under this Armistice pass into German and Italian control while fully armed. We note, of course, in the same Article the solemn declaration of the German Government that they have no intention of using them for their own purposes during the war. What is the value of that? Ask half a dozen countries what is the value of such a solemn assurance. Furthermore, the same Article 8 of the Armistice excepts from the operation of such assurances and solemn declarations those units necessary for coast surveillance and mine-sweeping. Under this provision it would be possible for the German Government to reserve, ostensibly for coast surveillance, any existing units of the French Fleet. Finally, the Armistice can at any time be voided on any pretext of non-observance, and the terms of Armistice explicitly provide for further German claims when any peace between Germany and France comes to be signed. Such, in very brief epitome, are the salient points in this lamentable and also memorable episode, of which, no doubt, a much fuller account will be given by history.

The House would naturally not expect me to say anything about the future. The situation at the present time is so uncertain and obscure that it would be contrary to the public interest for me to attempt to pronounce or speculate upon it, but I may well have more to say should the House permit me to make a further statement next week. In the meantime, I hope that the House will continue to extend their full confidence to His Majesty's Government and will believe that neither patience nor resolution will be lacking in the measures they may think it right to take for the safety of the Empire.

Mr Hore-Belisha: Has not the statement to which the House has just listened shown the absolute necessity in these times of carrying Parliament with us at every stage? Is it not inconceivable that this great surrender could have been made had the French Parliament been in session and public opinion, as expressed through the Press, not been subjected to a rigorous censorship? Will my right hon. Friend assure us, as I am sure he has this matter in mind, that in this country Parliament and a free Press will be maintained, so that the Government may not be cut off from the stimulus and inspiration of these patriotic elements in the country?

Mr Churchill: It was certainly not the fault of the French Parliament—

Mr Hore-Belisha: I agree.

Mr Churchill: – and it was certainly not the fault of the French Press, that they were not able to comment on these matters. They were driven, pell-mell, from their seat by the rapid advance of the enemy. I trust that the measures which we shall take will prevent any similar experiences overtaking my right hon. Friend or the British Parliament. Arrangements are being made – which I cannot conceive will be necessary, but are very carefully worked out – to enable Parliament to continue to be the guide, director and support of His Majesty's Government, and for the Press also to fulfil its function in all the grave vicissitudes which may lie before us.

Mr Maxton: The Prime Minister indicated that this was the only statement that we were to have on this particular happening until the historians came along. (Hon. Members: 'Next week.') Is the Prime Minister able, at this moment, to explain more fully what he dealt with only in a word, namely, how the Reynaud Cabinet was removed and from where the Pétain Cabinet derived its authority?

Mr Churchill: I could not explain that, and certainly not in a word. It is a very difficult matter to understand the politics of another country. It is sometimes even very hard to understand the politics of one's own country.

Mr Stokes[1]: The Prime Minister has told us on two occasions that it was due to lack of appreciation of the position by the French High Command that the British Expeditionary Force and the rest of the French Northern Armies were not withdrawn after the break-through at Sedan. Will the Prime Minister tell us whether General Gamelin was in favour of their withdrawal, or in favour of their maintenance in Northern France?

Mr Churchill: I do not think I could attempt to disentangle the relative responsibilities of the French High Command.

Sir Percy Harris: Can the Prime Minister give an assurance that, at an early date, there will be an opportunity for a full, free and frank discussion of the situation?

Mr Churchill: I am very much in favour of such a discussion. I hope it will be possible.

Mr Gallacher[2]: Is the Prime Minister aware of the fact that the events in France have given rise in this country to the most terrific demand for a further re-organisation of the Government, in order to bring about a real people's Government, and will he take any notice of that terrific feeling which exists in the country?

Mr Churchill: Our relations with Russia are in so agreeable a condition that I do not permit myself to make the obvious retort.

---

[1] Richard Rapier Stokes, 1897–1957. On active service in the Royal Artillery, 1915–18 (Military Cross and bar). Unsuccessful Labour candidate, 1935. Labour MP from 1938 until his death. Minister of Works, 1950–1; Minister of Materials, 1951. Privy Councillor, 1950.

[2] William Gallacher, 1881–1965. Began work as a grocer's delivery boy at the age of twelve. Chairman, Clyde Workers' Committee, 1914–18. Imprisoned four times for political activities, 1917, 1918, 1921 and 1925. Attended the 2nd Congress of the Communist International, Moscow, 1920 (where he met Lenin). Member of the Executive Committee of the Communist International, 1924, and again in 1935. Communist MP, 1935–50 (the only Communist MP 1935–45, then one of two). President of the Communist Party, 1953–63.

Winston S. Churchill to Marshal Stalin[1]
(*Churchill papers, 20/14*)

25 June 1940

At this time when the face of Europe is changing hourly, I should like to take the opportunity of your receiving His Majesty's new Ambassador[2] to ask the latter to convey to you a message from myself.

Geographically our two countries lie at the opposite extremities of Europe, and from the point of view of systems of government it may be said that they stand for widely differing systems of political thought. But I trust that these facts need not prevent the relations between our two countries in the international sphere from being harmonious and mutually beneficial.

In the past – indeed in the recent past – our relations have, it must be acknowledged, been hampered by mutual suspicions; and last August the Soviet Government decided that the interests of the Soviet Union required that they should break off negotiations with us and enter into a close relation with Germany. Thus Germany became your friend almost at the same moment as she became our enemy.

But since then a new factor has arisen which I venture to think makes it desirable that both our countries should re-establish our previous contact, so that if necessary we may be able to consult together as regards those affairs in Europe which must necessarily interest us both. At the present moment the problem before all Europe – our two countries included – is how the States and peoples of Europe are going to react towards the prospect of Germany establishing a hegemony over the Continent.

The fact that both our countries lie not in Europe but on her extremities puts them in a special position. We are better enabled than others less fortunately placed to resist Germany's hegemony, and as you know the British Government certainly intend to use their geographical position and their great resources to this end.

---

[1] Josef Vissarionovich Djugashvili, 1879–1953. Born in Georgia. A Bolshevik revolutionary, he took the name Stalin (man of steel). In exile in the Siberian Arctic, 1913–16. Active in Petrograd during the October revolution, 1917. Commissar for Nationalities, 1917–18. General Secretary of the Central Committee of the Communist Party, 1922. Effective ruler of Russia from 1923. Purged his opponents with show trials, 1936–8, murdering without compunction opponents and critics, and ordinary citizens who had committed no crime. Authorised the Nazi–Soviet Pact, August 1939. Succeeded Molotov as Head of Government, May 1941. Became a Marshal of the Soviet Union, May 1943. Buried beside Lenin in the Lenin Mausoleum, 1953. 'Downgraded' to the Kremlin wall, 1960. In 1989 Mikhail Gorbachev began the official process inside the Soviet Union of denouncing Stalin's crimes.

[2] Sir Stafford Cripps.

In fact, Great Britain's policy is concentrated on two objects – one, to save herself from German domination, which the Nazi Government wishes to impose and two, to free the rest of Europe from the domination which Germany is now in process of imposing on it.

The Soviet Union is alone in a position to judge whether Germany's present bid for the hegemony of Europe threatens the interests of the Soviet Union, and if so how best those interests can be safeguarded. But I have felt that the crisis through which Europe, and indeed the world, is passing is so grave as to warrant my laying before you frankly the position as it presents itself to the British Government. This, I hope, will ensure that in any discussion that the Soviet Government may have with Sir S. Cripps, there should be no misunderstanding as to the policy of His Majesty's Government or of their readiness to discuss fully with the Soviet Government any of the vast problems created by Germany's present attempt to pursue in Europe a methodical process by successive stages of conquest and absorption.

Winston S. Churchill to Anthony Eden
(*Churchill papers, 20/13*)

25 June 1940

DEFENCE WORKS

It is shocking that only 57,000 men are being employed on all these works.[1] Moreover, I fear that the troops are being used in large numbers on fortifications. At the present stage they should be drilling and training for at least eight hours a day, including one smart parade every morning. All the labour necessary should be found from civilian sources. I found it extremely difficult to arrange to see even a single battalion on parade in East Anglia during my visit planned to-morrow. The fighting troops in the Brigade Groups should neither be used for guarding vulnerable points, nor for making fortifications. Naturally a change like this cannot be made at once, but let me have your proposals for bringing it about as soon as possible.

---

[1] On 12 June 1940 Britain had been divided into lines of defence, with rivers, roads, canals, railways and villages to be defended by a system of pill-boxes and anti-tank devices. Ironside put his detailed plans to the Chiefs of Staff on 25 June: several thousand pill-boxes were to be constructed. A Home Guard corporal, J. Smith, is credited with the words 'Hitler has taken Poland. Hitler has taken Denmark and Norway. Hitler has taken Holland, Belgium and France. He will not take this pill-box!'

June 1940

Winston S. Churchill to Lord Lloyd
(*Churchill papers, 20/13*)

25 June 1940

The cruel penalties imposed by your predecessor[1] upon the Jews in Palestine for arming have made it necessary to tie up needless forces for their protection. Pray let me know exactly what weapons and organisation the Jews have for self-defence.

Winston S. Churchill to Herbert Morrison
(*Churchill papers, 20/13*)

25 June 1940

Thank you for your letter of June 22 about increasing the import of steel from the United States. I understand that owing to the transfer of the French contracts to us our volume of purchases for the coming month has more than doubled and that we are now buying at the rate of about six hundred thousand tons a month. This is satisfactory, and we should certainly get as much from the United States as we can while we can.

Winston S. Churchill to Lord Halifax
(*Foreign Office papers, 800/322*)

25 June 1940

It is quite clear to me from these telegrams and others that Butler held odd language to the Swedish Minister and certainly the Swede derived a strong impression of defeatism. In these circumstances would it not be well to find out from Butler actually what he did say. I was strongly pressed in the House of Commons in the Secret Session to give assurances that the present Government and all its Members were resolved to fight on to the death, and I did so taking personal responsibility for the resolve of all. I saw a silly rumour in a telegram from Belgrade or Bucharest and how promptly you stamped

---

[1] Malcolm MacDonald, Secretary of State for Dominion Affairs, 1935–9; for the Colonies, May 1938 to May 1940.

upon it, but any suspicion of lukewarmness in Butler will certainly subject us all to further annoyance of this kind.[1]

War Cabinet: Confidential Annex
(*Cabinet papers, 65/13*)

25 June 1940
6 p.m.
10 Downing Street

The War Cabinet were informed that the *Richelieu* had sailed from Dakar at 2.15 p.m. that afternoon.

After consideration of the various alternative courses, the War Cabinet authorised the Admiralty to take the best measures in their power to capture the *Richelieu*, and also the *Jean Bart* if she should put to sea. Every step should be taken to avoid bloodshed, and no more force should be used than was necessary. No communication should be made to the French Government until the operation had been completed.

John Colville: diary
(*Colville papers*)

25 June 1940

Dined with Seal[2] at the Travellers' wisely and well. He was interesting about Winston, explaining how much he had changed since becoming PM. He had sobered down, become less violent, less wild, less impetuous. Seal thinks that W believes in his mission, to extricate this country from its present troubles, and he will certainly kill himself, if necessary, in order to achieve his object. He is superstitious: Seal cited the case of the *Royal Oak*, which sank at the end of a day, Friday, November 13th, on which Winston had mistakenly put on a black tie instead of his usual spotted one – facts to which he attached great importance.[3]

---

[1] On 26 June 1940 R. A. Butler, then Under-Secretary of State for Foreign Affairs, wrote to Lord Halifax to explain that he had met the Swedish Minister, Bjorn Prytz, 'in the park and he came into the Office for only a few minutes; not being an arranged interview I did not keep a record'. Butler added: 'This instance of my private conversation can only be judged by the Swedish Minister, since no one else was present. I do not recognise myself or my conversation in the impression given.' Butler offered to resign, but Halifax rejected his offer. In his resignation offer, Butler wrote: 'Had I not been ready to subscribe to the Prime Minister's courageous lead in the House of Commons, I should have felt bound to inform you and to leave the administration.' (*Foreign Office papers, 800/322*.) Butler remained at the Foreign Office until July 1941, when Churchill appointed him President of the Board of Education (from 1944, Minister of Education).

[2] Churchill's Principal Private Secretary since September 1939.

[3] On 18 June 1940 John Peck wrote to Churchill: 'We did not invite Lord Salisbury to lunch today as he would have been the thirteenth at table. Shall we ask him for tomorrow (Friday)?' (*Churchill papers, 20/8*).

George Bernard Shaw[1] *to Winston S. Churchill*
(*Colville papers*)

26 June 1940

Dear Prime Minister,
Why not declare war on France and capture her fleet (which would gladly strike its colours to us) before AH[2] recovers his breath?
Surely that is the logic of the situation?

Tactically,
G. Bernard Shaw

Winston S. Churchill: recollection
(*'Their Finest Hour', page 148*)

26 June 1940

I visited our beaches in St Margaret's Bay, near Dover. The Brigadier informed me that he had only three anti-tank guns in his brigade, covering four or five miles of this highly-menaced coastline. He declared that he had only six rounds of ammunition for each gun, and he asked me with a slight air of challenge whether he was justified in letting his men fire one single round for practice in order that they might at least know how the weapon worked. I replied that we could not afford practice rounds, and that fire should be held for the last moment at the closest range.

General Ismay: recollection[3]
(*Churchill papers, 4/44*)

26 June 1940

I remember that the first visit you made to the troops was to a Corps commanded by General Massy[4] and that you made it by car. I well recall

[1] George Bernard Shaw, 1856–1950. Playwright, author and Fabian socialist, a friend of Churchill's mother, and an irrepressible wit. Nobel Prize for Literature, 1925. Churchill wrote of him: 'Mr Bernard Shaw was one of my earliest antipathies. Indeed, almost my first literary effusion, written when I was serving as a subaltern in India in 1897 (it never saw the light of day), was a ferocious onslaught upon him, and upon an article which he had written disparaging and deriding the British Army in some minor war' (*Pall Mall* magazine, August 1929, reprinted in *Great Contemporaries*).
[2] Adolf Hitler.
[3] Ismay set down his recollections of this visit to St Margaret's Bay in a letter to Churchill on 20 September 1948, for Churchill's war memoirs.
[4] Hugh Royds Stokes Massy, 1884–1965. Entered the Army, 1902. On active service, 1914–18 (Gallipoli and France, DSO, MC). Director of Military Training, War Office, 1938–9. Deputy Chief of the Imperial General Staff, 1939–40. Commander, North-Western Expeditionary Force (NWEF), Norway, April–June 1940. CB, 1940. Colonel Commandant, Royal Artillery, 1945–51.

your wrath on this occasion at being taken into the Corps War Room and introduced to all the staff. You told me that you had not come to see this sort of thing but to see troops exercising. We went down the front at some small seaside place, where practically every house was a boarding house which relied on the summer visitors for a living. It was a miserable rainy day, but all the old women who owned these boarding houses, and who had temporarily lost their livelihood, turned out and cheered you wildly and called God's blessing upon you.

Winston S. Churchill to General Ismay
(*Churchill papers, 20/13*)

26 June 1940

Have looked up in the records of the CID[1] my two papers written in 1913 entitled 'A bolt from the grey' and 'A time-table of a nightmare' respectively.[2]

Winston S. Churchill to Anthony Eden
(*Churchill papers, 20/13*)

26 June 1940

I don't think much of the name 'Local Defence Volunteers' for your very large new force. The word 'local' is uninspiring. Mr Herbert Morrison suggested to me to-day the title 'Civic Guard,' but I think 'Home Guard' would be better. Don't hesitate to change on account of already having made armlets, &c., if it is thought the title Home Guard would be more compulsive.[3]

---

[1] Committee of Imperial Defence.

[2] Both these papers gave details of a German invasion of the East Coast and of the measures that could be taken to counter it. Details of the first are in an earlier document volume of the Churchill biography (Randolph S. Churchill, *Winston S. Churchill*, volume 2, companion part 3, *1911–1914*, pages 1724–36). Churchill based his scenario on the landing of 20,000 German soldiers at Harwich, the Humber, Blyth, and Cromarty. The second paper is published in full in volume 2 of this biography (Randolph S. Churchill, *Winston S. Churchill*, volume 2, pages 613–27).

[3] Churchill had spent much of 26 June touring Home Defences, writing to Eden on the following day: 'I hope you liked my suggestion of changing the name "Local Defence Volunteers", which is associated with local government and local option, to "Home Guard". I found everybody liked this in my tour yesterday' (*Churchill papers, 20/13*).

June 1940

Winston S. Churchill to Alfred Duff Cooper
(*Churchill papers, 20/13*)

26 June 1940

The Press and broadcast should be asked to handle air raids in a cool way and on a diminishing tone of public interest. The facts should be chronicled without undue prominence or headlines. The people should be accustomed to treat air raids as a matter of ordinary routine. Localities affected should not be mentioned, with any precision. Photographs showing shattered houses should not be published, unless there is something very peculiar about them, or to illustrate how well the Anderson shelters work. It must be remembered that the vast majority of people are not at all affected by any single air raid, and would hardly sustain any evil impression if it were not thrust before them. Everyone should learn to take air raids and air raid alarms as if they were no more than thunderstorms. Pray try to impress this upon the newspaper authorities, and persuade them to help. If there is difficulty in this, I would myself see the Newspaper Proprietors' Association, but I hope this will not be necessary. The Press should be complimented on their work so far in this matter.

WSC

Winston S. Churchill to Captain Margesson
(*Churchill papers, 20/13*)

26 June 1940

If the Ministry of Information still desire that a wax record should be taken of future statements I may have to make in House of Commons on behalf of Government, it would be better that the Resolution authorising this should be agreed to the day before, so as not to have a wrangle about procedure on the occasion of some important declaration. If you agree, the Resolution might be discussed on Tuesday, and my statement could follow on Wednesday or Thursday.[1]

---

[1] The House of Commons declined to let any speech by Churchill in the Chamber be broadcast from the Chamber, or recorded as a gramophone record while being delivered.

Winston S. Churchill to Lord Halifax
(*Churchill papers, 20/13*)

26 June 1940

I am sure we shall gain nothing by offering to 'discuss' Gibraltar at the end of the war.[1] Spaniards will know that, if we win, discussions would not be fruitful; and if we lose, they would not be necessary. I do not believe mere verbiage of this kind will affect the Spanish decision. It only shows weakness and lack of confidence in our victory, which will encourage them the more.

Admiral Pound to Naval Commanders-in-Chief[2]
(*Premier papers, 3/179/4*)

26 June 1940
3.37 p.m.
Immediate

Supplementing instructions already sent regarding communication to be made to the *Richelieu*, it should be explained that we do not doubt Admiral Darlan's good faith and believe he would do his utmost to fulfil his pledge that no unit of French Fleet shall fall into enemy hands.[3] It must however be observed that under the armistices now signed with Germany and Italy, French naval vessels have to be demobilised and disarmed under German and

---

[1] On 24 June 1940, in a telegram to Lord Halifax distributed to the War Cabinet, Sir Samuel Hoare wrote: 'Neither Franco nor the Minister for Foreign Affairs has specifically raised Gibraltar with me. To both I have used the formula that there are no questions between Spain and Great Britain that cannot be settled amicably either during or at the end of the war. As events are moving very quickly, I suggest to you the wisdom of being more explicit and our telling them that whilst we will not discuss the future of Gibraltar during the war, we will discuss it with them at the end of war. I should propose not to say this in special interview but to introduce it into general discussion. I think that this would strengthen the Minister for Foreign Affairs's position particularly if faced with the Axis offer to secure Gibraltar for Spain. He has made it clear that he does not envisage the return of Gibraltar except as part of peace settlement' (*Foreign Office papers, 371/24515*).

[2] This signal was sent to the Commanders-in-Chief Mediterranean, South Atlantic and North Atlantic, also to HMS *Dorsetshire, Hermes, Resolution* and *Watchman*.

[3] The instructions, sent at 3.45 a.m. on 26 June 1940 to the naval Commanders-in-Chief Mediterranean and South Atlantic, as well as to Admiral Somerville at Gibraltar and to the principal warships in the area, stated: 'HMG have decided that *Richelieu* is to be captured and taken into a British port, and have instructed that every step should be taken to avoid bloodshed, that no more force should be used than necessary, and an unpleasant task carried out in as considerate a manner as possible.' A British naval officer was to go on board the *Richelieu* and inform its captain 'that HMG have instructed that force must be used if necessary but sincerely hope that this will not be the case' (*Premier papers, 3/179/4*).

Italian control, i.e. be handed over as fighting units to Germany and Italy. From that moment, Admiral Darlan will no longer have the power, though he would no doubt have the inclination, to carry out his promise, and we should have nothing to rely on but German and Italian declarations, which are obviously valueless.

Therefore, in taking steps to prevent French naval vessels from falling into German and Italian hands, HM Government are not only endeavouring to safeguard their vital interests, but are also giving Admiral Darlan the opportunity to fulfil his pledge.

HM Government are quite prepared to discuss the future of French naval units and are only concerned to make absolutely secure that in execution of the Armistice Terms no unit of French Fleet should fall into German or Italian hands.

Clementine Churchill to Winston S. Churchill
(*Baroness Spencer-Churchill papers*)

27 June 1940 10 Downing Street

My Darling,

I hope you will forgive me if I tell you something that I feel you ought to know.

One of the men in your entourage (a devoted friend) has been to me & told me that there is a danger of your being generally disliked by your colleagues & subordinates because of your rough sarcastic & overbearing manner – It seems your Private Secretaries have agreed to behave like school boys & 'take what's coming to them' & then escape out of your presence shrugging their shoulders. Higher up, if an idea is suggested (say at a conference) you are supposed to be so contemptuous that presently no ideas, good or bad, will be forthcoming. I was astonished & upset because in all these years I have been accustomed to all those who have worked with & under you, loving you – I said this & I was told 'No doubt it's the strain' –

My Darling Winston – I must confess that I have noticed a deterioration in your manner; & you are not so kind as you used to be.

It is for you to give the Orders & if they are bungled – except for the King, the Archbishop of Canterbury & the Speaker – you can sack anyone & everyone. Therefore with this terrific power you must combine urbanity, kindness & if possible Olympic calm. You used to quote: 'On ne règne sur les âmes que par le calme'. I cannot bear that those who serve the country & yourself should not love you as well as admire and respect you.

Besides you won't get the best results by irascibility & rudeness. They will breed either dislike or a slave mentality – (Rebellion in War time being out of the question!)

Please forgive your loving devoted & watchful

Clemmie

I wrote this at Chequers last Sunday tore it up, but here it is now.

John Colville: diary
(*Colville papers*)

27 June 1940

Went up to the PM's bedroom at about 10.00. He was lying in bed, in a red dressing-gown, smoking a cigar and dictating to Mrs Hill, who sat with a typewriter at the foot of the bed. His box, half full of papers, stood open on his bed and by his side was a vast chromium-plated cuspidor. His black cat Nelson, which has quite replaced our old No. 10 black cat, sprawled at the foot of the bed and every now and then Winston would gaze at it affectionately and say 'Cat, darling'.

Among this morning's minutes was one he wrote to the Secretary of State for Air about the shortcomings of the Air Ministry and the flaws in its organisation (criticisms based on a memorandum sent from the FO). He described the Air Ministry as 'a most cumbrous and ill-working administrative machine'.

War Cabinet: Confidential Annex
(*Cabinet papers, 65/13*)

27 June 1940
12 noon

The Chief of Naval Staff said that the *Richelieu* had been located by aircraft of HMS *Dorsetshire*. The aircraft had later had to make a forced landing, but the *Dorsetshire* had got in contact with the *Richelieu* at 3 p.m. the previous afternoon. At that moment, however, the *Richelieu* had altered course 180° and returned to Dakar, under orders from the French Admiral at Dakar.

The real question at issue was what to do as regards the French ships at Oran. One course would be at once to mine them in with magnetic mines, informing them that we were adopting this course. If this was to be done at once, it could only be done by aircraft from this country, which would have to land, say, in Tunisia when the operations had been completed. If we were prepared to wait three days, the operation could be carried out by aircraft from the *Ark Royal*.

By the 3rd July it would be possible for a British Fleet comprising the *Hood*, the *Nelson*, the *Valiant*, the *Resolution* and the *Ark Royal* to arrive outside Oran. This would be a far stronger force than the French Fleet. On arriving off the port the following courses would be open to us:–
  (1) We could demand that the ships should be demilitarised under our control;
  (2) We could ask the French ships to come to sea and proceed to British ports;
  (3) We could say that unless the ships had been sunk within three hours, we should bombard them.
    Another possibility was that we should leave two submarines outside the port, with orders to sink the ships if they came out.

The position of the ships in the harbour was explained. It was believed that they were moored with their sterns to the breakwater, so that they could not fire out to sea.

In discussion, the view was expressed that it was most important to take action to ensure that the French Fleet could not be used against us. Public opinion was strongly insistent that we should take action on the lines of the measures taken at Copenhagen against the Danish Fleet.[1]

In this connection, however, the references which were now appearing in the Press, as to measures which might be taken against the French Fleet, were greatly to be deprecated, and instructions should be sent to ensure that this matter was not discussed in the Press.

The Prime Minister summed up the discussion as follows: He thought that the War Cabinet approved in principle that the operation proposed should take place on the 3rd July. It might be combined with further operations in the Mediterranean, or with operations designed to secure the *Richelieu* and the *Jean Bart*.

The possibility that we might offer the French to agree to the ships being interned in American ports was also mentioned. This would require consideration from the political point of view. Meanwhile, plans for the operation should be drawn up, and should be considered later at a Meeting of the Ministers directly concerned, with their Advisers.

He was opposed to using aircraft based in this country to carry out magnetic mine-laying as he did not think it likely that the French ships would leave Oran immediately.

The War Cabinet approved in principle the operation on the lines indicated

---

[1] In 1800, following Denmark's adherence to the Russo-Swedish Armed Neutrality League, Britain sent Admirals Parker and Nelson to the Baltic where, on 2 April 1800, they destroyed the Danish fleet.

by the Prime Minister, and invited the First Lord of the Admiralty and the Chief of Naval Staff to arrange for the planning of the operation to be taken in hand at once. A report should be made at a Meeting of Ministers directly affected, under the Chairmanship of the Prime Minister, at which any detailed points involved could be settled. The proposal to lay magnetic mines forthwith by aircraft from the United Kingdom was however not approved.

Winston S. Churchill to A. V. Alexander
(<i>Churchill papers, 20/13</i>)</center>

27 June 1940

1. The French naval personnel at Aintree Camp numbering 13,600, equally with the 5,530 military at Trentham Park, the 1,900 at Arrow Park, and the details at Blackpool, are to be immediately repatriated to French territory, i.e., Morocco, in French ships now in our hands.

2. They should be told we will take them to French Africa because all French metropolitan ports are in German hands, and that the French Government will arrange for their future movements.

3. If, however, any wish to remain here to fight against Germany, they must immediately make this clear. Care must be taken that no Officer or man is sent back into French jurisdiction against his will. A short notice should be prepared which can be read to the above French personnel to-night.[1] The shipping is to be ready to-morrow. The troops should move under their own Officers, and carry their personal arms, but as little ammunition as possible. Some arrangements should be made for their pay. The French material on board ships from Narvik will be taken over by us with the ammunition from the *Lombardy*, and other ships as against expenses to which we are put.

4. Great care is to be taken of the French wounded. All who can be moved without danger should be sent back direct to France if possible. The French Government should be asked where they wish them delivered, and if at French metropolitan ports, should arrange with the Germans for their safe entry; otherwise Casablanca. All dangerous cases must be dealt with here.

5. Apart from any volunteers who may wish to stay in the above groups of personnel, there must be many individuals who have made their way here, hoping to continue to fight. These also should be given the option of returning to France, or serving in the French Units under General de Gaulle, who should be told of our decisions, and given reasonable facilities to collect his

---

[1] The notice read: 'You are being sent to North Africa (Casablanca) at the request of the French Government. Any officers and other ranks who wish to continue to fight against Germany may volunteer to remain in England.'

people. I have abandoned the hope that he could address the formed bodies as their morale has deteriorated too fast.

6. General de Gaulle is also to be consulted upon the immediate treatment of technical elements who wish to be of use to us. Whether they are or not can be found out later.

7. General Spears will act under War Office orders for the purposes of carrying out the above.[1]

WSC

Winston S. Churchill to General Smuts
(*Premier papers, 4/43B/1*)

27 June 1940
3 p.m.
Personal and Secret

Obviously we have first to repulse any attack on Great Britain by invasion, and show ourselves able to maintain our development of Air Power. This can only be settled by trial. If Hitler fails to beat us here, he will probably recoil eastwards. Indeed he may do this even without trying invasion, to find employment for his Army, and take the edge off the winter strain upon him.

2. I do not expect winter strain will prove decisive, but to try to hold all Europe down in a starving condition with only Gestapo and military occupation and no large theme appealing to masses is not an arrangement which can last long.

Development of our Air power particularly in regions unaffected by bombing, should cause him ever increasing difficulties, possibly decisive difficulties, in Germany no matter what successes he has in Europe or Asia.

4. Our large Army now being created for home defence is being formed on principle of attack and opportunity for large scale offensive amphibious operations may come in 1940 and 1941. We are still working on 55 Division basis here, but as our munitions supply expands and Empire resources are mobilised, larger numbers may be possible. After all we are now at least on interior lines. Hitler has vast hungry areas to defend, and we have the command of the seas. Choice of objectives in Western Europe is therefore wide.

5. I send you these personal notes in order to keep in closest contact with your thoughts which ever weigh with me.

WSC

[1] Of approximately 21,000 French troops who were on British soil at the time of the Armistice, some 7,000 elected to remain in Britain and join General de Gaulle: two battalions of the French Foreign Legion, 200 Chasseurs Alpins (who had fought in Norway), engineers, signallers, the officers and crews of two submarines and a patrol boat, and elements of the French air force.

Winston S. Churchill to General Smuts
(*Premier papers, 4/43B/1*)

27 June 1940
Personal and Secret

Your paragraphs from 6 onwards only just received.[1] We shall certainly give you all help in defending South Africa, but this would not be the moment to put British and Dominions Divisions into West or East Africa, and I do not see how they could be used or maintained if they got there. British Eastern Mediterranean fleet is well-placed to resist an attack on Egypt, as well as to cover east coast of Africa. We can also send forces from here by the Atlantic far quicker than any German force can traverse the immense land distances of Africa, if indeed they are traversable except by very small numbers. Possibility of air attack on South Africa appears remote at present time. We are attacking Germans ceaselessly and heavily in their homeland,[2] and are also being attacked ourselves, so far in a very unskilful fashion.

It would not be right to make any considerable detachment of Air Forces from Great Britain until we see what happens in the main trial of air strength now impending here.

Winston S. Churchill to General Ismay
(*Cabinet papers, 66/9*)

27 June 1940

It seems difficult to believe that any large force of transports could be brought to the Channel ports without our being aware of it, or that any system of mining would prevent our sweepers from clearing a way for attack on such transports on passage. However, it would be well if the Chiefs of Staff gave their attention to this rumour.

WSC

---

[1] In his telegram, Smuts expressed grave concern (paragraph 7) that Germany would join Italy in North Africa, 'conquer French Mediterranean colonies, capture Egypt and Suez, and then begin to drive down Africa until, if the war lasts long enough, they have mastered the African continent'. He therefore proposed (paragraph 9) 'a number of British or Dominion divisions flung in time into West and East Africa' which with air and sea power 'ought to hold out against the powerful Axis forces to the end of the war' (*Premier papers, 4/43/B/1*).

[2] On 17 June 1940 Bomber Command had begun a series of attacks on German aircraft factories, aluminium-making factories, and oil-producing plants. Beginning on that first day, the oil-producing factory at Leuna received the first of ten attacks over a two-month period. Among the aircraft factories bombed were the Focke-Wulf factory at Bremen, the Junkers 52 factory at Deichhausen and the Messerschmitt 110 factory at Gotha.

Winston S. Churchill to Anthony Eden
(*Churchill papers, 20/13*)

27 June 1940

Enclosed[1] makes me anxious to know how you propose to use these eight fine Regular battalions. Obviously, they will be a reinforcement for your shock troops. One would suppose they might make the infantry of two divisions, with five good Territorial battalions added to each division, total 18. Should they not also yield up a certain number of Officers and NCOs to stiffen the Territorial battalions so attached? You would thus have six brigades of infantry quite soon. Alas, I fear the artillery must lag behind, but not I trust for long.

Winston S. Churchill to Sir Archibald Sinclair
(*Foreign Office papers, 800/326*)

27 June 1940
Private and Personal

I should be glad if you would read the enclosed paper[2] which I have received from Lord Halifax before our talk this morning. It is, I am told, written by a highly competent person, who declares he is perfectly ready to be cashiered if necessary, and is evidently in a dangerous mood. The Foreign Secretary was much impressed by his arguments. I have been, as you know, for many months urging something like this policy, and everyone has been astounded at the failure of the Air Ministry to expand the Air Force on the outbreak of war, and recently at the proved failure to provide a proper supply of pilots when they have so long been crying out about the plethora of pilots, and 're-mustering' them for other duties. I am hoping that you will be able to make the same kind of practical changes at the Air Ministry as Lord Beaverbrook has made in the production of aircraft, from which we are deriving such inestimable relief in these dark days.

This document attached has nothing to do with Lord Beaverbrook, but you can see how much it confirms his many complaints of being hampered in production.

I note the supply of machines available at 48 hours' notice is growing every day, and also that the Air Ministry have abandoned the 96 hours' notice in preference to the 48. The figures of the 96 hours' notice are of course far more

---

[1] A letter from the Admiralty of 26 June 1940, giving the date of arrival in the United Kingdom of troop convoys arriving from India (15 July) in answer to Churchill's enquiry of 25 June 1940.
[2] Not found.

impressive in showing the large supply of aeroplanes than the 48 hours' notice recently adopted.

I do hope and pray that you will feel yourself able to effect radical reforms in what is, I am sure, a most cumbersome and ill-working administrative machine. I felt that with your new eye you would have a chance far greater than that enjoyed by persons compromised with the past.

Duke of Windsor to Winston S. Churchill
(*Churchill papers, 20/9*)

27 June 1940   Madrid
Personal

Regret that in view of your reply to my last message I cannot agree to returning until everything has been considered and I know the result.

In the light of past experience my wife[1] and myself must not risk finding ourselves once more regarded by the British public as in a different status to other members of my family.[2]

---

[1] Wallis Warfield, 1896–1986. Daughter of Teakle Wallis Warfield of Baltimore, Maryland. She married Edward, Duke of Windsor (as her third husband) on 3 June 1937: Randolph Churchill was one of the few guests at the wedding. Resident in the Bahamas, 1940–5; in France from 1945.

[2] On 28 June 1940 Sir Samuel Hoare telegraphed to Churchill from Madrid: 'I did my best in long conversation to persuade Windsors to return immediately, but I found him completely rigid on following lines. He says if he returns now he will probably not be able to leave England again during the war. This being so, his position must be regularised and he will not return unless it is. I asked him what he meant by this, and I found he had dropped the condition of receiving some post, and that it boiled down to both of them being received once only for quite a short meeting by the King and Queen, and notice of the fact appearing in the Court Circular. He said he did not ask to be received by Queen Mary as he did not wish to worry her. Nor did he raise any question about the title of Royal Highness' (*Churchill papers, 20/9*).

Winston S. Churchill to the Duke of Windsor
(*Churchill papers, 20/9*)

28 June 1940

Your Royal Highness has taken active military rank and refusal to obey direct orders of competent military authority would create a serious situation. I hope it will not be necessary for such orders to be sent. [Already there is a great deal of doubt as to the circumstances in which Your Royal Highness left Paris.][1] I most strongly urge immediate compliance with wishes of the Government.

R. V. Jones to Winston S. Churchill
(*Cabinet papers, 120/744*)

28 June 1940

On 22.6.1940, an unimpeachable source (who[2] had previously given the vital clue to the Knickebein solution) reported that he saw on 20.6.40, a request from Flakcorps I (AA Corps) for the following maps to be delivered, among others, immediately to their H.Q.:
(1) 800 copies England and Ireland, scale 1/100,000 and 1/300,000
(2) 300 copies France and England 1/1,000,000.[3]

---

[1] Churchill deleted this sentence in the telegram as finally sent to the Duke on 1 July 1940.

[2] Not 'who', but in fact a machine, Enigma (see page 800 n.1). To protect this most secret source, Enigma was always referred to as if it was an individual secret agent.

[3] In sending this decyphered German message (from Enigma) to Churchill, R. V. Jones added his own comment. 'It will be noticed,' he wrote, 'that this request is from a Flakcorps, and not from a Fliegercorps, possibly indicating an intention to land motorised AA units in both England and Ireland.' Churchill at once asked Professor Lindemann to study this report, and sent a copy to General Ismay for his scrutiny. What neither Churchill, Lindemann nor Ismay could know was that this top secret request for the distribution of maps was evidently an anticipation by the German Flakcorps Commander of Hitler's order, not issued until July 2, to prepare for the invasion of Britain. Flak, and later the paratroop formations, although both branches of army warfare, came under the German Air Force, and therefore used the German Air Force Enigma machine.

War Cabinet: minutes
(*Cabinet papers, 65/7*)

28 June 1940   10 Downing Street
Noon

The Prime Minister said that at a meeting the previous afternoon, it had been agreed that it was desirable to remove from this country as soon as possible all French personnel who did not volunteer to remain and carry on the fight. It was proposed to send them to North African ports in French ships. But it had since been pointed out that if we used French ships, they would be detained on reaching North Africa. It might therefore be better to use British ships. We could not afford to wait for French ships to be sent specially to this country to take back the troops.

The War Cabinet were informed that there would be about 20,000 men to transport. The first ship would be ready to leave that night with some 1,500 men.

There was general agreement that special measures should be taken in respect of the French wounded. Those who were fit to travel should if possible be sent back direct to France; the more serious would, of course, continue to be cared for in this country.

Winston S. Churchill to Lord Lloyd
(*Premier papers, 3/348*)

28 June 1940   10 Downing Street

This is the price we have to pay for the anti-Jewish policy which has been persisted in for some years.[1] Should things go badly in Egypt all these troops will have to be withdrawn. The position of the Jewish Colonists will be one of the gravest danger.

It is little less than a scandal at a time when we are fighting for our lives that these very large forces should be immobilized in support of a policy which only commends itself to a section of the Conservative Party.

[1] There were 20,000 British and Australian forces in Palestine in June 1940. The Jews had been forbidden arms for defence against Arab attacks on their villages, which since the Arab uprising in 1936 had been protected by the armed forces now needed for the defence of Egypt.

Winston S. Churchill to Lord Lothian
(*Churchill papers, 20/14*)

28 June 1940

No doubt I will make some broadcast presently, but I don't think words count for much now. Too much attention should not be paid to eddies of United States opinion. Only force of events can govern them. Up till April they were so sure the Allies would win that they did not think help necessary. Now they are so sure we shall lose that they do not think it possible. I feel good confidence we can repel invasion and keep alive in the Air. Anyhow we are going to try. Never cease to impress on President and others that if this country were successfully invaded and largely occupied after heavy fighting, some Quisling Government would be formed to make peace on the basis of our becoming a German Protectorate. In this case the British Fleet would be the solid contribution with which this peace government would buy terms. Feeling in England against United States would be similar to French bitterness against us now. We have really not had any help worth speaking of from the United States so far. We know President is our friend, but it is no use trying to dance attendance upon Republican and Democratic conventions. What really matters is whether Hitler is master of Britain in three months or not. I think not. But this is a matter which cannot be argued beforehand. Your mood should be bland and phlegmatic. No one is downhearted here.

Winston S. Churchill to Bernard Baruch[1]
(*Churchill papers, 2/392*)

28 June 1940

Am always hoping you are recovering fully from serious operation. Am sure we shall be all right here but your people are not doing much. If things go wrong with us it will be bad for them.

---

[1] Bernard Mannes Baruch, 1870–1965. Born in South Carolina, the son of a Jewish doctor who had emigrated from East Prussia in the 1850s. A self-made financier, he became a millionaire before he was thirty. As Chairman of the United States War Industries Board from 3 March 1918 until the end of the war eight months later he was in almost daily communication with Churchill (then Minister of Munitions). Accompanied President Wilson to the Paris Peace Conference, 1919. In 1929 and 1931 he was one of Churchill's hosts on his visits to the United States. From 1946 to 1951 he was United States Representative on the Atomic Energy Commission. When he presented his private archive to Princeton University in 1964 it contained 1,200 letters from nine Presidents, and 700 communications from Churchill.

Winston S. Churchill to Lord Halifax
(*Churchill papers, 20/13*)

28 June 1940

I hope it will be made clear to the Nuncio[1] that we do not desire to make any inquiries as to terms of peace with Hitler, and that all our agents are strictly forbidden to entertain any such suggestions.

Winston S. Churchill to the Chiefs of Staff Committee
(*Churchill papers, 20/13*)

28 June 1940

1. See papers by Vice-Chiefs of Staff and further papers by COS Committee.

2. It is prudent to block off likely sections of the beaches with a good defence and to make secure all creeks and harbours on the East Coast. The South Coast is less immediately dangerous. No serious invasion is possible without a harbour with its quays, &c. No one can tell, should the Navy fail, on what part of the East Coast the impact will fall. Perhaps there will be several lodgments. Once these are made all troops employed on other parts of the coastal crust will be as useless as those in the Maginot Line. Although fighting on the beaches is favourable to the defence, this advantage cannot be purchased by trying to guard all the beaches. Process must be selective. But if time permits defended sectors may be widened and improved.

3. Every effort should be made to man coast defences with sedentary troops, well-sprinkled with experienced late-war officers. The safety of the country depends on having a large number (now only nine, but should soon be fifteen) 'Leopard' brigade-groups which can be directed swiftly, i.e., within four hours, to the points of lodgment. Difficulties of landing on beaches are serious, even when invader has reached them; but difficulties of nourishing a lodgment when exposed to heavy attack by land, air and sea are far greater. All therefore depends on rapid, resolute engagement of any landed forces which may slip through the sea-control. This should not be beyond our means provided the field troops are not consumed in beach defences, and are kept in high condition of mobility, crouched and ready to spring.

4. In the unhappy event of the enemy capturing a port, larger formations with artillery will be necessary. There should be four or five good divisions

---

[1] There was no Papal Nuncio in Britain in 1940. The Apostolic Delegate, the Pope's senior representative, was Archbishop William Godfrey, subsequently Archbishop of Liverpool (1953) and of Westminster (1956). He was appointed Cardinal in 1958.

held in general reserve to deal with such an improbable misfortune. The scale of lodgment to be anticipated should be not more than ten thousand men landed at three points simultaneously, say, thirty thousand in all. The scale of Air attack not more than fifteen thousand landed simultaneously at two or three points in all. The enemy will not have strength to repeat such descents often. It is very doubtful whether air-borne troops can be landed in force by night; by day they should be an easy prey.

5. The tank story is somewhat different and it is right to minimise by local cannon and obstacles the landing-places of tanks. The Admiralty should report upon the size, character and speed of potential tank-carrying barges or floats, whether they will be self-propelled or towed and by what craft. As they can hardly go above seven miles an hour they should be detected in summertime after they have started, and even in fog or haze the RDF stations should give warning while they are still several hours from land. The destroyers issuing from the sally-ports must strike at these with gusto. The arrangement of stops and blocks held by local sedentary forces should be steadily developed, and anti-tank squads formed. Our own tank reserve must engage the surviving invader tanks, and no doubt is held in a position which allows swift railing to the attacked area.

6. Parachutists, Fifth-Columnists and enemy motor-cyclists who may penetrate or appear in disguise in unexpected places must be left to the Home Guard, reinforced by special squads. Much thought must be given to the trick of wearing British uniform.

7. In general I find myself in agreement with the Commander-in-Chief's plan, but all possible field-troops must be saved from the beaches and gathered into the 'Leopard' brigades and other immediate mobile supports. Emphasis should be laid upon the main reserve. The battle will be won or lost not on the beaches, but by the mobile brigades and the main reserve. Until the Air Force is worn down by prolonged air fighting and destruction of aircraft supply, the power of the Navy remains decisive against any serious invasion.

8. The above observations apply only to the immediate summer months. We must be much better equipped and stronger before the autumn.

Winston S. Churchill to General Ismay
(*Churchill papers, 20/13*)

28 June 1940

I want to see another General this week. Perhaps you would ask the General Commanding the southern side of the Thames Estuary, whoever he is,[1] if he could come to lunch to-morrow at Chequers.

Winston S. Churchill to General Ismay
(*Churchill papers, 20/13*)

28 June 1940
Secret

This is a very unsatisfactory figure.[2] When I mentioned 57,000 the other day in the Cabinet, I was assured that they represented a very small part of what were actually employed, and that 100,000 was nearer the mark, and that many more were coming in before the end of the week. Now, instead, we have a figure of only 40,000. Pray let me have a full explanation of this.

It is very wrong that fighting troops should be kept from their training because of the neglects to employ civilian labour.

The question must be brought up at the Cabinet on Monday.

Winston S. Churchill to General Ismay
(*Churchill papers, 20/13*)

28 June 1940

Although our policy about the French Navy is clear, I should like to have an appreciation by the Admiralty of the consequences which are likely to follow, namely: a hostile attitude by France, and the seizure by Germany and Italy of any part of the French Navy which we cannot secure. I should like to have this on Sunday next.

---

[1] Augustus Francis Andrew Nicol Thorne, 1885–1970. Joined the Grenadier Guards, 1904. On active service on the Western Front, 1914–18 (despatches seven times, DSO and two bars). Military Attaché, Berlin, 1932–5. Major-General Commanding the Brigade of Guards, 1938–9. Commanded the 48th Division, British Expeditionary Force, 1939–40 (despatches); the XIIth Corps, Kent, 1941; Scottish Command, 1941–5. Knighted, 1942. Commander-in-Chief, Allied Land Forces, Norway, 1945.

[2] Labour for defence works. Two days earlier General Brooke had been appointed General Officer Commanding-in-Chief, Southern Command. He had at once ordered the strengthening of coastal defences by means of anti-tank obstacles on the beaches, barbed wire, and pill-boxes. Tank traps and pill-boxes were also being built at points along which it was thought the Germans would advance.

Winston S. Churchill to General Ismay
(*Churchill papers, 120/3*)

28 June 1940

Mr Morrison seemed disquieted by the proposal,[1] thinking perhaps that it was derogatory to him that Mr Oliver Lyttelton should be on the Supply Council. I pointed out that it was intended to make it clear to him that he was under his orders. He seemed to prefer the idea that he should be a member of the Cabinet Secretariat.

You had better go and have a talk with Mr Morrison, and see if you can explain the position to him. I have asked him to make proposals of his own, as I must have an effective liaison with his Department, just as I have with the Services through you. Try to see Mr Morrison to-morrow, saying it was my wish you should ask him for an interview.

WSC

Winston S. Churchill to Sir John Anderson
(*Churchill papers, 20/13*)

28 June 1940

Let me see a list of prominent persons you have arrested.[2]

John Colville: diary
(*Colville papers*)

28 June 1940　　　　　　　　　　　　　　　　　　　　　　　　　Chequers

When the ladies had left the dining-room, Winston, Léger and Van[3] discussed the collapse of France. Winston told Léger he was speaking to a '*cercle sacré*' and must express himself frankly. He foresaw the possibility of France declaring war on us and he wanted to know how we could maintain the goodwill of the French people, for whose salvation we were the last hope, while we were obliged to starve them by blockade and destroy their towns by

---

[1] On 24 June 1940 Churchill had proposed Oliver Lyttelton for his 'liaison' with the Ministry of Supply, and a member of the Supply Council.

[2] This list remains secret, fifty-four years after the event. Two of those arrested were relatives by marriage of Clementine Churchill: Lady Mosley and Captain George Pitt-Rivers.

[3] Sir Robert Vansittart, Chief Diplomatic Adviser to the Government (a post to which he had been appointed in 1938 after his dismissal as Permanent Under-Secretary of State for Foreign Affairs).

bombs. How could we convince them that we were being cruel in order to be kind? It was essential to keep the French well disposed to us, even if their Government went to war with Great Britain. Léger replied that it was important to maintain contact with the Bordeaux Government, to send a chargé d'affaires to France and not to leave this country unrepresented there.

The Vansittarts and Léger left about 1.00 a.m. and afterwards the PM discussed with Ismay the organisation of the War Office and Air Ministry. The latter, in particular, disturbs him and it is the cause of serious differences between Sinclair and Beaverbrook. He told Ismay there was too much 'top hamper' in both departments: they would have to be simplified and useless officials must be ruthlessly eliminated.

Speaking of the Chiefs of Staff, W said he thought a lot of Pound, although he was slow; Newall had many good points (but Beaverbrook says 'he was an observer in the last war, and he has remained an observer ever since'); Dill had, unfortunately, aged a great deal in every way (cf. Weygand's sudden senility in the course of a few weeks).

Winston S. Churchill to Lord Halifax
(*Churchill papers, 20/13*)

29 June 1940

Monsieur Léger suggested to me last night that communication should be opened up with the Bordeaux Government on the subject of whether future representation is possible in unoccupied France, and how diplomatic ties could be maintained. To talk about this would at any rate seem a sort of contact. I mentioned to him about the wounded as another topic.

Winston S. Churchill to Professor Lindemann
(*Churchill papers, 20/13*)

29 June 1940

I have read this paper,[1] but I am not quite sure how to handle it. It seems to me that the blockade is largely ruined, in which case the sole decisive weapon in our hands would be overwhelming air attack upon Germany. At any rate, the facts of Mr Greenwood's paper should be considered by the Departments concerned with a view to making positive recommendations for action.

[1] Arthur Greenwood, 'Economic Aid from the New World to the Old' (War Cabinet Paper 209 of 1940).

If we assume that French resistance is negligible, we should gain great relief in the immediate future from not having to maintain an Army in France or sending supplies of beef, coal, &c., to France. Let me know about this.

How has the question of beef supplies been affected? We are freed from the obligation to supply the French Army with beef. There is really no reason why our Army at home should have rations far exceeding the heavy munitions workers'. The complications about frozen meat and fresh meat ought also to be affected by what has happened, although I am not sure which way.

Pray clarify these ideas for me, as I want to write a general paper for the Cabinet.

Winston S. Churchill to Professor Lindemann
(*Churchill papers, 20/13*)

29 June 1940

If we could have large supplies of multiple projectors and rockets directed by the RDF irrespective of cloud or darkness, and also could have the proximity fuse working effectively by day and to a lesser extent in moonlight or starlight, the defence against air attack would become decisive. This combination is therefore the supreme immediate aim. We are not far from it in every respect, yet it seems to baffle us. Assemble your ideas and facts so that I may give extreme priority and impulse to this business.

Winston S. Churchill to Professor Lindemann
(*Churchill papers, 20/13*)

29 June 1940

While we are hastening our preparations for air mastery, the Germans will be organizing the whole industries of the captured countries for air production and other war production suitable against us. It is therefore a race. They will not be able to get the captured factories working immediately, and meanwhile we shall get round the invasion danger through the growth of our defences and Army strength. But what sort of relative outputs must be faced next year unless we are able to bomb the newly-acquired German plants? Germany also being relieved from the need of keeping a gigantic army in constant contact with the French Army, must have spare capacity for the air and other methods for attacking us. Must we not expect this will be very great? How soon can it come into play? Hitherto I have been looking at the next three months because of the emergency, but what about 1941? It seems to me that only immense American supplies can be of use in turning the corner.

Winston S. Churchill to A. V. Alexander
(*Churchill papers, 20/13*)

29 June 1940

I trust there will be no slowing down on the work of the concrete ships,[1] and that not only small barges, but larger vessels will be constructed. We shall want these in 1942. I should like a special report on the concrete ships on the 7th of every month covering results to the last day of the preceding month.

Winston S. Churchill to A. V. Alexander and Admiral Pound
(*Premier papers, 3/179/1*)

29 June 1940
ACTION THIS DAY

THE FUTURE OF THE FRENCH FLEET AT ORAN

The three alternatives should be offered in the order set forth.[2] The first is infinitely preferable, and should be supplemented by a promise to repatriate the crews, to restore the ships at the peace, and to pay full compensation for any loss or damage during the war. If this offer is rejected, the second demand must be made. Only in case this is refused should the third be adopted, but the three alternatives would have to be put to them together. Some more general declaration explaining the position and our resolve to restore France, if we win, should also be made. If a Naval draft is prepared, Cabinet can improve upon it on Sunday night.

John Colville: diary
(*Colville papers*)

29 June 1940   Chequers

Beaverbrook and Brendan Bracken came down to lunch. The conversation began with a discussion on the evacuation of the Channel Islands and the food which had been left behind. Turning to me Winston said: 'Tell the Ministry of Food to evaluate it, and the Admiralty to evacuate it.' I carried out this peremptory order which, of course, led to much trouble – the cattle in Jersey

[1] Churchill noted in his memoirs: 'The development of concrete ships promised important relief to our vital war industries. It seemed that they could be built quickly and cheaply by types of labour not required in normal shipbuilding and would save large quantities of steel. These claims were found on examination to be based on false assumptions and many unforeseen technical difficulties arose. An experimental ship of 2,000 tons was built but was a failure and although experimental work continued, the use of concrete hulls was only successful in barges up to about 200 tons' (*The Gathering Storm*, page 595).
[2] The three choices were: demilitarisation, sailing to British ports, or being sunk.

had foot-and-mouth disease, etc., etc. Winston was obviously pleased with his epigram and did not look beyond.

In reply to a request from the PM, the Home Secretary sent a list of 150 'prominent people' whom he had arrested. Of the first three on the list two, Lady Mosley[1] and Geo Pitt-Rivers,[2] were cousins of the Churchills – a fact which piqued Winston and caused much merriment among his children!

Winston went to bed shortly after 1.00 a.m. and I resisted the now drunken Randolph's attempt to make me sit up with him and discuss the Fifth Column (which, incidentally, Winston thinks a much less serious menace than had been supposed). Randolph was in a horrible state, gross, coarse and aggressive. I felt ashamed of him for Winston's sake and yet W said, when he asked to be allowed some more active part in the war, that if R were killed he would not be able to carry on his work.

Winston S. Churchill to General Ismay
(*Churchill papers, 20/13*)

30 June 1940

The Admiralty charts of tides and state of the moon, Humber, Thames Estuary, Beachy Head, should be studied with a view to ascertaining on which days conditions will be most favourable to a seaborne landing. The Admiralty view is sought.

Winston S. Churchill to General Ismay
(*Premier papers, 3/88/3*)

30 June 1940

Let me have a report upon the amount of mustards[3] or other variants we have in store, and whether it can be used in air bombs as well as fired from guns. What is our output per month? It should certainly be speeded up. Let

---

[1] Diana Mitford (1910–). Third daughter of the 2nd Baron Redesdale. A cousin by marriage of Clementine Churchill, she married Oswald Mosley in 1936, was arrested with him in 1940, and imprisoned for the duration of the war. Her sister Unity, like her an admirer of Hitler, tried to commit suicide on the outbreak of war.

[2] George Henry Lane Pitt-Rivers, 1890–1966. A second cousin by marriage of Clementine Churchill. Landowner. On active service, 1914–18 (severely wounded). An anthropologist, he opposed mixed marriages between races and creeds; his book *Weeds in the Garden of Marriage* was published in 1931. In 1938 he expressed his dislike of Judaeo-Bolshevik influences on foreign policy in *The Czech Conspiracy* (on his deathbed, he urged me not to minimise or ignore those influences in my own work). 'Held a political prisoner by order of Home Secretary' (as he phrased it in *Who's Who*), 1939–45. On his release from prison, he inaugurated the Wessex Music Festival.

[3] Mustard gas.

me have proposals. Supposing lodgments were effected on our coast, there could be no better points for application of mustard than these beaches and lodgments. In my view there would be no need to wait for the enemy to adopt such methods. He will certainly adopt them if he thinks it will pay. Home Defence should be consulted as to whether the prompt drenching of lodgments would not be a great help. Everything should be brought to the highest pitch of readiness, but the question of actual employment must be studied by the Cabinet.

WSC

Winston S. Churchill to General Ismay
(*Churchill papers, 20/13*)

30 June 1940

It would be taking an undue risk to remove one of our only two thoroughly equipped divisions out of Great Britain at this juncture. Moreover, it is doubtful whether the Irish situation will require the use of divisional formations complete with their technical vehicles as if for Continental war. The statement that it would take ten days to transport a division from this country to Ireland, even though every preparation can be made beforehand, is not satisfactory. Schemes should be prepared to enable two or three lightly-equipped brigades to move at short notice, and in not more than three days, into Northern Ireland. Duplicate transport should be sent on ahead. It would be a mistake to send any large force of artillery to Ireland. It is not at all likely that a naval descent will be effected there. Air-borne descents cannot carry much artillery. Finally, nothing that can happen in Ireland can be immediately decisive.

WSC

Winston S. Churchill to Lord Woolton[1]
(*Churchill papers, 20/13*)

30 June 1940

CHANNEL ISLANDS

I think it will be necessary to evacuate the whole of the population, as the Germans will soon steal all the food left from the 80,000 remaining, and we

[1] Frederick James Marquis, 1883–1964. A successful businessman, statistician and economist. Chairman of Lewis's Investment Trust. Knighted, 1935. Director-General of Equipment and Stores, Ministry of Supply, 1939–40. Created Baron Woolton, 1939. Privy Councillor, 1940. Minister of Food, 1940–3. Companion of Honour, 1942. Member of the War Cabinet, and Minister of Reconstruction, 1943–5. Chairman of the Conservative and Unionist Central Office, 1946–55. Chancellor of the Duchy of Lancaster, 1952–5. Viscount, 1953. Earl, 1956.

shall have to feed them from here, the food again being stolen. I do not know on what principle 90,000 have been selected to come home, and 80,000 left. It would seem inevitable that all should go, and everything worth moving be taken away as soon as possible. A few watchers and scouts might be left to report any happenings. Fishermen would be good for this. General Ismay will bring this matter before the Joint Staff Committee.

Winston S. Churchill to Sir John Anderson
(*Churchill papers, 20/13*)

30 June 1940

I enclose you the list of suspected persons in the 55th Division Area which was given to me by the General Commanding[1] at my request. You will see Lord Swinton's[2] comment on it. In my view, the military authorities have a right to feel that suspected persons are removed from the zones which may soon be the subject of actual invasion.

Pray let me know in three days what action you find yourself able to take. I promised that prompt action should be taken.

John Colville: diary
(*Colville papers*)

30 June 1940   Chequers

Mr Amery and General Thorne (commanding XIIth Corps, south of the Thames) came to lunch. Randolph said something unpleasant about the former Government and claimed that its leaders ought to be punished. 'We

---

[1] William Duthie Morgan, 1891–1977. On active service, 1914–18 (despatches, DSO). On active service in France, 1939–40. Major-General Commanding the 55th Division (Hereford area), 1940–1. Chief of the General Staff, Home Forces, 1942–3. General Officer Commanding Southern Command, 1944. Chief of Staff to the Supreme Allied Commander, Mediterranean, 1945. Knighted, 1945. Supreme Allied Commander, Mediterranean, 1945–7. Army Member, Joint Staff Mission, Washington, 1947–50.

[2] Philip Cunliffe-Lister, 1884–1972. On active service, 1914–17 (Military Cross). Joint Secretary, Ministry of National Service, 1917–18. Conservative MP, 1918–35. President of the Board of Trade, 1922–3, 1924–9 and 1931. Secretary of State for the Colonies, 1931–5. Created Viscount Swinton, 1935. Secretary of State for Air, 1935–8 (when he advocated a larger Air Force expansion than the Government was prepared to accept). Brought back into Government on the outbreak of war as Chairman of the United Kingdom Commercial Corporation, responsible for pre-empting purchases of supplies and materials overseas that were needed by the German war machine. Appointed by Churchill in May 1940 to be Chairman of the Security Executive, concerned with measures against sabotage in Britain and overseas. Organised the supply route to the Soviet Union through the Persian Gulf, 1941–2. Cabinet Minister Resident in West Africa, 1942–4. Minister for Civil Aviation, 1944–5. Minister of Materials, 1951–2. Secretary of State for Commonwealth Relations, 1952–5. Created Earl of Swinton, 1955. His elder son died of wounds received in North Africa in 1943.

don't want to punish anyone now – except the enemy,' replied Winston. W is, however, less cautious about his criticism of Baldwin, etc., even though he never countenances a word against Chamberlain, and when I told him that the Germans had bombed the works of 'Guest, Keen and Baldwin', in South Wales, all he said was: 'Very ungrateful of them.'

We left Chequers about 4.00 p.m., I driving up to London with Mr Amery and General Thorne. We had a very pleasant conversation on every kind of subject. Amery said he thought Winston ought to be Minister of Defence and PM only in name: I said that this was in fact the case – he spent most of the day with the Chiefs of Staff. General Thorne said that that was as it should be: it was most desirable that one of the greatest students of military history and of war should himself play the leading part in the direction of this war's strategy. Winston was more vital to this country than Hitler to Germany, because the former was unique and irreplaceable and the latter had established a school of leaders. The obvious comment is that Hitler may be a self-educated corporal and Winston may be an experienced student of tactics; but unfortunately Germany is organised as a war machine and England has only just realised the meaning of modern warfare.

War Cabinet: Confidential Annex
(*Cabinet papers, 65/14*)

30 June 1940
7 p.m.
10 Downing Street

The Prime Minister reminded his colleagues that the date on which the proposed operation in regard to the French Fleet at Oran could take place depended on whether HMS *Nelson* was to take part in the operation. If it was decided to wait until HMS *Nelson* could reach the Western Mediterranean, the operation could not take place until the 5th July. If it was decided not to wait for the *Nelson*, the operation could take place two days earlier.

The Prime Minister said that the question whether the *Nelson* should be used in this operation depended in part upon the position in Home Waters. He had given considerable attention in the last two days to the state of our defences against invasion. The Prime Minister gave some details of the discussions which he had had on this matter in the previous two days. He had reached the conclusion that it would be wiser to keep HMS *Nelson* in Home Waters rather than to send her to the Western Mediterranean. This meant that the operation at Oran could take place on the 3rd July. On the whole, the sooner this operation was carried out the better.

The War Cabinet expressed general agreement with this view.

Discussion ensued on the importance of taking steps to ensure that the statement which we should make to the French naval authorities at Oran would become known to the ships' companies. The possibility of dropping leaflets had been considered. The Minister of Information was invited to consider whether it would be possible to broadcast a message on a wavelength which would be picked up by the crews of the French men-of-war at Oran.

The operation at Oran should be contemporaneous in regard to action with other French men-of-war. Thus steps should be taken to establish full control of all the French men-of-war in this country. Action should also be taken in regard to the *Emile Bertin*, and in regard to the ships under Admiral Godfroy[1] in the Eastern Mediterranean.

The action we were about to take would be enhanced if, before the operation was undertaken, a communication were handed to the French Admiral at Oran[2] on behalf of His Majesty's Government, making clear our determination to continue the war against Germany, and making the point that the interests of France, no less than those of this country, depended on our victory.

The War Cabinet:–
(1) Took note of the suggestion that the operation in regard to the French Fleet at Oran should take place on the 3rd July.
(2) Invited the Minister of Information to enquire into the possibility of broadcasting a message which would be picked up by the crews of the French men-of-war at Oran.
(3) Took note that the Prime Minister would prepare a draft of a communication to be made on behalf of His Majesty's Government to the French Admiral at Oran before the operation was undertaken.

John Martin: diary
(*Martin papers*)

30 June 1940

When I told Winston that six people had died of heart failure during the air raid warning, he said that <u>he</u> was more likely to die of over-eating, but he didn't want to die yet when so many interesting things were happening. I saw him this evening after his bath wrapped only in a huge towel, looking like one of the later Roman Emperors.

---

[1] Admiral Godfroy, commanding the French naval forces in the Eastern Mediterranean. Following the internment of his principal warships in Alexandria harbour by the British, he refused to respond to repeated appeals from the Gaullists to commit himself to the Free French movement. De Gaulle himself, visiting Alexandria in April 1941, recalled: 'I was able to see – and it wrung my heart – the fine French ships somnolent and useless in the midst of the British fleet cleared for action' (*The Call to Honour*, page 173).

[2] Admiral Gensoul, Flag Officer, French Battle Squadron, Oran.

July 1940

Winston S. Churchill to Neville Chamberlain[1]
(*Chamberlain papers*)

1 July 1940   10 Downing Street

My dear Neville,

I am v'y much obliged to you for y'r most inspiring & resolute broadcast wh I read with the greatest pleasure. I am sure it will do no end of good.[2]

Yours ever,
Winston S. Churchill

---

[1] For a facsimile of this letter, see page 450.

[2] In a broadcast on 30 June 1940, Chamberlain declared: 'The first thing I want to say is that all the members of the War Cabinet are working together in complete harmony and agreement. Anyone who lends himself to propaganda by listening to idle tales about disunion among us, or who imagines that any of us would consent to enter upon peace negotiations with the enemy, is just playing the Nazi game.' Later in his broadcast Chamberlain spoke with confidence of Britain's material strength. He then told his listeners: 'But we have something even stronger on our side. We shall be fighting for our own hearths and homes, and we shall be fighting with the conviction that our cause is the cause of humanity and peace against cruelty and persecution, of right against wrong; a cause that surely has the blessing of Almighty God. It would be a faint heart indeed that could doubt our success.'

10, Downing Street,
Whitehall.

2. VII. 40

My dear Neville,

I am so much obliged to you for yr most inspiring & resolute broadcast wh I read with the greatest pleasure. I am sure it will do no end of good

Yours ever,

Winston S. Churchill

War Cabinet: minutes
(*Cabinet papers, 65/8*)

1 July 1940   10 Downing Street
11.30 a.m.

The Chief of the Imperial General Staff said that General de Gaulle had addressed various bodies of French troops in this country on the previous day and had appealed for volunteers. Twenty-two Officers and 1,000 men of the Foreign Legion had volunteered, together with about 400 men from various miscellaneous units, and about 400 or 500 naval personnel. All these volunteers were being accommodated in the White City. General de Gaulle had wished the Senegalese troops to remain in this country. The War Office, however, had felt considerable anxiety about these troops and they had now sailed.

In discussion, it was pointed out that news had been received from several quarters of French personnel who were anxious to continue the struggle, but that the reception given to them had often been discouraging.

The Prime Minister said that it was of the utmost importance that we should have a French contingent. Too often, however, the British authorities had appeared hesitant about welcoming French volunteers on the grounds of lack of equipment or other difficulties. This attitude was most unfortunate, and must not be allowed to continue.

The Prime Minister drew attention to the scheme for evacuating children to North America. Many people were now expecting the scheme to develop on a considerable scale. A large movement of this kind encouraged a defeatist spirit, which was entirely contrary to the true facts of the position and should be sternly discouraged.

The Prime Minister was invited to consider issuing a circular to Heads of Departments instructing them to take drastic steps to put a stop to defeatist talk.

War Cabinet: Confidential Annex
(*Cabinet papers, 65/14*)

1 July 1940   10 Downing Street
6 p.m.

ORAN

The following were the main points dealt with in discussion:–
(1) The Vice Chief of Naval Staff had had a discussion with Admiral

Odend'hal[1] that morning. Admiral Odend'hal had said that he had had a telegram from Admiral Darlan asking that we should reserve final judgment until the details of the armistice conditions were known. Discussions on the armistice conditions were starting at Wiesbaden on the 1st July, and the conditions in regard to the French Fleet were to be dealt with first.

The Prime Minister said that discussions as to the armistice conditions could not affect the real facts of the situation.

Winston S. Churchill to General Ismay
(<i>Churchill papers, 20/13</i>)

1 July 1940

1. The Admiralty are retaining *Nelson* and her four destroyers in Home Waters, and the operation 'Catapult'[2] should go forward aiming at daybreak the 3rd.

2. During night of 2nd/3rd all necessary measures should be taken at Portsmouth and Plymouth, at Alexandria and if possible at Martinique, on the same lines as 'Catapult.' The reactions to these measures at Dakar and Casa Blanca must be considered, and every precaution taken to prevent the escape of valuable units. At the same time it would be desirable, if possible, to cut out and carry off the ships with the French politicians on board. Has this minor operation been studied.

3. It is most needful to gather together five to ten thousand or more French officers and men who are willing to go on with the fight with us. These should be collected from all parts, and I am very sorry to hear that General de Gaulle is dissatisfied with the way the French troops in Great Britain were given a choice of joining up. The political consequences of such a force under de Gaulle would be out of all proportion to its numbers. It is indispensable to have the nucleus of such a force for the operation known as 'Susan.'[3]

4. I am expecting to receive for submission to Cabinet at latest by tomorrow plans for 'Susan.' These plans should comprise approximately ten thousand Poles, five thousand British and as many French as can be got together. The operation cannot take place before the 15th, but should be considered for the last fortnight of July. The eight regular battalions from India will be here by then.

5. I attach great importance to the digging up of fields by local arrangement. This should be done simultaneously throughout the country in the next

[1] Admiral Odend'hal was head of the French Naval Mission in London. In June he had worked closely with the Admiralty in London to set up the machinery for getting French troops away from France, and protecting French ships in convoy.

[2] Operation 'Catapult', the British attack on French naval forces at Oran.

[3] Operation 'Susan', a possible amphibious landing in North Africa (no such landing proved possible until November 1942, Operation 'Torch').

48 hours. All that is needed is a trench across fields which are more than 400 yards long.

6. We are getting a lot of these pill-boxes made, and must become conscious of the danger of leaving them unguarded. If they fell into Fifth Column hands they would obstruct traffic on the roads. If enemy lodgments were effected and made progress inland, they would serve as a line of defensive posts to the invaders. I should be glad to receive to-day proposals for manning them forthwith, i.e., from to-night, with specially selected volunteers of the Home Guard.

7. See also my Minute about 'drenching' beaches as suggested.[1]

8. The Admiralty should endeavour to raise the flotillas in the narrow seas to a strength of forty destroyers, with additional cruiser support. An effort should be made to reach this strength during the next two or three days, and hold it for the following fortnight when the position can be reviewed. Losses in the WA[2] must be accepted meanwhile.

I should like also a daily return of the numbers of 'Dagger' craft on patrol or available between Portsmouth and the Tyne.

9. I should like also a daily return of new rifles issued to the troops and the Home Guard, observing that the American rifles must be now arriving in large numbers. The issue of these rifles should be made an evolution.

10. I was promised a Naval paper on the possibilities of mining-in a lodgment from the sea as an alternative or addition to our sea-borne counter-attack.

Pray let me have the assurance that all these matters are being dealt with forthwith by the Joint Staff, and give me precise details of the action taken as soon as possible.

WSC

Winston S. Churchill to General Wavell
(*Churchill papers, 20/14*)

1 July 1940

I am most anxious to gather together a force of five to ten thousand French officers and soldiers who volunteer to go on with the war either as British nationals or French. We are collecting from here. Others present themselves at Malta or in Tunis, but the bulk must come from Syria. Such a force under General de Gaulle may play a part in important operations outside the Mediterranean. Do not therefore on any account discourage the rallying of good men to our cause upon consideration local to your own command.

WSC

[1] See pages 444–5.
[2] Western Approaches.

Winston S. Churchill to Lord Beaverbrook
(*Churchill papers, 20/14*)

1 July 1940

Dear Minister of Aircraft Production,

I have received your letter of June 30,[1] and hasten to say that at a moment like this when an invasion is reported to be imminent there can be no question of any Ministerial resignations being accepted. I require you therefore to dismiss this matter from your mind, and to continue the magnificent work you are doing on which to a large extent our safety depends. Meanwhile I am patiently studying how to meet your needs in respect of control of the overlapping parts of your Department and that of the Air Ministry, and also to assuage the unfortunate differences which have arisen.

Yours ever sincerely,
Winston S. Churchill

War Cabinet: minutes
(*Cabinet papers, 65/8*)

2 July 1940 10 Downing Street
12 noon

The Prime Minister read telegrams from No. 8 (Salisbury-Jones[2]) Military Mission, to the effect that the Mission had received orders to close down and leave Syria. The movement of formed bodies of French troops across the frontier into Palestine had now ceased, and the French Authorities were anxious that movements of individuals should be stopped and that units

---

[1] On 30 June 1940 Beaverbrook had submitted his resignation to Churchill. With aircraft production having been 'immensely increased', he wrote, it had become 'imperative' that the Ministry of Aircraft Production 'should pass into the keeping of a man in touch and sympathy with the Air Ministry and the Air Marshals. I should be relieved of my duties after my successor has been informed of all our projects. In particular, the new Minister should be informed of my plans for carrying out a vigorous programme of development of new types of aircraft and engines. My decision to retire is based on my firm conviction that I am not suited to working with the Air Ministry or the Air Marshals. I am convinced that my work is finished and my task is over. I am certain that another man could take up the responsibilities with hope and expectation of that measure of support and sympathy which has been denied me.'

[2] Arthur Guy Salisbury-Jones, 1896–1985. On active service, 1915–18 (twice wounded; Military Cross and bar). Liaison officer in Syria during the Jebel Druze campaign, 1925–6. Commanded the 3rd Battalion, Coldstream Guards, Palestine, during the Arab revolt, 1938–9 (despatches). Mission to Syria, 1940. On active service, Somaliland, Greece and Crete, 1940–1 (despatches). Head of the British Military Mission to South Africa, 1941–4; to France, 1945. CBE, 1945. Military Attaché, France, 1946–9. Marshal of the Diplomatic Corps, 1950–61. Knighted, 1953. President of the English Vineyards Association, 1967–81.

July 1940

which had already crossed the frontier should be persuaded to return. Colonel Salisbury-Jones had stated that such action would have a disastrous effect on the remaining pro-British Frenchmen and suggested propaganda by radio from Palestine on the following lines:–

'The British have undertaken not to encourage desertion from the French Army. At the same time, it is false that volunteers whose honour forbids them to obey the dictates of the Bordeaux Government are not welcome, or that they are returned to the French Authorities. No volunteers have been or will be turned back.'

Such a broadcast might lead to a movement within the French Army which would result in the restoration of the situation under a younger leader.

Every encouragement should be given to French troops who were prepared to fight on, as it was from these elements that the proposed French Force for action in the Colonies would be formed. General de Gaulle had already formed three battalions in this country, and had collected 380 aviators, 1,000 young men anxious to serve, and a company of small tanks.

The Prime Minister then referred to a telegram from the General Officer Commanding Palestine,[1] saying that 15 train-loads of Poles had arrived in the country.

The Admiralty should consider whether these Allied troops could be brought from Syria, through the Mediterranean, to this country or elsewhere. Meanwhile, it was most important that the War Office should take the necessary steps to encourage French troops to cross into Palestine.

The Prime Minister thought that the General Officers Commanding-in-Chief of the Home Commands should have the right to remove suspected persons from those parts of the defended area which lay within their commands.

DIGGING UP OPEN SPACES

The Prime Minister said that it was difficult to carry out this work over the whole country, but steps were now being taken to increase the area round each aerodrome in which all open spaces were blocked.

In reply to a question by the Chief of Naval Staff, the Prime Minister said that it was our policy to encourage any French sailors, who were willing to continue to fight for us, to do so.

---

[1] General Barker, see page 681, note 1. Barker was succeeded as General Officer Commanding Palestine by General Philip Neame.

War Cabinet: Confidential Annex
(*Cabinet papers, 65/14*)

2 July 1940　　　　　　　　　　　　　　　　　　　　10 Downing Street
12 noon

... discussion ensued as to whether the Third Division should be sent to Northern Ireland.

The Prime Minister said that he thought that this Division was certainly required in this country, owing to the small number of fully trained and equipped Divisions at our disposal. He instanced the suggestion that our troops were very thin on the ground, particularly towards the South Coast.

The First Lord of the Admiralty expressed some anxiety as to the small number of troops in the South-west of this country available for the protection of Fleet bases.

The Prime Minister said that sedentary troops should suffice for this purpose, and that our trained troops must be kept in hand as a striking force. He had been speaking to the Commander-in-Chief, Home Forces, that morning, who reported that great progress had been made in the last five or six days with our arrangements for defence against invasion.

Winston S. Churchill to General Ismay
(*Churchill papers, 20/13*)

2 July 1940

DOVER GUN

I am glad that progress has been maintained as promised. Do I understand that this gun fires from a railway mounting, and is movable? Is the emplacement in a wood or well camouflaged? It might be in a big building or a shed. Can this gun go into action without calibrating trials? It is most important not to fire it from its new site till we have definite evidence that a number of enemy guns have been mounted on the French coast within its range or something else important happens. These could then be destroyed under aircraft observation. The whole position of the gun must be kept most secret. Is overhead cover being provided against air attack?

　　　　　　　　　　　　　　　　　　　　　　　　　　　　　　　　WSC

Winston S. Churchill to General Ismay
(*Churchill papers, 20/13*)

2 July 1940

If it be true that a few hundred German troops have been landed on Jersey or Guernsey by troop-carriers, plans should be studied to land secretly by night on the Islands and kill or capture the invaders. This is exactly one of the exploits for which the Commandos would be suited. There ought to be no difficulty in getting all the necessary information from the inhabitants and from those evacuated. The only possible reinforcements which could reach the enemy during the fighting would be by aircraft-carriers, and here would be a good opportunity for the Air Force fighting machines. Pray let me have a plan.

WSC

Winston S. Churchill to General Ismay
(*Churchill papers, 20/13*)

2 July 1940

See the letter[1] from Mr Wedgwood, MP, which is interesting and characteristic. What is the position about London? I have a very clear view that we should fight every inch of it, and that it would devour quite a large invading army.

General Bernard Montgomery[2]: *recollection*
(*'The Memoirs of Field Marshal the Viscount Montgomery of Alamein', pages 69–70*)

2 July 1940   South Coast

I showed him all that was possible in the time. I took him to Lancing College, inhabited by the Royal Ulster Rifles, and showed him a counter-attack on the small airfield on the coast below which was assumed to have been captured by the Germans; he was delighted, especially by the action of the Bren-gun carrier platoon of the battalion. We then worked our way along

---

[1] About the need to defend London street by street. For Churchill's reply to this, and to a second letter from Wedgwood, see 5 July 1940.

[2] Bernard Law Montgomery, 1887–1976. Entered the Army, 1903. On active service, 1914–18. Major-General, 1938. Commanded the 3rd Division, 1939–40; the 5th Corps, 1940; the 12th Corps, 1941. Knighted, 1942. Commanded the Eighth Army (including the Battle of El Alamein), 1942–3; the 21st Army Group (including the Normandy Landings), 1944–5. Field Marshal, 1944. Created Viscount, 1946. Knight of the Garter, 1946. Chief of the Imperial General Staff, 1946–8. Deputy Supreme Allied Commander, Europe, 1951–8.

the coast, finishing up in Brighton at about 7.30 p.m. He suggested I should have dinner with him and his party at the Royal Albion Hotel, and we talked much during the meal. He asked me what I would drink at dinner and I replied – water. This astonished him. I added that I neither drank nor smoked and was 100 per cent fit. This story is often told with embellishments, but the above is the true version.

From the window of the dining-room we could see a platoon of guardsmen preparing a machine-gun post in a kiosk on Brighton pier, and he remarked that when at school near here he used to go and see the performing fleas in the kiosk. Then we talked about my problems. The main thing which seemed curious to me was that my division was immobile. It was the only fully equipped division in England, the only division fit to fight any enemy anywhere. And here we were in a static role, ordered to dig in on the south coast. Some other troops should take on my task; my division should be given buses, and be held in mobile reserve with a counter-attack role. Why was I left immobile? There were thousands of buses in England; let them give me some, and release me from this static role so that I could practise a mobile counter-attack role. The Prime Minister thought this was the cat's whiskers.

I do not know what the War Office thought, but I got my buses.

Admiral Pound to Admiral Somerville
(*Premier papers, 3/179/1*)

2 July 1940
10.55 p.m.
Personal

ORAN

The War Cabinet will be impatiently awaiting news of 'Catapult'. I hope therefore you will be able to send short messages at intervals such as 'Emissary has made contact,' 'French ships in harbour,' etc.

You are charged with one of the most disagreeable and difficult tasks that a British Admiral has ever been faced with, but we have complete confidence in you and rely on you to carry it out relentlessly.

War Cabinet: Confidential Annex
(*Cabinet papers, 65/8*)

3 July 1940　　　　　　　　　　　　　　　　　　　　　　10 Downing Street
11.30 a.m.

The Prime Minister referred to the bombing which had been carried out on the previous day against oil refineries, aerodromes and marshalling-yards in

Germany. He said that there was a growing feeling that now that an attempt to invade this country might be imminent, our attacks should be directed against German ports.

The Chief of the Air Staff said that it had been generally acknowledged that invasion could only present a serious danger if the Royal Air Force had first been defeated. This defeat could only take place at the hands of the German Air Force, and the attacks which were being made on oil refineries, aircraft factories and aerodromes in Germany aimed at reducing the scale of air attack on this country. At the same time, there would be no hesitation in giving full priority to the attack of any assembly of transports which might be reported.

The Prime Minister appreciated the reasons for attacking objectives which would cripple the German Air Force, but considered that the coming week might well be so critical from the point of view of invasion that it justified transferring emphasis to the bombing of German ports.

The War Cabinet were informed that HMS *Foxhound* had arrived off Oran early that morning, but Captain Holland[1] had reported that the French Admiral[2] had refused to see him. A letter had therefore been handed in, setting out the terms offered.

Oran Chronology[3]

3 July 1940

12.16 p.m.	Message received from the Admiral Gensoul, that the French ships at Oran will fight if force is used against them.
12.32 p.m.	Admiral Somerville informed by the Admiralty that if the French ships try to leave harbour, he should open fire.
12.34 p.m.	Somerville informs the Admiralty that he is awaiting a reply from Gensoul (setting out the British terms) before opening fire.
1.01 p.m.	Somerville receives a message received from Gensoul, rejecting the British terms.
1.47 p.m.	Somerville gives Gensoul until 3 p.m. to accept the British terms.
2.40 p.m.	Somerville reports 'slight sign of weakening' on the part of Gensoul, and extends the deadline to 3.30 p.m.
3.09 p.m.	News from Alexandria that the French ships there were about to disable themselves in the harbour.

[1] The former British Naval Attaché in Paris, see page 714, note 2.
[2] Admiral Gensoul.
[3] Prepared by the author on the basis of material in the Churchill and Admiralty papers. The material in the Churchill papers was assembled by Captain G. R. G. Allen, R.N., one of Churchill's assistants when he was writing his war memoirs after the war.

3.30 p.m.   Oran deadline passes.

3.42 p.m.   Message from Somerville received in London: 'Am postponing action as I think they are weakening.'

4.14 p.m.   Gensoul instructed by French Admiralty not to accept the British terms.

5.55 p.m.   Somerville opens fire.

6 p.m.   Somerville reports to London, 'Am being heavily engaged.'

Defence Committee: minutes
(*Cabinet papers, 69/1*)

3 July 1940
11 p.m.

NAVAL SITUATION

The Committee discussed the situation in the light of the latest information of the action with the French ships at Oran. Further messages were received during the course of the meeting and the situation may be summarised as follows:–

(i) A heavy engagement had taken place between Force H[1] and the French warships in the harbour at Oran. All the French warships had been put out of action with the exception of one ship of the Strasbourg class which had succeeded in breaking out. This ship had subsequently been attacked by aircraft and was thought to have been hit by one torpedo; she had appeared to be shaping course for Toulon.

(ii) Admiral Somerville had reported that he did not intend to carry out a further attack that night owing to the danger from enemy submarines and in view of the destroyer situation. He had also stated that he was not in a position to chase and would signal the reasons for this on his return to Gibraltar.

(iii) The British destroyer patrolling off Casablanca had been fired on by the shore batteries.

(iv) The demilitarisation of defences at Bizerta had been held up.

(v) We had been referred to in one French message as 'the enemy'.

There was general agreement that there was a strong likelihood that the French Government would in the very near future declare war against us.

---

[1] The British naval force based on Gibraltar.

INVASION

The Chief of the Air Staff said that the Joint Intelligence Sub-Committee had reported that there were grounds for expecting that invasion was imminent. There was nothing that could be taken as definite evidence but there were indications from a number of directions which pointed to the imminence of invasion which it would be unsafe to ignore.

The Prime Minister asked for a full report of the facts, leading to the conclusion that invasion was imminent, to be placed before the War Cabinet at their meeting on the next day.

Winston S. Churchill to Sir Archibald Sinclair and Sir Cyril Newall
(*Churchill papers, 20/13*)

3 July 1940
ACTION THIS DAY

I hear from every side of the need for throwing your main emphasis on bombing the ships and barges in all the ports under German control.

WSC

Winston S. Churchill to Anthony Eden
(*Churchill papers, 20/13*)

3 July 1940
ACTION THIS DAY

I was disturbed to find the 3rd Division spread about 30 miles of coast, instead of being as I had imagined held back concentrated in reserve, ready to move against any serious head of invasion. But much more astonishing was the fact that the infantry of this Division, which is otherwise fully mobile, are not provided with the 'buses necessary to move them to the point of action. This provision of 'buses, waiting always ready and close at hand, is essential to all mobile Units, and to none more than the 3rd Division while spread about the coast.

I heard the same complaint from Portsmouth that the troops there had not got their transport ready and close at hand. Considering the great masses of transport, both 'buses and lorries, which there are in this country, and the large numbers of drivers brought back from the BEF, it should be possible to remedy these deficiencies at once. I hope, at any rate, the the GOC 3rd Division[1] will be told to-day to take up, as he would like to do, the large number of 'buses which are even now plying for pleasure traffic up and down the sea front at Brighton.

WSC

---

[1] General Montgomery.

John Colville: diary
(*Colville papers*)

3 July 1940

Before going to bed the PM rang for me and asked me to take down a telegram to the Duke of Windsor, offering him the Governorship of the Bahamas. Before dictating a sentence he always muttered it wheezingly under his breath and he seemed to gain intellectual stimulus from pushing in with his stomach the chairs standing round the Cabinet table! 'I think it is a very good suggestion of mine, Max,' he said to Beaverbrook, who was there.[1] 'Do you think he will take it?' 'Sure he will,' said B, 'and he'll find it a great relief.' 'Not half as much as his brother will,' replied W. When I gave him the dictated telegram he said: 'What a beautiful handwriting(!!), but, my dear boy, when I say stop you must write stop and not just put a blob.' (He is always pedantic about small things.)

Winston S. Churchill to the Dominion Prime Ministers
(*Churchill papers, 20/9*)

4 July 1940
Most secret and personal
Decypher yourself

The position of the Duke of Windsor on the Continent in recent months has been causing HM and HMG embarrassment as though his loyalties are unimpeachable there is always a backwash of Nazi intrigue which seeks to make trouble about him. The Continent is now in enemy hands. There are personal and family difficulties about his return to this country.

In all the circumstances it has been felt that an appointment abroad might appeal to him and his wife, and I have with HM's cordial approval offered him the Governorship of the Bahamas. HRH has intimated that he will accept the appointment. I think he may render useful service, and find a suitable occupation there.

I wished you to have the earliest possible advance information of this. You will appreciate how necessary it is to preserve complete secrecy. We here are of course doing all we can to ensure this.

---

[1] A different version of why the Duke of Windsor was sent to the Bahamas appears in the diary of Sir Ronald Storrs, who, after a talk with Lord Lloyd (the Colonial Secretary), reported that it was King George VI's idea, 'to keep him at all costs out of England' (Diary entry for 14 July 1940, *Storrs papers*).

July 1940

Winston S. Churchill to the Duke of Windsor
(*Churchill papers, 20/9*)

4 July 1940
Most immediate

I am authorised by the King and the Cabinet to offer you the appointment of Governor and Commander-in-Chief of the Bahamas. If you accept, it may be possible to take you and the Duchess there direct from Lisbon dependent on the military situation. Please let me know without delay whether this proposal is satisfactory to Your Royal Highness. Personally I feel sure it is the best open in the grievous situation in which we all stand. At any rate I have done my best.

Winston S. Churchill to General Ismay
(*Premier papers, 3/222/3*)

4 July 1940
ACTION THIS DAY
10 Downing Street

What is being done to encourage and assist the people living in threatened sea ports to make suitable shelters for themselves in which they could remain during an invasion? Active measures must be taken forthwith. Officers or representatives of the local authority should go round explaining to families that if they decide not to leave in accordance with our general advice, they should remain in the cellars, and arrangements should be made to prop up the building overhead. They should be assisted in this, both by advice and materials. Their gas masks should be inspected. All this must be put actively in operation from to-day. The process will stimulate voluntary evacuation, and at the same time make reasonable provision for those who remain.

War Cabinet: Confidential Annex
(*Cabinet papers, 65/14*)

4 July 1940
11.30 a.m.
10 Downing Street

FRENCH NAVAL FORCES AT ALEXANDRIA

The Prime Minister said that a quick solution of the problem must be reached. It was most important for the Eastern Mediterranean Fleet to regain its mobility and the spectacle of a deadlock in the harbour would do great harm to Egyptian opinion. For these reasons he deprecated the suggestion to starve out the French Forces.

Winston S. Churchill: letter to all civil servants
(*Harold Nicolson papers*)

4 July 1940

10, DOWNING STREET,

WHITEHALL.

ON what may be the eve of an attempted invasion or battle for our native land, the Prime Minister desires to impress upon all persons holding responsible positions in the Government, in the Fighting Services, or in the Civil Departments, their duty to maintain a spirit of alert and confident energy. While every precaution must be taken that time and means afford, there are no grounds for supposing that more German troops can be landed in this country, either from the air or across the sea, than can be destroyed or captured by the strong forces at present under arms. The Royal Air Force is in excellent order and at the highest strength it has yet attained. The German Navy was never so weak, nor the British Army at home so strong as now. The Prime Minister expects all His Majesty's servants in high places to set an example of steadiness and resolution. They should check and rebuke expressions of loose and ill-digested opinion in their circles, or by their subordinates. They should not hesitate to report, or if necessary remove, any officers or officials who are found to be consciously exercising a disturbing or depressing influence, and whose talk is calculated to spread alarm and despondency. Thus alone will they be worthy of the fighting men, who in the air, on the sea, and on land, have already met the enemy without any sense of being out-matched in martial qualities.

Winston S. Churchill

4th July, 1940.

July 1940

Winston S. Churchill: Oral Answers
(*Hansard*)

4 July 1940   House of Commons

HOME DEFENCE
Organisation

Colonel Arthur Evans[1] asked the Prime Minister whether, with a view to the efficient co-ordination of all military and civil Departments concerned with the defence of Great Britain, he will appoint a commander-in-chief with the necessary liaison staff for this purpose, who would come under the direct orders of the Minister of Defence?

The Prime Minister (Mr Churchill): A closely knit and necessarily elaborate organisation to ensure the effective concert of the whole apparatus of Home Defence has been over a considerable period of time gradually worked out by the combined staffs of the three fighting Services. This organisation, in the opinion of His Majesty's Government, supported by their professional advisers, gives to the Commander-in-Chief, Home Forces, the necessary control over not only the military but the civil sphere, subject, of course, to the fact that he has direct access to the Prime Minister or Minister of Defence for the time being, and can thus receive such guidance upon questions of high policy as may from time to time be required. It would be the greatest mistake, at the moment when it may well have to be put to the proof, to liquidate and remould this organisation, which at the present time is working to the satisfaction of all the principal executive persons concerned. It must, of course, be continually tested and improved. I cannot conceive that the proposal pressed in some quarters to appoint a super Commander-in-Chief over the whole field of the three Services and the civil power would not be a serious impediment to effective action; and I have never yet heard any practical suggestion as to who that officer should be.

Inspection by Members of Parliament

Mr Shinwell[2] asked the Prime Minister whether, in view of the desire of hon. Members to satisfy themselves that our defence against invasion is adequate, and that our production in arms and aircraft is being speeded up,

---

[1] Arthur Evans, 1898–1958. On active service, 1914–18. Conservative MP, 1922–3, 1924–9 and 1931–45. British Expeditionary Force, France, 1939. Lieutenant-Colonel commanding the Le Havre Defence Force and Garrison, 1940 (despatches). Leader of the Parliamentary Mission to President Roosevelt and the United States Congress, 1943. Knighted, 1944.

[2] Emanuel Shinwell, 1884–1986. Unsuccessful Labour candidate for Linlithgowshire, 1918; elected, 1922; re-elected, 1923. Defeated, 1924; re-elected at a by-election in April 1928 and again at the general election of 1929. Defeated in 1931. Parliamentary Secretary, Mines Department, 1924 and 1931. Financial Secretary, War Office, 1929–30. Labour MP for Linlithgow, 1928–31; for Seaham, 1935–50; for Easington, 1950–70. Minister of Fuel and Power, 1945–7. Secretary of State for War, 1947–50. Minister of Defence, 1950–1. Chairman of the Parliamentary Labour Party, 1964–7. Created Baron (Life Peer), 1970.

he will afford an opportunity for hon. Members to inspect defences and factories at an early date?

Colonel Wedgwood asked the Prime Minister whether he will allow Members of Parliament to inspect the civil and military defences of their country, will facilitate such inspection, and will welcome reports from them?

The Prime Minister: The Government would always desire to treat Members of the House with all possible consideration and courtesy, but no general right to inspect military defences, dockyards or secret munition factories has ever been claimed by the House for its individual Members, and I cannot think that any such departure should be taken at this time.

Mr Shinwell: Does the right hon. Gentleman appreciate that the purport of my Question was not to claim the right to inspect factories where operations are conducted in secret or defences which ought not to be inspected by other than military authorities, but that hon. Members should have some opportunity, other than the assurances given by the Government, to see that our defences are in an adequate condition? Is he also aware that hon. Members did have an opportunity of seeing the defences in their own areas and occasionally were disquieted by what they saw?

The Prime Minister: I hoped that aspect of the hon. Gentleman's Question would be covered by what I said about treating Members of this House with all possible consideration and courtesy, and I do not mean that to be an empty form. I think there are many contacts between Members of this House and the Ministers representing the different Departments, and I wish it to be clearly understood that it is desirable to facilitate the necessary work of Members of Parliament, especially in their own constituencies, so far as this may be done.

Colonel Wedgwood: Is the right hon. Gentleman not aware that during the last war he himself gave me and other Members frequent opportunities of visiting the front in France? Are we not to be allowed to do the same here?

Captain Bellenger: Does the right hon. Gentleman remember that when he was not in office himself he had very adequate facilities, more than other private Members, of going overseas, seeing the defences there and interviewing British generals?

The Prime Minister: I think that all these matters had better be decided in a spirit of the utmost good will.

MINISTERS (BROADCASTS TO AMERICA)

Mr G. Strauss[1] asked the Prime Minister whether he will take steps to ensure that only those Cabinet Ministers who are known to possess the confidence of the American people should broadcast to that country in future?

---

[1] George Russell Strauss, 1901–93. Labour MP, 1929–31 and 1934–79. Member of the London and Home Counties Traffic Advisory Committee, 1936. Parliamentary Secretary to the Minister of Aircraft Production (Sir Stafford Cripps), 1942–5. Minister of Transport, 1946–7. Privy Councillor, 1947. Minister of Supply, 1947–51. Introduced the Theatres Bill (for the abolition of stage censorship), 1968. 'Father of the House', 1974. Created Baron, 1979.

The Prime Minister: It was at my personal request that my right hon. Friend the Lord President of the Council delivered the excellent and inspiring broadcast to which the hon. Member refers. I have no doubt that it was widely welcomed both here and in the United States, and I am sorry that in this hour of peril the hon. Member should put upon the Notice Paper a Question which does the country so little good and himself so little credit.

Mr Strauss: Does not the Prime Minister consider that it is in the national interest that broadcasts from Ministers to America should be made by people who are *persona grata* with the American public – [Hon. Members: 'How do you know?'] – either by himself or other Ministers who are *persona grata* but not by those against whom there is strong feeling among the American public?

The Prime Minister: I have the greatest respect and regard for the American public, but I do not consider that we have any means of determining with any precision, which of us is *persona grata*, nor in the ultimate issue could I recognise their final right to judge.

BUSINESS OF THE HOUSE

Mr Lees-Smith: Will the Prime Minister state the Business for next week?

The Prime Minister: The Business for next week will be:

Tuesday – Committee stage of the Supplementary Vote of Credit for War Expenditure, 1940. Afterwards the Adjournment of the House will be moved, and a Debate will take place in Secret Session on the work of the Ministry of Economic Warfare.

Perhaps I might say about the Business to-day that after going formally into Committee of Supply the Adjournment of the House will be moved, and I shall make a statement on the War Situation. In view of the wish expressed last week for a full and frank Debate on matters relating to the war, it is proposed after my statement to move the necessary Resolution so that the House may continue the Debate in Secret Session.

Mr Cocks[1]: Will the right hon. Gentleman remember that it was never so true as to-day that we are the one voice in Europe and that we must speak freely to Europe and not in secret?

The Prime Minister: I hope that on some days we shall speak freely and sometimes in private.

---

[1] Frederick Seymour Cocks, 1882–1953. In 1918 he published *The Secret Treaties*, denouncing British policy during the First World War. Labour MP from 1929 until his death. Member of the Joint Select Committee on Indian Constitutional Reform, 1933–4. Member of the All-Party Committee on Parliamentary Procedure, 1945–6. Leader of the All-Party Parliamentary Delegation to Greece, 1946. CBE, 1950.

Sir H. Williams[1]: While fully appreciating what is in the Prime Minister's mind so far as to-day's Debate is concerned, I should like to ask whether he does not realise that there are certain dangers in speeches being made by Ministers and being published in respect of which there is no subsequent discussion published. Does he realise that there are essential dangers in a procedure of that kind?

The Prime Minister: It is very difficult to please everybody, but I understand that a Secret Session was felt to be desirable so that the House could get into the most intimate relationship with the Government and all views could be expressed without their having to be read next morning by the enemy; and at the next moment, when we are indulging in that procedure at the wish of the House, my hon. Friend raises the opposite point of view and claims that the discussions should be in public. It is a matter of total indifference to the Government if hon. Members would like to have the discussion in public. [Hon. Members: 'No.'] That could not be the case to-day, because we said last week that we would, if it was desired, have the discussion in secret.

Sir H. Williams: I do not think the Prime Minister quite appreciates the point I was trying to make. The point I am raising concerns the position when a statement is made by the Prime Minister and that statement alone is published, and the remainder of the Debate is not. I am entirely in favour of having Secret Sessions from time to time, but the question is whether it is desirable to have a Debate partly in public and partly in secret.

The Prime Minister: The statement which I shall make has certainly been considered from the point of view that it will be read abroad to-morrow.

Sir William Davison[2]: Is not the whole point that in a Secret Session certain suggestions may be made to the Government for amendments in tactics and so on, and that they would be useful to our enemies if they knew of them? Is not that the whole object in having a Secret Session?

Mr Godfrey Nicholson[3]: Will my right hon. Friend take steps to

---

[1] Herbert Geraint Williams, 1884–1954. A marine engineer. Secretary, Machine Tool Trades Association, 1911–28. Secretary, Machine Tool Department, Ministry of Munitions, 1917–18 (when Churchill was Minister). Conservative MP, 1924–9, 1932–45, and from 1950 until his death. Chairman of the Executive, London Conservative Union, 1939–48. Knighted, 1939. Member of the Select Committee on National Expenditure, 1939–44.

[2] William Henry Davison, 1872–1953. A company director, connected with several educational foundations. Chairman of the Improved Industrial Dwellings Company and the East Surrey Water Company. President of the Kensington Chamber of Commerce. Mayor of Kensington, 1913–19. Raised and equipped two battalions for territorial service, 1914. Knighted, 1918. Conservative MP, 1918–45. Chairman of the Metropolitan Division of the National Union of Conservative Associations, 1928–30. Created Baron Broughshane, 1945.

[3] Godfrey Nicholson, 1901–91. A distiller. Conservative MP, 1931–5 and 1937–66. Created Baronet, 1958. His daughter, Emma Nicholson, was elected to the House of Commons, as a Conservative, in 1978.

discourage organs of the Press giving entirely imaginary summaries of what may take place in Secret Session?

The Prime Minister: I have not seen any of that; very much to the contrary.

Winston S. Churchill: speech
(*Hansard*)

4 July 1940   House of Commons
3.54 p.m.

WAR SITUATION – FRENCH FLEET

The Prime Minister (Mr Churchill): It is with sincere sorrow that I must now announce to the House the measures which we have felt bound to take in order to prevent the French Fleet from falling into German hands. When two nations are fighting together under long and solemn alliance against a common foe, one of them may be stricken down and overwhelmed, and may be forced to ask its Ally to release it from its obligations. But the least that could be expected was that the French Government, in abandoning the conflict and leaving its whole weight to fall upon Great Britain and the British Empire, would have been careful not to inflict needless injury upon their faithful comrade, in whose final victory the sole chance of French freedom lay, and lies.

As the House will remember, we offered to give full release to the French from their Treaty obligations, although these were designed for precisely the case which arose, on one condition, namely, that the French Fleet should be sailed for British harbours before the separate armistice negotiations with the enemy were completed. This was not done, but on the contrary, in spite of every kind of private and personal promise and assurance given by Admiral Darlan to the First Lord and to his Naval colleague the First Sea Lord of the British Admiralty, an armistice was signed which was bound to place the French Fleet as effectively in the power of Germany and its Italian following as that portion of the French Fleet which was placed in our power when many of them, being unable to reach African ports, came into the harbours of Portsmouth and Plymouth about 10 days ago. Thus I must place on record that what might have been a mortal injury was done to us by the Bordeaux Government with full knowledge of the consequences and of our dangers, and after rejecting all our appeals at the moment when they were abandoning the Alliance, and breaking the engagements which fortified it.

There was another example of this callous and perhaps even malevolent treatment which we received, not indeed from the French nation, who have never been and apparently never are to be consulted upon these transactions, but from the Bordeaux Government. This is the instance. There were over 400

German air pilots who were prisoners in France, many of them, perhaps most of them, shot down by the Royal Air Force. I obtained from M. Reynaud a personal promise that these pilots should be sent for safe keeping to England, and orders were given by him to that effect; but when M. Reynaud fell, these pilots were delivered over to Germany in order, no doubt, to win favour for the Bordeaux Government with their German masters, and to win it without regard to the injury done to us. The German Air Force already feels acutely the shortage of high grade pilots, and it seemed to me particularly odious, if I may use the word, that these 400 skilled men should be handed over with the sure knowledge that they would be used to bomb this country, and thus force our airmen to shoot them down for the second time over. Such wrongful deeds I am sure will not be condoned by history, and I firmly believe that a generation of Frenchmen will arise who will clear their national honour from all countenance of them.

I said last week that we must now look with particular attention to our own salvation. I have never in my experience seen so grim and sombre a question as what we were to do about the French Fleet discussed in a Cabinet. It shows how strong were the reasons for the course which we thought it our duty to take, that every Member of the Cabinet had the same conviction about what should be done and there was not the slightest hesitation or divergence among them, and that the three Service Ministers, as well as men like the Minister of Information and the Secretary of State for the Colonies,[1] particularly noted for their long friendship with France, when they were consulted were equally convinced that no other decision than that which we took was possible. We took that decision, and it was a decision to which, with aching hearts but with clear vision, we unitedly came. Accordingly early yesterday morning, 3rd July, after all preparations had been made, we took the greater part of the French Fleet under our control, or else called upon them, with adequate force, to comply with our requirements. Two battleships, two light cruisers, some submarines, including a very large one, the *Surcouf*, eight destroyers and approximately 200 smaller but extremely useful minesweeping and anti-submarine craft, which lay for the most part at Portsmouth and Plymouth, though there were some at Sheerness, were boarded by superior forces, after brief notice had been given wherever possible to their captains.[2]

This operation was successfully carried out without resistance or bloodshed except in one instance. A scuffle arose through a misunderstanding in the submarine *Surcouf*, in which one British leading seaman was killed and two British officers and one rating wounded and one French officer killed and one

---

[1] Alfred Duff Cooper (later Britain's first post-war Ambassador to France) and Lord Lloyd.
[2] Churchill was informed that French ships taken over in British ports consisted of 2 battleships, 2 auxiliary cruisers, 2 light cruisers, 2 destroyers, 3 small minelayers, 6 torpedo boats, 4 gunboats, 7 submarines, 38 small minesweepers, 42 trawlers, drifters and patrol boats, 38 tugs and 39 small craft, a total of 185 (*Premier papers, 3/179/4*).

wounded. For the rest, the French sailors in the main cheerfully accepted the end of a period of uncertainty. A considerable number, 800 or 900, have expressed an ardent desire to continue the war, and some have asked for British nationality. This we are ready to grant without prejudice to the other Frenchmen, numbered by thousands, who prefer to fight on with us as Frenchmen. All the rest of those crews will be immediately repatriated to French ports, if the French Government are able to make arrangements for their reception by permission of their German rulers. We are also repatriating all French troops who were in this country, excepting those who, of their own free will, have volunteered to follow General de Gaulle in the French forces of liberation of whom he is chief. Several French submarines have also joined us independently, and we have accepted their services.

Now I turn to the Mediterranean. At Alexandria, where a strong British battle fleet is lying, there are, besides a French battleship, four French cruisers, three of them modern 8-inch gun vessels, and a number of smaller ships. These have been informed that they cannot be permitted to leave harbour and thus fall within the power of the German conquerors of France. Negotiations and discussions, with the details of which I need not trouble the House, have necessarily been taking place, and measures have now been taken to ensure that those ships, which are commanded by a very gallant Admiral,[1] shall be sunk or otherwise made to comply with our wishes. The anguish which this process has, naturally, caused to the British and French naval officers concerned may be readily imagined, when I tell the House that only this morning, in the air raid upon Alexandria by Italian aircraft, some of the French ships fired heavily and effectively with us against the common enemy. We shall, of course, offer the fullest facilities to all French officers and men at Alexandria who wish to continue the war, and will provide for them and maintain them during the conflict. We have also promised to repatriate all the rest, and every care in our power will be taken, if they allow it, for their safety and their comfort. So much for Alexandria.

But the most serious part of the story remains. Two of the finest vessels of the French Fleet, the *Dunkerque* and the *Strasbourg*, modern battle cruisers much superior to *Scharnhorst* and *Gneisenau* – and built for the purpose of being superior to them – lay with two battleships, several light cruisers and a number of destroyers and submarines and other vessels at Oran and at its adjacent military port of Mers-El-Kebir on the Northern African shore of Morocco. Yesterday morning, a carefully chosen British officer, Captain Holland,[2] lately Naval Attaché in Paris, was sent on in a destroyer and waited upon the French Admiral Gensoul. After being refused an interview,

---

[1] Admiral Godfroy.
[2] Cedric Swinton Holland, 1889–1950. On active service, 1914–18 (despatches). Naval Attaché, Paris, 1938–40. Commanded the aircraft carrier *Ark Royal*, 1940–1 (despatches). Director of the Signal Department, Admiralty, 1942–3.

he presented the following document, which I will read to the House. The first two paragraphs of the document deal with the general question of the Armistice, which I have already explained in my own words. The fourth paragraph begins as follows: This is the operative paragraph:

'It is impossible for us, your comrades up to now, to allow your fine ships to fall into the power of the German or Italian enemy. We are determined to fight on to the end, and if we win, as we think we shall, we shall never forget that France was our Ally, that our interests are the same as hers and that our common enemy is Germany. Should we conquer, we solemnly declare that we shall restore the greatness and territory of France. For this purpose, we must make sure that the best ships of the French Navy are not used against us by the common foe. In these circumstances, His Majesty's Government have instructed me' –

That is, the British Admiral –

'to demand that the French Fleet now at Mers-El-Kebir and Oran shall act in accordance with one of the following alternatives:

(a) Sail with us and continue to fight for victory against the Germans and Italians.

(b) Sail with reduced crews under our control to a British port. The reduced crews will be repatriated at the earliest moment.

If either of these courses is adopted by you, we will restore your ships to France at the conclusion of the war or pay full compensation, if they are damaged meanwhile.

(c) Alternatively, if you feel bound to stipulate that your ships should not be used against the Germans or Italians unless these break the Armistice, then sail them with us with reduced crews, to some French port in the West Indies, Martinique, for instance, where they can be demilitarised to our satisfaction or be perhaps entrusted to the United States and remain safe until the end of the war, the crews being repatriated.

If you refuse these fair offers, I must, with profound regret, require you to sink your ships within six hours.

Finally, failing the above, I have the orders of His Majesty's Government to use whatever force may be necessary to prevent your ships from falling into German or Italian hands.'

We had hoped that one or other of the alternatives which we presented would have been accepted, without the necessity of using the terrible force of a British battle squadron. Such a squadron arrived before Oran two hours after Captain Holland and his destroyer. This battle squadron was commanded by Vice-Admiral Somerville, an officer who distinguished himself lately in the bringing-off of over 100,000 Frenchmen during the evacuation from Dunkirk. Admiral Somerville was further provided, besides his battleships, with a cruiser force and strong flotillas. All day the parleys continued, and we hoped until the afternoon that our terms would be accepted without bloodshed.

However, no doubt in obedience to the orders dictated by the Germans from Wiesbaden, where the Franco-German Armistice Commission is in session, Admiral Gensoul refused to comply and announced his intention of fighting. Admiral Somerville was therefore ordered to complete his mission before darkness fell, and at 5.53 p.m. he opened fire upon this powerful French Fleet, which was also protected by its shore batteries. At 6 p.m. he reported that he was heavily engaged. The action lasted for some 10 minutes and was followed by heavy attacks from our naval aircraft, carried in the *Ark Royal*. At 7.20 p.m. Admiral Somerville forwarded a further report, which stated that a battle cruiser of the 'Strasbourg' class was damaged and ashore; that a battleship of the 'Bretagne' class had been sunk, that another of the same class had been heavily damaged, and that two French destroyers and a seaplane carrier, *Commandant Teste*, were also sunk or burned.

While this melancholy action was being fought, either the battle cruiser *Strasbourg* or the *Dunkerque*, one or the other, managed to slip out of harbour in a gallant effort to reach Toulon or a North African port and place herself under German control, in accordance with the Armistice terms of the Bordeaux Government – though all this her crew and captain may not have realised. She was pursued by aircraft of the Fleet Air Arm and hit by at least one torpedo. She may have been joined by other French vessels from Algiers, which were well placed to do so and to reach Toulon before we could overtake them. She will, at any rate, be out of action for many months to come.

I need hardly say that the French ships were fought, albeit in this unnatural cause, with the characteristic courage of the French Navy, and every allowance must be made for Admiral Gensoul and his officers who felt themselves obliged to obey the orders they received from their Government and could not look behind that Government to see the German dictation. I fear the loss of life among the French and in the harbour must have been heavy,[1] as we were compelled to use a severe measure of force and several immense explosions were heard. None of the British ships taking part in the action was in any way affected in gun-power or mobility by the heavy fire directed upon them. I have not yet received any reports of our casualties, but Admiral Somerville's Fleet is, in all military respects, intact and ready for further action. The Italian Navy, for whose reception we had also made arrangements and which is, of course, considerably stronger numerically than the Fleet we used at Oran, kept prudently out of the way. However, we trust that their turn will come during the operations which we shall pursue to secure the effectual command of the Mediterranean.

A large proportion of the French Fleet has, therefore, passed into our hands or has been put out of action or otherwise withheld from Germany by

---

[1] More than 1,250 French sailors lost their lives at Oran.

yesterday's events. The House will not expect me to say anything about other French ships which are at large except that it is our inflexible resolve to do everything that is possible in order to prevent them falling into the German grip.

I leave the judgment of our action, with confidence, to Parliament. I leave it to the nation, and I leave it to the United States. I leave it to the world and to history.

Now I turn to the immediate future. We must, of course, expect to be attacked, or even invaded, if that proves to be possible – it has not been proved yet – in our own island before very long. We are making every preparation in our power to repel the assaults of the enemy, whether they be directed upon Great Britain, or upon Ireland, which all Irishmen, without distinction of creed or party, should realise is in imminent danger. These again are matters upon which we have clear views. These preparations are constantly occupying our toil from morn till night, and far into the night. But, although we have clear views, it would not, I think, be profitable for us to discuss them in public, or even, so far as the Government are concerned, except under very considerable reserve, in a private session. I call upon all subjects of His Majesty, and upon our Allies, and well-wishers – and they are not a few – all over the world, on both sides of the Atlantic, to give us their utmost aid. In the fullest harmony with our Dominions, we are moving through a period of extreme danger and of splendid hope, when every virtue of our race will be tested, and all that we have and are will be freely staked. This is no time for doubt or weakness. It is the supreme hour to which we have been called.

I will venture to read to the House a message which I have caused to be sent to all who are serving in positions of importance under the Crown, and if the House should view it with sympathy, I should be very glad to send a copy of it to every Member for his own use, not that such exhortations are needed. This is the message:

'On what may be the eve of an attempted invasion or battle for our native land, the Prime Minister desires to impress upon all persons holding responsible positions in the Government, in the Fighting Services, or in the Civil Departments, their duty to maintain a spirit of alert and confident energy. While every precaution must be taken that time and means afford, there are no grounds for supposing that more German troops can be landed in this country, either from the air or across the sea, than can be destroyed or captured by the strong forces at present under arms. The Royal Air Force is in excellent order and at the highest strength it has yet attained. The German Navy was never so weak, nor the British Army at home so strong as now. The Prime Minister expects all His Majesty's servants in high places to set an example of steadiness and resolution. They should check and rebuke expressions of loose and ill-digested opinion in their circles, or by their subordinates. They should not hesitate to report, or if necessary remove, any officers or officials who are found to be consciously exercising a disturbing or depressing influence, and whose talk is calculated to spread alarm and despondency. Thus alone will they be worthy of the fighting men, who, in the air, on the sea, and on land, have already met the enemy without any sense of being outmatched in martial qualities.'[1]

In conclusion, I feel that we are entitled to the confidence of the House and that we shall not fail in our duty, however painful. The action we have already taken should be, in itself, sufficient to dispose once and for all of the lies and rumours which have been so industriously spread by German propaganda and Fifth Column activities that we have the slightest intention of entering into negotiations in any form and through any channel with the German and Italian Governments. We shall, on the contrary, prosecute the war with the utmost vigour by all the means that are open to us until the righteous purposes for which we entered upon it have been fulfilled.

SECRET SESSION

4.23 p.m.

The Prime Minister: Mr Speaker,[2] I beg to call your attention to the fact that strangers are present.

Mr Speaker: The Question is, 'That strangers be ordered to withdraw.'

Question put, and agreed to.

Strangers withdrew accordingly.

[The remainder of the Sitting was in Secret Session.]

Winston S. Churchill: recollection
(*'Their Finest Hour', page 211*)

4 July 1940

The House was very silent during the recital, but at the end there occurred a scene unique in my own experience. Everybody seemed to stand up all around, cheering, for what seemed a long time. Up till this moment the Conservative Party had treated me with some reserve, and it was from the Labour benches that I received the warmest welcome when I entered the House or rose on serious occasions. But now all joined in solemn stentorian accord.

---

[1] This letter is reproduced in facsimile on page 464.
[2] Captain E. A. Fitzroy, Speaker of the House of Commons from 1928 to 1943.

Harold Nicolson: diary
(*'Diaries and Letters, 1939–1945'*)

4 July 1940

The House is at first saddened by this odious attack but is fortified by Winston's speech. The grand finale ends in an ovation, with Winston sitting there with the tears pouring down his cheeks.

John Colville: diary
(*Colville papers*)

4 July 1940

The PM made a statement in the House, to which I listened. He told the whole story of Oran and the House listened enthralled and amazed. Gasps of surprise were audible but it was clear that the action taken was unanimously approved. When the speech was over all the Members rose to their feet, waved their order papers and cheered loudly. Winston left the House visibly affected. I heard him say to Hore-Belisha: 'This is heartbreaking for me.'

Cosmo Gordon Lang[1]*: diary*
(*J. G. Lockhart, 'Cosmo Gordon Lang'*)

4 July 1940

I am told that Winston Churchill's statement in the House of Commons was followed by the whole house rising to its feet and cheering, recalling the great scene when Neville Chamberlain announced that he was flying to Munich – a scene which seems to belong to another world.

E. A. Seal: private letter
(*Seal papers*)

4 July 1940

It was a tremendous success. The scene at the end was quite awe-inspiring – the whole crowded House rose, & cheered for a full two minutes. I had been nodding in the box – I always do – I know the speech by heart; but I was quite startled by the sudden burst of noise.

The PM was quite upset. He went pink, & there were certainly tears in his

---

[1] Cosmo Gordon Lang, 1864–1945. Fellow of All Souls College, Oxford, 1889. Bishop of Stepney, 1901–8. Archbishop of York, 1908–28; of Canterbury, 1928–42. Knighted, 1937. Created Baron, 1942.

eyes. What it was all about I still really don't know. The speech was good, but no better than the others; & the occasion – the outbreak of hostilities with our old ally – hardly one for rejoicing. I think that there had been a great deal more anxiety than we realised about the French Fleet, & there was general relief that such vigorous action had been taken.

Somerville, the Admiral, is an old friend of mine. It must have been a terrible order to give – to open fire on the French Fleet. But I think it was the only course to take. The reception in America seems to have been good, too.

What anxious & difficult times we do live in!

British Consul-General, Dakar,[1] to Foreign Office
(*Churchill papers, 20/13*)

4 July 1940 Dakar
Most Immediate

Mayor of Dakar considers that a show of force should be made by British Fleet if possible by 10th July. Later on the situation may be more difficult without considerable loss of life, whereas arrival in force in the near future might have the desired effect without much bloodshed. Best hour thought to be about 5 a.m. GMT. If date and hour made known to me in time measures could be taken to prevent as far as possible orders to fire reaching coastal defence artillery.

I know that semi-official groups of French European patriots are planning a *coup d'État* in various centres and would be ready to seize vital positions. Chief Mohammedan religious heads of Senegal have been in conference and are determined to join us. Two have visited me to convey this information. Black population would back action, but lack own leaders. I am exerting my influence, which is now tremendous among them, to prevent their movement turning anti-French.

Request early information as to whether a strong naval force could be available in the near future.

---

[1] Victor Vincent Cusden, 1893–1980. Studying for the Consular Service in Germany when war broke out in 1914. Interned at Ruhleben Camp (for civilian internees), 1914–18. Entered the Consular Service, 1919. Vice-Consul, Salonica, 1919; Antwerp, 1920; Valparaiso, 1924. Acting Consul General, Valparaiso, 1925; Barcelona, 1928; Malaga, 1929. Consul-General, Dakar, 1931–40; Luanda, 1941–5; Izmir, 1945–51. OBE, 1943.

478   JULY 1940

Winston S. Churchill to General Ismay
(*Churchill papers, 20/13*)

5 July 1940

This[1] appears to be of the utmost importance, and it should be possible for the Fleet to make contact almost by the date mentioned. The question is whether General de Gaulle should not go by flying-boat to Gibraltar, so as to embark with a small staff in one of our ships. There is no time to organize the movement of French troops from here. Arrangements might be dislocated if *Richelieu* put to sea, and the fleet was diverted in search. If she stays where she is, all would flow out quite smoothly. Let this be considered forthwith so that a report can be made to me at the Cabinet.

Winston S. Churchill to Josiah Wedgwood
(*Wedgwood papers*)

5 July 1940   10 Downing Street
Secret

My dear Jos,

Many thanks for your letters. I am hoping to get a great many more rifles very soon, and to continue the process of arming the Home Guard (LDV). You may rest assured that we should fight every street of London and its suburbs. It would devour an invading army, assuming one ever got so far. We hope however to drown the bulk of them in the salt sea.

Yours ever,
W

War Cabinet: minutes
(*Cabinet papers, 65/8*)

5 July 1940   10 Downing Street
12 noon

The Secretary of State for Foreign Affairs said that the main question was whether we should agree to the Japanese demand that we should close the Burma Road.[2] After giving full weight to the considerations urged by the Chiefs of Staff, he still felt that we should decline to agree to this demand. The advantages which we should gain by agreeing to this demand would be

---

[1] The telegram from Dakar, printed above.
[2] The Burma Road, along which military supplies from India could reach the Chinese Nationalists (under Chiang Kai-shek) at Chungking, without serious risk of Japanese attack.

insecure. Further, they would be obtained at the cost of betraying Chiang Kai-shek,[1] and of unfortunate political repercussions in the United States, in Russia, and in this country. The Secretary of State referred to the military measures which it would be open to the Japanese to take against us in the event of war. They might attack Hong Kong, but it seemed to him very doubtful whether they would take on the formidable proposition of attacking Singapore, or would start on some big adventure against the British Empire. He believed that there was a big element of bluff in their attitude.

The Prime Minister said that while acceptance by this country of Japan's demands might have a bad effect on public opinion in other countries, it looked as though the whole burden of the stand which it was suggested that we should take in this matter on behalf of China would fall on this country, which was already fully occupied in a military sense. He thought that the responsibility for the decision should be placed where it ought to lie, namely, with the United States. They should be asked flatly whether they would take any action whatever if, for example, Japan were to make lodgments in the Dutch East Indies. In the present state of affairs he did not think that we ought to incur Japanese hostility for reasons mainly of prestige.[2]

Sir Alexander Cadogan: diary
(*'The Diaries of Sir Alexander Cadogan'*)

5 July 1940

Cabinet at 12 and Winston took the wrong turning, dwelling on all the inconvenience of war with Japan. Well, we all see that, even if we *do* believe that Japan will declare war (which I still beg leave to doubt) . . . .

No decision – told to explore some half-way house. Don't mind doing that, but it's hopeless to do as Winston suggested – try to put the US on the spot. They simply won't stand there.

---

[1] Chiang Kai-shek, 1887–1975. Joined Sun Yat-sen's revolutionary party in 1907. A member of the revolutionary army, Shanghai, on the outbreak of the Chinese revolution, 1911. Served at Chinese General Headquarters, 1918–20. Visited the Soviet Union to study its military and social systems, 1923. Founder and Principal, Whanpoa Military Academy, Canton, 1924. Member of the Central Executive Committee of the Kuomintang, 1926. Commander-in-Chief, Northern Expeditionary Forces, 1926–8. Chairman of State, and Generalissimo of all fighting services, 1928–31. Resigned, 1931. Director-General of the Kuomintang Party, 1938. Chairman of the Supreme National Defence Council, 1939–47. President of the Republic of China, 1948. Retired, 1948. Formed a government on behalf of the Chinese Nationalists in Formosa (Taiwan), 1949.

[2] Under pressure from Japan, the War Cabinet agreed on 12 July 1940 to close the Burma Road for armament supplies being sent to the Chinese forces at Chungking. On 15 July 1940 Lord Halifax told the War Cabinet that he 'thought that the danger of war with Japan had passed for the time being' (*Cabinet papers, 65/8*).

Winston S. Churchill to General Ismay
(*Premier papers, 3/222/3*)

5 July 1940　　　　　　　　　　　　　　　　　　　　10 Downing Street
ACTION THIS DAY

General Ismay.

Clear instructions should now be issued about the people living in the threatened coastal zones: (1) They should be encouraged to depart voluntarily as much as possible, both by the pressure of a potential compulsory order hanging over them, and also by local (not national) propaganda through their Regional Commissioners or local bodies. Those who wish to stay or can find nowhere to go on their own, should be told that if invasion impact occurs in their town or village on the coast, they will not be able to leave till the battle is over. They should therefore be encouraged and helped to put their cellars in order so that they have fairly safe places to go to. They should be supplied with whatever form of Anderson shelter is now available (I hear there are new forms not involving steel). Only those who are trustworthy should be allowed to stay. All doubtful elements should be removed.

Pray have precise proposals for action formulated upon these lines forthwith for my approval.

WSC

Winston S. Churchill to General Ismay
(*Churchill papers, 20/13*)

5 July 1940

What has been done about air raid casualties?[1] I understood they were not to be published in any definite or alarming form, but I do not notice much difference in the procedure, or any sign of measures being taken.

WSC

---

[1] Following the War Cabinet on 3 July 1940, when Ministers were told press reports had appeared of 11 killed and 109 injured as a result of an air raid on the Newcastle area on the previous day, 'It was generally felt that it was undesirable to publish the exact number of air raid casualties. This gave the enemy information which should be withheld from him and might have a demoralising effect in this country' (*Cabinet papers, 65/8*).

July 1940

Winston S. Churchill to A. V. Alexander and Admiral Pound
(*Churchill papers, 20/13*)

5 July 1940
ACTION THIS DAY

1. It must be considered our settled policy to try to make French Units, naval, military and air, in the same way as we maintain Polish, Czech and Dutch Units. I hope the Admiralty will co-operate in this to the best of their ability.

2. It was understood that General de Gaulle and his Admiral[1] should have access to the evicted French sailors as soon as they had been sorted out into goers and stayers, and there was no danger of riot. Besides these there are, I believe, about four hundred sailors who had been collected at Aintree who have also expressed a wish to serve with us. In all, perhaps, there are already twelve hundred. Some may prefer to serve as British, and others as French Nationals. Close contact should be kept with the Vansittart Committee[2] through Major Morton, who will act as my liaison in the matter. Propaganda should be considered and organized, both among the goers and stayers. There would be no harm in our having two or three thousand French naval ratings.

3. Although I see your difficulties in making up a complete complement of Frenchmen because of the scarcity of technical ratings, nevertheless I think it important that de Gaulle should have one or two or even three ships, even perhaps a battleship, where the Frenchmen predominate and which fly the French flag. On these ships French routine should be followed, the Marseillaise played, &c. These ships may be of use in parleying with French Colonies and in getting into French harbours on one pretext or another. Even if it costs some inconvenience, I am sure the Admiralty will be able to make a success of it.

4. By all means take at once and commission under the White Ensign all French vessels that are of immediate practical use to us.

WSC

---

[1] Vice-Admiral Emile Muselier, of whom de Gaulle wrote in his memoirs that he 'had set many elements in the navy against him by the incidents of his career and the features of his personality, but whose intelligence and knowledge of the world offered advantages at that adventurous period, made it possible for me to give this embryo of our naval force a centre and a technical head' (*The Call to Honour*, page 90). In October 1940, at Brazzaville, he was a member of the newly established Defence Council of the Empire. Briefly imprisoned in error by the British, December 1940, after false allegations had been made of his alleged treacherous behaviour. On Christmas Eve 1941 he seized the French islands of St Pierre Miquelon (then under Vichy control), off Newfoundland, to the chagrin of the United States. See also p. 606, note 1.

[2] A committee set up by Churchill, with Sir Robert Vansittart at its head, to co-ordinate British policy and that of de Gaulle.

Winston S. Churchill to A. V. Alexander and Admiral Pound
(*Churchill papers, 20/13*)

5 July 1940
Most Secret

We must now use the ships in our power at Alexandria, first as a deterrent against a French declaration of war, and, second, if they do declare war, for our own service. As only skeleton crews will be on board, dependent on us for communication with the shore, it ought to be possible by every kind of means to secure their goodwill, or at least some trustworthy agents among them, so as to prevent scuttling. If the French declare war, we take the ships. Admiral Cunningham should be encouraged to work on these lines, so that in about a week he feels pretty sure we can get them if any excuse offers.

Winston S. Churchill to Admiral Phillips
(*Churchill papers, 20/13*)

5 July 1940

Could you let me know on one sheet of paper what arrangements you are making about the Channel convoys now that the Germans are all along the French coast? The attacks on the convoy yesterday, both from the air and by E-boats, were very serious, and I should like to be assured this morning that the situation is in hand, and that the Air is contributing effectively.

Winston S. Churchill to President Roosevelt
(*Premier papers, 3/462/2/3*)

5 July 1940   10 Downing Street

It has now become most urgent for you to give us the destroyers and motorboats. The Germans have the whole French coastline from which to launch U-Boat attacks upon our trade and food, and in addition we must be constantly prepared to repel threatened invasion by sea action in the narrow waters and also to deal with a break-out from Norway towards Ireland. Besides this we have to keep control of the exits from the Mediterranean [   ]¹ and prevent war spreading seriously into Africa. I know you will do all in your power. The consequences to the United States of our being hemmed in or overwhelmed are so grievous, [it seems to me very hard to

---

¹ Unclear words.

understand why]¹ this modest aid [is not given at the time when it] could be perhaps decisively effective. Pray let me know if there is [no] hope.

Situation in Ireland has deteriorated. De Valera and his Party are reconciling themselves to throwing in their lot with the Germans, [whom they think are bound to win]. They are in imminent danger of being invaded by Germany from the air, or possibly from the sea, if we cannot stop latter. They are quite unprepared. In these circumstances it may be necessary for us to forestall German action by a descent on certain ports, and I think it right to let you know this, even though you might feel unable to make any comment upon it.

Winston S. Churchill to A. V. Alexander, Anthony Eden and Sir Archibald Sinclair
(*Churchill papers, 20/13*)

5 July 1940

It has been represented to me that our colleagues not in the War Cabinet but above the 'line'² are depressed at not knowing more of what is going forward in the military sphere. It would be advantageous if each of the Service Ministers could in rotation have a talk with them, answer questions, and explain the general position. If a weekly meeting were instituted, this would mean that each Service Minister would meet them every three weeks. I trust this would not be too heavy a burden upon you. Nothing must ever be said to anybody about future operations. These must always be kept in the most narrow circles, but explanations of the past and expositions of the present offer a wide field. On the assumption that the above is agreeable to you, I am giving directions through Sir Edward Bridges.

Victor Cazalet³: diary
(*Robert Rhodes James, editor, 'Victor Cazalet, a Portrait'*)

5 July 1940

[Cazalet walked every Wednesday from the Dorchester Hotel to the Foreign Office with Lord Halifax]. We are disturbed somewhat about

---

¹ This and the subsequent passage in square brackets were deleted by the American Ambassador, Joseph Kennedy, when Lord Halifax showed him the final draft of this telegram. The last phrase in square brackets was deleted by Halifax. The telegram was never sent. (See Churchill's letter to Halifax of 7 July 1940).

² Cabinet Ministers with full ministerial office, as opposed to Junior Ministers within their departments (mostly Under-Secretaries of State, and Parliamentary Secretaries).

³ Victor Alexander Cazalet, 1896–1943. Educated at Eton and Christ Church, Oxford. Oxford half blue for tennis, racquets and squash, 1915. Served on the Western Front, 1915–18, when he won the Military Cross. A member of General Knox's staff in Siberia, 1918–19. Conservative MP for Chippenham from 1924 until his death. Parliamentary Secretary, Board of Trade, 1924–6. Political Liaison Officer to General Sikorski, 1940–3. Killed in the air crash in which Sikorski died.

Winston. He is getting very arrogant and hates criticism of any kind. H says it's almost impossible to get 5 mins conversation with him.

General Ironside: diary
(*'The Ironside Diaries'*)

5 July 1940

Late in the evening I was summoned up by Winston to show him our work map in the Cabinet War Room. He brought Beaverbrook with him and they both were pleased. One cannot help Winston enough, although he seems to have enough courage for everybody.

ON SATURDAY, 6 JULY 1940, Churchill, Anthony Eden and General Ironside visited the 1st Canadian Division, then stationed south of London, and saw a demonstration by the Canadian 2nd Brigade.

Winston S. Churchill to Colonel Jacob
(*Churchill papers, 20/13*)

6 July 1940

Obtain a most careful report to-day from the Joint Intelligence Staff of any further indication of enemy preparations for raid or invasion. Let me have this to-night. Thereafter I wish for daily reports till further notice.

E. A. Seal: private letter
(*Seal papers*)

6 July 1940

We went off early on Saturday to visit troops. It was raining miserably, & was altogether a beast of a morning. We went down to Limpsfield, & duly found the rendezvous but no one was there to meet us! So we had a drink, & then went out to try & find the General who was supposed to meet us. He unfortunately had gone the other way. However, after a very long wait in the rain, a junction was at length effected, & we went off & inspected some troops. Then they said the column we had inspected would move off past us: so we took up our stand at a convenient spot, & waited. It was very wet; & we waited & waited & waited. The troops had gone off down another road! However, after that we did see them doing some evolutionary rounding up imaginary parachutists & invaders, & things went somewhat better. Also after lunch the weather cleared up. The only real excitement was a Hun aeroplane overhead. No one seemed to worry about it, & it didn't worry about us, so even that wasn't too thrilling.

In the evening the PM, Mrs C & I went off to Chartwell, his house near Westerham. It is a wonderful spot, at the head of a private valley, with views from the house over the valley, & down it over the Weald. The gardens are lovely – not very well kept now, naturally – but designed as wild & natural gardens on the side of the hill, so that they don't look at all bad even if not fully maintained at concert pitch. One of the features of the place is a whole series of ponds, which are stocked with immense gold-fish – really a variety of carp. Some of them are well over a foot long; & there are hundreds of them. The PM loves feeding them: & we walked round with a bag of food on Sunday morning, watching them come to the surface & eat it up. One of his most amiable qualities is his obvious love of animals – he calls them all darlings, & shouts to the cat, & even the birds. The old swan on the lake knew his call, & answered back!

To lunch we had Lord Craigavon,[1] & Lord Beaverbrook. The latter & I went for a walk in the garden while the two Prime Ministers talked.

Winston S. Churchill to Lord Halifax: not sent[2]
(*Premier papers, 3/462/2/3*)

7 July 1940   10 Downing Street

My dear Edward,

I do not agree with the comments which Kennedy made upon my draft telegram. I fancy it was because it was not sent through him that he crabbed it.

I also have been studying your pencil corrections without quite understanding their purpose. Why for instance is it wrong to say – 'whom they think will win the war'? I should have thought this was another way of showing him

---

[1] James Craig, 1871–1940. A Protestant. Born in Dublin, the son of a wealthy distiller. A stockbroker by profession. Served in the South African War, 1899–1902. Unionist MP, 1906–21. A leading opponent of Irish Home Rule before 1914. On active service against the Germans in South-West Africa, 1914–15. Created Baronet, 1918. Parliamentary Secretary, Ministry of Pensions, 1919–20. Financial Secretary, Admiralty, 1920–1. First Prime Minister of Northern Ireland (under the Government of Ireland Act), from June 1921 until his death. Created Viscount Craigavon, 1927. In 1930 he was made an honorary member of the Other Club.

[2] Churchill decided not to send this letter, marking it 'Put by'.

the urgency of the business. As it now stands I do not see much use in sending any telegram. I am sure it is much better when I do to send them through the Ambassador whose help is then enlisted; and if Lothian gets a copy almost simultaneously he really has not much to complain of.

It is a long time now since I have sent any message to Roosevelt and I thought this was a good moment in view of the American approval of our treatment of the French.

Winston S. Churchill to A. V. Alexander and Admiral Pound
(*Churchill papers, 20/13*)

7 July 1940

1. Please see the marked paragraph in the attached report.[1] I cannot understand how we can tolerate the movement at sea along the French coast of any vessels without attacking them. It is not sufficient surely to use the Air only. Destroyers should be sent under Air escort. Are we really to resign ourselves to the Germans building up a large armada under our noses in the Channel, and conducting vessels through the Straits of Dover with impunity? This is the beginning of a new and very dangerous threat which must be countered.

2. I should be glad of a report not only on the points mentioned above, but also on the state of our minefield there, and how it is to be improved. Is it true the mines have become defective after ten months? If so, several new rows should be relaid. Why should not an effort be made to lay a minefield by night in the French passage, and lay in wait for any craft sent to sweep a channel through it? We really must not be put off by the fact that the Germans are holding the French coast from asserting our sea power. If German guns open upon us, a heavy ship should be sent to bombard them under proper Air protection.

WSC

[1] Cabinet War Room Interim Report No. 307A.

Winston S. Churchill to A. V. Alexander and Admiral Pound
(*Premier papers, 3/179/4*)

7 July 1940

It is undesirable to give the guarantee referred to in paragraph 2 of the attached;[1] above all, merely for the sake of expediting the departure of crews, or preventing scuttling by a promise. Please see my other Minute, addressed to you the other night, about wheedling the skeleton crews when they are on board. What action have you taken on this? We want all these ships very much, and we must not inhibit ourselves by needless undertakings. Now that we have got them in our power, we must certainly not let them go.

How are we to define a German breach of the Armistice? They will do whatever they think fit under its very elastic terms, and the Pétain Government will not dare to protest. We are not parties to the Armistice, and cannot relate any action of ours to a breach of its conditions. On no account let the Admiral give any further guarantees. I trust, indeed, he has not done so already.

Winston S. Churchill to Anthony Eden
(*Churchill papers, 20/13*)

7 July 1940

I have asked the Admiralty to make very special arrangements for bringing in your rifle convoys. They are sending four destroyers far out to meet them, and all should arrive during the 9th. You can ascertain the hour from the Admiralty. I was so glad to hear that you were making all preparations for the unloading, reception and distribution of these rifles. At least 100,000 ought to reach the troops that very night, or in the small hours of the following morning. Special trains should be used to distribute them and the ammunition according to a plan worked out beforehand exactly, and directed from the landing-port by some high Officer thoroughly acquainted with it. It would seem likely that you would emphasize early distribution to the coastal districts, so that all the Home Guard in the danger areas should be the first served. Perhaps you would be good enough to let me know beforehand what you decide.

WSC

[1] A telegram of 6 June 1940 from the Commander-in-Chief, Mediterranean, Admiral Cunningham, stating that he intended to use the proposed Admiralty offer 'of guarantee that French ships will not be seized unless Italy or Germany break armistice terms' as a means of 'expediting a departure of crews, and also to try and get an undertaking that ships will not be sunk at their moorings' (*Premier papers, 3/179/4*).

Winston S. Churchill to Anthony Eden
(*Churchill papers, 20/13*)

7 July 1940

You shared my astonishment yesterday at the statement made to us by General McNaughton that the whole of the 2nd Canadian Division was destined for Iceland. It would surely be a very great mistake to allow these fine troops to be employed on so distant a theatre. Apparently the first three battalions have already gone there. No one was told anything about this. We require two Canadian Divisions to work as a Corps as soon as possible.[1]

I am well aware of the arguments about training, &c., but they did not convince me. We ought to have another thorough re-examination of this point. Surely it should be possible to send second-line territorial troops to Iceland, where they should fortify themselves at the key points, and then to have, say, one very high-class battalion of the Gubbins[2] type in order to strike at any landing. I should be most grateful if you would deal with this.

WSC

Winston S. Churchill to Professor Lindemann
(*Churchill papers, 20/13*)

7 July 1940

I want my 'S' Branch[3] to make a chart of all the 30 Divisions, showing their progress towards complete equipment. Each Division would be represented by a square divided into numbers: Officers and men, rifles, Bren guns, Bren-gun carriers, anti-Tank rifles, anti-Tank guns, field artillery, medium ditto (if any), transport, sufficient to secure mobility of all three Brigades simultaneously, &c. As and when a proportion of these subsidiary squares is completed, a chart can be painted red. I should like to see this chart every week. A similar diagram can be prepared for the Home Guard. In this case it is only necessary to show rifles and uniforms.

---

[1] The original British suggestion that Canadian troops should be stationed in Iceland, to reinforce a British infantry brigade already there, had come from the Dominions Secretary (then Lord Caldecote) on 18 May 1940. Commanded by Brigadier L. F. Page and known as 'Z Force', its first elements reached Iceland on 16 June 1940. On 31 October 1940 they were transferred to Aldershot, to join the 2nd Canadian Division there. A small selection of the Cameron Highlanders of Ottawa spent the winter of 1940–1 in Iceland.

[2] Commando-type battalions, of the sort commanded by Colonel Gubbins in Norway in April and May 1940.

[3] The Statistical Branch, which Churchill had set up when he went to the Admiralty in September 1939, to scrutinise the statistics presented by other Government departments, and now continuing its work in the Prime Minister's Office, preparing charts on every aspect of war production, armaments supply, transatlantic convoys, and bombing.

July 1940

Winston S. Churchill to Herbert Morrison
(*Churchill papers, 20/13*)

7 July 1940

What is being done about designing and planning vessels to transport tanks across the sea for a British attack on enemy countries. This might well be remitted as a study to Mr Hopkins,[1] former Chief Contractor of the Navy, who must have leisure now that the Cultivator No. 6 is out of fashion. These must be able to move six or seven hundred vehicles in one voyage and land them on the beach, or, alternatively, take them off the beaches, as well, of course, as landing them on quays – if it be possible to combine the two.

WSC

Winston S. Churchill to General Ismay
(*Churchill papers, 20/13*)

7 July 1940
REPORT IN THREE DAYS

I was surprised not to have been consulted beforehand in the appointment of AGRM[2] which arose from various Minutes I had previously sent to the COS Committee. It is always better to mention a matter of this importance, involving the three Services, to me beforehand, especially when I myself am taking a great interest in it. However, I gladly approve, as a temporary and emergency measure, the interim steps which the COS Committee took. I have the highest opinion of General Bourne's[3] services as AGRM, and of his powers of emergency improvisation. The scope which I desire may be given to these operations is, however, far more extensive than is at present foreseen, and I have come to the conclusion that their planning must be entrusted to an Officer of seniority and proved war achievement. Three names naturally suggest themselves: Lord Trenchard, Lord Cork and Sir Roger Keyes, and I should be very glad to know what the Chiefs of Staff think of these Officers. I am at the present time considering an appointment for one of the first two in quite a different sphere, and my own judgment turns very strongly on Sir

---

[1] Charles James William Hopkins, 1887–1954. Assistant Constructor, Royal Navy, 1910; at the Admiralty, 1913–27; HM Dockyard, Simonstown, South Africa, 1930–4; Devonport, 1934–7. Chief Contractor for the Navy, 1937–9. Director of Naval Land Equipment, and later Deputy Controller, Ministry of Supply, 1939–44. Superintendent of Contract Work, Admiralty (Landing Craft), 1944; Director of Contract Work (Supplies), 1944–5. Deputy Director of Naval Construction (Production), 1946–51. CBE, 1949.

[2] Adjutant-General, Royal Marines.

[3] Alan George Barwys Bourne, 1882–1967. Entered the Royal Marine Artillery, 1899. On active service, 1914–18 (DSO). Adjutant-General, Royal Marines, 1939–43. Director of Combined Operations, 1940. Knighted, 1941.

Roger Keyes, who had a great deal to do with the planning and execution of Zeebrugge,[1] and has considerable experience of working with the Army and with the Air. He has also seen from the Belgian headquarters, moving freely about the battle zone, the opening phase of the present war. He would have to be supported by a strong Military or Marine staff. If General Bourne would care to work under him, that would be a very good arrangement – probably the best arrangement. But if he would prefer to continue to discharge the duties of AGRM, which he has performed with conspicuous success, I would not in the circumstances press him unduly.

It would be convenient if I could have the views of the Chiefs of the Staff early in the coming week.

War Cabinet: minutes
(*Cabinet papers, 65/8*)

7 July 1940 10 Downing Street
7 p.m.

The Secretary of State for the Colonies said that, speaking generally, the position in the French Colonies was not unfavourable to us; but he emphasised the vital need for taking effective action in the French Cameroons which occupied a nodal position.

The Prime Minister said that he was anxious not to give any impression, after the painful episode of the French Fleet, that we were endeavouring to grab the French Colonies. It was important that the step contemplated should receive the right publicity.

War Cabinet: Confidential Annex
(*Cabinet papers, 64/14*)

7 July 1940 10 Downing Street
7 p.m.

The Prime Minister said that he had discussed with the First Lord of the Admiralty and the First Sea Lord the question whether the time was now ripe for Fleet and Air action to be taken against the Italian Fleet. It had been decided that such action should be taken, and accordingly Force 'H' could not be spared to take action against the *Richelieu* at Dakar. It had been decided

---

[1] The attempt to block Zeebrugge harbour on 14 April 1918, with the aim of closing the canal exit from Bruges. Because of frequent bombardments of Zeebrugge from the sea, the Germans had turned Bruges into a submarine base. Keyes, then a Rear-Admiral, was in command of the Dover Patrol, which carried out the raid. During the blocking of the canal, 176 British troops were killed, and a destroyer lost. The raid served as a boost to British morale. A similar attempt to block Ostend harbour on 9 May 1918 failed.

that the *Hermes* should deal with the *Richelieu* by means of torpedo-bomber attack. The plan was that the *Hermes* should give a four hours' ultimatum offering the same alternatives as had been offered to the Fleet at Oran, with the exception that we should not include the offer that the *Richelieu* should be sailed to a British harbour and continue to fight with us.

The Prime Minister said that he had informed the First Lord that he approved action on these lines, which would take place that evening.

Winston S. Churchill to General Ismay
(*Churchill papers, 20/13*)

8 July 1940

Have any steps been taken to load the later portions of American ammunition, rifles and guns upon faster ships than was the case last time? What are the ships in which the latest consignments are being packed, and what are their speeds? Will you kindly ascertain this from the Admiralty?

War Cabinet: minutes
(*Cabinet papers, 65/8*)

8 July 1940　　　　　　　　　　　　　　　　　　　　　　10 Downing Street
11.30 a.m.

The Prime Minister thought that it was a mistake to publish detailed figures of the sinkings of merchant vessels. Even when the enemy thought he knew the facts, Press and broadcast reports gave him valuable confirmation. The enemy refrained from publishing information as to the effect of our mining operations, which we should be very glad to get.

The Prime Minister said that reports had recently been received to the effect that the Germans had been buying up land, removing hedges and filling up ditches at two or three places near Queenstown. This information had been passed to the Air Attaché at Dublin, and to Colonel Archer.[1] So far as War Office information went, however, no permanent guards had been left in the neighbourhood, and it seemed doubtful whether serious steps had been taken to frustrate a possible German landing in this district.

---

[1] Norman Ernest Archer, 1892–1970. Served in the Royal Navy, 1909–20; retired with the rank of Lieutenant-Commander, 1921. Colonial Office, 1921; Dominions Office, 1925. Private Secretary to the Secretary of State for Dominion Affairs, 1939–40. Principal Secretary, Office of the United Kingdom Representative to Eire, 1941, 1944–8. Assistant Under-Secretary of State, Commonwealth Relations Office, 1948–9.

The Prime Minister said that he thought it was implicit in the agreement to return the destroyers to Sweden, that we should make good any damage for which we were responsible.

The Prime Minister said that, as regards the Admiralty point, there would always be a channel of communication with the French Government as long as the Chargé d'Affaires remained here. He understood that no telegrams were, in fact, being received by Admiral Odend'hal. He thought that the segregation of the French Missions would form a useful topic for negotiations with the French Government, who would be informed frankly that it was necessary to retain certain persons and that, in the meanwhile, the remainder were being segregated pending discussion of the arrangements for their departure.

The Prime Minister read a letter from the Minister of Food[1] reporting that he had reached the conclusion that tea must be rationed, at a little below present consumption. It was impossible to give the public any notice, and he wished to make an Order that evening. He also proposed, in a fortnight's time, to ration margarine and cooking fats, in addition to butter. These were precautionary measures in case our supplies were badly disturbed by bombing. He was anxious to mention this in a broadcast that evening, but he thought that the War Cabinet should be aware of the proposed extension of the rationing system.

Winston S. Churchill to Lord Beaverbook
(*Churchill papers, 20/13*)

8 July 1940
Secret

I have been reading the correspondence leading up to the new aircraft programme about which we are to have a meeting at 5 o'clock this evening. I am very glad to see what a very large measure of agreement has been reached on the policy for the future, subject, of course, to your power to get the raw materials. In the fierce light of the present emergency, the fighter is the need and the output of fighters must be the prime consideration till we have broken the enemy's attack. But when I look round to see how we can win the war, I see that there is only one sure path. We have no continental army which can defeat the German military power. The blockade is broken and Hitler has

---

[1] Lord Woolton.

July 1940

Asia and probably Africa to draw from. Should he be repulsed here or not try invasion, he will recoil eastward, and we have nothing to stop him. But there is one thing that will bring him back and bring him down, and that is an absolutely devastating, exterminating attack by very heavy bombers from this country upon the Nazi homeland.[1] We must be able to overwhelm them by this means, without which I do not see a way through. We cannot accept any lower aim than air mastery. When can it be obtained?

It seems to me very likely that the PE fuze and other methods on the same lines will in the course of the next year greatly increase the effectiveness of fire from the ground against enemy aircraft, and I hope we shall find ourselves scientifically ahead in this respect.

I send this in order that you may know where I stand, before our discussion, by which I am quite prepared to be corrected.

Winston S. Churchill to William Wedgwood Benn[2]
(*Churchill papers, 2/392*)

8 July 1940   10 Downing Street

My dear Benn,

A splendid letter from your boy. We must all try to live up to this standard. Thank you for sending it to Brendan.[3]

Every good wish,

Yours very sincerely,
Winston S. Churchill

---

[1] When I first met Sir Arthur Harris ('Bomber' Harris) in 1969 he showed me a copy of this Churchill minute as his initial higher authority for the intense bombing of Germany that took, in the end, more than 500,000 German civilian lives.

[2] William Wedgwood Benn, 1877–1960. Liberal MP, 1906–27. A Junior Lord of the Treasury in Asquith's Government, 1910–15. On active service, 1915–19 (Royal Flying Corps, despatches twice). Joined the Labour Party, 1927. Labour MP, 1928–31 and 1937–42. Secretary of State for India in Ramsay MacDonald's second premiership, 1929–31. Created Viscount Stansgate, 1941. Secretary of State for Air in Clement Attlee's Government, 1945–6. One of his three sons was killed in action in 1944; another, Anthony (Tony) Wedgwood Benn, disclaimed his father's title and was a member of the Labour Governments of 1964 and 1974, but unsuccessful contender for the Deputy Leadership of the Labour Party (1981).

[3] David Wedgwood Benn, the eleven-year-old elder brother of the future Labour politician Tony Benn, and younger brother of Michael Benn (who died of wounds received on air operations in 1944), had written a letter to *The Times* explaining why he refused to be evacuated to Canada ('I would rather be bombed to fragments than leave England'). He remained in England, being subsequently head of the Yugoslav section of the BBC. I myself, then aged $3\frac{3}{4}$, and also about to be sent to Canada, was too young to be able to live up to the standard Churchill sought.

JULY 1940

General Freyberg[1]: *diary*
(*Paul Freyberg, 'Bernard Freyberg, VC'*)

8 July 1940   10 Downing Street

The Prime Minister was in the best of spirits with a bright seraphic smile, and a most engaging welcome. His opening remark to the gathering[2] was: 'I am tired; you're tired; we're all tired! Let's have some bubbly.' He talked buoyantly throughout the meal, with no hint of the critical and very precarious state of our position.

He was full of interest and enquiries. 'Were our men fit?' He would not ask about equipment, but he impressed upon me that 'there was no need to worry. The equipment would soon be there and then you will have guns galore.' He said that guns were arriving at all ports from the United States. Then the conversation switched.

'This is the most interesting government I have ever been in – far the most interesting.' He added that he had made himself Chairman of the Committee of Defence, and had purposely refrained from defining his duties, as he intended to do exactly what he considered necessary.

Towards the end of the dinner the Prime Minister took another line. 'This' (meaning England), he said, 'is the decisive theatre. If we are defeated here, the war is lost.' He repeated this remark many times during the evening. We all agreed on the need to defeat or prevent an invasion.

Mr Churchill also said to me that he was going to insist that convoys should come through the Mediterranean. It was evident that the dangers and difficulties of the situation were only acting as a spur to him. I had never seen him in better form, and he told me he was glad to have me in England with my men. I tried to turn the conversation to the Middle East, without much effect, and after one or two attempts I gave up the unequal struggle.

As we were saying goodbye, Mr Churchill said to me, 'I'm going to bring all your Anzacs[3] home through the Mediterranean.' To this impossible proposal I replied, 'You're not!' This was the first time I had been able to make any impression, but he was quite unmoved, and enquired: 'You don't

---

[1] Bernard Freyberg, 1889–1963. Born in London. Educated in New Zealand. Sub-Lieutenant, Royal Naval Division, 1914. On active service at Antwerp. 1914, the Dardanelles, 1915, and in France, 1916–18 (despatches six times, wounded nine times, DSO and two bars, Victoria Cross). He won the Victoria Cross for 'conspicuous bravery and brilliant leadership' at Beaumont Hamel, during the Battle of the Somme, 1916. General Staff Officer, War Office, 1933–4. Posted to India, 1937, but after a breakdown of his health invalided out of the Army. Passed fit for general service, September 1939. General Officer Commanding Salisbury Plain Area, October 1939. General Officer Commanding the New Zealand Forces from November 1939 until the end of the war. Commander-in-Chief, Allied Forces in Crete, 1941. Knighted, 1942. Awarded the third bar to his DSO, Italy, 1944. Governor-General of New Zealand, 1946–52. Created Baron, 1951.

[2] The other guests were Professor Lindemann, and Diana and Duncan Sandys.

[3] Australian and New Zealand Army Corps.

think they will attempt invasion?' to which I replied: 'I don't think they will succeed, but if you are not careful, you will lose Egypt.' He swept my remarks aside, and I felt that my counter-attack had not had any effect. Before leaving he said to me again, '*You* don't think they will attempt an invasion. Neither do I – but you must not say so.'

War Cabinet: Confidential Annex
(*Cabinet papers, 65/14*)

9 July 1940
12 noon
10 Downing Street

The Prime Minister said that the Fleet as disposed should be able to deal with what remained of the German Fleet if it endeavoured to escort an invading force. If any unescorted convoys endeavoured to make landings in this country, we should have sufficient small craft to deal with them. All round the coasts were some hundreds of armed trawlers, motor-torpedo boats and mine-sweepers which could take part in the *mêlée*, if invasion were attempted. In addition, the Admiralty had, with great speed, erected around the coast some 150 six-inch guns, in emplacements which would protect them from attacks by dive-bombers. These guns were manned by some 7,000 Naval ratings and marines. A number of land torpedo-tubes had also been fixed. Another deterrent would be the minefield in the Straits of Dover, which was being refreshed by the addition of further mines.

He did not think, however, that in the immediate future, at any rate, there was much possibility of an attack being launched from the French coast. According to the First Sea Lord's information, there was little shipping now in the Northern French ports, and only one old battleship and two destroyers at Calais. Nevertheless, the War Office were moving a number of troops to the South Coast.

General Ironside: diary
(*'The Ironside Diaries'*)

9 July 1940

My morning that I thought likely [for invasion] has come and gone without incident. Three Dutch Naval officers came over from Holland in a small boat. They all said that the Germans were all talking about the 11th as 'Der Tag'.[1]

---

[1] 'The day' (on which the Germans would invade Britain).

The Prime Minister has sent down an order, or what is practically an order, to withdraw two divisions from the beach-line. I have sent in to say that I can withdraw one in a few days. He has his son-in-law, now Captain Sandys, on his staff and he uses him as a go-between with my staff. It is difficult to tackle Winston when he is in one of his go-getter humours.

Winston S. Churchill to General Ironside and General Dill
(*Churchill papers, 20/13*)

10 July 1940

I am glad to know that the 3rd Division is coming out into reserve, and that you already have as many as 6 Divisions and 2 Armoured Divisions in reserve.

2. India was promised 12 battalions of Territorials in return for the 8 Regular. S of S for India[1] now agrees not to press for the immediate repayment of his 8 Regulars by the 12 Territorials, and the orders for their embarkation can be cancelled. On the other hand, if they had been able to go, the ships would have brought back a second 8 Regular battalions from India, making 16 in all. This second 8 we cannot now expect until we pay our debt at least to the extent of 8 out of the 12 battalions. I should like to effect this transference later on, but for the present it is impossible. I have agreed this arrangement with the S of S for India, and I trust it is satisfactory to you.

3. I find it very difficult to visualize the kind of invasion all along the coast by troops carried in small craft, and even in boats. I have not seen any serious evidence of large masses of this class of craft being assembled, and except in very narrow waters it would be a most hazardous and even suicidal operation to commit a large army to the accidents of the sea in the teeth of our very numerous armed patrolling forces. The Admiralty have over 700 armed patrolling vessels, of which two or three hundred are always at sea, the whole being well-manned by competent seafaring men. A surprise crossing would be impossible, and in the broader parts of the North Sea the invaders should be an easy prey, as part of their voyage would be made by daylight. Behind these patrolling craft are the flotillas of destroyers, of which 40 destroyers are now disposed between the Humber and Portsmouth, the bulk being in the narrowest waters. The greater part of these are at sea every night, and rest in the day. They would therefore encounter the enemy vessels in transit during the night, but also could reach any landing point or points on the front mentioned in two or three hours. They could immediately break up the landing-craft, interrupt the landing, and fire upon the landed troops, who, however lightly equipped, would have to have some proportion of ammunition and equipment carried on to the beaches from their boats. They would, however, need strong air support from our fighter aircraft during their

[1] L. S. Amery.

intervention from dawn onwards. This is being provided, and it would be well that you should reassure yourself on this point by direct inquiry, unless you are satisfied. The provision of the Air fighter escort for our destroyers is essential to their most powerful intervention on the beaches.

4. You should see the C in C's (Home Fleet)[1] reply to the question put to him by the desire of the Cabinet, i.e., what happens if the enemy cover the passage of their invading army with their heavy warships? The answer is that as far as we know at present they have no heavy ships not under long repair except those at Trondheim, which are closely watched by our very large superior forces. When the *Nelson* and *Barham* are worked up after refit in a few days' time (13th and 16th), it would be easily possible to make two forces of British heavy ships, either of which would be overwhelmingly strong, thus the danger of a Northern outbreak could be contained, and at the same time a dart to the South by the Trondheim ships could be rapidly countered. Moreover, the cruisers in the Thames and Humber are themselves strong enough with the flotillas to attack effectively any light cruisers with which the enemy could cover an invasion. I feel therefore that it will be very difficult for the enemy to place large well-equipped bodies of troops on the East Coast of England, whether in formed bodies or flung sporadically on the beaches as they get across. Even greater difficulties would attend expeditions in larger vessels seeking to break out to the northward. It may further be added that at present there are no signs of any assemblies of ships or small craft, except perhaps in Baltic ports, which are sufficient to cause anxiety. Frequent reconnaissance by the Air and the constant watching by our submarines, should give timely warning, and our minefields are an additional obstruction.

5. Even more unlikely is it that the South coast would be attacked. We know that no great mass of shipping exists in the French ports, and that the numbers of small boats there are not great. The Dover barrage is being replenished and extended to the French shore. This measure is of the utmost consequence, and the Admiralty are being asked to press it forward constantly and rapidly. They do not think that any important vessels, warships or transports, have come through the Straits of Dover. Therefore I find it difficult to believe that the South coast is in serious danger at the present time.

6. The main danger is from the Dutch and German harbours, which reflect principally upon the coast from Dover to the Wash. As the nights lengthen this danger zone will extend northwards, but then again the weather becomes adverse, and the 'fishing-boat invasion' far more difficult. Moreover, with cloud, the enemy Air support may be lacking at the moment of his impact.

7. I hope therefore, relying on the above reasoning, which should be checked with the Admiralty, that you will be able to bring an ever larger proportion of your formed Divisions back from the coast into support or

---

[1] Admiral Forbes.

reserve, so that their training may proceed in the highest forms of offensive warfare and counter-attack, and that the coast, as it becomes fortified, will be increasingly confided to troops other than those of the formed Divisions, and also to the Home Guard. I am sure you will be in agreement with this view in principle, and the only question open would be the speed of the transformation. Here, too, I hope we shall be agreed that the utmost speed shall rule.

Winston S. Churchill to Sir Archibald Sinclair
(*Churchill papers, 20/2*)

10 July 1940
Private and Confidential

My dear Archie,

I was very much taken aback the other night when you told me you had been considering removing Sir Hugh Dowding at the expiration of his present appointment, but that you had come to the conclusion that he might be allowed to stay on for another four months. Personally, I think he is one of the very best men you have got, and I say this after having been in contact with him for about two years. I have greatly admired the whole of his work in the Fighter Command, and especially in resisting the clamour for numerous air-raid warnings, and the immense pressure to dissipate the Fighter strength during the great French battle. In fact he has my full confidence. I think it is a pity for an officer so gifted and so trusted to be working on such a short tenure as four months, and I hope you will consider whether it is not in the public interest that his appointment should be indefinitely prolonged while the war lasts. This would not of course exclude his being moved to a higher position, if that were thought necessary. I am however much averse from making changes and putting in new men who will have to learn the work all over again, except when there is some proved failure or inadequacy.[1]

Yours always
W

Winston S. Churchill to A. V. Alexander
(*Churchill papers, 20/13*)

10 July 1940

Are you satisfied about the supply of anti-aircraft ammunition of all natures for the Fleet? Just before I left the Admiralty the use of ammunition by the destroyers had to be curtailed and I hope that these shortages have now been rectified.

[1] As Churchill wished, Dowding remained at Fighter Command, but he was removed in November 1940. Churchill's efforts in 1941 to have him recalled to an active command were in vain: in October 1941, Sinclair and the Air Staff rejected Churchill's suggestion that Dowding became Air Officer Commanding-in-Chief Middle East.

Winston S. Churchill to A. V. Alexander
(*Churchill papers, 20/13*)

10 July 1940

I should like to see a list of the completion dates of destroyers including the UBDs.[1] Has there been any falling off in these dates recently? It is important that we should keep the firms up to the mark.

WSC

Winston S. Churchill to General Ismay
(*Churchill papers, 20/13*)

10 July 1940

Have any plans been made in the event of large forces approaching the Egyptian border from Libya to cut the coastal motor road upon which they would be largely dependent for supplies of all kinds? It is not sufficient merely to bombard by air or from the sea. But if a couple of Brigades of good troops could take some town or other suitable point on the communications, they might, with sea power behind them, cause a prolonged interruption, require heavy forces to be moved against them, and then withdraw to strike again at some other point. Of course, such an operation would not be effective until considerable forces of the enemy had already passed the point of interception. It may be, however, that the desert itself affords free movement to the enemy's supplies. I wonder whether this is so, and if so, why the Italians were at pains to construct this lengthy road.

WSC

Winston S. Churchill to General Ismay
(*Churchill papers, 20/13*)

10 July 1940

OPERATION 'AMBASSADOR'[2]

General Bourne's operation cannot proceed until we know the strength of the German garrison on the Island. This follows the general rule that

---

[1] U-Boat Destroyers, originally called Fast Escort Vessels. In a minute on 12 December 1939, in changing their name, Churchill wrote to Admiral Fraser, the Controller of the Navy: 'They are, in fact, destroyers of medium size in every respect, and their prime function is to destroy U-boats. For the future they are to be called and classified destroyers, UBDs' (*Churchill papers, 19/3*).

[2] The plan to carry out a raid on the Channel Island of Guernsey, which had been taken by the Germans on 30 June 1940, and where 469 German troops were stationed. The raid took place on 14 July, when some demolitions were carried out, but one of the commandos was drowned and two were taken prisoner of war. Churchill commented, on reading a confidential account of the raid: 'Let there be no more silly fiascos like those perpetrated at Guernsey.'

reconnaissance must precede attack, and that the scale of attack should when possible be proportioned to the forces to be encountered. Any question of disappointment to the party prepared is irrelevant. If six more agents have been planted as a result of the permission given to-night, another submarine can be sent to make contact with them, and bring back the necessary information.

I do not consider that a mere raid upon an aerodrome is worth while. My Minute, on which the Cabinet decision is based, clearly referred to a plan for the elimination of the entire German force in the Island.

Pray show me before Cabinet to-morrow the orders that will be issued to give effect to this Minute of mine.

WSC

Winston S. Churchill to Sir Edward Bridges
(*Churchill papers, 20/13*)

10 July 1940

I think it would be well to set up a small standing Ministerial Committee, consisting of the Secretaries of State for War, India, and the Colonies, to consult together upon the conduct of the war in the Middle East (in which they are all three concerned), and to advise me, as Minister of Defence, upon the recommendations I should make to the Cabinet. Will you kindly put this into the proper form. The Secretary of State for War has agreed to take the chair.

WSC

Winston S. Churchill to Anthony Eden
(*'The Reckoning', page 120*)

10 July 1940

The same kind of intense Parliamentary pressure arose after the last war when I was in your shoes. The problem of demobilization raised not hundreds but thousands of questions which MPs had a right to ask. I protected myself by appointing my very able Parliamentary Private Secretary, Mr MacCallum Scott,[1] to be a kind of 'Members' friend'. I let him use my room at the House

---

[1] Alexander MacCallum Scott, 1874–1928. A journalist. Secretary, League of Liberals against Aggression and Militarism, 1900–3. In 1905 he published the first biography of Churchill, *Winston Spencer Churchill*. Called to the Bar, 1908. Liberal MP, 1910–20. In 1916 he published a revised biography, *With Winston Churchill in Peace and War*. Member of the Speaker's Committee on Electoral Reform, 1916–17. Parliamentary Private Secretary to Churchill (as Minister of Munitions), 1917–19; (as Secretary of State for War), 1919. Coalition Liberal Whip for Scotland, 1922. In 1924 he joined the Labour Party.

of Commons, and he sat there all the time for hours on end seeing Members and keeping them away from me.

This arrangement was commended to the House by me, and it was found to work very well. The precedent could be looked up, and might be of help to you. You have, however, also two Under-Secretaries in the House of Commons, and perhaps one of these could be nominated as the shock-absorber.

I entirely agree that you yourself should keep clear of minor business, so as to have plenty of time for the large issues of strategy, and the general problems of organizing the Army. I am afraid I have had to add to your labours by sending you numerous letters and Minutes.

Winston S. Churchill to Anthony Eden
(*Churchill papers, 20/1*)

10 July 1940
Strictly Private & Confidential

I am unhappy about the way in which the War Office handled this French business. Dill did not like the idea of getting as many Frenchmen as possible to stay, and I do not think the decision to which we came was carried out with thoroughness. I am also very much disappointed at the way in which the War Office have sent the whole of the French troops to be repatriated to Casablanca.[1] Although I said this should be considered in relation to the plans the Cabinet endorsed in principle for action in Morocco under de Gaulle, nothing was done to stop or divert this convoy, and we are now confronted with the fact that we have reinforced Morocco against ourselves. The Chiefs of the Staff Committee did not like this plan, and it has been effectually frustrated. There is nothing that can be done about either of these matters now, but I cannot feel that the views of the Cabinet have received the attention they deserve. I do not think we are having the help from General Dill which we hoped for at the time of his appointment, and he strikes me as being very tired, disheartened, and over-impressed with the might of Germany.

The above is for your most confidential consideration, and perhaps you will take occasion to talk to me about it.

Yours ever
WSC

---

[1] Duff Cooper and Lord Gort had just returned from Casablanca, where they had been sent by the War Cabinet to find out if the French authorities there might declare themselves for de Gaulle, but they were unwilling to turn their loyalty away from Vichy.

July 1940

War Cabinet: minutes
(*Cabinet papers, 65/8*)

11 July 1940   10 Downing Street
11 a.m.

The Prime Minister said that further consideration had been given to the question whether operations should be taken against the *Jean Bart*. The ship could not be made serviceable under many months and without being sent to a dockyard. In the circumstances the Admiralty took the view that we should now inform the French Naval Authorities that we proposed to take no further action in regard to the French ships in French Colonial or North African ports. We should, of course, reserve the right to take action in regard to French warships proceeding to enemy-controlled ports.

The Prime Minister said that he proposed to refer to this matter in his broadcast statement on Sunday.

It was pointed out that we should be taking a certain risk in delaying this announcement until the 14th July, and it was suggested that an interim communication might be made through Admiral Godfroy.

The Prime Minister said that it had now come to notice that one of the Attachés of the French Embassy had been circulating pamphlets describing His Majesty's Government in most opprobrious terms. Action must be taken to prevent occurrences of this nature.

The Prime Minister said that he proposed to broadcast on Sunday evening. In his speech he would refer to our relations with the French. He would say that it was not proposed to take any further action against units of the French Fleet, in particular the *Jean Bart*, and that His Majesty's Government regarded that phase of the war as being over. He proposed to strike a restrained and not unfriendly note, and might refer to the French as an oppressed people, who would be liberated by the defeat of Germany.

The Secretary of State for Foreign Affairs said that in any public statement it would be better to describe any Frenchmen who were well disposed towards us as anti-Nazi or anti-German, rather than as pro-Ally or 'free Frenchmen.'

The War Cabinet had before them a Memorandum by the Minister of Information (WP (G) (40) 178) urging reconsideration of the decision reached by the War Cabinet on the 3rd July that reports of casualties caused by German air-raids should in future be stated in general terms and should not give details of the precise number killed and injured.

In favour of the publication of the exact number, it was urged that the withholding of publication of facts known to a large number of people in this country created doubt and disquiet.

The Minister of Information and the Minister of Home Security[1] said that evidence in this sense was accumulating in reports from the Regions. Public opinion in this country could be relied upon to accept bad news, provided they knew that they were being given the full facts.

On the other hand, it was argued that the Home Front was now the front-line trench, and that there was no more reason to publish the detailed casualties inflicted on civilians each day than there would have been to publish the daily casualties inflicted in particular sectors of the battle front in Flanders. The day-to-day publication of the numbers of civilians killed must have a depressing effect on public opinion here, and must have some value to the enemy.

The Prime Minister suggested that, if it was necessary to publish information as to total civilian casualties sustained, this could be done periodically.

Winston S. Churchill to Neville Chamberlain
(*Churchill papers, 20/13*)

11 July 1940

You will see from the enclosed diagram how very necessary it is that these Departments which overlap so much, the bulk of which are already in Swinton's hands,[2] should be related to a common Chief. Experience shows that when Departments are under one head, they work together smoothly, but that wherever there is a departmental frontier line, friction, delay and jealousies arise. This might be particularly true in respect of the class of departments here involved, and of the people who manage them. For these reasons I thought it would be better if Swinton presided over the whole organization, having under him two 'chefs de cabinet,' of whom the overseas offensive one would be Vansittart. However, when I showed this paper and used these arguments to the Lord Privy Seal,[3] he seemed disappointed that Dalton was not to be the head of the Overseas Offensive Branch. I think he felt that, considering that our offensive against German rule must necessarily rest mainly on Left Wing revolutionary movements, someone connected with the

---

[1] Alfred Duff Cooper and Sir John Anderson.
[2] Lord Swinton was co-ordinating the Government's security services.
[3] Clement Attlee.

Labour-Socialist Party should have a hand in it. I thought myself that Left Wing elements could easily be supplied under Vansittart, and I am sure there will be difficulties between Dalton and some of the military departments concerned. Perhaps also Vansittart would not wish to serve under him. For these reasons, I still think the Swinton plan the better. It would be possible, none the less, to meet Attlee's views as indicated by me in ink, and make the bond of union between the grouped departments and two branches rest in you as Lord President, observing that you already preside over Swinton's affairs.

I should be grateful if you would talk this over with Halifax and Attlee during the day. I am perfectly clear that the Swinton arrangements will be the best in the public interest. However, there is also a duty to meet other points of view.

WSC

Winston S. Churchill to Sir Archibald Sinclair
(*Churchill papers, 20/13*)

11 July 1940

I am concerned at your heavy loss in Blenheims yesterday, and I trust that the inquiry made into the signal of HMS *Dainty*[1] will be accompanied by a drastic re-examination of the liaison at the Admiralty between the two Departments. It is inexcusable that an error of this kind should have been committed in respect of a considerable raid of 12 machines. This should surely have been known beforehand, and all forces concerned taken into consideration by the planning authority.

2. Generally speaking, the losses in the Bomber force seem unduly heavy, and the Bremen raid, of which only one out of six returned, is most grievous. At the present time a very heavy price may be paid (a) for information by reconnaissance of the conditions in the German ports and German-controlled ports and river-mouths, (b) for the bombing of barges or assemblies of ships thus detected. Apart from this, the long-range bombing of Germany should be conducted with a desire to save the machines and personnel as much as possible while keeping up a steady attack. It is very important to build up the numbers of the Bomber force, which is very low at the present time.

WSC

[1] A destroyer, commissioned in 1932, and sunk off Tobruk by enemy aircraft on 24 February 1941.

JULY 1940

John Colville: diary
(*Colville papers*)

11 July 1940

From Dover we drove to inspect the emplacement for a 14-inch gun which, owing to a caprice of Winston's, is being prepared at considerable risk, and with immense labour, for the purpose of bombarding the coast of France. It will require three valuable and vulnerable cranes to put it in position and will only last for 100 rounds: the military authorities call it 'a pure stunt'.

Jacob said he thought Winston was the only man who could hold the country united, but if he had a fault it was his inclination to go too much into detail. All these tours of defence areas, and his ceaseless output of minutes to Ministers and to Ismay, are the very antithesis of Chamberlain's practice; but they are not really the function of a Prime Minister.

Winston S. Churchill to A. V. Alexander and Admiral Pound
(*Churchill papers, 20/13*)

12 July 1940
ACTION THIS DAY

Let me see the answer it is proposed to send to this series[1] before it goes. I thought that *Illustrious* might well go to the Mediterranean and exchange with *Ark Royal*. (Note. – We have no air bases in Central Mediterranean, but all our Home bases are available for N Sea and Northern waters.) In this case *Illustrious* could take perhaps a good lot of Hurricanes to Malta. As we have a number of Hurricanes surplus at the moment, could not the Malta Gladiator pilots fly the Hurricanes themselves? This would not diminish our flying strength in this country.

The operation against Lulea has become less important now that the Germans have control of all the French and Belgian orefields. We must look to the Mediterranean for action.

2. You were going to let me have your plan for exchanging destroyers of more endurance with the Mediterranean flotilla. Could I have this with dates?

---

[1] Three telegrams on 11 July 1940 from Force H about the relocation of aircraft carriers.

JULY 1940

War Cabinet: minutes
(*Cabinet papers, 65/8*)

12 July 1940 10 Downing Street
11.30 a.m.

The Secretary of State for India said that he hoped the War Cabinet would approve in principle the following measures:–

(a) The Viceroy's plan to invite representative Indians to join his Executive Council and to associate with them in a wider War Advisory Council (which would meet at regular intervals) representatives of the Indian States and of other interests in the national life of India as a whole.

(b) The issue of a declaration on the general lines of that appended to WP (G) (40) 176.[1]

In the course of his statement, the Secretary of State made the following points:–

(1) The resignation of the Provincial Ministries in the early days of the war had not had the bad results which had been foretold at the time. The Provinces had been well administered, and the situation had been accepted with cheerfulness by the population as a whole. The Moslem element viewed the absence from office of the Congress Ministers with open satisfaction.

(2) But all was not well beneath the surface. The rift between the Hindu and the Moslem factions was widening. Mr Jinnah's[2] separatist programme was catching on with the Moslem masses, and there was real danger of a drift towards civil war. Competent judges, both Indian and European, took the view that we were exposing ourselves to the charge of insincerity by giving no indication of the time at which, or the

---

[1] The 'Revised Draft Statement' attached to War Cabinet Paper No. 176 of 1940, 'India and the War', circulated by L. S. Amery, stated: 'It is the firm intention of His Majesty's Government that India should attain, at the earliest practicable moment after the war, to her natural and rightful position as an equal partner-member in the British Commonwealth of Nations, as free to control her own affairs and shape her own destiny as the United Kingdom or the Dominions.' There was a caveat: the Government 'could not contemplate the transfer of their present responsibility for the peace and welfare of India to any system of government whose authority is directly denied by large and powerful elements in India's national life.' A timetable was proposed, 'to enable India's new self-devised self-governing constitution entering into force within a year of the conclusion of the war' (*Cabinet papers, 67/7*).

[2] Mohammed Ali Jinnah, 1876–1948. Born in Karachi, then part of British India. A graduate of Lincoln's Inn. Practised as a barrister in Bombay. Member of the Viceroy's Legislative Council from 1910. Joined the All-India Moslem League, 1913; President, 1916. Organised the Moslem League, 1934. Called for the partition of India and an independent 'Pakistan', March 1940. The first Governor-General of Pakistan, 15 August 1947. Known as *Quaid-i-Azam* ('Great Leader'). Died after thirteen months in office.

methods by which, we intended to fulfil our promise of Dominion status. A feeling was abroad that we were relying on the continued absence of agreement between the two main communities to free us from the performance of our pledges. Things in India were 'unpleasantly simmering.'

The Prime Minister said that, in his view, there was no real prospect that Indians would agree on a Constitution. The more we relaxed our control in India, the sharper would become the antagonism between Hindu and Moslem. The underlying trouble was that we were apt to deal with unrealities in India. Thus, in this case we promised something when agreement had been reached between Indians, but we did not really believe that there was any chance of agreement being reached. Again, we proposed to reject Congress's claim to dictate the future of India on the basis of a majority resting on adult suffrage. We did not adopt this attitude in regard to the other Dominions, but we had promised Dominion status to India.

The Secretary of State for India said that both the Viceroy and the Governor of Bombay[1] thought that an explanation as to how we proposed to carry through Dominion status would satisfy the majority of Indians. It was of the utmost importance to make a Declaration which would rally moderate opinion to our side.[2]

The Prime Minister doubted whether the present was a good time to make a far-reaching Declaration. First, many people who took an unduly gloomy view of the position would say that we had no power to carry out the very large task envisaged in this Declaration. Secondly, it would not be right, if it could be avoided, to take a step which led to a renewal in Parliament of the Indian discussions. He would prefer that we should make a heartening Declaration to India at a time when our growing strength was more evident, and when such a step would be a generous gesture made from strength. The Declaration which he had in mind would state the real facts of the position clearly, and would invite the co-operation of all Indian people in bringing the war to a successful conclusion. He suggested that the Viceroy should be told that the extension of

---

[1] Lawrence Roger Lumley, 1896–1969. On active service, 1916–18. Conservative MP, 1922–9 and 1931–7. Governor of Bombay, 1937–43. Parliamentary Under-Secretary for India and Burma, 1945. Succeeded his uncle as 11th Earl of Scarborough, 1945.

[2] The Viceroy of India, Lord Linlithgow, had proposed the issue of a new declaration affirming the British Government's intention to introduce Dominion status immediately after the war. For Churchill's letter to Linlithgow following this Cabinet meeting, see 16 July 1940.

the Executive Council and the establishment of a War Advisory Committee were approved; and that he should be invited to consider the preparation of a further Declaration making clear that we adhered to our existing promises and that there would be no avoidable delay in proceeding to make India a self-governing country.

Discussion ensued whether the two practical measures proposed by the Viceroy should be accompanied by the issue of a Declaration. No final decision was taken on this point. It was agreed that the first step would be for the proposed Declaration to be redrafted on the lines proposed, with a view to the Viceroy being consulted.[1]

Winston S. Churchill to General Ismay
(*Churchill papers, 20/13*)

12 July 1940

Will you bring the following to the notice of the Chiefs of Staff:–

It is the settled policy of His Majesty's Government to make good strong French contingents for land, sea and air service, to encourage these men to volunteer to fight on with us, to look after them well, to indulge their sentiments about the French flag, &c., and to have them as representatives of a France which is continuing the war. It is the duty of the Chiefs of Staff to carry this policy out loyally and effectively.

The same principle also applies to Poles, Dutch, Czech and Belgian contingents in this country, as well as to the Foreign Legion of anti-Nazi Germany. Mere questions of administrative inconvenience must not be allowed to stand in the way of this policy of the State. It is most necessary to give to the war which Great Britain is waging single-handed the broad, international character which will add greatly to our strength and prestige.

I hope I may receive assurances that this policy is being whole-heartedly pursued. I found the conditions at Olympia very bad, and there is no doubt

---

[1] Later that day, Amery wrote to Lord Halifax: 'Where, oh! where, were you this morning? I had an uphill battle with very little backing from anybody, except to some extent Attlee. Winston was full of eloquence, supported by George Lloyd, and John Simon rather left me in the lurch. That is, as regards the Declaration, for it was generally agreed that the enlarged Executive was all right.' Halifax replied three days later that the 'trouble' with Churchill was 'that it is not a matter of argument but instinct, which, in turn, is affected a good deal by his own past on the subject, and also, I suspect, by Lindemann'. (*Foreign Office papers, 800/318.*)

that the French soldiers were discouraged by some Officers from volunteering. An opportunity of assisting the French would be to make a great success of their function of July 14, when they are going to lay a wreath on the Foch statue.[1]

WSC

Winston S. Churchill to General Ismay
(*Churchill papers, 20/13*)

12 July 1940

1. The contacts we have had with the Italians encourage the development of a more aggressive campaign against the Italian homeland by bombardment both from air and sea. It also seems most desirable that the Fleet should be able to use Malta more freely. A plan should be prepared to reinforce the air defences of Malta in the strongest manner with AA guns of various types, and with airplanes. Malta was also the place where it was thought the aerial mine barrage from the 'Egglayer' would be useful. Finally, there are the PE fuzes which will be coming along at the end of August, which should give very good daylight results. If we could get a stronger Air Force there, we might obtain considerable immunity from annoyance by retaliation.

2. Let a plan for the speediest anti-aircraft reinforcement of Malta be prepared forthwith, and let me have it in three days with estimates in time. It should be possible to inform Malta to prepare emplacements for the guns before they are sent out.

WSC

Winston S. Churchill to General Ismay
(*Churchill papers, 20/13*)

12 July 1940

What is being done to reproduce and instal the small circular pill-boxes which can be sunk in the centre of aerodromes, and rise with an air bottle to two or three feet elevation, like a small turret commanding the aerodrome? I saw these for the first time when I visited Langley Aerodrome last week. This appears to afford an admirable means of anti-parachute defence, and it should surely be widely adopted. Let me have a plan.

---

[1] Marshal Foch's statue in Grosvenor Gardens, near Victoria Station.

Winston S. Churchill to Anthony Eden
(*Churchill papers, 20/13*)

12 July 1940

Now is the time to popularise your administration with the troops by giving to all Regiments and Units the little badges and distinctions they like so much. I saw the London Irish with their green and peacock blue hackles. We can easily afford the expense of bronze badges, the weight of which is insignificant in metal. All Regimental distinctions should be encouraged. The French Army made a great speciality of additional unofficial Regimental badges, which they presented to people. I liked this idea, and I am sure it would amuse the troops, who will have to face a long vigil. I am delighted at the action you have taken about bands, but when are we going to hear them playing about the streets? Even quite small parade marches are highly beneficial, especially in towns like Liverpool and Glasgow, in fact wherever there are troops and leisure for it there should be an attempt at military display.

WSC

John Colville: diary
(*Colville papers*)

12 July 1940   Chequers

At 6.00 p.m. I left with the PM, Ismay, Sandys, Seal and Elliot[1] (from the Cabinet Offices) for Kenley, to inspect the Hurricane squadron of which Winston is Honorary Air Commodore. Winston was arrayed in RAF uniform which, curiously enough, suited him well. We inspected the men and machines in pouring rain, watched twelve Hurricanes take off for patrol and went to see the operations room from which the activities of all aircraft in the area are directed. Then we got into a large machine, called a Flamingo, and flew very low, some 400 feet off the ground, to Northolt. The visibility was too bad for us to fly nearer Chequers.

---

[1] William Elliot, 1896–1971. On active service, 1914–18 (despatches; DFC and bar, 1918). Served in Russia, 1919. Assistant Secretary, Committee of Imperial Defence, 1937–9; War Cabinet, 1939–41. Secretary, Night Air Defence Committee, 1940. CBE, 1942. Director of Plans, Air Ministry, 1942–4. CB, 1944. Air Officer Commanding RAF Gibraltar, 1944; Balkan Air Force, 1944–5. Assistant Chief Executive, Ministry of Aircraft Production, 1945–6. Knighted, 1946. Assistant Chief of Air Staff (Policy), 1946–7. Commander-in-Chief, Fighter Command, 1947–9. Chief Staff Officer to Minister of Defence and Deputy Secretary (Military) to the Cabinet, 1949–51. ADC to King George VI, 1950–2; to the Queen, 1952–4. GCVO, 1953.

At dinner I sat between Ismay and Paget. The latter is charming and particularly easy to talk to. Winston began describing yesterday's tour of the South-East area and said that he had enjoyed a real 'Hun-hate' with one of the Generals there. 'I never hated the Germans in the last war, but now I hate them like . . . well, like an earwig.'

After the ladies had left the conversation became more serious and Paget and Auchinleck were put through their paces. They gave a good account of themselves. Winston then gave a brief account of what he thought might be the course of the war. He could not see much hope of a decision before 1942. For the next three months we must fight for the negative purpose of preventng invasion and defeating it if it comes. The winter will be terrible for Europe, but 'Hitler will take the other children's candy' and W does not think it will put an end to German resistance. Next year we shall be building up a great offensive army and we hope to have fifty-five divisions. We shall plan large-scale 'butcher and bolt' raids on the continent and Hitler will find himself hard put to it to hold 2,000 miles of coast line. Moreover we shall be approaching numerical equality in the air. By 1942 we shall have achieved air superiority and shall be ready for great offensive operations on land against Germany. But, said Winston, it is impossible to be precise: in the last war we kept on saying 'How are we going to win', and then while we were still unable to answer the question, we quite suddenly and unexpectedly found ourselves in a winning position.

The discussion turned to invasion. Winston does not think this is feasible in fishing boats from Norway, as is now said to be likely. Paget and Auchinleck thought that advance troops might arrive in this way in quite insignificant numbers. Simultaneously troop carriers, gliders and parachutists would be utilised to seize a port from which the main body could land. W does not believe in dispersing our troops along the beaches, but in concentrating effective and mobile divisions behind so that they may quickly be moved to any area where a serious threat materialises. He emphasised that the great invasion scare (which we only ceased to deride six weeks ago) is serving a most useful purpose: it is well on the way to providing us with the finest offensive army we have ever possessed and it is keeping every man and woman turned to a high pitch of readiness. He does not wish the scare to abate therefore, and although personally he doubts whether invasion is a serious menace he intends to give that impression, and to talk about long and dangerous vigils, etc., when he broadcasts on Sunday.

There followed an argument about encouraging the populace to fight. If they meet the invader with scythes and brickbats they will be massacred. Paget thinks they had better stay at home; Winston says they will not and Auchinleck says they ought not. W is sufficiently ruthless to point out that in war quarter is given, not on grounds of compassion but in order to discourage the enemy from fighting to the bitter end. But here we want every citizen to fight desperately and they will do so the more if they know that the alternative is massacre.

Winston S. Churchill to General Ismay
(*Premier papers, 3/372/1*)

13 July 1940								Chequers

Draw Admiralty attention to the importance of all these ships, especially *Western Prince*. What is her speed? It would be a disaster if we lost these 50,000 rifles. Draw attention also to the immense consequence of the convoy leaving New York between July 8 and 12. When will these various convoys be in the danger zone? When will they arrive? Let me have a report on the measures to be taken.

Most secret. Not to be mentioned even on green line.[1]

John Colville: diary
(*Colville papers*)

13 July 1940								Chequers

Winston showed greater animation and exuberance than I have seen before. He began by maintaining the arguable thesis that 'Human beings don't require rest; what they require is change or else they become bloody-minded'. He then went on to praise brass bands, to curse Hore-Belisha for abolishing them, to say they should return to every regiment and to ask what that large instrument was that he liked so much. I tentatively suggested a saxophone, whereupon he beamed philanthropically and said: 'You haven't been brought up in the army; you have been brought up in night-clubs', proceeding to tell the general company that I wanted to go and fight and desert him and he jolly well wasn't going to let me until the killing really began, etc., etc.

He reiterated his now familiar scheme of our future strategy and said it gave him confidence to be able to see clearly how this war could and should be won instead of groping forwards uncertainly. This week-end he felt more cheerful

---

[1] This was the scrambler telephone. On the following day Churchill received his answers. *Western Prince* was sailing 'independently' from New York to Liverpool at 14 knots, due at Liverpool on 20 July; the ships leaving New York between 8 and 12 July would join the Halifax convoy on 13 July and reach Liverpool on 30 July. Churchill was also told that these ships had 'an ocean Escort, HMS *Ranpura*'. He minuted at once: 'Not enough.' As for the unescorted *Western Prince*, he asked: 'Can she be met far out?' (*Premier papers, 3/372/1*).

than at any time since he took office. He spoke of the 'armoured panther springs' which our mechanised divisions would make on the continent next year and of the bombing supremacy we should attain. Even if 'that man' (as he always calls Hitler) were at the Caspian – and there was nothing to stop him from going there – we should bring him back 'to find a fire in his own backyard and we will make Germany a desert, yes a desert'. Hitler could do anything he liked where there was no salt water to cross, but it would avail him nothing if he reached the Great Wall of China and this Island remained undefeated. He could not survive if we devastated his homeland and if our excursions on the continent, made whenever we chose to land, were continually taxing his strength outside Germany. Therefore in the end he must probably be driven to attempt invasion, even if he decided against it now and went eastwards; and he would not succeed. Thus our vigil might be long and trying, and we shall have to be on our guard against surprise attack at any time of year and in any conditions. We should be put to the greatest test.

During dinner we talked of air matters. Winston said the last four days had been the most glorious in the history of the RAF.[1] Those days had been the test: the enemy had come and had lost 5 to 1. We could now be confident of our superiority. The discussion turned to technical questions of the superiority of the Hurricane, the defects of the Defiant, and the curious fact that the Germans had not yet put armour behind their engines. If they should do so, said Dowding, our tactics would become much more difficult. They also spoke of the new German beam, called 'Headache', which guides the enemy machines to their targets. The Germans do not know that we have discovered this, and Lindemann, who arrived this evening with all his albums of statistics, was horrified that Winston should mention it before Strakosch,[2] who is a chatterbox.

---

[1] On 10 July 1940, 120 German bombers and fighters attacked British shipping in the Channel, and a further 70 German aircraft raided the South Wales docks. This was the first large-scale German bombing raid on the United Kingdom, now considered the first day of the Battle of Britain. There were only 600 serviceable fighter planes to oppose these raiders; their success in doing so over the next four days was one of the heroic and morale-enhancing moments of British history.

[2] Henry Strakosch, 1871–1943. Entered a banking career in the City of London in 1891; from 1895 closely connected with industrial and gold mining development in South Africa. Author of the South African Currency and Banking Act, 1920. Knighted, 1921. Represented South Africa at the Genoa Conference, 1922, and at the League of Nations Assembly and the Imperial Conference, 1923. A Trustee for the League of Nations Loan for the Financial Reconstruction of Hungary, 1924. Member of the Council of India, 1930–7. Delegate of India at the Imperial Economic Conference, Ottawa, 1932. Adviser to the Secretary of State for India, 1937–42. Chairman of the Economist Newspaper Ltd. In March 1938 he gave Churchill (then in financial difficulties) a loan of £18,000 that enabled him to withdraw Chartwell from the market. Elected to the Other Club, 1939. In his will, published on 5 February 1944, he left Churchill £20,000.

We have reports, from Maisky[1] amongst others, that the Germans will use gas if they invade us. So perhaps Winston is wise to contemplate 'drenching' the beaches with mustard gas.

W started dictating his speech at midnight and I got leave to go to bed.

Winston S. Churchill to Lord Woolton
(*Churchill papers, 20/2*)

14 July 1940
Private

My dear Minister of Food,

Thank you very much for your letter. I am very glad to hear you are carrying the hotel proprietors with you, and that you are going to try to release larger quantities of frozen meat at cheaper prices for the poorer consumers.

I am surprised that the new situation has not produced more effect upon the beef position.

I am glad you do not set too much store by the reports of the Scientific Committee. Almost all the food faddists I have ever known, nut-eaters and the like, have died young after a long period of senile decay. The British soldier is far more likely to be right than the scientists. All he cares about is beef.

I do not understand why there should be these serious difficulties about food, considering the tonnages of food we are importing. The way to lose the war is to try to force the British public into a diet of milk, oatmeal, potatoes, etc., washed down on gala occasions with a little limejuice.

Yours sincerely,
Winston S. Churchill

[1] Ivan Mikhailovich Maisky, 1884–1975. Born in Omsk, the son of a Jewish doctor and a non-Jewish mother. A Menshevik, he was exiled by the Tsarist regime in Siberia, but escaped to Germany, and took a degree in economics at Munich University. Lived in London, 1912–17. Returned to Russia during the revolution. Became a Bolshevik, 1922. Counsellor at the Soviet Embassy in London, 1925–7. Soviet Ambassador to Britain, 1932–43. A Deputy Foreign Minister, 1943–5. Soviet member of the Reparations Committee, 1945–8. Arrested during one of Stalin's anti-Jewish purges, 1949. Imprisoned, 1949–53. Released from prison, 1953. Worked at the Soviet Academy of Sciences from 1957 until his death, writing his memoirs, and preparing various historical studies.

Winston S. Churchill to Anthony Eden
(*Churchill papers, 20/13*)

14 July 1940
Personal and Secret

This telegram[1] shows the dead-alive way in which the Middle East campaign is being run. It has been known for four months at least that Italy was on the verge of entering the war, or was in the war. Please bring this telegram before your Committee and let me know what you all think about it early in the present week. The storm will break here presently and the disasters which may follow may be very serious. Please try to draw up on one sheet of paper what you conceive should be the general plan. Meanwhile, I think it would be well if General Freyberg were consulted in this matter. He is comparatively young (50), very able, and has brilliant military achievements to his account.

WSC

PS – The news about Moyale[2] is bad this morning.

Winston S. Churchill to Admiral Pound
(*Churchill papers, 20/13*)

14 July 1940

When I was at the Admiralty I thought that the Submarine Department took an unduly pessimistic view of the number of U-boats we had sunk. Will you let me have the detailed calculations on which your increased estimate quoted in SR 40–185 of 60 or 65 U-boats is based, including particularly the last estimate which I had in detail before leaving the Admiralty, and the Admiralty account of what has happened since.[3]

WSC

Winston S. Churchill to General Ismay
(*Churchill papers, 20/13*)

14 July 1940

It seems to me very important that everybody should be made to look to their gas masks now. I expect a great many of them require overhauling, and

[1] Telegram No. 611 of 12 July 1940 from Cairo.
[2] On 13 July 1940 Italian forces had attacked the British garrison at Moyale in Abyssinia. Two days later the garrison withdrew, leaving the Italians in control.
[3] Only twenty-two U-boats had been sunk between the outbreak of war and Churchill's premiership, and a further three from 10 May to 14 July 1940.

it may well be Hitler has some gas designs upon us. Will you consider how the necessary overhauls can be set on foot. Action should be taken at once.

WSC

War Cabinet: minutes
(*Cabinet papers, 65/8*)

14 July 1940　　　　　　　　　　　　　　　　　　　　　10 Downing Street
7 p.m.

The Prime Minister read to the War Cabinet the passages in the broadcast which he was delivering that evening which referred to the French Nation, and the action which we had taken in regard to the French Fleet. The War Cabinet approved the proposed references.

Winston S. Churchill: broadcast
('*The Times*', *15 July 1940*)

14 July 1940

During the last fortnight the British Navy, in addition to blockading what is left of the German Fleet and chasing the Italian Fleet, has had imposed upon it the sad duty of putting effectually out of action for the duration of the War the capital ships of the French Navy. These, under the Armistice terms, signed in the railway coach at Compiègne, would have been placed within the power of Nazi Germany. The transference of these ships to Hitler would have endangered the security of both Great Britain and the United States. We therefore had no choice but to act as we did, and to act forthwith. Our painful task is now complete. Although the unfinished battleship the *Jean Bart* still rests in a Moroccan harbour and there are a number of French warships at Toulon and in various French ports all over the world, these are not in a condition or of a character to derange our preponderance of naval power. As long, therefore, as they make no attempt to return to ports controlled by Germany or Italy, we shall not molest them in any way. That melancholy phase in our relations with France has, so far as we are concerned, come to an end.

Let us think rather of the future. To-day is the fourteenth of July, the national festival of France. A year ago in Paris I watched the stately parade

July 1940

down the Champs Elysées of the French Army and the French Empire.¹ Who can foresee what the course of other years will bring? Faith is given to us, to help and comfort us when we stand in awe before the unfurling scroll of human destiny. And I proclaim my faith that some of us will live to see a fourteenth of July when a liberated France will once again rejoice in her greatness and in her glory, and once again stand forward as the champion of the freedom and the rights of man. When the day dawns, as dawn it will, the soul of France will turn with comprehension and with kindness to those Frenchmen and Frenchwomen, wherever they may be, who in the darkest hour did not despair of the Republic.

In the meantime, we shall not waste our breath nor cumber our thought with reproaches. When you have a friend and comrade at whose side you have faced tremendous struggles, and your friend is smitten down by a stunning blow, it may be necessary to make sure that the weapon that has fallen from his hands shall not be added to the resources of your common enemy. But you need not bear malice because of your friend's cries of delirium and gestures of agony. You must not add to his pain; you must work for his recovery. The association of interest between Britain and France remains. The cause remains. Duty inescapable remains. So long as our pathway to victory is not impeded, we are ready to discharge such offices of goodwill towards the French Government as may be possible, and to foster the trade and help the administration of those parts of the great French Empire which are now cut off from captive France, but which maintain their freedom. Subject to the iron demands of the War which we are waging against Hitler and all his works, we shall try so to conduct ourselves that every true French heart will beat and glow at the way we carry on the struggle; and that not only France, but all the oppressed countries in Europe may feel that each British victory is a step towards the liberation of the Continent from the foulest thralldom into which it has ever been cast.

All goes to show that the war will be long and hard. No one can tell where it will spread. One thing is certain: the peoples of Europe will not be ruled for long by the Nazi Gestapo, nor will the world yield itself to Hitler's gospel of hatred, appetite and domination.

And now it has come to us to stand alone in the breach, and face the worst that the tyrant's might and enmity can do. Bearing ourselves humbly before

---

¹ On 13 July 1939 Churchill had flown to Paris for the occasion as a guest of honour of the French Government. Consuelo Balsan (formerly Duchess of Marlborough), who was also present, later recalled that 'when I commented on the large tanks that had shaken the Champs Elysées in their progress', Churchill replied, 'The Government had to show the French that their economies had been transferred from the idleness of the stocking to the safety of the tank' (*The Glitter and the Gold*).

God, but conscious that we serve an unfolding purpose, we are ready to defend our native land against the invasion by which it is threatened. We are fighting *by* ourselves alone; but we are not fighting *for* ourselves alone. Here in this strong City of Refuge which enshrines the title-deeds of human progress and is of deep consequence to Christian civilisation; here, girt about by the seas and oceans where the Navy reigns; shielded from above by the prowess and devotion of our airmen – we await undismayed the impending assault. Perhaps it will come to-night. Perhaps it will come next week. Perhaps it will never come. We must show ourselves equally capable of meeting a sudden violent shock, or what is perhaps a harder test, a prolonged vigil. But be the ordeal sharp or long, or both, we shall seek no terms, we shall tolerate no parley; we may show mercy – we shall ask for none.

I can easily understand how sympathetic onlookers across the Atlantic, or anxious friends in the yet unravished countries of Europe, who cannot measure our resources or our resolve, may have feared for our survival when they saw so many States and kingdoms torn to pieces in a few weeks or even days by the monstrous force of the Nazi war machine. But Hitler has not yet been withstood by a great nation with a will power the equal of his own. Many of these countries have been poisoned by intrigue before they were struck down by violence. They have been rotted from within before they were smitten from without. How else can you explain what has happened to France? – to the French Army, to the French people, to the leaders of the French people?

But here, in our island, we are in good health and in good heart. We have seen how Hitler prepared in scientific detail the plans for destroying the neighbour countries of Germany. He had his plans for Poland and his plans for Norway. He had his plans for Denmark. He had his plans all worked out for the doom of the peaceful, trustful Dutch; and, of course, for the Belgians. We have seen how the French were undermined and overthrown. We may therefore be sure that there *is* a plan – perhaps built up over years – for destroying Great Britain, which after all has the honour to be his main and foremost enemy. All I can say is that any plan for invading Britain which Hitler made two months ago, must have had to be entirely re-cast in order to meet our new position. Two months ago – nay, one month ago – our first and main effort was to keep our best Army in France. All our regular troops, all our output of munitions, and a very large part of our Air Force, had to be sent to France and maintained in action there. But now we have it all at home. Never before in the last War – or in this – have we had in this island an Army comparable in quality, equipment or numbers to that which stands here on guard to-night. We have a million and a half men in the British Army under arms to-night, and every week of June and July has seen their organisation, their defences and their striking power advance by leaps and bounds. No praise is too high for the officers and men – aye, and civilians – who have made

July 1940

this immense transformation in so short a time. Behind these soldiers of the regular Army, as a means of destruction for parachutists, air-borne invaders, and any traitors that may be found in our midst (but I do not believe there are many – woe betide them, they will get short shrift), behind the regular Army we have more than a million of the Local Defence Volunteers, or, as they are much better called, the 'Home Guard.' These officers and men, a large proportion of whom have been through the last War, have the strongest desire to attack and come to close quarters with the enemy wherever he may appear. Should the invader come to Britain, there will be no placid lying down of the people in submission before him as we have seen, alas, in other countries. We shall defend every village, every town, and every city. The vast mass of London itself, fought street by street, could easily devour an entire hostile army; and we would rather see London laid in ruins and ashes than that it should be tamely and abjectly enslaved. I am bound to state these facts, because it is necessary to inform our people of our intentions, and thus to reassure them.

This has been a great week for the Royal Air Force, and for the Fighter Command. They have shot down more than five to one of the German aircraft which have tried to molest our convoys in the Channel, or have ventured to cross the British coast-line. These are, of course, only the preliminary encounters to the great air battles which lie ahead. But I know of no reason why we should be discontented with the results so far achieved; although, of course, we hope to improve upon them as the fighting becomes more widespread and comes more inland. Around all lies the power of the Royal Navy. With over a thousand armed ships under the White Ensign, patrolling the seas, the Navy, which is capable of transferring its force very readily to the protection of any part of the British Empire which may be threatened, is capable also of keeping open communication with the New World, from whom, as the struggle deepens, increasing aid will come. Is it not remarkable that after ten months of unlimited U-boat and air attack upon our commerce, our food reserves are higher than they have ever been, and we have a substantially larger tonnage under our own flag, apart from great numbers of foreign ships in our control, than we had at the beginning of the War?

Why do I dwell on all this? Not, surely, to induce any slackening of effort or vigilance. On the contrary. These must be redoubled, and we must prepare not only for the summer, but for the winter; not only for 1941, but for 1942; when the War will, I trust, take a different form from the defensive, in which it has hitherto been bound. I dwell on these elements in our strength – on these resources which we have mobilised and control – I dwell on them because it is right to show that the good cause *can* command the means of survival; and that while we toil through the dark valley we can see the sunlight on the uplands beyond.

I stand at the head of a Government representing all parties in the State –

all creeds, all classes, every recognisable section of opinion. We are ranged beneath the Crown of our ancient monarchy. We are supported by a free Parliament and a free Press; but there is one bond which unites us all and sustains us in the public regard – namely (as is increasingly becoming known), that we are prepared to proceed to all extremities, to endure them and to enforce them; *that* is our bond of union in His Majesty's Government to-night. Thus only, in times like these, can nations preserve their freedom; and thus only can they uphold the cause entrusted to their care.

But all depends now upon the whole life-strength of the British race in every part of the world and of all our associated peoples and of all our well-wishers in every land, doing their utmost night and day, giving all, daring all, enduring all – to the utmost – to the end. This is no war of chieftains or of princes, of dynasties or national ambition; it is a War of peoples and of causes. There are vast numbers not only in this island but in every land, who will render faithful service in this War, but whose names will never be known, whose deeds will never be recorded. This is a War of the Unknown Warriors; but let all strive without failing in faith or in duty, and the dark curse of Hitler will be lifted from our age.

Harold Nicolson: letter to his wife
(*'Diaries and Letters, 1939–1945'*)

14 July 1940

I dined ... at the Reform and we listened afterwards to Winston. I clapped when it was over. But really he has got guts, that man. Imagine the effect of his speech in the Empire and the USA. I felt a great army of men and women of resolution watching for the fight. And I felt that all the silly people were but black-beetles scurrying into holes. What a speech! One could feel after that as if the whole world might fall.

Si fractus illabatur orbis,
Impavidum ferient ruinae.[1]

Thank God for him. And for you. Winston's best phrase was, 'We shall show mercy, but we shall not ask for it.'

---

[1] Horace, *Odes*, III, iii: 'If the whole world were to crack and collapse about him, its ruins would find him unafraid.'

Anthony Eden to Winston S. Churchill
(*Churchill papers, 9/176*)

15 July 1940

My dear Winston,

You were magnificent last night, & gave us exactly what we all felt we needed, & what only you could give us.

Thank you.

Yours ever
Anthony

Defence Committee: minutes
(*Cabinet papers, 70/1*)

15 July 1940   10 Downing Street
11 a.m.

Mr Sinclair[1] said that he was satisfied that 1,023,000 was a very fair estimate of the rifles in the hands of the troops, and the total of 1,363,000 erred, if anything, on the small side.

The Prime Minister said he would have liked to have known exact figures to show our complete resources of rifles, but if the figures given were not exaggerated he would be satisfied with them for the time being. He enquired why 75,000 rifles were held in depots.

The Prime Minister thought that the Home Guard should also be given any rifles which, by reason of their unusual calibre, were unsuitable for use in mobile formations. If necessary, these could all be withdrawn from foreign Contingents, who should be issued with Service rifles. He would like to know what was being done in this matter.

Arising out of discussion of the last item, the Prime Minister enquired what steps were being taken to produce ammunition for the 75 mm field guns now being received from the United States. He was informed that plans had been made for the production of a limited quantity by turning over some of the capacity previously employed for 3-inch anti-aircraft ammunition. Discussion was also proceeding as to whether future production should take place in this country or the United States. No statement of requirements had yet been received by the Ministry of Supply from the War Office.

---

[1] R. J. Sinclair, Director-General of Army Requirements (War Office), Ministry of Supply.

Winston S. Churchill to Air Marshal Peirse
(*Cabinet papers, 120/300*)

15 July 1940
Secret
10 Downing Street

I am in full agreement with your proposal for bombing during the present moon-phase. I do not understand however why we have not been able to obtain results in the Kiel Canal. Nothing could be more important than this, as it prevents any movement of prepared shipping and barges from abroad for invasion purposes. I heard that you have dropped a number of bombs into this area, but that they did no good. Let me know what you have done about it in the past. How many raids, how many bombs, what kind of bombs, and what is the explanation that the Canal still works? Can you make any plans for bettering results in the future? This is surely a matter of the very highest importance and now is the time when it counts most.

WSC

Winston S. Churchill to Anthony Eden
(*Premier papers, 3/183*)

15 July 1940
ACTION THIS DAY

We ask repeatedly in Cabinet whether the 50,000 rifles on the lines of communications in France had in fact been brought home or not. We were finally assured by you that they had in fact come home, but I see in DC (S) (40) 22[1] of July 14 that it is stated 'we have no precise account of what happened to the reserves in France'. The authority you quoted to us was the Quarter Master General.[2] How is it he has no precise account of what has happened? Surely he must know how many rifles he sent to France and how many came back. I should be very much obliged if you would obtain from him a precise statement after the necessary inquiries have been made.[3]

WSC

---

[1] Defence Committee (Supply) Paper No. 22 of 1940.

[2] Walter King Venning, 1882–1964. Entered the Army, 1901. On active service, Europe, 1914–18 (Military Cross). Director of Movements and Quartering, War Office, 1934–8. Lieutenant-General, 1938. Knighted, 1939. Quartermaster–General to the Forces, 1939–42. General, 1940. Colonel Commandant, Army Catering Corps, 1941–5; Royal Electrical and Mechanical Engineers (REME), 1942–50.

[3] Eden replied: 'From recent reports there were, prior to the German advance, some 102,000 rifles in Base Depots in France, of which 95,848 were saved and 6,152 lost. I do not regard these figures as discreditable.' Eden added that the number of Reserve Rifles lost in France had been 24,557 (*Premier papers, 3/183*).

Winston S. Churchill to the Chiefs of Staff
(*Churchill papers, 23/4*)

15 July 1940
10 Downing Street

PLANS TO MEET A GERMAN INVASION

The Chiefs of Staff and Home Defence should consider these papers. The First Sea Lord's Memorandum may be taken as a working basis, although I personally believe that the Admiralty will in fact be better than their word, and that the invaders' losses in transit would further reduce the scale of attack, yet the preparations of the land forces should be such as to make assurance doubly sure. Indeed, for the land forces the scale of attack might well be doubled, namely, 200,000 men distributed as suggested by the First Sea Lord. Our Home Army is already at a strength when it should be able to deal with such an invasion, and its strength is rapidly increasing.

I should be very glad if our plans to meet invasion on shore could be reviewed on this basis so that the Cabinet may be informed of any modifications. It should be borne in mind that, although the heaviest attack would seem likely to fall in the North, yet the sovereign importance of London and the narrowness of the seas in this quarter make the South the theatre where the greatest precaution must be taken.

WSC

Winston S. Churchill to General Ismay
(*Churchill papers, 20/13*)

15 July 1940

THE DOVER GUN

Make sure that over-head cover against bombing attack is provided for the 14-inch gun. A structure of steel girders should be put up to carry sand-bag cover similar to that over the 6-inch guns which are mounted along the coast. All should be camouflaged. You will be told that it will be necessary to change the guns after 120 rounds. In that case the structure will have to be taken to pieces and put up again after the gun is changed. There should be no difficulty in this.

WSC

Winston S. Churchill to A. V. Alexander and Admiral Pound
(*Churchill papers, 20/13*)

15 July 1940

1. Your paragraphs 1 and 2 of your Minute of July 12.¹ I do not understand what is meant by 'reviewing the whole Mediterranean situation.' It is now three weeks since I vetoed the proposal to evacuate the Eastern Mediterranean and bring Admiral Cunningham's fleet to Gibraltar. I hope there will be no return to that project. Anyone can see the risk from Air attack which we run in the Central Mediterranean. From time to time and for sufficient object this risk will have to be faced. Warships are meant to go under fire. Our position would be very different if I had been assisted in my wish in October of last year to reconstruct the Royal Sovereign Class with heavy anti-aircraft armour on their decks at a cost to their speed through increased bulging. The difficulties which were presented at every stage were such as to destroy this proposal, and we are no further on than we were a year ago. If we had the Royal Sovereigns armoured, and their guns cocked up, or some of them, we could assault the Italian coasts by bombardment with comparative impunity. How does the reconstruction of these ships stand now? Will you kindly refresh my memory with the exact position in which I left the matter when I quitted the Admiralty? The various Boards of Admiralty which preceded the Great War altogether underrated the danger of air attack, and authorised sweeping statements to Parliament on the ability of ships of war to cope with it. Now there is a tendency to proceed to the other extreme, and consider it wrong to endanger His Majesty's ships by bringing them under air bombardment, as must from time to time be necessary in pursuance of operations.

I regret very much to have to record these facts, and I trust I need not infer from your first two paragraphs that there is a tendency to abandon the offensive against Italy on account of the air risk. It may be taken for certain that the scale of the enemy's air attack will increase in the Mediterranean as the Germans come there.

I should be glad if the First Lord could be shown my previous Minutes on the Royal Sovereigns in connection with 'Catherine'.² Other purposes were clearly held in view, and Italy was one of them.

2. Your paragraph 3. It becomes of high and immediate importance to build up a very strong anti-aircraft defence at Malta, and to base several squadrons of our best fighter aircraft there. This will have to be done under the fire of the enemy. I should be glad to know the full scale of defence which was proposed on various papers I have seen. The emplacements should be

¹ Not printed.
² Plan 'Catherine' was Churchill's scheme for a British naval entry into the Baltic. The scheme was prepared by Lord Cork during the winter of 1939–40.

made forthwith. I understand that a small consignment of AA guns and Hurricanes is now being procured, and that the main equipment is to follow later. It may well be possible at the end of this month to detach the larger consignment from our home defence. The urgent first consignment should reach Malta at the earliest moment. The stores may be divided between several ships so as to avoid losing all if one is hit. The immense delay involved in passing these ships round the Cape cannot be accepted. So far as Malta is concerned, it is not seen how the dangers will be avoided by this detour, the voyage from Alexandria to Malta being, if anything, more dangerous than the voyage from Gibraltar to Malta.

I should be glad to see the telegrams from the Admiralty to C-in-C, Mediterranean, and the reasons why he recommended the Cape route. If a large part of this consignment has anyhow to go from Gibraltar to Malta, it might be less hazardous to push right through with the rest than to leave the fleet at Alexandria in its present undefended position.

3. *Illustrious*. Considering that in the North Sea and Atlantic we are on the defensive and that no one would propose to bring *Illustrious* into the narrow waters, north and south of Dover, where we have already good shore-based aircraft, our aircraft-carriers in Home Waters will be able to operate some distance from the enemy's coast. In the Mediterranean, on the other hand, we must take the offensive against Italy, and endeavour especially to make Malta once again a Fleet base for special occasions. *Illustrious*, with her armoured deck, would seem to be better placed in the Mediterranean, and the *Ark Royal* in the home theatre. The delays in bringing this vessel into service have been very great, and I should be glad to know when the *Fulmar* will be embarked and she be ready to exchange with *Ark Royal*.

4. I am very glad that arrangements will be made to send out destroyers to Gibraltar of longer radius, and to bring home the short-radius vessels to the narrow seas.

5. I should be ready to discuss these matters with you this afternoon in the Upper War Room at 6.30 p.m.

WSC

Winston S. Churchill to Anthony Eden
(*Churchill papers, 20/13*)

15 July 1940

While General Freyberg is in England, fresh from the Middle East, it would be a good thing to ask him to give an appreciation of the situation there and his suggestions for action. For this purpose he ought to have the necessary information and assistance accorded him. He should report in one week so that we may have the benefit of his opinion, and also see what sort of opinions he holds.

WSC

Winston S. Churchill to General Ismay
(*Churchill papers, 20/13*)

15 July 1940

Let me know when the troop convoy from India is expected to come in. It is due to-night.

WSC

Defence Committee: minutes
(*Cabinet papers, 70/1*)

16 July 1940
11 a.m.

10 Downing Street

The Prime Minister pointed out that the present production of mortar ammunition was absurdly low, and would not justify the issue of the weapon to the troops. It would be necessary for the War Office and the Ministry of Supply to consult together, and see what could be done either to expand the output of ammunition, or else to restrict the output of mortars and to devote the capacity released to other more urgent work.

The Prime Minister said that the importance of the 3-inch mortar in the recent fighting had been demonstrated, and every effort should be made to improve the production. In the meanwhile, only those weapons which could be supplied with ammunition should be issued to the troops.

PRODUCTION OF ANTI-TANK GUNS

The Prime Minister said that the total requirement appeared to be in the neighbourhood of 7,000 guns, which, at the present rate of progress, would take years to reach. This was one of the most important articles of Army equipment, and strenuous efforts should be made to increase production by every possible means. It was a lamentable state of affairs that, after ten months of war, we could only produce 120 of these small weapons per month.

July 1940

TANK PRODUCTION. PLAN FOR PRODUCTION OF A NEW HEAVY TANK

The Minister of Supply[1] said that the Director General of Tanks and Transport[2] had reported to him that it would not be possible to produce 500 of the new heavy tanks by the end of March, 1941. He (the Minister) had called for a full report on the matter, which he proposed to lay before the Prime Minister at an early date. In the meanwhile, the Tank Board had approved the design, and production was in train.

The Prime Minister said that he was very concerned to hear this, in view of the statements previously made that expectations would probably be fulfilled. He would like to discuss the Report at a meeting on Friday morning at 11 a.m.

Defence Committee: minutes
(*Cabinet papers, 70/1*)

16 July 1940
5 p.m.
10 Downing Street

USE OF THE 3-INCH UP[3] FOR LONG-RANGE AA FIRE, AS DISTINCT FROM ITS USE AGAINST DIVE-BOMBING AIRCRAFT

The Prime Minister strongly emphasised the need for developing the 3-inch UP for long-range use against aircraft as distinct from its use, as at present envisaged, against dive-bombing aircraft.

It was pointed out that the main difficulty centred on the design of a suitable predictor. In order to produce the most suitable predictor, it would be necessary to modify the existing predictor to include some method of allowing the necessary wind correction to be fed into the normal operation of the predictor.

The Prime Minister directed:–

(a) That all possible steps should be taken forthwith to consider the problems involved in the use of the 3-inch UP for long-range anti-aircraft fire, as distinct from its use against dive-bombing aircraft, and that these steps should include the initiation of designs for a suitable projector and plans for the necessary modification of the predictor.

(b) That over and above the existing production arrangements, a shadow plan should be prepared to enable production to be put into operation on the widest possible basis, should this be justified by the outcome of the trials of the UP weapon.

[1] Herbert Morrison.
[2] Geoffrey Duke Burton, 1893–1954. Royal Engineers. Served at Gallipoli, in Egypt and in Palestine (despatches twice). Managing Director, Birmingham Small Arms Company, 1933–44. Director-General of Tanks and Transport, 1940–45. Knighted, 1942.
[3] The Unrotated Projectile anti-aircraft rocket.

John Colville: diary
(*Colville papers*)

16 July 1940

Speaking to Beaverbrook on the telephone the PM said: 'I feel better. The air boys have done it. We live on their wings.'[1]

Winston S. Churchill to Lord Linlithgow
(*Churchill papers, 20/14*)

16 July 1940

The Cabinet last week was entirely favourable to your two proposals. First, the expansion of your Council by the inclusion of representative Indians, not, however, including a representative of the Indian Princes; secondly, the setting up of a War Advisory Committee of leading Indians, including three representatives of the Princes, to give Indians an opportunity for full cooperation in India's war effort.

Paragraph 6 of your telegram of the 1st July was read by some as suggesting that you thought that, in order to make these two measures effective, they should be accompanied by some new declaration on the Constitutional issue.[2]

During the lifetime of the late Government I understood (see your telegram of 6th April, 1940) that you had reached the position that, in view of the attitude of the Congress and the widening rift between the Moslem League and Congress, the right course was to lie back and make no further gesture or pronouncement, relying on the declarations already made to give effect to the Cabinet decision of 14th October, 1939; as, for example, the statement which you made on the 17th October, your Orient Club speech delivered on the 10th January, 1940, and the various statements made here in Parliament.

I should be glad to know from you before the matter is again considered by the Cabinet (1) whether you consider that a further declaration is necessary to procure the acceptance of the two practical steps on which we are all agreed,

---

[1] No record was kept of Churchill's informal telephone conversations, although he frequently spoke on the telephone. Such records as do survive are mostly in recollections and diary entries such as this one.

[2] In paragraph 6 of his telegram of 1 July 1940 Linlithgow wrote that 'satisfied as I am that the case for expansion and popular representation of Central Government here is, in present circumstances, a very strong one, I should, as at present advised, be disposed, even if Congress refuse to co-operate, to take risks involved and to go ahead with the expansion of my Council'. He added: 'It would be necessary, if the Cabinet were disposed to approve that line, to consider very carefully the tactical handling of moves leading up to an announcement and the nature of any such announcement' (*Cabinet papers, 67/7*).

(2) if so, what are the new circumstances in the condition of India which have led you to this view, and (3) the actual form which you think the declaration should take. I should add that I see great difficulties in our agreeing upon a new Constitutional declaration at the present time when invasion appears imminent, when the life of the Mother-country is obviously at stake, and when in consequence the thrashing out in Parliament of the issues involved in such a far-reaching departure is impossible. If, however, you know exactly what you want to say, and feel that it is vital to the success of your new proposal, or still more to the internal peace and orderly government of India, it would obviously be our duty to give it immediate consideration.

Winston S. Churchill to L. S. Amery
(*Churchill papers, 20/2*)

17 July 1940
Secret

My dear Leo,

Thank you very much for your letter, which I have read and pondered upon.[1] You are seeking to make an immense departure from anything that Parliament or the public here have ever been asked to face. You propose to create what is virtually an independent India, and to regulate its relations with the Empire by a Treaty. All this is on the Egyptian model. There is no use in discussing such a change at the present time, and there are no means of thrashing it out in a constitutional way. I hope therefore you will not press me unduly at a time when all our thoughts should be devoted to the defence of the Island and to the victory of our cause.

Yours sincerely,
Winston S. Churchill

---

[1] In his letter to Churchill on 14 July 1940, Amery had argued that Dominion status was insufficient, and that he wished to move forward towards self-government, in view of 'the one fundamental agreement between all Indians, of all communities and castes, including, I think, also most of the Princes, and that is the desire that India as a nation should be regarded as an equal of the other nations in the British Commonwealth, and as such govern itself to the fullest extent that its peculiar circumstances allow'. Amery suggested an agreement 'perhaps by an enlargement of provincial powers which may satisfy the predominantly Moslem provinces; on the other hand by special concession to minorities'. He ended: 'In the present mood of India there is little chance for the acceptance of our idea of what might be the best form of government, before at any rate we have let Indians have a try at framing one. There remains the alternative of letting things slide into something like civil war, after which a partition of India, like the partition of Ireland and just as fruitful of future trouble, may be the only immediate solution. So let us at any rate make a sincere effort to secure agreement.'

Strube: cartoon
('Daily Express')

17 July 1940

"I DON'T LIKE THE LOOK OF THIS, ADOLF. YOUR MAP ONLY SHOWS 'TO SURRENDER ALL.'"

Winston S. Churchill to General Ismay and Sir Edward Bridges
(*Churchill papers, 20/13*)

17 July 1940

I have appointed Admiral of the Fleet Sir Roger Keyes as Director of Combined Operations. He should take over the duties and resources now assigned to General Bourne. Whether General Bourne or Captain Godfrey[1] should work under Sir Roger Keyes or fill the position of AGRM should be arranged with the parties concerned with the approval of the First Lord. General Bourne should be informed that, owing to the larger scope now to be given to these operations, it is essential to have an officer of higher rank in charge, and that the change in no way reflects upon him or those associated with him. Evidently he will have to co-operate effectively should he retain his present position of AGRM. I formed a high opinion of this officer's work as AGRM, and in any case the Royal Marines must play a leading part in this organization.

Pending any further arrangements, Sir Roger Keyes will form contact with the Service Departments through General Ismay as representing the Minister of Defence.

ON 17 JULY 1940 Churchill visited Gosport, on the South Coast, where he lunched with Admiral Sir William James, the naval Commander-in-Chief, Portsmouth Command, then went by car with General Brooke on a tour of inspection along the Hampshire and Dorset coasts.

Winston S. Churchill: recollections
(*'Their Finest Hour', page 233*)

17 July 1940

In mid-July the Secretary of State for War recommended that General Brooke should replace General Ironside in command of our Home Forces. On July 19, in the course of my continuous inspection of the invasion sectors, I visited the Southern Command. Some sort of tactical exercise was presented to me in which no fewer than twelve tanks(!) were able to participate. All the afternoon I drove with General Brooke, who commanded this front. His record stood high. Not only had he fought the decisive flank-battle near Ypres

---

[1] John Henry Godfrey, 1888–1971. A specialist in navigation. Served at the Dardanelles, off Smyrna, and in the Red Sea (in support of Arab forces), 1915–16. On the staff, C-in-C Mediterranean, 1916–18. Deputy Director, Plans Division, Admiralty, 1933–5. Commanded HMS *Repulse*, 1936–9. CB, 1939. Director of Naval Intelligence, 1939–42. Flag Officer Commanding the Royal Indian Navy, 1943–6.

during the retirement to Dunkirk, but he had acquitted himself with singular firmness and dexterity, in circumstances of unimaginable difficulty and confusion, when in command of the new forces we had sent to France during the first three weeks of June. I also had a personal link with Alan Brooke through his two gallant brothers – the friends of my early military life.[1]

General Brooke: diary
(*'The Turn of the Tide'*)

17 July 1940

He was in wonderful spirits, and full of offensive plans for next summer. We had a long talk together, mostly about old days and his contacts with my two brothers, Ronnie and Victor, of whom he was very fond.

Winston S. Churchill: interview with Edgar Ansel Mowrer[2]
(*Churchill papers, 2/396*)

17 July 1940

WC: Make no mistake: the position of the United States will, if Great Britain goes under, be one of dire jeopardy. Personally I shall never leave this country. But were we defeated – which I am confident we shall not be – I shall not hesitate to send the fleet to Canada. That is, always supposing I am able to. But suppose England were to be invaded and that further struggle in this country were useless. I myself shall never make peace with Germans – that is

---

[1] Victor Brooke had been a subaltern in the 9th Lancers when Churchill joined the 4th Hussars. 'I formed a warm friendship with him in 1895 and 1896,' Churchill wrote in his war memoirs. 'His horse reared up and fell over backwards, breaking his pelvis, and he was sorely stricken for the rest of his life. However, he continued to serve and ride, and perished gloriously from sheer exhaustion whilst acting as liaison officer with the French Cavalry Corps in the retreat from Mons in 1914' (*Their Finest Hour*, page 233, note 2). In the same footnote Churchill described Ronnie Brooke as follows: 'He was older than Victor and several years older than me. In the years 1895–98 he was thought to be a rising star in the British Army. Not only did he serve with distinction in all the campaigns which occurred, but he shone at the Staff College among his contemporaries. In the Boer War he was Adjutant of the South African Light Horse, and I for some months during the relief of Ladysmith was Assistant Adjutant, the regiment having six squadrons. Together we went through the fighting at Spion Kop, Vaal Krantz, and the Tugela. I learned much about tactics from him. Together we galloped into Ladysmith on the night of its liberation. Later on, in 1903, although I was only a youthful Member of Parliament, I was able to help him to the Somaliland campaign, in which he added to his high reputaton. He was stricken down by arthritis at an early age, and could only command a reserve brigade at home during the first World War. Our friendship continued till his premature death in 1925.'

[2] Edgar Ansel Mowrer, 1892–1977. A newspaper columnist, he joined the *Chicago Daily News* in 1914, and was their war correspondent on the French and Italian fronts. Subsequently in Berlin (for ten years) and Paris (until June 1940). Author of *Germany Puts the Clock Back* (1932). Winner of the Pulitzer Prize, 1932. Writer on foreign affairs from Washington, DC, 1940–2. Deputy Director of the Office of Facts and Figures (later called the Office of War Information), 1942–3.

not at all what I am here for. But others might take a different view. They might oust me and my friends and look around for the man who could get the best possible terms from Hitler. Their aim would be saving as many of our unfortunate people as circumstances would allow. Obviously they might well choose a man of the Mosley type. With such a man in power, my own plans could be frustrated and the fleet come into Hitler's hands. And do not forget that if we were beaten while you sat by and watched without lifting a finger to help us, some people might feel a sort of resentment. With the German, the Italian, the French and our great fleet massed in one armada, the situation would become very difficult for you. I don't say that three or four years from now you might not be in shape to defend yourself victoriously. But can you imagine a man with the energy of Hitler waiting so long? Make no mistake: if he got us down he would go for you at once. And then, as I said at the beginning, the position of the United States would be one of dire jeopardy.

Believe me, I am saying this with complete objectivity. I do not ask or expect you to come into the war to help us: we are primarily defending ourselves. But in your own interest, I cannot quite see how you could afford to fold your hands and take any risk of letting us go under without making a move to save yourselves through us.

EAM: But aren't we doing just that? Aren't you getting war material now? What further aid could we conceivably give you, short of actually going to war?

WC: Obviously we would benefit if you went to war. But we neither expect or ask anything of the sort. We do not need an American Expeditionary Force: we already have more men than we can immediately equip. But material aid we could use in unlimited measure.

EAM: For instance?

WC: Well, first, your destroyers – the obsolete ones. They are of little good to you: your needs are quite different. But just now we could use them for all sorts of minor tasks and have our modern ships free for actual fighting. Then there would be the possibility of your allowing your adventurous young men to enlist with us, if they cared to. After all, what more glorious thing can a spirited young man experience than meeting an opponent at four hundred miles an hour, with twelve or fifteen hundred horse power in his hands and unlimited offensive power? It is the most splendid form of hunting conceivable. Some of the inexperienced pilots go under. But the survivors grow skilful and hard and shoot down their adversaries and survive. You cannot overestimate the value to your country of a few thousand experienced veterans as the kernel of your own fighting force. Without any doubt you would profit immensely from allowing a few thousand of your young men to gain experience with us if they cared to do so.

Then we should like to take over immediately what war material your small army actually possesses while you are replacing it with better material from your factories. Finally we should like to know that from the vast new material that you are bound to produce within the near future for your own needs, you would save one segment for us on which we could count.

By allowing any or all of these things, you would be doing us an immense service and conceivably save both our countries from common ruin.

EAM: What will you do in case the Germans try to invade these islands?

WC: I shall answer you as I answered General Weygand when he asked me the same question when I last saw him in France: if we meet the Germans on the sea we shall drown them and if by chance they manage to land we shall knock them on the head.

EAM: It is difficult to knock a tank column on the head.

WC: Not if you are prepared and know how to meet them. One has to get over the idea of meeting tank columns with troops fighting in a line.

EAM: But surely Weygand tried defence in depth without much success.

WC: That isn't what I mean at all. One has to pit column against column. Why should tank columns, once they have gotten through and they always do, be permitted to lose themselves in the interior? After all, they can be followed and their crews never permitted to come out and rest, or refuel, or even sleep. No sleep – that's the worst. No, if they should manage to come we shall handle them in our own way. Sometimes I wish they would come at once. We have reached a high level of expectancy and it is rather a shame to let any of our fire subside. Never forget that we have a very large number of men under arms. Sometimes I think that we should now be in better shape if we had never had France on our side at all, since we never could foresee what happened. Poor France! But I have infinite faith in France. Give the French time. I just cannot see the French people going on submitting to the Nazis.

EAM: Your confidence is impressive. But that makes your attitude toward Japan in the matter of closing the Burma highway the more puzzling. What is the explanation?

WC: The key lies in America. You cannot expect this empire alone to take on any more enemies for the sake of defending those things which are dear to your country as much as to ourselves.

Brendan Bracken to Winston S. Churchill
(*Churchill papers, 2/396*)

17 July 1940

Prime Minister

This interview is awful.

Mowrer has agreed to suppress it. And as an additional assurance I asked Duff to instruct the censor that no interview with the PM should be passed without yr approval.

I think you ought to allow me to write to Mowrer in order that I may tell him that his summary of yr talk is inaccurate or inadequate.

He may try to publish it when he returns to America.

Who let him into Downing Street? He is a raucous bore.[1]

BB

Winston S. Churchill to Lord Halifax
(*Churchill papers, 20/13*)

17 July 1940
Urgent

I am afraid that it is not possible to ride these two horses hard at the same moment without running a great risk of the appearance of double-dealing. I have never liked the idea of our trying to make peace between Japan and China. I am sure that all this talk of a 'just and equitable settlement' is moonshine, and known to be so. I think it is a great pity to use it. It might serve as some palliation for the action which has been forced upon us[2] by the plight in which we lie. Thus I have yielded to it, but it is certainly not in our interests that China and Japan should end their quarrel, and I am delighted that Chiang Kai-shek should rest his objections to our conduct so largely upon our references to peace.

We, the Japanese and the Chinese all understand the true position perfectly, and I do not see any advantage in overlaying it with a veneer of utterly unreal diplomatic phrases. It is better to keep silent and let the truth plead its own cause. 'Qui s'excuse, s'accuse. Qui s'explique, se complique.'

By all means let us discuss it to-morrow in Cabinet.

WSC

I could say this to Chiang, if you think it would do any good:–

'I am sure you understand our action about the Burma road only too well. We shall never press you to any peace against your interests or your policy.'

WSC

---

[1] Mowrer had lunched at 10 Downing Street on 16 July 1940. The other guests included Lord and Lady Bessborough, and Oliver and Maureen Stanley (*Churchill Engagement cards*). Three days later Bracken wrote to Mowrer: 'I know how difficult it is to paraphrase a conversation which occurred at a large luncheon party.' Bracken added: 'I do not recognize my master's voice in parts of the record you sent him of his talk with you,' and went on to explain: 'I am quite sure that no one could give an exact summary of what a Prime Minister or a President might say at a party where many people were taking part in the conversation.'

[2] The closure of the Burma Road, preventing military supplies from reaching the Nationalist Chinese via India and Burma, see page 478, note 2, and pages 543–4.

Winston S. Churchill to General Ismay
(*Premier papers, 3/475/1*)

17 July 1940

I do not myself see what we are going to get out of this arrangement. Are we going to throw all our secrets into the American lap, and see what they give us in exchange? If so, I am against it. It would be very much better to go slow, as we have far more to give than they. If an exchange is to be arranged, I should like to carry it out piece by piece, i.e. if we give them our Asdics, they give us their Nordern bomb-sight; if we give them our RDF, they give us their highly-developed short-wave gadgets.

Generally speaking, I am not in a hurry to give our secrets until the United States is much nearer to the war than she is now. I expect that anything given to the United States Services, in which there are necessarily so many Germans, goes pretty quickly to Berlin in time of peace. Once it is war, very much better controls are operative.

What is the urgency of this matter? Who is making a fuss, and what happens if we do not give an immediate decision?

WSC

Winston S. Churchill to A. V. Alexander
(*Premier papers, 3/179/4*)

17 July 1940

The Commander-in-Chief has evidently committed us morally to agreement with his compact,[1] since the French have disarmed themselves largely in consequence.

We cannot tell what may arise, and perhaps the question may present itself in altogether different forms. I am therefore in no hurry to ratify, and I do not see what is to be gained by ratifying. We must not be in too great a hurry to have everything tied up very tight against ourselves.

---

[1] Admiral Cunningham's transmission to Admiral Gensoul of the British Admiralty's suggested guarantee of 7 July, a week earlier, that French ships would not be seized unless Italy or Germany broke the armistice terms. On 14 July Cunningham explained in a telegram to London that 'the undertaking not to seize French ships by force is set off against their guarantee not to scuttle, and to attempt regular hostile acts, nor try to leave harbour. The agreement moreover ceases automatically if war is declared between the British Empire and France, and is to be reconsidered if French ships elsewhere are taken over by Italians or Germans' (*Premier papers, 3/179/4*).

Winston S. Churchill to Lord Woolton
(*Churchill papers, 20/13*)

17 July 1940

I accepted and brought before the Cabinet, who agreed, your proposed reduction in the tea ration. I have since heard that it is causing a great deal of hardship, and I should be glad to receive your observations on the enclosed note, which has been prepared at my direction in my Statistical Department.[1]

WSC

Winston S. Churchill to his Private Office
(*Churchill papers, 20/9*)

17 July 1940
ACTION THIS DAY

Precise arrangements must be made for the Duke of Windsor's journey to Nassau. He should go by passenger ship to Bermuda, and be taken on thence by a cruiser. Thus there will be no need for him to tranship in the United States.

Let me have a plan worked out with details, so that I can give definite instructions on my return.

Of course if the Admiralty cannot spare a ship for military reasons, I must be informed, but I cannot believe this would be so in the present situation in American waters.

WSC

E. A. Seal: private letter
(*Seal papers*)

18 July 1940

We had a most interesting & enjoyable day yesterday – at Portsmouth in the morning up to lunch time, & thereafter visiting troops in Purbeck. We motored through to Sandbanks, Studley & Wareham from Gosport, via Cadnam. I felt quite sentimental at seeing so many of our old haunts! . . .

---

[1] In a note to Churchill on 15 July 1940, Lindemann wrote: 'It is undesirable to ration tea, 1, Because, like bread, it is one of the only substances which the poorer classes consume in greater amounts than the richer. 2, Because the incidence is most unequal, falling very heavily upon single men and women and not at all upon families containing many young children who do not take tea. 3, It is the only luxury of the working woman, whose morale should not be jeopardised.' Lindemann went on to explain that only a fragment of shipping space (65,000 tons a year) would be saved by not bringing in tea.

The beach is all cleared of people, & covered with wire netting. There are absolutely no visitors. Troops & guns are everywhere in evidence. . . .

We saw some very interesting exercises, with soldiers tanks guns & whatnot. We even had two sinister looking men in captured German uniform to impersonate the enemy! All ended well, with the defeat of the enemy, & a visit to the dressing station, with men on stretchers impersonating the wounded.

Then we came back by special train from Wareham.

War Cabinet: minutes
(*Cabinet papers, 65/8*)

18 July 1940　　　　　　　　　　　　　　　　　　　　　　10 Downing Street
11.30 a.m.

The Prime Minister said that he was still opposed to the daily publication of exact numbers of air raid casualties. He saw no objection to the casualties sustained in each locality being posted up in the Town Halls, but these lists should not be reproduced in the local Press. The whole population of this country was now in the front-line and should be treated in the same way as troops in the field whose casualties were not announced daily. Further, daily publication undoubtedly gave information to the enemy. He was willing, however, to agree to the publication of the total casualties sustained in the previous fortnight or month. If the Cabinet agreed, he himself would put this view in answer to a Private Notice Question that afternoon. The matter was primarily one of defence and there was no reason why the Minister of Information should bear the bulk of the criticism in this matter.

General agreement was expressed with the Prime Minister's view, emphasis being laid on the importance of publishing the total air raid casualties periodically.

War Cabinet: Confidential Annex
(*Cabinet papers, 65/14*)

18 July 1940　　　　　　　　　　　　　　　　　　　　　　10 Downing Street
11.30 a.m.

SABOTAGE AND OTHER POLITICAL ACTION

The Prime Minister said that new machinery was now in operation for co-ordinating action of the kind last mentioned.[1]

---

[1] This was the establishment of the Special Operations Executive (under Hugh Dalton).

The Prime Minister reminded his colleagues that the last few days had seen some slight improvement in Anglo-French relations. It was now the expectation that France would relapse into neutrality, in which event we should be precluded from attacking targets in unoccupied France.

Harold Nicolson: diary
(*'Diaries and Letters, 1939–1945'*)

18 July 1940

The Labour people say that they hope Winston will carry on after the war in order to inaugurate the New World. Brendan says that the moment the war is over, Winston will want to retire. He says that Winston is convinced that he has had all the fun he wants out of politics, and that when this is over he wants to paint pictures and write books.[1] He adds that in the twenty years he has known Winston, he has never seen him as fit as he is today, and his responsibilities seem to have given him a new lease of life. He adds that he is very determined not to become a legendary figure and has the theory that the Prime Minister is nothing more than Chairman of the Cabinet.

Winston S. Churchill: Oral Answers
(*Hansard*)

18 July 1940

INVENTIONS AND SUGGESTIONS

Major Milner[2] asked the Prime Minister what are the present arrangements in Departments for the consideration of ideas and suggestions, including inventions, for the more successful prosecution of the war; and whether he will take steps to obviate the difficulty of knowing to which Department to submit them and of obtaining their satisfactory consideration by Departments concerned, who are tied by preconceived notions?

The Prime Minister (Mr Churchill): An immense number of suggestions

---

[1] On the eve of becoming Prime Minister, Churchill had completed the final draft of a four-volume work, *A History of the English-Speaking Peoples*, which was to be partly re-written before it was published in 1956–8. He was also to write six volumes of war memoirs, published in six volumes between 1948 and 1954. He had also contracted before the war to write a History of Europe Between the Wars (for Harrap) and had written a synopsis of it while staying at the Château de l'Horizon early in 1939. The book was never written.

[2] James Milner, 1889–1967. On active service, 1914–18 (wounded, despatches, Military Cross and bar). Chairman, Leeds City Labour Party, 1926. Labour MP, 1929–51. Member, Indian Franchise Committee, 1932. Founder, Solicitors' Group, House of Commons. Chairman, History of Parliament Trust. Chairman of the Fire Committee (Civil Defence of the Houses of Parliament), 1943–5. Deputy Speaker, 1943-5 and 1945–51. Created Baron, 1951.

and inventions are sent in to the various Departments connected with the prosecution of the war. It is the duty of each Department to examine those suggestions which deal with matters with which they are concerned, and to refer the others to the appropriate Department. I believe that, on the whole, considering the extreme pressure of the times, this work is well done by the research branches of the Departments. I should deprecate the idea that the scientists at the disposal of the Government are tied by pre-conceived notions. I remember that, at the time when the magnetic mine appeared to be a menace, several hundred letters a day were received suggesting remedies. However, the Admiralty succeeded in solving the problem themselves almost as soon as they were able to deal with the correspondence about it. It would therefore be a mistake to assume that there is any lack of willingness or of ability to adopt new ideas. But this in no way implies that suggestions are not welcome. Correspondents in doubt about which Department to address should forward their suggestions to the Department of Scientific and Industrial Research, which is under the special care of the Lord President of the Council.

Major Milner: Is the right hon. Gentleman not aware that there is a great deal of dissatisfaction in regard to this matter? Would it not be well to set up some central organisation or committee which could call in expert evidence or knowledge from the Departments, and have an overriding right to make direct recommendations to himself, in cases where Departments would not take matters up?

The Prime Minister: It is very difficult indeed. I felt there was a good deal of force in the suggestion made, but when you come to apply it, it is very difficult, because some of the matters touch tremendous secrets which are being actively examined at this time, and it is not possible to come into consultation with outsiders about them. There are many difficulties of that kind. We are most anxious to examine any suggestions of a reasonable character, and a good many that come from the public can be attended to by the Department to which they are sent or transferred to the proper Department. If there is no particular Department, there is always the Lord President of the Council's general committee of scientific research, and application to him will be attended to.

ALIEN REFUGEES

Mr Wedgwood asked the Prime Minister whether he will give the pledge of His Majesty's Government that alien refugees from Hitler, now interned in this country will, under no circumstances, be handed back to Hitler, as in France?

The Prime Minister: Yes, Sir. It is inconceivable to me that His Majesty's Government, either now or at any future date, would hand over to their oppressors persons who had sought in this country a refuge from persecution.

MINISTERS (CONSULTATIONS)

Mr Davidson[1] asked the Prime Minister what arrangement has he made to ensure facilities of immediate consultation between himself and the Secretary of State for Foreign Affairs?

The Prime Minister: Sir, I have asked Ministers whose duties are intimately connected with the conduct of the war to arrange as soon as possible to sleep in their offices at the centre of Government. The reasons for this are sufficiently obvious. I regret to cause the Ministers concerned inconvenience. They certainly should not be obliged to incur expense. Full regard will be paid to economy in all the arrangements made, and the details will be subject to examination by the Public Accounts Committee in due course.

Mr Davidson: Does not the right hon. Gentleman think it advisable, in view of the necessity for immediate consultation with the Secretary of State for Foreign Affairs, that that gentleman should be established in No. 11?

The Prime Minister: I am very much obliged to the hon. Gentleman for the kindly and agreeable attention which he gives to our affairs. I can assure him that any suggestion that falls from him will receive attention.

DEFENCE OF GREAT BRITAIN

Mr Barnes[2] asked the Prime Minister whether he will provide an opportunity to every Member of Parliament to sign a declaration endorsing the Government's policy of defending every village, every town and every city?

The Prime Minister: I think that the resolve of the House has been expressed in a manner which needs, at the moment, no further emphasis.

CHILDREN'S OVERSEAS EVACUATION SCHEME

Mr Cocks asked the Prime Minister whether, in view of the fact that the large-scale evacuation of children overseas is an important factor in the military defence of Britain, he will reconsider the decision to postpone the scheme, bearing in mind that children can be evacuated in ships which are already being convoyed?

The Prime Minister: It is most undesirable that anything in the nature of a large-scale exodus from this country should take place, and I do not believe that the military situation requires or justifies such a proceeding, having regard to the relative dangers of going and staying. Nor is it physically

---

[1] John James Davidson. Labour MP for Glasgow Maryhill, 1935–45.
[2] Alfred Barnes, 1887–1974. Labour MP, 1922–31 and 1935–55. Chairman of the Co-operative Party (affiliated to the Labour Party), 1924–45. Lord Commissioner of the Treasury, 1929–30. Minister of War Transport, 1945–6. Privy Councillor, 1945. Minister of Transport, 1946–51.

possible. His Majesty's Government have been deeply touched by the kindly offers of hospitality received from the Dominions and the United States. They will take pains to make sure that in the use that is made of these offers there shall be no question of rich people having an advantage, if advantage there be, over poor. The scheme has been postponed, not abandoned, but any further emigration that may be possible, as opportunity serves, will be regulated, with a view to restoring the balance between classes, and not in pursuance of any policy of reducing the number of persons in this well-defended island. Furthermore, the scale of movement must necessarily be small in number and dependent in time upon naval facilities.

I must frankly admit that the full bearings of this question were not appreciated by His Majesty's Government at the time when it was first raised. It was not foreseen that the mild countenance given to the plan would lead to a movement of such dimensions, and that a crop of alarmist and depressing rumours would follow at its tail, detrimental to the interests of National Defence. I take full responsibility for the steps which were originally taken, but I ask for the indulgence of the House, on account of the many difficulties through which we have been passing.

Mr Cocks: Is it not possible, seeing that there are ships convoyed going out, to send children in small parties of, say, 50; secondly on the general question, is the right hon. Gentleman aware that this is the first time for the last seven years that I have disagreed with him?

The Prime Minister: It may be that opportunities will serve for sending, in accordance with what I have said in my answer, but I could give no guarantee at the moment of the time or the numbers. As to what the hon. Gentleman said last, a good deal of it is quite true, and I have felt myself greatly fortified by that approval. I shall still labour further to convince him.

Mr Benjamin Smith[1]: Will the right hon. Gentleman at some future date reconsider the possibility of evacuation of children by American and neutral ships getting these children away, as they are in no way connected with the Armed Forces?

The Prime Minister: Yes, of course; if a movement to send United States ships to these shores were set on foot from the other side of the Atlantic, it would immediately engage the most earnest attention of His Majesty's Government.

---

[1] Benjamin Smith, 1879–1964. Organiser of the Transport and General Workers' Union. Labour MP, 1923–31 and 1935–46. Labour Whip, 1925. Treasurer of the Household, 1929–31. Parliamentary Secretary, Ministry of Aircraft Production, 1942. Minister Resident in Washington for Supply, 1943–5. Knighted, 1945. Minister of Food (in Attlee's Government), 1945–6.

ANGLO-JAPANESE AGREEMENT
Transit of War Material to China

Sir John Wardlaw-Milne[1] (by Private Notice) asked the Prime Minister whether he can make a statement on the recent Japanese demand for the stoppage of supplies to China through Hong Kong and Burma?

The Prime Minister: On 24th June the Japanese Government requested His Majesty's Government to take measures to stop the transit to China via Burma of war material and certain other goods. A similar request was made in respect of Hong Kong. The continuance of the transit of these materials was represented as having a serious effect on Anglo-Japanese relations.

An agreement has now been reached with the Japanese Government as follows:

Hong Kong. – The export of arms and ammunition from Hong Kong has been prohibited since January, 1939, and none of the war materials to which the Japanese Government attach importance are in fact being exported.

Burma. – The Government of Burma have agreed to suspend for a period of three months the transit to China of arms and ammunition as well as the following articles: petrol, lorries and railway material.

The categories of goods prohibited in Burma will be prohibited in Hong Kong.

In considering the requests made by the Japanese Government and in reaching the agreement to which I have referred, His Majesty's Government were not unmindful of the various obligations accepted by this country, including their obligations to the National Government of China and to the British territories affected. His Majesty's Government were however also bound to have regard to the present world situation, nor could they ignore the dominant fact that we are ourselves engaged in a life and death struggle.

The general policy of this country towards the Far Eastern troubles has been repeatedly defined. We have persistently asserted our desire to see assured to China a free and independent future, and we have as frequently expressed our desire to improve our relations with Japan.

To achieve these objectives two things were essential – time and a relief of tension. On the one hand it was clear that the tension was rapidly growing owing to the Japanese complaints about the passage of war material by the Burma route. On the other, to agree to the permanent closure of the route would be to default from our obligations as a neutral friendly Power to China. What we have therefore made is a temporary arrangement in the hope that

---

[1] John Wardlaw-Milne, –1967. Member of the Bombay Municipal Corporation, 1907–17. Lieutenant-Colonel commanding the 4th (Bombay) Artillery, Indian Defence Force, 1914–19. President, Government of India's War Shipping Advisory Committee, 1914–18. Conservative MP, 1922–45. Knighted, 1932. Chairman, House of Commons Committee on National Expenditure, 1939–45. Chairman, Conservative Foreign Affairs Committee, 1939–45 (also the India and Anglo-Egyptian Committees).

the time so gained may lead to a solution just and equitable to both parties to the dispute, and freely accepted by them both.

We wish for no quarrel with any nation in the Far East. We desire to see China's status and integrity preserved, and as was indicated in our Note of 14th January, 1939, we are ready to negotiate with the Chinese Government, after the conclusion of peace, the abolition of extra-territorial rights, the rendition of concessions and the revision of treaties on the basis of reciprocity and equality. We wish to see Japan attain that state of prosperity which will ensure to her population the welfare and economic security which every Japanese naturally desires. Towards the attainment of the aims of both these countries we are prepared to offer our collaboration and our contribution. But it must be clear that if they are to be attained, it must be by a process of peace and conciliation and not by war or threat of war.

Sir J. Wardlaw-Milne: May I ask the Prime Minister whether, in view of that decision, to which apparently the Government have come with great reluctance, and in view of the possibility of far-reaching consequences, he will permit a very early opportunity for a full-dress Debate on the situation in the Far East?

The Prime Minister: If the House desires a Debate on foreign affairs, it might be convenient that we should finish certain matters which I will presently mention, but which have been adumbrated for next week. Then we could perhaps find some time for a Debate. If the House could wait until the week after, the Appropriation Bill would give an opportunity without a further addition to the labours of the House. It is my wish that the House should have a Debate on anything that may be desired.

Mr Noel-Baker: May we rightly interpret that statement as meaning that His Majesty's Government have no desire to impose peace terms on the Chinese people, or to urge them to accept peace terms which they regard as surrender to aggression?

The Prime Minister: I would not wish to add to my reply.

Mr Noel-Baker: May we correctly interpret the statement as meaning that His Majesty's Government still adhere to their attitude in the Far East of founding their policy on the Nine-Power Treaty, as well as on the other treaties by which we are bound?

The Prime Minister: I have read out a statement, which I have very carefully prepared and considered. My views in the past on this matter are well known. I should hesitate to try to improvise any addition to my statement now.

Mr Hore-Belisha: Is my right hon. Friend satisfied that this concession made to Japan will, in fact, secure the good will of that country towards this country; and has he operated throughout in consultation and, in so far as that may be possible, in agreement with the United States and Soviet Governments?

The Prime Minister: I can give no such assurance as is asked for in the first part of the question. I do not know at all. I think all that happens to us in the Far East is likely to be very much influenced by what happens over here. Naturally, we have made sure that what we have done has not been done without taking into full consideration the attitude of the two very important great Powers mentioned by my right hon. Friend.

AIR-RAID CASUALTIES (PUBLICATION)

Sir P. Harris (by Private Notice) asked the Prime Minister whether he can make any statement about the announcement of air-raid casualties?

The Prime Minister: I am sorry to see that my right hon. Friend the Minister for Information has been criticised for imposing this restriction. The truth is that I am primarily to blame in the matter. As Minister of Defence I do not consider that daily publication is desirable. First, we do not receive from the enemy any similar information about the effects of our attacks upon them, and I see no need to present them each day with the tabulated results of their raids. This information, when examined by the German Air Force, would enable them to lay their plans with more exactness than they have hitherto shown, and, by comparing it with the reports of their bombers, to ascertain to some extent which attacks were fruitful, and which were wide of the mark. Secondly, this country is now on active service so far as the whole mass of the people are concerned. It has been well said that the front line runs through the factories. It is not usual in war to publish the casualties which occur on the front as results of an artillery bombardment. If the casualties were heavy the enemy would be encouraged. If they were light he would strive to improve his aim. Thirdly, although each battalion of the line knows pretty well what its daily casualties are, it is not thought necessary to publish the totals daily in Army Orders, and read them out to the troops every morning. I do not see why these analogies do not apply to the aerial bombardment of the civil population under the new conditions of war.

I propose, therefore, that in future, as is already done to a large extent, all casualties from air raids shall be posted as soon as they are ascertained at the town hall or other convenient centre in any town or district; but that the reproduction of these figures in the Press, either individually or in the aggregate, shall be forbidden. I propose further that at monthly intervals the general total of the casualties in that period shall be announced to Parliament and published in the Press. This will give the public the satisfaction of knowing the worst without enabling the enemy to connect any particular attack with its results, and otherwise to gain information at our expense. It seems to be a good moment to make this change in procedure when, after a month's widespread, if ill-directed, bombardment our losses have been singularly slight.

BUSINESS OF THE HOUSE

Mr Hore-Belisha: Will my right hon. Friend find it possible at a reasonably early date to make a statement on the course of the war in Africa?

The Prime Minister: The Government are very much in the hands of the House. If the House wish it, that can be done. But I am not at all sure that a very full, frank and lucid description of the events which have taken place, or are impending, in that area would be likely to assist those who are immediately in charge of military operations.

Henry Channon: diary
(*'Chips'*)

18 July 1940

Winston was superb, magnificent, in the House as he answered Questions, and later made the very important statement about the Far East; and he successfully quashed the Leftist Opposition's eagerness for war in the East as well as everywhere else.

Winston S. Churchill to Sir John Anderson
(*Churchill papers, 20/13*)

18 July 1940

I certainly do not propose to send a message by the senior child to Mr Mackenzie King, or by the junior child either. If I sent any message by anyone, it would be that I entirely deprecate any stampede from this country at the present time. I cannot conceive why Mr Shakespeare[1] should leave his duties in London to see off a hundred children.[2]

---

[1] Geoffrey Hithersay Shakespeare, 1893–1980. Served in the Great War, at Gallipoli and in Egypt. President of the Cambridge Union, 1920. Private Secretary to Lloyd George, 1921–3. Called to the Bar, 1922. National Liberal MP for Wellingborough, 1922–3; Liberal MP for Norwich, 1929–31; Liberal National MP for Norwich, 1931–45. Liberal National Chief Whip, 1931–2. Parliamentary Secretary at the Ministry of Health, 1932–6; and at the Board of Education, 1936–7. Parliamentary and Financial Secretary, Admiralty, 1937–40. Parliamentary Under-Secretary of State, Dominions Office, 1940–2. Created Baronet, 1942.

[2] The children, including this author, were seen off at Liverpool, *en route* for Quebec.

July 1940

Winston S. Churchill to Sir Archibald Sinclair
(*Churchill papers, 4/201*)

18 July 1940

I am still concerned over the question of the employment of our pilots. According to figures which have recently been furnished by your Department, only three out of every ten pilots with Wings are operational. This seems a very low proportion. Of the remaining seven, two are pilots with Wings still under instruction, two are Instructors and the rest are Air Staff, Administrative, Technical or other non-operational duties. Thus more pilots are employed giving or receiving instruction than are actually serving as operational pilots in the Squadrons.

Our methods of training have produced such good results that we must interfere with them as little as possible, but I do think these figures require some further examination.

Winston S. Churchill to A. V. Alexander and Admiral Pound
(*Churchill papers, 20/13*)

18 July 1940

1. C-in-C's telegram 2259 of July 16. I have re-read my Minute of July 15,[1] and return it to you, as I wish it to remain on record.

2. Paragraph 8 of C-in-C's 2259[2] confirms the view I had formed, namely, that reinforcements and supplies, both to Malta and to Alexandria, should be passed through the Mediterranean as a major operation, possibly bringing about a general engagement, which is much to be desired.

3. For this purpose, the operation of flying Hurricanes from *Argus* to Malta is an admirable and indispensable preliminary. I should hope this might take place in less than a fortnight.

4. Thereafter, as soon as possible, *Illustrious* and Barham and two *Didos* should join Force 'H,' together with the two or three 16-knot transports required to carry the important supplies. *Dorsetshire* should join Force 'H,' and *Kent* should join C-in-C, Mediterranean, the latter being replaced if necessary by an R-class battleship.

5. The exchange of destroyers having taken place, and all being in readiness, Force 'H,' consisting of *Illustrious*, *Argus* and *Ark Royal* – an unprecedented floating Air concentration – with *Hood*, *Barham* and *Valiant*, with certain cruisers, including *Dorsetshire*, and at least a dozen good

---

[1] Printed earlier, under 15 July 1940.
[2] Not printed.

destroyers, should escort the convoy to Malta, the areas which they are to pass in darkness being carefully studied with a view to daylight action at the climax. The Malta Hurricanes should be nursed for this and an Air decision courted.

6. Meanwhile, in concert with the above, C-in-C, Mediterranean, should advance with all his force which may be suitable, plus *Kent*, towards Malta, taking care, however, not to get too far westward on account of his weak Air protection until Force 'H' is in the battle zone. Should the Italian fleet steam eastward to attack C-in-C, Mediterranean, he should draw them eastward as far as possible so that Force 'H' may either join him or get between the enemy and home. They are unlikely to run this risk.

7. A junction having been effected before, during or after a battle, or perhaps without any battle, and the convoy passed into Malta, *Illustrious* and *Barham* should remain with C-in-C, Mediterranean, together with any supply ships required for Alexandria, and Force 'H' should return to Gibraltar covered by *Ark Royal* and *Eagle*.

8. I should be much obliged if you would consider this general idea for the great operation, and return it to me this day with your comments. We can then discuss it together. As soon as we have reached agreement on the scheme, it should be telegraphed to C-in-C, Mediterranean, for his comments and modifications. Final decision can then be taken.

9. Meanwhile, it seems most undesirable to dispatch any stores or naval reinforcements round the Cape. We should only do this if we do not feel able to face the other.

Since writing the above I have seen C-in-C, Mediterranean's, 2301/17,[1] with which I am in close agreement.

WSC

Winston S. Churchill to A. V. Alexander and Admiral Pound
(*Churchill papers, 20/13*)

18 July 1940

It seems to me that the C-in-C, Mediterranean, should be complimented upon the whole of this series of operations. As we become more secure here against invasion through the great increase of the land forces and our shore defences, and also if our qualitative ascendancy in air fighting becomes pronounced, we must try to find him another good ship. Meanwhile, is there any reason why the *Dorsetshire* should not be sent him from Freetown round the Cape in exchange for one of his smaller cruisers? Why do we require an 8-inch cruiser off Freetown?

WSC

[1] Not printed.

July 1940

Winston S. Churchill to the Duke of Windsor
(*Churchill papers, 20/14*)

18 July 1940

A ship of the American Export line leaves Lisbon on August 1, and we are asking the United States Government to arrange for this vessel to make a special call at Bermuda, the additional expense being borne by us. This would bring Your Royal Highness to Bermuda on the 11th, and there is a Canadian National steamship of 8,000 tons, *Lady Somers*, due to call at Bermuda on August 13. We consider that this would be the most convenient arrangement. Should any hitch occur at Bermuda, and the military situation permit, the Commander-in-Chief, West Indies,[1] will be asked to arrange for a cruiser from Bermuda to Nassau.

Winston S. Churchill to General Ismay, General Dill and Sir Edward Bridges
(*Premier papers, 4/68/9*)

19 July 1940

Let it be very clearly understood that all directions emanating from me are made in writing, or should be immediately afterwards confirmed in writing, and that I do not accept any responsibility for matters relating to national defence, on which I am alleged to have given decisions, unless they are recorded in writing.[2]

WSC

Defence Committee: minutes
(*Cabinet papers, 70/1*)

19 July 1940　　　　　　　　　　　　　　　　　　　10 Downing Street
10 a.m.

The Prime Minister said that the choice which had to be made was not between a good tank and a better one, but between a fairly good tank and no tank at all. It was for this reason that a specification had been accepted which was not perfect in every particular, but which could be rapidly manufactured. He was not satisfied with the explanations which had been given, and would like to know definitely who had been responsible for altering the specification, and what the effect of the alterations had been upon the production forecast. In the meanwhile, work should proceed on the new plan.

[1] Admiral Sir Charles Kennedy-Purvis.
[2] This minute was also shown to the members of Churchill's Private Office: Eric Seal, Tony Bevir, John Martin, John Peck and John Colville.

Winston S. Churchill to Sir John Anderson
(*Churchill papers, 20/13*)

19 July 1940
ACTION THIS DAY

I have noticed lately very many sentences imposed for indiscretion by Magistrates' and other Courts throughout the country in their execution of recent legislation and regulation. All these cases should be reviewed by the Home Office, and His Majesty moved to remit the sentence where there was no malice or serious injury to the State. By selecting some of those cases which have recently figured in the public eye, and announcing remission publicly, you would give the necessary guidance without which it is difficult for local Courts to assess the lead and purpose of Parliament.

WSC

General Ironside: diary
(*'The Ironside Diaries'*)

19 July 1940

And so my military career comes to an end in the middle of a great war.[1] I have had 41 years and one month's service, and have reached the very top. I can't complain. Cabinets have to make decisions in times of stress. I don't suppose that Winston liked doing it, for he is always loyal to his friends.

Winston S. Churchill to Neville Chamberlain and Clement Attlee
(*Churchill papers, 20/13*)

20 July 1940

It might be worth while meeting Hitler's speech[2] by resolutions in both Houses. These resolutions should be proposed by private Peers and Members. On the other hand, the occasion will add to our burdens. What do you say?

---

[1] General Ironside was succeeded as Commander-in-Chief, Home Forces, by General Brooke. Ironside was sixty years old, Brooke fifty-seven on 23 July. On his retirement Ironside was made a Field Marshal and given a peerage, as Baron Ironside of Archangel and Ironside (in 1919, when Churchill was Secretary of State for War, Ironside had commanded the British forces at Archangel, in North Russia).

[2] On 19 July 1940, three days after his top secret 'Sea Lion' directive for the invasion of Britain, Hitler spoke publicly in Berlin of a 'peace offer' to Britain, and explained: 'If the struggle continues it can only end in annihilation for one of us. Mr Churchill thinks it will be Germany. I know it will be Britain.' Hitler continued: 'I am not the vanquished begging for mercy. I speak as a victor. I see no reason why this war must go on. We should like to avert the sacrifices that claim millions.' It was possible, Hitler added, 'that Mr Churchill will once again brush aside this statement of mine by saying that it is merely born of fear and doubts of victory. In this case I shall have relieved my conscience of the things to come.'

July 1940

Winston S. Churchill to Sir Alexander Cadogan
(*Churchill papers, 20/13*)

20 July 1940

I do not know whether Lord Halifax is in town to-day, but Lord Lothian should be told on no account to make any reply to the German Chargé d'Affaires'[1] message.[2]

Winston S. Churchill to Captain Beechman[3]
(*Premier papers, 4/37/4*)

20 July 1940   10 Downing Street

Thank you for the letter of July 11 signed by Mrs Tate,[4] Bartlett,[5] Acland, and yourself, in which you express concern at the lack of defensive preparation in the West Country.

I am assured that the possibility of the enemy attempting landings in that area has not been overlooked, and that precise plans exist to deal with such an eventuality.

You will of course appreciate that it is not possible or desirable for us to maintain troops along all the hundreds of miles of coastline which are now within reach of the enemy's seaborne raids.

In order to make the most effective use of our military resources it is necessary that a large proportion of the more highly-trained units should be held in the rear as a mobile reserve, disposed over the country in such a way that powerful forces can be rapidly brought to bear on any portion of these islands upon which the enemy may effect a landing, whether by sea or air.

Whilst you will not expect me to disclose the location of troops, I see no harm in informing you that some of our most seasoned and well-equipped

---

[1] Hans Thomsen. The German Government was helping to fund the America First isolationist movement by sending money through Thomsen.

[2] Regarding Hitler's 'peace offensive'.

[3] Nevil Alexander Beechman, 1895–1965. On active service, 1915–18 (Military Cross, wounded). Captain, 1917. President of the Oxford Union, 1921. Chairman of the Union of University Liberal Societies, 1922. Liberal National MP, 1937–50. Parliamentary Private Secretary to the Under-Secretary of State, Dominions Office, 1940; to the Minister of Health, 1941–2. Chief Whip of the Liberal National Party, 1942–5. A Lord Commissioner of the Treasury, 1942–5.

[4] Mavis Constance Tate, 1894–1947. National MP, 1931–5; National Conservative MP, 1935–45. Member of the Parliamentary delegation to Belsen concentration camp, 1945.

[5] Charles Vernon Oldfeld Bartlett, 1894–1983. On active service, 1914–16. Joined the *Daily Mail*, 1916; Reuters Agency, 1917; *The Times*, 1919. London director of the League of Nations, 1922–32. A regular broadcaster on foreign affairs from 1928. Staff of the *News Chronicle*, 1934–54. Independent Progressive MP, 1938–50. Author of some twenty-eight books. CBE, 1956.

mobile formations are so situated as to be able to engage the enemy with strong forces supported by aircraft in any part of the West Country within a very short space of time.

As the training and equipment of the Home Guard proceeds, these will provide a valuable addition to our regular troops, in particular along the coast, where they will be able to harass and impede the enemy at the critical moment of disembarkation.

In order to destroy or obstruct any seaborne expedition, heavy guns are being mounted and concrete defences and tank obstacles are being constructed in the vicinity of harbours and beaches in those parts of the island which are the most accessible to the enemy. Every effort is being made to expedite this work, and considering how recently these preparations were begun, the progress already achieved is most encouraging.

In estimating the strength of our defences, you must not underrate the part played by the Navy. We have many hundreds of armed craft constantly patrolling the seas around our coasts, and in the event of an attempted invasion larger naval vessels would immediately be available to intercept the enemy on the sea, or to fire upon his rear during or after landing.[1]

Winston S. Churchill to A. V. Alexander
(*Churchill papers, 20/13*)

20 July 1940

It is evident that Admiral Dudley North has not got the root of the matter in him, and I should be very glad to see you replace him by a more resolute and clear-sighted officer.[2]

Winston S. Churchill to Alfred Duff Cooper
(*Churchill papers, 20/13*)

20 July 1940

This is a cartoon which if published in Japan might be a great help to the War Party there. It is a singularly mischievous cartoon, and this paper has been most offensive. I wonder whether there is any possibility of a prosecution.

---

[1] At Churchill's request, his reply was redrafted by John Peck in the third person before being sent to the MPs.

[2] Admiral North was replaced as commander of Force H by Vice-Admiral Sir James Somerville, who was himself replaced six months later by Vice-Admiral Sir Neville Syfret (who held this command until 1943).

20 July 1940

'Daily Mirror': cartoon

Completing the Chain!

Winston S. Churchill to General Ismay
(*Churchill papers, 20/13*)

20 July 1940

It seems from these figures that very considerable efforts of employment of merchant shipping were needed to sustain over very short distances the German invasion of Norway by about 100,000 men. This has a direct bearing upon our invasion problem, and I should be glad to know that it has been considered.

Winston S. Churchill to Lord Halifax
(*Churchill papers, 20/13*)

20 July 1940

Don't you think we might go very slow on all this general and equitable, fair and honourable peace business between China and Japan? Chiang does not want it: none of the pro-Chinese want it: and so far from helping us round the Burma road difficulty it will only make it worse. I am sure that it is not in our interest that the Japanese should be relieved of their preoccupation. Would it not be a good thing to give it a miss for a month or so, and see what happens?

Winston S. Churchill to A. V. Alexander and Admiral Pound
(*Churchill papers, 20/13*)

20 July 1940

I have drawn attention to this danger before. I do not think *Hood* should be left lying in Gibraltar harbour at the mercy of a surprise bombardment by heavy howitzers. Both she and *Ark Royal* should go to sea for a cruise, with or without *Valiant* and *Resolution*, as may be thought fit. They could return to fuel or to carry out any operations provided the Spanish situation has not further deteriorated. Pray let me have your proposals.

Winston S. Churchill to Anthony Eden
(*Churchill papers, 20/13*)

20 July 1940

You may care to see this.[1] The only scale of attack which it seems to me need be contemplated for the centre of Government is, say, 500 parachutists

---

[1] A letter from Colonel Wedgwood, his third, about the need to defend London against a German parachute landing.

or Fifth Columnists. What is the present plan, and what is the scale against which it is being provided?[1]

You might do something for Jos. He is a grand hearted man.

Winston S. Churchill to Sir Archibald Sinclair and Sir Cyril Newall
(*Churchill papers, 20/13*)

20 July 1940

In case there is a raid on the centre of Government in London, it seems very important to be able to return the compliment the next day upon Berlin. I understand you will have by the end of this month a respectable party of Stirlings ready. Perhaps, however, the nights are not yet long enough. Pray let me know.[2]

WSC

Winston S. Churchill to the Duke of Windsor
(*Churchill papers, 20/9*)

20 July 1940   10 Downing Street
ACTION THIS DAY

Your Royal Highness' further telegram to Major Phillips.[3] I regret that there can be no question of releasing men from the Army to act as servants to your Royal Highness. Such a step would be viewed with general disapprobation in times like these and I should ill-serve your Royal Highness by countenancing it.

---

[1] Sand-bagged machine-gun posts had been set up in the Whitehall area, the main one at Admiralty Arch with a field of fire down the Mall, into St James's Park, and across Horse Guards Parade.

[2] Sinclair replied three days later that a Stirling light bomber squadron was in the process of formation, but would not be ready until 1 September 1940. With the heavy bombers then available, however, 17 tons of bombs could be dropped on Berlin each night for a week, with less than 24 hours' notice, and 35 tons 'on alternate nights' if given a full 24 hours' notice (*Premier papers, 3/14/2*).

[3] Gray Phillips, Comptroller to the Duke of Windsor from October 1939. 'He was six-and-a-half feet tall and had beautiful manners. He was something of a frustrated aesthete and intellectual; he had been a brilliant classical scholar at Eton, but the Great War had projected him reluctantly into the career first of a professional staff officer, later of comptroller to such great families as the Sutherlands. He was charming, resourceful, witty and kind; everybody liked him. He was a bachelor and had a strong artistic streak. He and the Duchess got on marvellously well' (Michael Bloch, *The Duke of Windsor's War*, page 44).

Winston S. Churchill to General Ismay
(*Churchill papers, 20/13*)

21 July 1940

These are most alarming proposals[1] when taken together. The anti-Japanese blockade might involve the destruction of the Dutch East Indies Refineries, or draw the Japanese down there to occupy them. Thus all that supply area would be closed against us. At the same time the second telegram marked 'B' would deprive us of all American supplies, and if, as well may be, Russia or Germany can lay hands upon the Iran and Iraq fields, we should be completely deprived of oil. It strikes me at first sight that all this is most dangerous, and should be immediately put a stop to. The Staffs and the Oil Executive should examine the matter to-day (Sunday), and furnish me with a report which can be brought before the Cabinet to-morrow (Monday).

WSC

Winston S. Churchill to General Ismay
(*Churchill papers, 20/13*)

21 July 1940

Let me have a statement showing the scheme of defence for the Central Government, Whitehall, &c. What was the scale of attack prescribed and who was responsible for taking the measures? What was the reason for attempting to put an anti-tank obstacle across St James's Park? Who ordered this? When was it counter-ordered?

WSC

Winston S. Churchill to A. V. Alexander
(*Churchill papers, 20/13*)

21 July 1940

I have now for ten days been awaiting the proposals of the Naval Staff with regard to attacking potential transports in Biscayan harbours. I have asked for a meeting with you and the First Sea Lord, CAS, and of course VCNS, for to-morrow (Monday) at 5 p.m., when this can be discussed.

---

[1] Proposals from Washington that Britain should be denied access to United States oil as part of a policy designed to prevent Japan from having access to American supplies: 'a complete ban on the export from the United States of oil, including lubricating oil, to all countries'. Lord Lothian, in setting out the proposals in a telegram on 19 July 1940, explained United States thinking: 'Figures indicate that the bulk of Japan's supplies come from California, Persian Gulf, and Dutch East Indies. If all these sources were closed, Japan itself would be almost completely denuded of petroleum, of which at present she has very small stock, while her consumption for purposes of war in China is high. She would then be unable to make war on us' (*Premier papers, 3/331/9*).

We can also deal with the situation at Gibraltar, about which I am becoming increasingly anxious. In view of the fact that the Dockyard is involved, I should be glad if the Controller[1] could also come.

You will have seen my Minute of yesterday about the risk to our capital ships lying in the harbour under threat of a sudden attack by shore batteries. There is no harm in Force 'H' going for a cruise into the Atlantic and thus being out of the enemy's sight. I entirely approve of your proposal to exchange *Renown* for *Hood* on account of *Renown*'s better protection. They might easily meet half-way at sea, and meanwhile we can reach definite decisions of principle and policy about Gibraltar.

WSC

Winston S. Churchill to Lord Linlithgow
(*Churchill papers, 20/14*)

21 July 1940

I am very much obliged to you for your 1430 S of July 18.[2] We await your draft statement and will give it immediate attention when it comes. You should know that the Cabinet were unaware of the correspondence referred to in para. 5 of your 1430 S, and that no decision has been taken by them making any departure from the declaration consequent upon the decision of Mr Chamberlain's Cabinet of October 14, 1939. The present War Cabinet who have been entrusted by Crown and Parliament with the sole responsibility for the general policy of the State would, however, be bound to take into consideration any request emanating from you for a new constitutional advance or declaration. I cannot attempt to pre-judge what the Cabinet decision would be.

Winston S. Churchill to Robert Menzies
(*Churchill papers, 20/14*)

21 July 1940

Please accept and also convey to Australian Naval Board my warmest congratulations upon brilliant action fought by HMAS *Sydney* in Mediterra-

[1] Rear-Admiral Bruce Fraser.

[2] In his telegram to Churchill, Linlithgow referred to discussions which he had had with Gandhi and Jinnah, as a result of his correspondence with Amery, which he (Linlithgow) had read 'as meaning that general feeling of His Majesty's Government and present Cabinet would be in favour of a further extensive and early, if not immediate, declaration of their intentions towards India, which would go a good deal beyond anything that had so far been said' (*Cabinet papers, 67/7*).

nean[1] which recalls the most opportune exploit of her predecessor in sinking *Emden* in the last War.

John Colville: diary
(*Colville papers*)

22 July 1940

The PM was in a cantankerous frame of mind, demanding papers which were not available.

War Cabinet: Confidential Annex
(*Cabinet papers, 65/8*)

22 July 1940　　　　　　　　　　　　　　　　　　　　　　　10 Downing Street
11.30 a.m.

The Prime Minister suggested that General Smuts' anxiety was premature.[2] In the first place, the Atlantic Islands projects related to a situation which might never develop. In the second place, further decisions by the War Cabinet would be required before our expeditions were given orders to sail. We should certainly take General Smuts into consultation at that stage. Thirdly, it by no means followed that we should at once be in a state of war with Portugal as a result of our action against the Atlantic Islands. Portugal might conceivably accept the situation under protest. In any event, it would be necessary to wait a few days, in order to see how the situation developed, before encouraging General Smuts to take action in South East Africa.

General Brooke: diary
(*'The Turn of the Tide'*)

22 July 1940

Just by ourselves at the end of a long day's work was rather trying. But he was very nice and I got a good insight into the way his brain is working. He is most interesting to listen to and full of the most marvellous courage considering the burden he is bearing. He is full of offensive thoughts, but I

[1] On 19 July 1940, off the north-west corner of Crete, the Australian cruiser HMAS *Sydney* sank the Italian light cruiser *Bartolomeo Colleoni*. The commander of the *Sydney*, Captain J. A. Collins, was awarded the CB for his part in the action. Just over a year later, on 19 November 1941, the *Sydney* was sunk in the Pacific by the German raider *Kormoran*, with the loss of all 645 officers and men. The *Kormoran* also sank, but most of her crew were saved.

[2] That a British move to control the Portuguese islands in the Atlantic might provoke a hostile reaction, detrimental to South Africa.

think he fully realises the difficulties he is up against. He said that he wondered if England had ever been in such straits since the Armada days. He refers to Hitler always as 'that man'!

Hugh Dalton: diary
(*'The Second World War Diary of Hugh Dalton'*)

22 July 1940

The War Cabinet agreed this morning to my new duties.[1] 'And now', said the PM, 'go and set Europe ablaze.'

Winston S. Churchill to Anthony Eden
(*Churchill papers, 20/13*)

23 July 1940
Most Secret

1. It is, of course, urgent and indispensable that every effort should be made to obtain secretly the best possible information about the German forces in the various countries overrun, and to establish intimate contacts with local people, and to plant agents. This, I hope, is being done on the largest scale, as opportunity serves, by the new organisation under MEW.[2] None of this partakes of the nature of military operations.
2. It would be most unwise to disturb the coasts of any of these countries by the kind of silly fiascos which were perpetrated at Boulogne and Guernsey.[3] The idea of working all these coasts up against us by pin-prick raids and fulsome communiqués is one to be strictly avoided.
3. Sir Roger Keyes is now studying the whole subject of medium raids, i.e., not less than five nor more than ten thousand men. Two or three of these might be brought off on the French coast during the winter. As soon as the invasion danger recedes or is resolved, and Sir RK's paper work is done, we will consult together and set the Staffs to work upon detailed preparations. After these medium raids have had their chance, there will be no objection to stirring up the French coast by minor forays.

---

[1] Dalton had been appointed head of the Special Operations Executive (SOE), to stimulate and co-ordinate action in German-occupied countries.

[2] Ministry of Economic Warfare.

[3] On 24 June 1940, 115 commandos had landed, briefly, at Boulogne; followed on 14 July 1940 by a raid on Guernsey, code name 'Anger' (reconnaissance) and 'Ambassador' (the raid itself) when 140 commandos landed and then returned. Four commandos were captured.

4. During the spring and summer of 1941 large armoured irruptions must be contemplated. The material for these is, however, so far ahead of us that only very general study of their possibilities is now necessary, and no directions need be given to the Staff upon them until the end of August.

WSC

War Cabinet: minutes
(*Cabinet papers, 65/8*)

23 July 1940
11.30 a.m.

The Prime Minister said that, while the Dominion demands for aircraft would probably have to be drastically scaled down, the Dominion requirements of munitions generally should be taken into account in the demands which we should make to the United States, at this juncture, when American industry was being turned over to munitions production.

The Postmaster-General[1] said that the postal arrangements with the United States and Canada had deteriorated, and it now took from ten to twelve days for a letter to reach this country from New York. The pay load of these two flying boats was 2,000 lbs, and all he asked for was an allocation of 250 lbs for urgent mail documents.

The Prime Minister said that he had considered that this question should come before the War Cabinet, as it involved the reversal of a previous War Cabinet decision. The case for reversal rested, he thought, not on the transport by air of passengers and mails for a period of six weeks, but on the Minister of Aircraft Production's need to send pilots by air across the Atlantic in order to pilot bombers back here. The fact that bombing planes were being flown from America here would make a great impression on the Germans.

The War Cabinet had before them a Memorandum by the First Lord of the Admiralty (WP (G) (40) 189) in regard to Naval measures proposed to effect Contraband Control off the West Coast of Europe and North-West Africa.

---

[1] William Shepherd Morrison, 1893–1961. Known as 'Shakes' Morrison. Served in the Royal Field Artillery, France, 1914–18 (wounded, Military Cross, despatches three times). Captain, 1919. President of the Edinburgh University Union, 1920. Called to the Bar, 1923. Conservative MP for Cirencester and Tewkesbury, 1929–59. King's Counsel, 1934. Financial Secretary to the Treasury, 1935–6. Privy Councillor, 1936. Minister of Agriculture and Fisheries, 1936–9. Chancellor of the Duchy of Lancaster and Minister of Food, 1939–40. Postmaster-General, 1940–3. Minister of Town and Country Planning, 1943–5. Speaker of the House of Commons, 1951–9. Created Viscount Dunrossil, 1959. Governor-General of Australia, 1960–1. A member of the Other Club from 1936. One of 'Shakes' Morrison's eight brothers, Alexander, had been killed in action at Loos in 1915.

The Prime Minister said he had grave doubts about the First Lord's proposals. In his view they amounted to an adoption of the German policy of unlimited submarine warfare, with the difference only that we should execute the policy with humanity. The Navy held the command of the sea and this should enable her to make prizes in the regular way according to International Law. The step suggested, if adopted, would mean that we were descending from a position which had been the turning point of great struggles in the past and we should be conceding a great principle without gaining any real advantage. Germany had endeavoured to gain command of the sea without paying the lawful price, which was a Fleet superior to that of the enemy. With command of the sea he did not see why it should be necessary for us to descend to German methods, which we should certainly be accused of doing if the proposed policy was adopted.

Winston S. Churchill to General Ismay
(*Churchill papers, 20/13*)

23 July 1940

Where is the South African Union Brigade of 10,000 men? Why is it playing no part in the Middle East? We have agreed to-day to send further reinforcements of Hurricanes and other modern aircraft to the South African Air Force. What is happening to the concert of the campaign in the Middle East? What has been done by the Committee of Ministers I recently set up? Now that large naval operations are contemplated in the Mediterranean, it is all the more essential that the attack on the Italian position in Abyssinia should be pressed and concerted by all means. Make sure I have a report about the position, which I can consider on Thursday morning.

WSC

Winston S. Churchill to General Ismay
(*Cherwell papers*)

23 July 1940

It seems to me that further and repeated warnings must be given about gas. Every mask must be tested, and civilians enjoined to use them and carry them everywhere. Gas-proofing of shelters, in so far as it exists, must be made efficient.

WSC

Winston S. Churchill to General Ismay
(*Churchill papers, 20/13*)

23 July 1940

OIL FUEL CAPACITY AT AERODROMES

I am told that the re-fuelling of fighter aeroplanes could be much more rapidly achieved if there were more tankers on the aerodromes, and considering that an attack by air would make every minute gained in returning the fighters to the air most precious, I should be glad if measures were taken at once to double it or greatly increase the fuelling facilities.

WSC

Winston S. Churchill to Anthony Eden
(*Churchill papers, 20/13*)

23 July 1940

I do not seem to have had any answer from you to my query about whether the 2nd Canadian Division and all it stands for is being frittered away in Iceland.[1]

WSC

Winston S. Churchill to Sir Archibald Sinclair and Lord Beaverbrook
(*Premier papers, 3/11/2*)

23 July 1940   10 Downing Street

From many quarters come reports of RAF bombs non-exploded. See attached telegram. What is being done about this? It would seem that the officers responsible should be provided with all the references to this in the Intelligence Reports, particularly from Switzerland, whence several cases have been mentioned. We ought to make sure of our bombs.

WSC

---

[1] Most of the Canadians left Iceland on 31 October 1940.

July 1940

Winston S. Churchill: Oral Answers
(*Hansard*)

23 July 1940 House of Commons
2.45 p.m. onward

RESTRICTIVE REGULATIONS

Mr Lindsay[1] asked the Prime Minister whether he is aware that the policy of the formation of silent columns,[2] of the regulation relating to the spreading of gloom and despondency, and the arbitrary arrest and release of British citizens is diminishing the bracing effects of his own speeches and broadcasts and belittling the loyalty and intelligence of the British people; and whether he will take suitable action in the matter?

The Prime Minister: The movement of forming silent columns was well-meant in its endeavour to discourage loose and ill-digested talk of a depressing character about the war. However, when this idea was put down in black and white it did not look by any means so attractive and seemed to suggest that reasonable and intelligent discussion about the war between loyal and well-disposed people ought not to take place. On the contrary, His Majesty's Government are glad that the general aspects of the war should be understood and discussed, provided that there is no breach, however inadvertent, of official secrecy, no precise references to the strength and disposition of our Forces, and no talk about future operations. This movement to create a silent column has, therefore, passed into what is called in the United States innocuous desuetude.

Upon the second part of my hon. Friend's Question, I would observe that we have been and are still passing through a most critical phase in the war, and that our Forces are now ranged and vigilant to strike at invasion. The House has accepted numerous regulations which, but for the gravity of the hour, would be extremely repugnant to all our ideas, and some of which might tend to encourage ill-natured tale-bearing and mutual suspicion in our midst. In the circumstances I have asked the Home Secretary to have every sentence imposed by the courts for loose or defeatist talk carefully and immediately reviewed, and that it should be reduced or remitted wherever it is clear that there was no evil wish, or systematic purpose to weaken the National Defence in the persons concerned. His Majesty's Government have no desire to make

---

[1] Kenneth Lindsay, 1897–1991. Educated at St Olave's school. On active service, 1916–18. At Worcester College, Oxford, 1921–2; President of the Oxford Union, 1922. Secretary, Political and Economic Planning (PEP), 1931–5. Independent National MP for Kilmarnock Burghs, 1933–45; Independent MP for the Combined English Universities, 1945–50. Civil Lord of the Admiralty, 1935–7. Parliamentary Secretary, Board of Education, 1937–40. Director of the Anglo-Israel Association, 1962–73. A Vice-President of the Educational Interchange Council (sometime Chairman), 1968–73.

[2] Groups of citizens, recruited by the Minister of Information, Alfred Duff Cooper, whose task was to report on disloyal or treasonable talk or activity. They were known as 'Cooper's snoopers'.

crimes out of silly vapourings which are best dealt with on the spur of the moment by verbal responses from the more robust members of the company. They desire only to curb, as it is their duty to do, propaganda of a persistent, organised and defeatist character. As these sentences come to be revised and their revision is made public, as it will be, the courts all over the country will have a good guide furnished them as to what are the intentions of Parliament and the requirements of the State in respect of these war-time regulations.

Mr Rhys Davies[1]: Is it possible for the Government to consider either withdrawing or amending this regulation?

The Prime Minister: No, Sir, I do not think so.

SUSPICIOUS POLITICAL ACTIVITIES (COMMITTEE)

Mr G. Strauss asked the Prime Minister whether the committee appointed by his predecessor, under the chairmanship of Lord Swinton, to report to him suspicious political activities, is still in existence; who its members are; and whether it is now making any reports?

The Prime Minister: It would not be in the public interest to give any information on the subject covered by the hon. Member's Question.

Mr Strauss: As this committee was set up without any public announcement, and its purpose seems to be rather peculiar, would it not be possible to allay public suspicion by some announcement in regard to its activities?

The Prime Minister: A great many committees and a good many enterprises, some of them of a peculiar character, are set up without any public announcement. I cannot see any advantage in this case in dealing with the matter across the Floor of the House.

AIR RAIDS (REPRISALS)

Mr Lewis[2] asked the Prime Minister whether he will undertake that, in the event of hostile air raids on London, prompt reprisals will be made not only on Berlin but also on Rome?

The Prime Minister: There is not much to be gained by putting Questions of this kind on the Paper. If the answer were in the negative, it would remove a deterrent upon the enemy. If it were in the affirmative, it might spur him to increase his preparations and add to the difficulties of our airmen. If it were non-committal, it would not add to the enlightenment of my hon. Friend.

---

[1] Rhys John Davies, 1877–1954. After elementary school, became a farm labourer, later a coal miner. A pacifist. A member of Manchester City Council. Secretary of the National Union of Distributive Workers' Approved Society. Labour MP, 1921–54. Under-Secretary for the Home Department in the first Labour Government, 1924.

[2] Oswald Lewis, 1887–1966. Younger son of John Lewis, founder of the Oxford Street firm of silk mercers and drapers. A partner in his father's firm. Called to the Bar, 1912. Member of the London County Council, 1913–19. On active service, 1914–16. Conservative MP, 1929–45.

Although the enemy frequently volunteers statements of his intentions through various channels, these are nearly always found to be untruthful and given for the purpose of misleading. I should be very sorry if my hon. Friend, by making inquiries about future military operations, were to tempt me into courses of that character.

Henry Channon: diary
('<i>Chips</i>')</center>

23 July 1940

Winston was in roaring spirits today, and gave slashing answers, which he had himself drafted, to foolish Questions, and generally convulsed the House. He is at the very top of his form now and the House is completely with him, as is the country, but he knows very little about foreign affairs. I sat behind him today and he was smiling and friendly, but I am always shy with him, and never get it quite right: I do not know why.

Defence Committee: minutes
(<i>Cabinet papers, 70/1</i>)</center>

23 July 1940
6.30 p.m.

The Prime Minister said there was a good case for arming the squadrons in the Middle East and Kenya with modern aircraft when the crisis here had passed, but he would like to know in detail how it would be done. He would not, however, consent to any modern aircraft going to South Africa other than the few which would be required to enable squadrons to train on the new type. It was only because the South African squadrons were actually engaged in battle that we could justify releasing equipment for their Air Force, and not for the Air Forces of other Dominions.

Winston S. Churchill to the Duke of Windsor
(<i>Churchill papers, 20/9</i>)</center>

24 July 1940
Secret

Arrangements have now been made for Your Royal Highness to leave by American Export vessel on August 1 for Bermuda, and proceed thence by Canadian National Steamship *Lady Somers* on the 13th direct to Nassau. His Majesty's Government cannot agree to Your Royal Highness landing in the

United States at this juncture. This decision must be accepted. It should be possible to arrange if necessary for the Duchess either to proceed from Bermuda to New York for medical reasons, or alternatively it will always be easy for her to go there from Nassau by sea or land.

Sir, I have now succeeded in overcoming the War Office objection to the departure of Fletcher,[1] who will be sent forthwith to join you.

Defence Committee: minutes
(*Cabinet papers, 70/1*)

24 July 1940 Upper War Room
11.30 a.m. Admiralty

The situation at Gibraltar was fully discussed, and the Prime Minister suggested that it would be advisable to examine the immediate action which might be taken against Spain in the event of any treacherous action on her part. He thought it might be worth while considering whether to draw the attention of the Spanish Government to the dangers to which they would expose themselves if they took any sudden action against Gibraltar.

Winston S. Churchill to Lord Halifax
(*Premier papers, 3/361/1*)

24 July 1940
Secret

All my reflections about the danger of our ships lying under the Spanish howitzers in Gibraltar lead me continually to the Azores. Must we always wait until a disaster has occurred? I do not think it follows that our occupation temporarily, and to forestall the enemy, of the Azores, would <u>necessarily</u> precipitate German intervention in Spain and Portugal. It might have the reverse effect. The fact that we had an alternative fuelling base to Gibraltar might tell against German insistence that we should be attacked there, or anyhow reduce German incentive to have us attacked. Moreover once we have an alternative base to Gibraltar, how much do we care whether the Peninsula is overrun or not? If it is not overrun at the present moment, that is only because Hitler shrinks from becoming embroiled in a war with the Spanish people. It does not follow that it would be a bad thing for us if he were

---

[1] The Duke of Windsor's soldier-servant.

so embroiled, as was Napoleon before him. There is much to be said on the other side, but I am increasingly attracted by the idea of simply taking the Azores one fine morning out of the blue, and explaining everything to Portugal afterwards. She would certainly have every right to protest.

WSC

Winston S. Churchill to General Ismay
(*Churchill papers, 20/13*)

24 July 1940

Apart from the Anti-Nazi Germans who can begin by being pioneers, rifles and ammunition should be issued to all these Foreign Corps.[1] Whether this should be from British Service rifles now in the possession of the Home Guard, but in process of being replaced by American rifles, or whether the Foreign Corps should be armed with American rifles direct, has no doubt been considered. On the whole I am inclined to the latter solution. It is most urgent to rearm the Poles and the French, as we may need them for foreign service in the near future. The armament of these Foreign Corps ranks after the armament of British troops so far as rifles are concerned, but they have priority over the Home Guard. They ought to have a small proportion of Bren guns, &c., even at the expense of our own men. What is being done to furnish them with artillery? Surely some of the '75s can be made to serve the purpose. The Polish Unit should be ripened as much as possible. Pray let me have a weekly report of numbers and weapons.

Winston S. Churchill to General Ismay
(*Premier papers, 3/372/1*)

24 July 1940

Draw the attention of the Admiralty to the great importance of the consignment due July 31. 100,000 rifles means 100,000 men.

WSC

---

[1] A total of 25,500 troops, made up of 14,000 Poles, 4,000 Czechs, 3,000 Anti-Nazi Germans, 2,000 French, 1,000 Poles, 1,000 Norwegians and 500 Belgians (War Cabinet Paper No. 281 of 1940).

John Colville: diary
(*Colville papers*)

24 July 1940

The PM's comment on a long telegram of July 22nd from the Viceroy (Linlithgow) about the proposals for new Indian constitutional measures is 'long-winded as ever and a piece of hypocrisy from beginning to end'.

On a note from Vansittart about a possible answer to the speech Hitler made last Sunday, Winston has written: 'I do not propose to say anything in reply to Herr Hitler's speech, not being on speaking terms with him.'

Winston S. Churchill to Sir Roger Keyes
(*Churchill papers, 20/13*)

25 July 1940
Secret

Pray let me have at your earliest convenience a list of all the men, material and establishments at present comprised in your sphere.[1] I am hoping that you will shortly present me in outline, not, of course, worked out in detail, with three or four proposals for medium-sized action (i.e., between five and ten thousand) of the kind which I mentioned to you verbally. I certainly thought we should be acting in September and October.

WSC

Winston S. Churchill to A. V. Alexander, Admiral Pound and Admiral Phillips
(*Churchill papers, 20/13*)

25 July 1940
ACTION THIS DAY

I cannot help feeling that there is more in the plan of laying mines behind an invader's landing than the Naval Staff felt when I mentioned the matter three weeks ago. In the interval, I sent a reminder asking that it should be further considered. If an invader lands during the night or morning, the flotillas will attack him in rear during the day, and these flotillas will be heavily

---

[1] Combined Operations, of which Keyes had just become the head.

bombarded from the Air, as part of the Air battles which will be going on. If, however, when night falls a curtain or fender of mines can be laid close inshore, so as to cut off the landing-place from reinforcements of any kind, these mines, once laid, will not have to be guarded from Air attack and, consequently, will relieve the flotilla from the need of coming back on the second day, thus avoiding losses of the Air and Air protection. At any rate, I think it improvident not to provide for the option whether to seal off the hostile landing by attack of flotillas or mines. There may be several landings, and you may want to leave one sealed off with mines in order to attack another. Of course, all the above will apply still more if the landing had got hold of a port instead of merely a beach.

Winston S. Churchill to Lord Halifax
(*Churchill papers, 20/13*)

25 July 1940
ACTION THIS DAY

I feel increasingly convinced that the kind of approach to Weygand I suggested yesterday should be made by me, and should be made now. I do not see any advantage in waiting until Mr Bland[1] reaches his post unless he can, in fact, be the bearer of the letter and can arrive in the next few days. Why does it take him so long to go? Moreover, I thought it would be better that it should not come through the official channels, since it clearly suggests a kind of friendly revolt against the Pétain–Laval policy.

2. Two further arguments have occurred to me. The Spaniards are casting covetous eyes on the French possessions in Africa. As soon as the French soldiers have been disarmed by the German–Italian Armistice Commission, said soon to be arriving, there is imminent danger of Moorish revolt and consequent anarchy. This will give Germans, Italians and Spaniards an opportunity of intervening to restore order. But by then the French will have lost their arms, and we much of our opportunity.

3. There will be great scarcity of food in unoccupied France. I think we should let them know that if there were a friendly French Government in Africa, and that Government were to ask us to send food into unoccupied France, even though a bad French Government were in power in the homeland, we should be willing to meet their need. In other words, we will

---

[1] Almost certainly J. W. Blanch, British Consul in Fez from April 1939 (and subsequently at Rabat).

allow food into France only if there is a French Government in North Africa which is continuing the war.

4. It will be a very good thing to put these possibilities before the French Government now without any more delay in order that it may work in their minds as the German and Italian ill-usage and the food shortage exert their pressures, and, if possible, before the Armistice Commission has completed the demilitarisation of North Africa.

5. To sum up, I want to promote a kind of collusive conspiracy in the Vichy Government whereby certain members of that Government, perhaps with the consent of some of those who remain, will levant to North Africa in order to make a better bargain for France from the North African shore and from a position of independence. For this purpose I would use both food and other inducements as well as the obvious arguments.

I regard all this as most important and urgent.

WSC

Winston S. Churchill to General Ismay
(*Cabinet papers, 65/14*)

25 July 1940

I personally feel that an attack on the Dutch East Indies by Japan is an even greater menace to our safety and interests than an attack upon Hong Kong, when it is admitted we shall have to fight. We should, in fact, be allowing ourselves to be cut off from Australia and New Zealand, and they would regard our acquiescence as desertion. I should hope the United States would not remain indifferent, as their position in the Philippines would also be affected. I was not aware that any such attack was imminent, and I do not quite understand the urgency for a decision. The American aspect might well be one to be discussed between the Staffs in the forthcoming conversations (when are these going to begin?).

Should a Japanese attack on the Dutch East Indies become imminent, we ought to tell Japan plainly that that will be war with us, and not wait until Singapore is directly menaced. We should have to rely mainly on submarines and a few fast cruisers at the outset. I doubt myself whether the Japanese would wish to run the risks of such an adventure while they are entangled in China.

If these observations should lead the Staff to agreement, there would be no need to trouble the Cabinet on the point till the Staff paper is completed. If, however, the difference persists, the case can be put to the Cabinet next week.

WSC

Winston S. Churchill to General Ismay
(*Churchill papers, 20/13*)

25 July 1940

I agree that no large scale exercise is possible except as a Staff ride. I approve of this latter taking place as proposed on the 29th. Cabinet cannot meet till 11.30, but may then meet in the War Room. We have not met there for some months, and it is useful to try it again. We might in fact move from No. 10 to the War Room as the result of a warning of a sham air raid, and see how long it takes us to get across. This should not occur till about one o'clock when the bulk of the business should have been disposed of.[1]

War Cabinet: minutes
(*Cabinet papers, 65/8*)

25 July 1940 10 Downing Street
11.30 a.m.

The Prime Minister thought that we might go a long way towards a real understanding with India if we could return to the use of plain and unambiguous language. We had been too much accustomed to hand the Indians lengthy documents full of high-sounding words such as 'Dominion Status' and independence – which were not always used in the same sense as they were by ordinary people. Let us now say exactly what we meant and thus remove the suspicions of which we ourselves had in part been the cause.

The Prime Minister thought it was important to recall the developments in Indian constitutional matters which had taken place, and the various Declarations which had been made, ending with the Statement made by the present Secretary of State for India on the 23rd May. In that Statement we had again said that the 'attainment by India of free and equal partnership in the British Commonwealth is the goal of our policy.' The Statement now proposed would involve an entirely new departure, namely, that we should undertake in advance to accept a Constitution framed by Indians. Further, the draft Statement proposed by the Viceroy went a long way towards pledging Parliament to ratify a Constitution framed in this way by Indians. The proposition that we should accept any Constitution upon which Indians themselves could agree went beyond the undertaking of Dominion status. The

---

[1] The War Cabinet did meet in the underground Cabinet War Room on the morning of 29 July 1940, when, contrary to Churchill's suggestion, the whole meeting took place underground, not just the final items.

proposal now put forward contained two elements of unreality: first, that the reservations on which we must insist cut at the root of Dominion status as commonly understood; secondly, that it was hard to believe that agreement on these matters among Indians themselves was possible.

The Prime Minister thought that to make a Statement at the present time on the lines proposed by the Viceroy was full of danger. If we did, opinion in the United States might well take the line that, having gone so far, we had better give Indians all that they asked for and have done with it. Further, to make a great Constitutional Declaration in a country like India was likely to give rise to acute controversy. Such a course was wholly unjustified at the present time.

The Prime Minister said that the practical measures to be adopted had already been agreed by the War Cabinet, namely, the expansion of the Viceroy's Executive Council and the establishment of a War Advisory Committee. He agreed that these measures should be accompanied by a further Statement which, he thought, should follow the general lines of the Statement made by the Secretary of State for India on the 23rd May, should emphasise that we were making a further forward movement, should speak generously of India's war effort, and should invite the Congress Ministries to take up office in the Provinces again. As regards Constitutional questions, the Statement might say that as soon as the war was over we were prepared to re-examine the basis of the 1935 Act, so far as concerned the Central Government.

Agreement was expressed with this suggestion and with the view that the Statement should include reference to re-examination of the Constitutional position when hostilities ceased.

War Cabinet: Confidential Annex
(*Cabinet papers, 65/14*)

25 July 1940
11.30 a.m.

10 Downing Street

The Prime Minister said that, in his opinion, the proposals which the Secretary of State for India had put forward represented so important a departure from previous policy that the War Cabinet should have been informed of the matter earlier. He thought that the Secretary of State would have been right to have consulted the War Cabinet before he had developed his ideas to the Viceroy.

In consequence of telegrams from the Secretary of State of the 2nd, 16th and 17th June, the Viceroy had been under the impression that the views put forward by the Secretary of State had in fact received the approval of the War Cabinet.

Furthermore, he thought that the War Cabinet had cause for complaint in that, at their Meeting on the 12th July, they had not been informed of the correspondence between the Secretary of State and the Viceroy in the period 1st to 22nd June. As a result, the War Cabinet had been under the impression that the proposals which they had considered at that Meeting had been made on the Viceroy's own initiative. In effect, these proposals had only been made by the Viceroy after considerable persuasion had been exercised upon him by the Secretary of State.

The Secretary of State for India said that he much regretted the misunderstanding which had occurred. In his Minute of the 19th July he had drawn attention to the various precautions which he had taken to make it clear to the Viceroy that his approach had been of a personal and exploratory character.

The Prime Minister said that he, of course, accepted the explanation which the Secretary of State had given. It was unfortunate that the discussion of this important matter should have been complicated by this misunderstanding. The position as to consultation with the Viceroy must necessarily be different under a small War Cabinet from the position in peace-time, when the Secretary of State was himself a member of the Cabinet.

The Prime Minister said that he had raised with the Foreign Secretary the previous day the importance of the North African coast line to us if we could only get a footing there. To obtain this should not be beyond the bounds of possibility. It was already clear from recent telegrams that the Vichy Government was not popular in France and he (the Prime Minister) was considering the possibility of promoting a kind of collusion conspiracy in the Vichy Government whereby certain members of it might levant to North Africa. It might be possible to negotiate with such a Government to allow food, of which there was a great scarcity, in to France on condition that the French Government in North Africa continued the war. Perhaps an approach to Marshal Weygand might be made as a first step in this direction.

The Prime Minister said he was seeing General de Gaulle that day and would sound him as to the possibility of his forming a rallying point in North Africa. In the meantime, he would be glad if his colleagues would watch events, with a view to the formation of a French Government in North Africa.

Winston S. Churchill to Lord Linlithgow
(*Churchill papers, 20/14*)

26 July 1940

Secretary of State has shown me telegrams which have passed on the Secret and Personal File, and for the first time I realise what has been going on. I must ask in the public interest and in justice to you to show these telegrams to the War Cabinet and the two or three other colleagues who have great Indian experience and whom I have consulted. It does not seem to me possible to withhold the facts from my colleagues.

Cabinet, Thursday, 25th, considered your new draft statement. We did not reach any conclusion going beyond the public declaration made by the Secretary of State in the House of Commons on the 23rd May, which defined the policy of the new Government in broad accordance with the views expressed by the late Administration in full knowledge of your views and wishes on the spot. Cabinet has left it to me to draft for your consideration an alternative statement in harmony with the only policies to which we are at present committed. I will send this to you as soon as I have completed it for your perfectly free consideration and suggestions.

You must remember that we are here facing constant threat of invasion with many strange novel features, and this is only held off and can only be mastered literally from day to day by the prowess of our Airmen at heavy odds and by the vigilance of the Royal Navy. In these circumstances, immense constitutional departures cannot be effectively discussed in Parliament, and only by the Cabinet to the detriment of matters touching the final life and safety of the State.

I am sure that I can count upon you to help us to the utmost of your power.

Defence Committee: minutes
(*Cabinet papers, 69/1*)

26 July 1940　　　　　　　　　　　　　　　　　　　　　Upper War Room
11.30 a.m.　　　　　　　　　　　　　　　　　　　　　　　　Admiralty

PROTECTION OF CONVOYS

The Prime Minister said he wished to discuss the action which should be taken to improve the system of protection for Channel convoys against air attack. We could hardly go on allowing the convoys to sustain casualties on the scale experienced on the previous day.[1]

---

[1] Five British merchant ships were sunk in the Channel on 25 July 1940: *Corhaven*, *Polgrange* and *Leo* off Dover, and *Henry Moon* and *Portslade* off Sandgate. Three more were sunk on the following day, the day of Churchill's minute.

JULY 1940

Air Marshal Peirse said that the point which seemed to stand out from recent actions was that our fighters were outnumbered by the enemy's. It was clear that at present the German aim was to harass our convoys. He suggested that it might be worth while concentrating our fighters in great strength, so as to teach them a lesson.

The Prime Minister agreed with this view. He thought that the move of a convoy should be treated as a tactical operation, and should be arranged in such a way that the defence would be used to the best advantage. More goods might be placed on the railways, and the sailing of convoys might be at irregular intervals.

Air Marshal Peirse expressed the opinion that the Germans would never be able to develop again the strength they had at their disposal at the beginning of the attack in the West.

The Prime Minister thought the Germans would have to remember that Russia was in the background, and they would hardly dare to throw in the whole of their forces.

THE UP WEAPON

Arising out of the discussion on the previous item, the Prime Minister enquired whether additional anti-aircraft guns had been placed at Dover.

Sir Hugh Dowding said that he was unable at present to find enough guns to cover all the vital objectives laid down by the Chiefs of Staff. By the end of August, however, he had been promised that the supplies of the UP weapon would begin. He was very anxious to receive these weapons without any refinements, such as a PE fuze, since he felt that a number of well-directed rockets bursting in the path of a dive bomber would spoil his aim. The provision of the UP weapon would also release a number of Bofors.[1]

The Prime Minister said that he was most anxious that the UP weapon in all its forms should be pressed on with the utmost vigour, and he instructed the Secretary[2] to obtain a report of the present situation, and a forecast of deliveries of projectors and projectiles.

ENGAGEMENT OF TANKS BY AIRCRAFT

The Prime Minister said that he had heard that at a demonstration of anti-tank devices held on the previous Monday (22nd July), great success had attended the firing from aircraft of cannon against a tank. He enquired whether aircraft were being equipped for this purpose.

---

[1] The British Army had adopted the Swedish 40mm Bofors gun in 1937. It was the most widely used anti-aircraft gun of the Second World War, in service with almost all the combatant armies. Its accuracy and rapid fire made it particularly effective against low-flying and dive-bombing aircraft.

[2] The Defence Committee Secretariat was headed by Colonel (later Major-General Sir) Leslie Hollis (see page 739, footnote 1).

Sir Hugh Dowding said that he was reserving the first few cannon fighters which he had received for this purpose, but his main intention was to put cannon in Lysander aircraft, which would be more suitable for the purpose than fighters. Tests had been most satisfactory, but what was now required was armour-piercing ammunition for the Hispano Suiza cannon. The present solid shot was stopped by about 20 mm of armour.

The Prime Minister said that this matter had been already mentioned to the Minister of Aircraft Production, and he instructed the Secretary to ascertain the position, and to report on the steps being taken.

Winston S. Churchill to Lord Lothian
(*Churchill papers, 20/14*)

26 July 1940

Need of American destroyers is more urgent than ever in view of losses and the need of coping with invasion threat as well as keeping Atlantic approaches open and dealing with Italy. All was clearly set out in FO telegram No. 1148.[1] There is nothing that America can do at this moment that would be of greater help than to send fifty destroyers, except sending a hundred. The flying-boats are also of the greatest importance now and in the next two months. As I have repeatedly explained, the difficulty is to bridge the gap until our new war-time production arrives in a flood. I append a note prepared in the Admiralty, and I propose also to send a personal message to the President.

Winston S. Churchill to Lord Lothian
(*Churchill papers, 20/14*)

26 July 1940

Owing to the withdrawal of British authorities from French ports, we are badly in need of accurate information as to the present state of readiness of units of the French Fleet.

We shall be most grateful for any assistance the United States Government are able to give us in this matter and, if you are prepared to agree, we propose the following procedure should be followed:–

The United States Consular representatives at Marseilles, Toulon, Bizerta,

---

[1] Lord Halifax to Lord Lothian, 15 July 1940. This was one of several telegrams sent to Lord Lothian in the third week of July, giving him advice as to the different points to be made in support of the British request for American destroyers.

Tunis, Bona, Philippeville, Algiers, Oran, Casablanca, Dakar, Saigon and other ports where French warships are based, to be instructed by the United States Ambassador in France[1] to send reports regarding movements, states of readiness, morale, &c., of French warships at their ports, direct to him; these reports then to be transmitted to Washington in cypher. The British Ambassador in Washington to be shown such reports and to be the means for passing the information so obtained to London.

By this method the United States Consular representatives would ostensibly be collecting information for the use of their own Government, and need have no knowledge that the reports they were making would eventually reach us.

Winston S. Churchill to General Ismay
(*Churchill papers, 20/13*)

26 July 1940
ACTION THIS DAY

It is most important to secure more volunteers from the French sailors and soldiers who are in this country, and the sinking of the *Meknès*[2] affords a good opportunity for enabling them to reconsider their view. Let a plan be proposed to-day by the Departments concerned, and let this plan be considered by Sir Robert Vansittart's Committee so that it gets fair treatment, and thereafter let it be put into operation. Make sure that proper Officers are chosen who are in sympathy with the plan.

WSC

Winston S. Churchill to General Ismay
(*Churchill papers, 20/13*)

26 July 1940
ACTION THIS DAY

TROOPS FROM NEW ZEALAND

We can hardly ask these people to come all this way and enter a war zone without giving them at least a minimum equipment of rifles and Bren guns. Arrangements must be made to send these by the Cape to meet them on arrival. What other items of equipment do they lack? Let me have a list, and let me see the telegram with paragraph 3 re-drafted accordingly.

[1] W. C. Bullitt.
[2] On July 24, a German motor torpedo boat sighted an unarmed French merchant steamer, the *Meknès*, sailing from Southampton at night with 1,179 repatriated French naval personnel on board, her French ensign spotlighted by a searchlight, her sides illuminated, her portholes lit up. She nevertheless attacked. When the Captain of the *Meknès* brought his ship to a standstill, signalled by a siren to that effect, and flashed her name and nationality by Morse, the only answer was a torpedo. The *Meknès* sank; 383 French sailors drowned.

578 JULY 1940

Winston S. Churchill to General Ismay
(*Churchill papers, 20/13*)

26 July 1940
ACTION THIS DAY

ERITREAN PORTS

Let the Joint Planning Committee prepare this day a plan for the capture of Assab and Massawah, using for the purpose whatever troops in the Middle Eastern theatre appear most convenient, and whatever ships are available and needed. Ample forces should be used and full advantage taken of our amphibious power. The action should take place at the earliest moment, and if *Eagle* is used she must be back in the Mediterranean by the middle of August. If it be necessary to employ any part of the Union Brigade, I will obtain permission from General Smuts. After capture, the places should either be thoroughly destroyed or left with small native garrisons.

Winston S. Churchill to A. V. Alexander
(*Churchill papers, 20/13*)

27 July 1940

The great consignments of rifles and guns, together with their ammunition, which are now approaching this country, are entirely on a different level from anything else we have transported across the ocean except the Canadian Division itself. Do not forget that 200,000 rifles mean 200,000 men, as the men are waiting for the rifles. The convoys approaching on the 31st July are unique, and a special effort should be made to ensure their safe arrival. The loss of these rifles and field guns would be a disaster of the first order.

Winston S. Churchill to the Duke of Windsor
(*Churchill papers, 20/9*)

27 July 1940
Secret

I send you this by Walter Monckton, who is flying out to see you before you leave, and who will talk over various matters upon which you should be verbally informed.

I am very glad to have been able to arrange for your Royal Highness and the Duchess a suitable sphere of activity and public service during this terrible time when the whole world is lapped in danger and confusion. I know Nassau, having stayed a month there recovering from my accident in New York,[1] and except for a few months in the year it has one of the most agreeable climates. Moreover, through its proximity to the United States, it presents a ceaseless flow of interesting people. I am sure that your Royal Highness and the Duchess will lend a distinction and dignity to the Governorship which will be to the best interests of the Island and its group, and may well have other results favourable to British interests.

It would of course be natural that from time to time your Royal Highness should ask for leave to visit the United States, or other Islands, or the United Kingdom. At the present time I do not think that a visit to the United States would be desirable, because as your Royal Highness sees, the Presidential Election and the critical character of the war here have created abnormal conditions. But you may surely rely upon me, as long as I hold my present position, to do all within my power to serve your Royal Highness' true interests, and to study your wishes.

Sir, may I venture upon a word of serious counsel. It will be necessary for the Governor of the Bahamas to express views about the war and the general situation which are not out of harmony with those of His Majesty's Government. The freedom of conversation which is natural to anyone in an unofficial position, or indeed to a Major-General, is not possible in any direct representative of the Crown. Many sharp and unfriendly ears will be pricked up to catch any suggestion that your Royal Highness takes a view about the war, or about the Germans, or about Hitlerism, which is different from that adopted by the British nation and Parliament. Many malicious tongues will carry tales in every direction. Even while you have been staying at Lisbon, conversations have been reported by telegraph through various channels which might have been used to your Royal Highness' disadvantage. In particular, there will be danger of use being made of anything you say in the United States to do you injury, and to suggest divergence between you and the British Government. I am so anxious that mischief should not be made which might mar the success which I feel sure will attend your mission. We are all passing through times of immense stress and dire peril, and every step has to be watched with care.

I thought your Royal Highness would not mind these words of caution from
Your faithful and devoted servant,
Winston S. Churchill

---

[1] Having been knocked down by a car in New York in December 1931, Churchill recuperated in the Bahamas before returning to the lecture circuit which the accident had interrupted.

General James Marshall-Cornwall[1]: recollection
(*Marshall-Cornwall papers*)

27 July 1940   Chequers

I reached Chequers about six o'clock and was told that the PM was resting. Two hours later we sat down to dinner. It was indeed a memorable meal. I was placed on the PM's right, and on my right was Professor Frederick Lindemann, Churchill's scientific adviser. The others around the oval table were Mrs Churchill, Duncan Sandys and his wife, 'Pug' Ismay, Jack Dill, Lord Beaverbrook, and one of the PM's private secretaries.

Churchill was bubbling over with enthusiasm and infectious gaiety. I marvelled how he could appear so carefree with the enormous load of anxieties on his shoulders, and I wish that I could remember some of the splendid sentences that rolled off his tongue.

As soon as the champagne was served he started to interrogate me about the condition of my Corps. I told him that when I had taken it over I had found all ranks obsessed with defensive tactical ideas, the main object of everyone being to get behind an anti-tank obstacle. I had issued orders that only offensive training exercises were to be practised, and that the III Corps motto was 'Hitting, not Sitting', which prefaced every operation order.

This went down tremendously well with the PM, who chuckled and chortled: 'Splendid! That's the spirit I want to see.' He continued: 'I assume then that your Corps is now ready to take the field?' 'Very far from it, Sir,' I replied; 'our re-equipment is not nearly complete, and when it is we shall require another month or two of intensive training.'

Churchill looked at me incredulously and drew a sheaf of papers from the pocket of his dinner-jacket. 'Which are your two Divisions?' he demanded. 'The 53rd (Welsh) and the 2nd London,' I replied. He pushed a podgy finger on the graph tables in front of him and said: 'There you are: 100 per cent complete in personnel, rifles and mortars; 50 per cent in field artillery, anti-tank rifles and machine-guns.' 'I beg your pardon, Sir,' I replied; 'that state

---

[1] James Handyside Marshall-Cornwall, 1887–1985. Entered Royal Artillery, 1907. Served as an Intelligence Officer in France and Flanders, 1914–18; awarded the Military Cross and mentioned in despatches five times. Lieutenant-Colonel, 1918. Attended the Paris Peace Conference, 1919. Officer Commanding the Dardanelles Defences, 1920. Intelligence Officer, Constantinople, 1920–2. British Delegate, Thracian Boundary Commission, 1924–5. Served with the Shanghai Defence Force, 1927. Military Attaché, Berlin, April 1928 to April 1932. Took the surname Marshall-Cornwall, 1929. Director-General, Air and Coast Defence, 1938–9. Knighted, 1940. General Officer Commanding the British Troops, Egypt, 1941; Western Command, 1941–2. Editor-in-Chief, Captured German Archives, 1948–51. President, Royal Geographical Society, 1954–8. Military historian.

may refer to the weapons which the ordnance depots are preparing to issue to my units, but they have not yet reached the troops in anything like those quantities.'

The PM's brow contracted; almost speechless with rage, he hurled the graphs across the dinner-table to Dill, saying: 'CIGS, have those papers checked and returned to me tomorrow.'

An awkward silence followed; a diversion seemed called for. The PM leant across me and addressed my neighbour on the other side: 'Prof! What have you got to tell me today?' The other civilians present were wearing dinner-jackets, but Professor Lindemann was attired in a morning-coat and striped trousers. He now slowly pushed his right hand into his tail-pocket and, like a conjuror, drew forth a Mills hand-grenade. An uneasy look appeared on the faces of his fellow-guests and the PM shouted: 'What's that you've got, Prof, what's that?' 'This, Prime Minister, is the inefficient Mills bomb, issued to the British infantry. It is made of twelve different components which have to be machined in separate processes. Now I have designed an improved grenade, which has fewer machined parts and contains a 50 per cent greater bursting charge.' 'Splendid! Splendid! That's what I like to hear. CIGS! Have the Mills bomb scrapped at once and replaced by the Lindemann grenade.'[1]

The unfortunate Dill was completely taken aback; he tried to explain that contracts had been placed in England and America for millions of Mills bombs, and that it would be impracticable to alter the design now, but the PM would not listen. To change the subject he pointed a finger at Beaverbrook across the table; 'Max! What have you been up to?' Beaverbrook replied: 'Prime Minister! Give me five minutes and you will have the latest figures.' He rose and went to a telephone box at the far end of the room; after a very few minutes he returned with a Puckish grin on his face. 'Prime Minister,' he said, 'in the last 48 hours we have increased our production of Hurricanes by 50 per cent.'

The brandy and coffee had now circulated and the PM lit his cigar. 'I want the Generals to come with me,' he said, and stumped off to an adjoining room, followed by Dill, Ismay and myself. On a large table was a rolled-up map, which the PM proceeded to spread out. It was a large-scale map of the Red Sea.

The PM placed his finger on the Italian port of Massawa.[2] 'Now, Marshall-Cornwall,' he said, 'we have command of the sea and the air; it is essential for us to capture that port; how would you do it?' I was in no way prepared to

---

[1] The Mills bomb (or Mills grenade) remained in production until the end of the war, with only minor modifications, and was essentially the same design as in the First World War. That Lindemann intended adding a greater bursting charge to the Mills bomb is unlikely, as one of its accepted failings was that it had too high an explosive charge.

[2] The principal port of Eritrea, occupied by Italy in 1885.

answer a snap conundrum of this kind, and indeed had no qualifications for doing so.

I saw Dill and Ismay watching me anxiously and felt that I was being drawn into some trap. I looked hard at the map for a minute and then answered: 'Well, Sir, I have never been to Massawa; I have only passed out of sight of it, going down the Red Sea. It is a defended port, protected by coast defence and anti-aircraft batteries. It must be a good 500 miles from Aden, and therefore beyond cover of our fighters. The harbour has a very narrow entrance channel, protected by coral reefs, and is certain to be mined, making an opposed landing impracticable. I should prefer to wait until General Wavell's offensive against Eritrea develops; he will capture it more easily from the land side.'

The PM gave me a withering look, rolled up the map and muttered peevishly: 'You soldiers are all alike: you have no imagination.'

We went to bed. I left the Wonderland of Chequers on the following afternoon, after a walk in the woods with Duncan Sandys, whom I have never found very communicative. On our way back to London Jack Dill said to me: 'I'm thankful, Jimmy, that you took the line you did last night. If you had shown the least enthusiasm for the project, I should have been given orders to embark your Corps for the Red Sea next week.'[1]

Winston S. Churchill to A. V. Alexander and Admiral Pound
(*Churchill papers, 20/13*)

28 July 1940

The attention of the Admiralty is drawn to the fate of the convoy attacked on 25th and 26th instant in the Channel. Five were sunk, one beached, four damaged, and afterwards three more sunk, making a total of 13 out of 21. It is evident that the precautions taken for the safety of this convoy were utterly ineffectual, and that both in its composition and escort it was unsuited to the task prescribed. I must consider this one of the most lamentable episodes of the naval war so far as it has yet developed.

---

[1] Massawa eventually surrendered, on 8 April 1941, to a Free French detachment of General William Platt's troops under Wavell's command, approaching from the hinterland. Had Marshall-Cornwall shown enthusiasm for the Massawa plan, it would first of all have been the task of the Joint Planning Committee to propose a detailed scheme, and then of the Chiefs of Staff Committee (of which Dill was a member) to give its approval. Had the Chiefs of Staff Committee rejected the plan, it could not have gone forward, however keenly Churchill might have favoured it.

Winston S. Churchill to Edith Bickford
(*Churchill papers, 2/392*)

28 July 1940

Dear Mrs Bickford,

It was with vy great sorrow that I learned that yr brave & brilliant son[1] was reported as Missing. I had the fortune to have two long talks with him after his famous exploits, & never do I remember meeting any young officer who seemed to embody all the finest attributes of mind & body in so excellent a degree. Yr loss is also your country's. I offer you my profound sympathy & that of my wife and daughter who also met yr son in all his splendour. May God help you to bear yr pain, & may he also bring comfort to a widow in her unspeakable grief & loneliness.

Yours very faithfully,
Winston S. Churchill

John Colville: diary
(*Colville papers*)

28 July 1940

Spent the morning at No. 10, where I was in constant touch with Chequers about India. The story, in brief, is that Amery has been telegraphing to Linlithgow about a public declaration which it is proposed the Viceroy should make concerning the attitude of HMG to India's status and Constitution after the war. Amery has tried to push his ideas (which would give a blank cheque to an Indian Constituent Assembly of the future) through without really consulting the Cabinet, and his telegrams, which Winston demanded to see on Friday and which may now be circulated as a Cabinet paper, contain a number of ill-advised references to Winston himself and complaints that he is driving the Cabinet to adopt his own views about the form this declaration should take. The Viceroy has been placed in an embarrassing position by Amery's impetuosity and now, as far as Amery is concerned, the fat is in the

---

[1] Edward Oscar Bickford, 1910–40. Served on the submarine *Salmon* from August 1938. Commander of the *Salmon* from December 1938. Awarded the DSO after torpedoing two German cruisers in December 1939. He was married, to Valerie Courtney, ten weeks before his death in action on 9 July 1940, when the *Salmon* was lost with all hands off Norway; she was thought to have struck a mine.

fire. Winston, after consultation with Lord Simon,[1] has redrafted the last paragraph of the declaration.[2]

Winston S. Churchill to Lord Linlithgow
(Churchill papers, 20/14)

28 July 1940

1. I was very glad to get your telegram, and I am sorry that intense pressure of business prevented me from entering into direct relations with you earlier.

2. Difficulties of draft statement dated July 24 begin at para. 7. Cabinet would not be able to promise in advance 'to accept, as a body to frame on the conclusion of the war, the main structure of the constitution, any body on which the representatives of the principal elements in India's national life can themselves meantime agree.' We should have to know beforehand what this body was, and feel assured that it truly represented the broad masses of the leading Indian communities, including, of course, not only Hindoos and Moslems, but the Princes, the Depressed Classes, the Sikhs, the Anglo-Indians and others.

3. It would further be quite impossible to pledge in advance the attitude of a future Parliament called into being in the unforeseeable conditions which will follow the war. Parliament must remain free to use its judgment and authority on the problems of that future day in the light of then existing circumstances. It would only be misleading our Indian friends if we led them to believe that we had any power under our free, democratic system to prescribe in advance the composition or temper of the future House of Commons, or that they would be likely to 'accept as they stood' whatever was set before them.

4. Objection was also taken by some of my colleagues to the fixing of a particular date for the achievement of Dominion Status. We are all agreed as to the earnestness of the effort to lead India forward on that path, and that no

---

[1] John Allsebrook Simon, 1873–1954. Educated at Fettes and Wadham College, Oxford. Fellow of All Souls. Liberal MP for Walthamstow, 1906–18; for Spen Valley, 1922–31. Solicitor-General, 1910–13. Knighted, 1910. Attorney-General, with a seat in the Cabinet, 1913–15. Home Secretary, 1915–16, when he resigned in opposition to conscription. Major, Royal Air Force, serving in France, 1917–18. Liberal National MP for Spen Valley, 1931–40. Secretary of State for Foreign Affairs, 1931–5. Home Secretary, 1935–7. Chancellor of the Exchequer, 1937–40. Created Viscount, 1940. Lord Chancellor, 1940–5.

[2] In 1930 Lord Simon (then Sir John Simon) had prepared a report on the future government of India which served as a basis for the India Act of 1935, whereby the Indians would be granted widespread provincial autonomy but not independence.

dilatory tactics should be tolerated. But that is quite different from fixing a date or a twelve months' time limit for the accomplishment of so vast a task.

5. The Cabinet therefore at their meeting on July 25 reached the following conclusions, which I take from the record:–
   (1) Reaffirmed their decision approving the expansion of the Viceroy's Executive Council, and the setting up of a War Advisory Committee.
   (2) Agreed that an announcement of these two measures should be accompanied by a further Declaration.
   (3) Invited the Prime Minister to draft, for consideration by the War Cabinet, a Declaration on the lines indicated by him in discussion, which should involve no departure in principle from the Declaration made on the 23rd May.

6. Pursuant to the above, I have ventured to recast for your consideration paras. 7 and 8, and I shall await your comments before bringing the appended alternative before the Cabinet.

7. There has, unfortunately, been a double misunderstanding in that you were led, quite naturally, to assume that the schemes proposed to you were in harmony with the wishes of the new Government, and that the Cabinet, for their part, were left under the impression that you were the initiator of a demand for a new departure of a far-reaching character. We both have cause to complain that these misunderstandings were not more successfully precluded, but the public interest must be our master. I shall ask the Cabinet to take steps to make sure that nothing of the kind can happen again. The Foreign Office and the Dominions Office conduct their affairs under the continual scrutiny of the Cabinet, and it seems to me that a similar superintendence must be exercised over the Indian sphere in respect of fundamental changes of policy. I sympathise keenly with you in the embarrassments in which you have been involved.

8. Appendix follows.

John Colville: diary
(*Colville papers*)

29 July 1940

It is being put about, Attlee has discovered, that Amery's liberal and statesmanlike proposals with regard to India are being sabotaged by Churchill. This is not true because Amery had merely wanted to make a woolly promise that HMG, after the war, would assent to whatever constitutional proposals a representative body in India should propose. It would be impossible to collect a really representative body and, secondly, such a wide and general promise would arouse expectations which might, and almost certainly would, be unfulfilled in the event.[1]

Winston S. Churchill to Anthony Eden
(Churchill papers, 20/13)

29 July 1940

I should have been glad to be consulted about General Pownall's new appointment.[2] It is only a few weeks since he was placed at the head of the Home Guard, and a great story made of the importance of this post. Now, while the Home Guard is most rapidly expanding, and at the moment when it may play a vital part in our defence against invasion, its Commander is to be dispatched on a mission of a totally different character. I have no doubt his qualifications are very good, but his name is quite unknown outside British military circles. I should be glad to hear from you about this before being committed, or having my name used as proposed in the enclosed telegram.

WSC

Cosmo Gordon Lang: diary
('Cosmo Gordon Lang')

29 July 1940

Winston Churchill continues to be the man of the hour. All his colleagues testify to his qualities of drive and courage, and his powers of glowing speech are a great public asset. Most of the team he has collected seem to be doing well – not least the two Labour men, Morrison and Bevin.

War Cabinet: minutes
(Cabinet papers, 65/8)

29 July 1940 Cabinet War Rooms
11.30 a.m.

The Prime Minister invited the Secretary of State for Air to give further consideration to the question whether suitable aircraft could not be made available for dropping leaflets in French Morocco.

---

[1] In all the constitutional promises made to India since 1930, none, even those made by Ramsay MacDonald and Stanley Baldwin at the Round Table Conference of 1931 and under the India Act of 1935, had involved full independence, which was specifically excluded from Dominion status.

[2] General Pownall had been appointed to command the British troops in Northern Ireland. In 1941 he was called back to London to become Vice-Chief of the Imperial General Staff.

The main consideration was felt to be that to send a letter in the terms proposed[1] to the Vichy Government might react unfavourably on General de Gaulle's cause. Before reaching a decision it would be very desirable that he should be consulted.

War Cabinet: Confidential Annex
(*Cabinet papers, 65/14*)

29 July 1940   Cabinet War Rooms
11.30 a.m.

The Prime Minister said that, to his mind, the central fact of the situation, if Japan obtained the mastery of the Netherlands East Indies, was that she would be able to prepare strong positions facing Singapore, including a base for her fleet. If we did not fight, she would be able to prepare these positions in peace, and to use them against us at the moment which suited her best.

If we made it clear that we should fight to preserve the integrity of the Netherlands East Indies, Japan might very well decide against attack. The danger of having to take on both this country and the United States of America was a powerful deterrent. Russia also might be added to the number of Japan's enemies.

On balance, the economic arguments told in favour of Japan's abstaining from war with the British Empire. Japan could not afford to see her shipping paralysed.

The First Lord of the Admiralty recalled the fact that only a week or two previously we had made a big concession to the Japanese, in closing the Burma road, on the principle that this country was not in a position to take on more than one war at a time.

The Prime Minister said that the present situation was different; we now had before us the possibility of a rival base being constructed over against Singapore. We could not afford to tolerate that.

The Prime Minister said that there was no question of deciding that morning to tell Japan that we would go to war with her if she interfered with the Dutch East Indies. The decision required was that a paper should be prepared showing our general plan of campaign if we went to war with Japan to prevent her interfering with the Dutch East Indies.

---

[1] An appeal to the French troops under Vichy command in Morocco to consider transferring their loyalties, and that of the Vichy Government, to the British cause. Hopes of a possible *rapprochement* with Vichy were to persist until the end of 1940.

The Prime Minister said that the Lord President of the Council, who was ill and could not be present that morning, had read the Chiefs of Staff Report, and had reached the conclusion that if the Dutch resisted Japanese aggression against the Dutch East Indies, we ought to go in with them and try to shame the United States into joining in; but that the first thing was to get a plan from the Chiefs of Staff on this assumption.

The Prime Minister said that he thought there was no disagreement that we should take all steps in our power to keep the Japanese out of the Dutch East Indies. The real question was the adequacy of the means at our disposal to effect this, and the consequences which would be involved to the general strategical position. If the need arose, we might have to withdraw our Fleet from the Mediterranean in order to station an adequate Fleet at Singapore. The first step was clearly that an appreciation should be prepared to show what action would be involved in resisting Japanese aggression against the Dutch East Indies.

The question of policy must be settled by the War Cabinet in the light of the appreciation which would now be prepared by the Chiefs of Staff. The final decision taken would, of course, take account of the means at our disposal to resist such aggression.

The First Sea Lord said that he had based his views on the situation as it stood today, and was likely to be in the next few months.

The Prime Minister agreed as to the importance of playing for time. In a few months our position might well be much stronger.

The trend of the discussion emphasised the importance of long-term projects. He thought that the Admiralty might well give further consideration to the question whether work should not be re-started on some at least of the Naval construction on which progress had been suspended.

Defence Committee: minutes
(*Cabinet papers, 69/1*)

29 July 1940　　　　　　　　　　　　　　　　　　　　　　　　10 Downing Street
5.30 p.m.

The Prime Minister said that he wished to consider the present phase of air operations in which it appeared that the enemy were concentrating against targets in the Dover area, and whether there were any further steps which should be taken. He thought it most important that we should not in any circumstances give up Dover. It seemed that a good opportunity was presented of inflicting heavy loss upon the enemy.

The Prime Minister suggested that it might be worth while making some dummy destroyers to put in the harbour at Dover as 'bait' for air attacks.

Winston S. Churchill: War Cabinet Memorandum[1]
(*Cabinet papers, 66/10*)

30 July 1940   10 Downing Street

I circulate herewith for the information of my colleagues my suggested remodelling of the draft statement prepared by the Viceroy and circulated to the War Cabinet as WP (40) 283.

Paragraphs 1 to 6 are reproduced unaltered from the Viceroy's draft.

I attach a new paragraph 7, which I propose should take the place of paragraphs 7 and 8 of the Viceroy's draft. I have used his words so far as possible. As will be seen from his telegram of the 30th July (WP (40) 294), the Viceroy accepts the new paragraph, subject to a drafting amendment which I have incorporated.

WSC

Winston S. Churchill: replacement paragraph seven
(*Churchill papers, 20/14*)

30 July 1940

7. The second point of general interest is machinery for building within the British Commonwealth of Nations the new constitutional scheme when the time comes. There has been very strong insistence that the framing of that scheme, *subject to provision for certain matters for which His Majesty's Government cannot divest themselves of responsibility, obligations arising out of their long connection with India*,[2] should be primarily the responsibility of Indians themselves, and should originate from Indian conceptions of the social, economic and political structure of Indian life. It is clear that a moment when the Commonwealth is engaged in a struggle for existence is not one in which fundamental constitutional issues can be decisively resolved. But His Majesty's Government authorize me to declare that they will most readily assent to the setting up after the conclusion of the war of a body representative of the principal elements in India's national life in order to devise the framework of the new constitution, and they will lend every aid in their power to hasten decisions on all relevant matters to the utmost degree. Meanwhile, they will welcome and promote in any way possible every sincere and practical step that may be

---

[1] Circulated as War Cabinet Paper No. 295 of 1940, 'India'.
[2] Words printed in italics in the paragraph as circulated by Churchill to the War Cabinet.

taken by representative Indians themselves to reach a basis of friendly agreement, first upon the form which the post-war representative body should take, and, secondly, upon the principles and outlines of the constitution itself. They trust, however, that for the period of the war (with the Central Government reconstituted and strengthened in the manner I have described, and with the help of the War Advisory Council) all Parties, communities and interests, will combine and co-operate in making a notable Indian contribution to the victory of the world cause which is at stake. Moreover, they hope that in this process new bonds of union and understanding will emerge, and thus pave the way towards the attainment by India of that free and equal partnership in the British Commonwealth which remains the proclaimed and accepted goal of the Imperial Crown and of the British Parliament.

John Colville: diary
(*Colville papers*)

30 July 1940

The PM and the First Lord are having a bit of a tiff, owing to the former's comments on the sinking of five ships and the damaging of six others in a raid on a Channel convoy last Friday. The PM complained that the Admiralty's precautions were 'utterly ineffectual', and said: 'I must consider this one of the most lamentable episodes of the naval war so far as it has yet developed.' A. V. Alexander flared up and wrote asking that this minute might be withdrawn. In his reply, refusing to do so, Winston said: 'I was naturally wounded to read of the massacre of all these poor little ships and I do not think I was wrong in describing the episode as "lamentable". The word lamentable expresses grief and not necessarily judgment.'

Winston S. Churchill to William Mackenzie King
(*Churchill papers, 20/14*)

30 July 1940

You will have seen from recent message conveyed to you by High Commissioner for United Kingdom[1] regarding Freetown, Sierra Leone, that in present circumstances the completion of the 9·2-inch battery at that port is becoming a matter of greatest urgency and importance. We have thus had to consider at once how the necessary two equipments can be provided with the

[1] Gerald Campbell, 1879–1964. Entered the Diplomatic Service, 1907. Consul-General, Philadelphia, 1920–1; San Francisco, 1922-31 (he welcomed Churchill to the city in 1929); New York, 1931–8. Knighted, 1934. High Commissioner for the United Kingdom in Canada, 1938–41. Director-General, British Information Service in New York, 1941–2. Minister in Washington (under Lord Halifax), 1942–5.

minimum of delay. As you will know, modern equipments for your battery at Halifax have been on order for some time and these are not far from being ready to ship. I want to be quite frank with you on the matter and I feel a personal responsibility because I discussed it when First Lord of the Admiralty with Mr T. A. Crerar,[1] your Minister of Mines and Resources, last November. As a result of those discussions, you were good enough to agree to the claims of Canada being postponed for a time in view of pressing needs elsewhere. I should have been most reluctant to suggest that once again Halifax should wait for new equipments, but I understand that the emplacements at Halifax will not be ready to receive the new mountings until the end of the year, and if you could agree to our sending to Freetown the equipments now becoming available we shall still have equipments coming forward in time to be shipped to Halifax, one in November and one in January.

Many difficult problems have presented themselves as a result of the recent change in our strategic situation. I should like to take this opportunity of telling you once again how profoundly grateful I am, and indeed all of us in this country are, to yourself and your colleagues for the many forms of assistance which you have given towards meeting our difficulties. I am anxious that you should not think that I under-estimate the importance or needs of Halifax. But you will recognise how imperative are the immediate claims of Freetown in relation to the Cape route, and if I am right in thinking that shipment of new equipment to Canada at once would not mean the immediate modernisation of the Halifax defences, I hope you will agree that the right course would be to send the equipment at once to Freetown.

Winston S. Churchill: speech
(*Hansard*)

30 July 1940   House of Commons
3.58 p.m.

SECRET SESSION

The Prime Minister (Mr Churchill): A week ago the Government were led to believe that there was a desire in the House to have a Debate about foreign affairs, and that it was the wish of the House for it to take place in secret, so that Members of all parties could say what they really felt about foreign countries without any danger of adding to the number of those countries with which we are at present at war. It is always the desire and also the duty of the

---

[1] Thomas Alexander Crerar, 1876–1975. A leading grain grower in Western Canada, fighting for low tariffs and low freight rates. Elected to the Canadian Parliament, 1917. Minister of Agriculture, 1917–19. Returned to private life, 1922–30. Minister of Railways and Canals, 1930. Minister of Mines and Resources, 1935–45. Senator, 1945–60.

Government, so far as possible, to meet the wishes of the House, and arrangements were accordingly made for this afternoon. However, it appears that some of the newspapers prefer that the Debate should take place in public, and we are assured that secrecy is undemocratic, especially in times of war, that it would be wrong for Members of Parliament to have privileges in matters of information not enjoyed by the whole mass of the nation, and that the Government should take the nation and the enemy fully into their confidence and let the whole world see plainly exactly how and where they stand in relation to all other countries in the present critical juncture. These arguments, or others like them, seem to have made an impression in various quarters of the House, and the Government are now in the embarrassing position of a servant receiving contradictory orders from those whom their only desire is to serve. We therefore have found means to give the House an opportunity of expressing by Debate and Division, the opinion whether the Debate should be secret or public. Also we have arranged that this preliminary Debate can itself take place under conditions of the fullest publicity. I conclude by moving,

> 'That the remainder of this day's Sitting be a Secret Session and that strangers be ordered to withdraw.'

This is a debatable Motion. The Government will not attempt to influence the opinion of the House on the issue. Unless provoked, we shall take no part in the discussion, and Ministers will take no part in the Division, which will be left to the free vote of the House. After that matter has been decided, my right hon. Friend the Under-Secretary of State for Foreign Affairs[1] will, at any point in the Debate that may be convenient, make his statement, either in public or in private as the House may have decided. He has already, I believe, taken the precaution of preparing two speeches, both, I am sure, excellent, but one somewhat longer than the other.

Henry Channon: diary
(*'Chips'*)

30 July 1940

At about 8, the PM himself rose and we had 40 minutes of magnificent oratory and artistry but he gave away no secrets and, indeed, talked from his heart rather than from his head. He stoutly defended our action in closing the Burma Road.[2]

---

[1] R. A. Butler.
[2] No record survives of Churchill's Secret Session speech on this occasion, unlike the outline notes of his previous Secret Session speech of 20 June 1940, and the full text of his next one, on 17 September 1940.

July 1940

Hugh Dalton: diary
('*The Second World War Diary of Hugh Dalton*')

30 July 1940

Secret session on foreign affairs. Winston in grand form, both before and during. He now leads the whole House, unquestioned and ascendant.

Harold Nicolson: private letter
('*Diaries and Letters, 1939–1945*')

30 July 1940

We had a Secret Session today. Mm. Hush. All that I can say is that Winston surpassed even himself. The situation is obscure. It may be that Hitler will first bomb us with gas and then try to land. At the same time, Italy and Japan will hit us as hard as they can. It will be a dreadful month. On the other hand, Hitler may feel that he cannot bring off a successful invasion and may seek to gain new, easy but sterile conquests in Africa and Asia. Were it not for this little island under a great leader, he would accomplish his desires. We may fail. But supposing we do not fail? That was their finest hour.

Winston S. Churchill to Lord Halifax
(*Premier papers, 3/462/2/3*)

30 July 1940

See Lothian's telegram that this is the moment to press the President about destroyers, &c. I have therefore drafted the attached (marked 'A' in red).

As I shall be away till after dark to-morrow, I send this urgently to you, hoping you will send it through Kennedy, informing and squaring Lothian. I am sure that this is the moment to plug it in, and it may well be that we were wise to hold back the previous draft. But pray let this go now.

WSC

Winston S. Churchill to President Roosevelt
(*Premier papers, 3/462/2/3*)

30 July 1940
Most Secret

It is some time since I ventured to cable personally to you, and many things both good and bad have happened in between. It has now become most urgent for you to give us the destroyers, motor-boats and flying-boats for which we have asked. The Germans have the whole French coastline from which to launch U-boat and dive-bomber attacks upon our trade and food, and in addition we must be constantly prepared to repel by sea action threatened invasion in the narrow waters, and also to deal with break-outs from Norway towards Ireland, Iceland, Shetlands and Faroes. Besides this we have to keep control of the exits from the Mediterranean, and if possible the command of that inland sea itself, and thus to prevent the war spreading seriously into Africa.

2. We have a large construction of destroyers and anti-U-boat craft coming forward, but the next three or four months open the gap of which I have previously told you. Latterly the Air attack on our shipping has become injurious. In the last ten days we have had the following destroyers sunk: *Brazen, Codrington, Delight, Wren*,[1] and the following damaged: *Beagle, Boreas, Brilliant, Griffin, Montrose, Walpole*, total ten. All this in the advent of any attempt which may be made at invasion. Destroyers are frightfully vulnerable to Air bombing, and yet they must be held in the Air bombing area to prevent sea-borne invasion. We could not keep up the present rate of casualties for long, and if we cannot get a substantial reinforcement, the whole fate of the war may be decided by this minor and easily remediable factor. I cannot understand why, with the position as it is, you do not send me at least 50 or 60 of your oldest destroyers. I can fit them very quickly with Asdics and use them against U-boats on the Western Approaches, and so keep the more modern and better gunned craft for the narrow seas against invasion. Mr President, with great respect I must tell you that in the long history of the world this is a thing to do now. Large construction is coming to me in 1941, but the crisis will be reached long before 1941. I know you will do all in your power, but I feel entitled and bound to put the gravity and urgency of the position before you.

3. If the destroyers were given, the motor-boats and flying-boats, which would be invaluable, could surely come in behind them.

4. I am beginning to feel very hopeful about this war if we can get round the next three or four months. The Air is holding well. We are hitting that man hard, both in repelling attacks and in bombing Germany. But the loss of destroyers by Air attack may well be so serious as to break down our defence of the food and trade routes across the Atlantic.

5. To-night the latest convoys of rifles, cannon and ammunition are coming in. Special trains are waiting to take them to the troops and Home Guard, who will take a lot of killing before they give them up. I am sure that

---

[1] HMS *Brazen* had been sunk on 20 July by German aircraft off Dover; HMS *Codrington* had been bombed and sank in Dover harbour on 27 July (Churchill had crossed the Channel in her a few months earlier, while First Lord); HMS *Wren* had been bombed and sank off Aldeburgh, Suffolk, on 17 July, and HMS *Delight* had been bombed and sank off Portland on 29 July. No further destroyers were sunk until 23 August, when HMS *Hostile* was mined and sank in the Mediterranean, off Cape Bon.

July 1940

with your comprehension of the sea affair, you will not let this crux of the battle go wrong for the want of these destroyers. I cabled to Lothian some days ago, and now send this through Kennedy, who is a grand help to us and the common cause.

WSC

AT 11.30 ON THE NIGHT of Tuesday, 30 July 1940, Churchill left London by train for North-East England, where he inspected Home Guard, Coastal and other defences, including those near Hartlepool. He returned to London by train on the evening of 31 July.

George Lambert[1] to Winston S. Churchill
(*Churchill papers, 2/396*)

31 July 1940

My dear Prime Minister,

Butler's speech amply justified the Secret Session yesterday. He gave facts impossible to disclose in public. As an old House of Commons man, I am glad you treat MPs as responsible individuals and not as irresponsible nobodies. Indeed, your leadership of the House is incomparably the most brilliant that I can remember, save perhaps that of Mr Gladstone. You have to-day the complete confidence of Parliament and the nation. God grant that you may be given the wisdom and strength to fulfil the great task that lies ahead.

Yours ever,
George Lambert

Winston S. Churchill to George Lambert: telegram
(*Churchill papers, 2/396*)

31 July 1940

Greatly cheered by your letter. Thank you so much.

Winston

---

[1] George Lambert, 1866–1958. Liberal MP for South Molton, 1891–1924, 1929–31. Civil Lord of the Admiralty, 1905–15. Privy Councillor, 1912. Chairman of the Liberal Parliamentary Party, 1919–21; Liberal National MP, 1931–45. Created Viscount, 1945.

August 1940

Winston S. Churchill to Sir Edward Bridges
(*Premier papers, 3/49*)

1 August 1940

There will have to be an inquiry into the methods by which people were selected for the *Arandora Star*,[1] and also into the conditions at a particular camp[2] which are complained of. The object of these inquiries is to find out the names of the officials who are responsible, with a view to their being punished by administrative action, should any case of laxity or mismanagement be proved against them. You should ask the Lord Privy Seal[3] to suggest the form of inquiry. It might be (1) a judge, (2) a member of the House of Commons not connected with the Government, or (3) a political Minister from another Department called upon specially for a report.[4]

WSC

---

[1] The *Arandora Star*, a former Blue Star ocean liner, taking civilian internees (including just under 700 Italians, and 473 Germans, of whom 123 were merchant seamen) to Canada, was torpedoed on 2 July 1940 by the German submarine ace Günther Prien off the coast of Ireland, with the loss of 714 lives. A Canadian destroyer rescued the remaining 868 passengers. Churchill minuted on 3 August 1940: 'The case of the brave German who is said to have saved so many, raises the question of his special treatment, by parole or otherwise' (*Premier papers, 3/49/1*). But the German was never identified.

[2] This was Huyton camp. Several of the would-be deportees there were later released, as being 'invalid or infirm', although the Home Office had instructed the police not to intern those that were sick or infirm.

[3] Clement Attlee.

[4] The inquiry into the sinking of the *Arandora Star* was conducted by Lord Snell, and presented to Parliament by Churchill himself. Snell was assisted by Sir Grattan Bushe, Legal Adviser to the Dominions and Colonial Office. In his covering note to Churchill, of 24 October 1940, Snell wrote, of one particular case: 'Among the Italians deported was Signor Anzani, who had lived in England for twenty years and was the Secretary of the Italian section of the League of the Rights of Men. His name, however, had been placed on the M15 list in error, as he was not a member of the Fascist Party' (*Premier papers, 3/49/1*).

August 1940

Winston S. Churchill to A. V. Alexander and Admiral Pound
(*Churchill papers, 20/13*)

1 August 1940
ACTION THIS DAY

In view of the threatening attitude of Japan, it is vitally important to know about *Bismarck* and *Tirpitz*. Pray let me have your latest information. It seems to me that a great effort will have to be made by the Air Force to disable these ships, as their apparition in the next few months would be most dangerous.

2. Assuming Japan goes to war with us, or forces us into war, I suppose you would send *Hood*, three 8-inch gun cruisers, 2 Ramillies and 12 long-radius destroyers to Singapore. Let me have the legends of the completed Japanese battle-cruisers.

War Cabinet: minutes
(*Cabinet papers, 65/8*)

1 August 1940
11.30 a.m.

The Prime Minister referred to a report that German aircraft were being fitted with an improved bomb sight, and invited the Chief of the Air Staff to examine the possibility of carrying out a certain operation.

The Prime Minister said he was glad that the supply of fighter aircraft was now much more satisfactory. He understood that in the near future the figures would show a still greater improvement.

The Secretary of State for Foreign Affairs said that the Japanese had arrested fourteen British subjects in Japan and two in Korea. Of the fourteen arrested in Japan, one had died and six had been released. Of these six, five had had their papers retained and one had been informed that he might be called up for further examination. Sir Robert Craigie[1] had now stated that he favoured the arrest of Japanese subjects in British territory as a reprisal and considered that, though the Japanese might reply by further reprisals, they would not regard our action as a *casus belli* (telegram No. 1409 from Tokyo). This coincided with his own view.

---

[1] Robert Leslie Craigie, 1883–1959. Entered the Foreign Office, 1907. British Representative, Inter-Allied Blockade Committee, 1916–18. First Secretary, Washington, 1920–3; transferred to the Foreign Office, 1923; Counsellor, 1928; Assistant Under-Secretary of State, 1934–7. Knighted, 1936. Privy Councillor, 1937. Ambassador to Japan, 1937–41. UK Representative to the United Nations War Crimes Commission, 1945–8.

The Prime Minister said that he was in favour of arresting a number of Japanese without prior notice. An additional method of reprisal was an unostentatious hampering by administrative action of Japanese shipping in our ports. By obstructing their trade in an inconspicuous manner we should involve them in financial loss, and give them perhaps a foretaste of how their trade would suffer in the event of war with this country.

ALIENS

The Prime Minister said that our position was now considerably more secure than it had been some two months earlier. At that time we had had very few trained and equipped troops in this country, and considerable numbers of aliens had been at large. He thought that it would now be possible to take a somewhat less rigid attitude in regard to the internment of aliens.

The Home Secretary agreed, but thought that it would be undesirable that there should be too violent a reaction from the policy previously enforced.

Winston S. Churchill to the Earl of Lytton[1]
(*Churchill papers, 20/6*)

2 August 1940
Private

My dear Victor,

Thank you so much for your letter. I am so glad you are going to help us in the Chairmanship of the important Committee about which Halifax spoke to you.[2] We were in great danger two months ago, and it was absolutely necessary for their own sake to round up a great number of aliens. I think my view and yours will not diverge on the way they should be treated and on the liberation by more refined processes of considerable numbers, now that we are feeling a good deal firmer on our feet.

---

[1] Victor Alexander George Robert Lytton, 1876–1947. Succeeded his father as 2nd Earl of Lytton, 1891. In 1902 he married Churchill's friend Pamela Plowden (whom Churchill once described to his mother as the only woman he could ever love). Civil Lord of the Admiralty, 1916 and 1919–20. Privy Councillor, 1919. Governor of Bengal, 1922–7. Leader of the Indian Delegation to the League of Nations Assemblies of 1927 and 1928. League of Nations Mission to Manchuria, 1932. In charge of the Council of Aliens (Foreign Office), 1940–1; of the Entertainments National Service Committee (Ministry of Labour), 1942–5. His eldest son was killed in a flying accident in 1933; his youngest son was killed in action in 1942.

[2] Lord Lytton had accepted the chairmanship of the Council of Aliens, under the Foreign Office.

I hope you will forgive me if I do not receive your deputation. Its object falls so clearly in the sphere of the Foreign Office, and I have to keep myself clear for Defence and other duties of my own.

Yours ever,
Winston S. Churchill

Winston S. Churchill to A. V. Alexander and Admiral Pound
(*Churchill papers, 20/13*)

2 August 1940
ACTION THIS DAY

I pray that we may never have to make this widespread distribution, but I am in full accord with the principles on which the Admiralty would propose to meet the strain. I should have thought that *Hood* would be a greater deterrent than *Renown*. Please let me have a report of the possibility of air attack on *Bismarck* and *Tirpitz*. This seems to me to be one of the most vital steps to take.[1] Apart from this, there is no need to make any new dispositions at the present time on account of Japanese war-risk.

I was much concerned to hear of the sinking of the three tankers off Tory Island. I should like to see you move some destroyers from the East Coast thither. We had better wait, however, until the August moon-phase is over. During this time also the American guns and rifles will be distributed to the troops.

Winston S. Churchill to General Ismay
(*Churchill papers, 20/13*)

2 August 1940
ACTION THIS DAY

Next week one of my principal tasks must be going through this scheme of the Air Ministry for increasing the pilots and for the training of pilots. Lord Beaverbrook should be asked for his views beforehand.

2. Let me have a report on the plans for lectures on tactical subjects for the troops in the autumn.

3. What has been done about the collection of scrap of all kinds. Let me have a short report on one page covering the progress made this year.

[1] In reply, Pound pointed out that *Renown* had 'a much better endurance' than *Hood*, 'which is of great importance in the Indian Ocean where ships may have to operate far from their base and remain at sea for a long time.' As to air attacks on the German capital ships, these would be carried out, when possible: *Bismarck* was 'apparently nearing completion' and *Tirpitz* 'being completed' but about three months behind *Bismarck* (*Admiralty papers, 205/6*).

4. When at the Admiralty I took a special interest in the work of the Salvage Department, and held a meeting there four months ago. A Naval Officer, Captain Dewar,[1] was then in charge. Let me have a report on what has happened to salvage since that day.

5. I am also expecting this week to reach a settlement about the functions of the ARP and the Police in the case of invasion. The Lord Privy Seal was dealing with this in the first instance. At the same time we must consider allowing transfers from ARP to the Home Guard, and their being made available for fighting purposes. To what extent has the payment of the ARP personnel been discontinued or restricted? It ought to be continually restricted.

6. Let me have a report on the progress and future construction of the tank divisions. There should be five armoured Divisions by March 31, and two more by the end of May. Let me know how far the present prospects of men and material allow of this. Let me know also what are the latest ideas for the structure and organisation of an armoured Division. This should be prepared on one sheet of paper, showing all the principal elements and accessories.

Winston S. Churchill to General Ismay
(*Churchill papers, 20/13*)

2 August 1940

It is very important to get on with the uniforms for the Home Guard. Let me have a forecast of deliveries.

WSC

Winston S. Churchill to Sir Edward Bridges
(*Churchill papers, 20/13*)

2 August 1940

The whole question of holidays and reduced hours should be considered by the Cabinet at an early date. It is far too soon to assume that the danger has passed. It is a great mistake to tell the work-people that they are tired. On the other hand certain easements are indispensable. Please communicate with Mr Bevin, Lord Beaverbrook and the Minister of Supply so that their views may be in readiness for Cabinet conversation. I should also like to know what is being done about holidays for the Civil Service and for Ministers, and persons in high Service positions. Something will have to be done about this, but we must be very careful not to be caught while in an August mood.

[1] A. Ramsay Dewar. Lieutenant, Royal Navy, 1907. A battleship gunnery officer, 1912. Rear-Admiral, retired, 1939. Head of the Salvage Department at the Admiralty, 1940.

August 1940

General Freyberg: diary
(*'Bernard Freyberg, VC'*)

3 August 1940   Chequers

The party for the weekend was a small one – Mr and Mrs Churchill, their kinsman Lord Ivor Spencer Churchill, General Ismay, the Military Secretary to the Prime Minister, and myself. I wondered what was in the wind, and sure enough after dinner the Prime Minister developed his theory upon the defence of Egypt. It was an ingenious one. Later he asked me to give an opinion upon the possibility – not the advisability – of a certain minor operation against the Italians should they advance from Libya. By this time I was placed in an even more difficult position than before, because the official advisers knew as well as I did that the only operation that we could contemplate in the defence of Egypt for many months was to hang on by every means possible and hope that the Germans in their madness would attempt an invasion of Great Britain. What we really dreaded was that she would switch all her air power to the Middle East to help the Italians turn us out of the Western Desert and consequently the Suez Canal and the Mediterranean.

Roughly his plan was to allow them to advance along the coast road in the direction of Mersa Matruh and then, when they had stretched their communications to the utmost, to land in force behind them from the sea and stop the flow forward of food, petrol and water to the fighting troops. He said that what he was after was 'Strangulatory Hernia'.

He was now a little more approachable on the question of the Middle East. I found out afterwards that the C-in-C, General Wavell, had cabled to the Cabinet that the way they were heading would end in the loss of Egypt and the Suez Canal and I made the most of what opportunities offered and kept at him about the great disadvantage we were working under, and the fact that to reinforce Egypt now took forty days by fastest surface ships while the slowest took as long as 120 days. The Axis could carry out their reinforcements by air in a week. He listened and brooded, muttered to himself, and then sought shelter behind the formula, 'This is the decisive theatre' – a general statement with which I did not agree. I kept on whenever I got the chance on the lines which did not appear to be congenial to the Prime Minister. I did not believe in the possibility of a German invasion of England; that it was the Middle East which was in peril; that we should send by the quickest route, through the Mediterranean if possible, all the aeroplanes, equipment and munitions possible – but above all aircraft.

I needed to get back to say farewell to some of my troops who were going out to the Middle East. I had to start before luncheon as they were to leave Aldershot at 4 p.m. I did not see the Prime Minister until 1 p.m. on 3 August, but when he came downstairs he walked up and down telling me how he visualised committing 'Strangulatory Hernia' upon the Italians in Libya. He was very pleased with the phrase. Just before I left he said that I must stay for lunch as General de Gaulle was coming. I wish I could have stayed on but one cannot be in two places at once. His parting shot dealt with the air situation in the Middle East. He said, 'We cannot increase the number of squadrons in Egypt but we can see that the pilots have good polo ponies.'

He liked that statement too because when I took leave, he added, 'Yes, we can mount them well, with the best polo ponies.'

Winston S. Churchill to Sir Edward Bridges
(Churchill papers, 20/13)

3 August 1940

1. I think the circular about work in the factories and holidays for whole establishments should, whatever the agreement of the Production Council, be brought before the Cabinet on Tuesday by the Minister of Labour. We must give holidays without creating a holiday atmosphere. It would therefore seem desirable to announce only that 'such local arrangements as are possible are being made for staggered holidays', or something like that.

2. I approve Sir Horace Wilson's letter to departments. It arose out of my instructions to him.

3. I shall be very glad if you will adjust the holidays of Ministers, and make sure that the Services arrange for similar relief in case of high military officers at the centre of government.

Winston S. Churchill to Clement Attlee and Sir John Anderson
(Premier papers, 3/359)

3 August 1940   10 Downing Street

The attached[1] raises a very difficult question, and one that must be speedily settled. We cannot surely make ourselves responsible for a system where the police will prevent the people resisting the enemy, and will lay down their arms and become the enemy's servant in any invaded area. I confess I do not see my way quite clearly to the amendments required in the

---

[1] A letter from Lord Mottistone, who as Jack Seely had been Secretary of State for War before the First World War and was now Lord Lieutenant of Hampshire, reporting on the confusion among senior Police and Home Guard officers as to what their forces were to do upon the arrival of German forces in the vicinity. The senior Home Guard officer in the Isle of Wight (where Seely lived) had told him 'that his men ought not to shoot in front of the village in the event of any considerable number of the enemy appearing, because he understood that in that event the Police were to surrender their arms and place themselves at the disposal of the enemy'.

regulations. In principle, however, it would seem that the police should withdraw from any invaded area with the last of His Majesty's troops. This would also apply to the ARP and the Fire Brigades, etc. Their services will be used in other districts. Perhaps on invasion being declared, the police, ARP, Fire Brigades, etc. should automatically become a part of the military forces.

It is most important that this matter should be settled in the next day or two, and I am asking Sir Edward Bridges to put it on the Agenda for Monday.

WSC

Winston S. Churchill to Lord Halifax
(*Premier papers, 4/100/3*)

3 August 1940

I should reply[1] as follows: 'On October 12th, 1939, His Majesty's Government defined at length their position towards German peace offers in a maturely considered statement made by the then Prime Minister, Mr Chamberlain, and by the present Foreign Secretary, in their respective Houses of Parliament. Since then a number of new hideous crimes have been committed by Nazi Germany against the smaller States upon her borders. Norway has been overrun, and is now occupied by a German invading army. Denmark has been seized and pillaged. Belgium and Holland, after all their efforts to placate Herr Hitler, and in spite of all the assurances given to them by the German Government that their neutrality would be respected, have been conquered and subjugated. In Holland particularly, acts of long-prepared treachery and brutality culminated in the massacre of Rotterdam, where many thousands of Dutchmen were slaughtered, and an important part of the city destroyed.

'These horrible events have darkened the pages of European history with an indelible stain. His Majesty's Government see in them not the slightest cause to recede in any way from their principles and resolves as set forth in October 1939. On the contrary, their intention to prosecute the war against Germany by every means in their power until Hitlerism is finally broken, and the world relieved from the curse which a wicked man has brought upon it, has been strengthened to such a point that they would rather all perish in the common ruin than fail or falter in their duty. They firmly believe, however, that with the help of God they will not lack the means to discharge their task. This task may be long; but it will always be possible for Germany to ask for an armistice, as she did in 1918, or to publish her proposals for peace. Before,

---

[1] To a proposal by the King of Sweden to act as an intermediary in peace talks between the belligerents.

however, any such requests or proposals could even be considered, it would be necessary that effective guarantees by deeds, not words, should be forthcoming from Germany which would insure the restoration of the free and independent life of Czecho-Slovakia, Poland, Norway, Denmark, Holland, Belgium and, above all, France, as well as the effectual security of Great Britain and the British Empire in a general peace.'

The ideas set forth in paragraph 5 of the Foreign Office memo[1] appear to me to err in trying to be too clever, and to enter into refinements of policy unsuited to the tragic simplicity and grandeur of the times and the issues at stake. At this moment, when we have had no sort of success, the slightest opening will be misjudged. Indeed, a firm reply of the kind I have outlined is the only chance of extorting from Germany any offers which are not fantastic.

I might add that the intrusion of the ignominious King of Sweden[2] as a peace-maker, after his desertion of Finland and Norway, and while he is absolutely in the German grip, though not without its encouraging aspects, is singularly distasteful.

Let me know what you think about all this.

Winston S. Churchill to General Ismay
(*Churchill papers, 20/13*)

3 August 1940

The 14-inch gun I ordered to be mounted at Dover should be ready in ample time to deal with this new battery. It certainly should not fire until all the guns are in position. The plan for the shoot may, however, now be made, and I should like to know what arrangements for spotting aircraft, protected by Fighters in strength, will be prepared for that joyous occasion. Also, when the two guns, 13·5's on railway mountings, will be ready, and whether they can reach the target mentioned. Several other camouflaged guns should be put up at various points, with arrangements to make suitable flashes, smoke

---

[1] Paragraph 5 of the Foreign Office draft reply read: 'It therefore lies with the German Government to make proposals by which the wrongs that Germany has inflicted upon other nations may be redressed. Moreover, as my Government indicated on October 12th, it would be necessary, before any such proposals could be considered, that effective guarantees by deeds, not words, should be forthcoming from Germany which would ensure in a general peace the restoration of freedom to France and to other countries which have been deprived of it, as well as the effectual security of Great Britain and the British Empire' (*Premier papers, 4/100/3*).

[2] Gustav V, born 1858. King of Sweden from 1906 until his death in 1950. In his telegram to King George VI he explained: 'As Head of one of the few neutral states in Europe remaining outside the present conflict, I consider it my duty at this moment to offer my bona officia to the Head of the States of Great Britain and Germany to enable contact to be made if these Powers should wish to establish such contact in order to examine the possibilities of making peace' (*Premier papers, 4/100/3*).

and dust. Let me know what arrangements can be devised. I presume work on the railway extensions for the 13·5's is already in hand. Please report.

2. The movement of the German warships southward to Kiel creates a somewhat different situation from that dealt with in C-in-C Home Fleet's appreciation asked for some time ago about an invasion across the narrow waters supported by heavy ships. The Admiralty should be asked whether C-in-C's attention should not be drawn to the altered dispositions of the enemy, in case he has anything further to say.

WSC

Winston S. Churchill to General Ismay
(*Churchill papers, 20/13*)

3 August 1940

All secret service reports about affairs in France or other captive countries are to be shown to Major Morton, who is responsible for keeping me informed. Make sure this instruction is obeyed.

WSC

Winston S. Churchill to Lord Lloyd
(*Churchill papers, 20/13*)

3 August 1940

DAKAR OPERATION

1. Major Morton and General Spears will explain to you what I have in mind and what is passing with General de Gaulle to which the utmost importance and urgency should be attached.

The matter will be brought before Cabinet on Monday, but meanwhile no time must be lost in preparation.

2. I am told that de Gaulle has difficulties in communicating with various people in West Africa and that his telegrams are sometimes held up for several days – and in fact have been held up in an important matter over the weekend. He ought to have facilities of telegraphing through British channels to his agents. This, of course, does not commit us to any particular course of action other than allowing him such facilities.

I shall be much obliged if you will make sure that these difficulties are disposed of.

WSC

Winston S. Churchill to Sir Archibald Sinclair and Sir Cyril Newall
(*Churchill papers, 20/13*)

3 August 1940
Secret

It will be necessary for you to find a flying-boat to take three emissaries of General de Gaulle on Monday next to Accra, West Africa, for purposes I will explain to you and to the Cabinet later.

It is evident that this will delay the starting of the Atlantic service by at least a week. Please make sure, however, that all arrangements are made, as the matter is of the highest importance.

Winston S. Churchill to Anthony Eden
(*Churchill papers, 20/13*)

3 August 1940

It seems quite possible that a portion of General de Gaulle's forces will be used in the near future. It therefore becomes of the utmost consequence and urgency to complete the equipment of his three battalions, Company of Tanks, Headquarters, &c. Evidently action is being taken already, but I shall be much obliged if you will accelerate this action by every means in your power, and also if you will let me know in what way the situation has improved since Major Morton's minute of yesterday.

WSC

Winston S. Churchill to A. V. Alexander
(*Churchill papers, 20/13*)

3 August 1940

It seems quite possible that a proportion of General de Gaulle's forces will be used in the near future, and I am asking S of S for War to accelerate their equipment to the uttermost. It will also be necessary for one or two French warships of Admiral Muselier's[1] Navy to be in readiness. They may have to start within ten days. Pray let me know the situation.

WSC

---

[1] Emile Henry Muselier, 1882–1965. Entered the French Navy, 1902. Captain, 1918. Admiral Commanding the Navy and Defences of Marseilles, 1938–40. Joined General de Gaulle, July 1940. Commander-in-Chief of the Free French Naval Forces, 1940–2; of the Free French Air Forces, 1940–1. Chief of the French Naval Delegation, Military Mission for German Affairs, 1944–5. Honorary British knighthood, 1946.

Winston S. Churchill to Lord Lothian
(*Premier papers, 3/462/2/3*)

3 August 1940
11.50 p.m.
Personal

My immediately preceding telegram and your telegram No. 1579.[1]

Second alternative, i.e. bases, is agreeable, but we prefer that it should be on lease indefinitely and not sale. It is understood that this will enable us to secure destroyers and flying boats at once. You should let Colonel Knox[2] and others know that a request on these lines will be agreeable to us. Admiralty have been asked about the lien to Canada on cruisers. This, however, does not seem a practicable arrangement because obviously we alone can be the judge of when our means of defence in the United Kingdom are exhausted, and ships in question might well be destroyed in the final effort. It is, as you say, vital to settle quickly. Now is the time when we want the destroyers. We can fit them with Asdics in about ten days from the time they are in our hands, all preparation having been made. We should also be prepared to give a number of Asdics sets to the United States Navy and assist in their installation and explain their working. Go ahead on these lines full steam.

Before taking action on this telegram please see my immediately following telegram.[3]

Winston S. Churchill to Neville Chamberlain
(*Churchill papers, 2/393*)

3 August 1940   Chequers
Private

My dear Neville,

I am so glad you are making swift progress, and to hear from Horder[4] that you will be back in a fortnight. We shall all be delighted to see you. I have

[1] As reported by Lothian in his telegram No. 1579, sent 1 August, received 2 August, the alternative to exchanging the American destroyers for British bases was for the United States to sell the destroyers to Canada 'and that Canada in return for sending them to Europe would get lien on some larger cruisers which in the event of British defeat would then become part of the Canadian contribution to North American defence' (*Premier papers, 3/462/2, 3*).

[2] United States Secretary for the Navy.

[3] Not printed.

[4] Thomas Jeeves Horder, 1871–1955. Consulting physician to St Bartholomew's Hospital, London. Knighted, 1918. Created Baron, 1933. Physician to King George VI, 1936–52. Chairman of the Empire Rheumatism Council, 1936–53. Chairman of the British Empire Cancer Campaign. Actively involved in recreative physical training schemes, marriage guidance, smoke- and noise-abatement, and physiotherapy. President of the Food Education Society (and adviser

added Max to the War Cabinet[1] in order to get more help in the supply side of the Defence Ministry. This will require delicate development, as H. Morrison is sensitive about his domain, and I must move output.

They bombed Great Missenden, five miles away, last night. Whether this was a personal compliment or not is uncertain.

Once more all good wishes,

Yours ever,
W

Winston S. Churchill: Press Statement
(*Premier papers, 4/68/9*)

3 August 1940

The Prime Minister wishes it to be known that the possibility of German attempts at invasion has by no means passed away. The fact that the Germans are now putting about rumours that they do not intend an invasion should be regarded with a double dose of the suspicion which attaches to all their utterances. Our sense of growing strength and preparedness must not lead to the slightest relaxation of vigilance or moral alertness.

Winston S. Churchill to A. V. Alexander and Admiral Pound
(*Churchill papers, 20/13*)

4 August 1940

The repeated severe losses in the North-Western Approaches are most grievous, and I wish to feel assured that they are being grappled with with the same intense energy that marked the Admiralty treatment of the magnetic mine.[2] There seems to have been a great falling off in the control of these Approaches. No doubt this is largely due to the shortage of destroyers through invasion precautions. Let me know at once the whole outfit of destroyers, corvettes and Asdic trawlers, together with aircraft available and employed in this area. Who is in charge of their operations? Are they being controlled from

---

to the Ministry of Food, 1939–45). Chairman of the Shelter Hygiene Committee (Ministry of Home Security and Ministry of Health).

[1] Churchill had brought Lord Beaverbrook into the War Cabinet on 2 August 1940.

[2] At the end of 1939 the Admiralty had succeeded in developing counter-measures for a devastating weapon, the magnetic mine, that was wreaking havoc with merchant shipping in the North Sea. This effort is described in detail in the previous volume of the Churchill War Papers, *At the Admiralty*.

Plymouth and Admiral Nasmith's[1] Staff? Now that you have shifted the entry from the south to the north, the question arises, is Plymouth the right place for the Command? Ought not a new Command of the first order to be created in the Clyde, or should Admiral Nasmith move thither? Anyhow, we cannot go on like this. How is the Southern minefield barrage getting on? Would it not be possible after a while to ring the changes upon it for a short time, and bring some convoys in through the gap which has been left? This is only a passing suggestion.

There were always increased dangers to be apprehended from using only one set of Approaches. These dangers cannot be surmounted unless the protective concentration is carried out with superior vigour to that which must be expected from the enemy. He will soon learn to put everything there. It is rather like the early days in the Moray Firth after the East Coast minefield was laid. I am confident the Admiralty will rise to the occasion, but evidently a great new impulse is needed. Pray let me hear from you.[2]

WSC

Winston S. Churchill to Professor Lindemann
(*Churchill papers, 20/13*)

4 August 1940

What are you doing to focus the discussions on food, shipping and agricultural policy for the second twelve months of the war? I thought it looked like 18,000,000 tons of shipping, plough up 1,500,000 more acres, and instruct the Food Department to submit a plan both for increasing rations and building up further food reserves. This should be possible on the above basis.

---

[1] Martin Eric Dunbar-Nasmith, 1883–1965. Entered the Royal Navy, 1897. Entered the submarine branch, 1904. In command of the submarine *E. 11* at the Dardanelles, he made the dangerous passage of the narrow waterway to spend ninety-six days in the Sea of Marmora, sinking ninety-six Turkish vessels including a battleship, a destroyer, and a large gunboat anchored off Constantinople. Churchill later wrote: 'This prodigious feat remains unsurpassed in the history of submarine warfare.' Awarded the Victoria Cross, 1915. Rear-Admiral Commanding the Submarine Branch of the Royal Navy, 1929–31. Knighted, 1934. Chief of Navy Personnel, 1935–8. Commander-in-Chief Plymouth and the Western Approaches, 1938–41. Flag Officer-in-Charge, London, 1942–5. Vice-Chairman, Imperial War Graves Commission, 1948–54.

[2] Churchill commented in his war memoirs: 'I encountered resistances. The Admiralty accepted my view in September of moving from Plymouth to the North, rightly substituting the Mersey for the Clyde. But several months elapsed before the necessary headquarters organisation, with its operations rooms and elaborate network of communications, could be brought into being, and in the meantime much improvisation was necessary. The new Command was entrusted to Admiral Sir Percy Noble, who, with a large and ever-growing staff, was installed at Liverpool in February 1941. Henceforward this became almost our most important station. The need and advantage of the change was by then recognized by all' (*Their Finest Hour*, pages 531–2).

August 1940

Winston S. Churchill to Sir Archibald Sinclair and Sir Cyril Newall
(*Cabinet papers, 120/300*)

4 August 1940

The danger of Japanese hostility makes it all the more important that the German capital ships should be put out of action. I understand that the Air Force intend to make heavy attacks on these ships as soon as there is sufficient moon. *Scharnhorst* and the *Gneisenau*, both in floating docks at Kiel, the *Bismarck* at Hamburg, and the *Tirpitz* at Wilhelmshaven, are all targets of supreme consequence. Even a few months' delay in *Bismarck* will affect the whole balance of sea power to a serious degree. I shall be glad to hear from you.

WSC

Winston S. Churchill to General Ismay
(*Churchill papers, 20/13*)

4 August 1940

Let me have the programme of new construction of the UP weapon and its ammunition, both wire and ordinary. A very large programme must be set on foot. Let me know what is now being done.

2. I am now happy about the new arrangement made for the Ministry of Supply to take over Mr Crow's[1] establishment. At the Admiralty I had him under my personal direction, all the other Departments having agreed. It now seems to be possible that he might be put under me as Minister of Defence, and be worked through your Secretariat. In the same way Tanks might possibly be withdrawn from the Ministry of Supply and placed under special Ministry of Defence control, when, after an interval, Lord Beaverbrook could get hold of it. Pray consider this this morning. I fear we shall not get the service we require. Anyhow, I am now satisfied with Crow's position, and wish to be given the material to write the Minister of Supply.

WSC

---

[1] Alwyn Douglas Crow, 1894–1965. On active service, 1914–17 (wounded, despatches, OBE). Joined the Proof and Experimental Establishment, Royal Arsenal, 1917; Director of Ballistics Research, 1919–39; Chief Superintendent, Projectile Development, 1939–40; Director and Controller of Projectile Development, 1940–5. Knighted, 1944. Director of Guided Projectiles, Ministry of Supply, 1945–6. Head of Technical Services, Joint Services Mission, Washington, 1946–53.

Winston S. Churchill to Sir Edward Bridges
(*Churchill papers, 20/13*)

4 August 1940

I circulate to my colleagues the enclosed report[1] on the first use of the UP weapon with the wire curtain at Dover. This appears to be of high importance, and may well inaugurate a decisive change in the relations of ground and air, particularly in respect of ships and ports exposed to dive-bombing attack.

WSC

General Ismay to Sir Cyril Newall
(*Cabinet papers, 120/300*)

4 August 1940

The Prime Minister wishes to have a report as soon as possible on the progress of the Air Route from Takoradi.[2] When will it be ready to use, and can anything be done to expedite it.

2. The Prime Minister also wishes to have your bombing programme for this moon. He tells me that you sent him a programme of this kind for the last moon and wishes it repeated.

Winston S. Churchill to Lord Halifax
(*Churchill papers, 20/13*)

4 August 1940

I don't think we ought to pay much attention to this account of the friendly French Counsellor at Washington. Whatever his intentions, he is only serving the Pétain Government by a side wind. Nothing can blind our eyes to the fact

---

[1] War Cabinet Paper No. 303 of 1940, 'Experience with the UP Weapon at Dover'. Written by A. D. Crow, this report described the two occasions on which Unrotated Projectiles had been fired, against a single German bomber on 4 July 1940, and against two waves of bombers, sixteen and twenty-two respectively, on 29 July 1940. 'The position appears to be,' Crow concluded, 'that in the two main engagements it is certain that the UP weapon destroyed one bomber, probable that it destroyed a second, and possible that it destroyed or crippled a third.'

[2] A town on the Atlantic Coast of Africa, on the Gold Coast (later Ghana). Its airport was being developed for the transit of war supplies from West Africa to the Sudan, and then south to Egypt, avoiding Vichy- and Italian-held territory in North Africa.

that we are (a) encouraging and aiding a revolt by de Gaulle, (b) that we are by our action, and indeed by our continued survival, making the Pétain Government look increasingly base and shameful, (c) that we must continue to bomb French ports and shipping, and (d) that we are keeping unoccupied France in the hunger zone for the present.

Compared to the above, leaflets and remarks about General Pétain are petty items. As for infuriating French Senators, I doubt if the Senate, or what is left of it, is capable of so strong an emotion. Anxious as I am to establish contacts of all kinds, official and unofficial, with defeated France, I hope we shall not be turned at all from the main lines of our war policy.

WSC

Winston S. Churchill to Lord Halifax
(*Churchill papers, 20/13*)

4 August 1940

Most of this is settled by numerous minutes and letters which I drafted for your consideration yesterday. I see no reason why General de Gaulle should not be informed of any fresh recruits for our Forces, though without having a right of veto.

It is not our policy to engage large numbers of Frenchmen or other friendly foreigners in our own Forces. We have not got enough weapons for ourselves, our Dominions, and the large Indian expansions which are in prospect. We have been drawn into offering employment in our Forces and raising foreign refugee Pioneer Battalions, not so much for our own sake, but to cater for the needs and wishes of these well-disposed and brave individuals. Our preference would be that intending recruits should join their appropriate national force. General Ismay will explain this point of view to the War Office, but I have no doubt they have it already. The Admiralty stand in a slightly different position, on account of the difficulty of making up ships' companies from French personnel, who do not correspond to the necessary technical ratings. The complements cannot therefore be balanced.

Subject to the above, I am in full agreement with your memo, and am quite willing to sign the letter to General de Gaulle. It is important, however, that the letter of interpretation should also be signed. These are secret and should be retained in the Foreign Office archives. The memorandum and my letter, and General de Gaulle's acceptance, will I presume be published in a White Paper to be laid before Parliament. I should like to see a proof of this when convenient.

WSC

Winston S. Churchill to Lord Lloyd
(*Churchill papers, 20/13*)

4 August 1940

Are you sure that the holding up of General de Gaulle's telegram by the Colonial Office for two or three days has not led to this unfortunate result?[1] I hope your department realises as keenly as you do the vital need of establishing a de Gaulle administration somewhere on the West Coast. This would be the prelude to a move to the Northern Coast.

War Cabinet: minutes
(*Cabinet papers, 65/8*)

5 August 1940　　　　　　　　　　　　　　　　　　　　10 Downing Street
11.30 a.m.

The Prime Minister informed the War Cabinet that General de Gaulle proposed to form a 'Council of Defence' of French Possessions beyond the seas, composed of those qualified authorities in French territories which decided to join the General for the purpose of pursuing the war against our common enemies. He proposed to reply that His Majesty's Government in the United Kingdom approved the plan of forming this Council of Defence, and would be glad to discuss with it all questions involving its collaboration with the British Empire, both in matters affecting the defence of such French colonies against the common enemies, and in those affecting the economic interests of those colonies.

The War Cabinet approved the despatch by the Prime Minister to General de Gaulle of a letter in the terms proposed.

The Prime Minister recalled that the War Cabinet had approved the terms of a draft letter for him to send to General de Gaulle covering a draft agreement. Difficulty had arisen in regard to two points. General de Gaulle had been anxious that the letter should include the words 'full restoration of the independence and greatness of France.' Again, General de Gaulle wanted a draft Article included specifying that his troops would not have to 'take up arms against France.'

From General de Gaulle's point of view, it was no doubt natural that he

---

[1] With Churchill's support, de Gaulle had telegraphed on 27 July 1940 to his representatives in the British Cameroons to recruit 2,000 Ivory Coast riflemen then in the Cameroons for the force to seize Vichy-controlled Libreville. Before his telegram was allowed through by the Colonial Office, the riflemen had been taken by the British commander in the Cameroons for his own force.

should press for this wording. On the other hand, it was undesirable that we should agree to phrases the interpretation of which might land us in difficulties. It was therefore proposed to accept the text proposed, but to safeguard the interpretation of these points by an exchange of letters. On the first point, it would be stated that the phrase in question had no precise relation to territorial frontiers. We had not been able to guarantee such frontiers in respect of any nation now acting with us, but, of course, we should do our best. On the second point, the phrase 'take up arms against France' must be interpreted as meaning 'a France free to choose its course without any direct or indirect duress from Germany.'

General de Gaulle was prepared to reply in a letter accepting these interpretations.

The War Cabinet approved the course proposed.

War Cabinet: Confidential Annex
(*Cabinet papers, 65/14*)

5 August 1940　　　　　　　　　　　　　　　　　　　　　　10 Downing Street
11.30 a.m.

The Prime Minister said that it had been one of our principal objects, since the defection of the Bordeaux Government, to establish the rule of a French Government friendly to His Majesty's Government and hostile to Germany in as many parts as possible of the French Empire. General de Gaulle with the Free French Forces now in the United Kingdom had the same object and it was right that we should give them every encouragement in carrying it out. Consideration had already been given to a number of possibilities, including projects for landing forces in Morocco, Algeria and Tunis. Each of these projects had, after examination, been dismissed for the sufficient reason that British land forces would be required to carry it out; we did not wish to embark on the course of active conquest of any part of the French Empire.

A plan had then been discussed for a landing by General de Gaulle in Algeria. General de Gaulle had himself taken the view that a landing in one of the French West African possessions would offer better prospects. Messages which had been received from the Governor General of Nigeria[1] afforded some confirmation of General de Gaulle's view. Accordingly the proposal now

---

[1] Bernard Henry Bourdillon, 1883–1948. Joined the Indian Civil Service, 1908. On active service in Mesopotamia, 1918. Acting High Commissioner, Iraq, 1925–6. Colonial and Chief Secretary, Ceylon, 1929–32. Governor and Commander-in-Chief, Uganda, 1932–5. Knighted, 1934. Governor and Commander-in-Chief, Nigeria, 1935–43. One of his two sons was killed while on duty in Jerusalem in 1946.

before the War Cabinet had been drawn up. The plan was that General de Gaulle's force should be ready to sail for West Africa on 15th August. They would embark in ships manned as far as possible by French crews, with a view to hoisting the Free French Flag in French territory in West Africa, the occupation of Dakar, and the consolidation under the Free French Flag of the French Colonies in West and Equatorial Africa.

Following this operation, the next objective would be to rally to the same cause the French Colonies in North Africa through the intervention of elements in those Colonies ready to continue the struggle.

In this connection, immediate arrangements would be made to transport General Catroux[1] from Indo-China to this country as quickly as possible.

If the War Cabinet approved the plan in principle, the first action would be to despatch to Nigeria three agents (two military officers and one civilian) selected by General de Gaulle. These would leave England for Accra on the following day in an Empire Flying Boat to confer with the Governor General, Nigeria, and the General Officer Commanding, West Africa,[2] and to make contact with French leaders in the French West African and Equatorial Colonies, thereafter reporting by telegram to General de Gaulle.

The intention was that only French forces should land in French West Africa. Our part would be to equip and transport and escort those forces. The report by the Chiefs of Staff (WP (40) 304) analysed the problem before us which was that of transporting and disembarking the forces of all arms, including guns, 13-ton tanks, Motor Transport vehicles and cased aircraft. The only French West African ports available for the disembarkation were Dakar, Konakri and Duala.

If a decision could be taken that day it was contemplated that the time table for the expedition might be roughly as follows:—

Forces mobilised at Aldershot	10th August
M/T and Store ships begin loading	11th August
M/T and Store ships sail	13th August
Troop ships sail	19th to 23rd August

---

[1] Georges Catroux, 1877–1969. A professional soldier, he spent most of his career in Syria, where in 1930 a young staff officer, Captain de Gaulle, was much impressed by his ability to rouse local sympathy and respect. As Governor-General of Indo-China in 1940, he was the only French pro-consul and the only Général d'Armée to join de Gaulle, for which he was condemned to death by Vichy. In 1941 he was appointed by de Gaulle to command the Free French forces against the Vichy forces in the Syrian campaign. Free French representative in Algeria, 1943. Ambassador to Moscow, 1945–8. Honorary British knighthood, 1946. Governor-General of Algeria, 1956.

[2] General Giffard, see page 699, note 2.

Winston S. Churchill to General de Gaulle
(*Foreign Office papers, 371/24360*)

5 August 1940
Secret

10 Downing Street

My dear General de Gaulle,

In answer to your letter of the 30th July, I wish to inform you that His Majesty's Government in the United Kingdom approve of your plan of forming as soon as possible a 'Council of Defence' of French possessions beyond the seas. This council is to be composed, as I understand from you, of those qualified authorities in the French colonies which decide to join you for the purpose of pursuing the war against our common enemies.

With reference to the declaration made on behalf of His Majesty's Government on the 28th June, I might add that His Majesty's Government would be prepared to discuss with such a 'Council of Defence' of French overseas possessions all questions involving its collaboration with the British Empire both in matters affecting the defence of such French colonies against the common enemies and in those affecting the economic interests of those colonies.

Yours sincerely,
Winston S. Churchill

Victor Cazalet: diary
(*'Victor Cazalet, a Portrait'*)

5 August 1940
1.30 p.m.

Polish Agreement[1] signed 10 Downing Street, inside Cabinet Room. Winston at last minute insisted on photographer coming into the Cabinet Room. We had all been told that was the one thing that was not to be done.

He was very distracted while we were in the garden and could not be got to do anything but smile. We all drank champagne and all the Polish officers, etc., whom I brought in, were very pleased as the whole Cabinet came down and made themselves pleasant.

---

[1] Under the Anglo-Polish Agreement of 5 August 1940, the Polish armed forces commanded by General Sikorski were to 'co-operate with the Allied armed forces'. Details were agreed for their arming, training (including training in Canada), participation in the war against Germany, and hospitalisation.

Sikorski, Zaleski[1] and I went to lunch – just us, the Churchills, Randolph and his wife, and Halifax. Winston's French quite good, very slow, very schoolboyish; one good phrase – 'si nos efforts sont blessés' – Clemmie intervened with 'I think you mean "bénis".'

He told us there were no signs of invasion yet. Hitler had us all guessing.

Anthony Eden to Winston S. Churchill
(*Premier papers, 3/498/1 and 2*)

5 August 1940

My dear Prime Minister,

You will remember that on Wednesday evening[2] the CIGS and I came over to discuss with you the question of the protection of vulnerable points. I attach a copy of the Note prepared on the subject.

At our meeting I understood that you accepted our proposals:–
(a) to appoint a general officer as a Vulnerable Points Adviser;
(b) that the Field Army should not be employed on Guard duties at vulnerable points;

and you said that you were prepared to issue an instruction on (b).

In order that arrangements may be made to put these two proposals into effect, I should be grateful if you could arrange for a copy of your instructions on this matter to be sent to me as early as possible.[3]

Winston S. Churchill: memorandum
(*Cabinet papers, 66/10*)

5 August 1940
Most Secret

Bearing in mind the immense cost in war energy and disadvantage of attempting to defend the whole west coast of Great Britain, and the dangers of being unduly committed to systems of passive defence, I should be glad if the following notes could be borne in mind:–

1. Our first line of defence against invasion must be as ever the enemy's ports. Air reconnaissance, submarine watching, and other means of obtaining

---

[1] Count August Zaleski, Polish Foreign Minister, 1926–32. In September 1939 there were plans in Warsaw to make him head of a national government. Following the German conquest of Poland, he became Foreign Minister of the Polish Government in exile (first in Paris, then in London), October 1939 to August 1941.

[2] Wednesday, 31 July 1940, following Churchill's return from a tour of inspection of defences on the North East coast.

[3] The officer appointed Vulnerable Points Adviser was Lieutenant-General M. G. H. Barker.

information should be followed by resolute attacks with all our forces available and suitable upon any concentrations of enemy shipping.

2. Our second line of defence is the vigilant patrolling of the sea to intercept any invading expedition, and to destroy it in transit.

3. Our third line is the counter-attack upon the enemy when he makes any landfall, and particularly while he is engaged in the act of landing. This attack, which has long been ready from the sea, must be reinforced by Air action; and both sea and air attacks must be continued so that it becomes impossible for the invader to nourish his lodgments.

4. The land defences and the home Army are maintained primarily for the purpose of making the enemy come in such large numbers as to afford a proper target to the sea and air forces above mentioned, and to make hostile preparations and movements noticeable to Air and other forms of reconnaissance.

5. However, should the enemy succeed in landing at various points, he should be made to suffer as much as possible by local resistance on the beaches, combined with the aforesaid attack from the sea and the air. This forces him to use up his ammunition and confines him to a limited area. The defence of any part of the coast must be measured not by the forces on the coast, but by the number of hours within which strong counter-attacks by mobile troops can be brought to bear upon the landing places. Such attacks should be hurled with the utmost speed and fury upon the enemy at his weakest moment, which is not, as is sometimes suggested, when actually getting out of his boats, but when sprawled upon the shore with his communications cut and his supplies running short. It ought to be possible to concentrate 10,000 men fully equipped within six hours, and 20,000 men within twelve hours, upon any point where a serious lodgment has been effected. The withholding of the reserves until the full gravity of the attack is known is a nice problem for the Home Command.

6. It must be admitted that the task of the Navy and Air Force to prevent invasion becomes more difficult in the narrow seas, namely, from the Wash to Dover. This sector of the coast front is also nearest to the supreme enemy objective, London. The sector from Dover to Lands End is far less menaced because the Navy and Air Force must make sure that no mass of shipping, still less protecting warships, can be passed into the French Channel ports. At present the scale of attack on this wide front is estimated by the Admiralty at no more than 5,000 men. Doubling this for greater security, it should be possible to make good arrangements for speedy counter-attack in superior numbers, and at the same time to achieve large economies of force on this southern sector in which the beach troops should be at their minimum and the mobile reserves at their maximum. These mobile reserves must be available to move to the south-eastern sectors at short notice. Evidently this situation can only be judged from week to week.

7. When we come to the west coast of Britain, a new set of conditions rules. The enemy must commit himself to the broad seas, and there will be plenty of time, if his approach is detected, to attack him with cruisers and flotillas. The Admiralty dispositions still conform to this need. The enemy has at present no warships to escort him. Should we, for instance, care to send 12,000 men unescorted in merchant ships to land on the Norwegian coast, or in the Skagerrak and Kattegat, in face of superior sea power and air power? It would be thought madness.

8. However, to make assurance triply sure, the Admiralty should pursue their plan of laying a strong minefield from Cornwall to Ireland, covering the Bristol Channel and the Irish Sea from southward attack. This minefield is all the more necessary now that by the adoption of the Northabout route for commerce we have transferred a large part of our patrolling craft from the Western Approaches which have become permanently more empty and unwatched.

9. The establishment of this minefield will simplify and mitigate all questions of local defence north of its point of contact with Cornwall. We must consider this sector from Cornwall to the Mull of Cantyre[1] as the least vulnerable to seaborne invasion. Here the works of defence should be confined to guarding by a few guns or land torpedo tubes the principal harbours, and giving a moderate scale of protection to their gorges. It is not admissible to lavish our limited resources upon this sector.

10. North of the Mull of Cantyre to Scapa Flow, the Shetlands and the Faroes all lies in the orbit of the main Fleet. The voyage of an expedition from the Norwegian coast would be very hazardous, and its arrival anywhere right round to Cromarty Firth would not raise immediately decisive issues. The enemy who is now crouched would then be sprawled. His advance would lie in difficult and sparsely-inhabited country. He could be contained until sufficient forces were brought to bear, and his communications immediately cut from the sea. This would make his position all the more difficult, as the distances to any important objective are much longer and he would require considerable wheeled transport. It would be impossible to fortify all landing points in this sector, and it would be a waste of energy to attempt to do so. A much longer period may be allowed for counter-attack than in the south-east opposite London.

11. From Cromarty Firth to the Wash is the second-most important sector, ranking next after the Wash to Dover. Here, however, all the harbours and inlets are defended, both from the sea and from the rear, and it should be possible to counter-attack in superior force within twenty-four hours. The Tyne must be regarded as the second major objective after London, for here

---

[1] Also spelt Mull of Kintyre: at the southern end of the promontory across the North Channel from Northern Ireland.

(and to a lesser extent at the Tees) grievous damage could be done by an invader or large-scale raider in a short time. On the other hand, the sea and air conditions are more favourable to us than to the southward.

12. The combined Staffs should endeavour to assign to all these sectors their relative scales of vulnerability and defence, both in the number of men employed in the local defence of beaches and of harbours, and also in the number of days or hours within which heavy counter-attacks should be possible. As an indication of these relative scales of attack and defence, I set down for consideration the following:–

Cromarty Firth to Wash inclusive	3
Wash to Dover promontory	5
Dover promontory to Lands End, and round to start of minefield	$1\frac{1}{2}$
Start of the minefield to the Mull of Cantyre	$\frac{1}{4}$
Mull of Cantyre north-about to Cromarty Firth	$\frac{1}{2}$

WSC

Winston S. Churchill to General Ismay
(*Churchill papers, 20/13*)

5 August 1940

What orders are extant for the future production of UP Multiple Projectors in groups of twenties, tens, fives, and also single projectors?

What amount of ammunition –

(a) of the ordinary rocket,
(b) of the aerial mine,
(c) of the PE fuze,
(d) of the radio fuze,

is on order? What are the forecasts of deliveries in the next six months in all cases?

Presently the PE fuze will probably supersede the aerial mine for use in multiple projectors mounted on HM ships. This will entail an alteration of the projector tubes. The Admiralty should be asked to study this betimes, so that the new tubes can be fitted on the existing mountings of HM ships with the least possible delay from the moment that this change appears desirable.

The Admiralty should also be asked to report whether any progress has been made on firing short aerial mines from ships' guns.

I wish to refresh my memory with what happened about this before I left the Admiralty.

August 1940

Winston S. Churchill to General Ismay[1]
(*Churchill papers, 20/13*)

5 August 1940

I am not satisfied with the volume or quality of information received from the unoccupied area of France. We seem to be as much cut off from these territories as from Germany. I do not wish such reports as are received to be sifted and digested by the various Intelligence authorities. For the present Major Morton will inspect them for me and submit what he considers of major interest. He is to see everything and submit authentic documents for me in their original form.[1]

Further, I await proposals from Colonel Menzies[2] for improving and extending our information about France and for keeping a continued flow of agents moving to and fro. For this purpose Naval facilities can, if necessary, be invoked. So far as the Vichy Government is concerned, it is not creditable that we have so little information. To what extent are Americans, Swiss and Spanish agents being used? Colonel Menzies should submit a report on what he has done and is proposing to do.

WSC

Winston S. Churchill to General Ismay
(*Churchill papers, 20/13*)

5 August 1940

I asked the other day for a forecast of the development of the armoured divisions which will be required in 1941 – namely, five by the end of March and one additional every month until a total of ten is reached at the end of August 1941; and also for the composition of each Division in armoured and ancillary vehicles of all kinds.

---

[1] Major Morton was responsible for taking all top secret intercepted German and Italian signals to Churchill. Morton's office was at Broadway, five minutes' walk from 10 Downing Street. These intercepts were kept were in a double-locked box: Churchill had one key and Morton another. Churchill's Private Secretaries had no idea what was in these daily boxes, other than that it was something of exceptional secrecy. Morton was helped by an assistant, Arthur (later Sir Arthur) Benson, and a secretary, Miss Gwynne.

[2] Stewart Graham Menzies, 1890–1968. A nephew of Muriel Wilson, to whom Churchill had proposed marriage in the late 1890s. Educated at Eton. Served in the Grenadier Guards, 1909–10; the Life Guards, 1910–39. On active service, 1914–18, involved from 1915 in counter-espionage and security duties at General Headquarters, France (despatches, DSO, Military Cross). Lieutenant-Colonel, 1919. Chief of the War Office Secret Service, 1919 (under Churchill). Military Representative of the War Office, Secret Intelligence Service, 1919. Personal Assistant to the Head of the Secret Intelligence Service (Admiral Sir Hugh Sinclair) from 1923. Colonel, 1932. Head of the Secret Intelligence Service, November 1939 to May 1952. CB, 1942. Knighted, 1943.

Pray let me know how far the War Office plans have proceeded and whether the numbers of tanks ordered correspond with a programme of these dimensions.

Let me further have a report on the progress of the means of transportation overseas which should be adequate to the movement at one moment of two armoured Divisions. Who is doing this – Admiralty or Ministry of Supply? I suggested that Mr Hopkins might have some spare time available.

WSC

On 6 August 1940 Churchill visited defences in Lincolnshire.

Winston S. Churchill to Anthony Eden
(*Premier papers, 3/498/1 and 2*)

6 August 1940   10 Downing Street

I entirely approve of your idea of withdrawing all troops of the mobile army from vulnerable points, and this operation should be completed before the end of August at latest. It will however be necessary for you to replace the mobile troops from your sedentary battalions or from specially organized units of the Home Guard, and I do not gather that the War Office in any way abandon its responsibilities in this respect. The 'Vulnerable Point Adviser'[1] so far as he is concerned merely in re-distributing War Office personnel is a matter purely for Departmental decision, but if he is to have authority to say that certain points need not be guarded, which hitherto have been regarded of importance, or only very weakly guarded, the Civil Departments must have their say.

WSC

Defence Committee: minutes
(*Cabinet papers, 70/1*)

6 August 1940   10 Downing Street
10.30 a.m.

The Prime Minister drew attention to the deplorable position regarding the supply of ammunition for trench mortars. This was to be attributed to the design of a fuze of such complexity that supply had been held up for three months and the troops consequently had only 15 rounds per mortar. He asked who was responsible for the various decisions which had led to this state of affairs.

---

[1] General Barker, see page 681, notes 1 and 2.

The Minister of Supply[1] said that steps had been taken to prevent a repetition of such mistakes by ensuring that there should in future be a closer association between the design and production staffs.

War Cabinet: minutes
(*Cabinet papers, 65/8*)

6 August 1940　　　　　　　　　　　　　　　　　　10 Downing Street
12 noon

The War Cabinet had before them a Memorandum by the Secretary of State for Dominion Affairs[2] (WP (G) (40) 204) reporting the upshot of the discussions in recent months with a view to making a comprehensive agreement with Eire on a number of trade questions. Substantial agreement had been reached on many points, but difficulties had arisen about the prices we should pay for butter, cheese and bacon from Eire.

The Prime Minister saw strong objection to subsidising a disloyal Dominion. In principle the proposal should be rejected. In any case, the concession should not be made unless we drove a hard bargain for it.

The Secretary of State for Foreign Affairs said that he had now had a telegram from our Ambassador in Tokyo (No. 1474) reporting that he favoured the withdrawal of the British garrisons in North China.

The Prime Minister agreed with the course proposed. He thought the two battalions withdrawn should be sent to Singapore, the garrison of which might perhaps also be reinforced by two more Indian Battalions. The result would be a heavy reinforcement of Singapore, and, if announced publicly, might help our prestige.

Winston S. Churchill to David Grenfell[3]
(*Churchill papers, 20/13*)

6 August 1940

I saw it stated that you were piling up large reserves of coal during the summer for use during the winter. I should be glad to know how far this very

[1] Herbert Morrison.
[2] Viscount Caldecote.
[3] David Rhys Grenfell, 1881–1968. A coal miner (underground) from the age of twelve to the age of thirty-five, Miners' Agent, 1916. Labour MP, 1922–59. Member of the Forestry Commission, 1929–42. CBE, 1935. Secretary for Mines, 1940–2. Chairman, Welsh Tourist Board, 1948. Privy Councillor, 1951. 'Father of the House', 1953–9 (though Churchill had first been elected 22 years earlier, in 1900, he had been out of the Commons from 1922 to 1924).

wise precaution has advanced. We were very short and anxious in January last, and I hope you are taking precautions.

WSC

The Dakar Operation[1]
(*Premier papers, 3/276*)

6 August 1940

... the Prime Minister saw General de Gaulle and evolved a new plan with him. This was, briefly, to land a force of infantry at a beach near Dakar: or land the whole force at Konakri, move on by rail across country to Bamako and thence to Dakar: or land at Freetown and thence overland to French Guinea. General de Gaulle made it quite clear that he would not be a party to a fight between Frenchmen.

General de Gaulle: recollection
(*'The Call to Honour', pages 114–17*)

6 August 1940

I found him, on August 6, as usual, in that large room in Downing Street which is used, by tradition, both as the Prime Minister's office and as the place where the government meets. On the enormous table which fills the room he had had some maps laid out, before which he paced up and down, talking with animation.

'We must,' he said to me, 'together gain control of Dakar. For you it is capital. For if the business goes well, it means that large French forces are brought back into the war. It is very important for us. For to be able to use Dakar as a base would make a great many things easier in the hard Battle of the Atlantic. And so, having conferred with the Admiralty and the Chiefs of Staff, I am in a position to tell you that we are ready to assist in the expedition. We mean to assign to it a considerable naval force. But we would not be able to leave this force on the coast of Africa for long. The necessity of bringing it back to help in covering England, as well as in our operations in the Mediterranean, demands that we should do things very quickly. That is why

---

[1] Part of a historical narrative printed for the War Cabinet on 5 February 1941. The War Cabinet reference for this, the first of a series of such narratives prepared by the Cabinet Office, was 'HIST (A) 1 (Revise)'. (*Premier papers, 3/276*).

we do not agree with your proposal for landing at Konakry and proceeding slowly across the bush – which would oblige us to keep our ships in the neighbourhood for months. I have something else to propose to you.'

Then Mr Churchill, colouring his eloquence with the most picturesque tints, set to work to paint for me the following picture: 'Dakar wakes up one morning, sad and uncertain. But behold, by the light of the rising sun, its inhabitants perceive the sea, to a great distance, covered with ships. An immense fleet! A hundred war or transport vessels! These approach slowly, addressing messages of friendship by radio to the town, to the navy, to the garrison. Some of them are flying the Tricolour. The others are sailing under the British, Dutch, Polish, or Belgian colours. From this Allied force there breaks away an inoffensive small ship bearing the white flag of parley. It enters the port and disembarks the envoys of General de Gaulle. These are brought to the Governor. Their job is to convince him that if he lets you land the Allied fleet retires, and that nothing remains but to settle, between him and you, the terms of his cooperation. On the contrary, if he wants a fight, he has every chance of being crushed.'

And Mr Churchill, brimming over with conviction, described and mimed, one by one, the scenes of the future, as they spurted up from his desire and his imagination.

'During this conversation between the Governor and your representatives, Free French and British aircraft are flying peacefully over the town, dropping friendly leaflets. The military and the civilians, among whom your agents are at work, are discussing passionately among themselves the advantages offered by an arrangement with you and the drawbacks presented, on the contrary, by a large-scale battle fought against those who, after all, are the allies of France. The Governor feels that, if he resists, the ground will give way under his feet. You will see that he will go on with the talks till they reach a satisfactory conclusion. Perhaps meanwhile he will wish, "for honour's sake," to fire a few shots. But he will not go further. And that evening he will dine with you and drink to the final victory.'

Stripping Mr Churchill's idea of the seductive ornaments added to it by his eloquence, I recognized, on reflection, that it was based on certain solid data. Since the British could not divert important naval forces to the Equator for long, a direct operation was the only means to be envisaged for making myself master of Dakar. This, short of taking on the character of a full-dress attack, was bound to involve some mixture of persuasion and intimidation. At the same time I judged it probable that the British Admiralty would be led, one day or another, with or without the Free French, to settle the question of Dakar, where the existence of a great Atlantic base and the presence of the *Richelieu* could not fail to arouse in it both desire and uneasiness.

I concluded that, if we were present, there would be some chance of the operation's becoming an adherence, though perhaps a forced one, to Free

France. If, on the contrary, we abstained, the English would want, sooner or later, to operate on their own account. In this case the place would resist vigorously, using the fortress guns and the artillery of the *Richelieu*, while the Glenn Martin bombers, the Curtiss fighters, the submarines – very dangerous for ships which were not, at that time, provided with any means of detection – would hold any transport armada at their mercy. And even if Dakar, crushed by shellfire, were finally forced to surrender with its ruins and its wrecks to the British, there would be reason to fear that the operation would end to the detriment of French sovereignty.

After a short delay I returned to Mr Churchill to tell him that I accepted his suggestion. I worked out the plan of action with Admiral Sir John Cunningham[1] who was to command the British squadron . . .

The Dakar Operation
(*Premier papers, 3/276*)

6 August 1940

The Chiefs of Staff, in the afternoon of the 6th, studied a report by the Inter-Service Planning Staff, which had been prepared after consultation with General de Gaulle, General Spears and the Vice-Chief of Naval Staff. At this meeting, General de Gaulle stated definitely that his object was to take possession of friendly territory and that if he met opposition, he would not consider going on with the operation. He felt that his reception could be much improved if the aircraft he took with him could be seen flying over the country as soon as possible.

General Spears pointed out that the Prime Minister had authorised the inclusion in the force of two Polish battalions.

---

[1] John Henry Dacres Cunningham, 1885–1962. Entered the Royal Navy as a cadet, 1900. Commander, 1917; served as navigator on HMS *Renown*, 1917, and HMS *Lion*, 1918. Assistant Chief of the Naval Staff (Air), 1937; Fifth Sea Lord and Chief of Naval Air Services, 1938. Commanded First Cruiser Squadron, 1938–41. Took part in the Norwegian campaign (evacuation of Namsos), May 1940. Naval Commander, Dakar expedition, September 1940. Fourth Sea Lord and Chief of Supplies and Transport, 1940–2. Knighted, 1941. Commander-in-Chief, Levant, 1943. Commander-in-Chief, Mediterranean, and Allied Naval Commander, 1943–5 (including the Anzio and South of France landings). First Sea Lord, 1946–8. One of his two sons, a submariner, was killed in action in 1941.

John Colville: diary
(*Colville papers*)

6 August 1940

Winston was in a nervous and irritable frame of mind in the evening, occupied with the question of obtaining from the US the fifty destroyers we so badly need. He refuses to contemplate a promise to give Canada, and thus the US, a lien on our warships if these islands are conquered and brands any such proposal as defeatism. We could only give such an undertaking in return for an Anglo-US Alliance. Thus Winston declares that the only *quid pro quo* we could give the US would be the lease of air and naval bases in the West Indies. This would be justifiable because it is in our interest to encourage a strong Anglo-American defence line in the Western Atlantic.

W protested strongly at the noise being made in the Private Secretaries' room and finally threatened to sack the next offender. This next offender was the Chief of the Air Staff, but the real culprit is Desmond Morton whose voice would penetrate the ramparts of a mediaeval castle.

ON 7 AUGUST 1940 Churchill inspected defences in East Anglia and the Nottingham area.

Winston S. Churchill to Anthony Eden
(*Churchill papers, 20/13*)

7 August 1940

Please let me know what is being done to train men in the use of the sticky bomb, which is now beginning to come through in quantity.

Winston S. Churchill to Lord Lothian
(*Premier papers, 3/462/2/3*)

7 August 1940

We need the fifty or sixty destroyers very much, and hope we shall obtain them. In no other way could the United States assist us so effectively in the next three or four months. We were, as you know, very ready to offer the United States indefinite lease facilities for naval and air bases in West Indian islands, and to do this freely on grounds of inevitable common association of naval and military interests of Great Britain and the United States. It was therefore most agreeable to us that Colonel Knox should be inclined to suggest action on these or similar lines as an accompaniment to the immediate sending of the said destroyers. But all this has nothing to do with any bargaining or declaration about the future disposition of the British Fleet. It would obviously be impossible for us to make or agree to any declaration being made on such a subject. I have repeatedly warned you in my secret telegrams and those to the President of the dangers United States would run if Great Britain were successfully invaded and a British Quisling Government came into office to make the best terms possible for the surviving inhabitants. I am very glad to find that these dangers are regarded as serious, and you should in no wise minimise them. We have no intention of relieving United States from any well-grounded anxieties on this point. Moreover, our position is not such as to bring the collapse of Britain into the arena of practical discussion. I have already several weeks ago told you that there is no warrant for discussing any question of the transference of the Fleet to American or Canadian shores. I should refuse to allow the subject even to be mentioned in any Staff conversations, still less that any technical preparations should be made or even planned. Above all, it is essential you should realise that no such declaration could ever be assented to by us for the purpose of obtaining destroyers or anything like that. Pray make it clear at once that we could never agree to the slightest compromising of our full liberty of action, nor tolerate any such defeatist announcement, the effect of which would be disastrous.

Although in my speech of June 4 I thought it well to open up to German eyes the prospects of indefinite oceanic war, this was a suggestion in the making of which we could admit no neutral partner. Of course if the United States entered the war and became an ally we should conduct the war with them in common, and to make of our own initiative and in agreement with them whatever were the best dispositions at any period in the struggle for the final effectual defeat of the enemy. You foresaw this yourself in your first conversation with the President, when you said you were quite sure that we should never send any part of our Fleet across the Atlantic except in the case of an actual war alliance.

Winston S. Churchill to Lord Halifax
(*Premier papers, 3/462/2/3*)

7 August 1940

The position is, I think, quite clear. We have no intention of surrendering the British Fleet, or of sinking it voluntarily. Indeed, such a fate is more likely to overtake the German Fleet – or what is left of it. The nation would not tolerate any discussion of what we should do if our Island were overrun. Such a discussion, perhaps on the eve of an invasion, would be injurious to public morale, now so high. Moreover, we must never get into a position where the United States Government might say: 'We think the time has come for you to send your Fleet across the Atlantic in accordance with your understanding or agreement when we gave you the destroyers.'

We must refuse any declaration such as is suggested, and confine the deal solely to the Colonial leases.

John Colville: diary
(*Colville papers*)

7 August 1940

Winston has gone off to East Anglia to inspect defences, taking with him Randolph and Major Jack Churchill.[1] I am afraid his naturally affectionate nature disposes him towards nepotism. He has given Duncan Sandys an important job at the Cabinet Offices, under Ismay, and a staff job is being arranged for Randolph.[2]

Marion[3] tells me that though the King and Queen appreciate Winston's qualities, and see that he is the man for the occasion, they are a little ruffled by the off-hand way in which he treats them. They much preferred Chamberlain's habit of going to the Palace regularly once a week and explaining the situation in a careful unhurried way. Winston says he will come at 6.00, puts it off by telephone till 6.30 and is inclined to turn up for ten hectic minutes at 7.00. Unfortunately the King, doubtless on the advice of Alec Hardinge, has chosen to oppose Winston on a number of questions, about which it would have been more tactful to remain silent, namely the appointment of Beaverbrook as Minister of Aircraft Production, the gift of a Privy Councillorship to Brendan, and the offer of a peerage to Ironside. But Winston, however cavalierly he may treat his sovereign, is at heart a most vehement Royalist.

---

[1] John Strange Spencer Churchill, 1880–1947. Churchill's younger brother, known as 'Jack'. Educated at Harrow. On active service in South Africa, 1900 (wounded). Major Queen's Own Oxfordshire Hussars, 1914–18. Served at Dunkirk, 1914; on Sir John French's staff, Flanders, 1914–15; on Sir Ian Hamilton's staff at the Dardanelles, 1915; on General Birdwood's staff, France, 1916–18. A stockbroker, he served as a partner with the City firm of Vickers da Costa, 1918–40. In 1931 he was elected to the Other Club; asked once why he so enjoyed his brother's company, Churchill is said to have replied: 'Jack is unborable'.

[2] In printing this extract from his diary forty-five years later, Colville noted: 'This is a libel. He was given a job in the Commandos but had a staff job later, before being parachuted into Yugoslavia.' Churchill always insisted that his son make his own way in the Army.

[3] Marion Hyde, a lady-in-waiting to Queen Elizabeth.

The Dakar Operation
(*Premier papers, 3/276*)

7 August 1940

... the Chiefs of Staff sent a minute to the Prime Minister on the 7th August, pointing out that there were implications of major policy, with which they were not competent to deal. There was a conflict between the policy of improving our relations with the Vichy Government and our interests in encouraging elements in the French Colonies to continue the fight against Germany. To encourage General de Gaulle's movements might lead to war not only with Metropolitan France, but also with the French Colonial Empire. If reports from General de Gaulle's agents on the spot and from our own civil and military representatives in the area were favourable, they recommended that the expedition should go forward.

Chiefs of Staff Committee: minutes
(*Cabinet papers, 79/6*)

7 August 1940　　　　　　　　　　　　　　　　　　10 Downing Street
11 p.m.

In the course of a full discussion there was general agreement that the only place at which a landing by General de Gaulle's force would be really effective was Dakar.

The Prime Minister expressed the view that the expedition should have sufficient backing by British forces to ensure its success, and he asked that a plan for the operation should be prepared as soon as possible.

Winston S. Churchill to General de Gaulle
(*Foreign Office papers, 371/24360*)

7 August 1940　　　　　　　　　　　　　　　　　　10 Downing Street
Secret

Dear General de Gaulle,

In regard to the letters between us, which are to be published, I think it necessary to put on record that the expression 'full restoration of the independence and greatness of France' has no precise relation to territorial frontiers. We have not been able to guarantee such frontiers in respect of any nation now acting with us, but, of course, we shall do our best.

The Article which specifies that your troops will not have to 'take up arms against France' must be interpreted as meaning a France free to choose her course without being under direct or indirect duress from Germany. For instance, a declaration of war by the Government of Vichy against the United Kingdom would not constitute a declaration of war by France, and there may be other cases of the same kind.

Perhaps you will confirm the above.

Yours sincerely,
Winston S. Churchill

Winston S. Churchill to General de Gaulle
(*Foreign Office papers, 371/24360*)

7 August 1940

Dear General de Gaulle,

You were good enough to give me your ideas as to the organisation, employment and conditions of service of the French volunteer force now being assembled under your command, in your capacity, in which you are recognised by His Majesty's Government in the United Kingdom, of leader of all free Frenchmen, wherever they may be, who rally to you in support of the Allied Cause.

I now send you a memorandum which, if you concur, will be agreed between us as governing the organisation, employment and conditions of service of your force.[1]

I would take this opportunity of stating that it is the determination of His Majesty's Government, when victory has been gained by the Allied arms, to secure the full restoration of the independence and greatness of France.

Yours sincerely,
Winston S. Churchill

John Colville: diary
(*Colville papers*)

7 August 1940

The First Lord told me on the telephone about 1.00 a.m. that a troopship[2] had been torpedoed off Ireland. This depressed Winston greatly; however he

[1] The third paragraph of the 'Memorandum of Agreement' read: 'His Majesty's Government will, as soon as practicable, supply the French force with the additional equipment which may be essential to equip its units on a scale equivalent to that of British units of the same type. As for French naval vessels in British ports, 'The French force will commission and operate as many vessels as it is able to man' (*Foreign Office papers, 371/24360*).

[2] This was the 7,500-ton *Mohammed Ali el-Kebir*, torpedoed off the Atlantic coast of Ireland with 732 military and naval personnel on board: 600 were rescued.

recovered when he heard that nearly all the men had been saved and that there were no valuable stores on board, merely remarking that the navy were not being as successful against U-boats as in the past. (We have lost much shipping lately.)[1]

Winston S. Churchill: directive to the Chiefs of Staff
(*Churchill papers, 20/3*)

8 August 1940

1. The telegram from the Governor of Nigeria shows the danger of German influence spreading quickly through the West African colonies of France with the connivance or aid of the Vichy Government. Unless we act with celerity and vigour, we may find effective U-boat bases, supported by German aviation, all down this coast, and it will become barred to us but available for the Germans in the same way as the western coast of Europe.

2. It is now six weeks since the Cabinet was strongly disposed to action at Casablanca, and Mr Duff Cooper and Lord Gort were dispatched. Nothing however came of this. The local French were hostile. The Chiefs of Staff were not able to make any positive proposals, and the situation has markedly deteriorated.

3. It would seem extremely important to British interests that General de Gaulle should take Dakar at the earliest moment. If his emissaries report that it can be taken peaceably so much the better. If their report is adverse an adequate Polish and British force should be provided and full naval protection given. The operation, once begun, must be carried through. De Gaulle should impart a French character to it, and of course, once successful, his administration will rule. But we must provide the needful balance of force.

4. The Chiefs of Staff should make a plan for achieving the capture of Dakar. For this purpose they should consider available: (a) de Gaulle's force and any French warships which can be collected; (b) ample British naval force, both to dominate French warships in the neighbourhood and to cover the landing; (c) a brigade of Poles properly equipped; (d) the Royal Marine Brigade which was being held available for the Atlantic islands, but might well help to put de Gaulle ashore first, or alternatively commandos from Sir Roger Keyes' force; (e) proper air support, either by carrier or by machines working from a British West African colony.

5. Let a plan be prepared forthwith, and let the dates be arranged in relation to the Mediterranean operation.

6. It is not intended, after Dakar is taken, that we shall hold it with British

[1] In the thirty days up to 7 August 1940, fifty-nine British merchant vessels had been sunk.

forces. General de Gaulle's administration would be set up, and would have to maintain itself, British assistance being limited to supplies on a moderate scale, and of course preventing any sea-borne expedition from Germanised France. Should de Gaulle be unable to maintain himself permanently against air attack or air-borne troops, we will take him off again after destroying all harbour facilities. We should of course in any case take over *Richelieu* under the French flag and have her repaired. The Poles and the Belgians would also have their gold, which was moved before the armistice to Africa by the French Government for safety, recovered for them.

7. In working out the above plan, time is vital. We have lost too much already. British ships are to be used as transports whenever convenient, and merely hoist French colours. No question of Orders in Council or legislation to transfer British transports to the French flag need be considered.

8. The risk of a French declaration of war and whether it should be courted is reserved for the Cabinet.[1]

War Cabinet: Confidential Annex
(*Cabinet papers, 65/14*)

8 August 1940　　　　　　　　　　　　　　　　　　　　　　10 Downing Street
11.30 a.m.

The Prime Minister thought that it would be premature to take a decision on the question of assistance to the Dutch in the event of Japanese aggression in the Netherlands East Indies.

The Prime Minister thought the situation could properly be unfolded to the Dominion Governments in the following manner which would inspire them with a much greater degree of confidence.
  (i) Our present policy was to beat the Italians in the Mediterranean for which purpose we required to keep a considerable fleet there.
  (ii) We had been handling our relations with Japan very carefully and hoped to avoid war with her.
  (iii) Nevertheless we might at any moment become involved in war with

---

[1] The War Cabinet's Dakar Operation Historical Narrative (compiled in February 1941) states: 'On receipt of the Prime Minister's directive, the Chiefs of Staff instructed the Joint Planning Sub-Committee to prepare a plan of the proposed operation. This was approved by them on the afternoon of the 9th August and submitted to the Prime Minister with certain comments, the chief of which was that they did not recommend the inclusion of Polish forces. These could not be trained in time; it was politically undesirable to mix the French and Poles, and General de Gaulle did not wish to have them associated with this project. The plan was based on the landing of six different parties at dawn and depended for its success on dispersing the effort of the defences.'

Japan. It did not follow that we must abandon our operations in the Mediterranean immediately Japan declared war. With China on her hands, it was unlikely that Japan's opening moves would be a full scale invasion of Australia and New Zealand.

Attacks on Hong Kong, Singapore and the Netherlands East Indies were more probable.
 (iv) If this appreciation of Japan's opening moves proved correct we should content ourselves with sending one battle cruiser and one aircraft carrier to the Indian Ocean, to be based on Ceylon, for the purpose of protecting our vital communications.
 (v) We assumed that Australia and New Zealand would not ask us to modify our strategy on account of the presence of Japanese raiders on their trade routes, or of small scale Japanese raids taking place on their coasts.
 (vi) If a full scale invasion of either Australia or New Zealand was threatened the situation could be retrieved by the intervention of the United States. Indeed, if the United States had previously made it clear that they would not tolerate the invasion of Australia or New Zealand, the Japanese would never take the plunge.
 (vii) In the last resort, however, our course was clear. We could never stand by and see a British Dominion overwhelmed by a yellow race, and we should at once come to the assistance of that Dominion with all the forces we could make available. For this purpose we should be prepared, if necessary, to abandon our position in the Mediterranean and the Middle East.

An assurance on these lines might form the basis of the telegram to the Dominions.

The Secretary of State for Dominion Affairs said that a declaration of the kind suggested by the Prime Minister would make a tremendous difference to Australia and New Zealand. It would put the whole Far Eastern situation in a different light.

Winston S. Churchill to A. V. Alexander
(*Churchill papers, 20/13*)

8 August 1940

I am impressed by the speed and efficiency with which the emplacement for the 14-inch gun at Dover has been prepared and the gun itself mounted. Will you tell all those who have helped in this achievement how much I appreciate the sterling effort they have made.

WSC

Winston S. Churchill to Admiral Pound
(*Churchill papers, 20/13*)

8 August 1940

Fighter Command tell me that the convoy to-day was very far out. I suppose it was steering from Beachy Head to Portland Bill. But since we are using these convoys as decoys surely they should creep in along the shore a good deal more than they do. Will you let me know about this.

2. I thought we arranged that only one convoy should be run at intervals of four or five days, and that Fighter Command should be all cued up for these occasions. It appears, however, there were no fewer than four convoys working at the same time. Pray let me know about this.

WSC

War Cabinet: minutes
(*Cabinet papers, 65/8*)

9 August 1940　　　　　　　　　　　　　　　　　　　　　10 Downing Street
12.30 p.m.

The Minister for Economic Warfare[1] said that he was satisfied that there would be no famine this winter in the 'enslaved territories' unless the Germans took food away from them to Germany. He was satisfied that the present policy of blockading 'unoccupied' as well as 'occupied' France should be maintained, and that we should take active steps to remove ignorance of the facts, particularly in America. He also favoured a declaration, first, that we were imposing the blockade in order to shorten the war; secondly, that, as soon as any area threw off Hitler's yoke, ample food would be available for it.

The Prime Minister said that we should have to pay regard to United States opinion in this matter. While at present that opinion was satisfactory, we might later find ourselves engaged in a rearguard action. He thought that we should take the following line: First, that there was plenty of food at the present time and that there could be no talk of famine immediately after the harvest. Secondly, that if there should be any talk of food shortage, this was due to the deliberate German policy of 'Guns, not Butter,' and to maldistribution of sources of food by the Germans. The third line of defence should be that, if any food was allowed into, say, unoccupied France, it was almost certain that the Germans would get hold of it. If, nevertheless, opinion in the United States should at some later date be strongly in favour of sending food into, say, unoccupied France, we should ask them to explain what administrative safeguards could be introduced.

[1] Hugh Dalton.

Winston S. Churchill to Alfred Duff Cooper
(*Churchill papers, 20/13*)

9 August 1940

It is important to keep General de Gaulle active in French on the broadcast, and to relay by every possible means our French propaganda to Africa. I am told the Belgians will help from the Congo.

Have we any means of repeating to the West African stations the agreement made between us and de Gaulle?

WSC

Winston S. Churchill: War Cabinet memorandum[1]
(*Churchill papers, 23/4*)

9 August 1940   10 Downing Street

BREVITY
Memorandum by the Prime Minister

To do our work, we all have to read a mass of papers. Nearly all of them are far too long. This wastes time, while energy has to be spent in looking for the essential points.

I ask my colleagues and their staffs to see to it that their Reports are shorter.

(i) The aim should be Reports which set out the main points in a series of short, crisp paragraphs.

(ii) If a Report relies on detailed analysis of some complicated factors, or on statistics, these should be set out in an Appendix.

(iii) Often the occasion is best met by submitting not a full-dress Report, but an *Aide-mémoire* consisting of headings only, which can be expanded orally if needed.

(iv) Let us have an end of such phrases as these: 'It is also of importance to bear in mind the following considerations . . .', or 'Consideration should be given to the possibility of carrying into effect . . .'. Most of these woolly phrases are mere padding, which can be left out altogether, or replaced by a single word. Let us not shrink from using the short expressive phrase, even if it is conversational.

[1] War Cabinet Paper No. 211 of 1940, 'Brevity'.

Reports drawn up on the lines I propose may at first seem rough as compared with the flat surface of officialese jargon. But the saving in time will be great, while the discipline of setting out the real points concisely will prove an aid to clearer thinking.

WSC

Winston S. Churchill to Anthony Eden and General Dill
(*Churchill papers, 20/13*)

9 August 1940

I was much concerned to find that the 1st Division which has an exceptionally high proportion of equipment, and includes a Brigade of Guards, should be dispersed along the beaches, instead of being held in reserve for counter-attack. What is the number of Divisions which are now free and out of the line, and what is the argument for keeping Divisions with a high equipment of guns, &c., on the beaches?[1]

WSC

Winston S. Churchill to Lord Beaverbrook
(*Churchill papers, 20/13*)

9 August 1940

If it came to a choice between hampering Air production or Tank production, I would sacrifice the Tank, but I do not think this is the case as the points of overlap are not numerous and ought to be adjustable. I gathered from you that you thought you could arrange with the Minister of Supply.

Winston S. Churchill to General Ismay
(*Churchill papers, 20/13*)

9 August 1940
ACTION THIS DAY

I am not getting the War Office telegrams as I should, or as I do the Naval telegrams. All the important Naval, Air and Military telegrams should come to the Defence Office immediately. They should be sifted by your Staff, and anything of interest or importance marked to me.

WSC

[1] The 1st Division was then guarding the beaches of Lincolnshire.

Winston S. Churchill to General Ismay
(*Churchill papers, 20/13*)

9 August 1940

Ask for a statement of the Ministry of Supply importation programme under various heads. Professor Lindemann should be consulted about these heads. Let me see them.

The programme for the second year of the war has not yet been presented to me in a coherent form.

WSC

Winston S. Churchill to General Ismay
(*Churchill papers, 20/13*)

9 August 1940

Get me a further report about the designs and types of vessels to transport armoured vehicles by sea and land on beaches.

WSC

John Colville: diary
(*Colville papers*)

9 August 1940   Chequers[1]

Pound suggested that the Germans had made a great mistake in going on, after they had proved the weakness of the French army, to strike a knock-out blow: they should have stopped after crossing the Somme and turned on us. Eden pointed out that the Germans probably thought, as did we, that the French would rally. The PM said that this mistake, if it was one, merely made the Germans slightly less admirable, but one could not detract from the brilliance of their strategy and of their unhesitating advance through Abbeville and Boulogne to Calais – and nearly to Dunkirk. The men of Calais were the bit of grit that saved us by stopping them as Sidney Smith stopped Napoleon at Acre.

[1] The guests at Chequers that weekend included five Generals (Dill, Wavell, Ismay, Gordon-Finlayson and Pownall), Air Marshal Sir Frederick Bowhill, Admiral of the Fleet Sir Dudley Pound, Eden, Lindemann and Ernest Bevin. Colville was the Duty Private Secretary and Colonel Jacob was there from the Defence Office. Two of Churchill's children, Randolph and Mary, were also present.

The conversation turned to home defence, and Winston and Eden both said that the only real worry was the acute shortage of small-arms ammunition. But think where we should have been if the fighting had begun in March and had still been going on in France! Dill said that might be true, but in actual fact people never ran out of small-arms ammunition. Their real requirements always fell below what they estimated. Eden said the new 'Molotov Cocktail' was a vast improvement on the old and the anti-tank mine on the beaches had been shown to be most devastating. In fact the latter had already accounted for too many of our own people: Winston instanced the golfer who recently drove his ball on to the beach; he took his niblick down to the beach, played the ball, and all that remained visible afterwards was the ball which returned safely to the green.

The PM said: 'Fancy, next year we shall have ten armoured divisions!' Eden and Dill dissented, saying that we should not have the equipment. 'Well,' said Winston, 'if you'll produce the men (cries of "Oh, we can do that") I'll see you get the weapons.' Then we should be able to undertake formidable raids on the continent. This autumn we should land small forces of 5,000 men (and all the Generals seemed enthusiastic about this idea of taking the offensive), thus giving valuable experience and training to individual brigades or battalions which would form a core for future operations. We had much open to us: a landing in Holland followed by a destructive raid into the Ruhr; the seizure of the Cherbourg peninsula; and invasion of Italy. Wavell suggested Norway: 'We shall need skis for that,' said Winston, 'and we don't want to go and get Namsosed again.[1] We've had enough of that.'

The PM, turning to Wavell, said that he promised he would not ask him to effect a landing in enemy territory until we could clear the air over the place of disembarkation.

Winston S. Churchill to General Ismay
(*Churchill papers, 20/13*)

10 August 1940

The Prime Minister would be glad to have a report from the COS Committee, after conference with the C-in-C Home Forces,[2] upon the small arms ammunition position on the beaches and with the Reserves.

---

[1] A reference to the British landing at Namsos, in Norway, in April 1940, which had to be abandoned as a result of German air superiority.
[2] General Brooke.

Winston S. Churchill to General Ismay
(*Premier papers, 3/457*)

10 August 1940
10 Downing Street

What arrangements are being made to receive this important United States mission?[1] I should see them almost as soon as they come, and I could give them a dinner at No. 10. Pray let me know in good time.

WSC

Winston S. Churchill to General Ismay
(*Churchill papers, 20/13*)

10 August 1940

Let me have a weekly return of the deliveries to troops of the American 75's and the ·300 rifles to Home Guard, with consequent liberation by them of Lee-Metfords. Begin at once.

WSC

Winston S. Churchill to General Ismay
(*Churchill papers, 20/13*)

10 August 1940

In COS (40) 247, page 4, Sir Alan Brooke is represented as saying: 'Yet the threat of invasion seems just as great on south coast towns as on the east coast.' This is surely contrary to the Admiralty paper signed by the First Sea Lord, which gives, as a maximum invading force that could at the present time be landed on the southern coast, not more than 5,000. Has Commander-in-Chief, Home Forces, been shown this paper?

I am not aware of any concentrations of enemy shipping between Calais and Brest, and it is certain, apart from a score of motor launches, there are no enemy warships for escort. Care should be taken not to disperse troops unduly

---

[1] A high-level military mission, sent by President Roosevelt, and disguised as a technical 'Standardisation of Arms' mission. It was headed by Admiral Robert L. Ghormley (Assistant to the Chief of Naval Operations), Brigadier General George V. Strong (Deputy Chief of the General Staff) and General Delos C. Emmons (Commanding General, General Headquarters, Air Force). It held the first 'Staff Conversations' of the war with senior British service personnel (*Premier papers, 3/457, folio 32*). The mission, too, had a hidden agenda: on its return to Washington, it reported favourably to General Marshall on Britain's chances of continued resistance.

August 1940 641

along the south coast, or to inflict needless hardship upon the inhabitants. General Ismay will place at Commander-in-Chief's, Home Forces, disposal any papers written about invasion during the present alarm before his appointment. In particular the Admiralty appreciation referred to should be made available.

Winston S. Churchill to General Ismay
(*Churchill papers, 20/13*)

10 August 1940
ACTION THIS DAY

Let me have a programme of the Somaliland reinforcements as finally decided, showing dates when each will arrive, &c., at Berbera. Let me also have a statement of the existing strength of the field force available for operations there, including men, Brens, artillery, Air Force, &c.

2. Let me also have a statement, quite short, of the strength in battalions, batteries and Air squadrons, with guns and bayonets, and other important equipment, of all the forces in the Middle East, specifying nationality.

3. Let me have the full scheme of reinforcements in the next three months from all quarters.

WSC

Winston S. Churchill to General Ismay
(*Churchill papers, 20/13*)

10 August 1940

Can anything be done to furnish the C-in-C, Middle East, with some fast reconnaissance machines, also a good machine for him to get about in. It occurred to me that the King's machine would be very suitable, being armed and fast, if, as I understand, HM has decided not to use it.[1]

WSC

---

[1] The King decided to keep his armed Lockheed-Hudson. In November 1940 he offered his De Havilland 'Flamingo', which was unarmed, to the Royal Air Force for normal duties, and this was accepted (*Royal Archives*).

Winston S. Churchill to General Wavell
(*Churchill papers, 20/13*)

10 August 1940

I am very much obliged to you for explaining to me so fully the situation in Egypt and Somaliland. We have yet to discuss the position in Kenya and Abyssinia. I mentioned the very large forces which you have in Kenya, namely, the Union Brigade of 6,000 white South Africans, probably as fine material as exists for warfare in spacious countries: the East African settlers, who should certainly amount to 2,000 men, thoroughly used to the country: the two West African Brigades, brought at much inconvenience from the West Coast, numbering 6,000: at least two Brigades of KAR;[1] the whole at least 20,000 men – there may be more. Why should these all stand idle in Kenya waiting for an Italian invasion to make its way across the very difficult distances from Abyssinia to the South, or preparing themselves for a similar difficult inroad into Abyssinia, which must again entail long delays, while all the time the fate of the Middle East, and much else, may be decided at Alexandria or on the Canal?

Without, of course, knowing the exact conditions locally, I should suppose that a reasonable disposition would be to hold Kenya with the settlers and the KAR, and delay any Italian advance southwards, it being so much easier to bring troops round by sea, than for the Italians to make their way overland. Thus, we can always reinforce them unexpectedly and swiftly. This would allow the Union Brigade and the two West African Brigades to come round at once into the Delta, giving you a most valuable reinforcement in the decisive theatre at the decisive moment. What is the use of having the command of the sea if it is not to pass troops to and fro with great rapidity from one theatre to another? I am sure I could persuade General Smuts to allow this movement of the Union Brigade. Perhaps you will let me have your views on this by tomorrow night, as time is so short.

Winston S. Churchill to Lord Halifax
(*Churchill papers, 20/13*)

10 August 1940
ACTION THIS DAY

While we do not want to keep a lot of discontented French soldiers, &c., in this Island, we ought to market their return as well as possible with the Vichy Government against proper treatment of our nationals and Allies in French territories, particularly Syria. We cannot have a one-sided return of military

[1] The King's African Rifles.

males to France while the kind of treatment described in Syria 78[1] is meted out to us.

2. I do not see why we should try to prevent economic distress developing in Syria. All this idea of 'subjugation without tears' is wrong. Nothing can be worse for us than the smooth and orderly submission of Syria to German or Italian influence. The economic distress is much more likely to make them turn to us, or important elements of them, than to be a help to the Germans. The maxim should be to help and feed our friends, to hinder our foes, and let indifferent or unhelpful neutrals suffer the full consequences of their pusillanimity. Pray consider this.

John Colville: diary
(*Colville papers*)

10 August 1940   Chequers

Later on, at lunch, Winston gave me his own views about war aims and the future. He said there was only one aim, to destroy Hitler. Let those who say they do not know what they are fighting for stop fighting and they will see. France is now discovering what she was fighting for. After the last war people had done much constructive thinking and the League of Nations had been a magnificent idea. Something of the kind would have to be built up again: there would be a United States of Europe, and this Island would be the link connecting this Federation with the new world and able to hold the balance between the two. 'A new conception of the balance of power?' I said. 'No,' he replied, 'the balance of virtue.'

I lunched *en famille* with the PM, Mrs C and Mary, and it could not have been more enjoyable. Winston was in the best of humours. He talked brilliantly on every topic from Ruskin to Lord Baldwin, from the future of Europe to the strength of the Tory Party. When he spoke of our lamentable lack of equipment, of that 'boob' Inskip,[2] etc., he said: 'We shall win, but we

---

[1] A telegram (No. 78) from the British Consul-General in Beirut, Godfrey Havard, on 8 August 1940, reported that the release of interned British sailors had twice been refused. In another telegram that day (No. 77) he reported that the French High Commissioner in Damascus had received instructions from Vichy 'to refuse exit permits from Syria and Lebanon to male subjects of the British Empire, and to Dutch, Belgian, Norwegian, Polish and Czecho-Slovak subjects capable of bearing arms, e.g. between the ages of 20 and 48' (*Foreign Office papers, 371/24593*).

[2] Viscount Caldecote, pre-war Minister for Co-ordination of Defence, and Secretary of State for Dominion Affairs from May to October 1940.

don't deserve it; at least, we do deserve it because of our virtues, but not because of our intelligence.' He said that the Tory Party was the strength of the country: few things need to be changed quickly and drastically; what conservatism, as envisaged by Disraeli, stood for was the gradual increase of amenities for an ever larger number of people, who should enjoy the benefits previously reserved for a very few (i.e. a levelling upwards, not a levelling downwards). The future depended not on the political system, but, once every man had sufficient, on the inner heart and soul of the individual.

At dinner I sat between Mary and Jacob and, when not discussing bloodsports with the former, listened to Winston. He mentioned the numerous projects, inventions, etc., which he had in view and compared himself to a farmer driving pigs along a road, who always had to be prodding them on and preventing them from straying. He praised the splendid *sang-froid* and morale of the people, and said he could not quite see why he appeared to be so popular. After all since he came into power, everything had gone wrong and he had had nothing but disasters to announce. His platform was only 'blood, sweat and tears'.

He sent Prof and me for some of his cherished graphs and diagrams and began to expound the supply position. Beaverbrook, he said, had genius and, what was more, brutal ruthlessness. He had never in his life, at the Ministry of Munitions or anywhere else, seen such startling results as Beaverbrook had produced; and Pownall, looking at the Aircraft Production charts, agreed that there had never been such an achievement. W regretted that the Ministry of Supply had shown themselves incapable of producing similar results for the army.

He proceeded to examine the statistics, calling on Prof for frequent explanations, and declaring that we were already overhauling the Germans in numbers (our production already exceeds theirs by one third). It was generally agreed that Hitler's aircraft position must be less good than we had supposed; otherwise why the delay, why the sparsity of attack?

After dinner (i.e. about 11.15!) we walked up and down beneath the stars, a habit which Winston has formed. When he came in I showed him a letter from Nelson to Lord Spencer (First Lord of the Admiralty), written a week after the Battle of the Nile, which I had found in one of the rooms. It began: 'My Lord, was I to die at this moment want of frigates would be found stamped on my heart. No words of mine can express what I have and am suffering for want of them . . .' I suggested to W that he might so begin a 'Former Naval Person' telegram to Roosevelt, substituting 'destroyers' for 'frigates'. He answered that we were certainly going to get the destroyers from America. But it is curious how history repeats itself even in small details.

August 1940

Colonel Jacob: recollection
('*Action This Day*', page 180)

10 August 1940   Chequers

Another characteristic that was of great importance to him was his capacity to sleep at once and at any time. He went straight to bed, and straight to sleep. This was well illustrated during my first visit to Chequers in 1940. The principal guest was General Gordon-Finlayson,[1] who had recently returned from commanding the British troops in Egypt, and who had been invited to Chequers to expound to the Prime Minister the problems of the Western Desert and the defence of Egypt. After the film there was an interesting discussion of all this, and, when at 2.30 a.m. the Prime Minister decided to go to bed, he asked General Gordon-Finlayson to put his views down on paper. We walked upstairs and dispersed. Almost immediately the General sought me out and asked whether I had a map of the Western Desert, as he couldn't write what he wanted to do without one. I said I hadn't, but that I would get the War Office to send one down first thing in the morning. I then groped my way downstairs again to the Private Secretaries' room to telephone to the War Office. There were a good many telephones there, and it was rather dark. Eventually I picked one up and unfortunately pressed the central knob. Almost at once a voice said, 'What is that? Is there any news?' I realised that it was the Prime Minister and apologised. He said, 'Well, please don't do it again, I was just dropping off.' It cannot have been more than five minutes after we had separated downstairs.

Winston S. Churchill to Robert Menzies and Peter Fraser
(*Premier papers, 4/43B/1*)

11 August 1940   10 Downing Street
Personal and Secret

The combined Staffs are preparing a paper on the Pacific situation, but I venture to send you in advance a brief foreword. We are trying our best to avoid war with Japan, both by conceding on points where the Japanese military clique can perhaps force a rupture, and by standing up where the ground is less dangerous, as in arrests of individuals. I do not think myself that Japan will declare war unless Germany can make a successful invasion of

---

[1] Robert Gordon-Finlayson, 1881–1956. Entered the Army, 1900. On active service, 1914–18 (despatches eight times, DSO). Served in North Russia, 1919. General, 1937. Knighted, 1937. Commander-in-Chief, British Troops in Egypt, 1938–9. Adjutant-General of the Forces, 1939–40. General Officer Commanding-in-Chief, Western Command, 1940–1. Retired, 1941. Special Commissioner, Imperial War Graves Commission, 1942.

Britain. Once Japan sees that Germany has either failed, or dares not try, I look for easier times in the Pacific. In adopting against the grain a yielding policy towards Japanese threats, we have always in mind your interests and safety.

Should Japan nevertheless declare war on us, her first objective outside the Yellow Sea would probably be the Dutch East Indies. Evidently the United States would not like this. What they would do we cannot tell. They give no undertaking of support, but their main Fleet in the Pacific must be a grave preoccupation to Japanese Admiralty. In this first phase of an Anglo-Japanese war, we should of course defend Singapore, which if attacked, which is unlikely, ought to stand a long siege. We should also be able to base on Ceylon a battle-cruiser and a fast aircraft-carrier, which, with the Australian and New Zealand ships which would return to you would exercise a very powerful deterrent upon hostile raiding cruisers.

We are about to reinforce with more first-class units the Eastern Mediterranean Fleet. This Fleet could of course at any time be sent through the Canal into the Indian Ocean or to relieve Singapore. We do not want to do this, even if Japan declares war, until it is found to be vital to your safety. Such a transference would entail the complete loss of the Middle East, and all prospect of beating Italy in the Mediterranean would be gone. We must expect heavy attacks on Egypt in the near future, and the Eastern Mediterranean Fleet is needed to help in repelling them. If these attacks succeed, the Eastern Fleet would have to leave the Mediterranean either through the Canal or by Gibraltar. In either case a large part of it would be available for your protection. We hope however to maintain ourselves in Egypt, and to keep the Eastern Fleet at Alexandria during the first phase of an Anglo-Japanese war, should that occur. No one can lay down beforehand what is going to happen. We must just weigh events from day to day, and use our available resources to the utmost.

A final question arises, whether Japan having declared war would attempt to invade Australia or New Zealand with a considerable army. We think this very unlikely, because Japan is first absorbed in China, secondly would be gathering rich prizes in the Dutch East Indies, and thirdly would fear very much to send an important part of her fleet far to the southward leaving the American fleet between it and home. If however contrary to prudence and self-interest, Japan set about invading Australia or New Zealand on a large scale, I have the explicit authority of the Cabinet to assure you that we should then cut our losses in the Mediterranean and proceed to your aid, sacrificing every interest except only the defence and feeding of this Island on which all depends.

We hope however that events will take a different turn. By gaining time with Japan, the present dangerous situation may be got over. We are vastly stronger here at home than when I cabled to you on June 16.[1] We have a large Army now beginning to be well-equipped. We have fortified our beaches. We have a strong reserve of mobile troops including our Regular Army and Australian, New Zealand and Canadian contingents, with several armoured Divisions or Brigades ready to strike in counter-attack at the head of any successful lodgments. We have ferried over from the United States their grand aid of nearly a thousand guns and 600,000 rifles with ammunition complete. Relieved of the burden of defending France, our Army is becoming daily more powerful and munitions are gathering. Besides this we have the Home Guard of 1,500,000 men, many of them war veterans, and most with rifles or other arms.

The Royal Air Force continues to show the same individual superiority over the enemy on which I counted so much in my aforesaid cable to you. Yesterday's important air action in the Channel showed that we could attack against odds of 3 to 1, and inflict losses of $3\frac{1}{2}$ to 1. Astounding progress has been made by Lord Beaverbrook in output of the best machines. Our Fighter and Bomber strength is nearly double what it was when I cabled you, and we have a very large reserve of machines in hand. I do not think the German Air Force has the numbers or quality to overpower our Air defences.

The Navy increases in strength each month, and we are now beginning to receive the immense programme started at the declaration of war. Between June and December 1940, over 500 vessels, large and small, but many most important, will join the Fleet. The German Navy is weaker than it has ever been. *Scharnhorst* and *Gneisenau* are both in dock damaged. *Bismarck* has not yet done her trials, *Tirpitz* is three months behind *Bismarck*. There are available now in this critical fortnight, after which the time for invasion is getting very late, only one pocket-battleship, a couple of 8-inch Hippers, two light cruisers, and perhaps a score of destroyers. To try to transport a large army, as would now be needed for success, across the seas virtually without Naval escort in the face of our Navy and Air force, only to meet our powerful military force on shore, still less to maintain such an army and nourish its lodgments with munitions and supplies, would be a very unreasonable act. On the other hand, if Hitler fails to invade and conquer Britain before the weather breaks, he has received his first and probably his fatal check.

We therefore feel a sober and growing conviction of our power to defend ourselves and the Empire successfully, and to persevere through the year or two that may be necessary to gain victory.

---

[1] Dictated on 15 June 1940, and sent on the following day (published as the penultimate document for 15 June 1940).

Winston S. Churchill to David Grenfell
(*Churchill papers, 20/13*)

11 August 1940

I felt sure you would take advantage of the breakdown of the export market to increase our stocks all over the country. I hope you will press on with this, especially as regards our essential gas, water, and electricity works. I note that the gas and electricity supplies are about 20 per cent up. We cannot go wrong in piling up such well-distributed stocks, which are sure to be used sooner or later.

I am sending a note to the Minister of Transport[1] to call his attention to the position of the railways.

The tremendous upset in your plans due to the collapse of France and the loss of three-quarters of our export markets must have put a great strain on your department. It must be very difficult after all your efforts to increase production to explain the sudden slump, but I have no doubt the men will understand. Indeed, what you tell me about the fortitude of the Kent miners is an encouraging sign of the spirit which I believe informs all the working men in the country.

Winston S. Churchill to Sir John Reith
(*Churchill papers, 20/13*)

11 August 1940
ACTION THIS DAY

I should be grateful for a full report on the steps taken by your Department to deal with the difficulties which may arise from the bombing and closing of ports.

One-quarter of our imports, it seems, normally comes in through the Port of London and one-fifth through the Mersey, with a tenth each through Southampton, the Bristol Channel and the Humber. We must envisage these entrances being wholly or partially closed, either one at a time or even several at a time, but I have no doubt you have worked out plans to take account of the various contingencies.

In view of our large accretions of shipping it may well be that port facilities and railway facilities may be a more stringent bottleneck than shortage of tonnage, so that the preparations you make to meet the various possible eventualities may well be of the greatest importance.

---

[1] Sir John Reith.

Winston S. Churchill to Anthony Eden
(*Churchill papers, 20/13*)

11 August 1940

I am sorry you have had to break up medium and heavy artillery regiments of the Field Army for the purpose of Coast Defence. I gather, however, that these were Regiments for which you had no guns, and who were being employed on infantry duty.

The First Lord apparently complains that Army gunners are being sent to the South and West coasts before the Batteries are ready for them. You do not seem, in your minute, to deal with this point. Would it not be well if you and the First Lord discussed the matter together? I have directed that a low priority should be given to the West coast defences. General Finlayson, Commanding the Western Area, expressed surprise to me at being asked to fortify a number of small ports in this area. I am asking for a review of the West coast position, and will call a Defence Committee meeting for the purpose.

Winston S. Churchill to General Ismay
(*Churchill papers, 20/13*)

11 August 1940

I cannot accept this proposal, which deprives us of invaluable resources (50 Infantry Tanks) during a most critical period, without making them available for the Middle East at the moment when they are most needed there. I must ask the Admiralty to make further proposals, and overcome the difficulties. If necessary, could not the personnel be distributed among the destroyers, a larger force of destroyers being sent through from Force H to the Eastern Mediterranean, and returned thereafter in the same way as the six destroyers are now being sent westward by Admiral Cunningham.

There is no objection to the 3rd Hussars going by the Cape, as General Wavell can make temporary arrangements for manning them in the meanwhile, so long as he gets their Light tanks. I am prepared to risk the 50 Infantry Tanks in the Mediterranean, provided their personnel is distributed among HM ships; but there can be no question of them or their personnel going by the Cape, thus making sure they are out of everything for two months. The personnel sent through the Mediterranean must be cut down to essentials; the balance going round.

Pray let me have further proposals by to-morrow (Monday).

Winston S. Churchill to Alfred Duff Cooper
(*Churchill papers, 20/13*)

11 August 1940

In view of certain activities we are planning for General de Gaulle, it is of the highest importance that the broadcasting of French news in North and West Africa should be carried to the highest point. Please make sure that the BBC conform to this requirement, and let me have a report on Monday to the effect that all is satisfactorily arranged.

I cannot emphasize too strongly that you have full authority to make the BBC obey.

Winston S. Churchill to General Ismay and Sir Edward Bridges
(*Churchill papers, 20/13*)

11 August 1940

The plan 'Scipio' as originally conceived, namely, of de Gaulle getting at it by peaceable means from behind, is the sole plan which is to be imparted to any others but the War Cabinet and the Service Ministers and Chiefs. Knowledge of later developments[1] is to be confined exclusively to the above, neither Minister of Information, nor Dominions Secretary nor Home Secretary being burdened with it.

John Colville: diary
(*Colville papers*)

11 August 1940   Chequers

Jacob thinks the PM should invite people from the War Office and Admiralty, as well as the Generals, down here so that they might realise how forceful and competent a person he is. At present the departments are driven to exasperation by the flow of enquiries, demands and commitments which reach them every morning from No. 10 and from Ismay's staff (now to be known as the Office of the Minister of Defence).

---

[1] On 9 August 1940 the original Operation 'Scipio', a landing at Dakar by troops loyal to de Gaulle, who, it had originally been expected, would be unopposed, was changed to Operation 'Menace', involving British naval and military units and commanders (the latter chosen on 10 August). It thereupon became an authorised British operation of war. The Cabinet Ministers who were not to be told of this change were Duff Cooper, Lord Caldecote and Sir John Anderson.

Air Marshal Bowhill[1] (C in C, Coastal Command) came to lunch, also the Randolph Churchills. The chief excitement was another big aerial engagement and I kept on having to ring up Fighter Command to discover 'the latest score'. W was very excited and kept on saying that 'the swine had needed three days in which to lick their wounds' before they came again and that their air superiority was clearly less than we had feared.

After tea I accompanied the PM to a rifle range nearby, where he fired with his Mannlicher rifle at targets 100, 200 and 300 yards away. He also fired his revolver, still smoking a cigar, with commendable accuracy. Despite his age, size and lack of practice, he acquitted himself well. The whole time he talked of the best method of killing Huns. Soft-nose bullets were the thing to use and he must get some. But, said Randolph, they are illegal in war; to which the PM replied that the Germans would make very short work of him if they caught him, and so he didn't see why he should have any mercy on them. He always seems to visualise the possibility of having to defend himself against German troops!

The PM asked me to come and talk to him while he was undressing and was most genial. He said Bevin was a good old thing and had 'the right stuff in him' – no defeatist tendencies. He expatiated on the debt we owed to our airmen and claimed that the life of the country depended on their intrepid spirit. What a slender thread, he exclaimed, his voice tremulous with emotion, the greatest of things can hang by! He has cause to be elated: today our fighters accounted for about seventy German planes over the Channel.

Winston S. Churchill to Herbert Morrison
(Premier papers, 3/359)

12 August 1940

The drafts submitted do not correspond with my view of the recent Cabinet decision. We do not contemplate or encourage fighting by persons not in the armed forces, but we do not forbid it. The police, and as soon as possible, the ARP services, are to be divided into combatant and non-combatant, armed and unarmed; the armed will co-operate actively in fighting with the Home

---

[1] Frederick William Bowhill, 1880–1960. An officer in the Merchant Navy, 1896–1912. Began flying in 1912. Lieutenant, Royal Navy, 1913; Royal Flying Corps (Naval Wing), 1917. On active service, 1914–18 (despatches six times; DSO and bar). Air Member for Personnel, Air Council, 1933–7. Knighted, 1936. Air Officer Commanding-in-Chief, Coastal Command, 1937–41. Commanded Ferry Command, 1941–3; Transport Command, 1943–5. Chief Aeronautical Adviser to the Ministry of Civil Aviaton, 1946–57.

Guard and Regulars in their neighbourhood, and will withdraw with them if necessary; the unarmed will actively assist in the 'stay put' policy for civilians. Should they fall into an area effectively occupied by the enemy, they may surrender and submit with the rest of the inhabitants, but must not in those circumstances give any aid to the enemy in maintaining order, or in any other way. They may, however, assist the civil population as far as possible.

Winston S. Churchill to Lord Simon
(*Churchill papers, 20/2*)

12 August 1940

My dear Chancellor,

I should be grateful if you would agree to place the services of Mr Justice Singleton[1] at the disposal of the Government for a short but important inquiry in connexion with the production of stabilized bombsights.

The stabilized bombsight has great advantages over the type now in service. A meeting was held on the 22nd December last at which it was decided to push forward the development of these improved bombsights as a matter of urgency. In spite of this decision none have yet been delivered to the operational squadrons.

I am very anxious to track down responsibility for this default. The matter is complicated, not merely on account of the difficult issues at stake and the complexity of the departmental organization, but also as a result of the separation of the Ministry of Aircraft Production from the Air Ministry.

I am also anxious that the findings should have the highest possible authority.

I trust therefore that you will be prepared to assist me by releasing Mr Justice Singleton for this purpose. I feel confident that he will probe the matter as I should wish.

The work would not take long nor the Judge's whole time.

Yours sincerely
Winston S. Churchill

---

[1] John Edward Singleton, 1885–1957. Called to the Bar, 1906. On active service, 1914–18; Captain, Royal Field Artillery. KC, 1922. Conservative MP, 1922–3. Recorder of Preston, 1928–34. Knighted, 1934. A Judge of the King's Bench Division, 1934–48. Headed two wartime enquiries, the first on bombsights, the second on German Air Force strength. Privy Councillor, 1949. A Lord Justice of Appeal from 1948 until his death.

Winston S. Churchill to Clement Attlee and David Margesson
(*Churchill papers, 9/173*)[1]

12 August 1940

It would probably be convenient for me to make a general statement on the war, covering the first year and also the first quarter of the new Government, before the House rises. This would be expected, and I suppose Tuesday the 20th would be the best day. This should of course be in Public Session. Perhaps you will let me know what you wish. An announcement could be made in good time this week.

It would save me a lot of trouble if a record could be taken at the time, so that the speech could be repeated over the wireless in the evening, or such parts of it as are of general interest. Can this be arranged without a Resolution? If not, could a Resolution be passed this week? I do not think the House would object.

Defence Committee: minutes
(*Cabinet papers, 70/1*)

12 August 1940　　　　　　　　　　　　　　　　　　　10 Downing Street
7 p.m.

THE UP WEAPON

The Prime Minister said that, as it was clearly impossible to produce the very large figures of heavy anti-aircraft guns which the Chiefs of Staff required, there was all the more reason for pressing on with the development and production of the UP weapon as a means of engaging high-flying as well as low-flying aircraft. He enquired what the present position was.

The Prime Minister said that every effort should be made to increase production of solventless cordite in the immediate future.

The Prime Minister said that it was essential that time and energy should not be wasted on trying to achieve perfection. If practical results could be achieved without a predictor or with some very simple instrument, then it would be better to devote to something else the man power and manufacturing capacity which would otherwise be spent on elaborate instruments.

---

[1] This minute was the first to be stamped by Churchill's Private Office 'Prime Minister's Personal Minute' and given a serial number, in this case, M1. The minute to Sir John Reith on the previous day was then given the number M0. Subsequent minutes, and later telegrams (T), were to be numbered consecutively. With General Ismay's staff being designated the Office of the Minister of Defence, Defence Office minutes were given the prefix 'D'. Professor Lindemann's Statistical Office minutes were given the prefix 'S'.

LIGHT ANTI-AIRCRAFT GUNS

Mr Morrison drew attention to the fact that in the case of the light gun there had also been a progressive stepping up of demands. Production was, however, continually increasing and he was confident that the forecast for 1940 would be well exceeded.

The Prime Minister summing up the discussion said that it was of great importance that anti-aircraft weapons should be produced in large numbers. There were limits to the production of guns, but the UP weapon which was an altogether simpler job and which in some respects had advantages over the gun, could supply the deficiency.

The Chiefs of Staff's proposal would have to be modified and it would be necessary for the whole programme of production of anti-aircraft weapons to be reviewed and demands co-related to the possibility of supply. A small committee representative of all the interests involved should be set up and should report the following week.

Winston S. Churchill to General Wavell and General Ismay
(*Churchill papers, 20/13*)

12 August 1940

1. I am not at all satisfied about the Union Brigade and the West African Brigade in Kenya. These forces as now disposed would play no part in the critical attacks now being developed against Egypt, Khartoum and Somaliland. It is always considered a capital blemish on military operations that large bodies of troops should be standing idle while decisions are reached elsewhere. Without further information, I cannot accept the statement that the South African Brigade is so far untrained that it cannot go into action. The Natal Carbineers were far further advanced in training before the war than our British Territorials, and they have presumably been embodied since the declaration. I cannot see why the Union Brigade as a whole should be considered in any way inferior to British Territorial units. Anyhow, they are certainly good enough to fight Italians. I have asked for full particulars of their embodiment and training in each case.

2. I do not consider that proper use is being made of the large forces in Palestine. The essence of this situation depends on arming the Jewish Colonists sufficiently to enable them to undertake their own defence, so that if necessary for a short time the whole of Palestine can be left to very small

British forces. A proposal should be made to liberate immediately a large portion of the garrison, including the Yeomanry Cavalry Division. I do not understand why the Australians and New Zealanders who have been training in Palestine for at least six months, should only be able to provide a Brigade for service in Egypt. How many of them are there, and what are the facts of their training? These men were brought at great expense from Australia, having been selected as the first volunteers for service in Europe. Many of them had previous military training, and have done nearly a year's training since the war broke out. How disgraceful it would be if owing to our mishandling of this important force, only one Brigade took part in the decisive operations for the defence of Egypt!

3. The two West African Brigades could certainly be brought to Khartoum via Port Sudan. It is a very good policy to mix Native Units from various sources, so that one lot can be used to keep the other in discipline. These two Brigades ought to be moved immediately to the Sudan, so that the Indian Division can be used in Egypt or Somaliland as soon as it arrives. I do not know why these Brigades were taken away from West Africa, if the only use to be made of them was to be a garrison of Kenya.

4. Let me have a return of the white settlers of military age in Kenya. Are we to believe they have not made any local Units for the defence of their own Province? If not, the sooner they are made to realise their position, the better. No troops ought to be in Kenya at the present time other than the settlers and the KAR. Considering the risks and trouble we are taking to reinforce Egypt from home, it cannot be accepted that forces on the spot should not be used to the highest capacity at the critical moment.

5. Let me have a full account of the two British Divisions in the Delta. It is misleading to think in Divisions in this area, nor can any plea that they are not properly equipped in every detail be allowed to prejudice the employment of these fine Regular troops.

6. Surely the statement that the enemy's armoured forces and vehicles can move just as easily along the desert as along the coastal road, requires further examination. This might apply to caterpillar vehicles, but these would suffer severely if forced to make long journeys over the rocky and soft deserts. Anyhow, wheeled transports would be hampered in the desert unless provided with desert-expanded indiarubber tyres of a special type. Are the Indian vehicles so fitted, and to what extent?

7. What arrangements have been made to 'depotibilize' for long periods any wells or water supplies we do not require for ourselves? Has a store of delay-action fuzes for mines in roadways, which are to be abandoned, been provided? Make sure that a supply of the longest delay-action fuzes, i.e., up to at least a fortnight (but I hope they run longer now) are sent to Egypt by the first ship to go through. Examine whether it is not possible to destroy the

asphalt of the tarmac road, as it is abandoned, by chemical action of heavy petroleum oil, or some other treatment.

8. Let me have a statement in full and exact detail of all Units in the Middle East, including Polish and French volunteers and arrivals.

I should be glad to discuss all these points to-night.

WSC

Defence Committee: minutes
(*Cabinet papers, 69/1*)

12 August 1940
10 p.m.

10 Downing Street

The Prime Minister said that, in the light of recent experiences of convoys passing between Malta and Egypt, the Admiralty appeared to be taking an unduly pessimistic view of the risks involved. In his opinion it should be possible to pass a convoy of three fast ships through to Egypt without great difficulty. The presence of these ships with the Fleet should act as 'bait' and should draw down upon them concentrations of Italian Naval Units, thereby affording the desired opportunity to inflict serious damage upon the Italian Navy. Nevertheless he felt bound to accept the opinion of the Naval Staff although he was not in agreement with it.

Hugh Dalton: diary
(*'The Second World War Diary of Hugh Dalton'*)

12 August 1940

Ministers meet at No. 10. PM says that he is feeling much more confident than two months ago. Our defences in this island have been immensely improved. The equipment is still short of what we should like, but is rapidly increasing. Our convoys in the Channel which the Nazis have been attacking have been decoys. We have deliberately invited these attacks and had our fighter aircraft suitably disposed to meet them. The convoys have consisted of small vessels only, all manned by naval ratings. We must speak and act on the basis of another year of war anyhow. Meanwhile, discussions of what is to happen afterwards are premature.

Anthony Eden: diary
(*Avon papers*)

12 August 1940

A very long and exhausting sitting with Winston beginning at 10 p.m. and finishing at 2 a.m. or later. First argument with Admiralty about armoured troops going through Mediterranean. Then long discussion about Wavell's dispositions. PM most anxious to move this battalion here and that battalion there. At the end he took me into the garden and we continued argument. He said we must concentrate on Egypt, move everything there, never mind about Kenya. Cairo was vital (incidentally, a very short time ago he maintained to Dill & I that Egypt didn't matter, only Sudan did). I replied that this did not square with urge to send troops, & material, to Somaliland.

Winston S. Churchill to Anthony Eden
(*Churchill papers, 20/2*)

13 August 1940
Secret and Personal

My dear Anthony,

I shall have to consult further with the Admiralty before reaching a conclusion upon the armoured reinforcement.

Upon the other matters we discussed last night, I have a clear view. I am favourably impressed with General Wavell in many ways, but I do not feel in him that sense of mental vigour and resolve to overcome obstacles, which is indispensable to successful war. I find instead, tame acceptance of a variety of local circumstances in different theatres, which is leading to a lamentable lack of concentration upon the decisive point.

I had a long talk with General Finlayson at the week-end and found him deeply informed upon the defence of Egypt. I have asked him for a paper, which I believe has just arrived.

I may want to see him to-morrow in order that we may have a fuller discussion of the problem. For this purpose I have cancelled my journey to the North.

The following changes in the Middle East dispositions must be considered as urgently needing settlement:–

1. The movement of the two West African Brigades to the Sudan.
2. The movement of the Union Brigade to the Canal Zone and Alexandria.
3. The release for the Field Army of the seven Regular Battalions there employed.
4. The movement into the Delta from Palestine of the six Regular

Battalions; of all the Australians who can be organized either for field or internal purposes; and of at least half of the Regular Cavalry Regiments. By this means only shall we provide in time the numbers which are necessary to meet the impending Italian attack. Even these may well be insufficient. Pray do not forget that the loss of Alexandria means the end of British sea power in the Eastern Mediterranean, with all its consequences.

I shall be very glad to see you and the CIGS at six.

Yours very sincerely,
Winston S. Churchill

Defence Committee: minutes
(*Cabinet papers, 69/1*)

13 August 1940 Upper War Room
10 a.m. Admiralty

The Prime Minister said he was very disturbed to read in paragraph 8 of the Memorandum the statement that it would be necessary to impose a temporary limitation on our operational strength during the autumn and winter.

The whole history of the expansion of the Royal Air Force had shown that a proper use of the aircraft available had not been made to expand the number of squadrons. We had not yet reached the figure of 125 which had been promised many months previously, and now it appeared there was to be a further check.

The Prime Minister said that in the past it had always been said that more aircraft were required in a squadron than there were pilots and that further reserves of aircraft should be held behind. Now, however, it appeared that more pilots were required than aircraft and there was a shortage of pilots. If this were so, why could not the aircraft which were now surplus be used to increase the output from operational training units?

The Prime Minister inquired what was the monthly wastage of pilots.

Air Marshal Garrod[1] said that the figure taken for planning was 746 per

---

[1] Alfred Guy Roland Garrod, 1891–1965. University College, Oxford, 1911–13. On active service, 1914–18, Infantry, August 1914; Royal Flying Corps, 1915 (Military Cross, Distinguished Flying Cross). Director of Equipment, Air Ministry, 1938–40. Air Vice-Marshal, 1939. Air Member for Training on the Air Council, 1940–3. Knighted, 1943. Deputy Allied Air Commander-in-Chief, South-East Asia, 1943–5. Air Marshal, 1945. Commander-in-Chief, Royal Air Force, Mediterranean and Middle East, 1945. Head of the RAF Delegation, Washington, 1946–8. Member, Advisory Panel, Official Histories of the War, 1949.

month. This was a figure which was constantly examined, as it determined the rate at which expansion of squadrons might be planned.

In further discussion it was pointed out that the wastage in July had been about 550 and that it seemed that the wastage rate assumed for planning purposes was too high.

The Prime Minister said he would like to see figures to show the expansion of operational squadrons which might be made in the next six months, taking as a basis first the assumed wastage rate and secondly the actual wastage rate for July as an average.

METHOD OF EXPANSION

The Prime Minister said he would like to examine further the method which might be employed for expanding operational strength. Recently, in the case of Fighter Command, it had been done by adding aircraft to the establishment of each squadron rather than by forming new squadrons. It might be better to keep the squadrons small and to use them to relieve each other. He was not sure which method was the best. He would like to hear further arguments.

The Prime Minister said he would like to know the full figures of aerodromes in this country, including those in use for various purposes, those which would be used for units about to be formed, those which would become available during the winter.

War Cabinet: Confidential Annex
(*Cabinet papers, 65/14*)

13 August 1940
12 noon
10 Downing Street

OPERATION 'MENACE'[1]

The Prime Minister said that the plans in regard to General de Gaulle's movements had now been changed. The original plan had been that General de Gaulle should land either at Duala, or at Freetown or Konakry, and from there should make his way inland by the railway and approach Dakar from the land side. This, however, would take a very long time to accomplish. Opinion had come round to the view that it was essential to take quicker

---

[1] On being enlarged, Operation 'Scipio', the landing at Dakar, was given the code name 'Menace'.

action. It would be an immense advantage to get General de Gaulle firmly installed on French territory.

The question had been discussed at length with the Chiefs of Staff, and agreement had been reached on a drastic change of plan. It was now proposed to establish General de Gaulle at Dakar by a *coup de main*.

This plan was based on the fact that there were only 2,500 Senegalese troops in Dakar. There were perhaps 200 French Officers. He proposed to put in two Brigades of well-trained troops (the 101st and 102nd Royal Marine Brigades) assisted by two independent Companies. A plan had been made, and it had been put to General de Gaulle by the Chiefs of Staff. General de Gaulle had said that the plan was a good one and that he agreed with it: but he had stipulated that some of the Foreign Legion should accompany each of the landing parties. Every endeavour would be made to secure the place without bloodshed, on the plea that an Allied force had come to prevent the Germans seizing Dakar, and to bring succour and help to the Colony. Aircraft would fly over and drop suitable messages promising food and freedom.

Before leaving, General de Gaulle would make a series of gramophone records which could be broadcast, disguising the fact that he had left this country. The forces which we sent would be sufficient to overcome the garrison if it came to a fight. The whole operation must be completed between dawn and dusk. General Irwin[1] would command the land forces, and Admiral John Cunningham the Fleet. Once General de Gaulle's forces had been successfully installed, our forces would withdraw.

What action would the Vichy Government take? It might be that they would declare war. It would not perhaps matter very much if they did: but, on the whole, it was unlikely that they would do so. General de Gaulle said that no doubt the Germans could make the Vichy Government declare war. But this would involve giving France a greater degree of coherence than the Germans wished. Their intention was to break up France.

Subject to the approval of the War Cabinet, the scheme – all preparations for which were going forward – would take place.

The Lord Privy Seal[2] said that he liked the scheme, but what would be the next step? If we could get Dakar, should we not then send the Expedition on and try to get control of the Cameroons?

---

[1] Noel Mackintosh Stuart Irwin, 1892–1972. Graduated from Sandhurst, 1912. On active service, 1914–18 (DSO and two bars, MC, despatches five times). Chief Instructor, Sandhurst, 1933–5. Major-General, 1940. CB, 1940. Commanding in France, West Africa, India, and Burma, 1940–5. Retired with the rank of Lieutenant-General, 1948.

[2] Clement Attlee.

The Prime Minister thought that this might be the next step: or that General de Gaulle might hope to get a footing in Algiers.

The Prime Minister added that the Germans were reported to have sent a flying-boat to Dakar. This had upset the United States a good deal, who thought it might be a jumping-off place for an attack on the Western Hemisphere.

THE MIDDLE EAST

The Prime Minister gave his colleagues an account of his discussions with General Wavell. Now that we were so much stronger, he thought that we could spare an armoured brigade from this country. He had asked the First Sea Lord if he could pass two armoured regiments (i.e. a light tank battalion and a cruiser tank battalion) through the Mediterranean on two fast motor transport ships, in conjunction with Operation 'Hats'.[1]

The Prime Minister said that later he had thought it would be a pity not to send a third armoured regiment of infantry tanks. He had asked the Chiefs of Staff to look into the matter, but they had thought that it was too risky to send MT ships through the Mediterranean, and proposed that the force should go round the Cape. He was now trying to persuade them to change their view on this matter.

The Prime Minister said that he had taken a great liking to General Wavell. In Somaliland we should stay on and fight it out, and a Brigade was being sent there as reinforcement.

In Kenya we had six Battalions of KAR, six Battalions from West Africa and a Brigade from the Union. These forces were not all required in Kenya at the present time, as no active operations could be started from Kenya into Abyssinia for some months. He thought that we should move a West African Brigade to Khartoum. He would also like to see the South African troops moved up to the Canal zone. The essential point was to make Egypt secure, and, if need be, we could run a risk in Kenya.

In Palestine we had six Regular Infantry Battalions, eleven Yeomanry or Cavalry Regiments, and 13,000 Australian troops. It was true that two Brigades of this force were earmarked as a reinforcement for Egypt, but he thought that a large force could be made available from Palestine for service in Egypt. At the present time we had four Regular Battalions at Mersa Matruh, and seven Battalions on the Canal and for internal security. The Union troops, if sent to the Canal, could relieve these seven Battalions for service on the Western frontier.

Generally, the Prime Minister thought that on the present lay-out we might find ourselves in serious difficulties in the Middle East. In the meanwhile,

[1] The operation to send ships in convoy through the Mediterranean, from Gibraltar, to Malta and Alexandria.

steps were being taken to accelerate the move of an Indian Division to Egypt, while further artillery was being sent to Somaliland, together with the Bikanir Camel Corps.

The Prime Minister gave details of the anti-tank guns and anti-aircraft guns which were being sent out to the Middle East. Regular batches of aircraft of modern types were also being sent out. We had fine pilots in the Middle East, at present operating with obsolete machines. As the supply of machines in this country had at present outstripped the supply of trained pilots, it was clearly right to send modern machines to the Middle East.

Winston S. Churchill: statement
(*Hansard*)

13 August 1940   House of Commons

AEROPLANE ACCIDENT, AUSTRALIA

The Prime Minister (Mr Churchill): We have all been shocked and grieved by the news of the lamentable and untimely loss which the Commonwealth of Australia and, indeed, of the whole Empire and its cause, has suffered in the deaths, like soldiers on duty, of the group of eminent Australian Ministers and high officers in the aeroplane accident of which we have this morning received the news. The sudden removal of these able and resolute men from the centre and summit of war direction in Australia inflicts an injury upon us all which I can be at no pains to conceal. In Brigadier Street[1] and Mr Fairbairn,[2] in Sir Henry Gullett[3] and Lieut.-General Sir Brudenell White,[4] Australia has been robbed of some of her best and ablest sons at a moment when the gifts

---

[1] Geoffrey Austin Street, 1894–1940. Born in Australia. On active service with the Australian forces, 1914–18 (Military Cross, Brigadier). Parliamentary Secretary for Defence, 1938. Minister for Defence, 1938–9. Acting Minister for the Navy, 1939. Minister for the Army from 1939 until his death.

[2] James Valentine Fairbairn, 1897–1940. Served first in the Royal Flying Corps, then in the Royal Australian Air Force, 1916–18. Entered the Australian Parliament, 1933. Minister for Air, and Minister for Civil Aviation, from 1933 until his death.

[3] Henry Somer Gullett, 1878–1940. Born in Australia. A journalist. Australian Official Correspondent with the British and French armies in France, 1916–17; with the Australian forces in Palestine, 1918. Director of Australian Immigration, 1920. Minister for Trade and Customs, Australia, 1928–9 and 1932–3. Knighted, 1933. Minister Directing Trade Treaties, 1934–7. Minister for External Affairs and Minister for Information, 1939–40. Vice-President of the Executive Council, and Acting Minister for Information, 1940.

[4] Cyril Brudenell Bigham White, 1876–1940. On active service in South Africa (1902) and in the Great War, including the Dardanelles (despatches, DSO). Knighted, 1919. Chief of the General Staff, Australia, 1920–3 and 1940 (recalled from the retired list).

they had to offer were most precious. The House will wish to extend its sympathy to their families and friends, and to the Prime Minister, Mr Menzies, whose burden is already heavy enough. In so doing, we shall give voice to the sorrow which in so many lands will be felt by all to whom the cause of freedom is dear. In this hour of battle there will be one other thought, equally spontaneous and equally widespread – Close the ranks, and carry on.

Winston S. Churchill to Anthony Eden
(*Churchill papers, 20/13*)

13 August 1940

If, owing to lack of equipment and other facilities, it is necessary to limit the numbers of the active Home Guard, would it not be possible to recruit a Home Guard Reserve, members of which would, for the time being, be provided with no weapons and no uniform other than arm bands? Their only duties would be to attend such courses of instruction as could be organised locally in the use of simple weapons like the 'Molotov cocktail,' and to report for orders in the event of invasion.

Unless some such step is taken, those who are refused enlistment will be bewildered and disappointed, and one of the primary objects of the Home Guard, which was to provide for the people as a whole an opportunity of helping to defend their homes, will be lost. I am anxious to avoid the disappointment and frustration which the stoppage of recruiting for the Home Guard is likely to cause to many people.

Please let me know what you think of this proposal.

WSC

Winston S. Churchill to Sir John Reith
(*Churchill papers, 20/13*)

13 August 1940

I should be glad to know what stocks of coal are now held by the railways and how they compare with those normally held. With the stoppage of our export trade to Europe there should be a great surplus just now, and no doubt you are taking advantage of this to fill up every available dump so that we shall have a well-distributed stock for the railway in case of any interruptions, or even in case of another very hard winter. Negotiations about price should not be allowed to hold up the process of re-stocking. If necessary, some form of arbitration will have to be employed to make sure that the prices paid are fair.

WSC

Winston S. Churchill to General Ismay
(*Churchill papers, 20/13*)

13 August 1940

I am greatly distressed at not having seen these original telegrams between the First Sea Lord and Commander-in-Chief Mediterranean; nor have I been permitted to see the very important Minute of the First Sea Lord. Instead of that I only had this feeble boil-down of the COS Committee.

On no account fail to let me see the actual documents on important transactions in which we are engaged.

WSC

John Colville: diary
(*Colville papers*)

13 August 1940

The PM is very much on edge, concerned with the quickest method of sending reinforcements to the Near East before the expected attack on Egypt. The War Office and the Admiralty want to send these via the Cape; Winston is intent on a dash through the Mediterranean (Operation 'Hats').

The long discussions on how to reinforce the Middle East continued after dinner, Winston (who did not have his sleep this afternoon) being in the worst of tempers.

Winston S. Churchill to A. V. Alexander
(*Churchill papers, 20/13*)

13 August 1940

1. Just before the French went out of the war Admiral Darlan bombarded Genoa in full daylight without any Asdic[1] destroyer protection, or any aircraft protection, and returned to Toulon unscathed. The Eastern Mediterranean Fleet has three times advanced to the centre of the Mediterranean and returned to Alexandria with only one ship – *Gloucester* – hit by one bomb. A few weeks ago a fast and a slow convoy were conducted uninjured from Malta to Alexandria – two days of their voyage being beset by Italian aircraft.

2. The Admiralty now propose to send six destroyers from Alexandria to

---

[1] An anti-submarine radar device.

meet Force H. These destroyers, which will certainly be detected from the air, will be within air-attacking distance of the very numerous, fast Italian cruiser forces in their home bases. This movement should be rightly condemned as hazardous in the extreme but for the just estimation in which Italian Naval enterprise is held by C-in-C, Mediterranean, and the Admiralty.

3. We are now told that it is too dangerous for the powerful forces we shall have in motion in the near future to carry through to the Eastern Mediterranean two MT ships steaming in company at only 15 knots. Yet at the same time we are asked to spend vast sums fortifying a large part of the Western coasts of Britain against what the Admiralty declare is a possible invasion by 12,000 men embarked and shipped in the *Gironde* and *St Nazaire*, who are to be escorted to their destination without any warship protection of any kind. If it is held to be a feasible operation to move 12,000 men unescorted on to the Irish or British Western coasts in the face of the full British sea power, can this be reconciled with the standard of danger-values now adopted in the Mediterranean?

4. No one can see where or when the main attack on Egypt will develop. It seems, however, extremely likely that if the Germans are frustrated in an invasion of Great Britain or do not choose to attempt it, they will have great need to press and aid the Italians to the attack of Egypt. The month of September must be regarded as critical in the extreme.

5. In these circumstances it is very wrong that we should attempt to send our armoured brigade round the Cape, thus making sure that during September it can play no part either in the defence of England or Egypt.

6. I request that the operation of passing at least two MT ships through with the Eastern reinforcements may be re-examined. The personnel can be distributed in the warships, and it is a lesser risk, from the point of view of the general war, to pass the MT ships through the Mediterranean than to have the whole armoured brigade certainly out of action going round the Cape. So long as the personnel are properly distributed among the warships, I am prepared to take the full responsibility for the possible loss of the armoured vehicles.

7. I am aware of the difficulty made about manoeuvring *Illustrious* while she is working her aircraft in conjunction with slower vessels. I suggest that further thought and ingenuity might find a manner of giving protection to the MT's with the forces at our disposal without compromising the modern capital units. I accept the condition of C-in-C, Mediterranean, that if either of the MT ships is so reduced in speed as to endanger the capital units it should be scuttled.

Pray let this be re-considered and an early effort made to meet a serious emergency, even though a certain measure of risk must be expected.

I shall be glad to discuss this in the Admiralty War-Room to-morrow, Wednesday, at 7 p.m.

War Cabinet: minutes
(*Cabinet papers, 65/8*)

14 August 1940　　　　　　　　　　　　　　　　　10 Downing Street
12.30 p.m.

The Prime Minister referred to the 11 Blenheim Bombers which had been lost on the previous day in an attack, unescorted by fighters, on Aalborg Aerodrome.[1] He thought that this raid ran counter to the directive in regard to bombing policy which had been issued on the 11th July.

The Prime Minister said that a Memorial Service to the Australian Ministers killed in the air liner disaster would probably be held on the 19th or 20th August, at 12.30 p.m., in Westminster Abbey. It would be appropriate that a number of Ministers, including one or more members of the War Cabinet, should attend the Service in person.

John Colville: diary
(*Colville papers*)

14 August 1940

In the afternoon I accompanied the PM to a meeting at the Admiralty Upper War Room. I walked back with him across the Horse Guards Parade and he confided to me that it was very difficult to make 'those fellows' (the First Lord and the First Sea Lord) be sensible about sending troops through the Mediterranean. They were so confoundedly cautious.

War Cabinet: minutes
(*Cabinet papers, 65/8*)

14 August 1940　　　　　　　　　　　　　　　　　10 Downing Street
6.30 p.m.

The Prime Minister read to the War Cabinet a document handed to him by the American Ambassador giving a personal message from the President of the United States. The substance of this message was that the President believed that it might be possible to furnish the British Government, as

[1] On raids over France and Holland on the night of 13/14 August, 'sixteen bombed but twelve were lost, eleven of the twelve aircraft from a formation provided by 82 Squadron which was caught by German fighters while attacking Aalborg airfield in Holland. This was the second time during the summer of 1940 that a formation from this squadron was almost completely destroyed' (Martin Middlebrook and Chris Everitt, *The Bomber Command War Diaries. An Operational Reference Book, 1939–1945*, page 73). Following an attack on the Dortmund–Ems Canal on the previous night, Flight-Lieutenant R. A. B. Learoyd had been awarded the first Bomber Command Victoria Cross of the war.

immediate assistance, with at least 50 Destroyers, Motor Torpedo Boats, and certain aircraft, provided the British Government found itself able and willing to take the two following steps: The first was an assurance that, if at any time the waters round these Islands became untenable for British ships of war, the latter would not be turned over to Germany or sunk, but would be sent to other parts of the Empire for the continued defence of the Empire. The second was an agreement on the part of Great Britain that the British Government would authorise the use of Newfoundland, Bermuda, the Bahamas, certain West Indian Islands and British Guiana as Naval and Air bases by the United States in the event of an attack on the American Hemisphere by any non-American nation; in the meantime, the United States should have the right to establish bases, the land for which should be acquired by purchase or through a lease.

The Prime Minister thought that, if the present proposal went through, the United States would have made a long step towards coming into the war on our side. To sell Destroyers to a belligerent was certainly not a neutral action. The 50 Destroyers would be of enormous value to the Admiralty, and the effect of the proposal as a whole on Germany would, he thought, be immense.

The crucial point was, he thought, what President Roosevelt would say publicly in regard to the first assurance asked for. The President said in his message that he did not contemplate any public statement by the Prime Minister, but only an assurance on the lines indicated, as, for example, reiteration to him (the President) of the Prime Minister's statement to Parliament on the 4th June. But it must be contemplated that the President might have to make some statement to Congress.

On the 4th June he (the Prime Minister) had said: 'We shall never surrender, and even if, which I do not for a moment believe, this island or a large part of it were subjugated and starving, then our Empire beyond the seas, armed and guarded by the British Fleet, would carry on the struggle. . . .' That statement had been made partly in order to reassure public opinion immediately after the collapse of France. Nothing must now be said which would disturb morale or lead people to think that we should not fight it out here.

The War Cabinet agreed that it was of the utmost importance to make it absolutely clear tht it was our firm resolve to fight it out here, and that even if, contrary to our belief, we should find ourselves being overwhelmed, we should retain, entirely unfettered, the right to decide when (if ever) we should send the Fleet away from these waters to defend our kith and kin overseas.

In discussion, the view was expressed that, if regarded from the point of view of the tangible assets which would pass, it could be contended that the

United States was making a hard bargain. In this connexion it was suggested that we should follow up a suggestion in Lord Lothian's telegram and press for more flying boats and rifles.

Winston S. Churchill to President Roosevelt
(*Churchill papers, 20/14*)

15 August 1940

I need not tell you how cheered I am by your message or how grateful I feel for your untiring efforts to give us all possible help. You will, I am sure, send us everything you can, for you know well that the worth of every destroyer that you can spare to us is measured in rubies. But we also need the motor-torpedo boats which you mentioned and as many flying boats and rifles as you can let us have. We have a million men waiting for rifles.

The moral value of this fresh aid from your Government and people at this critical time will be very great and widely felt.

We can meet both the points you consider necessary to help you with Congress and with others concerned, but I am sure that you will not misunderstand me if I say that our willingness to do so must be conditional on our being assured that there will be no delay in letting us have the ships and flying boats. As regards an assurance about the British Fleet, I am, of course, ready to reiterate to you what I told Parliament on June 4th. We intend to fight this out here to the end, and none of us would ever buy peace by surrendering or scuttling the fleet. But in any use you may make of this repeated assurance you will please bear in mind the disastrous effect from our point of view, and perhaps also from yours, of allowing any impression to grow that we regard the conquest of the British Islands and its naval bases as any other than an impossible contingency. The spirit of our people is splendid. Never have they been so determined. Their confidence in the issue has been enormously and legitimately strengthened by the severe air fighting in the past week. As regards naval and air bases, I readily agree to your proposals for 99-year leases, which is far easier for us than the method of purchase. I have no doubt that, once the principle is agreed between us, the details can be adjusted and we can discuss them at leisure. It will be necessary for us to consult the Governments of Newfoundland and Canada about the Newfoundland base in which Canada has an interest. We are at once proceeding to seek their consent.

Once again, Mr President, let me thank you for your help and encouragement, which mean so much to us.

War Cabinet: Confidential Annex
(*Cabinet papers, 65/14*)

15 August 1940   10 Downing Street
12 noon

The War Cabinet had a short discussion on the Military situation in the Middle East, following the receipt of a telegram from the Acting Commander-in-Chief, Middle East,[1] reporting that strong Italian forces had broken through our position at Tug-Argen, and that he had ordered evacuation.

The Prime Minister said that he was anxious as regards the defence of Egypt. General Wavell thought that a strong Italian concentration had been made in Libya, and that an attack might be launched while our position in the Middle East was still weak.

The Prime Minister said that part of our main defensive position in Egypt had been assigned to Egyptian forces, and was not as strongly fortified as the part of the line assigned to our forces. In effect, therefore, the weakest troops were holding the weakest part of the line. It had been suggested that Egyptian troops should hand over this part of the line to us, together with some of the weapons required for the defence of this sector. This suggestion had given rise to political difficulties and had been abandoned. Generally, it seemed that the disposition of our troops in the Middle East had often been determined, not on strategic, but on quite other grounds.

The Prime Minister then referred to the proposal that an Armoured Brigade should be sent to reinforce our troops in Egypt. The matter had been further discussed with the Admiralty, and it had been arranged to defer a decision until August 26th, when a decision could be reached in the light of the latest available information. Clearly there was a considerable risk in sending the Brigade through the Mediterranean, but the situation might make it necessary for us to run this risk. It was of the utmost importance that the fullest reconnaissance should be carried out between now and the 26th, so as to enable the decision to be taken on the best possible information.

Winston S. Churchill: Oral Answers
(*Hansard*)

15 August 1940   House of Commons
2.45 p.m.

The Prime Minister (Mr Churchill): I propose, with the permission of the House, to take advantage of the Questions of the hon. Members for East

---

[1] General Henry Maitland Wilson, see page 905, note 1.

Wolverhampton (Mr Mander)[1] and Ipswich (Mr Stokes) about the work and composition of the Swinton Committee, to make a few general observations on the subject. I submitted to the House some time ago the view that it was not in the public interest that Questions should be asked and answered about this Committee or other branches of Secret Service work, or about measures to deal with Fifth Column activities. It would be very wrong for a Government to plead the public interest as a reason for avoiding public and Parliamentary criticism and debate, and, personally, I would never do so. I am always anxious to give the House of Commons the utmost possible information, and to welcome debate. Therefore when I said it was not in the public interest that this matter should be pursued, I hoped that this would have been accepted by all Members of the House. However, I regret to say that a number of Questions have been put on the Paper day after day, quite disregarding the request which the Government made. It would have been possible for the Government, under the powers now accorded, to prevent these Questions from appearing on the Paper, and to prevent all reference to the subject in the newspapers; but I thought it would be much better to leave the putting down of Questions to the good will and sense of responsibility of Members, and I am very sorry that in a few cases this attitude has not been forthcoming.

Now why is it that we have thought it right to plead the public interest against the discussion of the Swinton Committee and its work? Not assuredly because we have anything to conceal which would reflect upon the loyalty, impartiality, and good faith of the Government, or anything which would do the Government harm as a Government, if it were all explained in the utmost detail. The reason is simply one of principle, namely, that matters of this kind, and Committees of this kind, are not fitted for public discussion, least of all in time of war. The House has recognised this principle for many years, and has always refused to allow any discussion of Secret Service funds, or to receive any return of how the money is expended, and similarly I am sure the House would wish the rule to be respected in the case of a Committee which, as I said, deals with Fifth Column activities and other cognate matters. No other country, when it is at war, gives information of this kind, and once the principle was admitted that a stream of Questions could be put about them, and that the Government would be bound to answer these Questions factually, there would be very serious injury done to our safety.

The House has, almost unanimously, recorded its confidence in the Government. That does not mean that the House is confident we shall do everything right, or that errors of policy and administration should not be

[1] Geoffrey Le Mesurier Mander, 1882–1962. Head of Mander Bros, paint and varnish manufacturers. Liberal MP, 1929–45. A leading Parliamentary critic of the Munich agreement, 1938. Parliamentary Private Secretary to the Secretary of State for Air (Sir Archibald Sinclair), 1942–5. Knighted, 1945. Joined the Labour Party, 1948.

freely criticised, and scandals or negligence exposed; but it does mean, I think that when such a Government pleads the public interest, it should be believed that it is acting fairly and honourably, and telling the truth, and not concerning itself with shielding any Ministerial or personal, or party interest. I hope very much we may be believed by the House, and that confidence will not be withdrawn from us, even in a small matter like this, at a time when we are making head, and making head successfully, against dangers as great as any that have ever threatened our national freedom and survival.

I am sorry indeed to have to say so much about this Committee, because it makes people think there is something mysterious in the whole affair. Nothing could be more straightforward. About 10 weeks ago, after the dark, vile conspiracy which in a few days laid the trustful Dutch people at the mercy of Nazi aggression, a wave of alarm passed over this country, and especially in responsible circles, lest the same kind of undermining tactics and treacherous agents of the enemy were at work in our Island. [An Hon. Member: 'Watch them.'] Several branches of State Departments are, of course, always charged with the duty of frustrating such designs. But they were not working smoothly. There were overlaps and underlaps, and I felt in that hour of anxiety that this side of the business of National Defence wanted pulling together. I therefore asked Lord Swinton to undertake this task. [Hon. Members: 'Why?'] Because he was the best man to do it. [An Hon. Member: 'He failed in another job.'] One has to be very careful how one judges failure, especially when one's own record of success is not to one's credit. I am glad to tell the House that a very great improvement has been effected in dealing with this Fifth Column danger. I always thought it was exaggerated in this Island, and I am satisfied now that it has been reduced to its proper proportions, and is being gripped and looked after with very high efficiency. It is important that this should be so, because although we feel, and are, very much stronger than in May, the danger of invasion has by no means passed away, and we are repeatedly assured from German circles in foreign countries that the performance is about to begin. I should not have felt I was doing my duty by the National Defence, if I had not taken these special steps to cope with Fifth Column activities, and I can assure the House that the powers that Parliament has given to the Executive will not be used consciously in any unfair, oppressive, or, if I may use the expression, un-British spirit. I trust therefore that the House will support me in declining, in the public interest, to answer any further Questions upon the subject.

Mr Austin Hopkinson[1]: There were two points made by the Prime Minister on which I should like further information, if I may have it. First,

---

[1] Austin Hopkinson, 1879–1962. On active service in South Africa (Lieutenant, Imperial Yeomanry), 1900 and 1914–18. Head of an engineering firm. Independent MP, 1918–29 and 1931–45. Lieutenant, Fleet Air Arm, 1940.

there was the statement that the Government have power to prevent Questions being put on the Order Paper. Surely not?

The Prime Minister: I am glad that Questions in the form which give away to the enemy matters which are essentially secret, and are against the public interest, are not accepted by the Clerks at the Table, and I think the views of Ministers would be considered in that respect.

Mr Hopkinson: Then I understand it is only Questions which in their form are adjudged to be against the public interest?

The Prime Minister indicated assent.

Mr Hopkinson: I am trying to elucidate further information, with your permission, Mr Speaker. We cannot understand why so much mystery was made about it. That is really what has given rise to all the trouble. When great mystery was made about it and names were refused, trade union opinion became very suspicious, whether justifiably or not is not the point. When the name of Lord Swinton was announced that suspicion was increased, owing to his activities on behalf of big business in politics.

Mr Speaker: The hon. Member is making a speech.

Mr Hopkinson: With your permission, Mr Speaker, I am endeavouring to elucidate from the Prime Minister the reason why—

Mr Speaker: If the hon. Member would ask a definite Question, the Prime Minister would no doubt answer it. Otherwise I cannot allow debate.

Mr Hopkinson: Why did the Prime Minister make such a mystery about it and refuse to give information which was perfectly harmless?

The Prime Minister: If my hon. Friend had paid half the attention to the full and very respectful statement which I have made to the House that he was accustomed to giving to obstructing my efforts to get this country properly defended before the war, I would not have had to answer this Question at all.

Mr Hopkinson: I ask for your protection, Mr Speaker, against this gross and lying innuendo?

Hon. Members: Withdraw.

Mr Hopkinson: May I ask the right hon. Gentleman to withdraw that statement? He is perfectly well aware that no man in this country has done more than I have.

The Prime Minister: Far from withdrawing what I said, I will take the liberty of sending the hon. Gentleman a copy of one of his interventions in Debate, which I looked up only last night, in which he did his utmost to discredit me when I was doing my utmost for the country.

SOMALILAND OPERATIONS

The Prime Minister: I have some unsatisfactory news for the House about Somaliland. The small British holding force which was occupying the Tug-Argen position to the North-East of Hargeisa has been driven back by greatly superior Italian forces, amounting to about two divisions, including armoured vehicles and considerable artillery. As operations are still in progress, I cannot say any more, but I shall be dealing generally with the Eastern situation next week.

John Colville: diary
(*Colville papers*)

15 August 1940

When the PM makes his own arrangements he is inclined to forget to tell any of us and then to forget himself. Thus today at 4.00 the room was full of military dignitaries, Eden, Dill, Wavell and Ismay, and the PM was quietly enjoying a whisky and soda in the smoking-room at the House.

Winston S. Churchill to Professor Lindemann
(*Churchill papers, 20/13*)

15 August 1940
Most Secret and Personal

The meeting this afternoon,[1] which is for Ministers only, is to try to get Herbert Morrison to accept necessary help. For this purpose we shall be considering bottle-necks at the Admiralty, at the MAP,[2] and generally in supply. Select me half a dozen of these, at least two of which must refer to the Admiralty and MAP. The difficulty of concerting the production of aeroplanes and tanks is also very serious. I must have this at four o'clock.

John Colville: diary
(*Colville papers*)

15 August 1940

Today there took place the greatest and most successful air battle of all. The figures of enemy planes destroyed kept on mounting and mounting until finally Winston, consumed with excitement, got into his car and drove off to Fighter Command at Stanmore. When he came back he told me the total was well over a hundred and asked me to ring up the Lord President, who is in the

---

[1] A 5.30 p.m. meeting with Beaverbrook, Bevin and Morrison.
[2] Ministry of Aircraft Production.

country recovering from an operation. I did so and found Mr Chamberlain somewhat cold at being disturbed in the middle of dinner. However he was overcome with joy when he heard the news and very touched at Winston thinking of him. It is typical of W to do a small thing like this which could give such great pleasure. 'The Lord President was very grateful to you,' I said to Winston. 'So he ought to be,' replied W, 'this is one of the greatest days in history.'

After dinner the PM sat down and dictated straight off a 'directive' about operations in the Middle East. I thought it a masterly document, long but clear and to the point.

Winston S. Churchill to Anthony Eden and General Dill
(*Churchill papers, 20/13*)

15 August 1940

GENERAL DIRECTIVE FOR THE COMMANDER-IN-CHIEF, MIDDLE EAST

A major invasion of Egypt from Libya must be expected at any time now. It is necessary, therefore, to assemble and deploy the largest possible army upon and towards the western frontier. All political and administrative considerations must be set in proper subordination to this.

2. The evacuation of Somaliland is enforced upon us by the enemy, but is none the less strategically convenient. All forces in or assigned to Somaliland should be sent to Aden, to the Sudan via Port Sudan, or to Egypt as may be thought best.

3. The defence of Kenya must rank after the defence of the Sudan. There should be time after the crisis in Egypt and the Sudan is passed to reinforce Kenya by sea and rail before any large Italian expedition can reach the Tana river. We can always reinforce Kenya faster than Italy can pass troops thither from Abyssinia or Italian Somaliland.

4. Accordingly either the two West African Brigades or two Brigades of the KAR should be moved forthwith to Khartoum. General Smuts is being asked to allow the Union Brigade, or a large part of it, to move to the Canal Zone and the Delta for internal security purposes. Arrangements should be made to continue their training. The Admiralty are being asked to report on shipping possibilities in the Indian Ocean and Red Sea.

5. In view of the increased air attack which may be expected in the Red Sea following upon the Italian conquest of British Somaliland, the air reinforcement of Aden becomes important.

6. The two Brigades, one of Regulars and the other Australian, which are held ready in Palestine, should now move into the Delta in order to clear the

Palestine communications for the movement of further reserves as soon as they can be equipped for field service or organized for internal security duties.

7. However, immediately three or four Regiments of British Cavalry, without their horses, should take over the necessary duties in the Canal Zone, liberating the three Regular battalions there for general reserve of the field army of the Delta.

8. The rest of the Australians, numbering six battalions, in Palestine, will thus be available at five days' notice to move into the Delta for internal security or other emergency employment.

The Polish Brigade and the French Volunteer Unit should move to the Delta from Palestine as may be convenient and join the general reserve.

9. The movement of the Indian Division now embarking or in transit should be accelerated to the utmost. Unless some of the troops evacuated from Somaliland and not needed for Aden are found sufficient to reinforce the Sudan, in addition to reinforcements from Kenya, this whole Division, as is most desirable, should proceed to Suez to join the Army of the Delta.

In addition to the above at least three Batteries of British Artillery, although horse-drawn, must be embarked immediately from India for Suez. Admiralty to arrange transport.

10. Most of the above movements should be completed between the 15th September and the 1st October, and on this basis the army of the Delta should comprise:–
   (a) The British Armoured Force in Egypt.
   (b) The Four British battalions at Mersa Matruh, the two at Alexandria and the two in Cairo – total eight.
   (c) The three Battalions from the Canal zone.
   (d) The reserve British Brigade from Palestine – total fourteen British Regular Infantry Battalions.
   (e) The New Zealand Brigade.
   (f) The Australian Brigade from Palestine.
   (g) The Polish Brigade.
   (h) Part of the Union Brigade from East Africa.
   (i) The Fourth Indian Division now in rear of Mersa Matruh.
   (j) The new Indian Division in Transit.
   (k) The 11,000 men in drafts arriving almost at once at Suez.
   (l) All the artillery (150 guns) now in the Middle East or *en route* from India.
   (m) The Egyptian army so far as it can be used for field operations.

The above should constitute by the 1st October at the latest ...[1]

---

[1] Churchill left the figure blank in his directive as dictated.

battalions and 150 guns together with the armoured forces, and exclusive of internal security troops of 55,000 bayonets and between 150 and 200 guns.
(Part II)

12. It is hoped that the armoured brigade from England of three Regiments of tanks will be passed through the Mediterranean by the Admiralty. If this is impossible their arrival round the Cape may be counted upon during the first fortnight in October. The arrival of this force in September must be considered so important as to justify a considerable degree of risk in their transportation.
(Part III)

Tactical employment of the above force:

13. The Mersa Matruh position must be fortified completely and with the utmost speed. The sector held by the three Egyptian battalions must be taken over by three British battalions, making the force homogeneous. This must be done even if the Egyptian Government wish to withdraw the artillery now in the hands of these three battalions. The possibility of reinforcing by sea the Mersa Matruh position and cutting enemy communications, once they have passed by on their march to the Delta, must be studied with the Naval Commander-in-Chief, Mediterranean Fleet. Alternatively a descent upon the communications at Sollum or further west may be preferred.

14. All water supplies between Mersa Matruh and the Alexandria defences must be rendered depotable. (A special note on this is attached.) No attempt should be made to leave small parties to defend the wells near the coast in this region. The 4th Indian Division should withdraw upon Alexandria when necessary or be taken off by sea. The road from Sollum to Mersa Matruh, and still more the tarmak road from Mersa Matruh to Alexandria, must be rendered impassable as it is abandoned by (a) delay action mines (see special note); or by chemical treatment of the asphalt surface (see special note).

15. A main line of defence to be held by the whole Army of the Delta, with its reserves suitably disposed, must be prepared (as should long ago have been done) from Alexandria along the edge of the cultivated zone and irrigation canals of the Delta. For this purpose the strongest concrete and sandbag works and pill-boxes should be built or completed from the sea to the cultivated zone and the main irrigation canal. The pipe line forward of this line should be extended as fast as possible. The Delta zone is the most effective obstacle to tanks of all kinds, and can be lightly held by sandbag works to give protection to Egypt and form a very strong extended flank for the Alexandria front. A broad strip, four or five miles wide, should be inundated from the flood waters of the Nile, controlled at Assouan. Amid or behind this belt a series of strong posts armed with artillery should be constructed.

16. In this posture then the army of the Delta will await the Italian invasion. It must be expected that the enemy will advance in great force limited only, but severely, by the supply of water and petrol. He will certainly

have strong armoured forces on his right hand to contain and drive back our weaker forces unless these can be reinforced in time by the armoured regiment from Great Britain. He will mask, if he cannot storm, Mersa Matruh. But if the main Line of the Delta is diligently fortified and resolutely held he will be forced to deploy an army whose supply of water, petrol, food and ammunition will be difficult. Once the army is deployed and seriously engaged, the action against his communications, from Mersa Matruh, by bombardment from the sea, by descent at Sollum, or even much further west, would be a deadly blow to him.

17. The campaign for the defence of the Delta therefore resolves itself into: *Strong defence with the left arm from Alexandria inland, and a reaching out with the right hand, using sea-power upon his communications.*[1] At the same time it is hoped that the reinforcements from Malta will hamper the sending of further reinforcements – Italian or German – from Europe into Africa.

18. All this might be put effectively in train by October 1, *provided we are allowed the time.* If not, we must do what we can. All trained or Regular units, whether fully equipped or not, must be used in defence of the Delta. All armed white men and also Indian or foreign units must be used for internal security. The Egyptian army must be made to play its part in support of the Delta front, thus leaving only riotous crowds to be dealt with in Egypt proper.

Pray let the above be implemented and be ready to discuss it in detail with me at 4.30 p.m. August 16.

War Cabinet: minutes
(*Cabinet papers, 65/8*)

16 August 1940　　　　　　　　　　　　　　　　　　　10 Downing Street
12.30 p.m.

The Minister[2] emphasised that, if speedy production of tanks was required, it would be necessary to give them priority 1 (a) along with the aircraft.

The Prime Minister said that this question should not be discussed as though the point at issue was whether we should have aircraft or tanks. We needed both. There could be no doubt that aircraft must have priority as far as

---

[1] The italicised passages were italicised in the directive as printed.
[2] Herbert Morrison, Minister of Supply.

678   August 1940

was necessary and until certain requirements were satisfied. The Fighter was our salvation and the Bomber offered means of victory. He could not admit, however, that, whilst giving aircraft first priority, we could not also produce large numbers of tanks, provided that the available resources were allocated to essential needs.

General Ismay: recollection
('*The Memoirs of Lord Ismay*', pages 179–80)

16 August 1940   Operations Room, No. 11 Group
Fighter Command

There had been heavy fighting throughout the afternoon; and at one moment every single squadron in the Group was engaged; there was nothing in reserve, and the map table showed new waves of attackers crossing the coast. I felt sick with fear. As the evening closed in the fighting died down, and we left by car for Chequers, Churchill's first words were: 'Don't speak to me; I have never been so moved.' After above five minutes he leaned forward and said, 'Never in the field of human conflict has so much been owed by so many to so few.' The words burned into my brain and I repeated them to my wife when I got home.

Winston S. Churchill to Sir Archibald Sinclair
(*Premier papers, 3/347*)

17 August 1940

I am very doubtful about the PAC rockets.[1] They are one of many suggestions which we took up at the Admiralty at the time when our small ships were being attacked on the East Coast, and we had nothing to put in them. I do not think they would be suitable for regular use; certainly it would be a great mistake to use up the wire which is needed for the aerial mines. I gathered from the conversation you had with Lord Beaverbrook the other day that your demands are reduced from 60,000 a month to 8,000, but even this latter figure appears to me to be altogether excessive. We must look to the regular UP weapon, with or without the new fuzes, as the future solution of

[1] Parachute and Cable rockets, a 2-inch rocket device. The rocket was fired vertically carrying a length of cable behind it, two parachutes and a small bomb. When deployed fully, the bomb was suspended on a long wire, supported by a parachute. If the aircraft struck the wire, the bomb was dragged up to the wing and exploded.

the protection of vulnerable points. Pray let me have a short note on the present position of this supply showing how it could be brought to a close in the course of the next month or six weeks, with a minimum waste of material already assigned to it.

WSC

Winston S. Churchill to Sir Cyril Newall
(*Churchill papers, 20/13*)

17 August 1940

While our eyes are concentrated on the results of the air fighting over this country we must not overlook the serious losses occurring in the Bomber Command. Seven Heavy Bombers last night[1] and also 21 aircraft destroyed now on the ground – the bulk at Tangmere – Total 28. These 28, added to the 22 Fighters, makes our loss 50 on the day and very much alters the picture presented by the German loss of 75. In fact, on the day we have lost two to three.

Let me know the types of machines destroyed on the ground.

WSC

Winston S. Churchill to Admiral Pound
(*Churchill papers, 20/13*)

17 August 1940

I am much concerned with the sinkings recorded in to-day's report attached.[2] They aggregate nearly 27,000 tons. This must be one of the worst days on record. Our losses have become most grievous in the last six weeks, and it seems to me that the whole position should be reviewed. I had hoped that the special measures you were taking to reinforce the protection of the North-Western Approaches would be effective. Apparently this is not the

---

[1] On the night of 16/17 August, 150 bombers attacked airfields in Holland and industrial targets in the Ruhr and Frankfurt, as well as more distant targets at Jena, Leuna and Augsburg. Seven bombers were lost.

[2] In the six weeks up to 17 August 1940 eighty-one British merchant ships had been sunk. On 16 August the sinkings had been *Clan Macphee* (6,600 tons), *Empire Merchant* (4,864 tons), *City of Birmingham* (5,309) and *Meath* (1,598 tons).

case. I still wonder whether the control can be effectively concerted from Plymouth.

Pray let me know what further measures you propose to grapple with losses of this kind, which seem to approach the April 1917 figure, and, if continued, could not fail to exercise a definite effect upon our war-making capacity.

WSC

Winston S. Churchill to General Ismay
(*Churchill papers, 20/13*)

17 August 1940

In Thursday's action, Lord Beaverbrook told me that upwards of 80 German machines had been picked up on our soil. Is this so? If not, how many?

I asked C-in-C Fighter Command if he could discriminate in this action between the fighting over the land and over the sea. This would afford a good means of establishing for our own satisfaction the results which are claimed.

WSC

Winston S. Churchill to Peter Fraser
(*Churchill papers, 20/14*)

17 August 1940

We are doing our utmost, but if we are attacked in Egypt soon, as seems likely, we shall all have to do our best with what we have got.

WSC

Winston S. Churchill to Sir Edward Bridges
(*Churchill papers, 20/13*)

17 August 1940
ACTION THIS DAY

Pray have a telegram drafted after this question[1] has been discussed with the Service authorities concerned. I see no reason why we should not ask for all we want, provided there is a reasonable chance of getting it.

WSC

---

[1] Supplies from the United States requested by the Ministry of Shipping.

Winston S. Churchill to Anthony Eden
(*Premier papers, 3/498/1 and 2*)

18 August 1940

My dear Anthony,

I have been thinking over the position of the newly appointed 'Vulnerable Points Adviser' (Lieutenant General M. G. H. Barker);[1] and it seems to me that the most satisfactory arrangement would be for him to work under me in my capacity as Minister of Defence.

Many Departments are closely concerned in the questions for which he will be responsible, and their interests are bound to be in conflict from time to time. It would therefore make for smooth working and expedition of business if General Barker were not attached to any of the interested parties.

Do you agree?[2]

Yours sincerely
WSC

Winston S. Churchill to General Ismay
(*Churchill papers, 20/13*)

18 August 1940

Ask for a report from the Air Ministry upon this extraordinary statement[3] which I saw in several newspapers.[4] If the facts are true, the officer concerned is highly blameworthy, both from the point of view of endangering a Hudson aircraft, and also of not having done his best against the enemy.

WSC

---

[1] Michael George Henry Barker, 1884–1960. On active service in South Africa, 1902, and on the Western Front, 1914–18 (despatches, DSO and bar). Director of Recruiting and Organisation, War Office, 1936–8. General Officer Commanding British Forces in Palestine and Transjordan, 1939–40. General Officer Commanding Aldershot Command, 1940. Vulnerable Points Adviser, 1940–1. A Deputy Regional Commissioner of Civil Defence, London, 1941.

[2] Within a month of General Barker's appointment he had both reduced the number of vulnerable points and, by careful use of Home Guard units, released 9,000 soldiers for army duties (*Premier papers, 3/498/1*).

[3] On 16 August 1940 the Air Ministry issued a statement, widely reported in the newspapers (e.g. ' "Sitting Bird" Insanity', *Sunday Dispatch*, 18 August 1940), that 'A Hudson aircraft of the Coastal Command on patrol near Borkum saw something reflected on the water in the moonlight. The Pilot went down, and found a Heinkel seaplane resting on the sea. The German would have been easy prey, but the British crew thought it unsporting to attack a "sitting bird". So our plane twice dived on the Nazi, with headlights on, to invite it to come up and fight. It did so and was destroyed.'

[4] Churchill tried to look through every daily newspaper either late at night (when he was sent the first editions) or first thing in the morning.

War Cabinet: minutes
(*Cabinet papers, 65/8*)

19 August 1940   10 Downing Street
12 noon

The Prime Minister said that there had been several air raid warnings in Central London in the last few days, although no air fighting had taken place over Central London. At his request, the Minister of Home Security was examining with the Commander-in-Chief, Fighter Command, whether the system of air raid warnings in London could be modified, possibly by dividing up London into a larger number of areas, so as to avoid unnecessary stoppages of work during the red warning.

In the meantime, pending his report, he asked Ministers, in their discretion, to give such instructions as they thought fit to the staffs in their Departments regarding the continuance of work after a red warning has been received, but before it becomes evident – by gunfire or otherwise – that an air battle is in progress.

The Prime Minister read a telegram from Mr Mackenzie King giving an account of a discussion he had had with President Roosevelt and Mr Stimson.[1] The main points in the discussion had been as follows:–

(i) President Roosevelt hoped to begin to supply us with destroyers before the end of the present week, and asked us to send over skeleton crews to take the destroyers across the Atlantic.

(ii) He hoped to let us have 50 destroyers in all. He hoped also to let us have 20 motor torpedo boats, 10 large flying boats, a further 250,000 rifles and 150–200 aircraft supplied with engines which were on order for Sweden.

(iii) The United States and Canada were setting up a permanent Joint Board on Defence.

(iv) The President would take up with the Government of this country matters pertaining to Newfoundland, on which there would have to be co-operation between the three Governments – United Kingdom, Canada and the United States.

(v) It was not the intention of the Canadian Government either to sell or to lease land to the United States Government. They might, however, arrange to permit the United States Army to enter some parts of Nova Scotia and New Brunswick in return for permission to the Canadian forces to hold manoeuvres in Maine.

(vi) The President would be quite satisfied if the Prime Minister would

---

[1] The United States Secretary of War.

make a public statement about the British Fleet, similar to his statement to Parliament of the 4th June. This would afford the assurance of which the President felt in need.

The Prime Minister said that he would deal with the last point in his speech on the following day.

Winston S. Churchill to General Ismay
(*Churchill papers, 20/13*)

19 August 1940

I have not felt entirely satisfied with the reports we have received about the way in which the action at Tug-Argen was broken off, when the Black Watch had not been engaged. The expression 'hopeless superiority' was not pleasing. The pursuit does not seem to have been pressed by the enemy. Reinforcements were on the way. I trust the Chiefs of the Staff will consider what further steps can be taken. Certainly a much fuller report must be called for.

Winston S. Churchill to Sir Malcolm Robertson[1]
(*Churchill papers, 2/404*)

19 August 1940

I find it hard to believe that the electors of Mitcham have been invited at this moment to divert their attention to a wholly unnecessary election contest.[2] There is only one issue before the country – the defeat of our enemies – and for that we must close the ranks and work together.

As however the contest has been forced on Mitcham, I feel certain that the electors will give you overwhelming support, and you will thus be able to give the House of Commons the benefit of your long and wide experience of public affairs.

---

[1] Malcolm Arnold Robertson, 1877–1951. Entered the Foreign Office, 1898. British High Commissioner, Rhineland, 1920–1. Consul-General, Tangier, 1920–5. Knighted, 1924. Ambassador to the Argentine, 1927–9. Chairman of Spillers Ltd, 1930–47. Conservative candidate for Mitcham, Surrey, 1940, following the death of the sitting member; MP, 1940–5. Chairman of the British Council, 1941–5.

[2] Sir Malcolm Robertson was returned unopposed. In 1945 he was defeated by the Labour challenger. A note on Churchill's letter by E. A. Seal states: 'Election now over. Destroy letter.'

Winston S. Churchill to General Ismay
(*Churchill papers, 20/13*)

19 August 1940

All this raises most grave questions. The Admiral cannot take up a position that only in ideal conditions of tide and moon can the operation be begun.[1] It has got to be begun as soon as possible, as long as the conditions are practicable, even though they be not the best. People have to fight in war on all sorts of days, and under all sorts of conditions. It would be a great misfortune if there were any delay beyond the first week of September.

Winston S. Churchill to A. V. Alexander, Admiral Pound and Admiral Power[2]
(*Churchill papers, 20/13*)

19 August 1940

I am distressed at the continued assertion of the Anti-submarine Warfare Department of the Admiralty that we have only got 25 U-Boats since the beginning of the war.[3] Considering that the Germans have got 20 of ours, this would be a lamentable reflection upon all our flotillas and hunting-craft, as well as upon the Asdic method. Indeed, it is an absurd conclusion, and the argument by which it is reached lies under the greatest suspicion. It is a fact that this argument would be vitiated if the Germans replaced sunken submarines by others which are given the same number. Surely this would be a very reasonable step for them to take, and which would help to conceal losses from their own people, and would baffle us. Anyhow, how can you contend that none of these hundreds of attacks recorded since the beginning of the war have been successful, but only the 20 or 25 in which there are actual corpses, prisoners or wrecks in our hands? I feel that the anti-submarine warfare department is rendering a poor service by the line they take of declaring futile all the efforts of our hunting craft.

I earnestly request this whole position may be made the subject of an independent inquiry.

WSC

---

[1] Operation 'Menace', the joint naval and military assault on Dakar. The naval action was to be commanded by Admiral John Cunningham.

[2] Vice-Admiral Arthur John Power, Assistant Chief of the Naval Staff.

[3] Between the outbreak of war and 19 August 1940, only twenty-seven U-boats had in fact been destroyed. A twenty-eighth, *U–51*, was sunk by the submarine HMS *Cachalot* fifty miles west of Belle Isle on 20 August 1940, after being spotted while on the surface.

Winston S. Churchill to Alfred Duff Cooper
(*Churchill papers, 20/13*)

19 August 1940

Could you let me have a report on the attached.[1] There is no shipping available for transporting anything like five Divisions across the Channel, and there could be no justification for such an irresponsible statement on so grave a matter.

Pray let me know what happened.

WSC

Winston S. Churchill to Alfred Duff Cooper
(*Churchill papers, 20/13*)

19 August 1940

I trust you will let me know at an early date the position with regard to the Reves[2] proposal for propaganda in the Americas.

His scheme for one central organisation powerful enough to fight the German machine had strong points, and I hope that you will not allow it to be weakened by official caution.

Please let me know how the matter stands.

WSC

[1] A cutting from the *Daily Telegraph* about invasion: an example of Churchill's diligent daily reading of the newspapers. A month later, on 19 September 1940, he wrote to the Postmaster-General, W. S. Morrison: 'There are, as you will see from *The Times* to-day, considerable complaints about the Post Office during Air raids. Perhaps you will give me a report on what you are doing' (*Churchill papers, 20/13*).

[2] Imre Revesz (later Emery Reves), 1904–81. Born in southern Hungary. Studied at the universities of Berlin and Paris. Doctorate in political economics, Zurich, 1926. Founded the Co-operation Press Service for International Understanding, 1930, and syndicated articles by public figures in some 400 newspapers in 60 countries. By 1937, when he first met Churchill, his authors included Austen Chamberlain, Clement Attlee, Anthony Eden, Léon Blum, Paul Reynaud, Eduard Beneš and Einstein. In February 1940 Revesz became a British subject. Concerned with propaganda to the USA and neutral countries, June-December 1940. Severely wounded by a bomb during the London Blitz, December 1940. In January 1941 he went to New York, where he published several important anti-Nazi works, including two books of his own, *A Democratic Manifesto* (1942) and *The Anatomy of Peace* (1945). Most of his relatives were murdered in German-occupied Yugoslavia. Helped to negotiate the American rights of Churchill's war memoirs, 1946. He himself purchased all the foreign-language rights to the war memoirs, as well as to the *History of the English-Speaking Peoples*. Between 1956 and 1960 Churchill was a frequent guest at his villa, La Pausa, in the South of France.

John Colville: diary
(*Colville papers*)

19 August 1940

The PM seems to have made an exception of Horace Wilson in the general forgiveness he has bestowed on the Men of Munich. Today HJ[1] sent a note attached to a letter: 'Mr Seal. The PM may be interested to see.' Winston put a red circle round the word 'interested' and wrote at the bottom 'Why?'.

Back at No. 10 I read the first edition of the speech which the PM is to make in the House tomorrow and on which he has spent many hours this afternoon. It is curious to see how, as it were, he fertilises a phrase or a line of poetry for weeks and then gives birth to it in a speech. On many occasions recently I have heard him speak of our bombing attacks on Germany and say that even if Hitler is at the Caspian these attacks will bring him back to defend his home. Now I see that the Caspian is featuring in the speech! The sentence I like most is that referring to the German air claims (which included a statement that we lost 150 machines yesterday); if these claims continue Hitler's 'reputation for veracity will be seriously impugned'.

The PM went to bed shortly after midnight expressing delight that the Germans had refrained from raiding on a big scale today and saying they were making a big mistake in giving us a respite.

Neville Chamberlain to Winston S. Churchill
(*Churchill papers, 2/396*)

20 August 1940

I shall see your statement tomorrow and have no doubt it will be a stirring one with such material as you know how to use to the utmost.

Yours ever
Neville Chamberlain

'Daily Mail': editorial
(*'Daily Mail', 20 August 1940*)

20 August 1940

Mr Churchill's surveys of the situation in the House of Commons seem to mark the closing of old and the opening of new chapters in the history of the war.

---

[1] Sir Horace Wilson (Horace John Wilson) was known as 'HJ' (and also as 'creeping Jesus').

His last speech to MPs was as long ago as July 4, when he said 'Finis' for the time being to the warfare of France and her Navy and opened the story of our preparations for defence.

To-day he speaks again.

Necessarily, his speech will range over a wide field, and must include a particular account of developments in the Near East. But its principal point will obviously be the glorious work of the RAF.

He will be able to close the chapter of our preparations to defeat invasion, whatever method the enemy may choose to try. They are complete and, we believe, invulnerable.

Winston S. Churchill: speech
(*Hansard*)

20 August 1940
3.52 p.m.
House of Commons

WAR SITUATION

The Prime Minister (Mr Churchill): Almost a year has passed since the war began, and it is natural for us, I think, to pause on our journey at this milestone and survey the dark, wide field. It is also useful to compare the first year of this second war against German aggression with its forerunner a quarter of a century ago. Although this war is in fact only a continuation of the last, very great differences in its character are apparent. In the last war millions of men fought by hurling enormous masses of steel at one another. 'Men and shells' was the cry, and prodigious slaughter was the consequence. In this war nothing of this kind has yet appeared. It is a conflict of strategy, of organisation, of technical apparatus, of science, mechanics and morale. The British casualties in the first 12 months of the Great War amounted to 365,000. In this war, I am thankful to say, British killed, wounded, prisoners and missing, including civilians, do not exceed 92,000, and of these a large proportion are alive as prisoners of war. Looking more widely around, one may say that throughout all Europe for one man killed or wounded in the first year perhaps five were killed or wounded in 1914–15.

The slaughter is but a fraction, but the consequences to the belligerents have been even more deadly. We have seen great countries with powerful armies dashed out of coherent existence in a few weeks. We have seen the French Republic and the renowned French Army beaten into complete and total submission with less than the casualties which they suffered in any one of half-a-dozen of the battles of 1914–18. The entire body – it might almost seem at times the soul – of France has succumbed to physical effects incomparably less terrible than those which were sustained with fortitude and undaunted will power 25 years ago. Although up to the present the loss of life has been mercifully diminished, the decisions reached in the course of the struggle are even more profound upon the fate of nations than anything that has ever happened since barbaric times. Moves are made upon the scientific and strategic boards, advantages are gained by mechanical means, as a result of which scores of millions of men become incapable of further resistance, or judge themselves incapable of further resistance, and a fearful game of chess proceeds from check to mate by which the unhappy players seem to be inexorably bound.

There is another more obvious difference from 1914. The whole of the warring nations are engaged, not only soldiers, but the entire population, men, women and children. The fronts are everywhere. The trenches are dug in the towns and streets. Every village is fortified. Every road is barred. The front line runs through the factories. The workmen are soldiers with different weapons but the same courage. These are great and distinctive changes from what many of us saw in the struggle of a quarter of a century ago. There seems to be every reason to believe that this new kind of war is well suited to the genius and the resources of the British nation and the British Empire and that, once we get properly equipped and properly started, a war of this kind will be more favourable to us than the sombre mass slaughters of the Somme and Passchendaele. If it is a case of the whole nation fighting and suffering together, that ought to suit us, because we are the most united of all the nations, because we entered the war upon the national will and with our eyes open, and because we have been nurtured in freedom and individual responsibility and are the products not of totalitarian uniformity but of tolerance and variety. If all these qualities are turned, as they are being turned, to the arts of war, we may be able to show the enemy quite a lot of things that they have not thought of yet. Since the Germans drove the Jews out and lowered their technical standards, our science is definitely ahead of theirs. Our geographical position, the command of the sea, and the friendship of the United States enable us to draw resources from the whole world and to manufacture weapons of war of every kind, but especially of the superfine kinds, on a scale hitherto practised only by Nazi Germany.

Hitler is now sprawled over Europe. Our offensive springs are being slowly compressed, and we must resolutely and methodically prepare ourselves for the campaigns of 1941 and 1942. Two or three years are not a long time, even in our short, precarious lives. They are nothing in the history of the nation, and when we are doing the finest thing in the world, and have the honour to be the sole champion of the liberties of all Europe, we must not grudge these years or weary as we toil and struggle through them. It does not follow that our energies in future years will be exclusively confined to defending ourselves and our possessions. Many opportunities may lie open to amphibious power, and we must be ready to take advantage of them. One of the ways to bring this war to a speedy end is to convince the enemy, not by words but by deeds, that we have both the will and the means, not only to go on indefinitely but to strike heavy and unexpected blows. The road to victory may not be so long as we expect. But we have no right to count upon this. Be it long or short, rough or smooth, we mean to reach our journey's end.

It is our intention to maintain and enforce a strict blockade not only of Germany but of Italy, France and all the other countries that have fallen into the German power. I read in the papers that Herr Hitler has also proclaimed a strict blockade of the British Islands. No one can complain of that. I remember the Kaiser doing it in the last war. What indeed would be a matter of general complaint would be if we were to prolong the agony of all Europe by allowing food to come in to nourish the Nazis and aid their war effort, or to allow food to go in to the subjugated peoples, which certainly would be pillaged off them by their Nazi conquerors.

There have been many proposals, founded on the highest motives, that food should be allowed to pass the blockade for the relief of these popualtions. I regret that we must refuse these requests. The Nazis declare that they have created a new unified economy in Europe. They have repeatedly stated that they possess ample reserves of food and that they can feed their captive peoples. In a German broadcast of 27th June it was said that while Mr Hoover's[1] plan for relieving France, Belgium and Holland deserved commendation, the German forces had already taken the necessary steps. We know that in Norway when the German troops went in, there were food supplies to last for a year. We know that Poland, though not a rich country, usually produces sufficient food for her people. Moreover, the other countries which Herr Hitler has invaded all held considerable stocks when the Germans entered and are themselves, in many cases, very substantial food producers. If all this food is not available now, it can only be because it has been removed to feed the people of Germany and to give them increased rations – for a change – during the last few months. At this season of the year and for some months to come, there is the least chance of scarcity as the harvest has just been gathered in. The only agencies which can create famine in any part of Europe now and during the coming winter, will be German exactions or German failure to distribute the supplies which they command.

There is another aspect. Many of the most valuable foods are essential to the manufacture of vital war material. Fats are used to make explosives. Potatoes make the alcohol for motor spirit. The plastic materials now so

---

[1] Herbert Hoover, 1874–1964. Chairman of the American Relief Committee, London, 1914–15; the Commission for Relief in Belgium, 1915–19. Food Administrator for the United States, 1917–19. United States Secretary of Commerce, 1921–8. President of the United States, 1929–33. In August 1940 he proposed a relaxation of the British naval blockade of Germany to enable food supplies to go to France, Belgium and Holland. In March 1946, at the request of President Truman, he undertook the co-ordination of world food supplies for thirty-eight countries.

largely used in the construction of aircraft are made of milk. If the Germans used these commodities to help them to bomb our women and children, rather than to feed the populations who produce them, we may be sure that imported foods would go the same way, directly or indirectly, or be employed to relieve the enemy of the responsibilities he has so wantonly assumed. Let Hitler bear his responsibilities to the full and let the peoples of Europe who groan beneath his yoke aid in every way the coming of the day when that yoke will be broken. Meanwhile, we can and we will arrange in advance for the speedy entry of food into any part of the enslaved area, when this part has been wholly cleared of German forces, and has genuinely regained its freedom. We shall do our best to encourage the building up of reserves of food all over the world, so that there will always be held up before the eyes of the peoples of Europe, including – I say it deliberately – the German and Austrian peoples, the certainty that the shattering of the Nazi power will bring to them all immediate food, freedom and peace.

Rather more than a quarter of a year has passed since the new Government came into power in this country. What a cataract of disaster has poured out upon us since then. The trustful Dutch overwhelmed; their beloved and respected Sovereign[1] driven into exile;[2] the peaceful city of Rotterdam the scene of a massacre as hideous and brutal as anything in the Thirty Years' War.[3] Belgium invaded and beaten down; our own fine Expeditionary Force, which King Leopold called to his rescue, cut off and almost captured, escaping as it seemed only by a miracle and with the loss of all its equipment; our Ally, France, out; Italy in against us; all France in the power of the enemy, all its arsenals and vast masses of military material converted or convertible to the enemy's use; a puppet Government set up at Vichy which may at any

---

[1] Wilhelmina, 1880–1962. Became Queen of the Netherlands at the age of ten, on the death of her father. A fluent speaker of English, French and German. Maintained the neutrality of Holland, 1914–18. Following the outbreak of war in September 1939, she reiterated the call for neutrality. Announced her willingness (with King Leopold of the Belgians) to use her good offices to negotiate a peaceful settlement, November 1939. Issued a 'flaming protest' at the German violation of Dutch neutrality, 10 May 1940. Brought to Britain by a British destroyer, 13 May 1940. Lived in London, 1940–5, narrowly escaping death in 1943 when a bomb fell near her home, killing two members of her household. Returned to Holland, 1945. Abdicated in favour of her daughter Juliana, 1948.

[2] On 13 May 1940, Queen Wilhelmina, warned that she might be kidnapped by the invading German forces and used as a hostage, left The Hague for Rotterdam, where she embarked on a British destroyer, HMS *Hereward*. Her aim was to join those of her armed forces still resisting in Zeeland. Heavy German bombardments made it impossible for her to land in Zeeland: she then crossed the North Sea to Harwich. After living in England as an exile, she returned to Holland as Queen in 1945.

[3] The bombing of Rotterdam on 14 May 1940 had created the same shock waves as the pre-war Japanese bombing of Shanghai and the German–Italian bombing of Barcelona and Guernica during the Spanish Civil War. In fact, relatively few people were killed: in all, 814 Dutch civilians (the figures mentioned at the time ranged from 25,000 to 30,000 dead).

moment be forced to become our foe; the whole Western seaboard of Europe from the North Cape to the Spanish frontier in German hands; all the ports, all the airfields on this immense front, employed against us as potential springboards of invasion. Moreover, the German air power, numerically so far outstripping ours, has been brought so close to our Island that what we used to dread greatly has come to pass and the hostile bombers not only reach our shores in a few minutes and from many directions, but can be escorted by their fighting aircraft. Why Sir, if we had been confronted at the beginning of May with such a prospect, it would have seemed incredible that at the end of a period of horror and disaster, or at this point in a period of horror and disaster, we should stand erect, sure of ourselves, masters of our fate and with the conviction of final victory burning unquenchable in our hearts. Few would have believed we could survive; none would have believed that we should to-day not only feel stronger but should actually be stronger than we have ever been before.

Let us see what has happened on the other side of the scales. The British nation and the British Empire finding themselves alone, stood undismayed against disaster. No one flinched or wavered; nay, some who formerly thought of peace, now think only of war. Our people are united and resolved, as they have never been before. Death and ruin have become small things compared with the shame of defeat or failure in duty. We cannot tell what lies ahead. It may be that even greater ordeals lie before us. We shall face whatever is coming to us. We are sure of ourselves and of our cause and here then is the supreme fact which has emerged in these months of trial.

Meanwhile, we have not only fortified our hearts but our Island. We have rearmed and rebuilt our armies in a degree which would have been deemed impossible a few months ago. We have ferried across the Atlantic, in the month of July, thanks to our friends over there, an immense mass of munitions, of all kinds, cannon, rifles, machine-guns, cartridges and shell, all safely landed without the loss of a gun or a round. The output of our own factories, working as they have never worked before, has poured forth to the troops. The whole British Army is at home. More than 2,000,000 determined men have rifles and bayonets in their hands to-night and three-quarters of them are in regular military formations. We have never had armies like this in our Island in time of war. The whole Island bristles against invaders, from the sea or from the air. As I explained to the House in the middle of June, the stronger our Army at home, the larger must the invading expedition be, and the larger the invading expedition, the less difficult will be the task of the Navy in detecting its assembly and in intercepting and destroying it on passage; and the greater also would be the difficulty of feeding and supplying the invaders if ever they landed, in the teeth of continuous naval and air attack on their communications. All this is classical and venerable doctrine. As in Nelson's day, the maxim holds, 'Our first line of defence is the enemy's ports.' Now air reconnaissance and photography have brought to an old principle a new and potent aid.

Our Navy is far stronger than it was at the beginning of the war. The great flow of new construction set on foot at the outbreak, is now beginning to come in. We hope our friends across the ocean will send us a timely reinforcement to bridge the gap between the peace flotillas of 1939 and the war flotillas of 1941. There is no difficulty in sending such aid. The seas and oceans are open. The U-boats are contained. The magnetic mine is, up to the present time, effectively mastered. The merchant tonnage under the British flag, after a year of unlimited U-boat war, after eight months of intensive mining attack, is larger than when we began. We have, in addition, under our control at least 4,000,000 tons of shipping from the captive countries which has taken refuge here or in the harbours of the Empire. Our stocks of food of all kinds are far more abundant than in the days of peace and a large and growing programme of food production is on foot.

Why do I say all this? Not assuredly to boast; not assuredly to give the slightest countenance to complacency. The dangers we face are still enormous, but so are our advantages and resources. I recount them because the people have a right to know that there are solid grounds for the confidence which we feel, and that we have good reason to believe ourselves capable, as I said in a very dark hour two months ago, of continuing the war 'if necessary alone, if necessary for years.' I say it also because the fact that the British Empire stands invincible, and that Nazidom is still being resisted, will kindle again the spark of hope in the breasts of hundreds of millions of down-trodden or despairing men and women throughout Europe, and far beyond its bounds, and that from these sparks there will presently come a cleansing and devouring flame.

The great air battle which has been in progress over this Island for the last few weeks has recently attained a high intensity. It is too soon to attempt to assign limits either to its scale or to its duration. We must certainly expect that greater efforts will be made by the enemy than any he has so far put forth. Hostile airfields are still being developed in France and the Low Countries, and the movement of squadrons and material for attacking us is still proceeding. It is quite plain that Herr Hitler could not admit defeat in his air attack on Great Britain without sustaining most serious injury. If, after all his boastings and blood-curdling threats and lurid accounts trumpeted round the world of the damage he has inflicted, of the vast numbers of our Air Force he has shot down, so he says, with so little loss to himself; if after tales of the panic-stricken British crouched in their holes cursing the plutocratic Parliament which has led them to such a plight; if after all this his whole air onslaught were forced after a while tamely to peter out, the Führer's reputation for veracity of statement might be seriously impugned. We may be sure, therefore, that he will continue as long as he has the strength to do so, and as long as any preoccupations he may have in respect of the Russian Air Force allow him to do so.

On the other hand, the conditions and course of the fighting have so far been favourable to us. I told the House two months ago that whereas in France our fighter aircraft were wont to inflict a loss of two or three to one upon the Germans, and in the fighting at Dunkirk, which was a kind of no man's land, a loss of about three or four to one, we expected that in an attack on this Island we should achieve a larger ratio. This has certainly come true. It must also be remembered that all the enemy machines and pilots which are shot down over our Island, or over the seas which surround it, are either destroyed or captured; whereas a considerable proportion of our machines, and also of our pilots, are saved, and soon again in many cases come into action.

A vast and admirable system of salvage, directed by the Ministry of Aircraft Production, ensures the speediest return to the fighting line of damaged machines, and the most provident and speedy use of all the spare parts and material. At the same time the splendid, nay, astounding increase in the output and repair of British aircraft and engines which Lord Beaverbrook has achieved by a genius of organisation and drive, which looks like magic, has given us overflowing reserves of every type of aircraft, and an ever mounting stream of production both in quantity and quality. The enemy is, of course, far more numerous than we are. But our new production already, as I am advised, largely exceeds his, and the American production is only just beginning to flow in. It is a fact, as I see from my daily returns, that our bomber and fighter strengths now, after all this fighting, are larger than they have ever been. We hope, we believe that we shall be able to continue the air struggle indefinitely and as long as the enemy pleases, and the longer it continues the more rapid will be our approach, first towards that parity, and then into that superiority in the air, upon which in a large measure the decision of the war depends.

The gratitude of every home in our Island, in our Empire, and indeed throughout the world, except in the abodes of the guilty, goes out to the British airmen who, undaunted by odds, unwearied in their constant challenge and mortal danger, are turning the tide of world war by their prowess and by their devotion. Never in the field of human conflict was so much owed by so many to so few. All hearts go out to the fighter pilots, whose brilliant actions we see with our own eyes day after day, but we must never forget that all the time, night after night, month after month, our bomber squadrons travel far into Germany, find their targets in the darkness by the highest navigational skill, aim their attacks, often under the heaviest fire, often with serious loss, with deliberate, careful discrimination, and inflict shattering blows upon the whole of the technical and war-making structure of the Nazi power. On no part of the Royal Air Force does the weight of the war fall more heavily than on the daylight bombers who will play an invaluable part in the case of invasion and whose unflinching zeal it has been necessary in the meanwhile on numerous occasions to restrain.

We are able to verify the results of bombing military targets in Germany, not only by reports which reach us through many sources, but also, of course, by photography. I have no hesitation in saying that this process of bombing the military industries and communications of Germany and the air bases and storage depots from which we are attacked, which process will continue upon an ever-increasing scale until the end of the war, and may in another year attain dimensions hitherto undreamed of, affords one at least of the most certain, if not the shortest of all the roads to victory. Even if the Nazi legions stood triumphant on the Black Sea, or indeed upon the Caspian, even if Hitler was at the gates of India, it would profit him nothing if at the same time the entire economic and scientific apparatus of German war power lay shattered and pulverised at home.

The fact that the invasion of this Island upon a large scale has become a far more difficult operation with every week that has passed since we saved our Army at Dunkirk, and our very great preponderance of sea power, enable us to turn our eyes and to turn our strength increasingly towards the Mediterranean and against that other enemy who, without the slightest provocation, coldly and deliberately for greed and gain, stabbed France in the back in the moment of her agony, and is now marching against us in Africa. The defection of France has, of course, been deeply damaging to our position in what is called, somewhat oddly, the Middle East. In the defence of Somaliland, for instance, we had counted upon strong French forces attacking the Italians from Jibuti. We had counted also upon the use of the French naval and air bases in the Mediterranean, and particularly upon the North African shore. We had counted upon the French Fleet. Even though metropolitan France was temporarily overrun, there was no reason why the French Navy, substantial parts of the French Army, the French Air Force and the French Empire overseas should not have continued the struggle at our side.

Shielded by overwhelming sea-power, possessed of invaluable strategic bases and of ample funds, France might have remained one of the great combatants in the struggle. By so doing, France would have preserved the continuity of her life, and the French Empire might have advanced with the British Empire to the rescue of the independence and integrity of the French Motherland. In our own case, if we had been put in the terrible position of France, a contingency now happily impossible, although, of course, it would have been the duty of all war leaders to fight on here to the end, it would also have been their duty, as I indicated in my speech of 4th June, to provide as far as possible for the Naval security of Canada and our Dominions and to make sure they had the means to carry on the struggle from beyond the oceans. Most of the other countries that have been overrun by Germany for the time being have persevered valiantly and faithfully. The Czechs, the Poles, the Norwegians, the Dutch, the Belgians are still in the field, sword in hand, recognised by Great Britain and the United States as the sole representative authorities and lawful Governments of their respective States.

That France alone should lie prostrate at this moment, is the crime, not of a great and noble nation, but of what are called 'the men of Vichy.' We have profound sympathy with the French people. Our old comradeship with France is not dead. In General de Gaulle and his gallant band, that comradeship takes an effective form. These free Frenchmen have been condemned to death by Vichy, but the day will come, as surely as the sun will rise to-morrow, when their names will be held in honour, and their names will be graven in stone in the streets and villages of a France restored in a liberated Europe to its full freedom and its ancient fame. But this conviction which I feel of the future cannot affect the immediate problems which confront us in the Mediterranean and in Africa. It had been decided some time before the beginning of the war not to defend the Protectorate of Somaliland, and when our small forces there, a few battalions, a few guns, were attacked by all the Italian troops, nearly two divisions, which had formerly faced the French at Jibuti, it was right to withdraw our detachments, virtually intact, for action elsewhere. Far larger operations no doubt impend in the Middle East theatre, and I shall certainly not attempt to discuss or prophesy about their probable course. We have large armies and many means of reinforcing them. We have the complete sea command of the Eastern Mediterranean. We intend to do our best to give a good account of ourselves, and to discharge faithfully and resolutely all our obligations and duties in that quarter of the world. More than that I do not think the House would wish me to say at the present time.

A good many people have written to me to ask me to make on this occasion a fuller statement of our war aims, and of the kind of peace we wish to make after the war, than is contained in the very considerable declaration which was made early in the Autumn. Since then we have made common cause with Norway, Holland and Belgium. We have recognised the Czech Government of Dr Beneš,[1] and we have told General de Gaulle that our success will carry with it the restoration of France. I do not think it would be wise at this moment, while the battle rages and the war is still perhaps only in its earlier stage, to embark upon elaborate speculations about the future shape which should be given to Europe or the new securities which must be arranged to

---

[1] Eduard Beneš, 1884–1948. Born in Bohemia, the son of a farmer. Educated in Prague, Berlin and London. A leading member of the Czechoslovak National Council, Paris, 1917–18. Czech Minister for Foreign Affairs, 1918–35; Prime Minister, 1921–2. President of the Czechoslovak Republic, 1935–8. In exile, 1939–45; President of the Czechoslovak National Committee in London, 1939–45. Re-elected as President of the Republic, Prague, 1945. Resigned, 1948. Author of many books and pamphlets on the Czech question.

spare mankind the miseries of a third World War. The ground is not new, it has been frequently traversed and explored, and many ideas are held about it in common by all good men, and all free men. But before we can undertake the task of rebuilding we have not only to be convinced ourselves, but we have to convince all other countries that the Nazi tyranny is going to be finally broken. The right to guide the course of world history is the noblest prize of victory. We are still toiling up the hill, we have not yet reached the crest-line of it, we cannot survey the landscape or even imagine what its condition will be when that longed-for morning comes. The task which lies before us immediately is at once more practical, more simple and more stern. I hope – indeed I pray – that we shall not be found unworthy of our victory if after toil and tribulation it is granted to us. For the rest, we have to gain the victory. That is our task.

There is, however, one direction in which we can see a little more clearly ahead. We have to think not only for ourselves but for the lasting security of the cause and principles for which we are fighting and of the long future of the British Commonwealth of Nations. Some months ago we came to the conclusion that the interests of the United States and of the British Empire both required that the United States should have facilities for the naval and air defence of the Western hemisphere against the attack of a Nazi power which might have acquired temporary but lengthy control of a large part of Western Europe and its formidable resources. We had therefore decided spontaneously, and without being asked or offered any inducement, to inform the Government of the United States that we would be glad to place such defence facilities at their disposal by leasing suitable sites in our Transatlantic possessions for their greater security against the unmeasured dangers of the future. The principle of association of interests for common purposes between Great Britain and the United States had developed even before the war. Various agreements had been reached about certain small islands in the Pacific Ocean which had become important as air fuelling points. In all this line of thought we found ourselves in very close harmony with the Government of Canada.

Presently we learned that anxiety was also felt in the United States about the air and naval defence of their Atlantic seaboard, and President Roosevelt has recently made it clear that he would like to discuss with us, and with the Dominion of Canada and with Newfoundland, the development of American naval and air facilities in Newfoundland and in the West Indies. There is, of course, no question of any transference of sovereignty – that has never been suggested – or of any action being taken, without the consent or against the wishes of the various Colonies concerned, but for our part, His Majesty's Government are entirely willing to accord defence facilities to the United States on a 99 years' leasehold basis, and we feel sure that our interests no less than theirs, and the interests of the Colonies themselves and of Canada and

Newfoundland will be served thereby. These are important steps. Undoubtedly this process means that these two great organisations of the English-speaking democracies, the British Empire and the United States, will have to be somewhat mixed up together in some of their affairs for mutual and general advantage. For my own part, looking out upon the future, I do not view the process with any misgivings. I could not stop it if I wished; no one can stop it. Like the Mississippi, it just keeps rolling along. Let it roll. Let it roll on full flood, inexorable, irresistible, benignant, to broader lands and better days.

John Colville: diary
(*Colville papers*)

20 August 1940

Although the gallery was crowded I made my way down to the House to hear the PM speak. It was less oratory than usual and the point of chief interest to the House was the account of the bargain with America about the lease of air-bases in the West Indies (he did not divulge what we hoped to get as a *quid pro quo*). On the whole, except for bright patches – like that about 'the Führer's reputation for veracity', which had a great success – the speech seemed to drag and the House, which is not used to sitting in August, was languid. The PM ended by comparing Anglo-American co-operation (will it one day be unity?) to the Mississippi river and saying, 'Let it roll on!' I drove back with him in the car and he sang 'Ole Man River' (out of tune) the whole way back to Downing Street.

Harold Nicolson: diary
(*'Diaries and Letters, 1939–1945'*)

20 August 1940

Winston makes his speech in the House. He deals admirably with Somaliland and the blockade. He is not too boastful. He says, in referring to the RAF, 'never in the history of human conflict has so much been owed by so many to so few'. It was a moderate and well-balanced speech. He did not try to arouse enthusiasm but only to give guidance. He made a curious reference to Russia's possible attack on Germany and spoke about our 'being mixed up with the United States', ending in a fine peroration about Anglo-American cooperation rolling on like the Mississippi.

Chiefs of Staff Committee: minutes[1]
(*Cabinet papers, 79/6*)

20 August 1940 10 Downing Street
10.30 p.m.

OPERATION 'MENACE'

The Prime Minister outlined the previous history of the plan for the above Operation. Originally it had been intended to land by day, but subsequently the Commanders had based their plan on a landing in the dark. As a result of the information about the defences of Dakar, it was now found that a night landing would be difficult and surprise would be forfeited. There would be no chance of parley and it was highly probable that the landing would meet with resistance.

He therefore proposed that we should revert to the original plan, and this should be carried out as follows. An Anglo-French armada would arrive off Dakar at dawn. Aircraft would drop steamers and leaflets over the town. The British Squadron would remain on the horizon and the French ships would advance towards the port. A picket boat flying the white flag and a tricolour would enter the harbour bearing a letter to the Governor[2] announcing the arrival of General de Gaulle and his Free French Troops. The letter would stress the fact that General de Gaulle had come to deliver Dakar from the possibility of imminent German aggression. They were bringing food and succour to the garrison and inhabitants. It would be emphasised that this was a French enterprise but that a British Squadron had accompanied it. There was no intention that the British would advance on the port provided the Governor was prepared to welcome General de Gaulle and his Free Frenchmen. It would then be necessary to await the results of this communication. Subsequent events might be as follows.

If the Governor proved amenable to General de Gaulle's entry all would be well. He might, however, refuse to receive General de Gaulle's emissary and this might possibly be followed by a formal show of resistance. Some of the coast defences might open fire. If the opposition was serious, General de Gaulle would request the British Squadron to close in. If the firing continued the British warships would open fire on the French gun positions but would use the utmost restraint in the initial stages. If it was clear that the coast batteries and possibly the battleship *Richelieu* were determined to make a fight, the British force would use all the force within their power to break down their resistance. It seemed unlikely however that French opposition would be severe in the face of the overwhelming force which would confront them. The action

---

[1] General de Gaulle, General Spears and Desmond Morton were present at this meeting.
[2] General Boisson, the Governor-General of French Equatorial Africa, and High Commissioner at Dakar, 'whom Roosevelt expected one day to open to him the gates of Africa', de Gaulle wrote in his memoirs (*The Call to Honour*, page 210).

outlined above would be carried out deliberately and without undue hurry so as to give the Frenchmen ashore time to realise the uselessness of resistance.

The next stage would be reached when General de Gaulle was established on shore. Parleys would take place and it was hoped that he would take control of Dakar in a peaceable manner. As soon as he announced that he was master of the fortress, the British Squadron would withdraw. He might, however, require help in the initial stages. In this event it might be necessary to put a British battalion, or possibly two battalions, on shore to support him.

In any event, it was essential that by nightfall General de Gaulle should be master of Dakar.

Summing up, the Prime Minister said that the important point to be borne in mind was that the British Squadron would only open fire if the French batteries offered resistance. Our fire should be directed with a view to subduing the fire of the enemy batteries. It was only in the event of really serious opposition that the full force at the command of the British Squadron would be employed.

General de Gaulle said that he was in general agreement with the above plan.

The Vice Chiefs of Staff[1] also fully agreed.

After further discussion, it was agreed that the Vice Chiefs of Staff should meet at 10.00 a.m. at Richmond Terrace the following morning, 21st August, and should inform Vice-Admiral John Cunningham and General Irwin of the plan as outlined above by the Prime Minister. A programme for the conduct of the operation should be worked out in consultation with General de Gaulle with a view to putting it into effect at the earliest possible moment. The plan should be submitted to the Prime Minister during the course of the day.

THE 'DUALA' OPERATION

A short discussion took place on the operation impending for the establishment of General de Gaulle's adherents at Duala.

There was general agreement that the operation as outlined in telegrams received that day from General Giffard[2] should proceed as soon as possible.

The Prime Minister instructed the Vice Chiefs of Staff to draft a telegram the following morning to General Giffard instructing him, and the local naval authorities, to give every assistance possible to the carrying out of the operation as outlined in his telegrams.

---

[1] Air Marshal Sir Richard Peirse, Vice-Admiral Tom Phillips and Lieutenant-General Sir Robert Haining.

[2] George James Giffard, 1886–1964. On active service in East Africa, 1913–14; on the Western Front, 1914–18 (wounded, despatches four times, DSO). Inspector-General, African Colonial Forces, 1938–9. Military Secretary to the Secretary of State for War, War Office, 1939. General Officer Commanding the Forces in Palestine and Transjordan, 1940. General Officer Commanding in West Africa, 1940 (Commanding-in-Chief, 1941–2). Knighted, 1941. General Officer Commanding-in-Chief, Eastern Army, India, 1943; 11th Army Group, South-East Asia, 1943–4.

700　August 1940

Winston S. Churchill to Neville Chamberlain
(*Churchill papers, 20/1*)

21 August 1940
Secret

My dear Neville,

I am delighted to hear your good news. Do not I beg you come back before you feel really fit. Parliament rises tomorrow and you can do a good deal of your work from the country. There has been very little Cabinet business. It would be the greatest mistake not to build up a proper reserve of strength.

When I brought Max into the War Cabinet I had the intention that he should relieve me of a very great part of the work I now have to do in Military Supply. This was not practicable while he himself retained MAP as he would have become inter-alia judge in his own case. I do not feel I can move him from MAP and make the new arrangement until the air battle shows very clear signs of being decided. Perhaps even now it has not reached its climax, but the Germans are showing various signs of weakness, and as soon as the battle is decided and the prospects of invasion become more remote with the winter weather, I have in mind to ask Greenwood to give up the Production Committee Chairmanship and let Max take this, giving up simultaneously MAP. Greenwood will not I think mind this as Attlee has a lot of work, some of which Greenwood could take. Herbert Morrison is, I understand quite agreeable to an arrangement whereby he will be on equal terms with MAP and the Controller's Department of the Admiralty. What he objected to was anything that looked invidious and suggested failure in the Ministry of Supply.

I thought Moore Brabazon would become MAP under Max's superintendence.[1] All this however must wait upon Military events.

All good wishes,
Yours ever,
Winston S. Churchill

Winston S. Churchill to Sir Archibald Sinclair
(*Churchill papers, 20/13*)

21 August 1940
ACTION THIS DAY

The important thing is to bring the German aircraft down and to win the battle, and the rate at which American correspondents and the American

---

[1] Moore-Brabazon succeeded Beaverbrook as Minister of Aircraft Production on 1 May 1941.

public are convinced that we are winning, and that our figures are true, stands in a much lower plane. They will find out quite soon enough when the German air attack is plainly shown to be repulsed. It would be a pity to tease the Fighter Command at the present time when the battle is going on from hour to hour and continuous decisions have to be taken about air raid warnings, &c. I confess I should be more inclined to let the facts speak for themselves. There is something rather obnoxious in bringing correspondents down to air squadrons in order that they may assure the American public that the Fighter pilots are not bragging and lying about their figures. We can, I think, afford to be a bit cool and calm about all this.

I should like you to see on other papers an inquiry I have been making of my own in order to check up on the particular day when MAP said they picked up no fewer than eighty German machines brought down over the land alone. This gives us a very good line for our own purposes. I must say I am a little impatient about the American scepticism. The event is what will decide all.

WSC

PS – You were admirable last night. I am so sorry not to have heard you.

Winston S. Churchill to Anthony Eden
(*Churchill papers, 20/13*)

21 August 1940

I am anxious to receive more precise reports about the action at Tug Argen Pass. Why was it so precipitately discontinued? How was the Black Watch used? Why did the General[1] speak of 'hopeless superiority' of the enemy? Why did he speak of heavy losses of the Black Watch when there are only fifteen killed and twenty wounded? The enemy pursuit does not seem to have been very severe. No doubt the evacuation has been well conducted, but I have not at all sustained the impression of obstinacy and vigour in resistance.

WSC

---

[1] Alfred Reade Godwin-Austen, 1889–1963. 2nd Lieutenant, 1909. On active service, Gallipoli and Mesopotamia, 1915–19 (Military Cross). Commanded the 14th Infantry Brigade, Palestine (Arab revolt), 1938–9 (despatches). Major-General, 1939. Commanding the 8th Division, on active service in East Africa and Abyssinia (for which he was awarded the CB), 1940. Principal Administrative Officer, India Command, New Delhi, 1945–6. Knighted, 1946. General, 1946. Chairman, South-Western Division, National Coal Board, 1946–8.

War Cabinet: minutes
(*Cabinet papers, 65/8*)

21 August 1940
12.30 p.m.
10 Downing Street

The Prime Minister reminded the War Cabinet that in his speech the previous day, he had announced that His Majesty's Government had some months previously come to the conclusion that the interests of the United States and of the British Empire both required that facilities should be placed at the disposal of the United States for the naval and air defence of the Western Hemisphere; and that we had now decided spontaneously, and without being asked or offered any inducement, to inform the Government of the United States that we were prepared to lease to them suitable sites in our transatlantic possessions. There was no question of any transfer of sovereignty.

The Prime Minister thought that our attitude in this matter, and that of the United States, should be that we were friends who were each prepared to do what was possible to help the other to gain added security, without receiving any *quid pro quo*. He thought that if we now made it plain that we would make available to the United States the facilities which they required, without payment, the United States Government would then find it possible to send us the Destroyers. If the United States Government wished to link the two transactions they could do so, but we should not do so.

General agreement was expressed with this view.

Defence Committee: minutes
(*Cabinet papers, 69/1*)

21 August 1940
6.15 p.m.
10 Downing Street

OPERATION 'MENACE'

Sir Richard Peirse said that as a result of the Meeting between the Prime Minister and the Vice Chiefs of Staff held the previous evening, the latter had held a Meeting the same morning with Admiral John Cunningham, General Irwin and General de Gaulle. The Vice Chiefs of Staff had explained the new conception of the Operation. The two Commanders and General de Gaulle had expressed their general agreement that the Operation as now conceived was feasible and an improvement on the previous conception.

Vice Admiral John Cunningham and General Irwin had been instructed to work out a plan in consultation with General de Gaulle, and this would be available later on that evening.

August 1940

War Cabinet: Confidential Annex
(*Cabinet papers, 65/14*)

22 August 1940   10 Downing Street
12 noon

In an explanatory statement, the Chancellor of the Exchequer[1] said that his colleagues should be fully aware of the existing position of our gold and exchange resources, and with the dangerous financial possibilities of the near future. There would be no difference of opinion as to the over-riding necessity of meeting our vital needs for the prosecution of the war. But he asked his colleagues to co-operate with him to the fullest extent of their ability in mitigating the financial situation.

. . . to lose gold at the rate we had experienced in the last six weeks, we should have none left by the end of December. It was not safe to reckon on a slower rate of loss and unless steps were taken it might prove higher. Moreover, to avoid complete financial dependence, it was most important that we should keep some minimum reserve in hand, even after American help had crystallised. When denuded of gold, our resources would be some £200 millions of securities, which were at present, and might then be, unsaleable in quantity.

Taking a longer view, a continuance of expenditure abroad at the present rate would mean that in the year July 1940 to June 1941, we should lose some £800 millions of gold and foreign exchange as compared with the previous estimate of £410 millions.

Turning to the policy of 'scraping the pot', described in part VI of his Memorandum, the Chancellor said that a requisition of wedding rings and other gold ornaments, would not produce more than some £20 millions.

The Prime Minister thought that this was a measure to be adopted at a later stage, if we wished to make some striking gesture for the purpose of shaming the Americans.

The Prime Minister read to the War Cabinet a letter which he had received from the Lord President of the Council.[2] The Lord President supported the general recommendations set out in paragraph VIII of the Chancellor's Memorandum.[3] He thought, however, that it would be necessary for us to gamble to some extent on the willingness of the United States to give us financial help on an extended scale.

---

[1] Sir Kingsley Wood.
[2] Neville Chamberlain.
[3] The Chancellor of the Exchequer's conclusion was that for 'the next six months at least the exchange position must be treated as a bottle-neck and dollar expenditure watched by the Treasury in conjunction with the departments concerned so as to limit it to vital needs, including vital munitions of war for delivery not too far ahead. The greater ease in the shipping position should be used to bring foods from more distant sterling parts of the Commonwealth rather than America' (War Cabinet Paper 324 of 1940, 21 August 1940, 'Gold and Exchange Resources', *Cabinet papers, 66/11*).

The Minister of Supply wondered whether anything further could be done to persuade the Dominions to restrict unnecessary imports from foreign countries, thereby increasing the difficulties of the British exchange control.

The Prime Minister thought it would be very difficult to put any further pressure on the Dominions in this direction.

Summing up, the Prime Minister said that he sympathised greatly with the Chancellor of the Exchequer in his difficulties. The Chancellor had done right to bring the financial dangers of the next few months so clearly before his colleagues. In his view, the Chancellor ought to be given the general support for which he asked, although there could be no question at the present critical stage of the war of stopping the development of the programme of the Supply Departments. After all, the greatest economy would be to shorten the war. Nothing could be more extravagant than to shape our course in such a way that we had to fight a prolonged war in a broken-backed condition.

He agreed, therefore, with the Supply Ministers that we should continue to place large scale orders in North America.

If the military position should unexpectedly deteriorate, we should have to pledge everything that we had for the sake of victory, giving the United States, if necessary, a lien on any and every part of British industry.

Winston S. Churchill to President Roosevelt
(*Churchill papers, 20/14*)

22 August 1940

I am most grateful for all you are doing on our behalf. I had not contemplated anything in the nature of a contract, bargain or sale between us. It is the fact that we had decided in Cabinet to offer you naval and air facilities off the Atlantic Coast quite independently of destroyers or any other aid. Our view is that we are two friends in danger helping each other as far as we can. We should therefore like to give you the facilities mentioned without stipulating for any return, and, even if to-morrow you found it too difficult to transfer the destroyers, &c., our offer still remains open because we think it is in the general good.

2. I see difficulties, and even risks, in the exchange of letters now suggested or in admitting in any way that the munitions which you send us are a payment for the facilities. Once this idea is accepted, people will contrast on each side what is given and received. The money value of the arrangements would be computed and set against the facilities, and some would think one thing about it and some another.

3. Moreover, Mr President, as you well know, each Island or location is a case by itself. If, for instance, there were only one harbour or site, how is it to

be divided and its advantages shared? In such a case we should like to make you an offer of what we think is best for both rather than to embark upon a close-cut argument as to what ought to be delivered in return for value received.

4. What we want is that you shall feel safe on your Atlantic seaboard so far as any facilities in possessions of ours can make you safe, and naturally, if you put in money and make large developments, you must have the effective security of a long lease. Therefore, I would rather rest at this moment upon the general declaration made by me in the House of Commons yesterday, both on this point and as regards the future of the Fleet. Then, if you will set out in greater detail what you want, we will at once tell you what we can do, and thereafter the necessary arrangements, technical and legal, can be worked out by our experts. Meanwhile, we are quite content to trust entirely to your judgment and sentiments of the people of the United States about any aid in munitions, &c., you feel able to give us. But this would be entirely a separate spontaneous act on the part of the United States arising out of their view of the world struggle and how their own interests stand in relation to it and the causes it involves.

5. Although the air attack has slackened in the last few days and our strength is growing in many ways, I do not think that bad man has yet struck his full blow. We are having considerable losses in merchant ships on the north-western approaches, now our only channel of regular communication with the oceans, and your fifty destroyers, if they came along at once, would be a precious help.

Winston S. Churchill to A. V. Alexander
(*Churchill papers, 20/13*)

22 August 1940
ACTION THIS DAY

In July you furnished the completion dates of the existing programme of construction for all its various vessels. Will you kindly let me know your proposed programme of replacements in the small craft. It is not necessary to look further ahead than March 31, 1941. In principle, I should concur in a policy of continuous replacements on the vacated slips of destroyers, corvettes, sloops and AS[1] trawlers. I should welcome a large development of anti-E-boat vessels. There should be a restricted but continuous production of submarines, equal certainly to our losses.

I cannot think that any cruisers, except the anti-aircraft cruisers, are

---

[1] Anti-submarine.

required to be sanctioned before the date mentioned, in view of the large programme already set on foot in this year.

I await your proposals about the resumption of the capital ship programme, which was approved by the late Cabinet on my initiative. This cannot be settled apart from the general demand upon steel and labour, but in principle I favour its resumption.

I hope opportunity will now be taken to repair the disastrous neglect to convert the Royal Sovereign class into properly armoured and bulged bombarding vessels with heavy deck armour. These will be needed next year for the attack on Italy. It is lamentable that we have not got them now. They should certainly take precedence over the resumption of battleship construction.

I shall be glad to hear from you soon, as early next week we shall be considering programmes and priority. I repeat that the only question now is concerned with the period between September 1 and March 31 next.[1]

WSC

Winston S. Churchill to General Ismay
(*Churchill papers, 20/13*)

22 August 1940

In conference last night with the S of S for War and Sir Roger Keyes, I came to the conclusion that the operation 'Menace' had best be entrusted to a smaller number of more highly mobile trained troops than is now proposed. It is a mistake to treat the Marine Brigades as trained for this purpose. They consist almost entirely of recruits brought in since the war and are only now beginning boat-work or manoeuvre. For training and mobility they cannot compete with many battalions of the Regular Army. Moreover, they can do very good work here, while they are maturing. One Regular Battalion and one Battalion of Marines may be sent as reserve.

The Director of Combined Operations, Sir Roger Keyes, will in three days

---

[1] In his reply to Churchill that day, A. V. Alexander reported that a plan was being made 'to meet your request for a programme of replacements of small craft', for the 'continuous replacement' of destroyers, corvettes, sloops and trawlers, and for the provision of twenty-four new submarines which, with other submarines then building, 'will more than replace losses up to date and will be some insurance against losses in the next twelve months'. As to cruisers, the eight whose building was suspended in May 1940 would now be built, but 'I should hesitate very much to put any of the Royal Sovereign class into reconstruction because we may need every one of them at any moment' (*Admiralty papers, 205/5*).

furnish 1,500 men from his Companies and commands, and these, with the reserve aforesaid, will constitute the fighting force of the expedition, apart from the French troops. Pray let me have your dates for the whole programme. There must be no delay.

WSC

John Colville: diary
(*Colville papers*)

22 August 1940

The PM is not unnaturally indignant because the gun – his gun – so laboriously installed at Dover was not ready to fire in reply to some shore batteries from the other side which bombarded first a convoy and then Dover today.

There is a double sting about air-raids at night. I gather that at No. 10 the PM strode about the house, having been aroused by gunfire in North London, wearing his flowery dressing-gown and a tin hat.

War Cabinet: minutes
(*Cabinet papers, 65/8*)

23 August 1940 10 Downing Street
11.30 a.m.

The Prime Minister said it was important to have as large a proportion as possible of highly-trained troops in mobile reserve, and he suggested that the Secretary of State for War should consider moving the First Division from the Coastal Area into mobile reserve.

The Prime Minister said that his view of the Cabinet decision to which the Home Secretary had referred[1] was that we did not contemplate or countenance fighting by persons not in the armed forces, but that we did not forbid it. What he had had in mind was that the police, and, he hoped, the ARP services, could be divided into combatant and non-combatant branches, armed and unarmed; those armed would co-operate actively in fighting with the Home Guard and Regulars in their neighbourhood, and would withdraw with them if necessary; the unarmed would assist in the 'stay put' policy for

---

[1] Instructions to the Police in the event of an invasion.

civilians. Should they fall into an area effectively occupied by the enemy, they might surrender and submit with the rest of the inhabitants, but must in no circumstances give any aid to the enemy in maintaining order, or in any other way. They should, however, assist the civil population as far as possible.

As regards the civil population, the order was 'not to join in the fight.' Nevertheless, the citizen retained his natural right to fight in defence of his family and his home. This might well result in civilians joining in the fight in support of the military. If this happened, the Government would certainly not desire to punish those responsible.

It was agreed that there was a growing demand for some statement of what we were fighting for. We must make our aims clear, not merely to our own people, but also to the peoples of Europe whom we were trying to free. In effect, Hitler said that, provided people were prepared to do without liberty and to sacrifice nationality, he could give them a good life. A time would come when it would be generally realised that this country was not only capable of maintaining the fight alone, but afforded the only real hope for the future. That would be the moment to 'put across' our conception of the new Europe. It was thought that there was in fact a considerable measure of agreement between members of all political parties, but time would be required to work out an adequate statement.

The Prime Minister outlined some of the points which he thought would be included in the scheme proposed. In addition to the five Great Powers of Europe, there should be three groups of smaller States – in Northern Europe, in Middle Europe, and in the Balkans. He also looked to see the five great nations and these three confederations linked together in some kind of Council of Europe. There should be a Court to which all justiciable disputes should be referred, with an international air force. There must be a scheme for a fair distribution of raw materials. It was also important that there should be no attempt at a vindictive settlement after the war.

War Cabinet: Confidential Annex
(*Cabinet papers, 65/14*)

23 August 1940　　　　　　　　　　　　　　　　　　　　　　10 Downing Street
11.30 a.m.

The War Cabinet had before them a Note by the Prime Minister covering a general directive to the Commander-in-Chief which had been drawn up in consultation with the Chiefs of Staff and despatched to General Wavell by telegram (WP (40) 330).[1]

[1] Churchill's directive to General Wavell (see pages 674–7), drafted by Churchill on 15 August 1940 and finalized on the following day.

The Prime Minister said that the directive was not intended as an order to be carried out without modification; rather it was intended to give the general position, and to stress the need for forming a big army in the Delta for meeting possible developments which might eventuate quite soon. The directive also emphasised the importance of subordinating the political to the strategic situation.

As regards the Armoured Brigade, the Prime Minister said that the War Cabinet had still got until the 26th August to decide the route which this unit should take. The Admiralty considered that a great risk would be run in sending it through the Mediterranean, and that the slow speed of the ships carrying the unit would hamper the Fleet in passing the *Illustrious* and the *Valiant* into the Mediterranean. Further the *Valiant* might be prevented from delivering vital equipment at Malta necessary for Malta's protection. It was a question of balancing risks and it might be that by the 26th August conditions in Egypt would be such that the risk of sending this unit through the Mediterranean would have to be run.

The Prime Minister said that he was very much in favour of the Australians and New Zealanders in this country joining their compatriots in Egypt, and thought they could well be spared from this country, in view of the increasing improvement of our defensive position at home.

Sir Alexander Cadogan: diary
(*'The Diaries of Sir Alexander Cadogan'*)

23 August 1940

About 5 telegram from Lothian to say Americans don't like PM's procedure and must stick to their exchange of letters idea. Lothian rang me up to emphasise that this was the only possible course. Went over about 6.30 with D. Scott and Dean[1] to see PM. He rather incensed and won't have exchange of letters. Says he doesn't mind if we don't get destroyers. Won't expose himself to a wrangle with Americans, having made us definite gift, haggling over the extent of ours. Dare say he is right. Sent provisional telegram to Lothian, and PM will dictate his own message in car on way down to Chequers.

---

[1] David Scott, Assistant Under-Secretary of State, Foreign Office, 1938–44; and Patrick Dean, Assistant Legal Adviser, Foreign Office, 1939–45. Both later rose to the heights of their profession, and both were knighted.

Winston S. Churchill to Sir Cyril Newall and Sir Richard Peirse
(*Churchill papers, 20/13*)

24 August 1940

It is of high importance to increase both the numbers of squadrons and the number of aircraft and crews immediately available. After a year of war we have only IE[1] operationally fit about 1,750, of which again only three-quarters are immediately available. You cannot rest satisfied with this which is less than the number we were supposed to have available before the war.

WSC

Winston S. Churchill to General Ismay
(*Churchill papers, 20/13*)

24 August 1940

Report to me on the position of Major Jefferis. By whom is he employed? Who is he under? I regard this officer as a singularly capable and forceful man, who should be brought forward to a higher position. He ought certainly to be promoted Lieutenant-Colonel as it will give him more authority.[2]

Winston S. Churchill to General Ismay
(*Churchill papers, 20/13*)

24 August 1940

The operation 'Scipio' was necessarily much talked about.[3] Being entirely a French project no doubt many in General de Gaulle's circle had to be consulted. The Poles, who were at one time to assist in manning de Gaulle's artillery, have also got to know.

Inside 'Scipio' another operation of a different kind has developed called 'Menace'. Although few people know the scope and character of 'Menace' yet

---

[1] Initial equipments (for Royal Air Force crews)

[2] Jefferis received his promotion, and was placed under the direct control of Churchill's Defence Office. Churchill was influenced in doing this as a result of a running feud between Jefferis and the Director of Artillery at the War Office, to which Jefferis was attached (see Churchill's minute to Eden of 10 November 1940).

[3] Lord Halifax had told Churchill that a member of the Polish Government-in-exile had told him that the destination of 'Scipio' was Dakar.

one may be sure that General de Gaulle will have been forced to consult his principal lieutenants, and, anyhow, there is bound to be a lot of talk centring on the place in question among the foreigners involved. This is shown by the General's wish to postpone repatriation of any Frenchmen from here pending events.

The question is whether we can assign some other purpose to the expedition as a blind. Perhaps Martinique might be used in talk. Let me have suggestions.

General de Gaulle should be warned in due course about his entourage. It does not look worse than pure indiscretion.

Winston S. Churchill to General Ismay and Sir Edward Bridges
(*Premier papers, 3/119/10*)

24 August 1940

The Joint Planning Committee will from Monday next work directly under the orders of the Minister of Defence, and will become a part of the Minister of Defence's Office – formerly the CID[1] Secretariat. Accommodation will be found for them at Richmond Terrace. They will retain their present positions in and contacts with the three Service Departments. They will work out the details of such plans as are communicated to them by the Minister of Defence. They may initiate plans of their own after reference to General Ismay. They will of course be at the service of the Chiefs of Staff Committee for the elaboration of any matters sent to them.

2. All plans produced by the Joint Planning Committee or elaborated by them under instructions as above, will be referred to the Chiefs of Staff Committee for their observations.

3. Thereafter should doubts and differences exist, or in important cases, all plans will be reviewed by the Defence Committee of the War Cabinet which will consist of the Prime Minister, the Lord Privy Seal and Lord Beaverbrook, and the three Service Ministers; the three Chiefs of the Staff with General Ismay being in attendance.

4. The Prime Minister assumes the responsibility of keeping the War Cabinet informed of what is in hand; but the relation of the Chiefs of the Staff to the War Cabinet is unaltered.

[1] Committee of Imperial Defence.

Winston S. Churchill to Sir Edward Bridges
(*Churchill papers, 20/13*)

25 August 1940

Papers dealing with future operations are to be circulated only to Members of the Defence Committee, as reconstituted, and to the Joint Planning Committee.

When such plans call for action by Departments other than the Service Departments, no more of the plan should be communicated than is necessary to enable such action to be taken. All papers connected with future plans are to be circulated under the arrangements appropriate to lock and key papers, i.e., in sealed envelopes in locked boxes.

Please submit to me the draft of an instruction to the Departments concerned, ordering them to take steps to see that documents relating to future operations are only communicated to such officers as must be acquainted with their contents.

Winston S. Churchill: Ministerial Directive
(*Churchill papers, 20/13*)

25 August 1940
Most Secret

We shall soon be engaged in preparing plans for offensive operations next Spring, the success of which will depend to an exceptional degree on surprise.

But surprise will be impossible of attainment if future plans are made known to a large number of officers who, in turn, pass them on and discuss them with their colleagues. In this way, what should be a closely guarded secret, becomes in a short time a matter of common knowledge and gossip throughout Whitehall and the Clubs of Pall Mall.

I have given instructions that the circulation of plans dealing with future plans shall be rigidly restricted to the Departments directly concerned. But this precaution will be of no avail unless each Minister takes steps to ensure that knowledge of future operations is only imparted to those individuals who must be acquainted with them, and only to the extent that is necessary to enable action to be taken.

For this to be effective, a change of outlook is wanted. No one, in whatever position, should regard it as in any sense a reflection on his prudence, if a plan is only communicated to him partially, or not at all. Everyone must be made to realise that the only way to keep a secret is to insist ruthlessly on the rule that only those are told who must be told. Everyone should take pride, not in how much knowledge of future plans he can acquire, but in carrying on with his work without asking unnecessary questions, or expecting to be told more than is required for the task he is called on to perform.

I ask that instructions in this sense may be issued by you to all concerned in your Department.

WSC

Winston S. Churchill to William Mackenzie King
(*Churchill papers, 20/14*)

25 August 1940

I and my colleagues have recently considered how we should deal with the gold, worth £70 millions, entrusted by the Bank of France to the Bank of England for custody. We have taken a different view from that which I understand you were disposed to take when Sir F. Phillips,[1] on our instructions, mentioned to you the analogous question of the gold entrusted to the Bank of Canada and the US dollars which we have to pay to the Bank of Canada for the credit of the State of France under the arrangements made for the assignment to us of French contracts in the USA. I should therefore like to explain our reasons fully.

The Bank of France, whose headquarters are in Paris, is in territory occupied by the enemy. Our Trading with the Enemy legislation (and I understand yours also) regards territory declared to be occupied by the enemy on the same footing as enemy territory. We therefore decided that the gold must be vested in the Custodian of Enemy Property, and this has been done.

The Custodian's duty is to protect the interests of the Bank of France in regard to this asset in any settlement after the war, but not to maintain it in the form of physical gold for the benefit of the Bank of France so long as it remains in occupied territory and under German domination. The Custodian's duty, in our view, does not make it improper for him to sell the gold to us for sterling, subject to a full obligation on our part to account for this asset at its full gold value in our settlement with France after it has been freed from German domination. This therefore is the course which we think it right to adopt.

It is true that we are not at war with France, but France is temporarily in enemy occupation and under enemy domination. The gold must therefore, in

---

[1] Frederick Phillips, 1884–1943. Entered the Treasury, 1908 (having taken first place in the Civil Service examination). Under-Secretary, 1932. Knighted, 1933. Joint Second Secretary, 1938. Chairman of the Financial Committee of the League of Nations. Represented the Treasury in the United States from 1940 until his death.

any event, remain blocked until France is free again. To allow gold to remain blocked instead of purchasing it for sterling would confer no benefit on the Bank of France, but would seriously prejudice the war effort of the Empire. There is no future hope for the French nation except through the victory for which we are all fighting, and our trusteeship for the future existence of a free France cannot be rated as less important than our trusteeship for the post-war financial interests of the Bank of France.

We have considered whether to buy this gold from our Custodian of Enemy Property now or to postpone this till later. We think it should be bought at once. That is the normal and natural procedure under our Trading with the Enemy legislation, and if it is not followed, some action at present unforeseen – whether technical or political – might be initiated by the Bank of France under German direction and render the purchase difficult or cause it to appear overbearing.

Moreover, we cannot long postpone the purchase without serious detriment to our own essential interests.

As you know, on the capitulation of France we decided to make every effort to increase our imports of munitions and war supplies from the United States. We met with a helpful response in many directions, and in addition we were enabled to take over the whole of the French contracts. The result has been that our resources in gold and United States dollars have in recent weeks been drawn upon at a much faster rate than hitherto, and it has become clear that they will be exhausted much sooner than had previously been expected. The magnificent help which we have received from Canada has also, of course, involved some additional drain on our resources, though much reduced by the generous way in which you are making dollars available for us.

The total of dollar securities owned by residents here, which we have requisitioned or shall requisition, though substantial, is small in relation to our total present and future commitments; moreover, owing in particular to the state and character of the American market, realisation is at present a difficult and tardy process, and affords only a modest alleviation of our immediate difficulties.

We are relying, therefore, on financial help from the United States in due course, and I am confident that we shall not look for this assistance in vain. We cannot, however, expect that this aid will take practical shape until perhaps some time after the election in November. On no account can we suffer our stock of gold and dollars to be reduced below the essential minimum working balance before this new fortification of our position can be solidly arranged.

It is for these reasons that I have come to the conclusion that our purchase of the gold should not be delayed. I have explained our views at length, as I want them to be in your mind when you are considering what course of action to adopt in regard to the French gold entrusted to the Bank of Canada. It is, I understand, worth some £90 millions, and lies in your jurisdiction. Should it seem right to you, in the light of the explanation I have given, to adopt the same course as we have adopted, it would be of great value to the cause for which we are both fighting. Our resources for obtaining supplies from the United States of America otherwise than as gifts are rapidly disappearing. No one can foresee what course events may take in the United States of America, and though I have good reason for feeling confident of their intention to give us all possible help, I am reluctant to leave anything undone by which our position may be made more secure. If you feel able to give your assent, I am anxious that this gold should be vested in your Custodian; that, except to the extent that you may wish the Canadian Exchange Control to purchase any part of it for your war effort, it should be sold by him for sterling and added to the War Chest here. There would, of course, remain an obligation to reach an appropriate settlement of this and many other matters when a free State of France will be restored after the war. That obligation will be ours.

I must refer, also, to the more complicated question which I understand Sir Frederick Phillips discussed with you at greater length, and which arises from the arrangement that we should pay United States dollars to the Bank of Canada in New York for the credit of the French State in respect of French payments made for goods which will, under the assignment of contracts, be delivered to us. These payments will be made gradually, and I am not suggesting that immediate action is called for in regard to them, but I would earnestly hope, for the reasons I have given, and notwithstanding the doubts which you have expressed and which I quite appreciate would be decisive in any but the extraordinary conditions in which we find ourselves, to receive your agreement in principle with the view that at the appropriate time these dollars should be sold for sterling and added to the War Chest by a procedure corresponding to that applicable to the gold.

I know you will do your utmost to help us, as you always have done in this great battle for our very existence. Nothing at this moment could do so much to strengthen our position as to enable us, with due regard to French interests and to her ultimate security, to use these financial resources for the common cause.

WSC

Winston S. Churchill to General Ismay
(*Churchill papers, 20/13*)

25 August 1940
ACTION THIS DAY

Address the War Office forthwith upon the situation disclosed at Slough and in General Haining's[1] letter to me. Point out the danger of this large concentration of vehicles; the desirability of dispersing and concealing the vehicles. Ask that a plan should be examined for de-centralizing this Depot as far as possible. We should also make sure that no sediment or surplus accumulates in the Depot. It would be a great pity if a thousand valuable vehicles were ruined in an air attack.

WSC

Winston S. Churchill to General Ismay
(*Churchill papers, 20/13*)

25 August 1940
ACTION THIS DAY

Ask the Air Ministry or whatever supply department is concerned for a report showing the numbers and character of the delay-action fuzes now in stock and under manufacture, and the programme for future production. What plans have been made for delay-action extending for weeks and even months. The Admiralty have a good deal of information on this. In addition what use has been made of delay-action bombs in Germany up to date? And what further action is proposed.

WSC

Winston S. Churchill to Anthony Eden
(*Churchill papers, 20/13*)

25 August 1940
ACTION THIS DAY

War Office have accepted from the War Cabinet the responsibility of dealing with delay action bombs. This may become a feature of the enemy

---

[1] Robert Hadden Haining, 1882–1959. 2nd Lieutenant, 1901; Major, 1915. On active service 1914–18 (despatches six times, DSO); Major-General, 1934. Commandant, Imperial Defence College, 1935–6. Deputy Director of Military Operations and Intelligence, War Office, 1936–8. Lieutenant-General, 1938. General Officer Commanding the British Forces in Palestine and Transjordan, 1938–9. Knighted, 1940. Vice-Chief of the Imperial General Staff, 1940–1. General, 1941. Intendant-General, Middle East, 1941–2.

attack. A number were thrown last night into the City, causing obstruction. They may even try them on Whitehall! It seems to me that energetic effort should be made to provide sufficient squads to deal with this form of attack in the large centres. The squads must be highly mobile so as not to waste men and material. They must move in motor lorries quickly from one point to another. I presume a careful system of reporting all unexploded bombs and the time at which they fell is in operation, and that this information will be sent immediately to the delay-action section of Home Defence, which has no doubt already been established, and also the various local branches. The service, which is highly dangerous, must be considered particularly honourable, and rewards should follow its successful discharge.[1]

I should be very glad to see your plans for the new section, together with numbers, and it will also be interesting to have a short account of the work done up to date and the methods employed. I presume you are in touch with all the scientific authorities you need.

On the other hand, I am asking the Air Ministry for information as to their reciprocating this process on the enemy.

Winston S. Churchill to A. V. Alexander
(*Churchill papers, 20/13*)

25 August 1940

I gathered that you now felt able to publish the fact that these four ships were sunk by three torpedoes, and that, consequently, the Fleet Air Arm shares credit with the RAF. It certainly seems to have been a most remarkable occurrence, and now that the Italians know how their ships were sunk publicity would seem advantageous.

WSC

---

[1] The first awards of the George Cross for bomb disposal work were announced on 30 September 1940, the three recipients being Thomas Hopper Alderson, Temporary Lieutenant Robert Davies and Sapper George Cameron Wylie. Alderson, a part-time worker (Detached Leader), Rescue Parties, at Bridlington, received the award 'for sustained gallantry, enterprise and devotion to duty during enemy air raids'. Davies was the Royal Engineer officer in charge of the party detailed to recover the bomb which fell in the vicinity of St Paul's Cathedral; Wylie was a member of the Bomb Disposal Section engaged upon the recovery of the same bomb.

AUGUST 1940

Winston S. Churchill to Sir Archibald Sinclair
(*Premier papers, 3/347*)

25 August 1940
Secret

I visited Kenley on Thursday,[1] saw the gunner in question and had a rocket fired off. Moreover it was the Admiralty Committee over which I presided early in the year which produced the idea of using these distress rockets. I am therefore well acquainted with the subject. The Air Ministry, not for the first time, spread itself into very large demands and using its priority barged in heavily into other forms of not less important production. I agree that PAC rockets may be a good interim defence against low-flying attack, but they have to take their place in the general scheme. I thought myself about 5,000 a month would be sufficient but I am willing to agree to 1,500 a week or 6,000 a month. This figure could be somewhat extended if the wire recovery projects you mention were further developed, and proved an effective economy. I am sending a copy of this Minute to MAP.

WSC

Winston S. Churchill to Anthony Eden
(*Churchill papers, 20/13*)

25 August 1940

It now appears that the casualties in British Somaliland were in the neighbourhood of 184, exclusive, of course, of dead and missing. This does not indicate any severe fighting. You are, I believe, making some inquiries into the conduct of the General. I certainly cannot feel that about five thousand troops should be driven out of strong fortified positions with a loss of only about 250, or about 5 per cent. If those sort of standards prevail we shall certainly find ourselves at grievous disadvantages.

WSC

Winston S. Churchill to Sir John Reith
(*Churchill papers, 20/13*)

25 August 1940

I have read with interest your memorandum on Port Clearance.
I note that the Minister of Shipping[2] doubts whether the country could be

[1] Churchill had visited Kenley aerodrome on Thursday, 22 August 1940.
[2] Ronald Hibbert Cross, 1896–1968. On active service, Royal Flying Corps, 1914–18. Conservative MP, 1931–45. Minister of Economic Warfare, 1939–40. Privy Councillor, 1940. Minister of Shipping, 1940–1. Created Baronet, 1941. High Commissioner in Australia, 1941–5.

supplied through the West Coast ports on the scale you envisage. I should be glad to have your views on this.

Does not the wide-spread dislocation caused by the cold spell last winter raise some doubts as to the ready adaptability of the railway system in case of sudden emergency?

No doubt arrangements have been made for the importation of oil, which is not included in the Food or Supply programme. It appears that over two-fifths of our oil imports come through London and Southampton in peace-time. Our stocks are high, but if road transport had to be used more fully to relieve the railways, our consumption would, of course, increase.

I presume that you have discussed their import programmes with the Ministers of Food and of Supply, so that alternative schemes will be ready in case of great diversions.

Winston S. Churchill to A. V. Alexander and Admiral Pound
(*Churchill papers, 20/13*)

25 August 1940

I shall be much obliged if you will make proposals for a shoot by *Erebus*[1] against the German batteries at Gris Nez. I was very glad to hear you thought this practicable. It is most desirable. There is no reason why it should wait for the railway guns, though, of course, if they were ready they could follow on with the 14-inch at daybreak. We ought to smash these batteries. I hope we have not got to wait for the next moon for *Erebus*, and I shall be glad to know what are the moon-conditions which you deem favourable.

WSC

Winston S. Churchill to Sir Cyril Newall
(*Churchill papers, 20/13*)

25 August 1940

MANSTON AERODROME

I gather that the evacuation of this aerodrome is only temporary because some unexploded bombs are on it. Can it not, however, be patched up in the meanwhile and dummy aircraft placed upon it?

Conservative MP, 1950–1. Chairman of the Public Accounts Committee, 1950–1. Governor of Tasmania, 1951–8.

[1] *Erebus* was the naval designation for the Dover long-range gun.

Winston S. Churchill to Anthony Eden
(*Churchill papers, 20/13*)

25 August 1940

I have been following with much interest the growth and development of the new guerilla formations of the Home Guard, known as 'Auxiliary Units.'

From what I hear these units are being organized with thoroughness and imagination, and should, in the event of invasion, prove a useful addition to the regular forces.[1]

Perhaps you will keep me informed of progress.

WSC

Winston S. Churchill to A. V. Alexander and Admiral Pound
(*Churchill papers, 20/13*)

25 August 1940

The enclosed returns show losses of over 40,000 tons reported in a single day.[2] I regard this matter as so serious as to require special consideration by the War Cabinet. Will you, therefore, have prepared a statement showing the recent losses, their cause, the measures which have been taken by the Admiralty to cope with the danger, any further measures which you feel it necessary to propose and whether there is any way in which the War Cabinet can assist the Admiralty.

I should be glad if you would make this report to the War Cabinet on Thursday next.

WSC

[1] In a minute to General Ismay four days earlier, Churchill commented: 'The prospects of invasion are rapidly receding' (Prime Minister's Personal Minute, D.17 of 21 August 1940, *Churchill papers, 20/13*).

[2] On 23 August 1940 six British merchant ships were sunk, *Cumberland* (10,939 tons), *Makalla* (6,677 tons), *Llanishen* (5,053 tons), *Severn Leigh* (5,242 tons), *St Dunstan* (5,681 tons) and *Brookwood* (5,100 tons). On the day that Churchill wrote this minute, eight British merchant ships were sunk, totalling a further 43,000 tons.

Winston S. Churchill to Sir Archibald Sinclair
(*Churchill papers, 4/201*)

25 August 1940
Private

My dear Archie,

I feel unhappy about your answers on the attached paper.[1] I cannot feel you are justified in maintaining the present scale of communication squadrons when we are fighting so heavily. The sole end should surely be to increase the reserve and operational strength of our fighting squadrons and to meet the problem of trainer aircraft. Surely your dominant idea should be STRENGTH FOR BATTLE. Everything should be keyed on to this, and administrative convenience or local vested interests must be made to give way. In your place I should comb and re-comb. I have been shocked to see the enormous numbers at Hendon, and I would far rather give up flying on inspections altogether for Members of the Government than that this should be made an excuse for keeping these forces out of the fight.

I should have thought that Hendon could provide at least two good squadrons of fighter or bomber aircraft of the reserve category, and that they should have the machines issued to them and practise on them as occasion serves. Then they could be thrown in when an emergency came.

Ought you not every day to call in question in your own mind every non-military aspect of the Air Force? The tendency of every Station Commander is naturally to keep as much in his hands as possible. The Admirals do exactly the same. Even when you have had a thorough search if you look around a few weeks later you will see more fat has been gathered.

I hope you will feel able to give some consideration to these views of your old friend

WSC

Winston S. Churchill to Anthony Eden
(*Churchill papers, 20/2*)

25 August 1940

My dear Anthony,

I have been thinking over our very informal talk the other night and am moved to write to you because I hear that the whole position of the commandos is being questioned. They have been told 'no more recruiting' and that their future is in the melting-pot. I thought therefore I might write to let

---

[1] Not printed: Sinclair had commented, in a letter of 22 August 1940, on a letter from Beaverbrook to Churchill of 15 August 1940, in which Beaverbrook criticised the number of aircraft being used by the Air Ministry solely for training purposes.

you know how strongly I feel that the Germans have been right, both in the last war and in this, in the use they have made of storm troops. In 1918 the infiltrations which were so deadly to us were by storm troops and the final defence of Germany in the last four months of 1918 rested mainly upon brilliantly-posted and valiantly-fought machine-gun nests. In this war all these factors are multiplied. The defeat of France was accomplished by an incredibly small number of highly equipped elite who, while the dull mass of the German Army came on behind, made good the conquest and occupied it. If we are to have any campaign in 1941 it must be amphibious in its character and there will certainly be many opportunities of minor operations all of which will depend on surprise landings of lightly equipped nimble forces accustomed to work like packs of hounds instead of being moved about in the ponderous manner which is appropriate to the regular formations. These have become so elaborate, so complicated in their equipment, so vast in their transport that it is very difficult to use them in any operations in which time is vital.

For every reason therefore we must develop the storm troop or commando idea. I have asked for 5,000 parachutists and we must also have at least 10,000 of these small 'bands of brothers' who will be capable of lightning action. In this way alone will those positions be secured which afterwards will give the opportunity for highly-trained regular troops to operate on a larger scale.

I hope therefore that you will let me have an opportunity of discussing this with you before any action is taken to reverse the policy hitherto adopted or to throw into uncertainty all the volunteers who have been gathered together.

I understood some decision was to be taken on Tuesday, so I add to the veritable budget I am sending you this week-end these few lines from

Yours ever,
Winston S. Churchill

Winston S. Churchill to President Roosevelt
(*Premier papers, 3/462/2*)

25 August 1940

I fully understand the legal and constitutional difficulties which make you wish for a formal contract embodied in letters, but I venture to put before you the difficulties, and even dangers, which I foresee in this procedure. For the sake of the precise list of instrumentalities mentioned, which in our sore need we greatly desire, we are asked to pay undefined concessions in all the Islands and places mentioned from Newfoundland to British Guiana 'as may be required in the judgment of the United States.' Suppose we could not agree to all your experts asked for, should we not be exposed to a charge of breaking our contract, for which we had already received value? Your commitment is definite, ours unlimited. Much though we need the destroyers, we should not wish to have them at the risk of a misunderstanding with the United States, or, indeed, any serious argument. If the matter is to be represented as a contract, both sides must be defined, with far more precision on our side than has hitherto been possible. But this might easily take some time. As I have several times pointed out, we need the destroyers chiefly to bridge the gap between now and the arrival of our new construction, which I set on foot on the outbreak of war. This construction is very considerable. For instance, we shall receive by the end of February new destroyers and new medium destroyers 20. Corvettes, which are a handy type of submarine-hunter adapted to ocean work, 60. MTBs[1] 37. MASBs[2] 25. Fairmiles, a wooden anti-submarine patrol boat, 104. 72-foot launches 29. An even greater inflow will arrive in the following six months. It is just in the gap from September to February inclusive, while this new crop is coming in and working up, that your 50 destroyers would be invaluable. With them we could minimise shipping losses in the North-Western Approaches and also take a stronger line against Mussolini in the Mediterranean. Therefore, time is all-important. We should not, however, be justified, in the circumstances, if we gave a blank cheque on the whole of our Trans-Atlantic possessions merely to bridge this gap, through which, anyhow, we hope we make our way, though with added risk and suffering. This, I am sure you will see, sets forth our difficulties plainly.

2. Would not the following procedure be acceptable? I would offer at once certain fairly well-defined facilities which will show you the kind of gift we have in mind, and your experts could then discuss these, or any variants of them, with ours – we remaining the final judge of what we can give. All this we will do freely, trusting entirely to the generosity and goodwill of the American people as to whether they, on their part, would like to do something for us. But, anyhow, it is the settled policy of His Majesty's Government to offer you, and make available to you when desired, solid and effective means of protecting your Atlantic seaboard. I have already asked the Admiralty and the Air Ministry to draw up in outline what we are prepared to offer, leaving your experts to suggest alternatives. I propose to send you this outline in two or three days and to publish in due course. In this way there can be no possible dispute, and the American people will feel more warmly towards us, because they will see we are playing the game by the world's cause and that their safety and interests are dear to us.

3. If your law or your Admiral requires that any help you may choose to give us must be presented as a *quid pro quo*, I do not see why the British Government have to come into that at all. Could you not say that you did not

[1] Motor Torpedo Boats.
[2] Motorised Anti-Submarine Boats.

feel able to accept this fine offer which we make, unless the United States matched it in some way, and that therefore the Admiral would be able to link the one with the other?

4. I am so grateful to you for all the trouble you have been taking, and I am so sorry to add to your burdens, knowing what a good friend you have been to us.

Winston S. Churchill: memorandum[1]
(*Cabinet papers, 66/11*)

26 August 1940

TRAINING OF RAF PILOTS

I have given a great deal of thought and time to the various Cabinet papers on this subject and have discussed them with the Ministers concerned, and with their expert advisers on numerous occasions. I trust it may be possible to reach agreement on the following conclusions:–

1. The air battle now proceeding over Great Britain may be a decisive event in the war and must dominate all other considerations. Until the issue of this battle becomes clear it would not be right to separate any large portion of our reserve of pilots or of potentially operational machines from the fighting strength of the RAF in this country. We cannot tell what new form the enemy's attack may take; nor what our losses will be; nor what damage will be done to our factories both of output and repair. We do not know with any certainty the size of the air force which the enemy may bring against us. It is certainly very much larger than our own. Therefore the scheme for moving a large part of our training establishments to Canada and South Africa should be postponed; and as uncertainty of date would be inconvenient, it would be well to postpone it for three months, i.e. until the beginning of December.

2. In the meanwhile every effort should be made to mitigate the evident difficulties of training in this Island under present conditions. Sir F. E. Smith[2] has prepared a note upon RDF congestion which intimates that there is no difficulty in trainers flying inland. It should be possible to secure,

---

[1] Circulated to the War Cabinet as War Cabinet Paper 338 of 1940.
[2] Frank Edward Smith, 1879–1970. Superintendent of the Electrical Department, National Physical Laboratory, 1901–20. OBE, 1918. Director of Scientific Research, Admiralty, 1920–9. CBE, 1922. Secretary, Department of Scientific and Industrial Research, 1929–39. Knighted, 1931. Director of Research, Anglo-Iranian Oil Company, 1939–55. Director of Instrument Production, and Controller of Bearings Production, Ministry of Supply, 1939–42. Controller of Telecommunications Equipment, Ministry of Aircraft Production, 1940–2. Chairman, Technical Defence Committee, M15, 1940–6. Chairman of the Road Research and Safety Research Board, 1945–54.

provide or enlarge their facilities for flying over the sea, but this will be undoubtedly restricted. Sir F. E. Smith has also mentioned the possibility of using infra-red rays for lighting aerodromes for night flying – these rays being invisible to anyone not provided with the special glasses that our trainer-pilots would have to have attached to their helmets. An alternative method is to have several training aerodromes lighted simultaneously to disperse the risks. The impediments to night flying arising from lighted grounds must be considered a very serious obstacle to training in this country.

3. Seventy-five additional air-fields are under construction and will, it is hoped, be completed by the end of the year. We shall certainly need more airfields than this, and another 50 should be at once selected and surveyed. Relief can, however, best be achieved by accelerating the construction of those already begun. I understand from General King,[1] the Chief Engineer of the Home Forces, that large numbers of concrete mixers, and digging machines and contract labour, can be released in the immediate future from the coastal sectors which are now rapidly nearing completion and these will be available for the construction of air-field tracks. Some five hundred excavators will be released (most of which will be suitable for work on the aerodromes), while 85 per cent of the cement mixers used for Home Defence work will be released by the end of October.

4. In this same three months' interval the utmost effort must be made to get the training establishments in Canada and South Africa ready as far as possible, and to utilise any local personnel, together with the small detachments who have already proceeded to these countries. I consider that the first Navigation School Unit should proceed to South Africa as now arranged, there being no doubt that practice in navigation is conducted under increasing difficulty at the present time in Great Britain.

5. Finally, the whole question must be reviewed at the beginning of November in the light of the fortunes of the battle, and of the progress made in overcoming difficulties obtaining at home.

6. Tables are appended showing –
(a) The estimated output of pilots under the Air Ministry scheme.
(b) The proposed despatch from this Island of men, and
(c) Machines.

WSC

---

[1] Charles John Stuart King, 1890–1967. 2nd Lieutenant, Royal Engineers, 1910. On active service, 1914–18 (despatches). Engineer-in-Chief, Home Forces, 1939–40. CBE, 1939. Engineer-in-Chief, 1941–4. Special Mission, India and South-East Asia Command, 1944. Knighted, 1945. Colonel-Commandant, Royal Engineers, 1946–56.

War Cabinet: minutes
(*Cabinet papers, 65/8*)

26 August 1940
12.30 p.m.
10 Downing Street

The Prime Minister drew attention to the heavy losses of merchant shipping. On two recent days these losses had amounted to 40,000 and 30,000 tons. If losses continued at this rate the position would become serious.

The First Sea Lord said that the heavy losses were believed to be due to the adoption of new tactics by the enemy. Suitable counter-measures were under consideration.[1]

In connection with the preceding Minute, it was again pointed out that if we could get 50 destroyers from the United States this would be a great help in fighting the submarine menace.

The Prime Minister referred to a further telegram which he had sent to Lord Lothian. The Chiefs of Staff had been invited to prepare a statement showing what British air and naval facilities the United States would wish to avail themselves of in the Western Atlantic. On the basis of this statement we should make a definite offer of facilities to the United States Government, but without inviting a specific *quid pro quo*.

The War Cabinet approved this suggestion.

War Cabinet: Confidential Annex
(*Cabinet papers, 65/14*)

26 August 1940
12.30 p.m.
10 Downing Street

The Prime Minister thought that the War Cabinet ought not to take the responsibility of over-ruling the judgment of the Commanders on the spot that the tank reinforcements should make the longer voyage by the Cape.

Nevertheless he acquiesced in this decision with regret, since in his judgment the dangers of sending the tank units through the Mediterranean had been exaggerated. On the other hand, under these arrangements, the *Valiant* would be able to deliver her cargo of guns at Malta.

---

[1] There was to be no fall in British merchant shipping losses. In August a total of 56 ships (278,323 tons) were sunk, in September 62 (324,030 tons), in October 63 (301,892 tons), in November 73 (303,682 tons), and in December 61 (265,314 tons).

Winston S. Churchill to General Ismay
(*Churchill papers, 20/13*)

26 August 1940

1. After 'Hats' and 'Menace'[1] are completed it should be possible about October 5 to pass a warship carrying AA stores into Malta. This would entail these stores leaving England about September 30. By that time we shall have at least 100 UP Projectors, some trained men and two or three thousand rounds of PE ammunition, together with a considerable quantity of ordinary fuze ammunition. Also some GPC gadgets[2] for searchlights. I propose that Malta shall be given the first call on these new weapons as the weather conditions are favourable, moreover we must regard the air defence of Malta as of the very first priority.

Advantage should be taken of this opportunity to send in as well any spare multiple projectors for the aerial mines not mounted in HM Ships or at Dover, together with suitable ammunition. Are there any? Where are they?

There should also be as large a consignment of Bofors as can be got together. Pray make me proposals on these lines.

WSC

Geoffrey Dawson[3]*: diary*
(*'Geoffrey Dawson and Our Times'*)

26 August 1940

To 10, Downing Street to lunch. The Cabinet was all emerging.

The luncheon party was a curious quartet – Winston, the Archbishop (Dr Lang), Henry Strakosch and I. Some talk with Winston about the Independent Companies or Commandos (storm troops). This partly in his Air Raid room, to which he and I adjourned on an early afternoon warning. He was in excellent form, fit and confident, and full of Beaverbrook's achievements in production.

---

[1] The operations to convoy ships through the Mediterranean from Gibraltar to Malta and Alexandria; and the amphibious landing at Dakar.

[2] Gel Permeation Chromatography.

[3] George Geoffrey Robinson, 1874–1944. Educated at Eton and Magdalen College, Oxford. Fellow of All Souls, 1896. Private Secretary to Milner in South Africa, 1901–5. Editor of the *Johannesburg Star*, 1905–10. Editor of *The Times*, 1912–19 and 1923–41. Took the surname Dawson, 1917.

Winston S. Churchill to General Ismay
(*Churchill papers, 20/13*)

26 August 1940

I approve the directives as amended by me. They should be circulated in a locked box to the War Cabinet Ministers only. I approve the telegram to General Giffard. There is no objection to the Memorandum on the Anglo-American standardization.

2. Reinforcements. Egypt and Palestine. It is undesirable to keep sixteen British Infantry and two machine-gun battalions for local internal security. These Infantry should form part of the three Infantry Divisions embodied in the Army Corps, their places being taken by other less highly trained white formations.

An Australian and New Zealand Army Corps (Anzacs) consisting of one Australian and one New Zealand Division should be formed at the earliest moment by the despatch of the Australians and New Zealanders from England and Australia. The big ships should be used, if possible, from England round the Cape.

We cannot send any more armoured vehicles at present owing to the very poor deliveries, except perhaps a small detachment for Kenya.

There are surely enough Generals and Staff Officers in Egypt to form the necessary Corps Headquarters.

Let me see a list of Generals.

Sudan requires further reinforcements. There can be no need to provide a British brigade for Crete.

Somaliland is already defunct and troops disposed of.

East Africa. Far from reinforcing East Africa, it should be reduced for the benefit of the Sudan and the Army of the Delta. There is no truth in the statement that the West African troops cannot be used in the Sudan for health reasons. They are admirably suited to the Sudan climate. Surely it is a misnomer to speak of 'South African Divisions (less two Brigade groups)' when what is meant is, in fact, only one Brigade group.

Every effort should be made to keep the Staffs at a minimum and in proper proportion to the rifle strength. A Divisional Staff should not be provided in addition to the Brigade Staff as long as the force is in fact only a Brigade.

AA. This must be gradually worked up, but Malta should take priority after Alexandria has been provided for.

West Africa. Is it really intended to send a British Infantry Brigade to West Africa? If this is necessary, would it not be better to bring back one of the West African brigades from Kenya? Who is going to invade West Africa, and how are they going to get there? If we have a British Brigade to spare, it had much better go to Egypt.

Far East. If the Australians send an additional Division to Malaya, we may accept this for the time being. It is hoped, however, that this Division will presently move out of the unhealthy climate of Singapore to join the Army of the Middle East. The immediate reinforcement of Singapore is provided by the two British Battalions withdrawn from China. It should be possible to send four more Indian Battalions, thus making two Brigades of one white and two native for garrison duty. There can be no question of sending an additional Division from England at the present time, and the 7th Australian Division can only be left in Malaya (after it gets there) until the tension with Japan relaxes.

Air Force. Unless some change of an adverse character occurs in the air battle over Great Britain, the complete remounting of our pilots in the Near East with Blenheims, Hurricanes and Glenn-Martins should go forward, as now arranged and with the utmost speed. However, this process must be reviewed constantly.

General. – Reductions should be sought in the Kenya Garrison and future reinforcements diverted as far as possible to the Delta. The number of troops allocated to internal security of Palestine must be regarded as far in excess of strategic requirements. The proposals in the directive recently given to General Wavell should be steadily pressed upon him, subject to settlement of the points now under discussion with him.

WSC

Winston S. Churchill to General Ismay
(*Churchill papers, 20/13*)

27 August 1940

It would not seem unreasonable that the enemy should attempt gradually to master the Dover promontory and command the Channel at its narrowest point. This would be a natural preliminary to invasion. It would give occasion for continued fighting with our Air Force in the hope of exhausting them by numbers. It would tend to drive our warships from all the Channel bases. The concentration of many batteries on the French coast must be expected. What are we doing in defence of the Dover promontory by heavy artillery? Ten weeks ago I asked for heavy guns. One has been mounted. Two railway guns are expected. Now we are told these will be very inaccurate on account of super-charging. We ought to have a good many more heavy guns lined up inside to smaller calibre with stiffer rifling, and a range of at least fifty miles and firing at twenty-five or thirty miles would then become more accurate. I do not understand why I have not yet received proposals on this subject. We must insist upon maintaining superior artillery positions on the Dover promontory, no matter what form of attack they are exposed to. We have to fight for the command of the Straits by artillery, to destroy the enemy's batteries, and to multiply and fortify our own.

I have sent on other papers a request for a surprise attack by *Erebus*, which should be able to destroy the batteries at Gris Nez. She has an armoured deck against air bombing. What is being done about this? When is she going into action? The Air Ministry should, of course, co-operate. The operation would take an offensive turn. We should require spotting aircraft by day. It may be that the first squadrons of Hurricanes fitted with Merlin 20 would be the best for this. If *Erebus* is attacked from the air, she should be strongly defended, and action sought with the enemy air force.

Pray let me have your plans.

War Cabinet: minutes
(*Cabinet papers, 65/8*)

27 August 1940　　　　　　　　　　　　　　　　　　10 Downing Street
12.30 p.m.

The Prime Minister said that General de Gaulle had asked him for a letter undertaking that His Majesty's Government would extend economic assistance to French Territories overseas which stood by the Alliance. He read out the draft of a letter which had been prepared in compliance with the above request.

The War Cabinet –
(i) Approved the guarantee of support to the Authorities of the Chad Territory which had been given by the Chiefs of Staff to General de Gaulle.
(ii) Approved the Prime Minister's proposed letter to General de Gaulle.

War Cabinet: Confidential Annex
(*Cabinet papers, 65/14*)

27 August 1940
12.30 p.m.

OPERATION 'MENACE', DAKAR

The Prime Minister informed the War Cabinet of the present position of the plans for Operation 'Menace'.

It was the general view of the War Cabinet that, having regard to the value of its objects, the Operation was one which we should be justified in undertaking. The danger of the Vichy Government declaring war as a result was not rated very highly.

The War Cabinet gave a general approval to the plans for Operation 'Menace'.

Winston S. Churchill to General de Gaulle
(*Cabinet papers, 65/8*)

27 August 1940

In pursuance of the various statements made on behalf of His Majesty's Government in the United Kingdom on the subject of economic assistance to French Colonial Territories, and upon the occasion of the declaration of the Chad Territory to adhere to the cause of the Allies, I wish to assure you on behalf of His Majesty's Government in the United Kingdom –
  (a) that, until such time as an independent and constitutional authority has been re-established on free French soil, we shall do everything in our power to maintain the economic stability of all French overseas territories, provided they stand by the Alliance;
  (b) that, so long as our pathway to Victory is not impeded, we are ready to foster trade and help the administration of those parts of the great French Empire which are now cut off from captive France.

These assurances apply with even greater force to those territories which rally to you as leader of all Free Frenchmen in support of the Allied cause. Therefore, subject to the needs of our own war effort, we are prepared to extend economic assistance on a scale similar to that which we should apply in comparable circumstances to the colonies of the British Empire. Plans are now being worked out for making such assistance rapidly effective.[1]

Winston S. Churchill to Lord Beaverbrook
(*Churchill papers, 20/13*)

27 August 1940

It was always understood that the Air Ministry should have these guns back when they were really needed for aeroplanes. Lewis guns[2] are no substitute for them. Rockets might be, and these are coming on with

---

[1] On the day Churchill sent this letter, Free French forces under Captain Leclerc seized Duala, in the Cameroons, attacking from the Gold Coast by native canoe. On the following day Leclerc took the train to the capital, Yaundé, where he was installed as Governor.

[2] The original Lewis gun had been invented by an American, Samuel Maclean, at the turn of the century, and developed and sold by a fellow American, Colonel Lewis. It was widely used in the First World War. After the loss of most of Britain's Lewis guns at Dunkirk, Britain purchased 40,000 aircraft Lewis guns from the United States. They were widely used as low-level anti-aircraft guns in single, double and quadruple mounts. During the Battle of Britain they accounted for 20 per cent of all aircraft shot down in the London area.

ammunition of the ordinary AD type.¹ I cannot denude the *King George V* and the Tyne at this most vital month in the battleship's completion. There was a very large surplus of Hispano Suiza guns² some time ago and the output is very large. While I think you are quite right to turn to the cannon-gun promptly, I hope you will not remove any that are actually in action until you have a machine waiting for them to be put into. I am sure you cannot want the whole lot back within a few days of your decision. In another two months it will be possible to replace these guns on the Tyne with rockets (UP Type)³ and the *King George V* will have got safely to sea. If we lost this ship or she were seriously set back, the *Bismarck* would be the fastest and strongest vessel afloat and could go wherever she wished with virtual impunity. Our only remaining exit to the oceans is much harassed at the present time.

Winston S. Churchill to Lord Beaverbrook
(*Churchill papers, 4/201*)

27 August 1940
Private

My dear Max,

Please see the attached.⁴ It is absolutely necessary to meet these facts. The reason why our aircraft are able to bomb Germany accurately by night is because they have superior navigational training. I do not see how we can possibly adopt the attitude that these Navigation Schools are to be brought to a standstill. I attach the greatest importance to your opinion, but you must either face the facts and answer them effectively and with a positive plan or allow the opinion of those who are responsible to prevail.

Yours ever,
WSC

---

¹ Air Defence type.

² The Hispano-Suiza gun, which fired a high-velocity shell, was the standard British fighter armament for the greater part of the Second World War. It was introduced in the summer of 1940 after many design and manufacturing difficulties had been overcome. It achieved impressive results in Hurricanes and Spitfires, as well as in Typhoons, Mosquitoes and Beaufighters.

³ Of the UP weapon, V. E. Tarrant writes in his book *King George V Class Battleships* (1991), page 27: 'This rather fanciful weapon, consisting of 20 smooth-bore barrels, used a 3-inch cordite-fired rocket to propel a 7-inch aerial mine to a height of 1000 ft. At this altitude the rocket exploded, releasing a parachute which supported the mine attached by a long trailing wire. Theoretically, if an attacking aircraft fouled the wire, the mine would be drawn against it where it would explode on contact. Only the two lead ships were thus fitted: One on top of the 'B' turret, two atop 'Y' turret, and one at the stern in *King George V*. *Prince of Wales* had only three fitted, including one instead of two on 'Y' turret. They were never used in action, and after the exposed UP ready-service lockers exploded in *Hood* during the Bismarck action they were removed.'

⁴ A note from the Air Ministry on the effect of operational restrictions on navigational training.

August 1940

Winston S. Churchill to Admiral Sir Andrew Cunningham
(*Churchill papers, 20/14*)

27 August 1940

Main object of directive was to safeguard Alexandria. Only a limited number of troops can be maintained at Mersa Matruh, as GOC, Middle East,[1] will inform you. Every effort is to be made to defend this position. If, however, it and intermediate positions are forced or turned, it will be necessary to hold the line from Alexandria southwards along the cultivated area. Air attack on the Fleet at Alexandria is not necessarily less effective from 120 miles distance than from 20 miles since aeroplanes often fly at 300 miles per hour, and have ample endurance. In practice it is usually thought better to hold aerodromes a little back of the actual fighting line. They do not move forward concurrently with the fronts of armies. Therefore I do not understand the point you make. Everyone here understood the grievous consequence of the fall of Alexandria, and that it would probably entail the Fleet leaving the Mediterranean. You are in error in supposing that Naval and Air aspect has not been fully examined by the Joint Staffs both from the Air and Naval points of view. If, however, you have any helpful suggestion to make for the more effective defence of Mersa Matruh or of any positions in advance of it, I should be obliged if you would tell me.

Winston S. Churchill to President Roosevelt
(*Churchill papers, 20/14*)

27 August 1940

Lord Lothian has cabled me the outline of the facilities you have in mind. Our Naval and Air experts studying the question from your point of view had reached practically the same conclusions except that, in addition, they thought Antigua might be useful as a base for flying boats. To this also you would be very welcome. Our settled policy is to make the United States safe on their Atlantic seaboard beyond a peradventure, to quote a phrase you may remember.[2]

2. We are quite ready to make you a positive offer on these lines forthwith. There would, of course, have to be an immediate conference on details, but for the reasons which I set out in my last telegram we do not like the idea of an arbiter should any difference arise because we feel that, as donors, we must

---

[1] General Wavell.
[2] The phrase was used by President Woodrow Wilson in the First World War. Another of Churchill's favourite phrases, on the same lines, was 'To make assurance double sure' (*Macbeth*).

734   AUGUST 1940

remain the final judges of what the gift is to consist of within the general framework of the facilities which will have been promised and always on the understanding that we shall do our best to meet United States wishes.

3. The two letters drafted by Lord Lothian to the Secretary of State[1] are quite agreeable to us. The only reason why I do not wish the second letter to be published is that I think it is much more likely that the German Government will be the one to surrender or scuttle its Fleet or what is left of it. In this, as you are aware, they have already had some practice. You will remember that I said some months ago in one of my private cables to you that any such action on our part would be a dastard act, and that is the opinion of every one of us.

4. If you felt able after our offer had been made to let us have the instrumentalities which have been mentioned or anything else you think proper, this could be expressed as an act not in payment or consideration for, but in recognition of, what we had done for the security of the United States.

5. Mr President, this business has become especially urgent in view of the recent menace which Mussolini is showing to Greece.[2] If our business is put through on big lines and in the highest spirit of goodwill, it might even now save that small historic country from invasion and conquest. Even the next forty-eight hours are important.

John Colville: diary
(*Colville papers*)

27 August 1940

The PM's system of working includes the enlistment of outside authorities to vet and supplement the labours of the officially responsible department. Thus today he sends over to P. J. Grigg at the War Office a batch of telegrams from India with the following mandate: 'I will from time to time send you other Indian telegrams in order that you may warn me if amid all their wordage there is anything being done counter to the policy now agreed.'

When I returned to No. 10 after an early dinner, there was a good deal to do and I was deeply involved in arranging papers when, at about 9.30, the sirens began. I went up to tell the PM that it was all due to one aeroplane and stayed

[1] Henry Stimson.
[2] Throughout August, British intelligence sources had been showing a continuing build-up of Italian preparations for a possible invasion of Greece. Publicly, on 15 August, the Greek cruiser *Helle* had been torpedoed by an unknown submarine. Italy denied responsibility. On 16 August Italian planes bombed two Greek destroyers: the Italian Government then apologised. Britain had signed a treaty with Greece on 13 April 1939. Italy invaded Greece, from Albania, on 28 October 1940. After heavy fighting the Italian forces were driven back into Albania.

to drink some coffee and smoke a cigar. Winston, to his obvious regret, refused brandy and demanded iced soda-water, saying that he was ashamed of the easy life he led and had never before lived in such luxury. Desmond Morton said that the PM's staff had different views on this question of an easy life! W went on to declare that his object was to preserve 'the maximum initiative-energy'. 'Every night,' he said, 'I try myself by court martial to see if I have done anything effective during the day. I don't mean just pawing the ground; anyone can go through the motions; but something really effective.'

On 28 august 1940 Churchill visited Manston Aerodrome in Kent, as well as coastal defences in the Dover and Ramsgate area.

Sir Alexander Cadogan: diary
(*'The Diaries of Sir Alexander Cadogan'*)

28 August 1940

No Cabinet today – Winston gone down to Dover to dispute the supremacy of the Straits.

Newspaper report
(*'Isle of Thanet Gazette'*, 30 August 1940)

28 August 1940

PREMIER IN RAMSGATE AIR RAID

Mr Winston Churchill, the Prime Minister, paid a visit to Ramsgate and Dover on Wednesday.

He was at Ramsgate at the time of an air raid. Accompanied by the Mayor (Alderman A. B. C. Kempe),[1] he visited the tunnel shelters and praised the town upon the fine protection they had provided.

---

[1] Arthur Bloomfield Courtenay Kempe. Mayor of Ramsgate, 1938–43. Encouraged workers from the Midlands and elsewhere to go to Ramsgate for their summer holidays. Known as the 'Top Hat Mayor' because of his penchant for wearing a top hat and frock coat around the town. Responsible, before the outbreak of war, for the building of a deep air raid tunnel shelter that could accommodate the entire population of the town. From May 1940 the German Army was only 28 miles away across the Channel. Military Welfare Officer (with the rank of Captain), 1940.

When he entered the tunnels he was smoking his inseparable cigar, and the Mayor reminded him that smoking was not permitted.

Discarding the cigar, the Premier remarked, 'There goes another good one.'

He chatted and shook hands with several people in the tunnel, and remarked to a warden, 'Keep your pecker up.'

Winston S. Churchill: recollection
('Their Finest Hour', page 308)[1]

28 August 1940

Another time I visited Ramsgate. An air raid came upon us, and I was conducted into their big tunnel, where quite large numbers of people lived permanently. When we came out, after a quarter of an hour, we looked at the still-smoking damage. A small hotel had been hit. Nobody had been hurt, but the place had been reduced to a litter of crockery, utensils, and splintered furniture. The proprietor, his wife, and the cooks and waitresses were in tears. Where was their home? Where was their livelihood? Here is a privilege of power. I formed an immediate resolve. On the way back in my train I dictated a letter to the Chancellor of the Exchequer laying down the principle that all damage from the fire of the enemy must be a charge upon the State and compensation be paid in full and at once. Thus the burden would not fall alone on those whose home or business premises were hit, but would be borne evenly on the shoulders of the nation. Kingsley Wood was naturally a little worried by the indefinite character of this obligation. But I pressed hard, and an insurance scheme was devised in a fortnight which afterwards played a substantial part in our affairs.

John Colville: diary
(Colville papers)

28 August 1940

The PM came back at about 11.00, having seen numerous air battles and been much affected by the plight of those whose houses have been destroyed or badly damaged by raids. He was, he said, determined that they should receive full compensation up to £1,000 and made a note to the effect that he would browbeat the Chancellor of the Exchequer on the subject next day.

---

[1] In the first edition of his war memoirs, published in 1948, Churchill described this visit as having been to Margate; following publication, the citizens of Ramsgate pointed out the error, which was corrected in subsequent editions.

Winston S. Churchill to General Ismay
(*Churchill papers, 20/13*)

28 August 1940
ACTION THIS DAY

1. Now that the long nights are approaching the question of the black-out must be reviewed. I am in favour of a policy not of black-out but of 'blackable-out.' For this purpose a considerable system of auxiliary electric street-lighting must be worked out. The whole of the centre of London now lighted by incandescent gas must be given priority. The best methods in the centres of other great cities must also be studied and local schemes must be examined. Thus the lights can be switched down and up and finally out on an air-raid warning being given. The lights themselves should not be of a too-brilliant character. The subdued lighting of shop windows must also be studied with a view to extending the facilities given last Christmas on a permanent basis. Where factories are allowed to continue working at night in spite of the black-out there can be no objection to extending blackable-out lighting to the surrounding districts, thus tending to make the target less defined. Consideration should also be given to decoy lighting and baffle lighting in open spaces at suitable distances from vulnerable points.

2. A Committee of three Officers plus a representative of Home Office should be formed. Professor Lindemann will represent me. It will not be necessary for him to attend except at intervals. Reports should be presented by September 15 at latest.

3. The Members of the Committee are to try to solve the problem and produce a practicable scheme. They need not concern themselves with policy, which will be settled by the War Cabinet, who will have the benefit of having their report showing exactly what is entailed before them.

4. It would be a good thing if we were to solve this problem so as to announce to the world that after a year of German air attack we felt strong enough to give a definite easement to our people.

General Ismay will submit a list of names for the Committee and I will see them myself in the early stages of their work.

WSC

Winston S. Churchill to Sir Cyril Newall and General Ismay
(*Churchill papers, 20/13*)

28 August 1940
ACTION THIS DAY

Pray let me have proposals for moving at least four heavy bombing squadrons to Egypt in addition to anything now in progress. These squadrons will operate from advanced bases in Greece as far as may be convenient should Greece be forced into the war by Italy. They would refuel there before attacking Italy. Many of the finest targets, including the Italian Fleet, will be open to such attacks. It is better to operate from Greece, should she come in, than from Malta in its present undefended state. The report should be brief and should simply show the method, the difficulties and the objectives together with a time table. It is not necessary to argue the question of policy which will be decided by the Defence Committee at the Cabinet. Making the best plan possible will not commit the Air Ministry or anyone else to the adoption of the plan, but every effort is to be made to solve its difficulties.

WSC

Winston S. Churchill to Herbert Morrison
(*Churchill papers, 20/2*)

28 August 1940
Secret

I understand that there is a chance of expanding greatly the output of the special cordite needed for the UP which has seemed likely to limit the use of this weapon. No doubt you will support Lord Weir[1] in all necessary steps to ensure that the greatest possible amount of it is produced at the earliest possible date. I am sure that if anyone can accelerate output he is the man to do so.

---

[1] William Douglas Weir, 1877–1959. Industrialist. Scottish Director of Munitions, 1915–16. Controller of Aeronautical Supplies, 1917–18. Knighted, 1917. Director-General of Aircraft Production, Ministry of Munitions (under Churchill), 1918. Created Baron, 1918. Secretary of State and President of the Air Council, April–December 1918. President of the British Employers Federation. Created Viscount, 1938. Director-General of Explosives, Ministry of Supply, 1939–40. Chairman of the Tank Board, 1942.

August 1940   739

Colonel Hollis¹: notes
(*Cabinet papers, 79/7*)

29 August 1940
Secret

At a meeting at No. 10 Downing Street this afternoon, attended by General de Gaulle, General Spears, and Major Morton, General de Gaulle enquired what assistance would be afforded by His Majesty's Government if French territory which had rallied to the de Gaulle standard were attacked by sea.

I am informed by Major Morton that the Prime Minister gave General de Gaulle a most formal undertaking that His Majesty's Government would, in the common cause, assume responsibility for the defence from the sea of any French Colonies which might declare their intention of continuing the fight under the de Gaulle standard, or might be forced to do so as a coup d'état, this undertaking including the defence against any attempted attack or landing organised by the Vichy Government.

This undertaking was given orally, but Major Morton informed me that it was none the less categorical and binding.

I am sure it would be the Prime Minister's wish that the Chiefs of Staff should be aware of the above undertaking so that its full implications can be appreciated, particularly from the naval point of view.

Neville Chamberlain to Winston S. Churchill
(*Churchill papers, 2/393*)

29 August 1940   Odiham
                                                                  Hampshire

My dear Winston,

When I last wrote I proposed to return on Sept 2nd. Your very kind reply encourages me now to ask if you can let me stop one more week, viz. till the 9th when just six weeks will have elapsed since my operation.

I am the last person to do any shirking but I am confident that the extra

---

[1] Leslie Chasemore Hollis, 1897–1963. Joined the Royal Marine Light Artillery as a probationer 2nd Lieutenant, 1914. Served with the Grand Fleet and Harwich Force, 1915–18. Captain, Royal Marines, 1922. Lieutenant-Colonel, 1937. Assistant Secretary, Committee of Imperial Defence, 1936. Senior Assistant Secretary, Office of the War Cabinet, 1939–46. Head of the Defence Committee Secretariat, 1940–5. Colonel (temporary Brigadier), 1941. Acting Major-General, 1943. Knighted, 1946. Chief of Staff to the Minister of Defence, and Deputy Secretary (Military) of the Cabinet, 1947–9. General, 1951. In 1956 he published *One Marine's Tale*, and in 1959 *War at the Top*.

time will give good value in increased capacity for work when I return. These last few days have registered more progress than the two preceding weeks; I am beginning to move about freely and though I still rest in the afternoons and go to bed early I no longer feel fatigue. Edward[1] has written to say that he can adapt his own plans to suit me, otherwise I should not have felt able to consider a further delay.

I get a pouch every day and so I am following affairs pretty closely. I should like to say that I am most heartily in accord with what you are doing about the American destroyers & the bases of British territory. The American attitude simply infuriates me but we can't win as we would wish without their help and I think your handling is admirable.

You must have had a most exciting visit to Dover, but I am glad you didn't get shelled. I see the invasion is now billed for Sept 1–10 but I didn't notice what year was specified.

We aren't getting any bombs very close here though I did hear a considerable roar when a time delayed bomb went off the other day. I see they are being 'dealt with' but I can't imagine how.

Best wishes to all my colleagues

Yours ever
Neville Chamberlain

Winston S. Churchill to Sir Archibald Sinclair, Sir Cyril Newall and General Ismay
(*Churchill papers, 20/13*)

29 August 1940

I was much concerned on visiting Manston Aerodrome yesterday to find that, although more than four clear days have passed since it was last raided, the greater part of the craters on the landing ground remained unfilled, and the aerodrome was barely serviceable. When you remember what the Germans did at the Stavanger aerodrome, and the enormous rapidity with which craters were filled, I must protest emphatically against this feeble method of repairing damage. Altogether there were 150 people available to work, including those that could be provided from the Air Force personnel. These were doing their best. No effective appliances were available, and the whole process appeared disproportionate to the value of maintaining this fighting vantage ground.

All craters should be filled in within 24 hours at most, and every case where

---

[1] Lord Halifax.

a crater is unfilled for a longer period should be reported to higher authorities. In order to secure this better service it will be necessary to form some crater-filling companies. You might begin with, say, two of 250 each for the South of England, which is under this intensive attack. These companies should be equipped with all helpful appliances and be highly mobile, so that in a few hours they can be at work on any site which has been cratered. Meanwhile, at every aerodrome in the attack-area, and later elsewhere, there must be accumulated by local contractors stocks of gravel, rubble and other appropriate materials sufficient to fill without replenishment at least 100 craters. Thus the mobile air-field repair companies would arrive to find all the material all ready on the spot.

I saw some time ago that the Germans filled in the shell holes by some process of having the gravel in wooden frameworks. The VCNS[1] drew my attention to it during the Norwegian operation, and he could perhaps put you on to the telegram referred to.

In what department of the Air Ministry does this process now fall?

After the craters had been refilled camouflage effort might be made to pretend they had not been, but this is a refinement.

WSC

Winston S. Churchill to General Ismay
(*Churchill papers, 20/13*)

30 August 1940

We must expect that many windows will be broken in the bombing raids, and during the winter glass may become scarce with serious resultant damage to buildings – if not replaced.

The utmost economy is to be practised in the use of glass. Where windows are broken they should, if possible, be boarded up except for one or two panes. We cannot afford the full-sized windows in glass. All glass not needed for hot-houses should be stored if the hot-houses are empty. I saw at Manston a large hot-house with a great quantity of glass, enough was broken to make it useless, and I directed that the rest should be carefully stored.

What is the condition of glass supply? It would seem necessary to press the manufacturers.

Government buildings should all be fitted with emergency windows, containing only one or two glass panes, which, when the existing frame-work is blown in, can be substituted. Let me have a full report on the position.

WSC

[1] The Vice-Chief of the Naval Staff, Admiral Phillips.

Winston S. Churchill to General Ismay
(*Churchill papers, 20/13*)

30 August 1940

Further to my previous Minute on defence of the Kentish promontory, we must expect that very powerful batteries in great numbers will be rapidly brought into being on the French coast. It would be a natural thought for the Germans to try to dominate the Straits by artillery. At present we are ahead of them with our 14-inch and two 13·5 railway guns. The Admiral at Dover[1] should be furnished, in addition, as soon as possible with a large number of the most modern 6-inch or 8-inch guns. I understand the Admiralty is considering taking guns from *Newcastle* or *Glasgow*, which are under long repair. A record evolution should be made of getting one or two of these turrets mounted. Report to me about this and dates. There is a 9·2 Army experimental gun and mounting and surely we have some 12-inch on railway mounting. If our ships cannot use the Straits the enemy must not be able to. Even if guns cannot fire on to the French shore they are none the less very valuable.

Some of our heavy artillery – the 18-inch howitzer and 9·2 – should be planted in position whence they could deny the ports and landings to the enemy and, as CIGS mentioned, support the counter-attack which would be launched against any attempted bridge-head. Much of this mass of artillery I saved from the last war has done nothing, and has been under reconditioning for a whole year.

Let me have a good programme for using it to support counter-strokes and deny landings, both north and south of the Thames: Further North I have seen already some very good heavy batteries.

I should like also to be informed of the real lines of defence drawn up between Dover and London and Harwich and London. Now that the coast is finished there is no reason why we should not develop these lines, which in no way detract from the principle of vehement counter-attack.

But the most urgent is one or two modern 6-inch to shoot all German craft up to 35,000 yards.

---

[1] Bertram Home Ramsay, 1883–1945. Entered the Royal Navy, 1898; commanded Monitor 25, Dover Patrol, 1915; HMS *Broke*, 1916–18. Chief of Staff, China Station, 1929–31. On the staff of the Imperial Defence College, 1931–3. Commanded HMS *Royal Sovereign*, 1933–5. Rear-Admiral and Chief of Staff, Home Fleet, 1935. Retired, 1938. Recalled, 1939. Flag Officer, Dover, 1939–42. Knighted, 1940. Naval Commander, Eastern Task Force, Mediterranean, 1943. Allied Naval Commander-in-Chief, Expeditionary Force, 1944–5. Killed in an aeroplane accident in France, January 1945. His 'finest hour' was as the naval officer in command of Operation 'Dynamo', the evacuation of the Dunkirk beachhead, from 26 May to 5 June 1940.

I am also endeavouring to obtain from United States at least a pair of their 16-inch coast-defence weapons. These fire 45,000 yards, throwing a ton and a quarter, without being super-charged. They should therefore be very accurate. General Strong,[1] United States Army, mentioned this to me as a promising line. He thought, without committing his Government, that United States Army might be prepared to take a couple of these guns and their carriages away from some of their twin batteries.

Let me know all details about these guns. It ought to be possible to make the concrete foundation in three months, and I expect it would take as long to get these guns over here. There are very few ships that can carry them on their decks.

WSC

Winston S. Churchill to General Ismay
(*Churchill papers, 20/13*)

30 August 1940

I gave directions that this officer[2] was to be provided for in consequence of General Ironside's retirement and I understood that you were looking after this. It would be quite suitable for him to be given suitable employment with the Home Guard in Oxfordshire.

2. I also drew attention to the foolishness of having a Cavalry Regiment stuck up on the cliffs at Shorncliffe. It is intolerable that the Jockey Club should raise objection to the use of Newmarket, which would be a first-class place to train such cavalry as we have. Pray see that action in both these respects is taken over the week-end and report to me if any difficulty is encountered and who is responsible for it.

WSC

---

[1] George Veazey Strong. 2nd Lieutenant, Cavalry, United States Army, 1904. Author of the *Japanese–English Military Dictionary*, 1911. United States Military Adviser, World Disarmament Conference, 1932–4. Brigadier-General, 1938. Assistant Chief of Staff, United States Army, 1938–41; Head of Military Intelligence, 1942–5.

[2] John Albert Edward William Spencer-Churchill, 1897–1972. Elder son of Churchill's cousin the 9th Duke of Marlborough and Consuelo Vanderbilt (Balsan). Marquess of Blandford. Captain, 1st Life Guards, 1916; retired, 1927. Succeeded his father as 10th Duke of Marlborough, 1934. Mayor of Woodstock, 1937–42. Aid-de-Camp to General Ironside, 1940. Home Guard, 1940–2. Military Liaison Officer to the Regional Commander, Southern Region, 1942. Lieutenant-Colonel, Liaison Officer, US Forces in Britain, 1942–5. In 1972, shortly before his death, he married, as his second wife, Mrs Laura Canfield, formerly Countess of Dudley and Viscountess Long.

Winston S. Churchill to Professor Lindemann
(*Churchill papers, 20/13*)

30 August 1940

If you have any points which I could put again to the Minister of Transport, pray assemble them. In addition there is the case of refrigerator trains. We lost last week an 11,000–ton meat ship[1] coming down the East Coast. If this ship could have been cleared at Bristol or Liverpool and the contents taken by refrigerated waggon to the London storage, the loss could have been avoided. I do not want to bring large ships down the East Coast needlessly.

War Cabinet: Confidential Annex
(*Cabinet papers, 65/14*)

30 August 1940　　　　　　　　　　　　　　　　　　　　　　　10 Downing Street
11.30 a.m.

In opening the discussion the Prime Minister referred to the latest developments in the battle for Great Britain. In the new phase of that battle the enemy had ceased using dive bombers. It had largely become a combat between fighters and fighters; and the German machines were now heavily armoured. The losses on the two sides were tending to approximate, and we were getting through our reserves of aircraft at a dangerous rate.

The Prime Minister said that there was no doubt that training at the Schools had been seriously interfered with, but he was extremely doubtful whether every effort had been made to overcome the difficulties of the existing conditions. It was absolutely imperative that the Air Staff should make further efforts in this direction. His suggestion of a three months delay before coming to a decision on the scheme would have the advantage of enabling it to be seen which way the present battle was going, and of allowing the Air Staff to overcome some at any rate of the training difficulties in this country.

John Colville: diary
(*Colville papers*)

30 August 1940　　　　　　　　　　　　　　　　　　　　　　　　　　　Chequers

At dinner, fortified by 1911 champagne, the PM talked brilliantly, though less epigramatically than usual. He said there were only three things that worried him: when, as yesterday, the proportion of our air losses was too high;

---

[1] The 11,445-ton *Remuera*, torpedoed from an aircraft east of Flamborough Head.

the startling shipping losses in the North-Western Approaches, where lay the seeds of something that 'might be mortal' if allowed to get out of hand; and the gun batteries at Griz Nez which would make the passage of our convoys through the Straits almost impossible and would mean that Dover might be 'laid in ashes'. He proposed to destroy those batteries – from the sea. (Captain Daniel[1] wants to do it by landing troops.)

The reason why he had brought the Joint Planners[2] down was to give them his general idea, which they could elaborate, of the campaign of 1941. He would not look as far as 1942, which must 'be the child of 1941', but would like to discuss the offensive action we should be able to take next year in order to turn the tables on the Germans and make them wonder, for a change, where they were going to be struck next. The essential prerequisite was the command of the air over the beaches where we should disembark our troops and armoured divisions. We had a large number of weapons, well on the road to development, which could help us in this: the AI,[3] which would for the first time be used in a Beaufighter plane tomorrow night and would soon be available in sufficiently large numbers to discomfort the enemy 'night prowlers', unescorted as they were by fighters; the 'Yagi' (now called 'Elsie') or wireless-controlled searchlights; and above all the PE fuze which was cheap, and easy to produce, and would shortly be given its trial in the clear atmosphere of Malta. Once these weapons were available, and the likelihood of being 'Namsosed' again had passed away, we could land on the continent.

He then outlined a number of possibilities which he wished the Joint Planners to study in the months to come: the capture of Oslo and the consequent undoing of Hitler's first great achievement; the invasion of Italy by sea; the cutting off of the Cherbourg peninsula (this might be used as a feint, because he did not wish to fight in France); and, most attractive of all, a landing in the Low Countries followed by the seizure of the Ruhr, or at any rate North German territory, so that the enemy might be made to experience war in his own land.[4] Forces of 100–120,000 men could be used, and if these operations were successful, who could tell to what they might lead?

---

[1] Charles Saumarez Daniel, 1894–1981. On active service with the Grand Fleet, 1914–18 (despatches). A specialist in signals and wireless. Captain, 8th Destroyer Flotilla, 1938–40. Director of Plans, Naval Staff, Admiralty, 1940–1; naval member of the Joint Planning Staff. CBE, 1941. Commanded HMS *Renown*, 1941–3. Flag Officer, Combined Operations, 1943. Rear-Admiral Commanding 1st Battle Squadron, British Pacific Fleet, 1944–5. CB, 1945. Third Sea Lord, 1945–9. Knighted, 1948. Commandant, Imperial Defence College, 1949–51. Admiral, 1950. Chairman, Television Advisory Committee, 1952–62.

[2] The three members of the Joint Planning Committee were Captain Daniel (Royal Navy), Brigadier Playfair (Army) and Group-Captain Slessor (Royal Air Force).

[3] Air Interception (airborne radar).

[4] This plan had attracted Churchill a quarter of a century earlier, in January 1915, when he wanted the German North Sea island of Borkum seized and used as a base for military assault on the Ruhr.

Brigadier Playfair[1] suggested it might be dangerous to use the PE fuze at Malta, in case its existence should become known and steps taken to parry it. But the PM said that there was no reason why it should be distinguished from accurate AA fire, and, moreover, if it were successful at Malta not only should we be able to plan our other operations with confidence, but also the fleet would once again have a secure base which would be fatal to Italy's communications with Libya and would alter the whole situation in the Mediterranean.

John Colville: diary
(*Colville papers*)

31 August 1940　　　　　　　　　　　　　　　　　　　　　　　　　Chequers

I had to break to the PM at 8.30 that three more big ships had been torpedoed off the Bloody Foreland (one of them 15,000 tons, carrying children to New York).[2] This distressed him particularly, because the North-Western Approaches are a very sore spot which shows no immediate sign of healing. On the other hand the news of our raids on Berlin last night is excellent: we seem to have found our objectives and damaged them severely.[3]

Winston S. Churchill to President Roosevelt
(*Premier papers, 3/462/2/3*)

31 August 1940

You ask, Mr President, whether my statement in Parliament on June 4th, 1940, about Great Britain never surrendering or scuttling her Fleet 'represents the settled policy of His Majesty's Government.' It certainly does. I

---

[1] Ian Stanley Ord Playfair, 1894–1972. On active service, 1914–18 (despatches, Military Cross and bar, DSO). General Staff Officer, Staff College, Quetta, 1934–7; Imperial Defence College, 1938. Commandant, Army Gas School, 1939. Director of Plans, War Office, 1940–1. Major-General, General Staff, South-East Asia Command, 1943. CB, 1943. Author of the four-volume official war history, *The Mediterranean and the Middle East, 1939–42*.

[2] On 28 August 1940 *Dalblair* (4,608 tons) and on August 29 the *Empire Moose* (6,103 tons) and the *Astra II* (2,393 tons) were sunk in the North-Western Approaches, west of the Bloody Foreland. A fourth merchant ship, the Palestinian registered *Har Zion* (2,508 tons), was sunk in the same area on 31 August. The 15,000-ton ship was a Dutch passenger liner, the *Volendam*. Although torpedoed by a U-boat on 30 August, she had not been sunk. All 884 passengers, including 317 children being evacuated to Canada, were rescued.

[3] During this air raid on Berlin, ten German civilians had been killed, and several military targets hit. On the road towards Tempelhof airport, the American journalist William Shirer noted in his diary: '200-lb bombs landed in the street, tore off the leg of an air raid warden standing at the entrance to his house, and killed four men and two women, who, unwisely, were watching the fireworks from a doorway.' (*Berlin Diary*).

must, however, observe that these hypothetical contingencies seem more likely to concern the German Fleet or what is left of it than our own.

Winston S. Churchill to General Ismay and Admiral Pound
(*Churchill papers, 20/13*)

31 August 1940
Secret

It becomes particularly urgent to attack the batteries on the French shore. Yesterday's photographs show guns being actually hoisted into position, and it will be wise to fire on them before they are able to reply. There are quite enough guns in position already. I trust therefore *Erebus* will not be delayed as every day our task will become harder.

It seems most necessary to damage and delay the development of the hostile batteries in view of the fact that we are so far behindhand with our own.

WSC

Winston S. Churchill to General Ismay
(*Churchill papers, 20/13*)

31 August 1940

If French India wish for trade they should be made to signify association with General de Gaulle. Otherwise no trade. This is not a matter upon which to be easy-going. Secretary of State for India to be informed.

The accession of any French possessions now is of importance.[1]

WSC

Winston S. Churchill to Herbert Morrison
(*Churchill papers, 20/13*)

31 August 1940

I am very glad to know that the chemical warfare stocks are piling up in this country. Let me know what the total now amounts to. The necessary containers should be brought level with supply. Do these stocks keep? Press on.

---

[1] On 9 September 1940 Louis Bonvin, the Governor of the French settlements in India (Mahé, Yanaon, Pondicherry and Karikal), announced their allegiance to the Free French. In the Pacific, New Caledonia had done so on 18 July, and the French settlement in Oceania on 2 September. The islands of St Pierre and Michelon, off Newfoundland, did so on 14 September, and the Pacific island of Nouméa on 20 September.

Winston S. Churchill to General Ismay
(*Churchill papers, 20/13*)

31 August 1940

I have not approved of any further Cruiser Tanks being despatched to the Middle East beyond those which have already gone. Although in principle it is desirable to contemplate the despatch of a full armoured division, further movements from this country can only be decided in relation to situation of Home forces. No decision of this importance must be taken without reference to me, and in this case I should have to consult the Cabinet.

WSC

Winston S. Churchill to Anthony Eden
(*Churchill papers, 20/13*)

31 August 1940

SOMALILAND

I am not at all satisfied with this story.[1] The losses sustained are not compatible with resolute resistance. It does not reflect well upon the Middle East Command that General Godwin-Austen should only have been sent at the last moment. Why was there not a competent commander in charge? The position of an officer who arrives to take over Command during an engagement is always difficult, and allowance must be made for that. The decision not to use the Black Watch to restore the situation was a grave one. The statement of the GOC[2] that they had suffered heavy losses was not true. The GOC threw his responsibilities upon the Middle Eastern Command, and they showed themselves very ready to cut the loss. If this is the sort of resistance that is to be expected and pass muster in the Middle East we must expect further tame and timely withdrawals.

I am of opinion that a Court of Inquiry should be set up without delay, and that the Middle East Command should be made aware that we are not accepting the account we have received up to the present as satisfactory. Pending the Court of Inquiry General Godwin-Austen should be suspended from duty.[3]

[1] A report on the Somaliland débâcle, sent to Churchill by General Wavell on 29 August 1940.

[2] General Godwin-Austen.

[3] On learning from Eden that no Court of Inquiry would be set up, Churchill minuted on 5 September 1940 (Prime Minister's Personal Minute, M.68): 'I understood from you that we were in full agreement that a formal inquiry should be held. Instead of this, all that is done is to ask for some further reports which cannot be of a character that would place us in a position where we can form an opinion. I have no doubt whatever that General Godwin-Austen should face a Court of Inquiry, and should be suspended meanwhile. It is only by taking formal action of this kind that the renewal of miserable episodes on a far larger scale can be prevented. I must beg you to act without delay' (*Churchill papers, 20/13*).

John Colville: diary
(*Colville papers*)

31 August 1940 Chequers
lunchtime

Sir Roger Keyes came to lunch and the Joint Planners stayed. The PM talked a lot. Pouring out another glass of brandy, and eyeing us all benevolently, he said that these Planners, on whose deliberation so much depended, could not afford to have more than one glass of brandy; but it was different for him who had only to take the responsibility. It was curious but in this war he had had no success but had received nothing but praise, whereas in the last war he had done several things which he thought were good and had got nothing but abuse for them.

Speaking of the Americans, who favoured many of the measures, such as violating Swiss neutrality in the air, which we are now taking, he said that their morale was very good – in applauding the valiant deeds done by others!

Sir R. Keyes then became the centre of conversation, the PM beginning by saying: 'I make myself detestable to everybody (i.e. by his refusal to let sleeping dogs lie or acquiesce in inactivity) except Roger whose dupe I am.' This is true because he has given Keyes a job out of loyalty and affection and in so doing has much angered the younger men in the navy. He told Keyes how he hoped that he would be able to undertake a raid on the Channel Islands soon, and Sir R. said that would be easy. The provision of air protection would however be difficult, insisted Slessor.[1]

Keyes said he hoped we should seize Casablanca when we took Dakar, but the PM replied that de Gaulle, who would have to be consulted, was now on the high seas.

Winston S. Churchill to Anthony Eden
(*Premier papers, 3/119/10*)

31 August 1940

The Minute of the Chief of the Imperial General Staff to you seems to be written under a misapprehension. There is no question of the Joint Planning Committee 'submitting military advice' to me. They are merely to work out

[1] John Cotesworth Slessor, 1897–1979. On active service, Royal Flying Corps, 1915–18 (despatches, wounded, Military Cross). Author of *Air Power and Armies* (1936). Waziristan Operations, 1936–7 (despatches, DSO). Air Commodore, 1939. Air Representative, Anglo-French Conversations, 1939; Anglo-American (ABC) Staff Conversations, 1941. Air Officer commanding 5 (Bomber) Group, 1941. Air Vice-Marshal, 1941. Assistant Chief of the Air Staff (Policy), 1942–3. Air Officer Commanding-in-Chief, Coastal Command, 1943. Knighted, 1943. Commander-in-Chief, Royal Air Force, Mediterranean and Middle East, 1944–5. Marshal of the Royal Air Force, 1950. Chief of the Air Staff, 1950–2.

plans in accordance with directions which I shall give. The advice as to whether these plans or any variants of them should be adopted will rest as at present with the Chiefs of the Staff. It is quite clear from paragraph 2 of my Minute of August 24 that the Chiefs of the Staff also have their collective responsibility for advising the Cabinet as well as the Prime Minister or Minister of Defence. It has not been thought necessary to make any alteration in their constitutional position. Moreover I propose to work with and through them as heretofore. There is therefore no need for the amendment proposed.

I have found it necessary to have direct access to and control of the Joint Planning Staffs because after a year of war I cannot recall a single plan initiated by the existing machinery. I feel sure that I can count upon you and the other two Service Ministers to help me in giving a vigorous and positive direction to the conduct of the war, and in overcoming the dead weight of inertia and delay which has so far led us to being forestalled on every occasion by the enemy.

It will of course be necessary from time to time to increase the number of the Joint Planning Staffs.

WSC

John Colville: diary
(*Colville papers*)

31 August 1940   Chequers
dinner time

Sir H. Dowding, C in C Fighter Command, and Sir C. Portal,[1] C in C Bomber Command, came to dinner. Dowding is splendid: he stands up to the PM, refuses to be particularly unpleasant about the Germans, and is the very antithesis of the complacency with which so many Englishmen are afficted.

There was a great discussion about the ethics of shooting down enemy pilots landing by parachute: Dowding maintaining it should be done and the PM saying that an escaping pilot was like a drowning sailor. Otherwise he was in a very ruthless frame of mind.

[1] Charles Frederick Algernon Portal, 1893–1971. Known as 'Peter'. On active service, 1914–18 (despatches, DSO and bar; Military Cross). As a 2nd Lieutenant, Royal Engineers, he was in both the advance to and the retreat from Mons in 1914. Seconded to the Royal Flying Corps, 1915. Major, commanding 16 Squadron, 1917 (working for the Canadian Corps, then carrying out night bombing tasks). Air Ministry (Directorate of Operations and Intelligence), 1923. Commanded the British Forces in Aden, 1934–5. Instructor, Imperial Defence College, 1936–7. Director of Organisation, Air Ministry, 1937–8. Air Member for Personnel, Air Council, 1939–40. Air Officer Commanding-in-Chief, Bomber Command, April–October 1940. Knighted, July 1940. Chief of the Air Staff, October 1940–November 1945. Created Baron, 1945; Viscount, 1946. Order of Merit, 1946. Knight of the Garter, 1946. Controller, Atomic Energy, Ministry of Supply, 1946–51. Chairman, British Aircraft Corporation, 1960–8.

After dinner the First Lord rang up from Brighton to say that enemy ships were steering westwards from Terschelling. The invasion may be pending (though I'll lay 10–1 against!) and all HM Forces are taking up their positions. If these German ships came on they would reach the coast of Norfolk tomorrow morning.

The PM and the Air Marshals, with Lindemann, looked at diagrams showing the working of the German Headache beam which, directed from Germany, guides the bombers to their objectives whatever the weather conditions or the visibility. We, having learnt of this, are in process of discovering how to jam and how to divert it. Diversion is more fun: it sends the enemy to wrong destinations.

Winston S. Churchill to Neville Chamberlain
(*Churchill papers, 2/393*)

31 August 1940

My dear Neville,

I showed your letter to the Cabinet. We were all delighted to learn of the improved progress you have been making.

I cannot conceal from you that there are several topics – like Railway Fares; Compensation in Rates to the Coastal Areas now under heavy attack; more generous treatment of individuals whose houses are smashed in these battered regions; – on all of which I should greatly welcome your counsel and assistance, apart from the general policy which we are pursuing. However we are fairly well on top of our job, and everyone was most determined not to allow you to come back until you are fit; and we beg you not to hesitate to take another week besides this one if you feel you will thereby gather more reserve. After operations of this kind, as I know from my own experience,[1] one very quickly recovers enough energy to do half a day's work but it takes some time to get to full efficiency. The great thing is not to try to start too soon and then have a set-back.

We are having fewer Cabinets now and the business often does not take more than an hour. This is not because many things are not going forward, but because we have got into a groove in which much action is outside our control.

---

[1] Churchill had three major operations before 1940 while he was in public life: in 1922 when he had an appendectomy in London and then had to travel to Dundee to fight the general election campaign (and lost 'my Office, my seat and my appendix'); in 1931, after he was knocked down by a car in New York (and had to curtail a coast-to-coast lecture tour); and in 1932, when he was taken ill with paratyphoid while in Salzburg, and had a serious relapse shortly after his return to Chartwell (thereby missing a crucial rearmament debate in the Commons).

A change seemed to be coming over the air attack. For some days they sent no dive bombers, and fewer bombers, and were trying to beat our fighters with their newly armoured craft. This tends somewhat to diminish our proportion of prizes, but we are all ready with our strong development of cannon guns, against which no armour will be any protection, and hope we shall be cutting into them pretty sharply in the near future. Yesterday they sent the bombers out again and the results were again good for us. We also hope that AI will be ready quite soon for the night prowlers.

There is a certain menace of invasion in the shipping gathering at Kiel and Emden, which we are looking after; but the new focus is upon the North Western Approaches where losses have become very heavy. I have been reading the Riot Act at intervals for the last ten days to the Admiralty, and I am satisfied they are exerting their full strength and ingenuity. I have never known them fail. The fifty American destroyers will be a godsend, and our own new construction is at last beginning to flow.

The spirit of the people is wonderful, but my heart bleeds for the little watering-places which are first impoverished and then badgered and battered. However when all is said and done I must say I feel pretty good about this war. It will be a long pull if we are to get a thoroughly good result.

My kindest regards to yourself and Mrs Neville.

Believe me,
Yours ever,
Winston S. Churchill

September 1940

Winston S. Churchill to General Ismay
(*Churchill papers, 20/13*)

1 September 1940

This[1] seems very long for a <u>daily</u> report, and the Joint Intelligence Sub-Committee may be setting themselves and others a needless task. A daily report should be limited to one page, and the weekly report should be a well-digested summary.

I see very little here that I have not read in the telegrams.

WSC

Winston S. Churchill to General Ismay
(*Churchill papers, 20/13*)

1 September 1940

The Joint Planning Staff will require the following reinforcements in order to cope with the additional duties which have recently been assigned to them:–
Naval Staff –
  1 Captain, RN
  2 Commanders.

---

[1] Report No. 1, 'French African Colonies', 30 August 1940.

General Staff –
1 GSO, 1st Grade.
2 GSOs, 2nd Grade.
Air Staff –
1 Group Captain.
2 Wing Commanders.

2. Very carefully selected officers must be made available for these important duties: but, other things being equal, officers who have been wounded, or at least seen service in this war, should be given preference.

WSC

Winston S. Churchill to General Ismay
(*Churchill papers, 20/13*)

1 September 1940

Ask C-in-C, Home Defence,[1] and C-in-C, Middle East,[2] for a weekly return of rifle, machine-gun and field artillery strength, and also of ration strength in their respective commands.

WSC

Winston S. Churchill to General Ismay
(*Churchill papers, 20/13*)

1 September 1940
Secret

I presume you will be thinking about what is to happen should 'Menace' succeed, with little or no bloodshed. It would seem that as soon as de Gaulle has established himself there and in the place a little to the north, he should try to get a footing in Morocco, and our ships and troops could be used to repeat the process of 'Menace,' if it has been found to work, immediately and in a more important theatre. This operation may be called 'Threat.'

WSC

[1] General Brooke.
[2] General Wavell.

September 1940

Winston S. Churchill to General Ismay
(*Churchill papers, 20/13*)

1 September 1940

Of course if the Glider scheme is better than parachutes, we should pursue it, but is it being seriously taken up? Are we not in danger of being fobbed off with one doubtful and experimental policy and losing the other which has already been proved? Let me have a full report of what has been done about the Gliders.[1]

WSC

Winston S. Churchill to A. V. Alexander and Admiral Pound
(*Churchill papers, 20/13*)

1 September 1940

I am deeply concerned at your news that you cannot attack these batteries[2] until the 16th. You are allowing an artillery concentration to be developed day after day, which presently will forbid the entry of all British ships into the Straits of Dover, and will prepare the way for an attack on Dover itself. Pray let me know what you propose to do about this.

Surely, while the big guns are actually being hoisted into position and cannot fire back, is the time for action. The general weakness of the defences of Dover itself in heavy guns is also a matter of great seriousness. We must not simply look at dangers piling up without any attempt to forestall them. *Erebus* will have to face double the fire on the 16th that she or any other ship would have to face in the next week.

I remember well that it was customary to bombard the Knocke and other German batteries on the Belgian coast very frequently during the late War. It was possible to fire most accurately by night after a buoy had been fixed and

---

[1] Gliders, engineless unarmed aircraft with the advantage of a silent approach, had first been used in war on 11 May 1940, when the Germans used them to send in troops to seize the Belgian fortress of Eben Emael (with the loss of only six men). They reached their maximum effectiveness in the war during the German attack on Crete in May 1941, but with heavy losses. It was not until the end of 1941 that the decision was finally made in Britain to form a glider division (the 1st Airborne Division). They were first used by night in the raid on the radar station at Bruneval near Le Havre in February 1942, and by day in July 1943 during the invasion of Sicily, at Syracuse, when 58 of their 300 pilots were killed. In 1944 the Germans sent glider-borne troops to fight the partisans in Yugoslavia. On 6 June 1944 the initial Normandy landings by parachutists were followed by glider-borne troops.

[2] The German long-range guns at Cap Gris Nez.

sound ranging used. I ask for proposals for action this week. Look at the photographs attached.[1]

WSC

Winston S. Churchill to Sir Archibald Sinclair and Sir Cyril Newall
(*Churchill papers, 20/13*)

1 September 1940

There must be no mistake about this expression 'South African allotment.' All Hurricane aeroplanes allotted to South Africa are allotted on the express condition that they are immediately put into action in East Africa or in the Middle East.

Would it not be well also to enter a caveat that the continued dispatch of operational Fighter aircraft must be reviewed from week to week in the light of the progress of the present grievous battle.

WSC

Winston S. Churchill to Anthony Eden
(*Churchill papers, 20/13*)

1 September 1940

I should be glad to have a full report of the arrangements being made to provide educational and recreational facilities for the troops during the coming winter. Who will be responsible for this important branch of work?

WSC

Winston S. Churchill: memorandum
(*Churchill papers, 20/13*)

1 September 1940

AIR RAID WARNINGS AND PRECAUTIONS

1. The present system of Air Raid warnings was designed to cope with occasional large mass raids on definite targets, not with waves coming over several times a day, and still less with sporadic bombers roaming about at nights. We cannot allow large parts of the country to be immobilised for hours every day, and to be distracted every night. The enemy must not be permitted

---

[1] Not printed. Churchill's daughter Sarah was later to work in the Photographic Reconnaissance Section.

to prejudice our war effort by stopping work in the factories which he has been unable to destroy.

2. There should be instituted, therefore, a new system of warnings:–
The Alert.
The Alarm.
The All Clear.

The Alert should not interrupt the normal life of the area. People not engaged on national work could, if they desired, take refuge or put their children in a place of safety. But in general they should learn, and they do learn, to adapt themselves to their dangers and take only such precautions as are compatible with their duties and imposed by their temperament.

3. The Air Raid services should be run on an increased nucleus staff, and not all called out every time as on a present red warning. The look-out system should be developed in all factories where war work is proceeding, and should be put into effect when the Alert is given; the look-outs would have full authority to give local factory or office alarms. The signal for the Alert might be given during the day by the hoisting of a display of yellow flags by a sufficient number of specially charged Air Raid wardens. At night, flickering yellow (or perhaps red) lamps could be employed. The use of electric street lighting should be studied, and the possibility of sounding special signals on the telephone.

4. The Alarm is a direct order to 'Take Cover' and for the full manning of all ARP positions. This will very likely synchronise with or precede by only a brief interval the actual attack. The routine in each case must be subject to local conditions.

The signal for the Alarm would be the siren. It would probably be unnecessary to supplement this by light or telephone signals.

5. The All Clear could be sounded as at present. It would end the Alarm period. If the Alert continued, the flags would remain hoisted; if the enemy had definitely turned back, the Alert flags and lights would be removed.

The use of the Alert and Alarm signals might vary in different parts of the country. In areas subject to frequent attack, such as East Kent, South and South-East London, South-East Anglia, Birmingham, Derby, Liverpool, Bristol, and some other places, the Alert would be a commonplace. The Alarm would denote actual attack. This would also apply to the Whitehall district. In other parts of the country, a somewhat less sparing use of the Alarm might be justified in order to keep the Air Raid Services from deteriorating.

6. In Government Offices in London, no one should be forced to take cover until actual firing has begun and the siren ordering the Alarm under the new conditions has been sounded. No one is to stop work merely because London is under Alert conditions.

WSC

Winston S. Churchill to L. S. Amery
(*Churchill papers, 20/13*)

1 September 1940

1. I am sorry to say that I cannot see my way to diverting aeroplanes or AA guns from the battle now raging here for the defence of India, which is in no way pressing; neither is it possible to divert American supplies for the building of an aircraft industry in India. We are already running risks which many might question in the reinforcement and re-equipment of the Middle East, and when the battle at home dies down, this theatre will absorb all our surplus for a long time to come.

2. It is very important that India should be a help and not on the balance a burden at the present time. The debit balance is heavy when you consider the number of British troops and batteries locked up there, and the very exiguous Indian forces which, after a year of war, have reached the field. I am glad you are making increased efforts to form Indian Divisions for the very large important operations which seem likely to develop in the Middle East in 1941.[1]

WSC

John Colville: diary
(*Colville papers*)

1 September 1940

At lunch the PM, talking of *Why England Slept*,[2] turned to me and said, 'You slept too, didn't you!' – a good-natured jibe at my professed 'Munichois' views!

In the afternoon I went with the PM, Lindemann and Ismay to Uxbridge, headquarters of No. 11 Group which controls all the Fighter Squadrons in the South-East. We talked to Air Marshal Park[3] who confirmed the PM's view

---

[1] Churchill hoped to have six Indian Divisions in the Middle East (also fifteen British and six Australian) by the spring of 1941.

[2] A book published shortly before the war by John F. Kennedy, son of the American Ambassador in London, and himself later President of the United States (1960–3). Kennedy had written the book while living in London with his father.

[3] Keith Rodney Park, 1892–1975. A New Zealander; Private, New Zealand Field Artillery, 1911. New Zealand Expeditionary Force, 1914. Royal Field Artillery, 1915 (on active service at Gallipoli, and in France). Seconded to the Royal Flying Corps, 1916. Captain, Royal Air Force, 1918 (Military Cross and bar; DFC). Senior Air Staff Officer, Fighter Command, 1938. Commanded No. 11 Fighter Group, April–December 1940. Air Officer Commanding No. 23 Group, Training Command, 1941. Commanded RAF Egypt, 1942. Knighted, 1942. Air Officer Commanding Malta, 1942–3; Middle East, 1944. Allied Air Commander-in-Chief, South East Asia, 1945–6. One of his two sons was killed in action in Korea, 1951.

that the Germans must already have developed their maximum attack and could not stand the strain much longer as far as an air offensive was concerned. The PM expressed delight at the success of our pilots, but said, 'It is terrible – terrible – that the British Empire should have been gambled on this.' He had already remarked at lunch, talking of Poland and the failure of France to maintain its position in Eastern Europe, 'This is one of the most unnecessary wars, and it will probably be one of the most terrible.' The Poles, he pointed out, had fought much better than the French and had shown infinitely greater spirit.

At dinner the PM, thinking of our new weapons, said that we could not hope to pile up sufficient men and munitions to outmatch the Germans. This was a war of science, a war that would be won with new weapons.

War Cabinet: minutes
(*Cabinet papers, 65/9*)

2 September 1940
12 noon

The Prime Minister said that on the 31st August[1] he had visited the Fighter Command during one of the big German air attacks. He had found it very instructive to watch the Officers of the Fighter Command deploying their forces and building up a front at the threatened points. He was sure that the Secretary of State for Air would welcome it if other Members of the War Cabinet were to pay similar visits.

The Prime Minister then reviewed the results of the last month of hard air fighting. We had every right to be satisfied with those results. He was tempted to ask why the enemy should continue attacks on this heavy scale – which included some days as many as 700 aircraft – if it did not represent something like their maximum effort. This might not, of course, be the explanation. But our own Air Force was stronger than ever and there was every reason to be optimistic about the 1940 Air Battle of Britain.

War Cabinet: Confidential Annex
(*Cabinet papers, 65/15*)

2 September 1940
12 noon

The proposal to send further armoured units out of this country as reinforcements for the Middle East gave rise to a short discussion as to the likelihood of invasion.

[1] According to Colville's diary, this visit took place on 1 September 1940.

The Prime Minister said that he regarded fog, which was more likely in the autumn, as a great ally to an invader, more especially as fog was usually accompanied by a calm sea.

As against this, the First Sea Lord said that in the winter the use of barges and small fishing craft, in regard to which there had been so many reports, was out of the question; or at least such craft could only be used on so few days that they could not form part of any expedition which started on a pre-arranged date.

It was difficult to give any date after which the weather would deteriorate seriously, but, after the equinoctial gales about 21st September, the weather was uncertain.

The Prime Minister pointed out that, as a result of the action which had been taken, our forces were now widely spread. He referred to the reinforcements sent to the Middle East (including the despatch of aircraft) and to Operation 'Menace'. He thought that it would be agreed that we had acted with determination in sending these forces out of the country at the present time.

The First Sea Lord said that the indications pointing to invasion had never been more positive than they were at the present time.

The Secretary of State for War said that he agreed with this view.

The Prime Minister asked what action was being taken to knock out the German batteries which were being installed on the French coast. He thought it was clear that the German High Command would think in terms of establishing artillery which could fire across the Straits of Dover, and make them impassable to our shipping. When this had been done, they would make a great effort to establish air superiority over the Channel, and win a bridgehead on English soil. The great need of the Germans to stage a successful invasion must not be overlooked.

The First Sea Lord described the steps which were being taken. The first stage was that a number of short-range guns were being established in the neighbourhood of Dover. These would be effective as coast defence weapons.

As a second stage, it was proposed to erect certain turrets which were available from battleships.

As a third stage, there was the possibility of erecting still larger guns of, say, 15-inch calibre. This, however, would take time.

Winston S. Churchill to General Ismay
(*Churchill papers, 20/13*)

2 September 1940

Endeavour to procure discreetly for me a photograph of Admiral Tovey,[1] Second-in-Command in the Mediterranean. I think I met this Officer several years ago, but have not seen him since the war began.

WSC

War Cabinet: minutes
(*Cabinet papers, 65/9*)

3 September 1940
12 noon

10 Downing Street

The Prime Minister suggested that, if a red warning was in operation when a Meeting of the War Cabinet was about to begin, there should be a standing arrangement that the Meeting should take place in the Cabinet War Room. If a red warning was given after a Meeting had begun at 10 Downing Street, he hoped that they would be able to continue their business without interruption.

The War Cabinet agreed to the standing arrangement proposed by the Prime Minister.

The Prime Minister informed the War Cabinet of the arrival of the *Valiant*, *Coventry* and *Calcutta* at Malta. They had transferred their stores during the daylight hours of the 2nd September and had sailed to join the Commander-in-Chief, Mediterranean.

He had it in mind to send a further message in a form suitable for publication to General Dobbie, who had ably and gallantly conducted the defence of Malta since Italy's entry into the war.

The War Cabinet approved this suggestion.

[1] John Cronyn Tovey, 1885–1971. On active service as a destroyer-captain, 1914–18 (despatches, DSO). Appointed Commander after the Battle of Jutland, 1916, for 'the persistent and determined manner in which he attacked enemy ships'. Rear-Admiral, Destroyers, Mediterranean, 1938–40. Vice-Admiral Second-in-Command, Mediterranean Fleet, 1940. Commander-in-Chief, Home Fleet, 1940–3 (his responsibilities included the Murmansk and Archangel convoys). Knighted, 1941. Admiral of the Fleet, 1943. Commander-in-Chief, the Nore, 1943–6. Created Baron, 1946.

Winston S. Churchill: memorandum[1]
(*Cabinet papers, 66/11*)

3 September 1940　　　　　　　　　　　　　　　　　　10 Downing Street

THE MUNITIONS SITUATION

I venture to submit to my colleagues the following points which suggest themselves to me in reading the deeply interesting survey of the Minister of Supply:–[2]

1. The Navy can lose us the war, but only the Air Force can win it. Therefore our supreme effort must be to gain overwhelming mastery in the Air. The Fighters are our salvation, but the Bombers alone provide the means of victory. We must therefore develop the power to carry an ever-increasing volume of explosives to Germany, so as to pulverise the entire industry and scientific structure on which the war effort and economic life of the enemy depends, while holding him at arm's length in our Island. In no other way at present visible can we hope to overcome the immense military power of Germany, and to nullify the further German victories which may be apprehended as the weight of their force is brought to bear upon African or Oriental theatres. The Air Force and its action on the largest scale must therefore, subject to what is said later, claim the first place over the Navy or the Army.

2. The weapon of blockade has become blunted and rendered, as far as Germany is concerned, less effectual on account of their land conquests and power to rob captive or intimidated peoples for their own benefit. There remain no very important special commodities the denial of which will hamper their war effort. The Navy is at present somewhat pressed in its task of keeping open the communications, but as this condition is removed by new Admiralty measures, by the arrival of the American destroyers, and by the increasing output of anti-U-Boat craft from our own yards, we may expect a marked improvement. It is of the utmost importance that the Admiralty should direct their attention to aggressive schemes of war, and to the bombardment of enemy or enemy-held coasts, particularly in the Mediterranean. The production of anti-U-Boat craft must proceed at the maximum until further orders, each slip being filled as it is vacated. The Naval

[1] Circulated to the War Cabinet as War Cabinet Paper 352 of 1940, 'The Munitions Situation'.
[2] On 29 August 1940, Herbert Morrison circulated to the War Cabinet a memorandum (War Cabinet Paper 339 of 1940), 'The Munitions Situation', in which he wrote: 'Though we cannot compete with Germany in sheer weight of metal, in a near future command of the sea and air may enable us to gain a considerable local superiority over Germany, in particular parts of Europe and elsewhere.' Since the beginning of June the supply of arms for the Army, 'which was desperately low two months ago, has greatly improved'. Britain's existing stock of weapons was, however, 'trifling, compared to the 15,000 to 20,000 field guns and the equivalent other arms of Germany' (*Cabinet papers, 66/11*).

Programme does not impinge markedly upon the Air, and should cede some of its armourplate to Tank production.

3. The decision to raise the Army to a strength of 55 Divisions as rapidly as possible does not seem to require any reconsideration. Within this, we should aim at 10 Armoured Divisions, 5 by the Spring, 7 by the Summer, and 10 by the end of 1941. The execution of these programmes of armament supply will tax our munitions factories to the full. I agree in principle with the proposals of the Minister of Supply for handling the ammunition supply problem, and also that firings on the 1917–18 scale are not to be expected in the present war.

4. The most intense efforts must be made to complete the equipment of our Army at home, and of our Army in the Middle East. The most serious weak points are Tanks and small arms ammunition, particularly the special types of anti-Tank guns and rifles, and even more their ammunition; trench mortars, and still more their ammunition; and rifles. We hope to obtain an additional 250,000 rifles from the United States, but it is lamentable that we should be told that no more than half a million additional rifles can be manufactured here before the end of 1941. Surely as large numbers of our Regular Army proceed abroad, the need of the Home Guard and of garrison troops for home defence on a far larger scale than at present will be felt. A substantial increase in rifle-making capacity is necessary.

5. The danger of invasion will not disappear with the coming of winter, and may confront us with novel possibilities in the coming year. The enemy's need to strike down this country will naturally increase as the war progresses, and all kinds of appliances for crossing the seas, that do not now exist, may be devised. Actual invasion must be regarded as perpetually threatened but unlikely to materialise as long as strong forces stand in this Island. Apart from this, the only major theatre of war which can be foreseen in 1940–41 is the Middle East. Here we must endeavour to bring into action British, Australasian and Indian forces, on a scale which should only be limited by sea transport and local maintenance. We must expect to fight in Egypt and the Sudan, in Turkey, Syria or Palestine, and possibly in Iraq and Iran. Fifteen British Divisions, 6 Australasian, and at least 6 Indian Divisions should be prepared for these theatres, these forces not being, however, additional to the 55 Divisions which have been mentioned. One would not imagine that the ammunition expenditure would approach the last War scale. Air power and mechanised troops will be the dominant factors.

6. There remain the possibilities of amphibious aggressive warfare against the enemy or enemy-held territory in Europe or North Africa. But the needs of such operations will be provided by the arms and supplies already mentioned in general terms.

7. Our task, as the Minister of Supply rightly reminds us, is indeed formidable when the gigantic scale of German military and aviation equipment is considered. This war is not, however, a war of masses of men hurling

masses of shells at each other. It is by devising new weapons, and above all, by scientific leadership, that we shall best cope with the enemy's superior strength. If, for instance, the series of inventions now being developed to find and hit enemy aircraft, both from the air and from the ground, irrespective of visibility, realise what is hoped from them, not only the strategic but the munitions situation would be profoundly altered. And if the UP weapon can be provided with ammunition, predictors and other aids which realise an accuracy of hitting three or four times as great as that which now exists, the ground will have taken a long step towards the re-conquest of the Air. The Navy will regain much of its old freedom of movement and power to take offensive action. And the Army will be able to land at many points without the risk of being Namsossed. We must therefore regard the whole sphere of RDF,[1] with its many refinements and measureless possibilities, as ranking in priority with the Air Force, of which it is in fact an essential part. The multiplication of the high-class scientific personnel, as well as the training of those who will handle the new weapons and research work connected with them, should be the very spearpoint of our thought and effort. Very great reliefs may be expected in anti-aircraft guns and ammunition, although it is at present too soon to alter present plans.

8. Apart from a large-scale invasion, which is unlikely, there is no prospect of any large expenditure or wastage of military munitions before the Spring of 1941. Although heavy and decisive fighting may develop at any time in the Middle East, the difficulties of transport, both of reinforcements and of supplies, will restrict numbers and expenditure. We have, therefore, before us, if not interrupted, a period of eight months in which to make an enormous improvement in our output of war-like equipment, and in which steady and rapid accumulations may be hoped for. It is upon this purpose that all our resources of credit, materials, and above all, of skilled labour, must be bent.

WSC

Winston S. Churchill to Sir John Anderson
(*Churchill papers, 20/13*)

3 September 1940
ACTION THIS DAY

In spite of the shortage of materials, a great effort should be made to help people to drain their Anderson shelters, which reflect so much credit on your name, and to make floors for them against the winter rain. Bricks on edge placed loosely together without mortar, covered with a piece of linoleum, would be quite good, but there must be a drain and a sump. I am prepared to help you in a comprehensive scheme to tackle this. Instruction can be given on

[1] Radio Direction Finding (radar).

the broadcast, and, of course, the Regional Commissioners and local authorities should be used. Let me have a plan.

WSC

John Colville: diary
(*Colville papers*)

3 September 1940
3 p.m.

Went to a service at Westminster Abbey to commemorate the first anniversary of the war. The King and Queen were to have gone, but an air-raid warning sounded just before the service began. However the PM and a good many Ministers attended.

Hugh Dalton: diary
('*The Second World War Diary of Hugh Dalton*')

3 September 1940

At 10.30 this evening I go to see PM at No. 10 Downing Street. I wished, before going on leave, to make an oral report to him, following upon a brief written report, of some of my proceedings. But I don't get much chance! He is much more anxious to talk than to listen, and walks up and down the room pouring forth a flow of his usual vigorous rhetorical good sense. 'This is a workmen's war . . . the public will stand everything except optimism . . . the nation is finding the war is not so unpleasant as it expected . . . the air attacks are doing much less damage than was expected before the war began . . . don't be like the knight in the story who was so slow in buckling on his armour that the tourney was over before he rode into the ring.' While I am there he also rings up Lord Portal[1] and asks him to become an additional Under-Secretary at the Ministry of Supply, to help Morrison with control of raw materials. Then he calls for Peck, a young man who is one of his secretaries, and demands that he shall show us air photographs on a screen. These show the guns at Cape Grisnez, the docks at Emden and Wilhelmshaven, etc. The PM is childishly pleased with these and also with the mechanism itself. He

---

[1] Wyndham Raymond Portal, 1885–1949. On active service, 1914–18 (DSO). Succeeded to his father's baronetcy, 1931. Chairman of the Coal Production Council. Created Baron, 1935. Regional Commissioner for Wales, Civil Defence Scheme, 1939. Additional Parliamentary Under-Secretary, Ministry of Supply, 1940–2. Minister of Works and Planning, 1942–4. Created Viscount, 1945. President of the Olympic Games, 1948.

says, 'Peck, you must get some new photographs every day and show them to me every evening.' He is a child of genius. When the Grisnez photograph comes on, he detects a German car travelling along the road, puts his finger upon it and cries, 'Look, there is a horrible hun. Why don't we bomb him?' He is very vexed at the difficulties of communication with France. He says, 'I can't even find an American who would take a letter from me to General Georges.[1] It would be quite a short letter. I should simply say, as Thiers[2] said, *"On pensez toujours! On parlez jamais!"* '[3] The PM's French is incorrect but intelligible and he rushes forward without hesitation or pedantry. 'He would understand that. I should need to say no more. I know that man and a message from me would make a difference to him. I know how he must be feeling.'

Winston S. Churchill to A. V. Alexander and Admiral Pound
(*Churchill papers, 20/13*)

4 September 1940

Before the end of the Gallipoli campaign very accurate long-range bombardment, both direct and indirect, was carried out at short notice by ships which lay in submarine-proof anchorage until the army called upon them. They then ran out, nosed a buoy in a fixed position and opened fire without any delay. They were previously registered on to their targets by aeroplane spotting. The preliminary work was done by hydrogaphers, who prepared bombarding charts and fixed aiming marks which could be lit at night, and thus our ships could open fire accurately when they were asked to do so by the army.

---

[1] General Georges, who was then in North Africa, joined the French Committee of National Liberation in Algiers in 1943. At the trial of Marshal Pétain in 1945, he told the court that when he met Churchill in North Africa in 1944, the Prime Minister had told him that Hitler 'made a great mistake in not going on to Africa' after the Franco-German armistice.

[2] Louis-Adolphe Thiers, 1797–1877. French statesman, historian and journalist. Prime Minister and Minister of Foreign Affairs, 1836 and 1840. Secured the return of Napoleon's body from St Helena, 1840. President of the Third Republic, 1871–3. Ruthless in his use of troops to defeat the Paris Commune, 1871.

[3] It was in fact the French patriot Gambetta who said, in regard to the German annexation of Alsace and Lorraine in 1871, 'Think of it always, speak of it never.' Churchill was to use this phrase, a favourite of his, in his broadcast to France on 21 October 1940. On that occasion, his Private Secretary John Peck confirmed that the remark was by Gambetta, not Thiers.

Off the Belgian coast during 1918 the same hydrographers produced target charts and devised a means for fixing by sound range positions off the enemy coast with great accuracy. They also produced a diagram, by means of which, given the position of a bombarding monitor, and the latitude and longitude of the target, the range and bearing could be determined, without reference to the chart. A gyro director enabled monitor guns to be laid on any true bearing, without the necessity of aiming marks, thus enabling them to fire at night, and under way, out of sight of land.

Three or four positions might be fixed which the *Erebus* could take up after dark for the bombardment of Gris Nez.

It might be necessary to register on to the targets by aeroplane spotting in daylight. Once this is done the *Erebus* could open fire accurately at night.

Captain E. Altham,[1] who designed the gyroscopic director and commanded one of the monitors on the Belgian coast in 1918, can give valuable advice. He thinks it might not be necessary to do the preliminary firing for ranging and testing the gyroscopic director actually on the spot, nor to visit a bombarding position in daylight. He is in touch with Captain Daniel, Director of Plans.

If it is approved to use the *Erebus*, a camouflaged anchorage should be made for the *Erebus* within a few hours' steaming of her bombarding position.

War Cabinet: minutes
(*Cabinet papers, 65/9*)

4 September 1940
11 a.m.
10 Downing Street

The Prime Minister referred to the suggestions outlined at the Cabinet two days earlier for modifying the warning system in regard to which discussions were proceeding.

For a year it had been impressed on workers that it was their duty to take cover when the sirens sounded. The habit had become ingrained, and a new outlook was wanted.

The Government had ample legal powers to compel men to remain at work.

---

[1] Edward Altham, 1882–1950. Commanded HMS *Wildfire* in the bombardment of the German Army's right wing off the Belgian coast, October 1914. Commanded the monitor *General Craufurd* off the Belgian coast, 1915. Senior Naval Officer, Archangel River expeditions, 1918–19. CB, 1919. Staff of Naval War College, 1920–1. Retired, 1922. Naval Editor, *Encyclopaedia Britannica*. Published *Jellicoe, a biography*, 1938. Recalled to active service, 1939. Chief Censor on Naval Staff, Admiralty, 1939–44.

But it would be a grave decision to apply compulsion to skilled workers in the aircraft industry.

A more suitable method would be the withdrawal of protection from service with the forces. But, before consideration was given to this or any other method, a full report should be obtained as to the local conditions in this factory,[1] and the Minister of Labour should be consulted.

It would be difficult to keep secret any measures found necessary to induce munition workers to continue at work; and there was a risk of affording encouragement to the enemy. The first step might well be that the men should be addressed by some national figure, who could bring them to a better realisation of the position.

The War Cabinet invited the Lord Privy Seal to investigate these matters, in consultation with the other Ministers concerned, in the course of the day, and to report to a Meeting of the War Cabinet to be held at 9.30 p.m. that evening.

The Foreign Secretary said that he had instructed his Department to consider, in consultation with the other Departments concerned, whether we could offer any economic inducements to Japan which would prove so attractive as to keep her on the paths of virtue.

The Prime Minister said that, if the present air battle went in our favour, it would greatly increase our prestige. But it would not materially affect the military position *vis-à-vis* Japan. A war with Japan would fundamentally affect our strategy in the Middle East. The right course was to go some way in offering inducements to Japan, and possibly also to go some way in using threats, but not to commit ourselves irrevocably to forcible action.

MANUFACTURE OF AIRCRAFT IN INDIA

The Prime Minister said that Germany was no doubt planning to organise aircraft production in all the enslaved countries of Europe. We must be prepared to meet aircraft production on a European scale. We could only do this if we used the most efficient centres of production and we must not dissipate our resources.

While the present air battle continued, we must direct all our energies to making ourselves as strong as possible; but if matters developed favourably for us, it might be possible to reconsider long term projects of this nature.

---

[1] Lord Beaverbrook had just told the War Cabinet that on Saturday, 31 August, 700 men had left the aircraft factory at Castle Bromwich that lunchtime 'without authorisation' and a further 700 at five that afternoon: '3,500 men had remained at work over the weekend, but there was a marked disinclination on the part of the men to continue at work after an air raid warning had been sounded. Production had already fallen off and prompt action was necessary if the situation was not to deteriorate further.' Beaverbrook told the War Cabinet that he would like to see the sounding of air raid sirens discontinued.

War Cabinet: minutes
(*Cabinet papers, 65/9*)

4 September 1940   Cabinet War Room
10.20 p.m.

The Prime Minister pointed out that the 'red' warning meant only that enemy aircraft were flying over a certain area. No one could tell whether the enemy aircraft intended to bomb that area or were on passage to some other place. Accordingly the 'red' warning bore no relation to the danger involved. He was sure that the people of this country would follow any clear and reasonable direction. The public would feel that there was an inherent contradiction between the continued sounding of the 'red' warning on the siren, which was associated with the official Government advice to take cover, and the directions that workers worth their salt should no longer obey these instructions but stay at work.

In reply to this, it was pointed out that there were two separate problems: the workers in factories, who were equivalent to troops in the front line, and the rest of the people in the country. It was argued that there was no inconsistency in giving the 'red' warning, which applied to the people of the country generally, and an instruction to the workers that their duty to continue production over-rode the duty to take cover unless danger was imminent.

A number of Members of the War Cabinet thought that the abolition of the 'red' warning could only come about gradually. To abolish it immediately might have bad effects on production. There should, however, be a general encouragement to munition workers to keep at work until the last possible moment, and to come back to it as soon as the danger was over and make up for lost time. The public must be educated to understand that the more we were attacked, the more important it was to increase production.

Another point dealt with in discussion was the importance of sleep for workers whether on day or night shifts.

The Prime Minister thought that everyone should be urged to sleep by day or by night in some place where he could stay put during air raid warnings.

General agreement was expressed with this view, although the Lord Privy Seal[1] pointed out that in certain poorer districts of London it was difficult to give effect to this principle.

---

[1] Clement Attlee.

Winston S. Churchill to A. V. Alexander
(*Admiralty papers, 199/1931*)

4 September 1940

No action is possible except to make sure the faults do not recur next time.[1]
The writer is granted protection by me, & must not be proceeded in any way.

WSC

War Cabinet: minutes
(*Cabinet papers, 65/9*)

5 September 1940

The Prime Minister read to the War Cabinet the main passages of the statement he was proposing to make in Parliament that afternoon.

The Prime Minister said that he proposed to deal with the question of air raid warnings very generally in order to prepare the way for changes, but not to indicate their nature. The changes would be discussed forthwith with the representatives of the organisations concerned, and an announcement made in the ensuing week.

The Minister of Labour had been informed of the discussion in the War Cabinet the previous night, and had expressed very strongly the view that time should be given to allow of further discussions with interested bodies before decisions were taken or announced on the new plans to be adopted.

Subject to amendments on one or two points, the War Cabinet approved the lines of the statement proposed.

The Prime Minister said that, at the meeting of the War Cabinet the previous evening, it had been contemplated that a further announcement should be made that Parliament would not adjourn when the 'red' warning was sounded. On reflection he thought that to make such an announcement would be asking for trouble. He suggested that arrangements should be made whereby if a 'red' warning sounded while the House was sitting he (or in his absence the Lord Privy Seal) would propose that the House should continue to sit, if that was the general sense of the House, until a further warning was received that an attack was imminent.

---

[1] Churchill had sent A. V. Alexander a letter from a naval lieutenant, R. T. Paget, criticising in detail some of the naval arrangements being made for the Dakar expedition. Paget, then aged thirty-two, was an Old Etonian and a barrister. He was later Labour Member of Parliament for Northampton, 1945–74, a QC (1947) and a Life Peer (1974).

This further warning would be received either by a message from the Fighter Command which would be passed to the Prime Minister's Private Secretary or from watchers specially posted by the authorities of the Houses.

This arrangement met with general approval.

The Prime Minister read out the draft passage in his speech dealing with compensation for damage resulting from air raids which had been settled in consultation with the Chancellor of the Exchequer. He intended to bring out the point that of some 12 million houses in this country only some 8,000 had been hit, of which very few had been totally destroyed. This was a far smaller percentage than that estimated before the war. The Treasury were prepared to review the decisions as to compensation for air raid damage which had been taken at the beginning of the war, more particularly in so far as those decisions affected small householders, providing that investigation showed that this class of case could be dealt with in isolation from other war losses.

The War Cabinet took note with approval of this suggestion.

The Prime Minister indicated briefly the line he proposed to take on a number of other topics. He proposed to announce the work being carried out by the Committee on Lighting Restrictions. He did not, however, propose to make any reference on this occasion to the question of aliens.

Winston S. Churchill: speech
(*Hansard*)

5 September 1940   House of Commons

WAR SITUATION

The Prime Minister (Mr Churchill): The memorable transactions between Great Britain and the United States, which I foreshadowed when I last addressed the House, have now been completed. As far as I can make out, they have been completed to the general satisfaction of the British and American peoples and to the encouragement of our friends all over the world. It would be a mistake to try to read into the official notes which have passed more than the documents bear on their face. The exchanges which have taken place are simply measures of mutual assistance rendered to one another by two friendly nations, in a spirit of confidence, sympathy and good will. These measures are linked together in a formal agreement. They must be accepted exactly as they stand. Only very ignorant persons would suggest that the transfer of American destroyers to the British flag constitutes the slightest violation of international law or affects in the smallest degree the non-belligerency of the United States.

I have no doubt that Herr Hitler will not like this transference of destroyers, and I have no doubt that he will pay the United States out, if ever he gets the chance. That is why I am very glad that the army, air and naval frontiers of the United States have been advanced along a wide arc into the Atlantic Ocean, and that this will enable them to take danger by the throat while it is still hundreds of miles away from their homeland. The Admiralty tell us also that they are very glad to have these 50 destroyers, and that they will come in most conveniently to bridge the gap which, I have previously explained to the House, inevitably intervenes before our considerable war-time programme of new construction comes into service.

I suppose the House realises that we shall be a good deal stronger next year on the sea than we are now, although that is quite strong enough for the immediate work in hand. There will be no delay in bringing the American destroyers into active service; in fact, British crews are already meeting them at the various ports where they are being delivered. You might call it the long arm of coincidence. I really do not think that there is any more to be said about the whole business at the present time. This is not the appropriate occasion for rhetoric. Perhaps I may, however, very respectfully, offer this counsel to the House: When you have got a thing where you want it, it is a good thing to leave it where it is.

The House has no doubt observed – to change the subject – that Rumania has undergone severe territorial mutilation. Personally, I have always thought that the Southern part of Dobrudja ought to be restored to Bulgaria,[1] and I have never been happy about the way in which Hungary was treated after the last war. We have not at any time adopted, since this war broke out, the line that nothing could be changed in the territorial structure of various countries. On the other hand, we do not propose to recognise any territorial changes which take place during the war, unless they take place with the free consent and good will of the parties concerned. No one can say how far Herr Hitler's empire will extend before this war is over, but I have no doubt that it will pass away as swiftly as, and perhaps more swiftly than, did Napoleon's Empire,[2] although, of course, without any of its glitter or its glory.

The general air battle, of which I spoke the last time we met together, continues. In July, there was a good deal of air activity, but August has been a real fighting month. Neither side has put out its full strength, but the Germans have made a very substantial and important effort to gain the mastery, and they have certainly put forth a larger proportion of their total air

---

[1] This was the Quadrilateral, the region of Southern Dobrudja (between the Danube and the Black Sea), which had been taken by Roumania from Bulgaria after the First World War. The northern limit of the Quadrilateral was a wall built by the Roman Emperor Trajan. The main port is Constanta (Kustendil).

[2] Napoleon's empire lasted for just over thirteen years, Hitler's Third Reich for just over twelve.

strength than we have found it necessary, up to the present, to employ against them. Their attempt to dominate the Royal Air Force and our anti-aircraft defences, by daylight attacks, has proved very costly for them. The broad figures of three to one in machines and six to one in pilots and crews, of which we are sure, do not by any means represent the total injuries inflicted upon the enemy. We must be prepared for heavier fighting in this month of September. The need of the enemy to obtain a decision is very great, and if he has the numbers with which we have hitherto credited him, he should be able to magnify and multiply the attacks during September.

Firm confidence is felt by all the responsible officers of the Royal Air Force in our ability to withstand this largely increased scale of attack, and we have no doubt that the whole nation, taking its example from our airmen, have been proud to share their dangers and will stand up to the position grim and gay.

Now is the chance of the men and women in the factories to show their mettle, and for all of us to try to be worthy of our boys in the air and not make their task longer or harder by the slightest flinching. That, I know, is the temper of the nation, and even if the average attack is doubled or trebled – which last is most unlikely – and however long it continues, we believe that we can stand it and that we shall emerge from it actually and relatively stronger in the air than we were before.

Our Air Force to-day is more numerous and better equipped than it was at the outbreak of the war, or even in July, and, to the best of our belief, we are far nearer to the total of the German numerical strength, as we estimate it, than we expected to be at this period in the war. I asked that the German claims of British aircraft destroyed during July and August should be added up. I was curious to see the total to which they would amount. I found them to make the surprising total of 1,921 British aircraft destroyed. That total is rather like the figures we heard about of losses among our Fleet, many ships of which have been sunk several times over. The actual figure of British losses, which we have published daily for these last two months, is 558. Our loss in pilots is, of course, happily very much less. I do not know whether Herr Hitler believes the truth of his own published figures. I hope he does. One is always content to see an enemy plunged in error and self-deception. How very differently this air attack which is now raging has turned out from what we imagined it would be before the war. More than 150,000 beds have stood open and, thank God, empty in our war hospitals for a whole year. When the British people make up their minds to go to war they expect to receive terrible injuries. That is why we tried to remain at peace as long as possible. So far as the air attack is concerned, up to the present we have found it far less severe than what we prepared ourselves to endure and what we are still ready, if necessary, to endure. One thousand and seventy-five civilians were killed during August in

Britain, and a slightly greater number seriously injured. Our sympathy goes out to the wounded and to those who are bereaved, but no one can pretend that out of 45,000,000 people these are losses which, even if multiplied as they may be two or three times, would be serious compared to the majestic world issues which are at stake. Apart from minor or readily reparable injuries, about 800 houses have been destroyed or damaged beyond repair. I am not talking of what can be put right very quickly or what is worth while to put right, but 800 houses were actually damaged beyond repair out of a total in this island of 13,000,000 houses.

This, of course, is very different from the estimate of damage which was given to the War Committee which considered and decided against the possibility of an insurance scheme against air-raid damage to property. It would, in my judgement, be worth while for a further examination of such a scheme, particularly as it would affect the small man, and to make this examination in the light of facts which we now know and also of future possibilities about which we are in a far better position to form an opinion that we were before the war began. I have therefore asked my right hon. Friend the Chancellor of the Exchequer to consider the best way of making such a review in the light of the facts as they are to-day. It is very painful to me to see, as I have seen in my journeys about the country, a small British house or business smashed by the enemy's fire, and to see that without feeling assured that we are doing our best to spread the burden so that we all stand in together. Damage by enemy action stands on a different footing from any other kind of loss or damage, because the nation undertakes the task of defending the lives and property of its subjects and taxpayers against assaults from outside. Unless public opinion and the judgment of the House were prepared to separate damage resulting from the fire of the enemy from all those other forms of war loss, and unless the House was prepared to draw the distinction very sharply between war damage by bomb and shell and the other forms of loss which are incurred, we could not attempt to deal with this matter; otherwise we should be opening up a field to which there would be no bounds. If, however, we were able to embark upon such a project as would give complete insurance, at any rate up to a certain minimum figure, for every one against war damage by shell or bomb, I think it would be a very solid mark of the confidence which after some experience we are justified in feeling about the way in which we are going to come through this war.

In the meanwhile, my right hon. Friend the Chancellor of the Exchequer, who has to give so many halfpence and take so many kicks, and upon whose wisdom and practical good sense those who have been his colleagues have learned to rely – and I can assure the House that it is no mere flattery in order to get the money out of him – has agreed to the following arrangements, in addition to the satisfactory provisions which have already been made in respect of the personal injuries and immediate needs of those smitten. At present in cases where the income of the claimant's household does not exceed £400 a year[1] and his resources are limited, payments are made to cover damage to essential household furniture up to a maximum of £50, and similar payments are made in respect of personal clothing up to £30, subject to income limits of £400 where there are dependants and £250 where there are no dependants. It is now proposed to abolish these upper limits of £50 and £30 respectively, so that payments for damage to the furniture or clothing of persons of limited means will now be made up to 100 per cent of the damage, whatever that amount may be. Hitherto there has been no provision to enable workmen to replace tools which are their personal property and the use of which is vital to their employment. It is proposed to remedy this hardship by making provision for payments for these purposes, subject to the same income limits which apply in the case of the clothing advances. Similar payments will be made to professional people within the same limits of income. Finally, there is the case of the small retailer who is not insured under the Board of Trade Commodities Insurance Scheme. Here payments up to £50 will be made within the same income limits as for clothing and tools, in order to enable those retailers to replace stocks essential to the continuance of trade. I may say that in all these three cases appropriate mitigating measures will be taken in the borderline cases lying just above the income limits.

Then there is the case of the coast towns which have been declared to be evacuation areas for the purpose of the Defence (Evacuated Areas) Regulations. Upon this a number of Members, as was their duty, have made representations to the Government. The Ministry of Health will be prepared, upon an application from the authorities of these areas, to make advances out of Exchequer funds to enable the authorities to meet liabilities for which collectable rate revenue will not suffice. These advances will be free of interest. The term 'advances' in this case is understood to mean that the Government retain the right to call for repayment, but the question how far this right will be exercised will be considered after the war in the light of the financial circumstances then prevailing, both in the areas interested and in the country generally. These advances must be conditional upon the examination of the estimates of expenditure and of revenue, and for this purpose my right hon. Friend the Minister of Health[2] will arrange for officers of the Ministry of Health to visit the towns concerned and to confer with the

---

[1] The 1994 equivalent of £400 in 1940 was almost £10,0000.
[2] The Minister of Health since May was Malcolm MacDonald, son of the former Labour Prime Minister, Ramsay MacDonald.

mayors and principal officials – very plucky fellows, some of them; one is proud to meet them. Such conferences will afford an opportunity for advising and assisting the local authorities upon the best means of securing reasonable economy consistent with the maintenance of essential services, and they will also advise them about the collection of revenue. These local authorities will not in the present circumstances be required to increase their existing rate of poundage as a condition of financial assistance. It is recognised that the shortage of rate income will involve a deficit in the sums collected by rates levied for meeting county council precepts. It is understood that some of the local authorities are, in fact, proposing to limit their payments in respect of county precepts to that proportion of the total rate which represents the county rate which they have been able to collect. The Government propose to recognise and validate these arrangements, and if in any case an unreasonable burden was thereby thrown upon the country's resources, the Government would not refuse to consider the possibility of extending to the county council some measure of assistance.

I think the House will see that we have been endeavouring to meet the cases both of individuals and of local authorities as they are affected by the conditions into which we have moved. We must expect for some time to come to have to live our lives and to carry on our work under these strange conditions, but they are conditions to which the fortitude and adaptiveness of the British people will not, we feel, be found unequal. If, as was suggested in a recent oration, there is to be a contest of nerve, will-power and endurance in which the whole British and German peoples are to engage, be it sharp or be it long, we shall not shrink from it. We believe that the spirit and temperament bred under institutions of freedom will prove more enduring and resilient than anything that can be got out of the most efficiently enforced mechanical discipline.

In the light of what we have learned so far with regard to the arrangements for air-raid warnings – here I come to the point on which I have been asked by the hon. and gallant Gentleman opposite me – we have come to the conclusion that the arrangements for air-raid warnings and what is to be done when they are given, which appears to be another question, require very considerable changes. There is really no good sense in having these prolonged banshee howlings from sirens two or three times a day over wide areas, simply because hostile aircraft are flying to or from some target which no one can possibly know or even guess. All our precaution regulations have hitherto been based on this siren call, and I must say that one must admire the ingenuity of those who devised it as a means of spreading alarm. Indeed, most people now see how very wise Ulysses was when he stopped the ears of his sailors from all siren songs and had himself tied up firmly to the mast of duty.

Now that we are settling down to the job, we must have different arrangements from those devised before the war. It is right that everyone should know now that the red warning is more in the nature of a general alert than a warning of the imminence of danger to any particular locality. In many cases it is physically impossible to give the alarm before the attack. Constant alarms come to be something in the nature of no alarm. Yet while they give no protection to very great numbers of people, who take no notice of them, they undoubtedly exercise a disturbing effect upon necessary war work. All our regulations, and much preaching, have taught people that they should take a whole series of steps, mostly of a downward character, when they hear the siren sound, and it is no use having official regulations which point one way and enjoin immediate respect for the alarm when exhortations are given, unofficially or officially, to disregard them and go on working. In our own case to-day, it was felt that the red warning should be taken merely as an alert, but that if special circumstances indicated the proximity of danger then the conditions of alarm should supervene. That is exactly what we did on receiving information that there was danger of a particular kind in the vicinity; and when that special condition departed we immediately resumed our work under the conditions of alert until the 'All Clear,' which has now sounded, restored us to normal. Something like this unrehearsed experiment may well give us guidance in our future treatment of the problem. All our regulations require to be shaped to the new basis which is being established by actual contact with events.

The responsibility to give clear guidance to the public in time of war is imposed upon His Majesty's Government. In order to preserve the confidence shown them by the House and by the public, the Government must act with conviction. I have, therefore, asked the various Departments concerned to review the whole position as a matter of urgency. In these matters one must expect to proceed by trial and error, and one must also try to carry public opinion along. What we want, on the one hand, is the greatest measure of real warning that is compatible with what all our people are resolved upon, namely, the active maintenance of war production. I will not make any specific announcement to-day, because we are in negotiation with very important bodies concerned, employers and employed, throughout the country. We want to move in these matters with sureness, precision and clarity, and no uncertainty or doubt, and I would like to have the opportunity of a little further consultation with the different bodies that are now in touch with the Government. This is a matter, of course, which affects scores of millions of people. Therefore, I will not attempt to make any specific announcement to-day, but such an announcement must be made within the next week, at the latest. I think I have given the House a pretty clear indication of what is in our thoughts, and of the direction in which we are thinking of moving at the present time.

There is another point which I should like to mention, and that is this business of lighting the streets, the centres of the cities of our country. [An Hon. Member: 'Motor cars.'] Well, it is a difficult question. When my hon. Friend says, 'Motor cars,' he does not simplify it, but raises a point which has to be borne in mind. Winter is coming along, and I hope we are not going through all that gloomy business that we went through last year. I have, therefore, asked a committee of persons, deeply versed in this matter, responsible people in the Departments, to meet together, and to see in what way we can make more light and cheer in the winter months, and at the same time subserve the purposes of alert and alarm. Such a course is not at all impossible, and I hope to come forward with some proposals, necessarily of a highly detailed character.

I do not mean to trespass at any length upon the time of the House this afternoon, because our affairs are evidently very largely in the region of action. No one must suppose that the danger of invasion has passed. My right hon. Friend the Secretary of State for War – to whom I would have gladly paid some compliments if he had not already forestalled me, in a very charming manner, and probably robbed any compliments of some of their intrinsic value – is absolutely right in enjoining the strictest vigilance upon the great and growing armies which are now entrusted in this country to the command of Sir Alan Brooke. I do not agree with those who assume that after the 15th September – or whatever is Herr Hitler's latest date – we shall be free from the menace of deadly attack from overseas; because winter, with its storms, its fogs, its darkness, may alter the conditions, but some of the changes cut both ways. There must not be for one moment any relaxation of effort or of wise precaution, both of which are needed to save our lives and to save our cause. I shall not, however, be giving away any military secrets if I say that we are very much better off than we were a few months ago, and that if the problem of invading Great Britain was a difficult one in June, it has become a far more difficult and a far larger problem in September.

Indeed, while all this preparation for home defence has been going forward on a gigantic scale, we have not hesitated to send a continuous stream of convoys with reinforcements to the Middle East. In particular, a few days ago we found it possible almost to double the effective strength of our Fleet in the Eastern Mediterranean by sending some of our most powerful modern vessels to reinforce the flag of Sir Andrew Cunningham, the admiral in the Eastern Mediterranean. This movement, while plainly visible to the Italians, was not molested by them. Some of our great ships touched at Malta on the way, and carried a few things that were needed by those valiant islanders and their garrison, who, under a remarkably resolute Governor, General Dobbie, are maintaining themselves with the utmost constancy. We must expect heavy fighting in the Middle East before very long. We have every intention of maintaining our positions there with our utmost strength, and of increasing our sea power, and the control which follows from sea power, throughout the Mediterranean, not only in the Eastern basin but in the Western basin. In this way, both at home and abroad, we shall persevere along our course, however the winds may blow.

Henry Channon: diary
('Chips')

5 September 1940

In the House, Winston, whom I had met in the passage with Clemmie and two of his daughters, spoke at some length, but he was not at his best, and invoked little enthusiasm; the House has become accustomed to his high-flown rhetoric and thinks that he jokes too much: it is true that he is rarely serious about even sacred things, such as loss of life, and he betrays too easily how he is enjoying power.

Winston S. Churchill to Lord Halifax
(Churchill papers, 20/13)

5 September 1940
ACTION THIS DAY

I have made a very close study of all the details connected with the Dardanelles bombardment referred to on page 3 of the enclosure of 3.9.40,[1] and I think the account given there is very far from being a correct appreciation. Indeed, it shows a great deal of the prejudice which was so largely responsible for the lamentable passivity to which the Navy was reduced. I trust the same prejudice has not animated the earlier pages. Very fine arguments are always given for doing nothing. The Admiralty will not have helped us very much if they allow these powerful batteries to come into existence at Gris Nez without any effort even being made to prevent their being erected.

WSC

[1] Vice-Admiral Dewar's memorandum 'Bombardment of Belgian Coast, 1914–18', in which Dewar wrote: 'Experience in the Dardanelles also proves the difficulty of ships attacking heavy modern batteries. The Allies brought a very powerful concentration of fire against relatively few Turkish guns on 18 March 1915. Some were temporarily silenced but none were put permanently out of action' (*Admiralty papers, 205/6*). Churchill's argument at the time was that the Admiral should make a second attempt to clear the minefields and push through the Dardanelles before the Turkish forts could be brought back into action. He also knew that the ammunition of the forts was almost exhausted (a fact which Stalin confirmed when they met in Moscow in 1942!).

Winston S. Churchill to Lord Halifax
(*Foreign Office papers, 371/24260*)

5 September 1940

Would it not be well to send a telegram to Lord Lothian expressing War Cabinet approval of the manner in which he handled the whole destroyer question, and paying him a compliment?

At the same time, what is being done about getting our 20 motor torpedo-boats, the 5 PBY,[1] the 150–200 aircraft, and the 250,000 rifles, also anything else that is going? I consider we were promised all the above, and more too. Not an hour should be lost in raising these questions. 'Beg while the iron is hot.'

Winston S. Churchill to A. V. Alexander and Admiral Pound
(*Churchill papers, 20/13*)

5 September 1940

I continue to be extremely anxious for KGV^2 to get away to the North. It would be disastrous if *Bismarck* were finished, and something happened to *KGV*. Surely the electricians, &c., can go North in her and finish up at Scapa. It would be most painful if you lost this ship now, after all these long, vexatious delays, just at the moment when she is finished and most needed. The Tyne is very ill-defended compared to Scapa.

Winston S. Churchill to A. V. Alexander
(*Churchill papers, 20/2*)

5 September 1940

My dear First Lord,

I understand that in the last four months of 1940 it is planned to lay down 107 thousand gross tons of tankers and only 177 thousand gross tons of other cargo vessels. In the last few months, as you are aware, there has been a large margin of tanker capacity, whereas every accession to our general cargo

---

[1] Catalina flying boats, which had first entered service with patrol-bomber squadrons of the United States Navy in 1936, under the designation PBY-1. In July 1939 the Air Ministry ordered one example, which was flown across the Atlantic to Britain. Thirty were then ordered, the first deliveries being in early 1941; they served in the Battle of the Atlantic and in the Indian Ocean. It was a Catalina that first spotted the *Bismarck* in May 1941. Later in the war, for courageous attacks on submarines, two Catalina pilots were awarded the Victoria Cross. The 196th and final U-boat sunk by Coastal Command was destroyed by a Catalina on 7 May 1945 at Sullom Voe.

[2] The battleship *King George V*, laid down in January 1937, and finally commissioned in October 1940. In the action in which the *Bismarck* was sunk, on 27 May 1941, she fired 339 rounds of her 14-inch shells.

vessels is welcome. Furthermore, I understand that the tanker takes longer to construct, so that the relief to the merchant fleet as a whole will come later in 1941 than it would if more capacity were devoted to non-tankers. No doubt this programme was approved before the great change in the tanker situation. Has it been reviewed in the light of recent events?

I am sending a copy of this letter to the Minister of Shipping.

Yours very sincerely,
Winston S. Churchill

General Freyberg: recollection
(*'Bernard Freyberg, VC'*, *page 230*)

5 September 1940

Mytchett Camp
near Aldershot

The Prime Minister also promised me that he would come and see them, and did so on the 5th of September in spite of the many calls on his time. His method was totally different from the C-in-C's. 'I don't want to see any training', he said, 'I just want to walk along the lines of men and look them in the eye.' It was arranged therefore that they should be drawn up in lines, and he went along line after line of men always looking them in the face, and he stopped at every few men and ran his fingers over the point of their bayonets. This was a source of great amusement to everybody.

One of the men in the rear rank 'lost his name for talking during inspection' and was duly crimed. 'What remark did he make?' said the Prime Minister, intensely interested in all the proceedings none of which were lost on him. He was told that he had made a highly improper remark, which was, 'He's a pugnacious looking b.....' This pleased the Prime Minister enormously and he chuckled away as he added, 'I hope that justice will be tempered with mercy in this case.'

Winston S. Churchill: speech
(*Freyberg papers*)

5 September 1940

Mytchett Camp
near Aldershot

We in these islands are now bearing the accumulated weight of the malice and tyranny of the enemy. We do not feel overweighted by it. When you first came here four months ago, a comparatively small army might have wrought much havoc before they were finished off.

But now we have very powerful armies, and if some people think that bad man is inclined to try his venture we feel sure that we shall give a good account of ourselves again.

We do not feel lonely when the sons from the Dominions overseas, where they breed the finest fighting races, come here or go to other parts of the British Empire to bear their part in this great contention.

Of all the wars we have ever fought, none has been more noble or righteous than this, and from none shall we emerge with a greater sense of duty done.

War Cabinet: minutes
(*Cabinet papers, 65/9*)

6 September 1940   10 Downing Street
11.30 a.m.

The Prime Minister pointed out that in several respects the army programme was not making satisfactory progress. The Minister of Supply clearly thought that satisfactory progress could not be made under the present arrangements. He (the Prime Minister) assumed, however, that the present system was only responsible for difficulties in so far as there were clashes between the needs of Departments. The new procedure proposed would not fundamentally alter the position of factories working wholly for the Ministry of Supply or the Admiralty.

The Prime Minister also referred to the very large demands made for production of army vehicles.

The Prime Minister said that he assumed that the Minister of Aircraft Production could not claim that the existing priority afforded to aircraft was meant to be an unlimited and indefinite priority. He thought it was important to define the programmes to which priorities should extend.

The Minister of Aircraft Production said that, provided the existing system could remain unchanged, he would submit particulars of his Department's requirements of steel of all types for the ensuing three months.

The Prime Minister thought that, while the discussion had been helpful towards elucidating the problem, a final decision could not be reached that morning. He would like rather longer to consider the matter. He therefore proposed that the Minister of Aircraft Production's suggestion that he should submit the particulars of his requirements of steel under various heads within the next three months should be accepted, and that discussion as to the procedure of priority should be adjourned for a fortnight.

The War Cabinet approved this suggestion.

War Cabinet: Confidential Annex
(*Cabinet papers, 65/15*)

6 September 1940
11.30 a.m.
10 Downing Street

Our dollar position would be considerably relieved if we could obtain possession of the French gold now held by the Bank of Canada. The Prime Minister said that the only answer which he had received to his telegram to Mr Mackenzie King had been that the matter had been referred to a Committee. He proposed in a few days' time to telegraph again to Mr Mackenzie King pressing for an early decision.

Winston S. Churchill to Sir Walter Citrine[1]
(*Churchill papers, 20/4*)

6 September 1940

I have been carefully considering your letter of August 31, and I am greatly obliged to you for inviting me to express an opinion upon your plans and movements.

There is no doubt that your standing as a national figure of the Labour movement here at home and your international reputation would make you the best representative of Labour who could visit the United States. On the other hand, there seem to me to be serious considerations which tell against you or anyone of the highest consequence going to the States in the last flurry of the Presidential Election. Our affairs are at once so hopeful and delicate in that vast community that I am personally of opinion that the less we intervene until the Election is over, the better. You will see how I kept all my references to the destroyers and bases *piano* yesterday. At the Presidential Election there are not only the perennial struggles between Capital and Labour, but now the all-absorbing issue of the war, and whether they should take a hand in it. This is a business for Englishmen to keep out of. The two Parties are striving for office and care little what they say or do to get it. They will turn with the greatest gusto on any foreigner out of whose presence, however unfairly, Election capital can be made.

Two months from to-day the whole situation will be changed, and if you

---

[1] Walter McLennan Citrine, 1887–1981. Secretary of the Electrical Trades Union, 1914–20; Assistant General Secretary, 1920–3. Assistant Secretary, Trades Union Congress, 1924–5; General Secretary, 1926–46. Director of the *Daily Herald*, 1929–46. Knighted, 1935. Visited Russia, 1936 and 1938. Privy Councillor, 1940. Member of the National Production Advisory Council, 1942–6 and 1949–57. Created Baron, 1946. Member of the National Coal Board, 1946–7. Chairman of the Central Electricity Authority, 1947–57. GBE, 1958.

can then be spared from this country, which always remains a serious question, a visit by you would do nothing but good, and HMG could aid it and weight it in every convenient way.¹

Yours very sincerely,
Winston S. Churchill

Winston S. Churchill to Sir Richard Peirse
(*Cabinet papers, 120/300*)

6 September 1940
ACTION THIS DAY

I never suggested any departure from our main policy,² but I believe that moral advantage would be gained in Germany at the present time if on two or three nights in a month a number of minor, unexpected, widespread attacks were made upon the smaller German centres. You must remember that these people are never told the truth, and that wherever the Air Force has not been, they are probably told that the German defences are impregnable. Many factors have to be taken into consideration, and some of them are those which are not entirely technical. I hope, therefore, you will consider my wish, and make me proposals for giving effect to it as opportunity serves.

WSC

General Brooke: diary
(*'The Turn of the Tide'*)

6 September 1940   Chequers

Party consisted of Dill, Ismay, PM and self. PM warmed up and was most entertaining for rest of evening. First of all he placed himself in the position of Hitler and attacked these shores while I defended them. He then revised the whole of the air-raid warning system and gave us his proposals to criticise. Finally at 1.45 a.m. we got off to bed.

---

¹ Two months later Citrine did go to the United States. Churchill wrote a letter of introduction for him to President Roosevelt (see 1 November 1940).
² Churchill had suggested to Bomber Command that they spread the bombing offensive as widely as possible over Germany.

Winston S. Churchill to A. V. Alexander
(*Churchill papers, 20/13*)

7 September 1940
Secret and Personal

1. The course of operation 'Hats' makes me quite sure that the First Sea Lord was wrong to recede from his original idea of passing the armoured vehicles through the Mediterranean. If you will read my Minute reciting all the reasons why this course should be adopted, you will see that they are reinforced by new facts now. Admiral Cunningham's ships moved about with perfect freedom for four days and were not seriously molested from the Air. They bombarded Rhodes and easily repulsed a sortie of E-boats. The storeship which was going to Malta from Alexandria, although damaged by a bomb affecting its steering, got in safely after two days in the most dangerous area. Admiral Somerville's force was not harmed or molested in any way. The *Valiant*, two cruisers, and several destroyers had no difficulty in landing stores or refuelling at Malta. The Italian fleet, although well aware of our movements, did not presume to interfere, but made for harbour at full speed. I have been told that the *Illustrious* cut a mine with her paravanes. This is what paravanes are for. Nevertheless, the incident shows that even a policy of 'safety first' pushed to extremes, does not exclude mortal risk to capital ships of the highest value. There is no doubt in my mind that it would have been quite easy to have transported the armoured brigade through the Malta channel, and that it would now have been in Egypt, instead of more than three weeks away. It may be that no serious disaster will occur in Egypt during those three weeks. That will in no way alter the fact that we might have been helped more effectively by the Admiralty without running appreciably more risks than were, in fact, incurred.

2. I am not impressed by the fact that Admiral Cunningham reiterates his views. Naturally they all stand together like doctors in a case which has gone wrong. The fact remains that an exaggerated fear of Italian aircraft has been allowed to hamper operations.

3. I do not feel that there is any good reason to extend Admiral Forbes' Command beyond October, when it normally expires. An effort will have to be made to bring younger Admirals to the front. Admiral Forbes has done extremely well, but the strain has been severe and prolonged, and it is time that a change should be made. After a year of war it is high time that the Service should be refreshed. Admiral Horton[1] is well spoken of by what are

---

[1] Max Kennedy Horton, 1883–1951. Entered the Royal Navy, 1900. Awarded the silver medal for saving life at sea. On active naval service, as a submarine commander, 1914–18, sinking two German cruisers and three destroyers (DSO and two bars). Vice-Admiral, commanding the First Cruiser Squadron, 1935–6; the Reserve Fleet, 1936–9; the Northern Patrol (flagship *Pyramus*), September 1939. Knighted, 1939. Vice-Admiral Submarines, from December 1939. Commander-in-Chief, Western Approaches, 1942–5.

called 'the new school of Naval Officers.' Admiral Phillips ought to have a chance in a great Command at sea.[1] Admiral Harwood[2] has proved his merit in action. I have never met Admiral Tovey, but I hear from many quarters the highest accounts of him. I should be glad to discuss all these points with you, and with you alone. Very likely you have the names of other younger men besides those I have mentioned.

WSC

Winston S. Churchill to Sir John Anderson
(*Churchill papers, 20/13*)

7 September 1940

Please propose me a hundred names for Civil Honours for bravery and good conduct up to the end of August 1940 during the Air raids. Another hundred names will be required during September unless the fighting slacks off. Show me how you propose to have these names collected and sifted. It is clear from your letter that practically nothing is being done on a scale appropriate to the conditions now prevailing. MAP and M of S,[3] as well as the Regional Commissioners, will be able to make you recommendations. The awards up to the end of August should be conferred and made public before the end of September, and thereafter monthly.

WSC

Winston S. Churchill to H. Ramsbotham[4]
(*Churchill papers, 20/13*)

7 September 1940

I have now examined in detail your memorandum on the Service of Youth and I approve your proposals. I am glad to see you are avoiding anything spectacular which might savour of the Hitler Youth Movement.

WSC

[1] In 1941, Phillips went to sea as Commander-in-Chief of the Eastern Fleet. He was drowned when his flagship, the *Prince of Wales*, was sunk by Japanese torpedo bombers on 10 December 1941, three days after Pearl Harbor.
[2] Henry Harwood, 1888–1950. Midshipman, 1904. Commodore Commanding South America Division, HMS *Exeter*, 1936–9. Knighted, 1939, and promoted Rear-Admiral (after the destruction of the *Graf Spee*). Rear-Admiral Commanding South America Division, 1940. Assistant Chief of the Naval Staff, 1940–2. Commander-in-Chief, Levant, 1943. Vice-Admiral Commanding Orkney and Shetland, 1944–5. Admiral, 1945.
[3] The Minister of Aircraft Production (Beaverbrook) and the Minister of Supply (Herbert Morrison).
[4] Herwald Ramsbotham, 1887–1971. Called to the Bar, 1911. On active service, 1914–18 (Military Cross). Conservative MP, 1929–41. Minister of Pensions, 1936–9. First Commissioner of Works, 1939–40. President of the Board of Education, 1940–1. Created Baron Soulbury, 1941. Chairman of the Assistance Board, 1941–8. Governor-General of Ceylon, 1949–54. Created Viscount, 1954.

Winston S. Churchill to Sir Richard Peirse
(*Churchill papers, 20/13*)

7 September 1940

Reports on recent attacks upon RAF Stations have contained reference to damage to hangars.

Such damage ought surely to be repaired with the least possible delay; but I am informed that damaged hangars have, in fact, been left unrepaired, for example, at North Weald, Tangmere, Croydon and Biggin Hill.

Pray let me have a report on this matter.

Winston S. Churchill to A. V. Alexander
(*Churchill papers, 20/13*)

7 September 1940
Secret

I should be glad if you would let me have a short résumé of the different occasions when I pressed, as First Lord, for the preparation of the 'Ramillies' Class ships to withstand Air bombardment by thick deck armour and larger bulges. If those ships had been put in hand when I repeatedly pressed for them to be, we should now have the means of attacking the Italian shores, which might be productive of the highest political and military results. Even now, there is a disposition to delay taking this most necessary step, and no substitute is offered.

I have not yet heard from you in reply to the Minute I sent you renewing this project of reconstruction in the hope that we may not be equally destitute of bombarding vessels next year. I shall be glad to have a talk with you on this subject when I have refreshed my mind with the papers.

I attach a note which Lord Halifax has handed me from Sir Percy Loraine, showing the importance of striking at Italy.

WSC

Winston S. Churchill to Admiral Pound and Admiral Phillips
(*Churchill papers, 19/1*)

7 September 1940

This correspondence[1] is of interest because it shows very clearly some of the issues involved in modern naval architecture. All the constructive genius and commanding reputation of the Royal Navy has been besmirched and crippled by Treaty restrictions for twenty years. A warship should be the

[1] Between Churchill and Admiral Henderson (not printed).

embodiment of a tactical conception. All our cruisers are the results of trying to conform to Treaty limitations and 'gentlemen's agreements.' The masterly letter of Admiral Henderson[1] throws a clear light on our policy and present position. As you will see, I was not convinced. Pray do not allow the reading of this to be a burden to you in your heavy work, but let me have it back when it has passed round.

WSC

On 8 September 1940, Churchill inspected the bomb damage in London's East End, following an air raid in which 300 Londoners had been killed and 1,337 seriously injured.

Samuel Battersby: recollection
(*Letter to the author, 6 April 1977*)

8 September 1940

At the time of the first big attack when the burning inferno of the London docks so illuminated the sky that 'at midnight one could read a newspaper in the city,' I was Government Censor in charge at the Commercial Cable Company in Wormwood St, and thinking – wrongly as I realised later – that to have a first-hand sight of the damage would help me in censoring the flood of cables that would be sent overseas, I joined an official party touring the devastated area.

The familiar figure of Churchill was there dabbing at his eyes from time to time with a large white handkerchief clutched in one hand. It was a harrowing sight, with the ARP and other officials digging out from the ruins injured people and bodies. From one forlorn little group alongside the remains of their homes an old woman shouted 'When are we going to bomb Berlin, Winnie?' Instinctively – without time for thought – Winston swung round, waving his fist clutching his handkerchief and, I think, an ebony, silver topped stick, and growled with menacing emphasis 'You leave that to me'! Morale rose immediately; everyone was satisfied and reassured. 'By God we're going to

---

[1] Reginald Guy Hannam Henderson, 1881–1939. Entered the Royal Navy, 1896. Naval Mission to Greece, 1913. On active service, 1914–19 (despatches). Commanded the aircraft carrier HMS *Furious*, 1926–8. Rear-Admiral Commanding Aircraft Carriers, 1931–3. Vice-Admiral, 1933. Third Sea Lord and Controller of the Navy, 1934–9. Knighted, 1936. Admiral, 1939. Churchill wrote in an unpublished draft of his second war memoirs: 'I also had a long and old friendship with Admiral Henderson, the Controller. He was one of our finest gunnery experts in 1912, and as I always used to go out and see the initial firings of battleships before their gun-mountings were accepted from the contractors, I was able to form a very high opinion of his work.'

knock hell out of them for this' was doubtless the general feeling. It was certainly mine.

Afterwards I pondered the incident and have done so countless times since. What could a Prime Minister at that time and in such desperate conditions say that was not pathetically inadequate – or even downright dangerous? 'When are we going to bomb Berlin?' 'As soon as we are able to' . . . 'In a year or two when we have built up a striking force' . . . 'Not just yet – you must be patient' . . . Almost anything – except what he did say – would have been wrong.

The incident typifies the uniquely unpredictable magic that was Churchill. Transformation of the despondent misery of disaster into a grimly certain stepping stone to ultimate victory. Captured in a brilliantly perceptive line from a verse of my old friend James Edward Holroyd,[1] he 'Unleashed the angered lions in the blood.'

General Ismay: recollection[2]
(*Churchill papers, 4/198*)

8 September 1940

On the day following the first serious night attack on the London Docks you had an early lunch and then visited the East End of London, particularly the London Docks. You took with you Jack Churchill, Duncan Sandys and myself. One of the first places to which you were taken was an air raid shelter which had had a direct hit. About 40 of the inmates had been killed and a very large number wounded. The place was full of people searching for their lost belongings when you arrived. They stormed you, as you got out of the car with cries of 'It was good of you to come, Winnie. We thought you'd come. We can take it. Give it 'em back'. It was a most moving scene, you broke down completely and I nearly did, and as I was trying to get to you through the press of bodies, I heard an old woman say 'You see, he really cares, he's crying'.

Later in the day we found many pathetic little Union Jacks flying on piles of masonry that had once been the homes of these poor people.

You made a very long visitation and the Luftwaffe returned to this blaze of light before you left the docks. We had a long job getting out through narrow streets, many of which were blocked by houses having been blown across them.

---

[1] James Edward Holroyd. Worked for many years as Press Officer at the Board of Trade. Best known for his books about Sherlock Holmes. President of the Sherlock Holmes Society.
[2] In a letter to Churchill in 1948, while Churchill was writing volume 2 of his war memoirs.

September 1940

Winston S. Churchill to Admiral Pound
(*Churchill papers, 20/13*)

8 September 1940

My idea was not that the President should build Winettes[1] as such, apart from any already arranged for, but that, out of the great number of merchant vessels being constructed in the United States for 1942, he would fit out a certain number with brows and side-ports to enable tanks to be landed from them on beaches, or into tank landing-craft which would take them to the beaches.

Please help me to explain this point to him, showing what kind of alteration would be required in the American merchant ships now projected.

Winston S. Churchill to Anthony Eden and General Dill
(*Churchill papers, 20/13*)

8 September 1940
ACTION THIS DAY

I am very pleased with this telegram.[2] It has been heartbreaking to me to watch these splendid Units fooled away for a whole year. The sooner they form machine-gun battalions, which can subsequently be converted into motor battalions, and finally into armoured Units, the better. Please let nothing stand in the way. It is an insult to the Scots Greys and Household Cavalry to tether them to horses at the present time. There might be something to be said for a few battalions of infantry or cavalrymen mounted on ponies for the rocky hills of Palestine, but these historic Regular regiments have a right to play a man's part in the war. I hope I may see your telegram approving this course before it goes.

---

[1] These were landing ships from which tanks could be put ashore during an amphibious landing (LSTs). The first version to be constructed consisted of three ships, each capable of landing twenty 25–ton tanks each. They were originally named Winettes, but soon renamed Boxer LST (1). In January 1941 the order for building them was awarded to Harland & Wolff in Belfast. The first three to be launched were HMS *Thruster* (September 1942), HMS *Bruiser* (October 1942) and HMS *Boxer* (December 1942). As insufficient facilities existed to build the numbers that would be needed, the United States agreed to build the next seven. The order was subsequently cancelled, and the vessels redesigned. These landing ships, eventually of several different types, were a prerequisite of the Allied landings in Sicily, Italy and Normandy. There is a full account of the landing ships, in preparation and in action, in Brian Macdermott, *Ships Without Names*, London, 1992.

[2] A telegram from General Wavell of 4 September 1940 concerning the use to be made of cavalry units then in the Middle East.

Winston S. Churchill to Anthony Eden
(*Churchill papers, 20/13*)

8 September 1940
ACTION THIS DAY

You told me that you were in entire agreement with the views I put forward about the Special Companies, and ending the uncertainty in which they were placed. Unhappily, nothing has happened so far of which the troops are aware. They do not know they are not under sentence of disbandment. All recruiting has been stopped, although there is a waiting list, and they are not even allowed to call up the men who want to join and have been vetted and approved. Although these Companies comprise many of the best and most highly-trained of our personnel, they are at present only armed with rifles, which seems a shocking waste should they be thrown into the invasion mêlée. I hope that you will make sure that when you give an order it is obeyed with promptness. Perhaps you could explain to me what has happened to prevent your decision from being made effective. In my experience, which is a long one, of Service Departments, there is always a danger that anything contrary to Service prejudices will be obstructed and delayed by Officers of the second grade in the machine. The way to deal with this, is to make signal examples of one or two. When this becomes known you get a better service afterwards.

Perhaps you will tell me about this if you can dine with me to-night.[1]

WSC

Winston S. Churchill to Admiral Sir Andrew Cunningham
(*Churchill papers, 20/13*)

8 September 1940

I congratulate you on the success of the recent operation in the Eastern and Central Mediterranean, and upon the accession to your Fleet of two of our finest Units with other valuable vessels. I am sorry, however, that the armoured brigade which is so necessary to the defence of Egypt and Alexandria is still separated by more than three weeks from its scene of action. I hope you will find it possible to review the naval situation in the light of the experience gained during 'Hats,' and the arrival of *Illustrious* and *Valiant*. Not only the paper strength of the Italian Navy, but also the degree of resistance which they may be inclined to offer, should be measured. It is of high

---

[1] Churchill dined at Chequers that Sunday night. His other guests included Air Marshal Sir Charles Portal, Sir Edward Bridges, Professor Lindemann and Pamela Churchill. John Martin was the Duty Private Secretary.

importance to strike at the Italians this autumn, because as time passes the Germans will be more likely to lay strong hands upon the Italian war machine, and then the picture will be very different. We intend to strengthen the anti-aircraft defences of Malta by every possible means, and some novel weapons of which I have high hopes will shortly be sent there for experiment. I trust that Malta may become safe for temporary visits of the Fleet at an earlier date than April 1941. If in the meanwhile you have any proposals for offensive action to make, they should be transmitted to the Admiralty. I shall be glad if you will also concert with the Army and Air Force, plans for an operation against the Italian communications in Libya, which at the right time could be used to hamper any large-scale offensive against Egypt. The advantages of gaining the initiative are obviously very great. I hope the Fulmars[1] have made a good impression. The battle here for Air mastery continues to be severe, but firm confidence is felt in its eventual outcome.

WSC

Winston S. Churchill to A. V. Alexander
(*Churchill papers, 20/13*)

9 September 1940

I have read your papers on the new programme. I understand you are going to redraft your Memorandum after reading the one I presented to the Cabinet in March. I am not content at all with the refusal to reconstruct the 'Royal Sovereign' Class.[2] I think these should have precedence over all battleships, except those which can finish by the end of 1942. This would mean that you could get on with the *Howe*.[3] The position of the other five capital ships being considered next year when the time for presenting the Navy Estimates comes. I see no reason why work should not proceed on the aircraft carrier *Indefatigable*, and on the eight suspended cruisers. I am quite ready to approve the refilling of all slips vacated by anti-submarine craft, provided that a

---

[1] The Fulmar was a British fighter aircraft, with a cruising speed of 228 miles an hour and an effective range 625 miles. It had an armament of eight machine guns, and was used for convoy escort duties.

[2] In a letter to A. V. Alexander, Pound pointed out that 'labour has not been available to convert one or more of these ships', but that had a Royal Sovereign class ship been converted as Churchill wished, and used to bombard the Italian coast, 'she would have to be escorted by other battleships and it would be preferable to use the fast battleships for the bombardment so as not to be hindered by the slow R class' (*Admiralty papers, 205/6*).

[3] The fleet carrier *Howe* was first in action in July 1943, during the Sicily landings, when it formed part of the reserve force to the west of the island. *Indefatigable*, ordered in 1938 and laid down in 1939, was first in action as part of the Pacific Fleet in March 1945.

maximum limit of 15 months is assigned to the completion of all new craft. All very large size destroyers taking over this period to build, must be excluded from the emergency war-time programme.

After your final proposals are ready, we can have a conference.

WSC

Winston S. Churchill to Herbert Morrison
(*Churchill papers, 20/13*)

9 September 1940

It falls upon us to provide armaments for General de Gaulle whose forces have been considerably increased by the rallying to him of French Equatorial Africa. We may expect a further enlargement of the Free French Army and Air Force if other African colonies follow suit.

All de Gaulle's forces are at present armed with French types of weapons and there is no reserve from which to maintain wastage and expenditure. Pray let me have your views as a matter of urgency on how we can best meet the difficulty. You should consider whether any contracts for French types of armaments placed in North America, and subsequently cancelled by us after the French armistice, can usefully be revived.

If we cannot manufacture somewhere a sufficient quantity of munitions of French types we shall be faced with the embarrassing problem of rearming the whole of de Gaulle's forces with our own types of weapons.

WSC

Winston S. Churchill to Anthony Eden
(*Churchill papers, 20/2*)

9 September 1940

My dear Anthony,

I am afraid I must ask that there should be a full Court of Inquiry, and that General Godwin-Austen should be suspended from duty meanwhile. Only in this way can the authorities concerned be apprised of the standards which we intend to enforce. Much valuable time has already been lost. I could not feel I was discharging my responsibility for the proper conduct of the war, or for the honour of the British arms, if a formal inquiry were not held. This alone can show whether a court-martial is or is not necessary.

Yours sincerely,
Winston S. Churchill

Winston S. Churchill to Neville Chamberlain
(*Churchill papers, 2/393*)

9 September 1940
Private

My dear Neville,

No. 11 Group, Fighter Command, which conducted this evening's action, have given me a very good report. Nearly 400 aircraft crossed the coast, and were met by at least 200 of our Fighters who broke them up into small parties, which fled after pursuit. The losses are not yet known.

I thought you would like to know.

I am so glad you are back to share our experiences. I have told them to see to the air conditioning of yr shelter.

Yours ever
W

Winston S. Churchill: recollection
(*'Their Finest Hour', page 335*)

10 September 1940

About this time the King changed his practice of receiving me in a formal weekly audience at about 5 o'clock which had prevailed during my first two months of office. It was now arranged that I should lunch with him every Tuesday.[1] This was certainly a very agreeable method of transacting State business, and sometimes the Queen was present. On several occasions we all had to take our plates and glasses in our hands and go down to the shelter, which was making progress, to finish our meal. The weekly luncheons became a regular institution. After the first few months His Majesty decided that all servants should be excluded, and that we should help ourselves and help each other. During the four-and-a-half years that this continued I became aware of the extraordinary diligence with which the King read all the telegrams and public documents submitted to him. Under the British Constitutional system the Sovereign has a right to be made acquainted with everything for which his Ministers are responsible, and has an unlimited right of giving counsel to his Government. I was most careful that everything should be laid before the King, and at our weekly meetings he frequently showed that he had mastered papers which I had not yet dealt with. It was a great help to Britain to have so good a King and Queen in those fateful years, and as a convinced upholder of constitutional and limited monarchy I valued as a signal honour the gracious intimacy with which I, as first Minister, was treated, for which I suppose there has been no precedent since the days of Queen Anne and Marlborough during his years of power.

[1] The first of these weekly lunches was on Tuesday, 10 September 1940.

Winston S. Churchill to Herbert Morrison
(*Churchill papers, 20/13*)

10 September 1940

Thank you for your letter. I am, indeed, distressed to see the falling off of Tracer[1] and De Wilde,[2] these being so important, and the latter vital to our Air fighting.

WSC

Winston S. Churchill to General Ismay
(*Churchill papers, 20/13*)

10 September 1940

1. The prime defence of Singapore is the Fleet. The protective effect of the Fleet is exercised to a large extent whether it is on the spot or not. For instance, the present Middle Eastern Fleet, which we have just powerfully reinforced, could in a very short time, if ordered, reach Singapore. It could, if necessary, fight an action before reaching Singapore, because it would find in that fortress, fuel, ammunition, and repair facilities. The fact that the Japanese had made landings in Malaya and had even begun the siege of the fortress would not deprive a superior relieving fleet of its power. On the contrary, the plight of the besiegers, cut off from home while installing themselves in the swamps and jungle, would be all the more forlorn.

2. The defence of Singapore must, therefore, be based upon a strong <u>local</u> garrison and the general potentialities of sea power. The idea of trying to defend the Malay Peninsula and of holding the whole of Malaya, a large country 400 by 200 miles at its widest part, cannot be entertained. A single Division, however well supplied with signals, &c., could make no impression upon such a task. What could a single Division do for the defence of a country nearly as large as England?

---

[1] The Tracer is a type of bullet which leaves a visible mark (or 'trace') while in flight, so that the gunner can observe the strike of the shot, and make adjustments in the event of a miss. It was originally developed for use by aerial machine gunners, who had otherwise no way of determining where their shots had gone in relation to the target. Its use was later extended to ground fire for machine guns.

[2] An improved incendiary bullet for the standard .303 rifle. Although the bullet was protected by a Swiss patent, de Wilde is believed to have been a Belgian: the British Government purchased the rights to his bullet in January 1939 and proceeded with its further development. The first version in use had the designation 'Cartridge S.A., Incendiary, .303 Inch, B Mark VI, Z'. The incendiary mixture caused a bright flash on impact, which was a valuable indication of where the bullet had struck. A common fault was the tendency of the base plug to break away from the bullet, causing premature explosion; this was addressed in a simplified version of the bullet, the B Mark VII.

3. The danger of a rupture with Japan is no worse than it was. The probabilities of the Japanese undertaking an attack upon Singapore which would involve so large a proportion of their fleet far outside the Yellow Sea, are remote; in fact nothing could be more foolish from their point of view. Far more attractive to them are the Dutch East Indies. The presence of the United States Fleet in the Pacific must always be a main pre-occupation to Japan. They are not at all likely to gamble. They are usually most cautious, and now have real need to be, since they are involved in China so deeply.

4. I should have preferred the Australian Brigade to go to India, rather than Malaya, but only because their training in India will fit them more readily for the Middle East.[1] I am delighted to know they can be trained in the Middle East, where all the advantages set forth on page 3 of COS (40) 725 will be reaped strategically by us.[2]

5. I do not, therefore, consider that the political situation is such as to require the withholding of the 7th Australian Division from its best station strategically and administratively. A telegram should be drafted to the Commonwealth Government in this sense.

WSC

---

[1] On 1 September 1940 Churchill had minuted to Ismay, with regard to reinforcements to be sent to Malaya: 'It is better to send the Australian Division to India where their training can be advanced, and to make some lesser additions to the garrison of Malaya. The two battalions from Shanghai plus four Indian battalions would seem a good reinforcement. We want to keep the Australian Divisions as free as possible for the Middle East' (*Churchill papers, 20/13*).

[2] A Chiefs of Staff Sub-Committee memorandum, 'Transfer of Australian Division to India or Malaya', by the Chief of the Imperial General Staff, contained a section on 'Arguments for sending Australians to Middle East'. The advantages of such a course were listed as 'to prevent the enemy from gaining successes' in the Middle East (which was likely to become an active theatre), the fact that the 7th Australian Division 'is not at present either fully equipped or fully trained to meet a first class European enemy', and that the facilities for training in Palestine were 'far better' than in Malaya (*Cabinet papers, 80/18*). Ironically, Lord Kitchener's argument for sending the Australians to Egypt in 1915 was that they were not sufficiently good to meet a 'first class' enemy (the Germans), but would do all right against a less efficient one (the Turks).

Bernard Partridge: cartoon
('*Punch*')

11 September 1940

SAILORS DO CARE

"The more we get together
The merrier we shall be."

War Cabinet: Confidential Annex
(*Cabinet papers, 65/15*)

11 September 1940
12.30 p.m.

10 Downing Street

The Prime Minister drew attention to the fact that the enemy was continuing to pass convoys of ships westward down the French coast, although a small number of ships had been successfully attacked off Ostend on the previous night. A powerful armada was thus being deployed along the coasts of France opposite this country. The argument of the naval authorities was that if we were to send our ships to attack these concentrations of barges and merchant vessels along the French coast, we might well throw away forces which would be invaluable to us if these barges and merchant ships attempted to cross the Channel.

He had had a conference the previous night to discuss our measures for defence against invasion with the First Lord, the Secretary of State for War and their advisers.

Continuing, the Prime Minister said that the vital stretch of coastline was from the North Foreland to Dungeness. If the enemy should succeed in getting lodgements of troops ashore on this coast, and could capture the guns deployed there, they would have, not only a bridgehead, but a sheltered passageway commanded by the coast defence guns from both sides of the Channel. Various steps were therefore proposed for strengthening this essential strip of coastline:–

(1) The gun positions should be intensively fortified.
(2) Consideration was being given to employing more highly trained troops in this sector. In particular, he hoped that the Special Companies would be made over to the Commander-in-Chief, Home Forces, and some of them employed in this sector. Behind the line for immediate counter attack would be the Australian Division, armoured troops and the London Division.
(3) It was also under consideration to deploy 30 to 40 Bofors guns in this area for the defence of the troops against low-flying attack.

The Secretary of State for War said that since the conference on the previous night he had seen the Commander-in-Chief, Home Forces, who pointed out that the extension of German shipping down the Channel gave him a longer front to defend. Nevertheless he agreed with the vital need for protecting the North Foreland–Dungeness sector. He was most grateful that the Special Companies were to be under his command. He would employ some of them in this sector, but he did not propose to move the companies now at Ryde and Rye. The Commander-in-Chief was also very anxious to get a regiment of Bofors guns. He preferred to keep the armoured troops and the

New Zealand troops in the Maidstone area, as this point was the best for internal communication to either Dover or Dungeness.

The Prime Minister said that he was proposing to visit this area on the following day in company with the First Lord of the Admiralty, the Secretary of State for War and their advisers, and the Commander-in-Chief, Home Forces.

The Prime Minister said that he understood that the First Lord of the Admiralty also agreed that the *Rodney* should remain at Rosyth.

As regards the likelihood of invasion, the Foreign Secretary referred to telegram No. 203 from Madrid, in which Sir Samuel Hoare reported a statement from a German source that the real enemy objective was Egypt.

The Prime Minister said he thought it was by no means impossible that the Germans would in the end decide not to launch an attack on this country because they were unable to obtain the domination over our fighter force.

The War Cabinet had before them a Memorandum by the Secretary of State for Foreign Affairs, setting out an exchange of telegrams from His Majesty's Minister in Stockholm[1] in regard to certain advances made by Dr Weissauer, said to be a secret emissary of Hitler, together with a draft reply to the last telegram from Stockholm.[2]

The Secretary of State for Foreign Affairs said that the Prime Minister proposed that the contents of these offers should be made known to President Roosevelt, who should be informed that we had sent a refusal to an offer of peace, made to us at a time when the threat of invasion was imminent.

Winston S. Churchill to General Ismay and his Private Office
(*Churchill papers, 20/13*)

11 September 1940

Please call for reports on whether any serious effects are being produced by the Air attack on –

(a) food supplies and distribution;

(b) numbers of homeless, and provision therefor;

[1] Victor Alexander Louis Mallet, 1893–1969. On active service, 1914–18. Entered the Diplomatic Service, 1919. Transferred to the Foreign Office, 1932. Counsellor at Washington, 1936–9. Minister at Stockholm, 1940–5. Knighted, 1944. Ambassador at Madrid, 1945–6; at Rome, 1947–53.

[2] On the previous day Lord Halifax and Sir Alexander Cadogan had seen Churchill twice, at 4 p.m. and 7.30 p.m., about what reply should be given to this initiative. 'He took the line I expected,' Cadogan noted in his diary, 'which doesn't differ from H's. It's a question not of what to reply but how to reply.' Of their second visit, Cadogan noted in his diary: 'He was in bed in flowered Chinese dressing gown, puffing large cigar. He read us his draft reply, which is all right' (*The Diaries of Sir Alexander Cadogan*).

(c) exhaustion of Fire Brigade personnel;
(d) sewage in London area;
(e) gas and electricity;
(f) water supplies in London area;
(g) General Ismay to find out what is the practical effect of the bombing on Woolwich production.

WSC

Winston S. Churchill to Sir Archibald Sinclair
(*Churchill papers, 20/13*)

11 September 1940

I understand that you are taking up with the Ministry of Information the possibility of getting additional personnel from the BBC for radio counter-measures. I know that the matter of the distribution of scientific personnel is to be considered as a whole in due course, but, in view of the extreme urgency of working these counter-measures to the full immediately, I trust there will be no difficulty in obtaining a few score, or even a hundred, technicians of the £300–£500 a year class even if only as a temporary measure.

WSC

Winston S. Churchill to Anthony Eden
(*Churchill papers, 20/13*)

11 September 1940

Please report what you have decided about 'A' – movement of the Special Companies towards the threatened beaches;[1] 'B' – plan for furnishing the troops in East Kent with mobile Bofors guns. I am willing to assist in this if you are having difficulty; 'C' – intensive fortification of gun positions.

---

[1] It was on 11 September 1940 that Churchill was sent details of a top secret German Air Force radio signal, decrypted at Bletchley Park on an Enigma machine. The Bletchley message read: 'We learn from a reliable source that a secret order has recently been issued by the German Air Force Command HQ in Western France that the transport of individual troops and units must be drastically curtailed during the current movement of armament and of engineer units connected therewith. Indents must in future be passed to the Command Transport Office and not direct to local transport office.' Military Intelligence commented: 'Although there are a number of possible reasons for this order, it cannot be overlooked that it may be in connection with the movement of troops and armament for invasion purposes' (*War Office papers, 199/911A*).

Winston S. Churchill: broadcast
('*The Listener*', 19 September 1940)[1]

11 September 1940
6 p.m.

When I said in the House of Commons the other day that I thought it improbable that the enemy's air attack in September could be more than three times as great as it was in August, I was not, of course, referring to barbarous attacks upon the civil population, but to the great air battle which is being fought out between our fighters and the German Air Force.

You will understand that whenever the weather is favourable, waves of German bombers, protected by fighters, often three or four hundred at a time, surge over this island, especially the promontory of Kent, in the hope of attacking military and other objectives by daylight. However, they are met by our fighter squadrons and nearly always broken up; and their losses average three to one in machines and six to one in pilots.

This effort of the Germans to secure daylight mastery of the air over England is, of course, the crux of the whole war. So far it has failed conspicuously. It has cost them very dear, and we have felt stronger, and actually are relatively a good deal stronger, than when the hard fighting began in July. There is no doubt that Herr Hitler is using up his fighter force at a very high rate, and that if he goes on for many more weeks he will wear down and ruin this vital part of his Air Force. That will give us a very great advantage.

On the other hand, for him to try to invade this country without having secured mastery in the air would be a very hazardous undertaking. Nevertheless, all his preparations for invasion on a great scale are steadily going forward. Several hundreds of self-propelled barges are moving down the coasts of Europe, from the German and Dutch harbours to the ports of Northern France; from Dunkirk to Brest; and beyond Brest to the French harbours in the Bay of Biscay.

Besides this, convoys of merchant ships in tens of dozens are being moved through the Straits of Dover into the Channel, dodging along from port to port under the protection of the new batteries which the Germans have built on the French shore. There are now considerable gatherings of shipping in the German, Dutch, Belgian and French harbours – all the way from Hamburg to Brest. Finally, there are some preparations made of ships to carry an invading force from the Norwegian harbours.

Behind these clusters of ships or barges, there stand very large numbers of German troops, awaiting the order to go on board and set out on their very

---

[1] This broadcast was also reprinted in the twenty-fifth birthday issue of *The Listener* on 14 January 1954.

dangerous and uncertain voyage across the seas. We cannot tell when they will try to come; we cannot be sure that in fact they will try at all; but no one should blind himself to the fact that a heavy, full-scale invasion of this island is being prepared with all the usual German thoroughness and method, and that it may be launched now – upon England, upon Scotland, or upon Ireland, or upon all three.

If this invasion is going to be tried at all, it does not seem that it can be long delayed. The weather may break at any time. Besides this, it is difficult for the enemy to keep these gatherings of ships waiting about indefinitely, while they are bombed every night by our bombers, and very often shelled by our warships which are waiting for them outside.

Therefore, we must regard the next week or so as a very important period in our history. It ranks with the days when the Spanish Armada was approaching the Channel, and Drake was finishing his game of bowls; or when Nelson stood between us and Napoleon's Grand Army at Boulogne. We have read all about this in the history books; but what is happening now is on a far greater scale and of far more consequence to the life and future of the world and its civilisation than these brave old days of the past.

Every man and woman will therefore prepare himself to do his duty, whatever it may be, with special pride and care. Our fleets and flotillas are very powerful and numerous; our Air Force is at the highest strength it has ever reached, and it is conscious of its proved superiority, not indeed in numbers, but in men and machines[1] Our shores are well fortified and strongly manned, and behind them, ready to attack the invaders, we have a far larger and better equipped mobile Army than we have ever had before.

Besides this, we have more than a million and a half men of the Home Guard, who are just as much soldiers of the Regular Army as the Grenadier Guards, and who are determined to fight for every inch of the ground in every village and in every street.

It is with devout but sure confidence that I say: Let God defend the Right.

These cruel, wanton, indiscriminate bombings of London are, of course, a part of Hitler's invasion plans. He hopes, by killing large numbers of civilians, and women and children, that he will terrorise and cow the people of this mighty imperial city, and make them a burden and an anxiety to the Government and thus distract our attention unduly from the ferocious onslaught he is preparing. Little does he know the spirit of the British nation, or the tough fibre of the Londoners, whose forebears played a leading part in the establishment of Parliamentary institutions and who have been bred to

---

[1] Churchill had just been informed by the Air Ministry that, as of 7 September 1940, the total pilot strength available to Britain was 3,835, of whom 3,495 were British pilots, 215 Poles, 91 Czechs, 22 Belgians, 7 French, 4 Americans and 1 Dutchman. This was an increase of 734 over the figure for 15 June 1940. (*Premier papers, 3/24/2.*) Of the 154 Polish pilots who fought in the Battle of Britain, 30 were killed (by the end of October 1940).

value freedom far above their lives. This wicked man, the repository and embodiment of many forms of soul-destroying hatred, this monstrous product of former wrongs and shame, has now resolved to try to break our famous island race by a process of indiscriminate slaughter and destruction. What he has done is to kindle a fire in British hearts, here and all over the world, which will glow long after all traces of the conflagration he has caused in London have been removed. He has lighted a fire which will burn with a steady and consuming flame until the last vestiges of Nazi tyranny have been burnt out of Europe, and until the Old World – and the New – can join hands to rebuild the temples of man's freedom and man's honour, upon foundations which will not soon or easily be overthrown.

This is a time for everyone to stand together, and hold firm, as they are doing. I express my admiration for the exemplary manner in which all the Air Raid precautions services of London are being discharged, especially the Fire Brigade, whose work has been so heavy and also dangerous. All the world that is still free marvels at the composure and fortitude with which the citizens of London are facing and surmounting the great ordeal to which they are subjected, the end of which or the severity of which cannot yet be foreseen.

It is a message of good cheer to our fighting Forces on the seas, in the air, and in our waiting Armies in all their posts and stations, that we send them from this capital city. They know that they have behind them a people who will not flinch or weary of the struggle – hard and protracted though it will be; but that we shall rather draw from the heart of suffering itself the means of inspiration and survival, and of a victory won not only for ourselves but for all; a victory won not only for our own time but for the long and better days that are to come.

Winston S. Churchill to Robert Menzies
(*Churchill papers, 20/14*)

11 September 1940

Most grateful for your inspiring message.[1] We have passed through anxious moments in the last twelve months, but the spirit of our people has withstood each shock with undaunted courage and the universal determination to destroy utterly the Nazi menace has only been strengthened. The magnificent support from you and the other Dominions has heartened and sustained us throughout. In the Australians of 1940 the valour of their fathers

---

[1] One of several messages from the Dominions, expressing support for Britain as the Blitz intensified.

lives again. The thrilling exploits of your sailors in the Mediterranean scene and of your airmen[1] round these shores give a foretaste of what the enemy may expect when all arms of the Australian forces get the chance which they are so eagerly awaiting. With the aid of such men we shall go on unflinchingly until final victory is won.

Winston S. Churchill to William Mackenzie King
(*Churchill papers, 20/14*)

12 September 1940

I am touched by the personal kindness of your telegram, and all our people are cheered and fortified to feel that Canada is with the Mother Country heart and soul. The fine Canadian Divisions which are standing on guard with us will play a notable part should the enemy succeed in setting foot on our shores. I am very glad to have this opportunity of thanking you personally for all you have done for the Common Cause and especially in promoting a harmony of sentiment throughout the New World. This deep understanding will be a dominant factor in the rescue of Europe from a relapse into the Dark Ages. On behalf of the Government and people of the United Kingdom I send you heartfelt thanks for your memorable message.

ON 12 SEPTEMBER 1940 Churchill visited the Southern and Eastern defences.

General Brooke: diary
(*'The Turn of the Tide'*)

12 September 1940

... proceeded to pick up Dill and then on to Holborn Viaduct Station which we reached with some difficulty owing to results of night's bombing. Here we joined the PM's train for Shorncliffe.[2] On the way had long talk with PM on the organisation of defences on the Narrows.

Proceeded to examine 9.2-in. railway guns, coast guns, defence to Dungeness. Then back to Dover for lunch in the castle with Bertie Ramsay. After lunch PM wanted to watch air-fight but there was none to see.

---

[1] Thirty-seven Australian pilots fought with the Royal Air Force in the Battle of Britain. Thirteen were killed. Their story is told in Denis Newton, *A Few of the Few* (London 1993).
[2] Churchill was also accompanied by A. V. Alexander, Admiral Pound and General Ismay.

Winston S. Churchill to Herbert Morrison
(*Churchill papers, 20/6*)

12 September 1940

What proportion of HE[1] and filling capacity was located at Woolwich? Surely we have much larger establishments elsewhere. Let us have a meeting to-morrow at 5 o'clock, in order to take stock of the situation.

WSC

Winston S. Churchill to Sir Edward Bridges
(*Churchill papers, 20/13*)

12 September 1940

Will you kindly convey to the Cabinet and Ministers the suggestion which I make that our hours should be somewhat advanced. Luncheon should be at 1 o'clock, and Cabinet times moved forward by half an hour. In principle it will be convenient if we aim at an earlier dinner-hour, say, 7.15 p.m. Darkness falls earlier, and for the next few weeks severe bombing may be expected once the protection of the Fighter aircraft is withdrawn. It would be a good thing if staffs and servants could be under shelter as early as possible, and Ministers are requested to arrange to work in places of reasonable security during the night raids, and especially to find places for sleeping where they will not be disturbed by anything but a direct hit.

I propose to ask Parliament when it meets at the usual time on Tuesday to meet in these occasional sittings at 11 a.m. and separate at 4 or 5 p.m. This will allow Members to reach their homes, and I hope their shelters, by daylight. We must adapt ourselves to these conditions, which will probably be accentuated. Indeed, it is likely we shall have to move our office hours forward by another half-hour as the days shorten.

WSC

Winston S. Churchill to General Ismay
(*Premier papers, 3/22/6*)

12 September 1940

The Professor thinks well of the project of using chemical searchlights from aeroplanes by night. I wish this matter to have a good trial. Make sure that this is done.

WSC

[1] High Explosive.

The Hon. Mrs Beckett[1] to Winston S. Churchill
(*Churchill papers, 2/416*)

12 September 1940 Hyde Park Hotel
London

When God wants a hard thing done he gets an Englishman to do it. This is what England tells of you, dear Winston

yrs affectionately
Muriel Beckett

No answer[2]

Winston S. Churchill to Anthony Eden
(*Churchill papers, 20/13*)

13 September 1940
ACTION THIS DAY

As I telephoned to you last night, it appears to be of high importance to cope with the UXB[3] in London, and especially on the railways. The congestion in the marshalling yards is becoming acute, mainly from this cause. It would be well to bring in clearance parties both from the North and the West, and also to expand as rapidly as possible General King's organization. I do not think he has planned it on large enough lines to cope with this nuisance, which may soon wear a graver aspect.

WSC

Sir John Reith: diary
(*'The Reith Diaries'*)

13 September 1940

I went up to my room to settle the minute for the Cabinet to which I went at 11.30 in the underground place. I was pressed by the PM on the subject of tube stations being used for refugees. I said that I thought it was inadvisable, admitting that as Minister of Transport I couldn't be completely impartial. A

---

[1] Muriel Helen Florence Paget, –1941. Daughter of Lord Charles Paget. A friend of Churchill in her youth. In 1896 she married Rupert Beckett, second son of the 1st Baron Grimthorpe. She was created CBE in 1918. In 1932 her daughter Pamela married Colonel Stewart Menzies, later head of the Secret Intelligence Service.

[2] Churchill ignored Muriel Beckett's injunction and replied by telegram: 'Thank you so much, dear Muriel. Winston.'

[3] Unexploded Bomb.

message was handed to him. Buckingham Palace had been dive-bombed. King and Queen safe. PM said he was sure that this indicated that they meant business.

John Martin: diary
(*Martin papers*)

13 September 1940

With PM to Chequers in afternoon, calling at Dollis Hill (where emergency headquarters had been prepared) and Uxbridge (11th Fighter Group) on the way.

John Martin: diary
(*Martin papers*)

14 September 1940

Returned to town in afternoon. Spent night at Central War Room.[1] More raids.

Chiefs of Staff Committee: minutes
(*Cabinet papers, 79/6*)

14 September 1940
9.30 p.m.

MALTA

The Prime Minister said he had been considering whether the garrison of Malta should not be increased by two battalions. He thought this matter should be examined by the CIGS. He invited the Chiefs of Staff to consider the possibility of passing reinforcements into Malta in October. He suggested that in addition to two battalions, a UP Battery and possibly some additional AA guns might be sent, the whole being carried in warships.

The Chiefs of Staff undertook to examine these proposals.

ACTION IN GOVERNMENT DEPARTMENTS DURING AIR RAIDS

The Prime Minister said that he had had several letters drawing attention to the unsatisfactory state of the present arrangements in Government Offices during air raid warnings. Lord Trenchard complained that it was three hours before he could get on to the War Office by telephone. Lord Beaverbrook had

[1] Also known as the Cabinet War Room. Churchill is known to have slept in the underground Cabinet War Rooms on only three occasions.

pointed out that whereas munition workers were being urged to remain at work during air attack, Civil Servants were instructed to take shelter in the basement as soon as there was the slightest danger. We had been subjected to air attack in London for a week and there had not been a single casualty in a Government Office, nor would there have been if everyone had remained at work in their ordinary rooms. Such a situation might not continue but it was clearly necessary to arrive at a reasonable solution which, on the one hand, would enable the work to proceed and on the other, prevent serious casualties in the event of a heavy attack. The problem was not confined to Government Offices but there was also the question of what Parliament should do and whether their meetings should be advertised in advance and whether any special protection could be afforded to their meetings. Considerable discussions ensued on these matters, and the Prime Minister invited the Chiefs of Staff:
- (a) to furnish him with their opinion as to the conditions under which Parliament should meet, having regard to the danger from air attack and the difficulty of giving special protection;
- (b) to give further consideration to the action to be taken by Government Departments during air raids and to express their views as to the suitability of a solution based on the following principles:
    - (i) the number of people employed in Departments in London to be reduced to a minimum;
    - (ii) work to be carried on and not to be interrupted except under conditions of exceptional danger. 'Business as Usual' and not 'Safety First' should be the governing principle to be aimed at;
    - (iii) the normal telephone service to be at all times operative;
    - (iv) no obstacle to be placed in the way of movement on legitimate business;
    - (v) a central system of responsible roof-watchers to be established and arrangements to be made to furnish them with information as to the scale of attack.

Sir John Reith: diary
(*'The Reith Diaries'*)

14 September 1940

Churchill rang me up again – 11.55 this time – to ask how I was getting on. Great confidence he said he had in me. Apropos the discomforts after fire he remarked that the adaptability of the English was one of our great assets. Odd.

Winston S. Churchill to Colonel Hollis
(*Churchill papers, 20/13*)

14 September 1940

DEFENCE OF FREETOWN

This matter can be reconsidered after the operation 'Menace' and its reactions are known. Meanwhile, preparations should be delayed. It is far more necessary to send two Battalions to Malta, as we do not there possess the command of the sea. It was evidently a mistake to send both West African Brigades away.

WSC

Winston S. Churchill to Anthony Eden
(*Churchill papers, 20/13*)

14 September 1940

I hear that there is a special type of auger manufactured in the United States which is capable of boring in the space of less than an hour a hole of such a size and depth as would take two to three days to dig manually.

You should I think consider ordering a number of these appliances for the use of the bomb disposal squads. The essence of this business is to reach the bomb and deal with it with the least possible delay.

These augers may, perhaps, be expensive, but they will pay for themselves many times over by the saving they will effect in life and property. Besides I consider that we owe it to these brave men to provide them with the very best technical equipment.

WSC

Winston S. Churchill to Anthony Eden
(*Churchill papers, 20/13*)

14 September 1940

I hope the Armoured Brigade will be in time. I have no doubt it could have been conducted safely through the Mediterranean and the present danger that it will be too late averted. It must, however, be remembered that General Wavell himself joined in the declaration of the Commanders-in-Chief of the Navy, Army and Air, that the situation in Egypt did not warrant the risk. It was this declaration that made it impossible for me to override the Admiralty objections, as I would otherwise have done.

WSC

Winston S. Churchill to Sir Edward Bridges, General Ismay, and the Private Office
(*Premier papers, 4/69/1*)

14 September 1940

1. I have not at any time contemplated wholesale movement from London of black or yellow[1] Civil Servants. Anything of this nature is so detrimental that it could only be forced upon us by Central London becoming practically uninhabitable. Moreover, new resorts of Civil Servants would soon be identified and harassed, and there is more shelter in London than anywhere else.

2. The movement of the high control from the Whitehall area to 'Paddock' or other citadels stands on a different footing. We must make sure that the centre of Government functions harmoniously and vigorously. This would not be possible under conditions of almost continuous air raids. A movement to 'Paddock' by echelons of the War Cabinet, War Cabinet Secretariat, Chiefs of the Staff Committee, and Home Forces GHQ must now be planned, and may even begin in some minor respects. War Cabinet Ministers should visit their quarters in 'Paddock' and be ready to move there at short notice. They should be encouraged to sleep there if they want quiet nights. All measures should be taken to render habitable both the Citadel and Neville Court.[2] Secrecy cannot be expected, but publicity must be forbidden.

We must expect that the Whitehall–Westminster area will be the subject of intensive air attack any time now. The German method is to make the disruption of the Central Government a vital prelude to any major assault upon the country. They have done this everywhere. They will certainly do it here, where the landscape can be so easily recognised and the river and its high buildings affords a sure guide both by day and night. We must forestall this disruption of the Central Government.

3. It is not necessary to move the Admiralty yet. They are well provided

---

[1] Black and yellow were categories of evacuation, according to function.

[2] In fact, Neville's Court, one of several buildings off Dollis Hill Lane, in north-west London, that made up the 'Paddock' complex of underground and above ground buildings, to be used by the Government as emergency headquarters in the event of the serious destruction of Whitehall. Accommodation had been prepared for Churchill himself (in Neville's Court), and for each individual member of the War Cabinet, their secretaries, Advanced HQ Home Forces, GHQ Reconnaisance, the War Office staff, a Dominions Liaison Officer, a Cabinet Room and a Map Room. The Admiralty and the Air Ministry were to be located half a mile from 'Paddock': the Air Ministry staff of 600 had plans to complete the move in six hours. Paddock was never used, except for one trial evacuation by the Cabinet later in September. The Citadel, the main building at Dollis Hill, much of it underground, had been built before the war by the Post Office as an emergency communications centre, and in 1940 prepared for use should the Government offices in Whitehall be evacuated. The London Transport Executive had also built an underground headquarters shortly before the war, at the discontinued Down Street station on the Piccadilly Line: Churchill slept there on four occasions at the height of the Blitz.

for.¹ The Air Ministry should begin to get from one leg to the other. The War Office and Home Forces must have all their preparations made.

4. Pray concert forthwith all the necessary measures for moving not more than two or three hundred principal persons and their immediate assistants to the new quarters, and show how it should be done step by step. Let me have this by Sunday night, in order that I may put a well-thought-out scheme before the Cabinet on Monday. On Monday the Cabinet will meet either in the Cabinet Room or in the Central War Room in accordance with the rules already prescribed.²

Winston S. Churchill to the Mayor of Tel Aviv³
(Churchill papers, 20/14)

15 September 1940

Please accept my deep sympathy in losses sustained by Tel Aviv in recent air attack.⁴ This act of senseless brutality will only strengthen our united resolve.

Winston S. Churchill to A. V. Alexander
(Admiralty papers, 205/5)

15 September 1940
Secret

1. Your new programme. I am very doubtful whether the Japanese figures are correct. The Naval Intelligence Branch are very much inclined to exaggerate Japanese strength and efficiency. I am not, however, opposed to the resumption of the battleship programme, provided it can be fitted in with more immediate wartime needs. Much of the battleship plant and labour

---

¹ The Admiralty had just finished building a large below- and above-ground bunker (now covered in ivy) at the Buckingham Palace end of the Admiralty building.

² On the following day, when Sir Edward Bridges showed Churchill the full Civil Service evacuation plans, Churchill approved them, but added: 'The time has not yet come to move' (*Premier papers*, 4/69/1).

³ Israel Rokach, 1896–1959. Born in Jaffa (then part of the Ottoman Empire). Educated in Switzerland as an electrical engineer. Elected to the first Tel Aviv Municipal Council, 1922. Mayor of Tel Aviv, 1937–53. Detained by the British for underground activities, 1947. A member of the Israeli Parliament (Knesset), 1949. Minister of the Interior, 1953–5. Deputy Speaker, 1957–9.

⁴ During the Italian air raid on Tel Aviv on 9 September 1940, 95 Jewish civilians were killed, among them 58 children. One Australian and 4 British soldiers were also killed. A further 27 civilians, all Arabs, were killed in the Arab village of Sommeil. Among those who witnessed this bombing was a seventeen-year-old Palestinian Jewish student, Yitzhak Rabin (whose father, a Russian-born Jew living in the United States in 1917, had joined the British Army in order to serve in Palestine, where he subsequently lived). Yitzhak Rabin was three times Prime Minister of Israel.

would not be useful for other purposes. Pray let me have a paper showing the demands these ships would make in each year they are under construction, in money, steel, and labour. Every effort must be concentrated upon *Howe*.

2. I should be content if two R Class vessels were taken in hand as soon as the invasion situation has cleared and we get *KGV* in commission. Meanwhile, material can be collected and preparations made. This should enable them to be ready in 18 months from now, i.e., the summer of 1942.

3. You should press on with *Indefatigable*, but we need not consider an additional aircraft-carrier until early next year. The drawings can, however, be completed.

4. I suppose you realise that the Belfast[1] type take over three years to build. Considering a large programme of cruisers is already under construction, I hope you will not press for these four to be added to the programme of this year.

5. I am all for building destroyers, and I do not mind how large they are, or how great their endurance, provided that they can be constructed in 15 months. This should be taken as the absolute limit, to which everything else must be made to conform. We were making destroyers which took three years to build, everyone thinking himself very clever in adding one improvement after another. I should like to discuss the destroyer designs with the Controller[2] and DNC.[3] They must be built only for this war, and have good protection from aircraft. Extreme speed is not so important. What you say about the U-Boats working continually further west is no doubt true, but the Corvettes, formerly called Whalers, have very fine endurance and range.

6. The Submarine programme is already very large, and makes inroads on other forms of war requirements. I think you would be wise to re-examine the demand for the 14 additional to the 24 to which the Treasury have agreed.

7. Great efforts should be made to produce the landing-craft as soon as possible. Are the Joint Planning Committee satisfied that these numbers are sufficient?

8. I am surprised you ask for only 50 anti-E-boats. Unless this is the utmost limit of your capacity, 100 would be more appropriate.

9. Speaking generally, the speed of construction and early dates of

---

[1] HMS *Belfast* was one of the Town class heavy cruisers, with six-inch guns, 9,100 tons displacement (later ships of 9,400 tons). The *Belfast*, commissioned in August 1939, is now moored as a museum ship in the Pool of London. She is the last survivor of her class.

[2] Rear-Admiral Bruce Fraser.

[3] Stanley Vernon Goodall, 1883–1965. Joined the Royal Corps of Naval Constructors, 1907. Constructor Commander, Royal Navy, 1919. Director of Naval Construction, Admiralty, 1936–44, and Assistant Controller (Warship Production), 1942–5. Knighted, 1938.

SEPTEMBER 1940 813

completion must at this time be considered the greatest virtues in new building. It is no use crowding up the order books of firms and filling the yards with shipping orders which everyone knows cannot be completed. You have, I presume, consulted Sir James Lithgow[1] about this programme, and have heard his views upon the consequences it will have upon merchant shipping building and our already reduced steel output. It is very wrong to trench too deeply upon the needs of other Services in time of war.

10. What has happened to the armoured torpedo ram which I asked the DNC to design?

It will be necessary to add a financial statement, as I did last time.

WSC

Winston S. Churchill: recollection
(*'Their Finest Hour'*, pages 293–7)

15 September 1940

We must take September 15 as the culminating date. On this day the Luftwaffe, after two heavy attacks on the 14th, made its greatest concentrated effort in a resumed daylight attack on London.

It was one of the decisive battles of the war, and, like the Battle of Waterloo, it was on a Sunday. I was at Chequers. I had already on several occasions visited the headquarters of No. 11 Fighter Group in order to witness the conduct of an air battle, when not much had happened. However, the weather on this day seemed suitable to the enemy, and accordingly I drove over to Uxbridge and arrived at the Group Headquarters. No. 11 Group comprised no fewer than twenty-five squadrons covering the whole of Essex, Kent, Sussex, and Hampshire, and all the approaches across them to London. Air Vice-Marshal Park had for six months commanded this group, on which our fate largely depended. From the beginning of Dunkirk all the daylight actions in the South of England had already been conducted by him, and all his arrangements and apparatus had been brought to the highest perfection. My wife and I were taken down to the bomb-proof Operations Room, fifty feet

---

[1] James Lithgow, 1883–1952. A shipbuilder. On active service, 1914–18 (despatches, wounded). Director of Shipbuilding Production, Admiralty, 1917. President, British Employers Federation, 1924. Created Baronet, 1925. Member of the Central Electricity Board, 1927–30. President of the Federation of British Industries, 1930–2. Chairman of the Scottish Development Council, 1931–9. Controller of Merchant Shipbuilding and Repairs, Board of Admiralty, 1940–6. President of the British Iron and Steel Federation, 1943–5.

below ground. All the ascendancy of the Hurricanes and Spitfires would have been fruitless but for this system of underground control centres and telephone cables, which had been devised and built before the war by the Air Ministry under Dowding's advice and impulse. Lasting credit is due to all concerned. In the South of England there were at this time No. 11 Group HQ and six subordinate Fighter Station Centres. All these were, as has been described, under heavy stress. The Supreme Command was exercised from the Fighter Headquarters at Stanmore, but the actual handling of the direction of the squadrons was wisely left to No. 11 Group, which controlled the units through its Fighter Stations located in each county.

The Group Operations Room was like a small theatre, about sixty feet across, and with two storeys. We took our seats in the Dress Circle. Below us was the large-scale map-table, around which perhaps twenty highly-trained young men and women, with their telephone assistants, were assembled. Opposite to us, covering the entire wall, where the theatre curtain would be, was a gigantic blackboard divided into six columns with electric bulbs, for the six fighter stations, each of their squadrons having a sub-column of its own, and also divided by lateral lines. Thus the lowest row of bulbs showed as they were lighted the squadrons which were 'Standing By' at two minutes' notice, the next row those at 'Readiness', five minutes, then at 'Available', twenty minutes, then those which had taken off, the next row those which had reported having seen the enemy, the next – with red lights – those which were in action, and the top row those which were returning home. On the left-hand side, in a kind of glass stage-box, were the four or five officers whose duty it was to weigh and measure the information received from our Observer Corps, which at this time numbered upwards of fifty thousand men, women, and youths. Radar was still in its infancy, but it gave warning of raids approaching our coast, and the observers, with field-glasses and portable telephones, were our main source of information about raiders flying overland. Thousands of messages were therefore received during an action. Several roomfuls of experienced people in other parts of the underground headquarters sifted them with great rapidity, and transmitted the results from minute to minute directly to the plotters seated around the table on the floor and to the officer supervising from the glass stage-box.

On the right hand was another glass stage-box containing Army officers who reported the action of our anti-aircraft batteries, of which at this time in the Command there were two hundred. At night it was of vital importance to stop these batteries firing over certain areas in which our fighters would be closing with the enemy. I was not unacquainted with the general outlines of this system, having had it explained to me a year before the war by Dowding when I visited him at Stanmore. It had been shaped and refined in constant action, and all was now fused together into a most elaborate instrument of war, the like of which existed nowhere in the world.

'I don't know,' said Park, as we went down, 'whether anything will happen to-day. At present all is quiet.' However, after a quarter of an hour the raid-plotters began to move about. An attack of '40 plus' was reported to be coming from the German stations in the Dieppe area. The bulbs along the bottom of the wall display-panel began to glow as various squadrons came to 'Stand By'. Then in quick succession '20 plus', '40 plus' signals were received, and in another ten minutes it was evident that a serious battle impended. On both sides the air began to fill.

One after another signals came in, '40 plus', '60 plus'; there was even an '80 plus'. On the floor-table below us the movement of all the waves of attack was marked by pushing discs forward from minute to minute along different lines of approach, while on the blackboard facing us the rising lights showed our fighter squadrons getting into the air, till there were only four or five left 'At Readiness'. These air battles, on which so much depended, lasted little more than an hour from the first encounter. The enemy had ample strength to send out new waves of attack, and our squadrons, having gone all out to gain the upper air, would have to refuel after seventy or eighty minutes, or land to rearm after a five-minute engagement. If at this moment of refuelling or rearming the enemy were able to arrive with fresh unchallenged squadrons some of our fighters could be destroyed on the ground. It was therefore one of our principal objects to direct our squadrons so as not to have too many on the ground refuelling or rearming simultaneously during daylight.

Presently the red bulbs showed that the majority of our squadrons were engaged. A subdued hum arose from the floor, where the busy plotters pushed their discs to and fro in accordance with the swiftly-changing situation. Air Vice-Marshal Park gave general directions for the disposition of his fighter force, which were translated into detailed orders to each Fighter Station by a youngish officer at the centre of the Dress Circle, at whose side I sat. Some years after I asked his name. He was Lord Willoughby de Broke.[1] (I met him next in 1947, when the Jockey Club, of which he was a Steward, invited me to see the Derby. He was surprised that I remembered the occasion.) He now gave the orders for the individual squadrons to ascend and patrol as the result of the final information which appeared on the map-table. The Air Marshal himself walked up and down behind, watching with vigilant eye every move in the game, supervising his junior executive hand, and only occasionally

---

[1] John Henry Peyto Verney Willoughby de Broke, 1896–1986. On active service, 1914–18 (Military Cross). Succeeded his father as 20th Baron, 1923 (the barony had been created in 1492). Commanded No. 605 (County of Warwick) Auxiliary Air Force Squadron, 1936–9. Lord Lieutenant of Warwickshire, 1939–68. Staff Officer, 11 Fighter Group, 1940 (despatches). Deputy Director, Public Relations, Air Ministry, 1940–4; Director, 1945–6. Steward of the Jockey Club, 1944–7 and 1964–7.

intervening with some decisive order, usually to reinforce a threatened area. In a little while all our squadrons were fighting, and some had already begun to return for fuel. All were in the air. The lower line of bulbs was out. There was not one squadron left in reserve. At this moment Park spoke to Dowding at Stanmore, asking for three squadrons from No. 12 Group to be put at his disposal in case of another major attack while his squadrons were rearming and refuelling. This was done. They were specially needed to cover London and our fighter aerodromes, because No. 11 Group had already shot their bolt.

The young officer, to whom this seemed a matter of routine, continued to give his orders, in accordance with the general directions of his Group Commander, in a calm, low monotone, and the three reinforcing squadrons were soon absorbed. I became conscious of the anxiety of the Commander, who now stood still behind his subordinate's chair. Hitherto I had watched in silence. I now asked: 'What other reserves have we?' 'There are none,' said Air Vice-Marshal Park. In an account which he wrote about it afterwards he said that at this I 'looked grave'. Well I might. What losses should we not suffer if our refuelling planes were caught on the ground by further raids of '40 plus' or '50 plus'! The odds were great; our margins small; the stakes infinite.

Another five minutes passed, and most of our squadrons had now descended to refuel. In many cases our resources could not give them overhead protection. Then it appeared that the enemy were going home. The shifting of the discs on the table below showed a continuous eastward movement of German bombers and fighters. No new attack appeared. In another ten minutes the action was ended. We climbed again the stairways which led to the surface, and almost as we emerged the 'All Clear' sounded.

'We are very glad, sir, you have seen this,' said Park. 'Of course, during the last twenty minutes we were so choked with information that we couldn't handle it. This shows you the limitation of our present resources. They have been strained far beyond their limits to-day.' I asked whether any results had come to hand, and remarked that the attack appeared to have been repelled satisfactorily. Park replied that he was not satisfied that we had intercepted as many raiders as he had hoped we should. It was evident that the enemy had everywhere pierced our defences. Many scores of German bombers, with their fighter escort, had been reported over London. About a dozen had been brought down while I was below, but no picture of the results of the battle or of the damage or losses could be obtained.

It was 4.30 p.m. before I got back to Chequers, and I immediately went to bed for my afternoon sleep.[1]

---

[1] But not before telephoning Desmond Morton in London (see the next document).

September 1940

Desmond Morton: note
(*Premier papers, 3/276*)

15 September 1940

The Prime Minister, at Chequers, telephoned Major Morton at 10 Downing Street, 1715, 15.9.40., and instructed him as follows:–

(1) To call together by 1800 the Chiefs of Staff or Vice-Chiefs, to consider the situation of 'Menace' as a result of the arrival at Dakar of French warship reinforcements, and to take action as under;

(2) The Prime Minister directs that 'Menace', as at present proposed, should be cancelled, in view of the arrival of the French reinforcements;

(3) In place of 'Menace', the original operation 'Scipio' should be carried out with the utmost despatch;

(4) By 'Scipio', the Prime Minister understands that the 'Menace' force, or part of it, will land at Conakry and make its way up the railway so as to cut the communications of Dakar from the land. At the same time, a sufficient naval force will blockade Dakar from the sea and cut all sea-borne communications between Dakar and Vichy France or other sources of supply or reinforcements.

(5) The Prime Minister considers that the land force proceeding from Conakry up the railway must be adequate, and that, therefore, some of the Commandos should accompany the Free French force. In his opinion, it is no longer essential to keep the operation wholly French. It is far more important that the operation should succeed.

(6) The Prime Minister considers that the utmost despatch is called for, since, if we do not get there first, the Vichy forces at Dakar may proceed, and may indeed already be proceeding, up their railway towards the frontier of French Equatorial Africa, which might produce a situation of great gravity.

(7) The Prime Minister directs that the necessary signals should be drafted by the Chiefs of Staff Committee, and that they should then be telephoned to him at Chequers for him to give his approval to them. If any further written appreciation or plan other than the signals is necessary, copy should be sent to him at Chequers by Special Messenger.

DM

Winston S. Churchill: recollection
(*'Their Finest Hour', page 297*)

15 September 1940

I must have been tired by the drama of No. 11 Group, for I did not wake till eight. When I rang, John Martin, my Principal Private Secretary, came in with the evening budget of news from all over the world. It was repellent. This had gone wrong here; that had been delayed there; an unsatisfactory answer had been received from so-and-so; there had been bad sinkings in the Atlantic. 'However,' said Martin, as he finished this account, 'all is redeemed by the air. We have shot down one hundred and eighty-three for a loss of under forty.'

Winston S. Churchill to Colonel Jacob
(*Churchill papers, 20/13*)

15 September 1940

More than a year ago it was considered possible that we should soon be able to develop RDF inland. Since then, however, we have relied entirely on the Observer Corps. These have done splendid work; but in cloudy weather like yesterday and to-day, they have the greatest difficulty in functioning accurately. If we could have even half a dozen stations which could work inland, I am assured that very great advantages would be reaped in interception. This is especially important over the Sheerness–Isle of Wight promontory, which is likely to be the main line of air attack on London. I am told that there are duplicate installations already at some of the stations on this sector of the coast as an insurance against bombing. These might be turned round and put in action. In other cases new stations could be made. I regard this matter as of the highest urgency.

2. To-morrow, Monday, Air Marshal Joubert will assemble all necessary scientific authorities and make a report that day to me on –
  (a) the desirability of the above.
  (b) its practicability and the time it will take to get even a few stations into action.

He should make proposals for putting into service at the earliest moment: six or twelve stations, and for rebuilding their reserves.

3. Should a feasible scheme emerge, I will myself bring it before the Minister of Aircraft Production.

WSC

Sir Archibald Sinclair to Winston S. Churchill
(*Churchill papers, 20/8*)

15 September 1940   Air Ministry
Personal

Winston,
  One thing worries me these days – that you stay at Downing Street without a proper shelter. This is sad backsliding since we last made war together,

September 1940   819

when you insisted on battalion headquarters having the best shelter that was available at Laurence Farm![1] You were right then but you <u>must</u> apply the same principle now & go and live in the War Room or somewhere where reasonable protection exists. You are making us ridiculous if you insist on us living in basements & refuse to do it yourself! Whether the country would agree about the rest of us I am not sure – but I am quite sure that they would be angry as well as amazed if they knew that you were not sleeping in reasonable safety.

                                                                   Yours ever,
                                                                      Archie

Winston S. Churchill to Colonel Jacob
(*Premier papers, 3/222/4*)

16 September 1940

Pray send a copy of this report[2] to the Chiefs of the Staff for C-in-C Home Forces, adding 'I consider that fog is the gravest danger, as it throws both Air Forces out of action, baffles our artillery, prevents organized Naval attack, and specially favours the infiltration tactics by which the enemy will most probably seek to secure his lodgments. Should conditions of fog prevail, the strongest possible Air barrage must be put down upon the invasion ports during the night and early morning. I should be glad to be advised on the proposed Naval action by our flotillas, both in darkness and at dawn, (a) if the fog lies more on the English than the French side of the Channel, (b) if it is uniform on both sides.

Are we proposing to use radio aids to nevigation?

Prolonged conditions of stand-by under frequent Air bombardment will be exhausting to the enemy. None the less, fog is our foe.'

                                                                         WSC

John Colville: diary
(*Colville papers*)

16 September 1940

At No. 10 there is a certain chaos caused by the fact that the building is thought to be unsafe. The basement is being fitted up for the PM to live and to

---

[1] The farm on the Western Front, at the Belgian village of Ploegsteert, which was Churchill's battalion headquarters from January to June 1916.
[2] Not printed.

work in, and meanwhile much of the time, both by day and by night, is being spent in the disagreeable atmosphere of the Central War Room.[1]

War Cabinet: Confidential Annex
(*Cabinet papers, 65/15*)

16 September 1940 Cabinet War Room
12 noon

The War Cabinet had before them a Report by the Chiefs of Staff (COS (40)4 (0)), relating to the situation of the Operation 'Menace', as a result of the arrival at Dakar of French warship reinforcements.

The Prime Minister said that the operation 'Scipio' was first conceived on the 4th August when it was proposed that General de Gaulle should land with a Free French Force in French West Africa where it was hoped he would be welcomed. This plan had been approved in principle by the War Cabinet. On the 7th August, 1940, General de Gaulle prepared a new plan, which entailed landing at a West African port, giving a revised date for reaching there as about the 10th September, 1940.

On the 8th August he (the Prime Minister) had asked for a plan to be prepared, in which British forces should be included, in order to put General de Gaulle ashore. In compliance with these instructions Operation 'Menace' was planned. The approximate date of arrival under this plan which was approved by the War Cabinet on the 13th August, 1940, was 8th September, 1940. Subsequently, this date was put back to the 12th September, 1940, but the delay of 24 hours in operation 'Hats' postponed it until the 13th.

When this plan was submitted to the Commanders they decided that it was essential that the expedition should go first to Freetown where certain refuelling and reloading would take place. This move added six days to the time at which the expedition could reach the rendezvous, i.e., the operation was then timed for the 18th September, 1940. This delay had been fatal. At the time the original 'Scipio' expedition had been conceived it had been necessary to take the Poles into our confidence as they were taking part in it, and gradually word got back to France, with the result that the Vichy

---

[1] On 21 October 1940 Churchill and his wife moved from 10 Downing Street to a group of adjacent rooms above ground in the former Board of Trade Building at Storey's Gate immediately above the Cabinet War Rooms, and overlooking St James's Park. The windows overlooking the park were fitted with metal shutters and the rooms were fortified with iron girders. Known as 'Number Ten Annexe' (though they had no direct connection to Downing Street), the rooms were given the code name 'The Barn'. For the rest of the war, while Churchill was in London, he slept there, and not underground.

Government had shown surprising resource and sent a force of warships, which, after refuelling at Casablanca and eluding our forces sent to intercept them, had arrived at Dakar. This event had altered the whole situation. To undertake the operation 'Menace' in these circumstances was, in his opinion, out of the question, and in view of the fact that the French warships might have troops on board would, if attempted, end in bloodshed.

The Prime Minister continuing said that a fiasco had undoubtedly occurred, and it was to be hoped that it would not too much engage public attention. The Chiefs of Staff now advised that General de Gaulle and his force should proceed at once to Duala, disembark there, and advance into Chad province. The British troops which had been sent out for the expedition would be brought back to this country, with the exception of one battalion of Marines which would remain at Freetown.

The War Cabinet:–
(a) Approved the recommendation of the Chiefs of Staff that General de Gaulle and his force should proceed at once to Duala, disembark there and advance into Chad province.
(b) Approved the despatch of the draft telegram to Admiral Cunningham giving effect to (a) above.
(c) Requested the Chiefs of Staff to consider how they would dispose of the British forces forming part of the force for Operation 'Menace'.

Winston S. Churchill to Combined Command, Dakar Force[1]
(*Churchill papers, 20/14*)

16 September 1940

You are fully at liberty to consider the whole situation yourselves and consult de Gaulle, and we shall carefully consider then any advice you may give. The whole question is largely affected by reference in your Part 3 as to whether arrival of cruisers has raised morale, and if this can be ascertained and how soon.

Have you considered the possibility of French cruisers having taken reinforcements to Dakar?

---

[1] General Irwin and Admiral John Cunningham.

War Cabinet: Confidential Annex
(*Cabinet papers, 65/15*)

17 September 1940   Cabinet War Room
12 noon

The First Lord of the Admiralty said that a telegram had been received the previous evening from the Senior Officer, Force 'M',[1] suggesting that until it was known to what extent the arrival of the Cruisers had raised the local morale, their presence did not alter the previous Naval situation.

The Prime Minister said that, on receipt of this message, he had authorised the despatch of a telegram to the effect that the Commanders were at liberty to consider the whole situation themselves and to consult General de Gaulle, and that we would carefully consider any advice they might give. His own view was that, if there was danger of having to use considerable force, it was better not to proceed with the Operation. But there could be no harm in hearing what the Officers in charge of the Operation had to say in regard to the situation. The telegram which had been despatched in no way committed us to a new course of action.

Winston S. Churchill: speech
(*Hansard*)

17 September 1940   House of Commons
4.20 p.m.

The Prime Minister (Mr Churchill): I do not feel it necessary to make any lengthy statement to the House to-day upon the general war position. Practically all the facts not of a secret nature have already been made public. The advance of the Italian army from Libya is in progress. The two British platoons which have been holding Sollum have been withdrawn. Sharp fighting is taking place upon the desert flank between the armoured vehicles of both sides. The enemy is still some distance from our position of resistance. We must see what happens.

The deployment of the German barges and ships in preparation for the invasion of Great Britain and Ireland continues steadily, and we must expect that he will make an attempt at what he judges to be the best opportunity. All our preparations must therefore be maintained in a state of vigilance. The process of waiting, keyed up to concert pitch day after day, is apt after a while to lose its charm of novelty. There is no doubt that it imposes a heavy strain

---

[1] Force M was the naval force carrying out Operation 'Menace' against the Vichy forces in Dakar: it was commanded by Admiral John Cunningham on board the battleship HMS *Barham*.

upon all concerned, but we must not under-rate the damage inflicted upon the enemy, who also has to wait, by the very heavy and prolonged nightly bombings upon his concentrations of ships and upon all the focal points of his assembly of troops. Undoubtedly serious injury has been done to his ships and barges, and meanwhile our own strength, I am able to assure the House, develops steadily by land, by sea, and above all in the air. Sunday's action was the most brilliant and fruitful of any fought upon a large scale up to that date by the fighters of the Royal Air Force. The figures have already been made public. To the best of my belief – and I have made searching inquiries and taken several cross checks – these figures are not in any way exaggerated. Neither side has yet employed more than a portion of its forces, but there are good reasons for believing at the present time that very grievous inroads are being made upon the enemy's superiority of numbers, and we may await the decision of this prolonged air battle with sober but increasing confidence.

The German attacks upon the civil population have been concentrated mainly upon London, in the hopes of terrorising its citizens into submission or to throw them into confusion, and, of course, in the silly idea that they will put pressure upon the Government to make peace. The deliberate and repeated attacks upon Buckingham Palace[1] and upon the persons of our beloved King and Queen are also intended, apart from their general barbarity, to have an unsettling effect upon public opinion. They have, of course, the opposite effect. They unite the King and Queen to their people by new and sacred bonds of common danger, and they steel the hearts of all to the stern and unrelenting prosecution of the war against so foul a foe.

I gave the House when I last addressed them the casualty figures up to the end of August and without prejudice to our habit of publishing the figures monthly. I may now mention that during the first half of September about 2,000 civilians – men, women and children – have been killed, and about 8,000 wounded by air bombardment. Four-fifths of these casualties have occurred in London. Many hospitals and churches and public monuments have been damaged, but the injury to our war-making capacity has been surprisingly small. We are only now beginning to get the increased flow of production from the great programmes which were started on the outbreak of the war, and it is very agreeable to see that the increases are maintained over so wide a field in spite of the enemy's fire. To show how indiscriminate and wanton is the enemy's attack, one has only to compare the figures of civilian

---

[1] On 9 September 1940 a bomb fell on the north side of Buckingham Palace, lodging itself under the stone steps of the Regency Room. It did not explode and the King continued to use his study immediately above it. It went off, however, at 1.25 the next morning. All the windows on all floors, including in the royal apartments, were shattered. The King and Queen had spent the night at Windsor. Only four days later the Palace was bombed again, by German aircraft flying up the Mall, while the King and Queen were in it: six bombs exploded, and four Palace workmen were injured. One of them, Alfred Davies, a plumber, died of his injuries a week later.

casualties in the first fortnight of this month with the military casualties. There were, as I have said, 10,000 civilian casualties from air attack, but only some 250 of these occurred in all the Fighting Forces.

The air-raid precautions organisation in all its branches has proved its efficiency, and the greatest discipline and devotion have been shown by all. The fire brigades are, of course, conspicuous, but in paying tribute to them there must be no disparagement to all the other forms of service which have been faithfully and punctiliously discharged. Of course, the task of preserving the health and well-being of this enormous community in the Thames Valley, exceeding 8,000,000 souls, living under artificial conditions of civilisation, and of supplying them with food and all other necessities and of making provision for those whose homes have been destroyed or who have had to be evacuated – all this and much else have, as the House will realise, cast a strain upon the machinery of government which calls for ceaseless exertion by all authorities concerned. I am glad to say that this heavy and intricate task is being efficiently and successfully discharged, and our whole system of life and labour is being rapidly adapted to conditions hitherto unknown to modern society. Constant adjustments have to be made and defects remedied in the light of experience. As I said last time, a great deal of our progress must be by trial and error. We have to feel our way and do our best to meet each defect as it reveals itself.

I had hoped, as I said when I last spoke during the week that has passed, to promulgate some new rules about air-raid warnings, but the intensification of the air attack has made it difficult to draw precise conclusions, and, in spite of my desire to make good my undertaking to the House, I feel that it is wiser for the moment to allow the process of local adaptation to run its course. Broadly speaking, our plan must be to use the siren, which, it may be noted, has been cut in two, as an alert and not as an alarm, and to have a system of highly trained what I may call Jim Crows or look-out men, who will give the alarm when immediate danger is expected at any point. Upon this basis everyone must endeavour to carry on his work and see that output and the public services do not suffer or suffer only the minimum interruption. No doubt, we shall work up to a much higher standard than we have at present attained in many respects, but I feel it better to proceed empirically than, at this moment, to try to make precise conditions; because, after all, we must expect that very much more intense examples of air fighting will be experienced in future than we have yet seen.

There are some matters connected with our arrangements under air attack which I should prefer to discuss in private. I must remind the House that every word spoken in public Session can be telegraphed all over the world; and that there is no reason why we should keep the enemy informed of the details of our arrangements, and thus enable him to inflict the maximum injury upon us. We do not receive any similar information from him about his way of life; although, I am sure, our military staffs would be very much convenienced thereby. There are several things that I wish to say to the House, and I dare say there are many things that hon. Members would like to say to the Government. Therefore, I propose that we should now move into Secret Session, and I declare to you, Mr Speaker that, casting my eyes around, I spy strangers.[1]

Winston S. Churchill: speech
(*'Secret Session Speeches', pages 17–23*)

17 September 1940　　　　　　　　　　　　　　　　　　House of Commons

The reason why I asked the House to go into Secret Session was not because I had anything particularly secret or momentous to say. It was only because there are some things which it is better for us to talk over among ourselves than when we are overheard by the Germans. I wish to speak about the Sittings of the House and how we are to discharge our Parliamentary duties.

A few days ago I had a notification from the Chiefs of the Staff. They considered that the date and time of this meeting of ours to-day had been so widely advertised that to hold it would be to incur an undue risk, and that it should be put off to some date and hour which had not been publicly announced. I felt, however, that Members would be offended if any course was taken which suggested for a moment that we should shirk our duty out of considerations of personal safety. And then there is all that argument which occurs to everyone of our setting an example, and of the incongruity of our ordering Government Departments, and urging factory workers to remain at work, while we ourselves did not assemble on particular occasions as we had resolved to do. Moreover, the rules of the House are such that we could only have avoided meeting at this hour by an earlier meeting on Monday, which would alter the hour, and a Monday meeting would have caused much inconvenience under the present conditions of travel.

I, therefore, took the responsibility of disregarding the very well-meant warning which we had received from those charged with the technical burden of national defence.

Nevertheless, this is a matter on which there should be clear thinking. We should fail in our duty if we went to the other extreme, and in a spirit of mettlesome bravado made it unduly easy for the enemy to inflict loss and inconvenience upon the public service. We ought not to flatter ourselves by imagining that we are irreplaceable, but at the same time it cannot be denied

---

[1] At this point, the *Hansard* reporters left and the public galleries were cleared for the start of a secret session.

that two or three hundred by-elections would be a quite needless complication of our affairs at this particular juncture. Moreover, I suppose that if Hitler made a clean sweep of the Houses of Parliament it would give widespread and unwholesome satisfaction throughout Germany, and be vaunted as another triumph for the Nazi system of Government. We must exercise reasonable prudence and a certain amount of guile in combating the malice of the enemy. It is no part of good sense to proclaim the hour and dates of our meetings long beforehand.

There are two kinds of air risks, the general and the particular. The general risk in air raids is largely negligible. It is at least a thousand to one. But the risk of staying in a particular building which the enemy undoubtedly regard as a military objective, is of a different order. Here we are sitting on the target. This group of well-known, prominent buildings and towers between three major railway stations, with the river as a perfect guide by night and day, is the easiest of all targets, and I have very little doubt that they will need extensive repairs before very long. We have seen how unscrupulous and spiteful the enemy is by his daylight attacks on Buckingham Palace. And anyone has only to walk to Smith Square or St Thomas's Hospital to see the kind of damage that a single aeroplane can do. We have not got to think only of ourselves in considering the matter. There is a large number of officials and staff attached to the House who have to be in attendance upon us when we are sitting. This building itself is not well constructed to withstand aerial bombardment. There is an immense amount of glass about the place, and the passages are long and narrow before the blast and splinter-proof shelters can be reached. There is no certain defence against the attacks which might so easily be made. There is no guarantee that the warning will be given in time. Even our watcher up aloft would very likely give his signal only at the moment when the bombs were already released. The firing of the artillery is no useful warning because it fires so often, and we should be hindered in our business if we attended to that.

If we are to do our duty properly we ought to adapt our arrangements to the peculiar conditions under which we live. Therefore, I am going to propose to the House three measures which they will find fully consonant with their dignity and with their duty, and with your permission, Mr Speaker, I now propose to outline their character.

The first is that the hours and dates of our sittings shall not be made public in the Press or announced beforehand, and that they shall be lapped in uncertainty. This is a very considerable protection, because it removes a large part of the incentive to the enemy. If we are not known to be gathered here, a large part of the attractiveness of the Palace of Westminster as a target will be gone, and we may have the use of the building and its conveniences for a longer period than is otherwise possible. Therefore I propose to move that when we adjourn to-day it will be to an hour and a date which will as far as possible be kept secret. The date should evidently be to-morrow, because it is inconvenient for Members to come from all over the country under present conditions merely for a single day's sitting.

But the Second Measure which I propose is that we should alter the hour of our sittings. We must expect that at any time after dark the nightly air raiding will begin. Our barrage will be firing, and, apart from bombs, great numbers of shell splinters usually described most erroneously as shrapnel, will be falling in the streets. It is better for Members and the officials and staff of the House to be in their homes or in their shelters before this begins. I shall therefore propose that we meet at eleven in the morning, and conclude our business at four in the afternoon, with half-an-hour for the Debate on the Adjournment.

This brings me to my third proposal. The fact that we meet in the mornings will be a great convenience to Members, but it only throws a heavier burden on Ministers and the Public Departments. Not only Cabinets but many scores of important meetings take place every morning, and the whole work of the Staffs and the Departments in the afternoon is affected by their decisions. If any large number of Ministers have to be in attendance upon the House, the whole progress of War Administration will be delayed or even deranged. Take the case of the Minister of Health, who is to-morrow to be in charge of a Debate upon the general health of the nation. That is a most interesting and important topic. But the Minister of Health is already working to the utmost limit of his strength on the many difficult situations created by the bombing of London; by its effects on drainage which is a serious problem, some of our great sewers having been broken; upon the rehousing of persons rendered homeless through their dwellings being destroyed or damaged, or because they have to be evacuated from districts on account of unexploded bombs or other special causes. He has also to deal with the dangers to national health arising out of people being crowded together in shelters, and contracting diseases which under these conditions, unless they are vigorously coped with, may foster epidemics of diphtheria, typhoid and influenza. In fact he is fighting the danger of pestilence.

Now I am first of all a Parliamentarian and House of Commons man. If I have any say in matters at the present time, it is due mainly to this House, and I therefore set Parliamentary duties above everything, subject, of course, to the leave of the House which I am sure would be generously given. My right hon. Friend will therefore carry out the programme as it has been arranged if the House so desires. But I must appeal to the House to show its consideration for Ministers, and for a Government in whom it has recorded its confidence almost unanimously. We are really doing our very best. There are no doubt many mistakes and shortcomings. A lot of things are done none too well. Some things that ought to be done have not yet been done. Some things have been done that had better have been left undone. But looking broadly at the whole picture as it is viewed by any impartial eye, the way in which our system of Government and society is standing up to its present ordeals, which will certainly increase in severity, constitutes a magnificent achievement, and has justly commanded the wonder and admiration of every friendly nation in the world. I ask therefore for the indulgence of the House, and for its support in not requiring too many sittings in the next month or two. I shall propose when we adjourn on Thursday that we adjourn until Tuesday, October 15. We shall, of course, meet a good deal earlier, but the House will be asked to leave the exact date unspecified and to be proposed by me as Leader of the House to Mr Speaker, giving sufficient notice to Members for their convenience. Of course if anything happens which raises any novel or fundamental issue, for which the authority of Parliament is required, we shall immediately summon Parliament even if it were only a few days after we have separated, and we shall make it our business to keep in touch with all parties and groups, not only through what are called 'the usual channels' but through any other channels which may be open.

Some ignorant people suppose that Members of Parliament are only doing their duty when they are sitting in this Chamber, either making or listening to speeches. But surely at this time of all others Members not otherwise occupied in national service may do invaluable work in their own constituencies. This is especially true of constituencies which have been knocked about by the enemy's fire, and where the people will have need of having their representative among them to share their dangers, resolve their perplexities, and if it were ever necessary, uphold their spirit.

These next few weeks are grave and anxious. I said just now in the Public Session that the deployment of the enemy's invasion preparations and the assembly of his ships and barges is steadily proceeding, and that at any moment a major assault may be launched upon this Island. I now say in secret that upwards of 1,700 self-propelled barges and more than 200 sea-going ships, some very large ships, are already gathered at the many invasion ports in German occupation. If this is all a pretence and stratagem to pin us down here, it has been executed with surprising thoroughness and on a gigantic scale. Some of these ships and barges, when struck by our bombing counter-attack and preventive attack, have blown up with tremendous explosions, showing that they are fully loaded with all the munitions needed for the invading armies and to beat us down and subjugate us utterly. The shipping available and now assembled is sufficient to carry in one voyage nearly *half* a million men. We should, of course, expect to drown a great many on the way over, and to destroy a large proportion of their vessels. But when you reflect upon the many points from which they could start, and upon the fact that even the most likely sector of invasion, i.e., the sector in which enemy fighter support is available for their bombers and dive-bombers, extending from the Wash to the Isle of Wight, is nearly as long as the whole front in France from the Alps to the sea, and also upon the dangers of fog or artificial fog, one must expect many lodgments or attempted lodgments to be made on our Island simultaneously. These we shall hope to deal with as they occur, and also to cut off the supply across the sea by which the enemy will seek to nourish his lodgments.

The difficulties of the invader are not ended when he sets foot on shore. A new chapter of perils opens upon him. I am confident that we shall succeed in defeating and largely destroying this most tremendous onslaught by which we are now threatened, and anyhow, whatever happens, we will all go down fighting to the end. I feel as sure as the sun will rise to-morrow that we shall be victorious. But I ask the House to assist us in solving these problems, worse than any that have ever threatened a civilized community before, by meeting the wishes of the Government in the arrangement of Parliamentary business and in lightening the burden which rests upon the men in charge.

Formal Resolutions in accordance with what I have said will be proposed to the House for their approval this afternoon while the House is still in Secret Session.

Harold Nicolson: diary
('*Diaries and Letters, 1939–1945*')

17 September 1940

Winston warns us that the bombing will get worse and that the Germans may seek to land 500,000 men in this country. I must say that he does not try to cheer us up with vain promises.

Winston S. Churchill to Sir Edward Bridges and General Ismay
(*Churchill papers, 20/13*)

17 September 1940
ACTION THIS DAY

Please report by to-morrow night the number of hours on September 16 that the principal offices in London were in their dug-outs and out of action through air alarm.

2. General Ismay should find out how the Air Ministry and Fighter Command view the idea that no red warning should be given when only two or three aircraft are approaching London.

WSC

Captain Berkeley: diary
(*Berkeley papers*)

17 September 1940

The onslaught against London continues by day and night. We have now all through the dark hours a tremendous firing of guns of all types. For this we have to thank the PM, who stamped and shouted a week ago that something must be done or morale would crack. The searchlights had proved quite useless, and people were getting desperate listening to the buzzing of the Boche wandering unopposed in the London sky, picking his targets. So the guns were brought in. There are now no lights but a sound detection system and a concentrated barrage on a likely patch. The effect is good: the Boche turns tail pretty quick. But he's apt to drop his load anywhere as he goes.

Winston S. Churchill to General Sikorski
(*Churchill papers, 20/14*)

17 September 1940

I deeply appreciated your telegram of the 14th September conveying the relief felt by the Polish Government, the Polish armed forces and the Polish people at the fortunate escape of the King and Queen from the recent German bombing of Buckingham Palace. As Their Majesties stated, these dastardly attacks have only strengthened the resolution of all of us to fight through to final victory.

Winston S. Churchill to General Ismay
(*Churchill papers, 20/13*)

17 September 1940

In all circumstances it would be impossible to withdraw the New Zealand Brigade from their forward position on the Dover promontory.[1] The two cruiser tank battalions cannot go. Would it not be better to keep the Australians back and delay the whole convoy until the third week in October. After all none of these forces going round the Cape can possibly arrive in time

---

[1] The minutes of a Chiefs of Staff Committee meeting at 10.30 that morning recorded: 'At a previous meeting the Committee recommended and the Prime Minister approved that the sailing of the Middle East convoy, consisting of the Australian and New Zealand Forces, two Cruiser Tank Battalions and other important reinforcements, should be postponed for one week, i.e. till 2nd October. After some discussion it was agreed to recommend that the convoy should sail on the 2nd October but that the two Cruiser Tank Battalions should remain in the United Kingdom' (*Cabinet papers, 79/6*).

to influence the impending battle in Egypt. But they may play a big part here. Perhaps by the third week in October the Admiralty will be prepared to run greater risks. Anyhow we cannot afford to make sure that the New Zealanders and the Tank Battalion are out of action throughout October in either theatre.

WSC

War Cabinet: Confidential Annex
(*Cabinet papers, 65/15*)

17 September 1940
9 p.m.

Cabinet War Room

DAKAR

The Prime Minister agreed that the accretion of strength resulting from the arrival of six medium-sized warships, was not great; but their arrival might strengthen the determination of the pro-Vichy Forces in Dakar. In particular, the coastal batteries at Dakar might now be resolutely manned. From our own point of view, the new factor in the situation was that Admiral Cunningham and General Irwin, after the close study of the plans for Operation 'Menace' for which the voyage had given them the opportunity, were anxious to proceed with the direct operation against Dakar. It must be assumed that they considered themselves to be in a position to deal with the coastal batteries. Were the War Cabinet prepared to say to them 'If you, the Commanders on the spot, are anxious, after due consideration, to proceed with the original plan, we will back you'?

The Prime Minister invited attention to the political aspects of the problem. Although we did not desire a state of war with the Vichy Government, the War Cabinet has so far been prepared to take strong action against that Government's warships. They had lived to bless the day on which they had decided upon the 'Oran' Operation, and they had been prepared to force their way by arms into Dakar, should peaceful persuasion fail. Similarly, only a few days previously, they had been prepared for our ships to sink the six warships which had sailed from Toulon rather than allow them to enter Dakar. It was clear, therefore, that the War Cabinet did not rate highly the dangers of any hostile reactions from Vichy.

The Prime Minister thought that insufficient attention had been paid to the moral effects of a failure of operation 'Menace'. If our expedition came back with its tail between its legs, we could hardly hope that the fact would escape notice.

War Cabinet: Confidential Annex
(*Cabinet papers, 65/15*)

18 September 1940 Prime Minister's Room
12 noon House of Commons

The First Sea Lord said that the *Renown* and six destroyers were west of Gibraltar patrolling off Casablanca. He asked what action should be taken to deal with French ships which passed through the Straits.

The Prime Minister thought that the right course was that the ships should be interrogated and asked where they were going. If they were only going to Casablanca, they should be allowed to proceed, but we should endeavour to prevent them from proceeding beyond that point.

Winston S. Churchill to Admiral John Cunningham and General Irwin
(*Admiralty papers, 205/6*)

18 September 1940 10 Downing Street

We cannot judge relative advantages of alternative schemes from here. We give you full authority to go ahead and do what you think is best, in order to give effect to the original purpose of the expedition. Keep us informed.

WSC

Winston S. Churchill to General Wavell
(*Premier papers, 3/309/1*)

18 September 1940

On the eve of what may prove to be one of the memorable battles of history[1] I send you every wish for good fortune and my assurance that all acts or decisions of valour and violence against the enemy will, whatever their upshot, receive the resolute support of His Majesty's Government.

---

[1] On 13 September, Italian forces, far superior in number to those under Wavell's command, had crossed from Libya into Egypt, occupying the port of Sollum. On the night of 17 September they took Sidi Barrani. During the battle, more than 400 Italian soldiers were killed, for 40 British deaths. The Italian forces then halted, having extended their lines of communication eastward by sixty miles, and did not in fact make a further advance, as Churchill had feared. In his memoirs, Churchill wrote: 'When I look back on all these worries, I remember the story of the old man who said on his deathbed that he had had a lot of trouble in his life, much of which had never happened . . . The Italians did not press their attack upon Egypt' (*Their Finest Hour*, page 418).

Winston S. Churchill to General Ismay
(*Premier papers, 3/22/6*)

18 September 1940
ACTION THIS DAY

Let precise orders be given for an experiment to be made with chemical searchlights without further delay. Professor Lindemann will draw up the general specification of the experiment which you should embody in a note and show me this day.

Report to me any officer or official who appears inclined to obstruct this experiment. Detail an officer from your Secretariat to make sure it gets fair play. We shall never get a move on unless examples are made.

WSC

Winston S. Churchill to General Ismay
(*Churchill papers, 20/13*)

18 September 1940
ACTION THIS DAY

Inquire from the COS Committee whether in view of the rough weather Alert No. 1 might not be discreetly relaxed to the next grade.

Report to me.

WSC

Winston S. Churchill to General Ismay
(*Premier papers, 3/264*)

18 September 1940
ACTION THIS DAY

Make inquiries whether there is no way in which a sheet of flaming oil cannot be spread over one or more of the invasion harbours. This is no more than the old fire-ship story with modern improvements that was tried at Dunkirk in the days of the Armada. The Admiralty can surely think of something.

WSC

Winston S. Churchill to Herbert Morrison
(*Churchill papers, 20/13*)

18 September 1940
ACTION THIS DAY

The De Wilde ammunition is of extreme importance. I was present at Headquarters of No. 11 Fighter Group, which covers all Kent, when the attached report[1] was made to the Commanding Officer.[2] All he said was: 'We fought without it before, we can fight without it again,' but it was evidently considered a great blow. I can quite understand the output dropping to 38,000 rounds in the week while you are moving from Woolwich and getting reinstated, but I trust it will revive again. Pray let me know your future forecast for the next four weeks. If there is revival in prospect, we might perhaps draw a little upon our reserve.

Winston S. Churchill to A. V. Alexander
(*Churchill papers, 20/13*)

18 September 1940
ACTION THIS DAY

When is *Erebus* coming into action, and what is the plan for her employment? These delays are very serious.

WSC

Winston S. Churchill to A. V. Alexander
(*Churchill papers, 20/13*)

18 September 1940

Surely you can run to a new Admiralty flag. It grieves me to see the present dingy object every morning.

WSC

Winston S. Churchill to Herbert Morrison
(*Churchill papers, 20/13*)

18 September 1940

The enemy will try by magnetic mines and other devices to smash as much glass as possible, and the winter is coming on. We must immediately revert to more primitive conditions in regard to daylight in dwellings. All glass in the

---
[1] Not printed.
[2] Air Vice-Marshal Park.

country should be held, and every effort made to increase the supply. Everyone should be encouraged or pressed to reduce window-glass to at least one-quarter of its present compass, keeping the rest as spare. Windows should be filled as may be most convenient with plywood or other fabric and the spare panes kept to replace the one to be preserved. The quicker this can be done in the target centres the better. Will you convene a meeting of the Departments concerned and reach decisions for action of a violent character and on the broadest lines, inviting me to assist you in suppressing obstruction.

WSC

Winston S. Churchill to Sir John Anderson
(*Churchill papers, 20/13*)

18 September 1940

Proceed as you have proposed, but let me have a report on Friday. The first task, apart from organising the stimulation and standardization of Honours, is the question of the new decoration. Lord Chatfield[1] should busy himself upon this and make proposals. At the moment I am inclined to a 'George Cross,' which may gradually come to hold its own with the Victoria Cross, and will be for the few outstanding deeds of *éclat*, and for a 'George Medal,' which will be given by thousands over the whole area of non-military good conduct and valour.[2]

Chiefs of Staff Committee: minutes
(*Cabinet papers, 79/6*)

19 September 1940   Cabinet War Room
5 p.m.

WEST AFRICA

A discussion took place on the action to be taken with French cruisers which had been apprehended off the West Coast of Africa.

The Prime Minister stressed the importance of preventing these cruisers from returning to Dakar.

---

[1] Alfred Ernle Montacute Chatfield, 1873–1967. Entered the Royal Navy, 1886. Served at the battles of Heligoland (1914), Dogger Bank (1915) and Jutland (1916). Fourth Sea Lord, 1919–20. Knighted, 1919. Rear-Admiral, 1920. Assistant Chief of the Naval Staff, 1920–2. Third Sea Lord, 1925–8. Commander-in-Chief, Atlantic Fleet, 1929–31. Vice-Admiral, 1930. Commander-in-Chief, Mediterranean, 1931–2. First Sea Lord, January 1933 to September 1938. Admiral of the Fleet, 1935. Created Baron, 1937. Privy Councillor, 1939. Minister for Co-ordination of Defence, 1939–40 (with a seat in the War Cabinet). Chairman, Civil Defence Honours Committee, 1940–6. Author of *The Navy and Defence* (1942), and *It Might Happen Again* (1947). In 1937 he was elected to the Other Club.

[2] The first George Cross awards were announced on 30 September 1940 (see page 717, note 1).

JAPAN

Sir Dudley Pound said that the despatch of a fleet, superior to the Japanese fleet, to the Far East would mean sending both our fleets at present stationed in the Mediterranean, together with a major portion of the Home Fleet. At the present time this would not be feasible.

Sir John Dill stressed the importance of denying the Malay Peninsula to the Japanese since if they obtained a firm foothold in the Peninsula they could establish air bases from which the fortress of Singapore could be threatened. Having established themselves firmly on the mainland, the Japanese would then be free to advance southwards and bring the fortress under artillery fire to which the coast defence batteries could make no reply. The GOC in C's[1] plan was to dispose his forces so as to prevent the Japanese seizing aerodromes in the Peninsula.

Sir Cyril Newall emphasized that the danger to Singapore lay not so much in its capture by the Japanese as the denial of its facilities for use by the fleet if the Japanese secured a firm foothold on the mainland.

The Prime Minister considered that the threat to Singapore had been overrated. In the first place, we were hoping to avoid hostilities with Japan and there was no reason to suppose that war with that country was a foregone conclusion. Even if Japan did declare war, it was, in his view, most unlikely that they would be inclined or be able to mount an attack against Singapore. The Japanese had shown themselves consistently reluctant to send their fleet far afield and if they were to embark on an expedition 2,000 miles from their homeland they would always have the fear of the American fleet on their flank[2] and of the arrival of the British fleet to cut them off before they had achieved their object of reducing the fortress. In the air the Japanese had not proved themselves formidable opponents and, judging by the resistance which the relatively unprotected and vulnerable city of London had put up to the heavy scale of attack of the German air force, it seemed illogical to assume that a fortress of the strength of Singapore could be seriously threatened by the Japanese from the air.[3] It seemed far more likely that the Japanese would first take on less formidable objectives e.g. – the Netherlands East Indies or Timor.

In present circumstances the despatch of a superior fleet to the Far East was doubtless out of the question but who could tell how the situation might develop, the Japanese could never be certain of what we might do.

---

[1] Lionel Vivian Bond, 1884–1961. Joined the Royal Engineers, 1903. Sessions Judge, Peshawar, 1910–11. On active service in Europe, 1914–18 (despatches). Commandant, School of Military Engineering, 1935–9. General Officer Commanding-in-Chief, Malaya, 1939–41. Colonel Commandant, Royal Engineers, 1940–50. Knighted, 1942.

[2] In the event, the Japanese eliminated this danger by destroying much of the United States Fleet while it was at anchor in Pearl Harbor.

[3] Churchill was right: the danger to Singapore came, as Sir John Dill had forecast, from Japanese land forces.

Sir Hastings Ismay pointed out that the inadequacy of the air force at Singapore made it temporarily necessary to increase the garrison as much as possible. When we had strong air forces there, the need for a large army garrison would not be so great.

The Prime Minister said that the discussion had been of great interest to him. In present circumstances we were forced to accept risks in all parts of the Empire, but in his view, and having regard to the greater dangers which existed on the home front and in the Middle East, the threat to Singapore could not be regarded as unduly alarming.

AIR ATTACK ON THE UNITED KINGDOM

Some discussions took place on the methods now being employed by the Germans of attacking us from the air with mines, oil canisters, Molotov bombs and similar sinister weapons.

The Prime Minister suggested that we should retaliate in like manner on the enemy and requested a report on what steps could be taken to produce similar or equally destructive types of explosives for dropping on Germany.

Anthony Eden to Winston S. Churchill
(*Premier papers, 3/372/1*)

19 September 1940 War Office

Prime Minister,

I am deeply exercised by our shortage of rifles. In recent months we have called up for training over half a million men, and many of these have now had two or three months training and have been formed into battalions, but I have not enough rifles to go round. I estimate that there may be some 100,000 of these soldiers without arms. With an invasion imminent, the Commander-in-Chief is naturally most anxious to arm these men immediately. There is no way of doing this except by withdrawing 303s from the Home Guard, and this I am most reluctant to do at the present moment.

The only way out that I can see is for the United States to release to us the balance of the 250,000 rifles which, you will remember, we originally hoped to receive from them. Do you think it would be possible for you to send a special appeal to the President about these rifles? This would greatly help us.[1]

AE

---

[1] Churchill noted on the bottom of Eden's minute, on 20 September: 'I will do so at once'. His telegram to Roosevelt was sent on 22 September (see page 854).

Winston S. Churchill to General Ismay
(*Churchill papers, 20/13*)

19 September 1940
Private

Be careful that the Glen ships[1] are not got out of the way so that it will be impossible to take the armoured reinforcements through the Mediterranean if the need is sufficient to justify the risk. I don't want to be told there are no suitable vessels available. The Admiralty are very wily when they don't want to do anything.

Let me know what other ships would be available if we should decide to run a convoy from West to East through the Mediterranean about the third week in October.

WSC

Winston S. Churchill to Sir Alexander Cadogan and General Ismay
(*Premier papers, 3/276*)

19 September 1940

We settled some time ago the dates when particular people were to be informed of 'Menace.' The zero hour has been retarded, but is now imminent. Pray, therefore, be ready to inform the Cabinet to-morrow what the dates will be. Sir Samuel Hoare will not know till then. When he knows, send the following Personal and Private Telegram from me:–

Begins: You will have heard by now of our Dakar intentions, after considering carefully all reactions in France and Spain. We are doing so much for France that, if de Gaulle's movement succeeds in Africa, we might easily make him spare something for Spain. You should explain to the Spaniards that none of our actions at Dakar is in the slightest degree inimical to them, and that we should be glad to see a satisfactory *modus vivendi* arranged between France and Spain over the zones. We are not contemplating anything at the present time about Morocco. But, of course, if de Gaulle establishes himself at Dakar and is master of Western and Central Africa, Morocco is next on the list. There is no use forming opinions or saying anything to the Spaniards until we see what are the results and reactions of Dakar. Your grasp of the situation is much appreciated here.[2]

WSC

---

[1] Three cargo ships of the Glen Line, the *Glenearn*, *Glengyle* and *Glenroy*, which had been converted to carry troops and landing craft for use in combined operations in the Mediterranean.

[2] This telegram was sent on 23 September 1940 as No. 781 to Sir Samuel Hoare at Madrid.

Winston S. Churchill to General Ismay
(*Premier papers, 3/314/2*)

19 September 1940

1. It was not solely on moral grounds that we decided against retaliation upon Germany. It pays us better to concentrate upon limited high-class military objectives. Moreover, in the indiscriminate warfare, his lack of skill in navigation, &c., does not tell against him so much.

2. However, the dropping of large mines by parachute proclaims the enemy's entire abandonment of all pretence of aiming at military objectives. At five thousand feet he cannot have the slightest idea what he is going to hit. This therefore proves the 'act of terror' intention against the civil population. We must consider whether his morale would stand up to this as well as ours. Here is a simple war-thought.

3. My inclination is to say that we will drop a heavy parachute mine on German cities for every one he drops on ours; and it might be an intriguing idea to mention a list of cities that would be black-listed for this purpose. I do not think they would like it, and there is no reason why they should not have a period of suspense.

4. The time and character of the announcement is a political decision. Meanwhile, I wish to know when the tackle could be ready. Let care be taken to make a forthcoming response to this. Let officers be set to propose the best method on a substantial scale in the shortest time. It would be better to act by parachute mines upon a number of German towns not hitherto touched, but if we have to use 1,000-lb air-bombs, which we have because otherwise the delay would be too long, let the case be stated.

5. I wish to know by Saturday night what is the worst form of proportionate retaliation, i.e., _equal_ retaliation, that we can inflict upon ordinary German cities for what they are now doing to us by means of the parachute mine. To-day we were informed that thirty-six had been dropped, but by tomorrow it may be 100. Well, let it be a hundred and make the best plan possible on that scale for action within, say, a week or ten days. If we have to wait longer so be it, but make sure there is no obstruction.

6. Pending the above information I agree that we should not make a wail or a whine about what has happened. Let me have practical propositions by Saturday night.

WSC

Winston S. Churchill to Anthony Eden
(*Churchill papers, 20/13*)

19 September 1940
ACTION THIS DAY

The armoured reinforcements are now in the Gulf of Aden. We have been assured that of course General Wavell has made all arrangements to get them into action as quickly as possible. I hope this is so. I am sorry that someone like Lord Beaverbrook is not waiting on the quay to do the job of passing them to the fighting line. We must do the best we can. Has it been considered whether it would be better to carry these vehicles through the Canal to Alexandria and debark them there close to the front, or have special trains and railway cars, cranes and other facilities been accumulated at Suez? Let the alternatives be examined here. Without waiting for this, let a telegram be drafted inquiring about the alternatives and the arrangements now made by General Wavell. Every day and even every hour counts in this matter.

Let me see draft to-morrow.

WSC

Cartoon
('*Daily Express*', 20 September 1940)[1]

20 September 1940

GIVE A SHIP A GOOD NAME
The first of the American destroyer flotilla is named H.M.S. Churchill.

[1] The destroyer USS *Herndon*, 1,190 tons, had been commissioned as a Royal Navy vessel on 9 September 1940 and renamed HMS *Churchill*. She was lent to the Russian Navy on 16 July 1944, renamed *Deiatelnyi*, and was sunk on 16 January 1945 in the Arctic Ocean by *U-956*.

842 September 1940

War Cabinet: minutes
(*Cabinet papers, 65/9*)

20 September 1940 10 Downing Street
12 noon

The Prime Minister said that, in the course of the negotiations with the United States Government in regard to the supply of munitions and the grant of base facilities, the United States Government had said that they wished to refer, in the exchange of correspondence, only to the supply of 50 Destroyers. But they had indicated clearly that we should receive the further 250,000 rifles, 20 motor torpedo-boats, the 150 aircraft on order for Sweden, and 10 large flying boats. He had instructed the Under-Secretary of State for Foreign Affairs[1] to telephone to Lord Lothian that day, and to explain to him that we regarded ourselves as having been promised these munitions, and that we felt the lack of them very severely. If need be, he (the Prime Minister) would send a personal message to President Roosevelt on the matter. He also attached importance to the rifles being despatched quickly. It had been stated that the Purvis Commission had insisted on re-packing the previous consignments, and had thereby caused considerable delay.[2]

The Prime Minister said that it was essential to give a lead in the direction of not allowing dislocation of production and of normal activities over wide areas, on account of a single aircraft.[3] The decision that the 'red' warning should not be given in the London area on account of a single aircraft must be adhered to. For the moment he was opposed to making any public statement on the subject. Later, if need be, the matter could be explained in Parliament.

The Prime Minister also stated that at a Meeting of Ministers held on Monday it had been arranged that weekly returns should be obtained from the principal Departments to show the working hours lost through air raid warnings. These returns should be circulated to all the Departments concerned, in order that each might see how its practice compared with that of others.

[1] R. A. Butler.
[2] General Strong had alleged that there had been a delay in the shipment of rifles previously released to Britain by the United States because the British Purchasing Commission had insisted on their being repacked. Commenting on this, Arthur Purvis reported (in paragrah 2 of a report prepared in the War Cabinet Offices on 21 September 1940), 'that a certain amount of difficulty had been caused by the handling of our request for further releases of rifles etc. through two different channels. By common agreement between all concerned in the United States, these releases (except of course the destroyers) were being handled between Mr Morgenthau, Mr Stimson and himself, and Mr Stimson rather resented a separate approach through other channels' (*Cabinet papers, 115/70*).
[3] In his diary, Sir John Reith noted another reason given by Churchill: 'PM said the streets and shops should be brightly lit for people going to cinemas and theatres.' (*The Reith Diaries*).

War Cabinet: Confidential Annex
(*Cabinet papers, 65/15*)

20 September 1940
12 noon
10 Downing Street

DAKAR

The Prime Minister said that he thought the result was by no means unsatisfactory. It was true that two of the three French Cruisers had got back to Dakar, but the *Primauguet* was no longer there. The French Naval forces were therefore only one ship up on balance.

The Minister of Information referred to the recent change which had taken place in French opinion. He thought that there was a risk of a setback in this change of opinion, if British ships once again had to fire on French ships. Indeed, some French journalists whom he had seen on the previous night, thought that such an action might finish the de Gaulle movement.

The Prime Minister said that the effect might well be the opposite. General Catroux, who had been informed of our intentions, was all in favour of the Operation going forward.

Later in the Meeting, a message was received to the effect that, at General de Gaulle's request, Operation 'Menace' was being postponed for 24 hours.

Winston S. Churchill to William Mackenzie King
(*Churchill papers, 20/14*)

20 September 1940

Message from Admiralty was as you rightly assume purely precautionary. Steps had to be taken to intercept certain French ships on their way to Dakar and Duala, with the object of frustrating the de Gaulle movement. Ships in question have now reached Dakar without any collision occurring. Some of these French ships have consented under duress to return to Casablanca. At the same time other steps will be taken shortly which it is hoped will not require any use of British force. You will be informed beforehand of this matter, which involves the highest operational secrecy, in a subsequent telegram. There is always a chance that Vichy may be made to declare war by the Germans, and they need not look far for a pretext on account of the blockade we are enforcing. I do not myself think that events will turn that way. Kindest regards.

Winston S. Churchill to Sir Archibald Sinclair
(*Churchill papers, 20/13*)

20 September 1940

Yours of September 18.[1] In your figures on page 3 please distinguish between metropolitan and overseas. It seems to me astonishing that with the supplies now reaching you, you should only produce 74 Squadrons of Fighters by April 1941. You now have 64½, though this includes foreign and Dominions, in the Metropolitan Force alone. You have reduced the additional equipment of the Fighter Squadrons from 16 to 12. It seems incredible that a greater expansion should not be achieved.

2. Even taking the Metropolitan strength for the summer of 1942 in para. 2 of your letter as 270 Squadrons at 12 each, this represents a front line strength of 3,240 aeroplanes. It would be interesting to see how many men, how many machines, and how much money this requires. I am sure an effective policy would secure at least 100 Bomber and 100 Fighter Squadrons by April 1941, and 80 of each by January 1941. Naturally during the fury of the battle expansion is arrested, but we need not expect that these conditions will last throughout the winter. Pray remember that we were supposed to have 125 Squadrons fully ready more than two years before the war in the Metropolitan Air Force alone. I am sure there must be something radically wrong with the organization, which with its enormous intake of machines, now over 1,700 a month, can only produce this limited and almost stagnant front. If you cannot produce more than 270 Squadrons by the summer of 1942, it will be necessary to examine the relation of all aircraft supplies to this restricted front.

WSC

Sir Alexander Cadogan: note
(*Cabinet papers, 115/70*)

20 September 1940
Most Secret

On the Prime Minister's instructions, I rang up Lord Lothian this afternoon to ask where we stood in regard to the 'other desiderata' promised to us at the time of the grant of naval bases and transfer of destroyers. I told him that the Prime Minister attached the greatest importance to the matter: he had been assured that this material was promised to us and could not but feel growing disappointment at its failure to materialise.

Lord Lothian said that, as we knew, owing to a ruling of the American

---

[1] Not printed.

Attorney-General,[1] the motor torpedo boats could not be transferred before January. As regards the rest of the material, the 250,000 rifles were arranged for and ready for shipment. I told him that I understood there had been some difficulty owing to the requirements of our own people in the matter of packing and I asked him to look into that matter and to do everything possible to expedite shipment. The Ambassador also said that the flying fortresses were arranged for, but that only one of these was at present ready. I asked him about the Curtiss aircraft and the aircraft on order for Sweden, but he had not up to date information on this aspect but promised to look into the matter immediately and to send me a telegram this afternoon stating exactly what the situation was.

I again impressed upon him that the Prime Minister regarded this as a matter of the greatest urgency and importance. He promised to do everything possible to expedite matters.

AC

Winston S. Churchill to Mrs Chamberlain
(*Churchill papers, 2/393*)

20 September 1940
Private

My dear Mrs Neville,

I am most obliged to you for taking my advice. I can't bear to think of Neville, while still recovering from a major operation, being under this continued bombardment in London. He must give himself a decent chance to recover full efficiency.

I have been very much worried about you both during the last ten days, though I have not ventured to interfere.

I should like to let you know that I do not think much will be left of Downing Street after a few weeks. I am having all the Government pictures and the few odd daubs we possess dumped in the vaults of the National Gallery, and all but the smallest personal effects of ours are being removed tomorrow. I propose to lead a troglodyte existence with several 'trogs'.

Meanwhile Rucker[2] will see that Neville is kept fully informed of all business.

Yours very sincerely
Winston S. Churchill

[1] Robert Jackson, later a Justice of the Supreme Court.
[2] Arthur Rucker, Chamberlain's Principal Private Secretary.

Lord Mottistone[1]: *note*
(*Camrose papers*)

20 September 1940

Mr Churchill told me at our last Dinner that he would appreciate a book with the signatures of his friends of the 'Other Club'.[2]

I have accordingly obtained a book, with a good binding, in which it is hoped all our members will be able to write their names, either at the Dinner on October 3rd or subsequently.

Since arranging this, two of our members, Lord Camrose and Mr Norman Holden,[3] have found a small gold snuff box, which it is known Lord Nelson owned and treasured for the last eight years of his life. Being sure that Mr Churchill would like so appropriate and historic a present, we have acquired it.[4]

John Colville: diary
(*Colville papers*)

20 September 1940

I motored down to Chequers with Randolph Churchill, who was pleasant but as usual talked a lot of vituperative nonsense about Horace Wilson, etc.

---

[1] John Edward Bernard Seely, 1868–1947. French gold medal for saving life at sea, 1891. On active service in South Africa, 1899–1900 (DSO). Liberal MP, 1900–6, 1906–10, 1910–22 and 1923–4. Secretary of State for War, 1912–14. On active service on the Western Front, 1914–18 (despatches, DSO, Major-General). Deputy Minister of Munitions (under Churchill), 1918. Under-Secretary of State for Air (under Churchill), 1919. Chairman of the National Savings Committee, 1926–43. Created Baron Mottistone, 1938. His eldest son, Frank, was killed in action on the Western Front in April 1917.

[2] The Other Club had been founded in 1911. The then Liberal Party stalwart Churchill and his Conservative friend F. E. Smith (later Earl of Birkenhead) had been among the prime movers. The aim was to bring together, at fortnightly dinners while Parliament was in session, political and other figures who had been caught up in the current acerbity of party politics, at the time of the crisis over the power of the House of Lords, and to maintain convivial relations. The club's meetings were held in the Pinafore Room at the Savoy Hotel. Churchill attended his last meeting on 10 December 1964. The only engagement in his desk calendar for the month after his death was to the Other Club on 4 February 1965.

[3] Norman Edward Holden, 1879–1946. On active service, South Africa (1899–1902), and in the First World War (Dardanelles, France). Major, Machine Gun Corps (wounded, despatches). Director-General, Mechanical Warfare Department, Ministry of Munitions, 1917–8 (while Churchill was Minister). OBE, 1918. Chairman of the British Industrial Corporation.

[4] More than sixty members of the Other Club paid £1 each towards the gift. The donors included Maurice Baring, Robert Boothby, Lord Camrose, Lord Chatfield, Alfred Duff Cooper, J. L. Garvin, David Lloyd George, Lord Gort, J. M. Keynes, Sir Edwin Lutyens, Sir Edward Marsh, Lord Moyne, James de Rothschild, Sir Archibald Sinclair, Lord Trenchard, Lord Tyrrell, Sir Robert Vansittart, H. G. Wells and the Duke of Westminster. The presentation was made when Churchill dined at the Other Club on the evening of 3 October 1940.

We followed the PM and Mrs Churchill to Dollis Hill where the Cabinet's emergency headquarters are. We inspected the flats where we should live and the deep underground rooms, safe from the biggest bomb, where the Cabinet and its satellites (e.g. me) would work and, if necessary, sleep. They are impressive but rather forbidding; I suppose if the present intensive bombing continues we must get used to being troglodytes ('trogs' as the PM puts it). I begin to understand what the early Christians must have felt about living in the Catacombs.

We talked about the possibility of the Germans using poison gas, but the PM and Ismay are confident that nothing new, or more devilish than mustard gas, is available. He is doubtful whether invasion will be tried in the near future, but says that there is no doubt every preparation has been made. He is becoming less and less benevolent towards the Germans (having been much moved by the examples of their frightfulness in Wandsworth which he has been to see: a landmine caused very great devastation there)[1] and talks about castrating the lot. He says there will be no nonsense about a 'just peace'. I feel sure this is the wrong attitude – not only immoral but unwise. We should aim at crushing them and then being firm but magnanimous victors.

Towards bedtime the PM, very animated, reminisced about the South African War (the last enjoyable war, he called it) and the beauties of the Veld. His thirst for talking military strategy is unquenchable.

Winston S. Churchill to Lord Beaverbrook
(*Churchill papers, 20/13*)

21 September 1940

The figures you gave me of the improvement in Operational types between May 10 and August 30 are magnificent. If similar figures could be prepared down to September 30, which is not far off, I would prefer to read them to the

---

[1] On 16 September 1940 the Germans had used aerial mines for the first time on land, against London (they had previously been dropped into the sea, where their magnetic properties attracted them to the hulls of ships; see index entry for 'magnetic mines' in the *At the Admiralty* volume of the Churchill War Papers). Known as land mines, and dropped by parachute, they had a high charge ratio of 60–70 per cent explosive, their 500 kilogram charge creating considerable blast damage in built-up areas. Should the mine not go off (as when its parachute was caught up in a building or other structure), any attempt to remove the rear casing to get at the magnetic or acoustic device exposed the photo-electric cell sitting under a glass window, and exploded the bomb. The existence of these parachute mines, which drifted to the ground without any conceivable means of being directed on to a specific target, was not officially disclosed to the public until 1944.

Cabinet rather than circulate them. If, however, the September figures cannot be got until late in October, I will read these to the Cabinet.

The country is your debtor, and of your Ministry.

WSC

Winston S. Churchill to Anthony Eden, General Dill and General Ismay
(*Churchill papers, 20/13*)

21 September 1940

1. This telegram[1] confirms my apprehensions about Malta. Beaches defended on an average battalion front of 15 miles, and no Reserves for counter-attack worth speaking of, leaves the Island at the mercy of a landing force. You must remember that we do not possess the command of the sea around Malta. The danger therefore appears to be extreme. I should have thought four Battalions were needed, but, owing to the difficulty of moving transports from the West, we must be content with two for the moment. We must find two good ones. Apparently there is no insuperable difficulty in accommodation.

2. What are the plans for the Malta convoy? When is it to start, and what is it to contain? What is the state of preparedness of the UP Batteries? If everything else were ready, I would not delay the convoy merely for the PE Fuzes. A destroyer could carry them in later.

Winston S. Churchill to Admiral Pound and Admiral Phillips
(*Churchill papers, 20/13*)

21 September 1940

How is the expenditure of Naval ammunition proceeding in the Middle East, as well as in the North Sea and Channel. Let me know of any weak points in the supplies which are emerging. Have you got over the difficulty of the 4·7 ammunition? Let me have a short note.

WSC

---

[1] A telegram from the Governor and Commander-in-Chief, Malta, General Dobbie, sent on 19 September 1940.

Winston S. Churchill to Sir Archibald Sinclair
(*Churchill papers, 20/13*)

21 September 1940

Pray have a look at the Air Ministry communiqué issued in this morning's papers. It includes the following:–

'The enemy formations were engaged by our fighters, but cloud conditions made interception difficult. Reports so far received show that four enemy aircraft were shot down. Seven of our fighters have been lost, the pilots of three being safe.'

It is very unwise to let the Germans know that their new tactics have been successful and that they resulted in our losing 7 fighters as against 4.

We do not of course want to conceal our losses, at the present time when we are prospering, but surely there is no need to relate them to any particular action.

WSC

Winston S. Churchill to Anthony Eden
(*Churchill papers, 20/13*)

21 September 1940

I am not happy about the equipment position of the commandos. It is a waste of this fine material to leave them without sufficient equipment for training purposes, much less for operations.

Pray let me have a statement showing:–

1. What equipment has already been issued to the various commandos.
2. What is the output scale of equipment which these units are to have.
3. What can be issued to them immediately for training purposes.

I should like to have a return each week showing the precise position as regards the equipment of the various commandos. The position is now very bad and far different from what you were led to believe.

Winston S. Churchill to General Brooke
(*Churchill papers, 20/13*)

21 September 1940

We often hear tales of how the Germans will invade on an enormous front, trying to throw, say, a quarter of a million men ashore anyhow, and trusting afterwards to exploit lodgments which are promising. For an attack of this kind, our beach defence system seems admirably devised. The difficulty of defending an island against overseas attack has always consisted in the power of the invader to concentrate a very superior force at one point or another. But if he is going to spread himself out very widely, the bulk of his forces, if they reach shore, will come up against equal or superior forces spread along the coast. It will be a case of one thin line against another, whereas I can readily imagine a concentrated attack pressed forward with tremendous numbers succeeding against our thin line. I find it difficult to see what would be the good of his landing large numbers of small parties, none of which would be strong enough to break our well-organized shore defence. If he is going to lose, say, 100,000 in the passage, and another 150,000 are to be brought up short at the beaches, the actual invasion would be rather an expensive process, and the enemy would have sustained enormous losses before we had even set our reserves in motion. If, therefore, there is anything in this alleged German plan, it seems to me it should give us considerable satisfaction. Far more dangerous would be the massed attack on a few particular selected points.

Perhaps you will talk to me about this when we next meet.

Winston S. Churchill to Sir Edward Bridges, Sir John Anderson and Sir John Reith[1]
(*Churchill papers, 20/13*)

21 September 1940
ACTION THIS DAY

1. When I asked at the Cabinet the other day why the Tubes could not be used to some extent, even at the expense of transport facilities, as Air Raid shelters, I was assured that this was most undesirable, and that the whole matter had been reviewed before that conclusion was reached. I now see that the Aldwych Tube is to be used as a shelter. Pray let me have more information about this, and what has happened to supersede the former decisive arguments.

2. I still remain in favour of a widespread utilization of the Tubes, by which I mean not only the stations but the railway lines, and I should like a short report on one sheet of paper showing the numbers that could be accommodated on various sections and the structural changes that would be required to fit these sections for their new use. Is it true, for instance, that 750,000 people could be accommodated in the Aldwych section alone? We may well have to balance the relative demands of transport and shelter.

3. I am awaiting the report of the Home Secretary on the forward policy of –
   (a) Making more shelters.

---

[1] Sir John Reith wrote in his diary: 'Silly "Action this day" memo from PM about Tubes to me and Anderson' (*The Reith Diaries*).

(b) Strengthening existing basements.
(c) Making empty basements and premises available.
(d) Most important. Assigning fixed places by ticket to a large proportion of the people, thus keeping them where we want them, and avoiding crowding.

WSC

Winston S. Churchill to Herbert Morrison
(*Churchill papers, 20/13*)

21 September 1940
Secret

The rapid disposal of unexploded bombs is of the highest importance. Any failure to grapple with this problem may have serious results on the production of aircraft, and other vital war material. The work of the Bomb Disposal Squads must be facilitated by the provision of every kind of up-to-date equipment. The attached Paper,[1] which I have received from the Secretary of State for War, shows the experiments on foot, and the equipment being planned. Priority 1 (a) should be allotted to the production of the equipment given in the Appendix, and to any further requirements which may come to light.

John Colville: diary
(*Colville papers*)

21 September 1940

'When we have abolished Germany,' said the PM, 'we will certainly establish Poland – and make them a permanent thing in Europe.' He suggested that one Pole was worth three Frenchmen.

The PM seems rather more apprehensive than I had realised about the possibility of invasion in the immediate future and he keeps on ringing up the Admiralty and asking about the weather in the Channel.

[1] Not printed.

General Pile[1]: *recollection*
('*Ack-Ack*', *pages 168–9*)

22 September 1940   Chequers

On Sunday, September 22, I had been invited to lunch at Chequers. Churchill, in great heart, said he had had a hot tip that the invasion was due at three o'clock that afternoon. However, I stayed to tea, and no invasion took place. ('If the Germans manage to land,' said Churchill, 'we shall show them no quarter.') So we talked a lot about all sorts of things – particularly about tanks and AA affairs.

Churchill announced his intention of coming round with me to see us in action. He adored guns. 'Cannon,' he used to call them, and he was more interested in questioning me as to the number of cannon I had in action in the various areas than in the other equipment so necessary to make those cannon useful. He liked to hear the noise of them, too, and, right up to the end of the War, he was always getting into trouble with his colleagues for going on to gun-sites in the middle of a raid when he ought to have been safe in a shelter.

Winston S. Churchill to Herbert Morrison
(*Premier papers, 3/200/3*)

22 September 1940
ACTION THIS DAY

GL SETS[2]

I will certainly send the note you wish, but I should be glad if you would give a draft showing exactly what I am to say on the details. Speed is vital.

WSC

---

[1] Frederick Alfred Pile, 1884–1976. Known as 'Tim'. Royal Artillery, 1904. On active service, 1914–18 (despatches, DSO, Military Cross). Succeeded his father as 2nd Baronet, 1931. Commander, Suez Canal Brigade, 1932–6; 1st Anti-Aircraft Division, Territorial Army, 1936–9. Lieutenant-General, 1939. General Officer Commanding-in-Chief, Anti-Aircraft Command, 1939–45. Knighted, 1941. Director-General, Ministry of Works, 1945. His son, in the Royal Tank Regiment, won the Military Cross in 1945.

[2] A ground-based radar device that could be mounted on anti-aircraft guns, and could reveal the course and height of bombers flying directly overhead. GL = gun-laying. They were codenamed 'George'. They were installed at searchlight posts, in direct radio communication with Fighter Command. The airborne equivalent were AI sets (air interception).

John Colville: diary
(*Colville papers*)

22 September 1940

The PM gave vent to a most horrific display of abusive epithets when he saw a telegram about Sir S. Symes,[1] Governor General of the Sudan, who is said to be 'bored with the war'. So strongly did he feel that he had to call me back and say, 'Don't put it to Cadogan in quite those terms.' (The report had come from Lampson at Cairo.)

Discuss the Egyptian battle which now seems to be opening. The PM is full of confidence and says that we have enough good troops out there to do what is necessary 'unless, of course, our men fight like skunks and the Italians like heroes'. But he feels the opposite is more likely to be the case.

Winston S. Churchill to Lord Halifax
(*Churchill papers, 20/13*)

22 September 1940

I am very sorry to read this telegram. What would be done to a Colonel who let his battalion down because he was bored with the war, or to a sentry who was bored on his beat? Here is the Governor-General of the Sudan, at the height of the greatest crisis in history, who has so far estranged all the loyalties which surround a man in a great position, as to lead to these reports being made about him. There is no need to make a scene on the spot, but he should be sent home forthwith, and on arrival here should be the subject of an enquiry with a view to disciplinary action being taken against him.

WSC

Sir Alexander Cadogan: diary
(*'The Diaries of Sir Alexander Cadogan'*)

22 September 1940

PM furious because, in sacking X on his instructions, I put some kind words into the telegram about his past services. After all, the man had given

[1] George Stewart Symes, 1882–1962. Entered the Army, 1900. On active service in South Africa (1902), Aden (1903–4, DSO), and on the Western Front (despatches). Assistant Director of Intelligence, Sudan, 1918–19. Governor of the Northern District, Palestine, 1920–5; Chief Secretary, Government of Palestine, 1925–8. Resident and Commander-in-Chief, Aden, 1928–31. Knighted, 1928. Governor and Commander-in-Chief, Tanganyika, 1931–3. Governor-General of the Sudan, 1934–40.

the whole of his life, and we are sacking him on hearsay evidence. Winston is very babyish in some ways.

Winston S. Churchill to General Ismay
(*Churchill papers, 20/13*)

22 September 1940

RIFLES FROM THE UNITED STATES

Make sure through every channel that all arrangements are made to bring these rifles over at full speed. They must be distributed in at least four fast ships. Could not some of them come by passenger liner. Let me know what Admiralty can do. Make sure there is no delay at Purco's[1] end through repacking as described by General Strong, USA.

Winston S. Churchill to President Roosevelt
(*Premier papers, 3/372/1*)

22 September 1940

I asked Lord Lothian to speak to you about our remaining desiderata. The 250,000 rifles are most urgently needed, as I have 250,000 trained and uniformed men into whose hands they can be put. I should be most grateful if you could arrange the necessary release. Every arrangement will be made to transport them with the utmost speed. They will enable us to take 250,000 ·303 rifles from the Home Guard and transfer them to the Regular Army, leaving the Home Guard armed with about 800,000 American rifles. Even if no ammunition is available these rifles will be none the less useful, as they can draw upon the stock which has already reached us.

Winston S. Churchill to Sir Alexander Cadogan
(*Premier papers, 3/72/1*)

22 September 1940
ACTION THIS DAY

RIFLES FROM THE UNITED STATES

If what Mr Purvis says is true, General Strong has been mischievous. I should like however to have some cross-check on the facts in view of the very positive and responsible character of the allegation.

---

[1] The Purvis purchasing mission in Washington.

I do not consider that Mr Purvis' comments in para. 2 should prevent my telegram being sent to the President. I presume this has been done. Considering the great importance of getting these rifles, etc., it is astonishing that Mr Purvis has not reported every few days the state of the negotiations and other arrangements for shipping. You must understand that the S of S for War presses me continually about these rifles, and that it is my duty to take action. Mr Purvis has only himself to thank if, when he leaves us for more than six weeks, totally in the dark about what he is doing and what is happening, other channels are opened up.

You should tell him to report daily what he is doing and what is the position.

WSC

Lord Lothian to Winston S. Churchill
(*Premier papers, 3/468*)

22 September 1940   Washington DC
11.15 p.m.

I read your telegram to the President to-night. He was delighted and repeatedly said 'splendid'. At the end he said he was 'happy' about it. He then asked what the Prime Minister would think of his sending a cruiser and a couple of destroyers to Monrovia, touching at Freetown and if possible at Dakar on the way purely as a friendly move. I said I thought the Prime Minister would welcome such a step, but would enquire. Of course ships could not arrive except after some delay. I then said that I thought the most important thing he could do would be to tell French Government [   ][1] was, announcing that a declaration of war on us would be derogatory to Franco-American relations. He said that he would do this through Henri Haye[2] and also say that it would inevitably mean a loss to Vichy of French possessions in West Indies and the Pacific.

---

[1] At this point in Lothian's telegram, two groups of letters were undecypherable.

[2] French (Vichy) Ambassador to Washington. On 5 August 1940 Roosevelt asked Lord Lothian if Britain had any information about Haye. Five days later Lord Halifax replied: 'M. Henri Haye is definitely a Fifth Columnist. He is a senator of the extreme right who has long been noted for his Fascist sympathies. He strongly opposed behind the scenes French support of the League of Nations in 1935. His friends are members of the Germanophile group in France. He is definitely a dangerous type and requires a lot of watching, more especially as he is a plausible rogue who gives the appearance of frankness and is thus the type of Frenchman who might appeal to the Americans. Mr Bullitt's appreciation of him would probably be endorsed by Ribbentrop, but certainly not by anyone who desires our victory.' Bullitt, the American Ambassador to France, had reported that Haye 'is not pro-German, though like many others, he had hoped for a settlement with the Germans without war.' (*Foreign Office papers, 371/24352.*)

Winston S. Churchill to General de Gaulle
(*Churchill papers, 20/14*)

22 September 1940

From every quarter presence of General Catroux was demanded in Syria. I therefore took the responsibility in your name of inviting the General to go there. It is, of course, perfectly understood that he holds his position only from you, and I shall make this clear to him again. Sometimes one has to take decisions on the spot because of their urgency and difficulty of explaining to others at a distance. There is time to stop him still if you desire it, but I should consider this was a very unreasonable act.

All good fortune in your enterprise to-morrow morning.

Winston S. Churchill to Admiral John Cunningham and General Irwin
(*Premier papers, 3/276*)

22 September 1940　　　　　　　　　　　　　　　10 Downing Street
Secret and Personal

Arrival of Vichy cruisers possibly with troops on board seems to me to destroy hope of a bloodless capture of Dakar, and must make its storm a far more severe operation with evil political consequences. You should with de Gaulle immediately reconsider the whole position, answering particularly the following questions:

(a) How can a strict unofficial blockade of Dakar be instituted in order to starve them out? Could both Bathurst and Freetown be used as re-fuelling bases? What is the minimum naval force required?

(b) Can we now revert to 'Scipio', observing that a Vichy force from Dakar will very soon work up the railway to Bamako and into the interior. At what point can the line be cut by the Free French forces to protect Central Africa?

(c) Can British troops be accommodated for a short time pending developments at Freetown? part sleeping on board?[1]

---

[1] Churchill decided not to send this telegram, marking it 'Show me later'. On 23 September 1940 E. A. Seal marked it 'Out of date' and it was set aside.

Winston S. Churchill to General Smuts
(*Premier papers, 3/276*)

23 September 1940
1 a.m.
Most Secret and Personal

You will have seen my message about Dakar. I have been thinking a great deal about what you said in your message in High Commissioner's[1] telegram of 22nd June No. 329 and in other messages since about not neglecting the African sphere. The de Gaulle movement to rescue the French Colonies has prospered in Equatoria and the Cameroons. We could not allow these solid gains to be destroyed by French warships and personnel from Vichy, sent probably at German dictation. If Dakar fell under German control and became a U-Boat base, the consequences to the Cape route would be deadly. We have therefore set out upon the business of putting de Gaulle into Dakar, peaceably if we can, forcibly if we must, and the expedition now about to strike seems to have the necessary force.

Naturally the risk of a bloody collision with the French sailors and part of the garrison is not a light one. On the whole I think the odds are heavily against any serious resistance, having regard to the low morale and unhappy plight of this French Colony, and the ruin and starvation which faces them through our sea control. Still, no one can be sure till we try. The argument that such a risk ought not to be run at a time when French opinion, encouraged by British resistance, is veering towards us even at Vichy, and that anything like a second Oran would be a great set-back, has weighed heavily with us. Nevertheless we came to the united conclusion that this objection might not turn out to be valid, and must in any case be surpassed by the dangers of doing nothing, and of allowing Vichy to prevail against de Gaulle. If Vichy did not declare war after Oran, or under the pressure of our blockade, there is no reason why they should do so if there is a fight at Dakar. Besides strategical importance of Dakar and political effects of its capture by de Gaulle, there are 60 or 70 millions of Belgian and Polish gold wrongfully held in the interior, and the great battleship *Richelieu*, by no means permanently disabled, would indirectly come into our hands. Anyhow the die is cast.

We do not intend to disturb Morocco at present on account of the German pressure on Spain and Spanish interests there. We are very hopeful about Syria whither General Catroux will go next week. An important battle is now

---

[1] Edward John Harding, 1880–1954. Entered the Colonial Office, 1904. Permanent Under Secretary of State, Dominions Office, 1930–40. Knighted, 1935. High Commissioner for the United Kingdom in the Union of South Africa, 1940–41. Cape Town Representative of the United Kingdom High Commission, 1942–45.

impending at Mersa Matruh and I hope our armoured reinforcements will arrive in time.

I am not particularly impressed with the dangers in Kenya, especially if we lie back and fight from the broad gauge railway, leaving the enemy the difficult communications. I am trying to send a few suitable Tanks to this theatre, which otherwise I feel is overstocked with troops needed in the Sudan and in the Delta.

It gives me so much pleasure and confidence to be trekking with you along the path we have followed together for so many years.

Winston S. Churchill to General Ismay
(*Churchill papers, 20/13*)

23 September 1940
ACTION THIS DAY

I think it better on the whole that the UP (PE) Battery should not go in the first instance to Malta. There are bound to be many teething troubles with the new Fuze, and these are better dealt with while the Battery is in close contact with Dr Crow's establishment. Moreover, very few PE's would be ready by the date fixed. After discussing the matter with General Loch[1] and General Pile I think it would be well if this Battery could take part in the defence of London, firing AD[2] ammunition. Indeed, I should welcome the entry of the rocket batteries into the fight at this juncture. Could they not be placed on some intercepting line, near the coast, before the enemy get too high? Let me have proposals from the authorities concerned.

Let me see the establishment and order of battle of the rocket batteries.

WSC

Winston S. Churchill to General Ismay
(*Premier papers, 3/222/4*)

23 September 1940

I have read this Fog paper, and discussed it with Sir Hugh Dowding and others.

It is pointed out that in a fog the enemy can point his beams very easily at

[1] Kenneth Morley Loch, 1890–1961. Entered the Army, 1910. On active service, 1914–18, including the retreat from Mons and the Battle of the Aisne (despatches twice, MC). Director, Anti-Aircraft and Coastal Defence, War Office, 1939–41. Master General of Ordnance, India, 1944–7. Knighted, 1946. British Control Commission, Germany, 1948–9.

[2] Anti-aircraft (Air Defence) ammunition, used by the Unrotated Projectile (UP) anti-aircraft rocket, equipped with the recently developed PE fuzes, one of the new weapons being developed at the Royal Aircraft Establishment at Farnborough.

one part of the coast, and switch off at the last stage to another. Also, could he not point at one part, and could his ships not steer so many degrees to the right or left of the beam? Therefore, it would seem that this security is not as good as is supposed, and also there would be danger in making concentrations in consequence of beam indications, which are the easiest feints in the world to make.

2. Let me have a separate note about the Admiralty dispositions in fog, and especially how fast the ASV sets[1] are being issued to flotillas in the narrow waters.

WSC

Winston S. Churchill to Anthony Eden and General Ismay
(*Churchill papers, 20/13*)

23 September 1940
ACTION THIS DAY

There is not much in the report referred to,[2] and what there is applies equally to the Sudan.

We are piling up troops and artillery in Kenya which are urgently needed in the Sudan.

With regard to what you say about the vast strategical front of the Kenya operation: If we lie back on the broad-gauge railway from Mombasa to the Lake, we have a lateral line of communication incomparably superior to any line by which we can be approached, and it should be possible to move our forces so as to have sudden superior strength at the point where the enemy advance develops.

Although no one can say for certain where the enemy's blow will fall, I am convinced that the true disposition would economise to the utmost in Kenya in order to reinforce the Sudan.

The one concession which is needed for Kenya is about ten Cruiser Tanks. If these were put on suitable vehicles on the railway, they could strike with deadly effect, and with surprise, at any Italian movement. But the mere piling up of guns and Brigades is a most painful process to watch.

In order to raise these points, I must ask that the move of the Mountain

---

[1] Air-to-Surface Vessel, an airborne radar device, the first to be used in action, with which aircraft could detect surface vessels in darkness or thick weather. An aircraft using ASV Mark 1 had to fly at only 200 feet to enable the radar operator to distinguish a U-boat from the 'clutter' of the sea's moving surface. At this height its range was limited to three and a half miles. The ASV sets were subsequently modified and improved, though with considerable delays in production (see Correlli Barnett, *Engage the Enemy More Closely*, London 1991, pages 479–80). Among the successful applications of ASV was the sinking of U-boats in pitch dark.

[2] Intelligence Summary No. 370, relating to the build-up of forces in Kenya against possible Italian attack.

Battery from Aden to Kenya shall be held up, and that instead the question of moving it or another Battery to the Sudan shall be considered.

WSC

PS – Please let me have a statement showing ration, rifle, mg and artillery strength of all troops in Kenya.

WSC

Winston S. Churchill to Sir Archibald Sinclair
(*Cabinet papers, 120/300*)

23 September 1940

What struck me about these photographs[1] was the apparent inability of the Bombers to hit these very large masses of barges. I should have thought that sticks of explosive bombs thrown along these oblongs would have wrought havoc, and it is very disappointing to see that they all remained intact and in order, with just a few apparently damaged at the entrance.

Can nothing be done to improve matters?

WSC

Winston S. Churchill to A. V. Alexander
(*Admiralty papers, 205/6*)

23 September 1940

It is very disappointing, as you say, that so much time should have been consumed, and the enemy given such excellent opportunities of mounting his guns.[2] One would have hoped for more alacrity.

With regard to the First Sea Lord's remarks at 'A,'[3] this runs entirely counter to the principle I laid down that the newest and best ships should be given matured crews, taken from older ships, and that the older ships should be worked up rather than encountering very long delays in the new ships which are of the greatest value. Take, for instance, the *King George V*; if a crew from, say, the *Revenge* had been turned over to her, it would have formed the

---

[1] On the morning of 23 September 1940 *The Times* published two photographs headed 'Bombing the barges at Dunkirk'. The caption read: 'The lower of these two pictures shows part of the dock area at Dunkirk a short time after the evacuation of the BEF had been completed. The upper one shows the same area taken this week-end, particularly the two docks in which barges of the German invasion fleet have been concentrated. Dock buildings round the upper of the two docks have been completely destroyed and unloading cranes and haulage gear smashed. Two big warehouses facing the other docks have been demolished and the one in the centre gutted by fire. Wharves, roads and railway sidings are pitted by bomb craters from the repeated attacks by RAF bombers. Damaged barges can be seen at the entrance of the upper dock.'

[2] At Cap Gris Nez, on the Channel coast opposite Dover.

[3] Not printed.

nucleus of her trained complement, and would have enabled *King George V* to come into service several weeks earlier. The Second Sea Lord's[1] Department has evidently sagged back into their old way of putting the rawest crews on the finest ships, with the result that we shall stand out of their aid for the longest possible time, while old vessels with well-seasoned complements will have to carry on. I know the complications which will be adduced by the Second Sea Lord's Department, but I am certain that with ingenuity they could be overcome, at any rate in a great many instances. It is nothing less than a scandal if the very best ships are to be manned largely, as the First Sea Lord says, 'by crews who are not seamen.'[2]

War Cabinet: minutes
(*Cabinet papers, 65/9*)

23 September 1940   Cabinet War Room
5 p.m.

The Prime Minister said that the operation 'Menace' had begun that morning. At the outset it had appeared that matters were progressing very favourably. Thus the first messages had stated that General de Gaulle's emissary had been received, and that our aircraft had landed at the aerodromes. Later a message had been received indicating that sporadic and formal resistance was being shown, and that our forces would have to interfere and open fire. The *Cumberland* had received a hit amid-ships by a shot from one of the batteries, and was out of action, and one destroyer had been damaged. The operation was now proceeding.

Later in the meeting a message was received, timed 1.58 p.m., stating that General de Gaulle was attempting a landing at Rufisque under cover of fog. It was also known that General de Gaulle had delivered an ultimatum to the Vichy forces and that they had been ordered to resist.

[1] Charles James Colebrooke Little, 1882–1973. Naval Cadet, 1897. Specialised in the Submarine Branch from 1903. Commanded the submarines of the Dover Patrol, 1914–16; the Grand Fleet Submarine Flotilla, 1916–18. Deputy-Chief of the Naval Staff, 1932–5. Knighted, 1935. Commander-in-Chief, China Station, 1936–8. Admiral, 1937. Second Sea Lord and Chief of Naval Personnel, 1938–41. Head of the British Joint Staff Mission, Washington, 1941–2. Commander-in-Chief, Portsmouth, 1942–5.

[2] In his reply, A. V. Alexander pointed out that in 1932 '87 out of every 100 ratings were trained, and even in 1937, when expansion was already well under way, the percentage was as high as 62. Given the present unavoidable high proportion of untrained men, almost any ship is bound to have a considerable number of men in her company who are not fully trained seamen.' In addition 'the large ships are in effect some of the largest sea-training estabishments under present conditions, so that they are constantly turning out trained ratings for all manner of new ships, and consequently always have a number of untrained ratings in their complement. To deprive a ship like the *Revenge* of the greater part of her trained complement at one stroke would thus seriously reduce her efficiency for a considerable period, a risk which I doubt whether we should be justified in taking at this crucial stage of the war' (*Admiralty papers, 205/6*).

John Colville: diary
(*Colville papers*)

23 September 1940

When I got back I found that 'Menace' was proceeding less favourably. The French had opened fire and all prospects of a peaceful landing had had to be abandoned. I told the PM who said, cheerfully, 'Let 'em have it. Remember this: never maltreat your enemy by halves. Once the battle is joined, let 'em have it.'

Chiefs of Staff Committee: minutes
(*Cabinet papers, 79/6*)

23 September 1940
9.30 p.m.

EVACUATION OF CHILDREN OVERSEAS

The Prime Minister said that in view of the recent disaster to the ship carrying women and children to Canada,[1] the further evacuation overseas of children must cease.[2]

Winston S. Churchill to Admiral John Cunningham
(*Premier papers, 3/276*)

23 September 1940
10.14 p.m.

Having begun we must go through to the end. Stop at nothing.

Winston S. Churchill to President Roosevelt
(*Premier papers, 3/468*)

24 September 1940
2.30 a.m.

I was encouraged by your reception of information conveyed by Lord Lothian about Dakar. It would be against our joint interests if strong German submarine and aircraft base were established there. It looks as if there might

---

[1] On 17 September 1940 the 11,000-ton *City of Benares* was torpedoed and sunk in the Atlantic on its way from Britain to Canada, and 77 of the children on board drowned, as well as 72 of the adults who accompanied them. Fifteen children and 18 women were saved.

[2] Churchill put this proposal to the War Cabinet at its next meeting, on 24 September 1940, the minutes recording: 'He was anxious that the scheme for evacuating children overseas should now be discontinued.' This was accepted without dissent.

be a stiff fight. Perhaps not, but anyhow orders have been given to ram it through. We should be delighted if you would send some American warships to Monrovia and Freetown and I hope by that time to have Dakar ready for your call. But what really matters now is that you should put it across to the French Government that a war declaration would be very bad indeed for them in all that concerns United States. If Vichy declares war that is the same thing as Germany, and Vichy possessions in the Western Hemisphere must be considered potentially German possessions. Many thanks also for your hint about invasion. We are all ready for them. I am vy glad to hear about the rifles.

War Cabinet: minutes
(*Cabinet papers, 65/9*)

24 September 1940   Cabinet War Room
12 noon

The First Sea Lord reported that the visibility at Dakar on the previous day had not exceeded two miles and the *Cumberland* had engaged the shore batteries at 4,000 yards. This explained the damage which she had received. General de Gaulle's emissary had landed at about 7.30 on the previous morning, but his proposals had been rejected and he had returned wounded, having encountered resolute opposition. About 2 p.m. General de Gaulle had attempted a landing at Rufisque, but owing to fog it had been impossible to carry out the operation before dark. The forces had therefore been withdrawn with the intention of resuming operations that morning. An ultimatum expiring at that time had been sent to the Dakar authorities. Later in the meeting the War Cabinet was informed that a French submarine had attacked the battle fleet, and, on being depth-charged, had surfaced and shown the white flag.

The Prime Minister referred to reports issued by the Germans that they had now dropped 22,000 tons of bombs on this country. It would be worth while for the Air Staff to calculate whether this statement was near the mark. It seemed clear that the air attack on this country had been most ineffectual in relation to the weight of the attack delivered.

September 1940

Winston S. Churchill to Anthony Eden
(*Churchill papers, 20/13*)

24 September 1940
Strictly Private

Many thanks for your interesting paper. There is no difference between us in principle; but the application of the principle raises issues of detail, and this is especially true of the denudation of this Island in the face of the imminent threat of invasion. Meanwhile, the General Staff continue to press for diversions from the Middle East, such as the Seventh Australian Division to be used for garrisoning the Malay Peninsula. This I stopped. Now the two Indian Brigades are to be employed in these jungles against a possible war with Japan, and a still more unlikely Japanese siege of Singapore. The paper on Indian reinforcements was considered last night by me and the Chiefs of Staff. You will see in it that a Division is to be provided for Malaya, another for Busra,[1] and a Corps for Iraq, thus absorbing all the Indian reinforcements available in 1941. This geographical distribution or dispersion of our forces shows the ideas prevailing, which are altogether erroneous in a strategic sense. However, it was explained to me that although all these forces were earmarked to particular theatres, they could all go to the Middle East if required. I therefore agreed to words being inserted making this clear. None the less, the impression produced by the paragraph dispersing these Divisions without regard to war needs made an unfavourable impression upon me.

We have next to consider the increasing waste of troops in Kenya, and the continued waste in Palestine. Some improvement has been made in Palestine, but Kenya, on the contrary, is at this moment to have a Mounted Battery sent there instead of to the Sudan. I fear that when General Smuts goes there he will naturally be influenced by the local situation. However, I hope to keep in touch with him by cable.

Lastly, there is the shocking waste of British regular troops on mere police duty in the Canal Zone, in Cairo, and at Alexandria, and the general slackness of the Middle East Command in concentrating the maximum for battle, and in narrowing the gap between ration strength and fighting strength. I have not had any answer to my request for figures on this point.

My idea, like yours, is to gather the strongest Army in the Middle East possible in the next few months, and I have indicated on other papers the number of Divisions I hope should be assembled there. But I think the first thing would be for the War Office and the Egyptian Command to make the

---

[1] Also spelt Bassorah and (more usually) Basra.

best use possible of the very large number of troops which they have already, and for which we are paying heavily.

Further, I am much disquieted about the position in Malta. It is now agreed that two Battalions shall be sent as reinforcements; but after how much haggling and boggling, and excuses that they could not be accommodated in the Island! Have you read General Dobbie's appreciation and his statement that he has his Battalions all spread on 15-mile fronts each, with no Reserves not already allocated to the defence of Aerodromes? Do you realise there is no command of the sea at Malta, and that it might be attacked at any time by an expeditionary force of 20,000 or 30,000 men from Italy, supported by the Italian Fleet? Yet it was proposed that these two Battalions should go to Freetown to complete the Brigade there, although no enemy can possibly attack Freetown while we have the command of the Atlantic Ocean. You will, I am sure, excuse my putting some of these points to you, because they illustrate tendencies which appear ill-related to the very scheme of war which you have in mind.

WSC

Winston S. Churchill to Lord Halifax
(*Churchill papers, 20/13*)

24 September 1940

Why do the British High Command in Egypt not want Egypt to declare war? I was not myself in a hurry for Egypt to do so when it was merely a question of Italy going to war with us. But now that the frontiers of Egypt have actually been violated, and an invasion is in progress, is it not absurd that war should not be declared by Egypt upon Italy? I understand that King Farouk[1] has money in Italian banks. This may explain his attitude, but not that of the British High Command. When have the High Command expressed the views attributed to them? Ought I to address this question to the Secretary of State for War, or do you know all about it?

Is it simply to prevent the bombing of Cairo? And will it do so?

WSC

[1] Farouk, 1920–65. Born in Cairo. King of Egypt from 1936 to 1952. Overthrown after displaying for many years a politically fatal combination of corruption and incompetence. Died in exile in Rome.

Winston S. Churchill to Neville Chamberlain
(*Churchill papers, 20/1*)

24 September 1940
Personal

My dear Neville,

I hope you will continue at your post, and give me your aid, which I so greatly value. You must however give yourself a fair chance to regain your strength after a serious operation. Therefore please make whatever arrangements are convenient, and let me know if I can be of any service.

The present conditions of bombardment are vexatious but I do not think that they will necessarily continue at their present height for many weeks. I have greatly admired your nerve and stamina under the cruel physical burden which you bear. Let us go on together through the storm. These are great days.

With kindest regards,
Believe me,
Yours ever
Winston S. Churchill

Winston S. Churchill to Admiral John Cunningham and General Irwin
(*Cabinet papers, 65/15*)

25 September 1940
Most Immediate
00.05 a.m.

Your signal 1417N/24 gives no indication of your plans. We asked you particularly to be full and clear in your accounts. Why have you not sent two or three hundred words to let us know your difficulties? and how you propose to meet them?

2. We do not understand conditions under which bombardment proceeded for some hours at 10,000 yards without grave damage to ships or fort unless visibility was so bad as to make targets invisible. Also if visibility bad, why is it not possible to force a landing at beaches near Rufisque in spite of fire from Goree Island.

3. Without this fuller information we can only ask why you do not land in force by night or in the fog or both on beaches near Rufisque and take Rufisque for a start observing that enemy cannot be heart-whole and force at Rufisque is comprised largely of native troops. At the same time if the weather

clears you could hold down batteries on Goree Island in daylight by long-range sea-fire and if there is fog you would not need to do so. It should be possible to feed the force, once ashore, by night. This force once landed ought to be able to advance on Dakar.

4. More ammunition is being sent from Gibraltar but evidently supplies will not stand many days firing like yesterday. Neither is there unlimited time as not only the French but German submarines will probably arrive in six or seven days.

5. Pray act as you think best, but meanwhile give reasoned answer to these points. Matter must be pushed to conclusion without undue delay.

War Cabinet: Confidential Annex
(*Cabinet papers, 65/15*)

25 September 1940   Cabinet War Room
11.30 a.m.

The Prime Minister summarised the situation which had developed at Dakar in the light of various telegrams.

The previous evening a telegram had been received showing that, in spite of a close-range bombardment, the forts had not been reduced, the fire of the French warships had not been neutralised and the morale of the garrison remained high. Fog had interfered considerably with operations.

A Meeting had been held the previous evening with the Service Ministers and the Chiefs of Staff to consider the position, and a telegram had been sent to the Commanders asking for a full account of the situation, and suggesting that a landing might be effected at Rufisque under cover of night or fog.

A further telegram had since been received from the Commanders reporting that a landing was impracticable in face of existing defences and that the only alternatives were either an immediate withdrawal or a continuation of systematic bombardment.

A reply had now been received (which was read out to the War Cabinet by the First Sea Lord) to the telegram despatched the previous evening giving the situation in greater detail. A landing by French fuselier marins had been carried out at Rufisque, but the troops had subsequently been withdrawn. HMS *Cumberland* had suffered damage from the guns of the fortress, our air reconnaissance had been hampered by AA fire and fighters, French resistance remained unimpaired and morale seemed to be high. In conclusion the Commanders had stated their intention to continue the bombardment that morning, and if it proved effective to carry out a landing should this be in any way possible.

Since this telegram had been received information had come through that HMS *Resolution* had been hit (after the bombardment had been resumed) and was withdrawing. The situation was, therefore, obscure and unsatisfactory.

The Prime Minister said that there were two courses open to the Cabinet. The first was to refrain from interfering with the orders of the Commanders on the spot and allow them to go forward with their present proposals to effect a landing if this should prove possible. He would have advised this course before receipt of the news that the *Resolution* had been put out of action; but the withdrawal of this ship added to the risk of the operations. The alternative course was to give orders for the operation to be brought to an end.

There was no doubt that the arrival of the French cruisers had changed the whole complexion of the situation. They had almost certainly brought to Dakar determined officers, who had been put on shore to stiffen the forces there. The landing of a force at this juncture would be a serious step for it might conceivably be cut off. Further, to keep our ships outside Dakar would be to expose them to the risk of attack from U-boats. There was also a report from Tangier that a number of German and Italian aircraft were flying south west, and they might be on their way to Dakar. Once it had been decided to put a force on shore, we might be involved in operations of an indefinite length. Further the fact that our ships were engaged at Dakar would mean delay to the reinforcement of the Mediterranean, and the *Ark Royal* would be unable to return to this country to pick up her new aircraft. A continuance of the 'Menace' operation would undoubtedly commit us to a great effort and great risks.

On the other hand, if it was decided to abandon the operation it was useless for General de Gaulle to proceed to Bathurst where we could not protect his force. In that event, he should be instructed to go to Duala where we could provide a force to safeguard him including, perhaps, the *Resolution*. We should also reinforce Freetown by detaching from the 'Menace' force one or two battalions of Marines.

The abandonment of this operation would undoubtedly mean that we should suffer a serious rebuff and would give a setback to the deterioration which was taking place in the Vichy Government's position. The public would also want to know why we had allowed the French cruisers to pass Gibraltar. The answer to this was that it had not been our policy to stop them proceeding as far as Casablanca. If it was asked why we had not intercepted them at Casablanca the answer was that they had eluded us.

The Prime Minister said that he thought it was essential to give the Commanders on the spot an indication of how we viewed the position, more especially since they might otherwise misinterpret the last sentence in the telegram despatched the previous night. The Prime Minister thereupon withdrew to draft a telegram.

The Prime Minister later returned to the War Cabinet with the draft of a telegram to the Commanders of the forces. This draft was approved, subject to one or two amendments.

The Prime Minister thought that a statement would have to be issued, setting out the reasons why the Expedition had been planned, and the sequence of events which had led to the three French Cruisers and three Contre-torpilleurs[1] passing through the Straits of Gibraltar and reaching Dakar. The statement should explain that the only action which we had taken had been to test the forts; that whereas we had been led to believe that Dakar was anxious to declare for General de Gaulle, we had met with stubborn resistance; and should indicate the reasons why we had decided not to proceed with the further use of force.

The War Cabinet:–
(1) Agreed to the despatch of the telegram attached to this Annex.
(2) Invited the Minister of Information, in consultation with the First Lord of the Admiralty, to prepare a draft Statement on the lines suggested, for consideration later by the Prime Minister and other Ministers concerned.

Winston S. Churchill to Admiral John Cunningham and General Irwin
(*Cabinet papers, 65/15*)

25 September 1940
Most Immediate
1.28 p.m.

On all the information now before us, including damage to *Resolution*, we have decided that the enterprise against Dakar should be abandoned, the obvious evil consequences being faced. Unless something has happened which we do not know which makes you wish to attempt landing in force, you should forthwith break off. You should inform us most immediate whether you concur, but, unless the position has entirely changed in our favour, you should not actually begin landing till you receive our reply.

Assuming enterprise abandoned, we shall endeavour to cover Duala by Naval Force, but we cannot safeguard de Gaulle's forces at Bathurst. Question of reinforcing Freetown with troops is being considered. Instructions regarding disposal of remainder of forces will be given on receipt of your reply.

[1] Torpedo-boat destroyers.

Admiral John Cunningham and General Irwin to Winston S. Churchill
(*Cabinet papers, 65/15*)

25 September 1940
Most Immediate
2.30 p.m.

Concur in breaking off.

On the afternoon of Wednesday, 25 SEPTEMBER 1940, Churchill visited the London docks.

Winston S. Churchill to President Roosevelt
(*Premier papers, 3/276*)

25 September 1940

Am deeply grateful for your action in securing release of rifles. We will use them well. I much regret we had to abandon Dakar enterprise. Vichy got in before us and animated defence with partisans and gunnery experts. All friendly elements were gripped and held down. Several of our ships were hit and to persist with landing in force would have tied us to an undue commitment when you think of what we have on our hands already.

Winston S. Churchill to Commander Cousins[1]
(*Churchill papers, 20/14*)

25 September 1940

Am delighted that your ship should be named after the great Duke of Marlborough, and I am sending you one of his handwritten letters for your Ward Room for luck.[2] Thank you so much for your kind message.

---

[1] Gerald Roger Cousins. Entered the Royal Navy as a Midshipman, 1911. On active service, 1914–18 (DSC). Commander RN, 1940.

[2] The ship was HMS *Churchill*, named after John Churchill, 1st Duke of Marlborough. She was one of the long-awaited American destroyers (see page 841, note 1).

Winston S. Churchill to Herbert Morrison
(*Churchill papers, 20/15*)

25 September 1940
ACTION THIS DAY

I must show you the comments made upon the latest returns of Small Arms Ammunition by my Statistical Department. They cause me the greatest anxiety. In particular the de Wilde ammunition, which is the most valuable, is the most smitten. It seems to me that a most tremendous effort must be made, not only on the whole field of Marks 7 and 8, but on de Wilde and armour-piercing. I am well aware of your difficulties. Will you let me know if there is any way in which I can help you to overcome them?

WSC

Winston S. Churchill to Lord Beaverbrook
(*Churchill papers, 20/13*)

25 September 1940

These wonderful results,[1] achieved under circumstances of increasing difficulty, make it necessary for me to ask you to convey to your Department the warmest thanks and congratulations from His Majesty's Government.

WSC

Neville Chamberlain to Winston S. Churchill
(*Churchill papers, 20/1*)

25 September 1940 Odiham
Personal Hampshire

My dear Winston,

Thank you very much for your kind letter. I will do as you suggest and hope presently to be well enough to return. But it is understood that I am at your disposal to go or stay without any reserve or qualification.

I am afraid Dakar has not gone too well, but I hope we shall succeed in capturing it. I am sure it was right to go for it.

---

[1] In August 1940 a total of 360 British combat aircraft had been destroyed. The production that month was 1,601. Aircraft losses in September totalled 361. The total production that month again exceeded 1,600.

I am glad to see that the Americans are now playing up with the rifles &c.
I am rather under the weather at present but your words have encouraged me to fight against my troubles.

Yours ever
Neville Chamberlain

War Cabinet: minutes
(*Cabinet papers, 65/9*)

26 September 1940   Cabinet War Room
12 noon

The Chief of the Air Staff reported that on the previous day enemy action had consisted of three main attacks – on Filton, Portland and Plymouth. The attack on the Bristol Company's works at Filton had been made by 27 bombers escorted by fighters, and considerable damage had been done to the works, and casualties amongst the staff had been heavy.

The Prime Minister suggested that Lord Chatfield should be invited to visit Filton to enquire whether there had been any outstanding examples of courage, which should be rewarded.

The attacks on Portland and Plymouth had been unsuccessful.

The Prime Minister mentioned that he had received a letter from Lord Trenchard – which he had referred to the Chiefs of Staff – in which he deplored that our bombers should be taken off attacking military objectives in Germany in order to bomb the invasion ports. The Prime Minister thought, however, that we should be assuming a great responsibility if we allowed invasion concentrations to accumulate in the Channel ports without taking action against them. But when the weather in the Channel was unfavourable for invasion, it might be possible to divert more aircraft to targets in Germany.

The Prime Minister said that he understood that the last of the armoured units which had recently been sent to Egypt would not be completely ready to go into action until the 14th October. He asked the Chief of the Imperial General Staff to report the reasons for the long period taken in getting all these units into action.

War Cabinet: Confidential Annex
(*Cabinet papers, 65/15*)

26 September 1940 Cabinet War Room
12 noon

The Prime Minister agreed that we should be careful of embarking upon new adventures with inadequate preparations. But nothing was easier or more fatal than to relapse into a policy of mere negation. He thought history would show that Dakar had failed as the result, not of rashness but of excess of care. It was not to be supposed that General de Gaulle had proposed a landing at Konakri without some assurances of support from French Guinea.

Winston S. Churchill to Lord Trenchard
(*Churchill papers, 20/2*)

26 September 1940
Secret

My dear Trenchard,

I have sent your letter to be considered by the Chiefs of Staff. I think everybody grudges the diversion of effort from Germany which has been imposed upon us by the heavy barge concentrations at the invasion ports; but I hope that this condition may diminish or pass away. Few people, I think, would care to court an invasion in the hopes of being able to deal with it satisfactorily once it had been launched.

You probably are aware that we are under conditions of Alert No. 1. Nevertheless, the weight of the heavy Bombers is kept on Germany in the main.

Yours very sincerely,
Winston S. Churchill

Winston S. Churchill to A. V. Alexander and Admiral Pound
(*Churchill papers, 20/13*)

26 September 1940

What is the speed of these ships?[1] When will they sail and in what convoy? When will they arrive? What special arrangements will you make for their safety? They are of the highest importance.

WSC

Winston S. Churchill to Sir Archibald Sinclair and Sir Cyril Newall
(*Churchill papers, 20/13*)

26 September 1940
Private

Considering that everything depends upon Lord Beaverbrook's success in obtaining the supply of aircraft and the heavy blows he is receiving at Bristol, Southampton and elsewhere, I earnestly trust you will see that his wishes are met fully and immediately in the matter of these spares.[2] I really could not endure another bickering over this, considering the gravity of the situation.

WSC

War Cabinet: minutes
(*Cabinet papers, 65/9*)

27 September 1940 Cabinet War Room
11.30 a.m.

The Prime Minister said that for the week ending the 21st September the number of aircraft repaired and new aircraft produced by the Ministry of Aircraft Production was nearly $2\frac{1}{2}$ times the number of machines that had been destroyed during that week. The output in new construction and repairs had also shown an increase on the output of the preceding week, which had

---

[1] Ships bringing rifles from the United States. These were the *Empire Audacity* (14–15 knots), the *Manchester Exporter* (12 knots), the *Harbury* (10 knots) and the *Biafra* (10 knots). The 5,000-ton *Harbury* was sunk in the mid-Atlantic on 5 May 1943. In his reply to Churchill, Alexander wrote: 'We anticipate that *Empire Audacity* will be ready to sail in Convoy HX 79, leaving Halifax on the 7th October and the other three ships in HX 80 on the 11th October. These convoys should arrive at West Coast ports on the 22nd October and the 26th October respectively. We shall do the best we can to reinforce from the Western Approaches two normal HX destroyer escorts as we have done previously when important cargoes of munitions have been included in the convoys' (*Premier papers, 3/372/1*).

[2] Lord Beaverbrook had asked for authority to order surplus stocks then in the Universal Equipment Depots.

been very satisfactory. He was sure that the War Cabinet would wish to congratulate the Minister of Aircraft Production on this fine achievement. The War Cabinet warmly endorsed this view.

The Prime Minister drew attention to telegram No. 784 from Madrid. According to the Spanish Minister for Foreign Affairs,[1] M. Laval[2] had asked the Spanish Government to allow the flight of French aeroplanes over Spanish and Moroccan territory for attack on Gibraltar. This request had been refused. M. Laval had also asked the German Government to take out of Toulon at once the *Strasbourg*, three 10,000-ton cruisers, three light cruisers, four destroyers and twelve submarines, presumably for the purpose of attacking the British Fleet.

The Prime Minister reported that the German wireless had just announced that a Three-Power Pact had been signed in Berlin between Herr von Ribbentrop,[3] Count Ciano[4] and the Japanese Ambassador,[5] to create a

[1] Colonel John Beigbeder. Spanish Foreign Minister, August 1939 to October 1940. Believed by General Franco to lack enthusiasm for the pro-German orientation of Spanish policy. In September 1940 Serrano Suñer, head of the Falange, was sent by Franco on a formal visit to Berlin to indicate the desire for closer Spanish–German links (Suñer replaced Beigbeder as Foreign Minister a month after this mission).

[2] Pierre Laval, 1883–1945. A lawyer. Socialist Deputy for the Seine, 1914–19 and (as an Independent) 1924–7. Independent Senator, 1927–44. Minister of Public Works, 1925; of Justice, 1926; of Labour, 1930 and 1932. Prime Minister and Foreign Minister, 1931–2 and 1935–6. Foreign Minister, 1934–5. Deputy Prime Minister and Minister of Information (under Pétain), July–December 1940. Prime Minister (under Pétain), April 1942 to August 1944 (also Foreign Minister, Minister of the Interior, and Minister of Information and Propaganda). Arrested by the Gestapo, 1944, and interned, 1944–5. Tried in Paris for treason, his trial began on 4 October 1945; he was sentenced to death on 10 October and executed on 15 October.

[3] Joachim von Ribbentrop, 1893–1946. Champagne salesman in Canada, 1910–14. Lieutenant, Western Front, 1914–18, when he was wounded, and won the Iron Cross, first class. Aide-de-camp to the German peace delegation in Paris, 1919. Head of a wine import-export business in Berlin, 1920–33. A National Socialist Deputy in the Reichstag, 1933. Ambassador to London, 1936–8. SS-Gruppenführer, 1936. Foreign Minister, 1938–45. Sentenced to death by the Allied Military Tribunal, Nuremberg, and hanged.

[4] Galeazzo Ciano, 1903–44. Entered the Italian diplomatic service, 1925. Married Mussolini's daughter Edda in 1930. Mussolini's Minister of State for Foreign Affairs, 1936–43. Ambassador to the Vatican, 1943, where he sought means of extracting Italy from the war. Voted for the dismissal of Mussolini at the Fascist Grand Council, 25 July 1943. Tricked into travelling to Germany, and arrested by the Gestapo. Handed over to a Fascist court in northern Italy, sentenced to death for treason, and shot, 11 January 1944.

[5] General Count Hiroshi Oshima, Japanese Ambassador in Berlin. His top-secret messages, sent by radio from Berlin to Tokyo, were systematically intercepted and read by British and American Signals Intelligence, giving vital information about German plans and intentions. It was through Oshima's message on 9 May 1944 that the Allies learned that the German High Command had no inkling that Normandy was the objective of the D-Day landing. His messages also revealed that the Germans believed, as late as 1 June 1944, when a Normandy landing had been suspected, that the true landing would be in the Pas de Calais: as late as 15 July 1944 Oshima reported that the Germans still thought that the Normandy landing was a feint for the main cross-Channel assault in the Calais area.

new order in Asia and Europe. A significant point of the Pact was that the three Powers would help each other if attacked by any Power not taking part in this war or in the Sino-Japanese war. The Pact, therefore, seemed to be directed against the United States of America.

The view generally expressed was that the Pact, which would probably anger the United States of America, left matters very much as they were, and did not affect the general situation. If anything, it was likely to accelerate the entry of the United States into the war. There was no support in the War Cabinet for the view, sometimes advanced, that the United States of America could lend us more help by staying out of the war.

The Prime Minister referred to telegram No. 2107 from Washington referring to a statement made by the President in conversation with our Ambassador, as to certain action in the event of Portugal being taken over by Germany.[1]

The Secretary of State for Air gave figures of the Hurricanes now available in this country which showed a considerable improvement on the position on the 1st September. He also gave figures showing our great numerical inferiority in fighters in the Middle East.

The Minister of Aircraft Production agreed that the position as regards fighters available in this country had considerably improved since the 1st September. Nevertheless he was strongly opposed to further withdrawals of either aircraft or pilots. The Battle of Britain was the only battle that counted.

The Prime Minister recommended that the situation should be kept constantly under review. The balance of argument was in favour of despatching from this country for the Middle East the aircraft shown in WP (40) 388 as awaiting despatch during the rest of September and during October.[2] In order that the programme of shipments should not be impeded, the packing of these aircraft should proceed immediately.

The question of the despatch of aircraft to the Middle East in November should be brought before the War Cabinet for decision in three weeks' time.

---

[1] On 25 September 1940 Lord Lothian telegraphed to Churchill: 'President last night said to me in casual conversation that if Portugal was taken over by the Germans he thought that it would be quite easy to provoke a revolution in the Azores separating the islands from Portugal, and that the best way of doing that would be for the British and the Americans immediately to send a gunboat each. Apparently he has met revolutionary leader who claims to have support of four-fifths of the population.' (*Foreign Office papers, 371/24522*).

[2] The aircraft involved were 66 Blenheims, 16 Wellingtons, 18 Hurricanes and 6 Lysanders. They were to be sent by sea to Takoradi, and then across Africa by air (*Cabinet papers, 66/12*).

John Colville: diary
(*Colville papers*)

27 September 1940

Overheard in the Cabinet: the PM – 'Personally I should like to wage war on a great scale in the Middle East. By next spring I hope we shall have sufficient forces there.' He has been taking tremendous pains lately about the despatch of reinforcements to Egypt and the position of the Australian and New Zealand contingents in that part of the world.

Winston S. Churchill to Herbert Morrison
(*Churchill papers, 4/201*)

27 September 1940

My dear Minister of Supply,

Some time has passed since two programmes of tank production, the 'target' programme and the 'reasonable expectations' programme, were presented to the Defence Committee (Supply), differing from one another by about 35%.

I should be glad to know if you are now in a better position to judge whether you will be able to reach the target during the next five quarters.

I understand that we are short of capacity for producing armour plate, alloy steel and drop forgings, but that at some sacrifice of other departmental requirements it ought to be just possible to meet the tank requirements for these materials in full.

If this is so, I should like to know if you are able to guarantee the target programme. Or are there still other shortages? Are you in a position to specify these precisely? Is your factory capacity organized so that, if the materials are forthcoming, the full programme can be completed? And has the Minister of Labour promised to meet your requirements of skilled labour for tank production in full?

Yours very sincerely,
Winston S. Churchill

Winston S. Churchill to the Dominion Prime Ministers[1]
(*Churchill papers, 20/14*)

27 September 1940

You will have seen from the Secretary of State's[2] message, sent through High Commissioner in telegram of 25th September, Circular Z, No. 258, that we decided to break off at Dakar. Situation there was changed by arrival of French cruisers from Toulon, which eluded our Naval forces and entered Dakar. There is no doubt that, apart from their own fighting power, these vessels brought some tough Vichy personnel to grip the garrison and townsfolk and man the batteries effectively. Having deposited this very important contingent at Dakar, French cruisers tried to go to Duala. They were intercepted by the Navy and two agreed to return to Casa Blanca. The other two went back into Dakar. On this serious change it seemed advisable to abandon the enterprise, but our Commanders on the spot and General de Gaulle pleaded to be allowed to test the defences and the morale of the garrison, on which all depended. We authorised them, therefore, to act as they thought best. It became clear, after the second day's operations, that the resistance of the fortress and of the French ships, including the heavy guns of the *Richelieu*, was most formidable. *Resolution* was torpedoed by a submarine and is making her way to Freetown. *Cumberland* was hit in the engine room by a large shell and is now in Bathurst. Both these ships will take some time to repair. *Barham* and *Australia* were hit without affecting their fighting efficiency. *Dragon* and *Inglefield* were slightly damaged. We sunk two French submarines which attacked us, capturing the crew of one. One destroyer was set on fire by *Australia*. It seems likely that *Richelieu* sustained further damage, but we have no proof yet. In view of new proportions which the operation had assumed, Commanders on the spot now advised discontinuance. In the circumstances we did not think it right to throw our troops on shore as we might thereby have been tied down and committed to a prolonged operation not against the Germans but against the French. This would have been detrimental politically to de Gaulle and also to our general position with the Vichy Government. Operations had miscarried through mis-chance and misfortune of prior arrival of French cruisers and reinforcements. Ships must return soon to Mediterranean. Troops also have other tasks. We decided to cut the loss, which is appreciable but should not be viewed out of proportion to the scale of events. I am sorry not to have a better tale to tell.

---

[1] William Mackenzie King (Canada), Robert Menzies (Australia), Peter Fraser (New Zealand) and General Smuts (South Africa).

[2] The Secretary of State for Dominion Affairs, Viscount Caldecote.

September 1940

Winston S. Churchill to General Ismay
(*Churchill papers, 20/13*)

28 September 1940

1. I approve the general dispositions proposed for the troops and transports of former M Force, with a view to being handy for 'Shrapnel' and 'Alloy'.[1] At the same time, these forces will give extra protection at various British West African ports.

2. I agree that it would be desirable in the circumstances for General de Gaulle to proceed to Duala and consolidate or extend his position in the Cameroons and Equatoria. But we must first of all allow him to disembark at Freetown, and we must await the fuller expression of his views and wishes. Nothing is to be done meanwhile which would prevent us from giving effect to his reasonable requests.

3. The commercial blockade of Dakar is to be intensified by every possible means, in order to put the utmost pressure upon that place by want of food and the ruin of its trade. No change must be made in our general policy towards the Vichy Government, and French trade and ships, until fresh decisions are taken by the Cabinet. It would be a great mistake to fall into a mood of being afraid of offending Vichy, or trying to 'kiss and make friends.' I do not doubt that the larger forces which are at work will soon efface the setback in French sentiment arising out of our fiasco at Dakar.

WSC

Winston S. Churchill to General Ismay
(*Churchill papers, 20/13*)

28 September 1940

1. These two papers cause me great anxiety.[2] I had understood that Randle had been working at full capacity as a result of the orders given by the War Cabinet on October 13, 1939, i.e., almost exactly a year ago. What is the explanation of the neglect to fulfil these orders, and who is responsible for it?[3]

2. Secondly, it appears that practically no steps have been taken to make

---

[1] 'Shrapnel' and 'Alloy' were the code names for the seizure of the Cape Verde Islands (Portuguese) and the Azores (Spanish) respectively.
[2] Not printed.
[3] A Chiefs of Staff Committee note, No. 787 of 1940, 'Chemical Warfare', of 29 September 1940, commented: 'The mustard gas plant at Randle has not been working at full capacity owing to lack of bulk storage arrangements. The original plant will now be worked to capacity to fill bombs, shells, and the new storage at Valley (Antelope)' (*Cabinet papers, 80/19*). Valley is in Anglesey, near Holyhead.

projectiles or containers, either for Air or artillery to discharge these various commodities. The programme now set out would clearly take many months before any results are realised. Let me have an immediate report on this. The highest priority must be given. I regard the danger as very great.

3. Thirdly, the possibility of our having to retaliate on the German civil population must be studied, and on the largest scale possible. We should never begin, but we must be able to reply. Speed is vital here.

4. Fourthly, instant measures should be taken to raise Randle to full production, and above all to disperse the existing stock.

5. What are the actual amounts in stock?

E. A. Seal to the Private Office
(*Premier papers, 4/80/3*)

28 September 1940

Will everybody please take note that from now on boxes will come regularly every day from 'C' marked 'Only to be opened by the Prime Minister in person'. This marking is not mere camouflage and is to be taken seriously. The boxes are to be put on the Prime Minister's desk and left for him to re-lock. They will be returned to 'C'.[1]

In any case of doubt as to whether a particular box comes within this category, it should be brought immediately to me.

EAS

Winston S. Churchill to Herbert Morrison
(*Churchill papers, 20/13*)

28 September 1940

Recent air raids have shown that the production of certain vital munitions, and particularly De Wilde ammunition, has been concentrated in one factory with the result that output has been seriously curtailed by one successful raid. Pray let me have a report on the distribution of the production of every important key munition. It will then be possible to assess the danger of serious reductions in output and to consider what can be done to distribute the risk more widely.

WSC

[1] This note marks the beginning of the daily scrutiny by Churchill of summaries of decrypted German top-secret radio messages, sent to him by Colonel Menzies ('C') from his offices in Victoria. The decrypted messages, mostly those sent between German headquarters and German units in the field by Enigma machine, were at this early stage principally German Air Force signals. Because the German Air Force acted in close co-operation with the German Army, the decrypts revealed a great deal about military as well as air operations and intentions.

Winston S. Churchill to Sir Horace Wilson
(*Churchill papers, 20/13*)

28 September 1940

I think there are very grave dangers in its becoming known that Civil Servants are only working four days and then one off. You say that this only applies to limited numbers; therefore there is nothing in the argument that this will relieve congestion on the London Transport system. You also say it is only of a temporary character; therefore I think you should bring it to an end at once.

Pray report to me how many are affected.[1]

WSC

Winston S. Churchill to Sir Edward Bridges and General Ismay
(*Churchill papers, 20/13*)

29 September 1940

I think it important that 'Paddock' should be broken in. Thursday next, therefore, the Cabinet will meet there. At the same time, other Departments should be encouraged to try a preliminary move of a skeleton staff. If possible, lunch should be provided for the Cabinet and those attending it.

WSC

Winston S. Churchill to Sir Edward Bridges
(*Cabinet papers, 115/70*)

29 September 1940

BRITISH MISSIONS IN THE UNITED STATES

I am sorry you are not able to make me a more clear-cut proposal about these missions.[2] I cannot feel that 'all is for the best in the best of all possible

---

[1] On 2 October 1940 Horace Wilson sent Churchill a report about the time that had been lost in Government departments owing to air raid warnings. Three days later Churchill asked Wilson to make a combined table for each Government office covering the previous six days 'and place the offices in order of merit. Let me see the result. At the same time circulate this Order of Merit and the attached table to all the Departments of State concerned, and follow this procedure every week. The Cabinet should also be apprised' (Prime Minister's Personal Minute, M151, *Churchill papers, 20/13*).

[2] In a minute on 28 September 1940, Sir Edward Bridges had explained that the Layton mission was temporary, that the 'difficulties and overlapping' of the Pakenham-Walsh mission had been 'straightened out', and that 'Purvis is on very intimate terms with Morgenthau, who is such an important means of approach to the President' (*Cabinet papers, 115/70*). Among the British missions then in the United States were those connected with Army, Navy, Air Force, raw materials and shipping needs.

worlds.' You had better consult with Sir Arthur Salter[1] with a view to outlining proposals for a considerable tidying-up. In the meanwhile, Sir Walter Layton should be asked through the Ministry of Labour to expedite his return, and the War Office should be asked to do the same by Pakenham-Walsh.[2] The Admiralty should also be asked about Missions 5 and 6. When can they be wound up, and are they already placed under the general control of Mr Purvis? When is Sir Henry Tizard's[3] mission coming to an end, and why does Sir Andrew Agnew[4] delay his return?

---

[1] James Arthur Salter, 1881–1975. Transport Department, Admiralty, 1904. Chairman, Allied Maritime Transport Executive, 1918. Knighted, 1922. Director, Economic and Finance Section, League of Nations, 1919–20 and 1922–31. Professor of Political Theory and Institutions, Oxford, 1934–44. Independent MP for Oxford University, 1937–50. Parliamentary Secretary, Ministry of Shipping, 1939–41; Ministry of War Transport, 1941. Head of the British Merchant Shipping Mission, Washington, 1941–3. Chancellor of the Duchy of Lancaster, 1945. Conservative MP, 1951–3. Minister of State for Economic Affairs, 1951–2. Minister of Materials, 1952–3. Created Baron, 1953.

[2] Ridley Pakenham Pakenham-Walsh, 1888–1966. Educated at Cheltenham College and the Royal Military Academy, Woolwich. 2nd Lieutenant, Royal Engineers, 1908; on active service at the Dardanelles, 1915–18 (Military Cross, despatches). British Representative, International Commission, Teschen, 1919–20. Instructor in Tactics, School of Military Engineering, 1923–6. Lieutenant-Colonel, 1928. Colonel, 1932. Churchill's travel companion and military adviser on the Marlborough biography, 1932. Assistant Adjutant-General, War Office, 1934–5. Brigadier, General Staff, Eastern Command, 1935–9. Major-General, June 1939. Commandant, School of Military Engineering, and Inspector, Royal Engineers, 1939. Engineer-in-Chief, British Expeditionary Force, 1939–40 (wounded, despatches). General Officer Commanding, Northern Ireland District, 1940–1; Salisbury Plain District, 1942. Lieutenant-General, 1941. Controller-General of Army Provision, 1943–6. Vice-Chairman, Harlow New Town Development Corporation, 1948–9.

[3] Henry Thomas Tizard, 1885–1959. Educated at Westminster School, Magdalen College, Oxford and Imperial College. Lecturer in Natural Science, Oxford, 1911–21. Royal Garrison Artillery, 1914; Royal Flying Corps, 1915–18. Lieutenant-Colonel, and Assistant Controller of Experiments and Research, RAF, 1918–19. Permanent Secretary, Department of Scientific and Industrial Research, 1927–9. Rector of Imperial College, 1929–42. Chairman, Aeronautical Research Committee, 1933–43. Knighted, 1937. Member of Council, Ministry of Aircraft Production, 1941–3. President of Magdalen College, Oxford, 1942–6. Chairman, Advisory Council on Scientific Policy and Defence Research Policy, 1946–52.

[4] Andrew Agnew, 1882–1955. A member of the Singapore Harbour Board, 1911–19. CBE, 1918. Subsequently Director of Shell Petroleum and Managing Director of the Shell Transport and Trading Company. Knighted, 1938.

Winston S. Churchill to Lord Halifax
(*Foreign Office papers, 800/323*)

29 September 1940

I think Sam[1] is doing very well in Madrid, and has established most valuable contacts. It would be a great pity for him to come home until or unless he is forced to do so.

I entirely agree with your letter to me of September 28 that we should delegate authority to our Embassy at Madrid to smooth the economic path, and settle minor blockade points out of hand. The Economic Warfare Ministry naturally do their best against the enemy, but they must be restrained, as you suggest, in regard to Spain. I would far rather we should pay our way with Spain by economic favours, and other favours, than by promises of giving up Gibraltar after we have won the war.

I do not mind if the Spaniards go into French Morocco. The letters exchanged with de Gaulle do not commit us to any exact restoration of the territories of France, and the attitude of the Vichy Government towards us and towards him has undoubtedly justified a harder feeling towards France than existed at the time of her collapse. I would far rather see the Spaniards in Morocco than the Germans, and if the French have to pay for their abject attitude, it is better that they should pay in Africa to Spain than in Europe to either of the guilty Powers. Indeed, I think you should let them know that we shall be no obstacle to their Moroccan ambitions, provided they preserve their neutrality in the war.

WSC

Winston S. Churchill to Sir Archibald Sinclair
(*Churchill papers, 20/13*)

29 September 1940
Private

I am very glad to find that you are as usual completely satisfied. I merely referred the Foreign Office telegram to you in order to test once more that impenetrable armour of departmental confidence which you have donned since you ceased to lead an Opposition to the Government and became one of its pillars. Either you must have been very wrong in the old days, or we must all have improved enormously since the change.

---

[1] Sir Samuel Hoare, British Ambassador to Spain. A former Foreign Secretary, Secretary of State for Air, and Secretary of State for India, Hoare was anxious to become Viceroy of India, but received no further public office after Spain.

This is, I think, at once the most reasonable and most gratifying conclusion.

I am not by any means convinced that the bombing of marshalling yards is not pushed too far. On the whole I believe the school who think it does very little harm except at moments when great troop movements are in progress, have reason on their side.

WSC

Winston S. Churchill to Neville Chamberlain
(*Churchill papers, 2/393*)

29 September 1940   Chequers

My dear Neville,

I must thank you for your letter placing yourself unreservedly in my hands, and I was grieved to learn from Edward how hard you have found the struggle to do your work under the severe conditions which prevail in London, – and will certainly become more marked as the dark hours lengthen. I do not feel in the circumstances that I ought to continue to press you further.

I find myself in need of help and must make arrangements to fill the gap and somewhat to enlarge our central instrument. A whole array of problems are bearing down upon us with the winter, which must be spent by millions under nightly bombardment. I propose therefore to make a number of changes in the Cabinet, and to accept the resignation of your office which you have proffered. In doing this let me express to you my admiration for the heroic effort you have made to do your duty and to see this grim business through, and my sincere sorrow that with nerve unshaken and mental prowess unimpaired, your physical strength no longer bears you up in a public station. I trust indeed that having put down this burden you will find life more endurable, and that a real improvement will set in.

I have greatly valued our comradeship and your aid and counsel during these five violent months, and I beg you to believe me your sincere friend,

Yours ever,
Winston S. Churchill

Winston S. Churchill to Lord Halifax
(*Churchill papers, 2/395*)

29 September 1940   Chequers
Private

My dear Edward,

I have decided to accept Neville's proffered resignation in view of the melancholy accounts I have received of his condition and of the impossibility of his continuing to work in London under the increasing severity of the enemy's attack. I have just written to him in this sense. Although our partnership has been short, it has travelled through the storms, and it is with sincere regret that I view its ending.

I now wish to ask you whether you would prefer to succeed him as Lord President in the second position in the Government, or to remain at the Foreign Office. If you will continue as you are, I propose to offer the Lord Presidency to Anthony. If you elect to change, then Anthony would take your place. I beg you to believe that either course is equally agreeable to me. I felt however that I ought to put the choice before you as both you and Anthony are a lap behind me in the march of time.[1]

Should you choose the Lord Presidency with the sphere of duties which Neville discharged, I should hope you would come to live at No. 11 (as long as it stands!) and of course you would have to lead the House of Lords.

Pray let me know what you will do, as other changes are consequential upon your decision.

Yours ever,
Winston S. Churchill

Anthony Eden: diary
(*'The Reckoning'*)

30 September 1940

Winston sent for me about 5 p.m. to ask me whether I would join his Cabinet as Lord President, or stay where I was. I asked which he would like me to do. He said that he preferred that I should decide for myself. I asked what the duties of Lord President would be. He said there might be some revision in an upward direction, but mainly those Neville had carried out and entirely domestic. He added that, as I knew, he had hoped to be able to offer me Foreign Office, but Edward clearly did not want to move to Lord President and he feared that if he suggested it, Edward would ask to go altogether, which Winston did not want at the moment Neville was leaving.

I asked for an hour or two to consider, but said that my present inclination was to stay where I was. Winston seemed to agree and said future was mine anyway. We then went to Cabinet where a noisy and discursive discussion on man-power and supply took place.

After dinner wrote Winston a note saying I would do as he wished, but if he left choice to me I was content to stay where I was. Winston sent for me before note was delivered and I took it over with me. Found him depressed because

---

[1] Churchill was born in 1874, Halifax in 1881 and Eden in 1897.

Max is suffering from asthma and will not take on Supply which is in a mess. This was holding up all his arrangements. I told him that if he wished for help in defence I was ready to do anything I could, even to give up War Office to be Lord President. I would then sit with Chiefs of Staff and him on Defence Committee, and could perhaps relieve him of much. Winston appeared to like this. He reiterated that he was now an old man, that he would not make Lloyd George's mistake of carrying on after the war, that the succession must be mine. John Anderson could clearly not 'be in the way' in this respect. He admitted that Kingsley's appointment would not be popular, but said the Chancellor must be in Cabinet if financial control was to be kept.[1]

Winston S. Churchill to Anthony Eden
(*Churchill papers, 20/1*)

30 September 1940

My dear Anthony,

You very kindly sent me the attached return dated 21.9.40 about the equipment of the Independent Companies and Commandos. I showed it to Sir Roger Keyes yesterday, the 29th, and he was very pleased to know that this was contemplated. It has not, however, materialized at present in any way. I had No. 7 Commando at Felixstowe rung up as a sample. It has no Bren guns, no Anti-Tank rifles, and though it has some Tommy guns, they have no ammunition. It is 100 men short of establishment, and enlistment is still shut down. I think you will probably wish to deal with the person who has sent you this misleading return. In your covering note to me, you say the figures deal with 'what has been sent them.'

I am sorry to be insistent upon these small points, but they have an alarming aspect.

WSC

---

[1] The Cabinet changes were announced on 3 October 1940. Sir John Anderson succeeded Neville Chamberlain as Lord President of the Council. Sir Kingsley Wood, the Chancellor of the Exchequer, joined the War Cabinet, as did the Minister of Labour and National Service, Ernest Bevin. Lord Cranborne succeeded Lord Caldecote (Sir Thomas Inskip) at the Dominions Office. Herbert Morrison succeeded Sir John Anderson as Home Secretary and Minister for Home Security. Sir Andrew Duncan succeeded Morrison as Minister of Supply. Oliver Lyttelton succeeded Sir Andrew Duncan as President of the Board of Trade. Sir John Reith became Minister of Works and Building, being succeeded by Moore-Brabazon as Minister of Transport. Eden, Halifax and Beaverbrook remained at the War Office, Foreign Office and Aircraft Production respectively.

September 1940

Winston S. Churchill to Herbert Morrison and Sir Andrew Duncan
(*Churchill papers, 20/13*)

30 September 1940
ACTION THIS DAY

I am sure we ought to increase our Steel purchases from the United States so as to save tonnage on ore. I should like to buy another couple of million tons, in various stages of manufacture. Then we should be able to resume the plan of the Anderson Shelters, and various other steel requirements which press upon us. I would if necessary telegraph to the President.

WSC

Winston S. Churchill to Sir Archibald Sinclair
(*Cherwell papers*)

30 September 1940

1. In my Minute No. 107 of September 20, I meant 16 instead of 12. I should have said you have reduced the initial equipment of the Fighter Squadrons from the temporary 20 to 16. I am sorry for this slip, but I was dictating from memory. My desiderata figures should therefore be corrected to 1,280 and 1,600 respectively for January and April 1941.

2. I see you calculate a wastage of Pilots from between 25 to 30 per cent first-line strength per month. Actually during these five months of very heavy fighting from May to September inclusive the loss has been only 14 per cent. I should have thought this realised result would be a firm foundation for the summer months, and that two-thirds of this rate might be assumed for the winter months. Will you kindly recalculate your position on this basis, assuming it is found correct, and showing what possibilities of expansion would be open.

3. I do not understand your figures in para. 4 about losses of eight-Gun Fighters. My information is that we are definitely stronger in Hurricanes and Spitfires than we were at the beginning of the five months' battle. You have no doubt seen Lord Beaverbrook's tables of loss and gain. For your convenience I attach a copy, which kindly return. You now state that during the heavy fighting of the last seven weeks you have eaten into your Reserves to the tune of 45 per cent. If this refers to the numbers in the ASUs,[1] you should consider that these Units were practically empty when the change of Government took place, and that if you look back over the five months' period, which is a truer basis than the arbitrarily selected seven weeks, you are far better off.

---

[1] Army Service Units: aircraft, more than a thousand in all, that were being used with army formations in Britain, for reconnaisance and transport.

4. You also say that you have only 288 eight-Gun Fighters in reserve, and that this represents no more than 11 days' supply. This implies that we are losing 26 eight-Gun Fighters a day, or roughly 800 a month in this category alone. This, of course, is entirely contrary to any figures you have ever disclosed to the public. Perhaps you will look into this, as I am sure your figures do not represent the facts. The published figures up to date for September amount to no more than 287 Fighter machines, or little more than 10 a day.

WSC

Winston S. Churchill: broadcast[1]
(*Churchill papers, 9/144*)

30 September 1940

To-day is the second anniversary of the Munich Agreement, a date which the world will always remember for the tragic sacrifice made by the Czecho-Slovak people in the interest of European peace. The hopes which this agreement stirred in the heart of civilized mankind have been frustrated. Within six months the solemn pledges given by the unscrupulous men who control the destiny of Germany were broken and the agreement destroyed with a ruthlessness which unmasked the true nature of their reckless ambitions to the whole world.

The protection which Hitler forced upon you has been a sham and a cloak for the incorporation of your once flourishing country in the so-called Greater Reich. Instead of protection he has brought you nothing but moral and material devastation, and to-day the followers of that great and tolerant humanitarian, President Masaryk,[2] are being persecuted with a deliberate cruelty which has few parallels in modern history.

In this hour of your martyrdom I send you this message. The battle which we in Britain are fighting to-day is not only our battle. It is also your battle, and, indeed, the battle of all nations who prefer liberty to a soulless serfdom. It is the struggle of civilized nations for the right to live their own life in the

---

[1] The text of Churchill's broadcast was published in *The Times* on 1 October 1940 with a note: 'On the occasion of the second anniversary of the Munich Agreement yesterday the following special message was broadcast to the Czecho-Slovak people from Mr Churchill.'

[2] Thomas Masaryk, 1850–1937. Professor of Philosophy, Prague, 1882–1914. Entered the Austrian Parliament as a member of the Young Czech Party, 1891. Active on behalf of Czech independence, he was in London, 1914–17, then in Russia, where he formed the Czech Legion. The founding father of Czech-Slovak unity. President of Czechoslovakia, 1918–35. His son Jan was the Czech envoy in London, 1925–38 and Foreign Minister, 1941–5 (in London) and 1945–8 (in Prague). A month after the Communist seizure of power, his body was found under an open window of the Foreign Ministry.

manner of their own choosing. It represents man's instinctive defiance of tyranny and of an impersonal universe.

Throughout history no European nation has shown a greater will to survive than yours, and to-day again your people have given countless proofs of their courage in adversity. Here in Britain we have welcomed with pride and gratitude your soldiers and airmen who have come by daring escapes to take part with ever-increasing success in that battle for Britain which is also the battle for Czecho-Slovakia.[1] And no less sincere is our admiration of those Czechs and Slovaks who on the home front are risking death, and worse than death, in order to foster resistance against a cruel and heartless oppressor.

It is because we both are fighting for the fundamental decencies of human life that we are determined that neither our struggle nor your struggle shall be in vain. It is for this reason that we have refused to recognize any of the brutal conquests of Germany in Central Europe and elsewhere, that we have welcomed a Czecho-Slovak Provisional Government in this country, and that we have made the restoration of Czecho-Slovak liberties one of our principal war aims. With firmness and resolution, two qualities which our nations share in equal measure, these aims will be achieved. Be of good cheer. The hour of your deliverance will come. The soul of freedom is deathless; it cannot, and will not, perish.

Winston S. Churchill to Neville Chamberlain
(*Churchill papers, 2/393*)

30 September 1940   10 Downing Street

My dear Neville,

Please write as you propose and I will reply. These letters can be published on Wednesday, by which time I expect to have settled the necessary changes.

I am deeply grieved that you must leave us.

I hope that I may submit your name to the King for the Garter. Austen[2] had it and was proud to wear it. Unless you forbid me this will be done.

Yours ever
Winston S. Churchill

---

[1] Two Czech squadrons fought in the Battle of Britain. It was a Czech pilot, Sergeant Josef Frantisek, who achieved the highest individual score of any pilot in the battle, with seventeen confirmed kills.

[2] Joseph Austen Chamberlain, 1863–1937. Educated at Rugby and Trinity College, Cambridge. Conservative MP, 1892–1937. Chancellor of the Exchequer, 1903–5. Unsuccessful candidate for the leadership of the Conservative Party, 1911. Secretary of State for India, 1915–17. Minister without Portfolio, 1918–19. Chancellor of the Exchequer, 1919–21. Lord Privy Seal, 1921–2. Foreign Secretary, 1924–9. Knight of the Garter, 1925. First Lord of the Admiralty, 1931. Half-brother of Neville Chamberlain.

October 1940

Neville Chamberlain to Winston S. Churchill
(*Churchill papers, 2/393*)

1 October 1940
Personal

My dear Winston,

Thank you so much. I enclose my letter which I hope you will approve.[1] I shant have time to see your reply before you publish, but I am quite happy to leave its terms to you.

It is kind of you to think of putting me forward for so great an honour as the Garter, but you will, I think, not misunderstand me when I say that I prefer to die plain Mr Chamberlain like my father before me, unadorned by any title. This applies to the Garter just as much as to a peerage which you once before suggested to me.

I shall continue to watch your conduct of affairs with anxious solicitude & the most earnest wishes for your success.

Yours ever
Neville Chamberlain

Anthony Eden: diary
(*'The Reckoning'*)

1 October 1940

Not having heard from Winston all day and having gone to bed, I was fetched round after midnight in pyjamas. I protested that I was in bed,

---

[1] In his formal letter of resignation to Churchill, Chamberlain wrote of his 'unshaken conviction that under your leadership this country with her Allies and associates will succeed in overcoming the forces of barbarism which have reduced a great part of Europe to a condition little better than slavery' (*Churchill papers, 2/393*).

October 1940

but W said he must talk over his list with me. I found David and KW[1] leaving.

Winston said that he had thought over defence suggestion[2] and had reluctantly decided to turn it down. It would make too many cogs in the machine and I should be in an uncomfortable position, which is perfectly true. He referred to my two letters, the latter written late Monday night after our talk. 'Your two very sweet letters, so generous and worthy of the occasion.' He lamented that he could not give me Foreign Office and thus bring me into War Cabinet and seemed distressed at this. 'It is not what I want', he repeated many times. He thought at Foreign Office I could help much with USA. I begged him not to worry about all this. Said with truth that I was happier where I was. He said: 'We shall work this war together' and began to talk of future projects and Smuts' view on Dakar, which I pointed out had been modified by a later telegram he had not seen. He said: 'You can keep your Dill!' So that is the end, I hope, of that long battle.[3] We parted in the early hours.

Hugh Dalton: diary
('The Second World War Diary of Hugh Dalton')

1 October 1940

A meeting of ministers to whom PM explains present situation. Invasion 'menace' still remains, and will, so long as Germans have in that long row of ports transport enough to put half a million men on board and in the Channel and North Sea on any night they choose. But, as the weather breaks and the season advances, the invasion must surely seem to them more and more difficult.

Sir John Reith: diary
('The Reith Diaries')

1 October 1940

Meeting with PM in Cabinet War Room. Told us about Dakar. A sorry story. Command of the seas doesn't mean what it ought – by a long way. He

---

[1] David Margesson (the Chief Whip) and Sir Kingsley Wood (Chancellor of the Exchequer).
[2] Eden had offered to help Churchill on defence matters as Lord President of the Council.
[3] As Eden wished, General Dill was to remain as Chief of the Imperial General Staff. A year later, on 16 November 1941, Churchill offered the post to General Brooke, who took up his duties, and became a member of the Chiefs of Staff Committee, on Christmas Day 1941.

didn't think it was such a sorry tale and was very indignant at press criticism. He thought things were going well – despite the destruction of London. Invasion by no means improbable.

War Cabinet: minutes
(*Cabinet papers, 65/9*)

1 October 1940 Cabinet War Room
11.30 a.m.

DAKAR

The Prime Minister read to the War Cabinet a personal telegram from Mr Menzies to the effect that the Australian Government were much disturbed over the failure of this operation, the conduct of which was strongly criticised. The telegram ended by expressing the hope that we had not underestimated the difficulties we should have to meet in the Middle East.

The Prime Minister read the terms of the reply which he proposed to send. This reply met with the complete approval of the War Cabinet.

War Cabinet: Confidential Annex
(*Cabinet papers, 65/15*)

1 October 1940 Cabinet War Room
11.30 a.m.

The Prime Minister said that we should not allow a particular incident to influence our judgment unduly. Dakar had been unfortunate, and had chilled and repressed a movement favourable to us, but that incident would not prevent the tides of opinion asserting themselves. The mere fact that M. Baudouin had made the approach mentioned in Sir Samuel Hoare's telegram, showed that the consequences of Dakar had not been so serious.[1] Strong forces were on our side, if we continued to survive in the battle for Britain. Again, we had recognised General de Gaulle and had entered into solemn

---

[1] On 29 September 1940 Paul Baudouin had sent a message to Sir Samuel Hoare in Madrid, to say that the Vichy Government, as he wrote in his diary, 'was in a better position than the English to assess the chances of success or the spreading of discontent in this or that colony. In other words, I was quite ready to discuss with the English Government the pros and cons of the spread of unrest in any particular colony' (*The Private Diaries of Paul Baudouin*, London 1948, pages 253–4).

engagements with him. De Gaulle had not behaved badly at or after Dakar, and had fallen in with our plans; his people were not discouraged and he was now proceeding to Duala with a view to seeing what he could do in French Equatorial Africa where it was essential for us to have a favourable French Administration. We should protect him there, and assist in any movement he started.

The Prime Minister said that he did not differ from the Foreign Secretary on the principle of talks with the Vichy Government, which should be encouraged, but only in the emphasis to be laid on them. He did not consider this a golden opportunity to come to an understanding.

The Prime Minister said that it would be necessary for the War Cabinet to decide:–

First, whether, if General de Gaulle wanted to make an expedition to some French colonial territory which had not yet declared for him, e.g. Libreville, he should be allowed to do so.

Secondly, whether French ships should be stopped proceeding from West Africa to Metropolitan France.

In regard to the second point, a discussion ensued as to the present disposition of the Naval forces which had been assembled for Operation 'Menace'. The view was expressed that the Admiralty should take steps to reconstitute a strong Naval force at Gibraltar as soon as possible.

The question arose whether the *Barham*, which was proceeding to Gibraltar for repairs, should continue to form part of the Naval force stationed at Gibraltar, or should be passed through to the Eastern Mediterranean. The First Sea Lord said that certain repairs had to be done to the *Malaya*. This matter was reserved for discussion by the Prime Minister with the First Lord of the Admiralty.

The Prime Minister said that he thought that the troubles and perplexities of France might well lead to developments in our favour. How could we refuse to back up General de Gaulle if he wished to make an attempt to gain over Libreville?

The Secretary of State for the Colonies saw nothing inconsistent in opening conversations with the Vichy Government and maintaining the pressure by continuing full support for General de Gaulle.

The Prime Minister thought that the reply to the message given to us by the French Ambassador at Madrid should certainly include the following:

First, that while we made no complaint of the action already taken by them against Gibraltar, which was in retaliation for the Dakar episode, we wished the Vichy Government to know that, if they bombed Gibraltar again, we should retaliate by attacking Casablanca and sinking the ships there.

Secondly, as regards Mediterranean traffic, we should make the point that ships were already passing from Algiers to Marseilles.

Thirdly, as regards the French request that merchant ships proceeding to unoccupied France should be allowed to pass through the Straits of Gibraltar, we should say that we were not satisfied that merchandise arriving in unoccupied France would not reach Germany. They would, no doubt, reply that they could give guarantees on this point, and an argument might follow.

As regards French merchant vessels passing through the Straits of Gibraltar, the present policy was that if these vessels were escorted they should not be interfered with, but if unescorted they should be subject to normal contraband control measures. (It was also our declared policy to prevent French warships proceeding to ports in enemy controlled France.)

The Prime Minister thought that these orders should stand for the moment, but the War Cabinet must realise that unless these orders were altered, or we reached an arrangement with the Vichy Government, the result would be to relax our economic pressure on Dakar.

Winston S. Churchill to Robert Menzies
(*Premier papers, 4/43B/1*)

2 October 1940

I am very sorry to receive your message of September 29, because I feel that the great exertions we have made deserve a broad and generous measure of indulgence, should any particular minor operation miscarry. You already have the information contained in my message of September 27, which is far more explicit than anything given to the British Parliament up to the present. A full secret report will be cabled to you when we ourselves hear the details from the Commanders on the spot.

The situation at Dakar was revolutionised by arrival of French ships from Toulon with Vichy personnel and the manning of the batteries by the hostile French Navy. Although every effort was made, the British Navy was not able to stop these ships on their way. After strongly testing the defences, and sustaining the losses I have already reported to you, the naval and military Commanders did not consider they had the strength to effect and support a landing, and I think they were quite right not to get us committed to a shore operation which could not, like the naval attack, be broken off at any moment, and might have become a serious entanglement.

With regard to your criticisms, if it is to be laid down that no attempt is to be made which has not 'overwhelming chances of success', you will find that a complete defensive would be imposed upon us. In dealing with unknown factors like the degree of French resistance, it is impossible to avoid uncertainty and hazard. For instance, Duala, and with it the Cameroons, were taken by twenty-five Frenchmen after their Senegalese troops had refused to march. Ought we to have moved in this case without having overwhelming force at hand?

Secondly, I cannot accept the reproach of making 'a half-hearted attack'. I hoped that you had not sustained the impression from these last five months of struggle which has excited the admiration of the whole world that we were 'a half-hearted Government' or that I am half-hearted in the endeavours it is my duty to make. I thought, indeed, that from the way my name was used in the Election that quite a good opinion was entertained in Australia of these efforts.

Every care will always be made to keep you informed before news is published, but we could not prevent the German and Vichy wireless from proclaiming the course of events as they occurred at Dakar before we had received any information from our Commanders.

With regard to what you say about the Middle East, I do not think the difficulties have been underestimated, but, of course, our forces are much smaller than those which the Italians have in Libya and Abyssinia, and the Germans may always help them. The defection of France has thrown the whole Middle East into jeopardy and severed our communications through the Mediterranean.

We have had to face the threat of invasion here and the full strength of Germany's air bombing attack on our cities, factories and harbours. Nevertheless, we have steadfastly reinforced the Middle East, and in spite of all our perils at home and scanty resources have sent over 30,000 men, nearly half our best tanks, many anti-aircraft guns needed to protect our vital aircraft factories, two of the finest units in the Fleet, the *Illustrious* and *Valiant*, and a considerable number of Hurricane fighters and Wellington bombers.

We have done this in the face of an accumulation across the Channel and the North Sea of barges and shipping sufficient to carry half a million men to these shores at a single voyage and in a single night. Therefore, if the Middle East difficulties and dangers have not been fully met, it is not because the Mother Country has shirked her share of perils and sacrifice. At present the situation in Egypt and the Sudan looks better than we feared some time ago.

Still, my dear Prime Minister and friend, as you have allowed me to deem you, I cannot guarantee 'clear-cut victory' in the Middle East, or that Cairo, Khartoum, the Suez Canal and Palestine may not fall into Italian or German hands. We do not think they will, and we are trying our utmost to resist the attacks which are massing against us. But I can make no promises at all of victory, nor can I make any promises that regrettable and lamentable incidents will not occur, or that there will not be disappointments and blunders. On the contrary, I think the only certainty is that we have very bad times indeed to go through before we emerge from the mortal perils by which we are surrounded.

I felt it due to your great position and the extremely severe tone of your message to reply with equal frankness.[1]

Winston S. Churchill: recollection
(*'Their Finest Hour'*, page 325)

3 October 1940

We held a Cabinet meeting at 'Paddock'[2] far from the light of day, and each Minister was requested to inspect and satisfy himself about his sleeping and working apartments. We celebrated this occasion by a vivacious luncheon, and then returned to Whitehall.

War Cabinet: minutes
(*Cabinet papers, 65/9*)

3 October 1940　　　　　　　　　　　　　　　　　　　　　　　Dollis Hill
11.30 a.m.

The War Cabinet had before them a Memorandum by the Secretary of State for Foreign Affairs (WP (40) 400).

It was argued in the Memorandum that, in view of the Japanese aggression in Indo-China, and of the German–Italian–Japanese Pact,[3] the question was not so much whether we should re-open the Burma Road, as when we should do so. Lord Lothian had made it clear that the case for refusing to renew the Burma Road agreement, as seen from Washington, was overwhelming; and he had reported Mr Cordell Hull as saying that he 'greatly hoped that we would re-open the Burma Road.'

In these circumstances, the Foreign Secretary suggested that the best and least provocative method of announcing our decision not to renew the agreement would be by means of a reply to a Parliamentary Question on Tuesday, the 8th October, in the sense that the agreement had been

[1] In his reply on 4 October 1940, Menzies wrote that 'Real point I make is that we, at this distance, will learn the lessons of events the more rapidly if information about those events can come to us as promptly and as fully as possible.' His telegram ended: 'Please, my dear Prime Minister, do not interpret anxieties arising from these facts as either fearful, selfish or unduly wrongheaded. And above all, please understand that whatever interrogative or even critical telegrams I may send to you in secret, Australia knows courage when it sees it and will follow you to a finish, as to the best of my abilities I certainly shall' (*Premier papers, 4/43B/1*).

[2] The Post Office underground headquarters at Dollis Hill (see page 989).

[3] With the agreement of Vichy France, Japanese forces entered French Indo-China on 22 September 1940; a ten-year-old pact between Japan, Germany and Italy was signed in Berlin five days later.

concluded for a definite period, and contained no provision for renewal, and that in any case in view of recent developments His Majesty's Government would have felt unable to agree to renewal, if this had been in question.

The Prime Minister was clear that this was the right decision. He did not believe that the Japanese would declare war upon us as a result. We should be justified in taking the line that, whereas we had expected the Japanese during the interval afforded by the currency of the Burma Road agreement to make a genuine effort to reach an all-round settlement, all they had done was to make the German–Italian–Japanese Pact. In these circumstances, we had no option but to carry out our duties as a neutral in the Sino-Japanese conflict.

The Prime Minister drew attention to a recent telegram No. 1901 from Sir Robert Craigie in which it had not been taken for granted, as it should have been, that the British Empire would be involved in the event of war between the United States and Japan.

The Foreign Secretary said that he would make it clear to Sir Robert Craigie that, if the United States were at war with Japan, we should certainly declare war on that country.

The Prime Minister drew attention to telegram No. 1905 from Tokyo in which it was suggested that a United States Naval Force might pay a visit to Singapore. He felt that this suggestion was one that we should follow up promptly. It might be possible to combine a courtesy visit to Singapore by an American Battle Squadron with the holding of the British–American–Dutch Technical Conversations which had been suggested by Mr Cordell Hull (Washington telegram No. 2147).

The War Cabinet invited the Chiefs of Staff to consider as a matter of urgency whether it was desirable that British–American–Dutch Technical Military Conversations should be held at Singapore, and to submit to the Foreign Secretary definite suggestion which he could communicate to Lord Lothian.

War Cabinet: Confidential Annex
(*Cabinet papers, 65/15*)

3 October 1940 　　　　　　　　　　　　　　　　　　　　　　　Dollis Hill
11.30 a.m.

The Prime Minister said that he did not think that incidents would prejudice our relations with the Vichy Government. The fact that the Vichy Government had made a démarche after Dakar went to show this. The conditions were such that the normal rules of conduct did not apply to our relations with France at the present time. While there was a lot to be said for not sending an expedition to, say, Réunion or Miquelon at the present time, it was quite another matter for the French to send a ship from Martinique to Cayenne, which had shown its willingness to declare for General de Gaulle. At the moment, until our Naval force had been re-constituted at the Western end of the Mediterranean, we could not interfere with French convoys coming from the African coast under escort. While he did not ask for a decision in that sense that morning, he thought that the time would shortly come when we should have to take this course.

Henry Channon: diary
(*'Chips'*)

3 October 1940

Winston is without doubt all-powerful now and, though he talks of resigning directly after the war to make room for younger men, he is at the moment, relishing to the full the fruits of power.

War Cabinet: minutes
(*Cabinet papers, 65/9*)

4 October 1940   Cabinet War Room
12 noon

The Prime Minister drew attention to the appreciation of the United States reactions to the Dakar incident contained in Washington telegram No. 2138.

Competent French-Americans said that the French people, including even Baudouin, were veering towards Great Britain and that the swing would have been strengthened had we sunk the French ships before they reached Dakar, success being now the one essential.

The Prime Minister referred to a number of indications from which we could draw encouragement, as to the forces at work in different parts of the French Empire.

His mind was moving in the direction of doing nothing to hamper either the French or the Spanish communications with North Africa, while maintaining our contraband control over the French and Spanish trade entering the Mediterranean by the Straits of Gibraltar. We might declare our policy on this matter in connection with the approach now being made to the Vichy Government through the French Ambassador in Madrid.[1] The matter was not ripe for decision that day.

The Secretary of State for Foreign Affairs said that he was studying a

[1] M. de La Baume.

Minute on these questions, which he had received from the Prime Minister. His first reactions to the suggested new policy were favourable, although he could not answer for the Minister of Economic Warfare, who might see great objections to the reopening of trade between France and North Africa, and to a less extent to the reopening of trade between Spain and Morocco.

The War Cabinet had before them Memoranda by the Minister of Shipping, the Minister of Food and the First Lord of the Admiralty (WP (40) 393, 401 and 403, respectively).[1]

The Prime Minister said that this matter had been discussed on the previous evening at a Meeting of the Defence Committee. The conclusion reached had been that, in view of the fact that suitable weather for an invasion was not likely to prevail on many occasions during the winter months, and taking into account the very heavy sinkings which were being sustained, it would be right to divert a number of destroyers and anti-submarine trawlers from anti-invasion duties, to reinforce the escorts to shipping in the North-West Approaches. Some of the vessels could be recalled at short notice, to assist in repelling any attempt to invade these Islands.

In addition to the vessels thus released, it was hoped to have ten further destroyers and six corvettes available for service in the next four weeks, including vessels received from the USA.

War Cabinet: Confidential Annex
(*Cabinet papers, 65/15*)

4 October 1940
12 noon

The Prime Minister said that he had held a Meeting of the Defence Committee (DO (40) 33rd Meeting) at which it had been agreed:–
(a) That preparations should be made for the sailing of a slow convoy, leaving on 1st November, and a fast convoy on 17th November, to include the remainder of the 2nd Armoured Division, an Australian Brigade, and the miscellaneous units and equipment as planned by the Secretary of State for War.

---

[1] The three memoranda were about the protection of merchant ships in convoy. The Minister of Food (Lord Woolton) expressed himself 'seriously disturbed by the extent of our food losses at sea'. The Minister of Shipping (R. H. Cross) wrote: 'I should be failing in my duty if I did not represent, in the strongest possible terms, the necessity for putting a stop to the present exorbitant risks to which our merchant shipping is being exposed.' The First Lord of the Admiralty (A. V. Alexander) explained that the lack of escorting vessels arose from 'the diversion from trade protection duties of considerable numbers of destroyers and anti-submarine trawlers to anti-invasion duties'. (*Cabinet papers, 66/12*.)

(b) That, in preparation for this move, the Armoured Fighting vehicles of the 2nd Armoured Division might now be withdrawn to be prepared for operating in the Middle East, on condition that careful plans should be made for their rapid reassembly and redeployment in case need should arise for them to take part in operations in this country.

(c) That the loading of the convoy should be so arranged that the two Cruiser Tank Regiments could be detached, and sent through the Mediterranean, if a decision to this effect were taken when the time came.

Careful thought had been given to the details of these sailing arrangements. The intention was to keep all the options open as long as possible, in view of the possibility of an invasion of the United Kingdom being staged during the month of October. Thus the remainder of the 2nd Armoured Division would not pass out of our control until 1st November. It would then have to be determined whether the two Cruiser Tank Regiments should proceed via the Mediterranean, where they would be in danger of attack by the Italian Fleet, or round the Cape, which would mean that they could not be in action in Egypt until towards the end of December. If the needs of the Middle East theatre were urgent, the Admiralty would be prepared to run the risks involved in sending them through the Mediterranean. The decision would be taken in the light of the situation existing in the Mediterranean at the beginning of November.

Winston S. Churchill to Lord Halifax
(*Churchill papers, 20/13*)

4 October 1940

I have been considering our Vichy position in the light of to-day's discussion at the Cabinet and these telegrams[1] and other data. I see no reason why we should embroil ourselves with the Spaniards about any traffic in the Mediterranean, either from Spain or from Vichy. We cannot control these waters at the present time, and therefore should for the time being make a virtue of necessity. There is no reason why we should not tell Vichy that we are not interfering with this traffic. On the other hand all the news from Dakar shows the importance of keeping the screw on there, and not allowing any West African trade that the Navy can stop to pass into the Mediterranean from the Atlantic, whether escorted or not. I suggest we should tell Vichy quite plainly that this is our line. Perhaps you will let me know your views.

WSC

---

[1] Telegrams 802, 809, 810 from Sir Samuel Hoare in Madrid.

Winston S. Churchill to Lord Halifax
(*Churchill papers, 20/13*)

4 October 1940

This[1] shows the very serious misconception which has grown up in Sir R. Craigie's mind about the consequences of the United States entering the war. He should surely be told forthwith that the entry of the United States into war either with Germany and Italy or with Japan is fully conformable with British interests.

2. That nothing in the munitions sphere can compare with the importance of the British Empire and the United States being co-belligerent. That if Japan attacked the United States without declaring war on us we should at once range ourselves at the side of the United States and declare war upon Japan.

It is astonishing how this misleading stuff put out by Kennedy that we should do better with a neutral United States than with her warring at our side should have travelled so far. A clear directive is required to all our Ambassadors in countries concerned.

WSC

Winston S. Churchill to President Roosevelt
(*Premier papers, 3/468*)

4 October 1940

After prolonged consideration of all the issues involved we to-day decided to let the Burma Road be re-opened when the three-months' period expires on October 17. Foreign Secretary and I will announce this to Parliament on Tuesday 8th. I shall say that our hopes of a just settlement being reached between Japan and China have not borne fruit and that the Three-Power Pact revives the Anti-Comintern Pact of 1939 and that it has a clear pointer against the United States. I know how difficult it is for you to say anything which would commit the United States to any hypothetical course of action in the Pacific. But I venture to ask whether at this time a simple action might not speak louder than words. Would it not be possible for you to send an American squadron, the bigger the better, to pay a friendly visit to Singapore. There they would be welcomed in a perfectly normal and rightful way. If

---

[1] In a telegram from Tokyo on 2 October 1940 (received on the following day), the British Ambassador, Sir Robert Craigie, wrote of 'the assumption on which I have hitherto proceeded, namely that the United States would be obliged to cease sending war materials to us in hostilities with Japan' (*Foreign Office papers, 371/24728*).

desired occasion might be taken of such a visit for a technical discussion of Naval and Military problems in those and Philippine waters and the Dutch might be invited to join. Anything in this direction would have a marked deterrent effect upon a Japanese declaration of war upon us over the Burma Road opening. I should be very grateful if you would consider action along these lines as it might play an important part in preventing the spreading of the war.[1]

In spite of the Dakar fiasco the Vichy Government is endeavouring to enter into relations with us which shows how the tides are flowing in France now that they feel the German weight and see we are able to hold our own.

Although our position in the air is growing steadily stronger both actually and relatively, our need for aircraft is urgent. Several important factories have been seriously injured and the rate of production is hampered by air alarms. On the other hand our losses in pilots have been less than we expected because in fighting over our own soil a very large proportion get down safely or only wounded. When your officers were over here we were talking in terms of pilots. We are now beginning to think that aeroplanes will be the limiting factor so far as the immediate future is concerned.

I cannot feel that the invasion danger is past. The gent has taken off his clothes and put on his bathing suit, but the water is getting colder and there is an autumn nip in the air. We are maintaining the utmost vigilance.

Winston S. Churchill to J. J. Tinker[2]
(*Churchill papers, 20/8*)

4 October 1940
Secret

Dear Mr Tinker,

I know there are others who favour the very bold strategy you mention.[3] The bulk of our effort is now against Germany; but he would be a very dangerous guide who deliberately courted an invasion of this Island because

---

[1] At the War Cabinet on 7 October 1940 Lord Halifax drew his colleagues' attention to two telegrams from Washington, one from the Navy Department, the other from the State Department, which 'reported Mr Cordell Hull's reactions, which had been very satisfactory, to His Majesty's Government's message about the reopening of the Burma Road and about the proposed joint technical discussions on defence in the Pacific'. Churchill commented, as the minutes of 7 October 1940 recorded, 'that this was a message of the highest importance. It showed how great a mistake Japan had made in affronting the Americans. The Navy Department's message had evidently crossed his own message to President Roosevelt' (*Cabinet papers, 65/9*).

[2] John Joseph Tinker, 1875–1957. A miners' agent in Lancashire. Labour MP, 1923–45. Parliamentary Private Secretary to the Secretary of State for War, 1924.

[3] A plan to encourage a German invasion, and then to seek to destroy the German forces.

we felt sure of being able to defeat it. They will not come unless they think they can make good, and we must not lay our country open to miseries from which we can shield them.

Yours sincerely,
Winston S. Churchill

Marshal of the Royal Air Force Sir John Salmond[1] to Winston S. Churchill
(*Premier papers, 3/22/1*)

5 October 1940

Dear Prime Minister,

I am most anxious to put to you the case for a change in the holder of the important position of C in C Fighter Command.[2]

Recently, on Lord Beaverbrook's instructions, I have carried out an enquiry into Night Air Defence, the result of which, together with what has since occurred, make a change, in my opinion, imperative.

This opinion is also very strongly held by most, if not all, Service members of the Air Council.

Yours sincerely,
John M. Salmond

Winston S. Churchill to General Ismay and Sir Edward Bridges
(*Churchill papers, 20/13*)

6 October 1940

1. Let me have the Cabinet Minutes of the discussion on October 13, 1939.[3] I am determined to proceed against whoever was responsible for disobeying War Cabinet orders without even reporting what was going on. Have you no machinery for seeing that orders are carried out?

2. Meanwhile, report date at which Randle is working to full capacity.[4]

---

[1] John Maitland Salmond, 1881–1968. Entered the Army, 1901; on active service in South Africa. Royal Flying Corps, 1912. On active service, 1914–18 (despatches five times, DSO). Commanded the Royal Flying Corps (later the Royal Air Force) in the field, 1918. Knighted, 1919. Air Officer Commanding British Forces in Iraq, 1922–4; Air Defence of Great Britain, 1925–9. Chief of the Air Staff, 1930–3. Marshal of the Royal Air Force, 1933. Director of Armament Production, Ministry of Aircraft Production, 1940–4. Director, General Flying Control and Air Sea Rescue, Air Ministry, 1944–5.

[2] Sir Hugh Dowding, whose grip on the Night Air Defence situation was believed to have slipped.

[3] Almost a year earlier, on 13 October 1939, the War Cabinet had 'approved the proposals for the provision of plant for the increased production of gas for chemical warfare' as recommended to it by Anthony Eden and Sir Archibald Sinclair.

[4] See page 879, footnote 3.

Report what has been done to disperse existing stocks more thoroughly. Report weekly the progress of supply both of the gases and their containers.

3. I feel this is a very great danger.

WSC

Winston S. Churchill to General Ismay
(*Churchill papers, 20/13*)

6 October 1940

Whenever the Fleet is moving from Alexandria to the Central Mediterranean, reinforcements should be carried in to Malta, which I consider to be in grievous danger at the present time. These reinforcements should be found by taking Battalions from the Canal zone and replacing them by dismounted Yeomanry or Australian details now in Palestine, or by South African Units presently to be moved from Kenya. Pray let me have proposals on these lines, and make sure that at least one Battalion goes to Malta on the next occasion. We cannot waste Regular Battalions on internal security duties in Egypt. If they were needed for the Field Army they would, of course, be irremovable, but that is not what they are being used for.

Winston S. Churchill to Sir Robert Menzies
(*Premier papers, 4/43B/1*)

6 October 1940
9.15 p.m.

I am deeply grateful for your generous message. Forgive me if I responded too controversially to what I thought was somewhat severe criticism. I am having an account prepared of the Dakar incident, in all its stages, which I will send for the confidential information of yourself and your colleagues.[1] I do not propose to defend myself at any length in Parliament, as such a

---

[1] The War Cabinet's Dakar Operation Historical Narrative was printed for the War Cabinet on 5 February 1941. The War Cabinet reference for this, the first of a series of such narratives prepared by the Cabinet Office, was 'HIST (A) 1 (Revise)' (*Premier papers, 3/276*).

spectacle would only gratify the enemy. I am deeply grateful for all that Australia has done under your leadership for the Common Cause. It has been a great comfort having some of the Australians here during these anxious months. I greatly admired their bearing and spirit when I inspected them. They had just received 24 good field guns. They are soon going to join the rest of the Australian Army in the Middle East, where they will probably be in the forefront of the fighting next year. We shall do everything in our power to equip them as they deserve. For the moment it seems that the situation in the Middle East is steady. Should the Armies engage near Mersa Matruh the forces available during the next month or six weeks would not appear to be ill-matched in numbers. This should give a good chance to General Wilson,[1] who is reputed a fine tactician, and the excellent troops he has. The Londoners are standing up magnificently to the bombing, but you can imagine the numerous problems which a ruthless attack like this upon a community of 8 million people creates for the administration. We are getting the better of our difficulties, and I feel confident that the act of mass terror which Hitler has attempted will fail, like his magnetic mines and other deadly schemes. All good wishes personally for yourself.

Night Air Defence Committee: minutes[2]
(*Cabinet papers, 81/22*)

7 October 1940
11.45 a.m.

The Prime Minister has instructed that a special report should be submitted by the Ministry of Aircraft Production with a view to increasing the order for mines to 1,000,000 and providing at least 24 aircraft to sow them.

---

[1] Henry Maitland Wilson, 1881–1964. Known as 'Jumbo'. On active service in South Africa, 1899–1902; on the Western Front, 1914–17 (despatches, DSO). General Officer Commanding-in-Chief, Egypt, 1939; in Cyrenaica, 1940; in Greece, 1941; in Palestine and Transjordan, 1941. Knighted, 1940. Commander-in-Chief, Allied Forces in Syria, 1941; Persia–Iraq Command, 1942–3; Middle East, 1943. Supreme Allied Commander, Mediterranean Theatre, 1944. Field Marshal, 1944. Head of the British Joint Staff Mission, Washington, 1945–7. Created Baron, 1946.

[2] The Night Air Defence Committee of the War Cabinet consisted of Churchill (in the Chair), Sir Archibald Sinclair, Beaverbrook, Sir Cyril Newall, Sir Frederick Pile, Sir John Salmond, General Loch, Sir Hugh Dowding. Admiral Fraser, Sir Philip Joubert de la Ferté, Commander Lawson (Naval Ordnance Department, Admiralty), Air Vice-Marshal W. S. Douglas (Deputy Chief of the Air Staff), Sir F. E. Smith (Ministry of Supply), Robert Watson-Watt (Air Ministry), Sir Edward Bridges and Professor Lindemann. The Secretary was Group Captain W. Elliot.

War Cabinet: minutes
(*Cabinet papers, 65/9*)

7 October 1940
5 p.m.
10 Downing Street

The Chief of the Imperial General Staff described our dispositions at Mersa Matruh and Siwa and the Italian dispositions at Sollum and Sidi Barrani, at each of which places two divisions were now present.

The Prime Minister said that this was the first occasion on which the War Cabinet had been informed that as many as four enemy divisions were in forward positions. It was important that they should be notified immediately of the arrival of any new enemy divisions at the Front.

The Prime Minister thought that we should tell the French now, through our Ambassador in Madrid, that the trade with the West African ports must stop although we would not interfere with any ships from these ports that were now on their way to French Mediterranean Ports. He was not worried about the trade inside the Mediterranean, which could proceed. The appeasement of Vichy was not worth while if it meant allowing this trade between West African ports and the unoccupied zones of France to go on. He doubted whether, if we stopped this trade, the Vichy Government would provoke an incident. If they bombed Gibraltar we would retaliate by bombarding Casablanca.

The Prime Minister said that he deprecated the conclusion that the French would react to our blockade of the West African trade by trying to bomb us out of Gibraltar. If we allowed this possibility to influence our policy, we should have to give way to the Vichy Government all along the line. He did not think that Government could carry the French people with it to-day in a policy of war with this country. There was an increasing longing among the people of France for our victory.

For the moment it was not necessary to reach any further decision, but we could not afford to allow trade to continue to pass through the Straits for any length of time while discussions with the Vichy Government continued. He wished to emphasise that, for his part, he was satisfied that we must face the threat of a French attack on Gibraltar if we interfered with their trade through the Straits.

The Prime Minister drew attention to an article in the *Sunday Pictorial* on the 29th September. This article, which had contained a lot of false information, had characterised the Dakar affair as 'another Blunder,' and had used language of an insulting character to the Government. In the issue of the same journal of the previous day (Sunday, the 6th October) great prominence had been given to an article published by Mr H. G. Wells[1] in an obscure pamphlet (the Bulletin of the Labour Book Service). This article had contained a slashing attack on Field-Marshal Sir Edmund Ironside and General Viscount Gort. The general tenor of Mr H. G. Wells's article, reproduced in the *Sunday Pictorial*, had been that, until the Army was better led, we stood no chance of beating the Germans.

The Prime Minister, summing up the discussion, said that the solution which he hoped to see adopted and which he thought was generally favoured, was that two members of the War Cabinet should see the Newspaper Proprietors' Association and explain the situation to them. The articles complained of should be shown to the Association, and it should be made clear that the Government was not prepared to allow continued publication of such articles. It should also be made clear that, if the Newspaper Proprietors' Association were not ready or able to take action to stop further publication of such articles, the Government would have to deal with the matter in some other way.

It was clear, however, that, before action could be taken on these lines, the War Cabinet must decide definitely that they were prepared to take action against these newspapers if necessary. In view, however, of the fact that the Home Secretary had a quasi-judicial function to perform, it would clearly be right to defer a decision in order to give him time for further consideration.

Sir Frederick Pile: recollection
(*'Ack-Ack'*, pages 168–70)

7 October 1940

Raids were in full swing, and it was a certainty that whenever one went to a gun-site there would be some action. Churchill, Dowding, and I dined that night at No. 10 and afterwards went to a gun-site at Richmond. The Prime Minister and Dowding drove down in the same car, and I followed. We had hardly reached Richmond Park when the alert was sounded, and very soon

---

[1] Herbert George Wells, 1866–1946. A prolific writer, author of more than seventy books, he published one of his best-known works, *The Time Machine*, in 1895. In 1923, in his book *Men Like Gods*, Churchill appears thinly disguised as Rupert Catskill, whose 'wild imaginings had caused the deaths of thousands of people'.

OCTOBER 1940

the guns were banging away. I had seen to it that a tin hat had been brought for the Prime Minister, but he would not wear it. He stayed in the Command Post while all around the Germans were dropping bombs and many fires were raging. Eventually, about 11 p.m., Dowding pointed out to me that we had laid on a programme for him to go down to Biggin Hill to see, first of all, the fighter station there, and then the searchlights. The first of the new radar sets for controlling searchlights had been fitted to an apparatus at Biggin Hill, and it was the intention to demonstrate it to the Prime Minister against enemy aircraft. In addition, some of the new rockets were available, and these too were to be demonstrated. When Churchill was pressed to leave he said: 'This exhilarates me. The sound of these cannon gives me a tremendous feeling.' However, after a few minutes he agreed to start.

By this time, except for the flashes of the guns and the blaze of the burning buildings, there was not a light anywhere. Dowding told me I was to take the Prime Minister with me, a thought that had never entered my head, and he said he would guide us down to Biggin Hill. We had not gone very far before we lost the guide, and very shortly afterwards we lost ourselves. The normal route was blocked by burning buildings, and after making half a dozen detours for all I knew we might have been going north instead of south. By this time the Prime Minister was, to say the least of it, a little impatient. He kept asking me whether we were near our destination, and I assured him that we were getting on, but it began to look more and more hopeless, until, after having been driving for two hours – the worst two hours of the War for me – I spotted the railway station which was to be our rendezvous.

We were taken, first of all, to the Air Force Operations Room, and then once more set sail, this time for the searchlight-site. Here we were met by Lieutenant-Colonel Harvie Watt.[1] He was commanding the searchlight regiment, and the moment I got out of the car I told him that the Prime Minister was feeling very cold, and asked if there was any hope of getting him a whisky-and-soda. He said there was about as much chance of getting a whisky-and-soda there as there was in the middle of the Sahara. But he promised to do his best to get one over from his own mess, ten miles away.

Matters became worse and worse. The field we were asked to enter in order to see the searchlight was about the wettest field in Europe, and the searchlight was at the far end of it. When we reached it there were half a dozen

---

[1] George Steven Harvie-Watt, 1903–89. Called to the Bar, 1930. Conservative MP, 1937–59. Assistant Government Whip, 1938–40. Lieutenant-Colonel commanding the 31st Battalion, Royal Engineers, Territorial Army, 1938–41; Brigadier, 6th Anti-Aircraft Brigade, 1941. Parliamentary Private Secretary to the Prime Minister (Churchill), July 1941 to July 1945. Created Baronet, 1945. He published his memoirs, *Most of My Life*, in 1980.

fitters working feverishly on the new apparatus,[1] while a very harassed technical officer looked on. I asked him whether we were likely to be able to see a demonstration or not, and he said that the so-and-so thing was working all right the day before, but that you could not get a spark out of it now. I told him to explain it to the Prime Minister, and if it was quite hopeless I would take him over and show him the rockets.[2] So in about five minutes we began trudging through the wet grass once more to see the rockets.

These were almost as disobliging as the radar. The first two refused to go off, but then one went screaming off into the sky, and Churchill at once said, shortly: 'Now, I think, we will go home.' Just as we arrived back at the car, Harvie Watt appeared with two glasses, one of which he handed to the Prime Minister, who, after thanking him politely, took one great mouthful, spluttered, and said: 'Good God, I have been poisoned. It is neat whisky.' I, however, was in such a state then that I was devoutly thankful and swallowed mine.

We then set off on the way home. I had warned my driver, Sergeant Macarthy, that, on pain of death, he was to find out the exact route, so that we could get back to Downing Street in the shortest possible time. When we had been travelling for about a quarter of an hour in complete and awful silence the PM said: 'My feet are very cold indeed. They are like ice.' Then I had my one brain-wave of the day. I said: 'There is only one thing to do. You must take off your shoes and wrap your feet up in the rug.' Somewhat to my astonishment, he said: 'That seems a good idea,' and in about two minutes he was leaning back, declaring that it was very comfortable indeed and that he had enjoyed his day.

I can't remember what we talked about, but as we got near London the bombs were still coming down, and once more I lost my nerve and produced his tin hat. He waved it away, but eventually, after I had put mine on firmly and said, 'Well, I'm going to wear mine, sir,' he said, 'All right; if you wish it, I will wear mine.'

By now it was about 4.30, and the Prime Minister suddenly said to me: 'Do you like Bōvril?' (the 'o' pronounced as in 'Hove'). I said I did. He pondered for a bit, and then he said: 'Bōvril and sardines are very good together.' I had never tried them, but I was ready to try anything at that time of morning. 'Well,' he said, 'we will see what the commissariat can do for us as soon as we get back to No. 10.' Very shortly afterwards we drew up in front of the door. The Prime Minister had a walking-stick with him with which he rapped the

---

[1] Searchlights fitted with radar, code name 'Elsie'.
[2] These were the Unrotated Projectile rockets of which Churchill had been a persistent advocate.

door sharply. When the butler opened it the Prime Minister said: 'Goering and Goebbels coming to report,' and added: '*I* am not Goebbels.' And so we went in. He tried to persuade me to stay the night, on account of the dangers outside, but as soon as I had had my Bovril and sardines I felt that honour was more than satisfied, and left.

Winston S. Churchill: Oral Answers
(*Hansard*)

8 October 1940   House of Commons

Captain Elliston[1] asked the Prime Minister, whether in view of recent developments of modern warfare, he will advise revision of the Royal Warrant so that the Victoria Cross may be awarded to any subject of His Majesty who displays supreme courage in countering enemy action?

The Prime Minister: The hon. Members will have learnt from His Majesty's broadcast speech on 23rd September, and subsequent announcements, that His Majesty has created the George Cross, which will rank next to the Victoria Cross. For this honour, men and women in all walks of civil life will be eligible. The George Medal, which has also been instituted, is a gallantry award for wider distribution.

Sir H. Morris-Jones[2]: Will my right hon. Friend consider the whole question of these awards, in view of the completely altered standard of risk as between civilians and the Services in this war? Why should not civilians get the Victoria Cross for heroism in the face of the enemy, just as did soldiers in the Army in the last war? The whole standard ought to be changed.

The Prime Minister: There is no difference in merit between the Victoria Cross and the George Cross; the George Cross ranks equal with the Victoria Cross, and after it in priority only. The whole question has been most carefully reconsidered, and the very far-reaching scheme which has been announced and the new decorations are the fruits of that reconsideration.

---

[1] George Sampson Elliston, 1874–1954. On active service, 1917–18 (Military Cross). A director of several printing and publishing companies. Conservative MP, 1931–45. Knighted, 1944. One of his two sons was killed in action in the Second World War.

[2] John Henry Morris-Jones, 1884–1972. On active service, 1914–18, serving as a doctor at Wimereux (Military Cross). A medical practitioner for twenty years. Liberal MP, 1929–31: Liberal National, 1931–50. Assistant Government Whip, 1932–5. A Lord Commissioner of the Treasury, 1935–7. Knighted, 1937. Chairman of the Welsh Parliamentary Party, 1941–2. Member of the Parliamentary Delegation to Buchenwald concentration camp, April 1945. Author of *Doctor in the Whips' Room*, 1955.

Parliamentary Report
(Hansard)

8 October 1940   House of Commons

NEW MEMBER SWORN

Randolph Frederick Edward Spencer Churchill, Esquire, for the Borough of Preston.[1]

Winston S. Churchill: speech
(Hansard)

8 October 1940   House of Commons

The Prime Minister (Mr Churchill): A month has passed since Herr Hitler turned his rage and malice on to the civil population of our great cities and particularly of London. He declared in his speech of 4th September that he would raze our cities to the ground, and since then he has been trying to carry out his fell purpose. Naturally, the first question we should ask is to what extent the full strength of the German bombing force has been deployed. I will give the House the best opinion I have been able to form on what is necessarily to some extent a matter of speculation. After their very severe mauling on 15th August, the German short-range dive bombers, of which there are several hundred, have been kept carefully out of the air fighting. This may be, of course, because they are being held in reserve so that they may play their part in a general plan of invasion or re-appear in some other theatre of war. We have, therefore, had to deal with the long-range German bombers alone.

It would seem that, taking day and night together, nearly 400 of these machines have, on the average, visited our shores every 24 hours. We are doubtful whether this rate of sustained attack could be greatly exceeded; no doubt a concentrated effort could be made for a few days at a time, but this would not sensibly affect the monthly average. Certainly there has been a considerable tailing off in the last 10 days, and all through the month that has passed since the heavy raids began on 7th September, we have had a steady decline in casualties and damage to so-called vulnerable points. We know, of course, exactly what we are doing in reply, and the size of our own bombing force, and from the many sources which are open to us we believe that the

---

[1] Randolph Churchill had been elected unopposed, according to the wartime custom. He was defeated at the general election of 1945, and failed to be re-elected (for Plymouth) in 1950 and 1951. On 26 September 1940 Lord Desborough had written to Churchill from Panshanger: 'My dear Winston, A thousand congratulations on having a son in Parliament. May he follow in the footsteps of his sire!' Desborough's grandfather, Charles Pascoe Grenfell (1790–1867), had represented Preston. (*Churchill papers, 2/393.*)

German heavy bomber pilots are being worked at least as hard as, and may be a great deal harder than, our own. The strain upon them is, therefore, very considerable. The bulk of them do not seem capable of anything beyond blind bombing.

I always hesitate to say anything of an optimistic nature, because our people do not mind being told the worst. They resent anything in the nature of soothing statements which are not borne out by later events, and, after all, war is full of unpleasant surprises. On the whole, however, we may, I think, under all reserve reach, provisionally, the conclusion that the German average effort against this country absorbs a very considerable part of their potential strength. I should not like to say that we have the measure of their power, but we feel more confident about it than we have ever done before.

Let us now proceed to examine the effect of this ruthless and indiscriminate attack upon the easiest of all targets, namely, the great built-up areas of this land. The Germans have recently volunteered some statements of a boastful nature about the weight of explosives which they have discharged upon us during the whole war, and also on some particular occasions. These statements are not necessarily untrue, and they do not appear unreasonable to us. We were told on 23rd September that 22,000 tons of explosives had been discharged upon Great Britain since the beginning of the war. No doubt this included the mines on the coast. We were told also, on last Thursday week, that 251 tons were thrown upon London in a single night, that is to say, only a few tons less than the total dropped on the whole country throughout the last war. Now, we know exactly what our casualties have been. On that particular Thursday night 180 persons were killed in London as a result of 251 tons of bombs. That is to say, it took 1 ton of bombs to kill three-quarters of a person. We know, of course, exactly the ratio of loss in the last war, because all the facts were ascertained after it was over. In that war the small bombs of early patterns which were used killed 10 persons for every ton discharged in the built-up areas. Therefore, the deadliness of the attack in this war appears to be only one-thirteenth of that of 1914–1918. Let us say 'less than one-tenth,' so as to be on the safe side. That is, the mortality is less than one-tenth of the mortality attaching to the German bombing attacks in the last war. This is a very remarkable fact, deserving of profound consideration. I adduce it, because it is the foundation of some further statements, which I propose to make later on.

What is the explanation? There can only be one, namely, the vastly improved methods of shelter which have been adopted. In the last war there were hardly any air-raid shelters, and very few basements had been strengthened. Now we have this ever-growing system of shelters, among which the Anderson shelter justly deserves its fame, and the mortality has been reduced to one-thirteenth, or, say, at least one-tenth. This appears, as I say, not only to be remarkable, but also reassuring. It has altered, of course, the whole of the estimates we had made of the severity of the attacks to which we should be exposed. Whereas, when we entered the war at the call of duty and honour we expected to sustain losses which might amount to 3,000 killed in a single night and 12,000 wounded, night after night, and made hospital arrangements on the basis of a quarter of a million casualties merely as a first provision – whereas that is what we did at the beginning of the war, we have actually had since it began, up to last Saturday, as a result of air bombing, about 8,500 killed and 13,000 wounded. This shows that things do not always turn out as badly as one expects. Also, it shows that one should never hesitate, as a nation or as an individual, to face dangers because they appear to the imagination to be so formidable. Since the heavy raiding began on 7th September, the figures of killed and seriously wounded have declined steadily week by week, from over 6,000 in the first week to just under 5,000 in the second, and from about 4,000 in the third week to under 3,000 in the last of the four weeks.

The destruction of property has, however, been very considerable. Most painful is the number of small houses inhabited by working folk which has been destroyed, but the loss has also fallen heavily upon the West End, and all classes have suffered evenly, as they would desire to do. I do not propose to give exact figures of the houses which have been destroyed or seriously damaged. That is our affair. We will rebuild them, more to our credit than some of them were before. London, Liverpool, Manchester, Birmingham may have much more to suffer, but they will rise from their ruins, more healthy and, I hope, more beautiful. We must not exaggerate the material damage which has been done. The papers are full of pictures of demolished houses, but naturally they do not fill their restricted space with the numbers that are left standing. If you go, I am told, to the top of Primrose Hill or any of the other eminences of London and look round, you would not know that any harm had been done to our city.

Statisticians may amuse themselves by calculating that after making allowance for the working of the law of diminishing returns, through the same house being struck twice or three times over, it would take 10 years at the present rate, for half the houses of London to be demolished. After that, of course, progress would be much slower. Quite a lot of things are going to happen to Herr Hitler and the Nazi regime before 10 years are up, and even Signor Mussolini has some experiences ahead of him which he had not foreseen at the time when he thought it safe and profitable to stab the stricken and prostrate French Republic in the back. Neither by material damage nor by slaughter will the people of the British Empire be turned from their solemn and inexorable purpose. It is the practice and in some cases the duty of many of my colleagues and many Members of the House to visit the scenes of destruction as promptly as possible, and I go myself from time to time. In all my life, I have never been treated with so much kindness as by the people who have suffered most. One would think one had brought some great benefit to them, instead of the blood and tears, the toil and sweat which is all I have ever promised. On every side, there is the cry, 'We can take it,' but with it, there is also the cry, 'Give it 'em back.'

The question of reprisals is being discussed in some quarters as if it were a moral issue. What are reprisals? What we are doing now is to batter continuously, with forces which steadily increase in power, each one of those points in Germany which we believe will do the Germans most injury and will most speedily lessen their power to strike at us. Is that a reprisal? It seems to me very like one. At any rate, it is all we have time for now. We should be foolish to shift off those military targets which the skill of our navigators enables us to find with a very great measure of success, to any other targets at the present stage. Although the bombing force that we are able as yet to employ is, as I have told the House on several occasions, much less numerous than that of which the enemy disposes, I believe it to be true that we have done a great deal more harm to the war-making capacity of Germany than they have done to us. Do not let us get into a sterile controversy as to what are and what are not reprisals. Our object must be to inflict the maximum harm on her war-making capacity. That is the only object that we shall pursue.

It must not be thought that the mists and storms which enshroud our Island in the winter months will by themselves prevent the German bombers from the crude, indiscriminate bombing by night of our built-up areas into which they have relapsed. No one must look forward to any relief merely from the winter weather. We have, however, been thinking about the subject for some time, and it may be that new methods will be devised to make the wholesale bombing of the civilian population by night and in fog more exciting to the enemy than it is at present. The House will not expect me to indicate or foreshadow any of these methods. It would be much better for us to allow our visitors to find them out for themselves in due course by practical experience. I think that is much the best way to handle that particular matter.

Meanwhile, upon the basis that this will continue and that our methods will also be improving, we have to organise our lives and the life of our cities on the basis of dwelling under fire and of having always this additional chance – not a very serious chance – of death, added to the ordinary precarious character of human existence. This great sphere of domestic organisation becomes the counterpart of our military war effort. The utmost drive and capacity of which we are capable as a Government and as a people will be thrown into this task. Nothing but the needs of the Fighting Services can stand in the way. We must try to have shelters with sleeping bunks for everyone in the areas which are liable to constant attack, and this must be achieved in the shortest possible time. As soon as it is accomplished, and in proportion as it is accomplished, people will have to go to their proper places, and, above all, we must prevent large gatherings of people in any shelters which only give illusory protection against a direct hit. People must be taught not to despise the small shelter. Dispersal is the sovereign remedy against heavy casualties. In my right hon. Friend the new Minister of Home Security[1] we have a man of warm sympathy, of resource and energy, who is well known to Londoners and has their confidence, and who will equally look after the other cities which are assailed. But do not let it be thought that the work of his predecessor, now Lord President of the Council,[2] has not been of a very high order. There is no better war horse in the Government. I am ashamed of the attacks which are made upon him in ignorant and spiteful quarters. Every one of his colleagues knows that he is a tower of strength and good sense, fearless and unflinching in storm and action. With my many burdens, I rely greatly upon him to take a part of the civil and domestic load from off my shoulders, setting me free for the more direct waging of the war. Large schemes are already on foot for providing food and hot drinks for those who sleep in shelters, and also for entertainment during the winter evenings. Far-reaching measures are being taken to safeguard the health of the people under these novel and primordial conditions. Widespread organisation and relief to those whose homes are smitten is already in being and is expanding and improving every day. All these matters will be unfolded at length, some in public, some in private Session, by the Ministers responsible for the various branches of action.

There is one scheme, however, upon which I must say a word to-day. The diminution of the damage done by blind bombing from what we had expected before the war, in the figures that I gave the House in the opening passage of my speech, enables us to take an enormous step forward in spreading the risk over the property of all classes, rich and poor. The Chancellor of the Exchequer,[3] as I indicated a month ago, is preparing, and in fact has virtually completed the preparation of, a Bill for nation-wide compulsory insurance against damage to property from the enemy's fire. Immediate needs of food and shelter are already provided for, so is loss of life and limb as far as it is possible for human beings to be compensated for such calamities, but why should we have the whole value of the buildings of the country simultaneously and universally discounted and discredited by the shadow of a sporadic sky vulture? Such a course would be financially improvident and also fiscally inane. An appropriate charge levied on the capital value of buildings and structures of all kinds will provide a fund from which, supplemented if need be by a State subvention, everyone can be covered, and covered with retrospective effect; and everyone can be made sure that compensation for his house and home and place of business will be paid to him in one form or another at the end of the war, if not sooner, and that, where necessity arises in the

---

[1] Herbert Morrison. The changes had taken place four days earlier.
[2] Sir John Anderson.
[3] Sir Kingsley Wood, since 3 October 1940 a member of the War Cabinet.

intervening period, means of carrying on will not be withheld. We also propose to provide insurance against the risk of war damage for all forms of moveable property, such as industrial plant, machinery, household effects and other personal possessions which are not at present protected by insurance. This will also be retrospective.

As I see it, we must so arrange that, when any district is smitten by bombs which are flung about at utter random, strong, mobile forces will descend on the scene in power and mercy to conquer the flames, as they have done, to rescue sufferers, provide them with food and shelter, to whisk them away to places of rest and refuge, and to place in their hands leaflets which anyone can understand to reassure them that they have not lost all, because all will share their material loss, and in sharing it, sweep it away. These schemes and measures, pursued on the greatest scale and with fierce energy, will require the concentrated attention of the House in the weeks that lie before us. We have to make a job of this business of living and working under fire, and I have not the slightest doubt that when we have settled down to it we shall establish conditions which will be a credit to our Island society and to the whole British family, and will enable us to maintain the production of those weapons in good time upon which our whole safety and future depend. Thus we shall be able to prove to all our friends and sympathisers in every land, bond or free, that Hitler's act of mass terror against the British nation has failed as conspicuously as his magnetic mine and other attempts to strangle our seaborne trade.

Meanwhile, what has happened to the invasion which we have been promised every month and almost every week since the beginning of July? Do not let us be lured into supposing that the danger is past. On the contrary, unwearying vigilance and the swift and steady strengthening of our Forces by land, sea and air which is in progress must be at all costs maintained. Now that we are in October, however, the weather becomes very uncertain, and there are not many lucid intervals of two or three days together in which river barges can cross the narrow seas and land upon our beaches. Still, those intervals may occur. Fogs may aid the foe. Our Armies, which are growing continually in numbers, equipment, mobility and training, must be maintained all through the winter, not only along the beaches but in reserve, as the majority are, like leopards crouching to spring at the invader's throat. The enemy has certainly got prepared enough shipping and barges to throw half a million men in a single night on to salt water – or into it. The Home Guard, which now amounts to 1,700,000 men, must nurse their weapons and sharpen their bayonets. [Interruption.] I have taken the trouble to find out very carefully how many hundred thousands of bayonets are at this time in their possession before I uttered such an adjuration; and for those who have not bayonets at the moment, I have provided for them by the phrase: 'They must nurse their weapons.' During the winter training must proceed, and the building of a great well-equipped army, not necessarily always to be confined to these islands, must go forward in a hardy and rigorous manner. My right hon. Friend the Secretary of State for War[1] will, in the course of the next few weeks, give a further account in Private Session of the tremendous strides which under his guidance our military organisation is making in all its branches. He will also announce in public the improvements which we have found it possible to make in the allowances for the dependants of the Fighting Services to meet the increased cost of living and to secure the proper nourishment and care of the wives and children of our fighting men. I shall not anticipate my right hon. Friend this afternoon.

But, after all, the main reason why the invasion has not been attempted up to the present is, of course, the succession of brilliant victories gained by our fighter aircraft, and gained by them over the largely superior numbers which the enemy have launched against us. The three great days of 15th August, 15th September and 27th September have proved to all the world that here at home over our own Island we have the mastery of the air. That is a tremendous fact. It marks the laying down of the office which he has held with so much distinction for the last three years by Sir Cyril Newall, and it enables us to record our admiration to him for the services he has rendered.[2] It also marks the assumption of new and immense responsibilities by Sir Charles Portal, an officer who, I have heard from every source and every side, commands the enthusiastic support and confidence of the Royal Air Force. These victories of our Air Force enable the Navy, which is now receiving very great reinforcements, apart altogether from the American destroyers now coming rapidly into service, to assert, on the basis of the air victories, its sure and well-tried power.

It is satisfactory for me to be able to announce that both in fighters and in bombers we are at this moment and after all these months of battle substantially stronger actually and relatively than we were in May when the heavy fighting began, and also to announce that the pilot situation is rapidly improving and that in many weeks our repaired aircraft alone, such is the efficiency of this organisation for repair, exceed by themselves or make good the losses which are suffered; so that in many weeks the new construction is ever expanding as a clear gain. No one has ever pretended that we should overtake the Germans, with their immense lead, in the first year or so of war. We have a long lap to make up. We must give ourselves a chance. Perhaps it will be possible to make a more satisfactory statement on this subject this time next year. But do not forget that the resources of the enemy will also be

---

[1] Anthony Eden.
[2] Air Chief Marshal Sir Cyril Newall was succeeded by Sir Charles Portal as Chief of the Air Staff. Newall was promoted Marshal of the Royal Air Force (the highest rank), received the Order of Merit, and went to New Zealand as Governor-General and Commander-in-Chief.

substantially increased by their exploitation of the wealth, of the plants and to some extent of the skilled labour of captive countries. If it were not for the resources of the New World, which are becoming increasingly available, it would be a long time before we should be able to do much more than hold our own.

Although we have had to face this continual, imminent threat of invasion by a military Power which has stationed 80 of its best divisions in Northern France, we have not failed to reinforce our Armies in the Middle East and elsewhere. All the while the great convoys have been passing steadily and safely on their course through the unknown wastes of the oceans, drawing from all parts of the Empire the forces which will, I trust, enable us to fill in time the terrible gap in our defences which was opened by the Vichy French desertion. I shall certainly not make any prophecies about what will happen when British, Australian, New Zealand, Indian, and Egyptian troops come to close grips with the Italian invaders who are now making their way across the deserts towards them. All I will say is that we are doing our best and that there as here we feel a good deal better than we did some time ago.

I do not propose to give the House a detailed account of the episode at Dakar. I could easily do so in private, but it would be out of proportion to the scale of events. Moreover, I do not relish laying bare to the enemy all our internal processes. This operation was primarily French, and, although we were ready to give it a measure of support which in certain circumstances might have been decisive, we were no more anxious than was General de Gaulle to get involved in a lengthy or sanguinary conflict with the Vichy French. That General de Gaulle was right in believing that the majority of Frenchmen in Dakar was favourable to the Free French movement, I have no doubt; indeed, I think his judgment has been found extremely sure-footed, and our opinion of him has been enhanced by everything we have seen of his conduct in circumstances of peculiar and perplexing difficulty. His Majesty's Government have no intention whatever of abandoning the cause of General de Gaulle until it is merged, as merged it will be, in the larger cause of France.

There is, however, one part of this story on which I should like to reassure the House, as it concerns His Majesty's Government alone and does not affect those with whom we have been working. The whole situation at Dakar was transformed in a most unfavourable manner by the arrival there of three French cruisers and three destroyers which carried with them a number of Vichy partisans, evidently of a most bitter type. These partisans were sent to overawe the population, to grip the defences and to see to the efficient manning of the powerful shore batteries. The policy which His Majesty's Government had been pursuing towards the Vichy French warships was not to interfere with them unless they appeared to be proceeding to enemy-controlled ports. Obviously, however, while General de Gaulle's enterprise was proceeding it was specially important to prevent any of them reaching Dakar. By a series of accidents, and some errors which have been made the subject of disciplinary action, or are now subject to formal inquiry, neither the First Sea Lord nor the Cabinet was informed of the approach of these ships to the Straits of Gibraltar until it was too late to stop them passing through. Orders were instantly given to stop them at Casa Blanca, or if that failed, to prevent them entering Dakar. If we could not cork them in, we could, at least, we hoped, have corked them out, but, although every effort was made to execute these orders, these efforts failed. The Vichy cruisers were, however, prevented from carrying out their further purpose of attacking the Free French Colony of Duala, and of the four French vessels concerned, two succeeded in regaining Dakar, while two were overtaken by our cruisers and were induced, persuaded, to return to Casa Blanca without any actual violence.

The House may therefore rest assured – indeed it is the only point I am seeking to make to-day – that the mischievous arrival of these ships, and the men they carried, at Dakar arose in no way from any infirmity of purpose on the part of the Government; it was one of those mischances which often arise in war and especially in war at sea. The fighting which ensued between the shore batteries at Dakar, reinforced by the 16-inch guns of the damaged *Richelieu*, and the British squadron was pretty stiff. Two Vichy submarines which attacked the Fleet were sunk, the crew of one happily being saved. Two of the Vichy French destroyers were set on fire, one of the cruisers was heavily hit and the *Richelieu* herself suffered further damage. On our part we had two ships, one a battleship and the other a large cruiser, which suffered damage – damage which, although it does not prevent their steaming and fighting, will require considerable attention when convenient.

What an irony of fate it is that this fine French Navy, which Admiral Darlan shaped for so many years to fight in the common cause against German aggression, should now be the principal obstacle to the liberation of France and her Empire from the German yoke, and should be employed as the tool of German and Italian masters whose policy contemplates not merely the defeat and mutilation of France, but her final destruction as a great nation. The Dakar incident reminds us of what often happens when a drowning man casts his arms around the strong swimmer who comes to his rescue and seeks in his agony to drag him down into the depths. Force in these circumstances has to be used to save life as well as to take life. But we never thought that what happened or might happen at Dakar was likely to lead to a declaration of war by the Vichy Government, although evidently such a step might be imposed upon them at any time by their masters. Whatever happens it is the tide and not mere eddies of events which will dominate the French people. Nothing can prevent the increasing abhorrence with which they will regard their German conquerors or the growth of the new-born hope that Great Britain will be victorious, and that the British victory will carry with it, as it must, the deliverance and restoration of France and all other captive peoples.

That is all I think it is useful to say at the present time, either about the Dakar affair or our relations with the Vichy Government, except this. We must be very careful not to allow a failure of this kind to weaken or hamper our efforts to take positive action and regain the initiative. On the contrary, we must improve our methods and redouble our efforts. We must be baffled to fight better and not baffled to fight less. Here let me say that criticism which is well meant and well informed and searching is often helpful, but there is a tone in certain organs of the Press, happily not numerous, a tone not only upon the Dakar episode but in other and more important issues, that is so vicious and malignant that it would be almost indecent if applied to the enemy. I know that some people's nerves are frayed by the stresses of the war, and they should be especially on their guard lest in giving vent to their own feelings they weaken the national resistance and blunt our sword.

I must now ask the House to extend its view more widely and to follow me, if it can find the patience, to the other side of the globe. Three months ago we were asked by the Japanese Government to close the Burma Road to certain supplies which might reach the Republic of China in its valiant struggle. We acceded to this demand because, as we told both Houses of Parliament, we wished to give an opportunity to the Governments of Japan and China to reach what is called in diplomatic language 'a just and equitable settlement' of their long and deadly quarrel – there were no doubt some other reasons, but that one is enough for my argument. Unhappily this 'just and equitable settlement' has not been reached. On the contrary, the protracted struggle of Japan to subjugate the Chinese race is still proceeding with all its attendant miseries. We much regret that the opportunity has been lost. In the circumstances His Majesty's Government propose to allow the agreement about closing the Burma Road to run its course until 17th October, but they do not see their way to renew it after that.

Instead of reaching an agreement with China, the Japanese Government have entered into a Three-Power Pact with Germany and Italy, a pact which, in many respects, is a revival of the Anti-Comintern Pact of a few years ago, but which binds Japan to attack the United States should the United States intervene in the war now proceeding between Great Britain and the two European dictators. This bargain appears so unfavourable to Japan that we wonder whether there are not some secret clauses. It is not easy now to see in what way Germany and Italy could come to the aid of Japan while the British and United States Navies remain in being, as they certainly do and as they certainly will. However, that is for the Japanese – with whom we have never wished to quarrel and to whom we have rendered great service in the past – to judge for themselves. Great services have been rendered to them by the peoples of the United States and Great Britain since their rise in the nineteenth century. We have never had a desire to quarrel with them. This is a matter on which they must judge for themselves. This Three-Power Pact is, of course, aimed primarily at the United States, but also in a secondary degree it is pointed against Russia. Neither of the branches of the English-speaking race is accustomed to react to threats of violence by submission, and certainly the reception of this strange, ill-balanced declaration in the United States has not been at all encouraging to those who are its authors. We hope, however, that all such dangers – and the dangers can plainly be seen – will be averted by the prudence and patience that Japan has so often shown in the gravest situations.

There is another country much nearer home which has for some months past seemed to hang in the balance between peace and war. We have always wished well to the Spanish people, and in a glorious period of our history we stood between the Spaniards and foreign domination. There is no country in Europe that has more need of peace and food and the opportunities of prosperous trade than Spain, which has been torn and tormented by the devastation of a civil war, into which the Spanish nation was drawn by a series of hideous accidents and misunderstandings, and from the ruins of which they must now rebuild their united national life of dignity, in mercy and in honour. Far be it from us to lap Spain and her own economic needs in the wide compass of our blockade. All we seek is that Spain will not become a channel of supply to our mortal foes. Subject to this essential condition, there is no problem of blockade that we will not study in the earnest desire to meet Spain's needs and aid her revival. Even less do we presume to intrude on the internal affairs of Spain or to stir the embers of what so lately were devouring fires. As in the days of the Peninsular war, British interests and policy are based on the independence and unity of Spain, and we look forward to seeing her take her rightful place both as a great Mediterranean Power and as a leading and famous member of the family of Europe and of Christendom, which, though now sundered by fearful quarrels and under the obsession of grievous tyrannies, constitutes the goal towards which we are marching and will march across the battlefields of the land, the sea and the air.

Because we feel easier in ourselves and see our way more clearly through our difficulties and dangers than we did some months ago, because foreign countries, friends or foes, recognise the giant, enduring, resilient strength of Britain and the British Empire, do not let us dull for one moment the sense of the awful hazards in which we stand. Do not let us lose the conviction that it is only by supreme and superb exertions, unwearying and indomitable, that we shall save our souls alive. No one can predict, no one can even imagine, how this terrible war against German and Nazi aggression will run its course or how far it will spread or how long it will last. Long, dark months of trials and tribulations lie before us. Not only great dangers, but many more misfortunes, many shortcomings, many mistakes, many disappointments will surely be our lot. Death and sorrow will be the companions of our journey; hardship our garment; constancy and valour our only shield. We must be united, we must be undaunted, we must be inflexible. Our qualities and deeds must burn and glow through the gloom of Europe until they become the veritable beacon of its salvation.

John Colville: diary
(*Colville papers*)

8 October 1940

I followed the speech from a flimsy of the PM's notes, which are typed in a way which Halifax says is like the printing of the psalms. Afterwards John Peck and I corrected the official report and altered the text in many places to improve the style and the grammar; for the PM's speeches are essentially oratorical masterpieces and in speaking he inserts much that sounds well and reads badly.

John Colville: diary
(*Colville papers*)

8 October 1940

The PM, dressed in his blue 'siren-suit',[1] dined with Eden in his new dining-room at No. 10 – formerly the typists' room in the basement and now redecorated and reinforced. He was in great form – as always after a speech has been successfully achieved – and amused Eden and me very much by his conversation with Nelson, the black cat, whom he chided for being afraid of the guns and unworthy of the name he bore. 'Try and remember,' he said to Nelson reprovingly, 'what those boys in the RAF are doing.'

---

[1] This is the first reference I have found during the war to Churchill's one-piece zip-up siren suit (not unlike a boiler suit) that he often wore on informal occasions.

War Cabinet: minutes
(*Cabinet papers, 65/9*)

9 October 1940 Prime Minister's Room
12 noon House of Commons

The Prime Minister said that when the 20,000 rifles which had been promised to Mr de Valera were handed over to him, he proposed to send a letter to Mr de Valera saying that he was confident that these rifles would be used in the defence of Irish hearths and homes and in the cause of freedom.

The Prime Minister said that the directions which had been given by the Cabinet in regard to gas preparations had not been fully implemented. He thought that this matter should be enquired into.

The Prime Minister said that the articles in the *Sunday Pictorial* and *Daily Mirror* constituted, in his view, a serious danger to this country. First, these newspapers were trying to 'rock the boat' and to shake the confidence of the country in Ministers. Secondly, the effect of the prominence given to Mr H. G. Wells's article must be to weaken discipline in the Army. Thirdly, an endeavour was being made to poison relations between members of the Government. It was intolerable that those bearing the burden of supreme responsibility at this time should be subject to attacks of this kind. He was determined to put a stop to these attacks and to obtain protection for the War Cabinet. It would be quite wrong that two members of the War Cabinet should be in the position of asking favours of the Newspaper Proprietors' Association.

The Prime Minister said that he was prepared to agree to the Minister of Aircraft Production and the Lord Privy Seal[1] sending for representatives of the Newspaper Proprietors' Association and speaking to them on the lines suggested. But he wished it to be clear that, for his part, he receded in no way from the view he had taken, that the Government must be prepared to take firm action to deal with this menace.

War Cabinet: Confidential Annex
(*Cabinet papers, 65/15*)

9 October 1940
12 noon

The Prime Minister said that it had been suggested that the Secretary of State for War should pay a personal visit to the Middle East. He was sure that such a visit would be of great value, especially as a Turkish Mission was

[1] Lord Beaverbrook and Clement Attlee.

shortly arriving in Egypt with a view, probably, to assessing our strength in that part of the world. It would be an advantage if the Secretary of State could meet this Mission. A meeting might perhaps also be arranged at Khartoum with General Smuts who would shortly be visiting Kenya.

The Prime Minister said that if Germany decided to throw her weight into an Eastward thrust, the countries immediately in her path, could not do more than greatly delay her progress. We should take advantage of such delay to develop our army in the Middle East.

The Foreign Secretary also reported that the attitude of the King of Egypt gave some cause for anxiety.

The Prime Minister said that it was for consideration whether we ought not to remind him that he was under the necessity of obeying our instructions. It was illogical that Egypt should not have declared war on Italy at a time when the Italians had invaded Egypt. We had possibly been remiss in allowing the fiction of Egyptian neutrality to continue. These matters might be discussed by the Secretary of State for War with Sir Miles Lampson and General Wavell on his arrival in Egypt.

Winston S. Churchill to Malcolm MacDonald
(*Churchill papers, 20/13*)

9 October 1940

This delay cannot be tolerated. Why do you not tell Admiral Evans[1] to get in touch with the Office of Works under my authority, and grasp the matter[2] with force and strength. Kindly have an inspection made every morning by one of your officers, and let me have a special report. If we cannot cope with a problem like this, we are certainly not going to be able to beat the Huns.

Let me also have a report about the traverses which are being put in for safety.

WSC

[1] Edward Ratcliffe Garth Russell Evans, 1881–1957. Entered the Royal Navy, 1897. Second-in-command, British Antarctic Expedition, 1909; returned in command of the expedition after the death of Captain Scott. On active service, 1914–18 (despatches twice). Rear-Admiral commanding the Royal Australian Navy, 1929–31. Knighted, 1935. Commander-in-Chief, the Nore, 1935–9. London Regional Commissioner for Civil Defence, 1939–45. Created Baron Mountevans, 1945.

[2] Preparation to get ready Churchill's above-ground rooms in the Board of Trade Building, later known as No. 10 Annexe (see page 979).

Winston S. Churchill to Lord Halifax
(*Premier papers, 3/184/1*)

9 October 1940

I see no reason why M. Chautemps should not be allowed to come here. He is a man of much distinction and though not a strong man was not I think a serious offender. Why should we mind Pétain's ex-ministers arriving here? The numbers cannot be very great and it all tends to show what a mistake they made at Bordeaux. I should like to see M. Chautemps and have a talk with him. Others will come here later. I hope you will consider this.[1]

WSC

Winston S. Churchill to Anthony Eden
(*Churchill papers, 20/13*)

9 October 1940
ACTION THIS DAY

The Chiefs of Staff should consider the matter to-morrow and make a recommendation to the Cabinet who must decide between the rival claims of Home Defence and Middle East. You seem to be rather optimistic about production and expansion here. You had better prepare a paper which should be printed and circulated for Cabinet on Friday. Anyone can see that aircraft are needed in the Middle East. What is not so easy is whether they can be spared here. Remember that we are still vastly inferior in numbers, both of fighters and bombers, to the German Air Forces, and that heavy losses have been sustained by our air production. The Chief of the Air Staff and Secretary of State must be asked for a precise recommendation.

WSC

Winston S. Churchill: speech
(*'Into Battle', pages 292–4*)

9 October 1940   Caxton Hall

I feel very much honoured that you have thought of calling me to assume the high and important task of leading the Conservative Party. The loss we have suffered and which I have suffered through the illness which has forced our late leader, Mr Neville Chamberlain, to withdraw from active public life is heavy and painful. The thoughts and the wishes with which we follow him

---

[1] On 22 October 1940 Lord Halifax wrote to Churchill: 'I spoke to you about this this morning & have in consequence prohibited Chautemps coming' (*Premier papers, 3/184/1*). See also page 957.

into his retirement are those of personal regard, and of respect and admiration for the courage and the integrity which have animated every action of his life.

It is now three years since I stood here and seconded the proposal that he should become our leader, and during the last thirteen months, some of which seem to count as if they were years, I was either his lieutenant or the head of the Government in which he so loyally and selflessly served. During that period our friendship, which was to some extent on both sides inherited, was welded in the fires of war into a comradeship of mutual trust and close identity of view. He has fallen out of our fighting ranks, and we must fill the gap in the Government and in the Party promptly and as best we may.

Before deciding to accept the trust and honour you wish to give me, I have asked myself two questions. The first is whether the leadership of a great party is compatible with the position I hold from King and Parliament as Prime Minister of an Administration composed of and officially supported by all parties. Unfortunately there are arguments both ways.

Considering, however, that I have to be in daily relations in matters of much domestic consequence with the leaders of the other two parties who are serving in the Government, I felt that it would be more convenient that I should be able to speak for the Conservative Party with direct and first-hand knowledge of the general position which they occupy upon fundamental issues, and also to speak with their authority. It also seems to me, that, as Leader of the House of Commons at a time when the Conservative Party enjoys a very large majority over all other parties, and when, owing to the war and the grave dangers and peculiar conditions amid which we live, no General Election is possible, I could discharge my task with less difficulty if I were in formal relation with the majority of the members of the House of Commons. If that, as I gather, Lord Halifax, from what you have said, is your opinion, I feel I need have no doubts as to either the wisdom or the propriety of the course which is now proposed.

The second question I have asked myself is much more personal. Am I by temperament and conviction able sincerely to identify myself with the main historical conceptions of Toryism, and can I do justice to them and give expression to them spontaneously in speech and action? My life, such as it has been, has been lived for forty years in the public eye, and very varying opinions are entertained about it – and about particular phases in it. I shall attempt no justification, but this I will venture most humbly to submit and also to declare, because it springs most deeply from the convictions of my heart, that at all times according to my lights and throughout the changing scenes through which we are all hurried I have always faithfully served two public causes which I think stand supreme – the maintenance of the enduring greatness of Britain and her Empire and the historical continuity of our island life.

Alone among the nations of the world we have found the means to combine

Empire and liberty. Alone among the peoples we have reconciled democracy and tradition; for long generations, nay, over several centuries, no mortal clash or religious or political gulf has opened in our midst. Alone we have found the way to carry forward the glories of the past through all the storms, domestic and foreign, that have surged about, and thus to bring the labours of our forebears as a splendid inheritance for modern progressive democracy to enjoy.

It is this interplay and interweaving of past and present which in this fearful ordeal has revealed to a wondering world the unconquerable strength of a united nation. It is that which has been the source of our strength. In that achievement, all living parties – Conservative, Liberal, Labour, and other parties like the Whigs who have passed away – all have borne a part and all today at the moment of our sorest need share the benefits which have resulted from it.

This is no time for partisanship or vaunting party claims, but this I will say – the Conservative Party will not allow any party to excel it in the sacrifice of party interests and party feelings which must be made by all if we are to emerge safely and victoriously from the perils which compass us about. In no other way can we save our lives and, what is far more precious than life, the grand human causes which we, in our generation, have the supreme honour to defend. It is because I feel that these deep conceptions lying far beneath the superficial current of party politics and the baffling of accidental events have always been yours and have always been mine, that I accept solemnly, but also buoyantly, the trust and duty you wish now to confide in me.

Mary Churchill: reflection
(*'Clementine Churchill', pages 299–300*)

9 October 1940

There were, and maybe still are, two views as to whether he was right to accept this invitation. Churchill himself had no doubt whatsoever; all his experience as a politician made him quite sure that he should grasp with a firm hand the Leadership of the party which held a commanding majority in both Houses of Parliament. The opposing view, which Clementine herself held with passionate conviction, was that Winston had been called by the voice of the whole nation, irrespective of party, at a time of grave national emergency to head a National Government, and that, although he might feel his position to be stronger in Parliament by accepting the Conservative Leadership, he would affront a large body of opinion in the country. Clementine put her view with vehemence, and all her latent hostility towards the Tory Party boiled over; there were several good ding-dong arguments between them. But Winston's view prevailed: he accepted the Leadership of the Conservative Party, and felt sustained through some tough times by the assurance of their solid support.

True to her custom, Clementine accepted her defeat 'hout recriminations. But she never altered her opinion that this step was a mistake, and that it alienated much of the support which Winston derived from the working-classes through the vindication of his pre-war prophecies and his record as a war leader. When about a year later she was invited to head the Red Cross Aid to Russia Fund, she accepted with alacrity, not only because of her wish to do something for the Russians, but also because she felt that in some way this might help to redress the balance.

Major Long[1] to Winston S. Churchill
(*Churchill papers, 2/3968*)

10 October 1940

470th Battery
Royal Artillery

My dear Prime Minister,

May I send you my warmest & sincere congratulations on your election as leader of the Conservative Party – God Bless you in your heroic work for England.

Yours ever
Eric Long

Sir Samuel Hoare to Winston S. Churchill
(*Templewood papers*)

10 October 1940
Private & Personal

British Embassy
Madrid

Dear Winston,

I feel that as one of the oldest Conservative MPs[2] I must write a line to congratulate you upon becoming leader of the Conservative Party. From

---

[1] Richard Eric Onslow Long, 1892–1967. Son of the 1st Viscount Long (Walter Long). Educated at Harrow. In business in the City, 1911–14. On active service in France and at the Dardanelles (despatches). Major, 1923. A Member of the London Stock Exchange. Conservative MP for Westbury, 1927–31. President, West Wiltshire Constitutional Association, 1927–33 and 1948. Officer Commanding the 75th Searchlight Regiment, Royal Artillery, 1939–43. His only brother was killed in action on 27 January 1917. His elder son, Lieutenant Walter Reginald Basil Long, was drowned while on active service in Greece, 28 April 1941, aged twenty-two. His nephew (whom he succeeded as 3rd Viscount) was killed in action in north-west Europe on 23 September 1944.

[2] Sir Samuel Hoare had been first elected to Parliament in 1910, as Conservative Member for Chelsea. At that time Churchill was sitting as a Liberal.

many points of view I am glad that the choice has now been made. You will yourself be much stronger with the Party machine behind you. This means that there need be no repetition of the LG collapse after the last war.[1] Besides this, it seems to me vital to the Party itself that it should have at once a popular leader at its head. The Party is still the greatest political instrument for the maintenance of the Empire and the preservation of its traditions. Without it the country will drift into the shallow waters of the ideologues. Both during the war and after it we must stop this drift and you with your personality and prestige will be able to stop it. Naturally, having myself been connected with Cabinet changes over a period of many years, I felt greatly isolated here whilst these last were being made. I daresay that you had the same kind of feelings when you were out of office after 1928. I do not believe that in either of our cases this feeling is chiefly due to personal ambition. We have both had our share of Government posts and the commendable desire to obtain them cannot be as keen as it was. It is rather, I think, a desire to play a part in the great events and the fear of frustration that makes us cling to public life. But here I am afraid that in my isolation I am becoming meditative and I must not on any account bore you with my reflections. I will therefore end this letter as I began it with my best wishes to you and the Party under your leadership.

Yours ever
Samuel Hoare

Chiefs of Staff Committee: minutes
(*Cabinet papers, 79/7*)

10 October 1940
10.15 a.m.

The Committee had before them a Note by the Secretary enclosing a Minute by the Prime Minister together with the relevant correspondence on the subject of increasing our air forces in the Middle East – circulated at the meeting.

The Prime Minister had called for the Chiefs of Staff recommendation to be put before the Cabinet the next day. It would not be possible for the Air Staff to put forward all relevant data within this time, nor was it desirable that the Chiefs of Staff should make a hasty decision on a major question of this type. It

---

[1] The collapse of the Liberal Party after 1918 had been dramatic, accelerated by the breach between the followers of Asquith and those of Lloyd George. In the second general election of 1910, the Liberal Party secured 272 seats. In 1918 the Liberal seats fell to 161 (133 of whom, including Churchill, were Lloyd George supporters), and in 1922 to 54 (when the Labour Party secured 142 seats, and Churchill, in his last election as a Liberal, was defeated at the polls).

was suggested that an interim reply should be submitted to the Prime Minister's Minute emphasizing the complexities of the problem and pointing out that certain preparations were already in hand and that therefore no time would be lost by deferring consideration of the problem until early the following week.

War Cabinet: minutes
(*Cabinet papers, 65/9*)

10 October 1940 Prime Minister's Room
11.30 a.m. House of Commons

The Prime Minister said that evidence was still accumulating that preparations for invasion were still going forward and that it would be premature to dismiss the possibility of an attempt being made.[1] Nevertheless, we should have to consider in the near future the extent to which we could afford to reinforce the Middle East at the expense of this country.

Winston S. Churchill to General de Gaulle
(*Churchill papers, 20/14*)

10 October 1940

I have received your telegram with great pleasure and I send my best wishes to you and to all other Frenchmen who are resolved to fight on with us. We shall stand resolutely together until all obstacles have been overcome and we share in the triumph of our cause.

---

[1] The decrypting at Bletchley of top-secret German Air Force signals had revealed, among other German instructions, the appointment in the first week of October of Air Force officers to embarkation staffs at Antwerp, Ostend, Dunkirk and Calais. Top secret instructions had also been decrypted with regard to a German air formation headquarters, which was known to be in charge of Air Force equipment in Belgium and Northern France, 'settling the details of loading of units and equipment into ships'. On 24 September 1940 the German 3rd Air Fleet had received orders, also decrypted at Bletchley, concerning the supply of air rescue vessels by seaplane bases off Norway and along the North Sea and Channel coasts 'in connection', as the message sent to Churchill explained, 'with the *Seelöwe* (Sea Lion) operation (presumed to be the invasion of Britain)'. On 9 October 1940 a further decrypt revealed that on the previous day the headquarters of the 2nd German Airfleet 'asked for provision of two tankers each filled with approximately 250,000 gallons of aviation fuel to be held in readiness for S + 3 day (presumably the third day of invasion operations against UK) at Rotterdam and Antwerp' ('German Preparations for Invasion', 4 and 9 October 1940, *War Office papers, 199/911A*).

John Colville: diary
(*Colville papers*)

10 October 1940

I talked to the PM while he was changing into his siren-suit for dinner and described what we had seen at the rest centre at Kentish Town. He told me to procure for him a full report on the subject of both rest centres and shelters, showing who was responsible for what. I asked Bridges to supply this. The PM went off after dinner to see AA and Searchlights at Richmond and Kenley.

John Colville: diary
(*Colville papers*)

11 October 1940

There are two unexploded bombs on the Horse Guards Parade. 'Will they do us any damage when they explode?' asked the PM lying in bed. 'I shouldn't think so, Sir,' I said. 'Is that just your opinion,' he replied, 'because if so it's worth nothing. You have never seen an unexploded bomb go off. Go and ask for an official report.' Such is the result of hazarding opinions to the PM if one has nothing with which to back them. But I was vindicated by the experts.

General Brooke: diary
(*Alanbrooke papers*)

11 October 1940

Flew to Old Sarum (Salisbury Plain) where Auchinleck met me and took me on to Monty's[1] HQ, where I attended part of his 'Officers' Week', and said a few words. Received message whilst there asking me to dine and sleep at Chequers. Flew back to London, changed and packed bag. Put in another hour in the office and then left for Chequers.

There I found the Prime Minister, Mrs Churchill, Randolph, Duncan Sandys, Mary, Pug Ismay and Tim Pile. Sat up till 2 a.m. PM in great form. Discussing probable course of the war, likelihood of German move in the Mediterranean. Also reasons for failure of the Dakar expedition. He has a wonderful vitality and bears his heavy burdens remarkably well. It would be impossible to find a man to fill his place at present.

---

[1] Major-General Montgomery, then commanding the 5th Corps.

Winston S. Churchill to Sir Gerald Campbell
(*Churchill papers, 20/14*)

11 October 1940

I am much distressed by the trouble and heat which has arisen about the JATC[1] and remembering our pleasant journey through the giant trees and your invaluable assistance at a critical moment, I address myself to you personally. I do not think that versions of private conversation, even if true, ought in these grievous times to play any part in great affairs. Your telegram therefore seems to me extravagant in tone, and I cannot believe that the passing of hot words to and fro is in any way helpful. I have sent a telegram to Mackenzie King which you should read. It is of course purely personal, but there is no reason why he should not show it to his colleagues, or why you should not talk it over with him. I hope to hear from you through the Secretary of State that you have managed to smooth it all down and remove any ill effects of tittle-tattle. The Canadian Government must rely upon the official communications which are made to them which represent the policy of His Majesty's Government. These have repeatedly shown how highly we value the JATC, and that we all realise the immense part it will play in the later stages of the war once we get there.

I cannot attempt to go into the technical issue about the aeroplanes which were diverted. There is repeated friction between the Air Ministry and MAP which I endeavour to soften as much as I can, always remembering that nothing but the marvellous expansion of supplies which Lord Beaverbrook has produced would have carried us through this crisis which is by no means ended.

Winston S. Churchill to William Mackenzie King
(*Churchill papers, 20/14*)

11 October 1940

Lord Beaverbrook informs me that no such conversation with Bishop[2] as has been attributed to him ever took place. Mr Bickell,[3] who was present on the only occasion when they met, confirms this statement in writing. Even if anything like it had taken place, it ought not to have been repeated out of its

[1] The Joint Air Training Corps training scheme, whereby British pilots and air crew were trained at flying schools in Canada. (See page 1188, note 1).

[2] William Avery Bishop, 1894–1956. Canadian aviator. Served in the Royal Flying Corps, 1915–18. Officially credited with bringing down 72 enemy aircraft (Victoria Cross, despatches, MC, DSO and bar, DFC). Air Marshal, 1938. Director, Royal Canadian Air Force, 1939–45.

[3] J. P. Bickell, of International Nickel. In charge of the ferrying of aircraft (ATFERO) from the factories in Canada to the squadrons in Britain. In the winter of 1940–1 a total of 160 aircraft were ferried across the Atlantic, with only one loss.

setting and out of its context. It is quite true, however, that Lord Beaverbrook is greatly distressed about the sending away of any fighting aeroplanes from this country at the present time.[1] We are fighting for our lives here, and he is feeding the fighting line from day to day in a truly marvellous manner. Factories are bombed almost nightly, and continuous readjustments and dispersions have to be made. One heavy blow is received after another. The repeated Air raid warnings coming upon workmen who perhaps in the same factory have seen a score of their comrades killed the week before, inevitably lead to shorter hours being worked and injury to output. Nevertheless, in spite of all, we are more than holding our own, largely thanks to the genius of this man. While I am sure he never said anything like what is so wrongly attributed to him, one must understand his point of view. Do not on any account, my friend, suppose that we do not value the great Empire training scheme, or that we are not going to push it with our utmost strength. But there is the inevitable conflict between the short-term and the long-term view. I hope we shall solve this problem satisfactorily, and pray cable to me if any difficulty arises in which I can be of assistance. Do not underrate the gravity of the pressure to which we are subjected here. Kindest regards.[2]

John Colville: diary
(*Colville papers*)

11 October 1940   Chequers

At dinner I sat between Mary and Diana. The PM was cheerful, despite the facts that our air results today and yesterday have been bad. He proclaimed that 'the man's effort is flagging'.

---

[1] Beaverbrook had objected to any further aircraft from Britain being sent at that time to the five flying training schools in Canada, but later agreed (at the War Cabinet of 15 October 1940) that fifty-seven aircraft that were already overseas could be sent to Canada.

[2] Churchill was so indignant at the 'derogatory charge against a member of the War Cabinet' (Beaverbrook) that he sought an apology from the Air Force officer concerned. When Sinclair declined to pursue the matter further, Churchill wrote to him (in a 'Private and Secret' letter): 'Do I understand from your Minute of 18.10.40 that you consider that an unfounded charge, accompanied by strictures of this kind, calls for no comment from you to the officer who has made them, and that no withdrawal or apology should be forthcoming from that officer? Even in private life, a gentleman who has made a derogatory charge against another and used language of censure about him on the strength of it, would be expected to withdraw and apologise when proved to have been wrongly informed' (*Churchill papers, 20/2*).

The conversation turned to General Hobart,[1] an erratic genius on tanks whose services are not being used. Brooke said he was too wild, but Winston reminded him of Wolfe standing on a chair in front of Chatham and brandishing his sword. 'You cannot expect,' he said, 'to have the genius type with a conventional copy-book style.'

Some apprehension was expressed about the vulnerability of Chequers, which would make an easy target for bombs. 'Probably,' said Winston, 'they don't think I am so foolish as to come here; but I stand to lose a lot, three generations at a swoop.' (Randolph's and Pamela's son[2] was born two days ago.) Certainly there is a danger: in Norway, Poland and Holland the Germans showed it was their policy to go all out for the Government, and Winston is worth more to them than the whole Cabinets of those three countries rolled into one. To bed at 2.15 a.m.

Winston S. Churchill to Sir Horace Wilson
(*Churchill papers, 20/13*)

12 October 1940

About a fortnight ago I directed that the talk about four days a week for Civil Servants should stop, because I feared the effect in the factories of such an announcement. I am, however, now coming round to the idea of a five-day week, sleeping in for four nights (and where possible feeding in), and three nights and two days away at home. This of course would only apply to people who work in London and live in the suburbs. I see such queues at the 'bus stops, and no doubt it is going to become increasingly difficult to get in and

---

[1] Percy Cleghorn Stanley Hobart, 1885–1957. Joined the Royal Engineers, 1904. Served on the North-West Frontier of India, 1908. On active service on the Western Front, 1915, and in Mesopotamia, 1916–18, when he was wounded, and taken prisoner. MC, DSO (1916) and OBE (1918). Served in Palestine, 1918; in Waziristan, 1921. Joined the Royal Tank Corps, 1923; Inspector, Royal Tank Corps, 1933–6. Commander, Tank Brigade, 1934–7. Deputy Director of Staff Duties, War Office, 1937. Major-General, 1937. Director of Military Training, War Office, 1937–8. Raised the 7th Armoured Division, Egypt, 1938–9; the 11th Armoured Division, 1941–2; the 79th Armoured Division, 1942 (commanding it in north-west Europe, 1944–5). Knighted, 1943. His sister married (in 1927) Bernard Montgomery (later Viscount Montgomery of Alamein). She died in 1937.

[2] Winston Spencer Churchill, 1940– . Born 10 October 1940, the son of Randolph and Pamela Churchill. Educated at Eton and Christ Church, Oxford. A newspaper correspondent from 1963 (Yemen, Congo, Angola). In 1964 he published *First Journey*. Author, with his father, of *The Six Day War* (1967). Conservative MP since 1967. Parliamentary Private Secretary to the Minister of Housing and Construction, 1970–2; to the Minister of State, Foreign and Commonwealth Office, 1972–3. Conservative Party front bench spokesman on defence, 1976–8. Author of *Defending the West*, 1981. Member of the Select Committee on Defence since 1983. A Governor of the English-Speaking Union, 1975–80. Published *Memories and Adventures*, 1989. In 1993 his mother was appointed United States Ambassador to France.

out of London quickly. Each Department should work out a scheme to suit their own and their Staff's convenience. The same amount of work must be crowded in to the five days as is now done. Efforts should also be made to stagger the hours of arrival and departure, so as to get as many away as possible before the rush hour and spread the traffic over the day.

Let me have your views on this, together with proposals for action in a circular to Departments.

WSC

Winston S. Churchill to Sir James Grigg
(*Churchill papers, 20/13*)

12 October 1940

Why should courts-martial be held in public on all occasions? Is this the law? Surely we have power to withhold publicity, on military grounds. In this case the military ground is that the publication of these cases will no doubt enhance our reputation here for the proper control of our own officers, but that the facts, detached from our treatment of them, will be used as dangerous propaganda, and also may react unfavourably upon the treatment of our numerous prisoners of war in German hands.

I have never heard of courts-martial being held in public as an ordinary rule, nor of reporters being admitted or wanting to be admitted to them.

WSC

Winston S. Churchill to General Ismay
(*Premier papers, 3/369/1*)

12 October 1940

This development of RDF with long-range coastal Batteries is serious. We have for a long time been on the track of this device, and I drew attention to it some weeks ago. I was then told that it had to have a low priority because of other even more urgent needs. Perhaps it may now be possible to bring it forward. Evidently it will turn night into day so far as defence against sea bombardment is concerned.

Pray see if some proposals can be made without injury to other radio projects.

WSC

John Colville: diary
(*Colville papers*)

12 October 1940   Chequers

At lunch we talked chiefly of the air-raids and their effects. The PM, sitting in his siren-suit and smoking an immense cigar, said he thought this was the sort of war which would suit the English people once they were used to it. They would prefer all to be in the front line, taking part in the Battle of London, than to look on helplessly at mass slaughters like Passchendaele.

The PM is obviously worried about the possibility of an attack on Chequers and says that he does not object to chance 'but feels it a mistake to be the victim of design'.

The accurate bombing much disturbed the PM, Attlee[1] and Dill who all feel that Whitehall – and particularly No. 10 – is extremely dangerous. The PM is thinking on authoritarian lines about shelters and talks of forcibly preventing people from going into the underground and allotting to each a place of safety so that the optimum dispersal may be achieved.

John Colville: diary
(*Colville papers*)

13 October 1940   Chequers

Winston's only noteworthy remark during lunch was, 'A Hun alive is a war in prospect.'

Winston S. Churchill to General Ismay
(*Churchill papers, 20/13*)

13 October 1940
Most Secret

REVIEW

1. First in urgency is the reinforcement of Malta –
(a) by further Hurricane aircraft flown there as can best be managed,
(b) by the convoy now being prepared, which should carry the largest anti-aircraft outfit possible, as well as the Battalions and the Battery. I understand another MT ship can be made available.

---

[1] A week later, a member of Attlee's Private Office wrote to Tony Bevir at 10 Downing Street: 'Would you be good enough to ask Colville (if he is about) whether he knows who has got Mr Attlee's tin hat? Mr Attlee took his to Chequers last week end and the one he brought back is several sizes too large.'

(c) by one or better still two more Battalions released from police duty on the Canal or in Palestine, and carried to Malta when next the Fleet moves thither from Alexandria. General Dobbie's latest appreciation bears out the grievous need of strengthening the garrison. Every effort should be made to meet his needs, observing that once Malta becomes a thorn in the Italian side, the enemy's force may be turned upon it. The movement of these reinforcements should therefore precede any marked activity from Malta,

(d) Even three I Tanks[1] at Malta would be important, not only in actual defence, but as a deterrent if it were known that they were there. Some mock-up Tanks also might be exhibited where they would be detected from the Air.

2. The movement of the Fleet to Malta must await this strengthening of the AA and Air defences. It is, however, a most needful and profoundly advantageous step. I welcome the possibility of even basing light Forces upon Malta, as they immediately increase its security. I understand it is intended they shall sally forth by day and only lie in harbour as a rule at night. It must be observed that a strong ship like the *Valiant* can far better withstand a hit from a bomb than light craft, and in addition she brings a Battery of 20 very high-class AA guns. Apart from the stake being higher, it is not seen why, if light Forces can be exposed in Malta Harbour, well-armoured and well-armed ships cannot use it too. The multiple aerial mine UP weapon gives considerable security against dive-bombing.

I should be glad to be more fully informed by the Admiralty about this.

Occasional visits by the whole Battle Fleet would be an immense deterrent on hostile attack, and also a threat to the Libyan communications while they lasted.

Let me have the number of AA guns now in position, and the whole maximum contents of the new convoy, together with estimated dates for their being mounted.

3. Relations with Vichy. We cannot accept the position that we must yield to the wishes of Vichy out of fear, lest they make Air raids upon Gibraltar; for there would be no end to that. We must reassert our blockade of the Straits, dealing with vessels whether escorted or unescorted, though without violating Spanish Territorial waters. We should assemble a sufficient force at Gibraltar for this purpose at the earliest date possible. Meanwhile, we must maintain as good a blockade of Dakar as possible, and protect Duala, &c., from a counter-stroke by the French cruisers in Dakar. The conversations with Vichy, if they

---

[1] 'I' Tanks: Infantry Tanks designed to provide close support for infantry during an advance. The Infantry Tank Mark II, the Matilda, was slow and heavily armoured. It had given a good account of itself in the battle for France and in the early campaigns in North Africa, but was withdrawn in 1942 after proving vulnerable to the latest German anti-tank weapons. It had a speed of 15 miles an hour, carried a crew of four, and was armed with a two-pounder gun and a machine gun. Nearly 3,000 were produced.

take place, may reach a *modus vivendi* falling somewhat short of these desiderata. Of course if we could be assured that Vichy, or part of Vichy, were genuinely moving in our direction, we could ease upon them to a very large extent. It seems probable that they will be increasingly inclined to move as we desire, and I personally do not believe that hard pressure from us will prevent this favourable movement. It is becoming more difficult every day for Vichy to lead France into war with us. We must not be too much afraid of checking this process, because the tide in our favour will master and overwhelm the disturbing eddies of the blockade, de Gaulle, and possible sea incidents. I do not believe that any trouble will arise with the French which will prevent the impending movement of our convoy to Malta. The chance is there, but it is remote and must be faced.

4. The greatest prize open to the Bomber Command is the disabling of *Bismarck* and *Tirpitz*. If *Bismarck* could be set back for three or four months, the *KGV* could go to the Eastern Mediterranean to work up, and could therefore play a decisive part in the re-occupation of Malta by the Fleet. This would speedily transform the strategic situation in the Mediterranean.

5. Should October pass without invasion, we should begin the reinforcement of the Middle East by the Cape route to the utmost extent our shipping permits, sending as arranged the Armoured Units, the Australians and New Zealanders in November, another British Division before Christmas, and at least four more during January, February and March. All this would be in addition to the necessary drafts. Let me know how far your present programme of sailings conforms to this.

6. The time has also come for a further strong reinforcement of the Middle East by Bombers and by Fighters. I should be glad to know how far the Chiefs of Staff would be prepared to go, observing that though the risk is very great, so also is the need.

7. Let me see the programme for reinforcing the Mediterranean Fleet during the next six months. It should be possible by the end of the year to send three flotillas of destroyers to the Eastern Mediterranean, and one additional to Gibraltar. If *KGV* must be kept to watch *Bismarck*, *Nelson* or *Rodney* should go to Alexandria, and either *Barham* or *Queen Elizabeth*. What cruiser reinforcements are contemplated? Will it be possible to send *Formidable* thither also and when?

8. Agreeably to the despatch of Divisions to the Middle East, the Home Army and the Home Guard will be developed to fill the gap. A minimum of 12 Mobile Divisions must lie in reserve, apart from the troops on the beaches, at any time.

9. It should be possible also to provide by the end of July a striking Force for amphibious warfare of six Divisions, of which two should be Armoured. The various alternative plans for the employment of such a Force are being studied.

John Colville: diary
(*Colville papers*)

13 October 1940   Chequers

I told the PM how much I admired this review, and he replied that it was by no means in a finished state: he had just written down what he had in his head. It shows great breadth of vision.

As the PM said goodnight to the Air Marshals,[1] he told them he was sure we were going to win the war, but he confessed he did not see clearly how it was to be achieved.

Winston S. Churchill to General Ismay
(*Churchill papers, 20/13*)

13 October 1940

I will preside at a Conference on India's war effort on Tuesday next at 5 p.m. in the Central War Room. Secretaries of State for India and Colonies should be invited, together with Minister of Supply,[2] Sir James Grigg, and the CIGS should let me know the War Office view during the course of Monday.

I am definitely of opinion that a great feature should be made of the armaments which India is making, though I know only too well that the limiting factor is supply.

General Ismay should implement this, see that all parties are informed, and circulate the necessary papers.

                                                                                                                           WSC

Winston S. Churchill to Colonel Jacob
(*Churchill papers, 20/13*)

13 October 1940

This return[3] is already a month behind the events. Let me know what has happened since, as far as it is possible to find out.

Let me know what are the monthly forecasts for every month up to and including March next year.

Finally, assuming expenditure continues on the September level, what will be our stocks in all types at March 31, 1941?

                                                                                                                           WSC

[1] Among Churchill's guests at Chequers that weekend were two airmen, Air Chief Marshal Sir Hugh Dowding and Air Marshal Sir Hugh Portal.
[2] L. S. Amery, Lord Lloyd and Sir Andrew Duncan.
[3] Of small arms ammunition production.

Winston S. Churchill to Lord Halifax
(*Cabinet papers, 120/300*)

13 October 1940

I am very glad to hear that the Foreign Office do not like the so-called 'offer' contained in 1061 from Mr Kelly.[1] It would simply result in a Committee under German influence or fear, reporting at the very best that it was six of one and half-a-dozen of the other. It is even very likely they would report that we had committed the major breaches. Anyhow, we do not want these people thrusting themselves in, as even if Germany offered to stop bombing now, we should not consent to it. Bombing of military objectives, increasingly widely interpreted, seems at present our main road home.

WSC

Winston S. Churchill to L. S. Amery
(*Churchill papers, 20/13*)

13 October 1940

Many thanks for your letter of October 7. I should have thought Walter Elliot would do very well.[2] He and his wife[3] make a strong combination. Cabinet and Parliamentary experience are very important qualifications. I think also he has been roughly served by the turn of events. Unless you have different views, I should like to talk to him about it, and make him the offer. I was very sorry indeed when the new Government was formed that he was a sufferer.

WSC

[1] David Victor Kelly, 1891–1959. On active service, 1915–18 (Military Cross). Entered the Diplomatic Service, 1919. Minister in Berne, 1940–2. Knighted, 1942. Ambassador to Argentina, 1942; to Turkey, 1946–9; to the Soviet Union, 1949–51. Chairman of the British Council, 1955.

[2] As Governor of Burma. Churchill also thought of sending Euan Wallace, but he was ill. In the event, Reginald Dorman-Smith, a member of Neville Chamberlain's pre-war Government (Minister of Agriculture), was appointed. Dorman-Smith had been one of the Cabinet Ministers who had threatened to go on 'strike' on the afternoon of 2 September 1939 if Chamberlain did not issue Britain's declaration of war against Germany that night.

[3] Walter Elliot, 1888–1958. On active service, 1914–18 (MC and bar). Conservative MP, 1918–23, 1924–45, 1946–50 and 1950 until his death. Minister of Agriculture and Fisheries, 1932–6. Secretary of State for Scotland, 1936–8. Minister of Health, May 1938 to May 1940. Director of Public Relations, War Office, 1941–2. In 1951 Churchill wanted to offer him the Ministry of Education, but he was away from his telephone when the call came from Downing Street. His second wife, Katherine Tennant, Chairman of the Women's National Advisory Committee of the Conservative Party, 1954–7, was created Baroness Elliot of Harwood, after failing to win her late husband's seat (Glasgow Kelvingrove) at the by-election following his death in 1958. She died in 1994.

Winston S. Churchill to Lord Cranborne
(*Churchill papers, 20/13*)

13 October 1940

1. These papers affect the position of the High Commissioner[1] more seriously than I at first thought. It appears that his charges against Lord Beaverbrook are entirely untrue, as both the witnesses present at the interview in question entirely confirm Lord Beaverbrook's account. Without in any way satisfying himself as to the truth of the matter, or apparently finding out from Colonel Bishop whether he endorsed the statements attributed to him, the High Commissioner adopted and identified himself with the story and used a tone which showed heat and prejudice, and was disrespectful to a Member of the War Cabinet under which he is serving.

2. This is not the first time that the High Commissioner has revealed animus against Lord Beaverbrook, and has lent a ready ear to gossip about Mr Mackenzie King's relations with him. In this case also he was entirely wrong.

3. More serious still is the complete misrepresentation by the High Commissioner of the facts about the Harvard aeroplanes, because in this case he had the telegrams in his possession which showed that the statement of the Air Officer concerned were untrue, or at the very least based upon an entire misunderstanding of the facts.

4. In these circumstances, you should call for a precise and full explanation from Sir Gerald Campbell. I ought not to leave you in doubt, however, that unless these explanations throw an entirely new light upon his conduct, he should be recalled and removed from his post. I have not the slightest doubt that the War Cabinet would take the gravest view of his behaviour. We shall surely also soon be hearing from Mr Mackenzie King.

Pray let me see by return the cable you will be sending. I am hoping that this matter can be brought before the Cabinet on Tuesday.

Winston S. Churchill to Sir James Grigg
(*Churchill papers, 20/13*)

13 October 1940

A hot discussion is raging in the ATS[2] about whether members who marry should, if they wish, be allowed to quit. Nearly everyone is in favour of this. It seems futile to forbid them, and if they desert there is no means of punishing

[1] Sir Gerald Campbell, High Commissioner to Canada.

[2] The Auxiliary Territorial Service. An all-women's service, in 1941 it provided the women's component of the Mixed Batteries deployed on anti-aircraft sites, starting with the one in Richmond Park. By 1943 the employment of women in Mixed Batteries (manned in proportion of two women to one man) freed some 28,000 soldiers for other duties.

them. Only the most honourable are therefore impeded. Pray let me have, on one sheet of paper, a note on this showing the pros and cons.

WSC

Winston S. Churchill to Lionel Barrymore[1]
(*Churchill papers, 20/4*)

13 October 1940

Dear Barrymore,

It was kind of you to write me such a charming letter[2] and I am touched by what you say. We feel confident of success over here but it cheers us to know that we can count on the sympathy and goodwill of people like yourself on the other side of the Atlantic.

Yours sincerely,
Winston S. Churchill

Winston S. Churchill to General Dill
(*Churchill papers, 20/13*)

14 October 1940

I saw General Hobart yesterday, and formed a very good opinion of him. I remember now that he came to me before the war to warn me of the terrible position which would arise through our neglect to make the Tanks and even decide upon the models.[3] I have now heard from four different sources quite spontaneously about him and his capacity. I was therefore very glad to hear

---

[1] Lionel Barrymore, 1878–1954. Brother of the actors John and Ethel Barrymore (to whom Churchill had once proposed marriage), and himself one of the most important twentieth-century character actors. His reputation was established on Broadway during the First World War. In Hollywood from 1926, he starred in (among other films) *Grand Hotel* (1932) and *Captains Courageous* (1937). Because of arthritis, from 1938 he usually performed in a wheelchair.

[2] Not found.

[3] Hobart had been introduced to Churchill in October 1936 by the writer and Member of Parliament A. P. Herbert, who described the General as 'top dog, I think, (or very nearly so) of Tanks, and has a lot of interesting things he wants to say to someone who like you knows about defence'. Herbert added: 'Probably the simplest thing would be if he could come and see you somewhere. He is one of the most intelligent and interesting soldiers I have met' (*Churchill papers, 2/267*).

that you propose to appoint him to one of the new Tank Divisions which is forming. I should be glad if this could be done this week, and if possible today.

Pray let me know.[1]

WSC

Winston S. Churchill to General Ismay
(*Churchill papers, 20/13*)

14 October 1940

Let a report be prepared on two sheets of paper only, showing what are the possibilities of Germany developing the munition industries, especially aircraft, of the countries she has overrun, and when these evil effects are likely to become manifest.

WSC

Winston S. Churchill to General Smuts
(*Churchill papers, 20/14*)

14 October 1940

Your No. 768.[2] As usual we are in agreement. Invasion danger has not yet passed, but I think the moment has come for further strong reinforcement of Mediterranean and Middle East. We are planning to build a great Army there by the summer of 1941, but transport is the limiting factor, and the voyage round the Cape is long. A continuous movement begins almost immediately. We are also rearming our Air Force with modern machines, and even

---

[1] With his reply, Dill enclosed a statement, which he asked Churchill to read, that Hobart had on various occasions 'been reported on as impatient, quick-tempered, hot-headed, intolerant and inclined to see things as he wished them to be instead of as they were'. After Churchill had seen Hobart, Dill agreed to appoint him to the next Armoured Division that would be formed, in a month's time. 'We can talk this over in the train,' Churchill minuted to Dill on 22 October 1940, 'but I wish this appointment to be made now. I have already told General Hobart' (*Premier papers, 3/220*).

[2] In his telegram to Churchill on 12 October 1940, Smuts warned of a possible German advance through Greece to Constantinople. To prevent this, and the subsequent overwhelming of British forces in the Middle East, he proposed 'a new powerful army' with Australian and Indian troops, Greeks and Turks. 'Our diplomacy should be so as to re-assure both Greece and Turkey in advance and give them promise of military support.' If Turkey could be certain 'of the Russians' benevolent neutrality, she might carry out her Treaty obligations to us and give us her very strong support in the field and to the end' (*Foreign Office papers, 371/25224*). In the event, Greece was overwhelmed in April 1941 and Turkey did not enter the war against Germany until February 1945.

reinforcing it with fresh Squadrons, although the attack on this Island has not died down. Lastly, we are continually building up the strength of the Mediterranean Fleet and increasing and strengthening the garrison at Malta. We must not keep too many troops in Kenya. I hope you will meet Eden somewhere and talk everything over with him. Kindest regards.

Winston S. Churchill: recollection
(*'Their Finest Hour'*, pages 305–7)

15 October 1940   10 Downing Street

Another evening (October 14[1]) stands out in my mind. We were dining in the garden-room of No. 10 when the usual night raid began. My companions were Archie Sinclair, Oliver Lyttelton, and Moore-Brabazon. The steel shutters had been closed. Several loud explosions occurred around us at no great distance, and presently a bomb fell, perhaps a hundred yards away, on the Horse Guards Parade, making a great deal of noise. Suddenly I had a providential impulse. The kitchen at No. 10 Downing Street is lofty and spacious, and looks out through a large plate-glass window about twenty-five feet high. The butler and parlourmaid continued to serve the dinner with complete detachment, but I became acutely aware of this big window, behind which Mrs Landemare,[2] the cook, and the kitchen-maid, never turning a hair, were at work. I got up abruptly, went into the kitchen, told the butler to put the dinner on the hot plate in the dining-room, and ordered the cook and the other servants into the shelter, such as it was. I had been seated again at table only about three minutes when a really very loud crash, close at hand, and a violent shock showed that the house had been struck. My detective came into the room and said much damage had been done. The kitchen, the pantry, and the offices on the Treasury side were shattered.

We went into the kitchen to view the scene. The devastation was complete. The bomb had fallen fifty yards away on the Treasury, and the blast had smitten the large, tidy kitchen, with all its bright saucepans and crockery, into

[1] In fact, 15 October 1940.
[2] Georgina Landemare. She had originally trained (as number six cook) and worked in the kitchen of a French chef, whom she later married. After his death (Grace Hamblin writes) 'she used her quite remarkable skills by cooking for weekend parties in various large country houses. Thus it was she was introduced to Mrs Churchill, and during the thirties she was often called upon to go to Chartwell in this capacity. She was both physically and by temperament a "large" person, and not only her cooking, but her very delightful personality, gave pleasure to the whole household. She was a truly wonderful cook, and even with wartime restrictions, she never failed to produce delicious meals' (*Letter to the author, 8 December 1992*). During the war Mrs Landemare went to Downing Street on a more permanent basis, and then stayed on with Mrs Churchill until her retirement in 1953, at the age of seventy. She later wrote a book, *Recipes from No. 10*, for which Mrs Churchill wrote a foreword.

a heap of black dust and rubble. The big plate-glass window had been hurled in fragments and splinters across the room, and would of course have cut its occupants, if there had been any, to pieces. But my fortunate inspiration, which I might so easily have neglected, had come in the nick of time. The underground Treasury shelter across the court had been blown to pieces by a direct hit, and the three civil servants who were doing Home Guard night-duty there were killed. All however were buried under tons of brick rubble, and we did not know who was missing.

As the raid continued and seemed to grow in intensity we put on our tin hats and went out to view the scene from the top of the Annexe buildings. Before doing so, however, I could not resist taking Mrs Landemare and the others from the shelter to see their kitchen. They were upset at the sight of the wreck, but principally on account of the general untidiness!

Archie and I went up to the cupola of the Annexe building. The night was clear and there was a wide view of London. It seemed that the greater part of Pall Mall was in flames. At least five fierce fires were burning there, and others in St James's Street and Piccadilly. Farther back over the river in the opposite direction there were many conflagrations. But Pall Mall was the vivid flame-picture. Gradually the attack died down, and presently the 'All Clear' sounded, leaving only the blazing fires. We went downstairs to my new apartments on the first floor of the Annexe, and there found Captain David Margesson, the Chief Whip, who was accustomed to live at the Carlton Club. He told us the club had been blown to bits, and indeed we had thought, by the situation of the fires, that it must have been hit. He was in the club with about two hundred and fifty members and staff. It had been struck by a heavy bomb. The whole of the façade and the massive coping on the Pall Mall side had fallen into the street, obliterating his motor-car, which was parked near the front door. The smoking-room had been full of members, and the whole ceiling had come down upon them. When I looked at the ruins next day it seemed incredible that most of them should not have been killed. However, by what seemed a miracle, they had all crawled out of the dust, smoke, and rubble, and though many were injured not a single life was lost. When in due course these facts came to the notice of the Cabinet our Labour colleagues facetiously remarked: 'The devil looks after his own.' Mr Quintin Hogg[1] had carried his father, a former Lord Chancellor, on his shoulders from the wreck,

---

[1] Quintin Hogg, 1907– . Barrister, Lincoln's Inn, 1932. Conservative MP, 1938–50. On active service, 1939–45 (wounded). Succeeded his father as 2nd Viscount Hailsham, 1950. First Lord of the Admiralty, 1956–7. Minister of Science and Technology, 1959–64. Disclaimed his peerage for life, 1963. Conservative MP, 1963–70. Secretary of State for Education and Science, 1964. Lord Chancellor, 1970–4 and 1979–87 (his father, Secretary of State for War in 1931–5, had been Lord Chancellor in 1928–9 and 1935–8). Created Baron, 1970. Chancellor, University of Buckingham, 1983–92. Knight of the Garter, 1988.

as Æneas had borne Pater Anchises from the ruins of Troy. Margesson had nowhere to sleep, and we found him blankets and a bed in the basement of the Annexe. Altogether it was a lurid evening, and considering the damage to buildings it was remarkable that there were not more than five hundred people killed and about a couple of thousand injured.[1]

Captain Pim: recollection
(*Pim papers*)

15 October 1940

In October, 1940, I had just left the Prime Minister one morning and had crossed the Horse Guards Parade when a 'stick' of bombs fell, demolishing part of the Paymaster General's Office next door to the Admiralty and the others hitt'r r the Horse Guards Parade. It was an example of Mr Churchill's consideration that he should ring up the Admiralty to enquire whether I had been clear of it and saying that he had been worried about my safety. For his own safety he never thought. The whole idea of precautions being taken for his safety while others were in danger was repugnant to him.

John Martin: private letter
(*Martin papers*)

15 October 1940

A high explosive bomb fell a few yards from No. 10. I was upstairs and dashed down to the shelter as I heard it fall, to the accompaniment of the most terrific explosion. It is difficult to remember exactly what happened; but I seemed to fly down with a rush of 'blast', the air full of dust and the crash and clatter of glass breaking behind. There was a rush of several of us into the shelter and we tumbled on top of one another in a good deal of confusion. Afterwards it was several minutes before the air cleared and, with the clouds of dust and the acrid, sooty smell, we thought that the house or the Treasury next door was on fire. Fortunately that was not so and by the light of torches we were able to survey the damage. The mess in the house was indescribable – windows smashed in all directions, everything covered with grime, doors off hinges and curtains and furniture tossed about in a confused mass.

[1] The night of 15 October 1940 saw the most intense bombing raid of the war thus far: 900 fires were started throughout London and dozens of air raid shelters were hit. A bomb above Balham underground station broke through to the platform below: of the 600 people sheltering there, 64 were killed. In all, 400 Londoners were killed that night.

Fortunately the PM has been using the basement and was dining there at the time at the opposite side of the house, with steel shutters closed, so was none the worse. Meanwhile incendiaries and HE were being dropped wholesale in the West End and there was a line of fire along the Pall Mall and Piccadilly direction. The Carlton Club was wrecked and burnt. The Reform Club had a fire, but was not (as far as I could see today) too badly damaged, though we can't use it. (During the night, I telephoned the hall porter at the Reform and asked how things were. A calm voice replied 'The Club is burning, Sir.') St James's Club in Piccadilly was burnt out. A big house in St James's Square was reduced to a heap of rubble – and so on. The hut of the soldiers who guard Downing Street was completely demolished: fortunately they had taken refuge elsewhere.

Winston S. Churchill: note[1]
(*Cabinet papers, 66/12*)

15 October 1940

PRIORITIES

The very highest priority in personnel and material should be assigned to what may be called the Radio sphere. This demands Scientists, Wireless Experts, and many classes of highly-skilled labour and high-grade material. On the progress made, much of the winning of the war and our future strategy, especially Naval, depends. We must impart a far greater accuracy to the AA guns, and a far better protection to our warships and harbours. Not only research and experiments, but production must be pushed hopefully forward from many directions, and after repeated disappointments we shall achieve success.

2. The 1A priority must remain with Aircraft Production, for the purpose of executing approved Target programmes. It must be an obligation upon them to contrive by every conceivable means not to let this priority be abused and needlessly hamper other vital Departments. For this purpose they should specify their requirements in labour and material beforehand, Quarter by Quarter, or if practicable, month by month, and make all surplus available for others immediately. The priority is not to be exercised in the sense that Aircraft Production is completely to monopolise the supplies of any limited commodity. Where the condition prevails that the approved MAP demands absorb the total supply, a special allocation must be made, even at prejudice to Aircraft Production, to provide the minimum essential needs of other

[1] Circulated to the War Cabinet as War Cabinet Paper 416 of 1940.

Departments or Branches. This allocation, if not agreed, will be decided on the Cabinet level.

3. At present we are aiming at five Armoured Divisions, and Armoured Brigades equivalent to three more. This is not enough. We cannot hope to compete with the enemy in numbers of men, and must therefore rely upon an exceptional proportion of armoured fighting vehicles. Ten Armoured Divisions is the target to aim for to the end of 1941. For this purpose the Army must searchingly review their demands for mechanized transport, and large purchases of MT must be made in the United States. The Home Army, working in this small Island with highly-developed communications of all kinds, cannot enjoy the same scale of transport which Divisions on foreign service require. Improvisation and makeshift must be their guides. A Staff Officer renders no service to the country who aims at ideal standards, and thereafter simply adds and multiplies until impossible totals are reached. A report should be furnished of MT, 1st, 2nd and 3rd Line of British Divisions –

(a) For Foreign Service,
(b) For Home Service,
(c) For troops on the beaches.

Any attempt to make heavy weather out of this problem is a failure to aid us in our need.

Wherever possible in England, horse transport should be used to supplement MT. We improvidently sold a great many of our horses to the Germans, but there are still a good many in Ireland.

4. Special aid and occasional temporary priorities must be given to the Laggard elements. Among these stand out the following:–

(a) Rifles.
(b) Small Arms Ammunition, above all the special types.

Intense efforts must be made to bring the new factories into production. The fact that scarcely any improvement is now expected until the end of the year, i.e., 16 months after the outbreak of war, is a grave reflection on those concerned. Twelve months should suffice for a cartridge factory. We have been mercifully spared from the worst consequences of this failure through the Armies not being in action as was anticipated.

Trench mortar ammunition and AT gun ammunition are also in a shocking plight, and must be helped.

All these Laggards must be the subject of weekly reports to the Production Council and to me.

5. The Navy must exercise its existing priorities in respect of small craft and Anti-U-Boat building. This applies also to merchant shipbuilding, and to craft for landing operations. Delay must be accepted upon all larger vessels that cannot finish in 1941. Plans must be made to go forward with all processes and parts which do not clash with prior needs. The utmost possible steel and armour-plate must be ordered in America.

Winston S. Churchill: Oral Answers
(*Hansard*)

15 October 1940   House of Commons

WAR AIMS

Mr Silverman[1] asked the Prime Minister whether, in anticipation of the time when this country and its Allies are in a position to resume the military offensive, he will take an early opportunity of stating, in general terms, our aims in this war, so that this country may take its rightful place as the leader of all those, wherever they may be found, who desire a new order in Europe, based not upon slavery to Germany but upon collective justice, prosperity, and security?

The Prime Minister (Mr Churchill): All this is being borne in mind, but the time has not come when any official declaration can be made of war aims beyond the very carefully considered general statements which have already been published.

Mr Silverman: Would the right hon. Gentleman bear in mind that the longer a purely negative attitude in this matter is maintained the greater grows the quite false impression that we are fighting this war merely to retain the *status quo*; and would the right hon. Gentleman, at any rate, say enough to indicate that that is not the position of this country?

The Prime Minister: I do not think anyone has the opinion that we are fighting this war merely to maintain the *status quo*. We are, among other things, fighting it in order to survive, and when our capacity to do that is more generally recognised throughout the world, when the conviction that we have about it here becomes more general, then we shall be in a good position to take a further view of what we shall do with the victory when it is won.

Mr Silverman: Would the right hon. Gentleman not agree that one important factor in enabling us, not merely to survive but to conquer, is to assure those who think with us all over the world that we are ready to lead the fight for the better world which we all want?

The Prime Minister: I think there is great danger in making statements which are not of a very general character upon this subject. Take, for instance, the attitude which we adopt towards the enemy when he is defeated – you will find very different opinions prevailing about that.

---

[1] Samuel Sydney Silverman, 1895–1968. A conscientious objector, 1916. Lectured in English at the National University of Finland, 1917–20. Admitted a solicitor, 1927. Labour MP from 1935 until his death. A member of the Parliamentary Delegation to Buchenwald concentration camp, 1945. Chairman of the World Jewish Congress, he was a fierce opponent of his Party's Foreign Secretary, Ernest Bevin, who maintained the pre-war Conservative restrictions (which Churchill had opposed) on Jewish immigration to Palestine. Member of the National Executive Committee of the Labour Party, 1956. For thirty years a campaigner against capital punishment; in 1964 the House of Commons, on a free vote, gave a majority of 185 to his Bill to free all types of murder from the death penalty.

950 October 1940

FRENCH WARSHIPS (PASSAGE OF STRAITS)

Rear-Admiral Beamish[1] asked the Prime Minister whether the formal inquiries into the failure to prevent French warships proceeding to enemy-controlled ports are yet complete; what disciplinary action has been taken, and against whom; whether full discretion to act was given to the officer commanding on the spot to prevent such ships passing the Straits; and whether he can now explain why the First Lord and Cabinet were not consulted before action was ordered or taken against potentially unfriendly ships?

The Prime Minister: As I indicated to the House last week, I do not think it desirable to answer any further questions upon this affair, for which, apart from technical mishaps, His Majesty's Government take full responsibility.

Rear-Admiral Beamish: Is my right hon. Friend aware that there is an impression that it was necessary for the officer commanding on the spot to communicate with the home authorities before taking action?

The Prime Minister: There may be a great many impressions, but I think I have said all that can safely be said on the subject at the present time, and, having regard to the difficulties of carrying on the war, I must ask for the support of the House in this.

War Cabinet: minutes
(*Cabinet papers, 65/9*)

15 October 1940　　　　　　　　　　　　　　　　　　　　　　Cabinet War Room
5 p.m.

The Prime Minister said that it would be premature to suppose that the danger of invasion had passed. Intelligence Reports indicated that enemy plans were still moving forward. In these circumstances it would not be possible for the Navy to withdraw any more of their forces from the invasion front in order to strengthen shipping escorts in the north-west approaches.

Discussion followed on the effect of night bombing on civilian morale. The view was advanced that the civilian population in London were beginning to wonder whether we were hitting back hard enough at Germany in our bombing operations. If this feeling was allowed to grow it might have an unfortunate effect on our war effort. It would be of the greatest advantage if

---

[1] Tufton Percy Hamilton Beamish, 1874–1951. On active service in East Africa, 1896. Assistant to the Chief of the Naval War Staff (set up by Churchill), Admiralty, 1912–13. Commanded HMS *Invincible*, Battle of the Falkland Islands, 1914; HMS *Cordelia*, Jutland, 1916. CB, 1917. Rear-Admiral, retired, 1925. Conservative MP, 1924–31 and 1935–45. One of his two sons was killed in action in 1945.

the public could be made to realise that a resolute effort was being made to check night bombing.

The Prime Minister said that those concerned were straining every nerve to improve means of countering night bombing. There were good prospects that our defensive measures would be greatly improved within the next two or three months. In the meantime we were retaliating as effectively as we could on Germany. But our Bomber Force was much smaller than that of the enemy, and had to make far longer journeys. Meanwhile the people of this country must stick it out. No doubt they realised that Hitler was trying to break morale over here. He (the Prime Minister) would consider whether it would be desirable for him to make another broadcast speech.

In further discussion, it was suggested that if more publicity could be given by way of photographs of the results of our bombing in Berlin, it would have a good effect.[1] Another suggestion was that it would be worth considering whether a document could be published containing extracts from the reports as to the effect of our bombing in Germany, without compromising the sources of this information.

The War Cabinet were reminded that, following the discussions on the 30th August, a revised programme had been agreed for the despatch of aircraft and pilots to Canada and South Africa. A number of moves had taken place in August, September and October, in accordance with the programme, and the Secretary of State for Air had undertaken to come to the War Cabinet early in October for authority to complete it (WP (10) 351).

The Prime Minister said that the Secretary of State for Air now wished to carry out a further instalment of the scheme. This involved a move of one School only, which involved only 10 pilots. Aircraft for this school would be supplied from America. In addition, it was proposed to send to Canada about 30 Ansons and 27 Battles required for the five schools already sent overseas. He understood that the Minister of Aircraft Production was still opposed to sending pilots and aircraft out of the country. It seemed, however, to him (the Prime Minister) that the arguments in favour of sending Flying Training Schools overseas had certainly not diminished since this proposal had first been made. The objection to sending pilots and aircraft out of this country, of course, remained; but if we did not adopt this course, we ran a great risk that we should not see the hoped-for increase in the Royal Air Force next spring.

After some discussion, the Prime Minister said that he thought the general feeling of the War Cabinet was that it would not be right to override the considered view of one of the Service Ministers in favour of the small further measure of transfer overseas now proposed.

---

[1] In the previous three weeks, Berlin had been bombed on the nights of 23/24 September, 24/25 September, 30 September, 1 October, 7/8 October (twelve individual targets), and 14/15 October.

The Prime Minister stated the case for the Army in the absence of the Secretary of State for War. The Army feared that the new Air Ministry demand for cement might result in some reduction of their own allocation. The proposed allocation for the Army itself for the period October to December, 1940, was only 205,850 tons, compared with requirements of 366,601 tons. If it were cut again, it would be at the cost of our coast defences, of the defences of Malta and Gibraltar, and of other vital works.

The Secretary of State for Air said that he would be in default if he failed to carry out the additional programme of 125 aerodromes. It was impossible for him to do so with his present allocation. His advice was that the cement requirement for perimeter tracks could not be further reduced. Tarmac was already largely used in constructing perimeter tracks.

The Minister of Home Security said that he must press for his original requirement of 514,000 tons. The heavy raids on London made it essential to speed up the shelter programme.

The Prime Minister did not question that the Air Ministry had a good case for their original requirement. Other Departments also had good cases, and it became a question of cutting one's coat according to one's cloth. He proposed that the War Cabinet should authorise the Minister without Portfolio[1] to make his adjudication. He would assess the competing claims of the Air Ministry, the Ministry of Home Security and the other Departments in the light of the strategic position.

Winston S. Churchill to A. V. Alexander
(Churchill papers, 20/13)

15 October 1940

If you wish to circulate the Naval Staff paper[2] of October 13, which I have now read, I do not demur. It is of course a most pessimistic and nervous paper which it is very depressing to receive from the Admiralty. Instances of the overdrawn character of the paper are found in para. 3, which claims that we must maintain 'general control in every sea,' whereas effective power of passage is all we require to do in many cases. And in para. 5, 'German strength in which from <u>now onwards</u> (October 15) must be counted the *Tirpitz* and the *Bismarck*.' This is not true, as even the *Bismarck* has I suppose to work

---

[1] Arthur Greenwood.
[2] 'The naval aspect of our policy towards the Vichy Government'.

up like the *King George V*, which should be ready as soon, or earlier. The *Tirpitz* is three months behind the *Bismarck* according to every statement I have received, and it is hoped by that time we shall have the *Prince of Wales* and *Queen Elizabeth*. If such statements are made to the Cabinet I should be forced to challenge them.

2. The whole argument is meant to lead up to the idea that we must submit to the wishes of Vichy because they have the power to drive us out of Gibraltar by bombing. I fully share the desire of the Naval Staff not to be molested in Gibraltar, but I do not think that the enforcement of the blockade will lead the French to do this, still less to declare war upon us. I do not believe the Vichy Government has the power to wage war against us, as the whole French nation is coming more and more on to our side. I have dealt with this in a Minute on general policy which is being circulated,[1] and of which I enclose you the relevant extract.

3. The redeeming point in this paper is the suggestion that we should tell the Vichy Government that if they bomb Gibraltar, we shall retaliate not against say Casablanca, but Vichy, to which I would add – or any other place occupied by the Vichy Government. This is the proper note to strike, and it is also important to bear in mind that while humbleness to Vichy will not necessarily prevent them being ordered to make war upon us by their German masters, a firm attitude will not necessarily deter them from coming over to our side.

These questions are not urgent because of the failure to intercept *Primaguet*.[2]

WSC

John Martin: private letter
(*Martin papers*)

16 October 1940

My birthday treat was to visit the ruins of the Carlton Club with the PM, who stumped in and wandered about among the wreckage, regardless of the impending roof. The dining room was like a bit of Pompeii, with unfinished meals and decanters of wine on the tables. At a bedroom door we found the Chief Whip David Margesson's bedroom slippers awaiting him. At the

---

[1] Minute of 13 October 1940, pages 836–8, section 3.
[2] A French merchant ship.

entrance steps the Prime Minister pointed to a piece of marble statuary half buried in rubble. Lifted up it was seen to be the head of Pitt.[1]

Winston S. Churchill to Sir Archibald Sinclair and Sir Cyril Newall
(*Premier papers, 3/314/2*)

16 October 1940
ACTION THIS DAY

I see it reported that last night a large number of land mines were dropped here, many of which have not yet gone off, and that great harm was done.

Let me have your proposals forthwith for effective retaliation upon Germany.

I am informed that it is quite possible to carry similar mines or large bombs to Germany, and that the Squadrons wish to use them, but that the Air Ministry are refusing permission. I trust that due consideration will be given to my views and wishes. It is now about three weeks since I began pressing for similar treatment of German military objectives to that which they are meting out to us. Who is responsible for paralysing action?

WSC

Winston S. Churchill to A. V. Alexander
(*Churchill papers, 20/13*)

16 October 1940
ACTION THIS DAY

This communiqué raises several questions. Why should the word 'gallant' be applied to the Italian destroyer just for towing a damaged sister-ship away, especially when, as the next two lines show, she made off the moment danger came?

Para. 8. Why should the position of the British Fleet be compromised by

---

[1] That month, in an introduction to the third edition of Pitt's speeches published by the Oxford University Press, Churchill wrote: 'No historical analogies can be exact, and in one respect our situation is very different from what it was in Pitt's day. A Nazi victory would be an immeasurably worse disaster for us and for all mankind than Napoleon's victory could ever have been. As modern France, and not France only, knows, Napoleon could construct as well as destroy. There can be no comparison, indeed, in the scale of civilization between the Nazi system and that of the Napoleonic empire; nor could the humane free-spirited French people ever have become the docile instruments of such barbarism as now issues from Berlin. All the firmer, therefore, must be our determination to fight on, as Pitt and his successors fought on, till we in our turn achieve our Waterloo' (Foreword dated October 1940 in R. Coupland, editor, *The War Speeches of William Pitt the Younger*, Oxford 1940).

wireless messages when everything possible and reasonable was done on the spot to save the Italians who had been shipwrecked? This kind of kid glove stuff infuriates the people who are going through their present ordeal at home, and this aspect should be put to the Admiral.

WSC

Winston S. Churchill to General Ismay
(*Churchill papers, 20/13*)

16 October 1940

I am astounded at the vast congregation who are invited to study these matters.[1] The Air Ministry is the worst offender and I have marked a number who should be struck off at once, unless after careful consideration in each individual case it is found indispensable that they should be informed. I have added the First Lord, who of course must know everything known to his subordinates, and also the Secretary of State for War.

A machinery should be constructed which makes other parties acquainted with such information as is necessary to them for the discharge of their particular duties. I await your proposals. I should also add Commander-in-Chief Fighter and Commander-in-Chief Bomber Command,[2] it being clearly understood that they shall not impart them to any person working under them or allow the boxes to be opened by anyone save themselves.

WSC

---

[1] This minute refers to the summaries and interpretations of decrypts of German top secret radio messages, then largely German Air Force messages, sent by Enigma machine from German headquarters to units in the field, which were decrypted at Bletchley and circulated to a limited number of recipients. On 8 November 1940 the thirty-one recipients of material from Bletchley were Churchill, Sir Edward Bridges, General Ismay, Lord Halifax, Sir Robert Vansittart, Sir Alexander Cadogan, Sir Orme Sargent, 'C' (Colonel Menzies), A. V. Alexander, Admiral Pound, Admiral Phillips, Anthony Eden, General Dill, General Haining, Sir Archibald Sinclair, Sir Charles Portal, Air Marshal Freeman, Sir John Anderson, Clement Attlee, Arthur Greenwood, Lord Beaverbrook, Ernest Bevin, Sir Kingsley Wood, Sir Alexander Hardinge (for the King), the Secretary of the Joint Intelligence Committee (Colonel Capel Dunn), the officer in charge of 'Secret Records', the Duty Officer at the Central War Room, Professor N. F. Hall (Ministry of Economic Warfare) and the Directors of Military, Naval and Air Intelligence.

[2] Air Chief Marshal Sir Hugh Dowding and Air Marshal Sir Richard Peirse (former Vice-Chief of the Air Staff). In December 1940 Judge Singleton was added to the list of those who knew about Enigma and saw the decrypts (see page 1201).

Winston S. Churchill to Anthony Eden[1]
(*Churchill papers, 20/14*)

16 October 1940

Have read all your telegrams with deepest interest and realisation of value of your visit. We are considering how to meet your needs. Meanwhile, continue to master the local situation. Do not hurry your return.[2]

War Cabinet: minutes
(*Cabinet papers, 65/9*)

16 October 1940　　　　　　　　　　　　　　　　　　　10 Downing Street
5 p.m.

The Secretary of State for Foreign Affairs read to the War Cabinet a summary of the reply received from the Vichy Government (telegram No. 862 from Madrid).

In a preliminary discussion the Prime Minister said that M. Baudouin's reply was not impressive, though it did not close the door to the suggested conversations. He thought the Vichy Government should be told that we were not proposing to take aggressive action against them; that we intended to support de Gaulle and maintain our rights of blockade; and that, whilst we should allow trade within the Mediterranean, we should intercept escorted convoys from French West African ports. We should add that, in the event of the Vichy Government retaliating by bombing Gibraltar, then not only should we bombard Casablanca but we would bomb Vichy itself. He was of opinion, however, that it would not be necessary to go to such extremes.

The Prime Minister said that, while it was no doubt desirable to have alternative quarters in the London area to which the nucleus of the Government could transfer in the event of some temporary emergency, he was more than ever satisfied that it was essential that the central nucleus of Government should not move. This, however, carried with it certain consequences. First, only the essential headquarters staff should remain in

---

[1] Eden had left London for Cairo on 11 October 1940. From Egypt, he went to Palestine to visit British troops there, then to Transjordan, back to Egypt, and to the Western Desert, and on to the Sudan. He was back in England on 8 November.

[2] In a telegram to Churchill that day, Eden wrote: 'Politically whole situation here would be immeasurably improved if we were able to gain some military success. Most hopeful field for this in the near future would appear to be Sudan and I trust that the "I" tanks for which I have asked can come in the November convoy. This is more important, since psychological moment for striking on that front may easily come shortly' (*The Reckoning*, page 153).

Central London. He agreed with a suggestion made by the Lord Privy Seal that the 'Grey' Move should proceed as rapidly as possible. Secondly, steps should be taken to ensure that accommodation for those working in Central London was as safe as possible. This might involve serious structural work to improve existing accommodation. He thought that there should be a survey of the protected accommodation of Government Departments, which varied considerably in quality. Thirdly, steps must be taken to enable the staff to adapt themselves to the new conditions. This would mean the provision of canteens and sleeping arrangements so that the staff could remain in their offices for several days on end before going away for a day or two days' rest.

Winston S. Churchill to Lord Halifax
(*Churchill papers, 20/13*)

17 October 1940

I am very sorry to read Sir Robert Vansittart's opinion which in no way convinces me. I do not see why it is thought proper to attempt so eagerly to build up relations with MM. Baudouin and Laval when this poor wretched old Chautemps is to be regarded as a pariah. I had rather hoped to learn something from him about the inner story from Bordeaux to Vichy. However, if it is felt that Chautemps as a refugee in England would be a cause of perturbation I could not press my view.[1]

John Martin: diary
(*Martin papers*)

17 October 1940

Another bomb in the yard at Downing Street. A large part of the Treasury demolished and four people killed in basement.

---

[1] Sir Alexander Cadogan noted on Churchill's minute: 'We have now sent instructions to suspend grant of visa to M. Chautemps. I should be the last to attempt to judge between him and MM. Baudouin and Laval. But, if we think there is anything to be got in the way of co-operation with Vichy, the latter might deliver some (soiled) goods. M. Chautemps has, I think, nothing to give us, and we shall do no good with any ex-Ministers of the last 20 years' (*Premier papers, 3/184/1*).

Winston S. Churchill: statement
(Hansard)

17 October 1940   House of Commons

CONDUCT OF A MEMBER

The Prime Minister (Mr Churchill): I beg to move,

'That a Select Committee be appointed to investigate the conduct and activities of Mr Boothby[1] in connection with the payment out of assets in this country of claims against the Government of and institutions in the Republic of Czecho-Slovakia: to report generally on these matters and in particular to consider and report whether the conduct of the honourable Member was contrary to the usage or derogatory to the dignity of the House or inconsistent with the standards which Parliament is entitled to expect from its Members.'

I have placed a Motion on the Paper, which is in possession of hon. Members, the terms of which they have no doubt studied. The House will require to know the grounds on which this Motion has been put down. It will be remembered that after the occupation of Prague certain Czech assets were blocked in this country, and there arose the question of payments from these assets to those who had claims against the Czech Government or institutions in that country. The hon. Member for East Aberdeen (Mr Boothby) took a very active part interviewing Ministers in this matter, pressing for legislation, and he spoke in this House on the Bill which was subsequently introduced. He became chairman of an informal committee of Czech claimants, and has pressed for the payment of claims. Evidence has recently been placed before the Government which indicates that the hon. Member had a financial interest in one large claim. This appeared to be inconsistent with a statement he had made to the former Chancellor of the Exchequer,[2] and, together with other evidence, it seemed to raise the question whether this action had been in accordance with the usages of Parliament, or the standards it is entitled to expect from its Members. When I communicated these apprehensions to the hon. Member it became clear that there was a conflict between the evidence in the possession of His Majesty's Government, and the facts as he described them. The matter, therefore, requires to be investigated by a Committee of this House. I considered whether I should then move that it should be referred

---

[1] Robert John Graham Boothby, 1900–86. Educated at Eton and Magdalen College, Oxford. Conservative MP for East Aberdeenshire, 1924–58. Parliamentary Private Secretary to the Chancellor of the Exchequer (Churchill), 1926–9. Elected to the Other Club, 1928. Parliamentary Secretary, Ministry of Food, 1940–1. A British delegate to the Consultative Assembly, Council of Europe, 1949–57. Knighted, on Churchill's recommendation, 1953. Created Baron, 1958. President of the Anglo-Israel Association. Rector of St Andrews University, 1958–61. Chairman, Royal Philharmonic Orchestra, 1961–3. Published *The New Economy* (1943), *I Fight to Live* (1947), *My Yesterday, Your Tomorrow* (1962) and *Recollections of a Rebel* (1978).

[2] Sir John Simon.

to the Committee of Privileges but, after obtaining guidance as to the precedents, I came to the conclusion that as the case appeared to raise other issues besides that of Privilege, it was better that it should go to a Select Committee, so that the truth could be ascertained and the conduct of the hon. Member considered.

The hon. Member has assured me that he concurs in the course proposed, and that he submits himself willingly to the Committee and will assist them in every way. I do not consider it fitting at this stage to call for the hon. Member's resignation of the office which he holds with distinction in the Government, as this might appear in the eyes of the public to prejudice the issue. The hon. Member has, however, asked to be suspended from his duties in the meanwhile, and I am prepared to make the necessary arrangements for this. I hope the course I have outlined will commend itself to the House, and that I shall not be pressed to elaborate it. It would be manifestly improper for me to enter into detail upon the matters which will be investigated by the Select Committee, and, still more, that we should debate matters which, if this Motion is accepted, will at once become *sub judice*. The terms of reference have been widely drawn, but when the evidence is heard I do not think the Committee will have any difficulty in deciding what matters are relevant to their inquiries.

Mr Bellenger: I agree that as the matter is *sub judice* it would be improper to go into the particular questions which form the basis of the Motion. The Prime Minister, however, has referred to making other arrangements to carry on the work which the hon. Gentleman is doing, and, I think, doing energetically and vigorously, while the investigation is taking place. He holds what is, in present circumstances, an important office, and could the Prime Minister say what are the arrangements which he has made for this work to be carried out while the hon. Gentleman is suspended?

The Prime Minister: I think that I might be given a little latitude.

Question put, and agreed to.

Harold Nicolson: diary
('*Diaries and Letters, 1939–1945*')

17 October 1940   House of Commons

I go to the smoking-room with Harry Crookshank[1] and Charles Waterhouse.[2] Winston is at the next table. He sits there sipping a glass of port and welcoming anyone who comes in. 'How are you?' he calls gaily to the most obscure Member. It is not a pose. It is just that for a few moments he likes to get away from being Prime Minister and feel himself back in the smoking-room. His very presence gives us all gaiety and courage. People gather round his table completely unawed. They ask him questions. Robert Cary[3] makes a long dissertation about how the public demand the unrestricted bombardment of Germany as reprisals for the raids on London. Winston takes a long sip at his port gazing over the glass at Cary. 'My dear sir', he says, 'this is a military and not a civilian war. You and others may desire to kill women and children. We desire (and have succeeded in our desire) to destroy German military objectives. I quite appreciate your point. But my motto is "Business before Pleasure".' We all drift out of the room thinking, 'That was a man!'

War Cabinet: Minutes
(*Cabinet papers, 65/9*)

18 October 1940   Cabinet War Room
11.30 a.m.

Discussion turned mainly on an amendment proposed to be made at the end of paragraph 7, to the effect that if we took reprisals against targets in unoccupied France we should direct our attention particularly to the seat of the Vichy Government wherever it might be.

The Prime Minister favoured an amendment in this sense, as the most likely means of deterring the Vichy Government from bombing Gibraltar. He

---

[1] Harry Frederick Comfort Crookshank, 1893–1961. On active service, 1914–18; Captain, 1919. Foreign Office, 1919–24 (Constantinople and Washington). Conservative MP, 1924–56. Secretary for Mines, 1936–9. Financial Secretary, Treasury, 1939–43. Postmaster-General, 1943–5. Minister of Health, 1951–2, and Lord Privy Seal, 1952–5 (Churchill's second premiership). In 1954 and 1955 he was one of the Conservative Cabinet Ministers most determined that Churchill should retire. Created Viscount (by Anthony Eden), 1956.

[2] Charles Waterhouse, 1893–1975. On active service, 1914–18 (Military Cross). Conservative MP, 1922, 1923, 1924–45, 1950–7. Assistant Postmaster-General, 1939–41. Parliamentary Secretary, Board of Trade, 1941–5. Privy Councillor, 1944. Chairman, National Union of Conservative and Unionist Associations, 1952. Chairman, Tanganyika Concessions, 1957–66.

[3] Robert Archibald Cary, 1898–1979. Educated at Sandhurst. On active service, 1916–18. General Staff, Iraq, 1920. Conservative MP, 1935–45 and 1951–74. Parliamentary Private Secretary to the Civil Lord of Admiralty, 1939; to the Secretary of State for India, 1942–4; to the Minister of Health, 1951–2; to the Lord Privy Seal and Leader of the House, 1951–64. Knighted, 1945. Created Baronet, 1955.

did not think they were likely to do this; but if we were to retaliate, we should retaliate effectively; and if the Vichy Government were driven out of Vichy, it would be a long step towards their final liquidation.

Winston S. Churchill to Sir Cyril Newall
(*Churchill papers, 20/13*)

18 October 1940

What arrangements have we got for blind landings for aircraft? How many aircraft are so fitted? It ought to be possible to guide them down quite safely as commercial craft were done before the war in spite of fog. Let me have full particulars. The accidents last night are very serious.[1]

WSC

Winston S. Churchill to J. T. C. Moore-Brabazon[2]
(*Churchill papers, 20/13*)

19 October 1940

One very definite opportunity presents itself to you. I see the queues waiting long hours for exiguous buses, yet all the time there are thousands of motor cars without petrol ration reposing in garages or back-yards, with thousands of men and women drivers who would be enchanted to come in and carry off this painful accumulation of hard-working folk. Of course it all wants organisation, but look at the way Lord Beaverbrook organises his private army and private defences for his factories and so forth, and see how he has made the figures for our production leap up. Here is a chance for you, but do not throw it away by playing small. Get 20,000 unused motor cars to ply in the rush-hours and not only in these hours, but staggered, and organise them into a regular corps. Prepare your appeal and the Ministry of Information will be

---

[1] Following bombing raids on Bremen, Kiel, Merseburg and Bordeaux on the night of 16/17 October by 73 bombers, 14 crashed on their return to England when fog covered their bases.

[2] Lieutenant-Colonel J. T. C. Moore-Brabazon had replaced Sir John Reith as Minister of Transport on 3 October 1940.

instructed to give you all facilities for publicity. See what can be done in one week. Think of it as if you were organising the motor cars of a big Division on Polling Day. If you fail there will be no great harm. If you succeed there will be great help in our need.

WSC

Winston S. Churchill to General Dill
(*Churchill papers, 20/13*)

19 October 1940

I was very much pleased last week when you told me you proposed to give an armoured Division to Major General Hobart. I think very highly of this officer, and I am not at all impressed by the prejudices against him in certain quarters. Such prejudices attach frequently to persons of strong personality and original view. In this case General Hobart's original views have been only too tragically borne out. The neglect by the General Staff even to devise proper patterns of tanks before the war has robbed us of all the fruits of this invention. These fruits have been reaped by the enemy with terrible consequences. We should therefore remember that this was an officer who had the root of the matter in him and also vision.

In my Minute last week to you I said I hoped you would propose to me the appointment that day, i.e., Tuesday, but at the latest this week. Will you very kindly make sure that the appointment is made at the earliest moment.

Since making this Minute I have carefully read your note to me and the summary of the case for and against General Hobart. We are now at war, fighting for our lives, and we cannot afford to confine Army appointments to persons who have excited no hostile comment in their career. The catalogue of General Hobart's qualities and defects in para. 2 of your Confidential Statement might almost exactly have been attributed to most of the great commanders of British history. Marlborough was very much the conventional soldier carrying with him the goodwill of the Service. Cromwell, Wolfe, Clive, Gordon and in a different sphere Lawrence, all had very close resemblance to the characteristics assembled in para. 2. They had other qualities as well and so I am led to believe has General Hobart. This is a time to try men of force and vision and not to be exclusively confined to those who are judged thoroughly safe by conventional standards.

I hope therefore you will not recoil from your proposal to me of a week ago, for I think your instinct in this matter was sound and true.

WSC

Winston S. Churchill to Herbert Morrison and Sir Andrew Duncan[1]
(*Churchill papers, 20/13*)

19 October 1940

There is no reason why, in a matter of this kind, production should not begin before experiments are complete, and the people frankly told that better helmets will be coming along later. The great thing is to avoid the awful process in which a certain class of officials are prone to indulge, of searching after perfection. This it was that ruined our Tank production, and has been the cause of the great delay in the Trench Mortar ammunition. I should strongly advise you to go ahead and make the best helmets possible as quickly as possible, and work up both quality and volume together. The matter is most urgent, and the issue would give widespread comfort and satisfaction to people in the bombarded areas.

WSC

Winston S. Churchill to Sir James Grigg
(*Churchill papers, 20/13*)

19 October 1940

PAY AND ALLOWANCES OF THE FREE FRENCH FORCES

It is no use offering the French nominal equality of conditions with us, if in fact they gain no benefit from the application of a principle which gives much to our people. I think therefore that equality should be interpreted as giving both classes of soldiers something worth while.

WSC

Winston S. Churchill to General Dill
(*Churchill papers, 20/13*)

19 October 1940

DIRECTOR-GENERAL, HOME GUARD

Are there no younger men available for this strenuous administrative appointment? The bringing back of retired Officers for these kind of posts causes much criticism, both in and out of Service circles. Why not try to find a man still in the forties, and give him temporary rank.[2]

WSC

---

[1] Since 3 October 1940, Minister of Home Security and Minister of Supply respectively.

[2] The officer eventually chosen, Major-General Ralph Eastwood, was only just fifty, having been born on 10 May 1890.

Winston S. Churchill to A. V. Alexander
(Churchill papers, 20/13)

19 October 1940

PASSAGE OF FRENCH WARSHIPS THROUGH STRAITS OF GIBRALTAR TO DAKAR

Captain ▬.[1] Can a letter of official displeasure be considered as a 'sentence,' barring all further action against an Officer for a most serious and disastrous failure in responsibility? I doubt it very much. The error or neglect committed by this Officer was contributory to a far worse misfortune than the hazarding of one of HM ships. It constituted a grievous breakdown in the Staff system at the Admiralty. Unless there is some definite legal bar, I would strongly press you to have the Officer put upon half-pay, unless he himself would wish to claim a court-martial.[2]

WSC

Winston S. Churchill to General Ismay
(Churchill papers, 20/13)

19 October 1940

SMALL ARMS AMMUNITION

In view of the forecasts of SAA, and the very great improvement in our position which will be effected from the factories coming into bearing in October, and the expanding output expected before the 31st March, 1941, and having regard to the fact that unless there is an invasion no operations are possible except in the Middle East, and then only on a comparatively moderate scale, I am of opinion that a very much larger issue may be made now to the Commander-in-Chief Home Forces for practice. I understand he has only 2 million rounds a week for this purpose, and that training is grievously hampered in consequence. Although it seems a risk to deplete our small War Office reserve, I think it should be considered whether, from the 1st November onwards, the amount issued for practice should not be doubled,

---

[1] I have struck out the name of this officer to avoid embarrassment to his family.
[2] Churchill's suggestion was not accepted. On 27 October 1940 he wrote to Alexander and Pound: 'The premature infliction of a minor and altogether inadequate punishment is now held to bar the proper disciplinary treatment of a gross case of neglect of duty in a Staff Officer. I greatly regret this result. WSC' (Prime Minister's Personal Minute, M234, Churchill papers, 20/13).

i.e., 4 million a week.[1] I shall be glad if you will consult the Chiefs of Staff immediately.

John Colville: Private Office note[2]
(*Churchill papers, 20/5*)

19 October 1940

Captain Harbord, the cypher king, has now been bombed and his telephone number at night will now be Victoria 2737. He will be glad to come at any hour in order to help decypher telegrams.

Should he be bombed again, and be once more unobtainable, Mr Wetherall, Home Forces, Extension 237, is an efficient substitute.[3]

JRC

John Peck to Winston S. Churchill
(*Churchill papers, 9/176*)

19 October 1940   10 Downing Street

BROADCAST TO THE FRENCH PEOPLE

The Ministry of Information say that at 10 p.m. on Monday it would only be possible to broadcast to France, and not to the French Colonial Empire, as for technical reasons connected with the synchronizing of the broadcasting stations it is only possible to reach the whole French Empire earlier in the evening. They ask whether you could broadcast instead at 8.35 p.m. when you could speak to the French Empire as well.

JHP

---

[1] On 3 November 1940, reading two consecutive weekly reports about the availability of small arms ammunition, Churchill minuted to Ismay that these reports 'altogether belie the confident statements which I queried three weeks ago, but which I was assured would be made good. Enemy action may account for 3,000,000, but even so, there is a great falling off from the promised yields of October. Yet it was upon the faith of these assurances that the larger issue was made to the C-in-C, Home Forces, for practice. Let me have revised forecasts. The position must be most carefully watched' (*Churchill papers 20/13*).

[2] This note was sent to John Martin, Tony Bevir, John Peck and Charles Barker.

[3] Harbord was the head of Churchill's personal cypher staff, responsible for encyphering and decyphering Churchill's personal telegrams. Wetherall was a member of the cypher staff of the Home Forces, who were co-located with Churchill's staff at the Cabinet War Rooms, and were thus at hand.

October 1940

Winston S. Churchill to John Peck
(*Churchill papers, 9/176*)

19 October 1940
ACTION THIS DAY

10 Downing Street

Tell Ministry of Information that I will broadcast from the CWR[1] at 10.0 p.m. Monday 21 to the French people. I shall only be about ten minutes and I shall speak once in English and once in French – total twenty minutes. Make all necessary arrangements, but it is not necessary to disclose the place beforehand. I may want help on Sunday or Monday about the translation. There is a Frenchman over here who did my translation for a speech I made to the Conference des Ambassadeurs in Paris in 1938. I believe he is in MOI. If not let someone else be found.

John Peck to Viscount Hood[2]
(*Churchill papers, 9/176*)

19 October 1940

Dear Hood,

I enclose the text of the broadcast which the Prime Minister proposes to make to the French people in English and French on Monday evening at 10 p.m. He would be glad of Mr Duff Cooper's comments and suggestions as soon as possible.

I am sending a copy of the broadcast with a similar request to Lawford.[3]

The Prime Minister would also like advice about publicity beforehand, i.e. whether arrangements should be made to let the French and English people know what is proposed.

As I also mentioned, the Prime Minister may want help on Sunday or Monday about the translation, and mentioned the name of Monsieur André David who translated a speech he made to the Conference des Ambassadeurs in Paris in 1938, and may now be working for the Ministry of Information. If he is not available would you have someone else standing by if required.[4]

[1] The Cabinet War Rooms.
[2] Samuel Hood, 1910–81. Succeeded his uncle as 6th Viscount, 1933. Assistant Private Secretary to the Secretary of State for India (Marquess of Zetland), 1936–9. Private Secretary to successive Ministers of Information (Lord Macmillan, Sir John Reith, Alfred Duff Cooper), 1939–41. Served in the Foreign Office, 1942–7. 1st Secretary, Madrid, 1947. Counsellor of Embassy, Paris, 1948. British Representative, Council of the Western European Union, 1956. Minister, Washington, 1957–62. Deputy Under-Secretary of State, Foreign Office, 1962–9. A Deputy Speaker, House of Lords, from 1971 until his death.
[3] Nicholas Lawford, Assistant Private Secretary to Anthony Eden.
[4] The translator chosen to help Churchill was Jacques Duchesne (see page 979).

The Prime Minister will deliver his broadcast from the CWR but does not want the place disclosed beforehand.

Yours sincerely,
J. H. Peck

PS Since I wrote this, the PM has said that he would like a translation prepared, following his sequence as closely as possible, & 'not too French French'.

Neville Chamberlain to Winston S. Churchill
(*Churchill papers, 2/402*)

20 October 1940

EXTRACT[1]

My thoughts are constantly with you in these anxious days. I hope you are taking some care of your own health.

Winston S. Churchill to Neville Chamberlain
(*Churchill papers, 20/2*)

20 October 1940

My dear Neville,

I do hope you are getting on and finding relief in repose. The weeks in London have become very hard now with the press of business and our numerous meetings having to be arranged under continued Alerts and Alarms. We have had two very near misses with big HE bombs at No. 10. They fell in the little yard by the Treasury passage, one in the corner and the other on the Treasury, the first killing one and wounding two, and the second killing four, including two principal clerks serving in the Home Guard. The effect of these explosions has been to shatter all our windows, doors, etc. on the exposed side, and render the greater part of the house uninhabitable.

---

[1] Chamberlain had written to Churchill, resigning as Chairman of the Conservative Research Department, suggesting that his successor should be someone of Cabinet rank and with 'a keen political insight', and proposing Sir Kingsley Wood.

However, the Cabinet Room is intact, and I am carrying on for the present in the downstairs rooms formerly used by the secretaries who dealt with correspondence.

I have moved everybody I can away, for really it is like living at a Brigade Headquarters in France.[1] We shall have to find some safer quarters soon. But where? For Edward told me about your five cows being killed, and the windows being sucked out at your house in the country. However, as I heard one of the Home Guard remark the other night, 'It's a grand life, if we don't weaken'.

The Germans have made a tremendous mistake in concentrating on London to the relief of our factories, and in trying to intimidate a people whom they have only infuriated. I feel very hopeful about the future, and that we shall wear them down and break them up. But it will take a long time.

It has occurred to me that while you are, I am sure, glad to be relieved of the mass of Papers which War Cabinet Ministers have to wade through, you might like to see occasional Papers or Telegrams on some points of special interest. In case you should feel any scruple about what is, perhaps, a somewhat unorthodox arrangement, I mentioned my intention to make this arrangement to the King the other day, and he most cordially approved it. I am telling Bridges to send you occasional Papers on matters which he thinks are likely to interest you especially, without sending so much as to become a burden.

Pray give my kindest regards to Mrs Neville,
and believe me,

Yours ever,
Winston S Churchill

PS Very bad news has just come in about our convoys in NW Approaches.[2] But we shall be stronger there in a month or so.

WSC

---

[1] In 1916, on the Western Front, Churchill had served as acting Brigadier for forty-eight hours at Brigade Headquarters, London Support Farm, Ploegsteert, in the temporary absence of the Brigadier of his Division (the 27th). 'It is not a vy satisfactory arrangement,' he wrote to Clementine on 8 February 1916, 'as of course I am only a caretaker and cannot attempt to take a grip of the whole machine. I do the office work and have prepared myself to meet any emergency; but otherwise I wait from hour to hour.'

[2] Eighteen British merchant ships were sunk in the North-West Approaches in forty-eight hours: on 18 October *Assyrian* (2,962 tons), *Sandsend* (3,612 tons), *Beatus* (4,885), *Empire Miniver* (6,055), *Creekirk* (3,917 tons), *Fiscus* (4,815 tons), *Shekatika* (5,458 tons), *Empire Brigade* (5,154 tons); on 19 October *Wandby* (4,947 tons), *Matheran* (7,653 tons), *La Estancia* (5,185 tons), *Caprella* (8,230 tons), *Ruperra* (4,548 tons), *Shirak* (6,023 tons), *Sulaca* (5,389 tons), *Uganda* (4,966 tons), *Clintonia* (3,106 tons) and *Sedgepool* (5,556 tons).

Kathleen Hill to Winston S. Churchill
(*Churchill papers, 9/176*)

20 October 1940

BROADCAST TO THE FRENCH PEOPLE

Prime Minister,

Major Morton suggests the following addition, (at an appropriate place), to your speech:–

'Do not believe the lies you hear on your Boche-controlled wireless, and in your Boche-controlled Press. We English are not trying to dismember the French Empire, or to steal the French Colonies for ourselves. On the contrary, we have promised when victory is ours to help restore the ancient glory of France. That promise must of necessity include the restoration of the French Empire overseas.'

KH

Winston S. Churchill to Sir Samuel Hoare
(*Premier papers, 3/186A/2*)

20 October 1940
Personal and Private

Thank you so much for your letter.[1] We admire the way in which you are dealing with your baffling task. I hope you will manage to convey to Vichy through the French Ambassador two root ideas. First that we will let bygones go and work with anyone who convinces us of his resolution to defeat the common foes. Secondly that as we are fighting for our lives as well as for a victory which will relieve simultaneously all the captive states, we shall stop at nothing. Try to make Vichy feel what we here all take for certain, namely that we have got Hitler beat and though he may ravage the Continent and the war may last a long time, his doom is certain. It passes my comprehension why no French leaders secede to Africa where they would have an Empire, the command of the seas and all the frozen French gold in the United States. If this had been done at the beginning we might well have knocked Italy out by now. But surely the opportunity is the most splendid ever offered to daring men. Naturally one would not expect precise responses to such suggestions, but try to put it in their heads if you see any opening.

---

[1] Sir Samuel Hoare's letter of congratulation of 10 October 1940, on Churchill becoming leader of the Conservative Party.

Winston S. Churchill: foreword[1]
(*Wedgwood papers*)

20 October 1940

Were I asked for the best evidence of the virtues of our democracy I would cite the whole political life of my old & gallant friend, Jos Wedgwood.

Had he achieved nothing more than the example he has set us of unselfish courage & constancy in the support of what he deemed the honour & interest of his fellow-countrymen, it would be enough.

But the distressed of the whole world have learnt to look to him, & through him to Parliament, for a patient hearing & the redress of wrongs.

There have been occasions when he & I have differed; but I have never doubted his single-minded pursuit of truth & justice.

WSC

Winston S. Churchill to Sir Archibald Sinclair and Sir Cyril Newall
(*Cabinet papers, 120/300*)

20 October 1940
Secret

1. After discussing the whole question of retaliating by parachute land mines on Germany with C-in-C, Bomber Command,[2] I have come to the conclusion that it would at the present time be an improvident use of our bomb-carrying capacity, except as a purely experimental, psychological feature, as proposed by you.

2. The use of the heaviest 1,000-pound and 2,000-pound bombs on Berlin is much to be desired. Would it not be well to save up for this, merely disturbing them meanwhile?

3. I am deeply concerned with the non-expansion, and indeed contraction, of our Bomber Force which must be expected between now and April or May next, according to present policy. Surely an effort should be made to increase our bomb-dropping capacity during this period. In moonlight periods the present arrangements for bombing are the best possible, and the only difficulty is our small numbers compared to the many attractive military targets. On no account should the limited Bomber Force be diverted from accurate bombing of military objectives reaching far into Germany. But is it not possible to organize a Second Line Bomber Force which, especially in the dark of the moon, would discharge bombs from a considerable and safe height upon the nearest large built-up areas of Germany, which contain military

---

[1] To Josiah Wedgwood's *Memoirs of a Fighting Life*.
[2] Air Marshal Sir Richard Peirse.

targets in abundance. The Ruhr of course is obviously indicated. The object would be to find easy targets, short runs and safe conditions.

4. How is such a Second Line or Auxiliary Bomber Force to be improvised during the winter months? Could not crews from the Training Schools do occasional runs? Are none of the Lysander and Reconnaissance pilots capable of doing some of this simpler bombing, observing that the Army is not likely to be in action unless invasion occurs? I ask that a whole-hearted effort shall be made to cart a large number of bombs into Germany by a Second Line organization such as I have suggested, and under conditions in which admittedly no special accuracy would be obtained. Pray let me have the best suggestions possible, and we can then see whether they are practical or not.

5. How is it that so few of our Bombers are fitted with blind landing appliances? MAP tells me that a number of Lorenz equipments[1] are available. The grievous losses which occurred one day last week ought not to be repeated. Not only do the Bombers need the blind landing facilities (which have been used in commercial aviation for years) but also if Fighter aircraft are to operate by night, as they must increasingly, such aircraft must also be furnished with the means of making safe landings. Pray let me have your observations.

6. I attach a singularly able paper which has been given to me privately, and which reinforces your paper on the Mine v. Bomb argument, but also contains other suggestive observations. Will you kindly let me have it back.

WSC

Winston S. Churchill to Sir Archibald Sinclair and Sir Cyril Newall
(*Cabinet papers, 120/244*)

20 October 1940

In connection with the plans now being developed for night fighting, not only by individual AI fitted machines, but by eight-gun Fighter Squadrons, it is worth considering whether in any area where our Fighters are operating and the guns have to remain out of action, these guns should not fire blank charges. This would (a) confuse the enemy by the flashing on the ground, and tend to make him less aware of the impending Fighter attacks. It would thus

---

[1] Early in the 1930s the Lorenz company had developed a blind approach system to help civil aircraft find landing grounds in bad weather. The system used two adjacent radio beams to mark out a path extending a distance of up to thirty miles from the airfield. One beam received morse code dots, the other dashes. Where the beams interlocked, a steady note was heard. Both the Royal Air Force and the German Air Force ordered the system. By the eve of the war the Germans had adapted the system to help aircraft bomb accurately, using what was known as the *X-Gerät* (the X-Device).

have a strictly military reason. (b) It would make a noise to drown the approach of our attacking Fighters, and also to avoid discouraging silence for the population. It would not be legitimate to fire blank merely for the second purpose, but if there is a military reason the objection disappears.

WSC

Winston S. Churchill to General Dill
(*Churchill papers, 20/13*)

20 October 1940

I am concerned by the very low state of equipment of the Polish troops, whose military qualities have been proved so high. I hope to inspect them on Wednesday this week.[1]

Pray let me have during Monday the best proposals possible for equipping them. I am most anxious they should not become disheartened.

WSC

Winston S. Churchill to General Dill and Sir James Grigg
(*Churchill papers, 20/13*)

20 October 1940

I have read this most valuable and sagacious report[2] with the greatest interest, and I find myself in almost complete agreement with its many conclusions of principle. All necessary action should be taken accordingly without further delay.

I note a few points on which I should be glad to have further information:–
(a) Would it be possible to make the grant of Commissions attach to the appointment rather than to the individual, i.e., a Home Guard officer filling a certain command and exercising its responsibilities would *ipso facto* receive the King's Commission and the appropriate rank. If, however, he ceased to fill that appointment, he would drop his Commission and fall back to the ranks of the Home Guard if he wishes,

---

[1] The inspection of the Polish forces, who were then in Scotland, took place on Wednesday, 23 October 1940. With Churchill on the train journey north were his wife, General Brooke, General Ismay, and the British liaison officer to General Sikorski, Victor Cazalet, MP. The Private Secretary on the journey, John Colville, recorded in his diary Churchill's remark 'People talk a lot of nonsense when they say nothing is ever settled by war. Nothing in history is ever settled except by wars' (*Colville papers*).

[2] On the Home Guard.

exactly as at present. I cannot pretend to have considered this as deeply as its importance deserves. It is, however, an attempt to compromise between the equality of status, and principle on which the Home Guard is founded, and the necessity of having Commissioned ranks and titles connoted to those of the Regular Army.

(b) Para. 79 (b). What will be the position of General Eastwood[1] under these changes, observing that he has only just been appointed?

(c) Para. 101. It is impossible to take away steel helmets from 'The Home Guard in Government offices.' Four were killed outside Downing Street on Thursday night. Whitehall is as heavily bombed as any part of the country. It will be difficult to take helmets away from anyone to whom they have been issued. I am astonished to see that the Army is aiming at 3 million helmets. I was not aware that we had 3 million men. Let me have a full return of all steel helmets in possession of the Regular Army, showing the different Branches, i.e., whether Field Army or Training or Holding Battalions, &c., or in store.

(d) I strongly favour the development out of the Home Guard of Special Home Guard Battalions on full time permanent duties.

(e) The number, 500,000 men employed in Home Guard factory protection, should be capable of marked diminution, in spite of the difficulty that most of them live and work on the spot.

WSC

Winston S. Churchill to General Dill
(*Churchill papers, 20/13*)

20 October 1940
ACTION THIS DAY

I see now you are forming the Field Army into a number of Army Corps. Nine are mentioned. But is this really necessary, for Divisions operating at home in the closest proximity to their respective Army Headquarters? Let me have a list showing the Staffs proposed for these Corps, and also the functions to be assigned to them. The multiplication of Generals and Staff Officers, and the setting up of glorified post offices interpolated between the Army Commanders and the Divisions are all dangers we must seek to avoid. Are there not already far too many Officers of junior and middle rank serving on the Staffs which already exist, which officers would be invaluable as Majors

---

[1] Ralph Eastwood, 1890–1959. Joined the Rifle Brigade, 1910. On active service at Gallipoli, in France and in North Russia, 1914–19 (Military Cross, DSO, despatches seven times). Commandant, Royal Military College, 1938–9. Director-General, Home Guard, 1940–1. General Officer Commanding-in-Chief, Northern Command, 1941–4. Knighted, 1943. Governor and Commander-in-Chief, Gibraltar, 1944–7.

and Seconds-in-Command of Battalions and Batteries. Have the Commanders-in-Chief of the various Commands under the Home Command been consulted about the establishment of Corps Headquarters? And do they not feel that they themselves should exercise the tactical and administrative functions now proposed to be devolved.

WSC

Winston S. Churchill to General Dill and Sir James Grigg
(*Premier papers, 3/318*)

20 October 1940

I have caused some inquiries to be made as to the necessity for the additional 35,000 MT vehicles which the War Office wish to have ordered from America (see War Cabinet minutes of September 30). If the figures given in the attached note are anything like correct, the War Office demands for MT seem to provide a bad example of over-estimating a military need without regard to any other consideration or competitive claim, e.g., Tanks and Aircraft.

2. We must be careful not to delay the equipment of the 55 Divisions; but I must insist on further information as to why this immense mass of transport is required, before agreeing to any further orders being placed in America.

3. To what strategic plan or plans is the War Office demand related? Whilst it might be possible that a force of 55 Divisions operating at the end of a 500-mile line of Communications, as it might have been doing if the French had not collapsed, might require transport on something like this scale, any such basis is now divorced from reality.

4. I must also have information as to (a) the specific units that require the remaining 327,000 tons of MT (see paragraph 3 of attached note) and (b) the basis on which the 300 Divisional months wastage were calculated, i.e., was it upon Divisions of 13,000 men, or upon a nominal figure of 33,000 men per Division? This question also applies to the basis for calculating the maintenance reserve.

5. Pray let me have a full report as soon as possible.

WSC

Winston S. Churchill to President Roosevelt
(*Churchill papers, 20/14*)

20 October 1940

We hear rumours from various sources that the Vichy Government are preparing their ships and Colonial troops to aid the Germans against us. I do not myself believe these reports, but if the French fleet at Toulon were turned over to Germany it would be a very heavy blow. It would certainly be a wise precaution, Mr President, if you would speak in the strongest terms to the French Ambassador[1] emphasizing the disapprobation with which the United States would view such a betrayal of the cause of democracy and freedom. They will pay great heed in Vichy to such a warning.[2]

You will have seen what very heavy losses we have suffered in the North-Western Approaches to our last two convoys. This is due to our shortage of destroyers in the gap period I mentioned to you. Thank God your fifty are now coming along, and some will soon be in action. We ought to be much better off by the end of the year, as we have a lot of our own anti-U-Boat vessels completing, but naturally we are passing through an anxious and critical period with so many small craft having to guard against invasion in the narrow waters and with the very great Naval effort we are making in the Mediterranean, and the immense amount of convoy work.

John Colville to Sir Arthur Salter
(*Premier papers, 3/483/2*)

20 October 1940

Dear Sir Arthur Salter,

The Prime Minister is so overwhelmed with work at present that he has had to cut down his interviews to a minimum. Without exaggeration it is true to say that he does not have five minutes of the day to himself. He therefore thinks that you will understand if he asks you to put in writing the point about which you wish to speak to him.[3]

---

[1] Henri Haye.
[2] For Roosevelt's reply, see the footnote to Churchill's telegram to Roosevelt on 26 October 1940.
[3] Salter replied to Colville on 22 October 1940 that what he had in mind was to put to Churchill 'certain general considerations as to the American position as affecting our supplies' rather than any specific points (*Premier papers, 3/483/2*).

Winston S. Churchill to Lord Beaverbrook
(*Premier papers, 3/33*)

20 October 1940

MAP

We must reinforce the ME,[1] & we must allow AM[2] to train their pilots for next year.[3]

I feel the force of yr arguments, but the others are overwhelming.

My task in adjudicating is difficult; but I do not regret any decision so far taken.

WSC

Winston S. Churchill to General Dill and Sir James Grigg
(*Premier papers, 3/276*)

21 October 1940

This very lengthy report on how General Irwin was carried out to Freetown and back, emphasizes all the difficulties of the operation in which he was concerned. He foresaw all the difficulties beforehand, and the many shortcomings in the preparations. He certainly felt throughout that he was plunged into the midst of a grave and hazardous undertaking on political rather than military grounds. All this makes it the more surprising that he should have wished to persist in this operation, with all its defects and dangers of which he was so acutely conscious, after these had been so formidably aggravated by the arrival through a Naval failure of the French cruisers and reinforcements in Dakar, and in the teeth of the considered opinion of the War Cabinet and the Chiefs of Staff that conditions had now so changed as to make the original plan impossible. However, any error towards the enemy, and any evidence of a sincere desire to engage, must always be generously judged. This Officer was commanding a Division very ably before he was selected for the Expedition, and I see no reason why he should not resume these duties now that he has returned. He would make a mistake, however, if he assumed either (a) that no enterprise should be launched in war for which lengthy preparation has not been made, observing that even in this connection 25

[1] Middle East.
[2] Air Ministry.
[3] In a letter to Churchill on 18 October 1940, Beaverbrook, as Minister of Aircraft Production, had protested at the Air Ministry having sent aircraft to the Middle East and elsewhere, writing: '1,164 aeroplanes, including 1,720 engines, have been shipped abroad since your Ministry was formed. In addition, vast quantities of spares have been dispatched here and there, all over the world.' Beaverbrook ended his letter, 'I hope you will stop it before long.'

Frenchmen took Duala, and with it the Cameroons, or (b) that ships can in no circumstances engage forts with success. This might well be true in the fog conditions which so unexpectedly and unnaturally descended upon Dakar. But it would not necessarily be true of the case where the ships' guns could engage the forts at ranges to which the forts could not reply, or where the gunners in the forts were frightened, inefficient, or friendly to the attacking force.

WSC

Winston S. Churchill to Lord Lloyd
(*Churchill papers, 20/13*)

21 October 1940

I am afraid I have been some time in studying your notes on the African Continent, and its strategic and political dangers in the present war. I should deprecate setting up a special Committee. We are overrun by them, like the Australians were by the rabbits. I see no reason to assume that we shall be at war with Vichy France or Spain, or that the South African position will develop dangerously. I should have thought that you would be able with your own military experience[1] and political knowledge to gather such Officials of the Colonial Office as you may need around you, and prepare yourself any reports you may think it right to present to the Defence Committee or the War Cabinet. If, however, you feel the need of being associated with a Committee, I suggest that the Middle East Ministerial Committee takes on the Agenda you have outlined as an addition to their present sphere.

WSC

PS – I am trying to move one of the West African Brigades back from Kenya to the West Coast.

Chiefs of Staff Committee: minutes
(*Cabinet papers, 79/7*)

21 October 1940
10.15 a.m.

Sir Cyril Newall said that the Prime Minister had in his speeches always drawn attention to the dangers of assuming that the threat of invasion had passed and supported the suggestion that the Prime Minister might, at a

---

[1] In the First World War Lord Lloyd had served in Egypt, at Gallipoli, in Mesopotamia, and in the Hedjaz.

favourable opportunity, again emphasise the dangers of over confidence in this respect. Any approach to the Press, however, should be done in such a way as to avoid alarming the public and thereby giving them another burden to bear.

Night Air Defence Committee: minutes[1]
(*Cabinet papers, 81/22*)

21 October 1940 Cabinet War Room
11.30 a.m.

At present German bombers can fly and bomb in weather when our Fighters are unable to leave the ground. It is desirable that where operationally possible our Fighters, and the aerodromes from which they operate, should be equipped with blind landing apparatus. The Lorenz apparatus cannot be carried in a single-seater fighter because its weight would affect the centre of gravity of the aircraft and necessitate a flat and dangerous landing approach with flaps down. It is, however, suitable for the Beaufighter, which is wired to carry it.

At present 1,000 air sets of Lorenz apparatus in the country are available for fitting in aircraft, fourteen Lorenz ground sets are installed at Bomber aerodromes, seven more ground sets are ready, and six more ground sets are being cabled for from America.

It was pointed out that the Lorenz apparatus would have to be used with great discretion to prevent the Germans from making use of it to guide them to our aerodromes. This could be overcome by choosing frequencies for which the German bomber receivers were not adapted.

It was agreed that immediate steps should be taken to fit all Beaufighters with Lorenz air sets, and to equip the Fighter aerodromes from which they would be working with Lorenz ground apparatus.

A shortcoming of the Lorenz apparatus is that it is not capable of completing the final process of 'touching down' the aircraft on its aerodrome. An improved method was under investigation before the outbreak of war but was not pursued after September, 1939.

The Prime Minister instructed that a report on this should be made, and proposals submitted for its development.

---

[1] For the members of this War Cabinet committee, see page 905, note 2. The committee met again on November 19, see pages 1109–10.

John Martin: diary
(*Martin papers*)

21 October 1940

We are in process of moving to 'Annexe' in old Board of Trade.[1]

John Peck: recollection
(*Letter to author, 13 March 1993*)

21 October 1940

It was a day of high drama with
(a) Winston insisting on composing it in French
(b) Winston admitting defeat and composing it in English
(c) The Ministry of Information sending to Chequers a terrified young Englishman with ? A-level French to translate (b) into French
(d) Winston fighting all the way in defence of his French version
(e) The young M of I man being shipped off to London
(f) A charming, avuncular, truly bilingual Frenchman[2] being unearthed from the BBC and rushed down to Chequers.

He very sensibly conveyed the impression that he was polishing up Winston's text while in fact virtually rewriting the whole thing, leaving Winston delighted with his masterpiece. It was perhaps a blessing that Jock[3] was not on duty as his French was good enough to be offered and add to the chaos.

---

[1] This was Number Ten Annexe, codenamed 'The Barn' (see page 820, footnote 1). On 22 October the War Cabinet urged Churchill to leave 10 Downing Street for 'a securer building'. This he was already doing.
[2] Jacques Duchesne was the wartime pseudonym of Michel Saint-Denis, 1897–1947, the distinguished French actor and producer, who was head of the French Section of the BBC from 1940 to 1944. He had fought on the Western Front in the First World War. From 1962 to 1966 he was a Director of the Royal Shakespeare Company.
[3] John Colville.

October 1940

John Colville: diary
(*Colville papers*)

21 October 1940

The PM made a gaffe. He is speaking on the wireless in French tonight, and just before dinner he came into the room, where the French BBC expert and translator, M. Duchesne, was standing, and exclaimed: 'Where is my frog speech?' M. Duchesne looked pained.

John Peck to Winston S. Churchill
(*Churchill papers, 9/176*)

21 October 1940

It was Gambetta who said it, in 1871. The exact words are:
'Pensons y toujours, n'en parlons jamais.'[1]

Winston S. Churchill: broadcast
(*BBC Written Archives Centre, recording*)[2]

21 October 1940   Cabinet War Room

Frenchmen! For more than thirty years in peace and war I have marched with you, and I am marching still along the same road. Tonight I speak to you at your firesides wherever <u>you</u> may be, or whatever your fortunes are. I repeat the prayer around the *louis d'or*, '*Dieu protège la France*', 'God Protect France'. Here at home in England, under the fire of the Boche, we do not forget the ties and links that unite us to France, and we are persevering steadfastly and in good heart in the cause of European freedom and fair dealing for the common people of all countries, for which, with you, we drew the sword. When good people get into trouble because they are attacked and heavily smitten by the <u>vile</u> and wicked, they must be very careful not to get at loggerheads with one another. The common enemy is always trying to bring this about, and, of course, in bad luck a lot of things happen which play into the enemy's hands. We must just make the best of things as they come along.

Here in London, which Herr Hitler says he will reduce to ashes, and which his aeroplanes are now bombarding, our people are bearing up unflinchingly.

[1] Normally translated 'Think of it always, speak of it never.' Gambetta was referring to the German annexation of the provinces of Alsace and Lorraine. In the versions of the speech as given to the press, and as later printed in Churchill's collected war speeches, the name is still Thiers; but in the spoken version Churchill said 'Gambetta'. John Peck's note had reached him just in time.

[2] The words underlined in the text are those on which Churchill laid emphasis when he spoke.

Our Air Force has more than held its own. We are waiting for the long-promised invasion. So are the fishes. But, of course, this for us is only the beginning. Now in 1940, in spite of occasional losses, we have, as ever, the command of the seas. In 1941 we shall have the command of the air. Remember what that means. Herr Hitler with his tanks and other mechanical weapons, and also by Fifth Column intrigue with traitors, has managed to subjugate for the time being most of the finest races in Europe, and his little Italian accomplice is trotting along hopefully and hungrily, but rather wearily and very timidly, at his side. They both wish to carve up France and her Empire as if it were a fowl; to one a leg, to another a wing or perhaps part of the breast. Not only the French Empire will be devoured by these two ugly customers, but Alsace-Lorraine will go once again under the German yoke, and Nice, Savoy and Corsica – Napoleon's Corsica – will be torn from the fair realm of France. But Herr Hitler is not thinking only of stealing other people's territories, or flinging gobbets of them to his little confederate. I tell you truly what you must believe when I say this evil man, this monstrous abortion of hatred and defeat, is resolved on nothing less than the complete wiping out of the French nation, and the disintegration of its whole life and future. By all kinds of sly and savage means, he is plotting and working to quench for ever the fountain of characteristic French culture and French inspiration to the world. All Europe, if he had his way, will be reduced to one uniform Boche-land, to be exploited, pillaged, and bullied by his Nazi gangsters. You will excuse my speaking frankly because this is not a time to mince words. It is not defeat that France will now be made to suffer at German hands, but the doom of complete obliteration. Army, Navy, Air Force, religion, laws, language, culture, institutions, literature, history, tradition – all are to be effaced by the brute strength of a triumphant Army and the scientific low cunning of a ruthless Police Force.

Frenchmen – rearm your spirits before it is too late. Remember how Napoleon said before one of his battles:[1] 'These same Prussians who are so boastful today were three to one at Jena, and six to one at Montmirail.' Never will I believe that the soul of France is dead. Never will I believe that her place amongst the greatest nations of the world has been lost for ever. All these schemes and crimes of Herr Hitler's are bringing upon him and upon all who belong to his system a retribution which many of us will live to see. The story is not yet finished, but it will not be so long. We are on his track, and so are our friends across the Atlantic Ocean, and your friends across the Atlantic Ocean. If he cannot destroy us, we will surely destroy him and all his gang, and all their works. Therefore, have hope and faith, for all will come right.

---

[1] The battle was Waterloo. Many British listeners were impressed that, in order not to offend French feelings, Churchill had discreetly omitted the name of Napoleon's defeat, speaking only of 'one of his battles'.

Now, what is it we British ask of you in this present hard and bitter time? What we ask at this moment in our struggle to win the victory which we will share with you, is that if you cannot help us, at least you will not hinder us. Presently you will be able to weight the arm that strikes for you, and you ought to do so. But even now we trust that Frenchmen, wherever they may be, feel their hearts warm, and a proud blood tingle in their veins, when we have some success in the air or on the sea, or presently – for that will come – upon the land.

Remember we shall never stop, never weary, and never give in, and that our whole people and Empire have vowed themselves to the task of cleansing Europe from the Nazi pestilence and saving the world from the new Dark Ages. Do not imagine, as the German-controlled wireless tells you, that we English seek to take your ships and colonies. We seek to beat the life and soul out of Hitler and Hitlerism. That alone, that all the time, that to the end. We do not covet anything from any nation except their respect. Those Frenchmen who are in the French Empire, and those who are in so-called unoccupied France, may see their way from time to time to useful action. I will not go into details. Hostile ears are listening. As for those to whom English hearts go out in full, because they see them under the sharp discipline, oppression, and spying of the Hun – as to those Frenchmen in the occupied regions – to them I say, when they think of the future let them remember the words which Gambetta, that great Frenchman, uttered after 1870 about the future of France and what was to come: 'Think of it always: speak of it never.'

Good night, then: sleep to gather strength for the morning. For the morning will come. Brightly will it shine on the brave and true, kindly on all who suffer for the cause, glorious upon the tombs of heroes. Thus will shine the dawn. *Vive la France!* Long live also the forward march of the common people in all the lands towards their just and true inheritance, and towards the broader and fuller age.

Winston S. Churchill: speech
(*'Into Battle', pages 298–300*)

21 October 1940   Cabinet War Room

Français! Pendant plus de trente ans, en temps de paix comme en temps de guerre, j'ai marché avec vous et je marche encore avec vous aujourd'hui, sur la même route. Ce soir je vous parle, au sein même de vos foyers, où que vous soyez, et quelque soit votre sort. Je répète la prière qui entourait vos Louis d'Or: 'Dieu protège la France.' Ici, chez nous, en Angleterre, sous le feu du Boche, nous n'oublions pas quels liens et quelles attaches nous unissent à la France: nous continuons à lutter de pied ferme et d'un cœur solide, pour que la liberté soit rétablie en Europe, pour que le peuple soit traité avec justice dans tous les pays, en un mot pour faire triompher la cause qui nous a fait ensemble tirer l'épée. Quand des honnêtes gens se trouvent déconcertés par les attaques et les coups que leur portent des coquins et des méchants, ils doivent faire bien attention de ne pas commencer à se quereller entre eux. C'est ce que l'ennemi commun essaie toujours de provoquer et naturellement quand la malchance s'y met bien des choses arrivent qui font le jeu de l'ennemi.

Je me rappelle toujours ce que dit Maître Labori[1] il y a bien des années, après qu'il fût blessé par un assassin: 'L'accident a beaucoup plus de place que l'intention dans les affaires humaines.'

Ici, dans cette ville de Londres que Herr Hitler prétend réduire en cendres et que ses avions bombardent en ce moment, nos gens tiennent bon. Notre aviation a fait plus que de tenir tête à l'ennemi. Nous attendons l'invasion promise de longue date. Les poissons aussi. Mais, bien sûr, nous n'en sommes encore qu'au commencement. Aujourd'hui en 1940, comme toujours, nous avons la maîtrise des mers. En 1941, nous aurons la maîtrise de l'air. N'oubliez pas ce que cela veut dire. Herr Hitler avec ses chars d'assaut et ses autres armes mécaniques et aussi grâce aux intrigues de sa cinquième colonne avec les traîtres, a réussi, pour le moment, à conquérir la plupart des races les plus belles de l'Europe et son petit complice italien, plein d'espoir et d'appétit, continue à trotter craintivement à son côté. Tous deux veulent découper la France et son Empire. L'un veut la cuisse, et l'autre l'aile.

Non seulement l'Empire Française sera dévoré par ces deux vilains messieurs, mais l'Alsace-Lorraine va une fois encore repasser sous le joug allemand – et Nice, la Savoie et la Corse – la Corse de Napoléon – seront arrachés du beau domaine de la France. Mais Monsieur Hitler ne songe pas seulement à voler le territoire des autres peuples et à en distraire quelques morceaux pour les lancer à son petit chien. Je vous dis la vérité et il faut que vous me croyiez. Cet homme de malheur, ce monstrueux enfant de la haine et de la défaite n'est résolu à rien moins qu'à faire entièrement disparaître la nation française, qu'à désagréger sa vie même et par conséquent à ruiner son avenir. Il se prépare par toutes sortes de moyens sournois et féroces, à tarir pour toujours les sources de la culture et de l'inspiration françaises dans le monde. S'il est libre d'agir à sa guise, toute l'Europe ne sera plus qu'une Bochie uniforme, offerte à l'exploitation, au pillage et à la brutalité des gangsters nazis. Si je vous parle aussi carrément, excusez-moi, mais ce n'est pas le moment de mâcher les mots.

---

[1] Ferdinand Labori, a distinguished French jurist. He defended Alfred Dreyfus during his second court martial in 1899. On the morning of 14 August 1899, in Rennes, while the Dreyfus trial was going on, he was shot at on his way to the courtroom.

Ce ne sont pas les conséquences de la défaite que la France doit aujourd'hui subir de la main des Allemands, mais toutes les étapes d'une annihilation complète. Armée, Marine, Aviation, Lois, Langue, Culture, Littérature, Histoire, Traditions, toutes vout être effacées par la force brutale d'une armée triomphante et par les ruses scientifiques et basses d'une police impitoyable.

Français! Armez vos cœurs à neuf avant qu'il ne soit trop tard. Rappelez-vous de quelle façon Napoléon disait avant une de ses victoires: 'Ces mêmes Prussiens qui sont aujourd'hui si vantards étaient à trois contre un à Jéna et à neuf contre un à Montmirail.' Jamais je ne croirai que l'âme de la France soit morte, ni que sa place parmi les grandes nations du monde puisse être perdue pour toujours.

Tous les complots et tous les crimes de Herr Hitler sont en train d'attirer sur sa tête et sur la tête de ceux qui appartiennent à son régime un châtiment que beaucoup d'entre nous verrons de leur vivant. Il n'y aura pas si longtemps à attendre. L'aventure n'est pas encore finie. Nous sommes sur sa piste; et nos amis de l'autre côté de l'océan Atlantique y sont aussi. Si Herr Hitler ne peut pas nous détruire, nous, nous somme sûrs de le détruire, avec toute sa clique et tous leurs travaux. Ayez donc espoir et confiance. Tout se rétablira.

Maintenant, nous autres Britanniques, que pouvons-nous vous demander aujourd'hui, dans un moment si âpre et si dur? Ce que nous vous demandons, au milieu de nos efforts pour remporter la victoire que nous partagerons avec vous, c'est que, si vous ne pouvez pas nous aider, au moins vous ne nous fassiez pas obstacle. En effet, vous devez renforcer le bras qui frappe pour vous. Nous croyons que les Français, où qu'ils soient, se sentiront le cœur réchauffé et que la fierté de leur sang tressaillera dans leurs veines chaque fois que nous remporterons un succès dans les airs, sur mer, ou, plus tard – et cela viendra – sur terre. N'oubliez pas que nous ne nous arrêterons jamais, que nous ne nous lasserons jamais, que jamais nous ne céderons et que notre peuple et notre Empire tout entier se sont voués à la tâche de guérir l'Europe de la pestilence nazie et de sauver le monde d'une nouvelle barbarie. Parmi les Français, ceux qui se trouvent dans l'Empire Colonial et ceux qui habitent la France soi-disant inoccupée peuvent, sans doute, de temps à autre, trouver l'occasion d'agir utilement. Je n'entre pas dans les détails. Les oreilles ennemies nous écoutent. Les autres, vers que l'affection anglaise se porte d'un seul mouvement, parce qu'ils vivent sous la stricte discipline, l'oppression et l'espionnage des Boches, je leur dis: Quand vous pensez à l'avenir, rappelez-vous les mots de ce grand Français que fut Gambetta: Il les prononça après 1870, à propos de l'avenir: 'Y penser toujours; n'en parler jamais.'

Allons, bonne nuit, dormez bien, rassemblez vos forces pour l'aube – car l'aube viendra. Elle se lévera brillante pour les braves, douce pour les fidèles qui auront souffert, glorieuse sur les tombeaux des héros. Vive la France! Et vive aussi la marche en avant des peuples de tous les pays qui veulent reconquérir le patrimoine qui leur appartient de plein droit.

October 1940

Paul Maze[1] to Winston S. Churchill
(*Churchill papers, 3/396*)

22 October 1940

My dear Winston,

I was so moved by your broadcast to the French people last night. Every word you said was like every drop of blood in a transfusion. I know that the French people will have risked everything to listen to you because you are irresistible to them & they need your human appeals. I love you for not despairing of them in these times.

Often in my Home Guard vigils I think of you – to us all you are our trusted pilot of whom we talk with admiration, gratitude & affection –

God bless you –
affectionately
Paul

F. W. Ogilvie[2] to Winston S. Churchill
(*Churchill papers, 20/6*)

22 October 1940   Broadcasting House

My dear Prime Minister,

I was very sorry I was not able to come for your broadcast last night. May I therefore be allowed to congratulate you most warmly upon it? It came through here superbly, in both languages, and it will obviously have a profound effect in France and all over the world.

---

[1] Paul Lucien Maze, 1887–1979. Born in Le Havre. Painter. On active service, 1914–18 (DCM, MM and Bar, Légion d'Honneur, Croix de Guerre). He first met Churchill in 1916, on the Western Front, and subsequently encouraged him with his painting. Churchill wrote the preface to Maze's war memoirs, *A Frenchman in Khaki*, published in 1934. Left France after the German invasion, 1940; subsequently resident in England. Served with the Home Guard, and then with the RAF (intelligence), 1940–5. In his Introduction to Paul Maze's war memoirs, Churchill wrote of Maze: '. . . he is an artist of distinction whose quick comprehension, keen eye and nimble pencil could record impressions with revealing fidelity. As a British private, who watched him one day sketching in a heavily bombarded trench, said, "Your pictures are done in shorthand." ' Churchill ended his Introduction: '. . . we have the battle-scenes of Armageddon recorded by one who not only loved the fighting troops and shared their perils, but perceived the beauties of light and shade, of form and colour, of which even the horrors of war cannot rob the progress of the sun. This volume should be acceptable alike to the artists and the soldiers of the two great nations whose cause of freedom its author so ardently and enduringly espoused.'

[2] Frederick Wolff Ogilvie, 1893–1949. Born in Chile, the son of a British engineer. Educated at Clifton and Balliol College, Oxford. On active service, 1914–18; severely wounded at Hill 60, as a result of which he lost his left arm. Demobilised with the rank of Captain, 1919. Lecturer in Economics, Trinity College, Oxford, 1920–6. Professor of Political Economy, Edinburgh, 1926–34. Principal and Vice-Chancellor, Queen's University, Belfast, 1934–8. Director-General of the BBC (in succession to Lord Reith), 1938–42. Knighted, 1942. Served with the British Council, 1942–4. Principal of Jesus College, Oxford, from 1944 until his death.

You will be sorry to learn that a bomb exploded right in the middle of our cake here last week, unhappily with the loss of seven lives, several other casualties, and the wrecking of most studio and other facilities above ground. All of our broadcast services, however, went on without interruption.

Yours sincerely,
F. W. Ogilvie

Winston S. Churchill to Harold Balfour
(*Balfour of Inchyre papers*)

22 October 1940
10 Downing Street

My dear Balfour,

I am obliged to you for the explanation which you have given of your committing us to the expenditure upon the aircraft in question, without consultation with the Ministry of Aircraft Production or sanction from the Treasury.[1] I cannot see why it was not possible to consult the Air Ministry, and through them the other Departments concerned, by cable or by telephone. You could surely have asked for the option to purchase to be delayed for, say, twenty-four hours while you did so. Your failure to do this has caused me a great deal of work and worry at a time when much else is happening.

I am glad to receive the expression of your regret, and your assurance through the Secretary of State for Air that such action on your part will not be repeated. I really do not see how the Government could be carried on if such unauthorised commitments were to be countenanced.

Yours sincerely,
Winston S. Churchill

[1] Balfour had purchased three Boeing Clippers of the six then under construction for Pan American Airways. In answer to Churchill's query, he explained that if anything had happened to Britain's two existing clipper flying boats, *Clyde* and *Clare*, 'we should have no load-carrying boats which could reach Bathurst. These clippers can fly a heavy load non-stop from England to West Africa. Other United States interests were negotiating for these boats, and at any time the offer of sale might have ceased to be open' (Harold Balfour, *Wings Over Westminster*, page 147).

Winston S. Churchill to Sir Samuel Hoare
(*Foreign Office papers, 800/323*)

22 October 1940

My compliments on your memo of October 18.[1] I felt Beigbeder's fate would distress you, but the relations you had with him played a valuable part. Now try to get Suñer.[2]

Winston S. Churchill to A. V. Alexander
(*Churchill papers, 20/13*)

22 October 1940

ACOUSTIC MINES[3]

It would seem that a very energetic effort should be made to cope with these new mines, and the fortnightly meetings proposed hardly seem adequate.

WSC

---

[1] In his memorandum, Hoare wrote: 'Colonel Beigbeder had a long and friendly meeting with Franco on Tuesday night, October 15th. When I saw him on the following day he was confident both of his own position and of the future of his own policy. He knew nothing more until he read in the official gazette of Thursday, October 17th, the brief notification of his dismissal and of his replacement by the Minister of the Interior, hitherto the most bitter opponent of his policy and a man who has gone out of his way through the medium of the Press Department to glorify Germany and Italy and to vilify Great Britain.' Hoare added: 'When I came here six months ago he was a germanophile to the point of believing that Germany must win the war. Our constant talks have left him an anglophile to the point that he detests the pagan methods of the Nazis and now believes that Great Britain cannot be beaten. It may be that his conversion has been too complete. With the fault of his quixotic qualities he has been incredibly indiscreet' (*Foreign Office papers, 371/24508*).

[2] On 17 October 1940 Ramon Serrano Suñer replaced Colonel Juan Beigbeder as Foreign Minister of Spain. He was himself replaced, in September 1942, by Count Francisco Jordana.

[3] A meeting on acoustic mines had been held at the Admiralty on 16 October 1940. The acoustic mine, which had first been used by the Germans in August 1940, was activated by the sound vibrations set up by ships' engines. Its existence, and hence its efficacy, was not revealed to the British public until the end of 1941, by which time minesweepers had been provided with the means of emitting a sound of sufficient intensity to detonate the mine at a safe distance.

Winston S. Churchill to A. V. Alexander
(*Churchill papers, 20/13*)

22 October 1940

I should be much obliged if you would let me have a record of the operation called 'Lucid'[1] from its inception to the present moment. This record need not occupy more than two or three sheets of paper.

WSC

Winston S. Churchill to Sir Edward Bridges
(*Premier papers, 4/69/1*)

22 October 1940

We now know the probable limits of the enemy air attack on London, and that it will be severe and protracted. It is probable, indeed, that the bombing of Whitehall and the centre of Government will be continuous until all old or insecure buildings have been demolished. It is therefore necessary to provide as soon as possible accommodation in the strongest houses and buildings that exist, or are capable of being fortified, for the large nucleus staffs and personnel connected with the Governing machine and the essential Ministers and Departments concerned in the conduct of the war. This becomes inevitable as a consequence of our decision not to be beaten out of London, and to release to the War Office or other Departments the accommodation hitherto reserved in the West of England for the Black Move.[2] We must do one thing or the other, and, having made our decision, carry it out thoroughly.

2. The accommodation at 'Paddock's' is quite unsuited to the conditions which have arisen. The War Cabinet cannot live and work there for weeks on end, while leaving the great part of their staffs less well provided for than they are now in Whitehall. Apart from the Citadel, there is no adequate

---

[1] At the end of June 1940, Desmond Morton had told Churchill of the possibility of sending fireships into German-controlled French ports (Operation 'Lucid') to 'scatter burning oil all over the harbour, possibly with most pleasing results'. With Professor Lindemann's approval, and the ministerial help of Geoffrey Lloyd, the Secretary for Petroleum, experiments had gone forward throughout July, August and early September. On 19 September 1940 all was set for a first venture to be carried out seven days later. The ships broke down, however, and the operation was postponed. On 4 October 1940 two fireships were sent against Calais and one against Boulogne, but the wind was blowing in the wrong direction for the burning oil to be squirted out successfully. During a renewed attempt three days later the escorting destroyer struck a mine, and the ships had to be recalled. The fireships then remained 'at seven days' notice' for action, but were never used again. (*Premier papers, 3/264.*)

[2] The Black Move was the plan for the evacuation of all Government departments to the West of England, in the event of the bombing of London making it impossible for work to be carried on in the capital. It was never carried out.

accommodation or shelter, and anyone living in Neville Court would have to be running to and fro on every Jim Crow warning.[1] 'Paddock' should be treated as a last resort to Citadel, and in the meantime should be used by some Department not needed in the very centre of London.

3. Nearly all the Government buildings and shelters beneath them are either wholly unsafe or incapable of resisting a direct hit. The older buildings, like the Treasury, fall to pieces, as we have seen, and the shelters beneath them offer no trustworthy protection. The Foreign Office and Board of Trade blocks on either side of King Charles Street are strongly built and give a considerable measure of protection in their basements. I have approved the provision of a substantial measure of overhead cover above the War Room and Central War Room offices, and Home Forces location in the Board of Trade building. This will take a month or six weeks with perpetual hammering. We must press on with this. But, even when finished, it will not be proof. Richmond Terrace is quite inadequately protected, and essential work suffers from conditions prevailing there. The Board of Trade have been invited to move to new premises, and certainly the bulk of their staff should find accommodation out of London. However, this move of the Board of Trade must be considered as part of the general plan.

4. There are several strong modern buildings in London, of steel and cement construction built with an eye to air raid conditions. These should immediately be prepared to receive the War Cabinet and its Secretariat, and also to provide safe living accommodation for the essential Ministers. We need not be afraid of having too much proof accommodation, as increasing numbers will certainly have to be provided for. It is essential that the central work of the Government should proceed under conditions which ensure its efficiency.

5. I have already asked for alternative accommodation for Parliament, but no satisfactory plan has yet been made. The danger to both Houses during their Sessions is serious, and it is only a question of time before these buildings and chambers are struck. We must hope they will be struck when not occupied by their Members. The protection provided below the Houses of Parliament is totally inadequate against a direct hit. The Palace of Westminster and the Whitehall area is an obvious prime target of the enemy, and I daresay already more than fifty heavy bombs have fallen in the neighbourhood. The Cabinet has already favoured the idea of a trial trip being made by the Houses of Parliament in some alternative accommodation. I propose to ask for an Adjournment from Thursday next for a fortnight, by which time it is hoped some plan can be made in London for their meeting.

6. I consider that a War Cabinet Minister, who should keep in close touch with the Chancellor of the Exchequer, should be entrusted with the general

---

[1] An early-warning air raid signal.

direction and supervision of the important and extensive works which are required, and that Lord Reith and his Department[1] should work for this purpose under Cabinet supervision. If my colleagues agree, I will ask Lord Beaverbrook, who has already concerned himself in the matter, to take general charge.

WSC

War Cabinet: minutes
(*Cabinet papers, 65/9*)

22 October 1940   Prime Minister's Room
12 noon   House of Commons

The Prime Minister said that he had examined the need for safer accommodation for essential Government staffs who would have to continue to work in London. A number of these staffs were now working in old buildings which were quite insecure, and should be moved to buildings which would provide greater safety and which would afford them reasonable means of carrying on their work. For many reasons 'Paddock' was an unsuitable solution to the problem. The Foreign Office Building and the 'New Public Offices' were strongly built, but were not constructed to withstand direct hits. He had given authority for part of the latter building to be strengthened so as to give a considerable measure of security, but the work would not be completed for six weeks. As part of the problem of providing adequate accommodation for central staffs, the Board of Trade had been invited to move to new premises. The Department was prepared to fall in with this arrangement, but this move must be considered in relation to the general scheme.

Continuing, the Prime Minister said that there were a number of stronger modern buildings in London of steel-framed construction, some of them still uncompleted, within a comparatively short distance of Whitehall, and he thought that Ministers and essential staffs should be distributed among these buildings when the necessary works had been completed. The Minister of Aircraft Production had concerned himself in the matter, and might be authorised to direct and supervise, on behalf of the War Cabinet, the important and extensive works required.

---

[1] Reith, newly created a Baron, had become Minister of Works and Building on 3 October 1940.

Reference was made to the Prime Minister's accommodation. The War Cabinet were unanimously of the opinion that it was wrong for the Prime Minister to continue to live or to transact business at No. 10, Downing Street. They urged him most strongly to agree to other arrangements being made forthwith for his accommodation in a securer building.

Defence Committee: minutes
(*Cabinet papers, 69/1*)

22 October 1940
3.30 p.m.
Cabinet War Room

Sir Cyril Newall said that General de Gaulle had asked for two further Blenheims from Takoradi but he was strongly against diverting any aircraft from the Middle East reinforcement programme. General de Gaulle already had six Blenheims and eight Lysanders.

The Prime Minister pointed out the dangers of inaction in the Libreville area and added that incidents were bound to arise in any case in the fulfilment of our pledge to defend General de Gaulle's sea communications. He was most anxious that, if the operation was to take place, it should be properly planned and that Vice Admiral Cunningham should assume responsibility for the planning and preparations.

On 22 OCTOBER 1940 Churchill travelled by train to Scotland, where he visited the Polish forces at Tentsmuir (Fife). He also visited the dockyard at Rosyth.

Victor Cazalet: diary
(*'Victor Cazalet, a Portrait'*)

22 October 1940

Up to Scotland in train with Winston, Dill, Ismay, Thompson[1] and Colville. W in great form and talked from 8 to 12. He asked me all sorts of questions about Polish Forces – very awkward in front of Dill. I made great friends with Ismay, who is firm friend of Poles. I did my best to get pay of Polish officers settled, but Winston would not attend. W in tremendous form.

---

[1] Commander C. R. ('Tommy') Thompson, Churchill's naval Flag Lieutenant at the Admiralty, who had stayed with him, and was to serve throughout his premiership as ADC.

Talked from 8 to 12 midnight. Dill getting v sleepy. I was thrilled. Even though I've known him for years, he has now assumed a world position, a positive dictator, whose slightest whims are of profound interest. W talked of the army, how officers should be trained. He quoted poetry and as always as the evening got later he got more and more jovial and genial. We arrived at Coupar about 9 a.m. on Wednesday 23rd. Generals galore to meet us.

Winston S. Churchill to Sir Samuel Hoare
(*Foreign Office papers, 800/323*)

23 October 1940
Personal and Private

My dear Sam,

I came to the conclusion some weeks ago that having regard to all the circumstances involved, it would be better not to break the continuity of Linlithgow's treatment of the immediate problems of Indian Government. I therefore offered him an extension of a year from March next, and he has accepted this proposal. The future clearly remains open, but I must in no wise be considered as committed to any particular solution of the personal and political issues involved in the selection of a new Viceroy.[1]

There was a sentence in one of your letters to Edward Halifax which seemed to indicate that you thought you might not be a suitable person to conduct our affairs with Suñer in view of the intimate relations you so skilfully built up with Beigbeder. From the accounts you have given us of the Spanish situation, I cannot feel that this will be so. We should all be very sorry if you wished to abandon your mission to Spain. I really do not think there is anyone who could serve us there so well as you, and the work that you have done already has given great satisfaction to the Cabinet. I hope therefore that you will persevere in your difficult task, standing as you do in one of the key posts of Imperial Defence.

Yours sincerely,
WSC

---

[1] Sir Samuel Hoare had been Secretary of State for India from 1931 to 1935. It was his ambition to be Viceroy, an ambition he was not to fulfil. Linlithgow was succeeded as Viceroy in 1943 by General Wavell, and Wavell in 1947 by Admiral Mountbatten. Hoare was raised to the Peerage, as Viscount Templewood, in 1944.

John Colville: diary
(*Colville papers*)

23 October 1940

We made an extensive tour of Rosyth dockyard and spent much time on the great new battleship, *King George V*, completing in dry dock before doing her trials. We saw the luxurious ward-room and sick-bay, officers' compartment, kitchens and turrets. In descending through the tiny hole into one of the 14-inch turrets both the PM and Lord Rosebery[1] all but got stuck. The PM had a long talk with the C in C, Home Fleet, Sir Charles Forbes, and then, dressed in his yachting cap and navy-blue brass-buttoned suit, addressed the ship's company about their ship and the necessity of having her in good trim before the *Bismarck* was out and at sea.

The PM talked to Dill and worked until 2.00 a.m. I heard the tail-end of a discussion in which Dill was being lectured on the desirability of employing General Hobart (who is disliked by the army – and by Dill): 'Remember,' said the PM with a meaning look at Dill, 'it isn't only the good boys who help to win wars; it is the sneaks and the stinkers as well.'

Winston S. Churchill to Ronald Cross
(*Churchill papers, 20/13*)

23 October 1940

I follow these losses[2] daily: and also the invasion risk. I have asked Admiralty for a large concentration of destroyers to be achieved by the middle of November. In repeated conferences with the Admiralty new plans have been made. Everything in our power will be done; and having regard to the large impending increases in destroyers, I do not think it necessary as yet to revise the programmes. By all means circulate your paper.

WSC

---

[1] Albert Edward Harry Meyer Archibald Primrose, 1882–1974. Son of the 5th Earl of Rosebery (Prime Minister, 1894) and Hannah, only daughter of Baron Meyer de Rothschild. Liberal MP, 1906–10. On active service, 1914–18 (wounded, DSO, MC). Succeeded his father as 6th Earl, 1919. A racehorse owner: President of the Thoroughbred Breeders Association, 1932–57. Regional Commissioner for Scotland, 1940–5. President of the National Liberal Party, 1945–7. Chairman of the Scottish Tourist Board, 1955–65.

[2] British merchant-shipping losses had been considerable, thirty-two ships in all, in the preceding week; two on the 15th, one on 16 October 1940, five on the 17th, eight on the 18th, twelve on the 19th, two on the 20th, and two on the 21st. No merchant ships were sunk on the 22nd or 23rd. One ship was sunk on the 24th.

Winston S. Churchill to Sir Archibald Sinclair
(*Churchill papers, 20/2*)

23 October 1940
Private

My dear Archie,

Yours of October 21, paragraph 2. My reference to 'what was not going on', implied no suggestion that Air Vice-Marshal McKean[1] was deliberately telling an untruth, but only that the facts were different from what he believed them to be.[2] But if a man, however honestly, accepts false facts and on them bases unfounded charges expressed in disrespectful language about his superior, undoubtedly he deserves censure, more especially if he does not mitigate this censure by an apology.

I am sorry that you brush aside what I wrote to you in my letter of the 19th instant. I will not renew my appeal.

I am having all the telegrams printed, and they should be ready by tomorrow. The Cabinet, happily, not I, must pronounce upon the issues which are open by the very serious and unfounded affront which has been offered to one of their Members. I hope you will not mind my saying that I feel I might have had a little more assistance from you in dealing with this difficult matter.

Yours sincerely,
WSC

John Colville: diary
(*Colville papers*)

24 October 1940

The train was very late and we had breakfast in comfort before reaching King's Cross. The PM passed the time in abusing the Foreign Office with Dill, who complained that the middle ranks in the Diplomatic Service were so poor. The PM said a large number should be pensioned off: 'What is wanted in that department is a substantial application of the boot.'

I drove back with him to No. 10. He said as the passers-by cheered, 'I

---

[1] Lionel Douglas Dalzell McKean, 1886–1963. Joined the Royal Navy, 1904. On active service with the Royal Naval Air Service, 1914–18; with the Royal Air Force, 1918. Air Vice-Marshal, 1939. Head of the Royal Air Force Mission to Canada, 1940–5. Knighted, 1945. His only son, a Pilot Officer, RAF, was killed on active service in 1940.

[2] Churchill was determined not to let Lord Beaverbrook be maligned, in the interests of fair play and the smooth working of aircraft production. The previous letter on this dispute which I have included is on page 941.

represent to them something which they wholeheartedly support: the determination to win. For a year or two they will cheer me.' He pointed out that we were not yet a nation in arms: it took four years for a nation to reach its peak in war production; Germany had reached that maximum state, while we were only at the end of the second year of our effort.

Winston S. Churchill to General Ismay
(*Churchill papers, 20/13*)

24 October 1940

1. I should like to know what the Chiefs of the Staff advise on the details of this operation[1] before I leave for the country to-morrow. I certainly think it should be postponed till we can see more clearly what the action of Vichy is going to be. At present I am very anxious about it.

2. I see rumours in the papers that they may cede the use of their bases or some of them to Germany and Italy. If anything like this were to come from Vichy immediate action would have to be taken. Let the Joint Planning Committee set to work at once upon a plan to capture Dakar as an important and purely British operation. It might be possible to treat the expedition as one of the convoys to the Middle East continually passing round the Cape. I should think myself that a landing by fifty or sixty tanks out of range of the guns of the fortress would very quickly bring about a decision. It must be recognised as quite intolerable that Dakar should become a strong German U-boat base. Time is very precious, and the sooner a plan is made the better. We can go into ways and means after.

3. If Vichy goes wrong, Libreville will have to be cleaned up. We must be masters of the West African coast at any rate south of Casablanca. If it should fall into bad hands the entanglement of the Navy would be most serious.

WSC

Winston S. Churchill to General Ismay or Colonel Hollis
(*Churchill papers, 20/13*)

24 October 1940

The water in St James's Park and Buckingham Palace Garden is undoubtedly a guide to enemy aircraft. Yet I am told it must be kept there as security against fire. Surely it would be possible to camouflage it by spreading wires

[1] A planned assault on Vichy-held Libreville, French Equatorial Africa, by British and Gaullist forces. Libreville was occupied by the Free French (led by General Koenig) on 9 November 1940. Some twenty French soldiers were killed on both sides.

across and steel wool camouflage nets, or by some other method. If it did not cost too much it would be worth trying.

WSC

John Colville: recollection
(*Colville papers*)

24 October 1940

In the autumn of 1940 Mr Boissier[1] wrote to me at 10 Downing Street asking whether I could persuade the Prime Minister to visit Harrow. I enquired and received a curtly negative reply. Shortly afterwards Mr Amery, who was Secretary of State for India, also made an effort but with equal lack of success. Then Harrow was bombed and the Prime Minister, who had never spoken of the School except with dislike, volunteered the statement that it was courageous to remain on the Hill and not to emigrate to more peaceful pastures.

Several days later an important telegram arrived from President Roosevelt just before dinner.[2] I took it upstairs to the Prime Minister who was in his bath, with the door wide open, and singing 'St Joles' at the top of his voice. After reading the telegram (still in his bath) and giving instructions about it, he continued cheerfully with 'St Joles' and then proceeded to tell me what an inspiration the Harrow Songs had been to him throughout his life. Indeed, he said, he was immensely grateful to Harrow on two accounts: the Songs and the fact that he had been well taught the beauties of the English language. He added, as an afterthought, that if the boys would sing him the songs he liked best – and he must be allowed to choose – he would after all go down to Harrow, where they were showing such courage under bombardment, even though he had long ago resolved never to set foot in the place again.

I asked why he had so resolved and (still in the bath) he told me the following story. In 1910 or 1911, when party passions were aroused over Irish Home Rule and the Parliament Bill to a degree which seems almost incomprehensible now, Mr Churchill, a member of the Liberal Cabinet, was motoring not far from Harrow with his personal friend but political opponent, F. E. Smith.[3] It suddenly occurred to him to divert the car and take 'FE' to

[1] Arthur Paul Boissier, 1882–1953. A master of the Royal Naval College, Osborne, 1905–19; at Harrow from 1919. Head Master of Harrow, 1939–42. Director of Public Relations, Ministry of Fuel and Power, 1943–4.

[2] This was the telegram in which Roosevelt informed Churchill that he had warned the Vichy Government not to allow its fleet to be used against its former ally, Britain.

[3] Frederick Edwin Smith, 1872–1930. Known as 'FE'. Conservative MP, 1906–19. With Churchill, he founded the Other Club in 1911. Head of the Press Bureau, August 1914; resigned, October 1914. Lieutenant-Colonel, attached to the Indian Corps in France, 1914–15. Solicitor-General, May 1915. Knighted, 1915. Attorney-General, November 1915 to 1919. Created Baron Birkenhead, 1919. Lord Chancellor, 1920–2. Created Viscount, 1921. Created Earl, 1922. Secretary of State for India, 1924–8.

see his old School. When they arrived Bill was in progress and the boys waiting in the yard recognised Winston Churchill. They booed him as loud and long as they could, so that even Churchill, who was seldom disconcerted, felt ashamed and humiliated. Above all he felt angry at being so boorishly received in the presence of his friend, and he turned on his heel vowing never to have anything more to do with Harrow. He sent his son to Eton and for thirty years he thought of the School, if he thought of it at all, with distaste and contempt.

The bombs and the songs changed all this. On Wednesday, December 18, 1940, he returned to the Hill, the most respected and the most powerful man in England, accompanied by the Old Harrovians in the Government.

Winston S. Churchill to Lady D'Abernon[1]
(*Churchill papers, 2/393*)

25 October 1940
Private

My dear Helen,

Thank you so much for your letter. Personally I think there will be a considerable abatement during the winter, and presently we shall have better means of dealing with the nuisance. Of course bombs may fall by accident on gas and water anywhere, but I should have thought it would be more prudent, as well as more comfortable, to stay where you are.

Love to you and Edgar,

Yours affectionately,
W

John Colville: diary
(*Colville papers*)

25 October 1940

At 4.00 a.m. a box was brought to me containing two Most Immediate telegrams from Hoare in Madrid. The French Ambassador had told him that the Vichy Government would, at a meeting today at noon, decide whether to hand over Toulon, their ports and their fleet to Germany. Pétain and Weygand were against it; Darlan and Laval in favour. It was suggested that a telegram from the King or the PM to Pétain might turn the scales.

---

[1] Lady Helen Venetia Duncombe, daughter of the 1st Earl of Feversham. In 1890 she married Edgar Vincent, later 1st Viscount D'Abernon. From 1914 to 1918 she served as a nurse on the Western and Italian Fronts. Their country house was at Stoke D'Abernon in Surrey, their London home at 20 St James's Place (which had been badly damaged by bombs early in the Blitz). She had asked Churchill whether it would be safe for her to stay in Surrey.

I got back into bed determined to leave the telegram till the PM, who was sleeping the night in the tube at Down Street,[1] should awake at 7.00. But when I thought of the short interval allowed us I got up, seized the telephone, rang up Alec Cadogan, arranged that the American Embassy should send a message through their Chargé d'Affaires at Vichy[2], spoke to Lord Halifax and was generally cold and hectic until about 7.30.

The PM came back and got into bed at No. 10 to draft a message from the King. He told me that he 'had an instinct' this was going to happen and that was why he had sent a telegram to Sam Hoare for communication to the French Ambassador last week. Brendan confirmed that the PM had been very uneasy about the whole question for the last few days – and particularly last night.

An air-raid alarm drove us all into the shelter and an influx of many people from the half-ruined Treasury caused such a disturbance that the PM could hardly concentrate on his drafting. Moreover I was dressing in the inner shelter and he had to sit in the outer. The alarm passed and he went back to bed in his room, but a few minutes later the 'Jim Crow' sounded once more and we all went scurrying for safety. Such were the conditions in which this vitally important document, in a race against time, had to be composed. Meanwhile, on the PM's instructions, I had arranged for the telegrams to be cabled to Washington for transmission to the President who, it is hoped, may encourage Pétain and Weygand to resist. But the wretched old Marshal has had to have an interview with Hitler – who has also been seeing Franco[3] – and it is doubtful whether there is much he can do, especially as Darlan and the navy are fanatically Anglophobe.

In three days' time we were to have backed de Gaulle in an assault on Libreville. This will now have to be postponed or cancelled.

---

[1] 'Until the early 1930s there had been a station at Down Street, off Piccadilly. The London Transport Executive converted it into a comfortable, indeed luxurious, air-raid shelter' (John Colville, *The Fringes of Power*, page 276, footnote 1).

[2] Robert D. Murphy. On 10 March 1942 he signed the Murphy-Weygand Agreement, providing limited United States economic assistance for French North Africa. The agreement was initialled at Vichy. The agreement was a contributory factor to the success of the American landings in North Africa in November 1942.

[3] Francisco Franco Bahamonde, 1892–1975. Entered the Spanish Army, 1907. Second-in-Command of the Spanish Foreign Legion, 1920. During the Republican regime he served abroad, in the Balearic Islands, Morocco and the Canary Islands. One of the leaders of the Nationalist revolt, July 1936. Head of State, 1939. Sent Spanish volunteers to fight with Germany against Russia, June 1941.

Winston S. Churchill to Anthony Eden
(*Churchill papers, 20/13*)

26 October 1940

Surely something should be said to General de Gaulle apprising him of the course we have taken, and of the fact we have communicated with General Weygand, or tried to.[1] In view of our relations with de Gaulle, and engagements signed, he has a right to feel assured we are not throwing him over.

Will you give your directions to Major Morton, who with or without the aid of his Committee will draft something for de Gaulle for your approval.

I have spoken to the First Sea Lord, and neither at Libreville nor in the Straits will any forcible action be taken for the next few days, or without definite prior sanction from here. *Devonshire* and *Delhi* are, however, ostentatiously showing themselves off Libreville to prevent reinforcements from Dakar being sent thither. The Admiral knows we do not want an incident, and I have little doubt that should reinforcements be intercepted they will be turned back by peaceful persuasion. The remote chance of a collision must, I think, be accepted in this particular theatre, as it is the French who would be seeking to alter the *status quo*.

WSC

---

[1] On the previous day, 25 October 1940, Churchill and Lord Halifax had seen Professor Rougier, an emissary from Vichy, who had suggested to them the possibility of an 'agreement' between Churchill and Pétain, whereby Vichy would agree not to attack any French Colony that had declared itself for de Gaulle, while for his part de Gaulle, at Britain's urging, would not attack any French colony loyal to Vichy. Churchill warned Rougier, however, that under any such quid pro quo, if a colony were to rally to de Gaulle spontaneously, 'we could not disavow General de Gaulle.' Churchill also told Rougier that if Vichy would 'resist German threats and blandishments', and at the same time organise 'a sphere of resistance' to North Africa, Britain would 'certainly consider relaxing the blockade'. (*Foreign Office papers, 371/24361*). On 1 November 1940 Sir Samuel Hoare wrote to Lord Halifax: 'It is an excellent thing that you and Winston have seen Rougier in London and still more important if he now sees Weygand' (*Foreign Office papers, 800/323*). Professor Louis Rougier, a French Canadian, was Professor of Political Economy. He published an account of his discussions in Vichy and London in *Les Accords Pétain–Churchill*, Montreal 1945.

Winston S. Churchill to Colonel Jacob
(*Churchill papers, 20/13*)

26 October 1940

Let me have particulars of the cargoes lost in the ships sunk in the Halifax convoys last week, mentioning particularly any war material. Answer limited to ten lines.[1]

WSC

Winston S. Churchill to President Roosevelt
(*Premier papers, 3/468*)

26 October 1940

Your cable with terms of splendid warning you gave the French[2] crossed mine to you about a suggested message to Pétain. Most grateful for what you have already done, but everything still in balance. Foreign Office tell me they have cabled you our latest information of German terms, which Pétain is said to be resisting. In this connection the surrender of bases on the African shores for Air or U-boats would be just as bad as surrender of ships. In particular Atlantic bases in bad hands would be menace to you and a grievous embarrassment to us. I hope therefore you will make it clear to the French that your argument about ships applies also to the betrayal of bases.

In spite of the invasion threats and Air attacks of the last five months, we have maintained a continuous flow of reinforcements round the Cape to Middle East, as well as sending modern aircraft and major Units of the Fleet. I do not think the invasion danger is yet at an end, but we are now augmenting our Eastern transferences. The strain is very great in both theatres, and all contributions will be thankfully received.

[1] That week, the Allied weekly tonnage losses were 198,000 tons, the heaviest since the war began.
[2] In his reply to Churchill's telegram of 20 October 1940, Roosevelt said that he had seen the French Ambassador and told him that in the opinion of the United States Government, 'The fact that a Government is a prisoner-of-war of another power does not justify such a prisoner in serving its conqueror in operations against its former ally.' Roosevelt added that, in the light of the 'most solemn assurances' given by the Pétain Government to the United States that the French Fleet would not be surrendered, 'If the French government now permits the Germans to use the French Fleet in hostile operations against the British Fleet, such action would constitute a flagrant and deliberate breach of faith with the United States Government' (Telegram received on 24 October 1940).

Winston S. Churchill to Anthony Eden
(*Churchill papers, 20/14*)

26 October 1940

Before leaving,[1] you should consider searchingly with your Generals possibilities of forestalling offensive. I cannot form any opinion about it from here, but it would not be sound strategy to await the concentration and deployment of overwhelming forces if any other course was open. I thought their existing plans for repelling an attack by a defensive battle and counter-stroke very good, but what happens if the enemy do not venture until the Germans arrive in strength? Do not send any answer to this, but go into it thoroughly and discuss it on return.

Secondly, satisfy yourself that the present policy of our favouring Egypt not declaring war is right.

Thirdly, please examine in detail the field state of the Middle Eastern Army so as to secure the largest proportion of fighting men and fighting Units for the great numbers on our ration strength. Study improvisation from White[2] details for the Canal Zone and internal security. All British battalions should be mobile and capable of taking part in battle. I fear that the proportion of fighting compared to ration strength is worse in ME than anywhere else. Please do not be content with the stock answers. Even ASC and AOC[3] depots and other technical details can all help in keeping order where they are, and should be organized for emergency use. Not only the best, but the second and third best, must be made to play their part.

Fourth, let me know your future plans, post-dating all dates by a number of days, which I will cable separately. Rumours of your going to Turkey or Iraq do no harm.

John Martin: private letter
(*Martin papers*)

27 October 1940   Chequers

We have had fewer visitors than usual; but a particularly interesting couple over the weekend – Lord Halifax and Lord Lothian. Lothian is very ready to talk and gave us a long account of the reactions in America to our battle. He was Private Secretary to the Prime Minister in Lloyd George's days and was

---

[1] Eden was on his way to Khartoum on 26 October 1940. He returned to Cairo on 1 November.
[2] Cecil Meadows Frith White, 1897–1985. Royal Field Artillery, 1915. On active service, 1915–18 (Egypt, Serbia, Greece and Palestine: despatches). Transferred to the Royal Signals, 1925. Lieutenant-Colonel commanding the 4th Indian Divisional Signals in Wavell's advance in the Western Desert, 1940 (DSO). Chief Signals Officer, East Africa campaign, 1941; 8th Army, 1941–3 (CBE). Signals Officer-in-Chief, 21st Army Group, 1944–5 (rank of Major-General, CB).
[3] The Army Service Corps and the Army Ordnance Corps.

here when Chequers was handed over to the nation. Archie Sinclair and his wife[1] have also been here today. She is a very natural, downright sort of person, whom I liked very much. I was introduced this morning to young Winston, Randolph's son. He is absurdly like his grandfather; but, as one of the daughters said, 'so are all babies'. (Some one else said that every baby resembles either Churchill or Max Beaverbrook.)

The talk at dinner here is quite the best entertainment I know. I feel peeved that I haven't the sort of memory that could treasure up the PM's obiter dicta to chuckle over afterwards.

For the moment we continue to sleep at No. 10 and with a waning moon the night raids have been less intense. It is extraordinary how little attention is paid to the occasional daytime raids: people mostly go about in the streets as if nothing was happening.

Nelson[2] has been evacuated to Chequers under the evacuation scheme; but Treasury Bill (alias the Munich Mouser) still prowls about the ruins of his home.

Winston S. Churchill to Admiral Pound
(*Churchill papers, 20/13*)

27 October 1940

How many submarines have we had in the Mediterranean, and how many have we lost since Italy came into the war?

I am pained to see in to-day's reports the loss of two submarines mentioned.[3]

WSC

Winston S. Churchill to L. S. Amery and Lord Lloyd
(*Churchill papers, 20/13*)

27 October 1940

Your Minute of October 24.[4] When Mr Eden returns in the early part of November, the whole position must be reviewed in the light of his information. Meanwhile it is useless to write as if nothing were being done. Every single ship that can be found and escorted is carrying a ceaseless stream of reinforcements to the Middle East. Seventy-two thousand men have already

---

[1] The former Marigold Forbes, whom Sinclair married in 1918. She died in 1975.
[2] Churchill's cat.
[3] HMS *Rainbow* had been sunk on 19 October 1940 off Calabria by gunfire from an Italian submarine, and HMS *Triad* sank on 20 October, also off Calabria, cause unknown.
[4] About the need for greater reinforcements to the Middle East.

been sent out since August, and, in addition, 53,000 are under orders before December 30. I had further proposed that one Division a fortnight should be sent from December 1. I am advised, however, that a Division a month from January 1 will be the utmost that our shipping can manage. (The loss of the *Empress of Britain* is a serious blow.)[1] Apart from this, we have already sent more than half our scanty store of superior Tanks. The Air Staff and the COS Committee have agreed to a very large movement of aircraft to rearm the Middle East Squadrons. This has been going on for several months. The sending of further reinforcements must depend upon the view taken of the Air struggle here. We could, of course, give up the bombing of Germany this winter.

I regret very much the use of expressions like 'gamble' when applied to the necessary precautions for the life of this country against far superior Air forces.

I do not agree with your suggestions that at the present time we should make any further promises to Greece and Turkey. It is very easy to write in a sweeping manner when one does not have to take account of resources, transport, time and distance.

With regard to what you say about it being 'vital so to reinforce Wavell without delay so that he can counter-attack and annihilate the Italian forces both in East Africa and Libya before the winter is over,' I should be as glad as you to see this done. This, however, also depends on the factors I have mentioned above, and also upon the judgment of the Generals on the spot. Up to the present they have been very glad to hold their own against heavy odds.

WSC

Winston S. Churchill to President Roosevelt
(*Premier papers, 3/468*)

27 October 1940

We have not yet heard what Vichy has agreed to. If, however, they have betrayed warships and African and other Colonial harbours to Hitler, our already heavy task will be grievously aggravated. If Oran and Bizerta become German–Italian Air and Submarine bases, our hopes of stopping or impeding the reinforcement of the hostile army now attacking Egypt will be destroyed, and the heaviest forms of German-organised Italian attack must be expected. The situation in the Western Mediterranean will also be gravely worsened. If

---

[1] The 42,348-ton ocean liner *Empress of Britain* had been attacked by German aircraft on 26 October 1940 and set on fire. Two days later she was torpedoed and sank off the Atlantic coast of Ireland.

Dakar is betrayed, very great dangers will arise in the Atlantic unless we are able to rectify the position, which will not be easy. On the other hand, the announcement of the Vichy terms may lead to the much-desired revolt in the French Empire, which we should have to aid and foster with further drains upon our slowly expanding resources. Either way, therefore, immense exertions will be required from us in the Mediterranean during the next year. We are endeavouring to assemble a very large Army in the Middle East, and the movement of troops thither from all parts of the Empire, especially from the Mother country, has for some months past been unceasing. The campaign which will develop there certainly in the New Year, and which may involve Turkey and Greece, makes demands upon our shipping and munitions output and resources which are enormous and beyond our power without your help to supply to a degree which would ensure victory. All the time we have to provide for the defence of the Island against an invasion, which is fully mounted and for which 60 of the best German Divisions and superior Air Forces stand ready. Lastly, the U-boat and Air attack upon our only remaining life-line, the North-Western Approaches, will be repelled only by the strongest concentration of our flotillas. You will see, therefore, Mr President, how very great are our problems and dangers. We feel, however, confident of our ability, if we are given the necessary supplies, to carry the war to a successful conclusion, and anyhow we are going to try our best. You will, however, allow me to impress upon you the extreme urgency of accelerating the delivery of the programme of aircraft and other munitions which has already been laid before you by Layton and Purvis. So far as aircraft is concerned, would it be possible to speed up the deliveries of the existing orders so that the numbers coming to our support next year will be considerably increased? Furthermore, can the new orders for the expanded programme also be placed so promptly that deliveries may come out in the middle of 1941? The equipment of our Armies, both for Home Defence and Overseas, is progressing, but we depend upon American deliveries to complete our existing programme, which will certainly be delayed and impeded by the bombing of factories and the disturbance of work. A Memorandum on technical details is being furnished you through the proper channels, and having placed all the facts before you, I feel confident that everything humanly possible will be done. The World Cause is in your hands.

October 1940

Chief of Staff Committee: minutes
(*Cabinet papers, 79/7*)

28 October 1940
10 a.m.

The Prime Minister informed the Committee that news had come through of the bombing of Athens.

A discussion took place on the counter-measures which we could take, and the Committee agreed –
(a) That our bombers should attack towns in Northern Italy the same night.
(b) That the Chief of the Air Staff[1] should submit a plan to the Prime Minister the same evening for operating bombers from Malta (which had flown from United Kingdom) against Rome and other targets in Southern Italy.
(c) That the Admiralty should instruct the Commander-in-Chief, Mediterranean, to consider and report –
  (i) What he could do during the next few days to harass Metropolitan Italy.
  (ii) If he could station an AA cruiser at Piraeus.
  (iii) If he is ready to seize the French ships at Alexandria should the necessity arise.

Hugh Dalton: diary
(*'The Second World War Diary of Hugh Dalton'*)

28 October 1940
4.45 p.m.

Greenwood and I then go to see the PM in his boudoir in the Cabinet War Room just before the 5 p.m. Cabinet. He comes in looking rather tired and apologises for keeping us waiting, saying, 'I have just had my sleep.' He has not much focused the point at issue but says at once that we cannot make a new ministerial job for Surpluses.

I say that Leith-Ross[2] can take on this job quite well in addition to what he is now doing for me, as I have a good deal de-centralised the work of MEW.

[1] Air Marshal Sir Charles Portal, who had just succeeded Sir Cyril Newall.
[2] Frederick William Leith-Ross, 1887–1968. Entered the Treasury, 1909. Deputy Controller of Finance, 1925–32. Member of the Economic Committee of the League of Nations (sometime Chairman), 1932–9. Knighted, 1933. Chief Economic Adviser to the Government, 1932–46. Director-General, Ministry of Economic Warfare, 1939–42. Chairman of the Inter-Allied Post-war Requirements Committee, 1941–3. Deputy Director-General, United Nations Relief Agency (UNRRA), 1944–5. Governor of the National Bank of Egypt, 1946–51. Deputy Chairman, National Provincial Bank, 1951–66.

The PM says, 'Tell him that he can have some extra staff and an additional Private Secretary.'

Winston S. Churchill to Anthony Eden
(*Churchill papers, 20/14*)

29 October 1940

You will have seen the various Service telegrams about Crete. It seems of prime importance to hold a Naval fuelling base at Suda Bay and the best airfield possible. Successful defence of Crete is invaluable aid to defence of Egypt. Loss of Crete to Italians grievous aggravation all Mediterranean difficulties. So great a prize is worth the risk and almost equal to successful offensive in Libya. Pray examine whole problem with General Wavell and Smuts and do not hesitate to make proposals for action on large scale at expense of other sectors, at the same time asking for any further aid you require from here, including aircraft and anti-aircraft. We are studying how to meet your need. Think your return to Cairo indispensable.[1]

War Cabinet: Confidential Annex
(*Cabinet papers, 65/15*)

29 October 1940　　　　　　　　　　　　　　　　　Cabinet War Room
12 noon

The Prime Minister said that certain military measures in support of Greece were in preparation. It would be best at the present stage not to discuss these operations, but the War Cabinet ought to be under no illusion as to the extent of the assistance that we could give. We were severely limited by the size of our forces in the Middle Eastern theatre.

In view of the risk of invasion at home, it was remarkable that we had been able to reinforce the Middle East by some 72,000 troops. Another 53,000 troops ought to reach the Middle East by the end of 1940. From the beginning of 1941 onwards, he would like to see a further division despatched each month to the Middle East. The provision of escorts and shipping presented formidable difficulties in the achievement of this programme. The whole question was being thoroughly examined.

---

[1] Eden was then at British General Headquarters in Khartoum. In a second telegram that day, sent to GHQ Cairo, Churchill told Eden: 'We here are all convinced an effort should be made to establish ourselves in Crete and that risks should be run for this valuable prize' (*Churchill papers, 20/14*).

The reinforcement of our forces in the Middle East had also to be balanced with the strength of the forces which must be retained in this country.

Winston S. Churchill to Sir Archibald Sinclair and Sir Charles Portal
(*Premier papers, 3/488/1*)

29 October 1940

This paper makes it easy for anyone to understand exactly what we are doing and what we want. It would therefore be of particular value for the purposes of Air Commodore Slessor's mission, as the American Ministers concerned will be able to take it in quickly. The whole movement of the argument leads up to the conclusion that we need the 'planes from them to carry out a carefully worked out plan, and that we have very nicely adjusted the balance between the pilots and the machines. It may be that some alterations in numbers or phrasing are necessary, but it would be a great pity if the movement and sequence of this orderly argument were in any way deranged. I shall be very glad to go through the paper at 5 p.m. to-day at the Central War Room, in order to settle with you the final form which you think it should assume.

It would certainly be a good thing to add to the end something to show how deeply the expansion will rise after June 1941.

WSC

Winston S. Churchill to Lord Beaverbrook
(*Churchill papers, 20/13*)

29 October 1940

I am shocked to read of the conditions of insecurity under which the Post Office is now working, which might easily prove deeply detrimental to national safety. I feel quite sure you will agree that it would not be suitable for us to stand between them and the absolutely necessary new security which is coming within their reach.

I am very much interested in the tunnel[1] they speak of, as it would be in such close proximity to the strengthened War Room, and might be made to

---

[1] The Whitehall Tunnel, which ran from just north of Trafalgar Square to Parliament Square, part of the Post Office's underground system of communications.

give much better security. Personally, I think security is much better achieved at these deep levels than above ground. Meanwhile, I am quite all right where I am as a part-occupier and guest.

Thank you so much for all the trouble you have been taking. I am quite ashamed to be such a burden.

WSC

Defence Committee: minutes
(*Cabinet papers, 69/1*)

29 October 1940   10 Downing Street
5.30 p.m.

PERIODICAL STATEMENTS REQUIRED BY UNITED STATES ADMINISTRATION

In the subsequent discussion, Lord Beaverbrook emphatically protested against giving detailed information on every aspect of our operations to the Americans.

The Prime Minister said that he was inclined towards a stiffer attitude than we had recently adopted. He thought that we should only furnish the Americans with periodical general reports on the progress of our expansion schemes, but should not give detailed figures of the kind demanded. He did not think the matter could be settled then and there, and he requested the Secretary of State for Air to discuss the matter again with Lord Lothian, and to make recommendations.

Defence Committee: Confidential Annex
(*Cabinet papers, 69/1*)

29 October 1940   10 Downing Street
5.30 p.m.

The Prime Minister said that though he realised it might be possible to change certain of the figures shown in the calculations, he felt that the Paper as it stood contained clear arguments leading inevitably to the desired conclusions. These were first that we could make good use of all the aircraft which we expected to get in America, and, secondly, that we would produce all the pilots required to man them. He suggested that a paragraph might be inserted drawing attention to the fact that there were many additional skilled pilots instructing in the training schools, who, in an emergency, could be made available for the battle; but he thought it would be a pity to spoil the general run of the Paper, which he found very convincing.

King George VI to Winston S. Churchill
(*Churchill papers, 20/1*)

29 October 1940
Windsor Castle

My dear Prime Minister,

I enclose the list of names I promised you.[1] I will not do any more re the Admiralty except to tell R. Adl. W. E. C. Tate[2] that you have got them. I have not put Dickie Mountbatten's[3] name down on purpose, but he can be borne in mind. I am so sorry that everything nowadays is so worrying for you; there is not a bright spot anywhere. But I am sure something bright will turn up one day.

I am
Yours very sincerely
George R.I.

Winston S. Churchill to General Dill
(*Churchill papers, 20/13*)

30 October 1940

What steps are we taking to get news from the Greek front? Have we observers there? What is our Attaché there doing?

Why do you not send one of your Generals from Egypt at the head of a Military Mission to be at the headquarters of the Greek Field Army? Let them go and see the fighting and give us some close-up information about the relative merits of the two Armies. I expect to have a good wire every day or so, telling us exactly what is happening, as far as the Greeks will allow it.

WSC

---

[1] The officers in the King's list were, with their seniority, Captain R. R. McGrigor (1933), Captain L. E. H. Maund (1934), Captain C. H. L. Woodhouse, CB (1934), Captain G. E. Creasy, DSO (1935), Captain H. P. K. Oram (1936), Captain C. E. Lambe (1937), Captain M. M. Denny, CB (1936) and Captain G. C. P. Menzies (1938).

[2] William Eric Campbell Tate, 1886–1946. Commodore in charge of the Royal Naval Barracks, Portsmouth, 1937–9. Rear-Admiral, 1938. Vice-Admiral, 1941. Director of Personnel Services, Admiralty, 1941. Commander-in-Chief, South Atlantic Station, 1942–4. Admiral, 1945.

[3] Prince Louis Francis Albert Victor Nicholas of Battenberg, 1900–79. Second son of Prince Louis of Battenberg. A naval cadet, 1913–15. Midshipman, 1916. His father was created Marquess of Milford Haven, and assumed the surname Mountbatten in 1917. Commander, 1932. Naval Air Division, Admiralty, 1936. Captain, 1937. Commanded HMS *Kelly*, 1939 (despatches twice). Chief of Combined Operations, 1942–3. Supreme Allied Commander, South-East Asia, 1943–6. Created Viscount Mountbatten of Burma, 1946. Viceroy of India, 1947. Created Earl, 1947. Governor-General of India, 1947–8. First Sea Lord, 1955–9. Admiral of the Fleet, 1956. Chief of the Defence Staff, 1959–65. Murdered by Irish terrorists of the Irish Republican Army (IRA), 27 August 1979, at Mullaghmore in the Irish Republic. Also murdered in the same explosion were his daughter's mother-in-law (aged eighty-two), his grandson Nicholas (aged fourteen), and a seventeen-year-old boatman. On the same day, eighteen British soldiers were killed in a landmine explosion in County Down, Northern Ireland.

Winston S. Churchill to General Ismay
(*Churchill papers, 20/13*)

30 October 1940

There is no objection to two Battalions going to Freetown, pending their relief by the West African Brigade, after which they can go on to Egypt. They are not to leave England until it is agreed that the West African Brigade is to go to West Africa.

Both Crete and Malta come before Freetown in AA guns, and I cannot approve of this diversion at the present time. Neither can I agree to the diversion of a Fighter Squadron at this stage. The Navy is responsible for preventing any sea-borne expedition attacking our West African Colonies. As to the Air attack, if the French bomb Freetown or Bathurst, we will bomb Vichy. I do not think this will happen.

WSC

Defence Committee: Confidential Annex
(*Cabinet papers, 69/1*)

31 October 1940   Cabinet War Room
11 a.m.

REVIEW OF THE SITUATION

The Prime Minister said that he was not satisfied that Commanders-in-Chief were at present kept sufficiently in touch with the general political and strategical situation. Measures to remedy this were under consideration, and, in addition, he proposed to invite Commanders-in-Chief to meetings round the table in London about once a month.

The Prime Minister then gave a general review of the strategical position. The last five months had shown our ability to continue the war indefinitely. There seemed to be little possibility of any major offensive in 1940 or 1941, but by 1942, we should have overtaken the lag in munitions production. We had only had two years of production on a National scale and had not yet reached the peak, while Germany had been hard at it for four years. With the passage of time, we would progressively make up the leeway. With the United States to help us, we might possibly reach peak production at the end of the third year.

In the meanwhile, we had first to defend ourselves here. With the advance of the season, and owing to our resolute defence, the invasion danger had greatly diminished. The Germans appeared to have relinquished the idea for the time being, but there was evidence that they had not abandoned it. In any event, they would undoubtedly maintain the threat in order to keep as many forces as possible pinned down in Britain. There must always be sufficient forces retained in this country to deal with invasion, but, subject to that proviso, it was intended to send reinforcements overseas to the maximum extent within the limits of shipping. We had already sent 72,000 men to the Middle East; and 53,000 more would arrive from this country and from other parts of the Empire by the end of the year. More than half our best tanks had been sent to the Middle East, and in spite of the great air battles over this country, we were in process of firstly re-equipping and then increasing our air forces overseas.

During 1941 we could not expect to undertake decisive operations. Germany was the master of Europe, and the German Army could move where it pleased. They would have ample forces for simultaneous campaigns in Spain and against Turkey and Russia, and, at the same time, to help Italy with men and munitions. The Germans would inevitably turn their eyes to the Caspian and the prize of the Baku oil fields. In that event, Russia would have to fight, as without oil for her agriculture, her people would starve. If Turkey resisted, she might greatly delay the German advance to the Suez Canal; and we should therefore back her up with all that we could send.

We were aiming at a total of 55 divisions ready by the end of 1941, and, in addition, we had accepted an offer from the United States to supply the equipment for an additional 10 divisions. Twenty-five to 30 divisions would be in the Middle East, which we hoped to reinforce at a rate of one division per month, or faster, if shipping was available. The Italians were finding difficulties in their Libyan Campaign, and our Commanders in the Middle East felt confident.

Our air strength would be greatly increased in 1941. We hoped to add 100 squadrons by June, after which the rate of increase would rise very steeply. We must bomb Germany and Italy to the greatest possible extent.

The question might be asked 'How are we to win the war?' This question was frequently posed in the years 1914–1918, but not even those at the centre of things could have possibly given a reply as late as August of the last year of the war.[1]

For the moment, all that we could do was to bank on the pressure of the blockade accompanied by the remorseless bombing of Germany and Italy. By 1941, however, we would be in a position to take on medium operations of an amphibious nature; and by 1942, we should be able to deliver very heavy oversea attacks.

Our power of survival depended on the maintenance of the life of this island. This postulated continued superiority in air defence and, in particular,

---

[1] As late as 7 October 1918 (a month and four days before the armistice), Churchill still thought that the war would not end until the autumn of 1919, and was making his munitions plans, and tank and aircraft production schedules, accordingly.

the successful countering of night bombing. That we must keep our sea communications open went without saying. There had been a serious recrudescence of submarine warfare, and recent losses had been heavy.[1] The United States destroyers were coming in, however, and a welcome amount of new construction would be available before the end of the year. It had been decided to bring up the destroyer strength in the Western Approaches to 60 by the 15th November.

The use of naval and air bases in Eire would greatly simplify our problems, but it would be most unwise to coerce Ireland until the danger was mortal. The United States might help us there, however; and after the Presidential elections it might be possible to persuade the Americans to send warships to Eire.

DISPOSITIONS DURING THE WINTER MONTHS

It was generally agreed that, although lodgements on our coast could not develop into a successful invasion in the face of our effective fighter force and unimpaired sea power, invasion would become a practical possibility if we were to relax essential precautions.

Sir Hugh Dowding said that although we had been successful in defeating the German air attacks by day, we had only done so with a narrow margin and it would be dangerous to assume that we could repeat this success in the face of sustained and determined German attacks unless the fighter force, and training organisation behind it, were both expanded.

Sir Charles Portal said that, in the formation of new squadrons, preference would be given during the next few months to fighter squadrons in order that we should be ready to meet a renewal of the German onslaught in the Spring. New bomber squadrons would be formed with a view to full employment during the longer nights of Autumn 1941.

Sir John Dill said that if the full burden of withstanding the initial shock of invasion were to fall on the Army, it was doubtful whether we could afford the continued flow abroad of the best trained units. We still had only an amateur army with an average of three pre-war officers per infantry battalion. Shortage of technical equipment would prevent the early formation of new divisions in place of those sent overseas.

Sir Alan Brooke agreed that the likelihood of serious invasion during the winter months was considerably reduced, except in the South East corner of England. Two divisions would be kept forward in the Dover area and one division in Norfolk. The remainder would be withdrawn into mobile reserve for training and the beaches would be held by lower category troops. The

---

[1] In the previous fortnight forty-three British merchant ships had been sunk.

reduction in light naval craft and patrols would mean surrendering 'no-man's land' i.e. the Channel, to the enemy, but he was prepared to accept this, provided the most thorough air reconnaissance of the invasion ports was maintained whenever weather conditions permitted.

The Prime Minister said that he agreed with most of the points made during the discussion. The danger of invasion had been reduced by the successful outcome of the air battles and by the increases in the strength of the Army. The threat of air-borne attack had been reduced by the raising and arming of the Home Guard. The danger during the winter months would remain relatively remote provided that we maintained our vigilance, and did not permit over-confidence in the country. The march of events in South East Europe compelled us to accept the risk of sending reinforcements to the Middle East to the limit of shipping capacity.

Note of an Informal Meeting
(*Cabinet papers, 127/14*)

31 October 1940   Cabinet War Room
12.30 p.m.

1. GREECE

The Prime Minister referred to various telegrams which had been received from Sir Michael Palairet,[1] and particularly to No. 1019 of the 30/31st October 1940. He said that we were doing all that we could to help Greece and that it would be wrong and foolish to make them promises which we could not fulfil.

The Prime Minister then read out a draft of a telegram which he suggested might be sent to Sir Michael Palairet as from the Prime Minister and Minister of Defence.

The Foreign Secretary agreed generally with the terms of the draft, but suggested that it would not be right to discourage Sir Michael Palairet too much. He asked whether it would not be possible for us to put a few aeroplanes in Greece itself at once.

The Prime Minister said that the Chief of the Air Staff had this idea under active consideration. It was also intended to operate from Crete, but this

---

[1] Michael Palairet, 1882–1956. Entered the Diplomatic Service, 1905. Minister to Roumania, 1929–35; to Sweden, 1935–7; to Austria, 1937–8; to Greece, 1939–42. Knighted, 1938. Assistant Under-Secretary of State, Foreign Office, 1943–5.

depended upon whether there were any aerodromes in the island from which modern aircraft could operate.

It was agreed that the telegram drafted by the Prime Minister should be despatched to Athens, subject to any addition or modifications which the Foreign Secretary might wish to make in order that the telegram might not be too discouraging to Sir Michael Palairet.

2. RELATIONS WITH THE VICHY GOVERNMENT

The Prime Minister said that he was very disturbed by the terms of Pétain's announcement.[1] From our point of view it would have been much better if he had either definitely accepted the most humiliating terms from Germany – in which event the French people would have probably thrown out the Government – , or alternatively if he had definitely rejected Hitler's terms. As it was, the position was neither one thing nor the other, thanks to Laval's machinations, and we ourselves were getting the worst[2] of both worlds. The collaboration which Pétain mentioned might only be represented as political and economic, but it could not help leading to collaboration in the military sphere.

The Prime Minister drew attention to the recent full and weightily-argued telegram from General de Gaulle, who was anxious to press on with operations in West Africa. We, however, were reluctant to take part in them until we knew more clearly how we stood with Vichy. We could not wait indefinitely, and it was essential to clear this matter up as soon as possible. He suggested that we should send something straight and stiff to our Ambassador in Madrid to be passed on to the Vichy Government.

The Foreign Secretary agreed in principle. He thought, however, that it would be unwise to prejudice the approach which was being made to General Weygand. It would be difficult to say to the French 'Unless you desist from collaboration with the enemy, we will treat you as hostile'.

The Prime Minister agreed. We should, however, be perfectly in order in telling them that it was no use their protesting that they were not going to allow the Germans the use of their bases. What we required was positive proof that there would be no possibility of the Germans taking them for themselves.

---

[1] In a speech on 30 October 1940, six days after meeting Hitler at Montoire, Pétain spoke of the policy of collaboration as an honourable one, aimed at maintaining 'the unity of France'. In a secret agreement reached at his meeting with Hitler, Pétain agreed that 'The Axis Powers and France have an identical interest in seeing the defeat of England accomplished as soon as possible. Consequently, the French Government will support, to the limits of its ability, the measures which the Axis Powers may take to this end.' On 27 October 1940, three days after the Montoire meeting, de Gaulle issued his Brazzaville Declaration, establishing a Council for the Defence of the French Empire, the effective governing body of all French territory loyal to the Free French cause.

[2] A note in the minutes at this point states: 'i.e. no favourable reaction in France or the French Colonial Empire on account of the enormity of the terms, and no backing of de Gaulle'.

At the present time the French Government were making capital out of our resistance, and hoped to get terms which they could never have got if we had thrown in our hands at the same time as they did.

He added that we should make it clear in any communication that we might make to the Vichy Government that in the event of any act of hostility on their part we should immediately retaliate by bombing the seat of the Vichy Government, wherever it might be.

The Secretary of State for Foreign Affairs undertook to prepare a draft telegram to Sir Samuel Hoare on the lines of the discussion which had taken place.

3. TURKEY

The Prime Minister referred to telegram No. 1016 from Athens. He thought it essential to ask the Turks to undertake to neutralise Bulgaria.

The Secretary of State for Foreign Affairs said that this had already been done. He had had a satisfactory interview with the Turkish Ambassador[1] who had told him that Turkey was going to make her position vis-à-vis Bulgaria perfectly clear, and that there was to be a statement (albeit not a very satisfactory one) in the Turkish Parliament tomorrow. M. Aras had spoken in robust terms and had made it clear that the Turks would fight if attacked.

Winston S. Churchill to General Ismay
(*Churchill papers, 20/13*)

31 October 1940
ACTION THIS DAY

These telegrams are of the greatest importance, and although two parts are missing, must be considered at once by the COS Committee. I fear the prolonged delay in reaching clear-cut decisions at Vichy, either one way or the other, and the probability that a middle course will be followed, which will deny us every advantage from French territory, and give the Germans many and increasing footholds. Another instalment will come later. Yet meanwhile we are held back from action. I am sure a far sterner message should now be sent to Vichy. Otherwise we are going to have the worst of both worlds, i.e., no favourable reaction in the French Colonies because of the enormity of the Axis terms, and no backing of de Gaulle.

WSC

[1] Tewfik Rushdi Pasha Aras, 1883–1972. Born in Chanak. Educated in Smyrna, Skopje, Constantinople and Beirut. A gynaecologist. Elected to the First Turkish National Assembly, 1920. Minister of Health, 1923–5. Foreign Minister of Turkey, 1925–38. Turkish Ambassador to London, 1939–42.

Winston S. Churchill to Sir Charles Portal
(*Cabinet papers, 120/300*)

31 October 1940

As long as they understand what we have in mind this seems all right.[1] It is not quite clear that so far as our means allow and opportunity serves we wish to place our fullest effort upon Italy, and that the morale of the Italian population may for the time being be considered a military objective.

I should be much obliged if I could have clearer copies of papers like this. I find them very difficult to read in the blurred style.

WSC

Hugh Dalton: diary
(*'The Second World War Diary of Hugh Dalton'*)

31 October 1940

The PM, I thought, was looking much better and less weary than two days ago. He is very pleased at reports that German aircraft are turning back and disliking the accuracy of our barrage even when it has to shoot at them through the clouds. We are getting our cat's eyes, it seems.

I said that I was glad that we were turning the main weight of our bomber attacks on to Italy for the next week, and told him that we had produced a very good leaflet, as I thought, to drop with the bombs – 'the curse of Garibaldi'. I said I hoped we should get as far as Rome but succeed in missing the Pope.[2] PM said, 'I should like to tell the old man to get down into his shelter and stay there for a week.'

John Colville: diary
(*Colville papers*)

31 October 1940

The PM felt ill, was sick, and went off to Down Street where he had no dinner.[3]

---

[1] An Air Ministry directive, 'Bombing programme – Objectives in Germany and Italy'.

[2] Eugene Pacelli, 1876–1958. Born in Rome. Ordained Priest, 1899. Cardinal, 1935. Elected Pope (as Pius XII), 1939. His papal messages were published in seventeen volumes, but his papacy remains the object of controversy for those who accuse him of not having spoken out sufficiently against Nazi atrocities during the war.

[3] The nature of Churchill's illness was unclear. Two days later the doctor whom he had consulted, H. Beckett-Overy, wrote to him: 'I wanted you to take the castor oil for I felt it was an opportunity to clear out whatever was irritating you' (*Churchill papers, 2/319*).

Winston S. Churchill to Private Office
(*Peck papers*)

31 October 1940
ACTION THIS DAY

Private Office

Pray let six new offices be fitted for my use, in Selfridge's, Lambeth Palace, Stanmore, Tooting Bec, the Palladium, and Mile End Road. I will inform you at 6 each evening at which office I shall dine, work and sleep. Accommodation will be required for Mrs Churchill, two shorthand writers, three secretaries, and Nelson. There should be shelter for all, and a place for me to watch air raids from the roof.

This should be completed by Monday. There is to be no hammering during office hours, that is between 7 a.m. and 3 a.m.

WSC[1]

---

[1] Although the initials 'WSC' appear at the bottom of this minute, typed on embossed 10 Downing Street paper, with a red ACTION THIS DAY label attached, and typed on a Downing Street secretary's typewriter, it is in fact a spoof minute, written by John Peck, one of Churchill's Private Secretaries. Half a dozen such minutes were circulated to members of the Private Office. One of them, which caused much hilarity in the Private Office, was addressed (as if by Churchill) to John Colville, asked for a meeting to discuss Colville's improper keeping of a diary. For more than twenty-four hours, Colville was on tenterhooks, and considered consigning his diary to the flames, before the spoof was revealed to him.

November 1940

Winston S. Churchill to President Roosevelt
(*Churchill papers, 20/4*)

1 November 1940

My dear Mr President,

This is to introduce to you my friend, Sir Walter Citrine. He worked with me three years before the war in our effort to arouse all parties in the country to the need of rearmament against Germany. At the present time he fills a position in the Labour movement more important to the conduct of the war than many Ministerial offices. As he is a Member of the Privy Council, you can count in every way upon his responsibility and discretion. He has the root of the matter in him, and I most cordially commend him to your consideration.

Believe me,
Yours very sincerely,
Winston S. Churchill

War Cabinet: minutes
(*Cabinet papers, 65/10*)

1 November 1940　　　　　　　　　　　　　　　　　10 Downing Street
12 noon

The Secretary of State for Foreign Affairs invited attention to telegram No. 1393 from our Ambassador at Cairo, referring to the non-co-operative and at times obstructive part played by the Palace and King Farouk. The Ambassador asked whether, if the matter of the King of Egypt came suddenly to a head, he might assume that he and the Service Commanders had authority to handle it as, in their judgment, the situation demanded, even to the extent of getting rid of King Farouk, preferably by way of abdication.

The Prime Minister suggested that Sir Miles Lampson should make quite clear to King Farouk, on a suitable occasion, that if he adopted an attitude which made it impossible for him to continue as King of Egypt, the alternative would probably involve internment in some place well out of harm's way.

The Foreign Secretary said that Dr Negrin's[1] continued presence in this country lent support to the view that we were intriguing in Spanish politics and plotting the overthrow of the existing *régime*. This provided admirable material for German propaganda. Sir Samuel Hoare was constantly being asked by our well-wishers in Spain why we permitted Dr Negrin to stay here. The Spanish Government represented that he was indulging in political activities, but there was no evidence that this was so.

If the Germans marched into Spain, the real hope of Spanish resistance turned on the attitude of the army. The army leaders were unlikely to fight the Germans if they thought that we were intriguing with the revolutionaries in Spain.

The Prime Minister wished it to be on record that, in his view, by keeping Dr Negrin here in this country we imposed a further strain on this country. Nevertheless, having regard to the conflicting views put forward, and since it was not clearly established that Dr Negrin's continued residence here involved us in any mortal hurt, he thought that a compromise solution should be reached.

War Cabinet: Confidential Annex
(*Cabinet papers, 65/16*)

1 November 1940 10 Downing Street
12 noon

The Prime Minister thought that we could not allow either the *Jean Bart* or the *Richelieu* to enter the Mediterranean. These two vessels when completed would be perhaps the most powerful capital ships in the world. It was a greater risk than we could accept to allow them to proceed to ports under German control (in which he included Toulon and French North African

---

[1] Juan Negrin, Spanish Minister of Finance, September 1936 to February 1938. Prime Minister, May 1937 to February 1938. In exile in London, 1938–45. Hoped to return to power in 1945, believing (wrongly) that Franco's regime could not long survive the fall of Hitler. Resigned as Prime Minister in exile in the hope of uniting all the Spanish exiles. Died in exile in Mexico, 1956.

ports) where they could be completed and made ready for action against us. The addition of these vessels to the German Fleet would go far to alter the balance of strength at sea.

The First Sea Lord said that the *Jean Bart* might perhaps take a year to complete. Questions of high policy as well as Naval factors had to be taken into account in reaching a decision. So far as the Naval factors went, there were risks on both sides. On the one hand the risk of the two new French battleships being added to the German Fleet. On the other hand the more immediate risk that our action in forbidding them to enter the Mediterranean might land us in hostilities with France. In that event the whole French Fleet as it now stood (which, normally speaking, was in readiness for sea) would pass under the control of our enemies. A very considerable part of that Fleet was now in Mediterranean waters.

The Prime Minister said that we must not allow ourselves to become obsessed with the idea that we must never in any circumstances offer provocation to the Vichy Government. That obsession might bring great dangers in its train.

The Foreign Secretary said that we were conducting our relations with the Vichy Government in a kind of twilight, in which we had to balance opposing risks. Our present suspicion of Vichy and all its works was natural and justified. Yet we had to remember that competent and friendly advisers such as the Polish Chargé d'Affaires at Vichy[1] (whom he had recently seen) viewed the position rather differently.

John Colville: diary
(*Colville papers*)

1 November 1940

After the PM had had his afternoon sleep we left for Chequers. I travelled with him in his car and after a sticky beginning found him most affable. He was dressed in his RAF uniform and we stopped at Northolt to inspect the Hurricane Squadron, No. 615, of which he is Honorary Air Commodore. They had been up four times today and told us of their experiences in the Mess while we drank whisky and soda. When we continued our journey the PM talked about the Italians, whose impertinence in sending bombers to attack this country has much annoyed him. He said he intended to attack Rome before long, as soon as we had enough Wellingtons at Malta. Last night our bombers successfully attacked Naples from there and today the press, ignorant of the truth, is chortling about the magnificent 3,000 mile flight from England to Naples and back. I said to the PM that I hoped if we bombed Rome we should be careful to spare the Coliseum. The PM answered that it

[1] Stanislaw Zabiello. In December 1942 he was arrested by the Germans, but survived the war.

wouldn't hurt the Coliseum to have a few more bricks knocked off it and then, becoming pensive, quoted:

> While stands the Coliseum Rome shall stand,
> When falls the Coliseum Rome shall fall . . .[1]

We talked about the Public Schools and he said he wished he had learned Greek. He said he would go down to Harrow to hear School Songs if I would arrange it, and then he reverted to his lament about the almost entire failure of Eton, Harrow and Winchester to contribute pilots to the RAF. I repeated Lord Bessborough's[2] condemnation of the de Gaulle headquarters and the PM said that de Gaulle was definitely an embarrassment to us now in our dealings with Vichy and the French people. I also told him what Louis Greig[3] had said about Weizmann's[4] discovery of 120 per cent octane oil and he said that if I could show him that the oil interests really were opposing this for their own ends, he would soon put a stop to their machinations.

He gave it as his view, emphatically, that Roosevelt would win the election by a far greater majority than was supposed and he said he thought America would come into the war. He praised the instinctive intelligence of the British press in showing no sign of the eagerness with which we desired a Roosevelt victory. He said he quite understood the exasperation which so many English people feel with the American attitude of criticism combined with ineffective assistance; but we must be patient and we must conceal our irritation. (All this was punctuated with bursts of 'Under the spreading Chestnut Tree').

'I should now like,' said the PM as we neared Chequers, 'to have dinner – at Monte Carlo – and then go and gamble!' He proceeded to expound the pleasures of chemin de fer and the exultation he found in gambling on the Riviera.

Despite his excellent humour, the PM was still suffering slightly from the effects of yesterday's sickness and he went straight to bed.

---

[1] Byron, *Childe Harold's Pilgrimage*.

[2] Vere Brabazon Ponsonby, Viscount Duncannon, 1880–1956. Conservative MP, 1910 and 1913–20. On active service at Gallipoli, 1915, and on the Western Front, on the Staff, 1916–18. Succeeded his father as 9th Earl of Bessborough, 1920. Governor-General and Commander-in-Chief, Canada, 1931–5. His wife Roberte was the daughter of Baron de Neuflize, of Paris.

[3] Louis Greig, 1880–1953. Royal Marine Brigade, on active service in France, 1914. Surgeon Lieutenant-Commander, Dover Patrol. Royal Air Force, 1918 (Major). Gentleman Usher in Ordinary to King George V, 1924–36. Knighted, 1932. Personal Air Secretary to the Secretary of State for Air, Sir Archibald Sinclair, 1940–5.

[4] Chaim Weizmann, 1874–1952. Born in Russia, educated in Germany. Reader in Biochemistry, University of Manchester, 1906. Naturalised as a British subject, 1910. Director, Admiralty Laboratories, 1916–19. President of the World Zionist Organisation, and of the Jewish Agency for Palestine, 1921–31 and 1935–46. Chairman, Board of Governors, Hebrew University of Jerusalem, 1932–50. Adviser to the Ministry of Supply, London, 1939–45. First President of the State of Israel from 1949 until his death. His eldest son, Flight-Lieutenant Michael Weizmann, RAF, was killed in action in 1942.

Winston S. Churchill to Sir Charles Portal
(*Churchill papers, 20/13*)

1 November 1940

How is it that when we have 520 crews available for Bombing Operations, and only 507 aircraft similarly available, we do not draw on the ASUs, where a large number are awaiting use?

WSC

Winston S. Churchill to Sir Archibald Sinclair and Sir Charles Portal
(*Premier papers, 3/25/1*)

1 November 1940

I much regret that no attempt will be made to expand the Bomber Force on the lines indicated in my paragraphs 3 and 4.[1] I must ask for more consideration of this need. I am not at all convinced by the replies given in your minute. It is a scandal that so little use is made of the immense masses of material provided. The discharge of bombs on Germany is pitifully small.

WSC

Winston S. Churchill to Sir Charles Portal
(*Churchill papers, 20/13*)

1 November 1940

I have minuted on other papers[2] to-day my extreme regret that you do not see your way at all to meet my wish for an expansion of the Bomber Command. The first offensive object of the Royal Air Force is the delivery of bombs overseas, and particularly on Germany. It is the rising scale of delivery of bombs which must be taken as the measure of the success of our policy. It is deplorable that so few Bombers are available even on good nights. I have made various suggestions for increasing the Bomber Force. If, instead of simply turning all these down, you and the Secretary of State[3] recognised the need of increasing the bomb delivery, and set to work to contrive the means of doing so, it would be a very great help.

I beg you to let me have some further proposals of a constructive character.

WSC

[1] Churchill's minute of 20 October 1940 to Sir Archibald Sinclair and Sir Cyril Newall, of which paragraph 3 began, 'I am deeply concerned . . .'
[2] The previous minute.
[3] Sir Archibald Sinclair.

Winston S. Churchill to Sir Charles Portal
(*Cabinet papers, 120/300*)

1 November 1940

Our need is to increase the bomb-dropping tonnage upon Germany. This is at present lamentably small, and it constitutes a serious reproach to the organisation of the RAF that only such limited results can be shown for so much money and material. I wish I could persuade you to realize that there is a great failure in quantitative delivery: no one should be content with the present delivery.

WSC

Winston S. Churchill to General Dill and Sir James Grigg
(*Premier papers, 3/318*)

1 November 1940

Your minute of October (undated) does not answer any of my questions. I therefore specify them more exactly.

1. The estimate of requirements abroad was increased last July by 27,428 vehicles, to allow for the short supply of materials (e.g., drop stampings). (Ministry of Supply No. 279/40, ERC[1]). Why could not the necessary stampings and alloy steel be bought abroad rather than whole vehicles?

2. Why, when field force formations had vehicles with a capacity of 51,000 tons on July 31, should the battalions on the beaches only have one lorry each?

3. Deliveries from home production in September alone were 6,167 load carrying vehicles (capacity 13,823 tons). This represents the unit equipment of about eight Divisions. What happened to it? Why shall we get nothing at all from production in the next few months?

4. You specify the maximum provision for reserves as 20 per cent. But the central 'maintenance' reserve given to me is 25 per cent, additional to the reserves allocated to each unit, e.g., 13 per cent to a Division. You do not mention this.

5. I asked the Secretary to account for the 327,000 tons of load carrying vehicles required in addition to the equipment and reserves of 55 Divisions, namely, for lines of communication, independent brigades, &c. Subtracting the wastage specified by CIGS, namely, one-twelfth of the total order and a 'maintenance reserve' consisting of 20 per cent of Divisional equipment, also

---

[1] The Economic Research Council.

specified by CIGS, there remains 278,000 tons for lines of communication, &c. This is nearly three times the equipment and reserves of 55 Divisions.

I cannot consent to the placing of new orders abroad unless some attempt is made to answer simple inquiries about the facts.

WSC

Winston S. Churchill to General Ismay, for Sir Charles Portal
(*Churchill papers, 20/13*)

1 November 1940

I should propose to make immediate arrangements to send four additional Heavy Bomber Squadrons (including the one already sent to Malta) to the Middle East at once, and also four Hurricane Fighter Squadrons, or if preferred a Defiant in part. Let me see plans for this movement. I should like to have a report on this to-day.

WSC

Winston S. Churchill to General Ismay
(*Churchill papers, 20/13*)

1 November 1940

Mr Eden has asked for 10,000 rifles for the Middle East. Can we not supply these out of the American packet, or is there any small parcel of rifles anywhere in the world to be picked up?

WSC

Winston S. Churchill to Air Vice-Marshal Longmore[1]
(*Churchill papers, 20/14*)

1 November 1940

Your A. 474.[2] You have taken a very bold and wise decision. I hope to reinforce you as soon as possible.

---

[1] Arthur Murray Longmore, 1885–1970. Lieutenant-Commander, Royal Navy, on active service 1914–18, including the Battle of Jutland (despatches, DSO). Royal Air Force, 1919. Air Officer Commanding Coastal Command, 1933–6. Knighted, 1935. Air Officer Commanding-in-Chief, Training Command, 1939. Air Officer Commanding-in-Chief, Middle East, 1940–1. Inspector-General of the Royal Air Force, 1941. Retired list, 1942. One of his three sons was killed in action in 1943.

[2] Proposing the despatch of a Blenheim Mark I Squadron to Greece.

November 1940

John Colville: diary
(*Colville papers*)

2 November 1940   Chequers

The First Lord, the First Sea Lord and the CIGS came to lunch. Speaking of Vichy, and their recent negotiations with the Germans, the PM said, 'Owing to our unexpected resistance they have been able to market their treachery at a slightly higher rate than would otherwise have been possible.' He referred to them with loathing and said that while he could understand people being wicked he could not understand their being so contemptible. He now thinks the invasion is off, but that can only be because of our constant vigilance. If we relaxed that, invasion would be an imminent danger. But of course this meant our keeping great forces immobilised at home, and similarly the North African threat meant our concentrating all the rest we possessed in Egypt. Thus the Axis powers could keep our forces concentrated in one or two spots while they amused themselves elsewhere.

Nevertheless the PM is determined that all possible, by land, sea and air, shall be done for Greece and when, after a long post-prandial discussion, Dill drove away at tea-time the PM's last words were, 'Don't forget – the maximum possible for Greece.' Similarly in a minute this morning to the CAS[1] about sending air support to the Greeks, the PM wrote: 'Perhaps you will say that all I propose is impossible. If so, I shall be very sorry, because a great opportunity will have been missed, and we shall have to pay heavily hereafter for it. Please try your best.'

The German fighters can outfly ours, but their pilots are very timid. We have some new bombers on the way, Halifaxes, Manchesters and Stirlings which will be most destructive, and by the end of next year the PM hopes to be bombing 'every Hun corner' every night. Peirse tells me that the much-vaunted American 'Flying Fortresses' are obsolete and we have refused to take them. As regards bombing Rome, the PM said to Peirse, as he said to me yesterday, 'We must be careful not to bomb the Pope; he has a lot of influential friends!' After dinner the PM with great pride showed the young air-force officers[2] some of his albums of aircraft production; he is never happier than when displaying the spectacular strides that have been made since Beaverbrook and the new government came into power.

---

[1] The Chief of the Air Staff (Sir Charles Portal).
[2] The two pilots were Squadron Leader Kayll and Squadron Leader Gaynor.

Squadron-Leader J. R. Kayll[1]: recollection
(*Letter to the author, 31 July 1982*)

2 November 1940

We talked about the Hurricane aircraft and especially about the supply of bullet proof petrol tanks. These were causing great concern to pilots as one incendiary bullet in the main tank, which was just in front of the pilot, was usually fatal. As far as I can remember it was a few months after this that I was sent to RAF Farnborough to see a demonstration of a bullet proof petrol tank which shortly after was put into production.[2]

Winston S. Churchill to Anthony Eden
(*Churchill papers, 20/14*)

2 November 1940

Having received your AE 45 Cipher of 1st November which is being studied by COS Committee.[3] Greek situation must be held to dominate others now. We are well aware of our slender resources. Aid to Greece must be attentively studied lest whole Turkish position is lost through proof that England never tries to keep her guarantees. I invite you to stay in Cairo for at least another week while these questions are being studied and we make sure we have done our best from both ends. Meanwhile, another 30,000 men are reaching you by November 15 which must affect local situation in Egypt.

---

[1] Squadron Leader J. R. Kayll was awarded the DSO and DFC in 1940. On 6 July 1941 he was shot down over France, near St Omer, and taken as a prisoner of war to Germany. In late 1942, with some 300 other RAF prisoners of war, he was sent to a prisoner-of-war camp in German-occupied Poland. In 1945 he was liberated by the British Army at Lübeck, on the Baltic Sea.
[2] On 6 November 1940 Squadron Leader Kayll wrote to Churchill: 'I had hoped that before I wrote to thank you, we would have been able to add to our score, but we have had no luck. We chased two lots of 109s yesterday, but were unable to catch them unfortunately' (*Churchill papers, 2/395*).
[3] In his telegram to Churchill, Eden stressed that because of a shortage of aircraft in the Western Desert, the first line of defence for Crete was the British Mediterranean Fleet, that infantry reinforcements should be sent to the island, but that no further air support should be sent. Eden concluded: 'We cannot, from the Middle East resources, send sufficient air or land reinforcements to have any decisive influence upon course of fighting in Greece. To send such forces from here, or to divert reinforcements now on their way or approved, would imperil our whole position in the Middle East and jeopardize plans for offensive operations now being laid in more than one theatre' (*The Reckoning*, page 168).

Winston S. Churchill to Sir Archibald Sinclair and Sir Charles Portal
(*Cabinet papers, 120/300*)

2 November 1940

Yours of the 31st.[1] I do not dissent from the general principles and statements which your Minute contains. In view, however, of the consensus of opinion among authorities on German and Italian morale, it is felt that a temporary diversion should be made to less precise objectives, especially in the case of Italy. This diversion is in the nature of an experiment. We have seen what inconvenience the attack on the British civilian population has caused us, and there is no reason why the enemy should be freed from all such embarrassments. Unless the results are seen to be good within a comparatively short time, the emphasis should be thrown again on to the precise objectives.

WSC

Winston S. Churchill to Sir Charles Portal
(*Churchill papers, 20/13*)

2 November 1940

1. I had in mind that the four Bomber Squadrons would fly to Crete or Greece via Malta. The personnel and ground stores would have to be carried through by cruiser. It is essential to have these Squadrons operating at the earliest from bases in Greek territory upon the Italian Fleet at Taranto, and generally against Southern Italy. For so vital an operation of war the Navy would have to make special exertions, and you should not assume that a ship will not be forthcoming. At any rate for such ground personnel, stores, &c., that are necessary to come into action at this very critical time. I see more difficulty in the vehicles, but perhaps some could come from Egypt, and the rest be improvised.

2. The Fighters are, of course, more difficult, but I should hope that they could fly from a carrier to Malta, as was done last time. If necessary, the *Furious* would have to help the *Ark Royal*. Could they fly from Malta to an aerodrome in Greece? If not, could they fly on to a carrier to refuel, and thence to Greece? In the case of the fighters the same arrangements would have to be made about stores, ground personnel, &c., as with the bombers.

3. I am interested to see your plans for the reinforcement of Egypt by

---

[1] Protesting at the diversion of bombing resources from Germany to Italy.

February 1, and I see no reason why this should not go forward quite independently of the emergency action required to aid Greece. I was a little distressed to see you describe as my proposal a movement which will not be effective till February 1. I am not at this moment at all interested in any such proposal of packing up aeroplanes in crates and sending them to Egypt round the Cape, though this may go forward in the ordinary way.

4. Perhaps you will say that all I propose is impossible. If so, I shall be very sorry, because a great opportunity will have been missed, and we shall have to pay heavily hereafter for it. Please try your best.

WSC

Winston S. Churchill to Admiral Pound
(*Churchill papers, 20/13*)

2 November 1940

DUMMY SHIPS

INFORMATION OBTAINED FROM A GERMAN PRISONER

The German Staff may know we are using dummies in particular harbours, but if the berths are shifted from time to time, enemy aircraft attacking will not know which is which, and their attack will consequently be dispersed. Thus there is some usefulness in our plan after all.

WSC

Winston S. Churchill to Admiral Pound
(*Churchill papers, 20/13*)

2 November 1940

When I went to the Admiralty in September 1939, I soon felt that I could not give proper attention to the Fleet Air Arm. I found my hands quite full with the Navy. I could not spare the time and energy to master the highly-specialised technique of what is virtually another Air Force, with some additional complications. I therefore obtained from the then Prime Minister permission to invite Colonel Moore-Brabazon, or alternatively Lord Lloyd, to undertake the specialised supervision of the Fleet Air Arm under my general directions. However, this scheme fell through, as Moore-Brabazon declined, and the Prime Minister changed his mind about Lord Lloyd. I therefore did the best I could in the circumstances. My experience, however, leads me to suggest to you something of the same sort.

The Fleet Air Arm is not expanding properly, either in men or machines. The figures of the training and personnel have not moved appreciably in the last six months. I suggest to you that you should let Lord Beaverbrook help you in this matter. He is quite ready to serve under your general direction for this purpose. He will, I have no doubt, be able to procure very rapidly a large number of pilots and machines, and to expand rapidly the number of your Shore Based Squadrons which work in conjunction with the Coastal Command. It would be quite impossible for the Admiralty to aspire to the Coastal Command, while their own expansion has been so very feeble. It would be far better to show drive and capacity, and thus have a case on merits for any further acquisitions.

No formal change appears necessary at the moment. It would be sufficient if you directed that all papers affecting the Fleet Air Arm pass to you through Lord Beaverbrook. You will find he will get a move on as no one else can.

Pray let me know your views, and if you think well, by all means talk it over with Beaverbrook first.

WSC

Winston S. Churchill to A. V. Alexander and Admiral Pound
(*Churchill papers, 20/13*)

2 November 1940

After the defection of France it was considered vital not to allow the *Jean Bart* and the *Richelieu* to fall into enemy hands, or to reach harbours where they could be completed. For this purpose you attacked the *Richelieu* and claimed to have disabled her to a very large extent. The *Jean Bart* is in an unfinished state, and neither ship can be fitted for action in the African harbours on the Atlantic, where they now lie. It is our decided policy not to allow these ships to pass into bad hands. I was, therefore, surprised to hear the First Sea Lord demur to the idea that the *Jean Bart* should be prevented from returning to Toulon, and argue in the sense that she might safely be allowed to do so. Toulon has always been judged by us to be an enemy-controlled harbour. It was for this reason that the most extreme efforts were made, unhappily without success, to prevent the *Strasbourg* reaching Toulon. I cannot reconcile this action with the apparent readiness to allow the *Jean Bart* to proceed there.

The Admiralty is held responsible for preventing the return of either of these two ships to French ports on the Atlantic, or to the Mediterranean, where they could be repaired and completed at Toulon, and then at any time betrayed to the Germans or captured by them.

WSC

Winston S. Churchill to Lord Halifax
(*Churchill papers, 20/13*)

2 November 1940

I do not know how imminent the movement of this ship[1] may be. I have informed the Admiralty that they are responsible for stopping her from entering the Mediterranean. It would seem, therefore, very important that you should give a clear warning to Vichy that the ship in question will be stopped, and if necessary sunk, if she attempts to go either to a German-controlled port in the Atlantic, or to a Mediterranean port which may at any time fall into German hands. My Private Office in London is sending you a copy of the Minute I have sent to the First Lord and the First Sea Lord.

WSC

Winston S. Churchill to Anthony Eden
(*Churchill papers, 20/14*)

3 November 1940

Do not return till you have received my telegram and considered it with your advisers in all its bearings. When I receive your answer I will consult Cabinet about your returning. It would be most unfortunate if at this juncture action were to be paralysed here and in Egypt by your being in transit. I do not understand why you cannot telegraph essential points you have in mind. The first decisions must be made now before you can possibly get back, and I wish to have your assistance in them on the spot.

---

[1] The *Jean Bart*.

Winston S. Churchill to Sir Edward Bridges and General Ismay
(*Churchill papers, 20/13*)

3 November 1940

What is the use of circulating a paper[1] like this to the Cabinet before it has been considered by the Defence Committee, or even been considered by me? What could the Cabinet do with the paper except to take note of it? The Members of the Cabinet must be advised by me and by the Defence Committee, and this is only possible after a preliminary discussion.

I appoint Tuesday, 5 p.m., for a meeting at the CWR of the Defence Committee.

Meanwhile take it off the Agenda for to-morrow's Cabinet.

WSC

Winston S. Churchill to Lord Elgin[2]
(*Churchill papers, 20/2*)

3 November 1940

Dear Lord Elgin,

I am sorry that you should have had the impression that when I went to Fife the other day some discourtesy was shown to you, as Lord Lieutenant of the County, in not informing you of my visit. I can assure you that nothing was further from my thoughts. The position of the Lord Lieutenant as His Majesty's representative in the County is one that should always be regarded with respect, but on this occasion my visit was solely to Naval and Military Establishments in the neighbourhood, and was of an entirely unofficial nature. I hope therefore that you will accept my assurance that no slight was intended either to you personally or to the Office of Lord Lieutenant.

Yours vy sincerely,
Winston S. Churchill

[1] War Cabinet Paper 431 of 1940, 'Possibility of Enemy Advance through the Balkans and Syria'. Enigma indications had shown a build-up of German Air Force facilities in Roumania and Bulgaria, on the Danube and the Black Sea.

[2] Edward James Bruce, 1881–1968. Succeeded his father as 10th Earl of Elgin in 1917. Landowner. Chairman of the Educational Endowments Commission, Scotland, 1926–36. Lord Lieutenant of Fife, 1935–65. Zone Adviser, Home Guard, 1940–6. President of the National Trust for Scotland, and of the Scottish Council (for Development and Industry). Churchill had been Under-Secretary of State at the Colonial Office while Elgin's father was Secretary of State, 1905–8.

John Colville: diary
(Colville papers)

3 November 1940   Chequers

The PM was upset by a broadcast made by the First Lord (A. V. Alexander) giving an extravagant picture of what we were doing, and would do, for Greece. 'Such a nice fellow – but, really . . .' he said. Of course the press have blazoned his remarks across their front pages and false hopes will be raised.

Then a telegram came from Eden saying he must return in order to discuss the position with the PM. I took it up to his bedroom, written in pencil, and waited while he drafted a reply telling Eden to wait till he had seen the PM's latest telegram – which the Chiefs of Staff are sending off this morning. He lay there in his four-post bed with its flowery chintz hangings, his bed-table by his side. Mrs Hill sat patiently opposite while he chewed his cigar, drank frequent sips of iced soda-water, fidgeted his toes beneath the bedclothes and muttered stertorously under his breath what he contemplated saying. To watch him compose some telegram or minute for dictation is to make one feel that one is present at the birth of a child, so tense is his expression, so restless his turnings from side to side, so curious the noises he emits under his breath. Then comes out some masterly sentence and finally with a 'Gimme' he takes the sheet of typewritten paper and initials it or alters it with his fountain-pen, which he holds most awkwardly halfway up the holder.

A note arrived from Lord Beaverbrook, announcing his resignation because of asthma (actually he is cross with the Air Ministry and piqued because the PM has thrown some cold water on his grandiose scheme for making Faraday House[1] the seat and centre of Government – thus upsetting all the Post Office arrangements). The PM smiled wryly when I gave him the note, knowing that Lord Beaverbrook resigns every few days; and then he rang him up and said if he did so there would be a public outcry, it would be called desertion, and anyhow why couldn't he just take a fortnight's or a month's holiday.

Lunch was a quiet meal: the family, myself and a Coldstream officer called Waddilove.[2] We listened to a Winstonian dissertation on Sadowa[3] and Austria and Bismarck. Waddilove said that Bismarck was the last German

[1] Post Office headquarters, in Queen Victoria Street, London E.C.4, a block of three substantial buildings completed in 1934. In 1942 a fourth building was added, Citadel Exchange, housing the central telephone exchange.

[2] Douglas Edwin Waddilove, 1918–76. Interrupted his university education to serve in the Coldstream Guards, 1940–5 (Egypt, North Africa, raiding forces Aegean Sea; despatches, MBE). Called to the Bar, 1947. A Circuit Judge from 1973 until his death.

[3] The Battle of Sadowa, 3 July 1866, in which the Prussian army under General Helmut von Moltke defeated the Austrians north-west of the Bohemian town of Königgrätz (by which name the battle is also known). As a result of the Prussian victory, Austria was excluded from the emerging Prussian-dominated Germany.

who knew where to stop; the PM said he would show these present Germans where they were to stop – in the grave.

After lunch I played backgammon with Mrs Churchill while the PM thought out the speech he is to make in the House on Tuesday to the accompaniment of Strauss waltzes on Mary's gramophone. Having received sufficient inspiration he went into the Hawtrey room to dictate the speech to Mrs Hill.

The PM is highly delighted by the Italian admission of their casualties in Africa which are more than ten times as great as ours. He says that 'the Italians are easier to kill than to catch'.

After dinner, before leaving the dining-room, projects for capturing Pantellaria ('by 300 determined men, with blackened faces, knives between their teeth and revolvers under their tails', as the PM envisaged the operation)[1] and Rhodes were discussed. The Pantellaria scheme could be left to Sir R. Keyes and his commandos.

Winston S. Churchill to General Wavell
(*Churchill papers, 20/14*)

3 November 1940

Gravity and consequence of Greek situation compels your presence in Cairo. However unjust it may be collapse of Greece without any effort by us will have deadly effect on Turkey and on future of war. Greeks probably as good as Italians and Germans not yet on the spot. Establishment of fuelling base and airfield in Crete to be steadily developed into permanent war fortresses indispensable. This is being done. But surely effort must be made aid Greece directly even if only with token forces. Quite understand how everyone with you fixed on idea of set-piece battle Mersa Matruh. For that very reason unlikely it will occur. Enemy will await completion pipe-line and development of larger forces than are now concentrated. Your difficulties in attacking across the desert obvious, but if you have no major offensive of your own in Libya possible during next two months then you should run risks to stimulate Greek resistance. Over 70,000 men sent to Middle East Command since June and 30,000 reaching you before November 15. 53,000 by end of the year. Armoured regiments have started in big convoy yesterday.[2] Cannot,

---

[1] Operation 'Workshop'.
[2] Churchill was determined to provide Wavell with sufficient reinforcements for an offensive, which was in fact able to begin on 9 December 1940, six months to the day after the Italian declaration of war. At that moment the Italian Commander-in-Chief, Marshal Graziani, was on the verge of launching his own further offensive towards Alexandria when Wavell gave the order for attack. Within a week, the Italians were driven from Egypt, and 40,000 British prisoners of war had been released from captivity.

therefore, believe that various minor offensives of which you speak, plus major defence at Mersa Matruh, will outvalue need of effective action in Greece. No one will thank us for sitting tight in Egypt with ever-growing forces while Greek situation and all that hangs on it is cast away. Loss of Athens far greater injury than Kenya and Khartoum, but no necessity for such a price to be paid. Read carefully Palairet's telegrams. New emergencies must be met in war as they come and local views must not subjugate main issue. No one expected Italy so late in the year would attack Greece. Greece resisting vigorously with reasonable aid from Egypt and England might check invaders. I am trying to send substantial bomber and fighter reinforcements to Crete and Greece, flying from England, with stores by cruiser. If this proves feasible details will be cabled to-morrow or Monday. Trust you will grasp situation firmly, abandoning negative and passive policies and seizing opportunity which has come into our hands. Safety first is the road to ruin in war, even if you had the safety which you have not. Send me your proposals earliest or say you have none to make.

Winston S. Churchill to General Wavell
(*Churchill papers, 20/14*)

3 November 1940

Your request for additional convoy end November has been carefully examined, but regret it is not possible. Moreover, as you know, any additional demands for shipping inevitably upset regular flow of convoys, which is most economical way of using available ships.

In view of departure from home of complete 2nd Armd. Div. it may be difficult to release balance of 'I' tank battalion, but in any case it cannot be sent till December convoy. Modified Brigade Recovery Section for 'I' tanks being prepared for despatch in WS 5.[1]

Two cruiser regiments of 2 Armd. Div. are now to go round Cape. As you say saving of time in light of naval considerations would be too small to warrant risk of passing through Mediterranean.

I am arranging for complete lists of equipment shipped in each convoy to be telegraphed as soon as loading is completed.

---

[1] Convoys of the WS series (together with a numerical suffix) took troops and equipment from Britain to the Middle East via the Cape of Good Hope, the Red Sea and Suez. This convoy route was inaugurated in June 1940 and ended in August 1943.

John Colville: diary
(*Colville papers*)

4 November 1940

The PM is much impressed by the slackening of air attacks and says it is not all due to the weather. The Germans have to continue them in order to try and hide their defeat, but evidently they do not like the reception they get or the retaliation on Berlin.[1]

Defence Committee (Supply): minutes
(*Cabinet papers, 70/1*)

4 November 1940   10 Downing Street
11.45 a.m.

TANK PRODUCTION

The Prime Minister said he was extremely concerned to find so great a failure in the realisation of the tank programme as revealed by the following figures, which were for Infantry and Cruiser Tanks added together:–

	June forecast 'Target'	August forecast 'Reasonable Expectation'	Actual Production
August	167	157	143
September	194	135	116
October	222	160	127

The Prime Minister enquired why a change from the Mark IV to the Mark V and VI had been undertaken at a time when we were so short of tanks in the Army. It was this continual introduction of fresh ideas into established programmes which was one of the main causes for our present deplorable situation.

Mr Burton[2] said that there was not sufficient capacity to produce further quantities of the engine installed in the Mark IV, and it had therefore been necessary to change. The main point, however, was that the Mark IV had been found to have insufficient armour for modern war. It had been thought that the design of the Mark VI would be very similar to the Mark IV, and

---

[1] In the previous two weeks, Berlin had been bombed on the nights of 20/21 October, 23/24 October, 26/27 October (to attack a power station), 29/30 October (but because of bad weather only four bombers reached the city), and 1/2 November.

[2] Geoffrey Duke Burton, 1893–1954. On active service with the Royal Engineers, Gallipoli and Palestine, 1915–18 (despatches twice). Managing Director, Birmingham Small Arms Company, 1933–44. Director-General of Mechanical Equipment (Tanks and Transport), Ministry of Supply, 1940–5. Knighted, 1942.

would therefore not have many teething troubles, but this had not proved to be so.

The Prime Minister said that there were three general requirements of tanks. The first for operations in distant countries like the Middle East, and second for possible future expeditionary forces, and the third for the defence of this country against invasion. A less mobile and less efficient machine could be accepted for the third category, and this should be borne in mind in deciding how to deal with relatively unsatisfactory products.

Sir Andrew Duncan said that he would bear this distinction in mind. He hoped that by the end of March a good deal of the time lost on the Cruiser Tank programme would have been regained, but he was quite unable to give any definite figures of production for Marks V and VI at present.

The Prime Minister said that he was shocked to hear that there would be so great a deficiency in tank production by the end of March, 1941, in comparison with the forecasts which had been given. He thought that the War Office should have been informed at once that there was to be this failure, as it would gravely affect their plans for raising Armoured Divisions. He enquired what were the figures which the War Office were now working on.[1]

The Prime Minister said that he was absolutely opposed to any alterations or modifications of design for any of the tanks now being produced. We had suffered too much in the past from continual changes of ideas, and attempts to achieve perfection. Everything should now be concentrated on getting the maximum production of approved types. He would like to meet again in a fortnight's time, and hear further about the tests of the Mark V and Mark VI Cruiser Tank, and the progress of the pilot model of the A22.

War Cabinet: Confidential Annex
(*Cabinet papers, 65/16*)

4 November 1940   10 Downing Street
5 p.m.

The Secretary of State for Foreign Affairs said that the Greek Minister[2] had been to see him that morning, and had made three requests. First, for aircraft, AA guns, anti-tank guns and rifles. Secondly, that we should,

[1] The minutes then noted that there 'was some discussion on this point', after which Churchill was told that the forecast made in August of 1,089 Cruiser tanks by March 1941 had fallen to 739 (because of the nil production of the 350 planned A22 Tanks), and the forecast of Infantry tanks had fallen from 282 to 167 (a total fall of 465 out of 1,371).

[2] Charalambos Simopoulos, 1874–1942. Educated in Greece, France and Germany. Greek Chargé d'Affaires in London, 1917–19. High Commissioner for Greece in Constantinople, 1922. Minister in Washington, 1924–25; in London from 1935 until his death. Under-Secretary of State for Foreign Affairs, Greek Government-in-exile, London, 1941–2.

through our Representative in Washington, give our support to requests the Greek Government would be making to the United States for the delivery of certain armaments. Thirdly, that we should allow the Greeks to use the machinery of our British Purchasing Commission in the United States for the purchase of arms.

The Foreign Secretary said that he had promised the Minister an answer as soon as possible.

The Prime Minister said that over the week-end he had been in consultation with the Chiefs of Staff over the military assistance which we could send to Greece. It had been decided to take certain steps, and action, which would take some time to carry out, was in train. This action could, of course, be cancelled if the War Cabinet did not agree with the decisions reached.

Looking at the matter from the military point of view, it was of the utmost importance to help Greece to resist the Italian attack. The Greeks were now mobilising 14 Divisions, and there was a reasonable prospect that a Greek front against Italy could be built up. Strategically, he thought that the loss of Athens would be as serious a blow to us as the loss of Khartoum, and a more irreparable one. If the Italians secured the Greek islands they would be in a position to dominate the Black Sea approaches with their air force, and to interfere more effectively with our shipping in the Mediterranean.

Our public opinion was most anxious for British intervention in Greece. If Greece was overwhelmed, it would be said that in spite of our guarantee we had allowed one more small ally to be swallowed up. We could answer such criticisms by pointing out that the guarantee had been a joint Anglo-French guarantee, and that the plans for implementing it had been in the hands of General Weygand. But no answer would really help if another small ally was overwhelmed.

The Prime Minister then read to the War Cabinet:–
(a) A telegram which he had sent to the Secretary of State for War, now in Cairo.
(b) A telegram which the Chiefs of Staff had sent to the Commanders-in-Chief, in the Middle East.

The substance of these telegrams was that it was only in the air that we were in a position to render sufficiently speedy assistance to Greece. It was impossible for anything from the United Kingdom to arrive in time, and the only course was to draw upon our resources in Egypt and to replace them from home as quickly as possible. The Air Officer Commanding-in-Chief, Middle East,[1] had already sent to Greece a composite squadron of Blenheims, consisting of nine Blenheim fighters and six Blenheim bombers. They had arrived on the previous day. His directive to the British authorities in the Middle East was that three more squadrons (one Gladiator and two

[1] Air Vice-Marshal Longmore.

Blenheims) were to be sent from the Middle East to Greece as soon as properly defended aerodromes were ready to receive them. Our immediate air reinforcements to Greece would thus amount to 4 squadrons in all. These would be followed by a second Gladiator squadron, as soon as the arrival of Hurricane reinforcements in Egypt made this possible.

The necessary ground staff and anti-aircraft guns would be sent to Greece and installed before any further squadrons were sent (over and above the composite squadron of Blenheims already despatched). At the best it would be a week or ten days (according to the availability of guns and shipping) before these were in position.

In addition to air operations from Greece, it was intended to increase the weight of attack from Malta by bringing the number of Wellingtons temporarily operating from there up to 24.

If necessary, a second British battalion was to be sent to Crete; one battalion had already arrived there. We should endeavour as rapidly as possible to establish a Naval base in Crete. Orders were being given for the despatch of the necessary anti-aircraft guns, boom defences, etc.

The Prime Minister made the following additional points:–
  (i) We could not foretell how the Italians would react to these moves. It was obviously essential to keep as secret as possible the strength and the origin of our reinforcements. Nevertheless, the Italian Intelligence Service would obtain at any rate part of the facts and this might decide the Italian Commander in Libya[1] to press his attack on the Western Desert Front.
  (ii) The British authorities in Egypt thought that we should not send more air reinforcements than the one composite Blenheim squadron. The Secretary of State for War endorsed this view. There had been no time to bring the Secretary of State home for consultation. Nevertheless, it was certain that the turn which events had taken made it necessary to accept a risk in the Middle East. That risk was of a temporary nature only, since large air reinforcements, which would more than make good the gap, were on the way to Egypt by various routes. These would include 34 Hurricanes which would be embarked at once in HMS *Furious*, disembarked at Takoradi, and flown onwards. The first of these Hurricanes should arrive in Egypt by about the 2nd December.
  (iii) The air was already our weakest point in Egypt. The decision now

---

[1] Marshal Graziani.

November 1940

taken would for the time being reduce by half our air strength in that country.

(iv) The idea of despatching to Greece a larger air contingent consisting of four squadrons of Hurricanes and four squadrons of Wellingtons had been considered and rejected. There was no prospect of improvising aerodromes to operate so many squadrons.

(v) We could not hope to preserve the Turkish Alliance if our reinforcements to Greece were on a smaller scale than now proposed.

The following were the main points made in discussion:–

(a) The Foreign Secretary welcomed the decisions taken by the Prime Minister. To have sent no help to Greece would have undermined the will to resist of the other Balkan countries.

(b) In reply to a question, the Chief of the Air Staff said that it would be possible to evacuate from Greece the aircraft now to be sent there if that course were later decided upon. But in that case the ground staff and ancillary Services would probably be left behind.

(c) In view of the dangers of leakage, we had not yet told the Greek Government what assistance we were sending to them. The difficulty was to find a way of heartening the Greeks, without disclosing our weakness in the Middle East. The King of Greece[1] and General Metaxas,[2] should be told in strict confidence the number of squadrons we were sending.

(d) Since our forces in the Middle East consisted largely of Dominion troops, it was essential that the Dominion Governments should be told, in strict confidence, of our decision and of the fact that we were making good with the utmost speed the resultant gap in the air defences of Egypt.

(e) There was no possibility whatever of providing, either from this country or from the United States, the munitions for which the Greek

---

[1] George II, King of the Hellenes, 1890–1947. Succeeded as King following the abdication of his father, January 1923. Deposed, December 1923, and lived in exile in England, a republic being proclaimed in Greece in 1924. Restored to the throne by plebiscite, November 1935. Following the German conquest of Greece in 1941, he temporarily resumed the duties of Prime Minister, setting up his headquarters on Crete. With the German conquest of Crete, he escaped to Egypt. Restored to the throne by plebiscite, September 1946 (69·7 per cent of the votes being in favour of a restoration of the monarchy). On his death he was succeeded as King by his brother Paul.

[2] Yanni Metaxas, 1870–1941. Fought in the Greek Army against the Turks, 1897. Chief of the General Staff, 1913. A rival and opponent of Venizelos, he was against the entry of Greece into the war, on the side of Britain and France, in 1915. Formed the Party of Free Opinion, 1923. Deputy Prime Minister, 1935. Prime Minister, 1936, at the head of a Cabinet of ex-army officers and non-politicians. Ruled Greece as an autocrat from 1936 until his death.

Government had asked. Any munitions provided from the United States would reduce the supplies available to us.
(f) The Minister without Portfolio[1] said that he would let the Foreign Secretary know in a few days what could be done to meet certain of the Greek demands.
(g) The Chief of the Imperial General Staff said that he was considering whether he could send a consignment of rifles to Greece. He had already sent 22 anti-tank rifles from Egypt, and he might be able to send 50 more from this country.
(h) The Chief of the Imperial General Staff undertook to send to Greece a number of instructors in dealing with unexploded bombs.

The War Cabinet:–
(i) Approved the instructions issued by the Prime Minister as to the despatch of five squadrons and AA protection to Greece from Egypt.
(ii) Approved the action proposed by the Chiefs of Staff to make good the resultant diminution in our air forces in Egypt by the despatch of air reinforcements from this country.
(iii) Invited the Foreign Secretary to instruct Sir Michael Palairet to inform the King of Greece and General Metaxas of the help which we had decided to send to their country, making it clear –
  (a) That this information was to be treated as strictly secret and personal, and that they would be endangering the common cause if they disclosed either the extent of the reinforcements or whence they came.
  (b) That the date of the arrival of the air reinforcements would depend in part on the date at which the Greeks would put adequately defended aerodromes at our disposal.
(iv) Invited the Dominions Secretary,[2] after consultation with the Service Departments, to inform the Dominion Prime Ministers in strict confidence of the decisions which had been taken, making it clear to them
  (a) That we had felt obliged to run certain risks in Egypt for the time being.
  (b) That the squadrons now being sent to Greece from Egypt were being replaced as quickly as possible.

---

[1] Arthur Greenwood.
[2] On 3 October 1940 Viscount Cranborne (later 5th Marquess of Salisbury) had succeeded Viscount Caldecote (formerly Sir Thomas Inskip) as Secretary of State for Dominion Affairs.

November 1940

Winston S. Churchill to Anthony Eden
(*Cabinet papers, 70/1*)

4 November 1940
1.25 p.m.

We are sending you Air reinforcements arriving as fully explained in accompanying message from Chiefs of Staff. Send at once to Greece one Gladiator squadron and two more Blenheim squadrons, three in all. If necessary send a second Battalion to Crete. Agreeably with arrival of our air reinforcements aforesaid and at earliest send one more Gladiator squadron. AA guns for airfields in Greece should precede arrival of squadrons. You should not abandon your special plan, though perhaps some postponement may be necessary.

Winston S. Churchill to Lord Lloyd and L. S. Amery
(*Churchill papers, 20/13*)

5 November 1940

These two telegrams[1] are very good examples of the undue burdening of the Cables and Ciphering Department by long essays of this character. Pray let me know how much these cables cost, and how long was spent approximately in enciphering and deciphering them.

WSC

Winston S. Churchill: Oral Answer
(*Colville papers*)

5 November 1940   House of Commons

Mr Craven-Ellis[2]: To ask the Prime Minister, what special steps are being taken to allay the growing feeling amongst the general public that the country is not being organised for total war as quickly as was anticipated following the change of Government.

PRIME MINISTER
You may wish to draft a reply yourself to the above question?[3]

---

[1] Two telegrams, sent on 28 and 29 October, from the Department of Supply of the Government of India to the Secretary of State for India (Amery).

[2] William Craven-Ellis, –1959. A director of several investment and property companies. Conservative MP, 1931–45. Chairman of the Parliamentary and Monetary Committee of the House of Commons, 1934–44.

[3] In answer to his Private Office question, Churchill drafted the answer (at the top of page 1042) in his own handwriting.

I am not in a position to measure the anticipations which were held by the general public at the time of the change of Government, & therefore I have no basis for judging whether the hon. Member is right in thinking there is a growing feeling that the country is not being organized for total war as quickly as was then expected. From what I can see going about the country there is a great deal of good will towards the Government; & many people are lucky not to have suffered worse. But there are always a few disgruntled ne'er-do-wells & busy bodies & croakers whom hon. Members must not mistake for the general public.[1]

Winston S. Churchill: speech
(*Hansard*)

5 November 1940　　　　　　　　　　　　　　　　　　House of Commons

WAR SITUATION

The Prime Minister (Mr Churchill): Since I last addressed the House on general topics about a month ago, the course of events at home has not been unexpected, nor, on the whole, unsatisfactory. Herr Hitler declared on 4th September that as we would not bend to his will, he would wipe out our cities. I have no doubt that when he gave the order he sincerely believed that it was in his power to carry his will into effect. However, the cities of Britain are still standing. They are quite distinctive objects in the landscape, and our people are going about their tasks with the utmost activity. Fourteen thousand civilians have been killed and 20,000 seriously wounded, nearly four-fifths of them in London. That has been the loss of life and limb. As against this, scarcely 300 soldiers have been killed and 500 wounded. So much for the attack on military objectives. A great deal of house property has been destroyed or damaged, but nothing that cannot be covered by our insurance scheme. Very little damage has been done to our munitions and aircraft production, though a certain amount of time has been lost through frequent air-raid warnings. This lost time will have to be made up as we get settled down to the new conditions. None of the services upon which the life of our great cities depends – water, fuel, electricity, gas, sewage – not one has broken down. On the contrary, although there must inevitably be local shortages, all

---

[1] Churchill's actual answer read: 'I do not know what is meant by the expression "total war" nor what exactly it conveys to the mind of my hon. Friend. I am not in a position to measure what the public anticipated when the present government was formed. I have no doubt it was something very unpleasant, and if so, they have not been far wrong. With regard to my hon. Friend's estimate of a "growing feeling in the country", I am obliged to him for bringing his opinion to my attention. But, of course, others may take a different view, and in the end it is only the House as a whole which can pronounce upon the feelings, growing or otherwise, of the general public' (*Hansard*).

the authorities concerned with these vital functions of a modern community feel that they are on top of their job and are feeling it increasingly as each week is passed.

Transport has been a greater difficulty, as may well be imagined when we think of the vast numbers who go in and out of our great cities every day. However, we are getting a good grip of that, and I say with some confidence that by one method or another, and probably by many methods at the same time, the problems connected with transport will be solved in a manner tolerable to the great numbers of people who are affected. Shelters are being multiplied and improved, and preparations on an extensive scale are in progress for mitigating the inevitable severities of the winter for those who are using the shelters. All this is going forward, and the House has received accounts of it from the different Ministers who are particularly concerned. In these vicissitudes the bearing of our people, not only in London, but in Birmingham, Liverpool, Manchester and other places, has gained the unstinted admiration of all classes throughout the British Empire, throughout the United States, and, so far as they have been allowed to hear about it, among the peoples of the captive countries. As I was going home the other night, I asked a group of steel-helmeted men who stood about the door what was going on, and a deep voice in the background said, 'It's a grand life, if we don't weaken.' There is the British watchword for the winter of 1940. We will think of something else by the winter of 1941.

There is no doubt that the full malice and power of the enemy and his bombing force have been employed against us. They have tried their best to obey Hitler's orders, but the scale of their attack has dwindled. The weekly average of the casualties killed and seriously wounded was, for September, 4,500, and, for October, 3,500. In the first week of intense bombardment in September there were 6,000 casualties; in the last week of October only 2,000 casualties. This diminution in the scale of the attack is not entirely due to the weather. The weather, no doubt, has a lot to do with it, but there are other things going on which play their part besides the weather and which, I believe, will play a greater part as the months pass by. The House will not wish me to go into technical details on these points.

Meanwhile, how have the attackers fared? Two months ago I hazarded the statement – I admit it was rather a shot – that we hoped over our own country to destroy three enemy machines to one, and six pilots to one. So far it seems I was almost exactly right about the machines, taking the whole period, and I was very nearly right about the pilots, but, of course, if you count the whole of the crews of the large enemy bombers which have been brought down, all highly trained personnel, then it would be more like ten to one. So I somewhat understated, from that point of view, the results which have been achieved. Obviously, this process, combined with our own rapidly increasing production and the production in the Empire and in the United States of aircraft and airmen, is much the quickest road to our reaching that parity in the air which has always been considered the minimum of our safety, and thereafter reaching that superiority in the air which is the indispensable precursor of victory. Surveying the whole scene, alike in its splendour and its devastation, I see no reason to regret that Herr Hitler tried to break the British spirit by the blind bombing of our cities and our countryside.

More serious than the air raids has been the recent recrudescence of U-boat sinkings in the Atlantic approaches to our islands. The fact that we cannot use the South and West Coasts of Ireland to refuel our flotillas and aircraft and thus protect the trade by which Ireland as well as Great Britain lives, is a most heavy and grievous burden and one which should never have been placed on our shoulders, broad though they be. Moreover, we have been during the last month at the lowest point of our flotilla strength. The threat of invasion has always to be met. The great forces which we are maintaining in the Mediterranean, in addition to the escorts necessary for the protection of our innumerable convoys, have imposed on the Royal Navy a gigantic task.

However, this period of stringency is perhaps passing. The 50 American destroyers are rapidly coming into service just when they are most needed, and the main flow of new construction started at the outbreak of war is now coming on. In spite of serious losses, we have still very nearly as much shipping tonnage as we had at the outbreak of the war, and a great deal of neutral tonnage which used to trade freely with us is now under our control. Moreover, our U-boat hunting is still having its successes. Two more German U-boats have been sunk in the last two or three days on the Western approaches, one of them the U-boat which sank the *Empress of Britain*. We have a number of their crews who have been saved, as prisoners of war. On the other hand, when I speak of our shipping tonnage not being appreciably diminished from the beginning of the war, it must be remembered that our shipping is not so fruitful in war as in peace time because ships have to go a long way round; they have often to zig-zag and there are delays in the marshalling of convoys and sometimes delays through congestion at the ports. Therefore, it would not be wise to suppose that a greater stringency has not been brought about, although the actual volume of shipping remains practically undiminished.

I need scarcely say that intense efforts are being made by the Admiralty – my right hon. Friend the First Lord gives the whole of his life and strength and high abilities to the task, and I am confident that he is aided by the ablest officers in the Service – and also by the Ministry of Shipping to cope with these difficulties, and having lived through a lot of it in this war and the last, I, personally, cannot doubt that they will be able to cope with them and will be able to bring in all the vital supplies of food and munitions which we shall require. Dangers in the air are sudden and might have become catastrophic, but the dangers to our sea-borne traffic mature much more slowly. They are none the less formidable however, and, if in any way neglected, they would touch the life of the State. We must expect that next year a still heavier U-boat attack will be made upon us, and we are making immense preparations to meet it.

We have to look a long way ahead in this sphere of the war. We have to think of the years 1943 and 1944 and of the tonnage programmes which we shall be able to move and which we shall have to move across the oceans then. Every endeavour must be made to use the time available to produce the greatest volume of food of which this fertile island is capable and so liberate our Navy and our merchant shipping for the movement of the considerable armies which will certainly be required in those years, if the enemy do not surrender or collapse in the meanwhile. Having dwelt upon this sea communications aspect rather openly and bluntly this morning, I should not like to leave it without assuring the House that I, personally, have no doubt whatever that we shall make our way through all right.

I turn to another of our dangers. Some of those very clever people who are sometimes wise after the event are now talking about 'the invasion scare.' I do not mind that, because it is true that the danger of invasion, particularly invasion by barges, has diminished with the coming of the winter months and the unpredictable uncertainty of the weather. It has also been diminished by the victories of the Royal Air Force and the ever-growing strength of the British Army. When I spoke at the end of June, I set forth in detail the well-known difficulties which would attend the invasion of these islands and which had been forgotten in years when we had not considered the matter at all. At that time, we had only a few brigades of well-armed and well-trained troops in this island. We had no Home Guard to deal with an invader or to deal with air-borne attacks behind the lines and the Royal Air Force had not then proved itself master of our own air by daylight.

Very different is the scene to-day. We have a very large Army here, improving in equipment and training continually. The main part of that Army is now highly mobile and is being constantly imbued with the spirit of counter-attack. We have 1,700,000 men in the Home Guard, all of whom will be in uniform by the end of this year and nearly all of whom are in uniform at this moment. Nearly 1,000,000 of the Home Guard have rifles or machine guns. Nearly half of the whole Home Guard are veteran soldiers of the last war. Such a Force is of the highest value and importance. A country where every street and every village bristles with loyal, resolute, armed men is a country against which the kind of tactics which destroyed Dutch resistance – tactics of parachutists or air-borne troops in carriers or gliders, Fifth Column activities – if there were any over here, and I am increasingly sceptical – would prove wholly ineffective. A country so defended would not be liable to be overthrown by such tactics. Therefore I agree with those who think that the invasion danger has for the time being diminished. But do not let us make the mistake of assuming that it has passed away, or that it may not occur in more acute form or in some other form.

What is it that has turned invasion into an invasion scare? It is the maintenance in Britain of strong forces and unremitting vigilance by sea, air and land. A mighty army crouches across the Channel and the North Sea, and substantial masses of shipping are gathered in all the harbours of the Western seaboard of Europe, from the North Cape to the Gironde River. We must not let our 'shallow-clevers' lead us into thinking that this is all pretence, a manoeuvre to tie us down here and prevent us redisposing our Forces. The vital realities of their duties must be borne in on the whole of our Home Forces and the whole of our Home Guard during these winter months. There must be no relaxation except for necessary leave, but let me say this, that the plain fact that an invasion, planned on so vast a scale, has not been attempted in spite of the very great need of the enemy to destroy us in our citadel and that all these anxious months, when we stood alone and the whole of the world wondered, have passed safely away – that fact constitutes in itself one of the historic victories of the British Isles and is a monumental milestone on our onward march.

Here let me say a word about the British Army. We are engaged in forming and training a very strong Army, and the like is being done in Canada, Australia, South Africa, New Zealand and India. We are now in the fifteenth month of the war and the British Army, of which I speak particularly now, is beginning to shape itself with precision. Although the sea and air will be the main elements of the war effort of the British Empire, we must have a strong Army, well equipped, well armed, well trained and well organised, capable of intervening as the war proceeds in the liberation of one or the other of the many countries which are yearning to throw off the odious Nazi yoke. Without such an Army, forged, tempered and sharpened, and the sea power which gives it so wide a choice, the action of this war might be needlessly prolonged and might drift towards disastrous stalemate. Nothing must be done which retards or hinders the development of our Army. What it lacks in numbers compared with the Nazi or Fascist hosts, it must make up in quality and equipment. This is a lengthy process, but we must persevere and not let ourselves be drawn from the task by passing distractions or temptations.

The British Army is quite ready in any emergency to give all possible help to Civil Defence forces in meeting local difficulties which might arise from exceptional air attack. To some districts which are overweighted by the burdens cast upon them they have given very great assistance and will, where necessary, give more, but to hear some people talk, one would think that we must begin almost immediately to draft a large portion of our Army into the civil and ARP Services. One would take its lorries, another would take its engineers and another would take its telegraphists; yet another would use man-power on a great scale to clear away ruins. Just as before this war it was a temptation not to make proper arrangements for Civil Defence, now there is this inclination, not unnaturally – it appears quite reasonable and rather seductive – to trench unduly on the efficiency of the military machine in order to meet day-by-day requirements. Let us be on our guard against this. All through this winter the Army has got to train itself and its fighting men in all the arts and manoeuvres of war. The House of Commons, the Press and public opinion must be active to ward off from our Army all demands and influences which would hamper or delay the preparation of a weapon of the highest quality. Only in this way should we reach a position where instead of being forced to suffer the measureless vexations of a widespread defensive attitude – hit here now and hit there then, often inevitably too late – we shall regain the initiative and make the enemy wonder where and how we are going to strike at them. I ask the House which is the foundation of our war-making effort to keep a careful eye on this aspect of our affairs.

During all this menace of invasion, so near and so deadly, we have never failed to reinforce our Armies in Egypt, almost to the limits of our shipping capacity, not only with men but with precious weapons which it was a wrench to take from our forces here. Scores of thousands of troops have left this Island month after month or have been drawn from other parts of the Empire for the Middle East. These troops have been streaming away from this Island during the months when some of those who now talk so gaily about the invasion scare were scared stiff themselves. Several times I have told the House that I could not guarantee a favourable result in the Middle East. After all, our position there was calculated on the basis that France was our Ally and that the powerful French Armies that General Weygand organised would stand side by side with us in the discharge of our joint obligations. The submission of the French Government to the German conquest and to the Italian exploitation has not only deprived us of those armies in Syria, Tunis, Algeria and Morocco, but has denied us the assistance of the fine French Navy and the use of the French naval and air bases in the Mediterranean. Such a frightful desertion and loss might well have confronted us with an insoluble problem. The Italian army in Libya, which some months ago far outnumbered the British and Imperial Forces in and around Egypt, seemed likely to roll forward irresistibly upon the Nile Valley and the Suez Canal.

I am thankful to be able to assure the House that the balance of forces on the frontiers of Egypt and in the Sudan is far less unfavourable than it was at the time of the French collapse. I can certainly not prophesy to the House about battles which have yet to be fought, but I think at the beginning of July, if we cast our minds back, the House would have been very glad to be assured that on 5th November we should still be holding in largely increased force every position of any importance. We have not had any serious collisions with the Italian forces, but we have every reason to be content with the results of the skirmishes and forays which have taken place on the ground and in the air.

Up to the end of September, the Italian official published casualties for the fighting in Libya amounted to 800 killed, 1,700 wounded and 860 missing; our own casualties for the same period and in the same theatre were 66 killed, 68 wounded, and 36 missing – a scale approaching something like 20 to 1. These facts speak for themselves and should be a good augury for the greater battles and engagements which certainly will develop, perhaps in the Winter, certainly in the Spring.

At the same time that the Navy is keeping open the sea routes under this very dangerous U-boat attack, and endeavouring to hunt down merchant raiders in the outer seas, and maintaining a strict blockade – at the same time as it is doing that we have ceaselessly strengthened the Fleet in the Eastern Mediterranean, and we are ready at any time to engage the Italian Navy in a general action. Time after time our Fleet has moved into close proximity to the main concentration of the Italian Fleet and we know that their presence has been detected from the air, but so far these cruises have not resulted in any decisive encounter. Still, the power of the British Fleet in the Eastern Mediterranean goes a long way to restore the situation created by the collapse of France and is a great guarantee to our friend and Ally, Turkey, of the unweakening power of Great Britain on the seas. Therefore, whether you look at the Home Front or at the Mediterranean theatre, I do not think it can be denied that we are far better off than anyone would have ventured to predict four or five months ago.

But now a new call has suddenly been made upon us. The Italian dictator, perhaps embarrassed by the somewhat florid flirtations of M. Laval with the German conqueror, or perhaps playing his part in some new predatory design, has, in his customary cold-blooded way, fallen upon the small but famous and immortal Greek nation. Without the slightest provocation, with no pretence at parley, Signor Mussolini has invaded Greece, or tried to do so, and his aircraft have murdered an increasing number of Greek civilians, women and children, in Salonika and many other open Greek towns. The Greek King, his Government and the Greek people have resolved to fight for life and honour, and lest the world should be too easily led in chains. France and Great Britain guaranteed to come to the aid of Greece if she were the victim of unprovoked aggression. It was a joint guarantee, and unhappily the Vichy Government is at this moment engaged in sincere and loyal collaboration with Herr Hitler in his schemes for establishing a so-called new order in Europe. At any rate, the Vichy Government is no longer in a position to play its expected part in the task it had accepted. We are, therefore, left alone.

We have most carefully abstained from any action likely to draw upon the Greeks the enmity of the criminal dictators. For their part, the Greeks have maintained so strict a neutrality that we are unacquainted with their dispositions or their intentions. I have already been at some pains to set forth to the House the very serious preoccupations which dominate us both at home and in the Middle East. We face one gigantic army across the waters of the Channel, we face another very powerful army, much more numerous, on the frontier of the Libyan Desert, and I must, as I say, approach the new task with a strong sense of the immense responsibilities which rest upon us both at home and in Egypt, and of the very great and continual dangers by which we are confronted. In the circumstances, there is only one thing we can do. We will do our best. We have already established a naval and air base in Crete which will enable us sensibly to extend the activities and radius of the Navy and of the Air Force. We have begun the bombing attack upon military objectives in the Italian cities and bases in the South of Italy. That will continue on an ever growing scale. I should also say that our forces are in movement with the desire and design to help the Greeks to the utmost of our capacity, having regard to our other obligations. I hope I shall not be asked by the House to give any definite account of such measures as we are able to take. If I were to set them high, I might raise false hopes; if I set them low, I might cause undue despondency and alarm; and if I stated exactly what they were, that would be exactly what the enemy would like to know. We shall do our best. That is all I can say. To that decision and declaration, generously and faithfully interpreted, I invoke with confidence the approval of the House.

Mr A. Bevan[1] (Ebbw Vale): I know it is very unusual to ask the Prime Minister a question at this stage, but can he arrange before the end of the Debate for some member of the Government to say a word about what is universally felt to be a great blunder in sending representations to the Soviet Union concerning the Danubian negotiations, and also a word about what is happening in Tangiers, which is also causing very considerable disquiet? I think the House is entitled to hear from the Government a statement to-day on these matters.

The Prime Minister: I can only speak for a moment with the leave of the House and I do not rise to answer these questions. I have selected very carefully the topics on which I thought a statement could be made with advantage, and I did not feel that on these two points there was anything which I could usefully say to-day. No doubt other opportunities will occur for the situation in both these quarters to be discussed, and at any time when it will be of advantage to do so I shall be very glad to be at the service of the House.

---

[1] Aneurin Bevan, 1897–1960. A coal miner from the age of thirteen. Miners' disputes agent, 1926. Labour MP from 1929 until his death. Forced in 1944 to give the Labour Party a written assurance of loyalty or be expelled (he gave the assurance). Minister of Health, 1945–51 (when he introduced the National Health Service). Minister of Labour and National Service, 1951: resigned in protest against defence spending and National Health Service charges (also resigning was the President of the Board of Trade, Harold Wilson, later Prime Minister). Treasurer of the Labour Party, and Deputy Leader of the Opposition, from 1956 until his death. His often acerbic manner (he was reported to have called the Conservatives 'lower than vermin') caused Churchill to dub him a 'merchant of discourtesy'.

Henry Channon: diary
(*'Chips'*)

5 November 1940

I admire the PM's pluck, his courageous energy and magnificent English: his humour too, although often in doubtful taste, is immense.

This morning one of his secretaries rushed up to me in the House, and asked me if I had seen him? He was apparently due to lunch at the Palace, and it was already 1.15. Luckily I had just seen him 'boozing' in the Smoking Room, and so I volunteered to remind him. I went up to him politely, but unsmilingly, and he got up ungraciously, after grunting at me. He can be very unattractive when he is in a bad temper. Neville, my poor dying Neville, was never like this.

Harold Nicolson: diary
(*'Diaries and Letters, 1939–1945'*)

5 November 1940

The Prime Minister makes a statement after Question-time. He is rather grim. He brings home to the House as never before the gravity of our shipping losses and the danger of our position in the Eastern Mediterranean. It has a good effect. By putting the grim side foremost he impresses us with his ability to face the worst. He rubs the palms of his hands with five fingers extended up and down the front of his coat, searching for the right phrase, indicating cautious selection, conveying almost medicinal poise. If Chamberlain had spoken glum words such as these the impression would have been one of despair and lack of confidence. Churchill can say them and we all feel, 'Thank God that we have a man like that!' I have never admired him more.

Thereafter he slouches into the smoking-room and reads the *Evening News* intently, as if it were the only source of information available to him.

Defence Committee (Operations): minutes
(*Cabinet papers, 69/1*)

5 November 1940   Cabinet War Room
5.30 p.m.

ASSISTANCE TO GREECE

The Prime Minister drew attention to the latest telegram received from Mr Eden in which he said that, in consultation with the Commanders-in-Chief, he had considered the plan sent out by the Chiefs of Staff for giving assistance to Greece. They agreed that the plan proposed was the best that could be done in the circumstances. They pressed, however, for the prompt fulfilment of the programme of air reinforcements for the Middle East so as to restore the position in Egypt as quickly as possible.

Sir Charles Portal said that he was having a programme prepared so that a watch could be kept on the progress of the air reinforcement scheme. Everything would be done to keep up to time.

The Prime Minister then referred to the telegram received from the three Service Attachés in Athens which gave a very favourable view of the present situation and of future possibilities. He hoped that such munitions as we could spare would be sent to the Greeks.

Sir Robert Haining said he would look into the possibility of sending some Anti-tank guns.

The Prime Minister said that he sympathised with the desire of the Admiralty to see the Coastal Command strengthened so as to grapple successfully with the strangle-hold which the enemy was trying to establish on our life line in the North Western approaches but he was surprised to see the extravagant demands which they now put forward for oversea requirements which could not possibly be met at a time when we were engaged on the task of increasing our power to bomb Germany.

The Prime Minister said that from his experience as First Lord of the Admiralty, he knew that there had, in the early days of the war, been some dissatisfaction with the co-operation between the Royal Navy and the Coastal Command; an improved liaison had been arranged but there was no doubt that there would be advantages in having the whole protection of trade under one operational control. The Coastal Command had not received the scale of equipment that they should have had. The question of whether the Royal Navy should take over Coastal Command had been fought out at the time when the Navy took over the Fleet Air Arm. At that time the Royal Air Force was still struggling to maintain its position. He had set out his views in a Paper which he had forwarded to Sir Thomas Inskip,[1] who was then Minister for Co-ordination of Defence, and these views had been adopted. He had not at that time recommended the taking over of Coastal Command because he had felt that there was no possibility of getting agreement on such a controversial point. The position now was very different, however. The Royal Air Force was expanding enormously and was forming itself into the leading element in bringing about our victory. The splitting off of Coastal Command would not, therefore, seriously harm them and might improve the operational control. It would be poor economy, however, to duplicate training grounds or to set up competition in the market for aircraft but it might be possible to tap new

[1] Viscount Caldecote.

streams of pilots and aircraft from Naval sources. He was not convinced that the Royal Navy were at present making the best use of the resources of the Fleet Air Arm. During a recent visit to Donibristle[1] he had noticed that though there were 170 aircraft on the station, there were only two squadrons capable of taking part in operations.

Mr Alexander said that there were cases where it seemed that the requirements of Coastal Command were not being met. For example it had been found necessary to keep back one Whitley squadron which was required for use in the Western Approaches. It was now suggested that Hampdens should be withdrawn from their mine-laying duties so as to replace the Whitleys being withdrawn from Bomber Command.

Sir Archibald Sinclair said that the Air Ministry were pressing forward with the provision of the programme asked for by the Chiefs of Staff and were ready to consider any proposals for improving the efficiency of Coastal Command.

Summing up the discussion, the Prime Minister said that it was not possible to reach a decision that evening on so important a matter. There appeared to be a case for a full examination by the Admiralty, the Air Ministry and the Ministry for Aircraft Production of how best to meet the requirements for reconnaissance and coastal duties and he would himself set out the heads for such a study in the course of the next few days. He would like to sound one note of warning. He had himself founded the Royal Naval Air Service before the last war. At first the Navy had not been keen on it but he had pushed it forward and on the outbreak of war, when the Royal Flying Corps went to France, the small Royal Naval Air Service was all that was left on the coasts of Britain. The Service was subsequently enormously increased and engulfed great quantities of men and material. The result was that at a time when the Royal Flying Corps was fighting for its life in France, large resources stood comparatively idle in this country. Such a thing must never be allowed to happen again.

Lord Reith: diary
(*'The Reith Diaries'*)

6 November 1940

I had to go to a Cabinet about Faraday House. Silly business, but interesting. The PM spoke most bitterly about the BBC – enemy within the gate; continually causing trouble; more harm than good. Something drastic must be done with them, he said. Duff Cooper (sitting next me) agreed – more control probably and they ought to be civil servants (!), but Broadcasting

---

[1] Two miles east of Rosyth.

House should not be commandeered; already a bomb there and seven people killed. He said this twice but fortunately the PM knew about the bomb and said it was their own fault that people had been killed. Anyhow the Broadcasting House point is to come up next week and meantime Faraday House is to be used as Beaverbrook and I were arranging.

Henry Channon: diary
(*'Chips'*)

6 November 1940

As raids are very much increasing in intensity there was a Secret Session today to discuss the House of Commons' future meeting place. Winston came in, 'spied strangers', and then made the Government statement. He told us that we are to meet in future at Church House in Westminster Cloisters, which has been converted by the Office of Works. He was humorous but dictatorial, and hinted at shutting down Parliament altogether if there was opposition to this decision, which on the whole seems a reasonable one. 'We must try the shoe, see where it pinches and perhaps return here later.' 'This procedure will confuse the enemy.' Such was his line. The House took none too kindly to this announcement, and there was chatter of 'funk holes' and 'bad example', etc. However, Winston stuck his ground, and at Church House we shall meet tomorrow, and probably rightly. Members are complaining openly that Winston trades on his position, on his immense following in the country, though his popularity is on the decline: but it is still high. Yet the country does not want a dictator.

President Roosevelt has had an even greater triumph than anyone anticipated. A real landslide, and I have yet to see anyone who is not delighted.[1]

Winston S. Churchill to President Roosevelt
(*Premier papers, 3/468*)

6 November 1940

I did not think it right for me as a Foreigner to express my opinion upon American politics while the Election was on, but now I feel you will not mind my saying that I prayed for your success and that I am truly thankful for it. This does not mean that I seek or wish for anything more than the full, fair and free play of your mind upon the world issues now at stake in which our

---

[1] President Roosevelt had been re-elected for an unprecedented third term.

two nations have to discharge their respective duties. We are entering upon a sombre phase of what must evidently be a protracted and broadening war, and I look forward to being able to interchange my thoughts with you in all that confidence and goodwill which has grown up between us since I went to the Admiralty at the outbreak. Things are afoot which will be remembered as long as the English language is spoken in any quarter of the globe, and in expressing the comfort I feel that the people of the United States have once again cast these great burdens upon you, I must avow my sure faith that the lights by which we steer will bring us all safely to anchor.[1]

War Cabinet: minutes
(Cabinet papers, 65/10)

6 November 1940
12 noon

Prime Minister's Room
House of Commons

The Prime Minister said that there had been a considerable decline in the output of munitions in the last two months. In particular, the Tank programme was seriously in arrear. This falling off was largely, but not, he thought, wholly, attributable to the effects of air raids.

The Foreign Secretary suggested that we should warn the Vichy Government that if they attempted to send such an expedition[2] we should, of course, resist it, and our forces would come into conflict – which we wished to avoid.

The Prime Minister thought that it would be a good thing to send a warning on these lines. We might, however, go rather further and add that we had no intention of launching another attack on Dakar; making it clear that if, for example, the port fell under German domination and our intentions changed, we would give them due notice. In exchange for this declaration of our intention not to attack Dakar we should invite the Vichy Government to refrain from action against the colonies which had declared for General de Gaulle.

[1] Two and a half weeks later, having received no answer to this telegram, Churchill telegraphed to Lord Lothian: 'Would you kindly find out for me most discreetly whether President received my personal telegram congratulating him on re-election. It may have been swept up in electioneering congratulations. If not I wonder whether there was anything in it which could have caused offence or been embarrassing for him to receive. Should welcome your advice' (*Premier papers, 4/171*).

[2] A possible Vichy naval expedition against the French colonies that had declared for de Gaulle. Halifax told the War Cabinet: 'There were indications that a force was being concentrated at Dakar, possibly for this purpose.' In fact, it was de Gaulle's forces who took the initiative, against the Vichy authorities in French Equatorial Africa, capturing the port-city of Libreville on November 9 and Port Gentil on November 12. They were assisted, at sea, by Admiral Cunningham.

Winston S. Churchill to General Dill
(*Churchill papers, 20/13*)

6 November 1940

HOME GUARD COMMAND

I still think General Eastwood is the best man. Moreover, his appointment would avoid the continued chopping and changing which is so injurious.

You impressed upon me how important it was to have a first-rate man in charge of the Home Guard, and what a compliment to them it would be if the former Chief of the Staff in France was chosen; so General Pownall was appointed. But a few weeks later I was astonished to learn he was to go to America on the Mission now discharged by General Pakenham-Walsh. With some difficulty I stopped this change. However, a little later Pownall was sent to Ireland, whereas I suppose he would have done very well for the Home Guard, both Direction and Inspection. Just as he got to know his job and men were beginning to look to him, he was whisked off to something else, and General Eastwood took his place. This is, I think, only a month ago. However, I dutifully set myself to work to make General Eastwood's acquaintance, and I suppose so did the principal officers of the Home Guard. I formed a favourable opinion of him, particularly on account of his age, which is under 50. I suppose he has been working very hard for the month, trying to learn his immense new task, and he certainly had begun to speak about it with knowledge. Now you propose to me to send him away, and to appoint a third new figure, all in four months.

All these rapid changes are contrary to the interests of the Service, and open to the most severe criticism. I am not prepared to agree to dismiss General Eastwood from the Home Guard Command. If you wish to set up this Directorate-General, he must have it, so far as I am concerned. However, the Secretary of State will be back in two days, if all goes well, and I am sending a copy of this Minute to him. I shall still expect to be consulted.

I also ought to let you know that I was much surprised and disconcerted by the removal of General Carr from the post he occupied in Supply. I can well believe that General Macready[1] is, perhaps, the better man, but the continuity of the work in this Department should never have been broken and all personal accountability removed by a change of this kind. Before you

---

[1] Gordon Nevil Macready, 1891–1956. Only son of General Sir Nevil Macready (one of Churchill's senior advisers at the War Office in 1919). On active service, 1914–18 (despatches six times). Special Mission (to organise a police force) in Poland, 1919. Chief of the British Military Mission to the Egyptian Army, 1938. Assistant Chief of the Imperial General Staff, 1940–2. Chief of the British Army Staff at Washington, 1942. Knighted, 1945. Regional Commissioner for Lower Saxony, 1946–7. Colonel-Commandant, Royal Engineers, 1946–56. Economic Adviser to the UK High Commissioner in Germany, 1949–51.

removed General Carr were you aware of the very serious breakdown in the Tank programme? I preside over the Committees on Supply from time to time, and it is extremely inconvenient when new figures are suddenly presented.

WSC

Winston S. Churchill to General Dill
(Premier papers, 3/109)

6 November 1940

It will be difficult to deny the Greeks the use of this Division in Crete. If that be so, we shall certainly have to put more troops on the Island. Perhaps the Polish Brigade might go there, and some of the British details, or some of the less trained Australians. It is important that there should be a certain number of troops, and that it should be thought by the enemy that we are landing considerable numbers. The area to be watched is very extensive, and the consequences of a counter-attack would be most disastrous.

Pray let me know your views.

WSC

Winston S. Churchill to Sir Charles Portal
(Churchill papers, 20/13)

6 November 1940

Last night at least seven of our planes crashed on landing or were lost.[1] The slow expansion of the bomber force is, as you know, a great anxiety to me. If bombing in this bad weather is imposing altogether undue risks and losses on the pilots, the numbers might be slacked down in order to accumulate our strength while at the same time keeping various objectives alive. I see in the paper circulated that the enemy last night used 210 bombers over Great Britain. Have they had losses similar to those we suffer? Or are our aerodromes far more weather-bound than theirs? I should be very glad to have your opinion about this in the course of the next few days.

WSC

---

[1] The three planes that were lost were among ninety-seven that struck at Hamburg (7 civilians killed and 236 'bombed out') and other targets. On the following night two out of eighteen bombers that attacked Berlin were lost.

Winston S. Churchill to Sir Edward Bridges
(*Churchill papers, 20/8*)

6 November 1940

I don't see much wrong with the telegram; but certainly, if you wish, acquaint Miss Maurice[1] that she must never send en clair communications without showing them to you, and if you wish banish her from Gwydwr House. I hope it will not be long before both General de Gaulle and General Spears are safely back in this country.

WSC

War Cabinet: minutes
(*Cabinet papers, 65/10*)

7 November 1940   Prime Minister's Room
12 noon   House of Commons (Annexe)[2]

A convoy passing Dover the previous night had been shelled by enemy coastal batteries, but no damage had been reported.

The Prime Minister said that these air attacks on convoys emphasised the necessity for further convoy protection by aircraft and guns, and made it all the more important that our fighter aircraft should work from the Irish coast.

The War Cabinet had before them a Report by the Chiefs of Staff on the possibility of a German advance through the Balkans and Syria to the Middle East (WP (40) 431).

The Prime Minister said that the Defence Committee (Operations) had recommended that the War Cabinet should give general approval to the Report, and in particular should authorise the following action:–

(i) The preparation of plans for giving assistance to Turkey.
(ii) Examination of methods of increasing supplies of armaments to Turkey.
(iii) The formation of a mission to Turkey which should be established in the Middle East as soon as possible and made ready to move into Turkey at once in the event of the Turks becoming involved in the war. The Turkish Government to be sounded as to whether they would receive this mission now.

---

[1] Nancy Maurice, daughter of General Maurice of the 'Maurice debate' in the First World War, and a direct descendant of Spencer Perceval, the Prime Minister assassinated in the House of Commons in 1812. Spears's secretary, and later second wife, she had sent him a telegram to Duala which had been stopped by the censor (who described it as 'indiscreet').

[2] Church House, Westminster.

(iv) The preparation of plans for the demolition of Turkish communications.
(v) The taking of measures on the lines suggested in paragraph 9 of the Report to prevent the French Authorities in Syria from menacing our interests.
(vi) The perfecting of plans for the destruction of Iraqi oil wells, and pipe lines in Iraq, Syria and Palestine.
(vii) The taking of firm measures towards Iraq, on the lines proposed in paragraph 10 of the Report.

Henry Channon: diary
(*'Chips'*)

7 November 1940

A dreadful day started with the House of Commons meeting for the first time in its new premises which Winston has dubbed 'The Annexe' – a large building, astonishingly well arranged, many Members turned up early to watch the proceedings: it is the first time since the big fire of 1834 that the Commons have met anywhere except at Westminster.

The Speaker was enthroned under his usual canopy, the Serjeant-at-Arms[1] on a camp chair at the Bar; Members found places as nearly as possible equivalent to where they usually sat at Westminster. The Hall was not too crowded, but the acoustics are indifferent and there was noise and muffled excitement, and ministers tumbling over one another. Winston watched the confusion with amusement.

Winston S. Churchill: Oral Answer
(*Hansard*)

7 November 1940   House of Commons (Annexe)
Church House

Mr Bevan: In announcing the Business, the Prime Minister made no reference to the Bill to implement the promise he made yesterday about supplementary old age pensions. In view of the fact that the promise was made and broadcast to the country, is it not highly undesirable that there should be any delay between the promise and the introduction of the Bill? May we have the Bill as quickly as possible?

The Prime Minister: There may be an interval of time, but there will be no delay.

[1] Charles Alfred Howard, 1886–1958. Entered the army, 1898. Wounded on the Somme, 1916. DSO, 1917 and bar, 1918. Commander of the Dover Garrison, 1932–5. Sergeant-at-Arms, House of Commons, 1935–56. Knighted 1944.

Chiefs of Staff Committee: minutes
(*Cabinet papers, 79/7*)

7 November 1940   Cabinet War Room
6.30 p.m.

ASSISTANCE TO GREECE

Sir John Dill read out the recent telegrams from Athens and the Middle East arising from the Greeks' wish to withdraw troops from Crete.

He said that although we should have to take risks in Crete, he did not consider them serious at present. The Italians had not even ventured an expedition to Corfu and as long as the Greeks held out, he thought the danger to Crete was slight. Even if they were driven back some of the Greek forces might withdraw to Crete.

Sir Dudley Pound thought that the capture of Crete would be a most difficult operation, particularly as we held Suda Bay.

There was general agreement that we could not object to the Greeks withdrawing some of their forces in Crete.[1]

Sir John Dill said that the responsibility for the defence of Crete must rest with the Commander-in-Chief, Middle East in conjunction with the other Commanders-in-Chief. He was anxious, however, about the withdrawal of the whole of the Greek artillery in the Island.

The Committee felt that a garrison of two battalions in Crete would not be sufficient. They therefore thought it necessary to ask the authority of the Government of Australia for permission to use their partially-trained and equipped troops in Crete if General Wavell thought it necessary.

The Prime Minister then entered the Meeting and agreed with the views of the Chiefs of Staff as outlined above. He suggested that the Greeks should be asked to leave in Crete 12 guns until we could replace them. He drew attention to the fact that General Wavell was receiving 48 more guns on the 16th November.

---

[1] Following this Chiefs of Staff Committee Meeting, the War Office telegraphed to the British Military Mission in Athens: 'We could not possibly raise any objection to the withdrawal from Crete of six Greek battalions and a proportion of their artillery. We are ready to assume responsibility for defence of Crete. We would be very grateful if Greeks could leave twelve guns in Crete which we will replace as soon as possible.' That same evening, General Wavell was informed by General Dill: 'Security of Crete must be your responsibility in conjunction naval and air Commanders-in-Chief.' (*Cabinet papers, 79/7.*)

Winston S. Churchill to General Dill
(*Premier papers, 3/109*)

7 November 1940

We shall render poor service to Greece if in consequence of our using Crete for our own purposes we deny them the use of two-thirds of their Fifth Division. The defence of Crete depends on the Navy, but nevertheless there must be a certain deterrent force of troops on shore. I doubt if the two Battalions of British and the three remaining Greek Battalions will be sufficient. I am much obliged to you for telegraphing as I asked to General Wavell. He must provide in meal or in malt:–

(a) Three or four thousand additional British troops and a dozen guns. These need not be fully equipped or mobile. Yeomanry from Palestine. Poles, even!

(b) He must do this from forces which he will not be using in the possibly impending battle.

(c) We must tell the Greeks we release the six Battalions and the Artillery of the Fifth Greek Division.

Every effort should be made to rush arms or equipment to enable a Reserve Division of Greeks to be formed in Crete. Rifles and machine guns are quite sufficient in this case. To keep a Greek Division out of the battle on the Epiraeus front would be very bad, and to lose Crete because we had not sufficient bulk of forces there would be a crime.

WSC

Winston S. Churchill to Sir James Grigg
(*Churchill papers, 20/6*)

7 November 1940

Kindly explain to General Macready, ACIGS, that the Minute referred to by him in his Minute of 1.11.40 was written by me in the train, and that the word should be 'by' and not 'to.' Tell him also not to use disrespectful expressions about the Minister of Defence under whom he is serving, even when that Minister's handwriting was not entirely plain.

The correspondence and the context make it perfectly clear that the word was 'by,' and not 'to,' and if the ACIGS had exercised his intelligence rather than his critical faculty, he would not have been led into a lapse of good manners. This Minute is to be shown to the Officer in question, and returned to me initialled by him.

WSC

John Colville: diary
(*Colville papers*)

7 November 1940

The PM was much displeased by a minute in a War Office file which referred to one of 'his scribbles' as being unintelligible. He sent a furious minute to P. J. Grigg demanding an apology and deploring that the officer in question (General Macready, ACIGS) should have made more use of his critical faculties than of his intelligence.

Seven bombs in succession shook our equanimity at the CWR.

Winston S. Churchill to General Ismay
(*Churchill papers, 20/13*)

7 November 1940

Although I bowed before the difficulties so industriously assembled by the Joint Planners in their report of 31st August,[1] and the general attitude of negation, I should be very much obliged to the COS Committee if they would very kindly read my Minute of 28th August and consider whether there was not something in it after all.

WSC

Lord Halifax to Winston S. Churchill
(*Churchill papers, 2/395*)

7 November 1940   Foreign Office

My dear Winston,

I'm just back from seeing Neville. He is pretty near the end. They talked about a week. But he was very steady and good – and I think not anxious for the time to be prolonged.

He was touched with the messages I gave him from you – and spoke with

---

[1] 'Proposals for the move of four heavy-bomber squadrons to Egypt with the object of operating against objectives in Italy from advanced landing grounds in Greece.' Report signed by the three Joint Planners, Daniel, Playfair and Slessor, on 31 August 1940. Churchill had asked them for a 'brief report setting out the method, difficulties, objectives and time factor' (*Cabinet papers, 84/18*).

much affection of you. Particularly touched by your having let him see papers, though that now must be at an end.

Anne Chamberlain did not wish the Press to know about his state.

Yrs ever
E

War Cabinet: minutes
(*Cabinet papers, 65/10*)

8 November 1940   Cabinet War Room
11.30 a.m.

The Prime Minister said that the Greeks wanted to withdraw six out of the nine battalions in Crete, together with all the artillery in the island. He had given instructions the previous evening that we should meet the Greek wishes, subject to their leaving one battery behind for the present. We should have to send further reinforcements to Crete. The Chief of the Imperial General Staff had telegraphed to General Wavell, pointing out that Crete was part of his Command, and that he would have to spare men to garrison it. It might be possible for General Wavell to spare some Australian units who had not yet completed their training. The Dominions Secretary had telegraphed to the Australian Government to inquire whether they would consent to a move of this kind.

For the present, Crete appeared to be in no great danger of Italian attack.

The Prime Minister said that we could not tolerate a continuance of shipping losses on the present scale.[1] He referred to Mr de Valera's statement, reported in the Press as follows:–

'There can be no question of handing over any of these ports on any conditions so long as this State remains neutral.'

It was now more unlikely than a few months ago that Eire would declare war on Germany, since Dublin was now within easy range of air attack from occupied France. Even assuming that the Irish wanted to go to war, they would certainly demand large quantities of munitions before consenting to abandon neutrality.

The Prime Minister thought that the only action which would be of any value would be an approach to President Roosevelt to see what pressure he

---

[1] Eight British merchant ships had been sunk on 5 November, two on 6 November and three on 7 November. Six of those sunk on 5 November had been sunk by the German pocket battleship *Admiral Scheer* in the South Atlantic.

could put on Mr de Valera. He might perhaps send a personal telegram on the following lines:–

'It will be at least two years before America can give us any effective help, since she is only now laying out her armament factories. The question is whether Great Britain can hold out for so long without the Treaty Ports. Anything which can be done to get for us the use of the Treaty Ports would thus be in defence of American interests.'

The War Cabinet invited the Prime Minister to send a personal message to President Roosevelt on the lines suggested.

The Prime Minister referred to the suggestion that General de Gaulle should go to Cairo. He feared that, if he went there, this might arouse the antagonism of General Weygand. He (the Prime Minister) would prefer that General de Gaulle should come home and consult on the general situation, when his position as regards General Weygand could be discussed.

The Prime Minister referred to a telegram which had been received from the Senior Naval Officer Commanding the Canal Zone[1] regarding the presence of a number of Vichy supporters in the Zone. It was essential to make certain that the military movements in the Zone were not betrayed by Vichy supporters. He had sent instructions on the subject to the Foreign Office.

OVERSEAS AIR SERVICES

The Minister of Economic Warfare[2] urged that a high priority should be given to the continuance of the service to Sweden, which was essential for certain activities with which he was charged. The Secretary of State for the Colonies said that evidence accumulated daily of the need for strengthening the Takoradi route.

On the other hand, the Prime Minister said that, while he appreciated the advantages of improved overseas air communications, he felt that, with the intensification of the war, we must direct all our efforts to first essentials. The attack on our merchant shipping was now a very grave danger, and if we were to deal with it adequately we must sacrifice many other needs. He might have taken a different view, if the strength of our Air Force had been increasing rapidly.

---

[1] Vice-Admiral Sir James Murray Pipon, 1882–1971. Admiral Superintendent, Gibraltar Dockyard, 1935–7. Retired from the Navy, 1937. Recalled, 1940: Senior British Naval Officer, Suez Canal, 1940–2. Flag-Officer in charge, Southampton, 1942–5.

[2] Hugh Dalton.

War Cabinet: Confidential Annex
(*Cabinet papers, 65/16*)

8 November 1940
11.30 a.m.

The Prime Minister stated that he did not think that the French had any intention of moving the *Jean Bart* and the *Richelieu*. So long as they were outside the Mediterranean the Vichy Government could always threaten Germany that they would turn these ships over to us. Once they had passed into the Mediterranean this card could not be used. In his opinion their passing into the Mediterranean would be a definite hostile act against us.

The Prime Minister said that President Roosevelt had always taken a great interest in the fate of these two French battleships and he thought that it might be desirable to telegraph to the President and suggest to him that he should warn the Vichy Government against moving them.[1]

Winston S. Churchill to Lord Halifax and General Ismay
(*Churchill papers, 20/13*)

8 November 1940

This telegram[2] reinforces my doubts about the wisdom of General de Gaulle flying to Cairo. His presence there will bring all the collision between Weygand France – of which I still have some hopes – and Free France, to a head. It would be much better for General de Gaulle to come home here as soon as the Libreville situation is cleared up. We must put frankly before him the facts which are developing, and the position of his Movement in relation to them. It is a good thing for him to have captured this South-Western African and Equatorial domain, and every effort must be made by us to hold it for him. But he and his Movement may now become an obstacle to a very considerable hiving off of the French Empire to our side. There is no doubt that men like Weygand and Noguès when searching their souls about their own misdeeds harden themselves against us by dwelling on the insubordination of de Gaulle. It will be much easier to point all these things out to de Gaulle at close quarters than when he is a distant potentate.

I suggest therefore that he should be urged to return here immediately after the Libreville operation without going to Egypt.

---

[1] For the telegram as eventually sent, see 10 November 1940.
[2] From the Senior Naval Officer, Suez Canal Area, Admiral Pipon.

2. On the other hand the very stiffest action should be taken to secure absolute control of the Canal, and the local French officials, including de Benoist,[1] should politely, but unmistakably, be made to see where they get off.

Paragraphs 3 (a) and (b) and paragraph 6[2] should surely be made effective as the SBNO, Suez Canal Area, desires.

I would much rather do this in the absence of de Gaulle than with him. The French will take from us what they will not take from him.

WSC

Winston S. Churchill to Sir Edward Bridges
(*Churchill papers, 20/13*)

8 November 1940

Many of the Executive Departments naturally have set up and developed their own Statistical Branches, but there appears to be a separate Statistical Branch attached to the Ministerial Committee on Production, and naturally the Ministry of Supply's Statistical Branch covers a very wide field. I have my own Statistical Branch under Professor Lindemann.

It is essential to consolidate and make sure that agreed figures only are used. The utmost confusion is caused when people argue on different statistical data. I wish all statistics to be concentrated in my own Branch as Prime Minister and Minister of Defence, from which alone the final authoritative working statistics will issue. The various Departmental Statistical Branches will, of course, continue as at present, but agreement must be reached between them and the Central Statistical Office.

Pray look into this, and advise me how my wish can be most speedily and effectively achieved.

WSC

[1] Baron de Benoist. He had been instrumental in forming a Free French group in Cairo on 18 June 1940, and had sought to rally those Frenchmen resident in Egypt to the Gaullist cause.
[2] In which Admiral Pipon stressed the need to take action against Vichy French supporters in the Canal Zone.

Winston S. Churchill to Sir Reginald Clarry[1]
(*Churchill papers, 20/2*)

8 November 1940
Confidential

Dear Clarry,

Your Committee will I hope believe that all these questions of high appointments are continually in my mind, and that I have many sources of information and opportunities of forming a right judgment. I have not only to try to make sure that the best men are chosen, but also to make officers discharging tasks of extreme difficulty feel confidence that they will be supported and protected while they do their duty. I do not think it would be at all a good thing for the 1922 Committee to become a kind of collecting house for complaints against serving Commanders-in-Chief or other important officials. This I am sure would be a function which the Members of the Committee would be the first to repudiate. Individual representations stand on a different footing.

Yours sincerely
Winston S. Churchill

Winston S. Churchill to King Zog[2]
(*Churchill papers, 20/2*)

8 November 1940

Sir,

I hope I shall not be thought discourteous if I say that in present circumstances the calls on my time are too pressing for me to have the honour of seeing Your Majesty. The necessity of giving constant and personal attention to the conduct of the war makes it inevitable that I should cut down

---

[1] Reginald Clarry, 1882–1945. A gas engineer; Engineer Manager and Secretary, Swansea Gas Company. Adviser to the Ministry of Munitions, 1916–18. Conservative MP, 1922–9 and from 1931 until his death. Knighted, 1936.

[2] Ahmed Zog, 1895–1961. A Muslim. The son of the head of a leading Albanian clan. Educated in Constantinople. Fought against the Turks in 1913. On active service in the Austro-Hungarian Army, 1914–18. Albanian Minister of the Interior, 1920. Commander-in-Chief of the Albanian forces, 1921. Minister of the Interior (for the second time), 1921. Prime Minister, 1921–4. After an attempt was made on his life, he retired with his colleagues to the mountains on the Serbian-Albanian border. Proclaimed Albania a republic, and elected President, 1925. Repressed the revolt of the northern Catholic tribes, 1926, and executed the Catholic priest who had inspired the revolt. Proclaimed King of Albania (as King Zog), 1928. Fled to Greece after the Italian invasion; and then to England (where he lived near High Wycombe). When Albania became Communist in December 1945, he went from England to Egypt, then to Long Island in the United States, and finally to Cannes. He died in hospital in Paris.

my interviews to the very minimum and I am thus prevented from seeing many persons with whom in easier circumstances I should have been only too glad to have had an interview.

May I express to Your Majesty my sympathy for You at a time when the soil of Albania is being used by the Italian aggressor for an attack on a peaceful neighbouring country and my conviction that Albania will soon be relieved from the sufferings which she at present endures.

Your Majesty's obedient servant,
Winston S. Churchill

Winston S. Churchill: recollection
(*'Their Finest Hour'*, page 479)

8 November 1940

The Secretary of State for War got back home on November 8, and came that evening after the usual raid had begun to see me in my temporary underground abode in Piccadilly.[1] He brought with him the carefully-guarded secret which I wished I had known earlier. Nevertheless no harm had been done. Mr Eden unfolded in considerable detail to a select circle, including the CIGS and General Ismay, the offensive plan which General Wavell and General Wilson[2] had conceived and prepared. No longer were we to await in our fortified lines at Mersa Matruh an Italian assault, for which defensive battle such long and artful preparations had been made. On the contrary, within a month or so we were ourselves to attack. The operation was to be called 'Compass'.

General Ismay: recollection
(*'The Memoirs of Lord Ismay'*, page 195)

8 November 1940

To a restricted meeting of the Defence Committee, at which only the Prime Minister, the three Service Ministers, the three Chiefs of Staff, Jacob and I were present, Eden disclosed that Wavell had decided not to await

---

[1] The discontinued Piccadilly Line underground station at Down Street, being used as an air raid shelter.
[2] General Sir Henry Maitland Wilson.

Graziani's[1] attack at Mersa Matruh, but to take the offensive himself at an early date; and he followed up this startling announcement with an explanation of Wavell's plans. Every one of us could have jumped for joy, but Churchill could have jumped twice as high as the rest. He has said that he 'purred like six cats'. That is putting it mildly. He was rapturously happy. 'At long last we are going to throw off the intolerable shackles of the defensive,' he declaimed. 'Wars are won by superior will-power. Now we will wrest the initiative from the enemy and impose our will on him.'

Needless to say, Wavell's plan was approved without a moment's hesitation, and even before the meeting broke up Churchill started estimating the spoils. He was always prone to count his chickens before they were hatched, and as a rule his estimates erred on the generous side. But on this occasion the results were to exceed his most optimistic expectations.

As THERE WAS a full moon that weekend, it was thought safer that Churchill should not go to Chequers, but to Ditchley, a house just over thirty miles further west.

Nancy Tree[2] to Winston S. Churchill
(*Churchill papers, 2/399*)

9 November 1940   Dytchley[3]

Dear Mr Prime Minister:–

I was horrified that I appeared as I did this morning on so momentous an occasion. I thought you were leaving very early or I would have been dressed & ready to wish you God speed. Like you, I do all my writing in bed but without the same happy results!

---

[1] Rudolfo Graziani, 1882–1955. A regular soldier, on active service in Libya, 1911, and on the Italian-Austrian front, 1915–18 (twice wounded, decorated for valour). Lieutenant-Colonel, Macedonian front, 1918. On active service (against rebel tribesmen) in Libya, 1921–31. Governor of Cyrenaica, 1931–5. Commanded the Italian forces which conquered Abyssinia from the south, 1935–6. Viceroy of Abyssinia 1936–7. Created Marquis of Neghelli, 1937. Commander of the Axis Forces in North Africa, 1940; defeated by the British in North Africa, 1941. Minister of War, 1943, in the Government of the Fascist Republic of Saló. Led the continuing Fascist armed resistance after the fall of Mussolini, 1943–4. Captured by Italian partisans near Lake Como, April 1945. Stripped of his rank, deprived of his decorations and sentenced to nineteen years' imprisonment for collaboration with the Germans, May 1950. Freed by Government amnesty, August 1950. Subsequently Honorary President of the neo-Fascist Italian Social Movement, from which he resigned in 1954, in protest against its opposition to the European Defence Community.

[2] Nancy Perkins, of Richmond, Virginia. The widow of Henry Field of Chicago, she married Ronald Tree in 1920. In 1948 she married, as her third husband, Colonel Claude Lancaster, a Conservative MP. Their marriage was dissolved in 1958.

[3] The printed notepaper spells Dytchley thus, with a 'y'. In her letter, Nancy Tree spelt it Ditchley (with an 'i'), the form most commonly used.

I have always been one of your greatest if most humble admirers – and I meant to tell you how delighted and honoured we all were to have you come to Ditchley. If it is convenient for you at any time to use no matter how short the notice – it is at your disposal.

I can only say that to be of even a small use to you on whom the hopes of so many depend – is a privilege and pleasure – and I trust you will feel that you can use the house as your own.

Very Sincerely Yrs
Nancy Tree

Winston S. Churchill to General Ismay and Sir Edward Bridges
(*Premier papers, 4/43B/1*)

9 November 1940

To whom has circular marked A[1] been sent? Who is responsible for drawing it up and sending it out? No one is entitled to be informed of impending movements of British ships, see paragraph marked B. It is intolerable that all these secret matters connected with operations should be scattered round the world. It may sometimes be necessary where Dominions forces are involved to give specific details, but more usually general statements should suffice. I had no idea such information was being circularized. Not only the lives of troops and sailors, but the success of operations are involved.

In future no such statements are to be issued without my written approval.

John Colville: diary
(*Colville papers*)

9 November 1940

The PM spent most of the morning dictating a speech he is to make at a Mansion House lunch today and with the composition of which he was so behindhand that he asked to be allowed to be half an hour late for lunch.

Desmond[2] also retailed two of the PM's latest remarks, one to General Sikorski who wanted foreign exchange: '*Mon Général, devant la vieille dame de Threadneedle Street je suis impotent*'; the other a 2.00 a.m. Parthian shot at the Chiefs of Staff: 'I am obliged to wage modern warfare with ancient weapons.'

---

[1] Circular Z, No. 345, to the United Kingdom High Commissioners.
[2] Desmond Morton, who, among other responsibilities, was Churchill's liaison officer with the governments-in-exile.

NOVEMBER 1940

Winston S. Churchill: speech
(*'Into Battle'*, *pages 310–13*)

9 November 1940
1 p.m.

I thank you, my Lord Mayor,[1] for the toast which you have proposed to his Majesty's Government and for what you have said about them and of the confidence felt in them. I thank you also for your reference to Mr Chamberlain, who was so recently one of our most active colleagues, under whom so many of us have served, and whose illness causes us all the greatest sorrow today. Things happen so quickly nowadays and there are such a lot of them going on that one finds it somewhat difficult to measure evenly the march of time. For myself, I can say there are weeks which seem to pass in a flash and then again there are others which are unutterably long and slow. At times it is almost difficult to believe that so much has happened and at another that so little time has passed.

It is now six months since the King and Parliament confided to me and to my colleagues the very grave and heavy task to which we have devoted ourselves, as I can assure you, to the best of our abilities. It is lucky that we did not make any extravagant optimistic promises or predictions, because a succession of melancholy disasters and terrible assaults and perils have fallen upon us. We have had to face these great calamities; we have come through the disasters; we have surmounted the perils so far; but the fact remains that at the present time all we have got to show is survival and increasing strength and an inflexible will to win.

The outside world which a little while ago took only a moderate view of our prospects, now believes that Britain will survive. But between immediate survival and lasting victory there is a long road to tread. In treading it, we shall show the world the perseverance and steadfastness of the British race and the glorious resilience and flexibility of our ancient institutions.

Let me remind you that, in spite of all the blows we have endured and under all the burdens we bear, and amid so many deadly threats, we have not abandoned one jot of any of our obligations or undertakings towards the captive and enslaved countries of Europe or towards any of those countries which still act with us. On the contrary, since we have been left alone in this world struggle we have re-affirmed or defined more precisely all the causes of all the countries with whom or for whom we drew the sword – Austria,

---

[1] George Henry Wilkinson, 1885–1968. An Alderman of the City of London, 1933–59. Chairman, Ministry of Home Security London Deep Shelter Committee, 1940–4. Lord Mayor of London, 1 October 1940 to 1 November 1941. Created Baronet, 1941. Chairman, National Greek Relief Fund, 1940–7; Lord Mayor's National Air Raid Distress Fund, 1941–54.

Czechoslovakia, Poland, Norway, Holland, Belgium; greatest of all, France; latest of all, Greece. For all of these we will toil and strive, and our victory will supply the liberation of them all.

The week that has now ended has brought us a message from across the ocean, a message of the highest encouragement and good cheer during the protracted tumult and controversy of the Presidential Election. Everyone in this island – Parliament, Ministers, the Press, the public – discreetly abstained from the slightest expression of opinion about the domestic, political, and party conflicts of the great democracy of the United States.

We were deeply touched by the words of kindness and goodwill and the promises of material aid which were uttered by Mr Willkie[1] on behalf of the Republican Party, which he captained so ably. But I am sure it will give no offence, now that all is over, if I offer in the name of HM Government, and, if you will allow me, my Lord Mayor, in the name of the citizens of London, our most heartfelt congratulations to the illustrious American statesman who has never failed to give us a helping hand, and who now, in the supreme crisis, has achieved the unprecedented mark of American confidence of being chosen for the third time to lead his mighty people forward on their path.

The help that we have been promised by the United States takes the form at the present time of a most abundant sharing with us of the fruits of the gigantic munitions production which has now been set on foot throughout the matchless workshops, furnaces, and foundries of the United States. This has no doubt been done primarily because our stubborn and unwavering resistance here will alone gain the time needed by the United States to convert its industry to a war basis and to build up the immense naval, military, and air forces which they have set on foot for their own purposes and for their own protection.

Their interest in our successful resistance and final victory has been proclaimed by all parties in America. But no one over here has been left in any doubt that, beyond this strong material help and foundation of common interest, there flows a tide of comprehension, of sentiment, and fierce, matchless sympathy for our cause which warms our hearts and strengthens our resolve.

People sometimes wonder why we are unable to take the offensive against the enemy, and always have to wait for some new blow which he will strike against us. The reason is that our production in munitions is now only in the

---

[1] Wendell Lewis Willkie, 1892–1944. Born in Indiana. A lawyer and a Democrat. Became a Republican in opposition to Roosevelt's New Deal. Unlike many Republicans, he was not an isolationist. Won the Republican Party nomination for the Presidency, 1940. Lost, but gained a larger Republican popular vote than any previous contender (a vote eventually exceeded by Eisenhower in 1952). Visited Britain, Russia and China as Roosevelt's personal emissary, 1940–1.

early part of its second year, and that enormous factories and plants which we laid down on or shortly before the outbreak of war are only now beginning to come into production. The Germans, on the other hand, have long passed the culminating point of munitions production, which is reached usually about the fourth year.

We have, therefore, a long and arduous road to travel in which our war industries must grow up to their full stature, in which our Navy must receive the reinforcements of the hundreds of vessels which we began on the outbreak of war, and which are now coming continuously into service; in which our Army must be equipped, trained, and perfected into a strong, keen offensive weapon; and, above all, our Air Force must add superiority of numbers to that superiority of quality which, in machines, and still more in manhood, they have so signally displayed. We are straining every nerve to accelerate our production, and with the ardent, resolute aid of British labour, guided by science and improving organisation, I do not doubt that we shall succeed.

But here is where the help from across the oceans is especially valuable, because in the United States, as in our great Dominions and in India, all the production of war materials and the training of pilots can proceed without any distraction or impediment. Therefore I welcome most cordially the aid which has been promised us from the United States as I do the important contributions which have already been received. There is one other point which must, however, be borne in mind in this survey. The enemy is naturally doing his utmost to cut us from these vital supplies and, therefore, the maintenance by sea-power of the ocean routes is an absolute necessity to our victory, and is of importance to all who need or who desire our victory.

It has been usual, on these occasions, for the Prime Minister to give a general survey of foreign policy and to refer to our relations with many countries in well-guarded, well-poised, and happily balanced terms. To-day I need not do that. It has been obvious to all that we are striving to the utmost of our strength for the freedom of nations against the oppressor, that we are striving for the progress of peoples through the process of self-government and for the creation of that wider brotherhood among men which alone will bring them back to prosperity and peace. We do not need to speak, therefore, of many of those nations.

But there is one small heroic country to whom our thoughts to-day go out in new sympathy and admiration. To the valiant Greek people and their armies – now defending their native soil from the latest Italian outrage, to them we send from the heart of old London our faithful promise that, amid all our burdens and anxieties, we will do our best to aid them in their struggle, and that we will never cease to strike at the foul aggressor in ever-increasing strength from this time forth until the crimes and treacheries which hang around the neck of Mussolini and disgrace the Italian name have been brought to condign and exemplary justice.

Winston S. Churchill to Sir Charles Portal
(*Churchill papers, 20/13*)

10 November 1940

Many thanks for all these figures, which kindly return.

Altogether, broadly speaking, 1,000 aircraft and 17,000 Air personnel in the Middle East provide 30½ Squadrons, with a total initial equipment of 395 Operational types, of which it is presumed 300 are ready for action on any date. Unhappily, out of 65 Hurricanes, only 2 Squadrons (apart from Malta) of initial equipment of 32 together are available, meaning in practice only 24. These are the only modern aircraft, unless you count the Blenheim IV's. All the rest of this enormous force is armed with obsolete or feeble machines. The process of replacement should, therefore, be pressed to the utmost, and surely it should be possible to utilize all this skilled personnel of pilots and ground staff to handle the new machines. Therefore 'remounting' the Eastern Air Force ought not in principle to require more personnel, except where new types are more complicated. However, as part of the reinforcements now being sent, i.e., four Wellington and four Hurricane Squadrons, we are sending over 3,000 additional personnel.

In the disparity between the great mass of men and numbers of aircraft on charge, and the fighting product constantly available, which is painfully marked both here and at home, lies the waste of RAF resources. What is the use of the 600 machines which are not even included in the initial equipment of the 30 Squadrons? No doubt some can be explained as Training Communication and Transport. But how is it that out of 732 Operational types, only 395 play any part in the fighting?

I hope that a most earnest effort will be made to get full value for men, material and money, out of this very large force: first by remounting, second by making more Squadrons out of the large surplus of machines not formed in Squadrons, third by developing local OTU's or other training establishments.

WSC

Winston S. Churchill to Malcolm MacDonald
(*Churchill papers, 20/13*)

10 November 1940

I see your total of homeless is down by 1,500 this week to about 10,000. Please let me know how many new you had in, and how many former went out. With such a small number as 10,000 you ought to be able to clean this up if you have another light week.

What is the average time that a homeless person remains at a rest centre?

WSC

1074   NOVEMBER 1940

Winston S. Churchill to Lord Halifax
(*Churchill papers, 20/13*)

10 November 1940

In the Chiefs of Staff's report recently about the Middle East, a more rough policy was suggested towards the Iraq Government. I do not know how you propose to handle this situation. It seems to me they ought to be made aware that we shall not hesitate to use force against them to the full if they intrigue with the Germans or Italians. We have treated them with extraordinary tenderness and consideration in the last few years, and they ought to be made to feel that in the pass to which things are come we are as much to be feared as anyone else. I should be grateful if you would let me have your views.

WSC

Winston S. Churchill to Anthony Eden
(*Churchill papers, 20/13*)

10 November 1940

This is the same Director of Artillery[1] who is always trying to crab this kind of thing. I hope you will look into this yourself. We had the greatest difficulty in carrying these bombs through, and there was every evidence they would not have received fair play had I not gone down myself to see the experiment. Now is the chance to let the Greeks try this method out, and it would seem that it might be very helpful to them.

What is this tale that they are dangerous to pack and handle? They are, of course, dispatched without their detonators, and therefore cannot explode.

As you know, there is a feud running between Major Jefferis's inventions and the D of A's Department, and I have had to take Jefferis under the protection of the Minister of Defence. When you think how disgraceful is the record of trench mortar and trench mortar ammunition so far as the D of A's Department is concerned, it is most vexatious to encounter this obstruction.

WSC

Winston S. Churchill to President Roosevelt
(*Churchill papers, 20/14*)

10 November 1940

1. We have been much disturbed by reports of intention of French Government to bring *Jean Bart* and *Richelieu* to Mediterranean for completion.

[1] Edward Montagu Campbell Clarke, 1885–1971. Entered the Royal Artillery, 1905. On active service, 1914–18. Major-General, 1938. Vice-President of the Ordnance Committee, 1938. Director of Artillery, 1938–41; Director-General of Artillery, 1942–5. Knighted, 1946.

It is difficult to exaggerate potential danger if this were to happen, and so open the way for these ships to fall under German control. We should feel bound to do our best to prevent it.

2. We conveyed a warning to French Government, through Ambassador at Madrid a few days ago, on the following lines:–

'Such a step would greatly increase the temptation to the Germans and Italians to seize the French Fleet. We doubt not the good faith of the French Government, but their physical ability to implement their assurances that they will not let the Fleet fall into enemy hands. We particularly wish to avoid any clash between British and French Naval Forces, and therefore hope that, if they had thought of moving the ships, they will now refrain from doing so.'

3. As we said to French Government, we should not question good faith of assurances, but even if we accept assurances we can feel no security that they will, in fact, be able to maintain them once the ships are in French ports in the power or reach of the enemy, and I must confess that the desire of French Government to bring these ships back, if this turns out to be well-founded, seems to me to give cause for some suspicion.

4. It would be most helpful if you felt able to give a further warning at Vichy on this matter, for if things went wrong it might well prove of extreme danger for us both.

Winston S. Churchill to General de Gaulle
(*Churchill papers, 20/14*)

10 November 1940

Further to my cable of yesterday, I feel most anxious for consultation with you. Situation between France and Britain has changed remarkably since you left. A very strong feeling has grown throughout France in our favour as it is seen that we cannot be conquered, and that war will go on. We know Vichy Government is deeply alarmed by the very stern pressure administered to them by United States. On the other hand, Laval and revengeful Darlan are trying to force French declaration of war against us and rejoice in provoking minor naval incidents. We have hopes of Weygand in Africa, and no one must underrate advantage that would follow if he were rallied. We are trying to arrive at some *modus vivendi* with Vichy which will minimize the risk of incidents and will enable favourable forces in France to develop. We have told them plainly that, if they bomb Gibraltar or take other aggressive action, we shall bomb Vichy, and pursue the Vichy Government wherever it chooses to go. So far we have had no response. You will see how important it is that you should be here. I therefore hope you will be able to tidy up at Libreville and come home as soon as possible. Let me know your plans.

Winston S. Churchill to Anne Chamberlain
(*Churchill papers, 20/2*)

10 November 1940   10 Downing Street

My dear Mrs Neville,

I heard the news of Neville's death and your grievous loss with deep sorrow.

During these long violent months of war we had come closer together than at any time in our twenty years of friendly relationship amid the ups and downs of politics. I greatly admired his fortitude and firmness of spirit. I felt when I served under him that he would never give in: and I knew when our positions were reversed that I could count upon the aid of a loyal and unflinching comrade.

I feel keenly for you in your grief, for I know what you were to one another, and I offer respectfully my most profound sympathy.

Believe me,
Yours very sincerely,
Winston S. Churchill

John Colville: diary
(*Colville papers*)

11 November 1940   10 Downing Street

The PM came back from Ditchley at lunch-time. Afterwards he went to sleep but had to be disturbed owing to the shriek of bombs nearby. He soon got tired of the shelter and returned to his bedroom, where he gave me a lecture on the excellence of his teeth-cleaning apparatus, an electrical appliance which spurts water at a high velocity into his mouth and removes the taste of cigars. He said that if young men like me were sensible enough to use them they would never have bad teeth.

He is very cross with Archie Sinclair who (after the attack in the Beer Cellar at Munich[1]) gave an interview to the *Daily Express* saying that dictators were military objectives. The PM thinks this may cause unpleasant reactions on himself and says such a statement almost amounts to incitement to assassination. But, if you are allowed to bomb Heads of States, surely you may shoot them?

Today we have shot down more raiders than usual and, for the first time over England, at least eight Italian planes among them. The PM gave a whoop of joy when I told him.

[1] On November 8 each year Hitler celebrated the anniversary of his 1923 attempt to seize power in Bavaria by a ceremony in the Beer Hall where the coup had begun. To avoid his speech being interrupted by British bombers that day, he had brought forward the ceremony by an hour. That night a total of 106 British bombers were over Germany, against several targets. The Beer Hall was untouched.

NOVEMBER 1940 1077

War Cabinet: minutes
(*Cabinet papers, 65/10*)

11 November 1940 Cabinet War Room
5 p.m.

The Prime Minister informed the War Cabinet that a telegram had now been received from General de Gaulle (No. 13 from Brazzaville) agreeing to return to this country for consultations, and adding that he counted on returning to French Equatorial Africa, where his presence was necessary. Arrangements should be made to facilitate the General's journey.

The Foreign Secretary also referred to telegram No. 1110 from Athens reporting the views of a Frenchman who had just arrived from Vichy to the effect that the French were with us, but that their courage was only now returning.

The Prime Minister expressed general agreement with the Foreign Secretary's suggestion. Matters at Libreville had gone well with us, but he thought that French opinion generally might well be veering in our favour, and that we should adopt a mixed attitude and not play out our hand against the Vichy French to the uttermost. As regards the blockade, we were not at the present stopping ships passing through the Straits of Gibraltar. While we must not allow that position to develop too far, he thought that it should continue, at any rate for the next few days.

The Prime Minister referred to a telegram which had been despatched, giving certain detailed information as to troop movements. While the Dominion Prime Ministers must, of course, be kept informed of the position generally, and, on occasions, of impending operations, it was undesirable that very specific information as to dispositions and future movements should be communicated to any person (including even Dominion Prime Ministers) other than those who must be acquainted with them to enable action to be taken.

The Prime Minister said that, since the War Cabinet had last met, they had suffered a severe loss in the death of Mr Chamberlain. This loss would be felt most deeply by all those who had worked with him. They had all admired the great courage he had shown in continuing at work for a fortnight, in failing health, after his severe operation. Mr Chamberlain's great grief in leaving life had perhaps been that he had not lived to see the end of the struggle in which we were engaged. But maybe he had lived long enough to feel confident as to the outcome.

On the following day, when the House met, tributes would be paid to Mr Chamberlain. It was usual, after these tributes had been made, for the House to adjourn. On this occasion, however, there would be no immediate adjournment, as a Service was to be held in Westminster Abbey on Thursday, and this would involve the adjournment of the House on that day.

Discussion then ensued whether the Prime Minister only should speak, on behalf of the whole Government and all the Parties comprised in it, or whether the Lord Privy Seal and the Secretary of State for Air as Leaders of the Labour and Liberal parties should also speak.

In discussion, it was argued that three speeches delivered from the same Bench might seem inappropriate. On the other hand, it was felt that there was no good reason to depart from the customary plan, whereby tributes were paid on these occasions by the party Leaders. Further, any departure from this procedure would be liable to misinterpretation.

The War Cabinet endorsed this view.

The Prime Minister said that no publicity should be given to the Service on Thursday. He would inform the House of Commons of the arrangements in Secret Session on the following day.

Defence Committee (Operations): minutes
(*Cabinet papers, 69/1*)

11 November 1940
9.30 p.m.

ASSISTANCE TO GREECE

The Committee had before them a Telegram from the Air Officer Commanding-in-Chief, Middle East,[1] and the Air Ministry's reply on the subject of despatch of air forces to Greece from Egypt.

The Prime Minister said that it was only natural that the Commanders-in-Chief on the spot should feel that they were being unduly weakened by the despatch of air forces to Greece, and that they should lodge a protest. At the same time, it was clear that there could be no question of countermanding the despatch of No. 80 Squadron which was due to leave for Crete on the 14th November.

As regards the second squadron of Gladiators, the instructions to the Air Officer Commanding-in-Chief, Middle East, were permissive, i.e. it was open to him to make representations if he felt that after the arrival of the Hurricanes on about the 2nd December he was still too weak in fighter aircraft to spare the second Gladiator Squadron.

The Secretary of State for War said that he was in Egypt when the instructions had arrived, and that he and all the Commanders had interpreted them as giving the AOC-in-C, Middle East, no option about the despatch of

[1] Air Vice-Marshal Sir A. M. Longmore.

the second Gladiator Squadron. It would ease their minds considerably if they could be told that it was open to them to make further representations if the situation in Egypt, even after the arrival of the Hurricanes, did not in their judgment justify the despatch of the second squadron.

It was agreed that a telegram should be despatched to the AOC-in-C Middle East in the above sense.

The Prime Minister said that there always seemed to be some doubt as to our actual air strength in the Middle East. It was most important that the arrival of reinforcements should be reported from day to day, and that we should at all times have a complete picture of our effective strength. He added that at present the Commanders in the Middle East were in the habit of sending most discursive telegrams explaining every little air action that had taken place and precisely where every bomb had been dropped, and omitted the item of information which it was necessary for us to know above all others, namely exactly how they stood as regards effective strength.

The Chief of the Air Staff undertook to telegraph to the AOC-in-C Middle East, requesting him to supply the information specified by the Prime Minister and to omit details of petty engagements.

The Prime Minister then drew attention to the large number of ground personnel (approximately 17,000) already in the Middle East, and to the fact that out of 1,000 aeroplanes in that area only about 40 were modern aircraft. The proper course was to scrap the obsolete machines as soon as possible and to concentrate the ground personnel on maintaining the machines that were worth maintaining.

Captain Berkeley: diary
(*Berkeley papers*)

12 November 1940

Winston flogs on, wildly but with the same genius. He is virtually a dictator and it is only seldom that some bold minister rebels. The COS, at any rate, are quite subservient and wholly engaged in ways and means. The invasion of Greece has started many new problems. They are putting up a stout resistance, but so did other such victims. And while the threat to Egypt subsides we can give them little help. Still, we have two squadrons operating in Greece, a force in Crete, and many attacks on Adriatic ports to our credit. And the Italian is by all accounts in low water, dispirited and afraid.

John Colville: diary
(*Colville papers*)

12 November 1940

Lord Lothian has drafted a telegram for the PM to send to Roosevelt. It stresses very frankly our need for American support in obtaining the Irish naval bases, in guarding Singapore, in getting more ships and above all in buying munitions and aircraft on credit. It is intended to make R feel that if we go down, the responsibility will be America's. Brendan tells me the PM thinks it so admirably written that he could not improve a word of it; but it will go before the Cabinet for consideration.

Anne Chamberlain to Winston S. Churchill
(*Churchill papers, 2/393*)

12 November 1940   Heckfield

Dear Prime Minister,
   I thank you for your letter.
   I find it hard to say more now.
   Neville shared your sense of comradeship & felt secure in the knowledge that you too would never give in –

Yours very sincerely
Anne Chamberlain

Winston S. Churchill: speech
(*Hansard*)

12 November 1940   House of Commons (Annexe)
                                                                        Church House

MR NEVILLE CHAMBERLAIN

The Prime Minister (Mr Churchill): Since we last met, the House has suffered a very grievous loss in the death of one of its most distinguished Members and of a statesman and public servant who, during the best part of three memorable years, was first Minister of the Crown.
   The fierce and bitter controversies which hung around him in recent times were hushed by the news of his illness and are silenced by his death. In paying a tribute of respect and of regard to an eminent man who has been taken from us, no one is obliged to alter the opinions which he has formed or expressed upon issues which have become a part of history; but at the Lychgate we may

all pass our own conduct and our own judgments under a searching review. It is not given to human beings, happily for them, for otherwise life would be intolerable, to foresee or to predict to any large extent the unfolding course of events. In one phase men seem to have been right, in another they seem to have been wrong. Then again, a few years later, when the perspective of time has lengthened, all stands in a different setting. There is a new proportion. There is another scale of values. History with its flickering lamp stumbles along the trail of the past, trying to reconstruct its scenes, to revive its echoes, and kindle with pale gleams the passion of former days. What is the worth of all this? The only guide to a man is his conscience; the only shield to his memory is the rectitude and sincerity of his actions. It is very imprudent to walk through life without this shield, because we are so often mocked by the failure of our hopes and the upsetting of our calculations; but with this shield, however the fates may play, we march always in the ranks of honour.

It fell to Neville Chamberlain in one of the supreme crises of the world to be contradicted by events, to be disappointed in his hopes, and to be deceived and cheated by a wicked man. But what were these hopes in which he was disappointed? What were these wishes in which he was frustrated? What was that faith that was abused? They were surely among the most noble and benevolent instincts of the human heart – the love of peace, the toil for peace, the strife for peace, the pursuit of peace, even at great peril and certainly to the utter disdain of popularity or clamour. Whatever else history may or may not say about these terrible, tremendous years, we can be sure that Neville Chamberlain acted with perfect sincerity according to his lights and strove to the utmost of his capacity and authority, which were powerful, to save the world from the awful, devastating struggle in which we are now engaged. This alone will stand him in good stead as far as what is called the verdict of history is concerned.

But it is also a help to our country and to our whole Empire, and to our decent faithful way of living that, however long the struggle may last, or however dark may be the clouds which overhang our path, no future generation of English-speaking folks – for that is the tribunal to which we appeal – will doubt that, even at a great cost to ourselves in technical preparation, we were guiltless of the bloodshed, terror and misery which have engulfed so many lands and peoples, and yet seek new victims still. Herr Hitler protests with frantic words and gestures that he has only desired peace. What do these ravings and outpourings count before the silence of Neville Chamberlain's tomb? Long and hard, hazardous years lie before us, but at least we entered upon them united and with clean hearts.

I do not propose to give an appreciation of Neville Chamberlain's life and character, but there are certain qualities, always admired in these Islands, which he possessed in an altogether exceptional degree. He had a physical and moral toughness of fibre which enabled him all through his varied career to endure misfortune and disappointment without being unduly discouraged or wearied. He had a precision of mind and an aptitude for business which raised him far above the ordinary levels of our generation. He had a firmness of spirit which was not often elated by success, seldom downcast by failure and never swayed by panic. When, contrary to all his hopes, beliefs and exertions, the war came upon him, and when, as he himself said, all that he had worked for was shattered, there was no man more resolved to pursue the unsought quarrel to the death. The same qualities which made him one of the last to enter the war, made him one of the last who would quit it until the full victory of a righteous cause was won.

I had the singular experience of passing in a day from being one of his most prominent opponents and critics to being one of his principal lieutenants, and on another day of passing from serving under him to become the head of a Government of which, with perfect loyalty, he was content to be a member. Such relationships are unusual in our public life. I have before told the House on the morrow of the Debate which in the early days of May challenged his position, he declared to me and a few other friends that only a National Government could face the storm about to break upon us, and that if he were an obstacle to the formation of such a Government, he would instantly retire. Thereafter, he acted with that singleness of purpose and simplicity of conduct which at all times, and especially in great times, ought to be a model for us all.

When he returned to duty a few weeks after a most severe operation, the bombardment of London and of the seat of Government had begun. I was a witness during that fortnight of his fortitude under the most grievous and painful bodily afflictions, and I can testify that, although physically only the wreck of a man, his nerve was unshaken and his remarkable mental faculties unimpaired.

After he left the Government he refused all honours. He would die like his father, plain Mr Chamberlain. I sought the permission of the King however to have him supplied with the Cabinet papers, and until a few days of his death he followed our affairs with keenness, interest and tenacity. He met the approach of death with a steady eye. If he grieved at all, it was that he could not be a spectator of our victory, but I think he died with the comfort of knowing that his country had, at least, turned the corner.

At this time our thoughts must pass to the gracious and charming lady who shared his days of triumph and adversity with a courage and quality the equal of his own. He was, like his father and his brother, Austen, before him, a famous Member of the House of Commons, and we here assembled this morning, Members of all parties, without a single exception, feel that we do ourselves and our country honour in saluting the memory of one whom Disraeli would have called an 'English worthy.'

John Colville: diary
(*Colville papers*)

12 November 1940

At 12.00 noon the PM rose in the unfamiliar surroundings of Church House and paid before the House of Commons his moving and eloquent tribute to Mr Chamberlain. The noise of Seal and Miss Watson[1] coming on to the dais (which takes the place of the official gallery), the coughs and creaks from members, were very disturbing in the small chamber used for debate, and I did not think the PM's delivery was equal to the magnificence of his language and the balance of his phrases.

War Cabinet: Confidential Annex
(*Cabinet papers, 65/16*)

12 November 1940   Cabinet War Room
5 p.m.

The Prime Minister said that the question of sending Defiants to the Middle East at a later date should be considered. He was satisfied, however, that the present reinforcement of the Middle East by Hurricane aircraft should not be interfered with. If it had been a question of parting with, say, 500 aircraft to the Middle East, he would not have favoured this course. As it was, we were only parting with aircraft on a scale which the Ministry of Aircraft Production was in a position immediately to make good. Again, we should enjoy a certain easement in the air during the next few months. The scale of the operations against this country had been diminishing for some time past.

The Prime Minister reminded the War Cabinet that the Admiralty, together with the Ministry of Shipping, had been invited to examine the possibility of using some of the large, fast ocean-going liners for transport purposes.

Later the Chiefs of Staff had initiated a Report on Basic Shipping Requirements with a view to ascertaining to what extent shipping would prove a limiting factor to our future plans (Chiefs of Staff 256th Meeting, Minute 4). It was important that both these Reports should be submitted as early as possible.

---

[1] Miss Watson, a former typist at 10 Downing Street, had been promoted to be a Private Secretary, with responsibility for Parliamentary Questions. Jock Colville writes: 'She seems to be a kind, efficient, unassuming and rather wizened old thing' (*The Fringes of Power*, page 31).

Winston S. Churchill to Herbert Morrison
(*Churchill papers, 20/13*)

12 November 1940

How are you getting on with the comfort of the shelters in the winter — flooring, drainage, and the like? What is being done to bring them inside the houses? I attach the greatest importance to gramophones and wireless in the shelters. How is that going forward? Would not this perhaps be a very good subject for the Lord Mayor's Fund? I should not be surprised if the improved lighting comes up again before many weeks are out, and I hope that the preparations for it will go forward.

WSC

Winston S. Churchill to Lord Hankey[1]
(*Premier papers, 3/214*)

12 November 1940
ACTION THIS DAY

Pray see the attached.[2] I am awaiting your proposals for assisting Greece with munitions. When you have made up the best packet you can, let me know, but not later than Friday next, so that I can then take up the question of transportation with the Admiralty.

WSC

Winston S. Churchill to Lord Halifax
(*Churchill papers, 20/13*)

12 November 1940

We shall most certainly have to obtain control of Syria by one means or another in the next few months. The best way would be by a Weygand or a de Gaullist movement, but this cannot be counted on, and until we have dealt with the Italians in Libya we have no troops to spare for a northern venture.

In the meanwhile, would it not be wise to raise a Turkish issue in Syria?

---

[1] On 7 November 1940 Sir Edward Bridges and General Ismay, in a note to Churchill about arms for Greece, had pressed upon him the need 'to get someone put in charge of this businees', and had suggested Lord Hankey (*Premier papers, 3/214*).

[2] Telegram No. 1119 from Greece, asking for ammunition.

The French have only a Mandate and the Turks have a vital interest. Can we not encourage the Turks to become active in their addresses to Vichy on the subject,[1] and to put pressure on locally by every means in their power? On no account must Italian or Caitiff–Vichy influences become or remain paramount in Syria.

WSC

Winston S. Churchill to Lord Cranborne
(*Churchill papers, 20/13*)

12 November 1940

I think it would be better, before sending this statement[2] to the Commonwealth, to await the further examination of the two batches of U-boat prisoners who have recently come into our possession. I am asking the Admiralty for their report on these, which should not take more than a fortnight or so to frame.

I suppose you realise that these figures, if true, constitute a most lamentable confession of failure on the part of the Navy? In over 60 weeks of war they only claim 25 U-boats, whereas Parliament and the Empire have been told that losses were proceeding at between two to four a week. Moreover, the Service has also been led to believe that a great many of their attacks have been successful.

Thousands of attacks have been made, and now we are told that only 35 have yielded results, mostly in the last few months. All this argument turns on the discovery of a captured order of battle in Norwegian operations of April, which showed about 30 U-boats by numbers. But, of course, if the Germans have chosen to give the same numbers to submarines built to replace those sunk, the whole argument would fall to pieces. I am very doubtful whether it is a good thing to fling this out to the Dominions at the present time. Unless there is a most insistent demand for it, in which case I should like to be further consulted, it would be much better to let sleeping statistics lie.

WSC

[1] The transit of war materials via Syria to Turkey, as revealed in a Foreign Office secret report.
[2] About the destruction of German submarines. The only U-boats sunk in the previous three months were *U–51* on 20 August 1940, *U–57* on 3 September, *U–32* on 30 October and *U–31* on 2 November. After the sinking of *U–104* on 21 November there were no further sinkings until 7 March 1941.

Winston S. Churchill to Anthony Eden
(*Churchill papers, 20/13*)

12 November 1940
Most Secret

Following on our conversation at Ditchley, I think you should ask General Pownall to study the question of a large increase in the garrison of Northern Ireland, with a view to a decisive move on a broad front, should this at any time become necessary. It should at the same time be made clear to General Pownall that this is merely an exercise in staff planning and in no way implies any decision of policy taken by His Majesty's Government.

It is assumed that the equivalent of six divisions lightly equipped, not on the Continental scale, but containing a number of independent mobile and mechanised brigades, would be employed, and that very large forces would be used so as to obviate serious opposition. A period of two months should be assigned for the concentration in the North, the effect of which in itself might produce the result desired. General Pownall should be given access to the facilities of the joint planning staff. The whole matter is especially secret, except that, of course, the movement of troops will become known locally and might have a salutary effect.

WSC

Winston S. Churchill to Sir Edward Bridges and General Ismay
(*Churchill papers, 20/13*)

12 November 1940

Please look at this mass of stuff[1] which reaches me in a single morning, most of it already having appeared in the Service and FO telegrams. More and more people must be banking up behind these different papers, the bulk of which defeats their purpose. Try now and simplify, shorten and reduce.

Make me proposals.

WSC

Winston S. Churchill to Sir Edward Bridges and General Ismay
(*Churchill papers, 20/13*)

12 November 1940

The Prime Minister has noticed that the habit of Private Secretaries and others addressing each other by their Christian names about matters of an

[1] Joint Intelligence Committee Intelligence Summaries, Cabinet War Room Reports and other reports.

official character is increasing, and ought to be stopped. The use of Christian names in inter-departmental correspondence should be confined only to brief explanatory covering notes or to purely personal and private explanations.

It is hard enough to follow people by their surnames.

WSC

Winston S. Churchill to Air Vice-Marshal Longmore
(*Churchill papers, 20/14*)

12 November 1940

I am trying every day to speed up the arrivals in your Command of Hurricanes, &c. This is especially important in the next three weeks. Pray report daily what you actually receive, and how many you are able to put into action.

I was astonished to find that you have nearly 1,000 aircraft and 1,000 pilots and 16,000 air personnel in the Middle East, excluding Kenya. I am most anxious to re-equip you with modern machines at the earliest moment; but surely out of all this establishment you ought to be able, if the machines are forthcoming, to produce a substantially larger number of modern aircraft operationally fit? Pray report through the Air Ministry any steps you may be able to take to obtain more fighting value from the immense mass of material and men under your command.

I am grieved that the imperative demands of the Greek situation and its vital importance to the Middle East should have disturbed your arrangements at this exceptionally critical time. All good wishes.[1]

Winston S. Churchill to Sir Miles Lampson
(*Churchill papers, 20/6*)

12 November 1940

Your private and personal telegram to Mr Eden was laid before me as soon as it had been decoded in the Foreign Office. You should not telegraph at Government expense such an expression as 'completely crazy' when applied by you to grave decisions of policy taken by the Defence Committee and the

---

[1] In his reply, Longmore told Churchill: 'Please rest assured I will continue to operate all available aircraft of types which will contribute to further depression of Italians, whilst not providing their numerous and quite efficient fighters with too easy prey.' Longmore added that while he was satisfied that everything possible was being done from home to reinforce, the time lag factor was 'very pronounced', and he was 'disappointed that deliveries American Curtiss' and Glenn Martins have been deferred from original estimate. These will not begin to filter through until January' (*Premier papers, 3/309/1*).

War Cabinet after considering an altogether wider range of requirements and assets than you can possibly be aware of.[1]

Lord Halifax to Winston S. Churchill
(*Churchill papers, 20/6*)

13 November 1940

I would be much relieved if you would reconsider your decision to send the attached message to Miles Lampson.

His telegram No. 1491 was addressed to Anthony Eden and marked 'Most Personal'. From the wording used by Lampson he clearly had no idea that it would receive any circulation in London. Through an error it was marked for Departmental (Secret) distribution and consequently a copy was sent to you. In the circumstances it would be unfair, I think, to penalise Lampson for a phrase used in the heat of the moment in what was a purely private and personal message to someone, who happens to be an old friend as well as a Minister, and with whom he had no doubt discussed everything on terms of complete confidence.[2]

John Colville: diary
(*Colville papers*)

13 November 1940

The PM frantically composed his speech and I drove down to Church House with him while he discoursed upon the difference this event makes to the whole of our naval disposition and the panic which the Italians, in their inner harbour, must have felt at the unexpected attack. His description of 'this glorious episode' to the House was greeted with enthusiastic cheers from an assembly hungry for something cheerful.

---

[1] Eden wrote to Lampson on 12 November 1940: 'I appreciate your feelings after air losses at Gallabat. But believe me we are not completely crazy. Only doing our best to balance conflicting demands.' In apologising to Churchill in a personal letter on 9 December 1940, Lampson explained: 'I can only plead that having just heard of the loss of a considerable number of machines at Gallabat and knowing that we were below safety level in Egypt, I felt it right to let the Secretary of State know my fears in the light of our many discussions when he was out here. The language was conversational and informal: and it was ill-judged.' (*Churchill papers, 20/6.*)

[2] For Churchill's reply to Lord Halifax, see page 1092.

Henry Channon: diary
(*'Chips'*)

13 November 1940

I met the PM coming in from behind the Chair. 'We've got some sugar for the birds this time,' he said; and even smiled at me. Questions seemed interminable but finally Winston rose and gave the electrified House the wonderful Nelsonian news.

Winston S. Churchill: statement
(*Hansard*)

13 November 1940

House of Commons (Annexe)
Church House

ATTACK ON ITALIAN NAVY

Fleet Air Arm Success

The Prime Minister: I have some news for the House. It is good news. The Royal Navy has struck a crippling blow at the Italian fleet. The total strength of the Italian battle fleet was six battleships, two of them of the 'Littorio' class, which have just been put into service and are, of course, among the most powerful vessels in the world, and four of the recently reconstructed 'Cavour' class. This fleet was, of course, considerably more powerful on paper than our Mediterranean Fleet, but it had consistently refused to accept battle. On the night of 11th–12th November, when the main units of the Italian fleet were lying behind their shore defences in their naval base at Taranto, our aircraft of the Fleet Air Arm attacked them in their stronghold. Reports of our airmen have been confirmed by photographic reconnaissance. It is now established that one battleship of the 'Littorio' class was badly down by the bows and that her forecastle is under water and she has a heavy list to starboard. One battleship of the 'Cavour' class has been beached, and her stern, up to and including the after-turret, is under water. This ship is also heavily listed to starboard. It has not yet been possible to establish the fact with certainty, but it appears that a second battleship of the 'Cavour' class has also been severely damaged and beached. In the inner harbour of Taranto two Italian cruisers are listed to starboard and are surrounded with oil fuel, and two fleet auxiliaries are lying with their sterns under water. The Italian communiqué of 12th November, in admitting that one warship had been severely damaged, claimed that six of our aircraft had been shot down and three more probably.

In fact, only two of our aircraft are missing, and it is noted that the enemy claimed that part of the crews had been taken prisoner.

I felt it my duty to bring this glorious episode to the immediate notice of the House. As the result of a determined and highly successful attack, which reflects the greatest honour on the Fleet Air Arm, only three Italian battleships now remain effective. This result, while it affects decisively the balance of naval power in the Mediterranean, also carries with it reactions upon the naval situation in every quarter of the globe.

The spirit of the Royal Navy, as shown in this daring attack, is also exemplified in the forlorn and heroic action which has been fought by the captain, officers and ship's company of the *Jervis Bay* in giving battle against overwhelming odds in order to protect the merchant convoy which they were escorting and thus securing the escape of by far the greater part of that convoy.

The Mediterranean Fleet have also continued to harass the Italian communications with their armies in Libya. On the night of 9th–10th November a bombardment was carried out at Sidi Barani, and, though the fire was returned by shore batteries, our ships sustained no damage and no casualties. Moreover, one of our submarines attacked a convoy of two Italian supply ships escorted by destroyers, with the result that one heavily laden ship of 3,000 tons sank and a second ship was certainly damaged and probably sunk. I feel sure that the House will regard these results as highly satisfactory and as reflecting the greatest credit upon the Admiralty and upon Admiral Cunningham,[1] Commander-in-Chief in the Mediterranean, and, above all, on our pilots of the Fleet Air Arm, who, like their brothers in the Royal Air Force, continue to render the country services of the highest order.

John Colville: diary
(*Colville papers*)

13 November 1940

A vile, hot and hectic afternoon, starting with a tour of the new building operations[2] – where the PM leapt deftly over girders and crawled through holes – and ending with great pressure of work.

---

[1] Admiral Sir Andrew Cunningham.

[2] John Colville later recalled: 'These excursions, of which I always seemed to be the victim, were made because Churchill, as a keen amateur builder, was fascinated by the work in progress to make the Central War Room more bomb-proof. He examined the plans and suggested alterations, including the construction of brick traverses' (*The Fringes of Power*, page 293, note 2).

Winston S. Churchill to General Wavell
(*Premier papers, 3/288/1*)

13 November 1940

Chiefs of Staff, Service Ministers and I have examined general situation in the light of recent events. Italian check on Greek front; British naval success against battlefleet at Taranto; poor showing Italian airmen have made over here; encouraging reports received of low morale in Italy; Gallabat;[1] your own experiences by contacts in Western Desert; above all the general political situation makes it very desirable to undertake operation of which you spoke to Secretary of State for War.

It is unlikely that Germany will leave her flagging ally unsupported indefinitely. Consequently it seems that now is the time to take risks and strike the Italians by land, sea and air. You should act accordingly in concert with other Commanders in Chief.

We should be prepared to postpone reinforcement of Malta in order to give you more aircraft for your operation if this can be done in time.

Telegraph latest date by which these should arrive in Egypt in order to be of use.

Winston S. Churchill to Herbert Morrison
(*Churchill papers, 20/13*)

13 November 1940

This[2] seems easy to explain and to put right. But I have had no answer to the enquiry I made about this case. Will you kindly let me know how it stands. I thought the man should have had the GM[3] after being told why he ought not to have done it.

WSC

---

[1] Gallabat, a Sudanese border town on the Ethiopian border, had been taken by the Italian Army on 6 July 1940, despite a stubborn defence by the Sudan Defence Force. It was counter-attacked on 6 November 1940, but in vain, by Indian Army units led by Brigadier (later Field Marshal) Slim. Italian fighter pilots, veterans of the Spanish Civil War, outclassed their British air adversaries in both speed and numbers.

[2] The £100 fine on Mr Leighton-Morris for removing a time bomb from a house without authorisation. In the Commons that day, Josiah Wedgwood had asked Churchill: 'In view of the courageous nature of the action, will he consider remitting the fine and arranging for some reward to be given?' (*Hansard*)

[3] The George Medal.

John Peck to R. H. Melville[1]
(*Premier papers, 3/488/1*)

13 November 1940

In reply to the Prime Minister's minute No. 265 of the 3rd November about the instructions to Air Commodore Slessor, your Secretary of State addressed a minute to Mr Churchill on the 8th November. He will like to know that, with reference to the last sentence, the Prime Minister has minuted as follows:

'Please do so. But keep it simple and do not try to tell everything, and safeguard yourselves at every point. No one will read it unless it is short and clear.'

Yours sincerely,
J. H. Peck

Winston S. Churchill to Lord Halifax
(*Churchill papers, 20/6*)

14 November 1940

Nothing cd be milder or more well merited than my rebuke. I expect to be protected from this kind of insolence. I request that my telegram may be sent. Indeed I thought it wd have gone by now.

WSC

Winston S. Churchill to Admiral Ryan[2]
(*Churchill papers, 20/2*)

14 November 1940

Dear Admiral Ryan,

I am distressed to hear that your son – Lieutenant Commander Ryan – was killed while endeavouring to make harmless a magnetic mine which had been dropped in the London area.[3]

---

[1] Ronald Henry Melville, 1912– . Entered the Air Ministry, 1934. Private Secretary to the Secretary of State, 1940. Deputy Under-Secretary of State, Air Ministry, 1958–60; War Office, 1960–3; Ministry of Defence, 1963–6. Knighted, 1964. Permanent Secretary, Ministry of Aviation, 1966.

[2] Frank Edward Cavendish Ryan, 1865–1945. Midshipman, 1881. On active service in Egypt, 1882. Chief of Staff to the Vice-Admiral, Second Fleet, 1914. Commodore, Portland, 1915–16. Rear-Admiral, retired, 1916. CBE, 1919.

[3] I have been unable to find any biographical details about Lieutenant Commander Ryan, or about the incident in which he was killed. His elder brother had gone to France with the Royal Scots in 1915 at the age of seventeen, and was wounded there a year later, winning the Military Cross.

I understand that he had done this work on many previous occasions and had actually rendered one harmless at Hornchurch on the same day.

I send you and his widow my sincere sympathy. His gallantry & devotion have rendered signal service to our country.

Yours very faithfully,
Winston S. Churchill

Henry Channon: diary
(*'Chips'*)

14 November 1940

The Abbey, as the Service had been kept so secret, was far from crowded.[1] There had been some uneasiness lest the Germans would stage a raid and get Winston and the entire Government with one bomb. However, nothing occurred, and there was no alert during the actual service, which was long, dignified and moving.

Winston S. Churchill: memorandum[2]
(*Cabinet papers, 66/13*)

14 November 1940

RELATIONS WITH VICHY

I have read Sir Ronald Campbell's comments in WP 437 about the state of affairs at Vichy.

Although revenge has no part in politics, and we should always be looking forward rather than looking back, it would be a mistake to suppose that a solution of our difficulties with Vichy will be reached by a policy of mere conciliation and forgiveness. The Vichy Government is under heavy pressure from Germany, and there is nothing that they would like better than to feel a nice, soft, cosy, forgiving England on their other side. This would enable them to win minor favours from Germany at our expense, and hang on as long as possible to see how the war goes. We, on the contrary, should not hesitate when our interests require it, to confront them with difficult and rough situations, and make them feel that we have teeth as well as Hitler.

It must be remembered that these men have committed acts of baseness on

---

[1] For Neville Chamberlain's funeral.
[2] Circulated to the War Cabinet as War Cabinet Paper 448 of 1940.

a scale which have earned them the lasting contempt of the world, and that they have done this without the slightest authority from the French people. Laval is certainly filled by the bitterest hatred of England, and is reported to have said that he would like to see us 'crabouillés,' which means squashed so as to leave only a greasespot. Undoubtedly, if he had had the power, he would have marketed the unexpected British resistance with his German masters to secure a better price for French help in finishing us off. Darlan is mortally envenomed by the injury we have done to his fleet. Pétain has always been an anti-British defeatist, and is now a dotard. The idea that we can build on such men is vain. They may, however, be forced by rising opinion in France, and by German severities, to change their line in our favour. Certainly we should have contacts with them. But in order to promote such favourable tendencies, we must make sure the Vichy folk are kept well ground between the upper and nether millstones of Germany and Britain. In this way they are most likely to be brought into a more serviceable mood during the short run which remains to them.

WSC

Winston S. Churchill to Sir Archibald Sinclair[1]
(*Churchill papers, 20/13*)

14 November 1940
Secret

I saw Sir Hugh Dowding this morning, and explained to him the importance of getting American war aviation developed on right lines, and lines parallel with ours. He expressed great doubts of his ability to fulfil this mission, but on my telling him I wished him to undertake it in the public interest, of which I was the judge, he accepted the task subject to the condition that if he wrote to me saying he was not getting on with it over there, he should be allowed to come home.

Personally I think he will perform the task very well, and I will give him a letter to the President. I have a very great regard for this Officer, and admiration for his qualities and achievements.

Let me see his instructions, please, in draft form.

WSC

---

[1] Sir Archibald Sinclair and the Air Staff had been emphatic that Dowding no longer had the stamina to be Commander-in-Chief of Fighter Command and must be replaced.

Defence Committee (Operations): minutes
(*Cabinet papers, 69/1*)

14 November 1940
12.45 p.m.

SHIPPING FOR THE MIDDLE EAST

The Prime Minister said that the urgent need during the coming months was to build up our strength in the Middle East. The great difficulty was shipping and if we were to take advantage of the opportunities offered to us to strike at Italy now or in the near future limitations of shipping must not be allowed to interfere with the urgent military necessity of concentrating such forces as we required in the Middle East.

The Minister of Shipping said that he fully appreciated the urgency of the problem. If military requirements were to be met in full, sacrifices would have to be made in our imports of food and other commodities.

The Prime Minister said that he would like to have a picture of what these sacrifices entailed.

John Colville: diary
(*Colville papers*)

14 November 1940

A typical incident happened just before lunch today. The PM had invited Cross, the Minister of Shipping, to lunch and was showing him great affability. Suddenly he charged back into the room at No. 10, where I was telephoning, and whispered hoarsely in my ear, 'What is the name of the Minister of Shipping?' 'Cross,' I whispered back furtively, because the Minister was standing in the doorway. 'Oh,' said the PM. 'Well, what's his Christian name?' Cross must have heard the whole conversation.

John Martin: diary
(*Martin papers*)

14 November 1940

False start for Ditchley. 'The moonlight sonata.'[1]

---

[1] Code name for the German bombing raids that night. These raids were at first believed, as a result of the interrogation of captured German air crew during the previous ten days, to be partly against the Birmingham area and partly against London. There was no knowledge at that point in the afternoon that the raid was in fact to be on Coventry.

NOVEMBER 1940

John Martin: recollection
(*Martin papers*)

14 November 1940

In the late afternoon of the 14th we set out from No. 10 for Ditchley. Just before starting from the garden gate I handed the Prime Minister a box with a top secret message. A few minutes later he opened this and read the contents – which I subsequently understood was a report that the German 'beam' seemed to indicate a raid on London.

The cars had now reached Kensington Gardens; but he immediately called to the driver to return to Downing Street. He was not going to sleep quietly in the country while London was under what was expected to be a heavy attack. I was informed by Miss Stenhouse and Miss Davies[1] – in 1977 – that they were sent to spend the night at the Dollis Hill headquarters, and the rest of the female staff sent home, by Brendan Bracken and Anthony Bevir, on the ground that the 'beam' pointed at Whitehall.

John Colville: diary
(*Colville papers*)

14 November 1940

It is obviously some major air operation – possibly stimulated by our success at Taranto – but its exact destination the Air Ministry find it difficult to determine. In any case we all decided to take the necessary precautions and to sleep in the safest place.

John Peck and I dined at Down Street Station ('the burrow', Winston calls it) where we fed excellently, and slept there in great comfort. The PM spent the night at the CWR to await the 'Moonlight Sonata', and became so impatient that he spent much of the time on the Air Ministry roof.[2]

Winston S. Churchill to Sir Charles Portal
(*Churchill papers, 20/13*)

15 November 1940

1. I am struck by the fact that the available bomber crews are barely two-thirds of the initial equipment.[3] This has a bearing on the other Minute I

---

[1] Miss Stenhouse and Miss Davies worked in the secretarial pool at 10 Downing Street. Based on the ground floor, in a room facing the garden, they were known as the garden room girls.

[2] The raid was, in fact, on Coventry. As soon as this became known, counter-measures were taken, the anti-aircraft barrage 'being greater than any put up on any one night by the London defences' (Chiefs of Staff Committee, Weekly Résumé, No. 64, 21 November 1940). No thought of protecting the source of the (belated) knowledge of the target inhibited any of the defensive measures.

[3] Churchill had been studying the Summarised Order of Battle for 11 November 1940.

sent you, showing the need to nurse them as much as possible. It is lamentable that our numbers are so small.

2. The fighters keep up at three quarters IE.[1]

3. The Army Co-Op seem to have 162 crews for a total IE of 156 machines, of which, however, only 109 are operationally fit. Why then are not some of the 122 aircraft in the ASU brought in to bring the 109 figure up to the level of the other two, namely, IE and crews available? Is there any chance of getting some pilots and crews for bombers out of this branch?

4. Coastal Command is again terribly below initial equipment, in fact it is barely half operationally fit. 157 is altogether inadequate for the duties of this force on the North-Western Approaches, &c. Every effort should be made to improvise greater numbers.

WSC

Winston S. Churchill to Lord Beaverbrook
(*Churchill papers, 20/13*)

15 November 1940

I do not think this could be said without the approval of the Air Ministry, and indeed of the COS Committee. My own feeling would be against giving these actual figures.[2] They tell the enemy too much. It is like getting one of the tail bones of the ichthyosaurus from which a naturalist can reconstruct the entire animal. The more I think about it the more I am against it.

WSC

Winston S. Churchill to Sir Archibald Sinclair and Sir Charles Portal
(*Churchill papers, 120/300*)

15 November 1940

This[3] amounts to a loss of eleven of our Bombers in one night. I said the other day by minute that the operations were not to be pressed unduly during these very adverse weather conditions. We cannot afford to have losses of this kind in view of your very slow replacements. If you go on like this, you will break the Bomber Force down to below a minimum for grave emergencies. No results have been achieved which would in any way justify or compensate for

[1] Initial equipments.
[2] Beaverbrook had sent Churchill the figures of aircraft strength that he proposed to use in a broadcast.
[3] The Cabinet War Room Record No. 439 for 15 November 1940, which showed that on the night of 14/15 November Bomber Command suffered the heaviest losses so far since the start of the war for a single night: ten aircraft shot down out of eighty-two, during raids on Berlin, Hamburg, and airfields in Holland.

these losses. I consider the loss of eleven aircraft out of 139, i.e., about 8 per cent, a very grievous disaster at this stage of our Bomber development.

Let me have the losses during the first half of November.

General Brooke: diary
(*'The Turn of the Tide'*)

16 November 1940

At 5 p.m. started for Ditchley Park, Enstone, where the PM was spending the week-end instead of Chequers owing to the full moon and the fear of night attacks by bombers. I dreaded the thought of being kept up till 2 a.m. by the PM in my sleepy mood. However, I slept in the car on the way out, and the evening went off better than I had hoped for and I was in bed by 2 a.m.[1]

Winston S. Churchill to Sir Andrew Duncan
(*Churchill papers, 20/13*)

16 November 1940

The rate of production of Bren guns shows a disquieting fall. Output in the week ending November 2 was only half the rate in July.

I understand that the reason for this fall is a shorter shift at Enfield. Pray inform me if there are special reasons for such a serious reduction in this particular factory, and whether it accounts for the whole of the fall.

WSC

Winston S. Churchill to President Roosevelt
(*Churchill papers, 20/14*)

16 November 1940

I am deeply obliged to you for the promptness of your action about the two big French ships.[2] I am sure you will have been pleased about Taranto. The three uninjured Italian battleships have quitted Taranto to-day, which

---

[1] Also at Ditchley that weekend were Admiral Tom Phillips, Walter Monckton, Brendan Bracken and Professor Lindemann.

[2] As a result of Roosevelt's initiative with regard to the *Jean Bart* and the *Richelieu*, Pétain had given an assurance 'that the French Fleet, including these two ships, shall never fall into the hands of Germany'. (Roosevelt to Churchill, 16 November 1940, *Churchill papers, 4/143*). On 23 November 1940 Roosevelt informed Churchill that Pétain had told Robert Murphy, the American Chargé d'Affaires in Vichy, 'that he would keep the vessels now at Dakar and Casablanca where they are and if there is any change in this plan he would give the Government of the United States previous notice' (*Churchill papers, 4/143*).

perhaps means they are withdrawing to Trieste. I am writing you a very long letter on the outlook for 1941, which Lord Lothian will give you in a few days. I hope you got my personal telegram of congratulation.

Winston S. Churchill to Vyvyan Adams[1]
(*Churchill papers, 20/13*)

16 November 1940
Private & Confidential

My dear Vyvyan Adams,

I have to acknowledge your letter of November 8, and I have now read your speech in the House.[2] I am very sorry you made it, as I do not think it helpful in any way. When you say that you trust my leadership that would seem to carry with it acquiescence at least in this important appointment, which of course was my unfettered decision. It has been my deliberate policy to try to rally all the forces for the life and death struggle in which we are plunged, and to let bygones be bygones. I am quite sure that Margesson will treat me with the loyalty he has given to my predecessors. The fault alleged against him which tells the most is that he has done his duty only too well. I do not think there is anyone who could advise me better about all those elements in the Tory Party which were so hostile to us in recent years. I have to think of unity, and I need all the strength I can get. Moreover I ought to tell you that even during the bitterest times I have always had very good personal relations with Margesson, and knowing what his duties were I never had any serious occasion to complain. Several times when I heard the Whips were putting stories about which were not true I spoke to him plainly and he stopped them. The Liberal and Labour Whips have the very highest opinion of his integrity and good faith in all House of Commons relations, and there is no doubt that he is the most efficient servant who could be found for these functions in a Three-Party Government.

[1] Samuel Vyvyan Trerice Adams, 1900–51. Educated at Haileybury and King's College, Cambridge. Called to the Bar, 1927. Conservative MP for West Leeds, 1931–45. Member of the Executive of the League of Nations Union, 1933–46. On active service, 1939–45 (Major, Duke of Cornwall's Light Infantry). In 1940, under the pen name 'Watchman', he published *Churchill: Architect of Victory*. Political researcher, 1946–51.

[2] In his letter to Churchill, in his remarks to the House of Commons, and in a letter published in the *Daily Telegraph* on 19 November 1940, Vyvyan Adams criticised the continued employment of Captain Margesson as Chief Whip on the grounds that, as Chief Whip under Neville Chamberlain, he had been a leading figure in the imposition of the pre-war policy of appeasement. In his reply to Churchill, Adams wrote from his Army camp in the Shetlands: 'Perhaps you will believe me when I say that my main object is to do what little I can to help you to win. And please do not think me impertinent if I add that I could not help believing that Margesson's masterful abilities would now be better employed elsewhere than in the Whips' Office. In the meantime, as I am proud that you are my leader, I should be glad if notices to attend the house could be sent me, as hitherto, from the Government Whips Office' (*Churchill papers, 20/3*).

Finally I may tell you in confidence that I have long had a very high opinion of Margesson's administrative and executive abilities, and that when I formed the new Government I offered him a Secretaryship of State. He declined this but offered in the frankest manner to go out altogether. I can assure you he has been a great help to me on many occasions since I became Prime Minister, and I am absolutely sure he will go on to the bitter end.

I write all this to you for your own private and secret information, and I hope you will find it possible to take a broader and more tolerant view of the situation, and of the measures I think it best to take in order to discharge my task.

Believe me,
Yours very sincerely,
Winston S. Churchill

Winston S. Churchill to General Wavell[1]
(*Premier papers, 3/288/1*)

17 November 1940   Dytchley

Secretary of State for War has given me full account of your plans and projects. We here fully appreciate limitations placed on your actions by many calls upon you.

You may however be assured that you will have our full support at all times in any offensive action you may be able to take against the enemy. Whether the outcome be well or ill we will sustain you in any well considered operation you may launch against the enemy.

Winston S. Churchill to Sir Charles Portal
(*Churchill papers, 20/13*)

17 November 1940

Thank you. I watch these figures every day with much concern. My diagrams show that we are now not even keeping level, and there is a marked downward turn this week, especially in the Bomber Command. Painful as it is not to be able to strike heavy blows after an event like Coventry,[2] yet I feel we should for the present <u>nurse</u> the Bomber Command a little more. This can

---

[1] The text of this telegram in Churchill's papers is written in Anthony Eden's handwriting, on Dytchley notepaper.

[2] Coventry had been bombed on 14 November, when 450 German bombers dropped 503 tons of high-explosive bombs and 881 incendiary canisters on the city, causing a fire storm and the destruction of the Cathedral: 554 people are believed to have been killed, and 865 seriously wounded.

be done (1) by not sending so many to each of the necessary objectives, (2) by not coming down too low in the face of heavy prepared batteries, and being content with somewhat less accuracy, and (3) by picking out soft spots where there is not too much organised protection, so as to keep up our deliveries of bomb content. There must be unexpecting towns in Germany where very little has been done in ARP and yet where there are military objectives of a minor order. Some of these could be struck at in the meanwhile.

2. I should feel differently about this if our Bomber Force were above 500, and if it were expanding. But having regard to the uncertainties of war, we must be very careful not to let routine bombing and our own high standards proceed without constant attention to our resources. These remarks do not apply, of course, to Italy, against which the full-scale risk should be run. The wounded Littorio is a fine target.

WSC

Winston S. Churchill to Sir Charles Portal
(*Churchill papers, 20/13*)

17 November 1940

Thank you very much for your full reply to my minute No. 289.

I am still struck by the astounding disparity between Operational fighting strength and the total ration strength personnel. The latest figures supplied by Longmore (on which before reading yours of to-day I sent you a minute) show about 220 operationally fit aircraft, for which he has, apart from approaching reinforcements, 17,000 personnel. This works out at about 77 Airmen for one serviceable Operational machine. Of course I know this is a very rough and ready way of looking at it, but I do not think anyone could be contented with such a result. Every saving that can be made of personnel, every successful combing of an establishment or branch, helps us to win the war almost as surely as bringing down enemy aeroplanes. It is clear to me that this Middle East establishment, growing up piecemeal, long necessarily deprived of good machines, has gathered to itself an amount of fat which bears no relation to its strength for practical purposes. What is required is a thorough overhaul. My only object is to increase the strength of the Air Force generally. I should have thought that at least 5,000 men could be combed from the Air Force in the Middle East, which could be used to service new Squadrons as better machines become available, or else, if they cannot be fitted in there and are only expert in handling obsolete types, brought home on the empty ships for further training.

2. The pilot question is even more pointed. Here we have just under 1,000 pilots for only 220 serviceable Operational machines, or between four and five pilots for every machine. It is surely not necessary, and when we see how very short we are of pilots at home, it would seem a duty to transfer some of these great numbers of pilots for whom there are no machines fit to fly, or any use for fighting, to home establishments.

3. All this makes me feel very much the need for an overhaul of the establishments. It may well be that the new and more complicated machines coming into service will require larger servicing staffs. All the more is it necessary that redundancy should be corrected. I earnestly hope you will help me in this.

4. It would seem that, in the first instance, a Committee of three (an Air Force officer, a business man and a Civil Servant) should be appointed at home to go into typical establishments, both here and the Middle East, on paper, so as to find out what every man is for. Or again, the Parliamentary Committee on Expenditure might be asked. The next step would be to compare these establishments with the actual staffs as they exist to-day at particular places. Out of this might come an Inspector-General of Establishments, who, with a proper staff, would travel about and continually correct and comb down to what is absolutely necessary. Has there, for instance, been any attempt to compare the establishments approved by the Air Ministry with the actual personnel who have accumulated in the Middle East? It is only by seeking efficiency and true economy that we shall come through our difficulties.

I should be very glad if you would think this over and discuss it with me.

WSC

Winston S. Churchill to Peter Fraser
(*Churchill papers, 20/14*)

18 November 1940

Your telegram is being dealt with departmentally. We dwell under a drizzle of carping criticism from a few members and from writers in certain organs of the Press. This has an irritating effect and would not be tolerated in any other country exposed to our present stresses. On the other hand, it is a good thing that any Government should be kept keen and made aware of any shortcomings in time to remedy them. You must not suppose everything is perfect, but we are all trying our best, and the war effort is enormous and morale admirable. All good wishes.

Winston S. Churchill to General Ismay
(*Churchill papers, 20/13*)

18 November 1940

I am informed that on the night of November 6/7 one of the German KG 100 squadron came down in the sea near Bridport. This squadron is the one known to be fitted with the special apparatus with which the Germans hope to do accurate night-bombing, using their very fine beams. Vital time was lost during which this aircraft or its equipment might have been salvaged because the Army claimed that it came under their jurisdiction, made no attempt to secure it, and refused to permit the Naval Authorities to do so.

Pray make proposals to ensure that in future immediate steps are taken to secure all possible information and equipment from German aircraft which come down in this country or near our coasts, and that these rare opportunities are not squandered through departmental differences.

WSC

Winston S. Churchill to General Ismay
(*Premier papers, 3/288/1*)

18 November 1940

OPERATION 'COMPASS': WESTERN DESERT

1. It becomes essential to know by to-morrow exactly the time-table of all appointed movements of aircraft, anti-aircraft and other reinforcements to the theatre by the new date, and also to consider whether anything else can get there by the time. This must be brought up at the Defence Committee Conference at 9.30 p.m. on Tuesday, the 19th.

In the meanwhile, all possible additions must be studied. The most precise information will be required about the conditions on the Takoradi route, also the movements of Air Force personnel in HM ships.

2. In view of General Wavell's telegram, the despatch to Greece of the additional Gladiator Squadron seems to be tolerable, but this, again, must be decided on the dates of the above movements.

3. While it is wrong to count upon success, every preparation should always be made to exploit it should it come. A Staff study should be available by to-morrow night to show how best amphibious power could be used in the event of a substantial success in the area now under scrutiny. If panic and large captures overtake the enemy, the sea power should be used to the utmost, and landings far behind the existing front might collect for almost nothing very large prizes. The lessons of the German armoured advance into

France and round to Calais must be appreciated and used in this connection. If of course we get a flop, the above does not apply. All the same it should be prepared, and all the troops in rear drawn upon for a rounding up movement on the remote communications.

WSC

Winston S. Churchill to A. V. Alexander and Admiral Pound
(*Churchill papers, 20/13*)

18 November 1940
ACTION THIS DAY

I was assured that 64 destroyers would be available for the North-Western Approaches by November 15. This return,[1] which goes to November 16, shows 60. But what is disconcerting is that out of 151 destroyers, only 84 are available for service, and out of 60 for the North-Western Approaches only 33 are available for service. When we held our conference more than a month ago, the Admiral was found with only 24 destroyers available, and all that has happened in the month that has passed is that another 9 have been added to his available strength. But meanwhile you have had the American destroyers streaming into service, and I was assured that there was a steady output from our own yards. I cannot understand why there has been this serious frustration of decisions so unitedly arrived at, nor why such an immense proportion of destroyers are laid up for one cause or another. Are the repairs falling behind? What has happened to the American destroyers? Is the Controller[2] failing in repairs and new construction?

I should be glad to have a special conference at 10 a.m. on Tuesday at the Admiralty War Room.

WSC

Winston S. Churchill to Sir Archibald Sinclair
(*Churchill papers, 20/13*)

18 November 1940

Please report on progress with operational use of LAM.[3]

I understand that the first experiment was very promising, though marred by a hitch in the release mechanism. It would be a great pity if this operation were held up by this when the need of some counter to the night bomber is so patent.

[1] A list of Royal Navy ships in Home Waters fitted with Asdic anti-submarine sonar detection devices.
[2] Rear-Admiral Bruce Fraser.
[3] Land Arm Mode, an automatic landing device.

Operational experiments should surely continue whilst improvements are being made, to avoid a recurrence of the trouble.

WSC

War Cabinet: minutes
(*Cabinet papers, 65/10*)

18 November 1940 Cabinet War Room
5 p.m.

GREECE

General Papagos[1] was very satisfied with the course of operations, but the urgent needs of the Greeks in ammunition and material were daily becoming increasingly obvious. They had made a further urgent request for air support, to counteract Italian air action, especially on the Epirus front.

The Prime Minister said that it was clear that we could not increase our air reinforcements beyond what we had already arranged to send. He had seen a report that the landing grounds in Albania were already so congested that the arrival of German air reinforcements on this front seemed improbable.

The Prime Minister reminded the War Cabinet that a Committee on Assistance to Greece was sitting under the Chairmanship of the Chancellor of the Duchy of Lancaster[2]. As a result of their first recommendations, which the Chiefs of Staff had accepted with certain modifications, four shiploads of munitions were about to be sent to Greece.

BOMBING OF COVENTRY

The Secretary of State for War said that he had listened on Saturday night to a special account of the effects of the air raid, given by the BBC. This had been a most depressing broadcast, and would have a deplorable effect on Warwickshire units.

Other Ministers confirmed this view.

---

[1] Alexander Papagos, 1883–1955. Born in Athens. In action during the Balkan Wars, 1912–13 (against the Bulgarians) and in Asia Minor, 1920 (against the Turks). Chief of the Army General Staff, 1936–40. Commander-in-Chief of the Greek Army, 1940–1. Held in various concentration camps as a hostage from 1943 until his release by the Americans in 1945. In 1949 he was recalled to his position as Commander-in-Chief to wage war against the Communist guerrillas in Northern Greece. Refused to take power in Athens after a military coup in his favour, May 1951. Headed the Greek Rally Party in Parliament, August 1951. Prime Minister from November 1952 until his death.

[2] Lord Hankey.

The Prime Minister said that he did not suggest that the decision to give prominence to the Coventry raid was wrong. The effect had been considerable both in the United States and, from a different point of view, in Germany. The enemy seemed to be alarmed at the publicity given to this raid, and to have taken the unusual course of announcing that they had lost 223 dead in our raid on Hamburg on the following night. Unless the publicity in the Press had had a bad effect on our morale, he doubted if it had done any harm. Nevertheless, he wished to be assured that the decision as to the degree of publicity given to raids of this character was entrusted to an officer of high standing. He would be glad if the Ministers concerned would consider the present procedure from this point of view.

VICHY FRANCE

In further discussion the Foreign Secretary said that it must be remembered that the Vichy Government were in a position in which it was very difficult for them to make an agreement with us on these matters. We might have to put them into a position in which they could say to the Germans that we had interfered with their trade by *force majeure*.

The Prime Minister said that the difficulties of the present situation arose from its indeterminate character. The consequences of allowing the present position to continue would be very serious. He recounted the steps by which the present position had been reached.

The present time, he thought, might well be favourable to action. The French were sore over the German action in Lorraine. We had had the naval success at Taranto, and General Weygand appeared to be indisposed to work in with the Germans. He thought, therefore, that we must be prepared to run some risks in order to interfere with the trade through the Straits. It would of course be very serious if we had a big naval clash with the French, but he did not think that this would happen. The French had made no response to the offers which we had made to them and in the meantime had continued to build up this trade. He thought that, as soon as a suitable opportunity offered, the Admiralty should try to make a *coup* and bring in for contraband control as many ships as they could lay their hands on. It would not be necessary to take such action continuously. The deterrent effect of a few seizures would be considerable. No doubt the Vichy Government would protest. If they did, we could then point out to them how badly they had behaved to us.

Discussion followed as to when the Navy would be able to make adequate forces available for this operation. The Prime Minister thought that this matter could conveniently be discussed at a Meeting of the Defence Committee (Operations).

Attention was drawn to the fact that numbers of French merchant ships were said to be passing through the Straits with almost nominal escorts, e.g., only a sloop or an armed trawler.

John Colville: diary
(*Colville papers*)

18 November 1940

When I got back to No. 10 Annexe[1] the PM was downstairs looking at Intelligence Reports, putting red ink circles round the names of Greek towns and chortling as he thought of the discomfiture of the Italians. Then, after expressing to me his disgust with Admiral Somerville who let twelve Hurricanes bound for Malta take off from an aircraft carrier too soon, so that eight came down in the sea and were lost, he went to bed and slept until the Cabinet was due.

Towards dinner-time, while I was desperately coping with mountainous papers on my desk, the PM appeared and, bidding me bring a torch, led me away to look at girders in the basement, intended to support the building. With astonishing agility he climbed over girders, balanced himself on their upturned edges, some five feet above ground, and leapt from one to another without any sign of undue effort. Extraordinary in a man of almost sixty-six who never takes exercise of any sort.

Defence Committee (Operations): minutes
(*Cabinet papers, 69/1*)

18 November 1940
9.30 p.m.

THE PROTECTION OF TRADE: NAVAL DISPOSITIONS

In reply to questions by the Prime Minister, the First Sea Lord explained the situation regarding destroyers in the north-western approaches. It had been found necessary to make rather extensive alterations to the American destroyers before they were fit for service. He gave details of the organisation of convoys and their escorts in the north-western approaches.

The current programme of convoys of overseas reinforcements was discussed.

The Prime Minister asked that he should be furnished with details of the troops being carried in convoy WS 5.[2]

[1] The set of rooms, above ground on the St James's Park side of the old Board of Trade Building at Storey's Gate, which were used by Churchill as his main sleeping, eating and working accommodation for the rest of the war. Whenever he could he would hold meetings in Downing Street, but his main base of operations, including his map room under Captain Pim, was situated in this Annexe. There was also a bedroom, a small dining-room, a study, and a room for the Private Secretaries. Immediately below were the underground Cabinet War Rooms.

[2] WS was the designation of military convoys (together with a numerical suffix) plying the route from Britain to the Middle East via the Cape of Good Hope. It was inaugurated in June 1940.

War Cabinet: Confidential Annex
(*Cabinet papers, 65/16*)

19 November 1940 House of Commons (Annexe)
11.30 a.m. Church House

The Prime Minister said that on the previous evening the Defence Committee (Operations) had considered what air reinforcements could be sent to Greece in response to their urgent requests contained in Telegrams Nos. 1154 of 17th November and 1159 of 18th November from Athens.[1] The Committee had been faced with the dilemma of conflicting claims, so common in war. In the end the Committee had decided to stick to the promises that had been made and to send five squadrons but no more. These would consist of two squadrons of fighters and three of Blenheims, the latter being capable of fulfilling a dual role. This would mean that some 74 aircraft in all would be despatched. Including the Blenheim aircraft already in Greece, three squadrons should have arrived by that evening and the other two would follow quite shortly. In addition to the above it had been decided that we should send 12 Gladiators for the use of the Greek Air Force itself. A telegram had already been sent to our Minister in Athens informing him of our decisions.

The Prime Minister added that he did not think that the practical difficulties in regard to the movement of aircraft from one country to another were quite realised by the lay mind and evidently they were not realised in Greece. It should be the business of our Air Attaché in Athens[2] to acquaint our Minister there with them and thus prevent impossible and unreasonable requests being put forward. As an instance of the amount of organisation that was necessary in order to keep a machine in the air, the Prime Minister said that in Egypt there were some 70 or 80 personnel on the ground for every machine that flew. This figure appeared much larger than was necessary, and he was inquiring into the matter with the Secretary of State for Air.

The assistance which we now proposed to give to Greece would mean that our Air Force in Egypt would be greatly depleted and might be barely sufficient to cover our requirements there should the enemy decide to stage an air offensive on that front.

---

[1] On the previous day Sir Michael Palairet, the British Minister in Athens, had telegraphed to London: 'President of the Council told me this evening that Greek request for 60 American fighters had been turned down because they were needed for us. He hopes very much that we will waive our claim for these in favour of Greece who needs them so urgently' (*Cabinet papers, 69/1*).

[2] Charles Edward Hastings Medhurst, 1896–1954. Entered the Royal Flying Corps. On active service in France and Palestine, 1915–18 (Military Cross). Deputy Director of Intelligence, Air Ministry, 1934–7. Air Attaché, Rome, Berne and Athens, 1937–40. Assistant Chief of the Air Staff (Intelligence), 1941. Commandant, RAF Staff College, 1943–4. Air Commander-in-Chief, RAF Mediterranean and Middle East, 1945–8. Knighted, 1945. Air Chief Marshal; Head of the Royal Air Force Staff, British Joint Services Mission, Washington, 1948–50.

The Secretary of State for Foreign Affairs said that he was seeing the Greek Minister that afternoon and, with the aid of the information contained in the telegram to our Minister in Athens, would inform him of the air assistance we proposed to send.

The War Cabinet approved of the decisions reached by the Defence Committee (Operations) in regard to air reinforcements for Greece.

Winston S. Churchill to Sir Michael Palairet
(*Cabinet papers, 65/16*)

19 November 1940
1.50 p.m.
Most Immediate

Promised Gladiator squadrons are being sent to Greece with utmost despatch as well as the remainder of the three Blenheim squadrons. The effectiveness of the Gladiators in the land battle is of course dependent on the serviceability of forward aerodromes. Information on this point should be communicated at once to Air Officer Commanding-in-Chief Middle East and repeated to London. In addition to Gladiator squadrons Air Officer Commanding-in-Chief is being requested to ferry over 12 more Gladiators for use of Greek Air Force. It is useless to talk about Hurricanes as immediate reinforcement since they cannot land at Crete en route and to fit extra tanks in place of guns and then reassemble them for operations would be a long business. Moreover we doubt whether Greek personnel could service or operate Hurricanes without special training. Air Officer Commanding-in-Chief Middle East is being informed by Air Ministry.

Night Air Defence Committee: minutes
(*Cabinet papers, 81/22*)

19 November 1940
5 p.m.

The Prime Minister expressed his wish to witness a demonstration with the PE fuze at some place within reasonable distance of London, and Major-General Loch undertook to make arrangements accordingly.

The Prime Minister directed that the trials and development of –
mine-laying aircraft,
mine-towing aircraft,

mine-carrying balloons
should be pressed forward with the utmost speed, regardless of expense.

Winston S. Churchill to Sir Archibald Sinclair
(*Churchill papers, 20/13*)

19 November 1940
ACTION THIS DAY
Secret

1. It is now, I think, more than three weeks since you very kindly promised to give me your new forecast of expansion, based on the adoption of the ascertained wastage during the five battle months. I cannot understand why it should be such a complicated business. It only means carrying different basic figure through whatever is the variety of calculations on which you depend.

2. I was very glad to read in your minute to me yesterday about appointments that you are pressing forward with the Egglayer proposal. I have so long and repeatedly urged this method, and have been so consistently baffled by delays and obstructions, that I almost despair of action. The paltry assignment of three Harrows to this vital task is characteristic of the process which has paralysed us. The fact that the enemy rely upon the Beam, and that we can ascertain beforehand the probable direction of his main attack, and to a very great extent can measure his altitude, should make this obvious method of intercepting and deterring him our first endeavour. But even now only 100,000 aerial mines have been ordered, and every kind of difficulty is made about the wires, &c. Everyone on the route heard the stream of enemy Bombers passing continuously for hours to and fro to bomb Coventry. There was plenty of time to put up 20 Egglayers in releases of 5, making a curtain of death through which these enemy machines would have had to pass coming and going. You might easily have had 20 or 30 brought down, with all the resulting deterrent in the future. Moreover, the enemy could not retaliate in the same way on our Bombers, which do not work on the Beam, but by navigational skill. If the enemy is driven off his Beam, he must go through a long process of training to reach a particular objective.

Pray let me have a report every three days on the progress you are making.

WSC

John Colville: diary
(*Colville papers*)

19 November 1940

I went with the PM to Down Street for the night and dined excellently, far beneath the level of the street, with Sir Ralph Wedgwood[1] (brother of the egregious Colonel Jos. and Chairman of the Railway Executive), Cole-Deacon[2] (the Secretary) and his wife. The LPTB[3] do themselves well: caviar (almost unobtainable in these days of restricted imports), Perrier Jouet 1928, 1865 brandy and excellent cigars.

After dinner the Defence Committee, consisting of the Chiefs of Staff, the service Ministers and Pug Ismay, met to discuss the unending topic of air-reinforcements for the Middle East and the difficulty of supplying Greece without dangerously weakening Egypt. That megalomaniac Sir R. Keyes was sent for in the armoured car to attend part of the meeting, presumably connected with 'special combined operations'.

After midnight I took in a long list of places bombed in London tonight and news of a heavy attack on Birmingham with streams of bombers passing over the country on their way there. 'Complete failure of all our methods,' commented the PM grimly. 'Four days have passed since Coventry and no remedy has been found.'

John Colville: diary
(*Colville papers*)

20 November 1940

Went to No. 10 where the PM worked in the Cabinet Room, demanding many things which were difficult to find and showing great reluctance to be photographed by Cecil Beaton[4] who was waiting patiently outside.

---

[1] Ralph Lewis Wedgwood, 1874–1956. Brother of Churchill's friend Josiah Wedgwood. Director of Docks, GHQ, France, 1916–19. Chief General Manager, London and North-Eastern Railway (LNER), 1923–39. Knighted, 1924. President, National Confederation of Employers' Organisations, 1929–30. Member of the Central Electricity Board, 1931–46. Chairman, Railway Executive Committee, 1939–41.

[2] Gerald John Cole-Deacon, 1890–1968. Assistant Solicitor, Great Northern Railway, 1914–20. Secretary, Railway Companies Association, 1930–48. Secretary, Railway Executive Committee, Ministry of War Transport, 1939–45. CBE, 1945.

[3] The London Passenger Transport Board.

[4] Cecil Walter Hardy Beaton, 1904–80. Photographer and designer. Held his first exhibition of photographs, and published his first photographic essay, in 1930. Photographer for the Ministry of Information, 1940–5. CBE, 1957. Knighted, 1972.

The PM feels that as we can hardly give any other sort of help to Greece we should do all we can financially. In a minute to the Chancellor of the Exchequer: 'I do hope that this will not be an occasion for the Treasury to do one of their regular departmental grimaces, which no doubt are very necessary in ordinary circumstances, but would be very much out of place now.' Another acrobatic tour of the girders.

Winston S. Churchill to Sir Kingsley Wood
(*Churchill papers, 20/13*)

20 November 1940
ACTION THIS DAY

The Greek Minister handed me this to-day.[1] It seems most necessary that as we can hardly give any other help, financial assistance should be given to Greece in the manner most likely to help them. I do hope that this will not be an occasion for the Treasury to do one of their regular Departmental grimaces, which no doubt are very necessary in ordinary circumstances, but would be very much out of place now. I gathered that you were in full agreement with the Cabinet wish that the Greeks should have prompt, effectual and adequate financial assistance. Remember that we can only give them a handful of aeroplanes and no troops.

WSC

War Cabinet: minutes
(*Cabinet papers, 65/10*)

20 November 1940　　　　　　　　　　　　　　　Prime Minister's Room
11.30 a.m.　　　　　　　　　　　　　　　　　　　House of Commons

The Prime Minister stressed the importance of conserving our bomber resources in present circumstances. The right course was, he thought, to combine heavy blows at particular objectives with attacks on a number of targets, thus interfering with production over wide-spread areas of Germany.

Ten Gladiators had arrived in Greece on the 18th November. They had already been in action and had destroyed ten Italian aircraft for certain and two probably. We had lost no machines, but one pilot had been hit.

The Prime Minister said that he had it in mind to make a further appeal to President Roosevelt in which he would point out the additional strain

[1] A Greek request, dated 19 November 1940, asking that the Bank of England be authorised to offer credit to the Greek Government for payment of supplies purchased outside Greece, and to facilitate other financial measures 'in order to render effective' the British economic aid that had already been granted to Greece.

involved on our resources, and would ask whether the United States could spare us some more destroyers.

Hugh Dalton: diary
(*'The Second World War Diary of Hugh Dalton'*)

20 November 1940

PM says that he is being pressed to make a statement on war aims. He is told that he will be given material to handle 'in what they call my own inimitable way'. He does not wish, however, merely to pronounce 'unctuous platitudes'. Can we do more just now? He will wait and see what is put up to him.

Anthony Eden: diary
(*'The Reckoning'*)

20 November 1940

Found telegram that Winston wanted to send to Wavell which is partly repetition of what I have already sent, with his approval. Telephoned and tried to persuade him to let me handle the business. Some acrimony, not much success.

Winston S. Churchill to Lord Halifax
(*Churchill papers, 20/13*)

20 November 1940

This is a very remarkable document,[1] and it is bound to have a great effect on the minds of Frenchmen on account both of its scope and its logic. It shows de Gaulle in a light very different from that of an ordinary military man.

WSC

---

[1] A declaration broadcast by General de Gaulle from Brazzaville on 17 November 1940.

November 1940

Winston S. Churchill to A. V. Alexander and Admiral Pound
(*Premier papers, 3/479/1*)

20 November 1940   10 Downing Street

These convoys are of the utmost consequence.[1] Let me know what will be done to protect them.

Has *Cameronia* arrived?[2]

WSC

War Cabinet: minutes
(*Cabinet papers, 65/10*)

21 November 1940   House of Commons (Annexe)
3 p.m.   Church House

The Prime Minister referred to telegram No. 319 from Sir John Maffey,[3] in Dublin. Sir John reported that Mr de Valera was in a very agitated and bitter mood. His attitude was that Irish sentiment towards this country had been steadily improving until we had suddenly raised the issue of the ports. This had let loose an abusive Press campaign.

The Secretary of State for Dominion Affairs said that a number of Members of Parliament had wished to put down a Question on this matter, but had been dissuaded. But it was doubtful how long the position could be held without answering a Question.

The Prime Minister suggested that one line of reply would be to say that this country had a very real appreciation of the fact that, if Eire was now at war with Germany, she would be exposed to the same perils as ourselves, but that at the moment she had no adequate defence. The last thing we wished to do was to lay Eire open to such attacks before adequate defence was available, and we were prepared to go to the limit of suffering. If, however, a time arrived when the use of Eire ports became a matter of life and death to this country, we might have to take another view. Clearly, however, no reply or statement should be made without further discussion in the War Cabinet.

The general opinion of the War Cabinet was that for the time being it would be better, if possible, to avoid making any statement. It was not clear,

---

[1] The convoys were bringing United States rifles to Britain.

[2] John Colville noted on this minute: 'Answer telephoned by First Lord to PM, 20/xi/40.'

[3] John Loader Maffey, 1877–1969. Entered the Indian Civil Srvice, 1899. Private Secretary to the Viceroy, 1916. Chief Political Officer with the forces in Afghanistan, 1919. Knighted, 1921. Chief Commissioner, North-West Frontier Province, 1921–3. Governor-General of the Sudan, 1926–33. Permanent Under-Secretary of State at the Colonial Office, 1933–7. United Kingdom Representative in Eire, 1939–49. Created Baron Rugby, 1947.

however, how long it would be possible to postpone making a statement, since public opinion in this country was becoming inflamed.

The Prime Minister added that every expedient must, of course, continue to be tried, both in the political field, in order to bring influences to work on Mr de Valera, and in the field of naval measures which might enable us to overcome the threat to our shipping without the use of the Eire ports.

The War Cabinet had before them a Note by the Minister without Portfolio, covering a Memorandum by the Chairman of the North American Supply Committee[1] as to the disclosure of secret information to the United States of America (WP (40) 441).

The Prime Minister thought that we should proceed cautiously in this matter, and vary our procedure according to the three main classes of secret information. The first comprised the details of our Supply programmes. Here the essential was that a full statement should be furnished to the United States Authorities in regard to each of the Supply programmes. A convincing case should be prepared for each programme, as had been done for the Aircraft programme. Once this statement had been made, all the other information supplied must be consistent with it.

The second class comprised details of technical devices. Here a distinction might be drawn between those which we wished to have manufactured in the United States for our own forces and those which the United States authorities wished to produce themselves for their own benefit. In the latter case we could demand a *quid pro quo* for disclosure.

The third class related to operational information. Here the main essential was to avoid giving away technical information which was intimately connected with operations likely to be undertaken in the near future.

Reference was made to the fact that during recent months the United States Air Attaché[2] had been supplied with a copy of the Air Ministry War Room Daily Summary. This document gave particulars of our own operations, and contained an Appendix giving details of the places in this country where enemy bombs had dropped and of the damage done.

It was explained that arrangements were being made to discontinue the supply of this Appendix to the United States Air Attaché.

The Prime Minister thought it undesirable to furnish the Attaché with a very detailed daily report of operations. It was obviously undesirable to cut off the supply of this information suddenly and entirely, and the best plan would

---

[1] Arthur Purvis.
[2] Captain G. Bryan Conrad.

be that the Summary should be reduced gradually in volume over the next two or three weeks.

Agreement was expressed with this view.

The Secretary of State for Foreign Affairs said that it would be disastrous if the United States authorities got it into their heads that we were treating them in these matters with a lack of confidence, and he suggested that Lord Lothian should discuss the position quite frankly with the President.

The Prime Minister said that he thought we should say that we did trust them, but that they would appreciate that we were fighting for our lives, and that it followed that there was certain secret information which we could not possibly divulge.

INDIA

The Prime Minister thought that a telegram should be sent to the Viceroy on the following lines:—

'We should make it clear that we were prepared to support him in whatever steps were necessary to maintain peace in India and India's effective part in the war. Before, however, we could agree to Congress being proclaimed we must know exactly what his programme involved. *Prima facie*, we thought it would give rise to an infinity of trouble if it was intended to make membership of the Congress party a criminal offence, and we found it difficult to see why it should be necessary to go further than proclaim the Working Committee. The War Cabinet would be glad to receive any new facts explaining how the situation was developing and which had a bearing on the need for taking immediate action.'

The Prime Minister added that he did not himself expect serious political trouble. He thought that agrarian trouble would be more likely to give rise to serious embarrassment. Congress were probably trying to keep themselves alive by a demonstration.

The Secretary of State for India concurred in this view.

Winston S. Churchill: speech
(*Hansard*)

21 November 1940 House of Commons (Annexe)
Church House

START OF THE NEW PARLIAMENTARY SESSION[1]

The Prime Minister (Mr Churchill): Even in times of the bitterest political controversy and party strife it has always been customary for all parties to listen with appreciation to the speeches of the Mover and the Seconder of the Address, and even when sometimes the circumstances have not entirely

[1] The previous Parliamentary Session had ended on the previous day, 20 November 1940.

sustained the compliments which were paid, those compliments have not been denied. But to-day I am sure that all the compliments which were paid by my right hon. Friend opposite,[1] who speaks for so many hon. Members who are not officially engaged in the work of Government, were not only sincere but were well deserved. We were very glad indeed to hear my hon. and gallant Friend the Member for North St Pancras (Squadron-Leader Grant-Ferris)[2] and I think it is gratifying to the House that one of our fighter-pilots who has taken part in severe actions, and will be engaged again, should be able to take his place here to-day to discharge his Parliamentary duties. I entirely agree with what has been said about the desirability of Members of Parliament serving not only in the military forces but in all other forms of warfare and discharging their Parliamentary duties at the same time or in alternation. No doubt difficulties arise, but I think they are well covered, and that the good sense of the House and of hon. Members will enable these dual and occasionally conflicting functions to be discharged.

In bygone days the House of Commons not only struggled for political power, but it did conduct a very great part of the business and activities of the country. Hon. Members led troops and squadrons of the Fleet and discharged all kinds of functions of Government at the same time as they conducted their work here. Some of the things that they did would not entirely commend themselves to our present higher standards of decorum, but, none the less, that this House should be a House of active, living personalities, engaged to the hilt in the national struggle, each according to the full strength that he has to give, each according to the aptitudes which he possesses is, I think, one of the sources of the strength of the Parliamentary institution, and will carry forward into the future the traditions which are inherent and the precedents which have come down to us from the past. I thought the House was absolutely right in the cordial welcome which it gave to their speeches, and we hope that we shall hear both hon. Members again on matters which they are particularly qualified to speak upon. The eloquence and oratorical gifts of the hon. Member for Bow and Bromley (Mr Key)[3] and the fervour with which he spoke of the tasks which we shall win the right to face when our warring days are over will, I am sure make the house feel that we have in him a Member who will be a very definite reinforcement of our ranks when we have important contributions to make to the problems which lie ahead.

[1] H. G. Lees-Smith, see page 179, note 1.
[2] Robert Grant Grant-Ferris, 1907– . Joined the Auxiliary Air Force, 1933. Unsuccessful Conservative candidate, 1935. Conservative MP, 1937–45. Flight-Commander, 1939–40; Wing-Commander, 1941. In charge of the fighter defences of Malta, 1941-2. Parliamentary Private Secretary to the Minister of Town and Country Planning, 1944–5. Created Baron Harrington, 1974.
[3] Charles William Key, 1883–1964. A schoolmaster. Labour MP from 1940 until his death. Regional Commissioner for the London Civil Defence Region, 1941–5. Parliamentary Private Secretary, Ministry of Health, 1945–7. Privy Councillor, 1947. Minister of Works, 1947–50.

My right hon. Friend,[1] if I may so call the one who sits in the place appointed for the main focus and spear thrust of Opposition, made us a very interesting speech, but I know that he and the House will forgive me if I do not attempt to deal with the war situation. I have on several occasions dealt with the issues as they arise, and I do not feel that this is a moment when it would be very convenient to make a statement on the war in the Mediterranean theatre – the two wars going on there, in both of which we have the very greatest interest. There is the defence of Egypt and the Canal, against greatly superior numbers of the enemy, which six months ago, at all events, looked rather a difficult affair, a doubtful affair, but which at the present time gives us a measure of confidence that we shall be able, as I said, to give a good account of ourselves when the invasion forces fall upon us – when they do fall upon us. And then there is the valiant, sudden uprising of the Greek nation, who, although taken by surprise and struck a felon's blow, have already almost entirely purged their soil of the conscript invaders, who were launched upon them upon an enterprise which cannot be described as other than pure, unmitigated brigandage. We have both those theatres to consider, and I can only say that we shall do our best. I feel that deeds, not words, are what are expected from us, and I certainly hope that we shall be able to give from our resources, which are always heavily strained, a helpful measure of assistance to the Greeks, and that we shall be able to discharge our responsibilities to Egypt in defending its soil and in guarding the vital artery of the Suez Canal.

It is customary for whoever leads the House on these occasions to give to hon. Members some account of the immediate Business which lies before them. The House will meet in the immediate future on the usual Sitting days. The Debate on the Address will be continued and will, I hope, be brought to a conclusion on the third Sitting day. Subject to your concurrence, Mr Speaker, I think we might devote ourselves to general topics on the first Sitting day and that we might, on the second Sitting day, debate production and man-power and, on the third Sitting day, the Army. My right hon. Friend the Secretary of State for War will be ready to give the House some account of his recent adventurous journey and the position generally of the great Armed Forces over which he presides and which are gaining in force, numbers and equipment as every week passes by; but that part of the discussion will clearly have to be in secret if the House is to be given the kind of account which it is entitled to receive, and would expect.

As to the immediate state of our work in this new Session, apart from the great Measures of finance, there are the two important Bills mentioned in the Gracious Speech. The War Damage (Compensation) Bill has perhaps lagged somewhat behind our hopes in its preparation. It is a Bill of great complexity and difficulty, but I can assure the House that every effort will be made to

---

[1] Lees-Smith.

bring it before Parliament at the earliest moment and that it will be a Measure of amplitude and scope which will deal effectively with the damage which now falls, now here and now there, upon individuals throughout the country. It will give effect to the feeling that there must be equality of risk and equality of treatment in respect of the damage done by the fire of the enemy. In other ways, many people have suffered material loss by the conditions of the war, but this Measure deals with damage done by the fire of the enemy and must be confined to that. Otherwise we should get into difficulties which would be beyond our powers to unravel. I feel that, because one man's home is smashed, that should be no special misfortune to him and that all whose homes are not broken up should stand in with him as long as the need may last; and even if all the homes of the country be levelled, then we shall still be found standing together to build them up again after the fighting is over.

There is the Means Test Bill on which I made a statement and which the House will, no doubt, await with interest. This Measure will to a very great extent end the question, which has been a subject of controversy between parties, but it will do more than that; I think it undoubtedly takes a step forward into those regions of social justice which are mentioned in the Gracious Speech. It is a step particularly adapted to the times in which we live, when households are situated very differently from what they are in peace, and when the means of individuals may not be the sole guide to the administration of relief in its various forms.

Mr Stephen[1] (Glasgow, Camlachie): Will the Bill be passed before Christmas?

The Prime Minister: That will depend to some extent upon the House, but it will certainly be pressed forward by the Government. There is one other Measure which requires to be dealt with before Christmas, and that is the Expiring Laws Continuance Bill. We also propose on the first Sitting day to set up the Select Committee on National Expenditure and the Select Committee on the Conduct of a Member. Any other necessary Business will, of course, be brought forward as and when required. I must also inform the House of the Government's intention to propose, on the next Sitting day, a Motion to give precedence to Government Business, to provide for the presentation of Government Bills only and to stop the Ballot for Private Members' Bills, following the precedents of the last Session and of the last war.

I have carefully considered this matter, and I feel sure that these proposals will receive, and certainly deserve, the general assent of the House. Anyone can see that in present circumstances our efforts must be concentrated upon those matters or measures which are vitally connected with the effective

---

[1] Campbell Stephen, 1884–1947. An 'ardent Socialist' (according to his *Who's Who* entry), and a Barrister-at-Law. Teacher of science and mathematics, 1919–22. Labour MP, 1922–31 and from 1935 until his death.

prosecution of the war at home and abroad. So far as opportunities for Debates are concerned, the House must have noticed how many general Debates we have had, and I see no reason why that process should not continue in the new Session. We are, in fact, instinctively reviving the ancient practice of the House, which was that the Government of the day got through its necessary Business with considerable expedition, and the House devoted itself to debating, usually on Petition, whatever were the topics of general public interest. I am wholly in favour of that. I believe, if this House is to keep its hold on the imagination and the interest of the public, that it is necessary that the great questions which interest the nation out of doors and occupy the Press should also be the questions subject to current discussion in this House. I very much deprecate the House falling unduly into the debating of details and routine, and losing sight of its larger duty of giving guidance and encouragement to the nation and administering when required the necessary corrective to the Executive. Therefore, I consider that this practice which we have of very often disposing of Business rapidly and then having an extensive Debate upon the Adjournment, although it appears to be an innovation after the quarrels of the last 20 or 30 years, is no more than a reversion, under forms very slightly different, to the process under which the House of Commons gained its great ascendancy in the public mind. I hope that there will be an agreement to adjourn the Debate on the Address in time to go into Secret Session for the purpose of considering a motion relating to the Sittings of the House and to the methods with which we transact our business and arrange our time table. We must have this Motion to-day if the work of the House is to be satisfactorily discharged in the coming week.

The time-honoured ceremonial and procedure in which Crown and Parliament have played their part to-day carry with them to anxious minds the balm of confidence and serenity. When our beloved Sovereign and the Queen come from their battered palace to a building which is not without evidence of the strokes of war, when the Sovereign comes to open Parliament in person and calls his faithful Commons to the discharge of their duties, at every step, in every measure, in every formality, and in every Resolution that we pass, we touch customs and traditions which go back far beyond the great Parliamentary conflicts of the seventeenth century; we feel the inspiration of old days, we feel the splendour of our political and moral inheritance.

We are frequently asked to make declarations about our war aims. Some may think that example is better than precept, and that actions speak louder than words. To-day, in inaugurating a new Session of Parliament, we proclaim the depth and sincerity of our resolve to keep vital and active, even in the midst of our struggle for life, even under the fire of the enemy, those Parliamentary institutions which have served us so well, which the wisdom and civic virtues of our forebears shaped and founded, which have proved themselves the most flexible instruments for securing ordered, unceasing change and progress; which, while they throw open the portals of the future, carry forward also the traditions and glories of the past and which, at this solemn moment in world history, are at once the proudest assertion of British freedom and the expression of an unconquerable national will.

His Majesty's Government are conscious with gratitude that they enter upon this new Session, not only with the formal and official support of all parties, but also, I trust and believe, with the general good will of the House. Immense surrenders of their hard-won liberties have been voluntarily made by the British people in order to serve in time of war the cause of freedom and fair play, to which, keeping nothing back, they have devoted all that they have and all that they are. Parliament stands custodian of these surrendered liberties, and its most sacred duty will be to restore them in their fullness when victory has crowned our exertions and our perseverance.

We have a long road to travel. I have never concealed from the nation or from the House the darker side of our dangers and burdens, because it is there and because I know that it is in adversity that British qualities shine the brightest, and it is under these extraordinary tests that the character of our slowly wrought institutions reveals its latent, invincible stength. Up to the present this war has been waged between a fully-armed Germany and a quarter- or half-armed British Empire. We have not done so badly. I look forward with confidence and hope to the time when we ourselves shall be as well armed as our antagonists, and beyond that, if need be, I look to a time when the arsenals and training grounds and science of the New World and of the British Empire will give us that material superiority which, added to the loyalty of constant hearts, will surely bring victory and deliverance to mankind.

Winston S. Churchill to Herbert Morrison
(*Churchill papers, 20/6*)

21 November 1940

My dear Home Secretary,

I must congratulate you on the excellence of your remarks today,[1] both about Italy and in reply to Kennedy's[2] vapourings.

The points could not have been better made and I am sure they will strike home.

Yours very sincerely,
Winston S. Churchill

[1] Morrison's remarks, made after the House had gone into Secret Session, were not recorded by *Hansard*.
[2] Joseph P. Kennedy, United States Ambassador.

November 1940

Winston S. Churchill to President Roosevelt
(*Churchill papers, 20/14*)

21 November 1940

You may be interested to receive the following Naval notes on the action at Taranto which I have asked the Admiralty to prepare:–

1. This attack had been in Commander-in-Chief, Mediterranean's, mind for some time; he had intended to carry it out on 21st October (Trafalgar Day), when the moon was suitable, but a slight mishap to *Illustrious* led to a postponement. During his cruise in the Central Mediterranean on 31st October and 1st November it was again considered, but the moon did not serve and it was thought an attack with parachute flares would be less effective. Success in such an attack was believed to depend on state of moon, weather, an undetected approach by the Fleet, and good reconnaissance. The latter was provided by flying boats and a Glenn Martin squadron[1] working from Malta. On the night of 11th/12th November all the above conditions were met. Unfavourable weather in the Gulf of Taranto prevented a repetition on 12th/13th.
2. Duplex pistols were used and probably contributed to the success of the torpedo attack.
3. The Greek Ambassador at Angora[2] reported on 11th November that Italian fleet was concentrating at Taranto in preparation for an attack on Corfu. Reconnaissance on 13th November shows that undamaged battleships and 8-inch-gun cruisers have left Taranto – presumably due to the attack on 11th/12th.

Thank you very much for your help and news about the two big French ships.

Harold Nicolson: diary
(*'Diaries and Letters, 1939–1945'*)

22 November 1940

Ronnie[3] says that Winston is convinced that the Germans will strive by every means to smash us before the spring. 'We are in for a very terrible

[1] These Glenn Martin reconnaissance aircraft had recently arrived in Malta from the United States.

[2] The Turkish capital, known today as Ankara (the Turkish as opposed to the Greek form of the name).

[3] Ronald Tree, 1897–1976. Son of Arthur Tree and Countess Beatty. Educated at Winchester. On active service in France and Italy, 1917–18. Managing Editor of *Forum* magazine, New York, 1922–6. Joint Master of the Pytchley Hounds, 1927–33. Conservative MP for Harborough division of Leicestershire, 1933–45. Parliamentary Private Secretary to Robert Hudson, 1936–8; to Sir John Reith, 1940; to Alfred Duff Cooper, 1940–1; and to Brendan Bracken, 1941–3.

ordeal.' After that we shall have a very strained summer and then supremacy in 1942. Meanwhile the Italian collapse in Greece is of great value to us. We may attack the Dodecanese shortly.

He says that someone complimented Winston upon his obituary oration on Neville Chamberlain. 'No', said Winston, 'that was not an insuperable task, since I admired many of Neville's great qualities.[1] But I pray to God in his infinite mercy that I shall not have to deliver a similar oration on Baldwin. That indeed would be difficult to do.'[2]

Then we get to Ditchley. The great mass of the house is dark and windowless, and then a chink in the door opens and we enter suddenly into the warmth of central heating, the blaze of lights and the amazing beauty of the hall.[3]

Winston S. Churchill to Lord Hankey and Lord Ismay
(*Premier papers, 3/214*)

22 November 1940
ACTION THIS DAY

The munitions which it is proposed to send to Greece seem very meagre. Briefly we seem only ready to spare about 1 per cent of the totals we have available here, if indeed we are ready to send anything. No field or anti-tank guns, only 8 anti-aircraft guns out of our total of 1,100 in this country, 12 Bofors and these without predictors out of 700 in England with a monthly output of 100. No mention is made of sending any ammunition except for the

---

Parliamentary Secretary, Ministry of Town and Country Planning, 1945. In 1920 he married, as his first wife, Nancy Perkins, of Richmond, Virginia, a niece of Nancy Astor, and widow of Henry Field of Chicago. In 1947 he married Mrs Mary Endicott Fitzgerald, daughter of the Rt Rev Malcolm Peabody of New York. Nancy Tree married, in 1948, as her third husband, Colonel Claude Granville Lancaster, a Conservative MP, 1938–70, and Chairman of the Tory Reform Committee, 1946.

[1] Kathleen Hill, to whom Churchill had dictated his Chamberlain tribute, later recalled: 'Then he showed it to Mrs Churchill. She said, "It is very good". "Well," he replied with a twinkle in his eye, "of course I could have done it the other way round" ' (Kathleen Hill, conversation with the author, 15 October 1982).

[2] In 1947, on Stanley Baldwin's eightieth birthday, Churchill wrote to the Principal Private Secretary at 10 Downing Street (declining to send a birthday message): 'I wish Stanley Baldwin no ill, but it would have been better for our country if he had never lived.'

[3] Churchill's other guests that weekend included his brother John, sister-in-law Lady Gwendeline Churchill and their daughter Clarissa, his daughter Mary, his son Randolph and daughter-in-law Pamela, Herbert Morrison, Richard Law (Bonar Law's son), Oliver and Lady Moira Lyttelton, Air Marshal Sir Richard Peirse, Air Marshal Sholto Douglas, Admiral of the Fleet Sir Dudley Pound, Rear-Admiral Fraser, General Hobart and Professor Lindemann. Eric Seal was the Duty Private Secretary.

anti-tank rifles, but presumably arrangements will be made to see that the Greeks have something to fire from the guns we do send.[1]

Question must be reconsidered in light of Greek achievements.

Winston S. Churchill to Sir Edward Bridges
(*Cabinet papers, 120/744*)

22 November 1940

This report and others like it should be steadily damped down, and its circulation restricted as far as possible. The reports given to the American Attaché should not be broken off suddenly but should become less informative and padding used to maintain bulk. This is not through any lack of confidence in him, but because the wild scattering of secret information must be curbed.

Report in one week what action has been taken.

WSC

Winston S. Churchill to Anthony Eden and General Dill
(*Premier papers, 3/288/1*)

22 November 1940

General Wavell's telegram to CIGS does not answer the question I put. The last sentence but one leaves everything unsettled. I had expected to hear either that the reinforcements of aircraft were insufficient, or that when they arrived he would act. It is not clear that he has made up his mind.

I presume he has been told of the additional two days' delay entailed by the need of giving destroyer protection to *Furious*. This cannot now arrive before 28th. Pray continue to press Air Ministry and Admiralty for utmost speed at both ends. Every day's delay endangers secrecy in Egypt, which must be full of Italian spies and agents.

See also No. 1013 from Sir Stafford Cripps.[2] Evidently we must now call upon Turkey to come in, or face the consquences in the future. Turkey will reply either by refusing, or by demanding as a condition immediate assistance in arms, men, ships and Air. A British victory in Libya would probably turn

---

[1] The text of Churchill's minute, with the exception of the final sentence, was sent to Churchill by Professor Lindemann.
[2] British Ambassador in Moscow.

the scale, and then we could shift our forces to the new theatre. How long would it be before the Germans could strike at Greece through Bulgaria? There might just be time for Wavell to act in Libya before the pressure becomes decisive. Anyhow, all his troops, except the barest defensive minimum, will be drawn out of him before long.

WSC

Winston S. Churchill to General Wavell
(*Premier papers, 3/288/1*)

22 November 1940
Personal and Secret

I had expected that you would answer my 89731 by saying either that the reinforcements of aircraft expected to arrive at end of first week of December were insufficient for 'Compass',[1] or that when they arrived you would act. Your 0–26780 to CIGS leaves this uncertain. I fully understand your difficulty, but you must also see mine. Read No. 1013 from Cripps at Moscow. If, as seems probable, Germany immediately attacks Greece through Bulgaria with or without Bulgarian aid, we shall certainly be bound to urge Turkey to the utmost to enter the war. Turkey will either refuse, in which case Greece will soon be ruined; or Turkey will come in, in which case she will make most heavy demands for arms, troops, ships and air. Importance of getting Turkey in, and perhaps Yugoslavia, would far outweigh any Libyan operation, and you would be relegated to the very minimum defensive role in Egypt. If, however, you could do 'Compass' in the first fortnight of December a new and very important event would occur, rendering more favourable alternatives possible. On the other hand, I do not wish to press you into precipitate action without the Air Force, which your judgement requires. We may be forced to abandon 'Compass' altogether, or there may be time to work it in before other things develop. I must, however, know what you are going to do, and when it would happen.

---

[1] 'Compass' was the code name given to the offensive that opened in the Western Desert on 6 December 1940, when Major-General Richard O'Connor's Western Desert Force attacked the Italian troops that had advanced into Egypt from Libya in September 1940. In the line-up of O'Connor's forces, Indian and New Zealand troops had a prominent place. The Italian general facing them was Lieutenant-General Annibale Bergonzoli, commanding the Italian XXIII Corps.

Winston S. Churchill to Lord Cranborne
(*Premier papers, 3/127/1*)

22 November 1940

I think it would be better to let de Valera stew in his own juice for a while. Nothing could be more harmless or more just than the remarks in the *Economist*. The claim now put forward on behalf of de Valera is that we are not only to be strangled by them but to suffer our fate without making any complaint. The paper you have written marked A should not, I think, be sent. It will do no good and is far too mild as an expression of our case.

Sir John Maffey should be made aware of the rising anger in England and Scotland, and especially among the merchant seamen, and he should not be encouraged to think that his only task is to mollify de Valera and make everything, including our ruin, pass off pleasantly. Apart from this, the less we say to de Valera at this juncture the better, and certainly nothing must be said to reassure him.

Let me see the Parliamentary Questions as they come in.

WSC

Winston S. Churchill to Lord Lloyd
(*Churchill papers, 20/13*)

22 November 1940

PROPOSAL TO SHIP TO MAURITIUS JEWISH REFUGEES WHO HAD ILLEGALLY EMIGRATED TO PALESTINE

As the action has been announced, it must proceed, but the conditions in Mauritius must not involve these people being caged up for the duration of the war. The Cabinet will require to be satisfied about this. Pray make me your proposals.

Winston S. Churchill to A. V. Alexander and Admiral Pound
(*Churchill papers, 20/13*)

22 November 1940

In my view Admiral Stark[1] is right, and Plan D[2] on page 2 is strategically sound and also most highly adapted to our interests. Evidently

---

[1] Harold Raynsford Stark, 1880–1972. Commissioned into the United States Navy, 1905. Served in European waters, 1917–18. Rear-Admiral, 1934. Commanding the Cruisers, Battle Force, 1938–9. Chief of Naval Operations, 1939–42. Commander, US Naval Forces in Europe, 1942–5. Honorary British knighthood, 1945.

[2] Plan D, as explained in Telegram 2750 from Washington, was for the 'Provision of all possible naval and military aid in European field to exclusion of any other interest. This would involve

this Admiral and the American Navy Board are working upon lines which would be likely to bring the United States into the war in the best possible manner for us. We should, therefore, so far as opportunity serves, in every way contribute to strengthen the policy of Admiral Stark, and should not use arguments inconsistent with it.

2. Should Japan enter the war on one side and the United States on ours, ample naval forces will be available to contain Japan by long-range controls in the Pacific. The Japanese Navy is not likely to venture far from its home bases so long as a superior battle-fleet is maintained at Singapore or at Honolulu. The Japanese would never attempt a siege of Singapore with a hostile, superior American fleet in the Pacific. The balance of the American fleet, after providing the necessary force for the Pacific, would be sufficient with our Navy to exercise in a very high degree the command of all the seas and oceans except those within the immediate Japanese regions. A strict defensive in the Far East and the acceptance of its consequences is also our policy. Once the Germans are beaten, the Japanese would be at the mercy of the combined fleets.

3. I am much encouraged by the American naval view. The paragraphs about our being incapable of winning alone are particularly helpful.

WSC

---

adoption of a strict defensive plan in Pacific and abandonment of any attempt seriously to reinforce Far East with accepted consequences. On the other hand, by full-scale concentration in European area, defeat of Germany was ensured with certainty, and if subsequently it was in American interest to deal with Japan, requisite steps would be possible.'

1128　November 1940

Winston S. Churchill to General Ismay
(*Churchill papers, 20/13*)

23 November 1940

I think it would be most undesirable for it to appear that the only people who dared raid the occupied coasts of France were black troops from Morocco. Moreover, I do not think the course of the war will be materially affected by a petty affair of 40 men.

WSC

Winston S. Churchill to A. V. Alexander and Admiral Pound
(*Churchill papers, 20/13*)

23 November 1940

1. I am somewhat disquieted by the dispositions foreshadowed in your No. 257. This is not the moment to withdraw any substantial force from the Eastern Mediterranean. The attitude of Turkey might be seriously prejudiced thereby. It is quite right to bring *Ramillies* home as part of 'Collar',[1] but I do not think *Valiant* should come now. You have only just passed *Barham* through, and the situation in the oceans has not changed so decisively, or so urgently, as to make such a complete change of policy justifiable. You have recently argued that the injuries to the Italian battle-fleet do not substantially alter the strategic situation.

2. I am very glad you are going to try to make *Malaya* carry on for the present. If she cracked up after you had sent *Valiant* and *Ramillies* away, Admiral Cunningham[2] would only have *Warspite* and *Barham*, and the whole aspect of a strong battle-fleet in the Eastern basin would have vanished, just at the moment when it is most needed.

3. The future employment of *Queen Elizabeth* cannot be settled till she is ready for action. I see the Germans announce both *Bismarck* and *Tirpitz* are 'in service.' This may be only to comfort Japan for the weakening of the Italian battle-fleet. But, anyhow, when are we going to get *Prince of Wales*?

---

[1] Operation 'Collar' was the convoy planned for 25/28 November to pass supplies from Gibraltar to Malta and Alexandria. The convoy of three fast merchantmen (two for Malta and one for Alexandria), two cruisers and four corvettes was to be escorted by Admiral Somerville's Gibraltar-based Force 'H' to a point south of Sardinia, where elements of Admiral Cunningham's Mediterranean Fleet would take over.

[2] Admiral Sir Andrew Cunningham, Commander-in-Chief, Mediterranean.

4. Now that we have Suda as well as Malta, a couple of cruisers might possibly be withdrawn for necessary convoy duties as proposed, and the occupation of Malta by light forces, on which you were so recently set, postponed.

5. I find it very difficult to understand how you can propose that *Formidable* with her armoured deck and latest equipment should be wasted outside the range of enemy aircraft, while a weak ship like *Eagle* is left exposed. I much regretted that *Formidable* should have to go all round the Cape to work up. If, however, you think it too dangerous to pass her into the Eastern basin and let her work up there, this disadvantage must be accepted. It would appear that *Formidable* should relieve *Eagle* by one route or the other as soon as possible. Both *Eagle* and *Argus* are suitable for the outer seas.

6. I am not aware of any evidence which justifies the belief that *Scheer* has proceeded into the South Atlantic. She is certainly not at Lorient and was never likely to go there. It is more probable that she has gone back northabout to Germany. *Renown* with *Ark Royal* are particularly well-placed at Gibraltar to deal with *Scheer* should she by any chance, as is not to be excluded, attempt some enterprise in the Azores. You may have a crisis there any day.

7. The losses caused by enemy surface raiders in the South Atlantic, Indian and Pacific Oceans can certainly not be cured by the very few hunter groups we have the means of forming at the present time. We must put up with them till the events impending in the Mediterranean theatre are more clear.

I shall be much obliged if you will give your consideration to these points, and discuss them with me to-night.

WSC

Winston S. Churchill to Herbert Morrison
(*Premier papers, 4/40/19*)

23 November 1940   10 Downing Street

There seems to be great disparity in these sentences, and I wonder whether any attempt is being made to standardize the punishments inflicted for this very odious crime. Five Years' penal servitude for stealing whisky for immediate consumption seems out of proportion when compared with sentences of three or six months for stealing valuables. Exemplary discipline is no doubt necessary as people must be made to feel that looting is stealing. Still I should be glad to know that these kind of cases are being reviewed and levelled out.[1]

WSC

Winston S. Churchill to Alfred Duff Cooper
(*Churchill papers, 20/13*)

23 November 1940

From time to time it might be possible to give my speech to the French[2] over the French radio. It is just as relevant to-day as when it was made, and I have a feeling that the audience would be more receptive. I understand a record was taken.

Pray let me know what you can do.

WSC

Winston S. Churchill to Sir Charles Portal
(*Churchill papers, 20/13*)

23 November 1940

Here is Lord Beaverbrook's reply to your complaint about the shortage of heavy bombers. You will see that he addresses himself to the subject in great detail. The high proportion of unserviceable machines in the Operational

---

[1] The *Daily Express* on 23 November 1940 reported a five-year prison sentence on six London firemen, three of whom had been caught near St Paul's, while in uniform, with canvas buckets filled with looted bottles of whisky and gin. In the same article it was reported that a labourer had received a six-month sentence for stealing two pairs of lace curtains. In reply to Churchill's minute, Herbert Morrison referred to 'the fact that the men concerned had taken advantage of their position as members of a public service'. The powers of sentencing so highly had been taken, Morrison explained, 'with a view to the possibility that the most drastic action might be necessary to suppress outbreaks of looting in an invaded area, or in an area where, owing to enemy action, there was a risk of a breakdown in the maintenance of public order' (*Premier papers, 4/40/19*).

[2] Churchill speech of 21 October 1940.

Units is remarkable. This is also true of the OTUs. The Air Ministry take very easily the idea that only about three-quarters of the Fighters, IE, and two-thirds of the Bombers, IE, should be available. These figures go even beyond this high proportion of unavailables.

I shall be very glad if you will go into this question of increasing the serviceability of machines, and also of making transfers of the machines of which there are shortages, and give me answers to the questions asked. If necessary more fitters and riggers should be supplied to the Operational and OT Units. Personnel should not be shown as unavailable if they are on leave and can be recalled at a few hours' notice. No one ever wrote down the strength of a Battalion of a ship's company because some of the officers and men were resting or on short leave.

Let me have also your views on the Hereford–Hampden point.

Could I also be informed about Points A, B and C, on page 2.

I do trust this matter may be dealt with. It is most painful for me to see the tremendous expenditure of machines and men which pour into the Air Force at one end, and the woefully small output for fighting purposes at the other. It is the duty of everyone concerned to try to reach a truer economy and give greater results in numbers without the diminishing of efficiency.

Even a 20 per cent improvement would be a godsend in these critical months.

WSC

Winston S. Churchill to Lord Woolton
(*Churchill papers, 20/13*)

23 November 1940
Most Secret

Do not circulate the attached[1] to your Department, but let me know exactly the effect that would be produced on your problems by the cutting off of Irish supplies of food for say six months.[2]

WSC

---

[1] A report sent to Churchill by the Dominions Secretary, Lord Cranborne.
[2] In his reply three days later, Lord Woolton stated: 'I believe that such a step would so profoundly disturb Irish agriculture during the next three months as to render negotiations possible with them subsequently on our terms' (*Premier papers, 3/128*).

E. A. Seal to all Private Secretaries
(*Premier papers, 4/80/3*)

23 November 1940

The logic of events has forced upon us an arrangement under which the Private Secretaries are in turn responsible for direct attendance upon the person of the Prime Minister. This is a result of the arrangements under which we work in three, four, or even five alternative places.

I think it would be of advantage that this arrangement should be frankly acknowledged and regularized. Up to the time of black-out and withdrawal for the night to the Barn,[1] CWR[2] etc., the 'Custos Corporis' ('CC') would be one of the three Junior Private Secretaries, (Mr Martin, Mr Colville and Mr Peck). It would be his duty to attend the Prime Minister wherever he might be, and to wait until relieved by one of the others. The 'CC' would keep the telephonists informed of his (and thus of the Prime Minister's) whereabouts, and would notify them immediately on relief. In this way we shall reap the maximum advantage from having our own telephone exchange.

The three Private Secretaries named should make arrangements between themselves for a suitable rota. The presence of Mr Bevir, Miss Watson, or myself with the Prime Minister would not relieve them of duty, unless a special arrangement to this end were made.

During lunch-time there would be no objection to Mr Barker[3] temporarily taking charge, a typist being left on watch at No. 10 Annexe[4] if the Prime Minister was not there. This is in fact the normal arrangement.

After withdrawal to the night retreat, the Private Secretary accompanying the Prime Minister (normally the Principal Private Secretary) would become 'CC'.[5]

---

[1] The former Piccadilly Line station at Down Street, in the underground rooms of which, belonging to the London Transport Executive, Churchill had already spent several nights during particularly heavy air raids on Central London.

[2] The underground Cabinet War Rooms (also known as the Central War Rooms) in the old Board of Trade Building, where Churchill was to spend at least three nights during heavy bombing raids, and where frequent meetings of the War Cabinet, the Defence Committee and the Night Air Defence Committee (all chaired by Churchill) were being held.

[3] Charles Barker, Chief Clerk at 10 Downing Street. Jock Colville writes: 'Efficient and entertaining, he was popular with the Private Secretaries. An expert on old silver' (*The Fringes of Power*, page 247, note 1).

[4] The above-ground rooms overlooking St James's Park in the old Board of Trade Building, where Churchill had begun to live and work. The Cabinet War Rooms were directly below.

[5] In the event, the appointment of Commander C. R. (Tommy) Thompson provided a form of Master of the Household to be in constant attendance (see page 1180), letter of 4 December 1940).

E. A. Seal: private letter
(*Seal papers*)

24 November 1940 Chequers

Last night was a 'Naval night' – the First Sea Lord, Fraser the Controller, & the First Lord. After dinner Alexander & Winston had a long & friendly discussion about socialism – the Prime Minister just scintillating on these occasions, & is full of fascinating sayings & anecdotes. All tremendous fun. But afterwards work went on until 2 am!

I do now believe that at long last we are on the verge of getting a good sensible organisation to cope with our difficulties – the principal of which is that the PM is never in one place for more than a few hours, & we therefore have to be ready to set up our tent almost anywhere.

The news from Greece ain't so bad – is it? It would be splendid if Musso's nose could really be put out of joint. What a silly bombastic old man he is! Anyway, the exploits of the Greeks have done something to cheer us in this most miserable of all months (the month of the dead) November.

Winston S. Churchill to Foreign Office and Chiefs of Staff Committee
(*Churchill papers, 20/13*)

24 November 1940

The moment is appropriate and the action needful, but I do not think Mr Campbell's draft[1] a very impressive document, it being conceived in a purely conventional, diplomatic style. One has to read it very carefully in order to understand what it means. I should hope that something could be re-drafted in plain, simple English, and much shorter, and that we could consider this at the Cabinet on Monday.

Meanwhile, the Chiefs of Staff should report at the same time their opinion on the last lines of paragraph 4 of Telegram 980.[2] Is there any aid and assistance we can give them, except by carrying on the war by ourselves as we are doing against the Germans and Italians? Attention should also be paid to the report of the Naval Attaché[3] that the Yugoslavs are contemplating in certain circumstances vacating their country altogether and sending their

---

[1] A proposed communication to the Yugoslav Government urging them to resist the demands of the Axis powers. Ronald Ian Campbell, 1890–1983, had been in the Diplomatic Service since 1914. From 1939 to 1941 he was British Minister in Belgrade, and from 1941 to 1945 in Washington. He was knighted in 1941. From 1946 to 1950 he was British Ambassador in Egypt.

[2] Containing a request by the Yugoslav Government for British military assistance, on the lines of that already being sent to Greece.

[3] Captain M. S. Despard, appointed to Belgrade on 8 August 1940.

Army to fight on with us wherever the war may lie, as they did last time. It would not, however, be wise to mention this in the proposed message.

If we cannot promise any effective material aid, we can at any rate assure them that, just as we did last time, we will see their wrongs are righted in the eventual victory.

WSC

Winston S. Churchill to Lord Halifax
(*Churchill papers, 20/13*)

24 November 1940
Secret

Yours of the 23rd.[1] I think everything is being done in the direction you indicate, but it is better at the present time to operate east of Malta and on the Italian communications.

I asked the Air Ministry some days ago to do all they could against Italy, but at this season of the year this can best be done from Malta.

I think it better to let the Dodecanese go for the present. They are being slowly starved, and the capture of either Rhodes or Leros is a big operation. Moreover, Greece and Turkey would quarrel over the prize if we won it. I have every reason to believe that what I told you about Egypt will come off soon. I greatly fear the German attacks threatened through Bulgaria. Every effort should be made to frame up Turkey and Yugoslavia against this. The impending fortnight is momentous.[2]

WSC

Winston S. Churchill to General Dill
(*Churchill papers, 20/13*)

24 November 1940

I sent you to-day two Foreign Office telegrams from Bucharest and Sofia respectively, which concur in an estimate of 30,000 Germans, or one full Division, as the maximum in Roumania at the present time. In view of this, your Intelligence Branch should carefully review the advice they gave to the effect that there were five Divisions in Roumania and that these could be

---

[1] Halifax had supported a plan drawn up by the Chiefs of Staff for the seizure of the Italian Dodecanese Islands (including Rhodes, Kos and Leros), Operation 'Mandibles'.

[2] On 1 November 1940, following the arrival of a German Air Force mission in Roumania, a top secret German Air Force radio message, decrypted at Bletchley as Enigma decrypt CX/JQ 417, had established the German intention to install aircraft warning systems in Roumania and Bulgaria.

November 1940   1135

assembled on the Bulgarian–Greek frontier in three or four days. I thought myself that this estimate was altogether too pessimistic, and credited the enemy with a rapidity of movement and a degree of preparedness which were perhaps more serious than the facts. Will you have the whole problem examined most carefully again? I had thought myself that it would be a fortnight before anything serious could happen on the Greek frontier, and that perhaps it might be a month. The great thing is to get the true picture, whatever it is.

WSC

Winston S. Churchill to General Ismay
(*Churchill papers, 20/13*)

24 November 1940

This paper[1] shows that we have completely failed to make Cruiser Tanks, and that there is no prospect of the present deficiency being made up in the next year. We must therefore equip our Armoured Divisions in the best possible way open to us in these melancholy circumstances. At this stage in Tank production numbers count above everything else. It is better to have any serviceable Tank than none at all. The formation and training of the Divisions can proceed, and the quality and character of the vehicles improved later on. The I Tank should not be disdained because of its slow speed, and in default of Cruisers must be looked upon as our staple for fighting. We must adapt our tactics for the time being to this weapon as we have no other. Meanwhile, the production of Cruiser Tanks and of A22 must be driven forward to the utmost limit.

WSC

Winston S. Churchill: recollection
(*'Their Finest Hour', page 333*)

24 November 1940

The next target was Birmingham, and three successive raids from the 19th to the 22nd of November inflicted much destruction and loss of life. Nearly eight hundred people were killed and over two thousand injured;[2] but the life and spirit of Birmingham survived this ordeal. When I visited the city a day or two later to inspect its factories, and see for myself what had happened,

[1] Defence Committee (Supply) Paper No. 89 of 1940, 'Tank Production'.
[2] In fact, 1,353 civilians had been killed in Birmingham on the night of 19/20 November. The total deaths in Birmingham during the Blitz were 2,241, with 6,629 injured and 12,391 houses and 302 factories destroyed, or damaged beyond repair.

an incident, to me charming, occurred. It was the dinner-hour, and a very pretty young girl ran up to the car and threw a box of cigars into it. I stopped at once and she said: 'I won the prize this week for the highest output. I only heard you were coming an hour ago.' The gift must have cost her two or three pounds. I was very glad (in my official capacity) to give her a kiss. I then went on to see the long mass grave in which so many citizens and their children had been newly buried. The spirit of Birmingham shone brightly, and its million inhabitants, highly organised, conscious and comprehending, rode high above their physical suffering.

John Colville: diary
(*Colville papers*)

25 November 1940

The PM returned at lunch-time and busied himself with picking holes in a FO telegram giving the pros and cons of pushing Turkey into war. He demanded a report on the subject while he was having lunch – an unreasonable request which caused much perturbation to me and the FO.

War Cabinet: minutes
(*Cabinet papers, 65/10*)

25 November 1940 Cabinet War Room
5 p.m.

The War Cabinet had before them a Report by the Lord Privy Seal[1] (WP (40) 450) as to why the direction given by the Cabinet in 1938 to increase the storage reserve of gas from 500 to 2,000 tons had not been fully carried out.

The Prime Minister said that it was of the utmost importance that Departments should press forward with the measures required to accumulate a thoroughly adequate reserve of gas weapons as quickly as possible. If the enemy could not beat down our resistance in any other way, he might well have recourse to gas, and we must be in a position to retaliate at once and effectively.

In connection with the preceding Minute, the War Cabinet were informed that schedules were circulated weekly to all Departments setting out –
    (a) The decisions reached by the War Cabinet in the preceding week, and
    (b) Decisions reached in earlier weeks in regard to which no notification

[1] Clement Attlee.

had been received by the War Cabinet Offices that action had been taken or, in the case of long-term projects, that the initial action was in hand.

The Prime Minister invited Ministers to consider whether some follow-up procedure should be set up in their own Departments, to make sure that effect was given promptly to Ministerial decisions on important matters.

War Cabinet: Confidential Annex
(*Cabinet papers, 65/16*)

25 November 1940   Cabinet War Room
5 p.m.

The Prime Minister thought that Mussolini might have been afraid that Hitler was doing a deal with France at his expense, and have given the order for the Italian ultimatum to Greece, contrary to Hitler's wishes. If this was so, it might be that Germany had no counter move ready to redress the position. But it would be rash to draw any conclusion favourable to ourselves. Germany might well be meditating a stroke on the lines which would be most embarrassing to us, namely, through Bulgaria to Salonika. Germany might count on inducing Bulgaria to give her right of passage and on persuading Turkey also to stand aside.

Discussion ensued as to how long it would take Germany to strike down from Roumania, on to the Aegean. It had been reported that Germany had only 30,000 troops in Roumania. Our General Staff put the figure higher, and thought that a move through Bulgaria could be operated in a matter of days, relying largely on rail transport. It was pointed out that German troops had been established in Roumania for some time, and that preparations for a rapid forward move might have been in hand for some time.

The Prime Minister referred to telegrams Nos. 1310 and 1311 to Turkey, which set out the arguments for and against bringing Turkey into the war at this stage.

The Foreign Secretary explained that these telegrams had been despatched after the Meeting of the War Cabinet held on Friday, 22nd November, when it had been decided to invite the Turkish and Yugoslav Governments to make a joint declaration to Bulgaria. (This suggestion now seemed unlikely to materialise, as Yugoslavia was afraid to commit herself so openly.) At the same Meeting it had been decided to communicate to our Ambassador at Ankara,[1] for his own information, the substance of the Chiefs of Staff's view

[1] Hughe Montgomery Knatchbull-Hugessen, 1886–1971. Entered the Foreign Office, 1908. British Minister to the Baltic States, 1930–4; in Teheran, 1934–6. Knighted, 1936. Ambassador to China, 1936–7; to Turkey, 1939–44; to Brussels, 1944–7. In 1949 he published his memoirs, *Diplomat in Peace and War*. Known, after secret documents in his possession had been stolen by the German spy Cicero in Turkey, as 'Snatch'.

on the question whether it would be to our advantage to bring Turkey into the war at this stage.

In discussion, the War Cabinet were reminded that the Chiefs of Staff, after very careful consideration, had come to the conclusion that the arguments on each side were nicely balanced. They had, however, considered that the balance was turned by one over-riding factor, namely, that if Turkey entered the war now we should be sure of her alliance, whereas if Greece was first over-run she might accede to Axis demands without fighting at all. It was suggested that it would be desirable that our Ambassador should be given clear and specific guidance as to the line he should take on this point.

At the suggestion of the Prime Minister, the War Cabinet agreed that the question whether it was to our advantage to bring Turkey into the war at this stage, and the instructions thereon to be sent to our Ambassador at Angora, should be further considered by the Defence Committee (Operations) that evening.

Winston S. Churchill to General Ismay
(*Premier papers, 3/214*)

25 November 1940

I cannot approve 20 Hurricanes going to Greece. They are all needed to augment our own force in ME. They must be disembarked in Egypt.

WSC

Winston S. Churchill to General Ismay
(*Churchill papers, 20/13*)

25 November 1940

The Chiefs of the Staff's report WP (40) 460 does not deal at all with the possibility of our landing an Army either to defend the approaches to Gibraltar or to attack Ceuta.[1] Plans, at any rate, should be made for this.

WSC

---

[1] Ceuta, a Spanish enclave on the African shore of the Strait of Gibraltar.

Anthony Eden: diary
(*'The Reckoning'*)

25 November 1940

Dined with Winston when we had some talk of future plans. We were alone. Champagne and oysters in his bedroom. I told him that if 'Compass' went reasonably well, we should need to determine future dispositions, after discussion with C-in-Cs on the spot and Greeks and possibly Turks. We could not leave an army inactive in Africa. Should we reinforce Greeks, if so where, Salonika? And what could these men achieve? I suggested I should pay another visit. We must continue to hammer Italians either in Africa, or Europe or both. Winston agreed generally. He felt that 'Compass' might influence attitude of all these countries; this is true, though one must not place too high hopes on 'Compass', which is at present a limited operation.

Winston S. Churchill to General Ismay
(*Churchill papers, 20/13*)

25 November 1940

'A'[1] must be discussed at a meeting with the Chiefs of the Staff and Service Ministers and myself to-night at 10 p.m. at the CWR.

WSC

Defence Committee (Operations): minutes
(*Cabinet papers, 69/1*)

25 November 1940   Cabinet War Room
9.30 p.m.

OPERATIONS IN EAST AFRICA

The Prime Minister drew attention to Telegram No. 945 of 23rd November, 1940, from the United Kingdom High Commissioner in the Union of South Africa (Annex).[2] He enquired why the projected operation against Kismayu had been postponed until May.

---

[1] Telegram No. 945 from the British High Commissioner in South Africa, reporting the distress of the South African Government that an imminent operation against the port of Kismayu in Italian Somaliland (Jubaland) had been postponed until May.

[2] A telegram of 23 November 1940 in which General Smuts reported that South Africa had sent a South African air squadron, of Hurricanes, from Kenya to Egypt 'in order to help situation caused by air reinforcements for Greece', but in which he then protested against the postponement of the planned expedition against Kismayu from January to May 1941 (*Cabinet papers, 69/1*).

Sir John Dill said that he had received a telegram from General Wavell saying that he would shortly be holding a Conference of Commanders, including General Cunningham,[1] to consider plans for the next six months, and that the latter had said that he would be unable to carry out this particular operation in January, but would undertake certain minor operations in Northern Kenya instead. The reason for this was not known at home, though it was believed that General Cunningham had not sufficient transport at his disposal.

Winston S. Churchill to Anthony Eden and General Dill
(*Churchill papers, 20/13*)

26 November 1940
ACTION THIS DAY

I understand we are to receive from you a full account of the reasons now alleged to prevent the Operation against K[2] before May, and that you will make a strenuous effort not to succumb to these reasons. If it should be decided that nothing can be done till May, the West African Brigade must go with the first set of empty transports to the West Coast, relieving the Battalion now at Freetown.

The proposal to keep the Brigade and not to fight is most depressing.

WSC

Winston S. Churchill: Motion
(*Hansard*)

26 November 1940   House of Commons

CONDUCT OF A MEMBER

The Prime Minister (Mr Churchill): I beg to move:

'That a Select Committee be appointed to investigate the conduct and activities of Mr Boothby in connection with the payment out of assets in this country of claims against the Government and of institutions in the

---

[1] Alan Gordon Cunningham, 1887–1983. On active service, 1914–18 (Military Cross, DSO, despatches five times). Major-General, 1938. General Officer Commanding East Africa Forces, 1940–1; 8th Imperial Army, Middle East, 1941. Knighted, 1941. Lieutenant-General, 1943. General Officer Commanding Northern Ireland, 1943–4; Eastern Command, 1944–5. General, 1945. High Commissioner and Commander-in-Chief, Palestine, 1945–8 (and the last British officer to leave Palestine, from Haifa port, when the Mandate came to an end).

[2] Kismayu (Chisimaio), the main port in Italian Somaliland, a hundred miles from the Kenyan border. It was occupied by South African and West African troops on 14 February 1941.

Republic of Czechoslovakia; to report generally on these matters and in particular to consider and report whether the conduct of the honourable Member was contrary to the usage or derogatory to the dignity of the House or inconsistent with the standards which Parliament is entitled to expect from its Members.'

Mr Shinwell (Seaham): On a point of Order. I understood that a Motion of this kind could be discussed. In any case, to put the matter in its proper perspective, I wish to inquire how long this Committee is to function? It seems to me to be invidious that the hon. Member whose conduct is under review should be kept in a state of suspense for a long period, and I want to ask how long it is likely to be before the matter has been fully reviewed?

The Prime Minister: I can answer that question immediately. That question lies entirely with the Committee itself; it is entirely out of my hands.

Mr Shinwell: In a matter of this kind, affecting the conduct of a Member, and particularly of a Minister, surely the House has some jurisdiction in the matter?

The Prime Minister: The House has no power of directing how the Committee shall conduct its business.[1]

Winston S. Churchill: speech
(*Hansard*)

26 November 1940   House of Commons

BUSINESS OF THE HOUSE

The Prime Minister (Mr Churchill): I beg to move,

'That, during the present Session, Government Business do have precedence at every Sitting and that no Public Bills other than Government Bills be introduced.'

I made it clear on Thursday, when I spoke on the Adjournment, that it would be necessary for the Government to move such a Motion as this. The course we are taking is agreeable with precedent, as set last Session, and also during the last war. Broadly speaking, it is felt that our deliberations must be

---

[1] The Select Committee found that Boothby had acted improperly in connection with the Czech assets in Britain. On 22 October 1940 he had resigned as Parliamentary Secretary at the Ministry of Food, and was never to hold political office again. He was succeeded by Lloyd George's son Gwilym. Boothby's sense of grievance against Churchill became more vocal with the passage of time, although he was later knighted, made a British delegate to the Consultative Assembly of the Council of Europe, and subsequently made a Peer. Despite his, and his biographer's, protestations that Churchill could have protected him against censure, it is not clear to me that this could have been done without impropriety on Churchill's part.

concentrated on those matters or Measures which are vitally connected with the effective prosecution of the war, and that the times are inappropriate for bringing forward controversial legislation or matters of academic interest. This was the justification made by Mr Asquith[1] on 3rd February, 1915. I have here a quotation from his speech. He pointed out that while such conditions prevailed it would be inappropriate for Members to introduce legislation of a party, or contentious, character, and that the Government must, for their part, confine their legislative programme to the Measures necessary for, in Mr Asquith's words, 'the successful prosecution of the war.' Mr Neville Chamberlain repeated this assurance last year, when a similar Motion was passed by the House.

The Prime Minister: My hon. Friend, who so ably represents the constituency of Ebbw Vale (Mr Bevan), was speaking in his most dulcet tones to-day and exercised to the utmost the persuasive and even seductive arts in which he is efficient, and it is not without regret that I find myself compelled to disappoint his hopes and resist his proposal. I think that if my hon. Friend, and the hon. Member who seconded the Amendment,[2] considered the position, they would see what a very impossible proposal they have submitted. On any day after Questions, if 40 Members rise, they can discuss anything they choose. [Hon. Members: 'No.'] Allow me to continue. Anything they choose, provided the Motion is already on the Paper.

Mr Bevan: My right hon. Friend has not seen the additional safeguard. The majority of the House, in Division, have to agree before it can be taken, but they cannot be asked unless 40 Members support the hon. Member's Motion.

The Prime Minister: Of course, I have only just seen the Amendment, but it is perfectly clear. It says that:

'if a Member rises in his place after Questions and proposes that a specified Notice of Motion standing on the Notice Paper be given precedence over Government business, and not less than 40 Members shall thereupon rise in their places in support of the proposal, Mr Speaker shall put the Question thereupon, and such Question shall be decided without Amendment or Debate.'

I submit to the House that this would be extremely inconvenient, and an impossible proposal. It would mean that any Question on the Paper might suddenly be subjected to the test of a Division as to whether or not it should be discussed. That is to force upon the Government of the day the need to meet what I imagine would amount to a Vote of Confidence. It would mean that

---

[1] H. H. Asquith, Prime Minister from 1908 until 1916.
[2] Vernon Bartlett, see page 551, note 5.

the most careful preparations would have to be made to secure a continuous majority at any moment. Think of the inconvenience which the House would suffer. Members travelling to the House ready to debate one subject would find themselves suddenly confronted with another.

Here is a list of some of the Questions on the Paper last Session, which is nothing to what there would be should the Amendment be accepted: Charity Commission Control, Abuse of the Privileges of the Courts of Law, Conduct of the War, Agriculture, Government Policy towards Nazi Germany and Austria, Equality of Sacrifice in War-time, Trading Profits on Food, Speech of a Member, Bottle Parties and other Activities on Licensed Premises, German and Austrian Civilian Internees, Bank of England, Proposals for Breaking the Blockade, Anglo-American Co-operation, Recording of Speeches, Dominions' Peace Terms, Joint Allied Plans, and so forth. At any moment during the day 40 Members could rise to demand a Division which would be a matter of consequence for the Government, and unless the Government were in a position to resist that at any moment, they would have to alter the whole course of Business so that Members arriving to discuss one matter could discuss another. Although there might be most urgent Government Business with regard to the carrying on of the war, that in itself would have to be side-tracked. It would be a far more severe procedure than anything which existed in peace-time. If the Amendment was carried or accepted, then Ministers would have to be ready at any moment to debate any one of this enormous panel of topics. They would not know until the actual Motion was moved what was coming on, and they would have to go about with their minds readily prepared for all these and many other varied topics.

I cannot conceive of a more inconvenient proposal, nor can I imagine that any Government would willingly subject itself to any force such as that. Conceive of the position at whatever hour the House meets. It would mean that the Government must have a majority which, in war-time, would be a matter of great inconvenience. Besides, what is the point of having all these Divisions? There would be Members saying that now was the time to discuss one or other of these matters, whether it was important, trifling or inconvenient, and it would be brought to the test of a Division. We might have a Division every day; in fact, there is nothing to prevent this procedure being invoked on any day on any question, and I regret it very much. We may have Divisions as Parliament has had from time to time. We have not had many so far. We were by way of being united, but to have this procedure, which would force the Government to reject Motions day after day, would mean an impossible impediment to, and a burden on, our duties, and would weaken the authority of the House. It would be a fertile cause of friction and disagreement, whereas under the procedure we have adopted almost any great question which either House hopes to discuss can receive early and proper attention.

Randolph S. Churchill: maiden speech[1]
(*Hansard*)

26 November 1940   House of Commons

EXTRACTS

Forty years ago, a young Member, concluding his maiden speech to this House, thanked the House for the kindness and patience with which it had listened to him, not on his own account but because of the splendid memory which many Members still preserved. I hope that the House will pardon me for striking this personal note, but I today have the personal privilege and satisfaction of having my father here. Therefore, I would like to ask an extra measure of indulgence, on account of the added embarrassment occasioned by paternal propinquity.[2]

One can see a number of hon. and right hon. Gentlemen who in a greater or lesser degree bear some measure of responsibility for the state of our Forces and for any shortage of equipment which might perhaps handicap those who plan our strategy. I have no wish to recriminate about the past. We have often been advised from different quarters against this evil tendency, but what about all this recriminating about the present from people whose conduct in the past has largely led up to the not altogether satisfactory position in which we find ourselves today?

I believe that the ordinary men and women of this country feel they have been misled by the caucuses of all three political parties. . . . When victory is won they will not be concerned with the easy shibboleths of reconstruction but will wish to breast the hills of the future without the burden of futile commitments and to be inspired instead by the enduring hope of their own genius and sacrifices.

Winston S. Churchill to Anthony Eden
(*Churchill papers, 20/13*)

26 November 1940
ACTION THIS DAY

I suggest the following to our Ambassador in Turkey:–
(Begins.) We have placed before you the various arguments for and against

[1] Randolph Churchill had taken his seat in the Commons on 8 October 1940 (two days before the birth of his son Winston at Chequers). When he made his maiden speech, dressed in his lieutenant's uniform, on 26 November, his mother, his wife Pamela, and his sister Mary were in the gallery; his father was on the front bench. He was introduced at the Bar of the House by his father, and the Chief Whip, David Margesson.

[2] A few moments later, while defending the Government, Randolph asked the House 'to overlook any relationship which I may perhaps have with a prominent member of the Administration'.

Turkish intervention which have occurred to the Staff Officers who have reported upon the matter, but we do not wish to leave you in any doubt of what our own opinion and your instructions are. We want Turkey to come into the war as soon as possible on the principle of 'a bird in the hand.' We are not pressing her to take any special steps to help the Greeks except to make it clear to Bulgaria that any move by Germany through Bulgaria to attack Greece, or any hostile movement by Bulgaria against Greece, will be followed by immediate Turkish declaration of war. We should like Turkey and Yugoslavia now to consult together so as, if possible, to have a joint warning ready to offer Bulgaria and Germany at the first sign of a German movement towards Bulgaria. In the event of German troops traversing Bulgaria with or without Bulgarian assistance, it is vital that Turkey should fight there and then. If she does not, she will find herself left absolutely alone, the Balkans will have been eaten up one by one, and it will be beyond our power to help her. You may mention that by the summer of 1941 we hope to have at least 15 Divisions operating in the Middle East, and by the end of the year nearly 25. We do not doubt our ability to defeat Italy in Africa.

WSC

6 p.m. – The Chiefs of the Staffs are in general agreement with the above.

Winston S. Churchill to General Wavell
(*Premier papers, 3/288/1*)

26 November 1940
11.20 p.m.

Importance of 'Compass' in relation to whole Middle East position, including Balkans and Turkey, to French attitude in North Africa, to Spanish attitude now trembling on the brink, to Italy in grievous straits, and generally to the whole war must be deeply borne in upon you by news from every quarter. Without being over-sanguine I cannot repress strong feelings of confidence and hope, and feel convinced risks inseparable from great deeds are fully justified.

2. Have asked Admiralty to inquire about part assigned to Fleet. Supposing success achieved, presume you have plans for exploiting it to the full. I am having a Staff study made here of possibilities open, if all goes well, for moving fighting troops and also reserve forward by sea in long hops along the coast, and establishing new supply bases to which pursuing armoured vehicles and Units might recur. Without wishing to be informed on details, I should like to be assured that all this has been weighed, explored, and as far as possible prepared.

It seems difficult to believe that Hitler will not be forced to come to rescue of his partner, and obviously plans may be far advanced for a stroke through Bulgaria at Salonika. From several quarters reports come in that Germans do not approve of Mussolini's adventure, and that they are inclined to let him pay the price himself. This makes me all the more suspicious that something bad is banking up ready to be let off soon. Every day's delay is in our favour. It might be that 'Compass' would in itself determine action of Turkey and Yugoslavia, and anyhow, in event of success, we should be in a position to make Turkey far greater assurances of early support than it has been in our power to do so far. One may, indeed, see possibility of centre of gravity in Middle East shifting suddenly from Egypt to the Balkans, and from Cairo to Constantinople. You are no doubt preparing your mind for this, and we are also having a Staff study made here.

As we told you the other day, we shall stand by you and Wilson in any well-conceived action irrespective of result, because no one can guarantee success in war, but only deserve it.

Tell Longmore how much I admire his calling in of the Southern Squadrons and accepting the risk of punishment there. If all is well *Furious* and her outfit should reach T[1] to-morrow. This should make amends for all the feathers we have had to pull out of him for Greece. Part played by RAF in Greek victories has been of immense military and political consequence. All good wishes to you both, and to the Admiral[2] who is doing so splendidly. I rejoice that he should feel Suda Bay 'an inestimable benefit.'

Winston S. Churchill to General Ismay
(*Premier papers, 3/288/1*)

26 November 1940

I am expecting to receive from the Admiralty some account of the part to be played in 'Compass' by the Fleet. In particular, I wish the Chiefs of the Staff to report upon the possibilities of exploiting a success, should one be gained, by moving troops and ships along the coast, establishing new bases of supply for our pursuing forces as well as cutting the enemy communications further back. The whole of this process should be studied here to-day, and then we can inquire with knowledge what, if any, preparations have been made by General Wavell.

As an alternative to this, it may be that, once 'Compass' has been decisively successful, we shall be called upon to go to the aid of Greece or Turkey, and that the centre of gravity will shift from Cairo to Constantinople, and that the

[1] Takoradi.
[2] Admiral Sir Andrew Cunningham.

Fleet will have some elements in the Black Sea. There is no need to decide which course will be best, or whether there will not be time to come to a final decision in Libya before having to move into Greece and Thrace, but both courses should be thoroughly explored, so that our minds may be prepared for the decisions which may be required in the near future.

A plan should also be made for landing a British Army of not less than four Divisions on the African shore of the Straits of Gibraltar, with a view to occupying Ceuta and the defences of the Straits.

Let me see any papers that have already been prepared. The Operations 'Shrapnel' and 'Workshop' should be timed to go off if desired in the current of any success resulting from 'Compass'.

WSC

Winston S. Churchill to Lord Lothian
(*Premier papers, 4/17/1*)

26 November 1940

We are so closely united in thought as in friendship that I feel you will not mind my making a few comments on your recent remarks.[1] I do not think it was wise to touch on very serious matters in newspaper interviews to reporters on the landing stage. It is safer to utter a few heartening generalities and leave the graver matters to be raised formally with the President or his chief lieutenants. The Chancellor of the Exchequer complains that he was not consulted about your financial statements, and Treasury does not like their form. While it is generally understood that you were referring wholly to dollar credits, actual words attributed to you give only too much foundation for German propaganda to broadcast that we are coming to the end of our resources.

I am still struggling with my letter to President, but hope to cable it to you in a few days.

Would you kindly find out for me most discreetly whether President received my personal telegram congratulating him on re-election. It may have been swept up in electioneering congratulations. If not I wonder whether there was anything in it which could have caused offence or been embarrassing for him to receive. Should welcome your advice.

---

[1] On 23 November 1940, having reached New York by Atlantic Clipper from England, Lord Lothian told journalists that there was 'no doubt there that Great Britain was going to win the war, but that people were not stupidly optimistic and everybody realised that the year 1941 would be hard and difficult'. Up till then, he said, Britain had paid in gold and by the sale of United States securities, for the purchase of war materials, 'but our securities on the American market will be used up before long and other means of payment will have to be found next year'.

Winston S. Churchill to the Duke of Abercorn[1]
(*Churchill papers, 20/14*)

26 November 1940

I have received with the deepest sorrow the news of the death of our old tried and valiant friend Craigavon.[2] His unswerving singleness of purpose was the mainstay, during many difficult years, of the life and integrity of Northern Ireland. He reaped his reward in the splendid and vital contribution which Ulster is making to the British Commonwealth of Nations and to the cause of freedom at this turning-point in world history. He was the first to hold out the hand of comradeship to the South in the troubled times which followed the last war. This also will bear its fruit in God's good time.

Winston S. Churchill: draft Parliamentary answer
(*Premier papers, 3/127/1*)

27 November 1940

Dr Little.[3] To ask the Secretary of State for Dominion Affairs whether all important decisions of the Cabinet are immediately conveyed to Eire as well as to the representatives of the other Dominions, in view of the fact that there are German and Italian legations in Dublin which are in constant touch with Berlin and Rome.

Proposed answer:–
'No, Sir'.

I sh'd say
'Discretion is always used in these matters & especial care is taken not to tell anyone secrets that might only embarrass them.'

WSC

---

[1] James Albert Edward Hamilton, 3rd Duke of Abercorn, 1869–1953. Succeeded his father as 3rd Duke, 1913. A Senator of Northern Ireland, 1921. Governor of Northern Ireland, 1922–45. Knight of the Garter, 1928.

[2] Lord Craigavon had died on 24 November 1940.

[3] James Little, 1868–1946. A Presbyterian minister since 1900. Author of several books on religious themes. Unionist MP (later Independent Unionist) for County Down from 1939 until his death.

Winston S. Churchill to Sir Charles Portal
(*Churchill papers, 20/13*)

27 November 1940
ACTION THIS DAY
Secret

1. I am told that about 30 Merlin engines have been fitted for some weeks past to Hurricanes or Spitfires, but that these machines, which are a great advance on any Fighters we have had so far, are all being used in OTUs. Will you very kindly explain this to me.

2. Pray see passage marked A.[1] We cannot tell quite how the political and military situation will work out in these quarters, but we should at once begin to establish in Greece ground staff and nucleus stores to enable at least two Squadrons of Wellingtons to bomb the Roumanian oilfields. We are late enough already in making these preparations. They certainly should not be put off any longer.

Pray let me have a report.

WSC

Winston S. Churchill to Lord Halifax and Lord Cranborne
(*Churchill papers, 20/13*)

27 November 1940

The only solution which I see is that Mr Purvis should divest himself of Canadian nationality and become a British subject.[2] Special facilities could perhaps be arranged for this. We clearly cannot confer any award upon a Canadian without the permission of his own Government. We should not think of conferring such a reward on a foreigner, without asking the Government of his own country whether it was agreeable to them, assuming of course that the country was friendly and allied. Mr Mackenzie King has an impregnable Parliamentary position in Canada. There is no use making trouble about Honours. They are meant to be a help and not a hindrance to the smooth working of our affairs.

WSC

[1] In the Joint Intelligence Committee's Summary No. 204, referring to an Enigma decrypt that revealed German Air Force Headquarters' concern about the possible basing of Royal Air Force Units within striking distance of Roumanian oilfields.

[2] Churchill saw Purvis at 10 Downing Street at 10.30 a.m. on 27 November 1940. Purvis remained a Canadian citizen until his death in an air crash in 1941, having up to that time received no Honour. Churchill had wanted him to have a knighthood, and on 30 November 1940 wrote to Eden: 'I had a long talk with Purvis yesterday, and thought him very able and zealous' (*Premier papers, 3/483/2*). On 7 December 1940 Churchill proposed Purvis for a Privy Councillorship (see his letter on that day to William Mackenzie King).

Winston S. Churchill to Lord Halifax
(*Churchill papers, 20/13*)

27 November 1940

PROPOSED DISCUSSION WITH GENERAL METAXAS

I was the author of this Plan of Pow-wow, but the Greek complication seems to me serious. It will be of enormous advantage to us if Germany delays or shrinks from an attack on Bulgaria through Greece. I should not like those people in Greece to feel that, for the sake of what is after all only a parade, we had pressed them into action which could be cited by Germany as a justification for marching. The only thing to do is to put the meeting off until we can see a little more clearly on this very confused chessboard of Eastern Europe.

I think the Dominions should be told that we are waiting for the Greek situation to define itself more clearly, and that this ought not to take more than a fortnight. I do not think it is necessary to give any reasons to the Allied Governments, except to assure them that the delay will be short.

WSC

Victor Cazalet: diary
(*'Victor Cazalet, a Portrait'*)

27 November 1940 Dorchester Hotel
1.30 p.m.

Winston promised to come to lunch to meet the Serving Members[1] of the House of Commons. Although there are over one hundred Members scattered in various parts of the country in the end about forty turned up. We had to have it at the Dorchester, as feeding arrangements, etc., at the House of Commons are very difficult.

I was rather anxious as to the sort of mood he would turn up in and carefully arranged my table so that we could have general conversation to start with. Winston is very bad at tête-à-tête talk. I was surprised he arrived punctually and I heard from Halifax afterwards that he had actually left the Cabinet saying, 'I must not keep these Serving Members waiting'.

When he arrived he was in very good form and was very agreeable to everybody. The lunch was excellent and we started straight in on general

---

[1] Members of Parliament who were on active service and who, when they attended Parliament, frequently did so in uniform.

conversation. I put Roger Keyes, Wedgwood Benn and Hamilton Kerr[1] opposite. We talked about Gladstone and the 1900 election when Winston got in for Oldham, and all went very well.

He had ordered his car about quarter past two, so at ten past, I asked him if he would mind my saying how pleased we were to see him to which he replied 'we have only just sat down', which made me think he was in a good mood and enjoying himself.

I got him a big cigar and some brandy and talk went on until about half past. I, who know him very well, found it difficult to know what to talk about. At half past, however, I got up and made a little speech in which I complimented Randolph on his maiden speech and said I had known Winston longer than even Randolph as I had been present at his wedding.

Then Winston got up and made, as he nearly always does when unprepared, rather a poor speech. He said one good thing. He was talking about the advisability of Members of Parliament taking an active part in the war. In the days of Arthur Wellesley[2] he said that while Wellesley was still Secretary for Ireland he was appointed Commander of the Forces in Portugal. A year or two later he was summoned home in order that his conduct of affairs might be inquired into. While this inquiry was going on, he continued his job as Secretary for Ireland on the Treasury Bench. Those were the days, Winston said, when we took a great man and made him a General – these are the days when we take a General and try to make him a great man.

After the speech he sat down again and let the Members ask him any questions they liked; why we didn't bomb Rome, why we did not take the Irish ports? etc. He was in the most benign mood and answered everything. He explained the quandary in which Hitler must be finding himself – whether to help Italy and perhaps start war in the Balkans or to allow his ally perhaps to be defeated. The Greek success had, at any rate, gone sufficiently far to alter the whole strategic course of the war. He did not leave until ten past three thereby making us half an hour late for our meeting with Anthony Eden. On the whole a very successful day.

He keeps very strange hours and is a very bad Chairman at Cabinet meetings. He takes no notice of the agenda until about the last five minutes of the meeting.[3]

[1] Hamilton William Kerr, 1903–74. A journalist. Conservative MP for Oldham (Churchill's first constituency), 1931–45 and for Cambridge, 1950–6. Parliamentary Secretary, Admiralty (to Duff Cooper), 1937–8; Air Ministry (to Harold Balfour), 1942–5; to the Minister of Health (H. Willink), 1945; to Harold Macmillan (as Minister of Defence, Foreign Minister and Chancellor of the Exchequer, 1954–6). Served in the Royal Air Force (Flying Officer, 1939; Flight-Lieutenant, 1941). Created Baronet, 1957.

[2] Later Duke of Wellington and Prime Minister (and the last commoner until Churchill to be given a state funeral).

[3] As Victor Cazalet did not attend Cabinet meetings, it is not clear who was the source for these last three lines, and for the following paragraph, but they indicate contemporary back-bench conversation.

Lastly, he is either very much under the influence or very frightened of Beaverbrook who has continued in the post of Minister of Aircraft Production and is now becoming a public danger. At the moment Beaverbrook is intriguing with Alexander of the Admiralty to take over the Coastal Command from the Air Ministry. Once, of course, you have people like B in the Government you are bound to have to pay the price.

After his speech and the two brandies and a cigar, I have never seen him in such good form. We all clustered round him and nothing pleases him more than admiring young men in uniform. He let us all ask any questions we liked and some of them were so foolish I thought he must be annoyed but not a bit of it. He did not finally go until ten past three.

War Cabinet: minutes
(*Cabinet papers, 65/10*)

27 November 1940　　　　　　　　　　　　　　　　　Cabinet War Rooms
5 p.m.

AIR RAIDS: REPAIR OF DAMAGE: MOBILE COLUMNS

The Lord President of the Council[1] gave an account of the Meetings which he had held with Ministers concerned and with representatives of the gas industry in order to make special arrangements to expedite the repair of public utility services. At all the three cities which had been subjected to recent heavy air attacks (Birmingham, Coventry and Bristol) the repairs to public utilities were now well in hand.

The Lord President of the Council said he would not be in a position to submit a full Report to the War Cabinet as to the establishment of a mobile column until he had obtained certain further data, e.g., as to the amount of skilled labour available capable of repairing public utilities.

In discussion, the Prime Minister explained that, in speaking of a mobile column, he did not mean that experts and workers would be withdrawn from their normal occupation and kept idle; but that they would be earmarked as ready to proceed to any centre at short notice and understudies instructed to take their places.[2]

---

[1] Sir John Anderson.
[2] A discussion had taken place at the War Cabinet of 27 November 1940 'on a proposal to establish a "mobile column" of experts and workers, who would be held in readiness to proceed to the scene of any heavy bombing in a munitions area, or other vulnerable area, with the object of getting public utilities restarted quickly and thus enabling production to be resumed'.

THE PRESS: LIBELLOUS CARTOON

The Prime Minister said that, in his considered view, no Minister was under an obligation to expose himself to the trouble of taking action in regard to a cartoon of this nature,[1] more especially in war time. In essence, the cartoon really amounted to no more than a vulgar insult. It would, of course, be a different matter if currency was given to a circumstantial account to which some credence might be attached. On the whole, his strong advice was that the Minister was under no obligation to take action in this case, and that the best course would be not to institute proceedings for criminal libel.

War Cabinet: Confidential Annex
(*Cabinet papers, 65/16*)

27 November 1940
5 p.m.
Cabinet War Rooms

The Prime Minister said he thought that preliminary arrangements should now be made so that, if the War Cabinet decided in favour of this course, we could bomb the Roumanian oilfields from air bases in Greece. Steps should be taken to examine the suitability of a number of aerodromes in Greece, both on the mainland and in the Greek islands. Lemnos was mentioned in this connection. If suitable aerodromes were not available, steps should be taken to make all the necessary preparations and to arrange for the servicing of the aircraft, so that action could be taken at very short notice if the War Cabinet decided that the Roumanian oilfields should be bombed.

John Colville: diary
(*Colville papers*)

28 November 1940

I got back to No. 10 by 9.30 and was disgusted to find that in my absence (on forty-eight hours' leave) the *Daily Express* had published an article by Mr Ingersoll[2] of the American paper *PM* who described his interview with Winston and added a large and inaccurate account of what I had told him. He described me as a 'dark, slim man in the middle thirties'![3] and proceeded to

---

[1] A cartoon in the *Daily Worker* of 18 November 1940 implied that the Minister of Labour, Ernest Bevin, had taken bribes from capitalist organisations.

[2] Ralph McAllister Ingersoll, 1900–85. Began work as a mining engineer, 1920. Entered journalism, 1923. A reporter on the *New Yorker*, 1925. Publisher of *Time*, 1937–9; of *PM* (a daily evening newspaper), 1940–5. In November 1940 his wartime articles were collected and published as *Report on England*. In 1941 he published *America is Worth Fighting For*.

[3] Colville was then twenty-five years old.

put into my mouth the cheapest account of a largely fictitious conversation. Winston was, I believe, furious and I feel both ashamed and angry.[1]

On 28 NOVEMBER 1940 Churchill spoke in London at a luncheon given by the Empire Press Union.[2]

Winston S. Churchill to Viscount Rothermere[3]
(*Churchill papers, 20/7*)

28 November 1940
10 Downing Street

My dear Esmond,

Your father[4] was a very close and old friend of mine, and I had the greatest regard for him. The news of his death came to me as a most painful shock in the midst of these hard times.

I send you my heartfelt sympathy in your immense loss. I felt deeply the death of my father of whom I had seen so little. But you had the happiness to live for many years as a companion and a colleague with one who loved you

[1] In an article on 26 November 1940 entitled ' "They keep trying to hit my house" said Winston Churchill to Ralph Ingersoll when they talked at 10 Downing Street', Ingersoll gave the *Daily Express* an account of his visit to Churchill. 'I found his voice and conversation milder than I had anticipated.' Ingersoll then explained that they had talked 'as one must talk with the President of the United States, not for publication', and commented on: 'He looked well and was nervously energetic. Several times during our conversation he got up and stood with his back to the fire, walked a step or two, came back and sat down, talking all the time. Finally he looked at the clock and said "I am afraid I have to go now." ' The rest of Ingersoll's article concerned his talk with Colville as the two of them waited for an air raid to pass. At one point Colville said, of his first master: 'I have never known a mind as brilliant as Chamberlain's. It was unbelievably quick, clear and incisive.'

[2] No record appears to survive of what Churchill said. Major Astor, owner of *The Times*, presided, and Brendan Bracken was also present, as were Alfred Duff Cooper (Minister of Information), S. S. Robertson (Canadian Press), G. L. Gilmour (Sydney Morning Herald Service), E. W. MacAlpine (Australian Consolidated Press), Trevor Smith (Australian Newspaper Service), R. I. Douglas (Australian Associated Press), E. R. Mackie (*The Statesman*, Calcutta), C. J. Saywell (Argus South Africa Newspapers), N. F. Grant, CBE (South African Morning Newspapers), G. R. Tonkin (*The Straits Times*), A. C. Cummings (Southam Newspapers of Canada) and L. W. Matters (*The Hindu*, Madras). (*Archives of 'The Times'*.)

[3] Esmond Cecil Harmsworth, 1898–1978. Only surviving son of the 1st Viscount Rothermere (whose other two sons were killed in action in the First World War). Royal Marine Artillery, 1917. ADC to the Prime Minister (Lloyd George) in Paris, 1919. Conservative MP, 1919–29. Newspaper proprietor. Chairman, Associated Newspapers, 1932–71. Chairman of the Newspaper Proprietors Association, 1934–61. Member of the Advisory Council, Ministry of Information, 1939.

[4] Harold Sidney Harmsworth, 1868–1940. Newspaper proprietor and philanthropist. Created Baron Rothermere, 1914. Director-General, Royal Army Clothing Department, 1916–17. Air Minister, 1917–18. Created Viscount, 1919. An advocate from 1933 of a large air force, in 1939 he published *My Fight to Rearm Britain*, with an introduction by Churchill (published on page 458 of the *At the Admiralty* volume in this series of documents).

very dearly, and who centred his hopes in you. The tie that is broken can never in any way be replaced. The world for you and your life in it will be different — more lonely. I know how vain words are in these moments. Nevertheless I venture to send you these few lines of sorrow and of friendship.

Always, dear Esmond,
Yours affectionately,
Winston S. Churchill

Winston S. Churchill to General Ismay
(Churchill papers, 20/13)

28 November 1940

It is of no use giving me these reports[1] five days late. The Admiralty know every day exactly the state of the flotillas. I do not know why this matter should go through the War Cabinet or Defence Ministry. Pray tell the Admiralty to send direct to me, every week, the state of their flotillas.

I am much concerned that the patrols on the Western Approaches should only have gone up to 30 effective. Let me see the chart showing previous weeks to-morrow.

WSC

Winston S. Churchill to Sir Kingsley Wood
(Churchill papers, 20/13)

28 November 1940

'A'[2] is surely a very dangerous admission to make. I do not want to be committed to the principle that this matter is in suspense and that the Poles must be consulted before action is taken. The position, as I understand it, is that the French have stolen the Polish gold, and the Poles now ask us to steal some of the French gold in Canada to pay them back. Our position is that we want to steal this gold for ourselves, and we hope eventually to get the power to do so. Meanwhile, however, Mr Mackenzie King is causing delay.

On the whole I think it will be better to wait until General Sikorski writes again.

WSC

---

[1] A list of Royal Navy ships fitted with Asdics.

[2] A proposed letter to General Sikorski, consulting him on the matter of the French gold reserves then in Canada, and their possible transfer, when acquired by Britain, to the Polish Government in London, which had no funds at all at its disposal.

November 1940

Defence Committee (Supply): minutes
(*Cabinet papers, 70/1*)

28 November 1940
3 p.m.
10 Downing Street

TANKS

There was a discussion on the speed required of the A22.

The General Staff would like the tank to be capable of maintaining a speed of 10 miles in the hour, which meant a maximum of about 15 mph. They would, however, rather have a high degree of reliability at the expense of a certain amount of speed, if this were essential.

The Prime Minister emphasised the importance of pressing forward with production. In our present situation, it was numbers that mattered. When we had got a reasonable amount of equipment at our disposal, we could afford to pay attention to refinements. It would be well worth sacrificing some of the speed of the A22 if by so doing its production could be simplified and accelerated. A constant study of new developments should proceed, and he hoped that the Ministry of Supply and the General Staff would keep in close contact for this purpose.

The formation of Armoured Divisions would have to go forward on the basis of the present programme of production. The result might not be ideal, but it would be necessary for us to adapt our tactics to suit the tanks we should have, rather than to try to change the programme.

Winston S. Churchill to President Roosevelt
(*Premier papers, 3/468*)

28 November 1940
Personal & Secret
10 Downing Street

Our accounts show that situation in Spain is deteriorating and that the Peninsula is not far from starvation point. An offer by you to dole out food month by month so long as they keep out of the war might be decisive. Small things do not count now, and this is a time for very plain talk to them. The occupation by Germany of both sides of the Straits would be a grievous addition to our naval strain already severe. The Germans would soon have batteries working by RDF which would close the Straits both by night and day. With a major campaign developing in the Eastern Mediterranean and the need to reinforce and supply our Armies there all round the Cape we could not contemplate any military action on the mainland at or near Straits. The Rock of Gibraltar will stand a long siege, but what is the good of that if we cannot use the harbour or pass the Straits? Once in Morocco the Germans will work south, and U-boats and aircraft will soon be operating freely from Casablanca and Dakar. I need not, Mr President, enlarge upon the trouble this will cause to us, or the approach of trouble to the Western Hemisphere. We must gain as much time as possible.

Winston S. Churchill: proposed paragraph to President Roosevelt
(*Colville papers*)

29 November 1940   Chequers[1]

While we will do our utmost, and shrink from no proper sacrifice to make payments across the Exchange, I should not myself be willing, even in the height of this struggle, to divest Great Britain of every conceivable saleable asset, so that after the victory was won with our blood and sweat, and civilization saved and the time gained for the United States to be fully armed against all eventualities, we should stand stripped to the bone. Such a course would not be in the moral or economic interests of either of our countries.[2]

Henry Channon: diary
(*'Chips'*)

29 November 1940

Dined . . . at the Dorchester, where Charles Peake[3] joined us, and was entertaining with his stories of Winston and Chequers, etc. It seems that Winston wearing an Air Force cap received the Halifaxes in particularly curious clothes and seemed rather put-out by Halifax's surprise; pointing to his strange garb he said 'Clemmie bought me these rompers!'

[1] Among those at Chequers was Arthur Purvis, with whom Churchill was discussing in detail the telegram to Roosevelt which Lord Lothian felt was essential if the President was to agree to a considerable increase in United States arms sales to Britain, to be paid for by some form of long-term loan or deferment. The inclusion of the paragraph printed here was strongly opposed by the Chancellor of the Exchequer, Sir Kingsley Wood.

[2] For the evolution of this telegram, see pages 1162, 1168–9 and 1179.

[3] Charles Brinsley Pemberton Peake, 1897–1958. On active service, 1916–18 (MC, despatches). Entered the Diplomatic Service, 1922. Head of the News Department, Foreign Office, and Chief Press Adviser, Ministry of Information, 1939. Personal Assistant to Lord Halifax (in Washington), 1942. British Representative to the French National Committee, 1942–4. Political Adviser to the Supreme Commander, Allied Expeditionary Force (General Eisenhower), 1944–5. Consul-General, Tangier, 1945. Ambassador in Belgrade, 1946–51. Knighted, 1948. Ambassador in Athens, 1951–7.

Lord Reith: diary
('*The Reith Diaries*')

29 November 1940

Meeting with Greenwood about cement. He said Beaverbrook was Public Enemy No. 1 and Churchill's Gestapo No. 2.

Dined with CIGS.[1] He is very fed up with Churchill and everybody loathes the whole Churchill entourage. PM goes away on Thursday now. Beaverbrook told me yesterday that he was in a highly nervous state. So I can well believe.[2]

Winston S. Churchill to General Wavell
(*Churchill papers, 20/14*)

29 November 1940

Actual place of Operation 'Workshop' must be kept utterly secret. Even high Staff Officers should only be told it is for an Operation on the Sicilian shore, and actual town in Sicily should never be mentioned. Alternatively, expedition might quite well go to Dodecanese, and if this leaked out it would not matter much. Pray make sure that Admiralty telegram 507 does not pass out of your personal control, and is not circulated to any branches. Fact should be confused and buried.

Winston S. Churchill to A. V. Alexander, Admiral Pound and General Ismay
(*Churchill papers, 20/13*)

29 November 1940
ACTION THIS DAY
Most Secret

1. I did not approve the sending of Hurricanes to the Greek Air Force. They must be used for the rearmament of our own Air Force first. This phrase marked A should be deleted.

2. Was it necessary to mention the word P[3] in a telegram?[4] Would it not

[1] The Chief of the Imperial General Staff, General Dill.

[2] Lord Reith, who had no knowledge of the secret war plans being evolved, or of the pressures on Churchill and his closest advisers, reflects in this diary entry the negative, and at times vitriolic, portrayal of Churchill and those closest to him by those on the fringes of power. 'Churchill's Gestapo' usually referred, principally, to Brendan Bracken, Lord Beaverbrook and Professor Lindemann.

[3] Pantelleria Island, the objective of Operation 'Workshop'.

[4] Admiralty Telegram to Commander-in-Chief, Mediterranean, sent at 3.32 a.m. on 28 November 1940.

have been better to have referred to 'Workshop' only, having already, in an earlier and separate telegram, given latitude and longitude of 'Workshop?' Thus there would be no single telegram which gave the clue or mentioned the name.

3. Beware of sending these plans by aeroplanes, which may fall into enemy hands.

4. Part II, paragraph (i). It was not intended to place these special troops under the command of the Commanders-in-Chief, ME, for them to decide their future activities in the event of their not being required for 'Workshop.'

5. Part III. What are the lessons of 'Collar'[1] which require withdrawal of *Barham* contrary to what we agreed last week? It is even claimed that the second Littorio is temporarily out of action.

6. Finally, it is terrifying to read the enormous list of people in the Admiralty alone who must be told the actual name of the Island. I suppose it will now be published to even wider circles throughout the three Services in the Middle East. There was no necessity to have allowed the name ever to have been breathed except to the highest authorities. Any Island would have sufficed to explain the bulk of the preparations to subordinates concerned.

WSC

Winston S. Churchill to Lord Woolton
(*Churchill papers, 20/13*)

29 November 1940

I should be much obliged if you would let me know the reasons which have made it necessary to stop the import of bananas altogether.

WSC

Winston S. Churchill to Anthony Eden and General Dill
(*Churchill papers, 20/13*)

29 November 1940

WEST AFRICA

There is no proposal for any Operation of the kind the General[2] suggests before us at the present time. It should, however, be remembered that if his negative advice had been taken, Duala might have been a German U-boat base to-day. He has yet to show himself fertile in resource and forward in action.

WSC

[1] The Gibraltar-Alexandria convoy of 25–28 November 1940 (see page 1128, note 1).
[2] The General Officer Commanding West Africa, Accra, General Giffard.

Winston S. Churchill to G. Spencer Summers[1]
(*Churchill papers, 20/2*)

29 November 1940

Dear Mr Summers,

It seems a pity that at a moment like this when all thoughts and energies should be bent upon the war, a contest should be forced upon you at Northampton. Nevertheless the issue which has been so foolishly raised by your opponent,[2] gives the electors of Northampton a chance to show their earnest zeal for the cause of freedom, and that they share with the British nation as a whole a firm resolve to wage this war till victory is won, and the foul tyranny of Nazi-ism is extirpated.

Yours faithfully,
Winston S. Churchill

Captain Harold Balfour to Winston S. Churchill
(*Churchill papers, 2/392*)

29 November 1940　　　　　　　　　　　　　　　　　　　　Air Ministry

My dear Prime Minister,

May I please be allowed to add my wishes for many happy returns of your birthday to those which you will be receiving in thousands from countless friends and supporters.

The lower members of your team do get a view of the load you have to carry. If we can lift it to any extent by our efforts, then we are lucky in our opportunity for at times I cannot help wondering how the human brain cells can accept, sift, and expel the thoughts of not only one man's brain but the thoughts brought to it by the so many you have to deal with.

– So I wish you health and strength to continue our War Leader to total victory.

Please, I ask no reply or acknowledgment.

Yours sincerely
Harold Balfour

ON 30 NOVEMBER 1940, at Chequers, Churchill celebrated his sixty-sixth birthday. He also attended church, for the christening of his grandson Winston.

[1] Gerard Spencer Summers, 1902–76. Chairman of the Sheet Makers Conference, 1936–9. Conservative MP, 1940–5 and 1950–70. Director-General of Regional Organisation, Ministry of Supply, 1941–4. Secretary, Department of Overseas Trade, 1945. Knighted, 1956.

[2] W. S. Seamark, who stood as a Communist. At the by-election, held on 6 December 1940, he secured 1,167 votes, against 16,587 cast for Summers.

Pamela Churchill: recollection
(*Letter to author, 6 January 1993*)

30 November 1940

Big Winston was at the christening. It was a very emotional day.

The four Godparents were also there: Lord Beaverbrook, Brendan Bracken, Lord Brownlow,[1] and Virginia Cowles.[2] I remember it as being one of the rare moments I had seen Winston in church. In fact, I think it was the first time any of us had been down to the church at Chequers. Winston was very emotional about the whole ceremony, and, with tears in his eyes, kept saying, 'Poor child. What a terrible world to be born into.' I remember it as being a somewhat important occasion for Winston. He had very much hoped to have a grandson that could bear his name.

Anthony Eden to Winston S. Churchill
(*Churchill papers, 2/394*)

30 November 1940   War Office

My dear Winston,

Many and happier returns of the day. Very few men in all history have had to bear such a burden as you have carried in the last six months. It is really wonderful that at the end of it you are fitter & more vigorous, and better able than ever to guide and inspire us all.

You do not know how you heartened me on Monday night by your comment that never in your life had you felt more equal to tackle your work. All the same, take care of yourself.

I have just read in a telegram a rumour that Italians in Libya are short of water & generally in trouble, and I feel better. So do we clutch at straws.

Bless you; thank you for all your kindness to me, and may we yet celebrate the last stage of a long hard road travelled *la main dans la main*.

                                                              Yours ever,
                                                              Anthony

PS No answer, of course.[3]

---

[1] Peregrine Francis Adelbert Cust, 1899–1978. Grenadier Guards, 1918–26. Succeeded his father as Baron Brownlow in 1927. Personal Lord-in-Waiting to King Edward VIII, 1936. Parliamentary Private Secretary to Lord Beaverbrook, 1940. Staff Officer, Bomber Command, 1941; to the Deputy Chief of Staff, 8th Air Force, 1943–4.

[2] Virginia Cowles, 1910–83. A newspaper correspondent from 1937, and friend of Randolph Churchill. Special Assistant to the American Ambassador, London, 1942–3. OBE, 1947. Popular historian; biographer of the Kaiser, the Rothschilds, and the last Tsar. In 1953 she published *Winston Churchill: The Era and the Man*.

[3] Churchill replied by telegram: 'I am very grateful to you for all your help and comfort.'

NOVEMBER 1940

Sir Archibald Sinclair to Winston S. Churchill
(*Churchill papers, 1/355*)

30 November 1940   Air Ministry

Dear Winston,

With all my heart I wish you a happy and victorious return of your birthday. Amid all your anxieties, you have much to gladden your heart this birthday – the successes against Italy, for example, which owe so much to your own judgement and action and Randolph's brilliant start in the House of Commons.

So good luck to you in the coming year – and take care of yourself, for you carry in your hands the destinies of us all.

Yours always,
Archie

PS Alas! No Stiltons this year – so I hope you will like these cigars!

Winston S. Churchill to A. V. Alexander, Admiral Pound and General Ismay
(*Premier papers, 3/205*)

30 November 1940

Furious should return home at once, and carry another load of aircraft and pilots as reinforcement for the Middle East. Every effort should be made to put off her refit till after she has carried this force. CAS[1] should say what composition of force is best. Every endeavour should be made to keep the number of Squadrons in this country undiminished by filling the gaps with new formations as part of the expansion scheme.

I presume the extension of Greek aerodromes is proceeding incessantly. I shall be glad to have a report on this. It is hoped that strong British Air Forces may be working from Greece in the near future.

WSC

John Colville: diary
(*Colville papers*)

30 November 1940   Chequers

The PM has at last completed his long letter to Roosevelt, on the lines suggested to him by Lothian. I was put to great exertions having the letter printed for the Cabinet, having it telegraphed to Washington and besieging the Treasury, Foreign Office and Admiralty with demands for comments.

[1] The Chief of the Air Staff, Sir Charles Portal, to whom a copy of this minute was sent.

Winston S. Churchill to Alfred Duff Cooper
(*Churchill papers, 20/13*)

30 November 1940
Secret

Read first the draft I have prepared of my letter to the President. It is all very secret, but does not differ materially from the sort of line you have in mind. I should like to know what Lothian's reaction to it is, and also, if possible, what the President feels about it, and I think it would be better for you to defer starting up your propaganda till we know where we are over there. I am a little uncertain as to whether requests emanating from London about placing American production on a war footing may not give offence.

Certainly also discuss these matters with Lord Halifax and the Chancellor of the Exchequer.

WSC

Winston S. Churchill to Admiral Pound[1]
(*Churchill papers, 20/13*)

30 November 1940

It is to me incomprehensible that with the 50 American destroyers coming into service, we should not have been able to raise the total serviceable to above 77 by November 23, when they stood at 106 on October 16. What happened between October 16 and October 26 to beat down serviceable destroyers by 28 vessels, and why did they go down from 84 to 77 between November 16 and November 23? – just at the very time when another dozen Americans were coming into service.

WSC

Winston S. Churchill to Arthur Greenwood
(*Churchill papers, 20/13*)

30 November 1940

Would you very kindly consider these points about Cement which have been assembled for me by Professor Lindemann. The failure of Departments even to use their allocation in October shows that the Cement position is not immediately serious, although the reserves are unduly small. The fact is,

---

[1] Admiral Pound had sent Churchill, as requested, a chart of Asdic-fitted ships in commission in Home Waters.

however, a disquieting sign of how far our programmes are falling behind the approved scale.

On no account must any capacity be idle this winter.

WSC

Winston S. Churchill to Sir James Grigg
(*Churchill papers, 20/13*)

30 November 1940

Lord De La Warr[1] spoke to me of the NAAFI[2] claiming to forbid troops to purchase cheap vegetables in the districts where they were quartered. From other quarters I hear complaints of their incompetence, and that the troops do not like them.

Pray give me a note upon the present position and the view taken of it by the War Office.

WSC

Winston S. Churchill to General Brooke
(*Churchill papers, 20/13*)

30 November 1940

I have authorized the ringing of church bells on Christmas Day, as the imminence of invasion has greatly receded. Perhaps, however, you will let me know what alternative methods of giving the alarm you would propose to use on that day, and, secondly, what steps would be taken to ensure that the ringing of the bells for church services and without any invasion do not, in fact, lead to an alarm. There must certainly be no relaxation of vigilance.

WSC

---

[1] Herbrand Edward Dundonald Brassey Sackville, Lord Buckhurst, 1900–76. Known as 'Buck'. Educated at Eton and Magdalen College, Oxford. Succeeded his father as 9th Earl De La Warr, 1915. Parliamentary Under-Secretary at the War Office in Ramsay MacDonald's second Labour Government, 1929–30. Parliamentary Secretary, Ministry of Agriculture and Fisheries, 1930–5; Board of Education, 1935–6. Chairman of the National Labour Party, 1931–43. Elected to the Other Club, of which he was Joint Secretary, 1935. Parliamentary Under-Secretary of State for the Colonies, 1936–7. Lord Privy Seal, 1937–8. President of the Board of Education, 1938–40. First Commissioner of Works, April–May 1940. Chairman of the Agricultural Research Council, and Director of Home Flax Production, 1943–9. Postmaster-General in Churchill's post-war Government, 1951–5. Chairman of the Joint East and Central African Board, 1956–9. His younger son was posted missing, presumed killed, on air operations in the Second World War, aged twenty.

[2] The Navy, Army and Air Force Institutes, established to provide servicemen with leisure facilities and extra food.

December 1940

Winston S. Churchill to General Ismay
(*Churchill papers, 20/13*)

1 December 1940
Secret

General de Gaulle told me[1] that he had in mind an attempt to recover Jibuti, hereinafter to be called 'Marie' in all papers and telegrams connected with the Operation. He would send three French Battalions from Equatorial Africa to Egypt, where General Gentilhomme[2] would meet them. These Battalions would be for the defence of Egypt, or possibly ostensibly as a symbolic contribution to the defence of Greece. There would be no secret about this. On the contrary, prominence would be given to their arrival. However, when the moment was opportune, these Battalions would go to Jibuti, being carried and escorted thither by the British Navy. No further assistance would be asked from the British. General de Gaulle believes, and certainly No. CO 581 (40) in the attached paper marked A[3] favours the idea, that Le Gentilhomme could make himself master of the place, bring over the garrison and rally it, and immediately engage the Italians. This would be a very agreeable development, and is much the best thing de Gaulle could do at the present time. It should be studied attentively, and in conjunction with

---

[1] Churchill had seen General de Gaulle at 10 Downing Street in the early afternoon of 25 November 1940.
[2] General Paul-Louis Le Gentilhomme. Commanding the French troops on the Somali coast, 1940, with his headquarters at Djibouti. He was one of only two commanders and Governors-General (the other being General Catroux in Indo-China) who maintained their opposition to Vichy. He was unable to persuade his subordinates to remain in the war. In April 1941 he led seven battalions of Free French troops against the Vichy forces in Syria, when, despite being severely wounded, he continued in action. A member of the Free French National Committee, 1941, in charge of the War Department.
[3] Colonial Office telegram No. 580 of 1940.

General de Gaulle. The importance of secrecy, and of never mentioning the name of the place, should be inculcated on all, remembering Dakar. I suppose it would take at least two months for the French battalions to arrive in Egypt.

Kindly let me have a full report, using the JP[1] as necessary.

WSC

Winston S. Churchill to General Ismay
(*Premier papers, 3/205*)

1 December 1940

I should be glad to have a return on one sheet of paper showing:
(a) what actually we have put into Malta in the last couple of months or so, both in guns and men,
(b) what we have carried through the Mediterranean to Egypt in AA guns and aircraft personnel,
(c) exactly what have we got and done at Suda Bay, i.e. troops, AA guns, CD guns, lights, wireless, RDF, nets, mines, preparation of aerodromes, etc.

I hope to be assured that many hundreds of Cretans are working at strengthening the defences and lengthening and improving the Aerodromes.

WSC

Winston S. Churchill to General Ismay
(*Premier papers, 3/288/1*)

1 December 1940
ACTION THIS DAY
Most Secret

My 90494[2] was Personal and Secret, and I do not see why it should prevent a telegram from the Chiefs of Staff on the lines of paragraph 3, Sub-Sections (i), (ii) and (iii). The continued retreat of the Italians in Albania, and the reports which we have received to-day of difficulties of feeding and watering their forces in the Libyan Desert, together with other reports of aircraft being moved back to Tripoli to be safer from our attacks, combined with safe arrival at Takoradi of 33 Hurricanes with first-class pilots, all constitute new facts entitling us to take a more confident view of the situation, which should be communicated to the General.

2. With regard to paragraph 2 of my 90494, I must attach the greatest

[1] The Joint Planning Staff.
[2] Churchill's telegram to Wavell of 26 November 1940.

importance to this. The enormous advantage of being able, once an enemy is on the run, to pull supplies and fighting troops forward 80 miles in a night by sea, and bring fresh troops up to the very advance guard, is very rarely offered in war. General Wavell's reply to my telegram does not seem to take any account of this, and considering how much we have ourselves at stake, I do not think we should be doing our duty if we did not furnish him with the results of the Staff study. It is a crime to have amphibious power and leave it unused. Therefore, I wish the study, if favourable, to be telegraphed. It must, however, be ready by the 3rd at latest.

3. Should any considerable success arise from 'Compass,' I propose to ask the War Cabinet to agree to the launching of 'Shrapnel'[1] hot foot upon it. The first will carry the second, and the second will emphasize the first. Without offering any explanations, therefore, 'Shrapnel' should be at 48 hours' notice from the third or fourth instant.

4. I must see the Staff study on the Ceuta project, hereinafter to be called 'Counterpoise,' early this week.

5. I take it as settled that 'Workshop'[2] goes forward, leaving here 18th.

6. I add the following general observation: The fact that we now have established ourselves at Suda Bay entitles us to feel much easier about Malta. While the Fleet is or may be at Suda, it will be most unlikely that any large landing would be attempted at Malta, which we have already reinforced by Tanks and guns. Therefore, it is not necessary to send the remaining two Battalions from ME. On the contrary, Malta can easily spare one Battalion to hold 'Workshop,' if needed. The possession of Suda Bay has made an enormous change in the Eastern Mediterranean.

I shall be very glad to receive your thoughts on the foregoing.

WSC

How does the Kismayu project stand?[3]

Winston S. Churchill to Lord Cranborne
(*Churchill papers, 20/13*)

1 December 1940

All this talk about Atlantic Operations and Atlantic Islands is most dangerous, and is contrary to the decision to describe such Operations as 'Shrapnel.' I see no need for these long and pointless telegrams, and it is becoming quite impossible to conduct military operations when everything has to be spread about the Departments and around the world like this.

Kindly give me the assurance that there will be no further discussion of

[1] The plan to seize the Cape Verde Islands from Portugal.
[2] The seizure of Pantelleria Island.
[3] The operation against Kismayu, in Italian Somaliland, was postponed until May 1941.

these matters by telegram without my seeing the messages before they are multiplied.

Let me also know exactly the lists of officials and Departments to whom these telegrams¹ have been distributed.

WSC

Winston S. Churchill to Sir Kingsley Wood
(<i>Premier papers, 3/128</i>)</div>

1 December 1940
ACTION THIS DAY
Secret and Personal

See attached.²

The straits to which we are being reduced by Irish action compels a reconsideration of these subsidies. It can hardly be argued we can go on paying them till our last gasp. Surely we ought to use this money to build more ships or buy more from the United States in view of the heavy sinkings off the Bloody Foreland.³

Pray let me know how these subsidies could be terminated, and what retaliatory measures could be taken in the financial sphere by the Irish, observing that we are not afraid of their cutting off our food as it would save us the enormous mass of fertilizers and feeding stuffs we have to carry into Ireland through the de Valera-aided German blockade. Do not assemble all the pros and cons for the moment, but show what we could do financially and what would happen. I should be glad to know about this to-morrow.

WSC

War Cabinet: minutes
(<i>Cabinet papers, 65/10</i>)</div>

2 December 1940   Cabinet War Room
5 p.m.

The War Cabinet had before them a draft letter from the Prime Minister to President Roosevelt (WP (G) (40) 466).

[1] Two telegrams which the Dominions Office had sent to South Africa (numbers 792 and 793).

[2] Official papers relating to the problems of the stoppage of Irish food supplies, in retaliation against the refusal of the Government of Eire to allow Britain to make use of Atlantic coast naval facilities at Berehaven and Loch Swilly (the British Treaty rights to which, negotiated by Churchill in 1921, had been given up in 1938 by Chamberlain's Government).

[3] The most recent of these merchant ship sinkings were the *Justitia* and *Bradfyne* on 22 November, the *Leise Maersk* and *King Idwal* on 23 November, the *Diplomat* and *Glenmore* on 27 November, the *St Elwyn* on 28 November and the *Aracataca* on 29 November, a total of more than 35,000 tons of shipping.

The Prime Minister said that Lord Lothian now thought that it would be better that the letter should not be delivered to the President, who was going on holiday, for about a week. There was thus more time to make any amendments.

The Prime Minister said that if the picture was painted too darkly, elements in the United States would say that it was useless to help us, for such help would be wasted and thrown away. If too bright a picture was painted, then there might be a tendency to withhold assistance. He had been rather chilled by the attitude of the United States since the Election; but it might well be that the President was waiting for the election atmosphere to disperse before taking any striking action.

Winston S. Churchill to Sir Archibald Sinclair and Sir Charles Portal
(*Cherwell papers*)

2 December 1940
ACTION THIS DAY
Secret

One cannot doubt that the Germans will be making tremendous efforts to increase their Air Force this winter, and that a far more serious attempt must be expected against us in the Spring. It is most necessary to form the best opinion possible about the potential scale of the German increase (a) by March 31, (b) by June 30 – these dates not being arbitrary if other dates are more convenient and equally illustrative. It is important not to exaggerate the German capacity, and therefore the limiting factors, e.g., engines, special raw materials, pilot training, effect of our bombing, are of special interest. On the other hand, full weight should be given to the German use of factories in the captive countries.

I should be glad if your Intelligence Branch would let me have a paper (not more than two or three sheets) upon this vital matter, and it would be convenient if they could keep in touch with Professor Lindemann while they are preparing this, so that we do not have to argue about the various bases of calculations adopted. While I want the report to be short, I want to be cognisant of the data and reasoning processes on which it has been built up. I am not sure to what extent MAP comes into this. It would be a comfort if an agreed view could be presented by the two Departments. Let me know how you will set about this. One week is all that can be spared.

WSC

Winston S. Churchill to A. V. Alexander and Admiral Pound
(*Churchill papers, 20/13*)

2 December 1940

Please see attached.¹ It must be remembered that a court martial or Court of Inquiry followed by removal of the Admiral will be taken as justifying the Italian claim that we ran away as well as they. I am not in favour of proceeding by disciplinary processes either in respect of the aeroplanes which were cast away, or of the late action. Admiral Somerville has clearly lost the confidence of the Board, and it is quite sufficient to tell him to haul down his Flag, and relieve him by Harwood without giving any other reason than that we think a change is necessary on general grounds. This is in fact true, because even before these last two episodes confidence in him had largely departed. Moreover, if a Court of Inquiry or a court martial is held, a considerable delay will occur while the Admiral is still *sub judice* and before his successor can be appointed. I do not therefore approve of sending Lord Cork and other Officers out to Gibraltar. The Service will suffer if the Fleet is not immediately entrusted to the best hand, and nothing must conflict with the interests of the Service.²

WSC

Winston S. Churchill to Lord Beaverbrook
(*Churchill papers, 20/13*)

2 December 1940

Pray see attached.³ Of course if articles appear in the *Evening Standard* which are observed to reflect the views you are pressing in Cabinet, the Air Force will start up their agitation the other way. It would be a great pity if this became a matter of public controversy. On the whole I am against duplicating the overheads.

---

[1] A BBC Report on Foreign Broadcasts, giving details of Italian claims that the British fleet turned and fled during the Battle of Taranto.
[2] On 10 January 1942 Admiral Somerville was succeeded as commander of Force H by Vice-Admiral Sir Neville Syfret, who held this command until 1943. Admiral Harwood was appointed Commander-in-Chief, Mediterranean, in April 1942.
[3] A letter from Sir Archibald Sinclair to Churchill (dated 29 November 1940) protesting about articles which had appeared in the *Evening Standard* advocating the transfer of Coastal Command to the Royal Navy.

Winston S. Churchill to General Wavell

2 December 1940

The Secretary of State has shown me your telegram about *Patria*.[1] Cabinet felt that, in view of the suffering of these immigrants and the perils to which they had been subjected through the sinking of their ship, it would be necessary, on compassionate grounds, not to subject them again immediately to the hazards of the sea. Personally, I hold it would be an act of inhumanity unworthy of the British name to force them to re-embark. On the other hand, Cabinet agreed that future consignments of illegal immigrants should be sent to Mauritius, provided that tolerable conditions can be arranged for them there. I doubt whether Cabinet will reverse these decisions.

2. I wonder whether the effect on the Arab world will be as bad as you suggest. If their attachment to our cause is so slender as to be determined by a mere act of charity of this kind, it is clear that our policy of conciliating them has not borne much fruit so far. What I think would interest them much more would be any kind of British military success. I therefore suggest that you should reconsider your statement about the Basra–Baghdad–Haifa road when we see which way the compass points. I am sorry you should be worrying yourself with such matters at this particular time, and I hope at least you will believe that the views I have just expressed are not dictated by fear of violence.[2]

---

[1] Early in November 1940 two ships (the *Milos* and the *Pacific*) with 1,771 Jewish immigrants on board had been escorted into Haifa by the Royal Navy. Being without Palestine certificates, they were transferred to a French passenger liner, the *Patria*, which the High Commissioner in Palestine had specially chartered to deport them to the Indian Ocean island of Mauritius. On 24 November, a third ship with 1,600 'illegals' on board was brought by the Royal Navy into Haifa. While the first few hundred were being transferred to the *Patria*, the Jewish self-defence force, the Haganah, tried to immobilise the *Patria* with a bomb. The explosion was much greater than intended and the ship sank within fifteen minutes: 250 refugees were drowned. The High Commissioner agreed that the 1,900 surviving refugees on board the *Patria* could stay in Palestine, but that the 1,600 on the *Atlantic* must be sent to Mauritius. On 30 November, Wavell protested to Eden about any of the 'illegals' staying in Palestine: 'From military point of view it is disastrous. It will spead all over Arab world that Jews have again successfully challenged decision of British Government' (*Premier papers, 4/51/2*).

[2] Churchill's intervention was decisive. The *Patria* deportees were allowed to remain in Palestine, first in an internment camp at Athlit on the coast, then, within a year, at liberty. On 14 December 1940 a Military Intelligence report on the incident concluded that the effect on the Arabs of allowing the refugees to stay had been 'remarkably small'. (Colonial Office papers, 733/430. I am grateful to Dr Ronald W. Zweig for this reference).

Winston S. Churchill to A. V. Alexander
(*Churchill papers, 20/26*)

2 December 1940

CAPTAIN LIDDELL HART[1]

It is out of date, and he seems more a case for a mental home than for more serious action.[2]

WSC

John Colville: diary
(*Colville papers*)

3 December 1940

The PM began by saying he would work at the Annexe, where he had breakfast, and then, maddened by hammering, transferred the seat of Government to No. 10. As always when these last-minute changes of mind take place, there was much confusion and a good deal of ill-temper.

Before lunch I listened to a little monologue by the PM, addressed to the Chiefs of Staff, on the means of helping Greece, by preparing advanced air bases, and on the desirability of putting severe economic pressure on Ireland in order to make her lend us the bases we so badly need. As regards Greece, Sir John Dill said: 'What is Germany doing?' 'They are preparing something terrible,' said the PM. He pointed out how carefully the attack on Poland had been planned, how Mussolini had been drawn into war by the sight of the overwhelming strength deployed against France, and how doubtful Pétain now is, having presumably been told something of Germany's might, about our ability to withstand the attack that is to come.

---

[1] Basil Henry Liddell Hart, 1895–1970. On active service, 1914–18 (wounded). Invalided out of the Army, 1924. Retired with the rank of Captain, 1927. Military Correspondent of the *Daily Telegraph*, 1925–35; of *The Times*, 1935–9. Military historian and analyst. A persistent advocate of the crucial importance of air power and armoured forces. Personal Adviser to the Secretary of State for War (Leslie Hore-Belisha), 1937–8. Author of more than thirty books: biographer of Sherman, Foch and T. E. Lawrence; editor of Rommel's papers. Knighted, 1966.

[2] Liddell Hart had been circulating privately a proposal in favour of peace with Germany, on the grounds that the war could lead only to stalemate, with exhaustion, disease and starvation on both sides, or to defeat. A. V. Alexander thought the proposal showed traces of German propaganda, and was not a spontaneous production. Alexander wrote to Churchill: 'Probably no technical correspondent has more responsibility than Liddell Hart for the accepted military theories propagated before the war and which were so disproved in the Battle of France. I should have thought he would have preferred to hide his head rather than produce still yet another theory as pregnant with defeat as his former theories, which are now proved heresies' (*Colville papers*).

Back at No. 10 I worked the epidiascope in the Cabinet Room and showed the PM and Sir R. Keyes large-scale photographs of the objective of Operation 'Workshop'.

The PM changed his mind at least eight times as to whether he would sleep and dine at No. 10 or at the Annexe and three times as to what time he would see Dr Dalton (whom he dislikes).

Winston S. Churchill to Admiral Sir Andrew Cunningham
(*Churchill papers, 20/13*)

3 December 1940
ACTION THIS DAY
Personal and Most Secret

Your 270.[1] We considered whole matter this morning with DCO Sir Roger Keyes who will execute it with full control of all forces employed, and final plans are now being prepared by him. His appointment will not be naval but limited to these combined operations. If necessary he will waive his naval rank. Cannot feel that Air counter-attack will be serious having regard to size Island, broken character, many houses and detached forts in which comparatively small attacking force will be intermingled with defenders. Enemy aircraft will not know who holds what till all is over, and even then Italian flags may be displayed on soft spots.

2. Capture of 'Workshop' no doubt a hazard but Zeebrugge[2] would never have got past scrutiny bestowed on this. Commandos very highly trained, carefully-picked volunteers for this kind of work. Weather and fixed date of Convoy may of course prevent attempt, in which case whole outfit will go to Malta or Suda for other enterprises. If conditions favourable, nothing will be stinted.

3. Apprehensions you have that AA guns, &c., will be diverted from Eastern Mediterranean and new commitment created, may be mitigated by capture of enemy AA which are numerous. Enemy unlikely attempt recapture, even though garrison left will be small. Commandos will come away after handing over to regular troops, and be available for further operations.

4. Comparing 'Workshop' with other Operation you mention in future

---

[1] About Operation 'Workshop', the seizure of Pantelleria Island from the Italians.
[2] The First World War raid, led by Admiral Keyes in 1918, on German fortifications at the Belgian port of Zeebrugge.

called 'Mandibles' (repeat 'Mandibles'),[1] kindly weigh following considerations:–

'Mandibles' requires ten or twelve thousand men and is far larger affair if the two big ones are to be taken. Little ones you mention would stir up all this area without any important reward unless process continued. Secondly, captures in 'Mandibles' area would excite keen rivalry of Greeks and Turks, which above all we don't want now. Thirdly, our reports show 'Mandibles' slowly starving and perhaps we shall get them cheaper later. Apart from the above, trying 'Workshop' does not rule out 'Mandibles' afterwards, unless ships and landing-craft are lost, which they may be. Also perhaps Operations on enemy's land communications along North African shore may present opportunities.

5. On strategic grounds 'Workshop' gives good Air command of most used line of enemy communications with Libyan Army, and also increased measure Air protection for our convoys and transports passing so-called Narrows. Joint Staffs here consider very high value attaches to removal of this obstruction to our East and West communications. Besides all this, we need to show ourselves capable of vehement offensive amphibious action. I call upon you therefore to use your utmost endeavours to procure success should conditions be favourable at zero hour.

WSC

Winston S. Churchill to Lord Beaverbrook
(*Churchill papers, 20/2*)

3 December 1940

My dear Max,

There is no question of my accepting your resignation. As I told you, you are in the galleys and will have to row on to the end. If, however, you wish for a month's rest, that I have no doubt could be arranged. Meanwhile I will certainly support you in carrying out your dispersal policy, which seems imperative under the heavy attacks to which we are subjected.

I am so sorry that your asthma returned yesterday, because it always brings great depression in its train. You know how often you have advised me not to let trifles vex and distract me. Now let me repay the service by begging you to remember only the greatness of the work you have achieved, the vital need of its continuance, and the goodwill of

Your old and faithful friend,
WSC

---

[1] The proposed seizure of the Italian Dodecanese island of Rhodes.

December 1940

Winston S. Churchill to General Ismay
(*Premier papers, 3/128*)

3 December 1940
ACTION THIS DAY
Secret

I gave you and each of the COS a copy of the Irish paper.[1] The Chancellor of the Exchequer's comments are also favourable, and there is no doubt subsidies can be withdrawn at very short notice.

We must now consider the military reaction. Suppose they invited the Germans in to their ports, they would divide their people, and we should endeavour to stop the Germans. They would seek to be neutral and would bring the war upon themselves. If they withdrew the various cable and watching facilities they have, what would this amount to, observing that we could suspend all connections between England and Southern Ireland? Suppose they let German U-Boats come in to refresh in West coast ports of Ireland, would this be serious, observing that U-Boats have a radius of nearly 30 days, and that the limiting factor is desire of crews to get home and need of refit, rather than need of re-fuelling and provisioning. Pray let me have your observations on these and other points which may occur to you.[2]

Winston S. Churchill to A. V. Alexander and Admiral Pound
(*Churchill papers, 20/13*)

3 December 1940

The new disaster which has overtaken the Halifax convoy[3] requires precise examination. We heard about a week ago that as many as thirteen U-boats were lying in wait on these approaches. Would it not have been well to divert the convoy to the Minches? Would this not have been even more desirable when owing to bad weather the outward-bound convoys were

---

[1] On the stoppage of Irish food supplies.

[2] On 6 December 1940 the Chiefs of Staff (Pound, Dill and Portal), in a memorandum on 'Measures to secure the use of Irish ports', set out what would be needed for Britain to take command of the defences of Eire: 288 heavy anti-aircraft guns, 318 light anti-aircraft guns and 312 searchlights. But they warned that the severe economic measures then being contemplated might lead to further anti-British IRA activity in Northern Ireland, the cutting of the Atlantic cable communications that came in through Southern Ireland, the closing of the transatlantic air routes at Foynes, and the loss of 'coast watching facilities'. Open Irish hostility would, they warned, give the Germans flying boat air bases and ports, as well as U-boat bases with which to extend their attacks against British trade (*Premier papers, 3/127/3A*).

[3] Eight merchant ships had been sunk in convoy in the North Atlantic on 2 December 1940: *Wilhelmina, Kavak, Tasso, Sterlingshire, Goodleigh, Victor Ross* (12,000 tons), *Lady Glanely, Victoria City* and *Pacific President*, totalling more than 72,000 tons.

delayed, and consequently the escort for the inward-bound could not reach the dangerous area in time?

WSC

Winston S. Churchill: recollection
(*'Their Finest Hour'*, page 536)

3 December 1940   Cabinet War Room

One evening in December I held a meeting in the downstairs War Room with only the Admiralty and the sailors present. All the perils and difficulties, about which the company was well informed, had taken a sharper turn. My mind reverted to February and March 1917, when the curve of U-boat sinkings had mounted so steadily against us that one wondered how many months' more fighting the Allies had in them, in spite of all the Royal Navy could do. One cannot give a more convincing proof of the danger than the project which the Admirals put forward. We must at all costs and with overriding priorities break out to the ocean. For this purpose it was proposed to lay an underwater carpet of dynamite from the seaward end of the North Channel, which gives access to the Mersey and the Clyde, to the 100-fathom line north-west of Ireland. A submerged minefield must be laid three miles broad and sixty miles long from these coastal waters to the open ocean. Even if all the available explosives were monopolised for this task, without much regard to field operations or the proper rearmament of our troops, it seemed vital to make this carpet – assuming there was no other way.

Winston S. Churchill to General Ismay
(*Churchill papers, 20/13*)

4 December 1940
ACTION THIS DAY

1. This is a very unsatisfactory and unresponsive telegram and I do not feel that it is at the level of events. Air Marshal Longmore stated that he had 35 Hurricanes fit for duty. We know that over 30 are traversing the Takoradi route, i.e., virtually doubling his force for the moment. All he says is that these 'comparatively small reinforcements' will no more than make good recent fighter wastage.

2. I do not think it was very helpful to ask them to express their opinion on

December 1940   1177

these hypothetical issues in your 90,210. It is better to wait the development of events, and then study the matter ourselves. General Wavell will have over a quarter of a million men under his command by the end of the year. Does he really suppose that action against the Dodecanese will be sufficient employment for these great armies, assuming that success attends the defence of Egypt?

WSC

Winston S. Churchill to General Ismay
(*Churchill papers, 20/13*)

4 December 1940

Two searchlights[1] seem very insufficient. What is going to be done to increase them?

2. In view of the torpedoing of the *Glasgow* by a seaplane while at anchor, ought not ships at anchor to be protected by nets at short range? I gather this was the Italian method at Taranto, but at the moment of the attack they had taken them off. Pray let me have a note on this.

WSC

Winston S. Churchill to Sir Archibald Sinclair
(*Churchill papers, 20/13*)

4 December 1940

1. I notice in the papers a speech by Sir Philip Joubert de la Ferté on war aims and other large political topics. It is quite wrong for serving officers to make speeches on political subjects, and I shall be glad if you will draw the Air Marshal's attention to this ruling which has indeed been long accepted in the Services.

2. Sir Philip Joubert de la Ferté's broadcasts no doubt give a great deal of pleasure to his audiences, but when I see how completely he has failed to produce any results in the night fighting against bombing attack, and how

---

[1] At the British naval base at Suda Bay, Crete, established under Operation 'Drink'.

unsatisfactory is the air action upon the North-Western approaches in respect of which he has most important liaison duties, I wonder if it would not be better if he confined himself more precisely to these professional duties upon which our safety so largely depends.

WSC

Defence Committee (Operations): minutes
(*Cabinet papers, 69/1*)

4 December 1940
9.30 p.m.
Cabinet War Room

The Prime Minister said that he had received a Minute drawn up by the First Sea Lord and the Chief of the Air Staff in agreement, containing short and medium term programmes for increasing the strength and efficiency of Coastal Command. This Minute was read to the Committee and it was pointed out by Sir Dudley Pound that the proposals contained in it were the best which could be made within the framework of the existing organisation.

The Prime Minister said that there were two conditions which must be satisfied in solving the problem of the control of the Coastal Command. The first was that the maximum possible force should be deployed for action in the North-Western approaches. The second was that a single authority should be responsible for bringing in the convoys.

Lord Beaverbrook urged that the Admiralty should take over the whole of the Coastal Command including the training of all the pilots from the beginning. The condition of the Coastal Command was a grave reflection on the Air Ministry who had starved it of equipment and had not given it the right type of aircraft. The Air Ministry were now promising reform, but there would be no satisfactory solution unless the Admiralty took over all flying over the sea.

Mr Alexander strongly supported this view. There would be no duplication of 'overheads' provided the Air Ministry handed over the whole of the Coastal Command complete. The Admiralty could not assume full responsibility for the protection of convoys unless they had control of the operations, equipment and training of these air squadrons employed on this work.

Sir Archibald Sinclair denied that the Air Ministry had starved the Coastal Command or that they were now trying to make a last minute reform.

Mr Alexander thought that if a proper lead were given from above the transfer could be effected without any difficulty. He wished to make it clear that in expressing his dissatisfaction with the present system he did not in any way wish to cast aspersions on the work of the Commander-in-Chief, Coastal Command, who had at all times co-operated to the full with the Admiralty.

The Prime Minister said that it might have been desirable, if he had been starting afresh in peacetime, to make the great change proposed. It would be disastrous at the present moment to tear a large fragment from the Royal Air Force. This was not the time for an inter-service controversy, but all were agreed that complete operational control over Coastal Command must be secured to the Admiralty. In the event of a difference of view between the Admiralty and the Air Ministry, it would be for the Defence Committee to decide on the resources to be devoted to the work of Coastal Command. It would then be for the Admiralty to make the best use of these resources. Administration and training must remain in the hands of the Air Ministry.

Anthony Eden: diary
(*'The Reckoning'*)

4 December 1940

W asked for news of 'Compass' and was indignant that I had not asked date. He was also critical of army and generals. 'High time army did something', etc. I made it plain that I did not believe in fussing Wavell with questions. I knew his plan, he knew our view, he had best be left to get on with it. This did not suit W. Dill was very angry at his attitude.

John Colville: diary
(*Colville papers*)

4 December 1940

I remarked to David[1] on the excellence of Winston's latest long letter to the President.[2] David answered that he wished W were as great an administrator as he is leader, orator and writer. The criticism is a fair one.

'This place,' said the Prime Minister, as he entered the Annexe after the evening Cabinet, 'is too hot. Tell them to turn off the central heading.' And the same man complained, on the hottest of June nights at Admiralty House, because his fire had not been lit!

---

[1] David Margesson, the Chief Whip (shortly to become Secretary of State for War).
[2] For the final version of the letter as sent, see 8 December 1940.

E. A. Seal: private letter
(*Seal papers*)

4 December 1940   10 Downing Street

Tomorrow I'm off to Chequers in the entourage. Bridges & Ismay are coming down, & we're going to have what the PM calls a staff evening – meaning a meeting of his own staff. What he's got in mind I don't really know. I expect that my affairs will be settled at some time or other during the weekend.

Today I have arranged for some substantial relief in the work of the office. We are going to get the Flag Commander from the Admiralty – Tommy Thompson – to act as a sort of Master of the Household. He'll fix up all the piddling details about where people sleep, & what telephones are required etc. etc. This is work which has nearly killed poor Tony Bevir.

Anthony Eden: diary
(*'The Reckoning'*)

5 December 1940

Winston unhappy at plan being turned down.[1] Sang Roger's[2] praises, and proposed I should go out to command in Middle East. Wellesley had gone straight from Parliament.[3] I declined very firmly.

Winston S. Churchill to A. V. Alexander
(*Churchill papers, 20/13*)

5 December 1940
ACTION THIS DAY

I hope this may be held up for the time being.[4] The gravest danger is in the North-Western Approaches and we cannot now spare the promised aid which the Coastal Command are expecting.

---

[1] The Chiefs of Staff had advised against Operation 'Workshop', the seizure of Pantelleria Island, which was to remain in Italian hands until after the fall of Tunisia in 1943, when it became a stepping-stone for the Allied invasion of Sicily. The Defence Committee discussed this advice four days later.

[2] Admiral Sir Roger Keyes.

[3] Arthur Wellesley, later Duke of Wellington.

[4] A request from Admiral Sir Andrew Cunningham, for reserve aircraft crews for the Mediterranean carrier squadrons, which would have to be provided from crews it was proposed to use to reinforce Coastal Command.

2. A very important munition convoy is approaching HX 91 and in addition the *Samaria* and *Consuelo*, both with most important cargoes.[1]

Pray let me know what arrangements are being made for these escorts.

WSC

Winston S. Churchill to Sir Kingsley Wood
(*Churchill papers, 20/13*)

5 December 1940

Pray convene a meeting to discuss the measures to be taken to reduce the burden on our shipping and finances in consequence of the heavy sinkings off the Irish coast, and our inability to use the Irish ports. The following Ministers should be summoned:–

Trade,
Shipping,
Agriculture,
Food,
Dominions.

Assuming there is agreement on principle, a general plan should be made for acting as soon as possible, together with a timetable and programme of procedure. It is not necessary to consider either the Foreign Affairs or the Defence aspect at this stage. These will have to be dealt with later. The first essential step is to have a good workable scheme, with as much in it as possible that does not hit us worse than it does the others.

WSC

Winston S. Churchill to L. S. Amery
(*Churchill papers, 20/13*)

5 December 1940
Personal and Secret

My dear Leo,

It was a pity that in your Speech you dealt with strategy and military policy, which are altogether outside the scope of your Department. Although it sounds quite harmless to say that when we have disposed of the Italians in Egypt, we shall transfer our forces to Greece or the Balkan Peninsula (I have

---

[1] Both the *Samaria* and the *Consuelo* reached Britain safely.

not the actual words), this might have unfortunate results. If the Germans thought we were establishing a land front in Greece, they would certainly be inclined to intervene against Greece. The longer this can be put off the better.

There are great dangers in speaking of these matters when one is not fully informed. We do not want to tell the enemy everything.[1]

John Colville: diary
(*Colville papers*)

5 December 1940

After dinner John Peck and I sat down to the three-hour task of sticking Lord Lothian's comments on the PM's letter to Roosevelt on pieces of paper next to the PM's original text. It was a complicated and laborious job but we thought we did it rather skilfully.

John Colville: diary
(*Colville papers*)

6 December 1940

The PM was not at all gracious about our handiwork and complained that we had had parts of the text retyped instead of sticking in every unamended word of the print. However his irritability was due to the fact that he did not care for many of Lothian's alterations and he described the whole thing as a 'bloody business'.

---

[1] Before sending this letter, Churchill deleted this last paragraph, and also the phrase 'which are altogether outside the scope of your department'. He often expressed his anger when dictating a letter, and then, on reading it for signature, caused it to be modified, to avoid unnecessary offence. At other times he decided, on re-reading, not to send such rebukes at all, on the principle, which he frequently enunciated: 'When in doubt whether to lay an egg or not – don't.'

Cartoon
('Daily Mail')

6 December 1940

Viscount Rothermere to Winston S. Churchill
(*Churchill papers, 20/7*)

6 December 1940

My dear Winston,

Thank you both for your charming letter of sympathy and your hospitality of last Sunday. My father had always the greatest admiration and affection for you at all times. When you were out of office he believed it to be a blot on the reputation of the country that your talents should be wasted whilst so many second raters should be in power.

How right he was in this as in so many other matters.

In his last letters he expressed his conviction that you would pull us through our present terrible difficulties and that we should win through to victory.

Yours ever
Esmond

Winston S. Churchill to General Dill
(*Premier papers, 3/288/1*)

7 December 1940
Secret

Naturally I am shocked at paragraph 2,[1] and I trust that your explanation of it will be realised. If, with the situation as it is, General Wavell is only playing small, and is not hurling on his whole available forces with furious energy, he will have failed to rise to the height of circumstances. I never 'worry' about action, but only about inaction.

WSC

Winston S. Churchill to Lord Cranborne and General Ismay
(*Churchill papers, 20/13*)

7 December 1940
Most Secret

I quite see how the matter occurred. As soon as the terms 'Shrapnel' and 'Brisk' were assigned to these particular operations,[2] General Smuts, who had already been apprised of them, should have been notified, and thereafter no mention of any other terms but these symbolic words should have appeared in any telegram. The topic, which in June was rather airy, has now become more dangerous, and I am greatly disturbed to see it circularised to so many Governments, none of whom are involved directly in it except that of General Smuts.

2. Should it at any time be decided to take action under 'Brisk' and 'Shrapnel,' it will not be possible to tell anyone beforehand except the War

---

[1] In a telegram from General Wavell about his forthcoming offensive in the Western Desert, Operation 'Compass'.
[2] Plans to take the Cape Verde Islands ('Shrapnel') and the Azores ('Brisk'), in order to provide air and naval bases for the closing of the Atlantic 'gap' in which U-boats were able to operate with little threat from British air attack.

Cabinet. It is not necessary to give any prior notification to General Smuts, as no action should be taken by him, or by Rhodesia, till the situation on the morrow of 'Brisk' and 'Shrapnel' can be surveyed. I do not myself think it would entail war with Portugal, and every effort will be made to assure them through diplomatic channels that none of their other possessions are in the slightest danger. It is of the utmost importance to avoid preparations against their African Colonies, which would stir their anger and alarm far more than the *fait accompli* involved in the successful conclusion of 'Brisk' and 'Shrapnel.'

3. I thank you for your assurances.

WSC

Winston S. Churchill to William Mackenzie King
(*Premier papers, 3/483/2*)

7 December 1940

Your telegram 5th December. I am most grateful to you for letting me know of the confidential communication you have received from Mr Morgenthau about our purchasing programme and the return of Mr Purvis. He will start very shortly and Layton is coming home at once.

I have now arranged after a good many personal adjustments that Purvis shall be under the Ambassador.[1] Purvis shall be the acknowledged head of all our supplies and technical Missions in the United States, whether permanent or temporary. This unity and focussing will be of high advantage. In order to raise and dignify Mr Purvis's status, I should propose to submit his name to the King for a Privy Councillorship. I was from many quarters pressed to confer an honour upon him, but this was impossible in view of the resolution of the Canadian Parliament. I am advised that that resolution does not cover Privy Councillorships, which are not honours but a sworn relationship necessary for the performance of highly confidential duties by persons of eminent station. I should however be very glad to know you have no objection to this step, which I regard not as a reward but as a necessary and appropriate war measure.

Precise date of Purvis's departure will be communicated to you as soon as possible.

[1] Lord Lothian.

Sir Charles Portal to Winston S. Churchill
(*Air Ministry papers, 20/5195*)

7 December 1940
Most Secret

You instructed me two days ago to prepare a plan for the most destructive possible bombing attack against a selected German town.

This has now been done, and the code name of the operation is 'Abigail'.

It is probable that over 200 aircraft will take part. The first attacks will be with incendiary bombs, and if weather permits it is intended to continue the bombing with HE and incendiary throughout the night.

1,000 lb and 500 lb bombs will be used in preference to 250 lb bombs, and a number of mines will also be dropped if conditions are suitable. All HE bombs will be fuzed for the best destructive effect against buildings, gas and water mains, and electric cables.

In order to take full advantage of the weather and to allow for different degrees of visibility it is necessary to select several alternative objectives. The following have been selected in order of priority:–

(a) Hanover.
(b) Mannheim.
(c) Cologne.
(d) Dusseldorf.

As soon as I receive your authority I will give instructions for the operation to be done on the first suitable night.

CP

Winston S. Churchill to Sir Charles Portal
(*Air Ministry papers, 20/5195*)

7 December 1940

Thank you. The War Committee should consider this at 9.30 p.m. Monday.[1]

WSC

[1] The War Cabinet considered, and approved, Portal's proposal, in Churchill's absence, at its evening meeting on Monday, 12 December 1940. The question of bombing civilian targets in Germany was considered so sensitive that it was not even put on the War Cabinet agenda, but, at Portal's insistence, was raised by him orally once the meeting had begun.

Winston S. Churchill to Robert Menzies
(*Premier papers, 3/156/6*)

8 December 1940

1. Your 1464. I am most grateful for your promised help at Singapore. The danger of Japan going to war with the British Empire is in my opinion definitely less than it was in June after the collapse of France. Since then we have beaten off the attacks of the German Air Force, and deterred the invader by our ever-growing land strength. Since then the Italians have shown their weakness by sea, land and air, and we no longer doubt our ability to defend the Delta and the Canal until or unless Germany makes her way through Turkey, Syria and Palestine. This would be a long-term affair. Our position in the Eastern Mediterranean is enormously improved by the possession of Crete where we are making at Suda Bay a second Scapa, and also by the victories of the Greeks and the facilities we now have for building up strong air bases in Greece from which Italy can be attacked.

2. The naval successes in the Mediterranean and our growing advantage there by sea and Air will not be lost upon Japan. It is quite impossible for our Fleet to leave the Mediterranean at the present juncture without throwing away irretrievably all that has been gained there and all the prospects of the future. On the other hand, with every weakening of the Italian naval power, the mobility of our Mediterranean Fleet becomes potentially greater, and should the Italian fleet be knocked out as a factor, and Italy herself broken as a combatant, we could send strong naval forces to Singapore without suffering any serious disadvantage. We must try to bear our Eastern anxieties patiently and doggedly until this result is achieved, it always being understood that if Australia is seriously threatened by invasion we should not hesitate to compromise or sacrifice the Mediterranean position for the sake of our kith and kin.

3. Apart from the Mediterranean, the naval strain has considerably increased. When *Bismarck* and *Tirpitz* join the German fleet, which they may have done already, the Germans will once again be able to form a line of battle. The *King George V* is ready, but we do not get *Prince of Wales* for several months, nor *Duke of York* till midsummer, nor *Anson* till the end of the year 1941. For the next six months we must keep more concentrated at Scapa Flow than has been necessary so far. The appearance of a raiding pocket battleship in the Atlantic last month has forced us to provide battleship escort again for our convoys, and we are trying to form hunting-groups for the raiders in the South Atlantic, and if necessary in the Indian Ocean. We have always to consider the possibility of the undamaged portion of the French fleet being betrayed by Laval and Darlan to Germany.

4. For all these reasons we are at the fullest naval strain I have seen either

in this or the former War. The only way in which a Squadron could be found for Singapore would be by ruining the Mediterranean situation. This I am sure you would not wish us to do unless or until the Japanese danger becomes far more menacing than at present. I am also persuaded that if Japan should enter the war, the United States will come in on our side, which will put the naval boot very much on the other leg, and be a deliverance from many perils.

5. I must tell you finally that we are sending enormous convoys of troops and munitions to the Middle East, and we shall have nearly 300,000 men there by Christmas. This again entails heavy escort duties. But great objects are at stake, and risks must be run in every quarter of the globe, if we are to emerge from all our dangers as I am sure we shall.

With all good wishes.

WSC

Winston S. Churchill to William Mackenzie King
(*Churchill papers, 20/14*)

8 December 1940

1. May I renew to you the deep satisfaction we feel over the offer which you are able to make to enlarge the Joint Training Scheme. There could not be a more striking testimony to the energy and efficiency with which the scheme has been operated. I send to you and your colleagues my admiration and my gratitude for an assistance which promises to be of major importance in the war.

2. I have now had the opportunity to review our training position. I find that it is not thought desirable to embark at present on an enlargement of the Joint scheme.[1] The decisive consideration is this: The Air Ministry is absorbed in current operations and in making ready for the Spring battle. Until that battle has opened it will not be possible for me to take decisions about an extension of the Joint scheme with the Secretary of State for Air. As soon as the situation has cleared, you may be sure that we will co-operate to the full in the admirable suggestion you make.

3. In the meantime the Secretary of State for Air will discuss plans at

---

[1] The British Commonwealth Air Training Plan was established on 17 December 1939. The training itself began in Canada on 29 April 1940. By the end of the war, 131,553 pilots, navigators, bomb aimers, air gunners and flight engineers graduated from 107 Canadian schools: almost half the total aircrew employed on British and Commonwealth flying operations.

length with Colonel Ralston[1] and Mr Howe.[2] He has arranged to meet Colonel Ralston on Tuesday next.

4. We should be most grateful if, in another direction, your Government could bring an additional measure of assistance to the training situation. It would be desirable to develop as swiftly as possible the production of Training aircraft in the Dominion. Any steps which your Administration might take to secure this object would have the complete co-operation and eager support of the Secretary of State.[3] In particular, the Secretary of State wishes to draw your attention to the possibilities of the Anson aircraft, particularly if Jacobs engines can be got from the United States. He understands further that it is possible that North American Harvards might be built in Canada. This would be a most desirable project provided only that engines are available. For you will understand how important it is that there should be no diversion of engines from the Harvards already on order in the United States, and destined for Canada.

5. The proposed extension of the productive capacity of the Dominion which I now put forward for your consideration would represent an important reinforcement of Canada's strategic rôle as a centre of training and supply. With complete confidence would we entrust it to an Administration which has so amply excelled promise by performance.

Winston S. Churchill to President Roosevelt
(*Churchill papers, 23/4*)[4]

8 December 1940
10 Downing Street

My dear Mr President,

As we reach the end of this year, I feel you will expect me to lay before you the prospects for 1941. I do so with candour and confidence, because it seems to me that the vast majority of American citizens have recorded their conviction that the safety of the United States as well as the future of our two democracies and the kind of civilization for which they stand, are bound up with the survival and independence of the British Commonwealth of Nations. Only thus can those bastions of sea power, upon which the control of the

[1] James Layton Ralston, 1881–1948. On active service in France, 1917–18; a noted battalion commander (DSO and bar). Privy Councillor, Canada, 1926. A Director of Canadian Vickers and the Montreal Locomotive Works. Minister for National Defence, 1926–30, of Finance, 1939–40, of Defence, 1940–4 (resigned because of his outspoken support of overseas conscription).

[2] Clarence Decatur Howe, 1886–1960. Canadian Minister of Transport, 1936–40, when he helped to create Trans-Canada Airlines. Minister of Munitions and Supply, 1940–4. Minister of Reconstruction, 1944. Minister of Trade and Commerce, 1956, when he sponsored a Trans-Canada pipeline.

[3] Viscount Cranborne, Secretary of State for Dominion Affairs.

[4] This letter was circulated to the War Cabinet on 8 December 1940 as War Cabinet Paper 466 of 1940, 'Final Revise'.

Atlantic and Indian Oceans depend, be preserved in faithful and friendly hands. The control of the Pacific by the United States Navy and of the Atlantic by the British Navy, is indispensable to the security and the trade routes of both our countries, and the surest means of preventing war from reaching the shores of the United States.

2. There is another aspect. It takes between three and four years to convert the industries of a modern state to war purposes. Saturation point is reached when the maximum industrial effort that can be spared from civil needs has been applied to war production. Germany certainly reached this point by the end of 1939. We in the British Empire are now only about half-way through the second year. The United States, I should suppose, was by no means so far advanced as we. Moreover, I understand that immense programmes of naval, military and air defence are now on foot in the United States, to complete which certainly two years are needed. It is our British duty in the common interest, as also for our own survival, to hold the front and grapple with the Nazi power until the preparations of the United States are complete. Victory may come before two years are out; but we have no right to count upon it to the extent of relaxing any effort that is humanly possible. Therefore, I submit with very great respect for your good and friendly consideration that there is a solid identity of interest between the British Empire and the United States while these conditions last. It is upon this footing that I venture to address you.

3. The form which this war has taken, and seems likely to hold, does not enable us to match the immense armies of Germany in any theatre where their main power can be brought to bear. We can, however, by the use of sea power and air power, meet the German armies in regions where only comparatively small forces can be brought into action. We must do our best to prevent the German domination of Europe spreading into Africa and into Southern Asia. We have also to maintain in constant readiness in this Island, armies strong enough to make the problem of an oversea invasion insoluble. For these purposes we are forming as fast as possible, as you are already aware, between 50 and 60 divisions. Even if the United States were our Ally, instead of our friend and indispensable partner, we should not ask for a large American expeditionary army. Shipping, not men, is the limiting factor, and the power to transport munitions and supplies, claims priority over the movement by sea of large numbers of soldiers.

4. The first half of 1940 was a period of disaster for the Allies and for Europe. The last five months have witnessed a strong and perhaps unexpected recovery by Great Britain fighting alone, but with the invaluable aid in munitions and in destroyers placed at our disposal by the great Republic of which you are for the third time the chosen chief.

5. The danger of Great Britain being destroyed by a swift, overwhelming blow, has for the time being very greatly receded. In its place, there is a long,

gradually-maturing danger, less sudden and less spectacular, but equally deadly. This mortal danger is the steady and increasing diminution of sea tonnage. We can endure the shattering of our dwellings, and the slaughter of our civil population by indiscriminate air attacks, and we hope to parry these increasingly as our science develops, and to repay them upon military objectives in Germany as our Air Force more nearly approaches the strength of the enemy. The decision for 1941 lies upon the seas. Unless we can establish our ability to feed this Island, to import the munitions of all kinds which we need, unless we can move our armies to the various theatres where Hitler and his confederate, Mussolini, must be met, and maintain them there, and do all this with the assurance of being able to carry it on till the spirit of the Continental Dictators is broken, we may fall by the way, and the time needed by the United States to complete her defensive preparations may not be forthcoming. It is therefore in shipping and in the power of transport across the oceans, particularly the Atlantic Ocean, that in 1941 the crunch of the whole war will be found. If, on the other hand, we are able to move the necessary tonnage to and fro across salt water indefinitely, it may well be that the application of superior air power to the German homeland and the rising anger of the German and other Nazi-gripped populations, will bring the agony of civilization to a merciful and glorious end.

But do not let us underrate the task.

6. Our shipping losses, the figures for which in recent months are appended, have been on a scale almost comparable to that of the worst year of the last war. In the five weeks ending the 3rd November losses reached a total of 420,300 tons. Our estimate of annual tonnage which ought to be imported in order to maintain our effort at full strength is 43 million tons; the tonnage entering in September was only at the rate of 37 million tons and in October at 38 million tons. Were this diminution to continue at this rate it would be fatal, unless indeed immensely greater replenishment than anything at present in sight could be achieved in time. Although we are doing all we can to meet this situation by new methods, the difficulty of limiting losses is obviously much greater than in the last war. We lack the assistance of the French Navy, the Italian Navy and the Japanese Navy, and above all of the United States Navy, which was of such vital help to us during the culminating years. The enemy commands the ports all around the north and western coast of France. He is increasingly basing his submarines, flying-boats and combat planes on these ports and on the islands off the French coast. We are denied the use of the ports or territory of Eire in which to organize our coastal patrols by Air and sea. In fact, we have now only one effective route of entry to the British Isles, namely, the Northern approaches, against which the enemy is increasingly concentrating, reaching ever farther out by U-Boat action and long-distance aircraft bombing. In addition, there have for some months been merchant ship raiders, both in the Atlantic and Indian Oceans. And now we have the

powerful warship-raider to contend with as well. We need ships both to hunt down and to escort. Large as are our resources and preparations, we do not possess enough.

7. The next six or seven months bring relative battleship strength in home waters to a smaller margin than is satisfactory. *Bismarck* and *Tirpitz* will certainly be in service in January. We have already *King George V*, and hope to have *Prince of Wales* in the line at the same time. These modern ships are of course far better armoured especially against Air attack, than vessels like *Rodney* and *Nelson* designed twenty years ago. We have recently had to use *Rodney* on Transatlantic escort, and at any time when numbers are so small, a mine or a torpedo may alter decisively the strength of the line of battle. We get relief in June, when *Duke of York* will be ready, and will be still better off at the end of 1941, when *Anson* also will have joined. But these two first-class modern 35,000-tons 15-in.-gun German battleships force us to maintain a concentration never previously necessary in this war.

8. We hope that the two Italian *Littorios* will be out of action for a while, and anyway they are not so dangerous as if they were manned by Germans. Perhaps they might be! We are indebted to you for your help about the *Richelieu* and *Jean Bart*, and I dare say that will be all right. But, Mr President, as no one will see more clearly than you, we have during these months to consider for the first time in this war a fleet action, in which the enemy will have two ships at least as good as our two best and only two modern ones. It will be impossible to reduce our strength in the Mediterranean, because the attitude of Turkey, and indeed the whole position of the Eastern basin depends upon our having a strong fleet there. The older, unmodernized battleships will have to go for convoy. Thus even in the battleship class we are at full extension.

9. There is a second field of danger: the Vichy Government may either by joining Hitler's New Order in Europe or through some manoeuvre, such as forcing us to attack an expedition dispatched by sea against the Free French Colonies, find an excuse for ranging with the Axis Powers the very considerable undamaged naval forces still under its control. If the French Navy were to join the Axis, the control of West Africa would pass immediately into their hands, with the gravest consequences to our communications between the Northern and Southern Atlantic, and also affecting Dakar and, of course, thereafter South America.

10. A third sphere of danger is in the Far East. Here it seems clear that Japan is thrusting southward through Indo-China to Saigon and other naval and air bases, thus bringing them within a comparatively short distance of Singapore and the Dutch East Indies. It is reported that the Japanese are preparing five good Divisions for possible use as an overseas expeditionary force. We have to-day no forces in the Far East capable of dealing with this situation should it develop.

11. In the face of these dangers we must try to use the year 1941 to build up such a supply of weapons, particularly of aircraft, both by increased output at home in spite of bombardment, and through ocean-borne supplies, as will lay the foundations of victory. In view of the difficulty and magnitude of this task, as outlined by all the facts I have set forth, to which many others could be added, I feel entitled, nay bound, to lay before you the various ways in which the United States could give supreme and decisive help to what is, in certain aspects, the common cause.

12. The prime need is to check or limit the loss of tonnage on the Atlantic approaches to our island. This may be achieved both by increasing the naval forces which cope with the attacks, and by adding to the number of merchant ships on which we depend. For the first purpose there would seem to be the following alternatives:–

(1) The reassertion by the United States of the doctrine of the freedom of the seas from illegal and barbarous methods of warfare, in accordance with the decisions reached after the late Great War, and as freely accepted and defined by Germany in 1935. From this, United States ships should be free to trade with countries against which there is not an effective legal blockade.

(2) It would, I suggest, follow that protection should be given to this lawful trading by United States forces, i.e., escorting battleships, cruisers, destroyers and air flotillas. The protection would be immensely more effective if you were able to obtain bases in Eire for the duration of the war. I think it is improbable that such protection would provoke a declaration of war by Germany upon the United States, though probably sea incidents of a dangerous character would from time to time occur. Herr Hitler has shown himself inclined to avoid the Kaiser's mistake. He does not wish to be drawn into war with the United States until he has gravely undermined the power of Great Britain. His maxim is, 'One at a time.'

The policy I have ventured to outline, or something like it, would constitute a decisive act of constructive non-belligerency by the United States, and more than any other measure, would make it certain that British resistance could be effectually prolonged for the desired period and victory gained.

(3) Failing the above, the gift, loan, or supply of a large number of American vessels of war, above all destroyers, already in the Atlantic is indispensable to the maintenance of the Atlantic route. Further, could not the United States Naval Forces extend their sea control of the American side of the Atlantic, so as to prevent the molestation by enemy vessels of the approaches to the new line of naval and air bases which the United States is establishing in British islands in the Western

Hemisphere. The strength of the United States Naval Forces is such that the assistance in the Atlantic that they could afford us, as described above, would not jeopardize the control of the Pacific.

(4) We should also then need the good offices of the United States and the whole influence of its Government continually exerted, to procure for Great Britain the necessary facilities upon the Southern and Western shores of Eire for our flotillas, and still more important, for our aircraft, working to the westward into the Atlantic. If it were proclaimed an American interest that the resistance of Great Britain should be prolonged and the Atlantic route kept open for the important armaments now being prepared for Great Britain in North America, the Irish in the United States might be willing to point out to the Government of Eire the dangers which its present policy is creating for the United States itself.

His Majesty's Government would of course take the most effective measures beforehand to protect Ireland if Irish action exposed it to German attack. It is not possible for us to compel the people of Northern Ireland against their will to leave the United Kingdom and join Southern Ireland. But I do not doubt that if the Government of Eire would show its solidarity with the democracies of the English-speaking world at this crisis, a Council for Defence of all Ireland could be set up out of which the unity of the Island would probably in some form or other emerge after the war.

13. The object of the foregoing measures is to reduce to manageable proportions the present destructive losses at sea. In addition, it is indispensable that the merchant tonnage available for supplying Great Britain and for the waging of the war by Great Britain with all vigour, should be substantially increased beyond the $1\frac{1}{4}$ million tons per annum which is the utmost we can now build. The convoy system, the detours, the zig-zags, the great distances from which we now have to bring our imports, and the congestion of our Western harbours, have reduced by about one-third the fruitfulness of our existing tonnage. To ensure final victory, not less than 3 million tons of additional merchant shipbuilding capacity will be required. Only the United States can supply this need. Looking to the future it would seem that production on a scale comparable to that of the Hog Island scheme[1] of the last War ought to be faced for 1942. In the meanwhile, we ask that in 1941 the

---

[1] Hog Island, New Jersey, was an area of marshland that had been transformed in 1918 into a shipyard containing fifty, as opposed to the normal five, building ways. It had its own bank, post office and weekly newspaper. The first ship was launched there on 5 August 1918.

United States should make available to us every ton of merchant shipping, surplus to its own requirements, which it possesses or controls, and to find some means of putting into our service a large proportion of merchant shipping now under construction for the National Maritime Board.

14. Moreover, we look to the industrial energy of the Republic for a reinforcement of our domestic capacity to manufacture combat aircraft. Without that reinforcement reaching us in substantial measure, we shall not achieve the massive preponderance in the air on which we must rely to loosen and disintegrate the German grip on Europe. We are at present engaged in a programme designed to increase our strength to 7,000 first-line aircraft by the Spring of 1942. But it is abundantly clear that this programme will not suffice to give us the weight of superiority which will force open the doors of victory. In order to achieve such superiority it is plain that we shall need the greatest production of aircraft which the United States of America are capable of sending us. It is our anxious hope that in the teeth of continuous bombardment we shall realise the greater part of the production which we have planned in this country. But not even with the addition to our squadrons of all the aircraft which, under present arrangements, we may derive from planned output in the United States can we hope to achieve the necessary ascendancy. May I invite you then, Mr President, to give earnest consideration to an immediate order on joint account for a further 2,000 combat aircraft a month? Of these aircraft, I would submit, the highest possible proportion should be heavy bombers, the weapon on which, above all others, we depend to shatter the foundations of German military power. I am aware of the formidable task that this would impose upon the industrial organisation of the United States. Yet, in our heavy need, we call with confidence to the most resourceful and ingenious technicians in the world. We ask for an unexampled effort, believing that it can be made.

15. You have also received information about the needs of our Armies. In the munitions sphere, in spite of enemy bombing, we are making steady progress here. Without your continued assistance in the supply of machine tools and in further releases from stock of certain articles, we could not hope to equip as many as 50 Divisions in 1941. I am grateful for the arrangements, already practically completed, for your aid in the equipment of the army which we have already planned, and for the provision of the American type of weapons for an additional 10 Divisions in time for the campaign of 1942. But when the tide of Dictatorship begins to recede, many countries trying to regain their freedom may be asking for arms, and there is no source to which they can look except to the factories of the United States. I must therefore also urge the importance of expanding to the utmost American productive capacity for small arms, artillery and Tanks.

16. I am arranging to present you with a complete programme of the munitions of all kinds which we seek to obtain from you, the greater part of

which is, of course, already agreed. An important economy of time and effort will be produced if the types selected for the United States Services should, whenever possible, conform to those which have proved their merit [in our hands][1] under the actual conditions of war. In this way reserves of guns and ammunition and of airplanes, become interchangeable, and are by that very fact augmented. This is, however, a sphere so highly technical that I do not enlarge upon it.

17. Last of all, I come to the question of Finance. The more rapid and abundant the flow of munitions and ships which you are able to send us, the sooner will our dollar credits be exhausted. They are already, as you know, very heavily drawn upon by the payments we have made to date. Indeed, as you know, the orders already placed or under negotiation, including the expenditure settled or pending for creating munition factories in the United States, many times exceed the total exchange resources remaining at the disposal of Great Britain. The moment approaches when we shall no longer be able to pay cash for shipping and other supplies. While we will do our utmost, and shrink from no proper sacrifice to make payments across the Exchange, I believe you will agree that it would be wrong in principle and mutually disadvantageous in effect if, at the height of this struggle, Great Britain were to be divested of all saleable assets, so that after the victory was won with our blood, civilization saved, and the time gained for the United States to be fully armed against all eventualities, we should stand stripped to the bone. Such a course would not be in the moral or economic interests of either of our countries. We here, would be unable, after the war, to purchase the large balance of imports from the United States over and above the volume of our exports which is agreeable to your tariffs and industrial economy. Not only should we in Great Britain suffer cruel privations but widespread unemployment in the United States would follow the curtailment of American exporting power.

18. Moreover, I do not believe that the Government and people of the United States would find it in accordance with the principles which guide them, to confine the help which they have so generously promised only to such munitions of war and commodities as could be immediately paid for. You may be certain that we shall prove ourselves ready to suffer and sacrifice to the utmost for the Cause, and that we glory in being its champions. The rest we leave with confidence to you and to your people, being sure that ways and means will be found which future generations on both sides of the Atlantic will approve and admire.

19. If, as I believe, you are convinced Mr President, that the defeat of the

---

[1] Churchill deleted this phrase before sending the telegram.

Nazi and Fascist tyranny is a matter of high consequence to the people of the United States and to the Western Hemisphere, you will regard this letter not as an appeal for aid, but as a statement of the minimum action necessary to achieve our common purpose.

I remain,
Yours very sincerely,
Winston S. Churchill

Winston S. Churchill to A. V. Alexander
(*Churchill papers, 20/13*)

8 December 1940

I should be grateful to receive in future a daily report showing the strength of our flotillas and anti-submarine vessels actively employed in each area of operations in Home Waters.

WSC

Winston S. Churchill to Sir Archibald Sinclair
(*Churchill papers, 20/13*)

8 December 1940

I regret to have to draw your attention to the article by Sir Philip Joubert de la Ferté appearing in to-day's *Sunday Express*.[1] What are the regulations governing the publication of articles by newspapers by Officers serving in the Air Force? Was he paid for this article? Who decided that he should write for any one particular paper? Disciplinary action in regard to this Officer is

---

[1] In a leader-page article in the *Sunday Express* on 8 December 1940 headed 'Will this winter weather stop the bomber?', Air Marshal Sir Philip Joubert de la Ferté answered his own question with the words: 'I say quite frankly that I do not think the winter weather is going to help us much in stopping the German bomber.' In the article he wrote about experiments that had been tried, including using television, for 'some means of enabling a pilot to see through cloud so that his bomb-aimer could sight his target'. He doubted that these experiments would succeed. He also wrote: 'The worst problem of bad weather flying is the formation of ice on the planes. We know that the Germans in peacetime maintained a very good civil air service with this country in extremely bad weather conditions, and that therefore they have had good experience in dealing with ice secretion.'

overdue. The very important, nay vital, work with which he is charged is not prospering, and he has no business to neglect it for the sake of advertisement and publicity. I understood you were to have had an interview with him following the Cabinet discussion on Friday.

WSC

Winston S. Churchill to Sir Archibald Sinclair
(Premier papers, 3/314/2)

8 December 1940

There is no doubt we have been much vexed by the German land mines, which have done grievous damage and much impressed the public with their power. If you cannot carry them over the Alps, why not make deliveries from Malta and also from the new aerodromes we are establishing in Greece?[1]

WSC

Winston S. Churchill to Anthony Eden
(Churchill papers, 20/13)

8 December 1940

I have had this looked into in consultation with Major Jefferis, who has convinced me that it is not the case that the Director of Artillery[2] had not had an opportunity of examining the ST bomb[3] in all its aspects. The detailed papers can be produced if desired.

What is wanted is to get this weapon used and tried. The ICI,[4] who know more about explosives than anyone else, are prepared to vouch for the explosive and the people, who have developed the weapon, have a man who is anxious to travel out with a consignment and demonstrate its use.

I should have thought that this was good enough to justify dispatching the bombs, which would be most valuable in Albania, without further delay.

WSC

---

[1] Sinclair replied: 'My own opinion is that the difference in moral effect between the heavy bombs we are now dropping on Italy and the land mine is not sufficient to justify sending Hampdens out to Malta, and so introducing a new type of heavy bomber (with the necessary personnel, equipment, spares, etc.) to the Middle East.' Sinclair added: 'Nevertheless it can, of course, be done if you so wish', to which Churchill noted on 10 November 1940: 'Not in view of y'r opinion' (*Premier papers, 3/314/2*).

[2] General E. M. C. Clarke.

[3] The Sticky Bomb, an anti-tank grenade, the adhesive outer covering of which was designed to stick to the surface of a tank.

[4] Imperial Chemical Industries.

December 1940

Michael Eden[1] to his mother[2]
(*Henley papers*)

8 December 1940　　　　　　　　　　　　　　　　　　　　　　Chequers

I dined last Sunday[3] with the Prime Minister. He sent you many messages and recalled especially the Manchester election of 1908. He asked much after you and asked me to remember him to you.

There were several distinguished people there. Air Marshal Sholto Douglas; Ld Louis Mountbatten, who had just fought an action off the Kent coast; a Professor Lindemann who is some sort of air statistical expert & showed us some very interesting graphs of various air activity. Another sailor and a secretary. The women were Mrs C; Mary C; Mrs Sandys; Winston's second daughter; Ly Louis Mountbatten;[4] and Mrs Randolph C.

Winston looked very small and round and chubby – indeed when Mary & Mrs R brought a pencil drawing of him out after dinner – I think by the Duchess of Rutland,[5] he said he had never been as good looking as that. They said it looked Angelic. He said no, he had looked like a cherub, but never like an angel.

I did not have much personal talk with him. He spoke to me at dinner and I sat next to him after the women had left and I had a word or two with him before I left at 11 to go round the sentries – I was the guard officer that night. I did not hear anything especially interesting about the war – I don't suppose he lets secrets out when anybody who isn't meant to hear them is there. He & Douglas & Mountbatten talked a good deal about the war in the summer house after dinner.

The American destroyers aren't much good – or won't be till the Spring as they are badly built. They roll 70° and there was apparently a domestic scandal about them in America & the naval under secretary & designer were sacked & the ships were never put into commission.

Winston looked full of vigour and bright of eye and seemed to be in a cheerful & confident frame of mind.

On Friday – yesterday – we had tea with Mary Churchill. General de

---

[1] Michael Francis Henley, 1914–77. A relative by marriage of Clementine Churchill's cousin Sylvia Henley. Captain, the Life Guards, 1940. In 1925 his father, the 6th Baron Henley, took the surname Eden. Succeeded his father as 7th Baron, 1962. President of the Liberal Party, 1966–7; Chairman from 1968.

[2] Lady Dorothy Georgiana Howard, third daughter of the 9th Earl of Carlisle. She had married the 6th Baron Henley in 1913.

[3] Sunday, 8 December 1940. This letter was written a week later.

[4] Edwina Cynthia Annette Ashley, daughter of the 1st Baron Mount Temple, and a granddaughter of Churchill's friend Sir Ernest Cassel. In 1922 she married Lord Louis Mountbatten. Superintendent-in-Chief, St John's Ambulance Brigade, 1942–60. President of the Save the Children Fund. She died in 1960 in North Borneo while on a tour on behalf of the St John's Ambulance Brigade, and was buried at sea from HMS *Wakeful* off Portsmouth.

[5] Lady Granby (Violet Lindsay), later Duchess of Rutland. Her drawing of Churchill is reproduced facing page 505 of volume 1 of the Churchill biography (by Randolph S. Churchill).

Gaulle & an English general[1] were there for a bit; but the Prime Minister & Mrs Churchill weren't there.

De Gaulle does not look nearly so gross & stupid & pompous as he appears in his photographs. He is certainly very ugly, but he has very dark & rather remarkable eyes, a pale, rather transparent skin & very dark hair.

He looked sad & seemed a shy and reserved man. He doesn't speak English and only stayed a very short time as he had to hurry off.

AT DAWN ON MONDAY, 9 DECEMBER 1940, British forces commanded by General Wavell had attacked the Italian positions in front of Sidi Barrani, thirty-five miles inside the Egyptian border, on the Gulf of Sollum.

John Colville: diary
(*Colville papers*)

9 December 1940

Motored from Hinchingbrooke back to London, where the great excitement is the beginning of our offensive against the Italian army in Egypt. The PM, who returned from Chequers after lunch with a cold in the head, said to the CIGS on the telephone: 'So we shan't have to make use of General Papagos[2] after all!' implying that at last our generals are living up to the Greek example of boldness and initiative.

Winston S. Churchill to Lord Reith
(*Premier papers, 3/18/1*)

9 December 1940
ACTION THIS DAY

I read with great interest your WP (G) (40) 321, and I am in general agreement with your proposals to set up machinery for the large-scale rebuilding which will be necessary after the war. Perhaps you will discuss with Sir Edward Bridges the best methods of obtaining a decision upon this – i.e., whether by the Home Policy Committee or by the Cabinet.

Your most urgent task however is to repair existing buildings which are not seriously but only slightly damaged. Sometimes I see a whole row of houses

---

[1] General Spears.
[2] Commander-in-Chief of the Greek armed forces.

whose windows are blown out, but which are not otherwise damaged, standing for weeks deserted and neglected. Active measures should be taken to replace tiles and to close up the windows with fabric, with one small pane for light, and to make such repairs as render the houses fit for habitation. In dealing with house casualties the least serious should claim priority. You ought to have a regular corps of workmen who would get this job done so that the people may get back into their homes, which are unlikely to be hit a second time. Branches of this corps should exist in all the great cities. Not a day should be lost. How the expense is met or divided can be settled with the Treasury. But this question must be no impediment on action.

Pray let me have your plans for dealing with this forthwith.

Winston S. Churchill to Sir Archibald Sinclair and Sir Charles Portal
(*Churchill papers, 20/13*)

9 December 1940

I spent four hours on Saturday[1] with the Officers of the Air Ministry Intelligence Branch and those of MEW. I have not been able to reach a conclusion as to which are right. Probably the truth lies mid-way between them. The subject is of capital importance to the whole future picture we make to ourselves of the war. It also would influence the use we make of our forces in the meanwhile. I am most anxious that the two Branches mentioned, whose Officers are in the most friendly relations, should sit together in an inquiry, to sift the evidence and ascertain the facts. There should be an impartial Chairman accustomed to weigh evidence and to cross-examine, and I wondered whether for this purpose Mr Justice Singleton, who had war experience as a Gunner and recently conducted an inquiry for me into bomb sights, would not be able to guide the discussions and throw a valuable light on the obscurities of this all-important scene. He would, of course, have to be told about the secret information.[2]

Before taking any decision, I should like to have your views.

Meanwhile, I have set out a statement of what I learned in our discussion on Saturday, as something for the Department to bite on. Every fact in it is open to question, modification or offset. I have sent a copy to each Branch, and it would form the staple of the investigations I contemplate.

WSC

[1] Saturday, 7 December 1940.
[2] The ability of the British to receive and then decrypt German top secret radio signals, using the Enigma machine. At that time the signals concerned were primarily the Enigma circuits being used by the German Air Force.

December 1940

Winston S. Churchill: statement
(*Churchill papers, 20/13*)

9 December 1940
Secret

1. Since the war began fifteen months ago, the German Air Force is believed to have received 22,000 aircraft of all types, and the British Air Force 18,000 of all types for use in all theatres and for all purposes. In the last eight months of hard fighting, the German Air Force has received from April to November inclusive 12,000 new machines, and the British Air Force 11,000, exclusive of 1,000 from overseas. In these eight battle months, when both Air Forces have been at full extension, the intake has been about equal, averaging 1,400 to 1,500 machines a month.

2. During these eight months, the front-line strength of the British Air Force of about 2,100 machines has scarcely changed. Thus, a monthly output of 1,400 machines has just sufficed in a period of active warfare to keep up a front-line strength of 2,100 machines.

If we reckon that of the 1,400 machines 500 were trainers, and another 200 were operational machines devoted to training, a very generous allowance in the heat of the battle, this implies that 700 operational machines, i.e., one-third of our front-line establishment, was written off every month. Actually the number is probably greater than this, at any rate in the Bomber Squadrons where a number of bombers equal to two-fifths of the front-line establishment is lost monthly.

3. The German losses have certainly not been less *pro rata*. Their battle losses between May and August were estimated by the Air Ministry as about 3,000, and from August to the end of October as 2,800 machines, i.e., 5,800 in all. Our battle losses in the equivalent period were less than half of this.

4. Information leads the Air Intelligence Branch at the Air Ministry to believe that the German front-line Air Force on the 1st May was about three times as great as ours, say, 6,000 machines. If this were so, and their *pro rata* losses were not higher than ours, their monthly wastage must have been at least 2,000 machines (on the two-fifths figure even higher). If our figures for their average output, i.e., 1,500 machines are correct, and if the statement that 1,100 of these were operational is accepted, the German Air Force must diminish at the rate of 2,000 minus 1,100, i.e., at least 900 machines in the first month. As the front line decreased, of course, the losses and the rate of drop would fall, but the strength would be well below 4,000 at the end of four months.

The only way of escaping this conclusion is to assume that the Germans carried an immense reserve of machines stored for such an eventuality. The pre-war output does not justify such an assumption. In any event it would be an uneconomical proceeding as the machines would rapidly become out of date. Any well-ranged Air Force reckons to have a reserve at the outbreak of war to tide it over the first two or three months while the war machine begins to operate and to run on production thereafter.

An investigation should be made showing exactly what proportion of our front-line establishment was written off each month, and what were the causes. It should be possible to make a fairly accurate estimate of our battle losses and the German battle losses, and the calculation should be made assuming that their other losses are *pro rata* the same as ours. It should be borne in mind that the Germans must send to the training establishments and write off therein an equivalent number of those which we have to devote to this purpose, OTUs counting as training establishments.

5. According to our information, only 400 German trainers are produced each month. This number seems most inadequate to replace the pilot wastage in such a huge Air Force as the Air Intelligence attribute to the Germans. We use considerably more, without counting those delivered direct to the training schools in Canada.

We are told that Germany had a huge reserve of pilots trained before the war, and that few pilots trained since have been found amongst the prisoners. If this were so, and if the huge reserves of machines also had really been in existence, it seems inconceivable that they should not have been brought together and the operational strength correspondingly increased for the duration of the great Air battles.

6. Every effort must be made to clear up the present contradiction. The MEW estimate for the output is incompatible with a front-line strength much higher than 3,000 machines. This figure is consonant with the weight of the German effort at Dunkirk and in the battle for Britain (taking account of the favourable geographical factors). The Air Intelligence estimate is nearly twice as great.

At present the only possible explanations seem to be –
(a) that MEW is wildly wrong, and that the German output is nearly twice as great as they believe. Further that the Germans did not make any very great effort in the battle for Britain or at Dunkirk.
(b) that the German Section have been misled, possibly intentionally, by the Germans, and are pinning their faith to an estimate far in excess of the real figure.
(c) that the units identified by the German Intelligence Section are not all of them what we should call front-line units, but that a considerable proportion of them (at least one-third) are non-operational, perhaps corresponding to OTUs.

WSC

1204 December 1940

Henry Channon: diary
(*'Chips'*)

9 December 1940

St Stephen's Cloister had been hit last night. I went into what was the Members' cloakroom and saw a scene of devastation; confusion, wreckage, broken glass everywhere, and the loveliest, oldest part of the vast building a shambles. Suddenly I came upon Winston Churchill wearing a fur-collared coat, and smoking a cigar; he was led by a policeman and followed by Seal, his secretary. 'It's horrible' he remarked to me without removing his cigar; and I saw that he was much moved, for he loves Westminster; I walked with him. 'They would hit the best bit' I said. 'Where Cromwell signed King Charles's death warrant' he grunted. I sensed the historic significance of the scene – Winston surveying the destruction he had long predicted, of a place he loved.

War Cabinet: minutes
(*Cabinet papers, 65/10*)

9 December 1940   Cabinet War Room
5 p.m.

The Prime Minister informed the War Cabinet that, as the result of his enquiry into the relations between the Admiralty and Coastal Command, a solution had been arrived at which was satisfactory both to the Admiralty and the Air Ministry. The issues involved were quite unsuitable for Parliamentary debate, and it would be necessary to resist a demand for such a debate which was to be made in the House of Lords on the following day. Least of all ought the Government to pledge itself that Parliament would always be consulted in advance before decisions were taken affecting the relationship between the three Defence Services.

War Cabinet: Confidential Annex
(*Cabinet papers, 65/16*)

9 December 1940   Cabinet War Room
5 p.m.

The Prime Minister reminded the War Cabinet of the main sequence of events. After the French defection our position in Egypt had looked precarious. Notwithstanding the risk of invasion at home, we had sent strong reinforcements to Egypt, including tanks and artillery. When the Secretary of State for War had visited Egypt some four or five weeks ago, he had found the condition of the Army so much improved that the High Command in Egypt were considering whether they could not take the offensive. Then had come the Italian attack on Greece, and we had had to deplete our air forces in Egypt in order to support the Greeks. Five squadrons had been sent to help them, and the King of Greece, in writing to the King, had said that this air help had constituted a decisive turning-point. Meanwhile we had taken steps to replace, from this country, the aircraft sent to Greece, while Air Marshal Longmore had withdrawn to Egypt two squadrons from Aden and another from the Sudan. In consequence, the Command in Egypt had felt able to proceed with their intention to take the offensive.

It had been necessary to observe the greatest secrecy in regard to this operation, and he (the Prime Minister) had therefore only sought the approval of the Defence Committee (Operations). General Wavell had been assured that if he cared to run the risk of undertaking offensive operations, he would be supported by those at home, even if the operation was unsuccessful.

The main British and Italian forces had, until three days ago, been separated by some 75 miles, although the advance parties were, of course, much closer. Three days ago we had started to move up large forces. It was a cause of satisfaction that we had been able to carry out these movements without any hindrance from the enemy. At dawn that morning our forces had attacked. So far, the only news received was that we had captured the camp at Mibiewa, some 15 miles South of Sidi Barrani, and had taken 500 prisoners, and that the enemy reaction had been slight.

Defence Committee (Operations): minutes
(*Cabinet papers, 69/1*)

9 December 1940
9.30 p.m.

Sir Dudley Pound read to the Committee Telegram No. 1513/9 from the Commander-in-Chief, Mediterranean.[1] This showed that in the opinion of the Commander-in-Chief, Middle East, there was no suitable objective at the present moment which the force destined for operation 'Workshop' could attack.

[1] In a telegram that day, Admiral Sir Andrew Cunningham told the Admiralty: 'It is highly undesirable for a force to arrive from UK and to be plunged directly into an operation without prior consultation and co-ordination with those concerned. Air Officer Commanding can provide local knowledge. Combined operations need more careful and detailed planning than any other situation and it appears these details should be worked out by those responsible for execution and subsequent support and maintenance of project. If any sea-borne operation is to take place in Libya or elsewhere the forces should first assemble in the Middle East area either in Egypt or Crete' (*Cabinet papers, 69/1*).

The Prime Minister said that when the operation had previously been discussed, it had been stated that it would not be possible to make available the large number of destroyers required. This point had not been mentioned by the First Sea Lord, who had now argued that the objection to the operation was that the chances of capturing the island with the forces available were three to one against.

Sir Dudley Pound explained that the two flotillas of destroyers were required to protect the Glen ships during the long period which would have been occupied in getting four flights of troops ashore. By the use of the *Royal Scotsman*, it had now been found unnecessary to keep the Glen ships so long, and the number of destroyers could therefore be reduced. On the other hand, under the new plan, it was still only reasonable to count on the first flight getting ashore, and this was why the possibility of success for the landing had been rated so low.

Sir John Dill said that the island was a large one – seven miles by three – about which we knew little. It had many guns, and might well have a fair sized garrison. We would be unable to give any fire support to the landing. The troops are excellent, and would be well led, but it was asking a lot of them to take on such a proposition unless the value of the Italians could be discounted.

The Prime Minister said that there were two questions to be decided. The first was whether the plan was feasible; and the second as to whether, taking account of the war situation as a whole, the plan, if feasible, should be carried out.

Discussion then took place as to whether the preparations should go forward and the force should sail.

Lord Beaverbrook thought that the force should sail, on the understanding that the execution of the operation could be reconsidered at a later stage in the light of developments in the situation.

Mr Eden agreed with Lord Beaverbrook.

Mr Attlee said that we were short of information about the island, and much would depend upon the outcome of the present battle in Libya. If this were successful, and following upon the events in Albania, the moral effect of a successful attack on the island would be very great, and he thought that it would be worth attempting.

Sir Archibald Sinclair said that the Chiefs of Staff only rated the chances of success at three to one. When the project was originally put forward, it was held that the island would be of little use to us if we captured it, and he had felt that it would be a pity to risk such fine troops for so meagre a prize. Now, however, that it appeared that the island would be of great use to us as a station for fighters, and since the operation could be called off if conditions proved unfavourable, he thought it would be well worth going ahead with it, provided the battle in Libya went well.

The Prime Minister said that he would be the first to call off the operation if it were found nearer the time that it would not fit harmoniously into the development of our strategic plans. The fact that the chances were judged by the Chiefs of Staff to be three to one against success (odds which he personally did not accept) could not be admitted as a valid argument against undertaking the operation. It was impossible for anyone to assess the precise chances of success in any military enterprise.

Winston S. Churchill to Anthony Eden
(*Churchill papers, 20/13*)

9 December 1940

ARMY ORGANISATION

1. I understand that you are asking for another big call-up shortly. The papers talk about a million men. This forces me to examine the distribution of the men you have. According to your paper, 27 British divisions are credited to Expeditionary Force and Middle East. These divisions are accounted for at 35,000 men each, to cover corps, army, and line of communications troops, etc., plus 70,000 security troops in ME.

2. The approved establishment of a British division at the present time is 15,500 men. It comprises only 9 battalions with an establishment of 850, i.e., about 7,500. The establishment of all battalions comprises a considerable proportion of servicing elements, and I doubt whether the rifle and machine-gun strength – i.e., fighting strength – amounts to more than 750. Thus the total number of men who actually fight in the infantry of a British division is 6,750. This makes the fighting infantry of 27 divisions, in what used to be called bayonet or rifle strength, 182,250. It used to be said that the infantry was 'the staple of the Army', to which all other branches were ancillary. This has certainly undergone some modification under new conditions, but none the less it remains broadly true. The structure of a division is built round its infantry of 9 battalions, with a battery to each battalion, the necessary proportion of signallers and sappers, the battalion, brigade, and divisional transport, and some additional elements, the whole being constituted as an integral and self-contained unit of 15,500 men.

3. When we look at the division as a unit, we find that 27 divisions at 15,500 official establishment require no less than 1,015,000 men. This gives an actual burden of 35,000 men for every divisional unit of 15,500 men, the units themselves being already fully self-contained. Nearly 20,000 men have therefore to be accounted for for each division of the EF or ME over and above the full approved establishment of 15,500.

This great mass, amounting to 540,000, has now to be explained. We are assured that the corps, army, L of C troops, etc., plus the 70,000 security troops in the ME, justify this enormous demand upon the manhood of the nation.

4. One would have thought, if this were conceded, that the process was at an end. On the contrary, it is only just beginning. There still remain nearly two million men to be accounted for, as are set out on the attached table and graph. No one can complain of 7 divisions for the Home Field Force, though it is surprising that they should require 24,000 men for divisional establishments of 15,500. This accounts for 170,000 men.

5. ADGB[1] 500,000 must be submitted to for the present, pending improved methods of dealing with the night-bomber and increased British ascendancy in the air.

6. 200,000 men for the permanent staffs and 'unavailable' at training and holding units is a distressing figure, having regard to the great margins already provided. Staffs, static and miscellaneous units, 'Y' lists,[2] etc., require 150,000 after all the 27 divisions and the 7 home divisions have been fully supplied with corps and army troops. Apart from everything necessary to handle an army of 27 divisions and 7 home divisions, there is this mass of 350,000 staffs and statics, living well off the nation as heroes in khaki.

7. Compared with the above, overseas garrisons, other than ME, of 75,000 seems moderate. India and Burma at 35,000 is slender.

8. 150,000 men for the corps, army, and L of C troops for divisions other than British requires to be explained in detail. I understand the Australian and New Zealand Forces had supplied a great many of their rearward services. At any rate, I should like to see the exact distribution of this 150,000 in every category behind the divisions which they are expected to serve.

9. The net wastage, 330,000, is of course a purely speculative figure. But it might well be supplied from the 350,000 permanent staffs, static and other non-availables already referred to.

10. Deducting for the moment the 330,000 men for wastage, which deals with the future up till March 1942, and 110,000 required for overseas garrisons other than ME, India, and Burma, we face a total of 2,505,000 required for the aforesaid 27 divisions plus 7 home divisions, equal to about 74,000 per division. If the 500,000 for ADGB is omitted we still have over 2,000,000 men – i.e., nearly 60,000 men mobilised for each of 34 divisions.

Before I can ask the Cabinet to assent to any further call-up from the public,

[1] Air Defence of Great Britain.
[2] The study of uncoded enemy wireless traffic, wireless traffic analysis, and the breaking of low-grade signals. By 1942 the British Army Y (wireless) service consisted of some forty Special Wireless Sections engaged in intercept work. About thirty of these sections were mobile and active in the field. A typical section had a total of seven officers, seventy-two Signals personnel and fifteen drivers serving with it at any one time. The historian of the Y service writes of how, after Dunkirk, the first systematically organised Intelligence Sections were created 'with three officers and sufficient personnel in the form of trained NCOs speaking fluent German or Italian to mount a three-shift twenty-four hour watch, moving with Corps HQ, and at Corps HQ itself and Army HQ' (Hugh Skillen, *Spies of the Airwaves*, London 1989, page ii).

it is necessary that this whole subject shall be thrashed out, and that at least a million are combed out of the fluff and flummery behind the fighting troops, and made to serve effective military purposes. We are not doing our duty in letting these great numbers be taken from our civil life and kept at the public expense to make such inconceivably small results in the fighting line.

Winston S. Churchill to General Ismay
(*Churchill papers, 20/13*)

9 December 1940

This matter[1] must be discussed by the Defence Committee before any proposals are formally set before the American Naval Authorities.

You will see on another telegram how strongly Admiral Stark has reacted against sending the whole American fleet to Singapore, and how he regards it as a purely British interest idea. There is no use in putting before them a naval policy which they will not accept, and which will only offend them and make it more difficult to bring them into the war. If they prefer Hawaii to Singapore, there is no more to be said.

Pray bring this minute to the notice of the Admiralty.

I wonder whether Admiral Bellairs[2] is the best representative who could be chosen to head a Mission from this country to the United States at this juncture.

WSC

Winston S. Churchill to Lord Halifax
(*Churchill papers, 20/13*)

9 December 1940
Secret

The passage at A[3] is not true, and there is now no reason why the true reason should not be given. We were on the verge of an offensive in Libya, and the British authorities in Egypt were naturally very loth to deprive themselves of the aeroplanes they needed to support it. They did so, however, and we have managed to carry on our offensive all the same. If we should be successful on a large scale in Libya, it will greatly relieve the whole situation in

[1] Asking the United States Navy to send warships from its Pacific Fleet, on a visit to the British naval base at Singapore.

[2] Roger Mowbray Bellairs, 1884–1959. Entered the Royal Navy, 1900. War Staff Officer, Grand Fleet, 1914–16 (despatches). CB, 1930. Retired with the rank of Rear-Admiral, 1932. Admiralty Representative, League of Nations Permanent Advisory Commission, 1932–9. Admiralty (including mission to USA), 1939–46; Head of the Historical Section, 1948–56.

[3] The statement in a draft letter being sent from King George VI to the King of Greece, stating that the naval action at Taranto had not been decisive, and that Egypt was still in danger.

the Eastern Meditrranean. We have asked for the improvement of aerodromes in Greece, and this is being done, but it is most important it should be pressed forward as fast as possible. This will give us the means of moving further reinforcments there rapidly if circumstances allow.

Perhaps these points might be worked in, in place of some of the padding.

If Kings have to write to each other in letters of equal length, I cannot suggest any abridgements.

WSC

Winston S. Churchill: Oral Answer
(*Hansard*)

10 December 1940　　　　　　　　　　House of Commons (Annexe)
　　　　　　　　　　　　　　　　　　　　　Church House

Mr Gallacher: Is the Prime Minister aware that the Imperial policy group with which the Secretary of State for India is associated is proposing a new order in Europe which will be dominated by the sterling and the dollar, and that statements of this kind are causing a lot of comment and confusion as far as the war aims of the Government are concerned?

The Prime Minister: There are such a lot of new orders in Europe that I really have to confine myself more directly to immediate business.

Winston S. Churchill to the Lord Mayor of Bristol[1]
(*Churchill papers, 20/2*)

10 December 1940

My Lord Mayor,

My thoughts have been much with the inhabitants of Bristol in the ordeal of these last weeks.[2] As Chancellor of the University I feel myself united to them by a special bond of sympathy and I have heard with pride of the courage, resolution and patience with which they have answered these detestable attacks on their families and their homes. It is a spirit such as theirs which makes certain the victory of our cause.

Yours very faithfully
Winston S. Churchill

[1] Thomas Henry Johnson Underdown, 1872–1953. President of the National Union of Teachers, 1917–18. Unsuccessful Liberal Parliamentary candidate, 1922. Chairman of the Bristol South Divisional Liberal Association, 1928–33. An Alderman at Bristol since 1938. Lord Mayor, 1940-1.

[2] German air raids had been severe on several provincial cities for some weeks: Bristol, Southampton, Portsmouth, Birmingham, Sheffield, Liverpool and Manchester. By the end of December, 3,793 civilians had been killed. The figure for November had been 4,588.

John Colville: diary
(*Colville papers*)

11 December 1940

The PM had been going down to Harrow today, with all the Old Harrovian members of the Government, to hear School Songs. However his cold is heavier and the trip had to be postponed.

In the Censorship Report (which incidentally shows a certain lower-class opinion, apparently worked on by propaganda, that the war is being engineered for financial and upper-class interests), I marked a number of passages which I thought particularly interesting and I noticed that the PM marked in red ink one phrase quoted from a letter: 'It's difficult to think politically, or socially, in classes any more . . . <u>there's a kind of warmth pervading England</u>.'

Winston S. Churchill to General Ismay
(*Premier papers, 3/124/2*)

11 December 1940
Secret

Let models be made of Rhodes and Leros. Report when they will be ready.

WSC

Winston S. Churchill to Alfred Duff Cooper
(*Churchill papers, 20/13*)

11 December 1940

I presume the German comments at A[1] are communicated to Mr Priestley.[2] Is he still employed in your organization? I see he has been writing critical articles in the newspapers. He has gained a vogue from the BBC which he might conceivably turn against the Government.

WSC

[1] German quotations from a J. B. Priestley broadcast, reported in the BBC's Report on Foreign Broadcasts for 9/10 December 1940. Priestley had upbraided Air Marshal Sir Philip Joubert de la Ferté as 'an ass' for urging Britons to go about their Christmas shopping as usual. It was obvious, Priestley said, that under conditions of total war, blackouts, bombing and rationing, it was only 'silly people' who pretended that life was normal: 'Life is clearly anything but normal. It is wildly and solidly abnormal, almost crazy.' (*BBC Written Archives Centre*)

[2] John Boynton Priestley, 1894–1984. On active service, 1914–18. A prolific and popular author, dramatist and broadcaster, he published his first book in 1922. Order of Merit, 1977.

Winston S. Churchill to Lord Halifax
(*Churchill papers, 20/13*)

11 December 1940
ACTION THIS DAY

1. Pray see the attached.[1] My minute and its postscript have reference not to the procedure in the House of Lords so much as to what should be said on behalf of the Government. The Air Ministry sent a Brief proving conclusively that it would never be possible to hand over the Coastal Command to the Admiralty. This would have resulted in a very grievous inter-Service wrangle. I therefore said that the Brief must be modified, and as a postscript I added a guide to the kind of way in which the Air Ministry argument could be worked in without committing the Government to a permanent negative. It was about this I was thinking, and not about the actual Debate. The most that the Government can say in public is conveyed in my answer. If there was a Secret Session there would be no harm in Lord Snell[2] putting the pros and cons.

2. With regard to the situation which has now developed, you have stated that I do not think the matter should be debated in public, and certainly I think it would be detrimental to the public interest if there should be a wrangle of this kind liable to start between the Services. I hope, therefore, that you will not fail to adhere to the line you have taken or leave me without support. If, however, you are not able to influence the House of Lords or procure a majority on behalf of the Government, the Debate will have to proceed in public. In that case, the Government representative must confine himself to the answer already given in the House of Commons, as I do not wish any Ministerial statement to go beyond these carefully-chosen words.

3. I hope, however, that you will be able to draw attention to the answer which I gave, which removes the whole purpose of the Debate by conceding Lord Trenchard's point in substance, and that, if the Lords wish to discuss the matter further, they should be asked to do so in Secret, and, if they refuse, that no further statement should be made on behalf of the Government.

4. With regard to your complaint that you, as Leader of the House of Lords, and that body were not treated with sufficient consideration, I should greatly regret if that were so. I only received the Air Ministry's brief when I began work at 7 o'clock on Tuesday morning. After reading it, I issued the Minutes which I enclose. I had then to do the work of the day and, in addition,

---

[1] Prime Minister's Personal Minute M.399, about Coastal Command.
[2] Henry Snell, 1865–1944. Farmworker, groom and ferryman. Speaker on labour and religious topics. Member of the London County Council, 1919–25; Chairman, 1934–8. Labour candidate, 1910 (twice) and 1918. Labour MP, 1922–31. Created Baron, 1931. President of the National Council of Social Service, 1938. Deputy Leader of the House of Lords from 1940 until his death. Vice-Chairman, Royal Institute of International Affairs, 1940–3.

to prepare the communiqué for the Statement in the House of Commons, of which I provided you with a copy. I had only just time to reach the House and read this out. Therefore, I hope you will excuse any defects in procedure which the conditions of the times entail.

WSC

John Colville: diary
(*Colville papers*)

11 December 1940

Just before dinner the PM rang up the King to tell him the glad news that Sidi Barrani had fallen. 'My humble congratulations to you, Sir, on a great British victory – a great Imperial victory.'

It is the first time since war began that we have really been able to make use of the word victory.

One of the PM's first reactions – a curious one – was to ask to see and peruse the two books General Wavell has written.[1]

Winston S. Churchill to General Ismay
(*Churchill papers, 20/13*)

11 December 1940

I believe there was a book written by Sir Archibald Wavell. Let me know what its name is and let me have a look at it.[2]

WSC

Winston S. Churchill to Sir Archibald Sinclair
(*Churchill papers, 20/13*)

11 December 1940
ACTION THIS DAY

Pray see attached.[3] What are we to do about para. 14?[4] What is the truth? Are you really going to use 7,000 brand-new combat airplanes in the training units? Considering that you put these words in my mouth and I cabled them accordingly, I hope you will be able to explain Air Commodore Slessor's amendments. Please return urgent.

WSC

[1] Wavell had written a First World War history, *The Palestine Campaigns*, and had edited an anthology of poetry, *Other Men's Flowers*.
[2] The book Ismay procured was *Other Men's Flowers*, the anthology of poetry.
[3] Telegram 2973 from Lord Lothian.
[4] Paragraph 14 of Churchill's telegram to Roosevelt of 8 December 1940.

Sir Frederick Phillips to the Treasury
(*Premier papers, 4/17/1*)

11 December 1940 Washington, DC
Most Immediate
Most Secret

1. Subject to the President's decision, which is expected within 24 hours, the way is clear to placing orders for Army programme B. Do you approve the financial proposals as regards capital expenditure set out in my immediately preceding telegram? You will appreciate that the scheme involves early, though not necessarily immediate payment of (a) dollars 57 million for capital, (b) about dollars 200 million in advance payments.

2. You will note that no corresponding release is given to shipping orders, whilst as regards Air, the financing of capital expenditure is still undetermined. This does not, however, preclude action on orders possible without capital expenditure estimated at dollars 673 million, with advance payments of dollars 168 million by the end of February. These orders were approved by MAP 1656 of 14th November.

3. The general effect of these Air orders (dollars 168 million), plus Army programme B (dollars 257 million), on top of existing programme of orders placed, or on the point of signing (dollars 580 million), is to involve expenditure in December, January and February of about dollars 1000 million.

4. Against this we have only dollars 574 million gold and United States dollars balance, and no assurance that Congress will have finished by the end of February. I do not know whether we can get the necessary assistance from the Administration in advance of Congressional action, and I am sure that we shall not get it unless we can either make use of the Allied, Dominion and French gold, or prove to their satisfaction that there are overwhelming reasons why we cannot do this.

General Ismay: recollection
(*'The Memoirs of Lord Ismay', page 155*)

11 December 1940 Chequers

I was walking with him in the garden at Chequers, after dinner. London was under bombardment, and we could see the glow of the fires from afar. Churchill was sad at all the suffering and said that he wished that he could do more 'for the poor people'. I reminded him that whatever the future held, nothing could rob him of the credit of having inspired the country by his speeches. 'Not at all,' he retorted, almost angrily. 'It was given to me to express what was in the hearts of the British people. If I had said anything else, they would have hurled me from office.'[1]

Anthony Eden: diary
('The Reckoning')

12 December 1940

Winston rang up early in morning and complained that we were not pursuing enemy and had much to say about missed opportunities. After an angry riposte from me, it emerged that he had not seen telegram that appeared during night giving details of further plans. But this is all symptomatic of his distrust of local leaders which to my disappointment is not abated at all. He even went so far as to say when I saw him later that this showed we should have held Somaliland. I replied: 'That is most ungenerous at this moment, you know that we had not a gun there.' 'Whose fault was that?' Winston retorted. Our talk was less cordial than usual.

Lord Halifax to A. V. Alexander
(Cabinet papers, 115/83)

12 December 1940

My dear Alexander,

Many thanks for your most secret letter of the 12th December in which you suggest that I should instruct Butler[2] to make a fresh approach to President Roosevelt about the 20 MTB's.[3]

Before I send a telegram to Butler, there are one or two considerations which, if I may, I would like to put before you. As I understand the position the President has always preferred to deal with questions of war supplies to us through the Morgenthau–Purvis channel. The 'Destroyer-Bases' deal was, of course, an exception, but then that was clearly a diplomatic and political question of the first importance and went far beyond the sphere of pure

---

[1] Reflecting on Churchill's words, General Ismay wrote: 'I had never attributed to him the quality of humility, and it struck me as odd that he failed to realise that the upsurge of the national spirit was largely his own creation. The great qualities of the British race had seemed almost dormant until he had aroused them. The people then saw themselves as he portrayed them. They put their trust in him. They were ready to do anything that he asked, make any sacrifice that he demanded, and follow wherever he led' (*The Memoirs of Lord Ismay*, page 155).
[2] Harold Butler, Minister at the British Embassy in Washington.
[3] Motor Torpedo Boats.

supplies. All arrangements for other releases (rifles, machine guns, etc.), have in fact been made through the Morgenthau–Purvis channel.

Further, I understand that Purvis, who is leaving for the USA to-day, has been instructed by the Prime Minister to launch a further wide scale attack following up the Prime Minister's letter to the President, over the whole field of supplies and that he has been fully briefed by all the departments concerned, your own included, to that end. I wonder whether the renewed approach on the MTB's would not most easily come as part of this large scale attack and whether it might not be a mistake to raise this one question in advance and through a different channel.

War Cabinet: minutes
(*Cabinet papers, 65/10*)

12 December 1940
11.30 a.m.

Prime Minister's Room
House of Commons (Annexe)
Church House

EIRE[1]

The Prime Minister said that this matter had been discussed with Sir John Maffey and with the Prime Minister of Northern Ireland.[2] The latter had seen no objection to the course of action proposed, and said that he would take the same line as that proposed by the Government in all public statements.

It was agreed that action on the line proposed should be justified on the ground of economic necessity; and that the strongest argument in favour of its adoption was that it afforded the best way of breaking the present *impasse*.

The Prime Minister said that, before taking action on the lines favoured by the War Cabinet at their last meeting, he thought it would be wise to consult President Roosevelt. He proposed to telegraph to him in the course of the next few days. Provided President Roosevelt did not react strongly against the proposal, there would be nothing to prevent action being taken. The War Cabinet would, however, be consulted before action was initiated.

---

[1] As one of the conclusions at its previous meeting the War Cabinet had decided to end the supply of foodstuffs from Britain to Eire, in view of the continued heavy sinkings of merchant ships bringing food to Britain. Churchill explained this to Roosevelt in his telegram on the following day (13 December 1940).

[2] James Miller Andrews, 1871–1956. A landowner and flax-spinner. Unionist MP, 1921–53. Minister of Labour in the Northern Ireland Cabinet, 1921–37; Minister of Finance, 1937–40; Prime Minister of Northern Ireland, 1940–3. Companion of Honour, 1943.

War Cabinet: Confidential Annex
(*Cabinet papers, 65/16*)

12 December 1940
9.45 p.m.

The Lord Privy Seal said that the Prime Minister, who was unable to be present that evening, was in favour of a modification of our bombing policy against Germany. He had asked that the matter should be discussed by the War Cabinet in order that action, if it was to be taken, should not be delayed.

The Chief of the Air Staff said that it was now widely appreciated that the Germans had altered their bombing policy against this country. The Prime Minister had given instructions for plans to be prepared for retaliation in kind.

Up to the present we had never sent more than 80 bombers to attack one town, and we had never concentrated on the destruction of a town as such. We had been faithful to our policy of picking out military targets. Usually a degree of dispersion had resulted from the fact that there had been three or four such targets in the towns which we had visited. The political question for decision by the War Cabinet was whether we were to concentrate as formidable a force of aircraft as we could command, with the object of causing the greatest possible havoc in a built-up area.

If the political decision was in favour of a 'crash concentration' against a single German town the following military considerations should be taken into account.

(1) The target chosen should be a town of some industrial importance.
(2) We should rely largely on fires, and should choose a closely built-up town, where bomb craters in the streets would impede the fire fighters.
(3) We should choose a town which we had not constantly visited, and where the ARP organisation was unlikely to be in good trim.
(4) To save fuel and increase our bomb load, the target should be as near to this country as possible.
(5) Since we aimed at affecting the enemy's morale, we should attempt to destroy the greater part of a particular town. The town chosen should therefore not be too large.
(6) In view of weather conditions there must be alternative targets.

The War Cabinet reached the following conclusions:–
(a) While confirming our existing air policy, agreed that the maximum scale of attack should, by way of experiment, be concentrated, on one night in the near future, against a single objective.[1]

---

[1] This plan, which Sir Charles Portal had submitted to Churchill in a 'Most Secret' memorandum on 7 December 1940, was given the code name 'Abigail'.

(b) In selecting this objective, preference should be given to a town which would be recognised as having a predominantly industrial character, was suitably located, and offered a target vulnerable to concentrated air attack.

(c) Hanover should accordingly be omitted for the present. A town might be chosen from the following list:–
Mannheim,
Frankfurt,
Duisburg,
Düsseldorf and perhaps
Hamburg.

(d) No previous announcement should be made that this attack was being carried out by way of reprisal for the German attacks on Coventry, Birmingham and Bristol, and no special publicity should be given to it afterwards.

Winston S. Churchill to A. V. Alexander
(*Premier papers, 3/369/5*)

12 December 1940

I understand that work is in progress on the production of false echoes to lessen the utility of the enemy RDF methods.[1]

In view of the fact that the Germans have something corresponding to GL in use and of the possibility that they may be using it from submarines, it is of the utmost importance to put these counter-measures into use at the earliest possible moment. I am informed that simple dipoles might perhaps suffice.

Please let me have a report immediately on the present position and prospects.

WSC

Winston S. Churchill: Statement
(*Hansard*)

12 December 1940

NORTH AFRICAN CAMPAIGN

Mr Lees-Smith (Keighley): May I ask the Prime Minister whether he has any statement to make about the war?

---

[1] Churchill had been informed of this by Professor Lindemann on 9 December 1940.

The Prime Minister (Mr Churchill): The House last Tuesday evidently appreciated the full significance of the fact, which I announced, without commenting upon it, that a British column had reached the coast between Buq-Buq and Sidi Barrani. This, of course, cut the principal road by which the main body of the Italian Army which had invaded Egypt could effect a retreat. The question then was whether the encircling positions which General Wilson's Forces had captured after their brilliantly executed desert march could be effectively maintained, and whether the net so drawn could be forced at all points to the sea-shore. The strong position of Sidi Barrani and various fortified posts in this neighbourhood appeared to be a considerable obstacle. However, as the House has learned from the newspapers and communiqués issued in Cairo, Sidi Barrani has been captured, and the whole coastal region with the exception of one or two points still holding out is in the hands of the British and Imperial troops. Seven thousand prisoners have already reached Mersa Matruh.

We do not yet know how many Italians were caught in the encirclement, but it would not be surprising if, at least, the best part of three Italian divisions, including numerous Black Shirt formations, have been either destroyed or captured. As Sidi Barrani was the advance base for all the Italian Forces which had invaded Egypt and were preparing for a further inroad, it seems probable that considerable masses of material may be found there. I may be able, on another occasion to make a fuller statement. In the meanwhile, the pursuit to the Westward continues with the greatest vigour, and the Air Force are bombing and the Navy are shelling the principal road open to the retreating enemy, and considerable additional captures have already been reported besides those which fell within the original encirclement.

While it is too soon to measure the scale of these operations, it is clear that they constitute a victory which, in this African theatre of war, is of the first order and reflects the highest credit upon Sir Archibald Wavell, Sir Maitland Wilson, the staff officers who planned this exceedingly complicated operation and the troops who performed the remarkable feats of endurance and daring which accomplished it. The whole episode must be judged upon the background of the fact that it is only three or four months ago that our anxieties for the defence of Egypt were acute. Those anxieties are now removed, and the British guarantee and pledge that Egypt would be effectually defended against all comers has been, in every way, made good.

Sir Alexander Cadogan: diary
(*'The Diaries of Sir Alexander Cadogan'*)

12 December 1940

News of Lothian's death.[1] A great blow. Who will succeed him? PM's list is Van,[2] Pound, Rob Hudson[3] and someone else (I can't remember). All catastrophic.

John Colville: diary
(*Colville papers*)

12 December 1940   Chequers

Mrs Churchill having a migraine, Mary and I dined alone with the PM. He began by saying he was going to read his book (Boswell's *Tour to the Hebrides*) – 'you children can talk' – but the tastelessness of the soup so excited his frenzy that he rushed out of the room to harangue the cook and returned to give a disquisition on the inadequacy of the food at Chequers and the fact that ability to make good soup is the test of a cook. Having mastered his indignation he began to lament the death of Lothian and to demand who he should put in his place. He would like to try LG[4] if he could trust him. I suggested Cranborne or Vansittart. He had thought of both and considered Cranborne particularly suitable. But as the evening wore on he 'sweetened to the idea of LG', as he put it, saying that his knowledge of munitions problems and his fiery personality marked him out. He thought LG would be willing to serve and in order to sweeten the pill of serving under Halifax (which I suggested would be an obstacle from LG's point of view) he would make him a member of the War Cabinet. He believed LG would be loyal to him; if not he could always sack him. The suitability of Cranborne, on which he had waxed eloquent, slowly receded into the background, and when I suggested that Cripps was being

---

[1] Lord Lothian, a Christian Scientist, had been taken ill, but refused to allow an operation. He was 58 years old.

[2] Sir Robert Vansittart, Chief Diplomatic Adviser to the Government since 1938.

[3] Robert Spear Hudson, 1886–1957. Educated at Eton and Magdalen College, Oxford. Attaché, Diplomatic Service, 1911; First Secretary, 1920–3. Conservative MP for Whitehaven, 1924–9; for Southport, 1931–52. Parliamentary Secretary, Ministry of Labour, 1931–5. Minister of Pensions, 1935–6. Secretary, Department of Overseas Trade, 1937–40. Privy Councillor, 1938. Minister of Shipping, April–May 1940. Minister of Agriculture and Fisheries, 1940–5. Created Viscount, 1952.

[4] David Lloyd George, Prime Minister from 1916 to 1922.

wasted in Russia, he replied that he was a lunatic in a country of lunatics and it would be a pity to move him.

Mary left us and I had a long tête-à-tête with Winston over the brandy. He grew very expansive, elated by the thought of our successes, continually growing in size, in North Africa. He spoke of the dignity of the Italians, who possessed every requisite for Empire except courage, and of the terrible miscalculation they had made about us. We had had a wonderful escape in these last months and it was now difficult to remember what we had been through.

Talking of the future he sketched the European Confederations that would have to be formed ('with their Diets of Worms') and shuddered as he thought of the intricate currency problems, etc. He did not understand such things and he would be out of it. He did not wish to lead a party struggle or a class struggle against the Labour leaders who were now serving him so well. He would retire to Chartwell and write a book on the war, which he already had mapped out in his mind chapter by chapter. This was the moment for him; he was determined not to prolong his career into the period of reconstruction. I said I thought he would be demanded by the people; there was no other leader. (This was not just Boswellian; there is not at present any man of the right calibre, nor any sign of one on the horizon.)

After a few slashes at Baldwin for not making better use of the sanctions period against Italy, he moved from the dining-room, with his multi-coloured dressing-gown over his siren-suit, rang up Gwilym Lloyd George[1] to sound him about his father, and then stood beaming in front of the fire in the Great Hall. He asked if I had heard LG during the debate in which the Chamberlain Government fell. I said I had, and deplored Chamberlain's mistake in saying 'I have my friends' to the hostile minority in the House.[2] The PM said it had been a wonderful opportunity for him: the stars in their courses had fought on his side. He had been able to defend his chief to the utmost and only to win esteem and support in so doing. No one could say he had been disloyal or had intrigued against Chamberlain – 'and I never have done that sort of thing'.

Remarking that tomorrow was Friday, 13th, I said that last year, on Friday, November 13th, the BBC had gloated over the date as having been a bad one

---

[1] Gwilym Lloyd George, 1894–1967. Second son of David Lloyd George. Educated at Eastbourne College and Jesus College, Cambridge. On active service in France, 1914–19 (Major, Royal Artillery; despatches). Liberal MP for Pembrokeshire, 1922–4 and 1929–50; for Newcastle North, 1951–7. Assistant Liberal Whip in the House of Commons, 1924. Parliamentary Secretary to the Board of Trade, 1931 and 1939–41. Parliamentary Secretary, Ministry of Food, 1941–2; Ministry of Fuel and Power, 1942–5; Ministry of Food, 1951–4. Secretary of State for the Home Department and Minister for Welsh Affairs, 1954–7. Created Viscount Tenby, 1957.

[2] Commenting with devastating effect on Chamberlain's remark, 'I have got my friends' (a remark Lloyd George had not actually been in the House to hear), Lloyd George declared (on 7 May 1940): 'It is not a question of who are the Prime Minister's friends. It is a far bigger issue. The Prime Minister must remember that he has met this formidable foe of ours in peace and war. He has always been worsted. He is not in a position to appeal on the grounds of friendship.'

for German submarines. Four hours later the *Royal Oak* was sunk. 'I wrote that communiqué,' replied Winston laconically. I subsided.

After some observations on the utility of his system of personal minutes to Ministers, and some praise by me of the effectiveness of 'Action this Day', the PM retired into the Hawtrey room and dictated telegrams to the Dominions and the US. To bed at 1.20 a.m.

Winston S. Churchill to Robert Menzies
(*Premier papers, 4/43B/1*)

12 December 1940
Personal and Secret

I am sure you will be heartened by the fine victory the Imperial Armies have gained in Libya. This coupled with his Albanian disasters may go hard with Mussolini. Remember that I could not guarantee a few months ago even a successful defence of the Delta and Canal. We ran sharp risks here at home in sending troops, tanks and cannon all round the Cape while under the threat of imminent invasion and now there is a reward. We are planning to gather a very large army representing the whole Empire and ample sea-power in the Middle East which will face a German lurch that way and at the same time give us a move eastward in your direction if need be. Success always demands a greater effort. All good wishes.

WSC

Winston S. Churchill to William Mackenzie King
(*Premier papers, 3/483/2*)

12 December 1940   10 Downing Street
Personal and Secret

Am very grateful to you for helping me about Purvis. Cabinet proposes to meet your point about his relations with Ambassador on the basis of independence but subject to harmonious consultation. Alas all this is now in flux. Lothian is grievous loss at this juncture.

I am sure you will be glad about Libya. We must be doubly thankful when we remember where we were four months ago. I am very glad we ran the risk in the teeth of the invasion menace of sending our best tanks to this distant battlefield. Consequences of the victory may be far-reaching. We must be worthy of them.

John Colville: diary
(*Colville papers*)

13 December 1940   Chequers

When the PM spoke to Halifax about the Washington appointment, H suggested Eden (who would not take it) and then Lord Dudley,[1] but seemed quite to approve of LG.

There was a question, much discussed on the telephone, whether the Duke of Devonshire[2] was to be given the Garter. The PM kept on repeating that he was not bad as Dukes go and that anyway there was 'no damned merit about it'.

General de Gaulle and Major Morton came to lunch. The PM held forth in his execrable but expressive French. There was a good deal of purring over Sidi Barrani, which de G said would make an excellent name for the battle. 'No,' said the PM, 'it should be called the Battle of Libya.'

Winston said he was inclined to lay stress on the fact that we were fighting the Nazis rather than Germany, even though many an Englishman now had murderous thoughts towards the whole German race. 'But,' objected de Gaulle, 'we fought the last war against the Hohenzollerns and German militarism; we crushed them both; and then came Hitler – *et toujours le militarisme allemand*. So there was something to be said for those who blamed the Germans as a whole.'

Winston S. Churchill to General Wavell
(*Premier papers, 3/309/1*)

13 December 1940

I send you my heartfelt congratulations on your splendid victory, which fulfils our highest hopes. House of Commons was stirred when I explained the skilful Staff work required and daring execution by the Army of its arduous task. The King will send you a message as soon as full results are apparent.

---

[1] William Humble Eric Ward, Viscount Ednam, 1894–1969. On active service, 1914–18 (MC, wounded). Conservative MP, 1921–4 and 1931–2. Succeeded his father as 3rd Earl of Dudley, 1932. President, Chambers of Commerce of the British Empire, 1937–45; of the British Iron and Steel Institute, 1938–40. Regional Commissioner for Civil Defence, No. 9 (Midland) Region, 1940.

[2] Edward William Spencer Cavendish, Marquess of Hartington, 1895–1950. A grandson of the 4th Marquess of Salisbury, Prime Minister at the turn of the century. On active service at the Dardanelles and France (despatches twice). Conservative MP from 1922 until he succeeded his father as 10th Duke of Devonshire in 1938. Parliamentary Under-Secretary of State for Dominion Affairs, 1936–40; for India and Burma, 1940–2; for the Colonies, 1943–5. He was made a Knight of the Garter in 1941.

Meanwhile, pray convey my thanks and compliments to Wilson and accept the same yourself.

The poet Walt Whitman says that from every fruition of success, however full, comes forth something to make a greater struggle necessary. Naturally, pursuit will hold the first place in your thoughts. It is at the moment when the victor is most exhausted that the greatest forfeit can be exacted from the vanquished. Nothing would shake Mussolini more than a disaster in Libya itself. No doubt you have considered taking some harbour in Italian territory to which the Fleet can bring all your stuff and give you a new jumping-off point to hunt them along the coast until you come up against real resistance. It looks as if these people were corn ripe for the sickle. I shall be glad to hear from you your thoughts and plans at earliest.

I am much inclined to Egypt declaring war on Italy at the moment when we have made her safe. Now is the appointed time.

As soon as you come to a full-stop along the African coast we can take a new view of our prospects and several attractive choices will be open.

Winston S. Churchill to General Smuts
(*Premier papers, 4/43B/1*)

13 December 1940

I know you will be pleased at the victory in Libya. Great credit is due to Wavell and Wilson for brilliant planning and execution. First, of course, pursuit till we come up against something solid. It looks as if these people were corn ripe for the sickle. Let us gather the harvest. I should like to know your view of action after that.

We were all much heartened here by your fine speech.[1] One has a growing feeling that wickedness is not going to reign. I remain always your faithful friend, and I wish Abe and Freddie[2] could rejoice with us to-night.

---

[1] Opening a by-election campaign in Wynburg, South Africa, General Smuts said: 'You can take it from me, as one who knows from the inside what is happening, that England today is immeasurably stronger than before the war. I come to the end of 1940 much more hopeful than I was at the end of 1939.' Later in his speech he said: 'When I speak of England I take off my hat. We who have been through something similar can appreciate it when nations stand fast as a wall.' Echoing Churchill's remarks in the Commons on 3 September 1939, Smuts said: 'The conflict is not about Poland. It is a question of which civilisation is to be eradicated and what civilisation is to be substituted' (*The Times*, 12 December 1940).

[2] Sir Abe Bailey (whose son had been briefly married to Churchill's daughter Diana) and the 1st Earl of Birkenhead, friends of both Churchill and Smuts from before the First World War.

Winston S. Churchill to President Roosevelt
(*Churchill papers, 20/14*)

13 December 1940

Am deeply grieved at loss of Lothian, who was our greatest Ambassador to the United States and who had established such intimate and cordial relations with you and your Executive. We have lost a good friend and high Interpreter.

Winston S. Churchill to President Roosevelt
(*Premier papers, 3/468*)

13 December 1940

1. I am sure you will be pleased about our victory in Libya. This, coupled with his Albanian reserves, may go hard with Mussolini if we make good use of our success. The full results of the battle are not yet to hand, but if Italy can be broken our affairs will be more hopeful than they were four or five months ago.

2. North Atlantic transport remains the prime anxiety.[1] Undoubtedly, Hitler will augment his U-boats and air attack on shipping and operate ever farther into the ocean. Now that we are denied the use of Irish ports and airfields our difficulties strain our flotillas to the utmost limit. We have so far only been able to bring a very few of your fifty destroyers into action on account of the many defects which they naturally develop when exposed to Atlantic weather after having been laid up so long. I am arranging to have a very full technical account prepared of renovations and improvements that have to be made in the older classes of destroyers to fit them for the present task, and this may be of use to you in regard to your own older flotillas.

3. In the meanwhile, we are so hard pressed at sea that we cannot undertake to carry any longer the 400,000 tons of feeding-stuffs and fertilizers which we have hitherto convoyed to Eire through all the attacks of the enemy. We need this tonnage for our own supply and we do not need the food which Eire has been sending us. We must now concentrate on essentials, and the Cabinet proposes to let de Valera know that we cannot go on supplying him under present conditions. He will, of course, have plenty of food for his people, but they will not have the prosperous trading they are making now. I am sorry about this, but we must think of our own self-preservation and use for vital

---

[1] The sinking of British merchant ships in the North Atlantic had continued without respite: one on 3 December, three on 5 December, three on 8 December, one on 9 December and one on 11 December (the 10,890-ton *Rotorua*). On the day after Churchill's telegram a U-boat torpedoed and sank the 10,926-ton *Western Prince*.

purposes our own tonnage brought in through so many perils. Perhaps this may loosen things up and make him more ready to consider common interests. I should like to know quite privately what your reactions would be if and when we are forced to concentrate our own tonnage upon the supply of Great Britain. We also do not feel able in present circumstances to continue the heavy subsidies we have hitherto been paying to the Irish Agricultural Producers. You will realise also that our merchant seamen, as well as public opinion generally, take it much amiss that we should have to carry Irish supplies through Air and U-boat attacks and subsidise them handsomely when de Valera is quite content to sit happy and see us strangled.

Winston S. Churchill to Sir Archibald Sinclair
(*Cherwell papers*)

13 December 1940

Your letter to Lord Beaverbrook of the 11th December.[1] Out of 1,800 estimated monthly German aircraft production, the Intelligence Branch of the Air Ministry consider that only 400 airplanes are provided for training. This seems very few considering that the Air Ministry's view is that the Germans are maintaining about $2\frac{1}{2}$ times our strength in the front lines. Alternatively, if the Air Ministry's requirement of Trainers is warranted, and if our Trainers are not profusely and unthriftily used, and large numbers kept about the aerodromes in an unserviceable state, the German front-line strength cannot well be maintained on such a small proportion of Trainers.

Mr Justice Singleton is coming to lunch with me on Sunday, and I will set him to work on the inquiry on which we are agreed.

WSC

Winston S. Churchill to Sir Andrew Duncan
(*Churchill papers, 20/13*)

13 December 1940

I am obliged to you for your note of December 3 on steel, and I hope that you are pushing forward with the necessary measures to give effect to your proposals.

In present circumstances it seems to me intolerable that firms should hold waggons up by delaying to unload them and action should certainly be taken to prevent this.

[1] About Trainer aircraft.

A sample shows that the average time taken by non-tanker cargo ships to turn round at Liverpool rose from 12½ days in February to 15 days in July and 19½ in October. At Bristol the increase was from 9½ to 14½ days, but at Glasgow the time remained steady at 12 days. To improve this seems one of the most important aspects of the whole situation.

WSC

Winston S. Churchill to Colonel Moore-Brabazon
(Churchill papers, 20/13)

13 December 1940

I see that oil imports during September and October were only half what they were in May and June, and covered only two-thirds of our consumption. I understand that there is no shortage of tankers, that the fall is the result of the partial closing of the South and East coasts to tankers, and that a large number had to be temporarily laid up in the Clyde and others held at Halifax, Nova Scotia. More recently some tankers have been sent to the South and East coasts, and oil imports increased during November.

From the reply your predecessor[1] made to my minute of August 26th (M38) I gathered that he was satisfied with the preparations in hand for the importation of oil through the West coast ports. His expectations do not appear to have been fulfilled.

There are two policies which can be followed to meet this situation. We can either expose oil tankers to additional risk by bringing them to South and East coast ports, and thus increase our current imports: or we can continue to draw upon our stocks, relying upon being able to replenish them from the West coast ports when arrangements have been completed for the handling of the cargoes and accepting the resulting inconvenience. I should be glad if you would consider, in consultation with the First Lord, to what extent each of these two policies should be followed.

I am sending a copy of this letter to the First Lord.

WSC

---

[1] Colonel Moore-Brabazon's predecessor as Minister of Transport (until 3 October 1940) was Sir John Reith.

David Low: cartoon
(*'Evening Standard'*)

13 December 1940

Winston S. Churchill to Lord Beaverbrook
(*Churchill papers, 20/4*)

13 December 1940

My dear Max,

The cartoon in today's *Evening Standard* against Greenwood will certainly make your path and mine more stony. I know the difficulty with Low, but others do not, and cartoons in your papers showing your colleagues in ridiculous guise will cause fierce resentment.

The cartoon the other day about 'butter fingers' also gave great offence, and all these Ministers conceiving themselves threatened will bank up against you and your projects, and owing to my friendship with you they will think that I am condoning the attacks made upon them.

Also, the matter may be raised in the House any day.

Would it not be possible for you to write a note to Greenwood explaining you had given orders that nothing like this was to appear in future?

Low is a great master of black and white, but he is a Communist of the Trotsky variety. He does you and your work disservice by these cartoons, and he is only too well aware of what he does.[1]

Yours ever
WSC

Winston S. Churchill to A. V. Alexander
(*Churchill papers, 20/13*)

13 December 1940

I do not think it worth while raising the question[2] over one single destroyer at this moment, but a report upon all the destroyers we have received so far would be valuable.

WSC

---

[1] In his reply on 14 December 1940 Beaverbrook wrote: 'On the one hand, you are constantly annoyed by the charge that I am interfering with the newspapers and that I should not do so. On the other hand, it is said by my colleagues in the Cabinet that I don't interfere with the newspapers and that I should do so.' Beaverbrook added: 'I do not agree with Low. I have rarely done so. I do not interfere with Low. I have never done so. In the Lords one day next week, I am going to say that I do not interfere with the newspapers, and possibly I will sustain attack because I neglect to do so. Don't you think that I could serve you much better outside the administration? I have held that view for a long time' (*Churchill papers, 20/4*).

[2] A suggestion by A. V. Alexander that the United States should be asked to replace the destroyer HMS *Buxton*, which was in poor condition, by a more sea-worthy vessel.

John Colville: diary
(*Colville papers*)

13 December 1940   Chequers

The VCNS (Tom Phillips) and Prof came to dinner. We began with talk of the Sidi Barrani operation, 'Compass' as it was called, the best-kept secret of the war. The PM said he had been living on hopes of it for five weeks and had been terrified some sandstorm would give the men on the spot a chance to back out. It had been well planned and brilliantly executed, unlike Narvik which of all the fiascos for which he had had any responsibility had been the worst – except for Dakar.

What a monstrous thing, exclaimed the PM, that Lothian should not have allowed a doctor to be called ('I had at last come to like Philip, after years of prejudice'). 'Is anyone here a Christian Scientist?' 'Well,' said Prof, 'I am if you divide the two words – a Christian and a Scientist.' 'I am willing to admit you may have some claim to be the latter.' 'Which is the only one of the two on which you have any qualifications to judge.'

The PM reverted, in some detail, to his ideas for the future. We had got to admit that Germany was going to remain in the European family. 'Germany existed before the Gestapo.' When we had won he visualised five great European nations: England, France, Italy, Spain and Prussia. In addition there would be four confederations: the Northern, with its capital at The Hague; the Mitteleuropa, with its capital at Warsaw or Prague; the Danubian, consisting of Bavaria, Württemberg, Austria, Hungary, etc., with its capital at Vienna; and the Balkan with Turkey at its head and Constantinople as its capital. These nine powers would meet in a Council of Europe, which would have a supreme judiciary and a Supreme Economic Council to settle currency questions, etc. Each power would contribute an air cohort – Prussia included – and boys of sixteen would be selected for it. Once enrolled they would be under no national jurisdiction, but they would never be obliged to co-operate in an attack on their own country. All air forces, military and civil, would be internationalised. As regards armies, every power would be allowed its own militia, because Democracy must be based on a people's army and not left to oligarchs or Secret Police. Prussia alone would, for a hundred years, be denied all armaments beyond her air contingent. The Council would be unrestricted in its methods of dealing with a Power condemned by the remainder in Council.

The English-speaking world would be apart from this, but closely connected with it, and it alone would control the seas, as the reward of victory. It would be bound by covenant to respect the trading and colonial rights of all peoples, and England and America would have exactly equal navies. Russia would fit into an Eastern re-organisation, and the whole problem of Asia would have to be faced. But as far as Europe was concerned, only by such a system of Confederations could the small powers continue to exist and we must at all costs avoid the old mistake of 'Balkanising' Europe.

There would be no war debts, no reparations and no demands on Prussia. Certain territories might have to be ceded and certain exchanges of population, on the lines of that so successfully effected by Greece and Turkey, would have to take place. But there should be no pariahs and Prussia, though unarmed, would be secured by the guarantee of the Council of Europe. Only the Nazis, the murderers of June 30th, 1934,[1] and the Gestapo would be made to suffer for their misdeeds.

But all this was a thing of the still distant future: we might have to give it one hundred years to work. At present he could utter no such ideals when every cottage in Europe was calling for German blood and when the English themselves were demanding that all Germans should be massacred or castrated.

We all liked this 'Grand Design', powerfully expounded as it was and I very much hope that Winston may live to lay its foundations.

We ended dinner by discussing a projected German operation, which seems aimed either at Ireland or Spain. The PM thinks Spain; he would go that way if he were Hitler. We discussed our strategy either in the event of Spain resisting or allowing German troops to pass.

The PM was much incensed by a request of Seal's that all the staff at No. 10 should be allowed a week's Christmas leave. He said that we should all go on working as usual with the exception of one and a half hours off for divine service! Continuity of work never harmed anyone.

A late despatch rider brought telegrams from Tangier announcing the intention of the Spanish Government to take over the International Zone. This together with their allowing two damaged Italian submarines to escape from Tangier has infuriated HMG and the FO have drafted a – for them – severe telegram threatening not to allow the Spaniards the cargoes of wheat they want and without which Spain, *'fier et misérable'*, will starve.

The PM thinks this a sign of big things to come and believes the projected German operation (called 'Felix'[2]), about which we know, will be in Spain. This may entail a drastic re-organisation of four or five of our own operations,

---

[1] The Night of the Long Knives, when the SS, on Hitler's orders, murdered the leaders of the Sturmabteilung (storm troopers), among them Ernst Röhm, and other political opponents of the Nazi regime, including Hitler's predecessor as Chancellor, General Kurt Schleicher.

[2] A German plan to seize Gibraltar and close the Strait to British shipping. Spanish support was presupposed, and General Franco was offered Oran and the French Zone of Morocco for his co-operation. A commander had been appointed, Field Marshal Walther von Reichenau, and troops chosen for the operation, including one of the best German Air Force Corps (the VIIIth Fliegercorps), through whose top-secret radio communications the plan had become known to British Signals Intelligence.

('Brisk', 'Shrapnel', 'Excess', 'Challenger'[1] etc.) which are pending, as he considers it would be undesirable to have our forces and our transports 'sprawled' about the world at such a moment.

Michael Eden to his mother
(*Henley papers*)

14 December 1940   Chequers

Winston is not here for the whole of this week end – he came on Thursday but left this afternoon, Saturday, so we shan't be lunching or dining there this weekend. We suspect that when the moon is up he spends his week ends somewhere else. Ditchley in Oxfordshire is suspected – Ronald Tree lives there.

John Colville: diary
(*Colville papers*)

14 December 1940   Chequers

The PM was amusing last night about the North African campaign. He said we had taken the right course: we had risked sending troops and material to Egypt when still under the threat of invasion at home, and we had sent substantial air assistance to Greece in spite of the fact that we were preparing for a 'Spring of the Lion' in North Africa. But if events had taken a different course, as they might have, what would history have said? He quoted dramatically from a mythical history book of the future, denouncing the criminal gambler who sent overseas the divisions which might have turned the scale against the German invasion at home, or the vacillators who sent to Greece the aeroplanes which could have turned the North African fiasco into a success. It was a good commentary on my favourite, and boring, thesis about the ease of being wise after the event.

Pound, Portal and Haining (the VCIGS) arrived at 11.00 and went into conference with the PM, Ismay and Phillips until lunch-time. Sir Roger Keyes arrived late and Lord Halifax, who thought we were at Ditchley and

---

[1] 'Brisk', the seizure of the Azores. 'Shrapnel', the seizure of the Cape Verde Islands. 'Excess' was the code name for a fast convoy planned for the Mediterranean between 6 and 11 January 1941, consisting of three supply ships to Piraeus and one to Malta, to be escorted by one cruiser and four destroyers from Gibraltar with further long-range escorts, including a battleship and a battle-cruiser (the cruiser *Solan*) for 'Challenger', the occupation of the Spanish African-coast port of Ceuta.

went there by mistake (the fault being the PM's) only reached Chequers at the end of lunch. There was the usual chortling over our North African exploits and the effect they would have on our prestige in the world. 'We have now reached the stage,' said Phillips, 'where we shall suddenly find we have got many more friends than we thought.' The PM enjoys mocking the Italians, whose civilisation and achievements he greatly admires but of whom he finds it easy and irresistible to make fun.

Winston S. Churchill to A. V. Alexander
(*Churchill papers, 20/13*)

14 December 1940

Let me have a full account of the condition of the American destroyers, showing their many defects and the little use we have been able to make of them so far. I should like to have the paper by me for consideration in the near future.

WSC

Winston S. Churchill to Sir Archibald Sinclair
(*Cherwell papers*)

14 December 1940
ACTION THIS DAY

There is one thing about the warfare between AM and MAP[1] which is helpful to the public interest, namely, that I get a fine view of what is going on and hear both sides of the case argued with spirit. Will you very kindly address yourself to the various statements made in this letter attached,[2] and especially to the one marked A, that on September 1 you had over 1,000 unserviceable Trainer aircraft? I have long suspected that the inefficiency which formerly ruled in the ASUs and left us with only 45 aeroplanes, when the new Government was formed, as against about 1,200 now, was reproduced in all the Trainer establishments and communication flights, and that a great mass of aeroplanes were kept in an unserviceable state, and I remember particularly the statement of one of your high Officers that the Training Command worked on a basis of 50 per cent unserviceable. Who is responsible

---

[1] The Air Ministry and the Ministry of Aircraft Production.
[2] From Lord Beaverbrook.

for Repair and Training Establishments? If I were you, I should throw the whole business of repair on to MAP, and then you would be able to criticise them, as you would readily do for any shortcomings.

See also the figures of how repaired aircraft and engines have increased since the change was made.

I recur to the point I made to you yesterday when you sent me your letter to MAP. The Air Ministry's view is that the Germans have nearly 6,000 airplanes in front-line action, and we have about 2,000. Air Ministry also believe that the German output is 1,800 a month, out of which they provide only 400 for Training Establishments, while we, out of 1,400 output, provide also 400. How do you, then, explain that the Germans are able to keep three times our establishment in front-line action with only an equal monthly subscription of Trainer aircraft? Apparently, on your figures, which I may say I do not accept (except for controversial purposes), the Germans can keep three times as large a force in action as you can for the same number of Trainer planes. I know that you will rightly say you are preparing for the expansion of the future, but they have to keep going on a threefold scale, and expand as well.

I await with keen interest further developments of your controversy.

WSC

Winston S. Churchill to Peter Fraser[1]
(*Churchill papers, 20/14*)

14 December 1940

Reference is to your telegram 20th November No. 485 and to Governor-General's[2] telegram 4th December No. 489.

Have been thinking constantly about your enquiries. But I deferred answering till results of Libyan battle were known. These may well be far-reaching if full use is made of success. We ran sharp risks at home in sending so many tanks and guns as well as troops all round the Cape to the Middle East when we were under heavy threat of invasion here. But now there is a reward. We are gathering in the Middle East a very large army representing the whole Empire in order with all Allies we can gather to meet what I

---

[1] Prime Minister of New Zealand.
[2] George Vere Arundell Monckton-Arundell, Baron Monckton, 1882–1943. A soldier from 1904. Unsuccessful Conservative candidate, 1910. On active service, 1914–18 (DSO). Commandant, Life Guards, 1925–9. Succeeded his father as 8th Viscount Galway, 1931. Governor-General of New Zealand, 1935–41.

apprehend will be a German onslaught. This army and the superior seapower which supports it obviously sustain your position in Eastern waters. If Italy should be broken Japan will become very cautious. Thus all hangs together and I hope you will have good confidence in us. It has been a great comfort to feel that the New Zealand Brigade Group under the Great St Bernard,[1] as General Wilson calls him, were well forward in all this brilliant operation. At the moment I do not know whether they have yet been engaged.

We will certainly send you some Hudsons for action against raiders but I know you would not wish to take more from the North Western Approaches to Great Britain than is absolutely necessary in these next few months.

When I spoke of our aircraft production being ahead of Germany it was true, but since then their bombing has somewhat damped down our factories and as we have had to lay off bombing their factories to bomb invasion ports, &c., their current output is now slightly ahead of ours. This is only a passing phase because our main expansion here and overseas is now on the threshold. We shall soon be better in the air.

The greatest anxiety is tonnage. When I mentioned the years 1943 and 1944 I was speaking of the slow processes of shipbuilding and agriculture which require to be set running in steady grooves. Of course this does not mean that I think the war will go on as long as that. I can truly say that, having lived through a very rough time, as you will remember, I feel we are more sure of the future than we have been since the war began. Every good wish.

Winston S. Churchill to Arthur Greenwood
(*Churchill papers, 20/4*)

14 December 1940

I was offended by a cartoon of Low's in Friday's *Evening Standard* ridiculing you, & I complained to Max. He had not seen it & was concerned about it. Low has always been a law to himself . . . a free hand for years past. Let me know how you feel & if I can do anything. I am sure this was not inspired by Max. But he just lets these papers run on their own.[2]

---

[1] General Freyberg.
[2] Arthur Greenwood replied: 'I never thought Max was in it & I have no personal feeling against Low as such, if it could be explained the cartoon was based on a misapprehension' (*Churchill papers, 20/4*).

John Colville: diary
(*Colville papers*)

14 December 1940   Ditchley

Ditchley is a lovely house and still kept up in pre-war style. On arrival, about an hour before the PM, I found Ronnie Tree and his very attractive wife, Mrs Churchill, Lady Cranborne[1] and Brendan. General Alexander,[2] the new C in C, Southern Command, an unusually delightful person, arrived to dine and sleep. The PM spent most of the time before dinner showing him the Prof's albums.

The Trees, who are very hospitable, put the house entirely at the PM's disposal. They are of course delighted to have him, but it must be something of a trial when he arrives with such a vast following.

There was a large dinner party, at which I sat between the Duchess of Marlborough[3] and Ronnie Tree, with both of whom I had very pleasant conversations. After dinner there was a film: Charlie Chaplin's *The Great Dictator* which has not yet been released in this country and which everyone has been eagerly awaiting.

The film, at which we all laughed a great deal, being over, Winston dictated to me a short telegram to Roosevelt, asking whether LG would be acceptable as Ambassador, and went to bed early. He twice complimented me on my 'beautiful handwriting', which he esteems far beyond its real merits. Roger Keyes, who has been scheming to come to Ditchley for the last two days, rang up and asked point blank. Winston, who is at long last becoming bored with his importunity, refused to speak to him and sent a snubbing answer through me.

---

[1] Elizabeth Vere Cavendish, 1897–1982. Granddaughter of the 8th Duke of Devonshire and of the 10th Duke of St Albans. She married Lord Cranborne (later 5th Marquess of Salisbury) in 1915. Their third son, Sergeant-Pilot Richard Hugh Vere Cecil, was killed during the Second World War, as a result of an accident, on 12 August 1944, aged twenty.

[2] General Sir Harold Alexander, like Churchill an Old Harrovian.

[3] Alexandra Mary Cadogan, 1900–61. Granddaughter of the 5th Earl Cadogan. In 1920 she married the Marquess of Blandford (10th Duke of Marlborough, 1934); Sarah Churchill, then aged six, was one of the child bridesmaids. Administered eight Red Cross auxiliary hospitals and convalescent homes, 1939–45. An executive committee member of the Red Cross from 1944. CBE, 1953. Mayor of Woodstock, 1946–51.

December 1940

Winston S. Churchill to President Roosevelt
(*Roosevelt papers*)

14 December 1940
Personal and Secret

I am thinking of proposing to Mr Lloyd George that he should undertake the task of filling Lothian's place at this juncture, and I should be very glad to know quite informally that this would be agreeable to you. I have reason to hope that he would not be unwilling to face the arduous responsibilities and I should be grateful if you would send me a message at the earliest possible moment as I am to see him on Monday[1] at noon, British time.

Sir Alexander Cadogan: diaries
(*'The Diaries of Sir Alexander Cadogan'*)

15 December 1940

I found PM had sent telegram last night to Washington telling them to sound President informally about appointment of LlG as Ambassador! I ascertained that H (who met PM at lunch yesterday) had agreed to this, but they had both forgotten to approach the King!

President Roosevelt to Winston S. Churchill
(*Roosevelt papers*)[2]

15 December 1940

Choice will be entirely agreeable. I knew him in world war.
I assume that over here he will in no way play into the hands of the appeasers.

Winston S. Churchill to Lord Cranborne
(*Churchill papers, 20/13*)

15 December 1940

You will see from my telegram to Mr Menzies that I do not view the situation in the Far East as immediately dangerous. The victory in Libya has reinforced, nay redoubled, the argument there set forth. I do not wish to commit myself to any serious dispersion of our Forces in the Malay Peninsula

[1] Monday, 16 December 1940. Churchill lunched that day with Lloyd George at 10 Downing Street.
[2] After Cordell Hull had jotted down these words in Roosevelt's presence, they were sent to London as a 'President to Former Naval Person' telegram. The code 'Former Naval Person' for Churchill (as a former First Lord of the Admiralty) had become fully established by the end of 1940, though it was not always used.

and at Singapore. On the contrary, I wish to build up as large as possible Fleet, Army and Air Force in the Middle East, and keep this in a fluid condition either to prosecute war in Greece and presently Thrace, or reinforce Singapore should the Japanese attitude change. I could not commit myself to the dispatch of many of the aircraft mentioned, certainly not the PBYs at this juncture when we have a major peril to face on the North-Western Approaches. I could not therefore agree to your telegram, and I should have thought my own (as amended in red) was quite sufficient at the present time.

WSC

Winston S. Churchill to Lord Beaverbrook
(*Churchill papers, 20/13*)

15 December 1940
Private

It is a magnificent achievement[1] in the teeth of the bombing. Quite apart from new production, the repaired aircraft has been your own creation after the failure of that fool Nuffield.[2] We now have 1,200 in the ASUs,[3] which is a great comfort. Dispersion has greatly hampered you, but was absolutely necessary as an insurance to spread the risk.

In addition, you have not confined yourself to mere numbers, but, on the contrary, have pushed hard into quality.

The reason why there is this crabbing, as at A,[4] is, of course, the warfare which proceeds between AM and MAP. They regard you as a merciless critic, and even enemy. They resent having had the MAP functions carved out of their show, and I have no doubt they pour out their detraction by every channel open. I am definitely of opinion that it is more in the public interest

---

[1] A table from Lord Beaverbrook comparing the actual output of aircraft with the programme.

[2] William Richard Morris, 1877–1963. Opened his first bicycle shop, 1893. Began manufacturing motor cars, 1911. Beginning in 1927 he made substantial charitable donations, mainly for medical causes (by the end of 1940 his charitable gifts had reached the then unprecedented total of more than £16 million). Created Baronet, 1929. Started manufacturing aero-engines, 1929. Created Baron Nuffield, 1934, Viscount, 1938. Began tank and armaments manufacture, 1938, including an aircraft factory at Castle Bromwich. Director-General of Maintenance, Air Ministry (responsible for the repair of aircraft), 1939–45.

[3] Air Storage Units. There were twenty-three of these, each consisting of five or more non-operational flying units. They were mainly located in the West Midlands and the West of England, adjacent to aerodromes, and within towing distance of operational airfields. On 20 May 1940 their control had passed from the Air Ministry to the Ministry of Aircraft Production.

[4] A paragraph in a minute from Beaverbrook to Churchill on the previous day, pointing out that it was sometimes said that the output of the Ministry of Aircraft Production would have been equalled by the Air Ministry if there had not been any change in May 1940.

that there should be sharp criticism and counter-criticism between the two Departments, than that they should be handing each other out ceremonious bouquets. One must therefore accept the stimulating but disagreeable conditions of war.

WSC

John Colville: diary
(*Colville papers*)

15 December 1940   Ditchley

The interminable wrangle between the MAP and the Air Ministry goes on, like The Brook, for ever. But Winston, in a minute this morning to Beaverbrook, says: 'I am definitely of the opinion that it is more in the public interest that there should be sharp criticism and counter-criticism between the two departments than that they should be handing each other out ceremonious bouquets.'

It was suggested that the Duke of Aosta,[1] now Viceroy of Abyssinia, might be used to head a movement against Mussolini. 'Yes,' said Winston, 'he would desert his tired and about-to-be-emasculated army, enter a sumptuous aeroplane and return to restore the soul of Italy to Democracy!' Mr Justice Singleton, who was lunching, thought that Mussolini might save his position by changing his régime. Winston said that he gave the blighter the credit for being a brave man who would go down with his ship, and, as far as changing his policy was concerned, 'I believe it is not in his character; I am sure it is not in his reach.'

After lunch the PM went off to Blenheim with Lady Cranborne.

Winston S. Churchill to Admiral Pound
(*Churchill papers, 20/13*)

15 December 1940

I should deprecate having *Malaya* immobilised in Gibraltar dockyard during the next month or so while her condenser tubes are being renewed. It would be much safer for her to be put right in the Middle East, or even at Singapore, and she certainly ought to be made to hold out until *Queen Elizabeth* is ready. We don't want to have an important Unit tied up in Gibraltar.

WSC

---

[1] Amadeo, Duke of Aosta, 1898–1942. A cousin of the King of Italy. Governor of Italian East Africa and Commander-in-Chief of the Italian Armies in Eritrea and Ethiopia. Undertook the invasion of British Somaliland, August 1940. Surrendered to the British, 16 May 1941. He died the following year while a prisoner of war in Kenya.

Winston S. Churchill to Sir Charles Portal
(*Premier papers, 3/205*)

15 December 1940
Secret

How are you getting on with the development on a large scale of Aerodromes in Greece to take modern Bombers and Fighters, and with the movement of skeleton personnel, spare parts, &c., there?

It is quite clear to me this is going to be most important in the near future, and we must try not to be taken by surprise by events.

I should be glad to have a fortnightly report.

WSC

E. A. Seal: private letter
(*Seal papers*)

15 December 1940

Winston's been very preoccupied, & a bit out of sorts lately. He has had a cold – which fortunately is now better. Also, the decision to take the offensive in Egypt weighed heavy upon him, although that, glory be, has been abundantly justified.

Winston S. Churchill to Lord Beaverbrook
(*Churchill papers, 20/4*)

15 December 1940

LOW CARTOON

My dear Max,

These are only minor difficulties, and are in no relation to the vast issues with which we have to deal. Part of my job is to try to smooth things down and keep the team pulling together. I think it would be a very good thing to make a short statement in the Lords about your position.

Everyone knows you are an owner of newspapers which have strongly marked characteristics. You did not seek to join the Government; you were asked by me to do so under circumstances of immense crisis in which it was impossible to refuse a call of this character. You have several times declared to me your willingness to retire from the Government if any difficulties arose. I have strenuously forbidden you to do so. In the meanwhile the newspapers must go on without being in any way under your supervision, and no doubt from time to time they will say things which will cause criticism here and there. You have given general instructions to your newspapers that while retaining their freedom and independence they are to give a general support to the Government, and of course, as they have always done, to the effective prosecution of the war. But you are far too busy with your public work, which takes your whole life and strength, to direct them or even in most cases read them, and you take no responsibility for them except for their general policy. What are they (your critics) going to do about it anyhow?

Or perhaps I might say something like the above if the occasion arose.

Anyhow, let us keep plodding on together and see how things look in another year. I think they will look much better.

Yours ever
W

John Colville: diary
(*Colville papers*)

15 December 1940   Ditchley Park

We saw *Gone with the Wind* which lasted till 2.00 a.m. I thought the photography superb. The PM said he was 'pulverised by the strength of their feelings and emotions'.

After some conversation between the PM and Eden about N Africa I got to bed at 3.00 a.m.; but the PM, throwing himself on a chair in his bedroom, collapsed between the chair and the stool, ending in a most absurd position on the floor with his feet in the air. Having no false dignity, he treated it as a complete joke and repeated several times, 'A real Charlie Chaplin!'

Winston S. Churchill to General Wavell
(*Churchill papers, 20/14*)

16 December 1940

The Army of the Nile has rendered glorious service to the Empire and to our cause, and rewards are already being reaped by us in every quarter. We are deeply indebted to you, Wilson and other Commanders whose fine professional skill and audacious leading have gained us the memorable victory of the Libyan desert. Your first objective now must be to maul the Italian Army and rip them off the African shore to the utmost possible extent. We were very glad to learn your intentions against Bardia and Tobruk, and now to hear of the latest captures of Sollum and Capuzzo. I feel convinced that it is only after you have made sure that you can get no farther that you will relinquish the main hope in favour of secondary action in the Sudan or Dodecanese. The Sudan is of prime importance, and eminently desirable, and it may be that the two Indian Brigades can be spared without prejudice to the Libyan pursuit battle. The Dodecanese will not get harder for a little waiting. But neither of them ought to detract from the supreme task of inflicting further defeats upon the main Italian army. I cannot, of course, pretend to judge special conditions from here, but Napoleon's maxim: 'Frappez la masse et tout le reste vient par surcroît' seems to ring in one's ears. I must recur to the suggestion made in my previous telegram about amphibious operations and landings behind the enemy's front to cut off hostile detachments and to carry forward supplies and troops by sea.

Pray convey my compliments and congratulations to Longmore on his magnificent handling of RAF and fine co-operation with the Army. I hope most of the new Hurricanes have reached him safely. Tell him we are filling up *Furious* again with another even larger packet of flyables from Takoradi. He will also get those that are being carried through in 'Excess'.[1] Both these should arrive early in January.

Winston S. Churchill to General de Gaulle
(*Premier papers, 3/288/2*)

16 December 1940

My dear General,

I thank you cordially on behalf of His Majesty's Government and myself for your most kind message of congratulation on the occasion of the capture of Sidi Barrani.

It must indeed be a source of great satisfaction to you, as it is to me, that the Forces of Free France have shared in the honours of this signal victory – a victory which may well be as far-reaching in its consequences as it is already so richly rewarding in its first fruits.

Yours sincerely
Winston S. Churchill

---

[1] 'Excess', the fast convoy planned for the Mediterranean between 6 and 11 January 1941 (three supply ships to Piraeus and one to Malta).

December 1940

Winston S. Churchill to Sir Edward Bridges
(*Churchill papers, 20/13*)

16 December 1940

Prepare minutes accordingly for my consideration to MAP and M of S.[1]

The vital need is the largest possible supply of aircraft gas containers for immediate retaliation. One would hardly expect the Army to be engaged in firing gas shells for the next few months. Only invasion would seem to render this necessary.

WSC

War Cabinet: Confidential Annex
(*Cabinet papers, 65/16*)

16 December 1940   Cabinet War Room
5 p.m.

The Prime Minister said that Hitler's next move was a matter of speculation. It looked as if he did not mean to make any effort in the Balkans where things were quiet. It might be that he would take charge of Italy, but that would not be a victory for him. The most menacing outlook was in Spain and there had been some indications that he might make a move in that direction with the object perhaps of occupying the N African coast.[2] Such a move would cause us great embarrassment. The Prime Minister continuing said that he had discussed the situation with the Foreign Secretary and the Chiefs of Staff on Saturday, and the conclusion had been arrived at that it would be advisable, in the circumstances, to delay certain operations and movements which had been contemplated.[3] By so doing we should have certain reserves in hand to meet Hitler's next move, should that move be towards the Iberian Peninsula and the N African coast. This postponement would have the advantage of leaving Admiral Cunningham free to assist General Wavell should the latter decide on further operations along the Libyan coast.

---

[1] Minutes to the Ministry of Aircraft Production and the Ministry of Supply about the supply of material for chemical warfare.

[2] This was Operation 'Felix', for the capture of Gibraltar and the closure of the Strait of Gibraltar to all British sea traffic.

[3] The capture of the Italian Dodecanese Islands, principally Rhodes, Kos and Leros.

Defence Committee (Operations): minutes
(*Cabinet papers, 69/1*)

16 December 1940
9.30 p.m.

OPERATION 'GRIND' AND OPERATION 'HUMOUR'

The Prime Minister said that there were a number of indications all pointing to the probability of a German move in the near future through Spain to gain control of the Western Mediterranean. A preliminary discussion of the possibilities had been held on Saturday, 14th December, and it had been thought that we should do well to suspend for a month projected operations which would occupy Force 'H' and the Mediterranean fleet, so as to leave our hands free to deal with any situation which might arise. In the meanwhile, we should see what we could do to secure Tangier, and possibly Morocco, and thus gain a foothold in North Africa. It was clear from the Report now before the Committee that operation 'Grind', which involved the landing of a force in Tangier only, could not be undertaken on the hypothesis of Spanish acquiescence in a German invasion. Operation 'Humour', which was the landing of a small force at the invitation of the Spaniards to help stiffen their resistance in Morocco, might be possible, but would hardly be sufficient. The Spaniards would no doubt expect us to help them in their resistance against Germany in Spain itself.

It was quite clear that if Germany made a move towards the Western Mediterranean, either with or without Spanish consent, we should have to take some action; and all possible methods of operation, whether in Spain or in North Africa, should be given thorough study, and plans and preparations should be made.

Anthony Eden: recollection
(*'The Reckoning', page 181*)

16 December 1940

On December 16th Mr Churchill held a conference at No. 10 Downing Street on our arms orders from the United States, with Lord Beaverbrook, Sir Archibald Sinclair, Mr A. V. Alexander, Sir Kingsley Wood and myself. Matters were not going well for the army and we all felt the time had come to air our discontent. We would rather not have programme 'B' at all than agree to it being placed before programme 'A'. Our point was taken and, in the event, the Americans did not enforce these priorities to our disadvantage.

After dinner the Prime Minister told me that Mr Lloyd George would not have the Washington Embassy, which he had offered him on the sudden death of Lord Lothian. Lord Horder, his doctor, had ruled him out, but he had been flattered by the invitation.

Winston S. Churchill to President Roosevelt: unsent draft
(*Premier papers, 4/17/1*)

17 December 1940
Personal. Secret
10 Downing Street

Our friend would much have liked to come but at his age he felt the strain would be too great.[1]

Am much puzzled by deadlock about programmes. We were told that we could have an extra ten Divisions equipment on American types and that our acceptance would enable American plants to be planned on a larger and more provident scale. Certainly this equipment would have enabled us to act and bleed on the front of another 200,000 men in 1942. We should welcome this opportunity, but we could not take it at the expense of the far-more urgent programmes needed for '41. We are now told that unless we accept the additional ten Divisions equipment and pay 257 millions of our rapidly-dwindling dollars as advance cover 'the Administration will wash its hands of us'. I feel sure there must be some misunderstanding and should be grateful for your advice. We could not sacrifice programme A to programme B, still less could we use for Programme B nearly half of the cash which is left to us without knowing broadly what you are going to give us over and above what we can pay for. If you were to 'wash your hands of us' i.e. give us nothing we cannot pay for with suitable advances, we should certainly not give in, and I believe we could save ourselves and our own National interests for the time being. But we should certainly not be able to beat the Nazi tyranny and gain you the time you require for your re-armament. You may be absolutely sure that whatever you do or do not feel able to do, we shall go on to the utmost limits of our resources and strength, but that strength unaided will not be sufficient to produce a world-result of a satisfactory and lasting character.[2]

---

[1] Lloyd George had declined the United States Embassy on the grounds of age (he was seventy-seven). Clementine Churchill noted after the war, 'I was in an agony of fear he should accept' (*Churchill papers, 4/175*).

[2] In anticipation of a public statement by Roosevelt that day, Churchill held back this telegram. As soon as he read Roosevelt's statement, he cancelled the telegram, for in his statement the President announced that the United States would take over Britain's munitions orders 'with the understanding that when the thing was over we would get repaid sometime in kind, thereby leaving out the dollar mark'.

Professor Lindemann to Winston S. Churchill
(*Premier papers, 4/17/1*)

17 December 1940

The fruits of victory which Roosevelt offers seem to be safety for America and virtual starvation for us. Not a very inspiring theme to set before the British people.

Two other points.

(1) We are putting between $\frac{1}{3}$ and $\frac{1}{2}$ our national effort into fighting Nazidom. 1000 million pounds worth of goods represents about $1/_{20}$ of the annual American national effort.

(2) The loss of our gold holdings will seriously jeopardise our power to attract Turkey and the Balkan states on to our side.

FAL

Hugh Dalton: diary
(*'The Second World War Diary of Hugh Dalton'*)

17 December 1940

The PM holds one of his ministers' meetings in the CWR and talks to us joyfully of the great victory in Africa. 'In Wavell we have got a winner', and Wilson, his Chief of Staff, has also done wonderfully well. They were most cautious in their forecasts of what they could do; they spoke only, at first, of a 'raid'. They did not know what they might find at Sidi Barrani. They might come up against a hard resistance there. In fact, they didn't, and so they went right on. The Italian Air Force was astonishingly ineffective. Obsolete machines and bad tactics. Many were bombed on the ground, so that we did to them from the air, though of course on a much smaller scale, what the Germans did to the Poles in the first weeks of the war. The battle, said the PM, is by no means over yet, and it has removed the threat to Egypt and will make repercussions all round the Mediterranean and through the whole Middle East and as far as Moscow.

The PM says that he is quite sure that Hitler cannot lie down under this. Perhaps within three weeks, and certainly within three months, he must make some violent counter-stroke. What will it be? An attempt, at long last, to invade us? Perhaps a gas attack on us on an immense scale, drenching our cities with mustard? Perhaps a blow through Spain, perhaps through Italy, perhaps to the Mediterranean through France, perhaps through Bulgaria to Salonika? Any of these might be awkward and troublesome, and we must be prepared to face difficult hours. There is nothing now to stop him coming through to Salonika. This is the easiest one of all. Why doesn't he do it? The

PM supposes because he fears that he might get wrong with both the Russians and the Turks.

The PM is very optimistic about US aid. They will soon, he thinks, be 'in the war in fact if not in form'. He would say to them, in effect, 'If you want to watch us fighting for your liberties, you must pay for the performance.'

Meanwhile, we shall follow 'that great imposter Triumph' as far as we can and apply all those Biblical injunctions which are also strategical principles: 'Knock and it shall be opened unto you; seek and ye shall find', etc.

He is in a happy, though not incautious, mood.

Captain Berkeley: diary
(*Berkeley papers*)

17 December 1940

We[1] discussed the PM's qualities and defects at great length. If only there were just a few more anything like him! Even the spectacularly successful campaign in Egypt would probably never have been launched if he had not ceaselessly urged Wavell on. Thank heavens he has been proved right.

Winston S. Churchill: Oral Answers
(*Hansard*)

17 December 1940　　　　　　　　　　　House of Commons (Annexe)
　　　　　　　　　　　　　　　　　　　　　　　　Church House

SIR ROBERT VANSITTART
(BROADCASTS)

Mr Stokes asked the Prime Minister whether the recent broadcasts by Sir Robert Vansittart were made with the approval of His Majesty's Government; and whether the declared policy, that this country desires nothing humiliating to the German people, has been changed?[2]

---

[1] Captain Berkeley and Anthony Bevir.
[2] While still holding the almost entirely sinecure position of Chief Diplomatic Adviser to the Foreign Secretary, Sir Robert Vansittart (a former Permanent Under-Secretary of State for Foreign Affairs) had broadcast a series of sweeping condemnations of Germany and the German people, later published in a pamphlet, *Black Record*. Considerable objection was taken to the harmful effect that these broadcasts might have in strengthening German hostility and resistance. Following his retirement at the beginning of 1941, Lord Vansittart, as he then became, intensified his public onslaught on the 'myth' of two Germanies, and sought to characterise all Germans as evil.

The Prime Minister: Many interesting points of view are put forward in our country from time to time without His Majesty's Government being committed to them, and this principle of free discussion within the limits of the law has the approval not only of the Government but of Parliament.

Mr Stokes: Arising out of that reply, is it not true that Tacitus described the Batavi as head of the German tribes, and is it not true that Sir Robert Vansittart is a descendant of the Batavi?

The Prime Minister: I think that is a very uncalled-for remark about a man who has had the root of the matter in his hands throughout this great controversy.

Mr Stokes: Arising out of that further answer, are not the Germans, in fact, much more our hereditary friends than anyone else?

Mr Granville[1]: Can the right hon. Gentleman say who selects the speakers? Is it the BBC or the Minister of Information?

The Prime Minister: The general authority must rest with the Minister of Information. Of course, tastes differ in these matters. It is impossible to give transmissions which please everybody or suit every audience by which they may be heard, but I think a difficult task is being discharged with considerable success.

Mr Henry Strauss[2]: Is it not necessary and desirable that the German people should suffer the humiliation of defeat?

The Prime Minister: Let us be content if they suffer defeat.

Defence Committee (Operations): minutes
(*Cabinet papers, 69/1*)

17 December 1940
10 p.m.

The Committee had before them the following Papers:–
(a) A Report by the Chiefs of Staff requesting a ruling as to the policy to be followed in disclosing secret information to the United States (COS (40)31(0)).

Some discussion took place upon the type of information which would be demanded, and illustrations were given from current operations.

[1] Edgar Louis Granville, 1899– . Served with the Australian Infantry Force, Gallipoli, Egypt and France, 1915–18. A Liberal MP, 1929–31; National Liberal, 1931–42; Liberal, 1942–51. Parliamentary Private Secretary to Herbert Samuel, 1931; to Sir John Simon, 1931–6. Captain, Royal Artillery, 1939–40. Created Baron Granville of Eye, 1967. He sat in the Lords as an independent.
[2] Henry George Strauss, 1892–1974. Enlisted in the army, 1914; invalided out. Called to the Bar, 1919. Conservative MP, 1935–45. Parliamentary Secretary to the Attorney General, 1936–42; to the Minister of Town and Country Planning, 1943–5. Resigned, February 1945, in protest against the Yalta Agreement. Created Baron Conesford, 1955.

The Prime Minister thought that it would be unwise to withhold pertinent information. The delegation should not give details of impending operations, but in discussing these should confine themselves to general explanations. He would like to know more about the type of questions which were being asked.

The Committee then turned to consideration of the draft instructions to the United Kingdom Delegation (COS (40) 1043). It was agreed that in the first paragraph of the enclosure on page 3 the words 'in dispute' in line 5 should be changed to 'unsettled'.

The Prime Minister said that he fully agreed with the instructions set out in the Paper, but it was most important that the attitude to be adopted by our delegation in the discussions on the naval strategy should be one of deference to the views of the United States in all matters concerning the Pacific theatre of war. It would be most unwise to try and force our views on naval strategy in that theatre upon the United States Naval authorities. Our delegation should open the discussion by saying that they recognised that the United States Navy would be in charge in the Pacific, and that the American views on strategy in that theatre must prevail. They would not be asking the Americans to come and protect Singapore, Australia, and India against the Japanese, but would offer the use of Singapore to the Americans if they required it.

If the delegation adopted this attitude, it might well be that as the war proceeded the Americans might spontaneously wish to enter more fully into the conflict against Japan, and thus be led of their own volition to send more considerable forces to Singapore. Nothing should stand in the way of the main principle, which was that all efforts should be directed to the defeat of Germany – the minimum force being left to hold Japan in check.

Winston S. Churchill to General Smuts
(*Churchill papers, 20/14*)

17 December 1940

I have read your message in High Commissioner's telegram No. 1001 of 7th December with the greatest interest, and am very glad to find how far you and I are in agreement on the broad issues. I share your view that there is some hope that, if it is necessary for us to take the action which we ourselves would undertake (now described as Operations 'Shrapnel' and 'Brisk'), we might do so without provoking active Portuguese hostility either in Portugal itself or in her African possessions. Let us therefore assume that there is a reasonable chance of our relations with Portuguese East Africa remaining unimpaired by what in the common interest we may have to do elsewhere. I have no doubt that you are right in thinking that if the matter does not turn out in that way you will still be able to deal with the situation in Portuguese East Africa.

There is, of course, the risk that if operations 'Dhqy' and 'Dhqz' are not undertaken simultaneously with operations 'Shrapnel' and 'Brisk,'[1] the Portuguese may sabotage the railways and petrol installations and so cause serious embarrassment to Southern Rhodesia. It seems to me, however, and I gather that you agree, that this is a risk that we must take in the hope of avoiding the greater risk of bringing Portugal and Spain (if we have to act in anticipation of Spanish hostility) into the war against us.

It is not possible to foresee the precise circumstances in which Operations 'Shrapnel' and 'Brisk' might have to be undertaken, and we had hoped to take you into consultation beforehand (see my telegram No. 348 of the 27th July). You will appreciate, however, that we may have to act quickly and in the greatest secrecy, and, in these circumstances, much as we should value your help and advice, time in which to exchange telegrams would be short, and it would be essential to avoid, at such a critical moment, all mention of our intentions. While we will do our best to keep you informed of any developments in the situation, it might not be practicable to consult you, but you may rest assured that no action would be taken without full and careful consideration by the War Cabinet. In any case, we should at once consult together in the light of reactions from Lisbon as to the desirability of undertaking operations 'Dhqy' and 'Dhqz,' referred to in High Commissioner's telegram No. 928 of the 21st November.

I feel that, in view of the extreme delicacy of the position and the dangers involved, it would be much better not to sound de Bettencourt,[2] even tentatively, as suggested in paragraph 8 of High Commissioner's telegram, and I hope that you will agree. I am most anxious that the potentialities of this situation should be discussed as little as possible.

As suggested in paragraph 7 of High Commissioner's telegram, we are communicating our views to the Prime Minister of Southern Rhodesia.[3]

---

[1] Operations against Portuguese East Africa (Mozambique) and Portuguese West Africa (Angola), the Azores, and the Cape Verde Islands (both also Portuguese).

[2] The Governor of the Azores.

[3] Godfrey Martin Huggins, 1883–1971. Born in Kent. Migrated to Southern Rhodesia, 1911. General practitioner and surgeon (on active service, Royal Army Medical Corps, France, 1916–17). Prime Minister of Southern Rhodesia from 1934. Created Viscount Malvern, 1955.

Winston S. Churchill: notes[1]
(*Churchill papers, 23/3*)

17 December 1940　　　　　　　　　　　　　　　10 Downing Street

Ambassador U.S.A.	Halifax
Foreign Office	Eden
War Office	O. Lyttelton
Board of Trade	Hudson ⎫
Agriculture & Food Production	L.G. ⎭
India Office	Cranborne (Lords)
Health	Amery
Dominions	D. Margesson
U.S. M.A.P.	R. A. Butler
U.S. Foreign Affairs	(Devonshire)
Chief Whip	Dugdale[2]
(Public Assistance Board) non-minsterial	Malcolm M.

Winston S. Churchill to Lord Halifax
(*Churchill papers, 20/11*)

18 December 1940　　　　　　　　　　　　　　　10 Downing Street[3]

My dear Edward,

Before proceeding further about the American vacancy I should like to know whether you yourself would care to undertake this high and perilous charge. I feel that I ought to put this question to you before considering lesser alternatives. In doing so let me assure you that I am in close personal and

---

[1] These notes were written out by Churchill in longhand. The first two changes, by far the most important, were made as he suggested. But it was David Margesson who went to the War Office and Oliver Lyttelton remained at the Board of Trade. Lloyd George once more declined to serve. Hudson remained at Agriculture, and Amery at the India Office, until the end of the war. Cranborne remained at the Dominions Office. MacDonald remained at Health, and Butler continued as an Under-Secretary at the Foreign Office (until becoming President of the Board of Education in July 1941). The Duke of Devonshire remained at the India Office and Sir C. Edwards remained Chief Whip. Thomas Dugdale became Deputy Government Chief Whip in Feburary 1941. No Under-Secretary of State was appointed at the Ministry of Aircraft Production.

[2] Thomas Lionel Dugdale, 1897–1977. On active service, 1917–18. Conservative MP, 1929–59. Parliamentary Private Secretary to Baldwin, 1935–7. A Lord of the Treasury, 1937–40. Deputy Chief Government Whip, 1941–2. Vice-Chairman, Conservative Party Organisation, 1941–2; Chairman, 1942–4. Created Baronet, 1945. Minister of Agriculture and Fisheries in Churchill's Conservative administration, 1951–4. Created Baron Crathorne, 1959.

[3] This copy of Churchill's letter to Halifax was written out on 10 Downing Street notepaper by John Martin.

political accord and sympathy with you & that I value and admire your work at the Foreign Office and wish for its continuance, and that only the issues now open between us and the United States on which our whole future depends incline me to contemplate the loss and disturbance which a change in our sphere of action would cause to the Cabinet.

Sir Alexander Cadogan: diary
(*'The Diaries of Sir Alexander Cadogan'*)

18 December 1940

H has had a letter from PM asking him to go to Washington. He doesn't want to, and I suggested how he should put his doubts to Winston. He and I went over to see Winston at 11.40 – about Portuguese suggestion for Staff talks. I then left them to discuss Washington. PM pressed him on Washington and would appoint Anthony in his place. H left at 7 to see A. A says he won't take FO. He may have to! H asks me to think of other candidates. There are very few. Mine would be Malcolm M but I gather PM regards him as ratpoison on account of his connexion with Eire ports.[1]

Winston S. Churchill to William Mackenzie King
(*Churchill papers, 20/14*)

18 December 1940

I am very grateful for your message and we fully appreciate all the work that you are doing for us in the smaller types of ships. The rapidity with which you have produced these craft has been a great help to us, and so has the personnel which you have provided for many vessels.

With regard to building larger vessels in Canada, such as destroyers and cruisers, there are two questions which must be considered.

Firstly, a considerable proportion of the special apparatus would in all probability have to come from the United Kingdom, and it is this part of the equipment which is nearly always the main difficulty here.

Secondly, the provision of a number of key men and constructors presents great difficulties. You will realise that there has necessarily been a great

---

[1] Malcolm MacDonald had been Colonial Secretary responsible for the 1938 negotiations that returned the British bases in Southern Ireland (including Berehaven and Loch Swilly) to Eire. Churchill also held against him the Palestine White Paper of 1939, which had restricted Jewish immigration and land purchase, and against which Churchill had been a persistent public critic.

expansion in this country, where technical experts have had to be spared for the supervision of the large programme which we have in hand, and also for all the small private yards. In addition to this we have had to establish bases and augment repair facilities in a large number of places abroad, such as Alexandria, Freetown, Gibraltar, Simonstown, Durban, Bombay and Calcutta. These commitments have used up all our key men and constructors, and although we are trying to obtain more from every available source we are still short of the requisite numbers. We have regretfully concluded, therefore, that it is impracticable to carry out your proposal exactly as you suggest in your paragraph 3.

I think, however, that it might be feasible, and would certainly be of the greatest assistance to the common cause, if you could undertake to build, say, a flotilla of destroyers to the latest American design, obtaining technical help from USA. It would probably also be possible to obtain from the same source, much of the special equipment for the ships. This is usually a bottleneck here and provision from USA would save shipping space.

I should be grateful for your views on this proposal. If you agree, would you desire to approach the American Government direct, or would you like me to make the suggestion in the first place?

Winston S. Churchill to General Wavell
(*Churchill papers, 20/14*)

18 December 1940

St Matthew, Chapter 7, Verse 7.[1]

Winston S. Churchill to Euan Wallace[2]
(*Churchill papers, 20/1*)

18 December 1940   10 Downing Street
Private

My dear Euan,

I am so sorry that you have been so ill and have had to have this painful operation. You must not mind giving up your job, because there will always be work for a man like you. Indeed at the time you fell ill I was wondering whether the Governor-Generalship of Burma would have been attractive to

[1] 'Ask, and it shall be given you; seek, and ye shall find; knock, and it shall be opened unto you.'
[2] David Euan Wallace, 1892–1941. Educated at Harrow and Sandhurst. Joined the 2nd Life Guards, 1911. On active service in France, 1914–18 (wounded, despatches four times, Military Cross). Captain, Reserve of Officers, 1919. Assistant Military Attaché, Washington, 1919–20. Conservative MP for Rugby, 1922–3; for Hornsey, 1924–41. Parliamentary Private Secretary to the First Lord of the Admiralty, 1922–3; to the Colonial Secretary, 1924–8. An Assistant

you. You may be sure I shall be on the look out for you in the future both in the public interest and because of our friendship and association.

The great thing now is for you to concentrate on getting quite well.

With kindest regards, Believe me
Yours sincerely,
Winston S. Churchill

Harrow School: songs
(*Harrow School archive*)

18 December 1940

'STET FORTUNA DOMUS'
EXTRA VERSE

Nor less we praise in darker[1] days
    The leader of our nation,
And Churchill's name shall win acclaim
    From each new generation.
While in this fight to guard the Right
    Our country you defend, Sir,
Here grim and gay we mean to stay,
    And stick it to the end, Sir.[2]

Government Whip, 1928–9. Civil Lord of Admiralty, 1931–5. Secretary, Department of Overseas Trade, 1935–7. Privy Councillor, 1936. Parliamentary Secretary, Board of Trade, 1937–8. Financial Secretary to the Treasury, 1938–9. Minister of Transport, 1939–40. In 1920 he married Barbara Lutyens (1898–1981), eldest daughter of Sir Edwin Lutyens, the architect. He already had two sons by his first wife, and they had three further sons. Of his first two sons, David was killed in action in Greece and Gerard was killed in a flying accident in Canada during the Second World War. Of their own three sons, Peter, a Battle of Britain pilot, was killed in action, and Johnny died in his early twenties as a result of a general anaesthetic during a nose operation. 'My poor boys,' Barbara Wallace used to say, 'only knew school and war.' Their third son, Billy (a friend of Princess Margaret), died of cancer in 1977, at the age of forty-nine.

[1] Churchill deprecated the word 'darker' and felt that 'sterner' would be more appropriate. 'Sterner' has been sung ever since.

[2] Sir Anthony Royle, who was present among the boys, later recalled: 'Winston wept copiously throughout the singing, which amused all of us small boys.' Royle was then thirteen. (*Letter to the author, 12 January 1983.*)

December 1940

John Colville: diary
(*Colville papers*)

18 December 1940 Harrow School
3.30 p.m.

The school sang well in spite of its depleted numbers, and Winston thoroughly enjoyed himself. An extra verse had been inserted into 'Stet Fortuna Domus' in his honour and he asked for two extra songs, 'Giants' and 'Boy'. He sang lustily, as did we all, and seemed to remember most of the words without referring to the book. Before 'Forty Years On' he made a brilliant impromptu speech to the school.

Winston S. Churchill: speech
(*Churchill papers, 2/336*)

18 December 1940
3.30 p.m.

It is a great pleasure, and a refreshing treat to myself and those of my Ministerial colleagues who have come to Harrow with me this afternoon, to join the School in singing Harrow Songs. When I was here as a boy, I was thrilled by them. I remember them well and mastered the words of many of them and they often come back to me. I feel they are one of the greatest treasures of the School, passing as they have done from one generation to another and pointing with bright hopes towards the future. We have sung of 'the wonderful giants of old,' but can anyone doubt that this generation is as good and as noble as any the nation has ever produced, and that its men and women can stand up against all tests; and can anyone doubt that this generation is in every way capable of carrying on the traditions of the nation and handing down its love of freedom, justice and liberty, and its message undiminished and unimpaired.

Although I like the song 'Boy', when I was at School I did not advance to that position of authority which entitled one to make that call. The songs and their spirit form a bond between Harrovians all over the world, and have played a great part in the influence which has been exercised in national affairs by men who have had their education here.

Herr Hitler, in one of his recent discourses, had declared that the fight was between those who had been through the Adolf Hitler schools and those who had been at Eton. Hitler had forgotten Harrow and he had also overlooked the vast majority of the youth of this country who have never had the privilege of attending such Schools, but who are standing staunchly together in the nation's cause and whose skill and prowess is the envy of the whole world.

When this war is won by this nation, as it surely will be, it must be one of our aims to work to establish a state of society where the advantages and privileges which hitherto have been enjoyed only by the few shall be far more widely shared by the men and the youth of the nation as a whole.

It is a great time in which you are called upon to begin your life. You have already had the honour of being under the fire of the enemy, and you acquitted yourselves with befitting courage and decorum. You are here at this most important period of your lives, at a moment when our country stands forth almost alone as champions of right and freedom all over the world. You, young men, will be the heirs of the victory which we shall surely achieve, and you in this Speech Room will perhaps derive from these songs and Harrow associations the impulse to render that victory fruitful and lasting.

L. S. Amery to Winston S. Churchill
(*Churchill papers, 2/392*)

19 December 1940

Your little speech to the boys couldn't have been bettered. As I listened I half wished I were one of the boys to carry it with me on my start in life. There will be some of them whose whole future will be shaped by it.[1]

Winston S. Churchill: Oral Answers
(*Hansard*)

19 December 1940   House of Commons (Annexe)
                                                              Church House

NEGOTIATIONS (HERR HITLER)

Mr Cocks asked the Prime Minister whether, in order to make it clear to the world that in no circumstances can there ever be any negotiations with Herr Hitler, His Majesty's Government will consider, after consultation with the Allies, issuing a declaration to the effect that Herr Hitler, having broken every pledge and treary, has placed himself outside the bounds of civil and social

---

[1] Among the boys at Harrow who heard Churchill's speech were Peter Green, who in 1944 served in the convoys to Russia and was later Chairman of Lloyd's; L. J. Verney, later a Circuit Judge; Anthony Royle, later Parliamentary Under-Secretary of State for Foreign and Commonwealth Affairs (1970–4); Robert Farquharson, later Ambassador to Yugoslavia (1977–80); Roger Dudley North, the son of Admiral North; John Lumsden, a member of the British Pentathlon team in the 1948 London Olympic Games; and Alastair McCorquodale, the fastest white man in the 1948 Olympics (he came fourth in the 100 yards, after three black runners). Other boys at the school in November 1940 included Ronald Mutter, later Lieutenant, Scots Guards, killed in action in Germany on 27 April 1945; Humphrey Bridgeman, killed in action in Italy on 28 May 1944, and Duncan Davidson, died of wounds in Burma on 2 March 1945.

relations and, as the general enemy and disturber of the peace of the world, is abandoned to public justice?

The Prime Minister: These admirable sentiments so happily expressed do not at this moment require to be embodied in a formal State declaration.

Mr Cocks: Would not those historic phrases apply more properly to Herr Hitler than to the much greater man to whom they were originally addressed – Napoleon.

The Prime Minister: I always deprecate comparisons.

MEMBERS OF PARLIAMENT (DETENTION)

Mr Mander asked the Prime Minister whether he will consider the advisability of amending Regulation 18B made under 1 (2) (a) of the Emergency Powers (Defence) Act, with a view to including the principles of the Act of 1715, which laid down that a Member of Parliament shall not be detained until the consent of the House has been obtained?

The Prime Minister (Mr Churchill): No, Sir. I hope it will not be necessary again to exercise this power in the case of a Member of Parliament, but if in the course of this war – a war in which Parliamentary liberties and all other liberties are at stake – it should be necessary for purposes of public safety to make an order for the detention of a Member, I do not think it would be right that the Minister charged with this grave responsibility should be powerless to take action – however urgent the need might be – unless Parliament were sitting or were specially summoned, and until after there had been a Parliamentary Debate and a disclosure of the information available to the Government, information which may possibly relate to matters of a most secret character.

Winston S. Churchill: speech
(*Hansard*)

19 December 1940   House of Commons (Annexe)
                                                              Church House

ADJOURNMENT (CHRISTMAS)

Motion made and Question proposed, 'That this House do now adjourn.' – (Captain Margesson.)

WAR SITUATION

The Prime Minister (Mr Churchill): Before I come to the immediate business which this Motion suggests, I take the opportunity of expressing the grief which the House has felt in all quarters at the untimely, sudden death of our Ambassador in the United States, Lord Lothian. He was a man of the very highest character and of far-ranging intellectual scope. All his life his mind played about broad issues of human progress, and, whether at home or abroad, he animated an ardent philanthropy with the keenest and brightest intellectual powers. In India his work is much respected. His work in the last war was already important, as my right hon. Friend the Member for Carnarvon Boroughs (Mr Lloyd George) – whom I am very glad to see here to-day – could no doubt remind us. But all the same, when he was appointed before the war to the Embassy in the United States, the most important of all the functions outside this country that can be discharged by any British subject, there were various opinions upon the wisdom of that choice. Very soon, however, it was seen that the new Ambassador was gaining in influence every day, that his stature rose with the greatness of the topics confided to him, and that the contacts which he established, the intimate relations which he developed, with the high personnel of the United States Administration, the friendship to which the President of the United States has himself testified, – all the evidence showed the remarkable efficiency and success with which he discharged his important and extremely delicate and difficult mission.

Suddenly, he is taken from us. He passes away. But I cannot help feeling that to die at the height of a man's career, the highest moment of his effort here in this world, universally honoured and admired, to die while great issues are still commanding the whole of his interest, to be taken from us at a moment when he could already see ultimate success in view – is not the most unenviable of fates. I feel that the House would have wished me to express, in these few words, the sorrow which we feel at his death, and also the very grievous and practical sense that we have of the loss we have suffered at this particular juncture in having been deprived of his invaluable services.

I should like to put rather frankly to the House a difficulty which I feel about making frequent statements on the war situation. I have to be much concerned in the conduct of the war in consequence of being called upon to occupy the offices which I do as Prime Minister and Minister of Defence, and there is a danger, if one gives full and frank and frequent statements, revealing one's own point of view, or the point of view of the Government or of those who are charged with the strategical and tactical decisions, that the enemy may gain an advantage. Certainly it would be very convenient if Herr Hitler or the important chiefs in Germany were to give us, every fortnight or so, an honest-to-God – if they were capable of it – statement. I am sure we should immediately set a dozen active and agile Intelligence Officers to study not only what was said but what was not said, and to read not only the lines but between the lines, and to collate any stray words with the other information which might perhaps afford a clue. Therefore, I hope the House will be indulgent to me if, although always at their service, I choose the occasions somewhat rarely, and, in the event of their desiring information at some period which I do not feel convenient, I hope the House will allow me to impart it to them as far as possible in Secret Session.

With this prelude, let me remind the House, in reinforcement of my plea for not making too many speeches, that I did say when we opened the Session, in a speech which I made on the Motion in reply to the Gracious Speech, that what was wanted was deeds, not words. Well, I do not think we have wholly failed to make good that hope. The Battle of the Libyan Desert is still proceeding, and I have no later news than that which is contained in the public Press at the moment. We are attacking the fort and town of Bardia with strong and increasing forces, and the situation there is not such that I can make any decided statement upon it. But I will go so far as to say that I have reason to believe it is developing favourably. Of course, of this memorable battle, spread over this vast extent of desert, with swiftly moving mechanised columns circling in and out of the camps and posts of the enemy, and with fighting taking place over an area as large, I have been told, as Yorkshire, it is not possible to give all the details at the present time. I am, however, sure that the figure of 30,000 prisoners is, even up to the present moment, a considerable under-statement, and 100 serviceable guns and 50 tanks, together with a great quantity of invaluable stores, have also been gathered by our troops. At Sidi Omar, the day before yesterday, operations resulted in another 800 prisoners and a battery of artillery being captured, and on the same day at Giarabub Oasis, West of the Siwa Oasis, that was being attacked by Australian Forces, it happened that an Australian cavalry squadron charged sword in hand and gathered both guns and transport as its trophies.

One cannot say that the Italians have shown a high fighting spirit, or quality, in this battle. In other periods of Italian history, we know, they have shown great courage; and I am certainly not going to frame a charge of lack of military qualities against a people with whom up to this time we have had – and God knows we never sought it now – no quarrel. But perhaps their hearts are not in their work. Perhaps they have been so long controlled and disciplined and ruled, and so much relieved of all share in the government of their own country, that they have not felt those virile emotions which are the foundation for the actions of brave armies, and which are best nourished by discipline imposed upon freedom. At any rate, we have seen the spectacle of at least one whole Italian division laying down its arms to far inferior forces; and our Air Force, which has been contending at odds of three or four or five to one, has been fighting with continued success. The House will be anxious to know what in this fighting the cost has been in life and limb to our troops. Up to the night of the 16th, which is the latest return I have, the British Army, a considerable Army, which was moved so rapidly into the desert, having continuous fighting the whole week, lost less than 1,000 killed and wounded of all ranks, British, Indians and Imperial troops. There, no doubt, have been other losses since. We must regard this event as highly satisfactory; and its reactions in other directions will be favourable, and should permit us to take bolder views than those which have been open to us before.

This is a case where risks have been well run. The risk in the desert was considerable. The movement across 70 or 80 miles of desert of this large force was open to very considerable hazards, and the assault upon Sidi Barrani had about it this cause of anxiety – with which I did not trouble the House at the time – that petrol and water were strictly limited in the attacking force, and that failure or delay would have entailed considerable curtailment of our operations. But these risks have been surmounted by the great skill of our Commander, General Wilson, who is reputed to be one of our finest tacticians; and General Wavell, whose figure grows upon the Eastern horizon, rises there to the very great pleasure and encouragement of all the people over here who look eagerly to see the arrival upon the scene of this great war of military, naval, and air figures to whom the Armies and the Fleets can give their enthusiasm. I must not forget the work which has been done in this battle by Air Chief Marshal Longmore, who at the most critical moment in their preparations had to have a very large part of his force taken away from him for Greece, but who, nevertheless, persevered, running additional risks, and whose handling of this situation, in co-operation with the Army, deserves the highest praise. It is, indeed, a pleasure to me personally, because when I was at the Admiralty in 1912, forming the Royal Naval Air Service, he was one of the first few fliers there, and in those days of very dubious machines he several times used to fly me about. We were personal friends as long ago as that.

I hope that the House will be contented with the present results achieved by this offensive. I do not consider that it is by any means at an end, but I think it will be better to let the future unfold as it will, without attempting to skip on ahead or in any way to forecast how the play may run. I have said that I considered that risks were well run there. They were also well run here by the General Staff of the British Army and by the War Cabinet and by the staffs who studied this matter; because it was not an easy thing in July and August – if we cast our minds back to that date – to send precious tanks of the best quality and cannon, of which we were then so short, on that long journey around the Cape of Good Hope, in order to enable us at first to defend ourselves, and later to assume the offensive. I can only say that those were hard decisions to take, and that my right hon. Friend the Secretary of State for War and I had many anxious days in coming to those conclusions. But you will not have any means of abridging this war, or, indeed, of emerging from it safely, unless risks are run. Risks do imply that when forfeit is exacted, as it may be when the great ship is sunk, or some great attack repulsed with heavy slaughter, the House will stand by the Government and the military commanders. I have endeavoured always to say that those who launch themselves against the enemy, in any action, with vigour and violence will, whatever the upshot, receive the support of His Majesty's Government and, I doubt not, also of the House of Commons.

Another reason which makes this victory gratifying to us is that the British Army has at last had an opportunity of showing its quality. We have had hard and unfortunate experiences in this war; but in the fighting around Dunkirk all the divisions which were engaged with the enemy had the consciousness that they were fully a match for their German opponents. Several battles fought on a front of one or two divisions showed that we had not the slightest reason to shrink from contact on anything like equal terms or even against a show of arms with the regular mass of the troops of the German Army. Now we have seen in Libya that our military science and staff officers are capable of planning and executing extremely complex and daring operations with efficiency – and it is not there only that we have such officers. Therefore, I renew my advice to the House to do all possible to cultivate and develop the strength and efficiency of the great British Army now building up at home. Certainly, it will give its help in any emergency when air-raid damage occurs, but we must have here an Army on a large scale – I carefully avoid saying what the numbers should be, but on a large scale – not only to defend this Island, but for action in other theatres should they suggest themselves at any time. We must have a large Army, well found, equipped with the very best weapons, and drilled, trained and practised in which I have ventured to call all the arts and manoeuvres of war.

I am sure the House will feel that is a wise and provident provision for the year 1941 in which we shall, I trust, find opportunities of using our Forces, if not in defence of this Island, in other theatres, where we may hope that they will be able to contend with their opponents on terms of a moderate equality in numbers and, I trust, in terms of equality of equipment. This is the first time that we have had equal equipment. As I have said, we are still only half armed. It is no good hoping and asking for immediate conclusions. We are still a half-armed nation, fighting a well-armed nation, a fully-armed nation, a nation which has already passed the saturation point in its armaments. But in the course of 1941 we shall become a well-armed nation too, and that will open possibilities to us which have not been opened up to the present. As my right hon. Friend the Member for Carnarvon Boroughs knows so well, it takes three or four years to put the industries of a country on to a war basis. The Germans reached the saturation point, the culmination point, certainly at the end of last year, and now we ourselves are still only in the second year; but by the efforts which are being made and by the great supplies which are reaching us and will reach us from the United States, we hope that we shall become well armed during the course of 1941. It is essential that every effort should be made in the armaments and munitions factories to improve the supplies not only of the Air Force but of the Army, and every risk well run there under the fire of the enemy, every loyal endeavour which our united nation can procure from the workmen in those factories, who themselves are whole-hearted in the vigorous prosecution of the war, everything that can be done to accelerate and to make a more abundant production, will be a step towards victory, and towards an earlier victory than would otherwise be possible.

The House is now separating. Hon. Members will be in their constituencies in many cases. Let them use their influence wherever they can to speed the good work, to sustain the morale, if ever it were necessary, and to speed the work of production in every way they possibly can. When we come back we can indeed debate these issues of man-power and production. We are not by any means content with the results, but they are certainly on a very great and very substantial scale. We must never be content. We must continue the drive to our utmost in order to see that our men have weapons placed in their hands worthy of the task that they have to perform and worthy of the qualities and sacrifice that they bring to the discharge of that task. What I have said in respect of munitions applies with equal force to food production in all its forms. When I spoke the other day of the years 1943 and 1944, I did not mean that I believed the war would go on then, but in matters like agriculture and shipbuilding you have to get on to steady grooves. You have to look ahead. If you do not make plans on that scale, you will not even get the first fruits in good time. Anything that can be done to increase the volume of our food production will be the wisest insurance for the later years of this war, assuming it should unhappily be prolonged to such a period, which is by no means certain.

We are separating, for a short Recess, and we may, I think, look with some sense of composure and even satisfaction at the progress which has been made and at the state of our affairs; but it would be a disaster if anyone supposed that the supreme dangers, the mortal dangers, are past. They are not. There are the dangers of prolonged deadlock, but there may be also more immediate dangers. The winter season offers some advantages to an invader to counterbalance those which belong to the summer season. It would be a very great lack of prudence, a lack of prudence amounting to a crime, if vigilance were relaxed in our Armies here at home, or if in any way it was assumed that the dangers of invasion had passed. Most careful preparations must continue to be made, and although it has been for some time past possible to give a proportion of leave to our troops to their homes which are close at hand, which are in this small Island, yet that should not in any way be taken as the slightest justification for supposing that we must not watch from hour to hour the dangerous menace which still exists in full force at so very short a distance away. I may say that, of course, our defence of the beaches is complete. From the North of Scotland right round the Island enormous masses of guns and machine guns and fortified posts, with every device of defence, have been erected and are guarded by large numbers of ardent and well-trained men.

But we are not making the mistake which was made by the French General Staff when they thought that holding the Maginot Line was all that was necessary. I remember well going to Paris at that dark moment after the first defeat and asking immediately, 'What are you going to do with your mass of manoeuvre or general reserve?' It was with the greatest sorrow that I learned that a general reserve did not exist and had to be drawn from different parts of the line. Well, we have now got a very large Army behind in this country which is capable of moving to any place with great rapidity and going into action in the strongest counter-offensive, and therefore, one may have good confidence in our power to beat the enemy, even supposing he should succeed in setting foot in any strength on these shores.

Nevertheless, the watchword which we must carry must be that vigilance must be unceasing. We must remember that Herr Hitler – and I certainly deprecate any comparison between Herr Hitler and Napoleon; I do not wish to insult the dead – who wields gigantic power and is capable of wielding it in a ruthless manner, has great need of doing something now, or soon – at any rate, in the next few months. When the war began he had his plans all ready for Poland, and he doubted whether Britain and France would come in, or, if they came in, would persist. When he had destroyed Poland, he found himself faced with the war effort of Britain and France. He waited a long time in complete quiescence, as it seemed, and then struck those terrible series of blows which shattered France. He then thought that in the fall of France would be involved the fall of Britain, but it did not turn out that way; it turned out differently, and one must suppose that he is making other plans which will be particularly directed to our benefit and our address. Therefore, I am using this opportunity of addressing the House to urge not only increasing vigilance but the increasing effort of all, wherever they may be.

We are not afraid of any blow which may be struck against us, but we must make increasing preparations. The attacks in the air have slackened, somewhat because of the weather, but they might easily have slackened in preparation for some other form of activity. I need hardly say, however, that the method of dealing with them and fighting by night is being studied with passion and zeal by a very large number of extremely able and brilliant scientists and officers. So far we have been no more successful in stopping the German night raider than Germans have been successful in stopping our aeroplanes, which have ranged freely over Germany. We have struck very heavy blows; the blows at Mannheim appeared to be of a very heavy character, and the enemy have not found any means of preventing them.[1] So

---

[1] On the night of 16/17 December Operation 'Abigail', the attack on the centre of a German city (Mannheim) agreed upon by the War Cabinet (in retaliation for the German air raids on Coventry, Southampton and Birmingham) was carried out by 200 bombers, the largest force sent to a single target up to that time. The raid was not a success, as the city centre was largely untouched, but 500 buildings were destroyed or damaged, 34 civilians (including 18 women and 2 children) killed and 1,266 bombed out of their homes. Three British bombers were lost on the raid, and four crashed on their return to England.

far we have not reached any satisfactory remedy, although we have noticed a considerable improvement in various directions. We must expect a continuance of these attacks and must bear them. The organisation of shelters, the improvement of sanitation, and the endeavour to mitigate the extremely painful conditions under which many people have to get their night's rest – that is the first task of the Government at home. The Air-Raid Precautions, the Home Office, and the Ministry of Health are just as much in the front line of the battlefield as are the armoured columns which are chasing the Italian columns about the Libyan desert. I hope and trust, indeed, that we shall succeed in mitigating increasingly the conditions which prevail in shelters. It will not be for the want of trying or for the lack of spending money. But the difficulties of handling such great numbers of people under conditions where materials are short and labour is so fully employed on this or that other task are very great. It is a matter in which we welcome the assistance of Parliament, in either Public or Secret Session. Complaints can be made, and should be brought to the notice of Ministers in order that everything possible may be done.

The only other point I would mention is the sinkings in the Atlantic. They still continue at a very disquieting level; not so bad as in the critical period of 1917, but still we must recognise the recrudescence of the danger which, a year ago, we seemed to have mastered. We shall steadily increase, from now on, our resources in flotillas and other methods of defence, but we must regard the keeping open of this channel to the world against submarines and the long-distance aircraft which are now attacking as the first of the military tasks which lie before us at the present time.

I have spoken rather longer than I had intended, but the interest of these topics is such that one is bound to refer to them. All I can say now is that if we look back to where we were in May and June, there is not one of us who cannot go away for Christmas – I would not say for holidays, because, so far as Ministers are concerned, any relaxation must only be the opportunity for making up arrears – or separate for the time being without a feeling of thankfulness that we have been preserved so far and that we have made progress after a moment when many in the world, including our best friends abroad, despaired of our continued power of resistance, that we have maintained ourselves, that our resistance has grown, that we have preserved ourselves secure in our Island home and reached out long and strong hands across the seas to discharge the obligations which we have undertaken to countries which have put their faith in us.

Anthony Eden: diary
(*'The Reckoning'*)

19 December 1940

Winston read his statement to the House in morning, which went well, including a picturesque description of a cavalry charge 'sword in hand' by Australians in desert.

Dined with Winston when we had talk of Edward[1] and Washington etc. W said that E had now made it clear to him that on personal grounds he did not want to go and that on public he was doubtful if it was right, but PM must decide. W was sure that it was right he should go, moreover he much wanted me back at FO. I asked if E had suggested anybody else. No, except hints that as result of my talking with E, I might like to go. I said NO! I had said no more to E than that in wartime all must go where sent.

Winston was tired but cheerful. We spoke of the dark days of the summer. I told him that Portal and I had confessed to each other that in our hearts we had both despaired at one time. Winston: 'Yes. Normally I wake up buoyant to face the new day. Then I awoke with dread in my heart.'

Winston S. Churchill to Lord Halifax
(*Churchill papers, 20/13*)

20 December 1940

This is a very unfortunate statement[2] for our Consul-General in New York[3] to have made (assuming he has been properly reported). We have not had anything from the United States that we have not paid for, and what we have had has not played an essential part in our resistance.

Can anything be done about it?

WSC

---

[1] Lord Halifax.

[2] According to a Reuters report: 'There would be no England resisting today were it not for the help America has sent, declared the British Consul-General in New York, Mr Godfrey Haggard, in a speech here.' Once more, Churchill's careful reading of the newspapers had led to a direct intervention.

[3] Godfrey Digby Napier Haggard, 1884–1969. Entered the Consular Service, 1908. Consul-General, Chicago, 1928–32; Paris, 1932–8; New York, 1938–44. Knighted, 1943. Director, American Forces Liaison Division, Ministry of Information, 1944–5.

Brendan Bracken to Winston S. Churchill
(*Churchill papers, 20/7*)

20 December 1940

Some of Air Chief Marshal Portal's colleagues say that he is grossly overworking.

The most of nights he sleeps for only five hours.

His colleagues believe that you are the only person who can bid him to get more rest.

BB

Winston S. Churchill to Sir Charles Portal
(*Churchill papers, 20/7*)

20 December 1940
Private and Personal

I hope you will try to take a few days' rest, and seize every opportunity of going to bed early. The fight is going to be a long one, and so much depends upon you. Do not hesitate to send your Deputy to any meetings I may call.

Pray forgive my giving you these hints, but several people have mentioned to me that you are working too hard.

WSC

Winston S. Churchill to General Dill
(*Churchill papers, 20/13*)

20 December 1940
Secret

Please let me know the earliest date when the 2nd Armoured Division –
(a) will land at Suez, and
(b) can be available for action in the Western Desert.

WSC

Winston S. Churchill to Lord Halifax
(*Churchill papers, 20/11*)

20 December 1940   10 Downing Street
Private

My dear Edward,

Your public spirit has prompted you to leave yourself in my hands in the matter of this great appointment.

I have no doubt whatever that the national interest will best be served at this juncture by your becoming our Ambassador in the United States. If you thought well to have Sir Gerald Campbell made Minister, you would be relieved of some of the pressure, and it would be possible for you to come back here for periodic visits. On such occasions I should wish you immediately to resume your position as a Member of the War Cabinet and sit with us for all purposes. The business we now have with the United States can only be handled by one who knows the whole policy of the Government and is in constant direct relation with us.

If New York and Washington were as near as Paris used to be, all important affairs would be transacted by personal meetings between Prime Ministers and Foreign Secretaries on both sides.

The Atlantic requires that this intimacy would be achieved by other processes, and you are I am sure the one person best qualified for this all-important duty.

Yours ever,
Winston S. Churchill

Sir Alexander Cadogan: diary
(*'The Diaries of Sir Alexander Cadogan'*)

20 December 1940

Picked up H at 11.45 to go to Lothian Memorial Service in Westminster Abbey. Dorothy[1] there, furious at Winston's letter. Declared she would see PM herself.

H – and Dorothy! – went off after to No. 10. Saw them on their return. They had found it useless. Dorothy recognised this – had realised PM's object really was to get rid of H. I said that had been my own conclusion. (When H had said to me this morning that it was *not* a plot to get rid of him, I didn't contradict him as, if in the end he stayed, it would have done no good to have injected poison into their relations). It's true, I'm afraid – and Winston is making a grave mistake – at this end.

---

[1] Lady Dorothy Onslow, 1885–1976. Younger daughter of the 4th Earl of Onslow. She married Edward Wood (later Earl of Halifax) in 1909. Lady of the Bedchamber to Queen Elizabeth, 1937–41.

John Colville: diary
(*Colville papers*)

20 December 1940

Before lunch the PM discoursed to me on the difficulty of his interview with Halifax, who told him yesterday that both his judgment and his inclination were against going to Washington. But, said the PM, he would never live down the reputation for appeasement which he and the FO had won themselves here. He had no future in this country. On the other hand he had a glorious opportunity in America; because unless the US came into the war we could not win, or at least we could not win a really satisfactory peace. If Halifax succeeded in his mission over there, he would come home on the crest of the wave. The PM's judgment has, I think, been considerably influenced by the monthly Censorship Reports which show Halifax to be unpopular over here and to have inherited the criticism that was Chamberlain's.

Everyone waited for the departure to Chequers, but when all was ready the PM suddenly went off to his bedroom and slept – keeping us all hanging about for hours.

Lord Halifax to Stanley Baldwin
(*Baldwin papers*)

20 December 1940

You can guess how mixed my feelings are. I don't think it is particularly my line of country and I have never liked Americans, except odd ones. In the mass I have always thought them dreadful! And then I have some misgivings – tho' this sounds egotistic – at leaving Winston! For there are not many of our colleagues who are prepared to stand up when the winds of fevered imaginings blow strongly. However when that really happens nobody can make much difference! Anyhow – there we are.

Winston S. Churchill to President Roosevelt
(*Churchill papers, 20/14*)

21 December 1940

I have now decided to ask for your formal *agrément* to the appointment of Lord Halifax as our Ambassador to the United States. I need not tell you what a loss this is to me personally and to the War Cabinet. I feel, however, that the transaction of business and the relationship between our two countries, and also contact with you, Mr President, are of such supreme consequence to the outcome of the war that it is my duty to place at your side the most eminent of my colleagues, and one who knows the whole story as it unfolds at the summit.

Winston S. Churchill to Admiral Pound
(*Premier papers, 3/462/1*)

21 December 1940

1. I am waiting for the reports on the American destroyers, showing defects that had to be remedied, improvements made, numbers brought into action, how long they were at sea, and what happened to each.

2. You are going to give me a statement to rebut the American fear that we have not been able to man these destroyers. I understood that all manning provision was made for the first 50. Unless this rumour can be well disposed of, it will set back our chances of getting more. I understand you could man 30 more in April. Both these reports should reach me at the earliest moment, as I want to send a cable to the President.

Winston S. Churchill to Sir Andrew Duncan
(*Churchill papers, 20/13*)

21 December 1940

What will be the effects of these changes[1] upon the rate of supply in time and numbers? It is characteristic of the War Office to change their types, without any new knowledge having come to hand in the middle of the war. How far has the design of the 7·2 progressed? Can we really be in production in September 1941? The new 9·2 looks a very fine weapon according to the performance set out. Shall we lose any capacity in jigs and gauges, spares or mountings, if we turn over to 7·2's? I must be assured that there is an improvement in production as a result of these changes before I can assent to them.

2. I thought we had a large reserve from the last war of 6-inch and 8-inch Hows, and certainly I have had returns bearing on these matters since the war began. Where have they all gone to?

3. Has the ammunition for the 9·2's, old and new patterns, been prepared? How does it stand? Will there be any waste or check in production in turning over to 7·2?

WSC

[1] A report by Anthony Eden on the new Heavy Artillery Howitzers.

Winston S. Churchill to Sir Andrew Duncan
(*Churchill papers, 20/13*)

21 December 1940
Secret

You will remember that the War Cabinet ordered an enquiry into the fact that bulk storage for 2,000 tons of mustard gas, which had been ordered by the Cabinet in October 1938, was still not ready in October 1940.

The latest information which I have received from your Ministry shows that the bulk stock of mustard gas on the 9th December was 1,485 tons. I was also informed through your Ministry that 650 tons of additional new storage was to have become available last week, and that production was being increased accordingly. Was this promise fulfilled?

Meanwhile, I note that the filling of the new 25-pdr base ejection shell has at last begun in earnest, and that 7,812 of this type of shell had been filled by December 9. I should be glad to know how this figure compares with the total reserve of this type of shell required by the Army, and when this reserve is likely to be attained.

None of the new 6-inch-base ejection shells has yet been filled. What reserve does the Army require of this type of shell, and when is this reserve expected to be ready?

I am sending a copy of this Minute to the Secretary of State for War.

WSC

Winston S. Churchill to Lord Cranborne
(*Premier papers, 3/156/6*)

21 December 1940

Why not add[1] –
'I should hope that these figures would not be made known outside the most secret circles; even telegraphing them has caused us anxiety. If our cyphers were penetrated, the success of our Operation and the safety of the Australian troops would be compromised.'

WSC

---

[1] In a telegram being sent to the Government of Australia about Middle East strength.

Winston S. Churchill to Lord Simon
(*Cherwell papers*)

21 December 1940
Secret

My dear Lord Chancellor,

I am anxious that an enquiry should be held into the strength of the German Air Force, about which there is a certain difference of opinion between the Air Ministry and the Ministry of Economic Warfare. In order that a prompt decision should be reached, it is desirable that an independent arbitrator should be appointed to preside over the discussions betwen the two Departments, and I have therefore asked Mr Justice Singleton, who did such useful work in connection with the bombsight enquiry last September, to undertake the task.

The call on Mr Justice Singleton's time in the present instance would not be heavy and I should be very grateful if you would agree to his helping me to solve this extremely important problem.

The matter is of the highest importance,

Yours v sincerely,
Winston S. Churchill

Winston S. Churchill to General Ismay
(*Churchill papers, 20/13*)

21 December 1940

I am anxious that the 'Brisk' and 'Shrapnel' Operations should be checked up with a view to preventing undue heavy weather being made about them. It would be a good thing, as we have a little time on hand, if DCO[1] and his Brigadier could confer with General Moorhouse[2] (if that is the Officer) and the Joint Planning Committee in order to see if any improvements or simplifications can be introduced.

2. What has been settled about leave for the Commandos?

WSC

---

[1] The Director of Combined Operations, Admiral Sir Roger Keyes.
[2] In fact, Major-General Charles Dawson Moorhead, 1894–1965. On active service, 1914–18 (Military Cross) and 1939–45 (despatches). DSO, 1940; CB, 1943.

December 1940

Winston S. Churchill to Lord Hugh Cecil
(*Quickswood papers*)

21 December 1940
Private

10 Downing Street

My dear Linky,

I hope you will give me the pleasure of submitting yr name to the King for a Barony.[1]

It wd be good to have you in the House of Lords, to repel the onset of the Adolph Hitler schools, to sustain the aristocratic morale, & to chide the Bishops when they err: and now that I read in the newspapers that the Eton flogging block is destroyed by enemy action, you may have more leisure & strength. Anyhow I shd like to see a brother Hughligan in the legislation & feel that yr voice was not silenced in the land.

Yours ever
Winston S. Churchill

Conversation between Winston S. Churchill and Pierre Dupuy[2]
(*Admiralty papers, 199/1928*)

21 December 1940

Mr Pierre Dupuy reported to Mr Winston Churchill that Marshal Pétain, Admiral Darlan and General Huntziger[3] had spoken to him about the sensibility of co-operation in North Africa and Continental France under this vital condition – that the present atmosphere of tension between Great Britain and France be maintained as a smoke screen, behind which contacts could be

---

[1] Cecil accepted, becoming Baron Quickswood. As Free Trade young Tories in 1903, they were part of a group of fellow-Tory MPs known, after Lord Hugh Cecil's name, as Hughligans (hooligans). Some followed Churchill into the Liberal Party, others, including Cecil, remained in the Conservative Party.

[2] Pierre Dupuy, 1896–1969. A French Canadian. First Secretary, Canadian Legation, Paris, 1928–40. Canadian Minister in Vichy, 1940. Canadian Chargé d'Affaires for Belgium, the Netherlands and France, 1940–3. CMG, 1943. Canadian Ambassador in The Hague, 1947–52; in Rome, 1952–8; in Paris, 1958–63.

[3] Charles Huntziger. The senior French negotiator at the armistice talks at Rethondes and on the French Armistice Commission at Wiesbaden, June 1940. A member of the Vichy Government, as Minister of War, September 1940 to April 1942. In May 1941 he and Darlan negotiated with the Germans the Paris Protocols, whereby Vichy agreed to give assistance to the anti-British rebellion in Baghdad, and to facilitate German air, road and rail links through Syria to Iraq. In November 1941 he was killed in an aircraft while returning from an inspection in North Africa. At the time of the Briare meeting (11–12 June 1940), de Gaulle, as Under-Secretary for War, had been so impressed by Huntziger's coolness under attack by General Guderian's armoured corps that he had wanted him to replace Weygand as Commander-in-Chief, and had gone so far as to inform Huntziger of this.

made and information exchanged. Mr Dupuy also said that if the Germans heard of such collaboration they would immediately crush the French and overrun the unoccupied part of French territory.

Mr Winston Churchill said he was ready to enter into a procedure along the lines suggested above; that he would like Mr Dupuy to inform the French Government of his readiness to send divisions to North Africa in case the French Government should decide to abandon the metropolitan territory or considered it opportune to receive British support in North Africa. Mr Winston Churchill said it was important that the question should be examined as soon as possible in order to avoid experiences similar to those of Norway, the Netherlands and Belgium.

He entrusted Mr Dupuy with the mission of presenting his point of view to the interested Department of the French Government, as well as to the French military authorities in North Africa.[1]

Winston S. Churchill to General Ismay
(*Churchill papers, 20/13*)

22 December 1940
ACTION THIS DAY

The work of the Joint Planners divides itself naturally into two parts:–
(a) all the current work they do for the COS Committee, and
(b) the long-term future projects which are indicated to them, and on which they are already at work.

It is to these latter that I now turn. I think it would be well to appoint a Director of Future Schemes, or some other suitable titles, who would guide and concert the preparation of the special schemes, who would preside over any meetings the Joint Planners engaged upon them, and have direct access to me as Minister of Defence. I think Major Oliver Stanley,[2] with his experience of foreign politics and Cabinet Government, would be able to

---

[1] Dupuy reported to the Canadian Prime Minister, William Mackenzie King, on 24 December 1940: 'Marshal Pétain still alert and hoping for a British victory.' In addition, and of particular importance to Britain, 'Pétain and Darlan also declare they are in a position to defend French naval bases which in case of risk would be handed over to us before the Germans could take hold of them' (*Admiralty papers, 199/1928*).

[2] Oliver Frederick George Stanley, 1896–1950. Son of the 17th Earl of Derby. Educated at Eton. On active service, France, 1914–18 (Military Cross, despatches). Major, 1918. Called to the Bar, 1919. Conservative MP for Westmorland, 1924–45; for Bristol West, 1945–50. Parliamentary Under-Secretary, Home Office, 1931–3. Minister of Transport, 1933–4; of Labour, 1934–5. Privy councillor, 1934. President of the Board of Education, 1935–7; of the Board of Trade, 1937–40. Secretary of State for War, January–May 1940; for the Colonies, 1942–5.

1274　December 1940

impart to all this work a liveliness which I cannot supply except at rare intervals. He would have to be given a temporary Army rank to make him senior.

Pray make me proposals for giving effect to this idea.

WSC

Winston S. Churchill to Colonel Jacob
(*Churchill papers, 20/13*)

22 December 1940
ACTION THIS DAY

SMALL ARMS AMMUNITION

Pray refresh your mind with the exchange of minutes on this subject over the last two months.

The forecasts, which you advised me were perfectly safe, should have yielded in the last week 11,600 plus a quarter of 45,000 from abroad, i.e., about 22,000. Actually the yield was 11,000, or less than half. How then do you contend that all is going forward as you expected? The position appears to me to be most disquieting, but before asking the Chiefs of the Staff to reconsider discontinuing the double practice issue to Home Forces, I should like to know what you say.

WSC

Winston S. Churchill to Sir Andrew Duncan
(*Churchill papers, 20/13*)

22 December 1940

I learn that the Central Priority Department has been conducting a special investigation into the requirements of materials likely to be short.

I am told that much the most serious case is that of drop-forgings, on which the production of aeroplanes, tanks, guns and transport all depend. Requirements for 1941 are estimated at 441,000 tons. Home production is now at the rate of 208,000. I am informed that there are orders in the United States for 7,000 tons, and that these are likely to rise to an annual rate of 25,000 by the end of 1941. Even if the requirements are considerably overstated, the deficiency is very serious.

Some moderate rate of expansion at home is expected, but we need to double the output. There are 14,000 workers in the industry, but it is reported that only 300 recruits have been received since August, that the industry alleges that it cannot absorb more than 1,000 new workers in each Quarter, and that it is difficult to get recruits. All this needs looking into.

Meanwhile, the only possible immediate action seems to be to increase purchases of drop-forgings in America, if necessary sending a special expert there for this purpose.

WSC

Winston S. Churchill to Lord Reith
(*Churchill papers, 20/13*)

22 December 1940

I understand that there is a serious shortage of accommodation for welfare services of all kinds to meet the needs of the homeless as well as of the evacuation schemes, and that you, in conjunction with the Minister of Health,[1] have undertaken to endeavour to find premises.

I hope that you will use your utmost endeavours to press on with this work.

I should be glad if you would let me have a return of commandeered premises which have not yet been used for war purposes, and which might be suitable for use of this kind.

WSC

Winston S. Churchill to Lord Beaverbrook
(*Churchill papers, 20/13*)

22 December 1940

I am disturbed to see from reports sent to me by the Ministry of Supply that deliveries to the Royal Air Force of bombs and containers charged with gas have dropped very noticeably during the past month – the total during the four weeks from the 11th November to the 9th December being:–

30-lb. bombs	Nil
250-lb. bombs	18
250-lb. containers	Nil
500-lb. containers	25
1,000-lb. containers	9

I understand that the reason for this decline is that factories have been bombed, and that difficulties have been encountered in the supply of certain component parts.

[1] Malcolm MacDonald.

Nevertheless, it is of vital importance that we should have the largest possible supply of aircraft gas containers for immediate retaliation if need be, and I would be glad to know what steps are being taken to improve the delivery of these containers and what the forecast of these deliveries will be over the next three months.

I am sending a copy of this Minute to the Secretary of State for Air.

WSC

Winston S. Churchill to Lord Chatfield
(*Churchill papers, 20/13*)

22 December 1940

I am grieved to find how very few George Medals have been issued. I had hoped there would be ten times as many. The idea was that you would go about and get into touch with local authorities where there has been heavy bombing, and make sure that recommendations were sent forward which could be sifted, and that you would stir the Departments on the subject. Can you not do something more in this direction? You ought by now to have a number of typical cases which could be circulated to the authorities and Departments concerned, who would thereafter be asked to match them from their experience.

Let me know if I can be of any assistance.

WSC

Winston S. Churchill to Herbert Morrison
(*Churchill papers, 20/13*)

22 December 1940

It must be remembered that these political *détenus* are not persons against whom any offence is alleged, or are awaiting trial or on remand. They are persons who cannot be proved to have committed any offence known to the law; but because of the public danger and the conditions of war have to be held in custody. Naturally I feel distressed at having to be responsible for action so utterly at variance with all the fundamental principles of British liberty, *Habeas Corpus* and the like. The public danger justifies the action taken, but that danger is now receding.

In the case of Mosley and his wife, there is much prejudice from the Left, and in the case of the Pandit Nehru[1] from the Right. I particularly asked that the rigorous character of the latter's imprisonment should be removed. In foreign countries such people are confined in fortresses, at least they used to be when the world was still civilised.

These reflections lead me to look into the details of Mosley's present confinement, as well as others of that category. Does a bath every week mean a hot bath, and would it be very wrong to allow a bath every day? What facilities are there for regular outdoor exercise and games and recreation under Rule 8? If the correspondence is censored, as it must be, I do not see any reason why it should be limited to two letters a week. What literature is allowed? Is it limited to the prison libraries? Are newspapers allowed? What are the regulations about paper and ink for writing books or studying particular questions. Are they allowed to have a wireless set? What arrangements are permitted to husbands and wives to see each other, and what arrangements have been made for Mosley's wife to see her baby,[2] from whom she was taken before it was weaned?

I should be grateful if you would let me know your own view upon these matters.[3]

WSC

Winston S. Churchill to Admiral Pound
(*Churchill papers, 20/13*)

22 December 1940

Very soon the Baltic will be frozen. Let me know its state and future prospects.

What has been happening to the Swedish ore during this summer? The Naval Staff should make the necessary inquiries.

What traffic has been moving down the Leads?

How has the position of German ore supplies been affected by the events of the last eight months? Is there any reason why we should not sow magnetic

---

[1] Jawaharlal Nehru, 1889–1964. Like Churchill, educated at Harrow. Barrister-at-Law, Inner Temple, 1912. Member of the All-India Congress Committee, 1918–47. President, Indian National Congress, 1929. Imprisoned several times, for his political activities, and calls for non-co-operation. Vice-President, Interim Government of India, 1946. Prime Minister of India from 1947 until his death. (Both his daughter Indira Gandhi, and his grandson, Rajiv Gandhi, were subsequently Prime Ministers of India.)

[2] Max Mosley, who was eleven weeks old when his mother was taken to prison.

[3] Churchill was later to arrange for married prisoners to be imprisoned together, to grow vegetables in the prison yard, and to do their own cooking. The Mosleys benefitted from this dispensation.

mines in the Leads, even if we do not lay a regular minefield? We seem to have forgotten all about this story.

I should be glad to have a note upon this, and whether anything can be done.

WSC

Winston S. Churchill to Sir Charles Portal
(*Churchill papers, 20/13*)

22 December 1940

In regard to your complaint that your Squadrons were hampered by lack of spares, and that the MAP have been piecing them together to increase the paper strength of their outputs, the following figures have been given to me by Lord Beaverbrook. Are they correct? If not, will you kindly give me the true figures as you believe them? If they are correct, then it does not seem to me that your complaint was valid; on the contrary, the achievement of MAP during the last six months appears astounding.[1]

WSC

Winston S. Churchill to Sir Archibald Sinclair and Sir Charles Portal
(*Premier papers, 3/445/1*)

22 December 1940

BRITISH AERODROMES IN GREECE

The Foreign Office must be asked to take this matter up with the Greek Government. It is not our interest to draw down German vengeance upon Greece. In any case, the Greeks would have to be the final authority as to the use made of their Aerodromes. They must be asked to allow us to develop at once all the Airfields which are effective against Italy, and we must let them know that the sending of any further Squadrons is dependent upon this.

---

[1] In the continuing dispute between the Air Ministry and the Ministry of Aircraft Production, Churchill was bombarded with conflicting statistics. According to Portal on 9 January 1941, because of the shortage of spare parts 'we are living very much from hand to mouth'. Nearly 42 per cent of all unserviceable aircraft were awaiting spares. On 1 January 1940 there had been 457 aircraft 'undergoing repair at home', and on 30 November 1940 there were 1,345. Portal added: 'I realise that this increase is partly due to this year's air battle, but it is important that these aircraft should be repaired as quickly as possible' (*Cherwell papers*).

With regard to the Aerodromes which would be effective against the Roumanian oilfields, &c., they should be told we should not use these without their permission for that purpose, but, in case they are attacked by Germany in the Spring, we must know about them. Perhaps, in the first instance, our Officers could reconnoitre them in plain clothes and report exactly what had to be done to fit them for the latest Fighters and Bombers. If you raise these matters with the Foreign Office, and mention them in the Cabinet, I shall be obliged, and will advise the Cabinet in this sense.

2. What is being done in Turkey? There surely a number of Aerodromes can be made of proper size, from which we could aid the Turkish defence if they are attacked.[1]

WSC

Winston S. Churchill to Lady Beatty[2]
(*Churchill papers, 2/392*)

22 December 1940
Private

Dear Lady Beatty,

I know that David[3] is very keen indeed upon serving actively afloat, and he now has a destroyer to command. If, however, after all these months of hard service his serious accident is telling upon him physically, and you think he would not be offended at the idea of coming ashore, I would then see what could be done to meet your wishes. I thought it was marvellous of him to keep going for so long, as I know how terrible were the injuries he received.

Perhaps you will write to me again.

Yours very truly,
Winston S. Churchill

---

[1] In a minute to Churchill that day, Portal noted that by April 1941 there could be two heavy bomber squadrons, five medium bomber squadrons and four fighter squadrons in Turkey. They would be stationed at ten different Turkish air bases, all of them in Turkey-in-Asia: 'Aerodromes in Thrace are not proposed, as the AOC-in-C considers them liable to too heavy a scale of air attack' (*Premier papers, 3/445/1*).

[2] Dorothy Power, of Virginia. In 1937 she married (as her second husband) the 2nd Earl Beatty (marriage dissolved by divorce in 1950). She died in 1966.

[3] David Field Beatty, 1905–72. Conservative MP, 1931–6. Succeeded his father (Admiral Beatty) as 2nd Earl, 1936. Chairman of the Navy League, 1937 (President, 1939–44). On active service in the Royal Navy, 1940–2 (DSC, 1942). Deputy Director of the Combined Operations Department, Admiralty, 1944–5. Joint Under-Secretary of State for Air, May–July 1945.

E. A. Seal to all Private Secretaries
(*Premier papers, 4/80/3*)

22 December 1940   Chequers

Two small points:
First I have learnt over the weekend that the Prime Minister can broadcast if necessary from Chequers, provided notice is given. Twelve hours at least.

Secondly, we must make arrangements with Butt[1] for a copious supply of Albums to be available here even when the Professor is not about.[2] Last night the Prime Minister wanted to show them to the Canadians[3] and they were not here. His annoyance was justified!

Winston S. Churchill to Pierre Dupuy
(*Churchill papers, 20/13*)

23 December 1940
Most Secret

Should you see Generals Weygand or Noguès you should explain that we now have a large, well-equipped army in England, and have considerable spare forces already well trained and rapidly improving, apart from what are needed to repel invasion.

The situation in the Middle East is also becoming good. If at any time in the near future the French Government decide to resume the war in Africa against

---

[1] David Miles Bensusan Butt, 1914–94. A student of J. M. Keynes. Served in the Prime Minister's Statistical Office, 1940–45; subsequently in the Cabinet Office and Treasury. Professor at the Australian National University, 1962–77. In 1980 he published *On Economic Knowledge*.

[2] The albums contained graphs relating to every aspect of war production and war losses. Roy Harrod, Lindemann's deputy, later recalled: 'Our graphs related to both economics and to defence matters. When still in the Admiralty we naturally provided a large amount of naval information. After Dunkirk, when most of our equipment was lost, we constructed charts showing for each division separately the gradual and slow build-up of its required complement of each of the main weapons. The Navy, the Air Force and the Army were assigned, as their special responsibility, to different members of the staff. We provided information about such economic matters as the distribution of manpower, the degree of utilization of machine tools, imports, etc. etc. After the fall of France the Prof's brother, Brigadier Lindemann, was attached to the British Embassy in Washington as adviser on scientific questions. Churchill asked us to have duplicate copies of his albums made, and these were sent to Washington in the Foreign Office bag; it was the duty of Charles Lindemann to pay a personal call on President Roosevelt from time to time and to place these volumes, as also the supplements which followed, in his hands. The United States was still neutral. The idea was that it would be a good thing for the President to know exactly how Britain was faring, for good or ill, and have the same information that Churchill himself used. It was desired to by-pass the State Department and any other "departments concerned". It would be for the President himself to use his direction in deciding to whom else, if anyone, he showed his precious information' (*The Prof*, London 1959, pages 191–2).

[3] The Canadians were Ralston (Minister of Defence), Howe (Minister of Munitions) and Dupuy (Minister in Vichy).

Italy and Germany we would send a strong and well-equipped Expeditionary Force to aid the defence of Morocco, Algiers, and Tunis. These divisions could sail as fast as shipping and landing facilities were available. The British Air Force has now begun its expansion, and would also be able to give important assistance. The command of the Mediterranean would be assured by the reunion of the British and French Fleets, and by our joint use of Moroccan and North African bases. We are willing to enter into Staff talks of the most secret character with General Weygand, or any officers nominated by him.

On the other hand, delay is dangerous. At any time the Germans may, by force or favour, come down through Spain, render unusable the anchorage at Gibraltar, take effective charge of the batteries on both sides of the Straits, and also establish their Air Forces in the aerodromes. It is their habit to strike swiftly, and if they establish themselves at Casablanca the door would be shut on all projects. We are quite ready to wait for a certain time, provided that there is a good hope of bold action, and that plans are being made. But the situation may deteriorate any day and prospects be ruined. It is most important that the Government of Marshal Pétain should realise that we are able and willing to give powerful and growing aid. But this may presently pass beyond our power.[1]

Winston S. Churchill to Admiral Sir Andrew Cunningham
(*Churchill papers, 20/13*)

23 December 1940
Secret

Although I am sure it was right to put off 'Workshop'[2] for a moon, I feel anxious lest it should fall under German control, when both its nuisance value and difficulty of capture would be multiplied manifold. Therefore we are still continuing preparations and training. Keyes wishes to come out with rank of Commodore; thus no awkward situations can arise between old comrades.

2. We are trying to adjust political difficulties of 'Mandibles'[3] with parties concerned. Their capture would certainly tidy up all that quarter.

3. Your dash into the Adriatic gave great satisfaction here.[4]

---

[1] On 27 December 1940 Dupuy informed Eden that Pétain, Darlan and Huntziger had suggested to him opening negotiations between Britain and Vichy, ostensibly on commercial matters, but 'with the hope that such negotiations might lead to closer collaboration between the two countries' (*Foreign Office papers, 371/24296*).

[2] The seizure of Pantelleria Island (Sicilian Channel) from Italy.

[3] The seizure of the Dodecanese Islands (Aegean Sea) from Italy.

[4] On 18 December 1940 the battleships *Warspite*, Admiral Sir Andrew Cunningham's flagship, and *Valiant* bombarded Valona (Vlone), the main supply port for the Italian Army in Albania.

Winston S. Churchill to Admiral Pound
(*Churchill papers, 20/13*)

23 December 1940

SHIPS FITTED WITH 'ASDICS' IN HOME WATERS

It seems extraordinary that only 23 should be available on the NW approaches out of 53. I should be glad to have details.

WSC

Winston S. Churchill to Lord Cranborne
(*Premier papers, 3/128*)

23 December 1940

IRISH PORTS

I do not think that a stray conversation of this kind should alter the very carefully considered conclusion to which the Cabinet came. Sir John Maffey naturally wishes to keep everything pleasant, but meanwhile we are suffering cruelly. The Cabinet decided this morning that the Chancellor of the Exchequer's Committee was to meet at once to take stock of the situation. As I pointed out the action requires notice and it may be that your visit would be more fruitful in its premonitory shadow. I do not see any reason for cooling down the Press. We must be very careful that inertia, delay and weakness do not dress themselves as 'patience'.[1] You have only just come into this business. I have been 'patient' for sixteen months. You are much more likely to get an invitation when they see there is something we can do and are going to do.

WSC

Winston S. Churchill to David Margesson[2]
(*Churchill papers, 20/13*)

23 December 1940

I was glad to see that your predecessor was interesting himself personally in the despatch of parcels to our prisoners of war. The causes of the delays which have to be overcome are evidently manifold, and many of them are outside the

---

[1] When Cranborne asked whether this was an accusation against himself, Churchill replied (having underlined the word we): 'The context as well as the pronoun makes it clear that this remark was of general application and includes myself in its scope. The next sentence [here Churchill underlined the word you] refers to you and is so addressed' (*Premier papers, 3/128*).

[2] On the previous day, David Margesson had succeeded Anthony Eden as Secretary of State for War.

control of the War Office; but I hope you will address yourself to this problem, and will keep me informed both of the progress you make and of anything I can do to help you overcome the obstacles.

WSC

Winston S. Churchill to General Ismay
(*Churchill papers, 20/13*)

23 December 1940

Please see that I have a good supply of photographs of war places. For instance, Sollum, Bardia, &c.

One of your Staff might be told off to give some attention to this.

WSC

War Cabinet: Confidential Annex
(*Cabinet papers, 65/16*)

23 December 1940   10 Downing Street
12 noon

Lord Halifax referred to telegram No. 1595 from our Minister at Berne[1] reporting that there would be no blackout in Switzerland on the night of 24th/25th December 'in the hope that our (Swiss) air space will not be violated on Christmas night'. Our Minister hoped that it would be possible to avoid impairing the goodwill of the Swiss people by flights over Switzerland on Christmas night or on Christmas eve.

The Secretary of State for Air said that from the Air Staff point of view, it would be unfortunate if we were to be debarred from carrying out operations on either of these two nights, since the number of nights which were suitable for bombing raids on Northern Italy were few. At the same time, he appreciated that there was a big political point involved, and that the War Cabinet might decide that it was better that we should not carry out bombing flights over Swiss territory on these two nights.

The Prime Minister said that he thought that this policy should be applied to bombing operations against Italy and Germany on both nights. We should not, of course, make any statement in advance as to our intentions in this matter. If, however, we did in fact refrain from bombing attacks on these two nights, we should get credit for it.

---

[1] David Kelly, see page 940, note 1.

The Prime Minister said that in accordance with the decision of the War Cabinet referred to in the margin,[1] he had despatched a telegram to President Roosevelt regarding our proposal to put economic pressure on Ireland. No reply had been received, but it was perhaps significant that he had taken no exception to the course proposed. He thought, however, that the War Cabinet Committee, under the Chairmanship of the Chancellor of the Exchequer, might now meet and discuss the action to be taken in this matter.

Winston S. Churchill to Sir Walter Citrine (Washington)
(*Churchill papers, 20/4*)

23 December 1940

We are watching with great interest all the good work you are doing for us. Kind regards. Winston Churchill.[2]

Winston S. Churchill to Sir Michael Palairet
(*Churchill papers, 20/13*)

23 December 1940

I have been deeply interested in the whole series of excellent telegrams you have sent from Athens since the Italian attack on Greece, and admire the deep and wide appreciation of the whole scene which they display.

Winston S. Churchill: broadcast
(*BBC Written Archives Centre*)

23 December 1940
9 p.m.

Tonight I speak to the Italian people and I speak to you from London, the heart of the British Islands and of the British Commonwealth and Empire. I speak to you what the diplomatists call words of great truth and respect. We are at war – that is a very strange and terrible thought. Whoever imagined until the last few melancholy years that the British and Italian nations would be trying to destroy one another? We have always been such friends. We were

[1] The decision to put economic pressure on Ireland, in the hope of being able to regain the use of the Irish ports (principally Berehaven and Loch Swilly) given up in 1938.

[2] At the request of the American Federation of Labour, Citrine was on a three-month tour of the United States, to give 'first hand, accurate, and definite information about the economic, social and labour situation in Britain under war conditions'. (Lord Citrine, *Two Careers*, London, 1967, page 64).

the champions of the Italian Risorgimento. We were the partisans of Garibaldi, the admirers of Mazzini and Cavour. All that great movement towards the unity of the Italian nation which lighted the nineteenth century was aided and was hailed by the British Parliament and public. Our fathers and our grandfathers longed to see Italy freed from the Austrian yoke, and to see all minor barriers in Italy swept away, so that the Italian people and their fair land might take an honoured place as one of the leading Powers upon the Continent and as a brilliant and gifted member of the family of Europe and of Christendom. We have never been your foes till now.

In the last war against the barbarous Huns we were your comrades. For fifteen years after that war we were your friends. Although the institutions which you adopted after that war were not akin to ours, and diverged, as we think, from the sovereign impulses which had commanded the unity of Italy, we could still walk together in peace and good will. Many thousands of our people dwelt with you in Italy. We liked each other; we got on well together. There were reciprocal services; there was amity; there was esteem. And now we are at war; now we are condemned to work each other's ruin. Your aviators have tried to cast their bombs upon London; our armies are tearing and will tear your African Empire to shreds and tatters. We are only now at the beginning of this sombre tale. Who can say where it will end? Presently we shall be forced to come to closer grips.

How has all this come about, and what is it all for? Italians, I will tell you the truth. It is because of one man. One man and one man alone has ranged the Italian people in deadly struggle against the British Empire, and has deprived Italy of the sympathy and intimacy of the United States of America. That he is a great man I do not deny, but that after eighteen years of unbridled power he has led your country to the horrid verge of ruin, can be denied by none. It is all one, one man, who, against the Crown and Royal Family of Italy, against the Pope and all the authority of the Vatican and of the Roman Catholic Church, against the wishes of the Italian people who had no lust for this war – one man has arrayed the trustees and inheritors of ancient Rome upon the side of the ferocious, pagan barbarians. <u>There</u> lies the tragedy of Italian history, and <u>there</u> stands the criminal who has wrought the deed of folly and of shame. What is the defence that is put forward for this action? It is, of course, the quarrel about Sanctions and Abyssinia. Let us look at that. Together, after the last war, Italy and Britain both signed the Covenant of the League of Nations, which forbade all parties to that Covenant to make war upon each other, or upon fellow members of the League, and bound all signatories to come to the aid of any member attacked by another. Presently Abyssinia came knocking at the door, asking to be a member. We British advised against it. We doubted whether they had reached a stage in their development which warranted their inclusion in so solemn a pact. But it was Signor Mussolini who insisted that Abyssinia should become a member of the

League, and who therefore bound himself, and bound you and us, to respect their Covenanted rights.

Thus the quarrel arose, it was out of this that it sprang; and thus, although no blood was shed between us, old friendships were forgotten. But what is the proportion of this Abyssinian dispute, arising out of the Covenant of the League of Nations, to which we had both pledged our word – what is it in proportion compared to the death-grapple in which Italy and Britain have now been engaged? I declare – and my words will go far – that nothing that happened in that Abyssinian quarrel can account for or justify the deadly strife which has now broken out between us.

Then the great war between the British and French democracies and Prussian militarism or Nazi overlordship began again. Where was the need for Italy to intervene? Where was the need to strike at prostrate France? Where was the need to declare war on Britain? Where was the need to invade Egypt, which is under British protection? We were content with Italian neutrality. During the first eight months of the war, we paid great deference to Italian interests. But this was all put down to fear. We were told we were effete, worn out, an old chatterbox people mouthing outworn shibboleths of nineteenth-century Liberalism. But it was not due to fear. It was not due to weakness. The French Republic for the moment is stunned. France will rise again, but the British nation and Commonwealth of Nations across the globe, and indeed I may say the English-speaking world, are now aroused. They are on the march or on the move, and all the forces of modern progress and of ancient culture are ranged behind them.

Why have you placed yourself, you who were our friends and might have been our brothers – why have you placed yourselves in the path of this avalanche, now only just started from its base to roll forward on its predestined track? Why, after all this, were you made to attack and invade Greece? I ask why – but you may ask too, because you were never consulted. The people of Italy were never consulted, the Army of Italy was never consulted. No one was consulted. One man, and one man alone ordered Italian soldiers to ravage their neighbour's vineyard. Surely the time has come when the Italian monarchy and people, who guard the sacred centre of Christendom, should have a word to say upon these awe-inspiring issues? Surely the Italian Army, which has fought so bravely on many occasions in the past, but now evidently has no heart for the job, should take some care of the life and future of Italy? I can only tell you that I, Churchill, have done my best to prevent this war between Italy and the British Empire; and to prove my words I will read you the message which I sent to Signor Mussolini in the fateful days before it began. Cast your minds back to the 16th of May of this year, 1940. The French front had been broken; the French Army was not yet defeated; the great battle in France was still raging. Here is the message which I sent to Signor Mussolini:

Now that I have taken up my office as Prime Minister and Minister of Defence, I look back to our meeting in Rome and feel a desire to speak words of good will to you as chief of the Italian nation across what seems to be a swiftly widening gulf. Is it too late to stop a river of blood from flowing between the British and Italian peoples? We can no doubt inflict injuries upon one another and maul each other cruelly, and darken the Mediterranean with our strife. If you so decree, it must be so; but I declare that I have never been the enemy of Italian greatness, nor ever at heart the foe of the Italian law-giver. It is idle to predict the course of the great battles now raging in Europe; but I am sure that, whatever may happen on the Continent, England will go on to the end, even quite alone, as we have done before; and I believe with some assurance that we shall be aided in increasing measure by the United States and indeed by all the Americans. I beg you to believe that it is in no spirit of weakness or of fear that I make this solemn appeal which will remain on record. Down the ages above all other calls comes the cry that the joint heirs of Latin and Christian civilization must not be ranged against one another in mortal strife. Hearken to it, I beseech you in all honour and respect, before the dread signal is given. It will never be given by us.

And this is the reply which I received:

I reply to the message which you have sent me in order to tell you that you are certainly aware of grave reasons of a historical and contingent character which have ranged our two countries in opposite camps. Without going back very far in time I remind you of the initiative taken in 1935 by your Government to organize at Geneva Sanctions against Italy engaged in securing for herself a small space in the African sun, without causing the slightest injury to your interests and territories, or those of others. I remind you also of the real and actual state of servitude in which Italy finds herself in her own sea. If it was to honour your signature that your Government declared war on Germany, you will understand that the same sense of honour and of respect for engagements assumed in the Italian–German Treaty guides Italian policy today and tomorrow in the face of any event whatsoever.

I make no comment upon this dusty answer. It speaks for itself. Anyone can see who it was that wanted peace, and who it was that meant to have war. One man and one man only was resolved to plunge Italy after all these years of strain and effort into the whirlpool of war, and what is the position of Italy today? Where is it that the Duce has led his trusting people after eighteen years of dictatorial power? What fell choice is open now? It is to stand up to the battery of the whole British Empire on sea, in the air, and in Africa, and the vigorous counter-attack of the Greek nation; on the other hand to call in Attila over the Brenner Pass with his hordes of ravenous soldiery and his gangs of Gestapo policemen to occupy, hold down and protect the Italian people, for whom he and his Nazi followers cherish the most bitter and outspoken contempt that is on record between races. There is where one man and one man only has led you; and there I leave this unfolding story until the day comes – as come it will – when the Italian nation will once more take a hand in shaping its own fortunes.

Harold Nicolson: diary
(*'Diaries and Letters, 1939–1945'*)

23 December 1940

Back in time to hear Winston's message to the Italian people. I had been bothered during the afternoon by people who urged me to stop him emphasising Italian links with America. I refused to intervene in any way, saying that I had confidence in Churchill's conception of great events. Then I listened with some trepidation. As a message to Italy, and to the Italians here and in the USA, it was magnificent. But even as a message to our own people it shows that he was not a war-monger but a heroic pacifist. He read out his letter to Mussolini of May last. It was tremendous. He read out Mussolini's reply. It was the creep of an assassin. Afterwards some of the American correspondents tell me that they think it is the best thing that Winston has ever done.[1]

Michael Eden to his mother
(*Henley papers*)

23 December 1940   Chequers

I haven't seen much of the Prime Minister – the weather is a bit cold for him and he doesn't come out. We've had much NE wind and frost. The cold out shooting was prodigious.

We don't yet know if he is staying here for Xmas. He was here yesterday, left this morning & returns tomorrow Xmas Eve. We rather believe he intends to stay here a week. I saw him this morning walking along the balcony in the hall smoking a cigar. I had gone in to get some of our money which is kept in their safe, a most inconvenient arrangement.

---

[1] An Italian version of Churchill's speech was telegraphed to Cairo, Athens and Jerusalem, to be broadcast from those stations, as well as from the BBC, throughout the following week. It was also relayed in Italian to the United States, and transmitted over the short-wave Boston station to Italy. (*Churchill papers, 9/176*.)

Margesson is a surprise at the War Office. From what I've heard of him I should say he was a regular Nazi in point of view & method. One of the creators of modern political machinery and a real dictating bureaucrat.

He has been the Tory drill sergeant since 1931. I am surprised Winston has much use for him as he organised the Nat Govt front against the opposition in the old appeasement days.

I suppose he is a very able man and an indispensable servant to the reigning power whatever it be.

John Colville: diary
(*Colville papers*)

24 December 1940   Chequers[1]

After lunch the PM signed a number of books, which he is giving us all as Christmas presents, and sent off presents to the King and Queen: a siren-suit for the King and Fowler's *English Usage* for the Queen! As he left the room he said, remembering our plea for a Christmas holiday, 'A busy Christmas and a frantic New Year.'

John Colville to H. A. Strutt[2]
(*Premier papers, 3/18/2*)

24 December 1940
Secret

Dear Strutt,

It has been suggested to the Prime Minister that on one or two occasions recently after a town had been severely bombed, the passage through the town of the relics of crashed German aircraft on lorries had had a noticeably good effect on public morale. He has therefore asked me to pass on to you the suggestion that if ever it seems desirable, it might be possible to arrange for German aircraft to be displayed in this manner. It would, of course, be

---

[1] With Churchill at Chequers over Christmas 1940 were his wife, his four children, Diana, Mary, Randolph and Sarah, his daughter-in-law Pamela, his sons-in-law Duncan Sandys and Vic Oliver, Clementine's cousin Maryott Whyte, Lord Woolton (to lunch on Boxing Day), and Professor Lindemann and Sir Wilfred Freeman (both to dine and sleep, Boxing Day).

[2] Henry Austin Strutt, 1903–79. Home Office, 1925–61; Principal Private Secretary to Herbert Morrison, 1940–3. Assistant Under-Secretary of State, Home Office, 1943–57. Knighted, 1953. Chairman of the Church of England Pensions Board, 1965–74.

essential to make it appear that the aircraft just happened to be passing through on their way to the disposal centre.
Would you please have this possibility considered?

Yours sincerely,
J. R. Colville

Winston and Clementine Churchill to Viscount and Viscountess Lee of Fareham[1]
(*Churchill papers, 2/396*)

24 December 1940   Chequers

We here in your lovely home send you Christmas Greetings, and think much of you and the inspiration which moved you to make this splendid gift to the nation.[2]

Winston S. Churchill to Sir Edward Bridges and General Ismay
(*Churchill papers, 20/13*)

25 December 1940   Chequers
Christmas Day

With the new year, a fresh effort must be made to restrict the circulation of secret matters in Service and other Departments. All the markings of papers in the Service Departments, Foreign Office, Colonial and Dominions Offices, &c., should be reviewed with a view to striking off as many recipients as possible.

The officials concerned in roneo-ing the various circulations should be consulted, and a return made for me showing how many are struck off of different secret documents.

Pray report to me how this object can be achieved.

WSC

---

[1] Arthur Hamilton Lee, 1868–1947. Military Attaché, Washington, 1899; that year he married Ruth Moore of New York. Conservative MP, 1910–18. Lloyd George's Personal Military Secretary, 1916. Created Baron, 1918. First Lord of the Admiralty, 1921–2 (when Churchill was Colonial Secretary). Created Viscount, 1922.

[2] Lord Lee had given Chequers to the nation, for the use of the Prime Minister of the day, on 8 January 1921. Churchill was one of the first people to be invited there by its first prime ministerial occupant, Lloyd George. In a letter to Clementine on 6 February 1921 he wrote: 'Here I am. You would like to see this place. Perhaps you will some day! It is just the kind of house you admire – a panelled museum full of history, full of treasures – but insufficiently warmed – Anyhow a wonderful possession' (*Baroness Spencer-Churchill papers*).

Winston S. Churchill to Lord Cranborne
(*Churchill papers, 20/13*)

25 December 1940 Chequers
Christmas Day

No departure in principle is contemplated from the practice of keeping the Dominions informed fully of the progress of the war. Specially full information must necessarily be given in respect of theatres where Dominion troops are serving, but it is not necessary to circulate this to the other Dominions not affected. However, on the whole an effort should be made not to scatter so much deadly and secret information over this very large circle. The Prime Ministers of every Dominion are bound to inform their colleagues, who again no doubt inform their wives and private secretaries. There is a danger that the Dominions Office staff get into the habit of running a kind of newspaper full of deadly secrets, which are circularised to the four principal Governments with which they deal. The idea is that the more they circulate, the better they are serving the State. Many other Departments fall into the same groove, loving to collect as much secret information as possible and feeling proud to circulate it conscientiously through all official circles. I am trying steadily to restrict and counteract these tendencies which, if unchecked, would make the conduct of war impossible.

While, therefore, there is no change in principle, there should be considerable soft-pedalling in practice.

I wish to be consulted before anything of a very secret nature, especially anything referring to Operations or current movements, is sent out.

WSC

Winston S. Churchill to Malcolm MacDonald and Herbert Morrison
(*Churchill papers, 20/13*)

25 December 1940 Chequers
Christmas Day

I enclose minutes of our meeting yesterday on which action is being taken.

I am convinced there should be only one authority inside the shelters, who should be responsible for everything pertaining to the health and comfort of the inmates. This authority should be charged with sanitation and storing of the bedding, &c. I cannot feel that the Home Security and Home Office, with all its burdens and duties under the enemy attack, ought to be concerned with questions affecting vermin and sanitation. These ought to be in the province of the Ministry of Health, who should be made responsible for the whole interior life of the shelters, big or small.

This would not affect the amended proposals of the Home Secretary's memorandum. The Regional Commissioner would be the executive hand carrying out the policy prescribed by the Ministry of Health inside the shelters, as well as his other duties. The assumption by the Regional Commissioner of his responsibilities must not be delayed by the transference of certain duties from Home Security to Health.

3. Pray let me know how effect can be given to the above.

WSC

John Martin: private letter
(*Martin papers*)

26 December 1940 Chequers
Boxing Day

The Prime Minister has made a great point of working as usual over the holiday and yesterday morning was like almost any other here, with the usual letters and telephone calls and of course many Christmas greeting messages thrown in. His present to me was an inscribed copy of *Great Contemporaries*.[1]

From lunch time on, less work was done and we had a festive family Christmas, with the three daughters, two sons-in-law and one daughter-in-law and no official visitors. For lunch we had the largest turkey I have ever seen, a present from Lord Rothermere's farm, sent in accordance with one of his last wishes before he died.[2]

Afterwards we listened to The King's speech and Vic Oliver played the piano and Sarah sang. It was the same after dinner. For once the shorthand writer was dismissed and we had a sort of sing-song until after midnight.

The PM sang lustily, if not always in tune, and when Vic played Viennese waltzes he danced a remarkably frisky measure of his own in the middle of the room. He then would sit up and talk till 2 a.m.; but I found him as brisk as ever this morning, cheerfully munching one of Lloyd George's apples from Churt.

[1] Churchill's volume of biographical essays, first appearing in various newspapers and magazines, and published in book form as *Great Contemporaries* in 1937.
[2] The 1st Viscount Rothermere had died on 26 November 1940.

Winston S. Churchill to Sir Edward Bridges and Professor Lindemann
(*Churchill papers, 20/13*)

26 December 1940
Boxing Day

I must examine the Import Programme for 1941 next week. 5 p.m. in the Lower War Room,[1] Monday, Tuesday and Wednesday. Agenda to be drawn up by you and Professor Lindemann. Let me see by Saturday night here. The immediate lay-out of the shipping programme in relation to food and supply and the demand for the Services in the face of present losses. Professor Lindemann will present me by Saturday night with the salient facts and graphs. To be summoned to the Meeting, the following:–
Lord President,
Lord Privy Seal,
Minister without Portfolio,
Minister of Aircraft Production,
Minister of Supply,
Ministers of Food, Transport and Shipping.[2]
(Ministers only.)

WSC

Winston S. Churchill to General Ismay
(*Churchill papers, 20/13*)

26 December 1940
Secret

I am in general agreement with COS (40) 818.[3] Tactical requirements must be paramount during invasion. I am deeply anxious that gas warfare should not be adopted at the present time. For this very reason I fear the enemy may have it in mind, and perhaps it may be imminent. Every precaution must be kept in order and every effort made to increase retaliatory power.

Sometimes I have wondered whether it would be any deterrent on the enemy if I were to say that we should never use gas ourselves unless it had first been used against us, but that we had actually in store many thousands of tons of various types of deadly gas with their necessary containers, and that we should immediately retaliate upon Germany. On the whole, I think it is perhaps better to say nothing unless or until we have evidence that the attack

[1] The Cabinet War Room.
[2] Sir John Anderson, Clement Attlee, Arthur Greenwood, Lord Beaverbrook, Sir Andrew Duncan, Lord Woolton, Colonel Moore-Brabazon and Ronald Cross.
[3] 'Plans for Employment of Gas from the Air in Retaliation for its use against us by the Enemy', a note by the Air Staff, circulated as Chiefs of Staff Paper 818 of 1940.

is imminent. After all, they can make the calculations to which Professor Lindemann refers for themselves. They would certainly say we had threatened them with gas warfare, and would soon invent a pretext. Thirdly, there would be too much bluff in any such statement. If anyone is of a different opinion, I shall be glad to know. The subject causes me much anxiety.

WSC

Winston S. Churchill to General Ismay
(*Churchill papers, 20/13*)

26 December 1940
Most Secret

PANTELLERIA ISLAND

I am becoming increasingly convinced of the need and urgency of 'Workshop,' and I am expecting to have conditions proposed to me which make it possible to carry it out before the middle of February.

WSC

Winston S. Churchill to General Ismay
(*Churchill papers, 20/13*)

26 December 1940
Most Secret

Now that there is more time to arrange about 'Workshop,' we should try to give them about four 3-inch Mortars, or if these are too heavy to manhandle, 2-inch Mortars. The Mortar is the only form of light artillery which can be used by a landing force, and something of this kind is necessary should resistance be maintained from buildings.

WSC

Winston S. Churchill to Sir Andrew Duncan
(*Churchill papers, 20/13*)

26 December 1940
ACTION THIS DAY

The discrepancy between weapons and ammunition is terrible in the case of the AT rifles, 2-inch and 3-inch Mortars, the climax being reached with the 3-inch Mortars. We have enough AT rifles to equip $23\frac{1}{2}$ Divisions, but only enough ammunition at 32,000 rounds per month to equip $5\frac{1}{2}$. We have enough 2-inch Mortars at 108 per Division to equip 33 Divisions, but ammunition at

32,400 rounds per month suffices only for 4½ Divisions. The worst of all is the 3-inch Mortar, where, oddly enough, we have at 18 per Division enough to equip nearly 40 Divisions, but at 14,000 rounds per month only enough ammunition for 1½ Divisions.

WSC

Winston S. Churchill to General Ismay
(*Churchill papers, 20/13*)

26 December 1940

What arrangements are being made to parade the Italian white prisoners to the best possible advantage? The bulk, I presume, will be led through the streets of Cairo or Alexandria. If they are to go to India, they will I suppose land at Bombay. The spectacle of large numbers of them moving through the streets of Bombay and other Indian cities would be highly beneficial. Every care should, of course, be taken to prevent their being insulted by the populace.

Films should be made and widely distributed by M of I.

WSC

Winston S. Churchill to A. V. Alexander
(*Churchill papers, 20/13*)

26 December 1940
Boxing Day

Provided that it can be arranged that four of the 15-inch can be cocked up[1] within six months from now, and all other repairs be completed, I agree to abandon my long-cherished hope, in which I have been so continuously frustrated, of making *Resolution* into an effective fighting ship for inshore action.

The story of these four ships since the war began ranks with the story of the two-gun turret of the KGV Class in the most melancholy pages of the Admiralty annals.

---

[1] 'Cocking up': alterations to improve the angle of elevation of the main armament. The four battleships were *Ramillies*, *Royal Sovereign*, *Revenge* and *Resolution*.

I hope I may have your positive assurance that the six months' condition will be fulfilled, barring enemy action, of course.[1]

WSC

Winston S. Churchill to Admiral Pound
(Churchill papers, 20/13)

26 December 1940
Secret

In view of what is stated in paragraph 5,[2] I consider a greater effort should be made to interrupt the ore traffic through the Leads during January and onwards. This should certainly come before the Iceland–Faroes Channel, which is a vast operation undertaken chiefly to use mines made for quite a different purpose, in conditions which have passed away. Now that we have not to give notice, and can lay secretly anywhere, conditions are much more favourable for mining the Norwegian coast than they were last year, but the need to act seems to be almost as great.

Pray let me have a further report.

WSC

Winston S. Churchill to President Roosevelt
(Premier papers, 3/462/1)

26 December 1940
Personal and Secret

I feel it my duty to send you the enclosed memorandum which has been prepared under my directions by the Admiralty. (Text in my immediately following telegram.[3]) Please do not suppose we are making any complaints

---

[1] Although it was almost certain in the later 1920s and early 1930s that the United States and Japan would build 16-inch gun battleships once the Washington Treaty expired on 31 December 1936, the Admiralty had felt that it could not wait that long for new designs to be developed, the lead time necessary for new armament, guns and mountings being from ten to fifteen years. They had therefore opted to make do with 15-inch guns. Churchill's irritation at having to make do with 15-inch guns was increased by the sacrifice of two even of these, coupled with the delay consequent upon the change of design.

[2] Of Admiral Pound's reply to Churchill's minute of 22 December 1940.

[3] This telegram repeated the text of an Admiralty memorandum listing defects that had been found in many of the United States destroyers. These defects, not 'our inability to man them', were the reason for the delay in bringing the destroyers into service, and to prepare them 'for the arduous conditions of the North Western Approaches'. Among the defects listed were weak bridge structure, unsatisfactory manoeuvring valves, and leaks in the hold and bulkheads. One of the destroyers, the renamed *Newmarket*, had a damaged manoeuvring valve which caused her 'to surge ahead into dock wall' at St John, Newfoundland, 'taking with her *Wells* and *Newark*', both of which had then to be further repaired. (*Premier papers, 3/462/1*.)

about the condition of these vessels. It may however be an advantage to your yards to know the kind of things that happen when ships that have been laid up so long are put into the hardest service in the Atlantic. We have of course been disappointed in the small number we have yet been able to get into service. It is not for want of trying, as our need can prove. Nor is it in any way for want of manpower. When we get a chance we are going to take two boilers out of some of them, reducing speed to 22 knots, and substituting oil fuel tanks for greater radius.

All good wishes for Christmas and the New Year.

War Cabinet: minutes
(*Cabinet papers, 65/10*)

27 December 1940   10 Downing Street
12 noon

The War Cabinet were reminded that up till now we had given full value for everything which we had obtained from the United States.

Of the fifty Destroyers which we had obtained from the United States, only nine were at present in action. A telegram was being sent to the President setting out the tale of the defects which had prevented more of these vessels from coming into immediate use.

EIRE

The Prime Minister said that it was a matter for consideration whether, in the first instance, the action taken should be limited to the withdrawal from Eire of shipping facilities which we urgently required for our own use. It was clear, however, that action in this matter must not be allowed to clash with the appeal which President Roosevelt would probably make to Congress in the near future about the financing of our munitions contracts in the United States.

War Cabinet: Confidential Annex
(*Cabinet papers, 65/16*)

27 December 1940
12 noon

The Prime Minister said that we had no wish to draw Germany down on Greece, although German intervention in the Balkans was to be anticipated in the long run. He thought, however, that we should proceed with the construction of aerodromes south of the line Olympus–Aerta. There could, of course, be no question of our bombing the Roumanian oilfields from Greek aerodromes without first having obtained the permission of the Greek Government.

The Prime Minister said that the construction of aerodromes in Turkey was also of importance. If the presence of Officers in uniform at these aerodromes presented difficulty, reconnaissance and supervision should be carried out by men in civilian clothing.

Winston S. Churchill to General Ismay
(*Churchill papers, 20/13*)

27 December 1940
ACTION THIS DAY

1. I do not recognize at all the account of my views given in the first paragraph of Section 3, 'Marie'.[1] I was under the impression that I had given a written minute. Pray let this be sought for. It is very unusual for me to give any directions other than in writing. To avoid further misunderstanding, the following is set forth:–

2. The Operation 'Marie' has been regarded by the Chiefs of the Staff, and is considered by me to be valuable and important. For this purpose, not only the Foreign Legion Battalion but two other French Battalions should be sailed in the January 4 convoy, and deposited at Port Sudan, where they can either intervene in 'Marie' or in Egypt. There is no use sending only the Foreign Legion without any other troops of the French forces. Therefore I have asked for proposals to sail transports capable of taking the other two Battalions empty from here to Freetown, so that the whole French Force can go round together.

Pray let me have to-day the proposals for giving effect to this.

There will be plenty of time to consider the political aspects when these troops have arrived at Port Sudan.

WSC

---

[1] Operation 'Marie' was the plan to enable the French forces under General de Gaulle to capture the Vichy French port of Djibouti, on the Red Sea. The first paragraph of section 3 of the Chiefs of Staff meeting minutes of 24 December 1940 read: 'Sir Robert Haining informed the Committee that the proposed transfer of Free French troops from West to East Africa had been discussed at a meeting the previous evening before the Prime Minister and the Secretary of State for War. The Prime Minister had said that if his military advisers were in favour of Operation "Marie" taking place in February, then the balance of General de Gaulle's force must be sent in convoy WS5(b), at the expense of British troops. If, on the other hand, it seemed better to postpone Operation "Marie" then the balance of the Free French troops could accompany Convoy WS6 early in February' (*Cabinet papers, 79/8*).

Winston S. Churchill to David Margesson and General Dill
(*Churchill papers, 20/13*)

27 December 1940
ACTION THIS DAY

1. Hitherto the production of AT rifles has been a bright spot, and we have nearly 30,000 already made. On the other hand, the ammunition for this weapon is deplorably in arrear, being, in fact, less than one-fifth of the proper proportion. The failure to 'marry' the ammunition and the AT rifle is one of the worst blots on our present munition programme. It is little less than a fraud to the troops to issue these large quantities of AT rifles, which would quickly become useless and worth no more than old iron through ammunition shortage. In many cases it has not been possible to allow any rounds for practice at all, these having to be saved for actual use against the enemy.

2. In these circumstances one would expect that the War Office would have concentrated their desires on ammunition, instead of increasing the already gigantic disproportion of AT rifles to ammunition. On the contrary, however, for reasons which I have never heard mentioned, the Army requirement of AT rifles is suddenly raised from 31,000 to 71,000 for the same number of Divisions. When was this decision taken; by whom; and what were the arguments? Was any attempt made at the time to make sure that the ammunition, already lagging so far behind, could catch up this enormous increase in rifles? Let me have a full report on this transaction.

3. However, the Germans have now twice bombed the Small Heath factory and checked the output of AT rifles, in a most decisive manner. There can be no possibility of fulfilling the increased War Office demand of 71,000 at the date desired. On the other hand, it is to be hoped that the ammunition supply will now have a chance of overtaking the weapons. It would therefore appear that a valuable and necessary readjustment of our programme has resulted from enemy action.

4. Arising out of the above, I wish to be informed when any large changes are made in the existing programmes for the Army, particularly when these necessitate setting up new plants, which can only be set up at the expense of other urgent work. All important modifications of the equipment tables set out in my diagrams are to be reported to me before action is taken.

WSC

Winston S. Churchill to Professor Lindemann
(*Churchill papers, 20/13*)

27 December 1940
Secret

Let me have a list showing any alterations in the approved equipment set forth in your Tables of Divisions.

You mentioned to me some weeks ago that the War Office had altered the bases. I must know about all important changes before they are sanctioned. The increase in the AT guns from 31,000 to 71,000 is a case in point.

See my minute of to-day on the subject.

WSC

Winston S. Churchill to Sir Kingsley Wood
(*Premier papers, 3/128*)

27 December 1940
Secret

Have you held your meeting on the Irish business? I propose to intimate to them that we cannot carry the 400,000 tons for them in 1941. If we do this, will not the question of the subsidies be otiose, as presumably they will not send anything back, or very little. Cutting off 400,000 tons is our strongest line, and it would be a pity to confuse it with other steps. Let me know exactly how this process is put into operation. Who gives notice and of what, and how much interval is there between the notice and the imports coming to an end?

I am not at all impressed with the favourable indications of which we have been told by the Dominions Secretary.[1] On the other hand, the timing of this action must be fitted in with President Roosevelt's financial performances and the Congress decision thereupon.

WSC

Winston S. Churchill to Colonel Moore-Brabazon
(*Churchill papers, 20/13*)

27 December 1940
Secret

It is said that two-fifths of the decline in the fertility of our shipping is due to the loss of time in turning round ships in British ports. Now that we are confined so largely to the Mersey and the Clyde, and must expect increasingly severe attacks upon them, it would seem that this problem constitutes the most dangerous part of the whole of our front.

[1] Lord Cranborne.

Would you kindly give me a note on:–
A. The facts.
B. What you are doing, and what you propose to do.
C. How can you be helped.

WSC

Colonel Hollis to Winston S. Churchill
(*Premier papers, 3/234*)

28 December 1940
Most Secret

The First Sea Lord spoke to you this afternoon about a plan which is being prepared for occupying Sicily. This is known as Operation 'Influx'. I mention the code name because I do not think you have yet been made aware of it.

The Directors of Plans submit the attached note, giving a very brief summary of the main feature of the plan. The plan itself is being considered by the Chiefs of Staff on Monday next, 30th December, and will be submitted to you early next week.

In the meanwhile, I think you would wish to see the attached summary in view of the mention which was made of it this afternoon by the First Sea Lord.[1]

Winston S. Churchill to Herbert Morrison
(*Churchill papers, 20/13*)

28 December 1940
Confidential

1. I was mildly surprised that you should have jumped to the conclusion that any leakage to *The Times* newspaper should have occurred from No. 10, and I was very glad you did not suggest that I could have been a party to such transactions. I have, however, gone into the question, and have satisfied

---

[1] Operation 'Influx' involved, in the first instance, the capture, by British forces then in the Middle East, of the Sicilian port of Catania, followed by an advance to Messina. The operation was to span twenty-five days. The forces needed would make it necessary to postpone the 'Mandibles' operation against the Dodecanese. The Joint Planners (Daniel, Playfair and Medhurst) wrote to Churchill on 27 December 1940: 'In continuation of our plans for the elimination of Italy from the war, we have now prepared a plan for the occupation of Sicily. It is based on an Italy reduced in morale but still capable of offering limited resistance. The essence of our plan is the time factor. We cannot afford to wait until Germany moves into Italy. We must take the initiative at the crucial moment' (*Premier papers, 3/234*).

myself, as you will see from the attached,[1] that there is no foundation for the suggestion which you made. If there had been leakage, it could only have been from some of those present at the meeting.

2. I do not, however, think it necessary to suppose that any leakage has taken place. The point is so obvious that anyone writing an article on Shelter Policy at the present time would naturally have referred to it. I have myself received from many quarters complaints about the overlapping, underlapping and conflict of authority in the shelters, and, when I called upon Sir Edward Bridges for a statement of what was happening, I was disturbed to see the facts, which, of course, are well known to everyone who is interested in the shelter problem.

WSC

Winston S. Churchill to Anthony Eden
(*Churchill papers, 20/13*)

29 December 1940

As you are dealing with Monsieur Dupuy I send you the enclosed,[2] of which the Admiralty should be kept informed. We should evidently continue our fitful efforts to maintain the blockade. General de Gaulle's troops are being sent to Egypt where they will be in a position either to carry out the Operation 'Marie' in March, or assist us in the Libyan campaign: we have plenty of time to consider which. If it is desired to maintain some causes of friction as a smoke screen (which will certainly not be difficult and is indeed inevitable anyhow), I should have thought the use of the term Vichy Government would be a harmless cause of resentment.

We are greatly indebted to Monsieur Dupuy for what he has done, and I am sending a cable to Mr Mackenzie King on the subject. The sooner he can get back to Vichy or North Africa the better. Vichy would be the better, in view of the turn events are taking, but we must leave it to him.

WSC

---

[1] A note by E. A. Seal, with a leading article in *The Times* of 27 December 1940 entitled 'Shelter Dangers', and a list of those who had been present at the meeting. According to the leading article, 'A great weakness in the provision of the shelter service is the division of responsibility between Government departments – the Ministers of Health and Home Security both having jurisdiction, and each being subject in some particulars to decisions by other departments – while the local responsibility rests with the borough councils. Central authority and responsibility ought to be concentrated in a single department endowed with all necessary powers and able to take and execute decisions with promptitude.'

[2] A note of the subjects examined at the talk between Churchill and Pierre Dupuy on 21 December 1940.

Winston S. Churchill to William Mackenzie King
(*Churchill papers, 20/14*)

29 December 1940

We are deeply grateful to you for Dupuy's magnificent work. We hope he will soon be back at Vichy. The Canadian channel is invaluable, and indeed at the moment our only line.

WSC

Winston S. Churchill to A. V. Alexander
(*Churchill papers, 20/13*)

29 December 1940

These ships[1] have been a great disappointment so far this war. The question of their alternative uses ought to be considered by the Admiralty. I expect they have a large number of skilled ratings on board. Could I have a list of these ships, their tonnage, speeds, &c. Could they not carry troops or stores while plying on their routes?

WSC

Winston S. Churchill to Sir Charles Portal
(*Churchill papers, 20/13*)

29 December 1940

It seems odd that only one machine should have been despatched from Takoradi during the week ending December 27, when no fewer than 44 are piled up there waiting. Is there a breakdown in the handling work at Takoradi? Could we have a special report on conditions there? Quite soon they will have the second instalment from the *Furious* upon them.

WSC

---

[1] Freighters being used as U-boat decoy ships.

Winston S. Churchill to Anthony Eden and General Ismay
(*Churchill papers, 20/13*)

30 December 1940
ACTION THIS DAY

It would seem that every effort should be made to meet the Emperor's[1] wishes.[2] We have already, I understand, stopped Erskine[3] and Brockelhurst[4] from entering the Galla country. It seems a pity to employ battalions of Ethiopian deserters, who might inflame the revolt, on mere road-making. We have 64,000 troops in Kenya, where complete passivity reigns, so they surely could spare these road-makers. On the first point I am strongly in favour of Haile Selassie entering Abyssinia. Whatever differences there may be between the various Abyssinian tribes, there can be no doubt that the return of the Emperor will be taken as a proof that the revolt has greatly increased, and will be linked up with the rumours of our victory in Libya.

I should be glad if a favourable answer could be drafted for me to send to the Emperor.

WSC

Winston S. Churchill to Sir Archibald Sinclair, Sir Charles Portal and Lord Beaverbrook
(*Churchill papers, 20/13*)

30 December 1940
ACTION THIS DAY
Secret

1. I am deeply concerned at the stagnant condition of our Bomber Force. The Fighters are going ahead well, but the Bomber Force, particularly crews, is not making the progress hoped for. I consider the rapid expansion of the

[1] Ras Tafari Makonnen, 1892–1975. Made Regent of Ethiopia after the death of his cousin King Menelek II, 1916. Crowned Emperor, 1930, taking his baptismal name Haile Selassie. Driven out by the Italians, 1936. Resident in Jerusalem, 1938–40. Re-entered Addis Ababa, May 1941. Deposed by a coup led by some of his Army officers, 1974. Died in his former palace less than a year later.

[2] The desire of the Emperor of Abyssinia, then in exile in Jerusalem, to be at the head of his own troops at the first crossing of Allied troops back into Abyssinia.

[3] Esmé Nourse Erskine, 1885–1962. On active service, 1914–18 (Military Cross). Anglo-Italian Boundary Commission, Kenya, 1925–8. Consul for Western Abyssinia, 1923–37; a botanist, he made several new botanical discoveries in Western Abyssinia which he contributed to Kew. CMG, 1937. Returned to the Foreign Office, 1939. Recalled to the Army, 1940. Political Service, Middle East, 1944.

[4] Henry Courtney Brockelhurst, 1882–1942. Entered the Army, 1908. Served in the Flying Corps in Palestine, Tanganyika and Murmansk (North Russia), 1916–19. Left the Army, 1919. Game Warden, Sudan Government, 1922. In charge of the 107 Military Mission, to Abyssinia, 1940–1. Officer Commanding Special Service Detachment, Burma, 1942. In 1918 he had married Clementine Churchill's cousin Lady Helen Mitford (from whom he was divorced in 1931). He was killed in action.

Bomber Force one of the greatest military objectives now before us. We are, of course, drawing upon the Bomber Force for the Coastal Command and for the Middle East. If the bottle-neck is, as I am told, crews, we must either have the pilots and personnel we are sending out to the Middle East returned to us after they have delivered their machines, or, what would be less injurious to formed Squadrons, have other pilots and personnel sent back from the Middle East in their place. The policy is to remount the Middle East, and this must be achieved before reinforcements of a permanent character can be indulged in. Even before the recent reinforcements, there were 1,000 pilots in the Middle East. Air Marshal Longmore must be told to send back an equal number of good men of the various classes, and not add to this already grossly distended personnel.

2. In order to increase the number of crews available, the training must be speeded up and a certain measure of dilution accepted.

3. The figures placed before me each day are deplorable. Moreover, I have been told on high authority that a substantial increase in numbers available for operations against Germany must not be expected for many months. I cannot agree to this without far greater assurance than I have now that everything in human wit and power has been done to avert such a complete failure in our Air expansion programme.

4. So far as aircraft are concerned, the question arises, from constant study of the returns, whether sufficient emphasis is put upon Bomber production. The Fighters are streaking ahead, and it is a great comfort we have so good a position in them. We must, however, increase our bomb deliveries on Germany, and it appears some of the types and patterns most adapted to this are not coming forward as we had hoped.

I am well aware of the damage done by enemy action, but I ask whether it cannot be remedied, and what further steps are possible.

5. I wish to receive a programme of expansion week by week, and also a plan set forth showing what measures can be taken to improve the position, which at present is most distressing and black.

WSC

Winston S. Churchill to General Dill
(*Churchill papers, 20/13*)

30 December 1940
Secret

We have had lately some figures of the Italian dispositions in Libya, for instance, the totals in Bardia, Tobruk and Benghazi have been mentioned. We have taken 40,000 prisoners, and it seems very probable another 10,000 men have perished in the Desert during the battle.

Altogether these figures would account for about 100,000 men.

What is the total estimated force of both black and white in the Province, and where are the rest distributed? What is known about the Italian garrison of Tripoli?

WSC

Winston S. Churchill to General Ismay
(*Churchill papers, 20/6*)

30 December 1940

STUDY OF POST-WAR PROBLEMS

Provision must now be made for the study of post-war problems. It is unnecessary to set up a grandiose Ministry of Reconstruction, but one Minister will be put in charge of the work, acting with a Committee of Ministers. This Minister will be the Minister without Portfolio. A small staff of five or six will be appointed, whose functions will be analytic and selective. They will, under instructions, obtain and sift practical reconstruction plans, to be given effect to in (say) the three years after the war. These plans should be worked out – (a) in the Departments and (b) by organisations such as Chatham House; and short statements of principle will be presented to the Ministerial Committee. Detailed implications will be worked out afterwards. The services of Junior and other Ministers will be utilised in this matter. The general aim will be to obtain a body of practical proposals which will command broadly the support of the main elements in all the political parties.

WSC

War Cabinet: minutes
(*Cabinet papers, 65/10*)

30 December 1940　　　　　　　　　　　　　　　　　　10 Downing Street
12 noon

The Prime Minister said that he thought that, although President Roosevelt's speech of the previous day had been in general terms, it had been satisfactory from our point of view, and he had been encouraged by it. It committed the United States to implacable hostility and resistance to the Three-Power Pact, while the phrase about keeping the United States out of a 'last ditch' war was, perhaps, significant.[1]

---

[1] Roosevelt began his 'Arsenal of Democracy' speech of 29 December 1940 with the words: 'This is not a fireside chat on war. It is a talk on national security; because the nub of the whole purpose of your President is to keep you now, and your children later, and your grandchildren much later, out of a last-ditch war for the preservation of American independence and all the things that American independence means to you and to me and to ours.' That was why, Roosevelt explained, the United States would serve as the arsenal for Britain and the democratic war against Nazism. (Samuel I. Rosenman, compiler, *The Public Papers and Addresses of Franklin D. Roosevelt*, 1940 volume, New York, 1941).

The War Cabinet were informed of the latest developments of the negotiations on this matter. It now seemed that the President might regard it as necessary to pass a Bill through Congress. The Chancellor of the Exchequer said that he thought that means could be found of staving off the immediate difficulty, without having recourse to the expedient proposed by President Roosevelt.

The Prime Minister asked the Chancellor of the Exchequer to discuss this matter with him later in the day, in connection with the telegram which he proposed to send to President Roosevelt thanking him for his speech.

War Cabinet: Confidential Annex
(*Cabinet papers, 65/16*)

30 December 1940
12 noon

The Prime Minister said that M. Dupuy who had already rendered invaluable services by establishing contacts with the Vichy Government was again returning to Vichy and hoped on his return journey to visit North Africa and see General Weygand. The Prime Minister said that he had prepared a Note, which had been submitted to and had received the approval of the Chiefs of Staff, for the guidance of M. Dupuy when he saw General Weygand. In this note M. Dupuy had been authorised to tell General Weygand that, if he unfurled his flag again in North Africa, we would support him to the extent of six divisions with proportionable Air Force assistance and Naval aid. (The Chiefs of Staff had felt that the allocation of such a force was not beyond our powers.) We would also be willing to enter into Staff Conversations to deal with the situation in the event of the Germans attempting to occupy Tangier.

Since this *aide-mémoire* for M. Dupuy had been written it had been suggested that Marshal Pétain was in need of support in his resistance to German demands and that it would help him if he was informed of what we were proposing to say to General Weygand. Similar information had, therefore, been sent to the Marshal on the previous Saturday.

The Prime Minister added that he now wondered whether it would be advisable to send a further message to both Marshal Pétain and General Weygand, to the effect that we would give every facility for the mobilisation and departure of the French Fleet from Alexandria should the situation demand it.

The Chief of the Imperial General Staff said that he ought to make it clear that the offer of six divisions to support the French in North Africa would be in diminution of the forces available to reinforce the Middle East.

The Prime Minister said that this was understood.

1308　December 1940

Nevile Butler[1] to Anthony Eden
(*Premier papers, 3/462/1*)

30 December 1940　　　　　　　　　　　　　　　　　Washington, DC
Most Immediate
received 9.20 p.m.

I venture to suggest that it would be undesirable to send in the Prime Minister's message to the President[2] today directly after the President's broadcast address last night. Despite the wording of the covering letter contained in your telegram No. 3738 President might feel that to deliver message just at this moment was rather ungrateful and it might have an unfortunate effect on him. I deliberately did not send in the message yesterday afternoon lest it upset the President just before his speech. I would suggest that it would be better to defer the delivery of the message for a few days until, say, January 2nd. Purvis shares this view fully.

Please inform me as soon as possible whether the Prime Minister agrees to this. If he does, he may desire to send his New Year wishes to the President in a separate telegram without delay.

On the night of Monday, 30 december 1940, the Germans dropped incendiary bombs on the City of London on an unprecedented scale, creating a swathe of fire on both banks of the River Thames. Many famous buildings were destroyed or severely damaged, including the Guildhall and eight Wren churches. Vigilant fire fighters were able to save St Paul's Cathedral from being engulfed in the flames. On the following morning Churchill visited the scenes of destruction.

Winston S. Churchill to President Roosevelt
(*Premier papers, 4/17/1*)

31 December 1940

We are deeply grateful for all you said yesterday. We welcome especially the outline of your plans for giving us the aid, without which Hitlerism cannot be extirpated from Europe and Asia. We can readily guess why you have not

---

[1] Nevile Montagu Butler, 1893–1973. On active service, 1914–18. Entered the Foreign Office, 1920. Minister at the Washington Embassy, 1940–41. An Assistant Under-Secretary of State, Foreign Office, 1944–47. Knighted, 1947. Ambassador to Brazil, 1947–51; to the Netherlands, 1952–54.

[2] This was the message about the defective destroyers, sent to the British Embassy in Washington (for transmission to the President) on 26 December 1940.

been able to give a precise account of how your proposals will be worked out. Meanwhile, some things make me anxious.

First, sending the warship to Capetown to take up the gold lying there may produce embarrassing effects. It is almost certain to become known.[1] This will disturb public opinion here and throughout the Dominions and encourage the enemy, who will proclaim that you are sending for our last reserves. If you feel this is the only way, directions will be given for the available Capetown gold to be loaded on the ship. But we should avoid it if we can. Could we, for instance, by a technical operation, exchange gold in South Africa for gold held for others at Ottawa and make the latter available for movement to New York? We must know soon, because the ship is on its way.

My second anxiety is because we do not know how long Congress will debate your proposals and how we should be enabled to place orders for armaments and pay our way if this time became protracted. Remember, Mr President, we do not know what you have in mind, or exactly what the United States is going to do, and we are fighting for our lives. What would be the effect upon the world situation if we had to default in payments to your contractors, who have their workmen to pay? Would not this be exploited by the enemy as a complete breakdown in Anglo-American co-operation? Yet, a few weeks' delay might well bring this upon us.

Thirdly, apart from the interim period, there arises a group of problems about the scope of your plan after being approved by Congress. What is to be done about the immense heavy payments still due to be made under existing orders before delivery is completed? Substantial advance payments on these same orders have already denuded our resources. We have continued need for various American commodities not definitely weapons: for instance, raw materials and oil. Canada and other Dominions, Greece and refugee Allies have clamant dollar needs to keep their war effort alive. I do not seek to know immediately how you will solve these later questions. We shall be entirely ready, for our part, to lay bare to you all our resources and our liabilities around the world, and we shall seek no more help than the common cause demands. We, naturally, wish to feel sure that the powers with which you propose to arm yourself will be sufficiently wide to deal with these larger matters, subject to all proper examination.

Sir Frederick Phillips is discussing these matters with Mr Secretary Morgenthau, and he will explain the war-commitments we have in many parts of the world for which we could not ask your direct help, but for which gold and dollars are necessary. This applies also to the Dutch and Belgian gold, which we may become under obligation to return in specie in due course.

---

[1] In an early draft of this message, Churchill had gone on to say: 'It would wear the aspect of a sheriff collecting the last assets of a helpless debtor' (*Premier papers, 4/17/1*).

They burned a large part of the City of London last night, and the scenes of widespread destruction here and in our provincial centres are shocking, but when I visited the still burning ruins to-day the spirit of the Londoners was as high as in the first days of the indiscriminate bombing in September, four months ago.

I thank you for testifying before all the world that the future safety and greatness of the American Union are intimately concerned with the upholding and the effective arming of that indomitable spirit.

All my heartiest good wishes to you in the New Year of storm that is opening upon us.

Winston S. Churchill to President Roosevelt: unsent sections[1]
(*Premier papers, 4/17/1*)

31 December 1940

There are great hopes here that you are going to invite the United States to give us substantial aid in the spirit of your declaration about the firehose.[2] But nothing of what this means has been imparted to us or to our representatives who are dealing with your financial authorities. For instance, no mention has been made of whether or how our interim payments are to be eventually covered, nor how the balance of payments under existing orders are to be met, nor do we know how long Congress will take in arriving at its decision. I feel sure from all you have said and from the general position

---

[1] Churchill made a number of stronger drafts of his letter to Roosevelt, but decided not to send them. They are printed here in the form in which they appear among his papers (*Premier papers, 4/17/1*).

[2] At a press conference in Washington on 17 December 1940, Roosevelt compared the proposed United States loan of munitions to Britain to the loan by a man of his garden hose to put out a fire in his neighbour's garden: 'Suppose my neighbor's home catches fire, and I have got a length of garden hose four or five hundred feet away: but, my Heaven, if he can take my garden hose and connect it up with his hydrant, I may help him put out the fire. Now, what do I do? I don't say to him before that operation, "Neighbor, my garden hose cost me $15; you have got to pay me $15 for it." What is the transaction that goes on? I don't want $15 – I want my garden hose back after the fire is over. All right. If it goes through the fire all right, intact, without any damage to it, he gives it back to me and thanks me very much for the use of it. But suppose it gets smashed up – holes in it – during the fire; we don't have to have too much formality about it, but I say to him, "I was glad to lend you that hose; I see I can't use it any more, it's all smashed up." He says, "How many feet of it were there?" I tell him, "There were 150 feet of it." He says, "All right, I will replace it" ' (Samuel I. Rosenman, compiler, *The Public Papers and Addresses of Franklin D. Roosevelt*, 1940 volume, New York, 1941).

adopted by the people of the United States that you have some scheme embracing all these issues.

If I have some word from you showing us where we stand and what you hope to do for us, I will gladly give directions for the gold in Capetown to be put on board any warships you may send or do anything else that may be just and fair.

It is not fitting that any nation should put itself wholly in the hands of another, least of all a nation which is fighting under increasingly severe conditions for what is proclaimed to be a cause of general concern. If I have some word from you showing us where we stand, and that the United States is going to supply us with the thousands of millions of dollars' worth of munitions which we shall need in 1941 and 1942 if Nazi-ism is to be beat, I will gladly give directions for any gold in Capetown to be put on board any warships you may send or do anything else that may be just and fair. I feel however that I should not be discharging my responsibilities to the people of the British Empire if, without the slightest indication of how our fate was to be settled in Washington, I were to part with this last reserve, from which alone we might buy a few months' food.

Whatever happens we shall certainly not give in, and I believe we can save ourselves and our own national interests for the time being. But you will not, I am sure, mind my saying that if you are not able to stand by us in all measures apart from war, we cannot guarantee to beat the Nazi tyranny and gain you the time you require for your rearmament. You may be absolutely sure that whatever you do or do not feel able to do, we shall go on to the utmost limit of our resources and strength. But I gravely fear that that strength unaided will not be sufficient to produce a world result of a satisfactory and lasting character.

Winston S. Churchill to Harold Butler
(*Premier papers, 3/462/1*)

31 December 1940
1 a.m.
Most Immediate

Message about destroyers is not urgent and you should let me know when an opportune moment arrives for imparting these facts. Any time in the next fortnight will do.

Winston S. Churchill to President Roosevelt
(*Premier papers, 3/462/1*)

31 December 1940
2.30 p.m.
Immediate

I believe you know that we have not yet been able to bring many of your destroyers into action. As I have seen it stated that this is due to our inability to man them I should like to tell you that this is not the case. Indeed, we could man another thirty destroyers from America from April next onwards, besides your first fifty. The main reason for delay has been the necessity for carrying out considerable dockyard work to fit them for service in the arduous conditions of the north western approaches. Extensive re-conditioning is, of course, inevitable in the case of ships laid up for long periods, and the Admiralty is giving your Naval Attaché here details of the work we have found necessary, as it may be valuable for you to have them in case you want to work up any of the destroyers lying in your yards.

John Colville: diary
(*Colville papers*)

31 December 1940

Spent much of the day in attendance on the PM, who was in mellow mood especially when inspecting two of Herbert Morrison's new domestic shelters (intended, I suspect, as rivals to Anderson's successful creation) upon the stresses and strains of which he could demonstrate his technical knowledge as a builder.

Winston S. Churchill to Marshal Pétain
(*Churchill papers, 20/14*)

31 December 1940

If at any time in the near future the French Government decide to cross to North Africa or resume the war there against Italy and Germany, we would be willing to send a strong and well-equipped Expeditionary Force of up to six Divisions to aid the defence of Morocco, Algiers and Tunis. These Divisions could sail as fast as shipping and landing facilities were available. We now have a large, well-equipped army in England, and have considerable spare Forces already well-trained and rapidly improving, apart from what are needed to repel invasion. The situation in the Middle East is also becoming good.

2. The British Air Force has now begun its expansion, and would also be able to give important assistance.

3. The Command of the Mediterranean would be assured by the reunion of the British and French Fleets and by our joint use of Moroccan and North African bases.

4. We are willing to enter into Staff talks of the most secret character with any military representatives nominated by you.

5. On the other hand, delay is dangerous. At any time the Germans may, by force or favour, come down through Spain, render unusable the anchorage at Gibraltar, take effective charge of the batteries on both sides of the Straits and also establish their air forces in the aerodromes. It is their habit to strike swiftly, and if they establish themselves on the Moroccan Coast, the door would be shut on all projects. The situation may deteriorate any day, and prospects be ruined unless we are prepared to plan together and act boldly. It is most important that the French Government should realise that we are able and willing to give powerful and growing aid. But this may presently pass beyond our power.

Winston S. Churchill to Anthony Eden
(Churchill papers, 20/13)

31 December 1940

One would think the Emperor would be the best judge of when to risk his life for his Throne. In your minute you speak of our being 'stampeded into premature and possibly catastrophic action.' I do not wish at all to be 'stampeded,' but I should like to know some of the reasons why nothing is to be done for some months yet for the Emperor. I should have hoped the telegram to him could have been more forthcoming, and the one to Sir Miles Lampson rather more positive. These are, however, only matters of emphasis, and if with your knowledge, gathered on the spot you are apprehensive of giving more clear guidance, I do not press for alteration of the telegrams.

The question of what pledges we give to Haile Selassie about his restoration, and what are our ideas about the Italian position in East Africa, assuming that our operations prosper, as they may, is one which I was glad to hear from you this morning is receiving Foreign Office attention.[1]

WSC

[1] On 20 January 1941 Haile Selassie flew from the Sudan to the Ethiopian border at Um Idla, where Orde Wingate, commander of Gideon Force (which had been formed for operations in Northern Abyssinia), awaited him with the 2nd Ethiopian Battalion. This battalion was formed of Ethiopian refugees led by British officers and NCOs. Gideon Force comprised a battalion of the Sudanese Defence Force, also with British officers and NCOs.

Winston S. Churchill to Sir Archibald Sinclair
(*Cabinet papers, 120/300*)

31 December 1940

This[1] is the most serious and precise of the many melancholy reports we are having of our Air bombing. I hope you will address yourself further to the matter, which causes me a great deal of anxiety, and also the Cabinet.

WSC

---

[1] Telegram No. 605 from the British Embassy in Budapest, reporting that the United States Naval Attaché in Berlin Commander A. E. Schrader, had stated that British air raids on Berlin had done 'little damage'.

Appendices

Appendix A

CODE NAMES

Abigail: a 200-bomber air raid on a German town
Alloy: plan to seize the Azores
Ambassador: a raid on German-occupied Guernsey
Brisk: plan to seize the Portuguese Azores
Catapult: the British attack on the French navy at Oran
Catherine: a British naval entry into the Baltic
Challenger: the occupation of Ceuta
Collar: ships in convoy Gibraltar–Malta–Alexandria (November 1940)
Compass: General Wavell's Western Desert offensive (November 1940)
Counterpoise: plan to seize Ceuta from Spain
Cultivator: a trench-digging machine
Dhqy: operations against Portuguese East Africa (Mozambique)
Dhqz: operations against Portuguese West Africa (Angola)
Drink: the setting up of a British naval base in Suda Bay, Crete
Egglayer: aerial mines
Excess: fast Mediterranean convoy (January 1941)
Felix: a German plan to seize Gibraltar and close the Strait
Force H: a British naval force based on Gibraltar, operating in the Mediterranean
Force M: the British naval force off Dakar (Operation 'Menace')
Grind: a British occupation of Tangier
Hats: ships in convoy through the Mediterranean
Headache: German beam for guiding planes to their target
Humour: a small British force to help the Spaniards resist the Germans in Spanish Morocco
Index: the establishment of British air bases on Crete
Influx: the occupation of Sicily
Leopards: Storm troops (British)
Lucid: a plan to send fireships into German-controlled French ports

1316

Mandibles: the seizure of the Italian Dodecanese Islands
Marie: Free French plan to take Jibouti from Vichy France
Marines/Royal Marine: mines for the Rhine
Menace: an Anglo-French landing at Dakar
Moonlight Sonata: German air raid on Coventry, 14 November 1940
Paddock: the emergency government centre at Dollis Hill
Paul: a plan to mine the approaches to Luleå
Scipio: a French landing at Dakar
Shrapnel: plan to seize the Cape Verde Islands
Susan: a possible amphibious landing in North Africa
Threat: a possible amphibious landing in Morocco
Workshop: the seizure of Pantelleria Island

Appendix B

ABBREVIATIONS

AA: anti-aircraft
AB: aerial bombsight
ACIGS: Assistant Chief of the Imperial General Staff
AD: anti-aircraft ammunition
ADC: Aide-de-Camp
ADGB: Air Defence of Great Britain
AFS: Auxiliary Fire Service
AFV; Armoured Fighting Vehicle
AGRM: Adjutant-General, Royal Marines
AI: air interception airborne night radar
AOC: Army Ordnance Corps
ARP: Air Raid Precautions
AS: anti-submarine
ASC: Army Service Corps
Asdic: anti-submarine detection
ASU: Air Storage Unit, aircraft in storage
ASV sets: air-to-surface vessel, an airborne radar device
AT: Anti-Tank (rifle, gun)
ATS: Auxiliary Territorial Service
BAFF: British Advanced Fighter Force
BEF: British Expeditionary Force
CAS: Chief of the Air Staff
CD guns: guns with radar direction finding attachments
CID: Committee of Imperial Defence
CIGS: Chief of the Imperial General Staff
CNS: Chief of the Naval Staff

C-in-C: Commander-in-Chief
COS: Chiefs of Staff
CWR: Central (or Cabinet) War Room(s)
DCO: Director of Combined Operations
DNC: Director of Naval Construction
EF: Expeditionary Force
FO: Foreign Office
GHQ: General Headquarters
GL sets: gun-laying sets, a ground based radar device that could be mounted on anti-aircraft guns
GM: George Medal
GOC: General Officer Commanding
GPC: Gel Permeation Chromatography
GQG: Grand-Quartier Général
HE: High Explosive
HE: His Excellency
H/L: House of Lords
HM: His Majesty
HMG: His Majesty's Government
HRH: His Royal Highness
HX: convoys leaving Halifax, Nova Scotia, for British ports
I Tanks: Infantry Tanks
ICI: Imperial Chemical Industries
IE: initial equipments (for Royal Air Force crews)
JATC: Joint Air Training Corps, for training British and Canadian pilots and aircrew in Canada
KAR: King's African Rifles
KGV: the battleship *King George V*
LAM: Land Arm Mode, an automatic aircraft-landing device
L of C: Lines of Communication
LDV: Local Defence Volunteers (later Home Guard)
LPTB: London Passenger Transport Board
MAP: Minister of Aircraft Production
MASB: Motorised Anti-Submarine Boat
ME: Middle East
MEW: Ministry of Economic Warfare
MGO: Master-General of Ordnance
M of I: Ministry of Information
M of S: Ministry of Supply
MT: motor transport
MTB: motor torpedo boat
mg: machine gun
NAAFI: The Navy, Army and Air Force Institutes

OTU: Officer Training Unit (Royal Air Force)
PAC: Parachute and Cable device, an anti-aircraft rocket
PBY: Catalina flying boats
PE fuzes: an anti-aircraft device, for ground fire against attacking aircraft
PF: Proximity fuze
RAE: Royal Aircraft Establishment (at Farnborough)
RDF: radio direction finding (radar)
SAA: small arms ammunition
SAP: sonic armour-piercing (ammunition)
SBNO: Senior British Naval Officer
ST bomb: Sticky Type bomb, an anti-tank grenade
SWC: Supreme War Council
UBD: U-Boat Destroyer
UP weapon: Unrotated Projectile, an anti-aircraft rocket
UXB: un-exploded bomb
VCNS: Vice-Chief of the Naval Staff
WA: Western Approaches
WP: War Cabinet Paper
WS: convoys from Britain to the Middle East via the Cape of Good Hope
Y list: the study of uncoded enemy wireless traffic
Z Force: the Canadian troops in Iceland

Appendix C

WAR CABINET, MAY–DECEMBER 1940

Prime Minister and Minister of Defence
  Winston S. Churchill (from 10 May 1940)
Lord President of the Council
  Neville Chamberlain (from 11 May 1940)
  Sir John Anderson (from 3 October 1940)
Lord Privy Seal
  Clement Attlee (from 11 May 1940)
Secretary of State for Foreign Affairs
  Viscount Halifax (from 11 May 1940)
  Anthony Eden (from 22 December 1940)
Minister without Portfolio
  Arthur Greenwood
Minister for Aircraft Production
  Lord Beaverbrook (in War Cabinet from 2 August 1940)
Chancellor of the Exchequer
  Sir Kingsley Wood (in War Cabinet from 3 October 1940)

Minister of Labour and National Service
   Ernest Bevin (in War Cabinet from 3 October 1940)

MINISTERS NOT IN THE WAR CABINET, MAY–DECEMBER 1940

First Lord of the Admiralty
   A. V. Alexander (from 11 May 1940)
Minister of Agriculture and Fisheries
   Robert Hudson (from 14 May 1940)
Secretary of State for Air
   Sir Archibald Sinclair (from 11 May 1940)
Minister for Aircraft Production
   Lord Beaverbrook (from 14 May 1940, War Cabinet from 2 August)
Secretary of State for Colonial Affairs
   Lord Lloyd (from 12 May 1940)
Secretary of State for Dominion Affairs
   Viscount Caldecote (from 14 May 1940)
   Viscount Cranborne (from 3 October 1940)
Minister for Economic Warfare
   Hugh Dalton (from 15 May 1940)
President of the Board of Education
   H. Ramsbotham (from 14 May 1940)
Chancellor of the Exchequer
   Sir Kingsley Wood (from 12 May 1940, War Cabinet from 3 October)
Minister of Food
   Lord Woolton (from 13 May 1940)
Minister of Health
   Malcolm MacDonald (from 13 May 1940)
Secretary of State, Home Office and Home Security
   Sir John Anderson (from 12 May 1940)
   Herbert Morrison (from 3 October 1940)
Secretary of State for India and Burma
   L. S. Amery (from 13 May 1940)
Minister of Information
   Alfred Duff Cooper (from 12 May 1940)
Minister of Labour and National Service
   Ernest Bevin (from 13 May 1940, War Cabinet from 3 October)
Chancellor of the Duchy of Lancaster
   Lord Hankey (from 14 May 1940)
Lord Chancellor
   Viscount Simon (from 12 May 1940)
Paymaster-General
   Viscount Cranborne (15 May to 2 October 1940)

Minister of Pensions
  Sir W. Womersley (from 15 May 1940)
Postmaster-General
  W. S. Morrison (from 15 May 1940)
Minister, Scottish Office
  Ernest Brown (from 14 May 1940)
Minister of Shipping
  Ronald Cross (from 14 May 1940)
Minister of Supply
  Herbert Morrison (from 12 May 1940)
  Sir Andrew Duncan (from 3 October 1940)
President of the Board of Trade
  Sir Andrew Duncan (from 12 May 1940)
  Oliver Lyttelton (from 3 October 1940)
Minister of Transport
  Sir John Reith (from 14 May 1940)
  J. Moore-Brabazon (from 3 October 1940)
Secretary of State for War
  Anthony Eden (from 11 May 1940)
  David Margesson (from 22 December 1940)

Appendix D

SENIOR OFFICERS AND CIVIL SERVANTS MENTIONED IN THE DOCUMENTS

First Sea Lord and Chief of the Naval Staff
  Admiral of the Fleet Sir Dudley Pound
Vice-Chief of the Naval Staff
  Vice-Admiral Tom Phillips
Second Sea Lord
  Admiral Sir Charles Little
Third Sea Lord and Controller
  Rear-Admiral Bruce Fraser
Fifth Sea Lord and Chief of Naval Air Services
  Vice-Admiral G. C. C. Royle
Assistant Chief of the Naval Staff
  Vice-Admiral A. J. Power

Chief of the Air Staff
  Air Chief Marshal Sir Cyril L. N. Newall
  Air Marshal Sir Charles Portal (from October 1940)

Vice-Chief of the Air Staff
 Air Marshal Richard Peirse (April–October 1940)
  (from October 1940)

Deputy Chief of the Air Staff
 Air Vice-Marshal W. S. Douglas
Assistant Chief of the Air Staff
 Air Marshal Sir P. B. Joubert de la Ferté

Chief of the Imperial General Staff
 General Sir Edmund W. Ironside
 General Sir John Dill (from 27 May 1940)
Commander-in-Chief, Home Forces
 General Sir Edmund W. Ironside (from 27 May to 23 July 1940)
 General Sir Alan Brooke (from 23 July 1940)
General Officer Commanding in Chief, Anti-Aircraft Command
 Lieutenant-General Sir Frederick Pile
General Officer Commanding British Troops in Ireland
 Lieutenant General Sir H. R. Pownall
Vice-Chief of the Imperial General Staff
 General Sir John Dill
 Lieutenant-General Sir R. H. Haining (from 27 May 1940)
Assistant Chief of the Imperial General Staff
 Major-General G. N. Macready
Director of Armoured Fighting Vehicles, War Office
 Major-General V. V. Pope
Director-General of Army Requirements
 R. J. Sinclair

Air Officer Commanding-in-Chief, Fighter Command
 Air Chief Marshal Sir Hugh Dowding
Air Officer Commanding in Chief, Bomber Command
 Air Marshal Sir Charles Portal (April–October 1940)
 Air Marshal Sir Richard Peirse (from October 1940)
Air Officer Commanding-in-Chief, Coastal Command
 Air Chief Marshal Sir Frederick Bowhill
Air Officer Commanding Northern Ireland
 Air Commodore C. Carr
Air Officer Commanding Middle East
 Air Vice-Marshal Longmore

Commander-in-Chief, Home Fleet
 Admiral of the Fleet Sir Charles Forbes
 Admiral J. C. Tovey (from November 1940)

Commander-in-Chief, Nore
  Admiral Sir Reginald Plunkett-Ernle-Erle-Drax
Commander-in-Chief, Portsmouth
  Admiral Sir William James
Commander-in-Chief, Rosyth
  Vice-Admiral C. G. Ramsey
Commander-in-Chief, Western Approaches
  Admiral Sir M. E. Dunbar-Nasmith
Vice-Admiral for Dover
  Vice-Admiral Sir Bertram Ramsay
Chief of Staff, The Nore
  Rear-Admiral H. C. Rawlings
Commander-in-Chief Mediterranean
  Admiral Sir Andrew Cunningham

Secretary of the War Cabinet
  Sir Edward Bridges
Permanent Under-Secretary of State for War
  Sir P. J. Grigg

MAPS

1. The Western Blitzkrieg
2. Dunkirk
3. The Fall of France
4. Awaiting invasion
5. The Thames Valley
6. Oran and Western Europe
7. The Blitz
8. Daker
9. West Africa
10. The Western Desert
11. The Mediterranean

1. The Western Blitzkrieg

2. Dunkirk

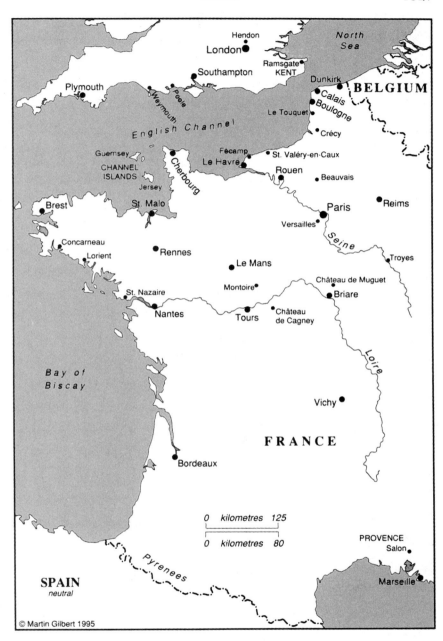

3. The Fall of France

4. Awaiting invasion

5. The Thames Valley

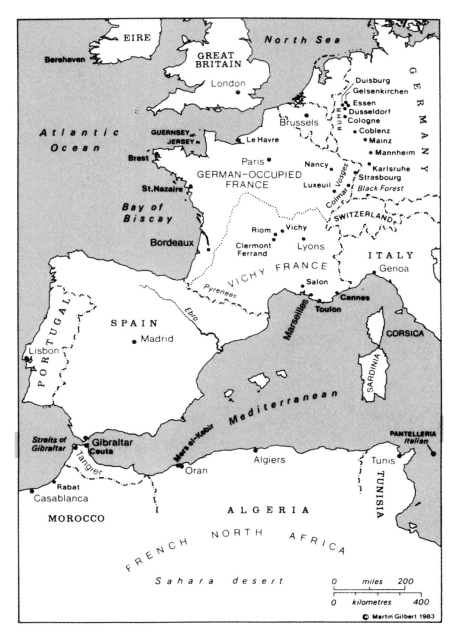

6. Oran and Western Europe

7. The Blitz

8. Daker

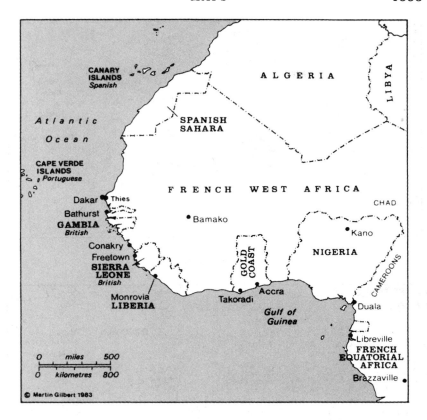

9. West Africa

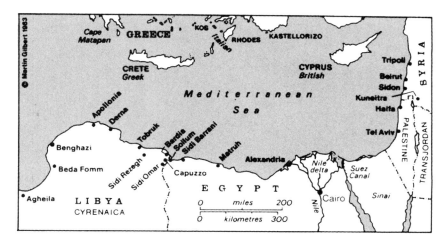

10. The Western Desert

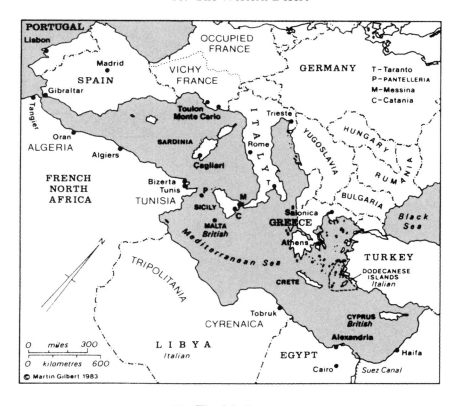

11. The Mediterranean

Index

Compiled by the Author
The subject entries appear under Churchill, (Sir) Winston Leonard Spencer

Abercorn, 3rd Duke of: 1148
Abrial, Admiral: 111, 209, 210, 211, 215, 223, 225, 395
Acland, Sir Richard: 22, 551
Adams, Vyvyan: 1099–1100
Aeneas: 946
Agnew, Sir Andrew: 882
Albery, Sir Irving: 23
Alderson, Thomas Hopper: 717 n.1
Alexander of Yugoslavia, King: 31 n.1
Alexander, A.V. (later Viscount): (in May 1940), 7, 13, 78, 82 n.2, 98, 99, 120, 133; (in June 1940), 250, 344, 359 n.1, 387, 393 n.1, 414, 428; (in July 1940), 456, 490, 590; (in August 1940), 649, 666, 751; (in September 1940), 799, 805 n.2; (in October 1940), 893, 899 n.1, 955 n.1; (in November 1940), 1025, 1032, 1052, 1133, 1152; (in December 1940), 1178, 1215–6, 1244; Churchill's minutes to (May 1940), 102, 201; (June 1940), 281–2, 354, 354–5, 373, 428–9, 443; (July 1940), 481, 482, 483, 486, 487, 498, 499, 505, 524–5, 536, 547–8, 548, 552, 554, 556–7, 558–9, 578, 582; (August 1940), 597, 599, 606, 608–9, 634, 664–5, 684, 705–6, 717, 719, 720; (September 1940), 755–6, 766–7, 770, 780–1, 785–6, 787, 792–3, 811–3, 834, 860–1, 874; (October 1940), 952–3, 954–5, 964, 987–8; (November 1940), 1029, 1104, 1114, 1126–7, 1128–9, 1158–9, 1162; (December 1940), 1170, 1172, 1175–6, 1180–1, 1197, 1218, 1229, 1233, 1295–6, 1303
Alexander, General Sir Harold (later Field Marshal Viscount): 59 n.1, 197, 210, 225, 1236
Allen, Captain G.R.G.: 459 n.2
Altham, Captain Edward: 767
Altmeyer, General René: 296 n.1
Altmeyer, General Robert: 296–7

Amery, L.S.: 29 n.2, 30, 184, 235, 368, 397–8, 446, 447, 496, 506–7, 508 n.1, 529, 557 n.2, 571–3, 574, 583, 585, 758, 939, 940, 996, 1002–3, 1041, 1181–2, 1210, 1251, 1256
Anchises: 946
Anderson, Sir John (later Viscount Waverley): 11, 40 n.3, 41, 106, 134 n.1, 144, 286, 444, 503, 598, 650 n.1, 682, 707, 886, 886 n.1, 915, 955 n.1, 1152, 1293, 1312; Churchill's letters and minutes to, 387, 399, 440, 446, 546, 550, 602–3, 764–5, 786, 835, 850–1
Andrews, James Miller: 1216
Anne, Queen: 794
Ansaldo, Giovanni: 276
Anzani, Signor: 596 n.4
Aosta, Duke of: 1239
Aras, Tewfik Pasha: 1015
Archer, Lieutenant-Commander (Colonel) Norman Ernest: 280 notes 1 and 2, 491
Asquith, H.H. (later Earl of Oxford and Asquith): 5 n.2, 1142
Astor, Major J.J.: 1154 n.2
Astrid, Queen (of the Belgians): 44 n.1
Attila the Hun (recalled), 1287
Attlee, Clement (later Earl): (pre-war), 365 n.1, 685 n.2; (in May 1940), 7, 18–19, 20, 21 n.1, 25, 29 n.2, 40, 41, 42, 120, 124–5, 156, 157, 159, 190, 203, 20_, 218; (in June 1940), 281, 320–1, 349, 350, 368; (in July 1940), 503–4, 508 n.1, 550, 585; (in August 1940), 596, 600, 602–3, 653, 660, 700, 711; (in September 1940), 768, 769; (in October 1940), 923, 936, 955 n.1, 957; (in November 1940), 1136; (in December 1940), 1206, 1293; Churchill's letters and minutes to, 550, 602–3, 653
Auchinleck, General (Sir) Claude: 330–1, 511, 931

Bailey, Sir Abe: 1224
Balbo, Italo: 155
Baldwin of Bewdley, Earl (Stanley Baldwin): 94, 248–9, 447, 586 n.1, 643, 1123, 1221, 1268
Balfour, A.J. (later Earl): 232
Balfour, Captain Harold (later Baron Balfour of Inchrye): 44, 986, 1160
Balsan, Consuelo: 517 n.1
Baring, Maurice: 846 n.4
Barker, Charles: 965 n.2, 1132
Barker, Lieutenant-General M.G.H.: 455, 617 n.3, 622, 681
Barnes, Alfred: 541
Barnes, Major-General Sir Reginald: 5–6
Barnett, Correlli: cited, 859 n.1
Barratt, Air Marshal (Sir) Arthur (later Air Chief Marshal): 37, 50 n.3, 66, 91, 100, 101, 234, 240, 265, 298–9, 300–1, 303
Barrymore, Lionel: 942
Bartlett, Vernon: 551, 1142
Baruch, Bernard: 'your people are not doing much', 436
Bastianini, Giuseppe: 186
Battersby, Samuel: 788–9
Baudouin, Paul: 54 n.2, 310, 317–8, 318 n.1, 892, 898, 956, 957
Beamish, Rear-Admiral Tufton: 950
Beaton, (Sir) Cecil: 1111
Beatty, 2nd Earl of: 1279
Beatty, Countess of (Dorothy Power): 1279
Beaverbrook, Lord (Sir Max Aitken): (in May 1940), 9 n.1, 15, 30, 34, 92; (in June 1940), 235, 248, 252 n.1, 255, 264, 274, 281, 331, 337 n.1, 388 n.2, 431, 441, 443; (in July 1940), 462, 485, 528, 560, 576, 580; (in August 1940), 599, 600; (a member of the War Cabinet, August 1940), 607–8, 610, 673, 680, 700, 711, 721 n.1; (September 1940), 768 n.1, 782, 807–8, 840, 874 n.2, 886 n.1; (October 1940), 903, 905 n.2, 923, 932–3, 941, 951, 955 n.1, 990, 1008; (November 1940), 1029, 1130, 1152, 1158, 1161; (December 1940), 1178, 1206, 1233 n.2, 1235, 1244, 1278, 1293; at Tours (13 June 1940), 314 n.1, 315, 413, and the King, 629; 'brutal ruthlessness of', 644; praise for 647, 693, 727, 961; ill, 885–6; and babies, 1002; resigns, 1032; his resignation refused, 1174; Churchill's minutes and letters to, 137–8, 258–9, 283, 454, 492–3, 637, 731–2, 732, 847–8, 871, 976, 1007–8, 1097, 1170, 1174, 1229, 1238–9, 1240–1, 1275–6, 1304–5
Beckett, Mrs Muriel: 806
Beckett-Overy, H.: 1016 n.3
Beechman, Captain N.A.: 551–2
Beigbeder, Colonel John: 424 n.1, 875, 987, 992

Beit, Sir Alfred: 206
Bellairs, Rear-Admiral R.M.: 1209
Bellenger, F.J.: 382, 466, 959
Beneš, Dr Eduard: 685 n.2, 695
Benn, David Wedgwood: 493
Benn, Tony: 493 n.2
Benn, William Wedgwood (later Viscount Stansgate): 493, 1151
Benoist, Baron de: 1065
Benson, (Sir) Arthur: 621 n.1
Bergeret, Colonel: 54 n.2
Bergonzoli, Lieutenant-General Annibale: 1125 n.1
Berkeley, Captain Claude: 30, 94, 140, 159–60, 205–6, 288, 298 n.1, 309 n.2, 350, 830, 1079, 1247
Bessborough, Lord and Lady: 535 n.1, 1021
Bevan, Aneurin: 1049, 1058, 1142
Bevin, Ernest: 7, 29 n.2, 131–2, 217, 371, 586, 600, 602, 638 n.1, 651, 673, 768, 770, 886 n.1, 949 n.1, 955 n.1
Bevir, (Sir) Anthony: 34, 123 n.2, 159, 336, 549 n.1, 936 n.1, 965 n.2, 1096, 1132, 1180, 1247
Bickell, J.P.: 932
Bickford, Edith: 583
Bickford, Commander E.O.: 583
Bickford, Valerie (Valerie Courtney): 583 and n.
Billotte, General Gaston: 83, 95, 104, 107, 111, 113, 171, 182
Birkenhead, 1st Earl of (F.E. Smith): 846 n.2, 996–7, 1224
Bishop, Air Marshal William ('Billy Bishop') VC: 932, 941
Bismarck, Otto von: 1032–3
Blakeney, Sir Percy (a character in fiction): 404 n.1
Blanch, Joseph William: 569
Blanchard, General: 111, 113, 125, 129, 131, 147, 151–2, 171, 172–3, 173, 182, 186, 209, 211, 215, 216, 223
Blennerhassett, Flight-Lieutenant: 303
Bloch, Michael: quoted, 555 n.3
Bloch-Lainé, J.F.: 372 n.2
Blum, Léon: 685 n.2
Boissier, Arthur Paul: 996
Boisson, General: 698
Bond, General (Sir) L.V.: 836
Bonham Carter, Violet (later Baroness Asquith of Yarnbury): 2–3
Bonvin, Louis: 747 n.1
Boothby, (Sir) Robert (later Baron): 45 n.1, 846 n.4, 958–9, 1140–1
Bourdillon, Sir Bernard Henry: 614, 632
Bourne, General (Sir) A.G.B.: 489, 490, 499, 531
Bowhill, Air Marshal Sir Frederick: 638 n.1, 651
Boyle, Air Commodore J.D.: 162

INDEX

Bracken, Brendan (later Viscount): 34, 123 n.2, 140, 206, 232, 248, 331, 443, 493, 534–5, 539, 629, 998, 1080, 1096, 1098 n.1, 1154 n.2, 1158 n.2, 1161, 1236, 1266
Braithwaite, (Sir) Joseph Gurney: 122
Bridgeman, Humphrey: 1256 n.1
Bridges, Sir Edward (later Baron): 10 n.2, 68, 136, 237, 483, 500, 531, 549, 596, 600, 602, 611, 650, 680, 711–12, 791 n.1, 805, 810–11, 811 n.2, 829, 850–1, 881, 881–2, 903–4, 905 n.2, 931, 955 n.1, 968, 988–90, 1031, 1057, 1065, 1069, 1084 n.1, 1086–7, 1124, 1180, 1200, 1243, 1290, 1293, 1302
Brocklehurst, Colonel H.C.: 1304
Brodrick, St John (later Viscount Midleton): 2
Brooke, General (Sir) Alan (later Viscount Alanbrooke): 327–30, 333–4, 356, 439 n.2, 531–2, 532, 550 n.1; Commander-in-Chief, Home Forces, 558–9, 639, 640, 754, 778, 784, 798–9, 804, 849–50, 934, 964, 972 n.1, 1012–3, 1098, 1164; Chief of the Imperial General Staff, 891 n.3; at Chequers, 931
Brooke, Ronnie: 532 n.1
Brooke, Victor: 532 n.1
Brownlow, 2nd Baron: 1161
Bryant, Sir Arthur: 329 n.1
Bullitt, William C.: 185, 307, 577, 855 n.2
Burton, (Sir) G.D.: 1035
Bushe, Sir Grattan: 596 n.4
Butler, Harold: 1215, 1308, 1311
Butler, R.A. (later Baron): 44–5, 419–20, 420 n.1, 592, 842, 1251
Butt, David Bensusan: 1280

Cadogan, Sir Alexander: 53, 159, 191, 200, 278, 314 n.1, 359, 360, 369, 401, 405, 479, 551, 709, 735, 799 n.2, 838, 844–5, 853, 853–4, 955 n.1, 957 n.1, 998, 1220, 1237, 1252, 1267
Caldecote, Viscount (Sir Thomas Inskip): 321, 488 n.1, 623, 634, 643, 650 n.1, 878, 886 n.1, 1040 n.2, 1051
Campbell, Sir Gerald: 590, 932, 941, 1267
Campbell, Mrs Patrick: 47 n.2
Campbell, Sir Ronald: 54 n.2, 110, 206, 217, 220, 240, 253, 266, 273, 280, 314 n.1, 315, 325, 341, 342, 346 n.1, 348, 349, 351, 357, 371, 1093
Campbell, (Sir) Ronald Ian: 1133
Camrose, 1st Baron (later Viscount): 43, 127–8, 846
Carr, General Laurence: 352, 370, 1055, 1056
Cartland, (Dame) Barbara: 128 n.2
Cartland, Ronald: 128
Cary, (Sir) Robert: 960
Catroux, General Georges: 615, 843, 857, 1165 n.2
Catskill, Rupert: his 'wild imaginings', 907 n.1
Cavour, Count: 1285

Cazalet, Victor: 483–4, 616–7, 972 n.1, 991–2, 1150–2
Cecil, Lord Hugh (later Baron Quickswood): 48, 1272
Chamberlain, Anne (Mrs Neville Chamberlain): 19, 845, 968, 1062, 1076, 1080
Chamberlain, Sir Austen: 685 n.2, 889, 1082
Chamberlain, Joseph: 890, 1082
Chamberlain, Neville: and the coming of war in 1939, 940 n.2, 1142; Churchill's letters to, 7–9, 49, 106, 449, 450, 503–4, 550, 607–8, 700, 751–2, 794, 866, 871–2, 884, 889, 967–8; his letters to Churchill, 9, 78, 399 n.3, 686, 739–40, 890, 967; becomes Lord President of the Council (10 May 1940), 9; (in May 1940), 10, 12, 15, 19, 20, 21 n.1, 24 n.2, 28, 40, 43, 70; (in June 1940), 386; and Churchill's visits to France, 53, 62 n.1, 109; and the withdrawal of the British Expeditionary Force, 68; and evacuation, 74; his notes for a Churchill broadcast, 75–6; and the fall of France, 154, 156, 157, 159, 167, 184, 191, 248, 322 n.1; and Lloyd George, 194–5, 255, 1221; and Churchill, 505, 1050, 1221; and Italy, 223; and internment, 237; and Norway, 278; and the United States, 333; and Sweden, 375; and Eire, 379; and a 'continuing vendetta', 281; and Munich and appeasement, 476, 1099 n.2, 1268; and de Gaulle, 401; and India, 557; and Japan, 588; no word against, 447; his broadcast (30 June 1940), 449, 467; and German peace offers, 603; and the King, 629; and the Battle of Britain, 673–4; and economic policy, 703; his illness, 845, 866, 871–2, 884, 886 n.1, 925–6, 1061–2, 1070; Churchill proposes Order of the Garter to, 889; his death, 1076, 1077–8, 1080–2; Churchill's obituary of, 1080–2, 1123; his 'brilliant mind' recalled, 1154 n.1
Champon, General: 172
Channon, (Sir) Henry: 44, 248, 546, 565, 592, 779, 898, 1050, 1053, 1058, 1089, 1093, 1204
Chaplin, Charlie: 1236, 1241
Charles I, King: 366 n.2, 1204
Chatfield, 1st Baron: 835, 846 n.4, 872, 1276
Chatham, Earl of (the elder Pitt): 934
Chautemps, Camille: 351, 925, 957
Chiang Kai-shek: 478 n.2, 479, 535, 554
Chollet, Fernand: 304 n.1
Churchill, Clarissa (later Countess of Avon): 1123 n.2
Churchill, Clementine (later Baroness Spencer-Churchill): (in May 1940), 4, 80, 127, 128, 193, 197, 205; (in June 1940), 440 n.2; (in July 1940), 485, 580; (in August 1940), 601, 643; (in September 1940), 779, 820 n.1, 847; (in October 1940), 931, 944 n.2, 968 n.1, 972 n.1, 1017; (in November

Churchill, Clementine—*contd.*
1940), 1033, 1157; (in December 1940), 1199, 1236, 1245 n.1, 1289 n.1, 1290 n.2, 1304 n.4; a word of warning from, 425–6; and her husband's leadership of the Conservative Party, 927–8

Churchill, Lady Gwendeline: 1123 n.3

Churchill, Major John S. ('Jack'): 629, 789, 1123 n.2

Churchill, Mary (later Lady Soames): 127, 638 n.1, 643, 644, 927–8, 931, 933, 1033, 1123 n.2, 1199, 1220, 1221, 1289 n.1, 1292

Churchill, Pamela (Mrs Averell Harriman): 231, 617, 651, 791 n.1, 934, 1123 n.2, 1144 n.1, 1161, 1199, 1289 n.1, 1292

Churchill, Lady Randolph: 47 n.2, 421 n.1, 598 n.1

Churchill, Randolph S.: 16, 70-1, 231, 248, 252, 377 n.2, 432 n.1, 444, 446, 617, 629, 638 n.1, 651, 846, 911, 931, 934, 1123 n.2, 1144, 1151, 1162, 1289 n.1

Churchill, Sarah (Mrs Vic Oliver, later Lady Audley): 4, 5, 756 n.1, 1199, 1236 n.3, 1289 n.1, 1292

Churchill, (Sir) Winston Leonard Spencer:
becomes Prime Minister, 1–6, 16, 19, 47–9; forms his Government, 7–8, 9–10, 13–15, 20–22, 30, 44–5, 68, 89, 255, 386–7; Government changes, 700, 884–6, 890–1, 1099–1100, 1251, 1253–4; and the opening of the battle in Belgium and Holland, 9, 11, 14, 24–5, 28, 39, 71–2, 101–2, 111; and the German invasion of France, 30–2, 35–9, 41, 43–4, 51, 52 et seq.; and British air support for France, 50–1, 52, 55–6, 80–1, 91, 97 n.1, 230, 234–5, 236, 252–3, 254, 256, 263–5, 268, 269–70, 279, 293–4, 300–1

as Minister of Defence, 46, 82 n.1, 447, 610, 681, 711, 1258

his broadcasts (19 May 1940), 75–6, 83–90, 91, 94; (14 July 1940), 516–20, 521; (11 September 1940), 801–3; to Czechoslovakia (30 September 1940), 888–9; to France (21 October 1940), 965–7, 969, 979–85, 1130; to Italy (23 December 1940), 1284–8

his Parliamentary speeches and statements (28 May 1940), 178–9; (4 June 1940), 240–7, 248, 250; (18 June 1940), 360–8; (20 June 1940), 379–87; (25 June 1940), 412–6; (4 July 1940), 469–74; (18 July 1940), 539–56; (23 July 1940), 563–5; (30 July 1940), 591–2; (15 August 1940), 669–73; (20 August 1940), 687–97; (5 September 1940), 771–9; (17 September 1940), 822–9; (8 October 1940), 911–22; (15 October 1940), 949–50; (17 October 1940), 958–9; (5 November 1941), 1041–50; (12 November 1940), 1080–3; (13 November 1940), 1088–90; (21 November 1940), 1116–21; (26 November 1940), 1140–4; (10 December 1940), 1210; (12 December 1940), 1218–9; (19 December 1940), 1256–65

and his Commons speeches *not* to be broadcast, 423

his speeches not in Parliament or over the BBC (5 September 1940), 781–2; (9 October 1940), 925–7; at Harrow School (18 December 1940), 996–7, 1021, 1211, 1254–6; at the Mansion House (9 November 1940), 1070–2; at the Empire Press Union (28 November 1940), 1154

his maiden speech (1901) recalled, 1144

his visits to France (16 May 1940), 53–65; (22 May 1940), 109–116; (31 May 1940), 205–20; (11–12 June 1940), 279, 285–6, 288–308; (13 June 1940), 308–24; (16 June 1940), in prospect, 342, 349, 350–1

his journeys inside Britain: to St Margaret's Bay (near Dover), 421–2; to Lancing College and Brighton, 457–8; to Limpsfield, 484–5; to Dover, 505, 735, 804; to Langley aerodrome, 509; to Kenley aerodrome, 510, 931; to the Hampshire and Dorset coasts, 531; to the South Coast, including Portsmouth, 537–8; to Lincolnshire, 622; to East Anglia, 629; to Manston aerodrome, 735, 740–1; to Ramsgate, 735–6; to Tidworth and Aldershot, 781–2; to the East End of London, 788–9; to Shorncliffe and Dungeness, 804; to Uxbridge, 813–6; to Dollis Hill, 847; to the London docks, 870; to Richmond, 907–10, 931; to Scotland, 991–2, 993; to Birmingham, 1135–6

his places of work: at Admiralty House, 33–4, 221; moves into Downing Street, 331; at Chequers, 336–7, 342, 440–1, 443–4, 446–7, 510–5, 580–2, 601–2, 638–9, 744–6, 749, 750–1, 807, 813, 852, 931, 933–4, 936, 939, 1021, 1025, 1032–3, 1160–1, 1199–1200, 1214–5, 1220–2, 1223, 1230–3, 1280, 1288–9, 1290, 1292; at Chartwell, 80–1, 485, 1221; in the Cabinet War Rooms, 819–20; above the Cabinet War Rooms (No. 10. Annexe, 'The Barn'), 820 n.1, 979, 989, 991, 1007, 1096, 1107; at Church House, Westminster (House of Commons Annexe), 1057

his places of refuge (from the bombing): at Down Street underground station, 810 n.2, 998, 1016, 1067, 1111, 1132; at Dollis Hill ('Paddock'), 847, 896, 988–9, 990; at Ditchley, 1068–9, 1076, 1086, 1098, 1123, 1236, 1239, 1241; at the Central (or Cabinet) War Rooms, 819–20, 924, 1090, 1107, 1112, 1246, 1293

'ashamed and humiliated' (in 1910), 996–7
'better days will come', 248
'close the ranks, and carry on', 663
'comb and re-comb', 721

INDEX

'confident of success', 942
'the dangers of inaction', 991
'delay is dangerous', 1313
'the forward march of the common people', 982
'hardship our garment', 922
'haunted and tortured', 297
'a Hun alive is a war in prospect', 936
'I awoke with dread in my heart' (in the summer of 1940), 1265
'keep your pecker up', 736
'a long and arduous road to travel', 1072, 1121
'the morning will come', 982
'my usual song', 219, 300, 312
'never in the field of human conflict . . .', 678, 693, 697
'never maltreat your enemy by halves', 862
'no one is downhearted here', 436
'sad at all the suffering', 1214
'safety first . . . the road to ruin', 1034
'we are waiting . . . so are the fishes', 981
'we must make increasing preparations', 1263
'we shall be victorious', 829
'we shall certainly not give in', 1311
'we shall . . . draw from the heart of suffering . . . survival', 803
'we shall fight on unconquerable', 358
'we shall go on to the utmost limit', 1311
'we shall never stop, never weary, and never give in', 982
'we shall never surrender', 247
'we shall not fail in our duty', 475
'we shall persevere along our course', 779
'we should stand stripped to the bone', 1157
'we will never cease to strike', 1072
'when this war is won', 1256
'wickedness is not going to reign', 1224
and 'an act of inhumanity', 1171
and 'another bloody country gone west', 371
and a 'carpet of dynamite', 1176
and a 'case for a mental home', 1172
and a 'dingy object', 834
and 'excess of care', 873
and 'a strong impression of defeatism', 419
and 'killing Huns', 651
'you should run risks', 1033
and 'the shame of defeat', 691
his 'great reluctance to be photographed', 1111
his love of animals, 485
sees *Gone with the Wind*, 1241
sees *The Great Dictator*, 1236
singing (in his bath), 996; (at Harrow), 1255; (at Chequers), 1292
his siren suit, 922, 931, 1157; and a siren suit gift, 1289
unwell, 1016, 1021, 1200
and adjudication, 952
and advice from George Bernard Shaw, 421
and aerial reconnaisance, 1051–2, 1283
and 'air mastery', 493

and air raid casualties, 480, 538, 545, 773–4, 823–4, 913, 1042
and air raid damage, 771, 774, 1118–9, 1152, 1200–1
and Air Raid Precautions (ARP), 144, 600, 651–2, 707, 756–7, 803, 1264
and air raid shelters, 144, 423, 463, 561, 764–5, 850–1, 886, 915, 924, 931, 988–90, 998, 1084, 1291–2, 1301–2, 1312
and aircraft production, 137–8, 581, 637, 644, 647, 673, 677–8, 693, 768, 782, 847–8, 871, 874–5, 902, 917–8, 947–8, 1025, 1083, 1130–1, 1195, 1226, 1233–4, 1238–9, 1278
and aircraft from the United States, 225, 255, 394, 607, 666–7, 668, 780, 845, 1195
and aircraft fuel, 562
and Allied governments-in-exile, 1309
and the choice of a new Ambassador (to the United States), 1220–1, 1223, 1236, 1237, 1244–5, 1251–2, 1265, 1266–9
and American munitions, 1071
and the proposed Anglo-French Union, 348–9, 349–50
and an apology, 1031
and the 'Arab world', 1171
and armaments and munitions supply (May 1940), 211, 213, 214; (June 1940), 355–6, 372, 373, 375, 392; (July 1940), 487, 491, 512, 521, 522, 526–7, 567, 578; (August 1940), 622–3, 639, 640, 647; (September 1940), 834, 854–5, 871, 880; (October 1940), 939, 948, 964–5; (November 1940), 1071–2, 1098; (December 1940), 1244, 1245, 1261, 1274, 1294–5, 1299
and assassination, 1076
and Australian troops, 191, 194, 227, 228, 251, 261, 647, 655, 658, 675, 796, 798, 830, 877, 899, 904, 918, 1208, 1259, 1270
and the BBC: 'more effective control over', 69; and a 'foolish broadcast', 399; and de Gaulle's broadcasts, 636, 650; personnel from, 800; and an 'extravagant picture', 1032; Churchill speaks 'bitterly' of, 1052; and J.B. Priestley, 1211; and a complaint in Parliament, 1247–8; and a 'depressing' broadcast, 1105–6; and a 'gloating communiqué', 1221–2; 'impossible . . . to please everybody', 1248
and 'badges and distinctions', 509
and bananas, 1159
and the Battle of Britain, 651, 673–4, 678, 679, 680, 682, 692–3, 721, 724, 744, 752, 758–9, 772–3, 787, 794, 801, 813–6, 818, 849
and the 'Battle of the Bulge' (May 1940), 66
and the Battle of Gallabat (November 1940), 1088 n.1, 1091
and the Battle of Jena (1806), 981
and the 'Battle of Libya' (December 1940), 1223, 1259

1340 INDEX

Churchill, (Sir) Winston L. Spencer—*contd.*
and the Battle of Montmirail (1814), 981
and the Battle of Passchendaele (1917), 688
and the Battle of Sadowa (1866), 1032
and the Battle of Sidi Barrani (December 1940), 1213, 1219, 1223, 1223–4, 1230, 1242, 1246
and the Battle of the Somme (1916), 688
and the Battle of Taranto (November 1940), 1089–90, 1098–9, 1106, 1122, 1177
and the Battle at Tug Argen (Somaliland), 683, 701
and the Battle of Waterloo (1815), 813, 981
and the Belgians, 9, 90, 368, 369, 508, 518
and the defeat of Belgium, 115, 122, 126, 134–6, 146, 151, 152, 161, 170–3, 176–7, 182, 242, 256
birthday greetings to (aged sixty-six), 1160–2
and the black-out, 737, 778
and the Blitz, 716–7, 773–4, 799–800, 802–3, 805, 806–7, 807–8, 810–11, 823–4, 830, 872, 907–10, 911–4, 936, 944–7, 950–1, 954, 967–8, 1035, 1042–4, 1111, 1135–6, 1235, 1264–5, 1289–90, 1310
and the blockade (of Germany), 307, 313, 441, 492; (of France), 440, 635; (of German-controlled Europe), 689, 697, 762, 1077
and bomb disposal, 806, 809, 851, 931
and bomb production, 1275–6
and the bombing of the Houses of Parliament, 1204
and bombing policy and operations, (May 1940), 17–19, 25–7, 41–3, 52, 55–6, 101, 216; (June 1940), 223, 226, 239, 253, 259, 265, 300–1, 304, 430, 441, 442; (July 1940), 458–9, 461, 492–3, 504, 513, 522; (August 1940), 666, 693–4, 738; (September 1940), 762, 784, 884; (October 1940), 938, 970–1, 1005, 1011–2, 1016; (November 1940), 1022–3, 1027, 1035, 1056, 1076, 1097–8, 1100–1, 1112, 1149, 1153; (December 1940), 1186, 1217–8, 1235, 1263, 1283, 1304–5, 1314
and the Bordeaux Government, 395, 404, 405–6, 410–11, 413, 440–1, 455, 614
and brass bands, 512
and the 'brave German', 596 n.1
and the British Army, 242, 376–7, 383, 391, 397, 418, 429, 431, 518–9, 580–1, 621–2, 637, 639, 691, 763, 782, 916, 948, 952, 973–4, 1011, 1023–4, 1034, 1045, 1046–7, 1072, 1195, 1207–9, 1261, 1299
and the British Commonwealth, 589, 696
and the British Expeditionary Force (BEF): in France, 9, 14, 20, 24–5, 51, 85–6, 91–2, 101, 111, 112–3, 126, 163, 178, 194, 242; reaches Britain, 198, 201, 203, 211–2, 213, 226–7; reconstitution of, in France, 227, 230, 233–4, 238–9, 254, 264, 268, 273, 287, 289, 291–2, 295, 307; in Britain, 228, 235–6, 340; final withdrawal of, from France, 325, 327–8, 329–30, 333–4; recalled, 361
and the British Fleet (future of), 93, 255, 270, 338, 341, 408, 409, 436, 627, 628–9, 667–8, 682–3, 746–7
and British prisoners-of-war, 1282–3
and brevity, 636–7, 1086, 1092
and a Cabinet leak, 1301–2
and the Cabinet War Rooms, 140, 571, 807, 819–20, 980, 1007, 1096, 1246, 1293
and the defence of Calais, 126, 133, 138–9, 141, 143, 148, 149–50, 160–1, 182, 241, 638
and camouflage (of two lakes), 995–6
and Canadian troops, 162, 194, 228, 230, 233, 262, 280, 328, 362, 409, 488, 562, 647, 804
and a car pool, 961–2
cartoons of, 29, 108, 267, 530, 797, 841, 1183
and cavalry units, 790; and a cavalry charge, 1259, 1265
and censorship reports, 1211, 1268
and the Channel ports (end May 1940), 116–7, 122, 124–5, 138–9, 140–1, 142–3, 241
characteristics of, and moods, as seen by his contemporaries: 'aggressively seeking to find out the exact state of affairs', 61; 'thrives on crisis and adversity', 78; 'buoyant spirits', 116; 'geniality and air of brisk confidence', 123; 'terrific, hurling himself about', 160; 'ceaseless industry', 192; 'confidence and energy', 196; 'encouragement and resolve', 198; 'bears no grudge', 222; 'a mountain of energy and good nature', 248; 'any amount of courage and experience', 359; 'less violent, less wild, less impetuous', 420; 'rough, sarcastic and overbearing', 425–6; 'getting very arrogant', 483–4; 'enough courage for everybody', 484; 'full of interest and enquiries', 494; 'animation and exuberance', 512; 'he has got guts, that man', 520; 'in wonderful spirits . . . full of offensive plans', 532; 'a cantankerous frame of mind', 558; 'full of offensive thoughts', 558–9; 'at the very top of his form', 565; 'bubbling over with enthusiasm', 580; 'his powers of glowing speech', 586; 'forceful and competent', 650; 'most genial', 651; 'vigorous rhetorical good sense', 765; 'a pugnacious looking b . . .', 781; 'most entertaining', 784; 'relishing to the full the fruits of power', 898; 'a wonderful vitality', 931; 'bears his heavy burdens remarkably well', 931; 'not despairing' (of the French), 985; 'his ability to face the worst', 1050; 'prone to count his chickens before they were hatched', 1068; 'flogs on, wildly but with the same genius', 1079; 'full of fascinating sayings and anecdotes', 1133; 'in the most benign mood', 1151; 'irritability', 1182; 'cheerful and confident', 1199; 'much moved', 1204; his 'humility',

INDEX 1341

1215 n.1; his ceaseless urging, 1247; tired but cheerful', 1265; 'working as usual over the holiday', 1292; 'in mellow mood', 1312
and chemical warfare, 747
and choosing 'the best men', 1066
and Christian names, 1086–7, 1095
and Christmas presents, 1289, 1292
and church bells (on Christmas Day), 1164
and HMS *Churchill*, 841 n.1, 870 n.2
and coal, 623–4, 663
and Coastal Command, 1051–2, 1097, 1170 n.3, 1178–9, 1204, 1212–3, 1305
and civilian traffic, 961–2
and the Coliseum (in Rome), 1020–1
and commandos, 457, 559, 721–2, 727, 791, 849, 886, 1033, 1173
and committees, 127–8, 136, 977
and 'the Common Cause', 288, 804
and complaints, 1066
and the Conservative Party, 49, 78, 435, 475, 643, 644, 1099
and the Conservative Party leadership, 925–9
and 'conventional standards', 962
and convoys, 574–5, 590, 635, 656, 657, 662, 664–5, 669, 676, 726–7, 761, 778, 785, 801, 899–900, 1000, 1033, 1034, 1057, 1107, 1114, 1175–6, 1181, 1194
his correspondence with Roosevelt, (May 1940), 45–6, 69–70, 71, 93, 204; (June 1940), 225, 285, 287–8, 307–8, 324, 333, 337–8, 341; (July 1940), 482–3, 593–5; (August 1940), 668, 704–5, 722–4; (September 1940), 733–4, 746–7, 870; (October 1940), 901–2, 974–5, 1000, 1003–4; (November 1940), 1018, 1053–4, 1063, 1064, 1074–5, 1080, 1098–9, 1122, 1156–7, 1162–3; (December 1940); 1168–9, 1179, 1182, 1189–97, 1216, 1225–6, 1236, 1237, 1245, 1268–9, 1284, 1296–7, 1308, 1308–11, 1312
and a Council of Europe, 708, 1230, 1231
and a critic protected, 770
and 'Cultivator No. 6' (a trench-crossing machine), 188
and the Czechs, 90, 368, 508, 567 n.1, 695
and Czech troops, 374–5
and the Danes, 90
and 'the darkest hour', 316
and decoys, 656
and 'defeatist talk', 451, 563–4
and the defence of Britain, (May 1940) 76–7, 99–100, 103–4, 124, 162; (June 1940), 221, 246–7, 249–50, 272, 353–5, 357, 370–1, 384, 398, 421–2, 430, 437–8, 439, 444–5; (July 1940), 452–3, 455–6, 457–8, 461, 463, 465–6, 480, 484–5, 488, 495–8, 509, 511–12, 523, 541, 551–2, 554–5; (August 1940), 602–3, 607, 617–20, 622, 639, 640–1, 643–5, 649, 681, 685, 691–2, 707–8, 720, 737, 742–3; (September 1940), 754, 778, 830, 833; (December 1940), 1262–3
and his Defence Secretariat, 403–4, 711
and delay-action bombs, 716–7
and 'departmental grimaces', 1112
and the deportation of internees, 596
and destroyers from the United States, 45, 69–70, 225, 255, 287–8, 338, 388, 407, 576, 594, 607, 627, 627–8, 629, 666–7, 682, 702, 704, 709, 722–3, 733–4, 752, 771–2, 780, 783, 842, 844–5, 1044, 1163, 1193–4, 1199, 1215–6, 1229, 1233, 1269, 1296–7, 1311–2
and directions (on national defence), to be in writing, 549
and a dispute with the Palace, 231–2
and the Dominions (Canada, Australia, New Zealand and South Africa), 118–9, 145, 162, 321, 339–4, 362, 430, 462, 560, 782, 1039, 1046, 1069, 1077, 1148, 1291, 1309
and the Dover guns, 251, 392, 456, 505, 523, 604–5, 634, 707, 719, 729–30, 742, 747, 755–6, 760, 766–7, 804
and dummy ships, 589, 1028
and economic problems, 68–9, 703–4, 713–5, 1069, 1118–9, 1147, 1157, 1196, 1214, 1308–11
and evacuation (before Dunkirk), 91, 96, 125, 126, 133, 138, 149, 153, 158, 178
and the Dunkirk evacuation, 126, 178, 179, 182, 184, 187, 188–91, 193–4, 196–7, 198–200, 201, 203, 208–11, 215–6, 223–4, 224–5, 241–4; and the aftermath of the evacuation, 226–8, 229–31, 232–5, 238–40, 244–6, 254–5, 268–9, 273, 276; recalled, 340, 361, 531–2
and the Dutch, 9, 24, 90, 368, 508, 518, 603, 625, 671, 690
and Egyptian troops, 918
and emergency powers, 74–5, 109
and enemy aliens, 40–1, 77, 134, 172, 237, 246, 392, 540, 598
and enemy pilots, 750
and the 'English-speaking world', 1230
and Enigma (later Ultra), 433, 800 n.1, 880 n.1, 930 n.1, 955 and n.1, 1031 n.1, 1134 n.2
and the evacuation of children (across the Atlantic), 391, 451, 493, 541–2, 546, 862
and an 'exterminating attack' (by British bombers), 493
and 'expressions of loose and ill-digested opinion', 464, 474–5
and Faith ('to help and comfort us'), 517
and Fifth Columnists, 77, 106, 246–7, 438, 446, 453, 475, 519, 554–5, 670, 1045
and fire-ships, 988
and the First World War recalled, 15, 236, 245, 293, 302, 307, 367, 386, 603, 687–8, 689, 763, 766–7, 779, 818–9, 912, 968, 1011, 1173, 1176, 1193

1342   INDEX

Churchill, (Sir) Winston L. Spencer—*contd.*
and the Fleet Air Arm, 257–8, 1028–9, 1051–2, 1089–90
and fog (an invasion hazard), 819, 858–9; (on airfields), 961
and 'food faddists', 514
and food production, 1262
and Force H (based on Gibraltar, for action in the Mediterranean), 547–8, 557, 665, 1244
and a Foreign Legion (of anti-Nazi internees), 391, 392, 508, 567
and the fall of France (June 1940), 275–6, 288–308, 308–29, 344–68, 394–5, 412–5, 440–1
and a Franco-British union, 321–2, 347–8
and the French Colonies, 351, 358, 400, 405, 481, 490
and the French Council of Liberation (de Gaulle), 400–1, 404–5; and the French Council of Defence (de Gaulle), 613–15, 616; and Britain's support for de Gaulle, 695, 698–9, 730, 731, 739, 747, 793, 856, 930, 956, 963, 991, 995, 999, 1014, 1015, 1063, 1064–5, 1075, 1077, 1113, 1165–6, 1298
and the French Fleet, 294 n.1, 306, 326, 335, 336–7, 337, 344, 346, 351, 354, 356–7, 373–4, 378, 390–1, 395–7, 400, 405–5, 408, 410–11, 414–5, 420, 421, 424–5, 426–8, 439, 443, 447–8, 451–2, 458, 459–60, 463, 469–74, 476–7, 482, 486, 502, 516–7, 536, 576–7
and French North Africa, 569–70, 573
and a French separate peace, 77, 149, 159, 169, 187, 219, 313, 317–8, 324, 326, 344–6, 351, 356–7, 394–5; the facts, recalled, 413–5
and French troops in Britain (June 1940), 428–9, 434, 451, 452, 453, 501, 508–9, 567 n.1; and French troops in Syria (July 1940), 454–5; and French sailors to be recruited by de Gaulle (July 1940), 481
and future 'European Confederations', 1221, 1230–1
and gas, 202, 444–5, 514, 515–6, 561, 593, 847, 879–80, 903–4, 923, 1136, 1243, 1270, 1275, 1293–4
and gas bombs, 1276
and gas masks, 515–6, 561
and the George Cross (GC), 717 n.1, 835, 910
and the George Medal (GM), 835, 910, 1276
and German air capacity (winter 1940–1), 1169, 1201–3, 1226, 1234, 1271
and the German air raid on Coventry, 1095–6, 1100, 1105–6, 1111
and the German drive to the sea, 81, 92, 95–6, 101, 103, 104, 106–7, 111–4, 116–8, 122, 123, 124–6, 129, 130–1, 140–1, 142–9, 151–72, 202–3, 211–89
and a possible German 'eastward thrust', 924
and German land mines (dropped by parachute), 970, 1198
and German munitions capacity, 943
and a new German weapon, 987
and his own 'Gestapo' (Bracken, Beaverbrook, Lindemann), 1158
and glass, 741, 834–5
and gliders, 755
and Goering, 910
and a possible gramophone recording, 423
and his grandson's christening, 1161
and 'heresy hunting', 281
and the historians ('when they have time'), 361
and history ('with its flickering lamp'), 1081; and the 'criminal gambler', 1232
and holidays, 600, 602, 1231, 1264
and the Home Guard (Local Defence Volunteers), 398, 422, 453, 478, 498, 519, 521, 567, 586, 600, 647, 651–2, 663, 707, 720, 802, 916, 963, 972–3, 1013, 1045, 1055–6
and the homeless, 1073, 1275
and Honours, 717, 786, 835, 910, 1091, 1149, 1185, 1272, 1276
and imports, 638, 648, 1227, 1293
and Indian troops, 918, 1242, 1259
and Intelligence reports and information, 562, 621, 753, 950
and the possibility of invasion, (May 1940), 71, 87, 99, 139, 162, 202, 218; (June 1940), 221, 226–7, 229, 238, 246–7, 248, 249, 272, 320, 339–40, 352, 353–4, 363–5, 384, 429, 430, 436, 437–8, 444–5, 446; (July 1940), 452–3, 455, 456, 457, 459, 461, 463, 474–5, 480, 484, 494–5, 495, 496–8, 511–2, 517–9, 523, 541, 551–2, 554, 554–5, 556, 576, 593, 594; (August 1940), 602–3, 608, 617–20, 640–1, 651, 687, 700, 707–8, 742; and an invasion scare (31 August 1940), 751, 752; and invasion prospects (September 1940), 759–60, 763, 798–9, 800, 801–2, 819, 822–3, 828–9, 851, 852, 858–9, 891, 895, 899, 930, 950, 977–8, 1004; and continuing preparations against (September 1940), 833, 849–50, 860, 873, 916–7; the prospect of, recedes (October 1940), 1010–11, 1045, 1046; and an invasion strategy, 902–3, 1293–4
and an invasion cartoon, 530
and Italian prisoners-of-war, 1259, 1295, 1305–6
and the Italians, 1107, 1221, 1233, 1259
and the Jews, 419, 435, 654, 1126, 1170
and the Joint Air Training Corps (pilot and aircrew training), 932, 1188
and the Joint Intelligence Sub-Committee, 753, 1149
and the Joint Planners, 745, 749–50, 753–4, 1061, 1166, 1273–4
and the Labour Party, 9, 49, 368, 503–4
and labour policy, 74–5, 131–2, 767, 769, 773, 776–7, 842
and the sinking of the *Lancastria*, 358
and landing-craft, 790, 812

INDEX 1343

and the League of Nations, 643
and leasing bases to the United States, 162–3, 607, 666–7, 696–7, 702, 704–5, 709, 722–4, 726, 733–4, 783, 842
his letter to Mussolini, 50, 1286–7
his letter to Stalin, 417–8
and loyalty (to Neville Chamberlain), 195; (to the administration), 387, 1099
and 'many melancholy reports', 1314
and mercy ('we shall ask for none'), 518; (justice to be 'tempered with'), 781
his messages of condolence and sympathy, 583, 811, 1076, 1092–3, 1148, 1154–5
and mining the Rhine, 11, 39, 274–5
and munitions supply, *see entry for* armaments
and new weaponry, 77, 124, 257, 266, 352, 372–3, 402, 442, 527, 575, 581, 610–11, 620, 627, 653–4, 678–9, 716, 718, 745, 746, 759, 852, 858, 935, 971–2, 1026, 1069, 1074, 1103, 1104, 1109–10, 1198, 1218, 1269
and New Zealand troops, 647, 655, 798–9, 830, 831, 877, 918, 1208, 1235
and the Night Air Defence Committee: 905, 978, 1009–10
and a 'nightmare' (May 1940), 93
and the Norwegians, 90, 368
and possible offensive action (after Dunkirk), 249–50, 251, 453, 486, 489, 499–500, 513, 532, 568, 639, 712–3, 745, 791–2, 1071, 1312–3
and offensive cartoons (of others), 552, 553, 1228, 1235, 1240–1
and offensive operations, 259, 389–90, 452, 513, 531, 532, 559–60, 568, 581–2, 639, 712–13, 745, 873, 1071–2, 1091, 1100, 1215, 1224, 1241–2, 1247, 1253
and oil, 181, 556, 719, 1227
and oil tankers (on aerodromes), 562
and Operation 'Abigail' (bombing a German city), 1186, 1263
and Operation 'Alloy' (seizure of the Azores), 879
and Operation 'Ambassador' (against Guernsey), 499–500
and Operation 'Brisk' (seizure of the Azores), 1184–5, 1232, 1249, 1250, 1271
and Operation 'Catapult' (against the French Fleet), 458–60, 469–75; recalled, 831
and Operation 'Challenger' (the occupation of Ceuta), 1232
and Operation 'Collar' (Mediterranean convoy), 1128–9, 1159
and Operation 'Compass' (Western Desert), 1103–4, 1125, 1139, 1145–7, 1167, 1179, 1184, 1205, 1213, 1219, 1222, 1230
and Operation 'Dhqy' (Portuguese East Africa), 1250
and Operation 'Dhqz' (Portuguese West Africa), 1250
and Operation 'Dynamo' (Dunkirk evacuation), 178
and Operation 'Excess' (a fast convoy), 1232, 1242
and Operation 'Felix' (a *German* plan to seize Gibraltar), 1231–2
and Operation 'Grind' (a landing in Tangier), 1244
and Operation 'Hats' (Mediterranean convoy), 661, 664, 727, 785, 791, 820
and Operation 'Humour' (help to Spanish resistance in Morocco), 1244
and Operation 'Influx' (Sicily), 1301
and Operation 'Lucid' (fire-ships), 988
and Operation 'Mandibles' (Rhodes), 1174, 1281
and Operation 'Marie' (Jibouti), 1165–6, 1298, 1302
and Operation 'Menace' (Dakar), 659–60, 684, 698–9, 706–7, 710–11, 727, 730–1, 754, 760, 817, 820–1, 822, 831, 843, 861–2, 866–70, 893
and Operation 'Paul' (mining the approach to Lulea), 32–3, 120, 129–30, 139, 256, 272
and Operation 'Royal Marine' (mining the Rhine), 11, 39, 274–5
and Operation 'Scipio', 650, 710–11, 817, 820, 856
and Operation 'Shrapnel' (seizure of Cape Verde Islands), 879, 1147, 1169, 1184–5, 1232, 1249, 1250, 1271
Operation 'Susan' (against French North Africa), 452
and Operation 'Threat' (against Morocco): 754
and Operation 'Workshop' (seizure of Pantellaria Island), 1033, 1147, 1158–9, 1167, 1172–3, 1180, 1205–7, 1281, 1294
and an opportunity 'of inflicting heavy loss', 588–9
and Parliamentary questions (in 1919), 500–1
and Party politics (after the war), 1221
and peace negotiations (prospects of, and proposals for), 93, 122, 144, 153, 156, 157–8, 166–70, 180–1, 182, 183, 185–7, 345, 409, 419–20, 437, 551, 603–4, 799, 940, 1256–7
and a Peerage, 629, 1272
and pilots, 235, 244, 257–8, 332, 431, 528, 547, 560, 599, 658–9, 724–5, 750, 951, 976, 1008, 1021, 1026, 1102, 1117, 1188–9, 1305
and the Poles, 90, 368, 508, 567 n.1, 759, 851, 1155
and Polish troops, 374, 567, 675, 972, 991, 1060
and the post-war world, 1230–1, 1306
praise from, 165, 177, 399, 412, 454, 493, 498, 512, 515, 528, 548, 761, 791, 871, 883, 942, 962–3, 970, 1090, 1121, 1146, 1238, 1281, 1284

Churchill, (Sir) Winston L. Spencer—*contd.*
and the Press, 423, 468–9, 491, 700–1, 906, 907, 923, 1153, 1197, 1301–2
and priorities, 652, 947–8, 1274–5
and the 'awful process . . . of searching after perfection', 963
and production, 237, 238, 245, 258–9, 1163–4, 1274–5, 1275–6
and the publication of casualties, 538, 545
and punishments, 550, 964, 1130
and 'the pursuit of peace, even at great peril', 1081
and the 'radio sphere', 947
and rationing, 492, 514, 537, 609
his reading of newspapers, 681, 685, 1130, 1265
rebukes by: 'delay is costing more . . . than vigorous action', 98; 'a feeble and weary Departmentalism', 262; 'doing nothing worth speaking of', 262; 'who was responsible for stifling action?', 283; a 'shocking example of costly over-caution and feebleness', 330–1; 'a serious default', 335; 'inadequacy bolstered up', 398; a 'foolish broadcast', 399; 'your people are not doing much', 436; and 'a defeatist spirit', 451; 'very much disappointed', 501; and 'the way to lose the war', 514; 'I entirely deprecate any stampede', 546; 'has not got the root of the matter in him', 552; and 'silly fiascos', 559; and 'an absurd conclusion', 684; and 'official caution', 685; and the conduct of a General, 718; and an 'emphatic protest', 740; and 'foolishness', 743; and an 'intolerable' objection, 743; and 'tame . . . withdrawals', 748; and a 'misapprehension', 749–50; and 'doctors in a case which has gone wrong', 785; and 'officers of the second grade', 791; and 'standards . . . we intend to enforce', 793; and the need to set examples, 833; and a sacking, 853–4; and 'haggling and boggling', 865; and a 'very serious misconception', 901; and 'misleading stuff', 901; and the Press, 923; and 'paralysing action', 954; and a friend's conduct, 958–9; and 'failure in responsibility', 964; caused me 'work . . . and worry', 986; and 'undue burdening', 1041; and 'disgruntled ne'er-do-wells', 1042; and 'shallow-clevers', 1046; and 'disrespectful expressions', 1060–1; and the 'general attitude of negation', 1061; and a 'disgraceful' record, 1074; and 'completely crazy' policy, 1087–8, 1093; and a 'thorough overhaul' needed, 1101; and 'a drizzle of carping criticism', 1102; and 'departmental differences', 1103; and 'negative advice', 1159; and 'complaints' of incompetence, 1164; and 'amphibious power . . . unused', 1167; and 'confidence . . . departed', 1170;
'more of a case for a mental home', 1172; 'not at the level of events', 1176; 'how completely he has failed', 1177–8, 1197–8; and an 'unfortunate' speech, 1181–2; 'failed to rise to the height of circumstances', 1184; 'missed opportunities', 1215; 'continuity of work never harmed anyone', 1231
and recompense (from bomb damage), 774–6, 914–6, 1118–9
and recreation for troops, 756
and regimental bands ('but when are we going to hear them playing . . .?'), 510
and Regulation 18B (arrest and imprisonment without trial), 440, 444, 563, 1257, 1276–7
and repair (of bomb damage), 1200–1
and reprisals (and retaliation), 564–5, 837, 839, 880, 893, 906, 914, 954, 956, 960, 970, 981, 1035, 1074, 1075, 1218, 1243
and retirement (to write 'a book on the war'), 1221
and rifles, 357, 372, 373, 487, 512, 522, 567, 578, 594, 599, 640, 647, 668, 763, 780, 837, 842, 845, 854–5, 870, 874 n.1, 923, 1024, 1114, 1299
and the later Roman Emperors, 448
and the Royal Air Force, 73, 97, 137–8, 163–5, 212–14, 223–4, 235, 243–4, 274, 283, 332, 335, 364–6, 401, 431–2, 498, 504, 513, 519, 547, 618, 647, 658–9, 700–1, 710, 762, 773, 844, 887–8, 917, 922, 1037–8, 1072, 1073, 1096–7, 1101, 1110, 1149, 1177–8, 1213, 1242
and the Royal Naval Air Service (recalled), 1260
and the Royal Navy, 46, 243, 259, 282, 338 n.1, 354–5, 363–4, 524, 525, 547–8, 618, 647, 692, 705–6, 792–3, 811–13, 860–1, 870, 948, 1072, 1104, 1128–9, 1155, 1239, 1252–3, 1282, 1295–6
and sabotage (overseas), 538, 559
and a 'Scarlet Pimpernel' organization, 404
and the search for troops, 76–7, 189, 214, 226–7, 261–2, 352
and secrecy, 263, 483, 670, 712–3, 826–7, 880, 935, 955, 1057, 1069, 1097, 1124, 1158–9, 1166, 1167–8, 1181–2, 1199, 1248–9, 1270, 1290
and the 'secret' war, 388–9, 751
and secrets (to be withheld), 536, 1148, 1248–9
and Secret Sessions (of the House of Commons), 379–87, 419, 591–3, 825–9, 1053
and the seizure of bases (in North Africa and the Atlantic Islands), 389–90
and the sharing of privileges (after the war), 1256
and 'silent columns' (of citizens), 563
and a son's encouragement, 231, 252
and the South African Brigade, 175, 561, 642, 654

INDEX 1345

and the Spanish Armada, 559, 833
and a spoof minute, 1017
and 'a statement . . . of the minimum', 1189–97
and statistics, 137, 238, 488, 513, 871, 913, 1065, 1169, 1300
and steel, 419, 813, 886, 1226
and Storm Troops ('Leopards'), 370–1, 372, 438
his strategic review (of 31 October 1940), 1010–12
and 'some sugar for the birds', 1089
and a Supreme Economic Council, 1230
and 'suspected persons', 446
and Swedish iron ore, 1277–8
and tanks, 137, 188, 228–9, 251, 257, 284, 370, 371, 393, 489, 527, 531, 549, 575–6, 600, 637, 649, 673, 677–8, 726, 748, 877, 942–3, 962, 1003, 1034, 1035–6, 1054, 1135, 1156, 1260
and the 'tragedy' of Italian history, 1285
and treason, 106
and truth (to 'plead its own cause'), 535; (to be the subject of an enquiry) 1201–3, 1271
and unexploded bombs, 806, 809, 851, 931
and a United States of Europe, 643
and the Victoria Cross, 835, 910
and a true 'victory', 1213
and 'a War of peoples and causes', 520
and 'a War of the Unknown Warriors', 520
and the war at sea, 338, 393, 394, 482, 486, 491, 494, 498–9, 505, 515, 547–8, 554, 557–8, 561, 568–9, 582, 590, 599, 608–9, 631–2, 656, 679–80, 684, 692, 717, 720, 726, 744, 745, 746, 752, 780, 787–8, 975, 993, 1000, 1044–5, 1048, 1051–2, 1063, 1085, 1175–6, 1178, 1180–1, 1187–8, 1190–3, 1197, 1225, 1235, 1264, 1300–1, 1303
and war aims, 22, 319, 643, 695–6, 949, 1113, 1120–1, 1160, 1177, 1256
and war crimes, 1231
and whistling, 337
woken (to learn of a new belligerent), 279
work methods of, 225–6, 426, 673, 686, 734–5, 1032, 1132
and the West African Brigade, 642, 654–5, 674, 728, 977, 1010, 1140
and West Indies Regiment, 352
and 'a word of serious counsel', 579
and 'The World Cause', 1004
and written orders, 549
and Abyssinia, 175, 561, 642, 1285–6, 1304, 1313
and the Adriatic, 1281
and Albania, 1066–7, 1166, 1198
and Alexandria, 471, 482, 642, 657, 728, 733, 1005, 1253, 1295, 1307
and Algiers, 1281, 1312
and Alsace-Lorraine, 981

and the Antwerp-Namur line (May 1940), 9, 54
and Athens, 1005, 1034, 1037
and the Atlantic Islands (of Portugal), 558
and Australia, 118, 634, 646–7, 662–3, 666, 728, 803–4, 892, 904–5, 1046, 1059
and Austria, 1070
and the Azores (and Cape Verde Islands), 558, 566, 876 n.1, 879, 1167–8, 1184–5, 1249–50, 1271
and the Baltic, 1277
and Barcelona, 366
and Bardia, 1242, 1259, 1283, 1305
and Belgium, 258, 260, 603–4, 695, 1071
and Belgium's colonies, 369
and Benghazi, 1305
and Berlin, 1314 n.1
and Birmingham, 1111, 1135–6
and Bizerta, 1003
and Blenheim, 1239
and Bombay, 1253, 1295
and Bristol, 1210
and British Guiana, 722
and Bulgaria, 772, 1015, 1031 n.1, 1125, 1134–5, 1137, 1145, 1146, 1150, 1246
and the Burma Road, 478–9, 534, 535, 543, 554, 896–7, 901, 920
and Cairo, 895, 1063, 1064, 1146, 1295
and Calcutta, 1253
and Canada, 145, 306, 590–1, 627, 668, 682, 694, 696, 713–5, 725, 782, 783, 804, 932–3, 941, 951, 1046, 1149, 1155, 1188–9, 1252, 1253, 1309
and Capetown, 1309, 1311
and Casablanca, 878, 893, 906, 918, 956, 1157, 1281
and Cayenne, 898
and Ceuta (Gibraltar Strait), 1138, 1147, 1232 n.1
and Ceylon, 646
and Chad, 731, 821
and the Channel Islands, 376, 443–4, 445–6, 457, 499–500
and Chartwell (Westerham, Kent), 43 n.1, 59 n.1, 80–1, 485, 1221
and the Cherbourg peninsula, 639, 745
and China, 479, 535, 543–5, 554, 570, 623, 646
and Constantinople (Istanbul), 1146, 1147
and Corsica, 981
and Coventry, 1095–6, 1100, 1105, 1106, 1110, 1111
and Crete, 301–2, 1006, 1010, 1027, 1041, 1049, 1056, 1059, 1060, 1062, 1166, 1187
and Cyprus, 302
and Czechoslovakia, 604, 888–9, 1071
and Dakar, 477, 478, 605–6, 614–5, 624–6, 630–1, 632–3, 650, 659–61, 684, 698–9, 702, 706–7, 710–11, 730–1, 754, 760, 817, 820–2, 831–2, 835, 838, 843, 856–8, 861–2, 862–3,

Churchill, (Sir) Winston L. Spencer—*contd.*
866–70, 878, 891–6, 906, 918–20, 931, 976–7, 995, 1054, 1157, 1166
and the Dardanelles, 779
and Denmark, 518, 604
and the Dobrudja (Roumania), 772
and the Dodecanese Islands (including Rhodes and Leros), 1123, 1134, 1158, 1174, 1177, 1211, 1242, 1281
and Duala (Cameroons), 659, 699, 731 n.1, 821, 843, 879, 893, 918, 937, 976–7, 1159
and Durban, 1253
and the Dutch East Indies, 479, 556, 570, 587–8, 633–4, 645, 836, 1192
and Egypt, 192, 283–4, 287, 495, 499, 601, 642, 646, 654–5, 656, 662, 674–7, 680, 728, 865, 895, 924, 1001, 1019, 1025, 1034, 1047, 1118, 1204–5, 1219, 1232, 1286
and Eritrea, 578, 582
and Freetown (Sierra Leone), 809, 820, 856, 868, 1140, 1253
and French Equatorial Africa, 793, 817, 893, 1064
and Germany, to be 'abolished', 851
and Gibraltar, 354, 398, 401, 424, 554, 557, 566, 646, 875, 953, 960, 1075, 1138, 1156, 1253, 1281, 1313
and Greece, 734, 738, 1003, 1009, 1013–4, 1024, 1025, 1026, 1027–8, 1033–4, 1036–40, 1041, 1048–9, 1050–1, 1056, 1059–60, 1062, 1071, 1072, 1074, 1078–9, 1084, 1103, 1105, 1107, 1108–9, 1112, 1123–4, 1125, 1134, 1137–8, 1149, 1150, 1153, 1158–9, 1162, 1172, 1181–2, 1198, 1205, 1232, 1238, 1240, 1278–9, 1286, 1297–8, 1309
and Guernsey, 559
and Hawaii, 1209
and Hog Island, 1194
and Holland, 259, 603, 639, 695, 1071
and Hong Kong, 479, 634
and Iceland, 355, 387, 391, 488, 562
and India, 262, 397–8, 506–8, 528–9, 557, 571–3, 574, 583–6, 589–90, 758, 939, 992, 1046, 1116
and Indo-China, 615, 1192
and Iran, 763
and Iraq, 334, 763, 864, 1058, 1074
and Ireland, 204–5, 342–3, 371, 379, 386, 390, 445, 483, 491, 623, 923, 1012, 1062–3, 1114–5, 1126, 1131, 1148, 1168, 1172, 1175, 1181, 1194, 1216, 1225–6, 1282, 1284, 1297, 1300
and Italy, 40, 50, 78, 146, 155, 156, 158, 175–6, 201, 216, 217, 259, 260–1, 286, 334, 356, 369, 490, 509, 561, 646, 669, 689, 738, 745, 1005, 1010, 1016, 1020–1, 1027, 1033, 1047–8, 1072, 1089–90, 1091, 1134, 1137, 1145, 1166, 1235, 1239, 1243, 1246, 1284–8
and Japan, 46, 478–9, 535, 543–5, 554, 556, 570, 587–8, 597–8, 610, 623, 633–4, 645–6, 729, 768, 796, 811, 836, 864, 897, 900, 920–1, 1127, 1187, 1192, 1235, 1249
and Jibouti (Djibouti), 695, 1165–6, 1298
and Kenya, 565, 642, 654, 655, 662, 674, 728, 858, 859–60, 864, 904, 1034, 1087, 1140, 1304
and Khartoum, 895, 1034, 1037
and the Kiel Canal, 522
and Kismayu (Italian Somaliland), 1139–40
and Korea, 597
and the Leads (Scandinavia), 1277–8, 1296
and Lemnos, 1153
and Leros, 1211
and Libreville, 613 n.1, 991, 999, 1064, 1075, 1077
and Libya, 499, 1224, 1241–2, 1259, 1264, 1305
and London: 'we should fight every inch of it', 457; 'could easily devour an entire hostile army', 519; a possible parachute raid on, 555, 556; plans to evacuate 'the high control' from, 810–11; anti-aircraft defence of, 830; bombing of, 892, 912–3, 980, 1042; a message from, 1072; 'widespread destruction in', 1310
and Londoners, 'the tough fibre of', 802–3; 'standing up magnificently to the bombing', 905
and Madrid, 302
and Malaya, 728–9, 795–6, 836, 864, 1237–8
and Malta, 259, 402, 509, 524–5, 656, 728, 738, 761, 792, 807, 809, 848, 865, 904, 936–7, 1010, 1091, 1166, 1167, 1198
and Mannheim, 1263
and Massawa, 581–2
and Mauritius, 1126, 1171
and the Mediterranean, 50, 354, 524–5, 547–8, 664–5, 785, 791–2, 838, 904, 938, 1034, 1089–90, 1187–8
and Mersa Matruh (Western Desert), 1033, 1067, 1067–8, 1219
and the Middle East, 500, 515, 525–6, 561, 565, 578, 601–2, 641–2, 657–8, 661–2, 664, 669, 674–7, 708–9, 733, 760, 778–9, 822, 832, 840, 848, 876–7, 895, 923–4, 925, 929–30, 938, 976, 1000–1, 1002–3, 1006, 1010, 1024, 1033–4, 1047–8, 1067–8, 1073, 1079, 1083, 1087, 1091, 1095, 1103–4, 1188, 1222, 1234–5, 1238, 1280, 1305
and the Mississippi, 697
and Morocco, 428, 501, 586, 754, 838, 857, 883, 1128, 1281, 1312–3
and Narvik, 32–3, 51, 67, 94, 96, 98–9, 107, 109, 120, 121, 129–30, 139, 145, 189, 190, 207–8, 218, 227, 231, 250, 260, 275, 281–2, 330–1, 428
and New Zealand, 577, 634, 645–6, 728, 1046
and Newfoundland, 667, 668, 696–7, 722
and Nice, 981

INDEX 1347

and Nigeria, 615
and the Nile Delta, 674–7, 728, 729, 1187, 1222
and Northampton, 1160
and Northern Ireland, 445, 1086
and Norway, 10, 120, 518, 604, 639, 695, 1071
and Oran, 458–60, 469–75; recalled, 831, 857; its future, 1003
and Oslo, 745
and the Pacific Ocean, 1126–7, 1194, 1209
and Palestine, 121, 122, 146, 189, 191, 227, 261, 334 n.1, 419, 454–5, 654–5, 662, 728, 729, 763, 790, 864, 895, 1058, 1060, 1187
and Pantellaria Island, 1033, 1158–9, 1172–3, 1180, 1205–7, 1281, 1294
and Paris, 302
and Poland, 518, 604, 616, 689, 851, 1071, 1172
and Port Sudan, 1298
and Portugal, 566–7, 876, 1185, 1249, 1252
and Portuguese East Africa, 1249
and Prussia, 1230, 1231
and Rhodes, 1173–4, 1211
and Rhodesia, 1185
and Rome, 287, 564, 1005, 1016, 1020, 1025
and Roumania, 772, 1031 n.1, 1134, 1149, 1153, 1279, 1297–8
and Rufisque (near Dakar): 861, 863, 867
and the Ruhr, 25, 27, 41–2, 639, 745
and Saigon, 1192
and Salonica, 1048, 1137, 1246
and Savoy (Savoie), 981
and Scandinavia, 11–12
and Sicily, 1158, 1301
and Sidi Barani (Libya), 1090
and Simonstown, 1253
and Singapore, 46, 479, 570, 587, 623, 634, 646, 729, 795–6, 836, 864, 897, 901, 1187, 1209, 1237–8, 1239, 1249
and Sollum (Libya), 822, 1242, 1283
and Somaliland, 641, 642, 654, 655, 661, 672–3, 674, 683, 694, 697, 701, 718, 728, 748
and South Africa, 561, 565, 642, 724, 756, 951, 1046, 1309
and Southern Rhodesia, 1250
and the Soviet Union, 72–3, 416, 417–8, 1011, 1221
and Spain, 354, 424, 566, 875, 883, 921, 987, 992, 1011, 1019, 1156, 1231–2, 1243, 1244, 1246, 1281, 1313
and Suda Bay (Crete), 1006, 1129, 1146, 1166, 1167, 1187
and the Sudan, 728, 859, 895, 1047, 1091, 1242
and the Suez Canal, 302, 895, 1001, 1011, 1047, 1063, 1065, 1118, 1187, 1222
and Sweden, 11–12, 46, 375, 492, 604
and Switzerland, 749, 1283
and Syria, 453, 454–5, 642–3, 763, 856, 857, 1031 n.1, 1058, 1084–5, 1187

and Takoradi, 1038, 1063, 1166, 1176, 1242, 1303
and Tangier, 1231, 1244, 1307
and Taranto, 1027, 1122
and Tel Aviv, 811
and Thrace, 1238
and Threadneedle Street, 1069
and Timor, 836
and Tobruk, 1242, 1305
and Toulon, 1029–30
and Trieste, 1098–9
and Tripoli, 1306
and Trondhjem, 277–8
and Tunis, 1281, 1312
and Turkey, 763, 1003, 1011, 1015, 1033, 1048, 1057–8, 1084–5, 1124, 1125, 1128, 1134, 1136, 1137–8, 1144–5, 1146, 1187, 1279, 1298
and the United States, (in May 1940), 71, 79–80, 92, 102, 162–3, 217–8; (in June 1940), 255, 270–1, 279, 304, 306, 312, 313–4, 316, 319–20, 322–5, 333, 335–6, 341, 345, 346, 375, 378, 385–6, 394, 407, 409, 419, 436; (in July 1940), 482–3, 485–6, 532–3, 536, 556, 576–7, 593–5; (in August 1940), 607, 627–9, 635, 640, 644, 647, 666–8, 682–3, 685, 696–7, 702, 714, 743, 749; (in September 1940), 782, 790, 809, 842, 854, 881–2, 886; (in October 1940), 897, 900, 1008, 1012, 1036–7, 1053–4, 1071, 1094; (in November 1940), 1112–3, 1115–6, 1121, 1126–7, 1147; (in December 1940), 1169, 1189, 1209–10, 1214, 1247, 1265, 1306–7
and the Vatican, 1025, 1285
and Vichy France, (in July 1940), 569–70, 573, 586–7; (in August 1940), 611–12, 621, 631, 632, 660, 690–1, 695; (in September 1940), 831, 856–7, 862–3, 875, 883; (in October 1940), 893, 897–8, 898, 900, 906, 919–20, 937–8, 953, 956, 960–1, 969, 974–5, 1000, 1003–4, 1014–5, 1015; (in November 1940), 1019–20, 1025, 1030, 1054, 1063, 1064, 1074–5, 1077, 1085, 1093–4, 1106; (in December 1940), 1192, 1272–3, 1280–1, 1302–3, 1307, 1312–3
and the West Indies, 352, 627
and the Western Desert, 601, 645, 1091, 1103–4, 1266
and Whitehall: vulnerability of, 556, 936, 973, 988–90
and Yugoslavia, 260–1, 1133–4, 1145
and Zeebrugge, 1173

Churchill, Winston S. (grandson): 231 n.2, 934, 1002, 1144 n.1, 1160, 1161
Ciano, Count G.: 50 n.2, 276 n.1, 875
Citrine, Sir Walter: 783–4, 1018, 1284
Clark, (Sir) Kenneth: 221 n.2

Clarke, Major-General (Sir) E.M.C.: 1074, 1198
Clarry, Sir Reginald: 1066
Clemenceau, Georges: 293 n.1, 310, 317 n.1
Clemenceau, Michel: 317
Clive, Lord (of India): 962
Cocks, Seymour: 467, 541–2, 1256–7
Cole-Deacon, G.J.: 1111
Coleridge, Lieutenant-Commander R.D. (later 4th Baron): 54 n.2, 206
Collins, Captain J.A.: 558 n.1
Colville, (Sir) John: (June 1940), 12, 19, 23–4, 28, 33–4, 45 n.1, 63–4, 65, 78, 80, 80–1, 83, 92, 106–7, 123, 130, 169, 175, 192, 200, 221–2, 248, 250, 256, 279, 308, 331, 335–7, 342, 358, 368–9, 371, 387, 420, 426, 440–1, 443–4, 446–7; (July 1940), 462, 476, 505, 510–12, 512–14, 528, 549 n.1, 558, 568, 583–4, 585–6, 590; (August 1940), 627, 629, 631–2, 638–9, 643–4, 650–1, 664, 666, 673, 673–4, 686, 697, 707, 734–5, 736, 744–6, 749, 750–1; (September 1940), 758–9, 765, 765–6, 819–20, 846–7, 851, 853, 862, 877; (October 1940), 922, 931, 933–4, 936, 939, 965, 972 n.1, 975, 979, 980 n.1, 991, 993, 994–5, 996–7, 997–8, 1016; (November 1940), 1020–1, 1025, 1032–3, 1035, 1061, 1069, 1076, 1080, 1083, 1088, 1090, 1095, 1096, 1107, 1111–2, 1113, 1132, 1136, 1153–4, 1162; (December 1940), 1172–3, 1179, 1200, 1211, 1213, 1220–2, 1223, 1230–2, 1232–3, 1236, 1239, 1241, 1255, 1268, 1289–90, 1312
Conder, Commander E.R.: 125 n.3
Conrad, Captain G. Bryan: 1115
Corbin, Charles: 348, 359, 374, 404, 406
Cork, Admiral of the Fleet the 12th Earl of (and Orrery): 33, 51, 67, 94, 98, 99, 107, 109, 120, 121, 145, 190, 227 and n., 250, 260; a possible job for, 489; and Plan Catherine, 524 n.2
Cornwall-Jones, Arthur: 64
Cornwallis-West, Major George: 47
Cousins, Commander G.R.: 870
Cowles, Virginia: 1161
Craigavon, 1st Viscount (Sir James Craig): 485, 1148
Craigie, Sir Robert: 597, 897, 901
Cranborne, Viscount (later 5th Marquess of Salisbury): 1, 886 n.1, 941, 1040, 1062, 1085, 1126, 1131 n.1, 1149, 1167–8, 1184–5, 1189, 1220–1, 1237–8, 1251, 1270, 1282, 1291, 1300
Cranborne, Viscountess (later Marchioness of Salisbury): 1236
Craven-Ellis, William: 1041
Crerar, Thomas Alexander: 591
Cripps, Sir Stafford: 72, 73, 417, 418, 1124, 1125, 1221
Cromwell, Oliver: 962, 1204
Crookshank, Harry (later Viscount): 960
Cross, (Sir) Ronald: 718, 781, 899 n.1, 993, 1095, 1293
Crow, (Sir) A.D.: 610, 611 n.1, 858
Cummings, A.C.: 1154 n.2
Cunningham, General (Sir) Alan: 1140
Cunningham, Admiral Sir Andrew (later Admiral of the Fleet, Viscount): 176, 217, 259, 482, 487 n.1, 524, 536, 547–8, 649, 664, 665, 733, 778, 785, 791–2, 1090, 1122, 1128, 1146, 1173–4, 1180 n.4. 1205, 1243, 1281
Cunningham, Admiral (Sir) John: 626, 660, 684, 699, 702, 821 n.1, 822 n.1, 831, 832, 856, 862, 866–70, 878, 991, 1054 n.2
Cusden, V.V.: 477

D'Abernon, Viscountess: 997
Dakar, Mayor of: 477
Daladier, Edouard: 54, 56–9, 60, 64, 65, 114
Dalton, Hugh (later Baron): 8, 69 n.1, 72, 182–4, 220, 227 and n., 238, 326, 368, 503–4, 538 n.1, 559, 593, 635, 656, 891, 899, 1005–6, 1016, 1063, 1173, 1246–7
Daniel, Captain (later Admiral Sir) C.S.: 745, 767, 1061 n.1, 1301 n.1
Darlan, Admiral: 210, 215, 216, 217, 280, 294 n.1, 300, 306, 307, 318 n.1, 320 n.2, 346, 359 n.1, 373–4, 383; and the fate of the French fleet, 395–7, 410–11, 424–5, 452, 469; recalled, 664; and Toulon, 997; 'revengeful', 1075, 1094; possible betrayal by, 1187; an approach from, 1272, 1273 n.1
David, André: 966
Davidson, Duncan: 1256 n.1
Davidson, J.J.: 541
Davies, Alfred: 823 n.1
Davies, Rhys: 564
Davies, Lieutenant Robert: 717 n.1
Davies, Miss: 1096
Davison, Sir William: 468
Davy, Lieutenant-Colonel G.M.O.: 178 n.1
Dawson, Geoffrey: 727
Dean, (Sir) Patrick: 709
De Gaulle, General Charles: (in June 1940), 273, 289 n.2, 290–1, 294–5, 300, 305, 307, 317, 322 n.1; (in London), 335, 347, 348–9, 348 n.2; (and the fall of France), 349–50, 351, 356, 369, 396; (British recognition for, and support of, June, 1940), 400–1, 404–5, 406–7, 408–9, 410 n.1, 428–9, 429 n.1, 448 n.1; (support for, July 1940), 451, 452, 453, 455, 471, 481; (August 1940), 602, 612–6, 695, 730, 731, 747; (September 1940), 793, 856, 879; (October 1940), 892–3, 930, 938, 956, 1014; (November 1940), 1021, 1054; (and Dakar), 478, 605, 606, 624–6, 630–1, 632–3, 636, 650, 659–61, 698–9, 702, 710–11, 730–1, 739, 754, 820–2, 838, 843, 856–7, 861–3, 868–9, 878, 893, 918–9, 991; and

INDEX 1349

North Africa, 573, 587; and Konakry, 873; and Duala, 879, 893; and Libreville, 893, 991, 995, 998, 1064; and Cayenne, 898; and Jibouti, 1165–6, 1298, 1302; broadcasting by, 636, 660; and British contacts with General Weygand, 999, 1014, 1063, 1064, 1075, 1077; and the Brazzaville declaration, 1014 n.1, 1113 n.1; and Syria, 1084; at Chequers, 1199–1200, 1223; and the victory of Sidi Barrani, 1242; and Libya, 1302

De La Baume, M.: 898 n.1

De Labilliere, Paul (Dean of Westminster): 144

De La Warr, 9th Earl: 1164

Denham, 1st Baron (George Wentworth Bowyer): 45 n.1

Desborough, 1st Baron: 911 n.1

Despard, Captain M.S.: 1133

De Valera, Eamon: 343, 371, 379, 390, 483, 923, 1063, 1114–5, 1126, 1168, 1225, 1226

Devonshire, 10th Duke of: 45 n.1, 1223, 1251

Dewar, Captain A. Ramsay: 600

Dewar, Vice-Admiral R.G.D.: 779 n.1

Dewing, General R.H.: 146

Dill, General (later Field Marshal) Sir John: Vice-Chief of the Imperial General Staff, 10 n.2, 51 n.1, 53, 54 n.2, 56, 57, 62, 65, 79, 95, 110, 112, 114, 125, 131, 134, 140–3, 146–8, 150; Chief of the Imperial General Staff, 163, 172, 174, 203, 205, 209, 214, 215–6; (in June 1940), 229, 273, 288, 293, 296, 302, 306, 327, 329, 350 n.4, 356, 370, 377–8, 378, 398, 441; and French troops, 501; and 'vulnerable points', 617; and artillery during an invasion, 742; and Australian troops, 796 n.2; and Singapore, 836; (in August 1940), 658, 673; (in September 1940), 804, 807, 872; (in October 1940), 891, 906, 936, 939, 942–3, 955 n.1, 991, 993, 994, 1012; (in November 1940), 1025, 1040, 1059, 1062; (in December 1940), 1140, 1158, 1172, 1175 n.2, 1206, 1307; Churchill's minutes to, 187, 188, 496–8, 637, 674–7, 790, 848, 962, 963, 972–4, 976–7, 1009–10, 1023–4, 1055–6, 1056, 1060, 1124–5, 1134–5, 1140, 1159, 1184, 1266, 1299, 1305–6; at Chequers, 580, 581–2, 582 n.1, 638 n.1, 639, 784

Disraeli, Benjamin (Earl of Beaconsfield): 644

Dobbie, Lieutenant-General (Sir) William: 402, 761, 778, 848, 865, 937

Dorman-Smith, (Sir) Reginald: 940 n.2

Douglas, R.I.: 1154 n.2

Douglas, Air Vice-Marshal (Sir) William Sholto: 216, 905 n.2, 1123 n.2

Dowding, Air Chief Marshal Sir Hugh (later Baron): 37, 38, 41, 80, 252 ns.1 and 2, 258, 263–4, 360, 372, 388 n.2, 498, 513, 575–6, 682, 750, 814, 816, 858, 903, 905 n.2, 907–8, 939 n.1, 955, 1012, 1094

Drake, Sir Francis: 802

Drew, Major-General (Sir) J.S.: 330

Duchesne, Jacques (Michel Saint-Denis): 979

Dudley, 3rd Earl of: 1223

Duff Cooper, (Sir) Alfred (later Viscount Norwich): (in May 1940), 29 n.2, 42–3, 67, 68, 118, 174, 177, 217; (in June 1940), 387, 391, 396, 407, 410, 448; (in July 1940), 470, 501 n.1, 503, 534, 545, 563 n.2; (in August 1940), 632, 650 n.1; (in September 1940), 843; (in October 1940), 966; (in November 1940), 1052, 1154 n.2; Churchill's letters and minutes to, 423, 552, 636, 650, 685, 1130, 1163, 1211

Dugdale, Thomas (later Baron Crathorne): 1251

Dunbar-Nasmith, Admiral Sir Martin Eric: 609

Duncan, Sir Andrew: 9 n.1, 245, 886 n.1, 887, 939, 963, 1036, 1226–7, 1269, 1270, 1274–5, 1293, 1294–5

Dunn, Colonel Capel: 955 n.1

Dupuy, Pierre: 1272–3, 1280–1, 1280 n.2, 1302, 1303, 1307

Eade, Charles: 379 n.1

Eastwood, Major-General (Sir) Ralph: 963 n.2, 973, 1055

Eden, Anthony (later Earl of Avon): (in May 1940), 11, 13, 24, 28, 34, 77 n.2, 79, 82 n.2, 92, 127, 140, 157, 160, 161, 190; (in June 1940), 233, 256, 288, 298, 299, 302, 306–7, 329, 335, 343, 345, 374–5, 391; (in July 1940), 484, 531; (in August 1940), 638, 639, 657, 673, 685 n.2, 706; (in September 1940), 760, 778, 798, 851, 855, 885, 885–6, 886 n.1; (in October 1940), 903 n.3, 917, 922, 923–4, 952, 955 n.1, 956, 1002, 1013–4; (in November 1940), 1032, 1050, 1067, 1087, 1088 n.1, 1100 n.1, 1113, 1118, 1139, 1151; (in December 1940), 1171, 1178, 1204–5, 1206, 1215, 1223, 1241, 1244–5, 1260, 1265, 1269 n.1, 1270, 1282, 1308; and the Cabinet changes of October 1940, 890–1; to go to the Foreign Office (December 1940), 1251, 1252, 1265; his letters to Churchill, 91, 521, 617, 837, 1161; Churchill letters and minutes to, (May 1940), 141, 187; (June 1940), 259, 261–2, 268, 330–1, 398, 418, 422, 431; (July 1940), 461, 483, 487, 488, 500–1, 501, 510, 515, 522, 525–6, 554–5, 559–60, 562, 586; (August 1940), 606, 622, 627, 637, 649, 657–8, 663, 674–7, 681, 701, 716–7, 718, 720, 721–2, 748, 749–50; (September 1940), 756, 790–1, 793, 800, 806, 809, 840, 848, 849, 859–60, 864–5, 886; (October 1940), 925, 999, 1001, 1006; (November 1940), 1026, 1030, 1041, 1070, 1086, 1124–5,

Eden, Anthony (later Earl of Avon)—*contd.*
  1140, 1144–5, 1159; (December 1940), 1180,
  1198, 1207–9, 1302, 1304, 1313
Eden, Michael (later 7th Baron Henley):
  1199–1200, 1232, 1288–9
Einstein, Albert: 685 n.2
Elgin, 10th Earl of: 1031
Elisabeth, Queen (of the Belgians): 44 n.1, 135
Elizabeth, Queen (later the Queen Mother):
  144, 321, 432 n.2, 629, 765, 794, 807, 823,
  830, 1120, 1289
Elles, Sir Hugh: 124, 399
Elliot, Katherine (later Baroness Elliot of Harwood): 940
Elliot, Walter: 940
Elliot, (Sir) William: 510, 905 n.2
Elliston, Captain (Sir) G.S.: 910
Emmons, General Delos C.: 640 n.1
Erskine, Esmé: 1304
Estéva, Admiral: 395–7
Evans, Colonel (Sir) Arthur: 465
Evans, Admiral Sir E.R.G.R. (later Baron Mountevans): 924
Evans, Major-General R.E.: 295, 297 n.1
Evill, Air Vice-Marshal (later Air Chief Marshal Sir) Douglas: 66

Fagalde, General: 111, 131, 134, 208
Fairbairn, James Valentine: 662
Farouk, King of Egypt: 865, 924, 1018–9
Farquharson, Robert: 1256 n.1
Fauvelle, Major: 151, 152
Fitzgerald, Admiral J.U.P.: 274
Fitzroy, Algernon: 21, 425, 475, 1058, 1118
Foch, Marshal Ferdinand: 31 n.1, 509 n.1
Forbes, Admiral of the Fleet Sir Charles: 6, 278, 497, 785, 993
Fortune, General (Sir) V.M.: 266, 308 n.1
Fournier, Colonel Pierre: 265
Franco, General Francisco: 424 n.1, 875 n.1, 987 n.1, 998, 1019 n.1
Fraser, Rear-Admiral (later Admiral Sir) Bruce (Baron Fraser of North Cape): 281, 393, 499 n.1, 557, 812, 905 n.2, 1104, 1123 n.2, 1133
Fraser, Peter: 118, 264, 339, 366, 645–7, 680, 878, 1102, 1234–5
Freeman, Air Chief Marshal Sir Wilfrid: 955 n.1, 1289 n.1
Frère, General: 141
Freyberg, General (Sir) Bernard (later Baron): 494–5, 515, 525–6, 601–2, 781, 1235

Gallacher, William: 416, 1210
Galway, 8th Viscount: 1234
Gambetta, Léon: 766 n.3, 980, 982
Gamelin, General Maurice Gustave: 24, 31, 32, 36, 37, 39, 44, 54–9, 60, 61, 65, 66, 110, 120, 171, 182, 241, 416

Gandhi, Mohandas Karamchand (Mahatma): 557 n.2
Garibaldi, Giuseppe: 1016, 1285
Garrod, Air Marshal (Sir) A.G.R.: 658–9
Garvin, J.L.: 846 n.4
Gaynor, Squadron Leader: 1025
Gensoul, Admiral: 448, 459, 471–3, 536 n.1
Gentilhomme, General Paul-Louis Le: 1165
George II, King (of Greece): 1039, 1040, 1205, 1209 n.3
George VI, King: 8, 21, 34, 126, 144, 152, 220, 232, 249, 425, 432 n.2, 462, 463, 604 n.2, 629, 641, 765, 794, 807, 823, 830, 889, 968, 997, 998, 1009, 1082, 1120, 1185, 1209 n.3, 1210, 1213, 1237, 1289, 1292
Georges, General Joseph: 31, 35, 36, 38–9, 55, 66, 78, 79, 101, 147, 193, 274–5, 290, 291, 292, 294, 300, 303, 307, 326, 766
Ghormley, Admiral Robert L.: 640 n.1
Giffard, General (Sir) G.J.: 455, 699, 728
Gilbert, Martin: 444 n.2, 493 notes 1 and 3, 546 n.2
Gilmour, G.L.: 1154 n.2
Giraud, General H-H.: 65
Gladstone, W.E. (1809–1898): 595, 1151
Godfrey, Captain J.H.: 531
Godfrey, Archbishop William: 437 n.1
Godfroy, Admiral: 448, 471
Godwin-Austen, Major-General (later General Sir) A.R.: 701, 748, 793
Goering, Hermann: 381
Goldsmith, Antony: 303, 309
Goodall, Sir Stanley: 812
Gorbachev, Mikhail: 417 n.1
Gordon, General (of the Sudan): 962
Gordon-Finlayson, General Sir Robert: 638 n.1, 645, 657
Gort, Field Marshal Viscount: (in May 1940), 36–7, 59, 79, 81, 83, 95, 102, 104, 112, 113, 114, 115, 116–7, 118, 126, 129, 131, 138, 140–1, 142–3, 147–8, 149, 150, 151, 152–3, 161, 163, 170–1, 173–4, 186, 189–90, 191, 196–7, 198, 200, 204, 209, 211, 215, 216; (after May 1940), 226, 246, 501 n.1, 632, 846 n.4, 907
Grandi, Dino: 155
Grant, N.F.: 1154 n.2
Grant-Ferris, Squadron-Leader Robert: 1117
Graziani, Marshal Rodolfo: 1033 n.2, 1038, 1067–8
Green, Peter: 1256 n.1
Greenwood, Arthur: 7, 9, 19, 25, 26, 42, 156, 157, 159, 170, 181, 334 n.1, 441, 700, 952, 955 n.1, 1040, 1115, 1158, 1163–4, 1228, 1229, 1235, 1293
Greig, Sir Louis: 1021
Grenfell, C.P.: 911 n.1
Grenfell, David: 623–4, 648
Grigg, Sir James (P.J. Grigg): 376, 734, 935,

INDEX   1351

939, 941–2, 963, 972–3, 974, 976–7, 1023–4, 1060, 1061, 1164
Gubbins, Colonel (later Major-General Sir) Colin: 488 n.2
Guest, Ivor (later 2nd Viscount Guest): 2
Guest, Ivor (later 2nd Baron Wimborne): 2
Gullett, Sir Henry: 662
Gustav V, King (of Sweden): 603 n.1, 604
Gwynne, Miss: 621 n.1

Haakon, King (of Norway): 120, 207
Haggard, (Sir) Godfrey: 1265
Haile Selassie, Emperor of Abyssinia: 1304, 1313
Hailsham, 1st Viscount: rescued, 945–6
Haining, Lieutenant-General Sir R.H.: 268 n.1, 370, 699, 716, 955 n.1, 1051, 1232, 1298 n.1
Halifax, 3rd Viscount: Foreign Secretary (in May 1940), 8, 9, 10, 12, 15, 40, 72, 79, 134–5, 144 n.3, 153, 431; and the fall of France, 156, 157–8, 159, 166, 168–9, 169–70, 180–1, 185, 186, 191, 192, 220, 230, 235–6, 253, 266, 346, 349, 369, 391; and 'mediation by Italy', 180–1, 185; and the French Fleet, 394, 396, 400; and 'free Frenchmen', 502; and a 'Fifth Columnist', 855 n.2; at 10 Downing Street, 617; at Chequers, 1001, 1232–3; and Holland, 259; and Italy, 260–1, 286–7, 787; and Belgium, 357; and Japan, 478–9, 479 n.2, 597, 623, 768, 896–7, 901; and the United States, 593, 628–9, 1116, 1215–6; and Vichy France, 898–9, 900, 925, 998, 1014, 1020, 1030, 1054, 1077, 1106; and Turkey, 1015; and Egypt, 1018–9; and Spain, 1019; and Greece, 1036, 1039, 1040, 1109; and Switzerland, 1283; and the Balkans, 1137–8; and Neville Chamberlain, 281, 740, 884–5, 968, 1061–2; at Tours (June 1940), 314 n.1, 315, 413; and de Gaulle, 400–1, 404–5, 406; and security, 504, 710 n.3; and a possible move to No. 11, 541; and Hitler's 'peace offensive' (July 1940), 551; and Swedish mediation, 603–4; and a German emissary (September 1940), 799; remains at the Foreign Office, 886 n.1; and a rebuke withdrawn, 1088; and Enigma, 955 n.1; and an important letter to Roosevelt, 1163; and the Washington Embassy, 1220, 1223, 1251, 1251–2, 1265, 1266–7, 1268; and Churchill's character, 483–4; and Churchill's 'rompers', 1157; and a Churchill remark, 1151; and Churchill's speech notes, 922; and Churchill's leadership of the Conservative Party, 926; Churchill's letters and minutes to, (June 1940) 192; (July 1940) 235–6, 259, 260–1, 283, 419, 424, 437, 441, 485–6, 535, 554, 566–7, 569–70; (August 1940), 603–4, 611, 612, 628–9, 642–3; (September 1940), 779, 780, 853, 865, 883, 884–5; (October 1940), 900, 901, 925, 940, 957; (November 1940), 1064–5, 1074, 1084–5, 1092, 1113, 1134, 1149, 1150; (December 1940), 1209–10, 1212–3, 1251–2, 1265, 1266–7
Halifax, Viscountess (later Countess of): 1267
Hall, Professor N.F.: 955 n.1
Hamblin, Grace: 944 n.2
Hankey, 1st Baron: 14–15, 280, 1084, 1105
Harbord, Captain: 965
Harding, Sir Edward John: 857
Hardinge, Sir Alexander (later 2nd Baron): 231–2, 629, 955 n.1
Harris, Sir Arthur: 493 n.1
Harris, Sir Percy: 179, 545
Harris, Robert: quoted, 93 n.1
Harrod, (Sir) Roy: 1280 n.1
Harvie-Watt, Lieutenant-Colonel (Sir) George: 908, 909
Harwood, Rear-Admiral (later Admiral) Sir Henry: 786, 1170
Havard, Godfrey: 643 n.1
Haye, Henri: 855, 975, 1000 n.2
Henderson, Admiral Sir Reginald: 787 n.1, 788
Herbert, (Sir) Alan (A.P. Herbert): 942 n.3
Herriot, Edouard: 320
Hill, Kathleen: 136, 342, 379 n.1, 426, 969, 1032, 1033, 1123 n.1
Hirsch, Georgette: 47 n.2
Hitler, Adolf: and Britain's war aims, 151, 156, 157–8, 319, 643; and the fall of France, 169, 269, 311, 312, 316, 320, 324, 326, 337, 338; and the fall of Belgium, 177; and Italian mediation, 180–1; and Britain's future, 183, 186, 246, 287, 308, 339, 593, 1191; and Britain's defeat, 271, 409, 533; his bleak prospect, 271, 341, 772; his aim, 313; and whistling, 337; and sea power, 338; and air power, 365, 385, 511, 644, 692, 801, 1043; and industrial power, 367; past forecasts, 365 n.1; the choice facing him, 368, 384; his triumph, 382; his dangers, 385; and possible peace negotiations with, 409, 550, 603–4, 799; and Russia, 429, 493; and Spain, 566, 1231, 1243, 1246; and Norway, 745; and the Czechs, 888–9; and the French fleet, 521, 516; and Marshal Pétain, 998, 1014; and Vichy France, 1003, 1014, 1048, 1192; and Churchill, 447, 493; and British bombing policy, 493, 513, 686, 694; and the bombing of British cities ('will fail'), 905, 911, 916, 980, 983, 1042, 1044; and the 'invasion' of 15 September 1940, 778, 802–3; and the British blockade, 635, 689; and the war at sea, 1225; and a bombing attempt on (November 1940), 1076 n.1; and gas, 515–6, 593; his 'gospel of hatred', 517; his past plans, 518, 1263; avoiding the Kaiser's mistake, 1193;

1352　INDEX

Hitler, Adolf—*contd.*
and the Night of the Long Knives (1934), 1231 n.1; his 'dark curse', 520; 'had us all guessing', 617; his offer to captive peoples, 708; and Mussolini, 1137, 1146, 1151; his future, 913; 'his doom is certain', 969; and 'retribution', 981; whither? (December 1940), 1246–7; forgets Harrow School, 1255; the 'general enemy', 1256–7; and an 'honest statement', 1258; and Napoleon, 1257, 1263; and Attila, 1287; 'that man', 559, 933; 'that bad man', 705; 'this wicked man', 803
Hoare, Brigadier-General Reginald: 16
Hoare, Sir Samuel (later Viscount Templewood): 14, 281, 391, 411–2, 424 n.1, 432 n.2, 799, 838, 883, 892, 900 n.1, 906, 969, 987, 992, 997, 998, 1014, 1019, 1075; his congratulations, 928–9
Hobart, Major-General (Sir) P.C.S.: 934, 942–3, 962, 993, 1123 n.2
Hogg, Quintin (later 2nd Viscount Hailsham, subsequently Baron Hailsham of St Marylebone): 945–6
Holden, Norman: 846
Holland, Captain C.S.: 459, 471, 472
Hollis, Colonel (later General Sir) Leslie: 575, 739, 809, 995–6, 1301
Holroyd, James Edward: 789
Hood, 6th Viscount: 966–7
Hoover, Herbert (former President): 689
Hopkins, C.J.W.: 489, 622
Hopkinson, Austin: 671
Horder, 1st Baron: 607, 1245
Hore-Belisha, Leslie (later Baron): 384, 415, 476, 512, 546
Horton, Vice-Admiral Sir M.K.: 785
Howard-Vyse, Colonel (Sir) John: 14, 327
Howe, Clarence Decatur: 1189, 1280 n.2
Hudson, Robert: 195, 1220, 1251
Huggins, Godfrey (later Viscount Malvern): 1250
Hull, Cordell: 322, 896, 897, 902 n.1, 1237 n.2
Huntziger, General Charles: 112, 1273
Hyde, Marion: 629

Illingworth (cartoonist): 1183
Ingersoll, Ralph: 1153–4
Ironside, General (later Field Marshal) Sir Edmund (later Baron): Chief of the Imperial General Staff, 10, 17, 20 n.1, 25, 27, 36, 40–1, 43, 67, 81–2, 83, 95, 97 n.1, 100, 104, 114, 117, 122, 125, 126, 130, 133, 139, 140, 150; Commander-in-Chief, Home Forces, 193, 202, 272, 359, 370, 372, 375, 438, 456, 484, 495–6; replaced by General Brooke, 531, 550; his peerage, 629; attacked, 907; Churchill's minutes to, 116–7, 141, 142, 149–50, 496–8
Irwin, Major-General (later Lieutenant-General) N.M.S.: 660, 699, 702, 821 n.1, 831, 832, 856, 866–70, 878, 976
Ismay, Major-General (Sir) Hastings (later Baron): (in May 1940), 10 n.2, 11, 34, 60, 62, 64, 65, 103, 110, 114, 140, 150, 172, 192, 205; (in June 1940), 263, 288, 314 n.1, 350, 441, 446; (in July 1940), 505, 510–11, 580, 581–2; (in August 1940), 601, 611, 612, 638 n.1, 673, 711; (in September 1940), 758, 784, 804 n.2, 837, 847; (in October 1940), 931, 939, 955 n.1, 972 n.1, 991; (in November 1940), 1111; (in December 1940), 1232; Churchill's minutes to, (May 1940), 32–3, 76–7, 91–2, 116–7, 121–2, 129–30, 138–9, 166, 175–6, 187, 188, 191–2, 204–5; (June 1940), 226–8, 249–50, 251, 252, 257, 272, 283, 352, 370–1, 392, 402–4, 404, 422, 430, 439–40, 444–5; (July 1940), 452–3, 456–7, 463, 478, 480, 489–90, 491, 499, 499–500, 509, 512, 515–6, 523, 526, 536, 549, 554, 556, 561, 562, 567, 570, 571, 577, 578; (August 1940), 599–600, 600, 604–5, 605, 610, 620–2, 637–8, 639, 640–1, 649, 650, 654–6, 664, 680, 681, 682, 684, 710–11, 712, 716, 720 n.1, 727, 728–30, 737, 738, 740–3, 747, 748; (September 1940), 753–5, 761, 795–6, 796 n.1, 799–800, 805, 810–11, 829, 830–1, 833, 838–9, 848, 854, 858, 858–9, 859–60, 879, 879–80, 881; (October 1940), 903–4, 904, 935, 936–8, 989, 943, 955, 964–5, 965 n.1, 995–6, 1010, 1015; (November 1940), 1024, 1031, 1061, 1064–5, 1069, 1084 n.1, 1086–7, 1103–4, 1128, 1135, 1138, 1139, 1146–7, 1155, 1158–9, 1162; (December 1940), 1165–7, 1175, 1176–7, 1184–5, 1209, 1211, 1271, 1273–4, 1283, 1290, 1293–4, 1295, 1298, 1304, 1306; his memoirs and recollections, 19, 206, 318, 678, 1067–8, 1214–5

Jackson, Robert: 844–5
Jacob, Lieutenant-Colonel (later Lieutenant-General Sir) Ian: 20 n.1, 198, 484, 505, 638 n.1, 644, 645, 650, 818, 819, 939, 1000, 1067, 1274
James, Admiral Sir William: 531
Jaspar, M.: 369
Jefferis, Major (later Major-General Sir) Millis: 402, 710, 1074, 1198
Jinnah, Mohammed Ali: 506, 557 n.2
Johnson, Dr.: 256
Johnson, Herschel V.: 92
Jones, R.V.: 387–8, 433
Jordana, Count Francisco: 987 n.2
Joubert de la Ferté, Air Marshal Sir Philip: 52, 54 n.2, 57, 58, 66, 388 n.2, 818, 905 n.2, 1177–8, 1197–8, 1211 n.1

Karslake, General Sir Henry: 148, 152

INDEX 1353

Kayll, Squadron Leader J.R.: 1025, 1026
Kelly, (Sir) David: 940, 1283
Kempe, Alderman A.B.C.: 735–6
Kennedy, Major-General (Sir) John: 330
Kennedy, John F.: 34 n.4, 758 n.2
Kennedy, Joseph: 34 n.4
Kennedy, Joseph P.: 34, 322, 324, 325, 337, 338, 483 n.1, 485–6, 593, 666, 901, 1121
Kennedy, Robert: 34 n.4
Kent, Duke of: 412
Kent, Tyler: 93 n.1, 106 n.1
Kerr, (Sir) Hamilton: 1151
Key, Charles William: 1117
Keyes, Admiral of the Fleet Sir Roger (later Baron): 39, 44, 101, 118, 126, 127, 128, 129, 130, 134, 135, 146, 147, 151, 152, 158–9, 161, 170, 173, 176–7; a possible job for, 489–90; Director of Combined Operations, 531, 559, 568, 632, 706–7, 749, 1033, 1111, 1151, 1173, 1180, 1232, 1271, 1281
Keynes, J.M. (later Baron): 846 n.4, 1280 n.1
King, General (Sir) C.J.S.: 725, 806
King, William Mackenzie: 145, 254–5, 264, 270, 280, 339, 366, 408, 409, 546, 590–1, 682, 713–5, 783, 804, 843, 878, 932–3, 941, 1149, 1155, 1185, 1118–9, 1222, 1252–3, 1273 n.1, 1302, 1303
Kirke, General Sir Walter: 128
Kitchener of Khartoum, Field Marshal Earl: 796 n.2
Knatchbull-Hugessen, Sir Hughe: 1137–8, 1144
Knox, Colonel W. Frank: 386, 607, 628
Koenig, General Pierre: 995 n.1

Labori, Ferdinand: 983
Lambert, George (later Viscount): 595
Lampson, Sir Miles (later Baron Killearn): 192 n.1, 287, 853, 924, 1019, 1087–8, 1313
Landemare, Georgina: 945–6
Lang, Sir Cosmo Gordon (later Baron): 425, 476, 586, 727
Laurencie, General de: 208
Laval, Pierre: 569, 875, 957, 997, 1014, 1048, 1075, 1094, 1187
Law, Richard (later 1st Baron Coleraine): 1123 n.2
Lawford, Nicholas: 966
Lawrence, T.E. ('Lawrence of Arabia'): 962
Lawson, Commander: 905 n.2
Layton, Sir Walter (later Baron): 403, 882, 1004, 1185
Leach, Captain, R.N.: 77
Learoyd, Flight-Lieutenant R.A.B.: 666 n.1
Lebrun, President: 359 n.1
Leclerc, Captain (Captain de Hautecloque): 731 n.1
Lee of Fareham, 1st Viscount: 1290
Lees-Smith, H.B.: 179, 467, 1117, 1218

Léger, Alexis Saint-Léger (St Jean Perse): 406, 440–1
Leighton-Morris, Mr.: 1091 n.2
Leith-Ross, Sir Frederick: 1005
Lelong, Colonel Albert: 407
Leopold, King of the Belgians: 44, 101–2, 113, 115, 126, 129, 135–6, 147, 151, 152, 158, 161, 171, 172–3; seeks armistice, 173, 176–7, 178–9, 182, 240, 242, 260; seeks negotiations (November 1939), 690 n.1
Lewis, Oswald: 564
Liddell, Lieutenant-General (later General) Sir Clive: 378
Liddell Hart, Captain (Sir) Basil: 1172
Lindemann, Brigadier Charles: 1280 n.1
Lindemann, Professor Frederick (later Baron Cherwell): (in May 1940), 77 n.2, 206; (in June 1940), 248, 336, 377, 388 n.2, 403, 433 n.z; (in July 1940), 494 n.2, 508 n.1, 513, 537 n.1, 580, 581; (in August 1940), 638, 644, 737, 751; (in September 1940), 758, 791 n.1, 805, 833; (in October 1940), 905 n.2, 988 n.1, 1065, 1098 n.1; (in November 1940), 1123 n.2, 1124 n.1, 1158 n.2, 1163; (in December 1940), 1169, 1199, 1218 n.1, 1230, 1246, 1280 n.1, 1289 n.1; Churchill's minutes to, 137, 237, 238, 266, 270, 441–2, 488, 609, 673, 744, 1293, 1300
Lindsay, Kenneth: 45 n.1, 563
Linlithgow, 2nd Marquess of: 397, 506–8, 528–9, 557, 568, 571–3, 574, 583, 584–5, 589, 992, 1116
Lithgow, Sir James: 813
Little, Admiral Sir Charles: 861
Little, James: 1148
Lloyd, Geoffrey (later Baron Geoffrey-Lloyd): 988 n.1
Lloyd, 1st Baron (George Lloyd): 121, 184, 217, 334 n.1, 359 n.1, 368–9, 374, 397, 400, 414, 419, 435, 462 n.1, 470, 490, 508 n.1, 605, 613, 939, 977, 1002–3, 1028–9, 1041, 1126
Lloyd George, David (later Earl Lloyd-George of Dwyfor): 5 n.2, 24, 194–6, 255, 314, 367, 846 n.4, 886, 929, 1220, 1223, 1236, 1237, 1244, 1251, 1258, 1261, 1292
Lloyd George, Gwilym (later Viscount Tenby): 1141 n.1, 1221
Loch, Major-General (Sir) Kenneth: 858, 905 n.2, 1109
Long, Major Eric (later 3rd Viscount Long): 928
Longmore, Air Vice-Marshal Sir A.M.: 1024, 1037, 1078–9, 1087, 1109, 1176, 1242, 1260, 1305
Loraine, Sir Percy: 40, 787
Lothian, 11th Marquess of (Philip Kerr): 79, 93, 162–3, 185, 270–1, 304, 374 n.1, 378, 436, 486, 551, 556 n.1, 576–7, 593, 607, 627–

Lothian, 11th Marquess of—*contd.*
8, 668, 709, 726, 733, 734, 780, 842, 844–5, 854, 855, 862, 876, 896, 1001–2, 1008, 1054, 1080, 1099, 1116, 1147, 1157 n.1, 1162–3, 1168, 1185; death of, 1220, 1225, 1257–8, 1267; successor to, 1230, 1237, 1244–5, 1267
Low, (Sir) David: 28 n.2, 29, 184, 1228, 1229, 1235
Lumley, Lawrence Roger (later 11th Earl of Scarbrough): 507
Lumsden, John: 1256 n.1
Lund, Brigadier (later General Sir) O.M.: 54 n.2, 288
Lutyens, Sir Edward: 846 n.4, 1253 n.2
Lyttelton, Lady Moira: 1123 n.2
Lyttelton, Oliver (later Viscount Chandos): 403, 404, 440, 886 n.1, 944, 1123 n.2, 1251
Lytton, 2nd Earl of: 598–9

MacAlpine, E.W.: 1154 n.2
Macarthy, Sergeant: 909
MacCallum Scott, Alexander: 500–1
McCorquodale, Alastair: 1256 n.1
MacDonald, Malcolm: 343, 352, 419, 775, 827, 924, 1073, 1251, 1252, 1275, 1291–2, 1302 n.1
MacDonald, Ramsay: 318 n.2, 586 n.1
McEwen, Captain: 45 n.1
McKean, Air Vice-Marshal (Sir) L.D.D.: 994
Mackesy, Major-General P.J.: 331
Mackie, E.R.: 1154 n.2
MacMichael, Sir Harold: 191
Macmillan, Harold (later Earl of Stockton): 410 n.3
Macmillan, Miss: 68 n.1
McNaughten, General A.G.L.: 133–4, 488
Macready, General (Sir) G.N.: 1055, 1060
Maffey, Sir John (later Baron Rugby): 1114, 1126, 1216, 1282
Maisky, Ivan: 514
Mallet, (Sir) Victor: 799
Mandel, Georges: 217 n.1, 309, 310, 320, 326, 345, 351
Mander, (Sir) Geoffrey Le M.: 670, 1257
Marchienne, Baron Emile Cartier de: 134–5
Margerie, Captain Roland de: 54 n.2, 110, 188, 219, 308
Margesson, David (later Viscount): 34, 331, 423, 653, 891, 945, 946, 953, 1099–1100, 1144 n.1, 1179, 1251, 1257, 1282–3, 1289, 1299
Marlborough, 1st Duke of (John Churchill): 794, 870, 962
Marlborough, 10th Duke of: 743
Marlborough, Duchess of (Lady Alexandra Cadogan): 1236
Marsh, Sir Edward: 846 n.4
Marshall, General George C.: 640 n.1
Marshall-Cornwall, General Sir James: 580–2

Martin, (Sir) John: 123, 137 n.1, 196, 225–6, 360, 448, 549 n.1, 791 n.1, 807, 817–8, 946–7, 953–4, 957, 965 n.2, 979, 1001–2, 1095–6, 1132, 1251 n.3, 1292
Marvell, Andrew: 366 n.2
Mary, Queen: 432 n.2
Masaryk, Dr. Thomas: 888
Massy, General H.R.S.: 421–2
Matters, L.W.: 1154 n.2
Maurice, Nancy (later Lady Spears): 1057
Maxton, James: 23, 416
Maze, Paul: 985
Mazzini, Giuseppe: 1285
Medhurst, Wing-Commander (later Air Chief Marshal Sir) C.E.H.: 1108, 1301 n.1
Melville, (Sir) R.H.: 1092
Menzies, (Sir) Robert: 118, 119–10, 162 n.2, 264, 339, 366, 557–8, 645–7, 663, 803–4, 878, 892, 894–6, 896 n.1, 904–5, 1187–8, 1222, 1237
Menzies, Colonel (Sir) Stewart Graham ('C'): 621, 880, 955 n.1
Metaxas, General: 1039, 1040, 1150
Michael, Prince (of Kent): 412 n.2
Michiels, Major-General (later Lieutenant-General) F.: 95
Middlebrook, Martin (and Chris Everitt): quoted, 666 n.1
Milner, Major James (later Baron): 539, 540
Mitford, Unity: 444 n.1
Molotov, Vyacheslav: 72, 417 n.1
Moltke, General Helmut von: 1032 n.3
Monckton, Sir Walter (later Viscount): 177–8, 578, 1098 n.1
Monnet, Jean: 263, 322 n.1, 347, 348, 374
Montagu, Venetia: 3
Montgomery, General (later Field Marshal Viscount) Bernard: 457–8, 931, 934 n.1
Moore-Brabazon, Lieutenant Colonel J.T.C. (later Baron): 380, 399, 700, 944, 961–2, 1028–9, 1227, 1293, 1300–1
Moorhead, Major–General C.D.: 1271
Morgan, Major-General (Sir) W.D.: 446
Morgenthau, Henry, Jr.: 225, 842 n.2, 1185, 1215–6, 1309
Morris-Jones, Sir John Henry: 910
Morrison, Herbert (later Baron): Minister of Supply, 7, 9 n.1, 29 n.2, 77 n.2, 184, 379 n.1, 422, 440, 586, 608, 610, 623, 654, 673, 677, 700, 704, 763, 765, 768, 782; Home Secretary and Minister of Home Security, 886 n.1, 915, 952, 1123 n.2, 1302 n.1, 1312; Churchill's minutes to, 257, 258, 355–6, 419, 489, 651–2, 738, 747, 793, 795, 805, 834, 834–5, 851, 852, 871, 877, 880, 887, 963, 1084, 1091, 1130, 1276–7, 1291–2, 1301–2; Churchill congratulates, 1121
Morrison, W.S.: (later Viscount Dunrossil): 560, 685 n.1

INDEX

Morton, (Sir) Desmond: 140, 159, 162, 206, 221, 270, 331, 348, 368–9, 377, 404, 481, 605, 606, 621, 627, 698 n.1, 735, 739, 816 n.1, 817, 969, 988 n.1, 999, 1069, 1223
Mosley, Lady (the Hon. Diana Guinness): 440 n.2, 444, 1277
Mosley, Max: 1277 n.2
Mosley, Sir Oswald: 183, 270, 1277
Mottistone, 1st Baron (Major-General Sir Jack Seely): 602 n.1, 846
Mountbatten, Admiral Lord Louis (later Earl Mountbatten of Burma): 992 n.1, 1009, 1199
Mountbatten, Lady (later Countess): 1199
Mowrer, Edgar Ansel: 532–4, 534–5, 534 n.1
Moyne, 1st Baron: 846 n.4
Munster, Captain Geoffrey, 5th Earl of: 196–7
Murphy, Robert D.: 998
Muselier, Vice-Admiral Emile: 481, 606
Mussolini, Benito: a neutral, 28 n.2, 40, 45, 50, 78, 144, 155 notes 1 and 2, 156, 157, 158, 159, 166–7, 180, 185, 186, 223; a belligerent (from 10 June 1940), 279, 283, 302, 363, 723, 734, 913, 981, 1048, 1072, 1133, 1137, 1146, 1151, 1172, 1191, 1222, 1224, 1225, 1239, 1285–7, 1288; Hitler's 'little confederate', 981
Mutter, (Lieutenant) Ronald: 1256 n.1

Napoleon Bonaparte: 246, 247, 567, 638, 766 n.2, 772, 802, 954 n.1, 981, 983, 984, 1242, 1257, 1263
Negrin, Juan: 1019
Nehru, Jawaharlal: 1277
Nelson, Admiral Horatio (of Bronte and the Nile): 427 n.1, 644, 691, 802, 846
Nelson (the cat): 426, 922, 1002, 1017
Newall, Air Chief Marshal Sir Cyril (later Baron): (in May 1940), 10 n.2, 17, 20, 37, 38, 43, 51, 58, 63, 67, 82 n.2, 97 n.1, 100, 101, 104, 106, 120, 144 n.1, 145, 165; (in June 1940), 222, 226, 258, 274, 277, 304, 345, 349, 350, 373, 388 n.2, 390, 441; (in July 1940), 461, 556; (in August 1940), 627; (in September 1940), 836, 872; (in October 1940), 905 n.2, 917, 977–8, 991, 1013; (in November 1940), 1079; Churchill's minutes to, 259, 282, 461, 555, 606, 610, 611, 679, 710, 719, 738, 740–1, 756, 874, 954, 961, 970–2
Nicholson, Brigadier C.N.: 139, 149, 160, 241
Nicholson, Emma: 468 n.3
Nicholson, Godfrey: 468–9
Nicolson, (Sir) Harold: 20, 68, 250, 476, 520, 539, 593, 697, 829, 960, 1050, 1122–3, 1288
Nicolson, Nigel: 68 n.1
Noble, Admiral Sir Percy: 609 n.2
Noel-Baker, Philip (later Baron): 381, 544
Noguès, General Auguste: 410, 1064, 1280

North, Admiral Sir Dudley: 410, 552
North, Roger Dudley: 1256 n.1
Northcliffe, 1st Viscount: 15 n.2
Nuffield, 1st Viscount: 1238
Nuri es-Said, General: 334

O'Connor, Major-General (later General Sir) Richard: 1125 n.1
Odend'hal, Admiral: 451–2, 492
Ogilvie, (Sir) F.W.: 985–6
Oliver, Vic (Victor Samek): 4–5, 1289 n.1, 1292
Orczy, Baroness: 404 n.1
Oshima, Count Hiroshi: 875

Page, Brigadier L.F.: 488 n.1
Paget, Major-General (later Lieutenant-General Sir) Bernard: 370, 511
Paget, Lieutenant (later Baron) R.T.: 770 n.1
Pakenham-Walsh, Major-General (later Lieutenant-General) R.P.: 882, 1055
Palairet, Sir Michael: 1013–4, 1034, 1040, 1108, 1109, 1284
Papagos, General Alexander: 1105, 1200
Park, Air Vice-Marshal (Sir) Keith: 758, 813–6
Parker, Admiral: 427 n.1
Partridge, Bernard: cartoon by, 797
Paul, Prince (later King) of Greece: 1039 n.1
Peake, (Sir) Charles: 1157
Pearman, Violet: 48–9
Peck, (Sir) John: 34, 123 n.2, 132, 420 n.3, 549 n.1, 552 n.1, 765, 766 n.3, 922, 965 n.2, 966–7, 979–80, 1092, 1096, 1132
Peirse, Air Marshal Sir Richard: 37, 38, 42, 110, 113, 115, 222, 252 n.1, 522, 575, 699, 702, 710, 784, 787; Commander-in-Chief, Bomber Command, 955, 970, 1025, 1123 n.2
Perceval, Spencer: 1057 n.1
Percival, General E.P.: 100
Pétain, Marshal Philippe: 31 n.1, 205, 206, 219, 222, 253, 256, 289 n.2, 293, 298, 300, 305, 307, 315, 351, 357, 359, 383; heads Vichy Government, 406, 410 n.1, 487, 569, 611–2, 925, 997, 998, 1000, 1014, 1094, 1098 n.2, 1172, 1272, 1273 n.1, 1281, 1307; Churchill's letter to (December 1940), 1312–3; his rival, 766 n.1
Phillips, Sir Frederick: 713, 715, 1214, 1309
Phillips, Major Gray: 555
Phillips, Sir Thomas: 74
Phillips, Rear-Admiral (Sir) T.S.V.: 138, 373, 393 n.1, 394, 397, 400, 451–2, 482, 556, 558–9, 626, 699, 741, 786, 787–8, 848, 955 n.1, 1098 n.1, 1230, 1232, 1233
Pierlot, Hubert: 173, 369 n.2
Pile, Lieutenant-General Sir Frederick: 852, 858, 905 n.2, 907–10, 931
Pim, Captain (Sir) Richard: 193, 946, 1107 n.1

Pimlott, Ben: quoted, 182 n.1
Pipon, Vice-Admiral Sir J.M.: 1063, 1064 n.2, 1065 n.2
Pitt, William (the Younger): 196, 953
Pitt-Rivers, Captain George: 440 n.2, 444
Pius XII, Pope (Eugene Pacelli): 1016, 1025, 1285
Platt, General William: 582 n.1
Playfair, Brigadier (later Major-General) I.S.O.: 745 n.2, 746, 1061 n.1, 1301 n.1
Pleven, René: 348
Plowden, Pamela (later Countess of Lytton): 598 n.1
Pontius Pilate: 315
Portal, 1st Baron (Wyndham Portal, later Viscount): 765
Portal, Air Marshal Sir Charles (later Viscount): 388 n.2, 750, 791 n.1, 917, 939 n.1, 1005, 1012, 1025, 1039, 1051, 1175 n.2, 1186, 1217, 1232, 1265; Churchill's minutes and letters to (in October 1940), 1007, 1016; (in November 1940), 1022–3, 1024, 1027–8, 1056, 1073, 1096–7, 1097–8, 1100–2, 1130–1, 1149, 1162; (in December 1940), 1169, 1186, 1201, 1240, 1266, 1278, 1278–9, 1303, 1304–5
Pound, Admiral of the Fleet Sir Dudley: (in May 1940), 10 n.2, 18, 20 n.1, 71, 77 n.2, 82 n.2, 96, 97 n.1, 98, 126, 145, 201; (in June 1940), 256, 272, 277, 279, 280 n.3, 305, 334, 349, 350, 359 n.1, 373, 390, 393 n.1, 394, 441; (in July 1940), 455, 490, 495, 523, 556, 560–1; (in August 1940), 631, 638, 661, 664, 666, 726; (in September 1940), 760, 785, 792 n.2, 798, 805 n.2, 832, 860, 867; (in October 1940), 893, 919, 955 n.1, 999; (in November 1940), 1020, 1025, 1029, 1044, 1059, 1107, 1123 n.2, 1133; (in December 1940), 1175 n.2, 1178, 1205–6, 1220, 1227, 1232, 1301; and the fate of the French fleet (June–July 1940), 395, 400, 414, 424–5, 426, 428, 443, 469; and Japan, 836; Churchill's minutes to, (in June 1940), 259, 260, 282, 373, 443; (in July 1940), 481, 486, 487, 505, 524–5, 547–8, 548, 554, 558–9, 582; (in August 1940), 597, 599, 608–9, 634, 679–80, 684, 719, 720, 747; (in September 1940), 755–6, 766–7, 780, 787–8, 790, 848, 874; (in October 1940), 964 n.2, 1002; (in November 1940), 1028–30, 1104, 1114, 1126–7, 1128–9, 1158–9, 1162, 1163; (in December 1940), 1170, 1175–6, 1239, 1269, 1282, 1296
Power, Vice-Admiral (Sir) Arthur: 684
Pownall, General (Sir) Henry: 81, 196, 198, 586, 638 n.1, 644, 1055, 1086
Prien, Günther: 596 n.1
Priestley, J.B.: 1211
Prioux, General: 111, 209
Prytz, Bjorn: 12, 419, 420 n.1

Purvis, Arthur: 70, 225, 372 n.2, 842 n.2, 854–5, 882, 1004, 1115, 1149, 1157 n.1, 1185, 1215–6, 1222

Quisling, Vidkun: 270

Rabin, Yitzhak: 811 n.4
Ralston, Colonel J.L.: 1189, 1280 n.2
Ramsay, Captain Archibald Henry Maule: 106 n.1
Ramsay, Vice-Admiral Sir Bertram: 742, 804
Ramsbotham, Herwald (later Viscount Soulbury): 786
Rashid Ali: 331 n.1
Redman, Lieutenant-Colonel (later Lieutenant-General Sir) Harold: 54 n.2, 61, 140, 206
Reichenau, General (later Field Marshal) Walther von: 117
Reith, Sir John (later Baron): 13, 648, 653 n.1, 663, 718–9, 806, 808, 842 n.3, 850–1, 886 n.1, 891–2, 961 n.2, 985 n.2, 990, 1052–3, 1158, 1200–1, 1227, 1275
Révész, Imre (later Emery Reves): 685
Reynaud, Paul: (in May 1940), 30–1, 32, 35–8, 41, 43, 54, 57, 59, 60, 61, 64, 65, 66, 79, 88 n.1, 93, 101, 102–3, 106, 109, 110, 113, 114, 117, 123, 125, 129, 130–1, 140–1, 141 n.1, 142–3, 147, 148, 150, 151–3, 151 n.2, 154–6, 158, 159–60, 163, 166–8, 174, 180–1, 185–7, 188, 190, 193–4, 199; and Churchill's visit to Paris, 31 May 1940, 205–9, 211–18, 219, 222, 229–30; and Dunkirk, 232, 236; and British assistance to France, 236, 238–9, 240, 252–3, 253–4, 262, 263, 265, 268, 267–70, 273, 275–6, 278, 280; and the battle for France, 285, 289–97, 298–302, 304, 307, 324, 326, 333–4, 337, 341, 344–5, 348–50; and Churchill's visit to Briare, 11–12 June 1940, 289–90, 293–7, 305–6; and Churchill's visit to Tours, 13 June 1940, 309–22, 413; and Cagney, 318 n.2; and Concarneau, 349–51; and the Franco-German armistice, 356–7, 383, 402, 413–4, 470; and the future of the French fleet, 405, 406, 410
Ribbentrop, Joachim von: 855 n.2, 875
Robertson, Sir Malcolm: 683
Robertson, S.S.: 1154 n.2
Rokach, Israel: 811
Rollin, Louis: 217
Romilly, Nellie (Mrs. Bertram Romilly): 3–4
Rommel, General (later Field Marshal) Erwin: 308 n.1
Roosevelt, President Franklin D.: (in May 1940), 25, 67, 79–80, 92, 118, 119, 144 n.3, 162, 167, 186, 203; (in June 1940), 255, 279, 286; and the fall of France, 285, 302, 306, 310, 311, 312, 314, 315–6, 319, 320–3, 320 n.2, 324–5, 333, 335–6, 337, 345–6; and the

French fleet, 378, 407; and destroyers for Britain, 304, 407, 482–3, 576, 593–5, 627–8, 644, 666–8, 682, 723, 975, 1112–3, 1269, 1296–7, 1308, 1311–2; and Ireland, 371 n.1, 1062–3, 1216, 1284, 1300; and rifles for Britain, 837 n.1, 854, 855, 870; and munitions, 842, 1214, 1297; and flying boats, 394, 407, 576, 682; and Britain's danger, 409, 436; and the future of the British fleet, 628, 682–3, 746–7; and bases on British territory, 696–7, 722–3; a naval gesture from, 855; and Dakar, 862–3, 870; and the Azores, 876 n.1; and the Burma Road, 901–2; and Vichy France, 996 n.2, 998, 1064, 1074–5, 1098–9; and the 1940 Presidential Election, 1021, 1053, 1169; a critical telegram to, 1080; and exchange of information, 1116; and Spain, 1127–8, 1156–7; and Britain's financial crisis (December 1940), 1245, 1246, 1247; and Lord Lothian, 1225, 1258; and Lord Halifax, 1268–9; statistics for, 1280 n.1; his 'Arsenal of Democracy' speech, 1306; Churchill pays tribute to, 385; his letters and telegrams to Churchill, (May 1940), 69–70, 204; (June 1940), 333; (October 1940), 996; (November 1940), 1098 n.2; Churchill's letters and telegrams to, (May 1940), 45–6, 71, 93; (June 1940), 225, 285, 287–8, 307–8, 324, 337–8, 341; (July 1940), 482–3, 593–5; (August 1940), 668, 704–5, 722–4, 733–4, 746–7; (September 1940), 854, 862–3, 870; (October 1940), 901–2, 974–5, 1000, 1003–4; (November 1940), 1018, 1053–4, 1074–5, 1098–9, 1122, 1147, 1156–7, 1162–3; (December 1940), 1168–9, 1179, 1189–97, 1225, 1225–6, 1236, 1237, 1245, 1268–9, 1296–7, 1308–11, 1312
Rosebery, 6th Earl of: 993
Rothermere, 1st Viscount: 1154, 1183–4; his posthumous gift, 1292
Rothermere, 2nd Viscount: 1154–5, 1183–4
Rothschild, James de: 846 n.4
Royle, Sir Anthony: 1254 n.2, 1256 n.1
Royle, Vice-Admiral (later Admiral Sir) Guy: 257–8, 274
Rucker, (Sir) Arthur: 64, 845
Ruskin, John: 643
Rutland, Duchess of (Lady Granby): 1199
Ryan, Rear-Admiral F.E.C.: 1092–3
Ryan, Lieutenant-Commander: 1092–3

Sackville-West, Vita: 250
Salisbury, 4th Marquess of: 420 n.3
Salisbury-Jones, Colonel (later General Sir) Guy: 454–5
Salmond, Marshal of the Royal Air Force Sir John: 903, 905 n.2
Salter, Sir Arthur (later Baron): 882, 975
Samuel, Sir Herbert (later Viscount): 365 n.1
Sandars, J.S.: 232
Sandys, Diana (Diana Churchill): 331 n.3, 336, 494 n.2, 580, 933, 1199, 1224 n.2, 1289 n.1, 1292
Sandys, Duncan (later Baron Duncan-Sandys): 331, 336, 403, 494 n.2, 496, 510, 580, 582, 629, 789, 931, 1289 n.1, 1292
Sargent, Sir Orme: 955 n.1
Saywell, C.J.: 1154 n.2
Schrader, Commander A.E. (U.S. Navy): 1314 n.1
Scott, (Sir) David: 709
Seal, (Sir) Eric: 23, 35 n.1, 64, 123 n.2, 420, 476–7, 484–5, 510, 537–8, 549 n.1, 683 n.2, 686, 880, 1083, 1123 n.2, 1132–3, 1180, 1204, 1231, 1240, 1280, 1302 n.1
Seamark, W.S.: 1160
Shakespeare, (Sir) Geoffrey: 546
Shakespeare, William: quoted, 733 n.2
Shaw, George Bernard: 421
Shinwell, Emanuel (later Baron): 45 n.1, 465–6, 1141
Shirer, William: 746 n.3
Sikorski, General Wladyslaw: 374, 483 n.3, 616 n.1, 830, 972 n.1, 1069, 1155
Silverman, Sidney: 949
Simon, 1st Viscount (John Simon): 508 n.1, 584, 652, 958, 1271
Simon, Colonel Paul: 110, 111
Simopoulos, Charalambos: 1036, 1112
Simpson, Captain D.J.R.: 125 n.3
Sinclair, Sir Archibald (later Viscount Thurso): Secretary of State of Air, (in May 1940), 8, 13, 21 n.1, 34, 41, 77 n.2, 80, 82 n.2, 165, 168; (in June 1940), 226, 252 n.1, 258, 281, 345, 350 n.4, 388 n.2, 441; (in July 1940), 586; (in October 1940), 903 n.3, 905 n.2, 944, 952, 955 n.1, 1002, 1008; (in November 1940), 1052, 1076; (in December 1940), 1170 n.3, 1178, 1188–9, 1206; Churchill's minutes to (June 1940), 235, 259, 282, 332, 335, 431–2; (July 1940), 461, 483, 493, 498, 504, 547, 555; (August 1940), 606, 610, 678–9, 700–1, 718, 721, 740–1; (September 1940), 756, 800, 844, 849, 860, 874, 883–4, 887–8; (October 1940), 933 n.2, 954, 970–2, 994, 1007; (November 1940), 1022, 1027, 1094, 1097–8, 1104–5, 1110; (December 1940), 1169, 1177–8, 1197–8, 1201, 1213, 1226, 1233–4, 1244, 1276, 1278–9, 1283, 1304–5, 1314; his warning to Churchill, 818–9; his birthday greetings, 1162
Sinclair, Admiral Sir Hugh: 621 n.2
Sinclair, Sir John: 14
Sinclair, (Sir) R.J. (later Baron): 376, 521
Singleton, Sir John Edward (Mr. Justice Singleton): 652, 1201, 1226, 1239, 1271

Skillen, Hugh: quoted, 1208 n.2
Slessor, Commodore (later Marshal of the Royal Air Force Sir) John: 745 n.2, 749, 1007, 1061 n.1, 1092, 1213
Slim, Brigadier (later Field Marshal Viscount) William: 1091 n.1
Smith, (Sir) Benjamin: 542
Smith, Charles Howard: rebuked, 387
Smith, Sir Frank Edward: 724–5, 905 n.2
Smith, Corporal J.: 418 n.1
Smith, Sir Sidney: defeats Napoleon (1799), 638
Smith, Trevor: 1154 n.2
Smuts, General (later Field Marshal) Jan Christian: 118–9, 175, 342–3, 366, 558, 578, 642, 864, 891, 924, 1006, 1139, 1185; Churchill's telegrams to, 271, 339, 429, 430, 857–8, 878, 943–4, 1224, 1249–50
Snell, 1st Baron: 596 n.4, 1212
Somerville, Vice-Admiral (later Admiral of the Fleet) Sir James: 143, 160, 160 n.1, 424 n.3, 458, 459–60, 460, 472–3, 477, 552 n.2, 1107, 1170
Southby, Sir Archibald: 1
Spaak, Paul-Henri: 260, 357
Spears, Major-General (Sir) Edward Louis: (in May 1940), 30 n.1, 130–1, 141, 147, 151–2, 151 n.2, 168, 172–3, 174, 193, 202, 206, 208 n.1, 219; (in June 1940), 238, 240, 263, 276, 289 notes 1 and 3, 342, 356, 405, 408, 429; (in August 1940), 605, 626, 698 n.1; (in September 1940), 739; (in November 1940), 1057 n.1; (in December 1940), 1165; his memoirs and recollections (of June 1940), 288–9, 290–1, 291 n.1, 294 n.1, 297–8, 299–300, 312 n.1, 314–5, 317–8; Churchill's letters to, 188, 236
Spencer, 2nd Earl (First Lord of the Admiralty, 1794–1801): 644
Spencer-Churchill, Lord Ivor: 47, 601
Spencer-Churchill, John George: 196–7
Stalin, Marshal J.V.: 417–8, 514 n.1
Stanley, Maureen (Lady Maureen Stewart): 535 n.1
Stanley, Oliver: 535 n.1, 1273–4
Stark, Admiral Harold S.: 1126–7, 1209
Stenhouse, Miss: 1096
Stephen, Campbell: 1119
Stern, Sir Albert: 284
Stewart, Andrew: 90 n.1
Stimson, Henry L.: 386, 682, 734, 842 n.2
Stokes, Richard: 416, 670, 1247–8
Storrs, Sir Ronald: 462 n.1
Strakosch, Sir Henry: 513, 727
Strauss, George (later Baron Strauss): 466–7, 564
Strauss, Henry George (later Baron Conesford): 1248
Street, Brigadier G.A.: 662

Strong, Brigadier-General George V.: 640 n.1, 743, 842 n.2, 854
Strube (cartoonist): 267, 530, 841
Strutt, (Sir) H.A.: 1289–90
Summers, (Sir) G. Spencer: 1160
Suñer, Ramon Serrano: 987, 992
Swayne, General (Sir) John: 66, 73, 95, 148, 152
Swinton, 1st Viscount (later Earl): 446, 503–4, 564, 671–2
Syfret, Vice-Admiral Sir Neville: 552 n.2, 1170 n.2
Symes, Sir Stewart: 853–4

Tacitus: 1248
Tarrant, V.E.: quoted, 732 n.3
Tate, Mavis: 551
Tate, Rear-Admiral (later Admiral) W.E.C.: 1009
Thiers, Louis-Adolphe: 766, 980 n.2
Thomas, J.H.: 132
Thompson, Commander C.R.: 205, 991, 1132 n.3, 1180
Thomsen, Hans: 551
Thorne, Major-General (Sir) A.F.A.N.: 439, 446, 447
Tinker, J.J.: 902–3
Tizard, Professor Sir Henry: 388 n.2, 882
Tonkin, G.R.: 1154 n.2
Tovey, Vice-Admiral (later Admiral of the Fleet, 1st Baron) J.C.: 761, 786
Tree, Nancy (later Mrs Lancaster): 1068–9, 1236
Tree, Ronald: 1122, 1232, 1236
Trenchard, Marshal of the Royal Air Force, 1st Baron: 127–8, 489, 807, 846 n.4, 872, 873, 1212
Trotsky, Leon: 1229
Truman, President Harry S.: 225 n.1, 689 n.1
Tudor, Major-General Sir Hugh: 5
Tyrrell, 1st Baron: 846 n.4

Ulysses: 776
Underdown, Thomas: 1210

Valon, Major-General A.R.: 370
Vansittart, Sir Robert (later Baron): 180, 322 n.1, 348, 368–9, 405, 408, 440–1, 481, 503–4, 568, 577, 846 n.4, 955 n.1, 957, 1220, 1247–8
Venizélos, Eleuthérios: 1039 n.2
Venning, General Sir Walter: 522
Verney, L.J.: 1256 n.1
Vickers, Lieutenant Noel: 137 n.1
Victor Emmanuel III, King of Italy: 369
Vuillemin, General Joseph: 54 n.2, 229, 254, 256, 304, 346

Waddilove, Lieutenant D.E.: 1032
Wake-Walker, Rear-Admiral (later Admiral Sir) William: 203
Wallace, Barbara (and her children): 1253 n.2
Wallace, Euan: 940 n.2, 1253–4
Wardlaw-Milne, Sir John: 543–4
Waterhouse, Charles: 960
Watson, Miss: 1083, 1132
Watson-Watt, Robert (Sir): 388 n.2, 905 n.2
Wavell, General Sir Archibald (later Field Marshal Earl): 261, 331 n.1, 412, 453, 582 n.1, 601, 638 n.1, 639, 642, 649, 654–6, 657, 661, 669, 673, 708, 733, 748 n.1; (in September 1940), 754, 790 n.2, 809, 832, 840; (in October 1940), 924, 992 n.1, 1006; (in November 1940), 1033–4, 1059, 1062, 1067–8, 1078, 1091, 1100, 1103, 1113, 1124–5, 1140, 1145–6, 1158; (in December 1940), 1167, 1177, 1200, 1205; rebuked, 1171; and a caveat, 1184; and a victory, 1213, 1219, 1223–4, 1247; future offensive by, 1241–2, 1243, 1246, 1253; his stature, 1260
Wedgwood, Josiah (later Baron): 121, 248, 457, 466, 478, 540, 554 n.1, 970, 1091 n.2, 1111
Wedgwood, Sir Ralph: 1111
Weir, 1st Viscount: 738
Weissauer, Dr.: 799
Weizmann, Dr. Chaim: 1021
Weizmann, Flig1.t-Lieutenant Michael: 1021 n.4
Wellesley, Arthur (later 1st Duke of Wellington): 5 n.2, 1151, 1180
Wells, H.G.: 846 n.4, 907, 923
Westminster, 2nd Duke of: 846 n.4
Wetherall, Mr.: 965
Weygand, General Maxime: (in May 1940), 95, 101, 102, 102–3, 104, 106, 109, 111–3, 114–6, 117, 118, 120, 122, 123, 125, 131, 134, 140, 142, 147, 151–2, 154, 156, 171, 172, 173, 190, 199, 202; and Churchill's visit to Paris (31 May 1940), 205, 209–11, 212, 215; and Dunkirk, 224–5, 236–7; and the battle for France (June 1940), 229–30, 236, 241, 252–3, 253–4, 256, 265, 269, 273; and Churchill's visit to Briare (11 June 1940), 289, 290, 291–3, 295, 296–7, 298, 302, 304, 305–6, 307; and Churchill's visit to Tours (13 June 1940), 310, 313, 315, 319, 324; and the Franco-German armistice, 326, 327, 328, 333, 351, 359, 368; and the Poles, 374; and French troops in Britain, 406–7; 'sudden senility of', 441; Churchill's earlier comment to, recalled, 534, 1047; possible 'collusive' action with, 573; and a crisis over Toulon, 997, 998; British contact with (October–December 1940), 999, 1014, 1063, 1064, 1075, 1084, 1106, 1280–1, 1307; and Greece, 1037; Churchill's messages to (May and June 1940), 129, 274–5, 303, 359

White, Lieutenant-General Sir Brudenell: 662
White, Lieutenant-Colonel (later Major-General) C.M.F.: 1001
Whitman, Walt: 1224
Whyte, Marriot: 1289 n.1
Wilhelmina, Queen, of the Netherlands: 259 n.2, 690
Wilkinson, (Sir) George Henry: 1070
William II, Kaiser: 1193
Williams, Sir H.G.: 468
Willkie, Wendell: 1071
Willoughby de Broke, 20th Baron: 815
Wilson, Sir Charles (later Baron Moran): 136
Wilson, (Sir) Harold (later Baron Wilson of Rievaulx): 1049 n.1
Wilson, General (Sir) Henry Maitland (later Field Marshal Baron): 668, 905, 1067, 1146, 1219, 1224, 1235, 1241, 1246, 1260
Wilson, Sir Horace: 123 n.2, 248, 602, 686, 846, 880, 934–5
Wilson, Muriel: 621 n.2
Wilson, President Woodrow: 436: n.1, 733 n.2
Wimborne, Alice Lady: 2
Windsor, Duchess of: 432, 555 n.3, 566, 578–9
Windsor, Duke of (formerly King Edward VIII): 375, 391, 399, 411–12, 432, 462, 463, 537, 549, 555, 565–6, 578–9
Wingate, Brigadier Orde: 372 n.1, 1313 n.1
Winkelman, General: 39
Wolfe, General (1727–1759): 934, 962
Wolkoff, Anna: 106 n.1
Wood, Sir Kingsley: 164, 703–4, 736, 771, 774, 886, 886 n.1, 891, 915, 955 n.1, 967 n.1, 1112, 1147, 1155, 1157 n.1, 1168, 1175, 1181, 1244, 1300, 1307
Woolton, 1st Baron (later Earl): 445–6, 492, 514, 537, 899 n.1, 1131, 1159, 1289 n.1, 1293
Wylie, Sapper George Cameron: 717 n.1

Zabiello, Stanislaw: 1020
Zaleski, Count August: 617
Zog, Ahmed (King of Albania): 1066–7